# McGILL UNIVERSITY THESIS DIRECTORY

VOLUME

I

1881-1959

Prepared for the

Faculty of Graduate Studies and Research

Frank Spitzer & Elizabeth Silvester, editors

MONTREAL 1976

ISBN 0-7735-0278-5
Legal Deposit 2nd Quarter 1976
Bibliothèque Nationale du Québec

Distributed for the Thesis Office, Faculty of Graduate Studies
and Research, McGill University, by
McGill–Queen's University Press
1020 Pine Avenue West
Montreal, Quebec, Canada H3A 1A2

All text processing was performed on the McGill University ATS System, and the McGill ATS–Composer System was used for all typesetting.

Printed in Canada

# Table of Contents

# Preface

Just a few months after offering Volume II (1960-1973) of this Directory to the public, I now warmly welcome Volume I which covers the years 1881 to 1959.

In the first half of this long period are the precious years in which the tradition for research and the design of graduate studies evolved in the University and became widely accepted within most of its Faculties. As the quality and size of these twin efforts were recognized, the Faculty of Graduate Studies and Research was established formally in 1922, and through its research supervisors and students it quickly became a major contributor to the character and reputation of the University. This book illustrates this happy development.

Several kinds of historical reflections on the contents of the Directory are suggested in the pleasing and interesting *Introduction* by Stanley B. Frost, a recent distinguished Dean of this Faculty, now deeply immersed in the study of rich historical material about McGill. Dr. Frost suggests the pleasures readers can find in browsing through the list; more seriously indicates that the material justifies systematic analysis from several different viewpoints.

This book contains some 4,600 listings (as compared to the nearly six thousand entries of Volume II), made up chiefly of some 3,150 Master's and 1,400 Ph.D. theses. For the period covered by both volumes, 1881-1973, the McGill contribution is about 14% of the Canadian total of 74,000; in comparison by most measures of size McGill is close to 5% of the Canadian university scene.

In Volume II, I had occasion to express our gratitude to the Editors, Mrs. Elizabeth Silvester and Professor Frank Spitzer, for the skilled judgement and devotion they brought this project. Our appreciation is even more appropriate with regard to the present volume, which since it deals with older and less homogeneous data obviously presented more problems. Most of these have been solved, I believe, but we will be grateful to be told of inaccuracies which may have escaped us.

W.F. Hitschfeld
Vice-Principal (Research)
Dean of Graduate Studies

Convocation Day
8 June 1976

# Foreword

This volume covers the years 1881-1959 while Volume II, in a similar format, covers 1959 to 1973.

These volumes show the names of authors, titles of their theses, names of their departments and their thesis supervisors, together with other details. A number of indices are attached.

Although a great deal of care has gone into the preparation of this material, inevitable errors will have occurred. Readers are invited to send suggestions for improvements or criticisms of the current publication to:


The Thesis Office
Faculty of Graduate Studies and Research
Dawson Hall
P.O. Box 6070, Station "A"
Montreal, Quebec H3C 3G1


For the benefit of those interested in particular areas, all the material is kept in a computerized data base. This and the existence of suitable application programs enable us to supply on request listings of theses selected by "specific keywords from the thesis title," "specific departments or programmes" or "specific supervisors."

# Introduction

## by

## S. B. Frost, Director, History of McGill Project

The commencement of the publication of this Directory, which is to be an on-going commitment of the Faculty of Graduate Studies and Research marks a very considerable development in the history of the University. The Directory gives both an overview and an access to the University's research programs more complete than any we have hitherto possessed.

McGill has long been characterised by an intense interest in research. As early as 1835, Frederick W. Hart, "defended in the presence of Principal G.J. Mountain and the Medical Faculty of the said University" a dissertation on the *Tic Doloureux* for the attainment of the Degree of Doctor in Medicine and Surgery, but the submission was in fact little more than a final year essay. This was probably true of other "dissertations" referred to in the early Minutes of the *Board and the Corporation*, as Senate used to be called. Like so much else, true research at McGill had its beginnings in the work of William Dawson, but what began as the personal interest of one man has now grown into such a vast and complex activity that the problems involved in the conservation of the results of this research, and the even greater problems involved in making it available to other researchers have at times appeared insuperable. Yet investigations which are not recorded, and results which are not readily accessible to others, are in practical terms a waste of effort and resources.

In 1968 and again in 1970, the Faculty published volumes entitled *The McGill Index of Researcn*, which listed work in progress across a wide range of university departments. By use of key-word designations and computer retrieval, the volumes sought to enable a researcher to become aware of what was being undertaken in his own and in contiguous areas. Those volumes are still worthy of consultation and are of considerable historical value, but now they have been supplemented if not superseded by the present project, which is the publication of the titles of all research theses accepted at McGill for the award of graduate degrees. From 1881 the record of post-graduate study and research is continuous, beginning appropriately enough for a university whose first professorial appointment was in Theology, with a thesis on a biblical subject, though it has to be remarked that it was accepted somewhat incongruously for the award of LL.D.

The present project is both more limited and more ambitious than the previous one in that it confines itself to the results of graduate student research, but it presents that record whole and entire. Since, however, the nature of graduate research at the University is that of the student working under the direction of a professor who is interested more or less closely in the same field, and who often incorporates into his own larger programme the results of his apprentice-collaborators, the presentation of the record of research theses accepted provides a remarkably full and representative account of university research in general. It is the achievement of these volumes that the research pursued in all the different departments of the University may be viewed for the first time in its development and multitudinous variety.

There are practical as well as intellectual benefits to be derived from these volumes. There has been from time to time uninformed criticism of university research, on the grounds that much of it is meretricious, that the money expended could have been better spent elsewhere or that the research interests of the professor have interfered with and distracted him from his first responsibility of teaching. The criticism is rightly called 'uninformed' for it has of necessity been based on vague impressions or isolated instances. Now the University's research record is in large measure (not wholly, for in some disciplines the professor's own research may be somewhat removed from that of his graduate students) laid out for all to see and judge. In research we are first creating the pieces and then fitting them together to form the ever-expanding jigsaw-puzzle of human understanding. No one ever knows which piece is going next to prove the critical one, but the backward look, now available to us through these volumes, enables us to see how the work in the University has contributed to the over-all growth of the macropattern of man's knowledge of himself and his environment. We venture to affirm, now that the evidence is laid out before us, that the University's achievement has been substantial, that it has over the years contributed to what have proved to be significant areas of research, and that it has been carried forward notably under the direction of just those professors who have gained high reputations as teachers both at the graduate and undergraduate levels.

Dictionaries, concordances, directories are made to be consulted rather than read, but they will always provide unlooked-for rewards to those who browse in them and the early years of the listing are rich in this respect. There were three doctoral degrees awarded before 1900, two in Divinity and one in Philosophy, but it was at the turn of the century that the Master's degree by thesis was made available, and it speedily became a hall-mark of academic excellence, and one which the University has proved well-able to maintain, despite tendencies elsewhere to allow its values to depreciate. It will surprise some that prior to the first World War, fully twenty percent of the successful candidates for post-graduate degrees were women, and this in a university which did not admit women to the Bachelor's degree until 1888. Pride of place goes to Harriet Brooks, for an M.A. in Physics conferred in 1901, and for which the thesis director was none other than Professor Ernest Rutherford. The first woman Ph.D. was Annie L. Macleod in Chemistry, in 1910, only one year after the University had conferred the degree for the first time. Miss Brooks went on to marry A.S. Eve, the distinguished Professor of Physics, who became Scientific Director of the Admiralty Experimental Research Station at Harwich during World War I, in succession to Sir William Bragg. Closely associated with Eve at that time was the recipient of the first McGill Ph.D., Robert W. Boyle. He played a notable role in the development of the submarine detection device which came to be known as "Asdic" and was later Director of the Division of Physics and Electrical Engineering, at the N.R.C. Laboratories in Ottawa. Eve had helped to direct Boyle's thesis in association with Howard Turner Barnes, who succeeded Rutherford as Macdonald Professor of Physics and who gained for himself and initiated for McGill an international reputation in ice-studies, an interest and a reputation which today flourishes as strongly as ever. Barnes' name occurs more often than anyone else's as thesis director in those early entries – fourteen times in the first twelve years – and among this students we note the names of Norman Shaw and Otto Maas. The McGill scientific tradition takes on a visible form as we read down these lists.

It is also salutary to discover that many of what we conceive to be the problems of our times have in fact been recognised as matters of great concern thirty, fifty even eighty years ago. In 1896, the first M.A. thesis of all concerned itself with "The Abolition of Capital Punishment according to the Hegelian Philosophy". In 1920, a thesis was presented on "The Status of Women in the Province of Quebec"; another in 1929 was a study of "The Negro in Canada" and this was followed in 1934 by "Transportation as a National Problem". Or we can watch the changing interests of departments and relate them to disciplinary developments, or to institutional or political events. This is illustrated by a

department like Psychology, which began its long series in 1907 with theses concerned with the personalist psychology of Freud and William James and moves steadily in later years to the more biological studies of experimental psychology; or like Geography, which recorded its first successful thesis in 1949 with a work on the polar north, thus indicating what was to be the dominating concern of the department down to the present. From the early sixties this has been varied by a succession of theses on the Caribbean and the humid tropics, interests arising from the opening of the University's Bellairs Research Institute in Barbardos. On the other hand, the impact of events like the loosening of ties with Britain, the Quiet and not-so-Quiet Revolutions in Quebec, the out-pouring in the past decade of North American "protest" literature, appear to have exerted comparatively little influence in the determination of thesis subjects, but it is noticeable that the reaction of departments in the humanities and the social sciences to these influential events varies quite markedly. The subject almost qualifies as the theme of a Master's thesis.

Another less serendipitous form of browsing is to take the listings by thesis supervisor and seek out some of the great names in a discipline and observe how many and on what themes theses are directed by them. In some instances, popular reputations are left somewhat insubstantial, whereas in others a solid body of results accummulated year after year confirms the general approbation. And if it be added – as it should be – that in research it is always quality not quantity which is significant, there is the further criterion to be applied of observing the later careers of those who were the students of these teachers. This book is indeed a valuable record of a vast endeavour, and it will, I am persuaded, grow in usefulness and significance as the years pass.

Now that the early years have been compiled, it will be a comparatively simple task to keep the record up to date, but few can ununderstand the immense amount of careful investigation and technological skill that have gone into the production of these first two volumes. The heavy burden of research has been undertaken by Elizabeth Silvester, Head of the Reference Department of the McLennan Library. Frank Spitzer, Associate Professor in the Department of Electrical Engineering has provided the technology which has made the organization and production of these volumes possible, and these two colleagues deserve our highest commendation, not only for their individual contributions but also for the way in which they have teamed together to produce these fascinating volumes. They also required the encouragement and resources provided by Vice-Principal Walter Hitschfeld, Dean of Graduate Studies and Research, without whose personal commitment to the project it would have never reached a successful conclusion.

All who seek to be aware of the wider implications of their own research, all who are concerned for the role of the University in Graduate Studies and all who have an interest in the intellectual history of McGill – and this is to say of our community and country, indeed of mankind – are greatly indebted to our colleagues for the recognition of a need and the splendid manner in which it has been met.

22 April, 1976

# Presentation of Data

The Annual Listing, the first section of this volume, contains in strict numerical order, corresponding approximately to alphabetical order, the theses accepted by the University each year, broken down by convocation and degree. A sample entry is given below:–

72-**047** **MacLeod**, Stuart M. (*Toronto*) Ph.D. "Hepatic microsomal drug oxidation and electron transport in immature rats, rabbits, and humans." (Pharmacology & Therapeutics: Eade, N.)

The first two digits indicate the calendar year in which the degree was awarded, superscript numerals indicating the 19th century.

The three subsequent bold numbers are the thesis reference number which combines to form a five digit code used throughout the indices. Numbers have been allocated in the sequences 1 to 499 for Spring and from 500 onwards for Fall convocations, resulting in a gap before the number 500.

The name of the candidate is given in bold characters in the form that was applicable at the time the degree was awarded; any subsequent name change has been ignored.

The name of the university granting the first degree is listed enclosed in parentheses after the author's name. Where this university is in North America, the name of the country has not been included. Every attempt has however been made to ensure that the names used are both clear and unambiguous.

The degree awarded appears next, followed by the title of the thesis within quotation marks.

The last component of the entry, enclosed in parentheses, identifies the name of the department or programme in which the student was registered and the supervisor of the thesis. The department name is given here as it was at the time the thesis was written. If there were several thesis supervisors, their names are listed in the sequence shown in the thesis. Only the first initial of each supervisor is given except where ambiguity might thereby result.

Each year starts a new page of the Annual Listing.

The 19th century theses in the Annual Listing are not included in the various indices in the Directory.

# Indices

The indices described below follow the annual listing.

1. **Alphabetical List by Author**

The index lists the authors of theses listed alphabetically without regard to year, department or degree. The thesis number and the degree awarded follow the author's name. Where students have submitted both a Master's and a Doctoral thesis within the index period of 1881 to 1959 there will be two entries for the same author. The thesis number is the key to the Annual Listing which gives full details of the thesis. Asterisks in any of the data fields are indicative of the unavailability of this element of information.

2. **Alphabetical List by Department**

This index provides a primary alphabetical listing of the department or programme and within each listing an alphabetical sequence of authors as well as the thesis number and the degree awarded. For fuller comments regarding the use of department or programme name, please see the comments on this topic.

3. **Alphabetical List by Supervisor**

This index provides an alphabetical list of students under each supervisory Professor together with the degree awarded and the thesis number. An asterisk preceding the author's name indicates that more than one Supervisor was responsible for the thesis; the other Supervisors may be ascertained by reference to the Annual Listing through the use of the thesis number.

4. **List of Theses by Department**

This index prints thesis titles sequenced by thesis number, but sorted by department in order to help researchers scanning the thesis listings. As it has not been possible to classify the theses by subject this index provides a means by which the titles are grouped together by discipline to facilitate searching by topic. For further comments regarding the use of department or programme name, please see the comments on this topic.

**Additional Lists**

The Faculty of Graduate Studies and Research maintains other indices in addition to those published here. These can be made available on demand.

# Departmental & Programme Nomenclature

The "Listing by Department" and the "Listing by Thesis Title" both provide access to thesis information arranged under the name of the department or programme in which the student was registered. The departmental names employed in the Directory have been taken from contemporary records. As departmental names have changed and varied over the years there are some inherent difficulties in employing them as headings for locating theses produced in a particular discipline. Hence, to facilitate the use of the indices, a list of all departmental and programme names used, grouped by related disciplines is provided here. It is essential to use this list in order to select the relevant headings for the names of authors in a particular field or for theses on a particular topic. Both specific and general headings should be checked – e.g. "Biology" should be scanned as well as "Botany" for Botany theses due to the recent amalgamation of the Botany, Genetics and Zoology Departments into the Biology Department. It may also be useful to check some of the related headings listed under *Agricultural Sciences* for some botanical topics, e.g. "Horticulture" or "Plant Pathology". Similarly, synonymous terms should be examined, e.g. "Bacteriology", "Bacteriology & Immunology" and "Microbiology" etc.

The Roman numerals which follow the names in the following lists refer to the volume number or numbers of the *McGill University Thesis Directory* in which the programme occurs.

## AGRICULTURAL SCIENCES

Agricultural Bacteriology, I & II
Agricultural Chemistry, I & II
Agricultural Economics, I & II
Agricultural Engineering, II
Agricultural Physics, II
Agricultural Science, II
Agronomy, I & II
Agronomy and Genetics, I
Agronomy & Plant Pathology, I
Animal Nutrition, I
Animal Nutrition & Breeding, I
Animal Science, II
Botany-Horticulture, I
Entomology, I & II
Horticulture, I & II
Horticulture-Botany, I
Horticulture-Genetics, I
Nutrition, I & II
Parisitology, I & II
Plant Anatomy, I
Plant Morphology, I
Plant Pathology, I & II
Plant Pathology & Botany, I
Poultry Husbandry, I
Renewable Resources, II
Soil Science, II
Woodlot Management, II

## BIOLOGICAL SCIENCES

Bacteriology, I & II
Bacteriology & Immunology, I & II
Biochemistry, I & II
Biology, I & II
Botany, I & II
Botany & Geological Sciences, I
Botany-Genetics, I
Botany-Horticulture, I
Entomology, I & II
Zoology-Genetics, I
Genetics, I & II
Invertebrate Morphology, I
Marine Sciences, II
Microbiology, II
Microbiology & Immunology, II
Organic Chemistry, I
Parisitology, I & II
Plant Pathology & Botany, I
Zoology, I & II

## ARCHITECTURE

Architecture, I & II

## ENGINEERING

Aerodynamics & Engineering, I
Applied Electricity, I
Chemical Engineering, I & II
Civil Engineering, I
Civil Engineering & Applied
  Mechanics, I & II
Computer Science, II
Electrical Communications, I
Electrical Engineering, I & II
Engine & Machine Design, I
Engineering, I
Hydraulics, I
Hydraulics & Hydrodynamics, I
Industrial Engineering, I
Machine Design, I
Machines & Machine Design, I
Mechanical Engineering, I & II
Metallurgical Engineering, I & II
Metallurgy, I
Mining & Metallurgy, I
Mining and Metallurgical Engineering,
  I & II
Mining Engineering, I & II
Mining Engineering & Applied
  Geophysics, II
Ore Dressing, I
Reinfoced Concrete Construction, I
Rock Crushing, I
Sanitary Engineering, I
Theory of Structures, I
Thermodynamics, I

## HUMANITIES

Classics, I & II
English, I & II
French, I & II
French & Italian, II
French Language & Literature, I
German, I & II
Greek, I
Islamic Studies, I & II
Italian, II
Italian & English, II
Latin, I
Linguistics, II
Music, I & II
Philosophy, I & II
Romance Languages, I & II
Russian, II
Spanish, II

## LAW

Air & Space Law, I & II
Civil Law, I & II
Comparative & Foreign Law, II
International Air Law, I
International Law, I
Law, I & II

## MATHEMATICS

Mathematics, I & II
Mathematics & Physics, I

## MEDICAL SCIENCES

Anatomy, I & II
Dentistry, II
Endocrinology, I
Epidemiology & Health, II
Experimental Medicine, I & II
Experimental Surgery, I & II
Human Communications Disorders, II
Investigative Medicine, I & II
Medicine, I
Neurology, I
Neurology & Neurosurgery, I & II
Neurosurgery, I
Otolarygology, II
Pathology, I & II
Pharmacology, I & II
Pharmacology & Therapeutics, II
Physiology, I & II
Psychiatry, I & II
Surgery, II

## PHYSICAL SCIENCES



## RELIGION



## SOCIAL SCIENCES

# Loans

Most McGill University theses may be borrowed through interlibrary loans from the university's libraries. The loan period is two weeks, without renewal option. A paper or microfilm copy may be purchased through:

Interlibrary Loans
McLennan Library
McGill University
3459 McTavish Street
Montreal, Quebec H2A 1Y1

Estimates are automatically provided by the Interlibrary Loans Service for theses for which circulating copies are not available.

Prepayment is not necessary if the order is placed through a recognized library, however, it is required for requests placed by individuals or corporate bodies.

Microform copies of McGill theses from 1967 onwards are available directly from:

Canadian Theses on Microfilm
National Library of Canada
Cataloguing Branch
Ottawa, Ontario K1A 0N4

Copies of McGill University theses are made available strictly for the purposes of consultation. The literary rights of the author must be respected. No part of a thesis may be copied, closely paraphrased, or reproduced in any way without the previous written consent of the author. If the reader obtains any assistance from the work, he is expected to give proper credit in his own production.

## ANNUAL LISTING

### LL.D. 1881

81-001 **Duff**, Archibald (*McGill*) LL.D.: "On the history of the idea of atonement among the Hebrews from the time of Amos (circa 800 B.C.) to the liberation by Cyrus from the Babylonian Exile (circa 540 B.C.)." (Divinity: **)

### LL.D. 1883

83-001 **Roy**, James ( ) LL.D.: "Law in language." (Philosophy: **)

### LL.D. 1886

86-001 **Krans**, Edward H. ( ) LL.D.: "Law in the spiritual life." (Divinity: **)

### M.A. 1896

96-001 **Internoscia**, Jerome (*McGill*) M.A.: "The abolition of capital punishment according to the Hegelian philosophy." (Philosophy: **)

### M.A. 1901

01-001 **Brooks**, Harriet ( ) M.A.: "Damping of the oscillations in the discharge of a Leyden jar." (Physics: Rutherford, E.)

01-002 **Duncan**, Gaylen R. ( ) M.Sc.: "The thermal conductivity of metals." (Physics: **)

01-003 **McClung**, Robert K. ( ) M.A.: "A preliminary account of an experimental investigation of the variation of the rate of recombination of gaseous ions with pressure." (Physics: Rutherford, E.)

01-004 **Newson**, William V. ( ) M.Sc.: "Certain gabbros and nephthaline syenites of the townships of Monmouth and Glamorgan, Ontario." (Geology: **)

## ANNUAL LISTING

### M.Sc. 1902

02-001 **Ried**, L. ( ) M.Sc.: "A petrographical study of the township of Wollaston, Ontario." (Geology: **)

### M.A. 1905

05-001 **Hadrill**, Margaret F. ( ) M.A.: "The ecclesiastical policy of Henry IV of France." (History: **)

05-002 **Henderson**, Ernest H. ( ) M.A.: "Observations into the development of an asterid closely allied to *Asternia gibbose*." (Zoology: McBride, **)

05-003 **McGregor**, Claire R. ( ) M.A.: "A study of Goethe's 'Faust'." (German: MacBride, *)

05-004 **Munn**, William C. ( ) M.A.: "Quebec in the seventeenth century, a study in social history." (History: **)

05-005 **Sheldon**, Ernest. W. ( ) M.A.: "Spherical trigonometry, orthogonal substitutes and elliptic functions." (Mathematics: **)

### M.A. 1906

06-001 **Brown**, Walter G. ( ) M.A.: "Socialism in British Columbia." (Political Science: **)

06-002 **Davidson**, MacFarlane B. ( ) M.A.: "Lee's invasion of the north in 1863." (History: **)

06-003 **Day**, Frank J. ( ) M.A.: "The religion of Israel in the eighth and seventh centuries B.C. with special reference to the work of the prophets." (Divinity: **)

06-004 **Henry**, Alice I. ( ) M.A.: "Gérard de Nerval." (French: **)

06-005 **Mingie**, George W. ( ) M.A.: "The influence of the geological structure of Palestine on the development of Jewish history." (Geology: **)

06-006 **Smith**, Esther M. ( ) M.A.: "Thomas de Quincey and his influence in literature." (English: **)

## ANNUAL LISTING

### M.A. 1907

07-501 **East**, Edith M. (*McGill*) M.A.: "The subconscious." (Psychology: Caldwell, W.)

07-502 **Hindley**, John G. (*McGill*) M.A.: "Stoic and Christian ethics." (Philosophy: Coussirat, D. & Scott, W. & Caldwell, W.)

07-503 **Kirsch**, Simon (*McGill*) M.A.: "On the development and function of certain structures in the stipe and rhizome of pterisaquihna and other pteridophytes." (Botany: Penhallon, D. & Adams, F.)

07-504 **Pearson**, Mary F. (*McGill*) M.A.: "Responsible government in Canada and its relation to English opinion 1759-1848." (Economics & Political Science: Flux, * & Tory, H. & Colby, C.)

07-505 **Pelletier**, Alexis D. (*McGill*) M.A.: "The schools of Manitoba." (Political Science: **)

07-506 **Rice**, Horace G. (*McGill*) M.A.: "The philosophy of the Book of Job." (Divinity: Coussirat, D.)

### M.Sc. 1907

07-507 **Brunner**, Godfrey H. (*McGill*) M.Sc.: "The distribution of stress in riveted connections." (Engineering: Bovery, H. & Brown, E. & Mackay, H.)

07-508 **Harrison**, Francis C. (*Toronto*) M.Sc.: "Published works." (Bacteriology: Adami, J.)

07-509 **Harvey**, John B. (*McGill*) M.Sc.: "Train resistance, its causes, measurement and value, and its bearing on locomotive rating and operation." (Engineering: McLeod, C. & Durley, R.)

07-510 **Lewis**, David S. (*McGill*) M.Sc.: "Some reactions of the monoamino acids." (Organic Chemistry: MacBride, E. & Walker, J.)

07-511 **Lyman**, Ruth D. ( ) M.Sc.: "Some points on the development of *Pleuragramma antarcticum*." (Zoology: Walker, J. & McBride, E.)

07-512 **Robertson**, Arthur F. (*McGill*) M.Sc.: "Notes on some reductions in the presence of finely divided nickel." (Chemistry: Walker, J. & Rutherford, E.)

## ANNUAL LISTING

### M.A. 1908

08-501 **Cousins**, George V. (*McGill*) M.A.: "The history of railway legislation in Canada." (Political Science: Colby, C. & Hemmeon, J.)

08-502 **Jamieson**, John S. ( ) M.A.: "The waterways of Canada in their international relations." (Political Science: Colby, C. & Hemmeon, J.)

08-503 **Parker**, David W. (*McGill*) M.A.: "Carleton and Burgoyne." (History: Moyse, C. & Colby, C.)

08-504 **Rorke**, Mabele L. (*McGill*) M.A.: "The negotiations between General Haldimand and the Allens of Vermont." (History: Colby, C. & Lafleur, P.)

08-505 **Salt**, Alexander E. (*Oxford*, England) M.A.: "Quarrels of the religious in the thirteenth century." (History: Colby, C. & Taylor, A.)

08-506 **Smith**, Ella L. (*McGill*) M.A.: "The dramas of Euripides in their relation to the life and thought of of his time." (Classics: Scott, W. & Taylor, A.)

08-507 **Vincent**, Irving O. (*McGill*) M.A.: "The relation between the theology of Clement of Alexandria and Greek philosophy." (Classics: Scott, W. & Taylor, A.)

### M.Sc. 1908

08-508 **Allan**, John A. ( ) M.Sc.: "(A) petrographical study of the rocks of Mount Royal." (Geological Sciences: Adams, F.)

08-509 **Graham**, Richard P. (*Oxford*, England) M.Sc.: "On the properties of krohndite, dausonite and some other Canadian minerals." (Geology & Mineralogy: Adams, F. & Evans, N.)

08-510 **Harrington**, John L. (*McGill*) M.Sc.: "The operating machinery for the lifting deck of the bridge over the Missouri River at Kansas City, for the Union Depot Bridge and Terminal Railroad Company." (Machines & Machine Design: Durley, R. & Mackay, H.)

08-511 **McFee**, Malcolm C. (*McGill*) M.Sc.: "The action of thionyl chloride on some organic compounds containing hydroxyl groups, and the physical properties of methyl mandelate." (Chemistry: Walker,J. & Adams, F.)

08-512 **McIntosh**, Donald S. (*Dalhousie*) M.Sc.: "On an occurence of tin ores and associated minerals in Nova Scotia, with a comparative study of tin deposits in other parts of the world." (Geological Sciences: Adams, F. & Walker, J.)

08-513 **Shearer**, George W. (*McGill*) M.Sc.: "The electromotive force developed between aluminium and magnesium in various electrolytes." (Physics: Barnes, H. & McIntosh, D.)

08-514 **Strangways**, Henry F. (*McGill*) M.Sc.: "The washing of bituminous coal, with notes on special experiments on certain Nova Scotian coals." (Ore Dressing: Porter, J. & Durley, R.)

## ANNUAL LISTING

Ph.D. 1909

09-001 **Boyle**, Robert W. (*McGill*) Ph.D.: "Absorption and adsorbtion with reference to the radioactive emanation." (Physics: Cox, J. & Barnes, H. & Eve, A.)

M.A. 1909

09-501 **Eaton**, Mary J. ( ) M.A.: "The element of satire in fiction written by Englishwomen from Miss Burney to George Eliot." (English: Moyse, C. & Colby, C. & Lafleur, P.)

09-502 **Gordon**, Nathan (*Cincinnati*) M.A.: "Capital punishment in the Bible and Talmud." (Semitic Studies: MacNaughton, J. & Brockwell, B.)

09-503 **Hayden**, Amy J. (*McGill*) M.A.: "Théophile Gautier as a prose writer." (French: Walter, H. & Lafleur, P.)

09-504 **MacCrimmon**, John R. (*Queen's*) M.A.: "The apology of slavery." (Political Science: Colby, C. & Hemmeon, J.)

09-505 **Rogers**, David B. (*McGill*) M.A.: "Metaphysical proofs for the existence of God." (Philosophy: Caldwell, W.)

09-506 **Tyndale**, Orville S. (*McGill*) M.A.: "François Villon et la poésie lyrique en France au XVe siècle." (French: Walter, H. & Lafleur, P.)

M.Sc. 1909

09-507 **Baird**, John B. (*McGill*) M.Sc.: "Approximate methods of longitude determination. An investigation of personal equation in astronomical observations with the Respold micrometer eyepiece." (Physics: McLeod, C. & Cox, J.)

09-508 **Day**, Franklin H. (*Boston*) M.Sc.: "Hygrometric conditions and their effect upon organic matter." (Physics: Barnes, H. & Starky, L.)

09-509 **Elliott**, Percy H. (*McGill*) M.Sc.: "Electrical conductivity of certain salts in acetanilid solution." (Physics: McIntosh, D. & Barnes, H.)

09-510 **Finlayson**, John N. (*McGill*) M.Sc.: "Tests on concrete columns." (Reinforced Concrete Construction: Mackay, H. & Durley, R.)

09-511 **Gillis**, Norman R. (*McGill*) M.Sc.: "An investigation into the extent and variation of water vapour in the sun's spectrum." (Physics: Barnes, H. & Cox, J.)

09-512 **Guillet**, George L. (*McGill*) M.Sc.: "The use of alcohol in an internal combustion engine: a comparative series of tests on a Blackstone oil engine using alcohol and coal oil." (Mechanical Engineering: Brown,E. & Durley, R.)

## ANNUAL LISTING

09-513 **Harvie**, Robert (*McGill*) M.Sc.: "The origin and relations of the Paleozoic breccia of the vicinity of Montreal." (Geological Sciences: Adams, F. & Penhallon, D.)

09-514 **Krieble**, Vernon K. (*Brown*) M.Sc.: "The investigation of amygdalin." (Chemistry: Walker, J.)

09-515 **Pitts**, Gordon M. (*McGill*) M.Sc.: "Secondary stresses in bridge trusses induced by riveted joints." (Engineering: Mackay, H. & Durley, R.)

09-516 **Roffey**, Myles H. (*McGill*) M.Sc.: "The design and construction of the modern transformer." (Electrical Engineering: Owens, R. & Barnes, H.)

09-517 **Sproule**, Gordon St. G. (*McGill*) M.Sc.: "The correlation and standardization of chemical, physical and microscopical methods of testing iron and steel." (Metallurgical Engineering: Stansfield, A. & Walker, J.)

09-518 **Vipond**, William S. (*McGill*) M.Sc.: "The evaporation of ice." (Physics: Barnes, H. & Walker, J.)

## ANNUAL LISTING

### Ph.D. 1910

10-001 **Bancroft**, Joseph A. ( ) Ph.D.: "Preliminary report on a portion of the coast of British Columbia and the islands adjacent thereto in the Nanaimo district." (Geological Sciences: Adams, F.)

10-002 **Kirsch**, Simon (*McGill*) Ph.D.: "The origin and development of resin canals in the coniferae with special reference to the development of thyloses and their correlation with the thylosal strands of the pteridophytes." (Botony: Penhallow, D.)

10-003 **Macleod**, Annie L. (*McGill*) Ph.D.: "A comparison of certain acids containing a conjugated system of of double linkages." (Chemistry: Walker, J. & Ruttan, R. & Barnes, H.)

### M.A. 1910

10-501 **Hatcher**, Albert G. (*McGill*) M.A.: "Numerical evaluation of elliptic functions." (Mathematics: Harkness, J. & Murray, *)

10-502 **Huntley**, Herbert W. (*McGill*) M.A.: "Inhibition." (Psychology: Caldwell, W. & Tait, W.)

10-503 **Huxtable**, Margaret (*McGill*) M.A.: "The attitude of Euripides to the traditional religion of Greece." (Greek: MacNaughton, J. & Walter, H.)

10-504 **King**, Lucile M. (*McGill*) M.A.: "Die Entwicklung des Romans und der Erzählung in der romantischen Schule." (German: Walter, H. & MacNaughton, J.)

10-505 **McDonald**, Jessie (*McGill*) M.A.: "The fairy element in English literature." (English: Moyse, C. & Walter, H.)

10-506 **MacKenzie**, John M. ( ) M.A.: "The span of attention." (Psychology:**)

10-507 **Maclean**, Herbert B. (*McGill*) M.A.: "Plato's *Republic* from the standpoint of philosophy and education." (Philosophy: Caldwell, W. & MacNaughton, J.)

10-508 **Macnaughton**, Ariel M. (*McGill*) M.A.: "The evolution of the fairy world, with special reference to its treatment in English literature." (English: Moyse, C. & Walter, H.)

10-509 **McNeil**, John T. (*McGill*) M.A.: "Partisan poetry of Roundhead and Cavalier." (English: Moyse, C. & Walton, F.)

10-510 **Smillie**, Eleanor A. (*McGill*) M.A.: "A comparative, historical and political study of the various schemes for the reconstruction of the relations of Great Britain and its colonies, 1764-1867." (Political Science: Leacock, S. & Fryer, C.)

## ANNUAL LISTING

M.Sc. 1910

10-511 **Arkley**, Lorne M. (*Swarthmore*) M.Sc.: "The design of a concrete block building with reinforced concrete floors for light manufacturing purposes." (Engineering: **)

10-512 **Bates**, Frederick W. (*McGill*) M.Sc.: "Penetrating radiation and the ionization of the atmosphere." (Physics: Barnes, H. & Eve, A.)

10-513 **Carmichael**, Henry G. (*McGill*) M.Sc.: "The mechanical purification of certain Canadian coals." (Mining Engineering: Porter, J.)

10-514 **Cheesbrough**, Arthur G. (*McGill*) M.Sc.: "Canadian turpentine, and its relation to the French and American varieties." (Chemistry: Walker, J. & Ruttan, R.)

10-515 **Dickieson**, Arthur L. (*McGill*) M.Sc.: "The flow of mercury in a magnetic field." (Physics: Barnes, H. & Wilson, H.)

10-516 **Fox**, Charles H. (*McGill*) M.Sc.: "Some reinforced concrete designs." (Engineering: Mackay, H. & Brown, E.)

10-517 **Hayes**, Albert O. (*McGill*) M.Sc.: "The petrography of some igneous rocks of Lexada Island." (Petrography: Adams, F. & Porter, J.)

10-518 **Meldrum**, William B. (*McGill*) M.Sc.: "The physical constants of some substituted malonic acids, with special regard to the influence of alkyl sustituents on the electrical conductivity of malonic acids." (Chemistry: Walker, J. & McIntosh, D.)

10-519 **O'Neill**, John J. (*McGill*) M.Sc.: "The diamond-bearing rocks of South Africa." (Geological Sciences: Adams, F. & Macmillan, C.)

10-520 **Richardson**, Lorne N. (*Toronto*) M.Sc.: "Algebraic configurations." (Mathematics: Harkness, J. & Murray, *)

10-521 **Shaw**, Albert N. (*McGill*) M.Sc.: "Clark and Weston standard cells." (Physics: Barnes, H.)

10-522 **Sullivan**, Charles T. ( ) M.Sc.: "The variation of the specific heat of metals with temperature; the specific heat of mercury by the water-cooled method of continuous flow calorimetry." (Physics: Barnes, H.)

10-523 **Weir**, Douglas (*Toronto*) M.Sc.: "An investigation into the nature and cause of certain plant malformations observed in the vicinity of Ste Anne de Bellvue, Que." (Plant Morphology: Lockhead, W. & Derick, C. & Simpson, J.)

10-524 **Yuill**, Harry H. (*McGill*) M.Sc.: "The concentration of lead-zinc sulphides in ores and their separation from one another." (Ore Dressing: Porter, J. & Durley, R.)

## ANNUAL LISTING

M.A. 1911

11-501 **Brittain**, Isabel E. (*McGill*) M.A.: "The development of the sense of beauty." (Education: Hickson, J. & Sinclair, S.)

11-502 **Cockfield**, Harry R. (*McGill*) M.A.: "Seneca and his Greek models." (Classics: MacNaughton, J.)

11-503 **Tremblay**, Joseph A. (*McGill*) M.A.: "Emile Zola et l'étude naturaliste des classes de la société." (French: Walton, F. & Walter, H.)

11-504 **Wilson**, Alice M. (*McGill*) M.A.: "The educational significance of suggestion." (Education: Dale, J. & Sinclair, S. & Hickson, J.)

M.Sc. 1911

11-505 **Ball**, Harry S. ( ) M.Sc.: "An investigation on the economics of tube milling." (Engineering: Durley, R.)

11-506 **Campbell**, Edmund E. (*McGill*) M.Sc.: "The exomorphic contact actions of acid igneous intrusions." (Geology & Mineralogy: **)

11-507 **Cox**, John R. (*McGill*) M.Sc.: "The efficiency of fine screening devices, with particular reference to the Callow revolving belt screen as a means of preparing crushed ore for treatment upon the Wilfley table." (Engineering: Mackay, H.)

11-508 **Dick**, William J. (*McGill*) M.Sc.: "The influence of igneous intrusions on the development of ore bodies of pneumatolitic origins." (Geology & Mineralogy: Adams, F. & Durley, R.)

11-509 **Drysdale**, George A. (*McGill*) M.Sc.: "Chemistry and metallurgy as applied to modern malleable and gray iron foundries." (Metallurgical Engineering: Stansfield, A.)

11-510 **Gibbins**, Gwynn G. (*McGill*) M.Sc.: "The classification of finely crushed ore with a view of further concentration on the Wilfley table." (Mining Engineering: Porter, J. & Mackay, H.)

11-511 **Gillies**, George A. (*McGill*) M.Sc.: "Stamp mill efficiency under varying conditions of feed, drop, water, and screen." (Ore Dressing: Porter, J. & Durley, R.)

11-512 **Harris**, Norman C. (*McGill*) M.Sc.: "The efficiency of production in industrial plants." (Engine & Machine Design: Durley, R. & Hemmeon, J.)

11-513 **Matheson**, Howard W. (*Dalhousie*) M.Sc.: " " (Chemistry: Walker, J. & Ruttan, R.)

11-514 **Munn**, David W. (*McGill*) M.Sc.: "The temperature - entropy diagram and its application to gas-engine cycles." (Thermodynamics: Durley, R. & Reay, *)

11-515 **Wheeler**, Nathaniel E. (*Colby*) M.Sc.: "The thermal expansion of rocks." (Physics: Barnes, H. & Adams, F.)

## ANNUAL LISTING

### Ph.D. 1912

12-001 **Boehner,** Reginald S. (*Dalhousie*) Ph.D.: "The hydrolysis of gelatin by baryta. The transformation of glutamine acid into proline." (Chemistry: Fischer, E.)

### M.A. 1912

12-501 **Howell,** Lucy M. (*McGill*) M.A.: "Sir Bartle Frere's policy in South Africa." (History: Fryer, C. & Walton, F.)

12-502 **Miller,** Clare B. (*McGill*) M.A.: "Fresh-water algae occurring in the vicinity of Montreal." (Botany: Derick, C. & Willey, A. & Walter, H.)

12-503 **Paterson,** Edith L. (*McGill*) M.A.: "State interference, theory and practice." (Economics & Political Science: Leacock, S. & Walter, H.)

12-504 **Potter,** James G. (*Queen's*) M.A.: "Biblical sociology." (Semitic Studies: Brockwell, B. & Walton, F.)

12-505 **Rowell,** Arthur H. (*McGill*) M.A.: "MacDougall's theory of instincts." (Psychology: Tait, W. & Dale, J. & Harkness, J.)

12-506 **Thorne,** Oliver (*McGill*) M.A.: "A study of the Church of England in its relation to the state, 1688-1760." (History: Fryer, C. & Harkness, J.)

### M.Sc. 1912

12-507 **Beagley,** Thomas G. ( ) M.Sc.: "Efficiency test of gasoline engines." (Engine & Machine Design: **)

12-508 **Galloway,** John D. (*McGill*) M.Sc.: "An investigation of the efficiency of certain rock-crushing machines." (Ore Dressing: Porter, J. & Durley, R.)

12-509 **Gillespie,** Peter (*Toronto*) M.Sc.: "The merits and defects of the concrete column, plain and reinforced, in the light of experimental research." (Engineering: Mackay, H. & Beullac, *)

12-510 **De Hart,** Joseph B. (*McGill*) M.Sc.: "Spontaneous combustion and weathering of coal." (Mining Engineering: Porter, J.)

12-511 **Lockhead,** Allan G. (*McGill*) M.Sc.: "Maple sugar sand." (Agricultural Chemistry: Snell, J.)

12-512 **Maass,** Otto (*McGill*) M.Sc.: "Phase rule studies; organic compounds, containing oxygen, with the halogens and halogen hydrides." (Chemistry: Barnes, H.)

12-513 **MacLean,** Allison R. (*McGill*) M.Sc.: "Optical studies of the asymmetric aliphatic acids." (Chemistry: Ruttan, R. & Barnes, H.)

## ANNUAL LISTING

12-514 **McNaughton**, Andrew G. (*McGill*) M.Sc.: "Dielectric strength of air, and suspension type insulators." (Applied Electricity: Mackay, H. & Durley, R. & Herdt, L.)

12-515 **Murray**, George E. (*McGill*) M.Sc.: "(a) The treatment of the ore from the Sullivan Mine, Kimberley, B.C. and (b) An investigation on the efficiency of the tube mill." (Mining Engineering: Porter, J. & Durley, R.)

12-516 **Nicolls**, Jasper H. (*McGill*) M.Sc.: "The hydrates of nickel sulphate." (Chemistry: **)

12-517 **Paterson-Smyth**, Marjorie E. (*McGill*) M.Sc.: "On the effect of rotating magnetic matter in a magnetic field." (Physics: Barnes, H. & Harkness, J. & Wilson, H.)

12-518 **Stansfield**, John (*Cambridge*, England) M.Sc.: "Contributions to the knowledge of the Monteregian petrographical province." (Geological Sciences: Adams, F.)

## ANNUAL LISTING

### Ph.D. 1913

13-001 **Krieble**, Vernon K. (*Brown*) Ph.D.: "Amygdalins and their inter-reactions with emulsin." (Chemistry: Walker, J.)

### M.A. 1913

13-501 **Brown**, Vera L. (*McGill*) M.A.: "The history of the Hay-Pauncefote treaty." (History: Fryer, C. & Walton, F.)

13-502 **Dewey**, Alexander G. (*McGill*) M.A.: "The first fifteen years of British administration in Montreal, 1760 to 1775." (History, **)

13-503 **Ellison**, Myra K. (*McGill*) M.A.: "The Asiatic immigration question in British Columbia." (Economics & Political Science: Leacock, S. & Walter, H. & Fryer, C.)

13-504 **Going**, Margaret C. ( ) M.A.: "Prisons and prison reform, with special reference to the United States." (Sociology: **)

13-505 **Grimes**, Evie M. (*McGill*) M.A.: "L'element lyrique dans les drames de Victor Hugo." (French: Walter, H. & Harkness, J. & Du Roure, R.)

13-506 **Irving**, William G. (*McGill*) M.A.: "Literary forgeries of the eighteenth century." (English: Lafleur, P. & Moyse, C. & Macmillan, C.)

13-507 **McBain**, Alexander R. (*Dalhousie*) M.A.: "Historical truth of English chronicle history plays." (English: Macmillan, C. & Moyse, C. & Walter, H.)

13-508 **Robinson**, Bernard S. ( ) M.A.: "The philosophy of religion as represented in Augustine." (Divinity: **)

13-509 **Schafheitlin**, Anna (*McGill*) M.A.: "Die deutsche Dorfgeschichte in ihren Haupttypen dargestellt." (German: Walter, H. & Harkness, J.)

13-510 **Stalker**, Archibald (*McGill*) M.A.: "The taxation of land values in Western Canada." (Economics & Political Science: Hemmeon, J. & Walton, F.)

13-511 **Steacy**, Frederick W. (*McGill*) M.A.: "St. Paul's philosophy of religion." (Classics: MacNaughton, J. & Fryer, C. & Harkness, J.)

13-512 **Thomson**, Herbert F. (*McGill*) M.A.: "Canada's relations with China." (History: Fryer, C. & Walton, F.)

## ANNUAL LISTING

M.Sc. 1913

13-513 **Billington**, Edward E. (*Liverpool*, England) M.Sc.: "The weathering of coal and lignite." (Mining Engineering: Porter, J. & Mackay, H.)

13-514 **Cooper**, Corin H. ( ) M.Sc.: "The work done by tube-mills in the wet reduction of ores." (Ore Dressing: Bell, J.)

13-515 **Cumming**, Charles L. (*Oxford*, England) M.Sc.: "Artesian wells of the Island of Montreal." (Chemistry: **)

13-516 **Dufresne**, Joseph A. (*Laval*) M.Sc.: "Geology of an area in the vicinity of Gull and Olga Lakes, northwestern Quebec." (Geological Sciences: Bancroft, J.)

13-517 **Kirkpatrick**, Robert (*Clark*) M.Sc.: "The action of nitric acid upon certain derivatives of gallic acid hi-methyl ether." (Chemistry: Ruttan, R. & Barnes, H.)

13-518 **Lamb**, Henry M. ( ) M.Sc.: "An experimental investigation of the secondary stresses in a fourteen foot Warren truss." (Engineering: **)

13-519 **Porter**, Cecil G. (*McGill*) M.Sc.: "The direct production of steel from iron ore by the Evans-Stansfield process." (Metallurgical Engineering: Durley, R. & Stansfield, A.)

13-520 **Scott**, Arthur A. (*McGill*) M.Sc.: "Electrical and magnetic properties of pure iron wire." (Physics: Barnes, H. & Herdt, L.)

## ANNUAL LISTING

### M.A. 1914

14-501 **Braeuer**, Mary A. ( ) M.A.: "Spencer and romanticism." (English: **)

14-502 **Common**, Frank B. ( ) M.A.: "The organization of Canadian labour and its relation to the labour movement of the United States." (Economics & Political Science: **)

14-503 **Dewey**, George F. ( ) M.A.: "English religious memoirs of the seventeenth and eighteenth centuries." (English: **)

14-504 **Hughes**, Frederick G. (*McGill*) M.A.: "Regulation of the English stage from the Restoration to the Licencing Act, 1737." (English: Macmillan, C. & Moyse, C. & Lafleur, P.)

14-505 **Lindsay**, William (*McGill*) M.A.: "Alliteration and assonance in Plautus." (Latin: MacNaughton, J. & Rose, * & Harkness, J.)

14-506 **McVittie**, Thomas J. (*McGill*) M.A.: "The relationships comprised by the Hebrew terms for Brother and Sister in the Old Testament." (Semitics: Brockwell, B. & Gordon, A. & Walter, H.)

14-507 **Powles**, Percival S. (*McGill*) M.A.: "The value of Bergson's intuitive method." (Philosophy: Caldwell, W. & Hickson, J. & Perdriau, M.)

### M.Sc. 1914

14-508 **Baily**, Philip P. (*McGill*) M.Sc.: "An investigation of certain chemical and physical phenomena affecting the solvent action of cyanide solutions upon gold and silver or upon their ores." (Ore Dressing: **)

14-509 **Cameron**, Alan E. (*McGill*) M.Sc.: "The slow combustion of coal." (Mining Engineering: Porter, J.)

14-510 **Davidson**, William A. ( ) M.Sc.: "The methods of laying out the underground workings and the haulage systems in the Crow's Nest district." (Mining Engineering: **)

14-511 **Duff**, Dorothy (*McGill*) M.Sc.: "Organization of a trematode." (Zoology: Willey, A. & Lloyd, F. & Macmillan, C.)

14-512 **DuPorte**, Ernest M. (*McGill*) M.Sc.: "Anatomy of *Gryllus pennsylvanicus* Burm." (Biology: Lockhead, W. & Willey, A. & Adams, F.)

14-513 **Hague**, Owen C. (*McGill*) M.Sc.: "Some notes on the measurement of conductivity in dielectrics." (Physics: Herdt, L. & Barnes, H.)

14-514 **Mitchell**, William G. (*McGill*) M.Sc.: "The mechanics of rock crushing. An instrumental investigation of disturbances produced by blasting and of vibrations due to street traffic." (Rock Crushing: Durley, R. & Porter, J.)

14-515 **Reilly,** Herschell E. (*McGill*) M.Sc.: "Some physical constants of ferry resistance wire, together with some measurements of the contact resistance of other metals and alloys." (Physics: Barnes, H. & McIntosh,D.)

14-516 **Ryan,** Charles C. (*McGill*) M.Sc.: "Internal cooling applied to a 12 h.p. gas engine." (Thermodynamics: McKergow, C. & Durley, R.)

14-517 **Scott,** Arthur P. ( ) M.Sc.: "On the open hearth process of steel manufacture: an investigation of the relative methods of an interrupted as distinguished from a continuous process." (Mining Engineering: **)

14-518 **Scott,** Joseph M. (*Queen's*) M.Sc.: "The ash constituents and organic acids of maple sugar." (Agricultural Chemistry: Snell, J. & Adams, F.)

14-519 **Shanly,** Eleanor (*McGill*) M.Sc.: "On the heat resistance of bacterial spores, with a consideration of the nature of the sporelike bodies seen in B. tuberculosis and allied forms." (Bacteriology: Adami, J. & Willey, A. & Harkness, J.)

## ANNUAL LISTING

### M.A. 1915

15-501 **Corbett**, Percy E. ( ) M.A.: " " (**: **)

15-502 **Forster**, David S. (*McGill*) M.A.: "Les principes de Molière sur l'éducation des femmes." (French: Morin, P. & Hurlblatt, * & Walter, H.)

15-503 **Honey**, Howard P. (*McGill*) M.A.: "The significance of a law of nature in modern science." (Philosophy: Caldwell, W. & Hickson, J. & Harkness, J.)

15-504 **MacSween**, Florence R. (*McGill*) M.A.: "L'orient musulman dans la littérature française au XVIIIe et XIXe siècles." (French: Morin, P. & Harkness, J.)

15-505 **Shearing**, Helen A. (*McGill*) M.A.: "The Montessori principles." (Education: Dale, J. & Tait, W. & Walter, H.)

15-506 **Sutherland**, Francis C. (*McGill*) M.A.: "The church school in the modern state: its province and problems." (Education: Dale, J. & Tait, W. & Macmillan, C.)

### M.Sc. 1915

15-507 **Cockfield**, William E. ( ) M.Sc.: "An investigation of the performance of certain rock crushing machines, with a view to finding a method for calculating their efficiency." (Mining Engineering: Porter, J.)

15-508 **James**, Clarke B. (*McGill*) M.Sc.: "A determination of the coefficient of expansion of mercury at low temperatures." (Physics: Barnes, H. & McIntosh, D.)

15-509 **Knight**, Frederic C. (*Dalhousie*) M.Sc.: "Report on the sewage disposal problem in Montreal." (Sanitary Engineering: **)

15-510 **Lathe**, Frank E. (*McGill*) M.Sc.: "Metal losses in copper slags." (Metallurgical Engineering: Stansfield, A. & Porter, J. & Adams, F.)

15-511 **Miller**, Iveson A. (*McGill*) M.Sc.: "The elementary theory of sets of points, with an introductory essay on irrational numbers." (Mathematics: Harkness, J. & Murray, *)

15-512 **Murphy**, William H. (*McGill*) M.Sc.: "The production of damped electric waves." (Electrical Engineering: Herdt, L. & Barnes, H.)

15-513 **Reid**, Hugh S. (*McGill*) M.Sc.: "Molecular weight determinations at low temperatures." (Chemistry: McIntosh, D. & Ruttan, R. & Barnes, H.)

15-514 **Spencer**, Roy A. (*McGill*) M.Sc.: "An investigation of the strength functions of Nova Scotia mine timbers." (Engineering: Mackay, H. & Porter, J. & Bates, *)

15-515 **Traversy**, Eric E. (*McGill*) M.Sc.: "Effect of small variations in the proportion of cement upon the strength of some standard mixtures of concrete." (Engineering: Mackay, H. & Brown, E.)

## ANNUAL LISTING

### Ph.D. 1916

16-001 **MacLean**, Allison R. (*McGill*) Ph.D.: "A colorimetric method for the estimation of amino acid alpha-nitrogen." (Chemistry: Ruttan, R. & Harding, V. & Barnes, H.)

### M.A. 1916

16-501 **Corbett**, Edward A. ( ) M.A.: "Some ethical aspects of modern charity problems." (Philosophy: Caldwell, W.)

16-502 **Goldstein**, Hildred M. ( ) M.A.: "Die patriotische Poesie der Deutschen im neunzehnten Jahrhundert." (German: **)

16-503 **Livinson**, Abraham J. (*McGill*) M.A.: "The pedagogical value and psychical influence of the motion picture on present day educational systems." (Education: Dale, J. & Hickson, J. & Mackay, H.)

16-504 **McCormack**, George J. (*McGill*) M.A.: "Some recent ethical tendencies." (Philosophy: Caldwell, W. & Hickson, J. & Lee, *)

16-505 **MacKenzie**, Francis S. (*McGill*) M.A.: "The virgin birth of Christ." (Classics: MacNaughton, J. & Fraser, * & Harkness, J.)

16-506 **Withey**, Albert N. (*McGill*) M.A.: "The invasion of Sennacherib." (Semitic Studies: Brockwell, B. & Gordon, A. & Adams, F.)

### M.Sc. 1916

16-507 **Cronk**, Francis J. (*McGill*) M.Sc.: "Concrete columns plain and reinforced." (Civil Engineering : Mackay, H. & Brown, E.)

16-508 **Dowler**, Vernon B. (*Toronto*) M.Sc.: "The partition of the blood supply in the liver." (Physiology: Mottram, * & Harding, V. & Mackay, H.)

16-509 **Fort**, Charles A. (*Middlebury*) M.Sc.: "Hydrolysis of certain proteins." (Chemistry: **)

16-510 **Gray**, Alexander M. (*Edinburgh*, Scotland) M.Sc.: "Heating and ventilation of electrical machinery." (Electrical Engineering: Adams, F. & Barnes, H. & Harkness, J.)

16-511 **Henry**, Elizabeth V. (*McGill*) M.Sc.: "Contact resistances of metals and alloys in oils and other media." (Physics: Barnes, H. & Skirron, *)

16-512 **Marshall**, Melville J. (*McGill*) M.Sc.: "Chemistry of adipocere." (Chemistry: Ruttan, R. & Barnes, H.)

16-513 **Moran**, James (*McGill*) M.Sc.: "Experiments in radioactivity." (Physics: Barnes, H. & Eve, A.)

16-514 **Van Barneveld**, Charles, E. ( ) M.Sc.: "Iron mining in Minnesota." (Mining Engineering: **)

16-515 **Wu**, Chow C. ( ) M.Sc.: "Geology and some of the mineral resources of China." (Geological Sciences: **)

## ANNUAL LISTING

### M.A. 1917

17-501 **Pelletier**, Annie H. (*McGill*) M.A.: "The relation between the home-maker and the state." (Education: Dale, J. & Colby, C.)

17-502 **Willis**, Helen A. (*McGill*) M.A.: "Piers Plowman as an interpretation of fourteenth century life, thought, and literature." (English: Moyse, C. & Lee, *)

17-503 **Worsfold**, Henry H. (*Cambridge*, England) M.A.: "The relation of school and university to life." (Education: Dale, J. & Harkness, J.)

### M.Sc. 1917

17-504 **Cromarty**, Robert P. (*Toronto*) M.Sc.: "On the influence of external secretions on the electrocardiogram." (Physiology: Barnes, H. & Downs, A.)

17-505 **Geldard**, Walter J. (*Clark*) M.Sc.: "The absorption of ammonia by alumina." (Chemistry: Barnes, H. & Ruttan, R.)

17-506 **Hatcher**, William H. (*McGill*) M.Sc.: "Studies in the compounds of phenol and pyridine." (Chemistry: Barnes, H. & Ruttan, R.)

17-507 **Sadler**, Wilfrid (*McGill*) M.Sc.: "Studies in marine bacteriology. (1) Bacterial destruction of Cofepods. (2) Bacteriology of swelled canned fish." (Bacteriology: Harrison, F. & Willey, A. & Barnes, H.)

D.C.L. 1918

18-001 **Mitchell**, Victor E. (*McGill*) D.C.L.: "Canadian commericial corporations." (Law: MacDougall, G.)

M.A. 1918

18-501 **Blackader**, Alexander D. ( ) M.A.: "Published works." (Medicine: **)

18-502 **Steed**, Joseph A. (*McGill*) M.A.: "The problem of moral education." (Education: Dale, J. & Caldwell, W. & Harkness, J.)

M.Sc. 1918

18-503 **Fritz**, Clara W. (*McGill*) M.Sc.: "Plankton diatoms in the vicinity of St Andrew's, N.B." (Botany: Lloyd, F. & Adams, F.)

18-504 **Howe**, Laura I. (*McGill*) M.Sc.: "Bog butter. Stearic and palmitic esters of propylene and glycol." (Chemistry: Harding, V.)

18-505 **Herzberg**, Otto W. (*McGill*) M.Sc.: "Study of the preparation and properties of hydrogen peroxide and its aqueous solution." (Chemistry: Mackay, H. & King, L. & Ruttan, R.)

18-506 **Russell**, John (*British Columbia*) M.Sc.: "(1) The effect of unsaturation on the formation of molecular compounds. (2) A method for the determination of the densities of gases." (Chemistry: Ruttan, R. & King, L. & Mackay, H.)

18-507 **Whitby**, George S. (*London*, England) M.Sc.: "The synthesis of mixed triglycerides of palmitic and stearic acids. Observations on the silver salts of the higher fatty acids." (Chemistry: Adams, F. & Harding, V. & Ruttan, R.)

18-508 **Wieland**, Walter A. (*McGill*) M.Sc.: "The properties of oxynitulase." (Chemistry: Ruttan, R. & Harding, V. & Adams, F.)

## ANNUAL LISTING

### Ph.D. 1919

19-001 **Lockhead**, Allan G. (*McGill*) Ph.D.: "Die Zersetzung der Cellulose durch Bakterien." (Agricultural Chemistry: Walter, H. & Mackay, H.)

### M.A. 1919

19-501 **Melvin**, Margaret G. (*McGill*) M.A.: "The ideal of courage in Plato." (Philosophy: Caldwell, W. & Hickson, J. & Harkness, J.)

### M.Sc. 1919

19-502 **Jull**, Morley A. (*Ontario Agricultural*) M.Sc.: "Studies in artifical incubation." (Physiology: Willey, A. & Mackay, H. & Lockhead, W.)

19-503 **Newton**, Margaret (*McGill*) M.Sc.: "The resistance of wheat varieties to *Puccinia graminis*." (Plant Pathology: Mackay, H. & Lockhead, W.)

## ANNUAL LISTING

### Ph.D. 1920

20-001 **Seyer**, William F. (*Alberta*) Ph.D.: "A chemical investigation of the asphalt in the tar sands of northern Alberta." (Chemistry: Ruttan, R. & Krieble, V.)

20-002 **Walker**, Osman J. (*Saskatchewan*) Ph.D.: "Investigation of natural and oxidised resins from herea rubber." (Chemistry: Ruttan, R. & Lloyd, F.)

20-003 **Whitby**, George S. (*London*, England) Ph.D.: "Contributions to the knowledge of the fats and fatty acids." (Chemistry: Ruttan, R. & Harding, V.)

### LL.M. 1920

20-500 **Rose**, Harold E. (*McGill*) LL.M.: "Acts of civil status in the province of Quebec." (Law: Lee, * & Lightboll, W.)

### M.Sc. 1920

20-501 **Anderson**, Clayton E. (*McGill*) M.Sc.: "The effect of changes in the design and adjustments of concentrating tables of the Wilfley type and the relation of such changes to the character and efficiency of operation." (Mining Engineering: Porter, J. & Bell, J.)

20-502 **Anderson**, Marian ( ) M.Sc.: "On the relative rate of dextrose fermentation of generations of colon bacteria grown on sugar-free media." (Bacteriology: **)

20-503 **Bierler**, Etienne S. (*McGill*) M.Sc.: "The capacity of high voltage porcelain suspension insulators." (Electrical Engineering: King, L. & Herdt, L.)

20-504 **Emmons**, William F. (*British Columbia*) M.Sc.: "Further immersion experiments and observations on some of the terrestrial *Crustaceae*." (Chemistry: Mackay, H. & Tait, J.)

20-505 **Jamieson**, Robert E. (*McGill*) M.Sc.: "Some considerations on the strength of built-up compression members." (Civil Engineering & Applied Mechanics: Mackay, H. & Brown, E. & Batho, C.)

20-506 **McKinney**, James W. (*Alberta*) M.Sc.: "An investigation of the kerogen in oil shells." (Chemistry: Krieble, V. & Ruttan, R. & Mackay, H.)

20-507 **Tousaw**, Albert A. ( ) M.Sc.: "The effect of changes in the design and adjustments of concentrating tables of Wilfey type, and the relation of such changes to the character and efficiency of operation." (Mining Engineering: Porter, J. & Bell, J.)

20-508 **Trimingham**, James H. (*McGill*) M.Sc.: "Electrical devices used in the anti-submarine campaign." (Electrical Engineering: Herdt, L. & Eve, A.)

20-509 **Weldon**, Richard L. (*McGill*) M.Sc.: "Internal cooling applied to an internal combustion engine." (Mechanical Engineering: Roberts, A. & Mackay, H.)

## ANNUAL LISTING

### M.A. 1920

20-510 **Blampin**, Caroline (*Bishop's*) M.A.: "Cicero's moral philosophy." (Latin: Slack, S. & MacLean, R.)

20-511 **Macdonald**, Isabella L. (*McGill*) M.A.: "The status of women in the province of Quebec." (Economics: Leacock, S. & Lee, *)

20-512 **Price**, Enid (*McGill*) M.A.: "Changes in the industrial occupations of women in the environment of Montreal during the period of the war, 1914-1918." (History: Leacock, S. & Lee, *)

## ANNUAL LISTING

Ph.D. 1921

21-001 **DuPorte**, Ernest M. (*McGill*) Ph.D.: "On the muscular system of *Gryllus assimilis* Fab. (*Pennsylvanicus* Burm)." (Invertebrate Morphology: Willey, A. & Macallum, A.)

21-002 **Hatcher**, William H. (*McGill*) Ph.D.: "The preparation and properties of pure anhydrons, and of pure concentrated solutions of hydrogen peroxide." (Chemistry: Ruttan, R. & Maass, O.)

21-003 **Wright**, Charles A. (*British Columbia*) Ph.D.: "Physical and chemical properties of the elementary hydrocarbons." (Chemistry: Maass, O. & Eve, A.)

M.Sc. 1921

21-501 **Boomer**, Edward H. ( ) M.Sc.: "An investigation of preparation and properties of ethylene oxide." (Chemistry: Ruttan, R. & Maass, O.)

21-502 **Dolid**, Jacob (*Yale*) M.Sc.: "Preliminary examination of the resins of herea rubber." (Organic Chemistry: Ruttan, R. & Whitby, G.)

21-503 **Douglas**, Allie V. (*McGill*) M.Sc.: "The beta-rays from radium E." (Physics: Eve, A. & King, L.)

21-504 **Douglas**, George V. (*McGill*) M.Sc.: "An investigation of a ball mill." (Ore Dressing: Mackay, H. & Porter, J.)

21-505 **Dowling**, Donaldson B. (*McGill*) M.Sc.: "33 papers and reports." (Geological Sciences: Mackay, H. & Kemp, J.)

21-506 **Edwards**, Gordon M. (*McGill*) M.Sc.: "Oil flotation: a study of the differential flotation of copper, iron, zinc and lead sulphides." (Ore Dressing: Porter, J.)

21-507 **Erlenborn**, Willi (*McGill*) M.Sc.: "Oil flotation." (Ore Dressing: Porter, J.)

21-508 **Harding**, Ellis G. (*South Africa*) M.Sc.: "An investigation of the mechanical efficiencies of rock crushing machines." (Mining Engineering: Porter, J. & Mackay, H.)

21-509 **Hill**, Eleanor M. (*McGill*) M.Sc.: "Autohydrolysis of fats." (Chemistry: Ruttan, R. & Simpson, G.)

21-510 **James**, William F. (*St. Francis Xavier*) M.Sc.: "The alteration of a quartz diabase dike at the Old Helen Mine." (Geology & Mineralogy: Adams, F. & Bancroft, J.)

21-511 **Kennedy**, Margaret E. (*Toronto*) M.Sc.: "The red colouration of dried codfish." (Bacteriology: Harrison, F.)

21-512 **McFarlane**, Nathaniel C. (*New Brunswick*) M.Sc.:"The estimation of malic acid." (Agricultural Chemistry: Johnson, F. & Ruttan, R.)

21-513 **Moe**, George G. (*McGill*) M.Sc.: "A study in Marquis wheat: a measure of its variability." (Botany: Lloyd, F.)

21-514 **Saunders**, Leslie G. (*McGill*) M.Sc.: "The anatomy of *Psyllia anali* Schneidberger." (Entomology: Willey, A. & Ruttan, R.)

21-515 **Smith**, Letha A. (*McGill*) M.Sc.: "1. A method of measuring the intensity of sound under water by means of the Rayleigh disc. 2. A problem in heat transmission." (Physics: Eve, A. & King, L.)

21-516 **Symons**, Jennie L. (*McGill*) M.Sc.: "Organisms which cause blackening in clams." (Bacteriology: Lloyd, F. & Adams, F.)

21-517 **Wallace**, George A. (*McGill*) M.Sc.: "Ratio and phase angle in current transformers." (Electrical Engineering: Herdt, L. & Eve, A.)

21-518 **Williams**, Frederick H. (*McGill*) M.Sc.: "The electric welding of iron and steel." (Metallurgical Engineering: Stansfield, A. & Eve, A. & Herdt, L.)

M.A. 1921

21-519 **Jones**, Thomas W. (*McGill*) M.A.: "Education and industry: their co-relation and development." (Education: Dale, J.)

21-520 **McBain**, Mary N. (*Cornell*) M.A.: "The myths and legends of the heroic cycle, and their use in Anglo-Irish literature." (English: Moyse, C. & Smith, H. & Macmillan, C.)

21-521 **Meyer**, Bertha (*McGill*) M.A.: "Theodor Fontane als Romanschriftsteller." (German: Walter, H. & Harkness, J.)

21-522 **Newnham**, May L. (*McGill*) M.A.: "Le sens historique et la couleur locale dans le drame romantique." (French: Walter, H. & Du Roure, R.)

21-523 **Nichol**, Helen R. (*McGill*) M.A.: "Investigation of labour conditions of children and young persons in Montreal." (Economics & Political Science: Mackay, I. & Hemmeon, J.)

21-524 **Noad**, Algy S. (*McGill*) M.A.: "Imaginary voyages in English literature: an essay in bibliography." (English: Walter, H. & Lomer, G.)

## ANNUAL LISTING

### Ph.D. 1922

22-001 **Dickson**, Bertram T. (*Queen's*) Ph.D.: "Studies concerning mosaic diseases." (Botany: Lloyd, F. & Harrison, F.)

22-002 **Von Abo**, Cecil V. (*Cape of Good Hope*, South Africa) Ph.D.: "A study of certain methods of computing secondary stresses in framed structures, with their adaptation to actual conditions of loading." (Engineering: Mackay, H. & Jacoby, H.)

### LL.M. 1922

22-500 **Renaud**, Paul E. (*Laval*) LL.M.: "De la personnalité: esquisse d'une théorie d'ensemble." (Law: Mackay, I. & Caldwell, W. & Howard, *)

### M.Sc. 1922

22-501 **Brow**, James B. (*McGill*) M.Sc.: "Investigation of the work of laboratory machines crushing Champion mine ore, and a comparison of their efficiency with the efficiency of the more inportant crushing machines in the Champion Mill." (Ore Dressing: Porter, J. & Eve, A.)

22-502 **Dewar**, Charles L. (*McGill*) M.Sc.: "Flotation of low grade copper nickel ores." (Ore Dressing: Eve, A. & Porter, J.)

22-503 **Dodd**, Geoffrey J. (*McGill*) M.Sc.: "The water factor in concrete." (Engineering: Brown, E. & Mackay, H.)

22-504 **Dustan**, Alan G. (*Toronto*) M.Sc.: "Studies on a new species of *Empusa*." (Botany: Harrison, F. & Haxter, R.)

22-505 **Eadie**, Robert S. (*McGill*) M.Sc.: "A study of the resistances developed in rivetted joints by friction and by rivet bearing." (Civil Engineering & Applied Mechanics: Mackay, H. & Batho, C.)

22-506 **Foran**, Herbert P. (*McGill*) M.Sc.: "The preparation and pharmacological behaviour of new salicyl derivatives." (Pharmacology: Tait, J. & Macallum, A. & Bonbour, H.)

22-507 **Gliddon**, William G. (*McGill*) M.Sc.: "(a) Aeroplane design. (b) The friction of sleigh runners on snow." (Aerodynamics & Engineering: Batho, C. & McKergow, C.)

22-508 **Godwin**, Kathleen F. (*McGill*) M.Sc.: "A preliminary report upon the organisms causing the deterioration of groundwood pulp with a view to ascertaining methods of control." (Plant Pathology: Lloyd, F. & Derick, C.)

22-509 **Greaves**, Clifford (*McGill*) M.Sc.: "Beryllium." (Chemistry: Ruttan, R. & Johnson, F.)

22-510 **Harrison**, Donald R. (*McGill*) M.Sc.: "The reduction of iron ores by solid and gaseous reducing reagents at temperatures below that of fusion." (Metallurgical Engineering: Evans, N. & Stansfield. A.)

## ANNUAL LISTING

22-511 **Hiebert**, Paul G. (*Manitoba*) M.Sc.: "Properties of pure hydrogen peroxide." (Chemistry: Ruttan, R. & Maass, O.)

22-512 **Howard**, Waldorf V. (*McGill*) M.Sc.: "Some outlines of the Monteregian hills." (Geological Sciences: Adams, F. & Cooke, H.)

22-513 **Macallum**, Alexander D. (*Toronto*) M.Sc.: "Ortho-substituted aromatic antimony compounds." (Chemistry: Whitby, G. & Ruttan, R.)

22-514 **Macdonald**, Albert E. (*Nova Scotia Technical*) M.Sc.: "The distribution of stress in a rivetted plate joint of variable section." (Civil Engineering & Applied Mechanics: Mackay, H. & Batho, C.)

22-515 **McGlaughlin**, William R. (*McGill*) M.Sc.: "Triglycerides and other fatty derivatives." (Chemistry: Ruttan, R. & Whitby, G.)

22-516 **Major**, Thomas G. (*McGill*) M.Sc.: "Cultural reactions of some dry root-rot organisms." (Botany: **)

22-517 **Morrison**, Donald M. (*British Columbia*) M.Sc.: "Tendency towards molecular compound formation of aromatic hydrocarbons with hydrobromic acid." (Chemistry: Ruttan, R.)

22-518 **Newton**, Dorothy E. (*McGill*) M.Sc.: "Marine spore forming bacteria." (Bacteriology: Dickson, B. & Harrison, F.)

22-519 **Richardson**, James K. (*McGill*) M.Sc.: "A study of bacterial soft rot of iris." (Botany: Dickson, B.)

22-520 **Saul**, Bernard B. (*Columbia*) M.Sc.: "Purification of coal gas with spent 'pickle liquor'." (Chemistry: Ruttan, R. & Evans, N.)

22-521 **Saunders**, James E. (*McGill*) M.Sc.: "An investigation of the principles and processes involved in differential flotation of copper nickel iron sulphide ores, and especially a comparison of sub aeration or 'Callow' methods as developed in the laboratory with standard type of intermittent mechanical agitators." (Ore Dressing: Eve, A. & Porter, J.)

22-522 **Shaw**, Thomas P. (*McGill*) M.Sc.: "The monobromstearic acid from oleic acid and the corresponding monohydroxystearic acids." (Chemistry: Ruttan, R. & Whitby, G.)

22-523 **Spier**, Jane D. (*McGill*) M.Sc.: "A preliminary report upon the organisms causing the deterioration of chemical pulps, with a view to ascertaining methods of control." (Plant Pathology: **)

22-524 **Vessot**, Charles U. (*McGill*) M.Sc.: "A solution for fibre flax manufacture in Canada." (Industrial Engineering: McKergow, C. & Adams, F.)

22-525 **Waldbauer**, Louis J. (*Cornell*) M.Sc.: "An investigation of the specific and latent heats of fusion at low temperatures." (Chemistry: Ruttan, R.)

M.A. 1922

22-526 **Davidson**, Winnifred H. (*McGill*) M.A.: "Wages and prices in the province of Quebec, with special reference to women workers." (Economics & Political Science: Caldwell, W. & Leacock, S. & Williams, B.)

22-527 **Harbert**, Eleanor (*Toronto*) M.A.: "Scottish sources of British liberalism." (History: Williams, B. & Macmillan, L.)

22-528 **Tidmarsh**, Clarence J. (*McGill*) M.A.: "Experiments on the contraction of white connective tissue fibres." (Physiology: Tait, J. & Macallum, A.)

22-529 **Troop**, George R. (*Toronto*) M.A.: "Socialism in Canada." (Economics: Hemmeon, J. & Mackay, I.)

## ANNUAL LISTING

Ph.D. 1923

23-001 **Boomer**, Edward H. (*McGill*) Ph.D.: "Vapour densities, molecular compound formation and the physical properties of certain organic compounds and their correlation in terms of molecular forces." (Chemistry: Maass, O. & Shaw, A.)

23-002 **Dolid**, Jacob (*Yale*) Ph.D.: "Contributions to the knowledge of the non-caoutchouc constituents of rubber. The resins of herea brasilensis." (Organic Chemistry: Whitby, G. & Macallum, A.)

23-003 **Greaves**, Clifford (*McGill*) Ph.D.: "Beryllium." (Chemistry: Stansfield, A. & Johnson, F.)

23-004 **Logan**, John F. (*Acadia*) Ph.D.: "The protein matter of bile." (Chemistry: Ruttan, R. & Macallum, A.)

23-005 **McKinney**, James W. (*Alberta*) Ph.D.: "The kerogen in pyrobituminous shale." (Chemistry: Ruttan, R. & Porter, J.)

23-006 **Stephens**, Henry N. (*McMaster*) Ph.D.: "Observations relative to the constitution of caoutchouc." (Chemistry: Maass, O. & Eve, A.)

23-007 **Waldbauer**, Louis J. (*Cornell*) Ph.D.: "An investigation of the specific heats and latent heats of fusion at low temperatures." (Chemistry: Maass, O. & Gray, J.)

LL.M. 1923

23-500 **Weibel**, Louise E. (*McGill*) LL.M.: "Jurisdiction in matrimonial causes in the Dominion of Canada." (Law: Greenshields, * & Wainwright, A.)

M.Sc. 1923

23-501 **Anderson**, Robert G. (*British Columbia*) M.Sc.: "Continuous differential flotation of the copper, nickel, iron, sulphide ores of the Sudbury district." (Ore Dressing: Porter, J. & Eve, A.)

23-502 **Armour**, John C. (*McGill*) M.Sc.: "Absorption of Chinese ink and of tubercle bacilli by the omentum." (Physiology: Oertel, H. & Bartown, H.)

23-503 **Bain**, George W. (*McGill*) M.Sc.: "The genesis of the deposits of dolomite and magnesite in Grenville and Olatham Townships, P.Q." (Geological Sciences: Adams, F.)

23-504 **Bickell**, William A. (*British Columbia*) M.Sc.: "Friction of a lubricated journal bearing." (Machine Design: Roberts, A. & McKergow, C. & Mackay, H.)

23-505 **Bissell**, Harold R. (*McGill*) M.Sc.: "The differential flotation of lead, zinc, iron, sulphide ores, employing sub-aeration, i.e. Callow methods, and a comparison of the above with methods based on intermittant mechanical agitation." (Geological Sciences: Eve, A. & Porter, J.)

23-506 **Cambron**, Adrien (*Laval*) M.Sc.: "The preparation of some organic sulphur compounds, and a study of their influence on vulcanization." (Chemistry: Whitby, G. & Barbour, H.)

23-507 **Carleton**, Everett A. (*Rhode Island State*) M.Sc.: "Soil acidity and lime requirement studies of Quebec soils." (Chemistry: Snell, J. & Harrison, F.)

23-508 **Carlyle**, Arthur W. (*McGill*) M.Sc.: "A study of the dyke rocks in Mount Royal Tunnel between Stations 260+00 and 283+00." (Geology & Mineralogy: Graham, R. & Evans, N.)

23-509 **Davies**, Vernon R. (*McGill*) M.Sc.: "Recent advances in hydraulic power development." (Hydraulics & Hydrodynamics: Brown, E.)

23-510 **Derick**, Russell A. (*McGill*) M.Sc.: "A study of the genotypic composition of a natural hybrid between *Avena sativa* and *Avena nuda*." (Genetics: Derick, C. & Macallum, A.)

23-511 **Dolan**, Everett P. (*St. Francis Xavier*) M.Sc.: "Metamorphic zone of Mount Royal." (Geology & Mineralogy: Bancroft, J. & Graham, R.)

23-512 **Humes**, Harold L. (*McGill*) M.Sc.: "The reduction of iron ores by solid and gaseous reducing reagents at temperatures below that of fusion." (Metallurgical Engineering: Stansfield, A. & Maass, O.)

23-513 **Jane**, Robert S. (*British Columbia*) M.Sc.: "Observations on the reaction product between caoutchone and sulphur." (Chemistry: Whitby, G. & Barbour, H.)

23-514 **Larose**, Paul (*McGill*) M.Sc.: "The diffusion of gases through metals." (Chemistry: Johnson, F. & Stansfield, A.)

23-515 **Lozinsky**, Ezra (*McGill*) M.Sc.: "The effects of dry and moist heat upon the body temperature and blood concentration of dogs." (Pharmacology: Barbour, H. & Simpson, G.)

23-516 **McClelland**, William R. (*McGill*) M.Sc.: "A study of the production of iron by electrolysis with special reference to its recovery from sulphide ores." (Metallurgy: Stansfield A. & Maass, O.)

23-517 **McPherson**, Anna I. (*McGill*) M.Sc.: "Radiotherapeutic measurements." (Physics: Eve, A. & Maass, O.)

23-518 **Thomson**, Walter W. (*McGill*) M.Sc.: "Some derivatives of the diquinolines." (Chemistry: Ruttan, R.)

23-519 **Weldon**, Thomas H. (*McGill*) M.Sc.: "The differential flotation of a complex head ore by the use of a single-cell, laboratory type apparatus for intermittant mechanical agitation; and a comparison of these results with those obtained with an 8-cell continuous agitation machine." (Ore Dressing: Porter, J. & Eve,A.)

M.A. 1923

23-520 **Birkett**, Winifred L. (*McGill*) M.A.: "The element of magic in west Highland folklore." (English: Latham, G. & Tait, J.)

23-521 **Davis**, Charles F. (*McGill*) M.A.: "Tendencies in English pulpit oratory from Hooker to Tillotson." (English: Lafleur, P. & Brockwell, C.)

23-522 **McGown**, Isabella W. (*McGill*) M.A.: "Imperial Federation Movement with special reference to Canada." (History: Waugh, W. & Leacock, S.)

23-523 **McGreer**, Edgar D. (*McGill*) M.A.: "The satirical aspect of Thackeray's work." (English: Oertel, H. & Lafleur, P.)

23-524 **Moore**, Dale H. (*McGill*) M.A.: "A portrayal of the clergyman in the fiction of Jane Austen, Mrs. Gaskell, the Brontë sisters, and George Eliot." (English: Lafleur, P. & Williams, B.)

23-525 **Pickel**, Margaret B. (*McGill*) M.A.: "Memoirs of the stage." (English: Sandwell, B. & Macmillan, C.)

23-526 **Renaud**, Paul E. (*Laval*) M.A.: "Du travail en la Nouvelle France." (Economics: Hemmeon, J. & Du Roure, R.)

23-527 **Wiseman**, Solomon (*McGill*) M.A.: "The three phases of Nietzsche's philosophy." (Philosophy: Mackay, I. & Hickson, J.)

## ANNUAL LISTING

### Ph.D. Spring 1924

24-001 **Hiebert**, Paul G. (*Manitoba*) Ph.D.: "The physical and chemical properties of pure hydrogen peroxide." (Chemistry: Maass, O.)

24-002 **Howard**, Waldorf V. (*McGill*) Ph.D.: "The Devonian volcanic series in the vicinity of Dalhousie, N.B." (Geological Sciences: Adams, F. & Ruttan, R.)

24-003 **Macallum**, Alexander D. (*Toronto*) Ph.D.: "Work on the chemistry of diolefines." (Chemistry: Stehle, R. & Whitby, G.)

24-004 **Morrison**, Donald M. (*British Columbia*) Ph.D.: "A study of molecular forces by means of the gas laws, molecular compound formation, and velocities of reaction." (Chemistry: Maass, O.)

### M.M.A. Spring 1924

24-500 **O'Neill**, Charles (*McGill*) M.M.A.: "A concert overture in F for orchestra. A choral and orchestral setting of 'The Ancient Mariner'." (Music: Perrin, H. & Macmillan, C. & Sanders, *)

### M.S.A. Spring 1924

24-501 **Bayfield**, Edward G. (*Alberta*) M.S.A.: "The comparative effect of several systems of fertilization on crop production and soil fertility." (Agronomy: Summerby, R. & Snell, J.)

24-502 **Cunningham**, Howe S. (*McGill*) M.S.A.: "Methods of checking and competition in relation to comparative crop tests." (Agronomy: Summerby, R.)

24-503 **Lamb**, Cecil A. (*British Columbia*) M.S.A.: "The effect of liming, manuring, and burning on certain peat soils, as measured by crop growth." (Agronomy: Summerby, R. & Dickson, B.)

24-504 **Parent**, Robert C. (*Toronto*) M.S.A.: "Thickness of planting in corn." (Agronomy: Raymond, L. & Snell, J.)

24-505 **Tinney**, Benjamin F. (*Toronto*) M.S.A.: "Methods of field crop experimentation, with special reference to the duration of the experiments." (Agronomy: Summerby, R. & Dickson, B.)

### M.Sc. Spring 1924

24-506 **Aylard**, Clara M. (*British Columbia*) M.Sc.: "Dykes encountered in Mount Royal tunnel." (Geological Sciences: Evans, N. & O'Neil, J.)

24-507 **Beaudet**, Lionel (*Ste. Anne de la Pocatière*) M.Sc.: "Phosphate deficiency in Quebec soils." (Chemistry: Snell, J. & Summerby, R.)

24-508 **Bishop**, Eric G. (*McGill*) M.Sc.: "The geology of the Outsider Mine, Portland, B.C." (Geological Sciences: Johnson, F. & O'Neil, J.)

24-509 **Bourne**, Wesley (*McGill*) M.Sc.: "The effects of anaesthetics on body temperature and blood solids at various environmental temperatures." (Pharmacology: Stehle, R. & Tait, J.)

24-510 **Buffam**, Basil S. (*McGill*) M.Sc.: "The oldest dykes of Mt. Royal, bostonites, tinguaites, etc., and their altered equivalents." (Geology & Mineralogy: Adams, F. & Evans, N.)

24-511 **Conklin**, Raymond L. (*Cornell*) M.Sc.: "A sporadic outbreak in cattle resembling tetanus." (Bacteriology: Oertel, H. & Harrison, F.)

24-512 **DeLong**, Walter A. (*Toronto*) M.Sc.: "Pentosan content in relation to winter hardiness in commercial varieties of the apple." (Chemistry: Bunting, T. & Snell, J.)

24-513 **Faith**, Willard V. (*McGill*) M.Sc.: "Some physical properties of copper-nickel mattes." (Metallurgical Engineering: Stansfield, A. & Maass, O.)

24-514 **Finley**, Frederick L. (*McGill*) M.Sc.: "The nepheline syenites and pegmatites of Mt. Royal." (Geology & Mineralogy: Graham, R. & Evans, N.)

24-515 **Fleet**, George A. (*McGill*) M.Sc.: "Growth-adhesive affinities of different forms of tissue, with special reference to peritoneal adhesions." (Physiology: Stehle, R. & Tait, J.)

24-516 **Gegg**, Richard C. (*McGill*) M.Sc.: "Sedimentation of finely divided rock material from water suspension, with especial reference to the theory of design of settling tanks and similar apparatus." (Ore Dressing: Porter, J. & Johnson, F.)

24-517 **Gordon**, William L. (*McGill*) M.Sc.: "Studies concerning injury to seed oats after smut disinfection." (Plant Pathology: Dickson, B. & Summerby, R.)

24-518 **Hammond**, George H. (*McGill*) M.Sc.: "The genitalia of Graphtolitha (sub-fam. Cucullianae, Noctudae)." (Entomology: DuPorte, E.)

24-519 **Holden**, George W. (*Bishop's*) M.Sc.: "Hydrogen peroxide as an oxidising agent in acid solution." (Chemistry: Stehle, R. & Hatcher, W.)

24-520 **Hunten**, Kenneth W. (*Bishop's*) M.Sc.: "On the examination of anomalous values of the Ramsey-Shields surface tension constant." (Chemistry: Maass, O. & Macallum, A.)

24-521 **Legg**, Roland E. (*McGill*) M.Sc.: "The applicability of gravity concentration and flotation as accessory to cyanidation in the treatment of a Porcupine ore." (Ore Dressing: Johnson, F. & Porter, J.)

24-522 **McLennan**, Logan S. (*McGill*) M.Sc.: "Net sections in riveted tension members." (Theory of Structures: Roberts, A. & Mackay, H.)

24-523 **Malcolm**, Robert B. (*McGill*) M.Sc.: "Some aspects of the physiology of the spleen." (Physiology: Tait, J. & Macallum, A.)

24-524 **O'Heir**, Hugh B. (*McGill*) M.Sc.: "Dykes of Mount Royal tunnel from the West Portal to Station 284+99." (Geological Sciences: Graham, R.)

24-525 **Patterson**, Arthur L. (*McGill*) M.Sc.: "The transformation of electronic energy (cathode and beta-rays) into electromagnetic radiations." (Physics: Eve, A. & Lynde, C.)

24-526 **Pelletier**, Rene A. (*McGill*) M.Sc.: "Absorption of inclusions of potsdam sandstone by alkalic magma, Mount Royal Heights, Montreal." (Geological Sciences: Adams, F. & Evans, N.)

24-527 **Perry**, Helen M. (*Massachusetts Agricultural*) M.Sc.: "Media for the lactic acid group of microorganisms." (Bacteriology: Harrison, F. & Oertel, H.)

24-528 **Scott**, Gordon A. (*Guelph*) M.Sc.: "Cultural characteristics of certain colletotrichum species." (Plant Pathology: Dickson, B.)

24-529 **Sivertz**, Christian (*British Columbia*) M.Sc.: "Reaction velocities and molecular compound formation." (Chemistry: Maass, O. & Shaw, A.)

24-530 **Smith**, Frederick M. (*McGill*) M.Sc.: "Relation between the chemical constitution of organic liquids and their ability to swell certain organic materials: the swelling of rubber." (Chemistry:Whitby, G. & Eve, A.)

24-531 **Squires**, Henry D. (*New Brunswick*) M.Sc.: "Dyke rocks of Mount Royal tunnel between East Portal and Station 182-90." (Geological Sciences: Bancroft, J.)

24-532 **Steacie**, Edgar W. (*McGill*) M.Sc.: "The viscosity of liquid haolgen." (Chemistry: Johnson, F. & Shaw, A.)

24-533 **Trueman**, James C. (*Manitoba*) M.Sc.: "Investigation of I-beams haunched with concrete with special reference to bond and sheer." (Engineering: Mackay, H. & Roberts, A.)

24-534 **Whittemore**, Carl R. (*McGill*) M.Sc.: "The production of pure titanium oxide." (Metallurgy: Stansfield, A. & Maass, O.)

24-535 **Yorston**, Frederic H. (*McGill*) M.Sc.: "A study of the constitution of hevea resin and serum." (Chemistry: Simpson, G. & Whitby, G.)

**M.A. Spring 1924**

24-536 **Berger**, Julius (*Western*) M.A.: "The education of the Jewish child in the light of Mishnaic and Talmudic law." (Oriental Languages: Brockwell, C. & Smith, H.)

24-537 **Fair**, Louisa M. (*McGill*) M.A.: "The transportation of Canadian wheat from the West to the sea." (Economics & Political Science: Leacock, S. & Viner, J.)

24-538 **Harris**, Richard C. (*McGill*) M.A.: "The plays and prefaces of George Bernard Shaw: a study of Shaw the dramatist and his criticism and interpretation of life." (English: Walter, H. & Macmillan, C.)

24-539 **Jones**, Randolph K. (*McGill*) M.A.: "Certain aspects of the economic development of the Dominion of Canada, with special reference to trade relations with the United Kingdom and the United States, and to the effect of tariff policies and investments on the expansion of British North America." (Economics and Political Science: Hemmeon, J.)

24-540 **Kydd**, Mary W. (*McGill*) M.A.: "Alien races in the Canadian West." (Economics: Leacock, S. & Viner, J.)

24-541 **MacOdrum**, Murdoch M. (*Dalhousie*) M.A.: "Survivals of the English and Scottish popular ballads in Nova Scotia: a study of folk song in Canada." (English: Mackay, I. & Macmillan, C.)

24-542 **Mathewson**, Dorothy R. (*McGill*) M.A.: "French-Canadian folk songs." (English: Macmillan, C. & Du Roure, R.)

24-543 **Peterson**, Frederick O. (*McGill*) M.A.: "Corporate finance in Canada." (Economics: Hemmeon, J. & Viner, J.)

24-544 **Reque**, A. Dikka (*Minnesota*) M.A.: "La critique française et le drame norvégien." (French: Du Roure, R. & Walter, H.)

24-545 **Silver**, Edith (*Columbia*) M.A.: "L'influence de Shakespeare sur le théâtre d'Alfred de Musset." (French: Du Roure, R. & Macmillan, C.)

24-546 **Walter**, Felix H. (*McGill*) M.A.: "Vicente Blasco Ibanez and his relation to the French naturalists." (English: Latham, G. & Du Roure, R.)

24-547 **Willard**, Eugene W. (*McGill*) M.A.: "The migration of people from Canada to the United States." (Economics: Hemmeon, J.)

24-548 **Wood-Legh**, Kathleen L. (*McGill*) M.A.: "Parliament in the time of Chaucer." (History: Waugh, W. & Smith, H.)

**M.S.A. Fall 1924**

24-549 **Rogers**, John T. (*Saskatchewan*) M.S.A.: "The relative yield and value of sweet clover under different methods of treatment." (Agronomy: McTaggart, A.)

**M.Sc. Fall 1924**

24-550 **Patton**, Isabelle J. (*McGill*) M.Sc.: "The relations existing between the degree of unsaturation of an organic compound and the amount of its adsorbtion by charcoal." (Chemistry: Shaw, A. & Johnson, F.)

24-551 **Snijman**, Johan J. (*South Africa*) M.Sc.: "Coarse grinding versus fine grinding in gold recovery by cyanidation." (Ore Dressing: Porter, J. & Mackay, H.)

## ANNUAL LISTING

### Ph.D. Spring 1925

25-001 **Chipman**, Harry R. (*Dalhousie*) Ph.D.: "The heats of solution of certain alkali halides and the specific heats of their solutions." (Biochemistry: Macallum, A. & Stehle, R.)

25-002 **Forbes**, John C. (*Saskatchewan*) Ph.D.: "The purification of pepsin and the determination of the chemical constitution and physical characters of the preparations obtained." (Biochemistry: Macallum, A. & Stehle,R.)

25-003 **Jane**, Robert S. (*British Columbia*) Ph.D.: "A study of the colloidal behaviour of rubber." (Chemistry: Whitby, G. & Keys, D.)

25-004 **Larose**, Paul (*McGill*) Ph.D.: "The diffusion of gases through metals." (Chemistry: Eve, A. & Johnson, F.)

25-005 **Mennie**, John H. (*British Columbia*) Ph.D.: "Vapor densities and molecular attraction." (Chemistry: Eve, A. & Maass, O.)

25-006 **Symons**, Jennie L. (*McGill*) Ph.D.: "Physiological variations in xanthium." (Botany: Lloyd, F. & Stehle, R.)

### Ph.D. Fall 1925

25-007 **Thomson**, Walter W. (*McGill*) Ph.D.: "The preparation and the properties of the margarines." (Chemistry: Ruttan, R. & Macallum, A.)

### M.S.A. Spring 1925

25-501 **Davidson**, James G. (*Saskatchewan*) M.S.A.: "The elimination of error in taking yields of forage crops." (Agronomy: Summerby, R.)

25-502 **Eaton**, Ernest L. (*Ontario Agricultural*) M.S.A.: "The effect of frost on germination of corn." (Agronomy: Raymond, L.)

25-503 **Hanlan**, Leamon H. (*Ontario Agricultural*) M.S.A.: "The variation in varieties and mixtures of cereal and forage crops with respect to border effect in comparative crop tests." (Agronomy: Summerby, R.)

25-504 **Lods**, Emile A. (*McGill*) M.S.A.: "A study of the influence of electric light used to supplement daylight on oats grown as breeding material in the greenhouse during the winter season." (Agronomy: Dickson, B. & Summerby, R.)

## ANNUAL LISTING

### M.Sc. Spring 1925

25-505 **Allan**, John M. (*McGill*) M.Sc.: "A. Preparation of compounds contributory to the study of the mechanism of vulcanization catalysis. B. Acid numbers in raw rubber samples." (Chemistry: Whitby, G. & Stehle, R.)

25-506 **Armstrong**, Thomas (*McGill*) M.Sc.: "The description, habits, and life history of the onion maggot, *Hylemyia antiga* Meit., with special reference to its control in the district of Montreal,Que." (Entomology: Willey, A. & DuPorte, E.)

25-507 **Atwell**, Ernest A. (*McGill*) M.Sc.: "Studies concerning the mosaic disease of tobacco." (Plant Anatomy: Harrison, F. & Dickson, B.)

25-508 **Baker**, Alexander D. (*McGill*) M.Sc.: "A comparative study of the male genitalia of the Canadian *Pentatomidae*." (Entomology: Willey, A. & DuPorte, E.)

25-509 **Barnes**, William H. (*McGill*) M.Sc.: "Some thermal constants of carbon dioxide." (Chemistry: Shaw, A. & Maass, O.)

25-510 **Becking**, John A. (*McGill*) M.Sc.: "Sizing on sieves." (Ore Dressing: Mackay, H. & Porter, J.)

25-511 **Bostock**, Hugh S. (*McGill*) M.Sc.: "A petrographic study of the dyke rocks of the Anyox district, B.C." (Geology & Mineralogy: Graham, R. & Johnson, F.)

25-512 **Brooke**, Richard O. (*Toronto*) M.Sc.: "A study of the fixation of phosphates by soils." (Chemistry: McCarthy, J.)

25-513 **Davidson**, Stanley C. (*McGill*) M.Sc.: "Petrographical study of rocks and ores from the Sullivan Mine, Kimberley, B.C." (Geological Sciences: O'Neill, J. & Johnson, F.)

25-514 **Elvidge**, Arthur R. (*McGill*) M.Sc.: "Injection of foreign particles into the blood stream." (Physiology: Tait, J.)

25-515 **Evans**, Arthur B. (*Birmingham*, England) M.Sc.: "The relation between the chemical constitution of organic liquids and their ability to swell rubber." (Chemistry: Whitby, G.)

25-516 **Fan**, Paul C. (*Nanyang*, Shanghai) M.Sc.: "Electric power transmission by alternating currents at high voltage." (Electrical Engineering: King, L. & Christie, C.)

25-517 **Fowler**, Grant M. (*McGill*) M.Sc.: "A method for the determination of halogens in the side chains of aromatic organic compounds." (Chemistry: Macallum, A. & Ruttan, R.)

25-518 **Green**, Frederick (*Naples*, Italy) M.Sc.: "Problems in immunity with special reference to the Wassermann reaction." (Physiology: Tait, J. & Rhea, L.)

25-519 **Hachey**, Henry B. (*St. Francis Xavier*) M.Sc.: "Resonence radiations." (Physics: Eve, A. & Johnson, F.)

25-520 **Harrison**, Kenneth A. (*Toronto*) M.Sc.: "Studies concerning bean anthraenose." (Plant Pathology: Dickson, B.)

25-521 **Illievitz**, Abraham B. (*McGill*) M.Sc.: "The relation of kidney activity in diabetes insipidus to the theories of urine excretion." (Biochemistry: Rabinovitch, I. & Macallum, A.)

25-522 **LeNeveu**, Arthur P. (*Manitoba*) M.Sc.: "Transmission of power at high voltages over long distances." (Electrical Engineering: King, L. & Christie, C.)

25-523 **McNally**, William J. (*Dalhousie*) M.Sc.: "Experiment on labyrinth of the frog." (Physiology: Tait, J. & Birkett, H.)

25-524 **Muir**, Allan K. (*McGill*) M.Sc.: "The settling of very finely divided material in water, and certain dilute akali solutions, with especial reference to decantation methods in ore dressing." (Ore Dressing: Porter, J. & Maass, O.)

25-525 **Powell**, Allan T. (*McGill*) M.Sc.: "The economic production of titanium oxide from ilmenite." (Metallurgy: Stansfield, A. & Johnson, F.)

25-526 **Robertson**, Carol E. (*McGill*) M.Sc.: "Conductivities of aqueous solutions of sulphur dioxide and other properties of sulphur dioxide." (Chemistry: Maass, O. & Stehle, R.)

25-527 **Robison**, Samuel C. (*McGill*) M.Sc.: "Isolation and identification of the flavouring principle of maple sugar." (Chemistry: Snell, J. & Ruttan, R.)

25-528 **Sweny**, George W. (*McGill*) M.Sc.: "The extraction of copper from its ores by simultaneous leaching and electrolysis." (Metallurgical Engineering: Stansfield, A. & Maass, O.)

25-529 **Vanterpool**, Thomas C. (*McGill*) M.Sc.: "Streak or Winter blight of tomato in Quebec." (Plant Pathology: Dickson, B. & Harrison, F.)

25-530 **Wilson**, Harold S. (*McGill*) M.Sc.: "The geology of the tin deposits of Cornwall." (Geological Sciences: Bancroft, J. & Johnson, F.)

**M.A. Spring 1925**

25-531 **Blumenstein**, Jacob H. (*McGill*) M.A.: "The taxation of corporations in Canada." (Economics & Political Science: Kemp, H. & Leacock, S.)

25-532 **Boyes**, Watson (*McGill*) M.A.: "The light shed by the Jewish-Aramaic papyri on contemporary Biblical literature." (Oriental Languages: Graham, W. & Brockwell, C.)

25-533 **Brownstein**, Charles (*McGill*) M.A.: "Taxation of income in Canada." (Economics & Political Science: Leacock, S. & Hemmeon, J.)

25-534 **Burns**, Dean K. (*Toronto*) M.A.: "Canadian orators and oratory." (English: Macmillan, C. & Mackay, I.)

25-535 **Foster**, Joan M. (*McGill*) M.A.: "Lord Carteret and the Hanoverian policy of the Georges." (History: Williams, B. & Corbett, *)

25-536 **Kelloway**, Warwick F. (*McGill*) M.A.: "The ethics of achievement." (Philosophy: Ritchie, D. & Mackay, I.)

25-537 **MacLennan**, Malcolm (*McGill*) M.A.: "Crime and criminals in English and French memoirs." (English: Du Roure, R. & Latham, G.)

25-538 **Nichol**, Jean (*McGill*) M.A.: "James Murray, the military initiator of British civil government in Canada." (History: Fryer, C. & Hemmeon, J.)

25-539 **Read**, Stanley M. (*McGill*) M.A.: "An account of English journalism in Canada from the middle of the eighteenth century to the beginning of the twentieth, with special emphasis being given to the periods prior to Confederation." (English: Leacock, S. & Macmillan, C.)

25-540 **Read**, Mary G. (*Bishop's*) M.A.: "The treatment of education in the novels of George Eliot, George Meredith and Thomas Hardy." (English: Tait, W. & Files, H.)

25-541 **Sharples**, Alice (*McGill*) M.A.: "'Théâtre en liberté' de Victor Hugo." (French: Du Roure, R. & Dombrowski, J.)

25-542 **White**, Harold (*McGill*) M.A.: "The treatment of immortality by poets of the ninteenth century." (English: Latham, G. & Waugh, W.)

**M.S.A. Fall 1925**

25-543 **Liebenberg**, Louis C. (*South Africa*) M.S.A.: "The relation of plot yields in one year to those of succeeding years." (Agronomy: Summerby, R. & Snell, J.)

25-544 **Maw**, William A. (*McGill*) M.S.A.: " " (Poultry Husbandry: DuPorte, E. & Rice, J.)

**M.Sc. Fall 1925**

25-545 **Burke**, Hugh E. (*McGill*) M.Sc.: "Injection of tissue extracts into the blood stream with special reference to blood coagulation." (Physiology: Tait, J. & Stehle, R.)

25-546 **Cassidy**, Gordon J. (*McGill*) M.Sc.: "The cause of death in cooled animals, with special reference to circulation and respiration." (Physiology: Meakins, J. & Tait, J.)

25-547 **Cave**, Allister E. (*McGill*) M.Sc.: "An experimental study of mechanical filtration, with special reference to the use of rotary drum filters on slimes from ore dressing plants." (Ore Dressing: Johnson, F. & Porter, J.)

25-548 **Home**, Maurice S. (*British Columbia*) M.Sc.: "The striated electric discharge in nitrogen and helium." (Physics: Shaw, A. & Gillson, A..)

25-549 **Shaw**, Gerald E. (*McGill*) M.Sc.: "Continuity in steel I-beams haunched with concrete." (Civil Engineering & Applied Mechanics: Roberts, A. & Mackay, H.)

25-550 **Zoond**, Alexander (*British Columbia*) M.Sc.: "The influence of green manures upon the growth and physiological efficiency of cyotobacter." (Bacteriology: Harrison, F. & McTaggart, A.)

## M.A. Fall 1925

25-551 **Wilkinson**, George (*Vermont*) M.A.: "What is the metaphysic of ethics? " (Philosophy: Caldwell, W. & Ritchie, D.)

## ANNUAL LISTING

### Ph.D. Spring 1926

26-001 **Chataway**, Helen D. (*Manitoba*) Ph.D.: "The sulphuration of fatty oils." (Chemistry: Whitby, G.)

26-002 **Douglas**, Allie V. (*McGill*) Ph.D.: "Spectroscopic magnitudes and parallaxes of A-type stars." (Physics: Gillson, A. & Young, R.)

26-003 **Hunten**, Kenneth W. (*Bishop's*) Ph.D.: "Investigation of anomalous values of the Ramsey-Shields constant from the point of view of surface orientation." (Chemistry: Maass, O.)

26-004 **Sivertz**, Christian (*British Columbia*) Ph.D.: "Reaction velocities and molecular attraction in related systems." (Chemistry: Maass, O. & McIntosh, D.)

26-005 **Sivertz**, Victorian (*Washington*) Ph.D.: "Effect of molecular attraction on the total pressure of gas mixtures." (Chemistry: Maass, O. & McIntosh, D.)

26-006 **Steacie**, Edgar W. (*McGill*) Ph.D.: "The absorbtion of gases in metals." (Chemistry: Johnson, F.)

### Ph.D. Fall 1926

26-007 **Munro**, Lloyd A. (*Dalhousie*) Ph.D.: "The sorption of vapors by alumina." (Chemistry: Johnson, F. & Shaw, A.)

### M.S.A. Spring 1926

26-501 **Clark**, John A. (*Toronto*) M.S.A.: "A study of the influences of several rotations on yield and cost of producing farm crops." (Agronomy: Snell, J. & Summerby, R.)

26-502 **Schurman**, David C. (*Toronto*) M.S.A.: "Methods of experimentation with corn: elimination of error in plot tests." (Agronomy: Snell, J.)

### M.Sc. Spring 1926

26-503 **Atkinson**, Hammond J. (*New Brunswick*) M.Sc.: "The detection of adulteration in butter." (Agricultural Chemistry: Snell, J. & Maclean, R.)

26-504 **Campbell**, Alexander (*McGill*) M.Sc.: "An investigation of the secondary stresses in a roof truss having unsymmetrical members." (Civil Engineering: Mackay, H. & Sullivan, C.)

26-505 **Cashin**, Martin F. (*McGill*) M.Sc.: "Perfusion of surviving organs with particles in suspension." (Physiology: Tait, J. & Macallum, A.)

26-506 **Chalk**, Mary L. (*McGill*) M.Sc.: "Potential distributions in the Crooke's dark space and relative intensities of Stark effect components of H-beta and He-lamda." (Physics: Eve, A. & Maass, O.)

26-507 **Cleland**, John G. (*McGill*) M.Sc.: "The nervous connections of the spleen." (Physiology: Tait, J.)

26-508 **Draper**, William B. (*McGill*) M.Sc.: "The unity or multiplicity of the autocoids responsible for the pressor, oxytocic, and renal activities of the posterior lobe of the pituitary gland." (Pharmacology: Tait, J. & Stehle, R.)

26-509 **Ellis**, David H. (*McGill*) M.Sc.: "A study of the genesis of the copper and other ores of the Eastern Townships of Quebec." (Geology & Mineralogy: Graham, R. & Adams, F.)

26-510 **Gibbs**, Ronald D. (*London*, England) M.Sc.: "Effect of ultra-violet light on spirogyra." (Botany: Lloyd, F. & Stehle, R.)

26-511 **Graham**, Archibald R. (*McGill*) M.Sc.: "A morphological study of the genitalia of some *Ipidae*." (Entomology: Willey, A. & DuPorte, E.)

26-512 **Henderson**, Jean T. (*McGill*) M.Sc.: "The lethal temperatures of *Lamellibranchiata*." (Zoology: Willey, A. & Macallum, A.)

26-513 **Howes**, Frederick S. (*McGill*) M.Sc.: "Valve oscillator design and characteristics." (Electrical Engineering: Christie, C. & Wallace, G.)

26-514 **Johns**,Cyril K. (*Alberta*) M.Sc.: "A rapid method for the determination of mould and yeast counts in creamery butter." (Bacteriology: Hood, E. & Harrison, F.)

26-515 **Leduc**, Joseph A. (*Alberta Agricultural Institute*) M.Sc.: "Turbidity tests on butterfat and its substitutes." (Agricultural Chemistry: Hatcher, W. & Snell, J.)

26-516 **Macrae**, Ruth (*McGill*) M.Sc.: "The *Cyanophyceae*: pigments and structure." (Botany: Lloyd, F. & Macallum, A.)

26-517 **Matheson**, George L. (*McGill*) M.Sc.: "Some properties of pure hydrogen peroxide." (Chemistry: Maass, O.)

26-518 **Miller**, George G. (*McGill*) M.Sc.: "A study of cerebral concussion." (Physiology: Archibald, E.)

26-519 **Mills**, Edward S. (*McGill*) M.Sc.: "The vascular arrangements of the spleen." (Physiology: Tait, J. & Howard, C.)

26-520 **Morrison**, James E. (*McGill*) M.Sc.: "A study of titaniferous blast furnace slags." (Metallurgical Engineering: Stansfield, A. & Maass, O.)

26-521 **Pasternack**, David S. (*Queen's*) M.Sc.: "The relation between the polarity of isomeric benzine derivatives and other substances and (a) inhibition by organic colloids; (b) their solvent power." (Chemistry: Whitby, G. & Scarth, G.)

26-522 **Popp**, William (*Manitoba*) M.Sc.: "Studies on *Puccinia coronata* - the crown rust of oats." (Plant Pathology: Dickson, B.)

26-523 **Priestman**, Bryan (*Cambridge*, England) M.Sc.: "Derivation of the law of electromagnetic induction for any linear conductor." (Physics: Eve, A. & Gillson, A.)

26-524 **Rosenbaum**, Saul B. (*McGill*) M.Sc.: "A study on the histology of the lung." (Pathology: Tait, J. & Oertel, H.)

26-525 **Rowles**, William (*Saskatchewan*) M.Sc.: "The Stark effect for silver in the visible and ultra-violet regions." (Physics: Foster, J.)

26-526 **Stewart**, Kenneth E. (*McGill*) M.Sc.: "A study of the biology and control of the onion maggot." (Entomology: DuPorte, E.)

26-527 **Sutherland**, Brian P. (*British Columbia*) M.Sc.: "Study of the propylene-halogen hydride reaction." (Chemistry: Maass, O. & Keys, D.)

26-528 **Terroux** Fernand R. (*Loyola of Montréal*) M.Sc.: "Striated discharge in mixed gases, with special reference to the spectra emitted by various parts of the discharge." (Physics: Eve, A. & Maass, O.)

26-529 **Toole**, Francis J. (*McGill*) M.Sc.: "Studies in the oxidation of organic compounds by hydrogen peroxide." (Chemistry: Hatcher, W.)

26-530 **Townsend**, Charles T. (*British Columbia*) M.Sc.: "A study of bacteria isolated from cases of bovine mastitis." (Bacteriology: Harrison, F. & Hood, E.)

26-531 **Walter**, Albert J. (*McGill*) M.Sc.: "Studies in the reduction of telluride ores, with special reference to the ores of Kirkland Lake district, Ontario." (Mining Engineering: Porter, J. & Stansfield, A.)

26-532 **Warren**, Thomas E. (*Queen's*) M.Sc.: "Dissociation pressures of the orthophosphates of ammonia." (Chemistry: Snell, J.)

26-533 **Watson**, Edmund E. (*McGill*) M.Sc.: "The development of an improved type of cathode ray oscillograph." (Physics: Eve, A. & Brown, E.)

26-534 **White**, Roy M. (*Manitoba*) M.Sc.: "The external anatomy of *Camnula pellucida* scudder in its various stages." (Entomology: DuPorte, E.)

**M.A. Spring 1926**

26-535 **Aikman**, Cecil H. (*McGill*) M.A.: "The automobile industry in Canada." (Economics & Political Science: Sandwell, B. & Farthing, J.)

26-536 **Armstrong**, Charles A. (*McGill*) M.A.: "The psychology of mysticism." (Psychology: Tait, W. & Files, H.)

26-537 **Boden**, Quinibert P. (*Poitiers*, France) M.A.: "La vie intellectuelle des noirs de la Caroline du Nord." (French: Messac, R.)

26-538 **Creighton**, Edith M. (*Dalhousie*) M.A.: "Jeanne d'Arc dans le théâtre moderne anglais et français." (French: Noad, A. & Du Roure, R.)

26-539 **Di Florio**, Pasquale (*McGill*) M.A.: "Peter Martyr: a study in Italian influence upon the English Reformation principally in the reign of Edward VI." (History: Fryer, C. & Latham, G.)

26-540 **Edwards**, Margaret C. (*Vassar*) M.A.: "Canadian drama, dramatists, and players." (English: Macmillan, C.)

26-541 **Forsey**, Eugene A. (*McGill*) M.A.: "Economic and social aspects of the Nova Scotia coal industry." (Economics & Political Science: Hemmeon, J. & Kemp, H.)

26-542 **Gower**, Douglas L. (*Edinburgh*, Scotland) M.A.: "The question of a separate Secretary of State for Scotland from the Union of 1707 to the Liberal administration of 1880." (History: Fryer, C.)

26-543 **Gurd**, Jean M. (*McGill*) M.A.: "The use of the fairy element in the Elizabethan and modern drama: a contrast with special reference to Shakespeare and Barrie." (English: Fryer, C. & Macmillan, C.)

26-544 **Knechtel**, Max U. (*McMaster*) M.A.: "The psychology of fire." (Psychology: Dawson, C. & Tait, W.)

26-545 **Layhew**, John H. (*McGill*) M.A.: "Public utilities in the Province of Quebec." (Economics: Day, J.)

26-546 **Levy**, Gordon W. (*McGill*) M.A.: "The 'Lemieux' Act and the Privy Council decision of 1925." (Economics: Hemmeon, J. & Sandwell, B.)

26-547 **McFarlane**, Duncan H. (*McGill*) M.A.: "The sociology of Rouville County." (Social Science: Dawson, C. & Hemmeon, J.)

26-548 **MacLaren**, Margaret J. (*McGill*) M.A.: "Robert Louis Stevenson and romance: his attitude toward life and his confidence in the essential goodness of man as revealed in his romances." (English: Latham, G.)

26-549 **MacLeod**, Elmer D. (*McGill*) M.A.: "Personality and bodily structure." (Psychology: Tait, W. & Bridges, J.)

26-550 **MacVicar**, Donald H. (*McGill*) M.A.: "The psychology of Gestalt." (Psychology: Tait, W. & Mackay, I.)

26-551 **Preston**, George P. (*Colgate*) M.A.: "The men and women of Thomas Hardy." (English: Dawson, C. & Files, H.)

26-552 **Reich**, Nathan (*McGill*) M.A.: "The pulp and paper industry in Canada." (Economics & Political Science: Leacock, S.)

26-553 **Ross**, Dorothy V. (*McGill*) M.A.: "British naval obligations to France involved in the Entente of 1904." (History: **)

26-554 **Smith**, Arthur J. (*McGill*) M.A.: "The poetry of William Butler Yeats." (English: Mackay, I. & Files, H.)

26-555 **Smith**, Henry L. (*McGill*) M.A.: "Tennyson: his relation to Romanticism, with special reference to his political views." (English: Tait, W. & Latham, G.)

26-556 **Stager**, Drucilla N. (*Wilson*) M.A.: "La légende napoléonienne dans l'oeuvre de Béranger." (French: Dombrowski, J. & Messac, *)

26-557 **Tombs**, Laurence C. (*McGill*) M.A.: "The port of Montreal." (Economics & Political Science: Leacock, S.)

**M.Sc. Fall 1926**

26-558 **Dimmock**, Frederick (*McGill*) M.Sc.: "A comparison of first generation corn hybrids with their parent types." (Agronomy: Raymond, L.)

26-559 **Shotwell, John S.** (*McGill*) M.Sc.: "Action of caustic on cellulose: effect of variations in the conditions of manipulation." (Chemistry: Ruttan, R. & Hibbert, H.)

## ANNUAL LISTING

### Ph.D. Spring 1927

27-001 **Barnes**, William H. (*McGill*) Ph.D.: "Some thermal properties of carbon dioxide and of ice." (Chemistry: Maass, O. & Boyle, *)

27-002 **Bishop**, Eric G. (*McGill*) Ph.D.: "The geology of a section of the Wunnummin Lake area." (Geology & Mineralogy: Young, G. & Bancroft, J.)

27-003 **Elvidge**, Arthur R. (*McGill*) Ph.D.: "Experimental anaemia." (Physiology: Tait, J.)

27-004 **Emmons**, William F (*British Columbia*) Ph.D.: "Pernicious anaemia." (Physiology: Macallum, A. & Tait, J.)

27-005 **Holden**, George W. (*Bishop's*) Ph.D.: "Hydrogen peroxide as an oxidising agent in acid solution." (Chemistry: Hatcher, W.)

27-006 **Lipsett**, Solomon G. (*Manitoba*) Ph.D.: "The surface energy and heat of solution of solid sodium chloride." (Chemistry: Maass, O.)

27-007 **Maass**, Carol E. (*McGill*) Ph.D.: "An investigation of the properties of pure sulphur dioxide and its aqueous solutions." (Chemistry: Johnson, F.)

27-008 **McNally**, James G. (*Trinity*) Ph.D.: "Some colloidal and elastic properties of meta styrene and rubber." (Chemistry: Whitby, G.)

27-009 **Pelletier**, Rene A. (*McGill*) Ph.D.: "Geology of the Thurso area, Quebec and Ontario." (Geology & Mineralogy: Bancroft, J.)

27-010 **Russell**, John (*British Columbia*) Ph.D.: "Molecular attraction." (Chemistry: Maass, O.)

### M.S.A. Spring 1927

27-501 **Russell**, Mary G. (*McGill*) M.S.A.: "The relation of plot yields of one period with those of another." (Agronomy: Summerby, R.)

### M.Sc. Spring 1927

27-502 **Airey**, Henry T. (*McGill*) M.Sc.: "The flotation and concentration of certain complex auriferous ores of northern Canada (Kirkland Lake and Porcupine areas)." (Mining Engineering: Porter, J. & Stansfield, A.)

27-503 **Cuthbertson**, Arnold C. (*McGill*) M.Sc.: "Preparation and properties of pure hydrogen peroxide." (Chemistry: Maass, O.)

27-504 **Gough**, William F. (*British Columbia*) M.Sc.: "The colon count as a substitute for the numerical count in the examination of a city milk supply." (Bacteriology: Harrison, F. & Sanborn, *)

27-505 **Greenberg**, Harry (*McGill*) M.Sc.: "1.The action of potassium cyanide on certain disulphides. 2.Some aspects of the behaviour of pure caoutchouc, with special reference to the influence of protien." (Chemistry: Whitby, G. & Bliss, S.)

27-506 **Hill**, Hinson (*McGill*) M.Sc.: "Cultural studies of certain fungi to determine whether 'Phage' occurs as in bacteria." (Plant Pathology: Dickson, B.)

27-507 **Houghton**, Edward O. (*McGill*) M.Sc.: "Cyclic acetal formation and polymerisation." (Chemistry: Hibbert, H. & Stehle, R.)

27-508 **Johnston**, Harry W. (*McGill*) M.Sc.: "Fractional distillation on the large laboratory scale as applied to the separation into their components of the binary systems Butanol(1)-Propanol(1), Butatone(2)-Propanone(2) and (2)Butenal(1)-Paraethanal." (Chemistry: Hibbert, H.)

27-509 **Katz**, Morris (*McGill*) M.Sc.: "A study of some polymerizable substances, especially connamylidene fluorene and similar compounds." (Chemistry: Whitby, G. & Bliss, S.)

27-510 **Lane**, Cecil T. (*McGill*) M.Sc.: "An absolute determination of the magnetic susceptibility of potassium in the pure state." (Mathematics & Physics: Maass, O. & Bieler, *)

27-511 **Maytum**, Helen E. (*California*) M.Sc.: "The inorganic chemistry of the nerve fibre as revealed by microchemical methods." (Biochemistry: Rabinovitch, I. & Macallum, A.)

27-512 **Morrison**, Carson F. (*Saskatchewan*) M.Sc.: "The effect of the manner of support and of certain details of construction on the secondary stresses in a roof truss." (Civil Engineering: Mackay, H.)

27-513 **McCurdy**, Lyall R. (*McGill*) M.Sc.: "Journal bearing friction characteristics." (Machine Design: Roberts, A.)

27-514 **Perreault**, Champlain (*McGill*) M.Sc.: "A study of a common leaf spot of iris in Quebec." (Plant Pathology: Dickson, B.)

27-515 **Pomerleau**, Rene (*Ste. Anne de la Pocatiere*) M.Sc.: "Some pyrenomycetes of Quebec." (Plant Pathology: Dickson, B.)

27-516 **Press**, Abraham (*Cooper Institute of New York*) M.Sc.: "Consequences of a matrix mechanics and a radiating harmonic oscillator without the quantum postulate." (Physics: Eve, A. & Gillson, A.)

27-517 **Riordon**, Charles H. (*McGill*) M.Sc.: "A study of some of the igneous rocks and ores of the Slocan Mining District, B.C." (Geology & Mineralogy: Graham, R. & Porter, J.)

27-518 **Ross**, Dudley E. (*McGill*) M.Sc.: "Relation of para-thyroids to fracture healing as controlled by X-rays." (Physiology: Tait, J. & Archibald, E.)

27-519 **Ross**, William B. (*McGill*) M.Sc.: "A laboratory investigation of the principles governing the sizing of crushed ores and minerals in sieves." (Mining Engineering: Porter, J. & Mackay, H.)

27-520 **Watson**, Horace G. (*Toronto*) M.Sc.: "The application of the Piezo-electric effect to the measurement of pressures in internal combustion engines." (Mathematics & Physics: Keys, D. & Brown, E. & Maass, O.)

27-521 **White**, Thomas N. (*McGill*) M.Sc.: "Application of methods of X-ray crystal analysis to a problem in organic chemistry: effect on the X-ray diffraction pattern of stretching meta styrene, as compared with the effect obtained on stretching rubber." (Mathematics & Physics:Hibbert, H. & Eve, A.)

**M.A. Spring 1927**

27-522 **Bissett**, Alice M. (*McGill*) M.A.: "Lord Palmerston's policy of opposition to the project and to the construction of the Suez Canal." (History: Fryer, C. & Hemmeon, J.)

27-523 **Bogante**, Jack R. (*McGill*) M.A.: "Government guarantee of bank deposits in Canada." (Economics: Day, J. & Pierce, *)

27-524 **Brown**, Richard C. (*McGill*) M.A.: "The English versions of the Bible, and the various linguistic influences which affected their language and style." (English: Howard, * & Latham, G.)

27-525 **Brown**, Wilfred H. (*McGill*) M.A.: "The Slovakian community in Montreal." (Sociology: Dawson, C. & Prince, S.)

27-526 **Claxton**, John W. (*Queen's*) M.A.: "An introduction to the philosophy of religion." (Philosophy: Caldwell, W. & Welsh, R.)

27-527 **Culliton**, John T. (*Saskatchewan*) M.A.: "Assisted immigration and land settlement with special reference to Western Canada." (Economics: Leacock, S. & Sandwell, B.)

27-528 **Davies**, Thomas R. (*McGill*) M.A.: "Twelve years of the Westminster Review." (English: Leacock, S. & Noad, A.)

27-529 **Davis**, Richard E. (*Toronto*) M.A.: "The Montreal Young Men's Christian Association as a religious and social organization." (Sociology: Dawson, C. & Best, E.)

27-530 **Forbes**, Frederic J. (*Dalhousie*) M.A.: "Canada in the League of Nations." (Economics & Political Science: Leacock, S. & Sandwell, B.)

## Ph.D. Spring 1928

28-001 **Butler**, Keith H. (*Dalhousie*) Ph.D.: "The preparation and properties of the persulphides of hydrogen." (Chemistry: Maass, O.)

28-002 **Cambron**, Adrien (*Laval*) Ph.D.: "A study of the preparation and reactions of some organic sulphides, with special reference to the conversion of dithio carbolkyl disulphides into the corresponding mono sulphides." (Chemistry: Whitby, G.)

28-003 **Carpenter**, Gilbert B. (*British Columbia*) Ph.D.: "Aberrations from the ideal gas laws in systems of one and two components." (Chemistry: Maass, O.)

28-004 **Chalk**, Mary L. (*McGill*) Ph.D.: "Observed relative intensities of Stark components in hydrogen." (Physics: Foster, J.)

28-005 **Crozier**, Robert N. (*British Columbia*) Ph.D.: "An investigation of the constitution of caoutchouc with special reference to the mode of polymerization." (Chemistry: Whitby, G.)

28-006 **Machacek**, John E. (*Saskatchewan*) Ph.D.: "Studies on the association of certain phytopathogens." (Plant Pathology: **)

28-007 **Rowles**, William (*Saskatchewan*) Ph.D.: "Stark effect in complex spectra." (Physics: Foster, J.)

28-008 **Sutherland**, Brian P. (*British Columbia*) Ph.D.: "Viscosity of gases, and the effect of molecular attraction on the total pressure of gas mixtures." (Chemistry: Maass, O.)

## Ph.D. Fall 1928

28-009 **Greenberg**, Harry (*McGill*) Ph.D.: "A study of the constituents of the serum of *Herea latex*." (Chemistry: Whitby, G.)

28-010 **Pasternack**, David S. (*Queen's*) Ph.D.: "The action of sulphur and sulphur halides on certain unsaturated substances, especially fatty oils." (Chemistry: Whitby, G.)

28-011 **Patterson**, Arthur L. (*McGill*) Ph.D.: "The application of X-rays to the study of organic substances." (Physics: Eve, A.)

28-012 **Yorston**, Frederic H. (*McGill*) Ph.D.: "The rotary dispersion of non-tautomeric organic compounds." (Chemistry: Whitby, G.)

## M.S.A. Spring 1928

28-501 **Raynauld**, Robert (*Montréal*) M.S.A.: "Study of factors influencing the percentage of hull in oats." (Agronomy: Lods, E.)

## ANNUAL LISTING

**M.Sc. Spring 1928**

28-502 **Burton**, Frederick R. (*McGill*) M.Sc.: "A petrographic study of a zinc prospect in Bouchette Township, Que." (Geological Sciences: O'Neill, J.)

28-503 **Crowe**, Marguerite (*Chicago*) M.Sc.: "The temperature coefficients of electrical conductivity for concentrated solutions of calcium chloride, with precision measurements of conductivity for the higher concentrations." (Physics: Shaw, A. & Maass, O.)

28-504 **Daviault**, Lionel (*Montréal*) M.Sc.: "The anatomy, histology and physiology of the digestive canal of crickets." (Entomology: DuPorte, E.)

28-505 **Davies**, Frank T. (*Wales*) M.Sc.: "1.The measurement of surface temperature, with special reference to surfaces undergoing evaporation. 2.The construction and testing of a hygrostat. 3.The relation of indoor to outdoor humidities and the determination of a correlation factor between them for certain periods of the year."(Physics: Shaw, A. & Maass, O.)

28-506 **Dworkin**, Simon (*McGill*) M.Sc.: "Temperature control in the animal body." (Physiology: Tait, J. & Stehle, R.)

28-507 **Dyce**, Elton J. (*Ontario Agricultural*) M.Sc.: "A study of the swarm control of bees." (Entomology: Willey, A. & DuPorte, E.)

28-508 **Finney**, William H. (*McGill*) M.Sc.: "The mechanism of hibernation." (Physiology: Tait, J. & Meakins, J.)

28-509 **Fowler**, Donald E. (*New Brunswick*) M.Sc.: "A study of the interactions of solutions of maple syrup and basic lead acetate, with particular reference to the Canadian lead number." (Agricultural Chemistry: Whitby, G. & Snell, J.)

28-510 **Gallay**, Wilfred (*McGill*) M.Sc.: "Some studies of elastic organic colloids." (Organic Chemistry: Whitby, G.)

28-511 **Henderson**, John T. (*McGill*) M.Sc.: "A study of the time-pressure curves of explosions in gaseous mixtures at constant volume by the Piezo-electric method." (Physics: Keys, D.)

28-512 **Holbrooke**, George L. (*McGill*) M.Sc.: "Petrographic study of the Aldermac mine." (Geological Sciences: O'Neill, J. & McBride, W.)

28-513 **Hou**, Hsiang-Ch'uan (*Peking Medical*,. China) M.Sc.: "Study of *glandula uropygialis* in birds." (Physiology: Willey, A. & Tait, J.)

28-514 **Irwin**, Marion L. (*British Columbia*) M.Sc.: "The bacteriology of 'process' cheese." (Bacteriology: Harrison, F. & Sanborn, *)

28-515 **Kearns**, Peter J. (*McGill*) M.Sc.: "Anatomy and pathology of placental circulation." (Pathology: Oertel, H. & Chipman, W.)

28-516 **MacDonald**, James L. (*McGill*) M.Sc.: "The stark effect in the secondary spectrum of hydrogen." (Physics: Foster, J. & Gillson, A.)

28-517 **MacLeod**, Malcolm D. (*McGill*) M.Sc.: "A study of relaxation oscillations in different gases." (Physics: Keys, D. & Christie, C.)

28-518 **McRae**, Duncan R. (*McGill*) M.Sc.: "The absorption of infra-red rays by water, ice and other substances." (Physics: Eve, A. & Maass, O.)

28-519 **Maltais**, Jean B. (*Laval*) M.Sc.: "Thoracic sclerites of muscoid diptera." (Entomology: DuPorte, E.)

28-520 **Mitchell**, Claude R. (*McGill*) M.Sc.: "The influence of the composition of basic lead acetate on the Canadian lead number of maple products." (Chemistry: Snell, J. & Johnson, F.)

28-521 **Montserin**, Blazini G. (*McGill*) M.Sc.: "Studies on culture media." (Plant Pathology: Coulson, J. & Sanborn, *)

28-522 **Phillips**, John B. (*McGill*) M.Sc.: "Nature of lignin." (Chemistry: Hibbert, H.)

28-523 **Sankey**, Charles A. (*Toronto*) M.Sc.: "Identification of lignin constituents." (Chemistry: Hibbert, H.)

28-524 **Snelgrove**, Alfred K. (*McGill*) M.Sc.: "The geology of the central mineral belt of Newfoundland: a collation and contribution." (Geological Sciences: O'Neill, J. & McBride,W.)

28-525 **Vineberg**, Arthur M. (*McGill*) M.Sc.: "Amino acids of blood in pathological conditions." (Biochemistry: Rabinovitch, I. & Stehle, R.)

28-526 **Young**, John M. (*McGill*) M.Sc.: "Radical changes in rarified gases." (Physics: Keys, D. & Gillson, A.)

**M.A. Spring 1928**

28-527 **Alward**, Frederick P. (*McGill*) M.A.: "Le sport dans le roman francais d'après la guerre." (French: Benoit, * & Du Roure, R.)

28-528 **Banford**, Jean E. (*McGill*) M.A.: "Supernatural influence in classical tragedy." (Latin: Latham, G. & Carruthers, C.)

28-529 **Boos**, Albert W. (*McGill*) M.A.: "The financial arrangements between the provinces and the Dominion." (Economics: Hemmeon, J.)

28-530 **Clark**, Peter A. (*McGill*) M.A.: "The actual and projected legislation of Julius Caesar and its treatment by his successors." (Latin: Thompson, A. & Corbett, P. & Carruthers, C.)

28-531 **Edel**, Abraham (*McGill*) M.A.: "Literary decadence and the Alexandrian Callimachus." (Greek: Carruthers, C. & Files, H.)

28-532 **Edel**, Joseph L. (*McGill*) M.A.: "Henry James and some recent psychological fiction." (English: Kellogg, C. & Files, H.)

28-533 **Goforth**, John F. (*Toronto*) M.A.: "The economic and ethnological basis of Canadian confederation." (Economics & Political Science: Leacock, S.)

28-534 **Gordon**, Thomas M. (*McGill*) M.A.: "The Canadian sales tax." (Economics: Hemmeon, J.)

28-535 **Hague**, Helen (*McGill*) M.A.: "Heresy in England in the fifteenth century." (History: Latham, G. & Waugh, T.)

28-536 **Harris**, Theodore H. (*McGill*) M.A.: "Economic aspects of the Crow's Nest Pass rates agreement." (Economics & Political Science: Hemmeon, J.)

28-537 **Hasley**, Isabel J. (*McGill*) M.A.: "Dramatic criticism by playwrights and players." (English: Walter, H. & Macmillan, C.)

28-538 **Hayakawa**, Samuel I. (*Manitoba*) M.A.: "Literary criticism of Matthew Arnold." (English: Carruthers, C. & Files, H.)

28-539 **Hayes**, Saul (*McGill*) M.A.: "Good times and hard times in Canada and their economic environment." (Economics: Leacock, S.)

28-540 **Henderson**, Thomas G. (*McGill*) M.A.: "The concept of mind in recent thought." (Philosophy: Caldwell, W. & Stanley, C.)

28-541 **Hudson**, James C. (*McGill*) M.A.: "The social ideals of William Langland." (English: Latham, G. & Dawson, C.)

28-542 **Little**, John W. (*McGill*) M.A.: "Credit and credit facilities in Canada, with special reference to current commercial practice and merchandising methods." (Economics: Goforth, W.)

28-543 **McCall**, Muriel B. (*Manitoba*) M.A.: "A study of family disorganization in Canada." (Sociology: Dawson, C. & Best, E.)

28-544 **McCullagh**, Paul F. (*Toronto*) M.A.: "The idea of evolution in politics in the political writings of Aristotle." (Greek: Stanley, C. & Caldwell, W.)

28-545 **McInnis**, Sarah (*Montréal*) M.A.: "Les caractères ecclesiastiques dans l'oeuvre d'Anatole France." (French: Du Roure, R. & Macmillan, C.)

28-546 **MacLean**, Mary W. (*McGill*) M.A.: "Psychological aspects of myth and folk lore." (Psychology: Tait, W. & Latham, G.)

28-547 **MacPherson**, John T. (*Mount Allison*) M.A.: "A critical examination of the theories of emotion." (Psychology: Kellogg, C. & Slight, *)

28-548 **Murray**, Mae F. (*McGill*) M.A.: "Influence of the French naturalists on the work of George Moore." (English: Files, H. & Du Roure, R.)

28-549 **Nelson**, Eda M. (*Dalhousie*) M.A.: "The literature of the Maritime Provinces of Canada and its bearing on the struggle for education and political freedom." (English: Mackay, I. & Macmillan, C.)

28-550 **O'Brien**, Margaret T. (*Syracuse*) M.A.: "The influence of Irish folk-songs and folk-lore on English literature." (English: Macmillan, C. & Sullivan, C.)

28-551 **Robert**, Percy A. (*Loyola of Montréal*) M.A.: "Dufferin district: an area in transition." (Sociology: Dawson, C.)

28-552 **Schleien**, Donna S. (*McGill*) M.A.: "Arthur Schnitzler: eine Studie." (German: Walter, H.)

28-553 **Silverman**, Beatrice I. (*McGill*) M.A.: "P. Heyse und seine Falkentheorie." (German: Graff, W. & Latham, G.)

28-554 **Smith**, Lawrence L. (*Mount Allison*) M.A.: "Life and letters during the age of Pope:the *Dunciad*." (English: Messac, R. & Files, H.)

28-555 **Smyth**, Desmond H. (*McGill*) M.A.: "Memory, with special reference to affective aspects." (Psychology: Tait, W. & Dawson, C.)

28-556 **Turner**, Alice W. (*McGill*) M.A.: "Plücker's numbers in the theory of algebraic plane curves." (Mathematics: Sullivan, C.)

28-557 **Wickenden**, Marguerite H. (*Aldelphi*) M.A.: "La presse Franco-Americaine." (French: **)

28-558 **Young**, Charles H. (*McGill*) M.A.: "The population expansion of the French in Canada." (Sociology: Hemmeon, J. & Dawson, C.)

M.Sc. Fall 1928

28-559 **Coleman**, Charles L. (*McGill*) M.Sc.: "Treatment of complex copper-zinc ores of the Rouyn District." (Mining Engineering: McBride, W. & Graham, R.)

28-560 **Freedman**, Nathan (*McGill*) M.Sc.: "The age period changes in the cervix uteri, with special reference to cancer development." (Physiology: Oertel, H. & Ruttan, R.)

28-561 **Hamilton**, William B. (*McGill*) M.Sc.: "Gum production by *Azotobacter chroococcum* and its physiological significance." (Bacteriology: Sanborn, * & Harrison, F.)

M.A. Fall 1928

28-562 **Duckworth**, John M. (*McGill*) M.A.: "Some psychological considerations on the education of superior children." (Psychology: Tait, W. & Best, E.)

28-563 **Gray**, Leona (*McGill*) M.A.: "The development of stage costuming in England." (English: Mackay, I. & Macmillan, C.)

28-564 **Israel**, Wilfred E. (*Acadia*) M.A.: "The Montreal negro community." (Sociology: Dawson, C. & Best, E.)

28-565 **Mullaly**, Jessie R. (*Montréal*) M.A.: "Religious experience of Francis Thompson." (English: Files, H. & Mackay, I.)

28-566 **Scott**, Mary E. (*Montréal*) M.A.: "The novel of manners as written by women, from Sarah Fielding to Jane Austin." (English: Files, H. & Dawson, C. & Macmillan, C.)

## ANNUAL LISTING

Ph.D. Spring 1929

29-001 **Burke**, Hugh E. (*McGill*) Ph.D.: "Blood platelets." (Physiology: Miller, * & Tait, J.)

29-002 **Campbell**, William B. (*McGill*) Ph.D.: "Proprties of sulphur dioxide solutions above room temperatures." (Chemistry: Maass, O.)

29-003 **Carter**, Neal M. (*British Columbia*) Ph.D.: "The structural and geometrical isomerism of cyclic acetals of glycerol and the migration of groups in glycerol esters and ethers." (Chemistry: Kohler, E & Hibbert, H.)

29-004 **Coffin**, Carl C. (*Dalhousie*) Ph.D.: "The effect of molecular attraction upon the velocity of chemical reactions." (Chemistry: Maass, O.)

29-005 **Cuthbertson**, Arnold C. (*McGill*) Ph.D.: "Preparation and properties of hydrogen peroxide." (Chemistry: Maass, O.)

29-006 **Hill**, Allan C. (*Dalhousie*) Ph.D.: "Oxidation of organic compounds, with special reference to hydrogen peroxide." (Chemistry: Hatcher, W.)

29-007 **Jahn**, Edwin C. (*New York State*) Ph.D.: "Nature of the supermolecular state of certain aldehyde and ethylene oxide derivatives. 1:The action of sodium on crotonaldehyde. 2: The ethylene oxide ring in relation to the supermolecular state." (Cellulose Chemistry: Hibbert, H.)

29-008 **Johnston**, Harry W. (*McGill*) Ph.D.: "The penetration of wood by liquids." (Chemistry: Maass, O.)

29-009 **Marion**, Leo E. (*Queen's*) Ph.D.: "Isolation and identification of some lignin constituents." (Chemistry: Hibbert, H.)

29-010 **Matheson**, George L. (*McGill*) Ph.D.: "Properties of hydrogen peroxide." (Chemistry: Maass, O.)

29-011 **Pidgeon**, Lloyd M. (*Manitoba*) Ph.D.: "Adsorption of water by wood." (Chemistry: Maass, O.)

29-012 **Rowley**, Harry J. (*Queen's*) Ph.D.: "A study of the chemistry of spruce wood lignin and a new method of isolation." (Chemistry: Hibbert, H.)

29-013 **Stansfield**, John (*Cambridge*, England) Ph.D.: "Assimilation and petrogrenesis; separation of ores from magmas." (Geological Sciences: Adams, F.)

29-014 **Taylor**, Kenneth A. (*Mount Allison*) Ph.D.: "The action of hypochlorous acid on lignin and related compounds." (Chemistry: Hibbert, H.)

29-015 **Toole**, Francis J. (*McGill*) Ph.D.: "The absorption of gases by metals." (Chemistry: Johnson, F.)

29-016 **Whelen**, Myron S. (*Saskatchewan*) Ph.D.: "Studies on the ring structure of cyclic acetals from glycerols." (Chemistry: Hibbert, H.)

Ph.D. Fall 1929

29-017 **Katz**, Morris (*McGill*) Ph.D.: "Further observations on the polymerization of indene. The polymerization of styrene, iso-safrole, iso-eugenol and related substances." (Chemistry: Whitby, G.)

29-018 **Lane**, Cecil T. (*McGill*) Ph.D.: "The determination of the magnetic susceptibility of sodium, potassium, and caesium." (Physics: Bieler, E. & King, L.)

29-019 **Priestman**, Bryan (*Cambridge*, England) Ph.D.: "Propagation of quanta." (Physics: Adams, F. & Gillson, A.)

29-020 **White**, Thomas N. (*McGill*) Ph.D.: "The X-ray investigation of certain substitution products of cyclohexane." (Physics: Patterson, E.)

M.S.A. Spring 1929

29-501 **Bird**, Joseph N. (*Toronto*) M.Sc.: "Competition between adjacent rows of corn." (Agronomy: Raymond, L. & McRostie, *)

M.Sc. Spring 1929

29-502 **Bain**, Archie M. (*Manitoba*) M.Sc.: "Distribution of stress in welded joints." (Engineering: Mackay, H.)

29-503 **Blau**, Abraham (*McGill*) M.Sc.: "Studies on microbic dissociation in vibrio comma." (Bacteriology: Harrison, F.)

29-504 **Blumberg**, Perry (*City College of New York*) M.Sc.: "The inorganic constituents of egg yolk." (Biochemistry: Collip, J. & Macallum, A.)

29-505 **Bray**, Alton C. (*McGill*) M.Sc.: "A petrographic study of certain corderite-bearing rocks ." (Geological Sciences: Graham, R.)

29-506 **Bruger**, Moses (*McGill*) M.Sc.: "The effects of solutions of dextrose and various electrolytes, introvenously administered, on the rate of secretion and composition of the urine." (Pharmacology: Stehle, R. & Scarth, G.)

29-507 **Dobridge**, Ronald W. (*McGill*) M.Sc.: "Theory and practice of resistivity measurements for earth and other materials." (Physics: Wallace, G. & Eve, A.)

29-508 **Gerson**, Harold S. (*McGill*) M.Sc.: "Investigation of lead-zinc replacements in limestone where there is no apparent connection with igneous activity." (Geological Sciences: O'Neill, J. & Bell, J.)

29-509 **Helwig**, Gerald V. (*McGill*) M.Sc.: "Piezoelectricity and its application. The variation of the Peizoelectric effect of tourmaline with temperature." (Physics: Keys, D. & Maass, O.)

29-510 **Hopper**, Ronald V. (*McGill*) M.Sc.: "The manganese deposits of Tchiatonsi, Georgia, Russia." (Geological Sciences: Clark, J. & McBride, W.)

29-511 **Kamm**, Josephine J. (*McGill*) M.Sc.: "Comparative anatomy of the great horned owl and whistling swan." (Zoology: Willey, A.)

29-512 **Mirsky**, Isadore A. (*McGill*) M.Sc.: "Studies on the effect of rate and rhythm of the heart on the coronary circulation." (Physiology: Tait, J. & Stehle, R.)

29-513 **Mueller**, William H. (*Alberta*) M.Sc.: "The oxidation of organic compounds." (Chemistry: Hatcher, W. & Snell, J.)

29-514 **Painter**, Richard H. (*Toronto*) M.Sc.: "The biology of the tarnished plant bug *Lygus pratensis* L." (Entomology: Brittain, W. & Willey, A.)

29-515 **Perry**, Stanley Z. (*McGill*) M.Sc.: "(a) Constitution of the so-called tetrabromobutyralt-chyde. (b) An investigation into the 'super-molecular' structure of polyethyleneoxide and dirinylether." (Cellulose Chemistry: Hibbert, H. & Stehle, R.)

29-516 **Platt**, Muriel E. (*Smith*) M.Sc.: "Ring migration and isomerism in the glycerol cyclic acetals." (Chemistry: Hibbert, H.)

29-517 **Pugsley**, Leonard I. (*Acadia*) M.Sc.: "Studies of bovine amnionic fluid." (Agricultural Chemistry: McCarthy, J. & Collip, J.)

29-518 **Starrock**, Murray G. (*Alberta*) M.Sc.: "Cyclic acetal formation." (Chemistry: Hibbert, H.)

29-519 **Silver**, Ralph C. (*McGill*) M.Sc.: "Electrical power transmission and stability in electrical systems." (Electrical Engineering: Christie, C. & King, L.)

29-520 **Sutherland**, Hugh S. (*Mount Allison*) M.Sc.: "A study of the butylene halogen hydride reactions." (Chemistry: Maass, O.)

29-521 **Thompson**, Robert R. (*Toronto*) M.Sc.: "The bacterial flora of the pregnant bovine uterus." (Bacteriology: Conklin, R.)

**M.A. Spring 1929**

29-522 **Auld**, Jean M. (*Colorado*) M.A.: "The inter-relation between Attic tragedy and Greek art of the Classical period." (Greek: Traquair, * & Woodhead, W.)

29-523 **Banfill**, Gladys M. (*McGill*) M.A.: "La theâtre de Marie Lenéru." (French: McCullagh, * & Furness, L.)

29-524 **Brierley**, James G. (*McGill*) M.A.: "A study of literature in English produced in the province of Quebec prior to Confederation with its historical background." (English: Macmillan, C.)

29-525 **Cardonsky**, Mary (*McGill*) M.A.: "The problem of the education of exception children in the province of Quebec." (Psychology: Tait, W. & Kellogg, C. & Derick, C.)

29-526 **Cheasley**, Clifford H. (*McGill*) M.A.: "The chain store movement in Canada." (Economics: Kemp, H. & Hemmeon, J.)

29-527 **D'Hauteserve**, Louis (*Paris*, France) M.A.: "La crise de l'adolescence telle qu'elle apparait dans les romans français parus depuis la guerre de 1914-18." (French: Du Roure, R.)

29-528 **Draper**, Herbert L. (*Manitoba*) M.A.: "Alberta coal." (Economics & Political Science: Kemp, H. & Hemmeon, J.)

29-529 **Epstein**, Elsie (*McGill*) M.A.: "The minimum wage for women and its application in Canada." (Economics & Political Science: Freeman, * & Hemmeon, J.)

29-530 **Featherston**, Florence E. (*McGill*) M.A.: "Some contributions of psychology to industry." (Psychology: Tait, W. & Dawson, C.)

29-531 **Ferrand**, Lucy M. (*Michigan*) M.A.: "La revendication des femmes chez Brieux." (French: Du Roure, R. & Macmillan, C.)

29-532 **Garland**, Sidney G. (*McGill*) M.A.: "The Church in the changing city." (Sociology: Best, E. & Dawson, C.)

29-533 **Goldenberg**, Hyman C. (*McGill*) M.A.: "The Canadian budgets (1867-1928)." (Economics: Kemp, H. & Hemmeon, J.)

29-534 **Gruchy**, Allan G. (*British Columbia*) M.A.: "Collective bargaining in the building, coal-mining and transportation industries of Canada." (Economics: Hemmeon, J. & Kemp, H.)

29-535 **Hodgins**, Samuel R. (*McGill*) M.A.: "The status of the familiar essay in Canadian literature." (English: Macmillan, C.)

29-536 **Howat**, David (*Cambridge*, England) M.A.: "A critical study of the teaching of mathematics in the schools of Montreal and the surrounding district." (Psychology: Sullivan, C. & Kellogg, C.)

29-537 **Jahn**, Helen L. (*Syracuse*) M.A.: "The American novel since 1910." (English: Latham, G. & Dawson, C.)

29-538 **Jefferis**, Jeffrey D. (*Bishop's*) M.A.: "Literary indecency in certain Roman satirists." (Latin: Thompson, A. & Noad, A.)

29-539 **Johnston**, Agnew H. (*McGill*) M.A.: "Diplomatic relations between Canada and Japan, with special reference to underlying economic and political conditions." (Economics: Kemp, H. & Goforth, W.)

29-540 **Kelland**, Frank J. (*McGill*) M.A.: 'Public and private ownership in the hydro electric industry of Canada." (Economics: Hemmeon, J.)

29-541 **Kirschberg**, Abraham (*McGill*) M.A.: "American investments and control of capital in Canada." (Economics: Hemmeon, J. & Kemp, H.)

29-542 **Knowles**, Eustace C. (*McGill*) M.A.: "The English philosophical radicals and Lower Canada, 1822-40." (History: Fryer, C. & Johnson, W.)

29-543 **Lyman**, Beatrice M. (*McGill*) M.A.: "The attitude of the Middle Ages towards animals." (History: Waugh, W. & Willey, A.)

29-544 **Mackay**, Robert de W. (*McGill*) M.A.: "The philosophy and poetry of Robert Browning with special reference to his philosophy of immortality; its sources and some conclusions." (English: Stanley, C. & Noad, A.)

29-545 **McLetchie**, James K. (*McGill*) M.A.: "Germany's acquisition of South-West Africa: a study in British imperial policy, 1880-1885." (History: Fryer, C. & Lighthall, W.)

29-546 **Mendels**, Morton M. (*McGill*) M.A.: "The asbestos industry in Canada." (Economics: Kemp, H. & Hemmeon, J.)

29-547 **Reed**, John G. (*McGill*) M.A.: "The milling industry in Canada." (Economics: Hemmeon, J. & Freeman, *)

29-548 **Townsend**, Eleanor H. (*New Brunswick*) M.A.: "Anatole France critique litteraire." (French: Du Roure, R. & Graff, W.)

29-549 **Traver**, Lillie A. (*Queen's*) M.A.: "Early negotiations for the acquisition of the Hudson's Bay territory by the Union government of Canada." (History: Fryer, C.)

29-550 **Troop**, William H. (*Toronto*) M.A.: "The political and constitutional implications of the 1926 Imperial Conference." (Economics: Hemmeon, J. & Freeman, *)

29-551 **Edwards**, Lyford P. (*Chicago*) M.A.: " " (**: **)

**M.S.A. Fall 1929**

29-552 **Cox**, Kenneth (*Toronto*) M.Sc.: "A study of the effect of competition on the comparative yields of varieties." (Agronomy: Summerby, R.)

**M.Sc. Fall 1929**

29-553 **Daniels**, Eli (*McGill*) M.Sc.: "Effects of certain hormones and electrolytes on the circulation." (Physiology: Tait, J.)

29-554 **Godbout**, Fernand (*Laval*) M.Sc.: "A study of seed treatments." (Plant Pathology: Coulson, '. & Lods, E.)

29-555 **Harkness**, Harold W. (*Queen's*) M.Sc.: "The development of high precision in absorption hygrometry, with new methods and applications." (Physics: Shaw, A. & Maass, O.)

M.A. Fall 1929

29-556 **Kiefer**, Elsie B. (*Kansas*) M.A.: "The development of stage lighting in England and America." (English: Noad, A. & Tait, W.)

29-557 **Phelan**, Lewis J. (*Loyola of Montréal*) M.A.: "Sir Edmund Gosse and the critical portrait." (English: Woodhead, W. & Noad, A.)

## ANNUAL LISTING

### Ph.D. Spring 1930

30-001 **Chalmers**, William (*British Columbia*) Ph.D.: "Influence of structure upon the ability of organic compounds to polymerize." (Chemistry: Allen, C. & Whitby, G.)

30-002 **Currie**, Balfour W. (*Saskatchewan*) Ph.D.: "Adsorption of ions at a water surface." (Physics: McTaggart, A. & Eve, A.)

30-003 **Gallay**, Wilfred (*McGill*) Ph.D.: "Studies in polymerization." (Chemistry: Hibbert, H. & Whitby, G.)

30-004 **Harkness**, Harold W. (*Queen's*) Ph.D.: "The Stark effect in xenon." (Physics: Foster, J.)

30-005 **Langstroth**, George O. (*Dalhousie*) Ph.D.: "Relative intensities of the stark components in helium." (Physics: Foster, J.)

30-006 **MacKay**, Margaret E. (*Dalhousie*) Ph.D.: "The action of histamine on secretory and motor phenomena in different digestive glands." (Physiology: Babkin, B.)

30-007 **McRae**, Duncan R. (*McGill*) Ph.D.: "The effect of fine structure on the Stark component of H-alpha." (Physics: Saunders, F. & Foster, J.)

30-008 **Morgan**, Oliver M. (*Western*) Ph.D.: "An investigation of equilibria existing in gas-water systems forming electrolytes." (Chemistry: Maass, O.)

30-009 **Mueller**, William H. (*Alberta*) Ph.D.: "Comparative studies in oxidation." (Chemistry: Hatcher, W.)

30-010 **Peiker**, Alfred L. (*Trinity*) Ph.D.: "The mechanism for the hydrolysis of hydrogen cyanide." (Chemistry: Kreible, V. & Maass, O.)

30-011 **Phillips**, John B. (*McGill*) Ph.D.: "The nature of the resins of Jack pine." (Chemistry: Hibbert, H.)

30-012 **Pinhey**, Kathleen F. (*McGill*) Ph.D.: "Investigations on invertebrate blood." (Zoology: Redfield, A. & Willey, A.)

30-013 **Sankey**, Charles A. (*Toronto*) Ph.D.: "The mechanism of the action of sulphurous acid on lignin and related compounds." (Chemistry: Hibbert, H.)

30-014 **Sturrock**, Murray G. (*Alberta*) Ph.D.: "The mechanism of organic oxidation." (Chemistry: Hatcher, W.)

### Ph.D. Fall 1930

30-015 **Buxton**, Kenneth S. (*Clark*) Ph.D.: "Colorimetric measurements in relation to surface phenomena." (Chemistry: Johnson, F. & Maass, O.)

# ANNUAL LISTING

## Mus.D. Fall 1930

30-016 **Treharne**, Bryceson (*McGill*) Mus.D.: "Musical compositions." (Music: Clarke, D. & Perrin, H.)

## M.Sc. Spring 1930

30-501 **Baxter**, Hamilton A. (*McGill*) M.Sc.: "The nervous control of the salivary secretion." (Physiology: Tait, J.)

30-502 **Campbell**, Herbert N. (*McGill*) M.Sc.: "Kinetics of chemical change in gaseous systems." (Chemistry: Steacie, E. & Foster, J.)

30-503 **Gottlieb**, Rudolf (*McGill*) M.Sc.: "Haemolytic jaundice, with special reference to icterus neonatorum." (Physiology: Tait, J. & Waugh, T.)

30-504 **Hardy**, Robert M. (*Manitoba*) M.Sc.: "Further investigations of the distribution of stresses in welded joints." (Engineering: Sullivan, C. & Mackay, H.)

30-505 **Katzman**, John (*McGill*) M.Sc.: "On the double striations in hydrogen." (Physics: Keys, D.)

30-506 **L'Hérisson**, Camille (*Haiti*) M.Sc.: "Experimental culture and reactions of paramecium." (Zoology: Willey, A.)

30-507 **Linton**, Everett P. (*Mount Allison*) M.Sc.: "The preparation and properties of pure hydrogen peroxide." (Chemistry: Maass, O.)

30-508 **MacRae**, Norman A. (*Queen's*) M.Sc.: "Studies in the biology of loose smut of barley." (Plant Pathology: Lods, E. & Coulson, J.)

30-509 **Moore**, Leonard P. (*Minnesota*) M.Sc.: "The action of sulphurous acid and bisulphites on cellulose." (Chemistry: Hibbert, H. & Scarth, G.)

30-510 **Paquet**, Arthur (*Laval*) M.Sc.: "Mechanism of cyclic formation." (Chemistry: Hibbert, H.)

30-511 **Skazin**, Lev (*Crech*, Russia) M.Sc.: "Studies on maple syrup and maple sugar." (Agricultural Chemistry: Allen, C. & Snell, J.)

30-512 **Taylor**, Bertram W. (*McGill*) M.Sc.: "Investigations on invertebrate digestion." (Zoology: Berrill, N. & Scarth, G.)

30-513 **Webster**, Donald R. (*Dalhousie*) M.Sc.: "Variations in the acidity of pure gastric juice." (Physiology: Babkin, B. & Collip, J.)

30-514 **Weldon**, Frederick E. (*McGill*) M.Sc.: "The treatment of gold ore by flotation." (Mining Engineering: McBride, W. & Stansfield, A.)

30-515 **Williamson**, John T. (*McGill*) M.Sc.: "A detailed petrographic study of ten mile rock occurrence, Hall's Bay Road, Nfld." (Geological Sciences: Graham, R.)

30-516 **Wright**, Robert H. (*British Columbia*) M.Sc.: "On the vapour density of hydrogen sulphide gas." (Chemistry: Maass, O.)

## ANNUAL LISTING

### M.A. Spring 1930

30-517 **Best**, Kathleen E. (*McMaster*) M.A.: "Old age pension legislation in Canada." (Economics: Kemp, H. & Hemmeon, J.)

30-518 **Blouin**, Wilhelmine E. (*Seton Hill*) M.A.: "Le catholicisme de M. Paul Bourget etudié dans ses principaux romans et nouvelles." (French: Du Roure, R. & Graff, W.)

30-519 **Burk**, Christopher A. (*McGill*) M.A.: "Capital and financial organization in Canada." (Economics: Leacock, S. & Kemp, H.)

30-520 **Camerlain**, Homer H. (*McGill*) M.A.: "Economic relations of Canada with the British West Indies." (Economics: Freeman, *)

30-521 **Carroll**, Lovell C. (*McGill*) M.A.: "Provincial public finance in Canada." (Economics: Hemmeon, J. & Kemp, H.)

30-522 **Chait**, Rachel (*McGill*) M.A.: "The Cynewulf question." (English: Graff, W. & Latham, G.)

30-523 **Cohen**, Bernard B. (*McGill*) M.A.: "The federal income tax in Canada." (Economics: Kemp, H. & Hemmeon, J.)

30-524 **Dawes**, Charles H. (*McGill*) M.A.: "The question of marriage in the novels of 1880-1900." (English: Tait, W. & Files, H.)

30-525 **Donald**, Henry G. (*McGill*) M.A.: "A critical analysis of the writings of Aphra Behn." (English: Dawson, C. & Files, H.)

30-526 **Frank**, Harold (*McGill*) M.A.: "The psychology of behaviourism." (Psychology: Tait, W. & Dawson, C.)

30-527 **Gough**, Roger W. (*McGill*) M.A.: "The political philosophy of Thomas Carlyle, with special emphasis upon his theory of the hero." (English: Hendel, C. & Noad, A.)

30-528 **Greaves**, Ida C. (*McGill*) M.A.: "The Negro in Canada." (Economics: Leacock, S. & Kemp, H.)

30-529 **Hamilton**, Andrew W. (*Saskatchewan*) M.A.: "Migration of population between Canada and the United States." (Economics & Political Science: Leacock, S. & Kemp, H.)

30-530 **Heard**, Jack F. (*Western*) M.A.: "The striated discharge in gases." (Physics: Keys, D.)

30-531 **Japp**, Robert (*St. Andrews*) M.A.: "A critical study of the teaching of English in the Protestant schools of Montreal and the surrounding district." (Psychology: Tait, W. & Clarke, F.)

30-532 **Jenkins**, Lloyd H. (*Acadia*) M.A.: "Dramatic technique and tragic values in the works of Eugene Gladstone O'Neill." (English: Hendel, C. & Files, H.)

30-533 **Lande**, Harold B. (*McGill*) M.A.: "Economic factors affecting the trend of language in the Province of Quebec." (Economics: Hemmeon, J.)

30-534 **Lawrence**, Gertrude R. (*Montréal*) M.A.: "The role of Goldsmith and Sheridan in eighteenth century comedy." (English: Files, H.)

30-535 **Legge**, Katharine B. (*California*) M.A.: "Labour legislation in Canada affecting women and children." (Economics: Hemmeon, J.)

30-536 **MacMillan**, Donald N. (*McGill*) M.A.: "The relation between religion and ethics." (Philosophy: Hendel, C. & Stanley, C.)

30-537 **MacSporran**, Maysie S. (*McGill*) M.A.: "James McGill, a critical biographical study." (History: Lightall, W. & Fryer, C.)

30-538 **Moore**, Ruth E. (*McGill*) M.A.: "Patriotism and political propaganda in the plays of Euripides." (Classics: Woodhead, W. & Noad, A.)

30-539 **Munroe**, David C. (*McGill*) M.A.: "The jurisdiction over merchant shipping within the British empire." (Economics: Leacock, S.)

30-540 **Parthenais**, J. Theodore (*Boston*) M.A.: "Les origines du journalisme Canadien-Français." (French: Furness, L. & Forsey, E.)

30-541 **Pollard**, Samuel L. (*McGill*) M.A.: "Fifty years of industrial transition in the British Navy - from sail to steam from wood to iron (1820-70)." (History: **)

30-542 **Pursley**, Robert (*McGill*) M.A.: "The psychological implications of Mr. Bertrand Russell's philosophy." (Psychology: Tait, W. & Hendel, C.)

30-543 **Radler**, Ruth (*McGill*) M.A.: "British and American influences on Canadian news content as shown by a study of two Montreal newspapers." (Sociology: Dawson, C. & Latham, G.)

30-544 **Savage**, Mae L. (*McGill*) M.A.: "Bank credit in Canada." (Economics: Day, J. & Kemp, H.)

30-545 **Smith**, Gladys L. (*Alberta*) M.A.: "The regional basis of news distribution in the prairie provinces." (Sociology: **)

30-546 **Spence**, Kenneth W. (*McGill*) M.A.: "An experimental study of the maze with special reference to its reliability." (Psychology: Tait, J. & Kellogg, C.)

30-547 **Talpis**, Clarence (*McGill*) M.A.: "Lucretius and his times." (Latin: Stanley, C. & Waugh, W.)

30-548 **Tanner**, Lea E. (*Queen's*) M.A.: "Le travail dans l'oeuvre de Pierre Hamp." (French: Lemaitre, G. & Hemmeon, J.)

30-549 **Zitzmann**, Irene J. (*Omaha*) M.A.: "Greek influence on Shakespeare." (English: Macmillan, C. )

M.Sc. Fall 1930

30-550 **Evans**, Joseph P. (*Harvard*) M.Sc.: "Experimental epilepsy.A study of the effects of cerebral wounds and cerebral excisions, with a review of the literature of post traumatic epilepsy."

30-551 **Baxter**, Stewart G. (*McGill*) M.Sc.: "The nervous control of the pancreatic gland in the rabbit." (Physiology: Babkin, B. & Tait, J.)

30-552 **Stavrakis**, George V. (*Odessa*, Russia) M.Sc.: "Studies on the motor mechanism of the salivary glands." (Physiology: Babkin, B. & Stehle, R.)

30-553 **Wyman**, Harold R. (*Dalhousie*) M.Sc.: "Surface energy relationships." (Chemistry: Maass, O. & Shaw, A.)

M.A. Fall 1930

30-554 **Grant**, Elizabeth R. (*McGill*) M.A.: "Studies in glycogen metabolism." (Biochemistry: Collip, J. & Long, C.)

30-555 **McHarg**, Muriel S. (*Bishop's*) M.A.: "The pauperization of the Roman populace during the Later Republican period, with special reference to frumentation laws and distributions." (Latin: MacDermot, J. and Woodhead, W.)

30-556 **Wilson**, Evelyn C. (*McGill*) M.A.: "The Seat of Government question,1839-1859." (History: Fryer, C. & Stanley, C.)

## ANNUAL LISTING

Ph.D. Spring 1931

31-001 **Allardyce**, William J. (*British Columbia*) Ph.D.: "Chemical and physiological studies of the parathyroid hormone." (Biochemistry: Collip, J.)

31-002 **Ball**, Ralph H. (*British Columbia*) Ph.D.: "Cellulose ethers." (Chemistry: Hibbert, H.)

31-003 **Beatty**, Stanley A. (*Queen's*) Ph.D.: "The chemistry of the soluble proteins of fish muscle and its probable relation to muscular movement and to rigor mortis." (Biochemistry: Collip, J.)

31-004 **Bedford**, Robert H. (*Alberta*) Ph.D.: "The vertical distribution of marine bacteria in the northern Pacific Ocean." (Bacteriology: Murray, E.)

31-005 **Cooper**, Douglas L. (*King's*) Ph.D.: "Aberrations from the ideal gas laws and a precision method for the determination of the densities of gases." (Chemistry: Maass, O.)

31-006 **Grace**, Nathaniel H. (*Saskatchewan*) Ph.D.: "The sorption of vapors by wood and cellulose." (Chemistry: Maass, O.)

31-007 **Howlett**, Leslie E. (*British Columbia*) Ph.D.: "The Raman effect." (Physics: Eve, A.)

31-008 **Sutherland**, Hugh S. (*Mount Allison*) Ph.D.: "A study of the reactions between unsaturated hydrocarbons and the halogen hydrides." (Chemistry: Maass, O.)

31-009 **Tarr**, Hugh L. (*British Columbia*) Ph.D.: "Studies in bacterial metabolism." (Bacteriology: Hibbert, H.)

31-010 **Wright**, Robert H. (*British Columbia*) Ph.D.: "The nature and properties of aqueous solutions of hydrogen sulphide." (Chemistry: Maass, O.)

Ph.D. Fall 1931

31-011 **Barker**, Walter E. (*Queen's*) Ph.D.: "1,5-Diketones: addition reactions of phenyl vinyl ketone." (Chemistry: Allen, C.)

31-012 **Helwig**, Gerald V. (*McGill*) Ph.D.: "The structure of certain optically active dithionates." (Physics: Barnes, W.)

31-013 **Sawyer**, William R. (*Queen's*) Ph.D.: "Studies in photochemistry." (Chemistry: Johnson, F.)

M.Sc. Spring 1931

31-501 **Brodie**, Maurice (*McGill*) M.Sc.: "Active immunization against poliomyelitis in monkeys." (Physiology: Tait, J.)

31-502 **Brown**, Alexander B. (*Edinburgh*, Scotland) M.Sc.: "Effects of temperature on stomata of excised leaves of *zebrina pendula*." (Botany: Scarth, G.)

31-503 **Bynoe**, Evan T. (*McGill*) M.Sc.: "A systematic study of the genus mycobacterium." (Bacteriology: Gray, P.)

31-504 **Cooper**, Lawrence O. (*McGill*) M.Sc.: "Cavitation phenomena and the flow in diverging tubes." (Hydraulics: Brown, E.)

31-505 **Doubilet**, Henry (*McGill*) M.Sc.: "Studies in cholesterosis." (Experimental Medicine: Archibald, E.)

31-506 **Edelstein**, Leo J. (*New York*) M.Sc.: "The structure and function of the lateral line and development of the vertebral column in aquatic amphibia." (Zoology: Willey, A.)

31-507 **Howatt**, John L. (*McGill*) M.Sc.: "Studies on the mosaic disease of tobacco." (Plant Pathology: Coulson, J.)

31-508 **Hutt**, Gordon M. (*Manitoba*) M.Sc.: "The whitemud sediments of southern Saskatchewan." (Geological Sciences: Graham, R.)

31-509 **Melville**, Kenneth I. (*McGill*) M.Sc.: "Some aspects of the pharmacology of mercury." (Pharmacology: Stehle, R.)

31-510 **Morehouse**, Fred R. ( ) M.Sc.: "The preparation of ethyl acetylene and a determination of some of its physical constants." (Chemistry: Maass, O.)

31-511 **Morrison**, Thomas J. (*McGill*) M.Sc.: "Cavitation phenomena and flow in diverging tubes." (Hydraulics: Brown, E.)

31-512 **O'Connell**, Francis J. (*McGill*) M.Sc.: "The investigation of slime settling in Dorr thickeners." (Mining Engineering: McBride, W.)

31-513 **Richardson**, Ronald E. (*Alberta*) M.Sc.: "Penetration studies: the circulation of alkali reagents into and of reaction products out of the fibre cavity." (Chemistry: Maass, O.)

31-514 **Ross**, Douglas A. (*McGill*) M.Sc.: "Experiments on the sense of hearing in fishes." (Physiology: Tait, J.)

31-515 **Ross**, William B. (*McGill*) M.Sc.: "The measurement of specific inductive capacity in irregularly shaped bodies." (Physics: Keys, D.)

31-516 **Thomas**, William F. (*McGill*) M.Sc.: "The investigation of slime settling in Dorr thickeners." (Mining Engineering: McBride, W.)

31-517 **Whitehead**, Walter E. (*McGill*) M.Sc.: "The morphology of the head-capsule of some coleopterus larvae." (Entomology: DuPorte, E.)

31-518 **Wykes**, Eric R. (*McGill*) M.Sc.: "The petrology of some crystalline rocks of the Perth Sheet, Ontario." (Geological Sciences: Osborne, F.)

M.A. Spring 1931

31-519 **Allen**, Marguerite Z. (*Omaha*) M.A.: "The Christian implications in Beowulf." (English: Latham, G.)

## ANNUAL LISTING

31-520 **Bergithon**, Carl (*McGill*) M.A.: "The problem of social insurance in Canada." (Economics & Political Science: Forsey, E.)

31-521 **Berman**, Alfred (*Manitoba*) M.A.: "The construction industry in Montreal, with special reference to seasonal unemployment." (Economics & Political Science: Marsh, L.)

31-522 **Brown**, George (*McGill*) M.A.: "The influence on English literature of the 'Edinburgh Review' under Francis Jeffrey." (English: Noad, A.)

31-523 **Burton**, Garland G. (*McGill*) M.A.: "The social ethics of the Prophets." (Oriental Languages: Brockwell, C.)

31-524 **Caplan**, Benjamin (*McGill*) M.A.: "Theories of value from David Hume to John Stuart Mill: a critical study." (Economics & Political Science: Hemmeon, J.)

31-525 **Connors**, Vara M. (*Tulsa*) M.A.: "Maurice Maeterlinck devant la critique Americaine." (French: Furness, L.)

31-526 **Cruikshank**, Marion G. (*Middlebury*) M.A.: "The influence of the university on the development of drama in the United States and Canada." (English: Macmillan, C.)

31-527 **Detlor**, W. Lyall (*McGill*) M.A.: "The development and influence of Newman's ecclesiastical views." (English: Latham, G.)

31-528 **Estall**, Henry M. (*McGill*) M.A.: "The doctrine of the will as consent." (Philosophy: Porteous, A.)

31-529 **Etziony**, Mordecai (*McGill*) M.A.: "The problem of 'emotions' with particular reference to the emotional life of the child." (Psychology: Kellogg, C.)

31-530 **Feiner**, Abraham (*McGill*) M.A.: "Factors entering into the use of Canadian wheat in foreign countries." (Economics & Political Science: Leacock, S.)

31-531 **Flahault**, Elizabeth (*Montréal*) M.A.: "La Bretagne dans les lettres contemporaines." (French: Furness, L. & King, L.)

31-532 **Gold**, Samuel (*McGill*) M.A.: "Elementary theory of quadratic forms." (Mathematics: Sullivan, C.)

31-533 **Hewitt**, Frank S. (*McGill*) M.A.: "Philosophy in George Eliot's novels." (English: Files, H. & Hendel, C.)

31-534 **Lang**, John G. (*St. Andrews*) M.A.: "Educative activities outside the school programme." (Education: Clarke, F. & Dawson, C.)

31-535 **MacGachen**, Freda K. (*McGill*) M.A.: "The history and development of scenery on the English stage from mediaeval times to the year 1700." (English: Macmillan, C.)

31-536 **MacLaggan**, Marjorie F. (*Dalhousie*) M.A.: "Shakespeare's use of sound and colour." (English: Macmillan, C.)

31-537 **Morton**, Nelson W. (*McGill*) M.A.: "The psychology of evidence." (Psychology: Tait, W. & Corbett, P.)

31-538 **Norris**, Kenneth E. (*McGill*) M.A.: "Characterisitcs and abilities of evening high school students." (Psychology: Kellogg, C. & Clarke, F.)

31-539 **Pattison**, Irma E. (*Toronto*) M.A.: "The manufacture and marketing of knitted goods in Canada." (Economics & Political Science: Leacock, S. & Goforth, W.)

31-540 **Rhoades**, Winifred (*Illinois*) M.A.: "La representation de la guerre de 1914-1918 et ses consequences directes par le theatre frençais." (French: Lemaitre, G. & MacDermott, J.)

31-541 **Rubin**, Lionel L. (*McGill*) M.A.: "The transfer of natural resources to the Prairie Provinces." (Economics & Political Science: Hemmeon, J.)

31-542 **Shlakman**, Vera (*McGill*) M.A.: "Unemployment in the men's clothing industry of Montreal." (Economics & Political Science: Marsh, L.)

31-543 **Stansfield**, Ellen E. (*McGill*) M.A.: "The wonderland in English literature." (English: Noad, A. & Hughes, E.)

31-544 **Sullivan**, Norah E. (*McGill*) M.A.: "The purpose and development of the dance in the English drama from 1590 to 1642." (English: Macmillan, C.)

31-545 **Tuttle**, Harry G. (*McGill*) M.A.: "Frontier religious organization, with special reference to the Peace River area." (Sociology: Dawson, C. & Latham, G.)

31-546 **Wade**, Margaret M. (*Manitoba*) M.A.: "A sociological study of the dependent child." (Sociology: Dawson, C. & Best, E.)

31-547 **Warldeworth**, Eleanor S. (*McGill*) M.A.: "Francois Marie Perrot and the Ile Perrot." (History: Adair, E.)

31-548 **Willis**, Stewart W. (*Saskatchewan*) M.A.: "Agricultural credit in Western Canada." (Economics & Political Science: Culliton, J.)

31-549 **Woods**, Harry D. (*New Brunswick*) M.A.: "Economic relations of the Maritime Provinces to Central Canada." (Economics & Political Science: Hemmeon, J. & Goforth, W.)

**M.Com. Spring 1931**

31-550 **Smith**, Greig B. (*Queen's*) M.Com.: "Inter-imperial trade in cotton textiles, 1914-1928." (Economics & Political Science: Day, J.)

**M.Sc. Fall 1931**

31-551 **Gage**, Everett L. (*Pennsylvania*) M.Sc.: "The effect of vasomotor nerve section on experimental epilepsy." (Experimental Medicine: Russel, C. & Babkin, B.)

31-552 **Glynn**, John H. (*Chicago*) M.Sc.: "The mechanism of staphylococcus aureus localization in rabbit tissues." (Bacteriology: Murray, E. & Rhea, L.)

31-553 **Hicks**, Arthur J. (*McGill*) M.Sc.: "A study of diseases of narcissi." (Plant Pathology: Coulson, J.)

31-554 **Komarov,** Simon A. (*Kharkov,* Russia) M.Sc.: "Organic constituents of gastric juice." (Physiology: Babkin, B. & Collip, J.)

31-555 **McDougall,** John F. (*Alberta*) M.Sc.: "The initial stresses in welded joints." (Civil Engineering & Applied Mechanics: Jamieson, R. & Sullivan C.)

31-556 **Morton,** Richard (*McGill*) M.Sc.: "The kinetics of chemical change in gaseous systems." (Chemistry: Steacie, E. & Keys, D.)

31-557 **Reeve,** Herbert A. (*McGill*) M.Sc.: "The kinetics of gas reactions." (Chemistry: Steacie, E. & Foster, J.)

31-558 **Snell,** Arthur H. (*Toronto*) M.Sc.: "The comparison of gaseous densities by the method of balancing columns, with applications." (Physics: Shaw, A. & Maass, O.)

31-559 **Stewart,** William W. (*Dalhousie*) M.Sc.: "The viscosity of sulphur dioxide." (Chemistry: Maass, O.)

31-560 **Wells,** Franklin B. (*Illinois*) M.Sc.: "The preparation of certain organic compounds of nitrogen." (Chemistry: Allen, C. & Worrall, D.)

**M.A. Fall 1931**

31-561 **Bisson,** Margaret M. (*McGill*) M.A.: "Le théâtre français à Montréal 1878-1931." (French: Du Roure, R.)

31-562 **Coade,** Emma L. (*Manitoba*) M.A.: "La doctrine de l'unanimisme dans les oeuvres de M. Jules Romains." (French: Du Roure, R. & Celieres, A.)

31-563 **Gilmore,** Laura B. (*New Hampshire*) M.A.: "La France d'après-guerre, jugee par le roman américain." (French: Du Roure, R. & Dombrowski, J.)

31-564 **Lawley,** John D. (*Mount Allison*) M.A.: "The attitude of the Roman satirists towards foreigners." (Latin: Thompson, A.)

31-565 **Longan,** Virginia L. (*Park*) M.A.: "L'Alsace-Lorraine dans le roman français entre les deux guerres." (French: Du Roure, R. & Celieres, A.)

31-566 **Lowry,** Hope (*Albrion*) M.A.: "L'influence française sur les poètes hispano-américains de l'école 'modernista'." (French: Du Roure, R. & Dombrowski, J.)

31-567 **Tapp,** James S. (*Western*) M.A.: "Investigation of density of vapors in equilibrium with liquids." (Chemistry: Maass, O. & Shaw, A.)

## ANNUAL LISTING

**Ph.D. Spring 1932**

32-001 **Browne**, John S. (*McGill*) Ph.D.: "Chemical and physiological properties of crystalline oestrogenic hormones." (Biochemistry: Collip, J.)

32-002 **Filby**, Edgar A. (*Saskatchewan*) Ph.D.: "The specific volume of cellulose and wood and the density of adsorbed water vapour." (Chemistry: Maass, O.)

32-003 **Frame**, Gordon F. (*Dalhousie*) Ph.D.: "Some reactions of gamma ketonic esters." (Chemistry: Allen, C.)

32-004 **Gallaugher**, Arthur F. (*British Columbia*) Ph.D.: "The physical and chemical properties of the polyethylene glycols and their derivatives." (Chemistry: Hibbert, H.)

32-005 **Gurd**, George W. (*Western*) Ph.D.: "Equilibria in the three component system: calcium oxide - sulphur dioxide - water over the temperature range 25$^{0}$C to 130$^{0}$C." (Chemistry: Maass, O.)

32-006 **Harwood**, Robert U. (*Alberta*) Ph.D.: "A study of methods for the analysis of bile." (Biochemistry:Thomson, D.)

32-007 **Heard**, Jack F. (*Western*) Ph.D.: "The Stark effect in the red region of the xenon spectrum." (Physics: Foster, J.)

32-008 **Linton**, Everett P. (*Mount Allison*) Ph.D.: "An investigation of the resonance method for the measurement of dielectric constant." (Chemistry: Maass, O.)

32-009 **McPhail**, Murchie K. (*British Columbia*) Ph.D.: "Hormonal studies of the placenta and the anterior lobe of the pituitary body." (Biochemistry: Collip, J.)

32-010 **Macklin**, Lionel S. (*Manitoba*) Ph.D.: "The penetration of sodium hydroxide solutions into spruce wood and the cooking of spruce wood by concentrated sodium hydroxide solutions." (Chemistry: Maass, O.)

32-011 **Morehouse**, Fred R. (*McGill*) Ph.D.: "Preparation and study of the physical properties of aliphatic acetylenes." (Chemistry: Maass, O.)

32-012 **Platt**, Muriel E. (*Smith*) Ph.D.: "Cyclic acetal formation, the ring-partition principle, and their relation to the structure of carbohydrates." (Chemistry: Hibbert, H.)

32-013 **Powell**, Edward C. (*Saskatchewan*) Ph.D.: "Studies in organic peracids." (Chemistry: Hatcher, W.)

32-014 **Pugsley**, Leonard I. (*Acadia*) Ph.D.: "Studies in calcium and phosphorus metabolism." (Biochemistry: Meakins, J.)

32-015 **Saunderson**, Hugh H. (*Manitoba*) Ph.D.: "The penetration of aqueous sulphite solutions into spruce wood." (Chemistry: Maass, O.)

32-016 **Sutherland**, John W. (*Alberta*) Ph.D.: "Penetration studies: the entry of liquids into the fibre cavity." (Chemistry: Maass, O.)

32-017 **Williams**, Alan R. (*Queen's*) Ph.D.: "The surface energy and heat of solution of solid rhombic sulphur and the heat of reaction of S (monoclinic) -- S (rhombic)." (Chemistry: Maass, O.)

## ANNUAL LISTING

### Ph.D. Fall 1932

32-019 **Allen**, John S. (*British Columbia*) Ph.D.: "I. The nature of polymerization and its relation to the dielectric constant. II. The electric moment in relation to the structure of organic compounds." (Chemistry: Hibbert, H.)

32-020 **Baxter**, Stewart G. (*McGill*) Ph.D.: "The role of the sympathetic nervous system in the secretory processes of the digestive glands." (Physiology: Babkin, B.)

32-021 **Grant**, Elizabeth R. (*McGill*) Ph.D.: "Studies in glycogen metabolism." (Experimental Medicine: Lang, C.)

32-022 **Greig**, Margaret E. (*McGill*) Ph.D.: "Studies in hydrogen migration." (Chemistry: Hibbert, H.)

32-023 **Grieve**, Arthur D. (*Western*) Ph.D.: "Equilibria in the three-component system: water - calcium oxide - sulphur dioxide over the temperature range $0^{o}$C to $25^{o}$C." (Chemistry: Maass, O.)

32-024 **Howland**, Frances (*Mount Holyoke*) Ph.D.: "The mechanism of organic reactions in the gaseous state: the kinetics of the oxidation of gaseous acetaldehyde." ((Chemistry: Hatcher, W. & Steacie, E.)

32-025 **Munro**, Ferdinand L. (*British Columbia*) Ph.D.: "The relation between particle size and light absorption by suspended particles." (Chemistry: Maass, O.)

32-026 **Thompson**, Robert R. (*Toronto*) Ph.D.: "A study of the distribution of *Brucella abortus* (Bang) in reacting cows and its isolation from sex organs and from glands." (Agricultural Bacteriology: Murray, E.)

32-027 **Watson**, Horace G. (*Toronto*) Ph.D.: "A new device and method for electromagnetic geophysical prospecting." (Physics: Keys, D.)

### M.Eng. Spring 1932

32-500 **Arcand**, Louis J. (*McGill*) M.Eng.: 'Some investigations in reinforced concrete: experimental research on concrete columns with transverse and longitudinal reinforcement." (Civil Engineering & Applied Mechanics: French, R.)

32-501 **Crawford**, James M. (*McGill*) M.Eng.: "Stability of generation and transmission systems." (Electrical Engineering: Christie, C.)

32-502 **Jacobsen**, Eric R. (*McGill*) M.Eng.: "Kane system of composite construction." (Civil Engineering & Applied Mechanics: Brown, E.)

32-503 **Moore**, William H. (*McGill*) M.Eng.: "Generation and reception of ultra short radio waves." (Electrical Engineering: Eve, A.)

32-504 **Ogilvy**, Robert F. (*McGill*) M.Eng.: "The value of planning in the establishment of large industrial enterprises." (Industrial Engineering: McKergow, C.)

32-505 **Stobart**, Walter T. (*McGill*) M.Eng.: "Flotation of gold and copper in Noranda ore." (Mining Engineering: McBride, W.)

32-506 **Vasilkioti**, Nikolai (*Czechoslovakia Technical*) M.Eng.: "Eccentricity and attitude of a full journal bearing." (Mechanical Engineering: Roberts, A.)

M.Sc. Spring 1932

32-507 **Adair**, Thomas H. (*Queen's*) M.Sc.: "Sponge iron: some conditions essential for its production." (Metallurgical Engineering: Stansfield, A.)

32-508 **Boothroyd**, Raymond A. (*McGill*) M.Sc.: "Studies concerning mosaic diseases of plants." (Plant Pathology: Coulson, J.)

32-509 **Buckland**, Francis C. (*British Columbia*) M.Sc.: "The geology and petrography of a section along the tramway, Mount Royal, Montreal, P. Que." (Geological Sciences: Osborne, F.)

32-510 **Cameron**, James W. (*McGill*) M.Sc.: "The morphology of *Halictus lerouxi*, Le P." (Entomology: DuPorte, E.)

32-511 **Chorobski**, Jerzy (*Cracow*, Poland) M.Sc.: "Origin, distribution and function of cranial vascular nerves. Part I. A vasodilator nervous pathway to the cerebral vessels from the central nervous system. Part II. On the occurrence of afferent nerve fibres in the internal carotid plexus." (Experimental Medicine: Cone, W.)

32-512 **Eardley**, Eric A. (*McGill*) M.Sc.: "Investigations of the secondary tumour formation by *Pseudomones tumefaciens* sm. and towns on herbaceous hosts." (Plant Pathology: Suit, R.)

32-513 **Grimes-Graeme**, Rhoderick C. (*McGill*) M.Sc.: "The petrology of certain igneous rocks of Newton township, Ontario." (Geological Sciences: Gill, J.)

32-514 **Halet**, Robert A. (*British Columbia*) M.Sc.: "A study of the geology in the vicinity of Corporation Quarry, Mt. Royal, Montreal." (Geological Sciences: Graham, R.)

32-515 **Hampton**, William F. (*Dalhousie*) M.Sc.: "Heat capacity of gelatin gels." (Chemistry: Mennie, J.)

32-516 **Johnson**, Robert E. (*McGill*) M.Sc.: "Cytological studies in the genus *Hordeum*." (Botany: Huskins, C.)

32-517 **Kay**, Muriel G. (*McGill*) M.Sc.: "Studies in polymerization." (Chemistry: Hatcher, W.)

32-518 **Lavallée**, Edouard (*Oka*) M.Sc.: "Investigations on some diseases of the pea plant in the Gaspé district, Que." (Plant Pathology: Coulson, J.)

32-519 **Lyons**, Walter (*McGill*) M.Sc.: "Experiments on electromagnetic shielding at frequencies between one and thirty kilocycles." (Physics: King, L.)

32-520 **McMaster**, Norman B. (*McGill*) M.Sc.: "The microbiology of air-dried cultivated soils." (Bacteriology: Gray, P.)

32-521 **Prebble**, Malcolm L. (*New Brunswick*) M.Sc.: "The biology of *Podisus serieventris*, with especial reference to its predatory habits." (Entomology: Brittain, W.)

32-522 **Rawlinson**, Herbert E. (*Alberta*) M.Sc.: "Histo-physiological studies on secretion in the salivary gland." (Physiology: Babkin, B.)

32-523 **Reeks**, Wilfrid S. (*McGill*) M.Sc.: "Morphology of the spruce saw-fly, *Diprion polytomum Hartig*." (Entomology: DuPorte, E.)

32-524 **Sutherland**, George F. (*McGill*) M.Sc.: "Auditory sense in dogs." (Physiology: Tait, J.)

M.A. Spring 1932

32-525 **Benning**, Paulette (*McGill*) M.A.: "The question of sex-differentiation in education." (Education: Clarke, F.)

32-526 **Edgar**, William S. (*McMaster*) M.A.: "Old age pensions: a study of opinion on the subject of state aid to necessitous old age in Great Britain." (History: Fryer, C.)

32-527 **Goforth**, William W. (*Toronto*) M.A.: "The Canadian tariff: a political instrument and an economic expedient, or, Post-war Canadian tariff." (Economics: Leacock, S.)

32-528 **Goodman**, Samuel J. (*McGill*) M.A.: "The planned economy in the capitalist state." (Economics: Hemmeon, J.)

32-529 **Heaton**, Phyllis (*McGill*) M.A.: "Standard of living studies and their significance, including a study in Montreal." (Sociology: Dawson, C.)

32-530 **Hebb**, Donald O. (*Dalhousie*) M.A.: "Conditioned and unconditioned reflexes and inhibition." (Psychology: Kellogg, C.)

32-531 **Kaplan**, Florence R. (*McGill*) M.A.: "Max Beerbohm: an appreciation." (English: Files, H.)

32-532 **Lees**, David (*Glasgow*, Scotland) M.A.: "The training of teachers: a comparison between Scotland and the province of Quebec." (Education: Clarke, F.)

32-533 **LePage**, Inez M. (*Manitoba*) M.A.: "Group organization and development of the adolescent girl." (Sociology: Cressey, P.)

32-534 **McCracken**, Edward J. (*St. Francis Xavier*) M.A.: "The steel industry of Nova Scotia." (Economics: Forsey, E.)

32-535 **McIntyre**, George D. (*McGill*) M.A.: "The cellophane industry in Canada and its relations to allied and inter-related industries." (Economics: Day, J.)

32-536 **MacKinnon**, Patrick A. (*Edinburgh*, Scotland) M.A.: "Classification in secondary schools." (Education: Clarke, F.)

32-537 **Matthews**, Florida L. (*Atlanta*) M.A.: "Edmond Rostand aux Etats-Unis." (French: Du Roure, R.)

32-538 **Picard**, Robert I. (*McGill*) M.A.: "Triangular preferential trade." (Economics: Leacock, S.)

32-539 **Prowse**, Alice R. (*McGill*) M.A.: "L'eau dans l'oeuvre de Lamartine." (French: Du Roure, R.)

32-540 **Rand**, Frank H. (*Queen's*) M.A.: "Dramatic censorship in France and England, 1843-1909: a study in comparative literature." (English: Macmillan, C.)

32-541 **Reid**, Ewart P. (*McGill*) M.A.: "The Doukhobors in Canada." (Economics: Hemmeon, J.)

32-542 **Roberts**, Gwen R. (*McGill*) M.A.: "Popular recreation in the Middle Ages." (History: Waugh, W.)

32-543 **Rollit**, John B. (*McGill*) M.A.: "The taxation of motor vehicles." (Economics: Hemmeon, J.)

32-544 **Ross**, Dorothy J. (*McGill*) M.A.: "The position and functions of the Justices of the Peace in England, 1600-1642." (History: Adair, E.)

32-545 **Ross**, Herman R. (*Princeton*) M.A.: "Juvenile delinquency in Montreal." (Sociology: Cressey, P.)

32-546 **Schwab**, Jean G. (*Vassar*) M.A.: "Migration between Canada and the United States with particular reference to professional and intellectual classes." (Economics: Leacock, S.)

32-547 **Thorpe**, Benjamin J. (*McGill*) M.A.: "The Old Testament in English satire." (English: Macmillan, C.)

32-548 **Tough**, David L. (*McGill*) M.A.: "Chaucer's interest in the problem of free will." (English: Latham, G.)

32-549 **Weeks**, Marie S. (*Swarthmore*) M.A.: "Les moeurs americaines jugées par les français d'après-guerre." (French: Du Roure, R.)

32-550 **Werry**, Wilfrid W. (*McGill*) M.A.: "The theories of Gordon Craig and their relation to the contemporary theatre." (English: Macmillan, C.)

32-551 **Woodley**, Elsie C. (*McGill*) M.A.: "The history of education in the province of Quebec: a bibliographical guide." (Education: Clarke, F.)

**M.Com. Spring 1932**

32-552 **Trotter**, Wallace S. (*McGill*) M.Com.: "Fluctuations in the exchange value of the Canadian dollar, 1919-1931." (Economics: Day, J.)

M.Eng. Fall 1932

32-553 **Pimenoff**, Clement J. (*McGill*) M.Eng.: "Theory and application of photo-elasticity." (Civil Engineering & Applied Mechanics: Jamieson, R.)

M.Sc. Fall 1932

32-554 **Dunn**, William K. (*McGill*) M.Sc.: "The influence of temperature gradients on thermoelectric effects in metals." (Physics: Shaw, A.)

32-555 **Ferguson**, William (*McGill*) M.Sc.: "Some studies on the physiology of cold resistance in plants." (Botany: Scarth, G.)

32-556 **Findlay**, Gordon H. (*Bishop's*) M.Sc.: "Studies on maple sap and syrup." (Agricultural Chemistry: Snell, J.)

32-557 **Pelletier**, Joseph R. (*Laval*) M.Sc.: "Methods of sub-sampling cigar leaf tobacco in relation to accuracy." (Agronomy: Summerby, R.)

32-558 **Tarlov**, Isadore M. (*Clark*) M.Sc.: "The structural and functional relationships of the cerebrospinal nerve roots." (Experimental Medicine: Penfield, W.)

M.A. Fall 1932

32-559 **Ballantyne**, Murray G. (*McGill*) M.A.: "Laud and the Church of England." (History: Adair, E.)

32-560 **Copland**, Edward B. (*McGill*) M.A.: "Traces of the influences of the Russo-Japanese War upon the the Chinese revolutionary movement, from 1904-1911." (History: Fryer, C.)

32-561 **Hall**, Clifton L. (*Bishop's*) M.A.: "Washington Irving et la France." (French: LeMaitre, G.)

32-562 **Snyder**, John K. (*McGill*) M.A.: "Franklin and Canada." (History: Fryer, C.) s,

**Ph.D. Spring 1933**

33-001 **Armstrong**, John M. (*Saskatchewan*) Ph.D.: "Cyto-genetic studies in *Matthiola* and *Triticum*." (Botany: Huskins, C.)

33-002 **Barsha**, Jacob (*McGill*) Ph.D.: "The structure of synthetic polysaccharides." (Chemistry: Hibbert, H.)

33-003 **Boyer**, Raymond (*McGill*) Ph.D.: "The action of sulphuric acid on cyclopropane ketones." (Chemistry: Allen, C.)

33-004 **Burton**, Frederick R. (*McGill*) Ph.D.: "Geology of the district about Lake Aylmer, Eastern Townships, Province of Quebec: a report on a detailed investigation of a typical part of this section of the Appalachian region." (Geological Sciences: Clark, J.)

33-005 **Cressman**, Homer W. (*Muhlenberg*) Ph.D.: "Addition reactions of vinyl phenyl ketone III, malonic ester." (Chemistry: Allen, C.)

33-006 **Hallonquist**, Earland G. (*British Columbia*) Ph.D.: "Synthesis, structure and properties of cyclic and bicyclic acetals." (Chemistry: Hibbert, H.)

33-007 **Hampton**, William F. (*Dalhousie*) Ph.D.: "The heat capacity of gelatin gels." (Chemistry: Mennie, J.)

33-008 **Haslam**, Robert N. (*Saskatchewan*) Ph.D.: "The Stark effect in the ultra-violet region of the mercury spectrum." (Physics: Foster, J.)

33-009 **Hess**, Ernest (*Polytechnicum*, Switzerland) Ph.D.: "Effects of sub-optimal temperatures on marine bacteria." (Bacteriology: Gray, P.)

33-010 **Holcomb**, Robert K. (*McGill*) Ph.D.: "The application of densimetric methods to quantitative analysis." (Chemistry: Johnson, F.)

33-011 **Katzman**, John (*McGill*) Ph.D.: "The growth of space charge in the Crooke's dark space of a Geissler discharge at low pressures." (Physics: Keys, D.)

33-012 **Kutz**, Russell L. (*Alberta*) Ph.D.: "Studies on the physiology of the adrenal cortex." (Biochemistry: Collip, J.)

33-013 **Massey**, Ernest E. (*Bishop's*) Ph.D.: "Delta-ketonic esters." (Chemistry: Allen, C.)

33-014 **Moore**, Leonard P. (*Minnesota*) Ph.D.: "Action of sulphurous acid on cellulose." (Chemistry: Hibbert, H.)

33-015 **Price**, Aubrey F. (*Dalhousie*) Ph.D.: "An investigation of the reaction between unsaturated hydrocarbons and the halogen hydrides." (Chemistry: Maass, O.)

33-016 **Price**, Peter (*British Columbia*) Ph.D.: "The geology and ore deposits of the Horne Mine, Noranda, Quebec." (Geological Sciences: O'Neill, J.)

33-017 **Reeve**, Herbert A. (*McGill*) Ph.D.: "A comparison of the kinetics of homogeneous and heterogeneous gas reactions." (Chemistry: Steacie, E.)

33-018 **Richardson**, Ronald E. (*Alberta*) Ph.D.: "The sorption of sodium hydroxide from liquid phases by various celluloses; and related researches." (Chemistry: Maass, O.)

33-019 **Snell**, Arthur H. (*Toronto*) Ph.D.: "The Stark effect in the molecular spectrum of hydrogen." (Physics: Foster, J.)

33-020 **Spanagel**, Edgar W. (*Lawrence*) Ph.D.: "Anhydroacetonebenzil." (Chemistry: Allen, C.)

33-021 **Stewart**, William W. (*Dalhousie*) Ph.D.: "The viscosity of gases and its relationship to the gas laws." (Chemistry: Maass, O.)

33-022 **Tapp**, James S. (*Western*) Ph.D.: "An investigation of the density of a vapour in equilibrium with a liquid near the critical temperature." (Chemistry: Maass, O. & Steacie, E.)

33-023 **Thornton**, Robert L. (*McGill*) Ph.D.: "(a) The Stark effect for krypton. (b) Stark intensities in hydrogen and helium." (Physics: Foster, J.)

33-024 **Webster**, Donald R. (*Dalhousie*) Ph.D.: "The gastric secretion under normal and some pathological conditions." (Physiology: Babkin, B.)

33-025 **Williamson**, John T. (*McGill*) Ph.D.: "The origin and occurrence of the chromite deposits of the Eastern Townships, Quebec." (Geological Sciences: O'Neill, J.)

33-026 **Wilson**, Charles V. (*Saskatchewan*) Ph.D.: "Part I. The stereochemistry of certain tertiary amines. Part II. Studies on lactols." (Chemistry: Allen, C.)

33-027 **Winkler**, Carl A. (*Manitoba*) Ph.D.: "Investigation of the continuity of state in one and two component systems." (Chemistry: Maass, O.)

**Ph.D. Fall 1933**

33-028 **Hearne**, Edna M. (*Queen's*) Ph.D.: "Chromosome studies on the mechanism of meiosis in *Melanoplus femur-rubrum*." (Botany: Huskins, C.)

33-029 **Lusby**, George R. (*Mount Allison*) Ph.D.: "Alkali cooking studies." (Chemistry: Maass, O.)

33-030 **Morton**, Nelson W. (*McGill*) Ph.D.: "The industrial quality of the unemployed with particular reference to occupational classification." (Psychology: Kellogg, C.)

33-031 **Ross**, William B. (*McGill*) Ph.D.: "Investigation on the Kennelly-Heaviside and Appleton layers." (Physics: Eve, A.)

33-032 **Venning**, Eleanor M. (*McGill*) Ph.D.: "Experimental study of blood fats in health and disease." (Experimental Medicine: Browne, J.)

33-033 **Vineberg**, Arthur M. (*McGill*) Ph.D.: "Some aspects of the mechanism of gastric secretion." (Physiology: Babkin, B.)

33-034 **Wells**, Franklin B. (*Illinois*) Ph.D.: "Part I. The cyanocyclopropanes. Part II. Trivalent asymmetric arsenic." (Chemistry: Allen, C.)

## ANNUAL LISTING

### Ph.D. Spring 1934

34-001 **Anderson**, Evelyn M. (*Carleton*) Ph.D.: "The inter-relationship of the anterior pituitary and the thyroid gland." (Biochemistry: Collip, J.)

34-002 **Atkinson**, Hammond J. (*New Brunswick*) Ph.D.: "Organic matter and acidity in podsol soils." (Agricultural Chemistry: Snell, J.)

34-003 **Bell**, Adam C. (*Dalhousie*) Ph.D.: "The addition reactions of phenyl vinyl ketone." (Organic Chemistry: Allen, C.)

34-004 **Buckland**, Irene K. (*Smith*) Ph.D.: "Phenol derivatives of lignins." (Chemistry: Hibbert, H.)

34-005 **De Montigny**, Raimbault (*McGill*) Ph.D.: "Penetration in sulphite cooking." (Chemistry: Maass, O.)

34-006 **Halet**, Robert A. (*British Columbia*) Ph.D.: "The geology and mineral deposits of the Beattie-Galatea area." (Geological Sciences: O'Neill, J.)

34-007 **Morris**, Herbert E. (*Alberta*) Ph.D.: "The discontinuity at the critical temperature: adsorption, density and dielectric constant." (Chemistry: Maass, O.)

34-008 **Normington**, James B. (*McGill*) Ph.D.: "The condensation of gamma ketonic esters with aromatic aldehydes; ring-chain tautomerism in gamma ketonic acids." (Chemistry: Allen, C.)

34-009 **Okulitch**, Vladimir J. (*British Columbia*) Ph.D.: "The geology of the Black River group in the vicinity of Montreal." (Geological Sciences: Clark, J.)

34-010 **Plewes**, Argyle C. (*Queen's*) Ph.D.: "The kinetics of the oxidation of mixtures of gaseous hydrocarbons with other substances." (Chemistry: Steacie, E.)

34-011 **Rollit**, John B. (*McGill*) Ph.D.: "Transportation as a national problem." (Economics: Hemmeon, J.)

34-012 **Ross**, Douglas A. (*McGill*) Ph.D.: "Physiological analysis of eighth nerve reception." (Physiology: Tait, J.)

34-013 **Russell**, John K. (*Dalhousie*) Ph.D.: "A study of the nature of vapour sorption on cellulose." (Chemistry: Maass, O.)

34-014 **Sallans**, Henry R. (*Saskatchewan*) Ph.D.: "1,5 - diketones: cyclic compounds containing a carbonyl group; a mechanism for the formation of pyrylium salts." (Chemistry: Allen, C.)

34-015 **Scarrow**, James A. (*Western*) Ph.D.: "Addition reactions of alpha-methoxybenzalacetophenone." (Chemistry: Allen, C.)

34-016 **Schindler**, Norman R. (*Rhodes*, South Africa) Ph.D.: "Igneous rocks of Duprat Lake and Rouyn Lake areas, Quebec." (Geological Sciences: Gill, J.)

34-017 **Solomon**, Ernest (*Manitoba*) Ph.D.: "Kinetics of homogeneous gas reactions at high pressures." (Chemistry: Steacie, E.)

34-018 **Trister**, Saul M. (*McGill*) Ph.D.: "Cyclic acetal formation and the 'Hibbert-Michael' partition principle, and its relation to polysaccharide chemistry." (Chemistry: Hibbert, H.)

Ph.D. Fall 1934

34-019 **Findlay**, Gordon H. (*Bishop's*) Ph.D.: "Maple flavour, its nature and origin." (Agricultural Chemistry: Snell, J.)

34-020 **Gray**, Kenneth R. (*British Columbia*) Ph.D.: "The structure and properties of glycol lignin." (Chemistry: Hibbert, H.)

34-021 **King**, Ellis G. (*British Columbia*) Ph.D.: "The structure and properties of spruce wood lignin and derivatives." (Chemistry: Hibbert, H.)

34-022 **Marshall**, Harry B. (*British Columbia*) Ph.D.: "The structure and properties of alkali lignin." (Chemistry: Hibbert, H.)

34-023 **Plunguian**, Mark (*New York State*) Ph.D.: "Preparation, properties and structure of humic acids. Part I. The properties and structure of lignite humic acid. Part II. The preparation, properties and structure of sugar humic acid." (Chemistry: Hibbert, H.)

34-024 **Rawlinson**, Herbert E. (*Alberta*) Ph.D.: "Certain histophysiological aspects of gland secretion." (Physiology: Babkin, B.)

34-025 **Sheps**, Louis J. (*Manitoba*) Ph.D.: "Hexendones." (Chemistry: Allen, C.)

M.Eng. Spring 1934

34-500 **De Angelis**, Marius L. (*McGill*) M.Eng.: "Regenerative braking of electrical cars and locomotives: a study of its fundamental principles and applications." (Electrical Engineering: Wallace, G.)

34-501 **Goode**, Robert C. (*Cambridge*, England) M.Eng.: "Probable chemical reactions and their effect on sulphide flotation." (Mining Engineering: Bell, J.)

34-502 **Jehu**, Llewellyn (*McGill*) M.Eng.: "An investigation of stress in welded joints." (Civil Engineering & Applied Mechanics: Jamieson, R.)

34-503 **Muir**, William L. (*Glasgow*, Scotland) M.Eng.: "Efficiency in the ventilation of metal mines by mechanical means." (Mining Engineering: McBride, W.)

34-504 **Richards**, Victor L. (*Queen's*) M.Eng.: "The re-design of an iron foundry." (Mechanical Engineering: McKergow, C.)

34-505 **Savage**, Palmer E. (*McGill*) M.Eng.: "Experiments on cavitation." (Civil Engineering & Applied Mechanics: Brown, E.)

**M.C.L. Spring 1934**

34-506 **Charlap**, Gregory (*Liège*, Belgium) M.C.L.: "The legal status of the worker in Quebec." (Civil Law: Scott, F.)

**M.Sc. Spring 1934**

34-507 **Baxt**, Lawrence M. (*McGill*) M.Sc.: "The investigation of gaseous oxidation processes by the method of dilute flames." (Chemistry: Steacie, E.)

34-508 **Cohen**, Arthur (*McGill*) M.Sc.: "The source of cells in regeneration and growth." (Zoology: Fantham, H.)

34-509 **Erickson**, Theodore C. (*Minnesota*) M.Sc.: "Neurogenic hyperthermia." (Experimental Medicine: MacKay, F.)

34-510 **Finlayson**, Duncan A. (*McGill*) M.Sc.: "The effect of fertilization on the nutritive value of pasture grass." (Animal Nutrition & Breeding: Crampton, E.)

34-511 **Hunter**, Albert W. (*McGill*) M.Sc.: "A karyo-systematic investigation in the *Gramineae*." (Botany: Huskins, C.)

34-512 **Hurst**, Donald G. (*McGill*) M.Sc.: "Photoelectric currents in irradiated rocksalt crystals." (Physics: Watson, W.)

34-513 **MacVicar**, Roderick M. (*McGill*) M.Sc.: "Inheritance of seed colour in alfalfa." (Agronomy: Raymond, L.)

34-514 **Peck**, Oswald (Alberta) M.Sc.: "Some *Ichneumonidae* of Alberta: a survey of the subfamily *Joppinae*." (Entomology: DuPorte, E.)

34-515 **Rosenberg**, Solomon (*McGill*) M.Sc.: "The kinetics of the oxidation of gaseous propionaldehyde." (Chemistry: Steacie, E.)

34-516 **Shaw**, George (*Saskatchewan*) M.Sc.: "The geology and petrography of Viewmount Ave., Westmount." (Geological Sciences: Osborne, F.)

34-517 **Simard**, Lionel R. (*Manitoba*) M.Sc.: "Pyrrhotite in rocks and mineral deposits." (Geological Sciences: Osborne, F.)

34-518 **Stobbe**, Peter C. (*Manitoba*) M.Sc.: "The effect of some commercial fertilizers on the chemical composition of pasture herbage in the Eastern Townships of Quebec." (Agronomy: Raymond, L.)

34-519 **White**, Elwood V. (*Toronto*) M.Sc.: "The structure of beech-wood lignin: an investigation into the isolation of lignin by the direct acetylation of beech-wood meal." (Chemistry: Hibbert, H.)

34-520 **Workman**, E. Walter (*McGill*) M.Sc.: "The effect of partial tracheal occlusion on the compensatory hypertrophy of autotransplants and remnants of the thyroid gland." (Experimental Medicine: Scrimger, F.)

M.A. Spring 1934

34-521 **Baker**, Carrie E. (*Boston*) M.A.: "La participation de la France à l'expédition de Rhode Island en 1778." (French: Du Roure, R.)

34-522 **Barnett**, Elizabeth S. (*Saskatchewan*) M.A.: "The memoirs of pioneer women writers in Ontario." (English: Latham, G.)

34-523 **Brenhouse**, Samuel E. (*McGill*) M.A.: "Control of the profit system." (Economics: Hemmeon, J.)

34-524 **Craig**, Grace L. (*Smith*) M.A.: "A comparison of some European ballads." (English: Macmillan, C.)

34-525 **Gill**, Dorothy A. (*British Columbia*) M.A.: "The drama in secondary education." (Education: Clarke, F.)

34-526 **Gilroy**, Geoffrey S. (*McGill*) M.A.: "A historical survey of economic fluctuations, 1800-1914." (Economics: Hemmeon, J.)

34-527 **Hagerman**, Verna B. (*Mount Allison*) M.A.: "The English literature of the Maritime Provinces of Canada: influences and trends." (English: Latham, G.)

34-528 **Holland**, Catherine N. (*Queen's*) M.A.: "The relation between arithmetic in the elementary school and mathematics in the secondary school." (Education: Clarke, F.)

34-529 **Howie**, Ruth J. (*McGill*) M.A.: "L'évolution des idées de Romain Rolland sur la vie internationale." (French: Lemaitre, G.)

34-530 **Johnson**, John S. (*McGill*) M.A.: "History and organization of the Montreal Stock Exchange." (Economics: Hemmeon, J.)

34-531 **Kent**, Josephine P. (*New York State*) M.A.: "Le roman regionaliste depuis la guerre." (French: Du Roure, R.)

34-532 **Kinnear**, Mary E. (*Mount Allison*) M.A.: "Les animaux dans Colette." (French: Lemaitre, G.)

34-533 **Lunn**, Alice J. (*McGill*) M.A.: "Economic development in French Canada, 1740-1760." (History: Adair, E.)

34-534 **Macphail**, Moray S. (*Queen's*) M.A.: "On the location in the complex plane of the zeros of a polynomial." (Mathematics: Williams, W.)

34-535 **Michel**, Lina J. (*Wells*) M.A.: "La jeune fille de la bourgeoisie française dans le roman d'après-guerre." (French: Du Roure, R.)

34-536 **Milburne**, Kathleen E. (*McGill*) M.A.: "The stream of consciousness in recent English fiction by women." (English: Files, H.)

34-537 **Owen**, George R. (*McGill*) M.A.: "La liberté d'opinion: une etude des libertés publiques en France et au Canada." (Economics: Hemmeon, J.)

34-538 **Rexford**, Laura H. (*William Smith*) M.A.: "Pierre Loti et la Turquie." (French: Du Roure, R.)

34-539 **Weston**, Grace E. (*Colby*) M.A.: "Quelques intérieurs dans les romans d'Honoré de Balzac." (French: Furness, L.)

**M.Eng. Fall 1934**

34-540 **Craig**, Carleton (*McGill*) M.Eng.: "Temperatures and thermal stresses in welded plates." (Civil Engineering & Applied Mechanics: Jamieson, R.)

34-541 **Denny**, Denison (*McGill*) M.Eng.: "A study of certain phases of fine grinding." (Mining Engineering: McBride, W.)

**M.Sc. Fall 1934**

34-542 **Gray**, Nelson M. (*McGill*) M.Sc.: "The influence of natural chemical stimuli on the motility of the small intestine." (Physiology: Babkin, B.)

34-543 **Savile**, Douglas B. (*McGill*) M.Sc.: "Histologic changes induced by certain phytopathogens." (Plant Pathology: Coulson, J.)

**M.A. Fall 1934**

34-544 **Bois**, Joseph S. (*Laval*) M.A.: "Some objective aspects of temperament." (Psychology: Tait, W.)

34-545 **Devenney**, Hartland M. (*Springfield*) M.A.: "A critical survey of current opinion on the development of character in physical education." (Education: Clarke, F.)

34-546 **Dodds**, Margaret R. (*McGill*) M.A.: "A critical review of Piaget's contributions to child psychology." (Psychology: Tait, W.)

34-547 **Gibbard**, Harold A. (*British Columbia*) M.A.: "The means and modes of living of European immigrants in Montreal." (Sociology: Hughes, E.)

34-548 **Mamchur**, Stephen W. (*Saskatchewan*) M.A.: "The economic and social adjustment of Slavic immigrants in Canada, with special reference to the Ukrainians in Montreal." (Sociology: Dawson, C.)

**M.Com. Fall 1934**

34-549 **Heiber**, Sol P. (*Toronto*) M.Com.: "Job-finding and methods of industrial recruitment: a study of a selected group of persons and firms in Montreal." (Economics: Marsh, L.)

35-033 **Spier**, Jane D. (*McGill*) Ph.D.: "Observations upon chromosome associations." (Genetics: Huskins, C.)

M.Eng. Spring 1935

35-500 **Clarke**, George F. (*McGill*) M.Eng.: "The redesign of the sugar mill." (Mechanical Engineering: Roberts, A.)

35-501 **Hicks**, Henry B. (*McGill*) M.Eng.: "A photoelectric method of measuring the surface of small particles with particular regard to its application to the problems of ore dressing." (Mining: McBride, W.)

35-502 **Howe**, Lawrence M. (*Manitoba*) M.Eng.: "A study of some problems in radio interference." (Electrical Engineering: Howes, F.)

M.Sc. Spring 1935

35-503 **Dore**, William G. (*Queen's*) M.Sc.: "Ecological aspects of the pasture-conditioned climax in the Eastern Townships of Quebec." (Agronomy: Raymond, L.)

35-504 **Gobeil**, Antoine R. (*Laval*) M.Sc.: "Biology of *Ips perturbatus* Eichh." (Entomology: DuPorte, E.)

35-505 **Griffiths**, Henry J. (*McGill*) M.Sc.: "The liver fluke of sheep in eastern Canada." (Parasitology: Cameron T.)

35-506 **Gutteridge**, Harry S. (*British Columbia*) M.Sc.: "The effect of feeding deaminized vs. untreated cod liver oils upon growth, egg production, and mortality of poultry." (Animal Nutrition & Breeding: Conklin, R.)

35-507 **Herzer**, Richard W. (*Manitoba*) M.Sc.: "The recovery of copper, gold and silver from sulphide ores and concentrates by processes including roasting, leaching and electrolysis." (Metallurgy: Stansfield, A.)

35-508 **Jones**, Trevor L. (*Toronto*) M.Sc.: "Some observations on the bionomics of ascaris lumbricoides." (Parasitology: Cameron, T.)

35-509 **MacCallum**, William J. (*New Brunswick*) M.Sc.: "The kinetics of the oxidation of gaseous hydrogen iodide." (Chemistry: Steacie, E.)

35-510 **Monro**, Hector A. (*McGill*) M.Sc.: "Ecology of the pine sawfly *Diprion simile* Htg." (Zoology: Fantham, H.)

35-511 **Neeland**, William D. (*McGill*) M.Sc.: "The petrology of Grenville limestone contacts with certain intrusives." (Geology: Osborne, F.)

35-512 **Nicholls**, John V. V. (*McGill*) M.Sc.: "The motility of the gastro-intestinal tract of Elasmo branch fishes." (Physiology: Babkin, B.)

35-513 **Nicholls**, Robert V. V. (*McGill*) M.Sc.: "Tetrachlorophthalimide as a reagent in qualitative organic analysis." (Chemistry: Allen, C.)

35-514 **Oldham**, Frances K. (*McGill*) M.Sc.: "The action of the preparation from the posterior lobe of the pituitary gland upon imbibation of water by frogs." (Pharmacology: Stehle, R.)

35-515 **Richmond**, Hector A. (*Oregon State*) M.Sc.: "The morphology of the bark beetle *Dendroctonus monticolae* Hopk." (Entomology: DuPorte, E.)

35-516 **Sanders**, H. L. (*McGill*) M.Sc.: "A study of the antimony electrode." (Chemistry: Mennie, J.)

35-517 **Scoggan**, Homer J. (*McGill*) M.Sc.: "Food reserves in trees with special reference to the paper birch *Betula alba var. Papyrifera*" (Botany: Gibbs, R.)

35-518 **Walker**, Forestier (*British Columbia*) M.Sc.: "Light absorption as a means of measuring particle size and consistency." (Chemistry: Maass, O.)

**M.A. Spring 1935**

35-519 **Bassinov**, Saul (*Clark*) M.A.: "The romantic and realistic in the contemporary British and American drama." (English: Macmillan, C.)

35-520 **Berry**, William G. (*Mount Allison*) M.A.: "Sir William Davenant and the 17th century theatre." (English: Files, H.)

35-521 **Blakely**, Sister Claire (*Seton Hill*) M.A.: "L'idée religieuse dand l'oeuvre dramatique de Paul Claudel." (French: Du Roure, R.)

35-522 **Bloomfield**, Morton W. (*McGill*) M.A.: "'Piers Plowman', annotated, together with an introductory essay." (English: Latham, G.)

35-523 **Blumenthal**, Estelle H. (*McGill*) M.A.: "Some recent tendencies in the short story (1914-1934)." (English: Files, H.)

35-524 **Clark**, Edgar H. Jr. (*McGill*) M.A.: "French economic self-sufficiency." (Economics: Hemmeon, J.)

35-525 **Cox**, Mary D. (*New Brunswick*) M.A.: "Les idées dans le théâtre de François de Curel." (French: Lemaitre, G.)

35-526 **Dubé**, Claudia M. (*New Hampshire*) M.A.: "La survivance française dans la Nouvelle-Angleterre." (French: Du Roure, R.)

35-527 **Grant**, Mary J. (*McGill*) M.A.: "The exposure of infants in ancient Greece from Homeric to Christian times." (Classics: Carruthers, C.)

35-528 **Jennings**, Thomas J. (*Hobart*) M.A.: "L'histoire du nouveau théâtre à New York." (French: Du Roure, R.)

35-529 **Khaner**, Miriam (*McGill*) M.A.: "Some entozoa found in certain amphibia in Quebec Province." (Zoology: Fantham, H.)

35-530 **Luxton**, Edward A. G. (*British Columbia*) M.A.: "Large-scale merchandising in Canada: some economic implications." (Economics: Hemmeon, J.)

35-531 **Mazza**, Sister Maria S. (*Seton Hill*) M.A.: "L'idée religieuse dans les oeuvres de Charles Peguy." (French: Du Roure, R.)

35-532 **Moellmann**, Albert (*Saskatchewan*) M.A.: "The Germans in Canada: occupational and social adjustment of German immigrants in Canada." (Sociology: Hughes, E.)

35-533 **Robertson**, Barbara M. (*British Columbia*) M.A.: "Occupational traits in clerical work: a study of employed and unemployed women in Montreal." (Psychology: Tait, W.)

35-534 **Ross**, Mary C. M. (*McGill*) M.A.: "La préciosité dans l'oeuvre dramatique d'Edmond Rostand." (French: Furness, L.)

35-535 **Styles**, Arthur D. (*McGill*) M.A.: "The interest of Canada in the silver question." (Economics: Leacock, S.)

35-536 **Thompson**, Winifred (*McGill*) M.A.: "Preliminary work in science in the junior school." (Education: Hughes, J.)

35-537 **Ulrichsen**, Barbara A. (*McGill*) M.A.: "Democratic tendencies in American poetry of the 19th century." (English: Latham, G.)

**M.Sc. Fall 1935**

35-538 **Haymaker**, Webb (*South Carolina*) M.Sc.: "Tissue culture of the pituitary." (Neurology: Penfield, W.)

35-539 **Shaw**, Hampden C. (*McGill*) M.Sc.: "The correlation of the sciences, with reference to psychology." (Psychology: Tait, W.)

35-540 **Thatcher**, Frederick S. (*McGill*) M.Sc.: "Studies on the parasitism of *Uromyces fabae* (Pers.) de Bary." (Plant Pathology: Conlson, J.)

**M.A. Fall 1935**

35-541 **Clark**, Samuel D. (*Saskatchewan*) M.A.: "The role of metropolitan institutions in the formulation of a Canadian national consciousness, with special reference to the United States." (Sociology: Dawson, C.)

35-542 **Graham**, Gordon B. (*Broaddus*) M.A.: "The sorption of gases by solids: the solubility of water vapour in solid inorganic compounds at high temperatures." (Chemistry: Steacie, E.)

35-543 **Hamilton**, Marion M. (*British Columbia*) M.A.: "The history of impressionism in English criticism up to the year 1900." (English: Files, H.)

35-544 **Jackson**, Naomi C. (*McGill*) M.A.: "Gottfried Keller als Erzahler." (German: Walter, H.)

35-545 **Lennox**, Robert (*McGill*) M.A.: "Typical flights of classical Hebrew oratory." (Oriental Languages: Brockwell, C.)

35-546 **Peden**, Gwendolyn W. (*McGill*) M.A.: "A study of reading disability." (Psychology: Tait, W.)

35-547 **Reid**, William S. (*McGill*) M.A.: "The struggle of the Church of Scotland for equal rights and privileges with the Church of England in Canada." (History: Fryer, C.)

35-548 **Roy**, William J. (*New Hampshire*) M.A.: "The French-English division of labour in the Province of Quebec." (Sociology: Hughes, E.)

35-549 **Walker**, Margaret G. (*Fisk*) M.A.: "L'histoire dans le théâtre d'Alexandre Dumas père." (French: Lemaitre, G.)

## ANNUAL LISTING

### Ph.D. Spring 1936

36-001 **Bois**, Joseph S. (*Laval*) Ph.D.: "The graphic signs of introversion-extraversion." (Psychology: Tait, W.)

36-002 **Byers**, Alfred R. (*McGill*) Ph.D.: "The geology and mineral deposits of the Night Hawk Lake area, Ont." (Geology: Gill, J.)

36-003 **Cohen**, Arthur (*McGill*) Ph.D.: "Studies on morphogenesis and differentiation." (Zoology: Fantham, H.)

36-004 **Corey**, Alfred J. (*New Brunswick*) Ph.D.: "A study of the method of the delignification of wood in aqueous acid media." (Chemistry: Maass, O.)

36-005 **Fowler**, Frances L. (*British Columbia*) Ph.D.: "The structure of dextran." (Chemistry: Hibbert, H.)

36-006 **Geddes**, Amos L. (*Dalhousie*) Ph.D.: "An investigation of the pressure, volume and temperature relations of one component systems near the critical point, system ethylene." (Chemistry: Maass, O.)

36-007 **Gilman**, Lucius (*Illinois*) Ph.D.: "The action of the Grignard reagent on polynuclear ketones." (Chemistry: Allen, C.)

36-008 **Horn**, Wallace R. (*Queen's*) Ph.D.: "Calorimetric measurements on gels." (Chemistry: Mennie, J.)

36-009 **Hurst**, Donald G. (*McGill*) Ph.D.: "Optical absorption by the alkali metals in the Schumann region." (Physics: Watson, W.)

36-010 **Marsden**, James (*Mount Allison*) Ph.D.: "The discontinuity at the critical temperature; reaction velocity; dielectric constant." (Chemistry: Maass, O.)

36-011 **Rosenberg**, Solomon (*McGill*) Ph.D.: "The kinetics of the homogeneous decomposition of diethyl ether at high pressures and other gas reactions." (Chemistry: Steacie, E.)

36-012 **Shaw**, Geoffrey T. (*McGill*) Ph.D.: "The kinetics of the thermal decomposition of alkyl nitrites." (Chemistry: Maass, O.)

36-013 **Steeves**, William H. (*Mount Allison*) Ph.D.: "The structure of lignin." (Chemistry: Hibbert, H.)

36-014 **Webster**, Edward C. (*McGill*) Ph.D.: "Vocational guidance in relation to school training and the distribution of mental abilities." (Psychology: Tait, W.)

36-015 **White**, Elwood V. (*Toronto*) Ph.D.: "Action of chlorine and its derivatives on lignin." (Chemistry: Hibbert, H.)

36-016 **Young**, Donald M. (*McGill*) Ph.D.: "Indol formation and dipyrrols." (Chemistry: Allen, C.)

## ANNUAL LISTING

### Ph.D. Fall 1936

36-017 **Brown**, Robert S. (*McGill*) Ph.D.: "A new adiabatic calorimeter and some thermal properties of deuterium oxide." (Chemistry: Maass, O. & Barnes, W.)

36-018 **Moore**, Ralph G. (*British Columbia*) Ph.D.: "Degradation products of lignin." (Chemistry: Hibbert, H.)

36-019 **Nicholls**, Robert V. V. (*McGill*) Ph.D.: "The action of basic reagents on a highly phenylated ketolactone." (Chemistry: Allen, C.)

36-020 **Panter**, Shraga F. (*McGill*) Ph.D.: "Stark effect in iron." (Physics: Foster, J.)

36-021 **Peck**, Oswald (*Alberta*) Ph.D.: "The genetalia in the *Ichneumonidae*." (Entomology: DuPorte, E.)

36-022 **Wrenshall**, Charlton L. (*Saskatchewan*) Ph.D.: "The condition of the phosphorous of soils." (Agricultural Chemistry: McKibbin, R.)

### M.Eng. Spring 1936

36-500 **Hamilton**, Donald M. (*Edinburgh*, Scotland) M.Eng.: "Preheating effects on residual stresses in arc-welded steel plates." (Civil Engineering & Applied Mechanics: Jamieson, R.)

36-501 **Lindsay**, Victor C. (*McGill*) M.Eng.: "The composition and properties of modern refractory cements." (Metallurgical Engineering: Stansfield, A.)

36-502 **Lupton**, Mac J. (*Manitoba*) M.Eng.: "Tension tests for residual stresses in arc-welded steel plates." (Civil Engineering & Applied Mechanics: Jamieson, R.)

36-503 **MacKay**, Donald M. (*McGill*) M.Eng.: "A study of certain phases of fine grinding." (Mining Engineering: McBride, W.)

36-504 **Pidoux**, John L. (*Alberta*) M.Eng.: "Physical properties of clay and clay-salt mixtures." (Civil Engineering & Applied Mechanics: French, R.)

36-505 **Poole**, Gordon D. (*McGill*) M.Eng.: "An investigation of timber tension splices." (Civil Engineering & Applied Mechanics: Jamieson, R.)

36-506 **Schippel**, Walter H. (*McGill*) M.Eng.: "Electrical power system stability." (Electrical Engineering: Christie, C.)

36-507 **Wadge**, Norman H. (*McGill*) M.Eng.: "A study of certain phases of fine grinding." (Mining Engineering: McBride, W.)

### M.Sc. Spring 1936

36-508 **Boldrey**, Edwin B. (*De Pauw*) M.Sc.: "The architectonic subdivision of the mammalian cerebral cortex." (Neurology: Petersen, J.)

36-509 **Brown**, Robert A. (*McGill*) M.Sc.: "The Sillery Formation in the vicinity of Granby, Quebec." (Geology: Clark, T.)

36-510 **Cameron**, Colin D. (*McGill*) M.Sc.: "The nutrative value of pasture grasses." (Animal Nutrition & Breeding: Crampton, E.)

36-511 **Gfeller**, Frederick (*Toronto*) M.Sc.: "Inheritance studies of earliness, bunt resistance, awns and phenol colour reaction in a spring wheat cross." (Genetics: Huskins, C.)

36-512 **Malouf**, Stanley E. (*Saskatchewan*) M.Sc.: "The petrology of a part of Westmount Mountain near Summit Circle, Montreal." (Geology: Osborne, F.)

36-513 **Miller**, Max J. (*Saskatchewan*) M.Sc.: "The parasites of pigeons in Canada." (Parasitology: Cameron, T.)

36-514 **Norcross**, Nathan C. (*Harvard*) M.Sc.: "Studies of cerebral circulation." (Neurology: Penfield, W.)

36-515 **Pickett**, Allison D. (*McGill*) M.Sc.: "Studies in *Trypetidae* with special reference to the genus *Rhagoletis*." (Entomology: Brittain, W.)

36-516 **Puddington**, Ira E. (*Mount Allison*) M.Sc.: "A study of carbonaceous matter of maple syrup which is precipitated by basic lead acetate." (Agricultural Chemistry: Snell, J.)

36-517 **Smith**, Stanley G. (*McGill*) M.Sc.: "Cyto-genetic studies of compactoid and speltoid mutations in *Triticum vulgare Host*." (Genetics: Huskins, C.)

36-518 **Smith**, Philip D. (*McGill*) M.Sc.: "Geiger-Muller counters for induced radioactivity." (Physics: Keys, D.)

36-519 **Stothart**, John G. (*McGill*) M.Sc.: "An analysis and interpretation of feeding and carcass data of hogs tested under the Canadian Advanced Registry Policy for swine." (Animal Nutrition & Breeding: Crampton, E.)

36-520 **Twinn**, Cecil R. (*Ontario Agricultural College*) M.Sc.: "The blackflies of eastern Canada (*Simuliidae, Diptera*)." (Entomology: DuPorte, E.)

36-521 **White-Stevens**, Robert H. (*McGill*) M.Sc.: "Physiological and pathological aspects of celery in cold storage and their possible relation to culture and variety." (Plant Pathology: Scarth, G.)

36-522 **Williams**, Sydney B. (*McGill*) M.Sc.: "The comparative nutrative values for poultry of barley, corn, wheat, oats and rye." (Animal Nutrition & Breeding: Conklin, R.)

M.A. Spring 1936

36-523 **Bartlett**, Harry (*Hamilton College*) M.A.: "Guy de Maupassant: sa vie, son oeuvre, et la critique américaine." (French: Du Roure, R.)

36-524 **Bloomfield**, Arthur I. (*McGill*) M.A.: "Canadian wheat marketing policy: 1929-1936." (Economics: Hemmeon, J.)

36-525 **Bly**, Elsie R. (*Middlebury*) M.A.: "L'enfant dans le foyer de la bourgeosie française d'après le roman moderne." (French: Du Roure, R.)

36-526 **Bonis**, Margaret E. (*Toronto*) M.A.: "Tennyson as the voice of Victorian England." (English: Latham, G.)

36-527 **Brown**, Margaret F. (*New Hampshire*) M.A.: "The sincerity of the Roman satirists." (Latin: Thompson, A.)

36-528 **Conroy**, Mary P. (*Montréal*) M.A.: "A history of the theatre in Montreal prior to Confederation." (English: Macmillan, C.)

36-529 **Frey**, Flavian F. (*St. Joseph's College*) M.A.: "L'art unanimiste dans les oeuvres en prose de Jules Romains." (French: Du Roure, R.)

36-530 **Hamilton**, Robert A. (*McGill*) M.A.: "American poetry from 1910 to 1935." (English: Latham, G.)

36-531 **Harvie**, Jean E. (*McGill*) M.A.: "Imprisonment in Greece." (Classics: Carruthers, C.)

36-532 **Hetherington**, Elizabeth M. (*Toronto*) M.A.: "Spain and the English Romanticists." (English: Noad, A.)

36-533 **Heyman**, Madeleine C. (*Hunter College*) M.A.: "Henri Barbusse et son champ de bataille." (French: Du Roure, R.)

36-534 **Klein**, Jenny (*Columbia*) M.A.: "The history of Johnson's Preface to Shakespeare, 1765-1934." (English: Files, H.)

36-535 **Klineberg**, Beatrice A. (*McGill*) M.A.: "A discussion of the problem of relativity in morals." (Philosophy: Maclennan, R.)

36-536 **Leathem**, Ronald M. (*McGill*) M.A.: "State control of civil aviation in the British Empire." (Economics: Leacock, S.)

36-537 **MacQueen**, David J. (*McGill*) M.A.: "Allegorical interpretation of Homer." (Classics: Woodhead, W.)

36-538 **Mallin**, Estelle C. (*Saskatchewan*) M.A.: "Conceptions of consciousness in contemporary philosophy." (Philosophy: Hendel, C.)

36-539 **Paist**, Gertrude W. (*McGill*) M.A.: "The political theories of Alfred Tennyson." (English: Macmillan, C.)

36-540 **Paour**, Peter J. (*St. Mary's Seminary*) M.A.: "L'influence de St. Vincent de Paul sur l'eloquence de la chaire." (French: Du Roure, R.)

36-541 **Perrigard**, Elma E. (*McGill*) M.A.: "The development of properties in drama on the English-speaking stage." (English: Glassford, N.)

36-542 **Vineberg**, Philip F. (*McGill*) M.A.: "The French franc and the gold standard, 1926-1936." (Economics: Day, J.)

36-543 **Williams**, Katharine R. (*McGill*) M.A.: "Social conditions in Nova Scotia, 1749-1783." (History: Adair, E.)

M. Com. Spring 1936

36-544 **McGill**, John J. (*McGill*) M.A.: "The minimum wage and its proposed application in the Dominion of Canada." (Economics: Hemmeon, J.)

M.Eng. Fall 1936

36-545 **Kirk**, William D. (*Queen's*) M.Eng.: "The development of bond between a steel beam and a superposed concrete slab." (Civil Engineering & Applied Mechanics: Jamieson, R.)

M.Sc. Fall 1936

36-546 **Dorman**, Robert W. (*Dalhousie*) M.Sc.: "Development of a method for the identification of hydroxyl groups in organic compounds." (Chemistry: Hibbert, H.)

36-547 **Gibson**, William C. (*British Columbia*) M.Sc.: "A morphological study of interneuronal connections." (Neurology: Penfield, W.)

36-548 **Lathe**, Grant H. (*McGill*) M.Sc.: "The determination of iodine in the blood." (Biochemistry: Collip, J.)

36-549 **Riddell**, John E. (*McGill*) M.Sc.: "The geology of the Buffalo Ankerite Gold Mines, Ltd." (Geology: Gill, J.)

36-550 **Stevens**, Robert L. (*Alberta*) M.Sc.: "Effects of unbalanced voltage on synchronous motor operation." (Electrical Engineering: Christie, C.)

36-551 **Wallace**, Alexander B. (*Edinburgh*, Scotland) M.Sc.: "The lymphatics of the lower urinary and genital tracts: an experimental study with some special reference to renal infections." (Experimental Medicine: MacKenzie, D.)

M.A. Fall 1936

36-552 **Rexford**, Orrin B. (*McGill*) M.A.: "Teacher training in the Province of Quebec: a historical study to 1857." (Education: Hughes, J.)

## ANNUAL LISTING

**Ph.D. Spring 1937**

37-**001** **Beazley**, Warren B. (*Dalhousie*) Ph.D.: "Equilibria existing in the system calcium oxide - sulphur dioxide - water." (Chemistry: Maass, O.)

37-**002** **Bell**, Alan (*British Columbia*) Ph.D.: "Fission products and properties of lignin." (Chemistry: Hibbert, H.)

37-**003** **Broughton**, James W. (*Manitoba*) Ph.D.: "Sorption and heat measurements near the critical temperature: a correction equation for the quartz spring balance." (Chemistry: Maass, O.)

37-**004** **Buckland**, Francis C. (*British Columbia*) Ph.D.: "The dolomitic magnesite of Grenville Township, Argenteuil Co., P. Que." (Geology: Osborne, F.)

37-**005** **DeLuca**, Horace A. (*Western Ontario*) Ph.D.: "The measurement of the dielectric constant of cellulose and that of adsorbed vapour." (Chemistry: Maass, O.)

37-**006** **Findlay**, Robert A. (*British Columbia*) Ph.D.: "The development of a method for measuring heat conductivity of colloidal systems under constant humidity conditions. Thermal conductivities of cellulosic materials." (Chemistry: Maass, O.)

37-**007** **Giguere**, Paul A. (*Laval*) Ph.D.: "The preparation and properties of pure hydrogen peroxide solutions." (Chemistry: Maass, O.)

37-**008** **Halley**, Leroy F. (*Illinois*) Ph.D.: "Aryl iododihalides as halogenating agents." (Chemistry: Allen, C.)

37-**009** **Hebb**, Catherine O. (*Dalhousie*) Ph.D.: "The secretory activity of the pancreatic gland in relation to carbohydrate metabolism." (Physiology: Babkin, B.)

37-**010** **Horton**, Cyril A. (*Acadia*) Ph.D.: "The Stark effect in argon and krypton." (Physics: Foster, J.)

37-**011** **Hunter**, Albert W. (*McGill*) Ph.D.: "The direction of coiling in the chromonemata of *Trillium erectum* L." (Genetics: Huskins, C.)

37-**012** **Jones**, Donald C. (*New Brunswick*) Ph.D.: "Stark effect in the spectrum of the HD molecule." (Physics: Foster, J.)

37-**013** **Katz**, Sidney (*Manitoba*) Ph.D.: "The effect of configuration on unimolecular reaction rates." (Chemistry: Steacie, E.)

37-**014** **Keating**, Bernard J. (*St. Francis Xavier*) Ph.D.: "Geology of the augmentation of Grenville Township, Que." (Geology: Osborne, F.)

37-**015** **MacIntosh**, Frank C. (*Dalhousie*) Ph.D.: "Humoral and hormonal mechanisms regulating the activity of the digestive glands." (Physiology: Babkin, B.)

37-**016** **Morrison**, John L. (*Saskatchewan*) Ph.D.: "Measurement of the heats of wetting of liquids and electrolytes on standard cotton and mercerized cotton in relation to theories of mercerization and adsorption." (Chemistry: Maass, O.)

37-017 **Neamtan**, Samuel M. (*McGill*) Ph.D.: "Stark effect on the molecular spectrum of deuterium." (Physics: Foster, J.)

37-018 **Pounder**, Elton R. (*McGill*) Ph.D.: "The influence of crossed electric and magnetic fields on the helium spectrum." (Physics: Foster, J.)

37-019 **Ross**, Archibald S. (*Western Ontario*) Ph.D.: "The physical properties of chlorine and of its aqueous solutions with a view to the elucidation of the equilibria existing in the latter." (Chemistry: Maass, O.)

37-020 **Rudoff**, Hyman (*McGill*) Ph.D.: "Cyclopentenolones." (Chemistry: Allen, C.)

37-021 **Sair**, Louis (*Manitoba*) Ph.D.: "The chloroform soluble constituents of maple syrup." (Agricultural Chemistry: Snell, J.)

37-022 **Sanders**, Herbert L. (*McGill*) Ph.D.: "Phase boundary potentials." (Chemistry: Mennie, J.)

37-023 **Swartz**, Joseph N. (*McGill*) Ph.D.: "Bleaching studies." (Chemistry: Hibbert, H.)

37-024 **Walker**, Forestier (*British Columbia*) Ph.D.: "The effects of surrounding media on cellulose." (Chemistry: Maass, O.)

**Ph.D. Fall 1937**

37-025 **Billingsley**, Lawrence W. (*McGill*) Ph.D.: "Factors affecting the metabolism of small mammals." (Biochemistry: Collip, J.)

37-026 **Denstedt**, Orville F. (*Manitoba*) Ph.D.: "An examination of the lipids of the anterior pituitary." (Biochemistry: Collip, J.)

37-027 **Evans**, Joseph P. (*Harvard*) Ph.D.: "A study of the cerebral cicatrix." (Neurology: Penfield, W.)

37-028 **Friedman**, Mac H. (*McGill*) Ph.D.: "Gastric secretion and motility in certain vertebrates." (Physiology: Babkin, B.)

37-029 **Johannson**, Oscar K. (*Saskatchewan*) Ph.D.: "Vapour density of sulphur dioxide at 0.0 degrees C." (Chemistry: Maass, O.)

37-030 **MacLauchlan**, Donald W. (*Mount Allison*) Ph.D.: "Properties of hydrogen peroxide." (Chemistry: Hatcher, W.)

37-031 **Wendling**, André V. (*Sorbonne*, France) Ph.D.: "An X-ray study of the structure of rubidium dithionate." (Physics: Barnes, W.)

**M.Eng. Spring 1937**

37-500 **Fraser**, Gordon E. (*McGill*) M.Eng.: "Fine grinding of ores with particular reference to the surfaces produced." (Mining Engineering: Bell, J.)

## ANNUAL LISTING

M.Sc. Spring 1937

37-501 **Adams**, James R. (*McGill*) M.Sc.: "Some observations on certain animal communities in the environs of the Island of Montreal: the ecology of two freshwater ponds." (Zoology: Fantham, H.)

37-502 **Boulet**, Lucien J. (*Manitoba*) M.Sc.: "Plant ecology and a comparative study of methods of reproduction of certain pasture plants, with an investigation of the soil viable seed flora." (Agronomy: Raymond, L.)

37-503 **Cox**, Harold A. (*McGill*) M.Sc.: "Physiological studies of *Venturia inaequalis* (Cke.Wint.)." (Plant Pathology: Coulson, J.)

37-504 **Davis**, Charles W. (*McGill*) M.Sc.: "The petrography of a section of Westmount Mountain." (Geology: Osborne, F.)

37-505 **Eaves**, Charles A. (*McGill*) M.Sc.: "Physiology of apples in artificial atmospheres." (Botany: Scarth, G.)

37-506 **Folkins**, Hillis O. (*Mount Allison*) M.Sc.: "The kinetics of heterogeneous gas reactions: the decomposition of nitrous oxide on a silver catalyst." (Chemistry: Steacie, E.)

37-507 **Graham**, Kenneth (*British Columbia*) M.Sc.: "Development of the confused flour beetle as effected by saturation deficiency and temperature." (Entomology: Brittain, W.)

37-508 **Gray**, Richard H. (*McGill*) M.Sc.: "The Sydney coalfield." (Geology: Clark, T.)

37-509 **Howlett**, John G. (*McGill*) M.Sc.: "Study of water balance in the 'alarm reaction'." (Experimental Medicine: Browne, J.)

37-510 **McEvoy**, Edward T. (*McGill*) M.Sc.: "Seed transmission of plant viruses." (Plant Pathology: Brodie, H.)

37-511 **Moss**, Albert E. (*Saskatchewan*) M.Sc.: "Microscopical investigation of certain Quebec ores. Part A. Technique of investigation." (Geology: Osborne, F.)

37-512 **Rankin**, Robert A. (*Glasgow*, Scotland) M.Sc.: "The design of refractory furnace linings subjected to high temperature and erosion with special reference to oil fired steam generators." (Metallurgy: Stansfield, A.)

37-513 **Rose**, Bram (*McGill*) M.Sc.: "The determination of histamine in the blood and tissues under various conditions." (Experimental Medicine: Browne, J.)

37-514 **Sproule**, William K. (*McGill*) M.Sc.: "Relations between graphite and cementite in pure iron-carbon alloys." (Metallurgy: MacEwan, J.)

37-515 **Steeves**, Allison E. (*Mount Allison*) M.Sc.: "An investigation of the iodine content of potatoes and potato soils of the Province of Quebec." (Agricultural Chemistry: DeLong, W.)

M.A. Spring 1937

37-516 **Allen**, Gertrude E. (*McGill*) M.A.: "Three women letter writers of eighteenth century England: Mrs. Montagu, Mrs. Thrale and Fanny Burney." (English: Files, H.)

37-517 **Bronner**, Frederic J. (*Queen's*) M.A.: "La survivance française." (French: Du Roure, R.)

37-518 **Chapman**, Antony D. (*McGill*) M.A.: "English folk-carols and the dance." (English: Latham, G.)

37-519 **Collard**, Edgar A. (*McGill*) M.A.: "The origins of the Oxford Movement, with special reference to contemporary English social and intellectual conditions." (History: Fryer, C.)

37-520 **Craig**, Isabel F. (*McGill*) M.A.: "Economic conditions in Canada, 1763-1783." (History: Adair, E.)

37-521 **Dillon**, Sister Marie de Lourdes (*Marymount*) M.A.: "Etude sur Antoine Frédéric Ozanam." (French Language and Literature: Du Roure, R.)

37-522 **Falle**, George G. (*McGill*) M.A.: "The political fiction of Benjamin Disraeli." (English: Files, H.)

37-523 **Kleiner**, George (*McGill*) M.A.: "Capital accumulation in Canada since Confederation." (Economics: Forsey, E.)

37-524 **Lamal**, Mary L. (*Rosary College*) M.A.: "L'étude du paysan dans l'oeuvre de René Bazin." (French Language and Literature: Du Roure, R.)

37-525 **Lumsden**, Stanley G. (*McGill*) M.A.: "Humour in Virgil." Classics: Thompson, A.)

37-526 **MacKenzie**, Mary E. (*Dalhousie*) M.A.: "The fairness of Byron's judgments." (English: MacMillan, C.)

37-527 **Morgan**, Mildred A. (*Western Ontario*) M.A.: "The office of Receiver-General and its tenure by deputy in the Province of Quebec, 1763-1791." (History: Fryer, C.)

37-528 **O'Brien**, Michael V. (*Loyola*) M.A.: "Early Canadian historical literature: the journals of the traders of the North West Co. of Merchants from Canada." (English: MacMillan, C.)

37-529 **Pellerin**, Evelyn (*Louisiana State Normal College*) M.A.: "La langue française en Louisiane." (French Language and Literature: Du Roure, R.)

37-530 **Pick**, Alfred J. (*McGill*) M.A.: "The municipal and financial administration of Paris and Montreal: a comparative study." (Economics: Hemmeon, J.)

37-531 **Roy**, Esther M. (*Smith*) M.A.: "L'écolier et le lycéen dans la littérature française contemporaine." (French Language and Literature: Du Roure, R.)

37-532 **Stock**, Marie L. (*Queen's*) M.A.: "Les histoires d'animaux dans la littérature canadienne anglaise." (French Language and Literature: Du Roure, R.)

M.Sc. Fall 1937

37-533 **Ayers**, George W. (*McGill*) M.Sc.: "Studies on celery storage disorders." (Plant Pathology: Coulson, A.)

37-534 **Boone**, Charles S. (*New Brunswick*) M.Sc.: "A study of the nature of the sulphur compounds in a Quebec peat soil." (Agricultural Chemistry: McFarlane, W.)

37-535 **Bourque**, Leopold (*Laval*) M.Sc.: "Some investigations with regard to the effect of nitrogen on the storage qualities of celery." (Horticulture-Botany: Murray, H.)

37-536 **Dyer**, William J. (*McGill*) M.Sc.: "Photoelectric colorimetry of phosphorus in soil extracts." (Agricultural Chemistry: Wrenshall, C.)

37-537 **Lead**, Harry D. (*McGill*) M.Sc.: "Some observations on the animal ecology of Molson's Creek, Montreal East." (Zoology: Fantham, H.)

37-538 **Parker**, William E. (*McGill*) M.Sc.: "A study of the distribution of iron in plant tissue." (Agricultural Chemistry: McFarlane, W.)

37-539 **Schacher**, Josephine (*McGill*) M.Sc.: "Metabolism of the sterols related to the female sex glands." (Experimental Medicine: Browne, J.)

37-540 **Shewell**, Guy E. (*McGill*) M.Sc.: "The *Lauxaniidae* of eastern Canada." (Entomology: DuPorte, E.)

37-541 **Siminovitch**, David (*McGill*) M.Sc.: "A study of the mechanism of cold injury to plants." (Botany: Scarth, G.)

M.A. Fall 1937

37-542 **Aikman**, Mary E. (*McGill*) M.A.: "The nature of women's employment with special reference to Montreal." (Sociology: Dawson, C.)

37-543 **Dike**, Mary E. (*McGill*) M.A.: "Studies of some English mystical poets in the seventeenth and eighteenth centuries." (English: Files, H.)

37-544 **Hall**, Oswald (*Queen's*) M.A.: "A study of the size and composition of the Canadian family." (Sociology: Dawson, C.)

37-545 **Lovelock**, Margaret K. (*Manitoba*) M.A.: "Le cadre et le milieu dans les romans d'Edouard Estaunié." (French Language and Literature: LeMaitre, G.)

## ANNUAL LISTING

**Ph.D. Spring 1938**

38-001 **Alexander**, Wendal A. (*Queen's*) Ph.D.: "Free radicals in organic decomposition reactions." (Chemistry: Steacie, E.)

38-002 **Brown**, Arthur G. (*Saskatchewan*) Ph.D.: "An investigation of olefine halogen-hydride reactions in the liquid state." (Chemistry: Maass, O.)

38-003 **Calhoun**, John M. (*Alberta*) Ph.D.: "A study of the mechanism of the delignification of wood in aqueous sulphite solutions." (Chemistry: Maass, O.)

38-004 **Cameron**, James W. (*McGill*) Ph.D.: "The reactions of the housefly, *Musca domestica* Linn. to light of different wavelengths." (Entomology: Brittain, W.)

38-005 **Denis**, Bertrand T. (*McGill*) Ph.D.: "Guillet Township map area." (Geology: Osborne, F.)

38-006 **Eliot**, Charles G. (*McGill*) Ph.D.: "2,3 - diphenylbutadiene." (Chemistry: Stevens, P.)

38-007 **Harlow**, Charles M. (*Acadia*) Ph.D.: "A haematological and chemical study of the blood during the alarm reaction." (Biochemistry: Selye, H.)

38-008 **Hawkins**, Walter L. (*Rensselaer*) Ph.D.: "The structure of lignin obtained from hard woods." (Chemistry: Hibbert, H.)

38-009 **Howard**, Alma C. (*McGill*) Ph.D.: "The relation between chromosome behaviour and susceptibility to mammart gland cancer in mice." (Genetics: Huskins, C.)

38-010 **Leger**, Francis J. (*Alberta*) Ph.D.: "Some fission products of furans and lignin." (Chemistry: Hibbert, H.)

38-011 **Lieff**, Morris (*Queen's*) Ph.D.: "The structure of lignin and its relation to other plant constituents." (Chemistry: Hibbert, H.)

38-012 **McCarthy**, Joseph L. (*Washington*) Ph.D.: "The mechanism of bleaching kraft pulp." (Chemistry: Hibbert, H.)

38-013 **Marshall**, James (*Washington State College*) Ph.D.: "Inverted spray mixtures and their development with reference to codling moth control." (Entomology: Brittain, W.)

38-014 **O'Donovan**, Denis K. (*University College*, Ireland) Ph.D.: "A specific metabolic hormone of the pituitary gland and its relation to the melanophore-dilating hormone." (Biochemistry: Collip, J.)

38-015 **Phillips**, Norman W. (*British Columbia*) Ph.D.: "Primary processes in the reactions of gaseous hydrocarbons." (Chemistry: Steacie, E.)

38-016 **Shipley**, John H. (*Alberta*) Ph.D.: "The heat content of water sorbed on cellulose." (Chemistry: Maass, O.)

38-017 **Smith**, Stanley G. (*McGill*) Ph.D.: "Further studies in the cyto-genetics of compactoid and speltoid mutations in *Triticum vulgare* host." (Genetics: Huskins, C.)

38-018 **Smith**, Walter M. (*New Brunswick*) Ph.D.: "The kinetics of organic decomposition reactions." (Chemistry: Steacie, E.)

38-019 **Stovel**, Henry V. (*McGill*) Ph.D.: "The kinetics of the sorption of gases by solid substances." (Chemistry: Steacie, E.)

**Ph.D. Fall 1938**

38-020 **Cooper**, John I. (*Western Ontario*) Ph.D.: "French-Canadian Conservatism in principle and in practice, 1873-1891." (History: Fryer, C.)

38-021 **Guest**, Gordon H. (*Saskatchewan*) Ph.D.: "A study of pyrroles in biological materials." (Agricultural Chemistry: McFarlane, W.)

38-022 **Perry**, Stanley Z. (*McGill*) Ph.D.: "Nature and mechanism of the polymerization of ethyleneoxide." (Chemistry: Hibbert, H.)

38-023 **Puddington**, Ira E. (*Mount Allison*) Ph.D.: "The thermal decomposition of hydrocarbons." (Chemistry: Steacie, E.)

38-024 **Whyte**, James H. (*Edinburgh*, Scotland) Ph.D.: "A study of factors affecting stomatal movement in the dark." (Botany: Scarth, G.)

**M.Eng. Spring 1938**

38-500 **Brissenden**, William G. (*McGill*) M.Eng.: "A study of certain phases of fine grinding." (Mining: Bell, J.)

38-501 **Griffiths**, George H. (*Manitoba*) M.Eng.: "Residual stresses in butt-welded steel plates." (Civil Engineering & Applied Mechanics: Jamieson, R.)

38-502 **O'Shaughnessy**, Martin D. (*McGill*) M.Eng.: "Phases of fine grinding." (Mining: Bell.J.)

**M.Sc. Spring 1938**

38-503 **Beaulieu**, André A. (*Laval*) M.Sc.: "Biologie de *Carpocapsa pomonella* L. en relation avec la température et l'humidité." (Entomology: Brittain, W.)

38-504 **Campbell**, James A. (*Ontario Agricultural College*) M.Sc.: "Studies on the relative ability of steers and rabbits to digest pasture herbage." (Animal Nutrition & Breeding: Crampton, E.)

38-505 **Cannon**, Douglas G. (*McGill*) M.Sc.: "Some trematode parasites of ducks and geese in eastern Canada." (Parasitology: Cameron, T.)

38-506 **Cleveland**, Courtney E. (*British Columbia*) M.Sc.: "The geology of the vicinity of Bralorne Mines, B.C." (Geology: Osborne, F.)

38-507 **Forshaw**, Robert P. (*British Columbia*) M.Sc.: "The intra-seasonal changes in the nutrative value of pasture herbage." (Animal Nutrition & Breeding: Crampton, E.)

38-508 **Gilbert**, Margaret R. (*Acadia*) M.Sc.: "Part I. The structure of dipyrroles and indole formation from pyrroles. Part II. Stereochemistry of linalool." (Chemistry: Stevens, P.)

38-509 **Greig**, Edmund W. (*Saskatchewan*) M.Sc.: "A description of the Kaniapiskau Series, upper Hamilton River, Newfoundland-Labrador: with a petrographic description of the Dyke Lake volcanics." (Geology: Osborne, F.)

38-510 **Harrison**, Sybil M. (*McGill*) M.Sc.: "Homologues of acetoacetic acid." (Biochemistry: Thomson, D.)

38-511 **MacDonald**, Murray V. (*Saskatchewan*) M.Sc.: "The Aldermac syenite porphyry stock, Que." (Geology: Osborne, F.)

38-512 **Maughan**, George B. (*McGill*) M.Sc.: "A quantitative study of glucuronic acid excretion." (Experimental Medicine: Meakins, J.)

38-513 **Miles**, Henry J. (*McGill*) M.Sc.: "Microfloral and soil treatment studies relative to the control of common scab of potato, due to *Actinomyces scabies*." (Plant Pathology: Coulson, J.)

38-514 **Morley**, Peter M. (*Toronto*) M.Sc.: "Factors influencing the attractiveness of logs to oviposition by barkbeetles and woodborers." (Entomology: Brittain, W.)

38-515 **Reid**, William L. (*Adelaide*, Australia) M.Sc.: "The physiology and pathology of herniation of the cerebrum through the incisura tentorii." (Neurology: Cone, W.)

38-516 **Robinson**, Raymond F. (*Union*) M.Sc.: "The geology of the Orland property, Beauchastel Township, P.Que." (Geology: O'Neill, J.)

38-517 **Robinson**, William G. (*Saskatchewan*) M.Sc.: "The geology of a section of Mount Royal, near the new building of the University of Montreal." (Geology: Osborne, F.)

38-518 **Riordon**, Peter H. (*McGill*) M.Sc.: "The geology of a section of Beauchastel Township, Que." (Geology: Osborne, F.)

38-519 **Rosenthall**, Edward (*McGill*) M.Sc.: "Generalized quaternions and the representation of numbers in certain ternary quadratic forms." (Mathematics: Pall, G.)

38-520 **Ross**, Henry U. (*McGill*) M.Sc.: "Beneficiation of a pyritic siderite ore." (Metallurgy: MacEwan, J.)

38-521 **Shane**, Gerald (*McGill*) M.Sc.: "The kinetics of polymerization of iso-butene." (Chemistry: Steacie, E.)

38-522 **Sutherland**, Angus J. (*McGill*) M.Sc.: "Studies on the problem of improving the vitamin A value of winterproduced milk." (Agricultural Chemistry: McFarlane, W.)

38-523 **Wishart**, George (*Toronto*) M.Sc.: "A study of the factors governing the sex ratio in *Chelonus annulipes* Wesm. a braconid parasite of the European corn borer." (Entomology: Brittain, W.)

38-524 **Yuen**, Henry B. (*McGill*) M.Sc.: "Chrysene and derivatives." (Chemistry: Stevens, P.)

## ANNUAL LISTING

### M.A. Spring 1938

38-525 **Bishop**, Annetta C. (*Queen's*) M.A.: "Lady Morgan and her circle." (English: Noad, A.)

38-526 **Boulkind**, Mabel (*McGill*) M.A.: "Vocational training facilities for women in Montreal." (Education: Southam, H.)

38-527 **Bourget**, Adeline E. (*Colby*) M.A.: "Le sentiment de la nature dans le romans du XVIIIe siècle." (French: Du Roure, R.)

38-528 **Cumming**, Robert S. (*Dalhousie*) M.A.: "Industrial relations of a typical Canadian company." (Economics: Hemmeon, J.)

38-529 **Duncan**, Albert S. (*Alberta*) M.A.: "Unemployment relief in the Prairie Provinces, 1930-1937." (Economics: Hemmeon, J.)

38-530 **Henry**, Arthur M. (*London*, England) M.A.: "Noegentic abstraction as an essential principle of learning and intelligence." (Education: Hughes, J.)

38-531 **Hilkert**, Marjorie B. (*Ohio*) M.A.: "Le développement de la biographie romancée en France." (French: Du Roure, R.)

38-532 **Irwin**, Nora F. (*McGill*) M.A.: "Le christianisme de Mauriac dans toute son oeuvre." (French: Lemaitre, G.)

38-533 **Jamieson**, Stuart M. (*British Columbia*) M.A.: "French and English in the institutional structure of Montreal: a study of the social and economic division of labour." (Sociology: Hughes, E.)

38-534 **Jones**, Margaret (*Rosary College*) M.A.: "La justice au théâtre en France à partir de 1800." (French: Du Roure, R.)

38-535 **Kelly**, Ignatius (*Propagondaé* Italy) M.A.: "L'influence de François de Sales sur la prédication du dix-septième siècle." (French: Du Roure, R.)

38-536 **Kibbe**, Doris E. (*Vermont*) M.A.: 'Les relations de famille dans le roman de François Mauriac." (French: Du Roure, R.)

38-537 **Lennon**, Sister Mary George (*Rosary College*) M.A.: "Le théatre chrétien d'Henri Ghéon." (French: Du Roure,R.)

38-538 **McDonald**, Cyril P. (*Toronto*) M.A.: "The co-operative movement in Nova Scotia." (Economics: Culliton, J.)

38-539 **Munroe**, David C. (*McGill*) M.A.: "The fur trade of New France, down to 1663." (History: Adair, E.)

38-540 **Murray**, Sydney G. (*Harvard*) M.A.: 'Theories of money, value and trade fluctuations suggested by Canadian monetary and banking history." (Economics: Hemmeon, J.)

38-541 **Noyes**, Harry A. Jr. (*Vermont*) M.A.: "The history and development of the Committee for Industrial Organization in the United States." (Economics: Hemmeon, J.)

38-542 **Solin**, Cecil D. (*McGill*) M.A.: "Representation of numbers in certain regular and irregular ternary quadratics forms." (Mathematics: Pall, G.)

38-543 **Winkler**, Louis (*McGill*) M.A.: "The Canadian balance of international payments, 1900-1936." (Economics: Marsh, L.)

M.Sc. Fall 1938

38-544 **Bedoukian**, Paul (*McGill*) M.Sc.: "Hydrogenation of geraniol and related compounds." (Chemistry: Phillips, J.)

38-545 **McGibbon**, Ralph W. (*Alberta*) M.Sc.: "Action of phenylmagnesium bromide on anthraquinones." (Chemistry: Hatcher, W.)

38-546 **Minshall**, William H. (*Toronto*) M.Sc.: "Comparison of the pH requirements of certain lawn grasses and weeds, together with a study of the related physiological differences." (Botany: Scarth, G.)

38-547 **Nichols**, Walter M. (*Glasgow*, Scotland) M.Sc.: "Changes in the circulation of the brain and spinal cord associated with nervous activity." (Neurology: Penfield, W.)

38-548 **Pattee**, Chauncey J. (*Bishop's*) M.Sc.: "The role of the sex hormones in the luteal phase of the menstrual cycle." (Experimental Medicine: Meakins, J.)

38-549 **Sergeyeva**, Maria A. (*State Institute of Medical Science*, Leningrad, Russia) M.Sc.: "Effects of sympathetic and para-sympathetic stimulation on the acinous and island tissue of the pancreatic gland." (Physiology: Babkin, B.)

M.A. Fall 1938

38-550 **Astbury**, John S. (*Mount Allison*) M.A.: "Examinations, with particular reference to their place in secondary schools." (Education: Hughes, J.)

38-551 **Kennedy**, Judith (*McGill*) M.A.: "Two New England writers of children's books: Jacob Abbott and Louisa Alcott." (English: MacMillan, C.)

38-552 **Rittenhouse**, Charles B. Jr. (*Manitoba*) M.A.: "Educational dramatics in England in the sixteenth century." (English: MacMillan, C.)

38-553 **Reed**, Ernest S. (*Manitoba*) M.A.: "A criticism of the naturalistic ethics of Hume." (Philosophy: MacLennan, R.)

38-554 **Self**, George M. (*McGill*) M.A.: "The Chartist incident on Kennington Common, April 10th, 1848, critically examined, more particularly in the light of the Home Office Papers at the Public Records Office, London." (History: Fryer, C.)

38-555 **Stevenson**, James A. (*McGill*) M.A.: "The measurement of scientific aptitude in the field of student personnel work." (Psychology: Kellogg, C.)

## ANNUAL LISTING

### Ph.D. Spring 1939

39-001 **Adams**, Alfred Byron (*British Columbia*) Ph.D.: "Adiabatic vacuum calorimeter and the precision measurement of specific heats of liquids." (Chemistry: Maass, O.)

39-002 **Brown**, Robert A. (*McGill*) Ph.D.: "The geology of a portion of the Granby Sheet, Que." (Chemistry: Clark, T.)

39-003 **Cannon**, John J. (*Queen's*) Ph.D.: "A study of the mechanism of sulphite cooking." (Chemistry: Maass, O.)

39-004 **Cramer**, Archie Barrett (*Manitoba*) Ph.D.: "Structure of lignin." (Chemistry: Hibbert, H.)

39-005 **Dorland**, Rodger M. (*Western*) Ph.D.: "The ozonization and structure of lignin in relation to solubility in bisulphite solution." (Chemistry: Hibbert, H.)

39-006 **Erickson**, Theodore C. (*Minnesota*) Ph.D.: "The nature and spread of the epileptic discharge." (Neurology: Penfield, W.)

39-007 **Folkins**, Hillis Otty (*Mount Allison*) Ph.D.: "Free radicals in the decomposition of hydrocarbons." (Chemistry: Steacie, E.)

39-008 **Fordyce**, Reid George (*British Columbia*) Ph.D.: "The synthesis of polyoxyethylene glycols and the relation of their viscosities to chain length." (Chemistry: Hibbert, H.)

39-009 **Griffiths**, Henry J. (*McGill*) Ph.D.: "Studies on the nematode genus *Strongyloides* Grassi, 1879." (Parasitology: Cameron, T.)

39-010 **Holder**, Clinton Howard (*Mount Allison*) Ph.D.: "An investigation of reaction velocity and solubility in the critical temperature region." (Chemistry: Maass, O.)

39-011 **Hunter**, Melvin J. (*Antioch*) Ph.D.: "Ethanolysis of maple wood." (Chemistry: Hibbert, H.)

39-012 **McIntosh**, Robert Lloyd (*Dalhousie*) Ph.D.: "An investigation of the transition region of liquid to gas." (Chemistry: Maass, O.)

39-013 **Mason**, Stanley George (*McGill*) Ph.D.: "Transition phenomena in the critical region." (Chemistry: Maass, O.)

39-014 **Morrison**, Frank Orville (*Alberta*) Ph.D.: "A revision of the American species of Gonia Meigen (*Diptera: Tachinidae*) together with a study of the male genetalia in calyptrate Diptera based on the same genus." (Entomology: DuPorte, E.)

39-015 **Newcombe**, Howard B. (*Acadia*) Ph.D.: "Chromosome studies in the *Liliaceae*. I. Chromatid and chiasma interference in *Trillium erectum* L." (Genetics: Huskins, C.)

39-016 **Norris**, Kenneth E. (*McGill*) Ph.D.: "The permanence of school learning as indicated by a study of unemployed men." (Psychology: Kellogg, C.)

39-017 **Pall**, David Boris (*McGill*) Ph.D.: "The heat capacity and surface tension of ethylene in the critical region." (Chemistry: Maass, O.)

39-018 **Parlee**, Norman Allen Devine (*Dalhousie*) Ph.D.: "The elementary reactions of the hydrocarbons." (Chemistry: Steacie, E.)

39-019 **Peniston**, Quintin Pearman (*Washington*) Ph.D.: "The occurrence, isolation, structure and properties of red oak lignin." (Chemistry: Hibbert, H.)

39-020 **Potvin**, Roger (*Ironside*) Ph.D.: "Cadmium photosensitized reactions." (Chemistry: Steacie, E.)

39-021 **Pyle**, James Johnston (*British Columbia*) Ph.D.: "Structure of lignin." (Chemistry: Hibbert, H.)

39-022 **Rose**, Bram (*McGill*) Ph.D.: "The metabolism of histamine." (Experimental Medicine: Browne, J.)

39-023 **Ross**, Dorothy J. (*McGill*) Ph.D.: "The country justice in English local government during the first half of the seventeenth century." (History: Adair, E.)

39-024 **Sander**, Hans G.F. (*McGill*) Ph.D.: "Chromosome mutations in avena." (Genetics: Huskins, C.)

39-025 **Siminovitch**, David (*McGill*) Ph.D.: "Studies on the mechanism of frost injury to plant cells." (Botany: Scarth, G.)

39-026 **Thatcher**, Frederick S. (*McGill*) Ph.D.: "The water and permeability relationships in the parasitism of certain phytopathogenic organisms." (Plant Pathology: Coulson, J.)

39-027 **Wilson**, George Bernard (*Acadia*) Ph.D.: "The structure and behaviour of chromosomes during meiosis in *Trillium erectum* L." (Genetics: Huskins, C.)

39-028 **Wilson**, Norman L. (*Saskatchewan*) Ph.D.: "An investigation of the metamorphism of the Orijarvi type with special reference to the zinc-lead deposits at Montauban-les-Mines, Que." (Geology: Osborne, J.)

**M.A. Spring 1939**

39-029 **Bayley**, Charles Melville (*British Columbia*) Ph.D.: "The social structure of the Italian and Ukrainian immigrant communities in Montreal." (Sociology: Dawson, C.)

39-030 **Boger**, Dellie Lee (*Howard*) M.A.: "Le noir dans le roman français." (French: Du Roure, R.)

39-031 **Clark**, Jocelyn Godfrey (*Antwerp*) M.A.: "The price of gold since 1931." (Economics: Hemmeon, J.)

39-032 **Farrell**, Amelia Mary (*Vermont*) M.A.: "Les juifs dans les oeuvres des frères Tharaud." (French: Furness, L.)

39-033 **Fleer**, Edward Herman (*Princeton*) M.A.: "The nature and meaning of historical knowledge." (Philosophy: Hendel, C.)

39-034 **Fraser**, David Robert (*McGill*) M.A.: "L'évolution des chemins de fer français et le problème canadien." (Economics: Hemmeon, J.)

39-035 **Godine**, Morton Robert (*McGill*) M.A.: "The origin and development of fascist political theory." (Economics: Forsey, E.)

39-036 **Henry**, Eleanor May (*McGill*) M.A.: "Byron: a study of his political theories." (English: Macmillan, C.)

39-037 **Kerry**, Esther Wilson (*McGill*) M.A.: "The role and function of the volunteer in social work." (Sociology: Hughes, E.)

39-038 **Kieffer**, Michael Ignatius (*St. Louis*) M.A.: "L'école littéraire de Montréal." (French: Du Roure, R.)

39-039 **Lewis**, James Neilson (*Acadia*) M.A.: "The human ecology of the St. John River Valley." (Sociology: Dawson, C.)

39-040 **Lipman**, Julian A. I. (*New York*) M.A.: "The relation of the American government to railroads in recent times." (Economics: Culliton, J.)

39-041 **Lipton**, Charles (*McGill*) M.A.: "A critique of materialism in social and political ethics." (Philosophy: Hendel, C.)

39-042 **Murphy**, Florence Elizabeth (*McGill*) M.A.: "L'influence de Jean-Jacques Rousseau sur la littérature enfantine de 1762 à 1830." (French Language and Literature: Furness, L.)

39-043 **Ratelle**, Ruth M. (*Cornell*) M.A.: "Défense et illustration des femmes au quinzième siècle: 'Le champion des dames' de Martin Le Franc." (French: D'Hauteserve, L.)

39-044 **Ross**, Charles Alexander (*McGill*) M.A.: "The Canadian dollar, its' valuation and control." (Economics: Day, J.)

39-045 **Scotcher**, Charles W.D. (*New Brunswick*) M.A.: "The aetiological interest of Euripides." (Classics: Woodhead, W.)

39-046 **Urbain**, Joseph V. (*Xavier*) M.A.: "Le traditionalisme de René Bazin." (French Language and Literature: Du Roure, R.)

39-047 **Coughlin**, Clifton Rexford (*Queen's*) M.Com.: "The newsprint industry in Canada." (Economics: Hemmeon, J.)

39-048 **Hall**, George Birks Alexander (*McGill*) M.Com.: "The demand for and the supply of currency in Canada, as bearing on ultimate credit control." (Economics: Day, J.)

## ANNUAL LISTING

### M.Eng. Spring 1939

39-049 **Giddings**, E. W. Garner (*Toronto*) M.Eng.: "The analysis of classified fractions of certain pulps." (Chemistry: Phillips, J.)

39-050 **Gribbins**, Gordon Henry (*McGill*) M.Eng.: "The recovery of sodium sulphite cooking liquor." (Chemistry: Phillips, J.)

39-051 **Hum**, Thed Klung (*McGill*) M.Eng.: "The effects of certain factors on the properties of Portland cement concrete." (Civil Engineering & Applied Mechanics: Jamieson, R.)

39-052 **Kennedy**, Taylor James (*McGill*) M.Eng.: "Studies in fine grinding of ores." (Mining Engineering: Bell, J.)

39-053 **Moss**, Bernard B. (*McGill*) M.Eng.: "Recovery of gold from arsenical gold ores." (Mining & Metallurgy: MacEwan, J.)

### M.Sc. Spring 1939

39-054 **Bychowsky**, Victor ( ) M.Sc.: "Optical absorption by thin barium films in the Schumann region." (Physics: Watson, W.)

39-055 **Byrne**, Joseph Lawrence (*McGill*) M.Sc.: "The differentiation of *salmonella pullorum* by fermentation and agglutination reactions." (Bacteriology: Smith, J.)

39-056 **Dolan**, Desmond Daniel (*McGill*) M.Sc.: "An investigation of certain storage disorders of celery." (Plant Pathology: Coulson, J.)

39-057 **Gilbert**, Harold Adrian (*McGill*) M.Sc.: "The external morphology of the adult of *Hydroecia immanis* Guenee, with notes on the biology." (Entomology: DuPorte, E.)

39-058 **Hall**, James Dickie (*McGill*) M.Sc.: "The geology of the lower 'A' ore-body, Waite-Amulet, as disclosed by diamond drilling." (Geology: Osborne, F.)

39-059 **Hart**, Edward Arthur (*Saskatchewan*) M.Sc.: "The geology of the Fontana Gold Mines Property, Duverny Township, Quebec." (Geology: Gill, J.)

39-060 **Humphreys**, Storer Plumer (*Norwich*) M.Sc.: "Study of the vascular and cytological changes ir. the cerebral cicatrix." (Neurology & Neurosurgery: Penfield, W.)

39-061 **Lachance**, Rene O. (*Laval*) M.Sc.: "Pathological anatomy of boron deficient plants." (Plant Pathology: Coulson, J.)

39-062 **Lange**, Eugene Hausknecht (*Manitoba*) M.Sc.: "The relative ability of steers and rabbits to digest pasture herbage." (Animal Nutrition & Breeding: Crampton, E.)

39-063 **Logan**, Vaughn Stewart (*McGill*) M.Sc.: "Milk production in dairy cattle: factors affecting total yield and rate of secretion during lactation period, with particular reference to effect of pregnancy." (Animal Nutrition & Breeding: Crampton, E.)

39-064 **Lyster**, Lynden Laird (*McGill*) M.Sc.: "*Apophallus imperator* sp. nov., a heterophyid trematode encysted in trout with a contribution to its life history." (Parasitology: Cameron, T.)

39-065 **Maxwell**, Charles Wilmot Brown (*McGill*) M.Sc.: "Studies of the toxicity of nicotine in combination with various adjuvants." (Entomology: DuPorte, E.)

39-066 **Neish**, Arthur Charles (*McGill*) M.Sc.: "Studies on the isolation of chloroplasts and their composition." (Agricultural Chemistry: McFarlane, W.)

39-067 **Ounsworth**, Leslie Frank (*McGill*) M.Sc.: "Some aspects of the nutrition and storage of celery." (Horticulture-Botany: Murray, H.)

39-068 **Schlemm**, Leonard G.W. (*McGill*) M.Sc.: "Geology of the Lake Rowan Gold Mines." (Geology: Gill, J.)

39-069 **Selmser**, Calbert (*Union*) M.Sc.: "The petrology of a part of Mount Royal near Côte des Neiges Village." (Geology: Osborne, F.)

39-070 **Trenholm**, Laurence Stuart (*Saskatchewan*) M.Sc.: "Geology of the Amm Gold Mine, Cadillac Township, Quebec." (Geology: Gill, J.)

**Ph.D. Fall 1939**

39-500 **King**, Thomas Elston (*Laval*) Ph.D.: "The equilibrium existing in the three component system, magnesium oxide - sulphur dioxide - water, over temperature range 25° to 130° C." (Chemistry: Maass, O.)

39-501 **Moss**, Albert E. (*Saskatchewan*) Ph.D.: "The geology of the Siscoe Gold Mines, Siscoe, Quebec." (Geology: Gill, J.)

39-502 **Schwartz**, Harry (*McGill*) Ph.D.: "The colouring matter in Kraft pulp." (Chemistry: Hibbert, H.)

39-503 **Skey**, Arthur James (*Toronto*) Ph.D.: "Heats of wetting of cellulose materials." (Chemistry: Maass, O.)

39-504 **Smith**, George Ransom (*Dalhousie*) Ph.D.: "The fractionation of soil phosphorus." (Agricultural Chemistry: DeLong, W.)

39-505 **Walker**, Laurence Richard (*McGill*) Ph.D.: "The scattering of alpha particles by carbon." (Physics: Foster, J.)

**M.A. Fall 1939**

39-506 **Hunter**, Jean Isobel (*McGill*) M.A.: "The French invasion of the Eastern Townships: a regional study." (Sociology: Dawson, C.)

39-507 **Laxer**, Robert Mendel (*McGill*) M.A.: "Problems in the origin of the family." (Psychology: Kellogg, C.)

39-508 **Seidel**, Judith (*McGill*) M.A.: "The development and social adjustment of the Jewish community in Montreal." (Sociology: Dawson, C.)

39-509 **Shecter**, Una (*Columbia*) M.A.: "Three women autobiographers of the English Civil War period: Mrs. Lucy Hutchinson, Lady Ann Fanshawe, and Margaret, Duchess of Newcastle." (English: Noad, A.)

39-510 **Thompson**, Helen Muriel (*McGill*) M.A.: "Edmond Demolins: propagateur de l'éducation anglaise en France." (French: Du Roure, R.)

M.Sc. Fall 1939

39-511 **Ashton**, Gordon Clemence (*Toronto*) M.Sc.: "The utilization of feed for body weight maintenance and for body weight increase by growing bacon-type swine." (Animal Nutrition & Breeding: Crampton, E.)

39-512 **Cannon**, Frederick Merriet (*McGill*) M.Sc.: "Studies in the toxicity of nicotine." (Entomology: Brittain, W.)

39-513 **Echlin**, Francis Asbury (*McGill*) M.Sc.: "Cerebral ischaemia and its relation to epilepsy." (Neurology: Penfield, W.)

39-514 **Graham**, Annie Philathea (*McGill*) M.Sc.: "The air-bladder and pulmonary and systemic circulation of *Aoia calva* L., together with a general description of the fish." (Zoology: Wynne-Edwards, V.)

39-515 **Knight**, Enid P. (*Acadia*) M.Sc.: "A study of the effects of impurities on the accuracy of various methods of sugar analysis." (Agricultural Chemistry: McFarlane, W.)

39-516 **McKay**, Kenneth Gardiner (*McGill*) M.Sc.: "Cyclotron ion sources." (Physics: Foster, J.)

39-517 **McNiven**, Neal Lindsay (*McGill*) M.Sc.: "Reactions of tetrahydrolinalool." (Chemistry: Stevens, P.)

39-518 **Matthewman**, William Grenfell (*Toronto*) M.Sc.: "The external anatomy of the four-lined leaf bug *Poecilocapsus lineatus* Fab." (Entomology: Brittain, W.)

39-519 **Purdy**, Thomas Lenton (*Saskatchewan*) M.Sc.: "A statistical study of the characteristics of the body fat of bacon pigs and some factors which affect them." (Animal Nutrition & Breeding: Crampton, E.)

39-520 **Salisbury**, Herbert Frederick (*British Columbia*) M.Sc.: "A study of the organic fraction of some Quebec soils." (Agricultural Chemistry: DeLong, W.)

39-521 **Weil**, Paul Gregory (*North Carolina*) M.Sc.: "The metabolism of the hormone of the adrenal cortex." (Experimental Medicine: Browne, J.)

## ANNUAL LISTING

### Ph.D. Spring 1940

40-001 **Bjorklund**, Gordon Herbert (*McGill*) Ph.D.: "The chemical and physical properties of hydrogen peroxide nitric acid solutions." (Chemistry: Hatcher, W.)

40-002 **Brickman**, Leo (*Manitoba*) Ph.D.: "The structure of lignin." (Chemistry: Hibbert, H.)

40-003 **Brown**, Douglas Frederick (*New Brunswick*) Ph.D.: "The dielectric constants of cellulose and of water sorbed thereon." (Chemistry: Maass, O.)

40-004 **Brown**, Ernest A. (*Manitoba*) Ph.D.: "Elementary reactions of the lower paraffins." (Chemistry: Steacie, E.)

40-005 **Cleveland**, Courtney E. (*British Columbia*) Ph.D.: "The geology of the Empire Mine, Bralorne, B.C." (Geology: Osborne, F.)

40-006 **Cunningham**, Robert Leonard (*Dalhousie*) Ph.D.: "The mercury photosensitized reactions of ethane." (Chemistry: Steacie, E.)

40-007 **Dacey**, John Robert (*Dalhousie*) Ph.D.: "Pressure, volume, temperature, and density relations in the critical region." (Chemistry: Maass, O.)

40-008 **Dewar**, Donald James (*Queen's*) Ph.D.: "The mercury photosensitized reactions of propane." (Chemistry: Steacie, E.)

40-009 **Dyer**, William (*St. Francis Xavier*) Ph.D.: "Chemical composition and biological behavior of soil organic phosphorus." (Chemistry: Wrenshall, C.)

40-010 **Gray**, Richard Heath (*McGill*) Ph.D.: "The Sydney coalfield." (Geology: O'Neill, J.)

40-011 **Harvey**, Ross Buschlen (*Saskatchewan*) Ph.D.: "The heat capacity of ethylene and carbon dioxide in the critical temperature region." (Chemistry: Maass, O.)

40-012 **Howells**, William Crompton (*Alberta*) Ph.D.: "The Windrum Lake area, Saskatchewan." (Geology: Osborne, F.)

40-013 **Hughes**, Robert Edward (*Laval*) Ph.D.: "Physical properties and chemical reactions of hydrogen peroxide, nitric acid mixtures." (Chemistry: Hatcher, W.)

40-014 **Lachance**, Rene O. (*Laval*) Ph.D.: "Pathological anatomy of boron-deficient plants." (Plant Pathology: Coulson, J.)

40-015 **Lovell**, Edwin Lister (*British Columbia*) Ph.D.: "Some properties of long-chain molecules and their solutions." (Chemistry: Hibbert, H.)

40-016 **Marsh**, Leonard C. (*London*, England) Ph.D.: "The Canadian working population: an analysis of occupational status divisions and the incidence of unemployment." (Economics: Hemmeon, J.)

40-017 **Milner**, Robert Leopold (*Dalhousie*) Ph.D.: "Geology and Ore deposits of Barry Lake map-area, Northern Quebec." (Geology: Osborne, F.)

40-018 **Naldrett**, Stanley Norman (*Alberta*) Ph.D.: "An investigation of the state of aggregation of a one component system in the critical temperature - critical pressure region." (Chemistry: Maass, O.)

40-019 **Prebble**, Malcolm L. (*New Brunswick*) Ph.D.: "The diapause and related phenomena in *Diprion polytomum* (Hartig)." (Entomology: Brittain, W.)

40-020 **Richmond**, James Hugh (*McGill*) Ph.D.: "The decomposition of quaternary ammonium bases and of xanthate esters." (Chemistry: Stevens, P.)

40-021 **Scott**, Donald Burton (*Toronto*) Ph.D.: "The Stark effect in zinc." (Physics: Foster, J.)

40-022 **Shane**, Gerald (*McGill*) Ph.D.: "Thermal reactions of the lower hydrocarbons." (Chemistry: Steacie, E.)

40-023 **Shugar**, David (*McGill*) Ph.D.: "Stark effect in copper and nickel." (Physics: Foster, J.)

40-024 **Soley**, Russell Clyne (*Mount Allison*) Ph.D.: "The influence of environment on the apparent specific volume of cellulose." (Chemistry: Maass, O.)

40-025 **Taylor**, William Dixon (*Mount Allison*) Ph.D.: "The effect of surrounding media on the apparent volume of cellulose." (Chemistry: Maass, O.)

**M.A. Spring 1940**

40-026 **Faurot**, Jean Hiatt (*Park*) M.A.: "Augustine's philosophy of the state." (Philosophy: Maclennan, R.)

40-027 **Fulford**, Lloyd G. (*McGill*) M.A.: "The history and development of scenery, costumes and lighting of the English stage from Medieval times to the year 1700." (English: Macmillan, C.)

40-028 **Goldberg**, Simon Abraham (*McGill*) M.A.: "The French-Canadians and the industrialization of Quebec." (Economics: Hemmeon, J.)

40-029 **Kirchschlager**, Hellmuth (*Swarthmore*) M.A.: "The new trade agreement between the United States and Canada, signed, November 17, 1938." (Economics: Hemmeon, J.)

40-030 **Lieff**, Pearl (*McGill*) M.A.: "The urbanization of the French-Canadian parish." (Sociology: Hughes, E.)

40-031 **McNamara**, Mary F.C. (*Toronto*) M.A.: "L'histoire dans la poésie canadienne-française de 1860-1900." (French Language and Literature: Du Roure, R.)

40-032 **Tetrault**, Claude Moncel (*McGill*) M.A.: "La législation ouvrière dans la Province de Québec." (Economics: Hemmeon, J.)

## ANNUAL LISTING

### M.Com. Spring 1940

40-033 **Fullerton**, Douglas Henderson (*McGill*) M.Com.: "The public debt of the Dominion of Canada and associated problems of public finance." (Economics: Culliton, J.)

### M.Eng. Spring 1940

40-034 **Grassby**, James Neil (*McGill*) M.Eng.: "The cyanidation of gold ores, with varying oxygen concentrations." (Mining & Metallurgy: Bell, J.)

40-035 **Leblanc**, Raymond F. (*McGill*) M.Eng.: "The influence of certain factors and impurities on the precipitation of gold from cyanide solutions by zinc dust." (Mining and Metallurgical Engineering: MacEwan, J.)

40-036 **Seto**, Kin (*Illinois*) M.Eng.: "Particle interference in Portland cement concrete." (Civil Engineering & Applied Mechanics: Jamieson, R.)

40-037 **Anderson**, Ernest Grant (*Toronto*) M.Sc.: "Changes in germination capacity of weed seeds in storage, and factors influencing it, with special reference to *Chenopodium album* L." (Botany: Scarth, G.)

40-038 **Bertrand**, Paul (*Montreal*) M.Sc.: "Physiological changes in stored celery." (Horticulture-Botany: Scarth, G.)

40-039 **Bray**, Richard Charles Elliott (*Queen's*) M.Sc.: "A comparison of the non-opaque minerals of certain parts of the Waite-Amulet area, Quebec." (Geology: Osborne, F.)

40-040 **Brossard**, Leo (*Ecole Polytechnique*) M.Sc.: "Geology of the Beaufor Mine." (Geology: Gill, J.)

40-041 **Cann**, Donald Bruce (*McGill*) M.Sc.: "The acid solubility of the inorganic phosphate of Quebec soils." (Agricultural Chemistry: Wrenshall, C.)

40-042 **Denton**, William Ernest (*Saskatchewan*) M.Sc.: "The metamorphism of the Gordon Lake sediments, Northwest Territories." (Geology: Osborne, F.)

40-043 **Genereux**, Henri G. (*Laval*) M.Sc.: "Soil treatment with mercurials for the control of common scab of potatoes (*Actinomyces scabies* (Thax.) Gussow)." (Plant Pathology: Coulson, J.)

40-044 **Grant**, Edwin Parkhurst (*McGill*) M.Sc.: "A study of carbohydrate and protein metabolism in relation to blossom-end rot in tomatoes grown under different cultural treatments." (Agricultural Chemistry: De Long, W.)

40-045 **Hill**, Lawrence Stanley (*Saskatchewan*) M.Sc.: "A petrographic study of a basic intrusive sheet in the Yellowknife area, Northwest Territories." (Geology: Osborne, F.)

40-046 **Marcello**, Louis S. (*Toronto*) M.Sc.: "The availability and fixation of potassium in pasture soils." (Agricultural Chemistry: Wrenshall, C.)

40-047 **Nauss**, Arthur William (*New Brunswick*) M.Sc.: "The origin and economic possibilities of Canadian manganese deposits." (Geology: Gill, J.)

40-048 **Stewart**, Gordon Stafford (*McGill*) M.Sc.: "Ketosis." (Biochemistry: Collip, J.)

40-049 **Strean**, Lyon P. (*McGill*) M.Sc.: "Active and passive immunization with *Haemophilus pertussis*." (Bacteriology & Immunology: Smith, F.)

40-050 **Thorson**, Erling (*Saskatchewan*) M.Sc.: "Rocks and rock alteration in part of the Malartic area, Quebec." (Geology: Gill, J.)

**Ph.D. Fall 1940**

40-500 **Adams**, James Russell (*McGill*) Ph.D.: "The biotic cycles in northern pond communities." (Zoology: Wynne-Edwards, V.)

40-501 **Frankton**, Clarence (*McGill*) Ph.D.: "Agronomical and ecological research with special reference to the pastures of the Eastern Townships of Quebec." (Agronomy & Genetics: Scarth, G.)

40-502 **Greenwood**, Sydney Hugh John (*McGill*) Ph.D.: "The mechanism of intramolecular rearrangements." (Chemistry: Stevens, P.)

40-503 **McCoubrey**, James Addison (*Alberta*) Ph.D.: "The Grignard reagent and ethylene oxides." (Chemistry: Stevens, P.)

40-504 **Reid**, Evans Burton (*McGill*) Ph.D.: "Dimeric ketenes and cyclobutanediones." (Chemistry: Stevens, P.)

40-505 **Shaw**, John Leslie Dickinson (*Manitoba*) Ph.D.: "Studies on the determination of tryptophane." (Agricultural Chemistry: McFarlane, W.)

40-506 **Tomecko**, Joseph Wesely (*Saskatchewan*) Ph.D.: "An investigation of the 'leak effect' in measuring dielectric constants." (Chemistry: Hatcher, W.)

**M.A. Fall 1940**

40-507 **Avison**, Henry Reade Charles (*McGill*) M.A.: "The social and political ideas of John Ruskin." (English: Macmillan, C.)

40-508 **Beebe**, Mary Elizabeth (*Russell Sage*) M.A.: "Les sources de l'oeuvre de Marcel Proust." (French: Du Roure, R.)

40-509 **Branchaud**, Sister Mary (*Clarke*) M.A.: "Henri Bremond, critique original des mystiques." (French: Du Roure, R.)

40-510 **Guyton**, Pauline (*Wittenberg*) M.A.: "La révolte sociale dans le roman d'après-guerre." (French: Larivière, H.)

40-511 **Rowley**, Marie Rita (*Marymount*) M.A.: "Le satanisme dans les oeuvres des auteurs modernes: de Chateaubriand à Georges Bernanos." (French: Du Roure, R.)

40-512 **Stevens**, Valeria Dean (*Smith*) M.A.: "The critic on the hearth; biography as written by the wives of some famous novelists." (English: Macmillan, C.)

40-513 **Weyl**, Salom (*Cologne*, Germany) M.A.: "A study of the life and works of Conrad Ferdinand Meyer." (German: Beck, J.)

40-514 **Woo**, Wesley Stewart (*McGill*) M.A.: "Thiamin (Vitamin B1), and its effect upon learning ability." (Psychology: Kellogg, C.)

## M.Eng. Fall 1940

40-515 **Cameron**, Douglas Alastair (*McGill*) M.Eng.: "Effect of oxygen on the rate of dissolution of gold in cyanide solution." (Metallurgy: Bell, J.)

40-516 **Stidwell**, William Francis (*Queen's*) M.Eng.: "An investigation in the recovery of sodium bisulphite cooking liquor." (Chemical Engineering: Phillips, J.)

## M.Sc. Fall 1940

40-517 **Boothroyd**, Eric R. (*Bishop's*) M.Sc.: "The interlocking of non-homologous bivalents in *Trillium erectum* L." (Genetics: Huskins, C.)

40-518 **Feeny**, Harold Francis (*McGill*) M.Sc.: "The Stark effect in cobalt and zinc." (Physics: Foster, J.)

40-519 **King**, Robert Henry (*British Columbia*) M.Sc.: "The relative ability of sheep and rabbits to digest pasture herbage." (Animal Nutrition & Breeding: Crampton, E.)

40-520 **Manning**, Kenneth Raymond (*Acadia*) M.Sc.: "Studies in lignin: the lignin content of some common vegetables, with observations on methods for the determination of lignin." (Agricultural Chemistry: DeLong, W.)

40-521 **Morehouse**, Clarence Kopperl (*Tufts*) M.Sc.: "A study of some methods of separation and determination of molybdenum." (Chemistry: Mennie, J.)

40-522 **Ogilvie**, James D. (*McGill*) M.Sc.: "Kinetics of some gas reactions." (Chemistry: Winkler, C.)

40-523 **Sackston**, Waldemar Esi (*Manitoba*) M.Sc.: "Studies on the significance of the microflora of wilt affected clover plants." (Plant Pathology: Crowell, I.)

40-524 **Udow**, Alfred Bernard (*McGill*) M.Sc.: "The general factor in suggestibility." (Psychology: Tait, W.)

40-525 **Watts**, Humphrey Stanley (*Alberta*) M.Sc.: "The action of ring opening reagents on cyclopropane dicarboxylic acid-1,2." (Chemistry: Nicholls, R.)

## Ph.D. Spring 1941

41-001 **Bedoukian**, Paul (*McGill*) Ph.D.: "I. Cyclization of 1,5-hexadienes. II. Inactivity of bromine in Bromacetal." (Chemistry: Ross, J.)

41-002 **Cooke**, Lloyd Miller (*Wisconsin*) Ph.D.: "High pressure hydrogenation studies of lignin and related materials." (Chemistry: Hibbert, H.)

41-003 **Duncan**, Robert Daman (*Mount Allison*) Ph.D.: "Heat of reaction of gaseous sulphur dioxide on moist wood." (Chemistry: Maass, O.)

41-004 **Fisher**, John Henry (*British Columbia*) Ph.D.: "The synthesis and properties of glycosides related to lignin plant constituents." (Chemistry: Hibbert, H.)

41-005 **Forsey**, Eugene A. (*McGill*) Ph.D.: "The royal power of dissolution of Parliament in the British Commonwealth." (Economics & Political Science: Hemmeon, J.)

41-006 **Geldart**, Lloyd Philip (*Mount Allison*) Ph.D.: "Stark effect in cadmium." (Physics: Foster, J.)

41-007 **Gobeil**, Antoine R. (*Laval*) Ph.D.: "La diapause chez les tenthrèdes." (Entomology: DuPorte, E.)

41-008 **Godard**, Hugh Phillips (*British Columbia*) Ph.D.: "The hydrogenation of lignin and wood." (Chemistry: Hibbert, H.)

41-009 **Habeeb**, Herbert (*New Brunswick*) Ph.D.: "Zinc photosensitized reactions of ethylene." (Chemistry: Winkler, C.)

41-010 **MacInnes**, Alexander S. (*British Columbia*) Ph.D.: "A comparison of the lignins of plant materials by ethanolysis." (Chemistry: Hibbert, H.)

41-011 **Matthews**, Fred White (*Mount Allison*) Ph.D.: "X-ray diffraction analysis applied to certain war problems." (Chemistry: Barnes, W.)

41-012 **Pearce**, Jesse Arthur (*Queen's*) Ph.D.: "(1) Water in silica gels. (2) Sodium silicate in water." (Chemistry: Maass, O.)

41-013 **Petrie**, Richards J. (*New Brunswick*) Ph.D.: "The tax systems of Canada." (Economics: Hemmeon, J.)

41-014 **Robinson**, William G. (*Saskatchewan*) Ph.D.: "The Flavrian Lake map area and the structural geology of the surrounding district." (Geological Sciences: Gill, J.)

41-015 **Schneider**, William George (*Saskatchewan*) Ph.D.: " (1) (a) The preparation and properties of cyanogen fluoride. (b) Measurements of the service time of respirator charcoals for poison gases. (2) The investigation of the physical properties of a two component system in the critical temperature - critical pressure region." (Chemistry: Maass, O.)

41-016 **Sparrow**, Arnold H. (*Saskatchewan*) Ph.D.: "Studies on the chromosome spiralization cycle in *Trillium*." (Genetics: Huskins, C.)

41-017 **Topp**, Allan C. (*Dalhousie*) Ph.D.: "(1) The preparation and solubility of phosphorous trifluoride. (2) The preparation of arsine and calcium arsenide. (3) The adsorption of gases by respiratory charcoals." (Chemistry: Maass, O.)

41-018 **Weil**, Paul Gregory (*North Carolina*) Ph.D.: "The adrenal cortex and its role in resistance." (Experimental Medicine: Browne, J.)

M.A. Spring 1941

41-019 **Bercuson**, Leonard (*Alberta*) M.A.: "Education in the bloc settlements of western Canada." (Education: Hughes, J.)

41-020 **Birchard**, Lucile (*McGill*) M.A.: "Madame de Segur, vie, oeuvre et influence sur la litterature enfantine en France." (French: Furness, L.)

41-021 **Dwyer**, Florence Mary (*New Rochelle*) M.A.: "L'Aviation dans la littérature contemporaine." (French: Furness, L.)

41-022 **Gay**, Alice Grace (*Russell Sage*) M.A.: "Les livrets d'opera du XIXme siècle tirés des chefs-d'oeuvre de la littérature française." (French: Furness, L.)

41-023 **Heisler**, John Phalen (*British Columbia*) M.A.: "The county sheriff, 1600-1642." (History: Adair, E.)

41-024 **Henderson**, Harold Lloyd (*McGill*) M.A.: "The innovation theory of the trade cycle." (Economics: Hemmeon, J.)

41-025 **Kelly**, Marie Ste. Anne (*Marymount*) M.A.: "Le sentiment religieux de Maurice Barres." (French: Du Roure, R.)

41-026 **Letichevsky**, Jack (*McGill*) M.A.: "Foreign exchange control." (Economics: Hemmeon, J.)

41-027 **Levitt**, Bella (*McGill*) M.A.: "Supreme political power in Greek literature of the fifth century, B.C." (Classics: Woodhead, W.)

41-028 **McDonald**, Elizabeth (*McGill*) M.A.: "A pre-Shakesperian drama in pre-Shakesperian and in modern times." (English: Macmillan, C.)

41-029 **Von Cardinal**, Clive H. (*McGill*) M.A.: "Maltesches in Rilkes vor-Malteschem Werk." (German: Graff, W.)

41-030 **Whitehead**, Jean V.H. (*McGill*) M.A.: "Twentieth century poetic drama in English." (English: Files, H.)

41-031 **Wykes**, Neville George (*McGill*) M.A.: "The highway transportation problem in Quebec." (Economics: Culliton, J.)

**M.Eng. Spring 1941**

41-032 **Brown**, George Osburn (*McGill*) M.Eng.: "The effect of oxygen on the cyanidation of gold." (Mining Engineering: Bell, J.)

41-033 **Dembicki**, Steve (*Alberta*) M.Eng.: "Concentration of chromite ores by flotation." (Mining Engineering: Bell, J.)

**M.Sc. Spring 1941**

41-034 **Baxt**, Judith Brainin (*McGill*) M.Sc.: "An investigation into experimental neurosis and its treatment." (Physiology: Dworkin, S.)

41-035 **Beaupre**, Thomas Norbert (*McGill*) M.Sc.: "Sand culture experiments with spinach." (Botany-Horticulture: Scarth, G.)

41-036 **Bezeau**, Louis Manning (*Toronto*) M.Sc.: "The relation between chemical composition of ration and its feeding value for bacon hogs." (Animal Nutrition & Breeding: Crampton, E.)

41-037 **Douglas**, John MacDonald (*Saskatchewan*) M.Sc.: "Mineralography of contrasting mineralization at Gaspé, Québec." (Geology: Osborne, F.)

41-038 **Fortier**, Yves (*Queen's*) M.Sc.: "Geology of chromite." (Geology: Osborne, F.)

41-039 **Fraser**, Frank C. (*Acadia*) M.Sc.: "The effects of X chromosome inversions on crossing-over in the third chromosome of *Drosophila melanogaster*." (Genetics: Steinberg, A.)

41-040 **Friedman**, Sydney M. (*McGill*) M.Sc.: "The influence of hormones on renal structure and function." (Anatomy: Selye, H.)

41-041 **Fu**, Cheng-Yi (*National Hsing Hua*, China) M.Sc.: "The determination of the thickness of overburden by geophysical methods." (Physics: Keys, D.)

41-042 **Kerr**, Ernest A. (*McMaster*) M.Sc.: "On the behaviour of the univalents of certain aberrant wheats during microsporogenesis." (Genetics: Huskins, C.)

41-043 **Lessard**, Henri-Louis (*Montréal*) M.Sc.: "Comparative digestibility by rabbits of ether extract and true fats of feeds." (Animal Nutrition & Breeding: Crampton, E.)

41-044 **MacIntyre**, Thomas Martin (*McGill*) M.Sc.: "Some factors affecting fat and vitamin A metabolism of fowl with specific reference to the effect of the anterior pituitary." (Animal Nutrition & Breeding: Maw, W.)

41-045 **Mauffette**, Pierre (*Queen's*) M.Sc.: "Geology of Calumet Mines Ltd." (Geology: Osborne, F.)

41-046 **Poole**, John B. (*British Columbia*) M.Sc.: "Development and effects of *Strongyloides papillosus* in rodents." (Parasitology: Cameron, T.)

41-047 **Roche**, Mary Nora (*McGill*) M.Sc.: "Studies in blood coagulation." (Biochemistry: Denstedt, O.)

41-048 **Schiessler**, Robert Walter (*Pennsylvania State*) M.Sc.: "The nitration of paraffin hydrocarbons." (Chemistry: Ross, J.)

41-049 **Sheffield**, Edward Fletcher (*McGill*) M.A.: "College for employed adults." (Education: Hughes, J.)

41-050 **Wahl**, William G. (*Michigan State*) M.Sc.: "Geology of a part of the north limb of the Marquette syncline." (Geology: Gill, J.)

41-051 **Wood**, Charles Rowell (*Toronto*) M.Sc.: "A study of pigment metabolism in the wheat kernel during ripening." (Agricultural Chemistry: McFarlane, W.)

41-052 **Wright**, Annie Mary (*New Brunswick*) M.Sc.: "The expression of rhino, hairless and naked genes in the house mouse." (Genetics: Huskins, C.)

Ph.D. Fall 1941

41-501 **Buckley**, Bernard P. (*St. Francis Xavier*) Ph.D.: "The effect of temperature on the sorption of water vapor by cellulosic materials." (Chemistry: Maass, O.)

41-502 **Dunbar**, Maxwell John (*Oxford*, England) Ph.D.: "Studies in the Arctic plankton, comprising a faunistic survey of certain of the marine planktonic groups collected in the Canadian eastern arctic, and an investigation of the breeding cycles of five of the most important species in the eastern Arctic and in west Greenland." (Zoology: Wynne-Edwards, V.)

41-503 **Evans**, Taylor H. (*Alberta*) Ph.D.: "The chemical structure and antigenicity of Dextran II." (Chemistry: Hibbert, H.)

41-504 **Malouf**, Stanley E. (*Saskatchewan*) Ph.D.: "The geology of the Francoeur-Arntfield district, Beauchastel Township, Quebec." (Geology: Gill, J.)

41-505 **Minshall**, William H. (*Toronto*) Ph.D.: "Effects of acidity on growth, structure, and physiology of plants with special reference to root cells." (Botany: Scarth, G.)

41-506 **Parker**, William E. (*Acadia*) Ph.D.: "Studies on vitamin A and carotene." (Chemistry: McFarlane, W.)

41-507 **Rotenberg**, Avrahm Benjamin (*Toronto*) Ph.D.: "The construction and some applications of an electrically driven ultracentrifuge." (Physics: Foster, J.)

41-508 **Schiffrin**, Milton Julius (*Rochester*) Ph.D.: "Relationship between the parathyroid and gastric glands in the dog. The experimental production of peptic ulcer." (Physiology: Babkin, B.)

41-509 **Weaver**, William Strathern (*McGill*) Ph.D.: "(1) The ozonization of unsaturated acids. (2) A course in mavstrial organic analysis. (3) The characterization of mink oil." (Chemistry: Hatcher, W.)

M.A. Fall 1941

41-510 **Allard**, Wilfred Philip (*New York State*) M.A.: "Le roman d'aventure humoristique de Jean Martet." (French: Darbelnet, J.)

41-511 **Barrett**, Doris Pearl (*Vermont*) M.A.: "La pensée religieuse dans le théâtre de François de Curel." (French Language and Literature: Furness, L.)

41-512 **Denton**, Dorothy May (*McGill*) M.A.: "Studies in humanism: Babbitt, More, and American criticism." (English: Files, H.)

41-513 **Dolan**, John Philip (*Colby*) M.A.: "The influence of adversity on the career of Henry Wadsworth Longfellow." (English: Files, H.)

41-514 **Dooling**, Sister Margaret (*D'Youville*) M.A.: "Deux philosophes français et le renouveau thomiste: l'esprit médiéval dans les oeuvres de M. Gilson et de M. Maritain." (French Language and Literature: Larivière, H.)

41-515 **Fortier**, Mireille (*Montréal*) M.A.: "Le conflit des générations tel que l'illustre le roman français d'aprèsguerre." (French: Darbelnet, J.)

41-516 **Gallagher**, John (*Toronto*) M.A.: "A study of French influence on Canadian education with special reference to Quebec." (Education: Hughes, J.)

41-517 **Gillies**, Elizabeth Webster (*Wellesley*) M.A.: "The asbestos industry since 1929." (Economics: Hemmeon, J.)

41-518 **Hardy**, Norah Woodbury (*McGill*) M.A.: "La peinture de l'amour dans les premiers romans de Paul Bourget." (French: Larivière, H.)

41-519 **Lapin**, Murray (*McGill*) M.A.: "British participation in the sanctions against Italy arising out of the Abyssinian War." (History: Adair, E.)

41-520 **Orlick**, Emanuel (*Western*) M.A.: "A psychological study of dictators." (Psychology: Tait, W.)

41-521 **Parsons**, Clarence Reuben (*McGill*) M.A.: "André Gide et le communisme." (French: Furness, L.)

41-522 **Stovel**, John Archibald (*McGill*) M.A.: "A study in war finance." (Economics: Hemmeon, J.)

M.Sc. Fall 1941

41-523 **Armstrong**, John Grant (*Alberta*) M.Sc.: "Studies on the hemicellulose fraction of plant tissue." (Agricultural Chemistry: DeLong, W.)

41-524 **Asbury**, Winfred Nowers (*McGill*) M.Sc.: "Faulting and ore deposition in the Rouyn-Bell River region." (Geology: Gill, J.)

41-525 **Bridgers**, William Henry (*Duke*) M.Sc.: "A study of epileptogenic lesions of the brain." (Neurosurgery: Penfield, W.)

41-526 **Chapman**, Ross A. (*Ontario Agricultural*) M.Sc.: "Studies on the determination of thiamine and riboflavin in foods." (Agricultural Chemistry: McFarlane, W.)

41-527 **Cownie**, Douglas Heron (*McGill*) M.Sc.: "The mental factors in leadership." (Psychology: Tait, W.)

41-528 **Hope-Simpson**, David (*McGill*) M.Sc.: "Petrogenesis of the silicate minerals associated with copper ores, Gaspé, Quebec." (Geology: Osborne, F.)

41-529 **Kenalty**, Brendan Joseph (*St. Francis Xavier*) M.Sc.: "The reaction of hydrogen atoms with iso-butane." (Chemistry: Maass, O.)

41-530 **Lorrain**, Paul (*McGill*) M.Sc.: "The Southworth UHF panel antenna." (Physics: Foster, J.)

41-531 **MacDougall**, Daniel (*Bishop's*) M.Sc.: "Studies on lignin: the effect of methods of preparation of plant tissue and of conditions of determination on the yield and nature of the apparent lignin obtained." (Agricultural Chemistry: DeLong, W.)

41-532 **McLean**, James Douglas (*New Brunswick*) M.Sc.: "(1) The hydrolysis of propionitrile by strong acids. (2) Some reactions of SF6." (Chemistry: Winkler, C.)

41-533 **McNaughton**, Francis Lothian (*McGill*) M.Sc.: "The distribution of sensory nerves to the dura matter and cerebral vessels." (Anatomy: Martin, C.)

41-534 **Munroe**, Eugene Gordon (*McGill*) M.Sc.: "A study of the genera *Callarctia* and *Apantesis* (*Lepidoptera: Arctiidae*)." (Entomology: DuPorte, E.)

41-535 **Pudenz**, Robert Harry (*Duke*) M.Sc.:"The prevention of meningocerebral adhesions." (Neurosurgery: Penfield, W.)

41-536 **Telford**, William M. (*McGill*) M.Sc.: "Automatic rangefinder for 10 cm. radar." (Physics: Foster, J.)

**Ph.D. Spring 1942**

42-001 **Allenby**, Owen C. (*McGill*) Ph.D.: "The reduction of alpha-bromoisobutyrophenone with aluminium isopropoxide; the nitrartion of p-cymeme." (Chemistry: Nicholls, R.)

42-002 **Arnell**, John C. (*Dalhousie*) Ph.D.: "The mechanism of the sorption of gases by charcoal and other research in chemical warfare." (Chemistry: Maass, O.)

42-003 **Black**, James M. (*British Columbia*) Ph.D.: "The Bell River igneous complex." (Geological Sciences: Osborne, F.)

42-004 **Blizzard**, Ronald H. (*Washington*) Ph.D.: "1. Aromatization of petroleum hydrocarbons. 2. Synthesis of cyclopentenedions." (Chemistry: Nicholls, R.)

42-005 **Brais**, Roger ( ) Ph.D.: "Study of the action of ammonia on phosphorous trifluoride." (Chemistry: Maass, O.)

42-006 **Briggs**, Janet B. (*Sarah Lawrence*) Ph.D.: "The effect of a water-soluble carcinogen on the early development of the frog." (Zoology: Berrill, N.)

42-007 **Davis**, John (*British Columbia*) Ph.D.: "Sorption of gases by charcoal and researches in chemical and explosive warfare." (Chemistry: McIntosh, R.)

42-008 **Davis**, Stuart G. (*Alberta*) Ph.D.: "1. The proknock activity of verious compounds. 2. The dynamic sorption of ammonia and butane on charcoal. 3. The reaction of hydrogen atoms with propylene." (Chemistry: Winkler, C.)

42-009 **Deans**, Sidney A. (*McGill*) Ph.D.: "1. The catalytic conversion of p-cymene into toluene. 2. Polyvinyl nitrates." (Chemistry: Nicholls, R.)

42-010 **Dosne**, Christiane (*McGill*) Ph.D.: "The role of the adrenals in general resistance." (Anatomy: Selye H. )

42-011 **Edward**, John T. (*McGill*) Ph.D.: "The preparation of RXD by the McGill process." (Chemistry: Boyer, R.)

42-012 **Gillies**, Archibald (*Alberta*) Ph.D.: "1. Effect of proknock substances on butane oxidation. 2. A study of the cyclonite reaction - McGill process." (Chemistry: Winkler, C.)

42-013 **Hewson**, William B. (*Mount Allison*) Ph.D.: "Mechanism of wood ethanolysis and the structure of lignin." (Chemistry: Hibbert, H.)

42-014 **Josephson**, Vernal (*Utah State Agricultural*) Ph.D.: "The mesotron component in cosmic rays." (Chemistry: Watson, W.)

42-015 **Levi**, Irving (*Manitoba*) Ph.D.: "The chemical structure of dextran I." (Chemistry: Hibbert, H.)

42-016 **Lin**, Wei-cheng (*Nanking*, China) Ph.D.: "Anode potentials of lead and lead alloys." (Chemistry: Mennie, J.)

42-017 **Lossing**, Frederick P. (*Western*) Ph.D.: "1. The preparation of disulphur decafluoride. 2. The density and viscosity of disulphur decafluoride. 3. The preparation and hydrolysis of aluminium and zinc arsenides." (Chemistry: Maass, O.)

42-018 **Mowat**, John H. (*Maine*) Ph.D.: "The action of sodium upon highly branched chain ketones." (Chemistry: Boyer, R.)

42-019 **Mungen**, Richard (*Saskatchewan*) Ph.D.: "Studies on the compounds of sulphur and fluorine, and the preparation of S2F10, and work on problems in chemical warfare." (Chemistry: Maass, O.)

42-020 **Neish**, Arthur C. (*McGill*) Ph.D.: "Studies on the metabolism of normal and tumor tissue of beet-roots." (Chemistry: Hibbert, H.)

42-021 **Ogilvie**, James D. (*McGill*) Ph.D.: "1. A study of pro-knock activity. 2. The dynamic sorption of ammonia and butane on charcoal." (Chemistry: Winkler, C.)

42-022 **Rabinovitch**, Benton S. (*McGill*) Ph.D.: "1. Studies in chemical kinetics. 2. The detection of vesicants." (Chemistry: Winkler, C.)

42-023 **Scoggan**, Homer J. (*McGill*) Ph.D.: "Ecological studies of the Arctic-alpine flora of the Gaspé peninsula and of Bic." (Botany: Scarth, G.)

42-024 **Stuart**, Allan P. (*New Brunswick*) Ph.D.: "Specific surface measurement of particulate and fibrous materials, and problems of chemical warfare." (Chemistry: Maass, O.)

42-025 **Wang**, Sheng-Nien (*Central*, China) Ph.D.: "The thermal decomposition of vinyl ethyl ether." (Chemistry: Winkler, C.)

42-026 **Wasson**, Burton K. (*Mount Allison*) Ph.D.: "1. Bentonite as a vapour phase catalyst. 2. The conversion of p-cymene into toluene with ammonium chloride. 3. Synthesis of proknocks." (Chemistry: Nicholls, R.)

42-027 **West**, Kenneth A. (*British Columbia*) Ph.D.: "Studies on lignin building units." (Chemistry: Hibbert, H.)

**M.A. Spring 1942**

42-028 **Bolger**, Josephine Augusta (*Boston*) M.A.: "A comparative study of the educational traditions of New England with those of French Canada." (Education: Currie, A.)

42-029 **Erskine**, John Steuart (*Acadia*) M.A.: "Les historiens canadiens-français." (French: Larivière, H.)

42-030 **Fry**, Margaret Exie (*Wittenberg*) M.A.: "Gertrude Bell as a literary artist." (English: Noad, A.)

42-031 **Gagnon**, Aurele (*Montréal*) M.A.: "An evaluation of the psychological examining in the Youth Training Plan." (Psychology: Kellogg, C.)

42-032 **Heller**, Mildred (*McGill*) M.A.: "The significance of Henry Fielding's dramatic works." (English: Files, H.)

42-033 **Hollinger**, Martin (*McGill*) M.A.: "The price system, inflation and price control in total war." (Economics: Hemmeon, J.)

42-034 **Johnston**, Charles Franklin (*McGill*) M.A.: "Deux predicateurs Français: Adolphe et Wilfred Monod." (French: Furness, L.)

42-035 **Koenig**, Sister Mary Gregoire (*Notre Dame*) M.A.: "Les Etats-Unis de 1919 à 1939 vus par les écrivains français contemporains." (French Language and Literature: Darbelnet, J.)

42-036 **Peck**, Robert Alfred (*McGill*) M.A.: "L'Anglicisme dans les grands quotidiens de Québec." (French: Darbelnet, J.)

42-037 **Ponticello**, Eva Edith (*St. Lawrence*) M.A.: "Les idées dans les préfaces de François de Curel." (French: Furness, L.)

42-038 **Price**, Frederick William (*McGill*) M.A.: "The use of radio in the school." (Education: Currie, A.)

42-039 **Reisman**, Sol (*McGill*) M.A.: "Internal economic control in wartime: Canada." (Economics: Hemmeon, J.)

42-040 **Ross**, Sally Chipman (*Manitoba*) M.A.: "Huxley's novels of ideas: a study in values." (English: Giles, H.)

42-041 **Rossiter**, Maryellen (*McGill*) M.A.: "Le théâtre de George Sand: sources et influences." (French: Furness, L.)

42-042 **Schiffers**, Tania (*Paris*, France) M.A.: "Paris, source d'inspiration dans la poésie française des origines à Baudelaire." (French: Larivière, H.)

42-043 **Shane**, Gerald S. (*Sir George Williams*) M.A.: "The relief of monotony in industry." (Psychology: Kellogg, C.)

42-044 **Smith**, Stanley Alfred (*McGill*) M.A.: "The vocabulary of the non-literary papyri of the Hîbeh collection in relation to New Testament language." (Classics: Carruthers, C.)

42-045 **Solomon**, David N. (*McGill*) M.A.: "The Young Men's Hebrew Association of Montreal: a study of the formal and informal in an ethnic institution." (Sociology: Laviolette, F.)

42-046 **Taylor**, Margaret Ellen Bresee (*McGill*) M.A.: "Le roman historique Canadien français, des origines jusqu'à 1914." (French: Furness, L.)

42-047 **Williams**, Ivor David (*McGill*) M.A.: "Freedom in Kantian ethics." (Philosophy: Maclennan, R.)

M.Eng. Spring 1942

42-048 **Chang**, Lo-ching (*Chekiang*, China) M.Eng.: "The beneficiation of siderite ores." (Metallurgical Engineering: MacEwan, J.)

42-049 **Faucher**, Joseph Arthur Roland (*Laval*) M.Eng.: "Treatment of Lake Rowan gold ore." (Mining Engineering: Bell, J.)

42-050 **Yao**, Yu-Lin (*Chekiang*, China) M.Eng.: "Copper losses in slags." (Metallurgy: MacEwan, J.)

M.Sc. Spring 1942

42-051 **Croll**, Diane (*Manitoba*) M.Sc.: "Glucuronic acid metabolism." (Experimental Medicine: Browne, J.)

42-052 **Entin**, Martin A. (*Temple*) M.Sc.: "Cytology and growth of normal and malignant tissues." (Zoology-Genetics: Huskins, C.)

42-053 **Graham**, Walter Donald (*Toronto*) M.Sc.: "Studies on the determination of vitamin D." (Agricultural Chemistry: McFarlane, W.)

42-054 **Henry**, James P. (*Cambridge*, England) M.Sc.: "The effects of irradiation of protein antigenicity." (Experimental Medicine: Meakins, J.)

42-055 **Kennedy**, John Edward (*Queen's*) M.Sc.: "Stark effect in lead and tin." (Physics: Foster, J.)

42-056 **Kent**, George Adrian (*Alberta*) M.Sc.: "Problems connected with war research: preparation of calcium arsenate and of arsine and the determination of flourine in urine." (Chemistry: Mennie, J.)

42-057 **Lajoie**, Paul (*Montréal*) M.Sc.: "Studies on the acid-oxalate fraction of some podzolic soils." (Agricultural Chemistry: DeLong, W.)

42-058 **Leblond**, David (*Laval*) M.Sc.: "Studies of speckled leaf-blotch of oats (*Septoria avenae* Frank)." (Plant Pathology: Crowell, I.)

42-059 **Lin**, Shu-Chang (*Nanking*, China) M.Sc.: "Organ specific growth factors in the frog tadpole." (Zoology: Berrill, N.)

42-060 **Livingstone**, Constance A. (*McGill*) M.Sc.: "The adaptation of kidney tests to small laboratory rodents." (Anatomy: Selye, H.)

42-061 **MacLean**, Alister Joseph (*McGill*) M.Sc.: "Chemical studies in soil variability." (Agronomy: Summerby, R.)

42-062 **MacLennan**, Louise Isabel (*McGill*) M.Sc.: "A study of the microorganisms of the genera *Staphylococcus* and *Micrococcus*." (Bacteriology: Kelly, C.)

42-063 **Mitchell**, Mary Verity Ross (*Columbia*) M.Sc.: "Mental development as related to institutional and foster home placement." (Psychology: Kellogg, C.)

42-064 **Robinson**, Harold Ross (*Saskatchewan*) M.Sc.: "A study of the genus *Baculites* in the bearpaw formation of Western Canada." (Geology: Clark, T.)

42-065 **Shuh**, John Edward (*Ontario Agricultural*) M.Sc.: "I. Fertility studies with the Greensboro loam soil. II. Establishment and succession of seeded pastures as affected by the climatic and biotic factors." (Agronomy: Raymond, L.)

42-066 **Stern**, Herbert (*McGill*) M.Sc.: "Micrurgical studies in the physiology of cell division." (Botany-Genetics: Scarth, G.)

**Ph.D. Fall 1942**

42-500 **Hay**, Alden Wendell (*New Brunswick*) Ph.D.: "(a) The mercury photosensitized decomposition of n-butane. (b) The kinetics of the factors influencing the stability of S." (Chemistry: Winkler, C.)

42-501 **Kulka**, Marshall (*Alberta*) Ph.D.: "Structure of lignin: isolation of new ethanolysis products from maple wood." (Chemistry: Hibbert, H.)

42-502 **Livingston**, William Rodger (*Manitoba*) Ph.D.: "A study of the mechanism of the sorption of phosgene by charcoal and other research in chemical warfare." (Chemistry: Maass, O.)

42-503 **Lunn**, Alice J. (*McGill*) Ph.D.: "Economic development in New France - 1713-1760." (History: Adair, E.)

42-504 **Masson**, Georges Marie Charles (*Paris*, France) Ph.D.: "Experimental investigations on the effect of steroid compounds on the uterus." (Anatomy: Selye, H.)

42-505 **Patterson**, Ralph Francis (*British Columbia*) Ph.D.: "The ultraviolet absorption spectra of lignins and related compounds." (Chemistry: Hibbert, H.)

42-506 **Strean**, Lyon P. (*McGill*) Ph.D.: "Active and passive immunization with *Haemophilus pertussis*." (Bacteriology & Immunology: Smith, F.)

42-507 **West**, Einar (*Iowa*) Ph.D.: "The ethanolysis of spruce wood and the structure of lignin." (Chemistry: Hibbert, H.)

**M.A. Fall 1942**

42-508 **Beauvais**, Roxane (*Paris*, France) M.A.: "Saint François de Sales, directeur de conscience." (French: Larivière, H.)

42-509 **Carter**, Alfred Edward (*British Columbia*) M.A.: "Baudelaire devant la critique de 1857 à 1917." (French: Darbelnet, J.)

42-510 **Firestone**, Otto Jack (*Vienna*, Austria) M.A.: "Development of Mercantilism, a study in government intervention in trade, industry and agriculture in England and France during the sixteenth to eighteenth centuries." (Economics: Hemmeon, J.)

42-511 **Gold**, Rosalynd (*McGill*) M.A.: "Occupational selection and adjustment in the Jewish group in Montreal, with special reference to the medical profession." (Sociology: Dawson, C.)

42-512 **Graham**, C. R. (*McGill*) M.A.: "Unemployment insurance in Canada." (Economics: Hemmeon, J.)

42-513 **McGarry**, Ave Marie (*Smith*) M.A.: "Marie le Franc, romancière de la Brétagne et du Canada." (French: Furness, L.).

42-514 **Murphy**, Sister Marie Magdalen (*St. Mary's*) M.A.: "Ducis, essai sur l'influence de Shakespeare en France jusqu'à l'époque romantique." (French: Larivière, H.)

M.Eng. Fall 1942

42-515 **Gauvin**, William (*McGill*) M.Eng.: "The effect of gelatin on cathode polarization during the electrodeposition of copper." (Chemical Engineering: Winkler, C.)

M.Sc. Fall 1942

42-516 **Allen**, Della Elizabeth (*McGill*) M.Sc.: "The influence of phenothiazine on cellular metabolism." (Biochemistry: Thomson, D.)

42-517 **Bornstein**, Murray Bernard (*Dartmouth*) M.Sc.: "The effect of stimulation of the vestibular apparatus on gastric motility in the dog." (Physiology: Babkin, B.)

42-518 **Choquette**, Laurent P. E. (*Montréal*) M.Sc.: "Studies on Ascariasis in pigs. The seasonal incidence and the effects of infection on growth, with special attention to factors of resistance to harmful infection." (Parasitology: Cameron, T.)

42-519 **Collier**, Barbara Catherine (*Acadia*) M.Sc.: "Observations on the guinea pig growth method of vitamin C assay." (Nutrition: Crampton, E.)

42-520 **Doyle**, J. André (*Montréal*) M.Sc.: "External morphology of the tarnished plant bug (*Lygus pratensis* Linn.)" (Entomology: DuPorte, E.)

42-521 **Duncan**, Joseph (*Laval*) M.Sc.: "Studies on the *Pentatomidae* of Quebec (*Hemiptera: Heteroptera*)." (Entomology: DuPorte, E.)

42-522 **Filman**, Conrad Colton (*Toronto*) M.Sc.: "Sand culture experiments with celery." (Horticulture-Botany: Murray, H.)

42-523 **Gilbey**, John Alfred (*Ontario Agricultural*) M.Sc.: "Anthracnose rot of tomatoes due to *Colletotrichum phomoides* (Sacc.) Chester." (Plant Pathology: Coulson, J.)

42-524 **Hall**, Charles E. (*McGill*) M.Sc.: "Geographical variation and distribution of the Johnny darter (*Boleosoma nigrum olmstedi*) in Quebec." (Zoology: Wynne-Edwards, V.)

42-525 **Hecht**, Maurice (*McGill*) M.Sc.: "A statistical analysis of speltoid wheat (heights and number of culms)." (Physics: Huskins, C.)

42-526 **More**, Robert Hall (*Toronto*) M.Sc.: "A study of the arterial and arteriolar architecture in normal and diseased human kidneys by means of neoprene injections." (Pathology: Duff, G.)

42-527 **Morrison**, Mary F.M. (*Acadia*) M.Sc.: "Studies on the ascorbic acid content of dehydrated vegetables and its retention in cooking." (Nutrition: Crampton, E.)

42-528 **Payette**, Albert (*Montréal*) M.Sc.: "The effect of growth substances on certain phytopathogenic fungi." (Plant Pathology: Coulson, J.)

42-529 **Rochlin**, Isidore (*McGill*) M.Sc.: "*Haemoglobin* - a study of its stability in preserved blood." (Biochemistry: Denstedt, O.)

42-530 **Savard**, Kenneth F.G. (*Laval*) M.Sc.: "A study of guanyl-nitrourea." (Chemistry: Hatcher, W.)

42-531 **Schachter**, Melville (*McGill*) M.Sc.: "Experimental studies on motion sickness." (Physiology: Melville, K.)

Ph.D. Spring 1943

43-001 **Ashford**, Walter R. (*British Columbia*) Ph.D.: "Starch nitrates: preparation, properties, and structure." (Chemistry: Hibbert, H.)

43-002 **Boothroyd**, Eric R. (*Bishop's*) Ph.D.: "Differential reactivity in the chromosomes of *Trillium* species." (Genetics: Huskins, C.)

43-003 **Bower**, John R. (*Montana State*) Ph.D.: "High pressure hydrogenation of wood and related carbohydrates." (Chemistry: Hibbert, H.)

43-004 **Creighton**, Robert H. (*Swarthmore*) Ph.D.: "The oxidation of lignin and related compounds." (Chemistry: Hibbert, H.)

43-005 **Eastham**, Arthur M. (*British Columbia*) Ph.D.: "Studies on lignin progenitors." (Chemistry: Hibbert, H.)

43-006 **Grummitt**, William E. (*Alberta*) Ph.D.: "A.) Viscosity instability in high polymeric systems. B.) Molecular weights from osmotic pressure measurements. C.) The behaviour of various pro-knock compounds." (Chemistry: Maass, O.)

43-007 **Hoffman**, Martin M. (*Mount Allison*) Ph.D.: "Some aspects of the metabolism of the steroid hormone." (Experimental Medicine: Browne, J.)

43-008 **Jack**, Lawrence B. (*British Columbia*) Ph.D.: "Control of municipal finance in three federal countries: Canada, the United States, and Australia." (Economics: Hemmeon, J.)

43-009 **MacGregor**, Warren S. (*Idaho*) Ph.D.: "Oxidation of lignins: structural significance." (Chemistry: Hibbert, H.)

43-010 **Mead**, Bruce R. (*British Columbia*) Ph.D.: "Lignin: structure, extraction, and intratability." (Chemistry: Hibbert, H.)

43-011 **Morrison**, James A. (*Alberta*) Ph.D.: "The viscosity instability of solutions of high polymers." (Chemistry: Maass, O.)

43-012 **Robinson**, Donald B. (*Mount Allison*) Ph.D.: "1. Reactions of tetrahydrolinalool. 2. The conversion of N.N. diethyniline to N. ethylaniline. 3. The preparation of picric acid by the oxynitration of benzene. 4. The preparation of RDX." (Chemistry: Nicholls, R.)

43-013 **Thompson**, Allan L. (*Bishop's*) Ph.D.: "War research problems. A.) The chemistry of methyl-bis B-chlorethylamine and related compounds. B.) Various aspects of pro-knock activity." (Chemistry: Winkler, C.)

43-014 **White**, W. Harold (*Western*) Ph.D.: "Part I. The reaction of hydrogen atoms with isobutane and butadiene. Part II. The effect of temperature treatment and moisture content on the quality of dried whole egg powder." (Chemistry: Winkler, C.)

43-015 **Williams**, Harry L. (*Western*) Ph.D.: "A.) Nickel impregnated respirator charcoals. B.) An x-ray investigation of H.M.X. crystals. C.) The kinetics of the reactions to produce R.D.X." (Chemistry: Winkler, C.)

43-016 **Yaffe**, Leo (*Manitoba*) Ph.D.: "Studies on aerosol filtration." (Chemistry: Campbell, W.)

**Ph.D. Fall 1943**

43-017 **Baker**, Samuel B. (*Sir George Williams*) Ph.D.: "Lignin polymers and building units." (Chemistry: Hibbert, H.)

43-018 **Brewer**, Charles P. (*British Columbia*) Ph.D.: "High pressure hydrogenation of maple wood." (Chemistry: Hibbert, H.)

43-019 **Darwent**, Basil de B. (*McGill*) Ph.D.: "The mercury photosensitized reactions of 2-methylpropane (iso-butane)." (Chemistry: Winkler, C.)

43-020 **Fisher**, Herbert E. (*British Columbia*) Ph.D.: "Studies on lignin progenitors." (Chemistry: Hibbert, H.)

43-021 **Hay**, Eleanor C. (*Queen's*) Ph.D.: "Morphological studies of steroid metabolism." (Anatomy: Selye, H.)

43-022 **Millman**, Thomas R. (*Toronto*) Ph.D.: "Jacob Mountain, first Lord Bishop of Quebec, 1793-1825: a study in Church and state." (History: Cooper, J.)

43-023 **Pepper**, James M. (*British Columbia*) Ph.D.: "High pressure hydrogenation of maple wood." (Chemistry: Hibbert, H.)

43-024 **Zuckerman**, Abraham (*McGill*) Ph.D.: "Wood tissue lignification, plant metabolism and phenol formation." (Chemistry: Hibbert, H.)

**M.Eng. Spring 1943**

43-500 **Farmer**, Eric W. (*McGill*) M.Eng.: "The design of matching networks for antennas and transmission lines." (Electrical Engineering: Howes, F.)

**M.Sc. Spring 1943**

43-501 **Alarie**, Albert M. (*Laval*) M.Sc.: "Nitrification and nitrifying organisms in some Quebec soils." (Agricultural Bacteriology: Gray, P.)

43-502 **Andreae**, Wolfgang A. (*McGill*) M.Sc.: "Vitamin C fortification of apple juice." (Agricultural Chemistry: McFarlane, W.)

43-503 **Bauer**, Donald de F. (*Dartmouth*) M.Sc.: "*Situs inversus viscerum completus*: significance and etiology." (Genetics: Huskins, C.)

43-504 **Harding**, Stanley R. (*Saskatchewan*) M.Sc.: "The geology of the lower Lorraine in the vicinity of Montreal." (Geological Sciences: Clark, T.)

43-505 **MacLeod**, Donald M. (*McGill*) M.Sc.: "The calcium-boron ratio as an important factor in the growth of the plant cell." (Plant Pathology: Coulson, J.)

43-506 **McLeod**, William S. (*Alberta*) M.Sc.: "Further refinement of a technique for testing contact insecticides." (Entomology: Brittain, W.)

43-507 **Narod**, Milton (*British Columbia*) M.Sc.: "The biological assay of vitamin D." (Nutrition: Maw, W.)

43-508 **Paquette**, Joseph P. (*Montréal*) M.Sc.: "The preparation of 2, 4, 6-trinitrotolyl-3-methyl nitramine from the waste liquor obtained in the purification of T.N.T." (Chemistry: Boyer, R.)

43-509 **Stevens**, Thelma V. (*Acadia*) M.Sc.: "Ovule development and parthenocarpy in *Polygonum natans*." (Botany: Roscoe, M.)

43-510 **Whiting**, Frank (*Alberta*) M.Sc.: "Factors affecting the reliability of digestibility coefficients of livestock feeds." (Nutrition: Crampton, E.)

**M.A. Spring 1943**

43-511 **Jackson**, Joan S. (*McMaster*) M.A.: "An analysis of Elizabethan and some twentieth century methods of producing Shakespeare's 'Hamlet'." (English: Macmillan, C.)

43-512 **Mooney**, Elizabeth S. (*McGill*) M.A.: "The reaction to war and militarism as reflected in the British and American theatre from 1918 to 1942." (English: Files, H.)

43-513 **Pitt**, Edith S. (*Wellesley*) M.A.: "The political relationship between Caesar and Cicero to the conclusion of the civil war." (Classics: Woodhead, W.)

43-514 **Royer**, France M. (*McGill*) M.A.: "Contes populaires et légendes de la province de Quebec." (French: Darbelnet, J.)

43-515 **Sirken**, Irving A. (*McGill*) M.A.: "Wartime labour problems and policies." (Economics: Hemmeon, J.)

43-516 **Stabler**, Ernest (*Queen's*) M.A.: "Bernard Shaw: socialist, reformer and creative evolutionist." (English: Files, H.)

**M.Com. Spring 1943**

43-517 **Fox**, Lester L. (*Queen's*) M.Com.: "Prices and wages in Canada since the beginning of the Second World War." (Economics: Hemmeon, J.)

**M.Sc. Fall 1943**

43-518 **Douglas**, Donald E. (*McGill*) M.Sc.: "The action of hydrogen with amino acids." (Chemistry: Winkler, C.)

43-519 **Eiger**, Irena Z. (*McGill*) M.Sc.: "The synthesis of unsymmetrically disubstituted ethanes." (Chemistry: Nicholls, R.)

43-520 **James**, Allen P. (*McGill*) M.Sc.: "An investigation of the cytology of native and Russian species of the genus Taraxacum." (Genetics: Sander, G.)

**M.A. Fall 1943**

43-521 **Clarke**, Douglas B. (*Sir George Williams*) M.A.: "The effects of a cognitive set on the affective aesthetic experience." (Psychology: Kellogg, C.)

43-522 **Egan**, Marie J. (*Marymount*) M.A.: "Le sentiment religieux et le sentiment de la nature dans l'oeuvre de Francis Jammes." (French: Furness, L.)

43-523 **Finestone**, Harold (*McGill*) M.A.: "Trends in the population stucture of the Sherbrooke subregion." (Sociology: Dawson, C.)

43-524 **McQuillan**, Marie B. (*Marymount*) M.A.: "L'enfant dans l'oeuvre des écrivains catholiques modernes." (French: Frances, M.)

43-525 **Magee**, Arch W. (*McMaster*) M.A.: "The work of the Baptists in Canadian education." (Education: Currie, A.)

43-526 **Poirier**, Mary A. (*D'Youville*) M.A.: "L'étude du caractere anglais dans l'oeuvre d'André Maurois." (French: Darbelnet, J.)

43-527 **Randolf**, John H. (*McGill*) M.A.: "Some theories of interest." (Economics: Day, J.)

43-528 **Spearman**, Donald (*McGill*) M.A.: "Psychology and war." (Psychology: Kellogg, C.)

**Ph.D. Spring 1944**

44-001 **Bourns**, Arthur N. (*Acadia*) Ph.D.: "The vapour-phase dehydration of butaniols." (Chemistry: Nicholls, R.)

44-002 **Courtright**, Mary N. (*McGill*) Ph.D.: "Investigation of a method of fractionation of anterior pituitary." (Endocrinology: Collip, J.)

44-003 **Fineman**, Manuel N. (*McGill*) Ph.D.: "Influence of structural factors on the adsorption of gases by charcoal." (Chemistry: McIntosh, R.)

44-004 **Foran**, Michael R. (*Saskatchewan*) Ph.D.: "War research; the sorption of cyanogenchloride on charcoals." (Chemistry: Winkler, C.)

44-005 **Friedman**, Orrie M. (*Manitoba*) Ph.D.: "An investigation of the chemistry of some polymethylene nitramines." (Chemistry: Boyer, R.)

44-006 **Gardner**, Joseph A. (*British Columbia*) Ph.D.: "Studies on lignin progenitors." (Chemistry: Purves, C.)

44-007 **Guest**, Rex M. (*Western*) Ph.D.: "The apparent density and internal structure of activated charcoal." (Chemistry: McIntosh, R.)

44-008 **Holmes**, James M. (*New Brunswick*) Ph.D.: "The viscosity stability of high polymers." (Chemistry: McIntosh, R.)

44-009 **Knight**, Enid P. (*Acadia*) Ph.D.: "Nutritional requirements of trout." (Agricultural Chemistry: McFarlane, W.)

44-010 **Lips**, Alair (*British Columbia*) Ph.D.: "Studies on anti-oxidants for lipids and related substances." (Agricultural Chemistry: McFarlane, W.)

44-011 **MacDougall**, Daniel (*Bishop's*) Ph.D.: "Studies on the chemical determination of plant lignin." (Agricultural Chemistry: DeLong, W.)

44-012 **Mitchell**, Leonard (*British Columbia*) Ph.D.: "Studies on lignin progenitors." (Chemistry: Purves, C.)

44-013 **Robertson**, Ross E. (*Mount Allison*) Ph.D.: "Characterization of polyvinylacetate by molecular weight determination." (Chemistry: McIntosh, R.)

**Ph.D. Fall 1944**

44-014 **Armstrong**, John G. (*Alberta*) Ph.D.: "Studies on the hydrogenation of linseed oil in relation to flavour reversion." (Agricultural Chemistry: McFarlane, W.)

44-015 **Bishinsky**, Charles (*McGill*) Ph.D.: "The preparation of disulphur decafluoride." (Chemistry: McIntosh, R.)

44-016 **Chapman**, Ross A. (*Ontario Agricultural*) Ph.D.: "A study of incipient chemical changes in dried milk powder during storage." (Agricultural Chemistry: McFarlane, W.)

44-017 **Epstein**, Samuel (*Manitoba*) Ph.D.: "The relation between RDX and HMX production in the Bachmann reaction." (Chemistry: Winkler, C.)

44-018 **Gilpin**, Victor (*Western*) Ph.D.: "A.) Thermal decomposition of rossite and picrite in aqueous media. B.) Rate of transition of H.M.X. polymorphs. C.) Thermochemistry of the R.D.X. reactions." (Chemistry: Winkler, C.)

44-019 **Hardwick**, Thomas J. (*McGill*) Ph.D.: "A.) The chemistry of methyl bischloroethylamine and related compounds. B.) The deacidifation of RDX-B." (Chemistry: Winkler, C.)

44-020 **McLeod**, Lloyd A. (*Alberta*) Ph.D.: "The preparation of disulphur decafluoride." (Chemistry: McIntosh, R.)

44-021 **Schenker**, Victor (*McGill*) Ph.D.: "Nitrogen metabolism in damage and convalescence." (Experimental Medicine: Browne, J.)

44-022 **Siminovitch**, Louis (*McGill*) Ph.D.: "The preparation of disulphur decafluoride." (Chemistry: McIntosh, R.)

44-023 **Sowden**, Frederick J. (*Toronto*) Ph.D.: "Studies on lignin and related compounds in forage and in animal excreta." (Agricultural Chemistry: DeLong, W.)

**M.Eng. Spring 1944**

44-500 **Salman**, Mehmet T. (*McGill*) M.Eng.: "Flotation of chromite." (Mining Engineering: O'Shaughnessy, M.)

**M.Sc. Spring 1944**

44-501 **Beaudry**, Jean-Romuald (*Montréal*) M.Sc.: "The interaction of variaties of crop plants grown in Quebec to localities and seasons." (Agronomy: Summerby, R.)

44-502 **Farmer**, Florence A. (*McGill*) M.Sc.: "A study of diets intended for use in vitamin C bio-assay, using the guinea pig growth method." (Nutrition: Crampton, E.)

44-503 **Jackson**, Ivan R. (*Alberta*) M.Sc.: "The seasonal trend of the chemical composition and digestibility of mixed pasture herbage." (Nutrition: Crampton, E.)

44-504 **Korenberg**, Sarah M. (*McGill*) M.Sc.: "The chemical composition of urinary calculi and its significance." (Biochemistry: McIntosh, J. & Thomson, D.)

44-505 **Menzies**, Robert G. (*Alberta*) M.Sc.: "The relation of pH to base saturation in some Quebec soils." (Agronomy: DeLong, W.)

44-506 **Montgrain**, Clement (*Montréal*) M.Sc.: "The freezing of celery and its effect upon water loss." (Horticulture-Botany: Murray, H.)

44-507 **Morrison**, Earl S. (*New Brunswick*) M.Sc.: "The use of adsorbents in refining linseed oil." (Agricultural Chemistry: McFarlane, W.)

44-508 **O'Reilly**, Henry J. (*Toronto*) M.Sc.: "Nutrient levels as affecting stringiness in celery." (Horticulture-Botany: Murray, H.)

44-509 **Privett**, Orville S. (*Toronto*) M.Sc.: "The preparation and antioxidant properties of vitamin E concentrates from wheat-germ oil." (Agricultural Chemistry: McFarlane, W.)

44-510 **Sainte-Marie**, Dorothée L. (*McGill*) M.Sc.: "On the synthesis of the 12-oxygen analogs of corticosterone." (Biochemistry: Heard, R.)

44-511 **Simard**, Thomas (*Montréal*) M.Sc.: "Studies on tuber rot of potatoes due to *Phytophthora infestans* (Mont.) De By." (Plant Pathology: Coulson, J.)

44-512 **Weisz**, Paul (*McGill*) M.Sc.: "Part I. Growth and metamorphosis of the frog intestine in relation to body size. Part II. A qualitative and quantitative analysis of the plankton from two Laurentide lakes." (Zoology: Berrill, N.)

44-513 **Woolsey**, Lloyd D. (*Toronto*) M.Sc.: "Incisor tooth assay of vitamin C: micrometric measurement of the odontoblast cells." (Nutrition: Crampton, E.)

**M.A. Spring 1944**

44-514 **Dubensky**, Alexander (*Western*) M.A.: "Some aspects of labour problems in Canadian post-war industry." (Economics: Day, J.)

44-515 **Lumsden**, Jean G. (*McGill*) M.A.: "The political and social satire of Thomas Love Peacock." (English: Mason, G.)

44-516 **Panos**, Dimitrios (*McGill*) M.A.: "The concept of moral freedom with special reference to Nicolai Hartmann." (Philosophy: Maclennan, R.)

44-517 **Williams**, Christine S. (*Bryn Mawr*) M.A.: "The arithmetic of generalized quaternions." (Mathematics: Pall, G.)

**M.Sc. Fall 1944**

44-518 **Anderson**, Joan C. (*McGill*) M.Sc.: "(I) Parasites found in the frog *Rana pipiens* from the province of Quebec. (II) Experiments on the Wolffian duct of amphibia." (Zoology: Berrill, N.)

44-519 **Heller**, Nathan (*McGill*) M.Sc.: "The bio-assay of DCA-like substances." (Experimental Medicine: Browne, J.)

44-520 **Lusena**, Charles V. (*McGill*) M.Sc.: "Studies on the processing of wheat germ." (Agricultural Chemistry: McFarlane, W.)

44-521 **Pelletier**, Real (*Montréal*) M.Sc.: "Studies on some market diseases of tomatoes with special reference to anthracnose (*Colletotrichum phomoides* (Sacc.) Chester)." (Plant Pathology: Coulson, J.)

44-522 **Rosten**, Jean (*McGill*) M.Sc.: "The synthesis of 1, 1-diphenylethane from benzene and acetaldehyde." (Chemistry: Nicholls, R.)

44-523 **Trottier**, Bernard (*McGill*) M.Sc.: "War research. Kinetic studies on the conversion of D.T.P. and P.H.X. to H.M.X." (Chemistry: Winkler, C.)

**M.A. Fall 1944**

44-524 **Hemsley**, Stuart D. (*McGill*) M.A.: "English satire since Swift." (English: Files, H.)

44-525 **Kidd**, James R. (*Sir George Williams*) M.A.: "A study of the influence of Dr. H.M. Tory on educational policy in Canada." (Education: Currie, A.)

## ANNUAL LISTING

**Ph.D. Spring 1945**

45-001 **Alarie**, Albert M. (*Laval*) Ph.D.: "A systematic study of amylolytic bacteria, that decompose cellulose, isolated from Quebec soils." (Agricultural Bacteriology: Gray, P.)

45-002 **Betts**, Robert H. (*Alberta*) Ph.D.: "Pilot plant studies on the preparation of RXD-B by the Bachmann reaction." (Chemistry: Winkler, C.)

45-003 **Boyer**, Thomas W. (*Alberta*) Ph.D.: "The recovery of glacial acetic acid from the residual liquors of the Bachmann process. The development of a continuous reactor with which to investigate the Bachmann reaction; a) the U tube reactor, b) the rotating tube reactor." (Chemistry: Winkler, C.)

45-004 **Fraser**, Frank C. (*Acadia*) Ph.D.: "The expression and interaction of hereditary factors affecting hair growth in mice." (Genetics: Steinberg, A.)

45-005 **Garmaise**, David L. (*McGill*) Ph.D.: "A.) The preparation of 1, 1-Di(4-chlorophenyl) -2, 2, 2-trichloroethane (DDT). B.) The role of hexamine dinitrate in the formation of RDX in the McGill or Ross reaction." (Chemistry: Boyer, R.)

45-006 **Gauvin**, William (*McGill*) Ph.D.: "Investigation of polarization and effects of addition agents during the electrodeposition of copper." (Chemistry: Winkler, C.)

45-007 **Kirsch**, Milton (*McGill*) Ph.D.: "Kinetic studies of the nitrolysis of hexamine in acetic acid and in chloroform and the detonation velocity of axially cavitated cylinders of cast dina." (Chemistry: Winkler, C.)

45-008 **Legge**, Norman R. (*Alberta*) Ph.D.: "Pilot plant and laboratory studies of the Bachmann reaction for the production of cyclotrimethylenetrinitramine (RDX)." (Chemistry: Winkler, C.)

45-009 **Morton**, Maurice (*McGill*) Ph.D.: "The pyrolysis of 1, 1-diphenylethane over bentonite, tertiary mercaptans as modifiers in butadiene-styrene co-polymerization." (Chemistry: Nicholls, R.)

45-010 **Nelson**, John A. (*Alberta*) Ph.D.: "Studies on the determination of amino acids in protein hydrolysates: a new micro-colorimetric method for the determination of lysine." (Agricultural Chemistry: McFarlane, W.)

45-011 **Papineau-Couture**, Gilles (*McGill*) Ph.D.: "War research: A.) Thermal decomposition of rossite and picrite in aqueous media. B.) Velocity of detonation of tubular dina." (Chemistry: Winkler, C.)

45-012 **Stern**, Herbert (*McGill*) Ph.D.: "Physiological and physical changes of protoplasm during meiosis and mitosis in pollen mother-cells of *Trillium*." (Botany-Genetics: Scarth, G.)

45-013 **Vroom**, Alan H. (*McGill*) Ph.D.: "War research: The mechanism of the direct nitrolysis of hexamine." (Chemistry: Winkler, C.)

## ANNUAL LISTING

**Ph.D. Fall 1945**

45-014 **Andreae**, Wolfgang A. (*McGill*) Ph.D.: "Studies on vitamin metabolism." (Agricultural Chemistry: McFarlane, W.)

45-015 **Blain**, Auray (*Montréal*) Ph.D.: "The sexual reproduction of trillium, *T. erectum* L., *T. grandiflorum* (Michx) Salisb." (Genetics: Huskins, C.)

45-016 **Bowen**, William G. (*McGill*) Ph.D.: "A nitroguanidine-formalehyde explosive polymer of resin type." (Chemistry: Boyer, R.)

45-017 **Douglas**, Donald E. (*McGill*) Ph.D.: "The reaction of H with amino acids." (Biochemistry: Heard, R.)

45-018 **Hawkes**, Arthur S. (*British Columbia*) Ph.D.: "The thermal detonation of lead azide." (Chemistry: Winkler, C.)

45-019 **Humphrey**, John P. (*McGill*) Ph.D.: "The functions of government and the nature of laws." (Political Science: Brady, A.)

45-020 **Smart**, George N. Russell (*McGill*) Ph.D.: "The mechanism of RDX fromation in the Bachmann reaction." (Chemistry: Nicholls, R.)

**M.Eng. Spring 1945**

45-500 **Clark**, Robert H. (*McGill*) M.Eng.: "Experiments on water hammer using a Piezo-electric pressure indicator." (Civil Engineering & Applied Mechanics: Wood, D.)

45-501 **Nevitt**, Henry J. (*Toronto*) M.Eng.: "Design of linear electrical networks to produce waves of given shape from impressed square waves." (Electrical Engineering: Howes, F.)

**M.Sc. Spring 1945**

45-502 **Auclair**, Lucien (*Montréal*) M.Sc.: "Biological studies of the Mexican bean beetle, *Epilachna varivestis* Mulsant, in the province of Quebec." (Entomology: DuPorte, E.)

45-503 **Bell**, John M. (*Alberta*) M.Sc.: "Feeding value and digestibility of oats by swine as affected by fineness of grinding." (Nutrition: Crampton, E.)

45-504 **Boulet**, Marcel (*Montréal*) M.Sc.: "A study of the reaction between copper and dithiocarbamic acid, as applied to the determination of copper and amino acids." (Agricultural Chemistry: McFarlane, W.)

45-505 **Brogden**, Clarence L. (*McGill*) M.Sc.: "Variations in the composition of forage plants with special reference to phosphorus and calcium." (Agricultural Chemistry: DeLong, W.)

45-506 **Cameron**, Harcourt L. (*Acadia*) M.Sc.: "The gold deposits of Fifteen Mile Stream, Nova Scotia." (Geological Sciences: Gill, J.)

45-507 **Carlton**, Lucille (*McGill*) M.Sc.: "The fate of intravenously injected colloids." (Biochemistry: Denstedt, O.)

45-508 **Chalmers**, A. Edith (*McGill*) M.Sc.: "The effect of storage on the vitamin A content of mixed rations as determined by growth of rats." (Nutrition: Crampton, E.)

45-509 **Clarkson**, Scott F. (*McGill*) M.Sc.: "A storage rot of apples due to *Gloeosporium album* Osterw." (Plant Pathology: Coulson, J.)

45-510 **Leduc**, Real A. (*Montréal*) M.Sc.: "The stabilization and concentration of vitamin A in cod-liver oil." (Agricultural Chemistry: McFarlane, W.)

45-511 **Morgan**, Cecil V. (*British Columbia*) M.Sc.: "The life history and morphology of the green spruce looper, *Semiothisa granitata* Gn." (Entomology: DuPorte, E.)

**M.A. Spring 1945**

45-512 **Duncan**, Agnes P. (*McMaster*) M.A.: "Some aspects of Ernest Hemingway in his relation to American literary naturalism." (English: Files, H.)

45-513 **Ferencz**, Agnes M. (*McGill*) M.A.: "The impact of urbanization on French Canadian medical attitudes." (Sociology: **)

45-514 **Hamilton**, Lorne D. (*McGill*) M.A.: "The education of Canadian service men." (Education: Hughes, J.)

45-515 **Homer**, Kenneth C. (*Mount Allison*) M.A.: "James Branch Cabell: an interpretation." (English: Files, H.)

45-516 **Howe**, Margaret G. (*Hobart*) M.A.: "The place of Robert Frost in modern American poetry." (English: Files, H.)

45-517 **MacLean**, Mona G. (*McGill*) M.A.: "A survey of the education of British women to the nineteenth century." (Education: Hughes, J.)

45-518 **Woolner**, Evelyn F. (*Acadia*) M.A.: "Humour in the Wessex novels." (English: Files, H.)

**M.Eng. Fall 1945**

45-519 **Chadillon**, Francois J. (Montréal) M.Eng.: "The effect of pulsating air on the rate of drying of porous material." (Chemical Engineering: Phillips, J.)

**M.Sc. Fall 1945**

45-520 **Barker**, Clifford A. (*Toronto*) M.Sc.: "The effect of low temperatures on certain nematodes of sheep." (Parasitology: Cameron, T.)

45-521 **Bishop**, Robert F. (*Acadia*) M.Sc.: "The effect of lime, manure, and certain fertilizers on soil colloids." (Agricultural Chemistry: DeLong, W.)

45-522 **Chapman**, Douglas G. (*Toronto*) M.Sc.: "The chemical determination of free, combined and total choline in biological materials." (Agricultural Chemistry: McFarlane, W.)

45-523 **Chen**, Chao-jen (*Cheeloo*, China) M.Sc.: "The perineural space of the peripheral nerve." (Neurology & Neurosurgey: Cone, W.)

45-524 **Cohen**, Herman (*McGill*) M.Sc.: "Some aspects of nitrogen metabolism in the rat." (Medicine: Hoffman, M.)

45-525 **Corona**, Carlos (*Guadalajara*, Mexico) M.Sc.: "Acute aseptic leptomeningitis postoperative." (Neurology & Neurosurgey: Penfield, W.)

45-526 **Forest**, Bertrand (*Laval*) M.Sc.: "Effects of fertilizer levels on potatoes with respect to yields, specific gravity of tubers and discoloration after cooking." (Horticulture-Botany: Murray, H.)

45-527 **Galinsky**, Irving (*McGill*) M.Sc.: "A developmental comparison of the normal and wild type floret in avena." (Genetics: Stephens, S.)

45-528 **Glickman**, Irwin (*McGill*) M.Sc.: "An investigation of the relationship of body colour and susceptibility to D.D.T. in *Drosophilia melanogaster*." (Genetics: Huskins, C.)

45-529 **Gold**, M.M.A. (*McGill*) M.Sc.: "Studies on the mechanism of renal failure associated with the release of haemoglobin or related pigments in the blood plasma." (Pathology: **)

45-530 **Gold**, Simon (*McGill*) M.Sc.: "Physiological studies on the nature of toxemia of pregnancy." (Physiology: Hoff, H.)

45-531 **Halpern**, Philip E. (*McGill*) M.Sc.: "The nutritive requirements of penicillin notatum." (Agricultural Chemistry: McFarlane, W.)

45-532 **Hughes**, Muriel I. (*Acadia*) M.Sc.: "The relation between the odontoblast development in the guinea pig tooth and the intake of vitamin C." (Nutrition: Crampton, E.)

45-533 **Kaufman**, Hyman (*McGill*) M.Sc.: "New methods for the derivation of thermodynamical relations for certain complex systems." (Mathematics: Shaw, A.)

45-534 **Morantz**, Daniel J. (*McGill*) M.Sc.: "The reaction of trichloromethylparachlorophenylcarbinol to 1, 1-Di(p-chlorphenyl)-2, 2, -trichloraethane (DDT)." (Chemistry: Winkler, C.)

45-535 **Pringle**, Ross B. (*Alberta*) M.Sc.: "Studies on antibiotics." (Agricultural Chemistry: McFarlane, W.)

45-536 **Robinson**, John (*British Columbia*) M.Sc.: "The isolation and culture of fungi that produce antibacterial substances." (Agricultural Bacteriology: Thatcher, F.)

45-537 **Savage**, Marion C. (*McGill*) M.Sc.: "Enteritis in children." (Bacteriology: Smith, F.)

45-538 **Shapiro**, Stanley K. (*McGill*) M.Sc.: "Studies on the toxicity of D.D.T. to mice." (Genetics: Huskins, C.)

45-539 **Sinclair**, George W. (*Sir George Williams*) M.Sc.: "Some Ordovician lingulid brachiopods from Ontario and Quebec." (Zoology: Wynne-Edwards, V.)

45-540 **Smith**, Melvin J. (*McGill*) M.Sc.: "The nitration of polyamides." (Chemistry: Nicholls, R.)

45-541 **Stinton**, Arthur W. (*Alberta*) M.Sc.: "The vapor phase dehydration of ketones and glycols." (Chemistry: Nicholls, R.)

45-542 **Welt**, Isaac D. (*McGill*) M.Sc.: "Influence of dietary constituents upon renal size and structure." (Anatomy: Selye, H.)

**M.A. Fall 1945**

45-543 **Dando**, John A. (*McGill*) M.A.: "Some aspects of social drama in America during the thirties." (English: Macmillan, C.)

45-544 **Edwards**, Clifford E. (*Acadia*) M.A.: "La survivance de la culture française en Nouvelle-Ecosse." (French: Darbelnet, J.)

45-545 **Meyer**, Paul H. (*McGill*) M.A.: "La vie de l'époque dans les lettres de Mme. de Sevigne." (French: Darbelnet, J.)

45-546 **Penrose**, George H. (*McGill*) M.A.: "The educational significance of the Home and School movement." (Education: Currie, A.)

45-547 **Reid**, Allana G. (*McGill*) M.A.: "The importance of the town of Quebec - 1608-1703." (History: Adair, E.)

## ANNUAL LISTING

**Ph.D. Spring 1946**

46-001 **Barry**, James G. (*Sir George Williams*) Ph.D.: "(a) The action of sulfuric acid on D.D.T. and some related compounds. (b) the synthesis and derivatives of 1-4 chlorophenyl 2,2,2-trichloroethanol." (Chemistry: Ross, J.)

46-002 **Beland**, Eleanor (*California*) Ph.D.: "The renotropic action of various hormones." (Anatomy: Selye, H.)

46-003 **Boyd**, Mary L. (*Manitoba*) Ph.D.: "Kinetic studies on the formation of hexamine." (Chemistry: Winkler, C.)

46-004 **Cragg**, Gerald R. (*Toronto*) Ph.D.: "The Church and transition, 1660 to 1695." (History: Adair, E.)

46-005 **Devins**, John C. (*Dalhousie*) Ph.D.: "The mechanism of popcorn polymer formation." (Chemistry: Winkler, C.)

46-006 **Eastwood**, Thomas A. (*Western*) Ph.D.: "The kinetics of 1,1,1-trichloro-2,2-bis(4-chloro -phenyl)ethane formation." (Chemistry: Winkler, C.)

46-007 **Friedman**, Sydney M. (*McGill*) Ph.D.: "The living anatomy of the abdominal alimentary tract." (Anatomy: Martin, C.)

46-008 **Grassie**, Vernon R. (*British Columbia*) Ph.D.: "Possible mechanisms for the thermal decomposition of nitrocellulose." (Chemistry: Purves, C.)

46-009 **Guptill**, Ernest W. (*Acadia*) Ph.D.: "A linear accelerator for electrons." (Physics: Foster, J.)

46-010 **Hall**, Charles E. (*McGill*) Ph.D.: "The hormonal production of cardiovascular lesions." (Anatomy: Selye, H.)

46-011 **Hugill**, John T. (*Alberta*) Ph.D.:"The production and study of compounds of sulphur and fluorine for use in chemical warfare, with special reference to disulfur decafluorine, and the physical properties of disulfur decafluorine." (Chemistry: Maass, O.)

46-012 **Marcus**, Rudolph A. (*McGill*) Ph.D.: "Studies on the conversion of PHX to AcAn." (Chemistry: Winkler, C.)

46-013 **Novack**, Lazare (*Sir George Williams*) Ph.D.: "The chemistry, the identification, and the quantitative estimation of nitrodicyancliamicline." (Chemistry: Boyer, R.)

46-014 **Sobel**, Harry (*Temple*) Ph.D.: "The correlation between neutral urinary reducing lipids and adrenal cortical function." (Biochemistry: Heard, R.)

46-015 **Sylvester**, Elizabeth M. (*McGill*) Ph.D.: "The hormonal control of electrolyte metabolism." (Anatomy: Selye, H.)

46-016 **Weisz**, Paul (*McGill*) Ph.D.: "Part I. Studies on the development of the young of the South African clawed toad, *Xenopus laevis*. Part II. Studies on development and growth of the brine shrimp, *Artemia salina*." (Zoology: Berrill, N.)

46-017 **White**, Howard L. (*McGill*) Ph.D.: "The resolution of 1-(4-chlorophenyl) -2,2,2-trichloroethanol. Some chemical and insecticidal studies on the separated alcohols." (Chemistry: Boyer, R.)

46-018 **Wiggins**, Ernest J. (*Queen's*) Ph.D.: "Specific surface of fibrous materials and problems of explosives production." (Chemistry: Maass, O.)

46-019 **Wise**, Louis M. (*Queen's*) Ph.D.: "A critical study of osmometers used for macromolecules and the changes of polyvinyl acetate in oxygen." (Chemistry: Maass, O.)

**Ph.D. Fall 1946**

46-020 **Brown**, Robert K. (*Alberta*) Ph.D.: "Effects of the accessible fraction of cellulose on some properties of its nitrates." (Chemistry: Purves, C.)

46-021 **Cann**, Everett D. (*McGill*) Ph.D.: "Fractionation of soil organic matter." (Agricultural Chemistry: DeLong, W.)

46-022 **Christian**, William R. (*McGill*) Ph.D.: "The isometric cis-trans trinitrates of pyrogallitol." (Chemistry: Purves, C.)

46-023 **Cox**, Lionel A. (*British Columbia*) Ph.D.: "Preparations and properties of methyl allyl cellulose." (Chemistry: Purves, C.)

46-024 **Foxlee**, Frank H. (*Alberta*) Ph.D.: "Factors influencing the nitration on polyvinyl alcohol." (Chemistry: Purves, C.)

46-025 **Glegg**, Ronald E. (*McGill*) Ph.D.: "Studies on the accessible fraction of cellulose." (Chemistry: Purves, C.)

46-026 **Graham**, Wilfred (*Saskatchewan*) Ph.D.: "Studies on butadiene polymerization." (Chemistry: Winkler, C.)

46-027 **Henery-Logan**, Kenneth R. (*McGill*) Ph.D.: "Studies on the combining ratios of monomers in copolymerization." (Chemistry: Nicholls, R.)

46-028 **Lemieux**, Raymond U. (*Alberta*) Ph.D.: "Hindrance effects in cellulose substitution reactions." (Chemistry: Purves, C.)

46-029 **MacLean**, David B. (*Acadia*) Ph.D.: "Some studies on tertiary hexadecylmercaptan as a modifier in butadiene-styrene corpolymerizations." (Chemistry: Nicholls, R.)

46-030 **Moir**, Robert Y. (*Queen's*) Ph.D.: "Synthesis of a substituted centralite." (Chemistry: Purves, C.)

46-031 **Polley**, John R. (*Western*) Ph.D.: "Studies on the formation of hexamine from formaldehyde and ammonium salts in aqueous solution." (Chemistry: Nicholls, R.)

46-032 **Segall**, Gordon H. (*Alberta*) Ph.D.: "The selective denitration of cellulose nitrates." (Chemistry: Purves, C.)

46-033 **Sirianni**, Aurele F. (*Mount Allison*) Ph.D.: "Molecular weight measurements of macromolecules with an improved osmometer." (Chemistry: Maass, O.)

46-034 **Toby**, Charlotte G. (*Toronto*) Ph.D.: "Studies on experimental shock." (Endocrinology: Collip, J.)

**M.C.L. Spring 1946**

46-500 **Cuevas Cancino**, Francisco M. (*Mexico*) M.C.L.: "La nullité des actes juridiques." (Civil Law: Scott, F.)

46-501 **Lussier**, Claude (*Montréal*) M.C.L.: "The revision of international conventions." (International Law: Humphrey, J.)

**M.Eng. Spring 1946**

46-502 **Freeman**, Paul O. (*McGill*) M.Eng.: "Triaxial residual stresses in arc-welded steel plates." (Civil Engineering & Applied Mechanics: Jamieson, R.)

46-503 **Legendre**, Rosaire (*Laval*) M.Eng.: "The refining and hydrogenation of fish oils." (Chemical Engineering: Gauvin, W.)

**M.Sc. Spring 1946**

46-504 **Andreae**, Shirley R. (*McGill*) M.Sc.: "Chemical changes in stored blood." (Biochemistry: Denstedt, O.)

46-505 **Atkinson**, James T. (*McGill*) M.Sc.: "Studies with the Haring cell." (Chemistry: Winkler, C.)

46-506 **Ayoub**, Raymond G. (*McGill*) M.Sc.: "Transfinite numbers." (Mathematics: Sullivan, C.)

46-507 **Berry**, Verne H. (*Saskatchewan*) M.Sc.: "A modified Kennelly-Velander bridge for the measurement of low frequencies." (Physics: Watson, H.)

46-508 **Black**, Percy (*Sir George Williams*) M.Sc.: "Systematized unreason and science: a socio-psychological interpretation of magic, mysticism, religion, and science." (Psychology: Kellogg, C.)

46-509 **Black**, Robson H. (*Toronto*) M.Sc.: "Examination of fibres by electron microscopy." (Physics: Keys, D.)

46-510 **Chan**, Allan P. (*McGill*) M.Sc.: "Mineral nutritional effects on head lettuce." (Horticulture-Botany: Murray, H.)

46-511 **Chaplin**, Charles E. (*McGill*) M.Sc.: "The microflora of the rhizosphere with special reference to the oxidation of manganese." (Agricultural Bacteriology: Thatcher, F.)

46-512 **Chin-Yee**, Harold R. (*McGill*) M.Sc.: "Kinetics of the sulphonation of chlorobenzene." (Chemistry: Winkler, C.)

46-513 **Collins**, Vernon K. (*Acadia*) M.Sc.: "Chemical changes in the lipid fraction of wheat germ during storage." (Agricultural Chemistry: McFarlane, W.)

46-514 **Cordukes**, William E. (*McGill*) M.Sc.: "Chemical evaluation of the nutrient status of soils with respect to phosphorus and potassium." (Agronomy: Summerby, R.)

46-515 **Davidson**, Margaret E. (*McGill*) M.Sc.: "Regeneration in hydroids." (Zoology: Berrill, N.)

46-516 **Dodds**, John W. (*McGill*) M.Sc.: "Some characterisitcs of slots in ultra-high frequency wave guides." (Physics: Watson, H.)

46-517 **Drapala**, Walter J. (*Manitoba*) M.Sc.: "Lignification studies with red clover." (Agronomy: Raymond, L.)

46-518 **Gertler**, Menard M. (*Saskatchewan*) M.Sc.: "The physiological basis of neurocirculatory asthenia." (Physiology: Hoff, H.)

46-519 **Hall**, Octavia (*McGill*) M.Sc.: "Hormonal production of arthritis." (Anatomy: Selye, H.)

46-520 **Hanson**, Angus A. (*British Columbia*) M.Sc.: "Investigations of brown heart in swedes." (Agronomy: Raymond, L.)

46-521 **Hawboldt**, Lloyd S. (*McGill*) M.Sc.: "*Bessa selecta* (Meigen) as a parasite of *Gilpinia hercyniae* (Hartig)." (Entomology: DuPorte, E.)

46-522 **Hinds**, Henry E. (*McGill*) M.Sc.: "Studies in renal haemoglobin precipitation." (Pathology: Duff, G.)

46-523 **Hymovitch**, Bernard (*Sir George Williams*) M.Sc.: "Mental factors in leadership from early to late adolescence." (Psychology: Webster, E.)

46-524 **Lachance**, Francois de S. (*McGill*) M.Sc.: "Black spot of bass." (Parasitology: Cameron, T.)

46-525 **Lambek**, Joachim (*McGill*) M.Sc.: "A non-distributive calculus of numerical functions." (Mathematics: Pall, G.)

46-526 **Mamelak**, Joseph S. (*McGill*) M.Sc.: "Survey of electromagnetic theories." (Mathematics: Gillson, A.)

46-527 **Mills**, Margaret F. (*McGill*) M.Sc.: "A study of the effect of varying the type and level of shortening on the nutritive value of baked diets." (Nutrition: Crampton, E.)

46-528 **Nichol**, Charles A. (*Toronto*) M.Sc.: "A study of an enzymatic method for determination of nicotinic acid in foods." (Agricultural Chemistry: McFarlane, W.)

46-529 **Parsons**, John G. (*Fordham*) M.Sc.: "A study of the guidance needs of rural schools." (Psychology: Kellogg, C.)

46-530 **Pazur**, John H. (*Toronto*) M.Sc.: "Estimation of lignin in red clover forage: application of trisodium periodate oxidation." (Agricultural Chemistry: DeLong, W.)

46-531 **Proverbs**, Maurice D. (*McGill*) M.Sc.: "Studies on the insecticidal action of DDT (1,1,bis(4,4-dichlorophenyl) 2,2,2-trichloroethane) and related compounds, with a view to correlating this action with chemical structure." (Entomology: Morrison, F.)

46-532 **Quinn**, Hubert F. (*McGill*) M.Sc.: "Electron diffraction in thin metallic films." (Physics: Keys, D.)

46-533 **Robb**, James P. (*McGill*) M.Sc.: "A study of the effect of cortical excision on speech in patients with previous cerebral injuries." (Neurology & Neurosurgery: Penfield, W.)

46-534 **Robertson**, Florence E. (*Mount Allison*) M.Sc.: "A study of liver function tests on rabbits." (Biochemistry: Denstedt, O.)

46-535 **Schachter**, Ruth (*McGill*) M.Sc.: "Analysis of frog metamorposis by means of thiouracil." (Zoology: Berrill, N.)

46-536 **Tagiuri**, Renato (*McGill*) M.Sc.: "Comparison of results obtained from the Wechsler-Bellevue vocabulary test with those from the Stanford-Binet vocabulary, using a population of normal subjects and mental patients." (Psychology: Malmo, R.)

**M.A Spring 1946**

46-537 **Amsel**, Abram (*Queen's*) M.A.: "The effect of anxiety state upon intra-serial interference in rote learning of nonsense syllables." (Psychology: Malmo, R.)

46-538 **Beresford-Howe**, Constance (*McGill*) M.A.: "The heroines of Virginia Woolf." (English: Files, H.)

46-539 **De Jersey**, Murray G. (*McGill*) M.A.: "The prediction of engineering aptitude." (Psychology: Kellogg, C.)

46-540 **Layton**, Irving (*McGill*) M.A.: "A critical examination of Laski's political doctrines." (Political Science: Tuck, R.)

46-541 **Macdonald**, Roderick R. (*McGill*) M.A.: "A revision of Grassmann's law." (Classics: Carruthers, C.)

46-542 **MacKeen**, Frances C. (*McGill*) M.A.: "L'actualité politique dans 'Les hommes de bonne volonté' (volumes I à XIV) de Jules Romains." (French: Darbelnet, J.)

46-543 **Macpherson**, John (*McGill*) M.A.: "The origin and development of the Prometheus myth." (Classics: Woodhead, W.)

46-544 **Munroe**, William M. (*McGill*) M.A.: "The function of music in education." (Education: Hughes, J.)

46-545 **Nakashima**, Kimiaki (*Washington*) M.A.: "Economic aspects of Japanese evacuation from the Canadian Pacific coast." (Economics: Day, J.)

46-546 **Reid**, David B. (*McGill*) M.A.: "Some applications of modern statistical methods to psychometric data." (Psychology: Kellogg, C.)

46-547 **Seywerd**, Henry (*Sir George Williams*) M.A.: "A case study of community consensus with respect to emerging delinquent behaviour." (Sociology: LaViolette, F.)

46-548 **Sloat**, Annie P. (*McMaster*) M.A.: "La survivance française au Nouveau Brunswick." (French: Darbelnet, J.)

**M.Com. Spring 1946**

46-549 **Rothschild**, Fred (*McGill*) M.A.: "Business taxes and investment." (Economics: Higgins, B.)

**M.Eng. Fall 1946**

46-550 **Bastin**, Douglas H. (*British Columbia*) M.Eng.: "Problems encountered in the development of a standard test for microphones." (Electrical Engineering: Howes, F.)

46-551 **Bott**, Raoul H. (*McGill*) M.Eng.: "The design of wide-band matching networks for U.H.F. antennae." (Electrical Engineering: Howes, F.)

46-552 **De Stein**, Joseph L. (*Saskatchewan*) M.Eng.: "The structural value of light alloy sections in the plastic range." (Civil Engineering & Applied Mechanics: Jamieson, R.)

46-553 **Epstein**, Norman (*McGill*) M.Eng.: "Non-isothermal friction drop for gas." (Chemical Engineering: Gauvin, W.)

46-554 **Filman**, Norman J. (*British Columbia*) M.Eng.: "A study of the peak values of transient voltages present in the radio-frequency and intermediate-frequency amplifiers of a communication type receiver." (Electrical Engineering: Howes, F.)

46-555 **Ives**, Walter J. (*Manitoba*) M.Eng.: "The development of a logarithmic indicating instrument for the measurement of radio noise voltages encountered in radio receivers." (Electrical Engineering: Howes, F.)

46-556 **Perrault**, Charles H. (*McGill*) M.Eng.: "The effect of aluminum additions on the graphitization rate of white cast iron." (Metallurgical Engineering: Sproule, G.)

M.Sc. Fall 1946

46-557 **Askonas**, Brigitte A. (*McGill*) M.Sc.: "Detoxication in psychiatric disorders." (Biochemistry: Thomson, D.)

46-558 **Berman**, Doreen (*McGill*) M.Sc.: "Hormonal effects on fat deposition in the liver." (Anatomy: Selye, H.)

46-559 **Birmingham**, Marion K. (*Bennington*) M.Sc.: "The effect of damage on *in vitro* protein metabolism." (Experimental Medicine: Venning, E.)

46-560 **Burch**, George N. (*Mount Allison*) M.Sc.: "Canadian tall oils and their fatty acids." (Chemistry: Nicholls, R.)

46-561 **Burrow**, Martin D. (*McGill*) M.Sc.: "The application of conformal mapping to the solution of electrostatic problems." (Mathematics: Rosenthall, E.)

46-562 **Burton**, Barbara W. (*Acadia*) M.Sc.: "Some factors affecting the bioassay of vitamin C by the odontoblast method." (Nutrition: Crampton, E.)

46-563 **Dussault**, H.P. (*Ottawa*) M.Sc.: "A study of the microflora of sheeps' rumen with special reference to cellulose-decomposing bacteria." (Agricultural Bacteriology: Gray, P.)

46-564 **Ellington**, Alton C. (*McGill*) M.Sc.: "Studies on the isolation and quantitative determination of amylose from wheat and oat starch." (Agricultural Chemistry: McFarlane, W.)

46-565 **Ewart**, Mervyn H. (*Toronto*) M.Sc.: "Production of 2,3-butanediol and the nature of the *Bacillus soli* fermentation." (Agricultural Chemistry: McFarlane, W.)

46-566 **Gillies**, Norman B. (*Dalhousie*) M.Sc.: "The geology of the Formaque property, Bourlamaque township, Quebec." (Geological Sciences: Osborne, F.)

46-567 **Gillingham**, John T. (*British Columbia*) M.Sc.: "Studies on the availability of potassium in podzol soil." (Agricultural Chemistry: DeLong, W.)

46-568 **Girdwood**, Barbara M. (*Toronto*) M.Sc.: "The effect of extraneous elements in the micro-quantitative analysis of boron." (Physics: Foster, J.)

46-569 **Gurd**, Frank R. (*McGill*) M.Sc.: "Changes in the lipoproteins of human blood serum during processing." (Biochemistry: Denstedt, O.)

46-570 **Hardie**, Robert H. (*McGill*) M.Sc.: "The design and construction of a spectroscopic isotope detector and its application to the isotopes of radioactive lead." (Physics: Keys, D.)

46-571 **Karp**, Dorothy (*McGill*) M.Sc.: "The effect of quinine and atabrine on gastric secretory function in the dog." (Physiology: Babkin, B.)

46-572 **Lee**, Burdett (*Toronto*) M.Sc.: "The place of experimental work in the study of rock structures." (Geological Sciences: **)

46-573 **McMillan**, Gardner C. (*McGill*) M.Sc.: "The effect of alloxan diabetes mellitus on experimental cholesterol arteriosclerosis in the rabbit." (Pathology: Duff, G.)

46-574 **Perlin**, Arthur S. (*McGill*) M.Sc.: "Studies on the decomposition of cellulose by micro-organisms." (Agricultural Chemistry: McFarlane, W.)

46-575 **Pinsky**, Alex (*McGill*) M.Sc.: "The determination and synthesis of riboflavin in cultures of microorganisms." (Agricultural Chemistry: McFarlane, W.)

46-576 **Russell**, Gordon D. (*McGill*) M.Sc.: "The reaction of tertiary hexadecyl mercaptan with a butadiene-styrene copolymer." (Chemistry: Nicholls, R.)

46-577 **Sabin**, Israel M. (*McGill*) M.Sc.: "The metabolism of testosterone." (Medicine: Hoffman, M.)

46-578 **Saffran**, Murray (*McGill*) M.Sc.: "The clearance of injected citrate from the blood." (Biochemistry: Denstedt, O.)

46-579 **Sourkes**, Theodore L. (*McGill*) M.Sc.: "The nutritive value of the proteins of stored livestock rations." (Nutrition: Crampton, E.)

46-580 **Stultz**, Harold T. (*Acadia*) M.Sc.: "The bionomics of the codling moth, *Carpocapsae pomonella* L., in the Annapolis Valley, Nova Scotia." (Entomology: DuPorte, E.)

46-581 **Wallace**, Raphael H. (*Dalhousie*) M.Sc.: "Nutritional requirements of cellulolytic bacteria isolated from Quebec soils." (Agricultural Bacteriology: Gray, P.)

M.A. Fall 1946

46-582 **Albert**, Ruth R. (*McGill*) M.A.: "A critical evaluation of the theories of economic change of Smith, Ricardo, Marx and Schumpeter." (Economics: Keirstead, B.)

46-583 **Barry**, Rexford G. (*McGill*) M.A.: "Some aspects of Spencer, Bishop of Norwich." (History: Bayley, C.)

46-584 **Bradford**, Florence E. (*Toronto*) M.A.: "L'histoire du Canada dans l'oeuvre de Maurice Constantin-Weyer." (French: Woodhead, W.)

46-585 **Culver**, Eleanor A. (*Cornell*) M.A.: "Etude critique de la traduction anglaise du livre de Jules Romains 'Le six octobre'. (Premier volume de 'Les hommes de bonne volonté')." (French: Launay, J.)

46-586 **Friedlander**, John B. (*McGill*) M.A.: "The effect of the War on Canadian foreign trade." (Economics: Day, J.)

46-587 **Hunter**, Gerald F. (*McGill*) M.A.: "The reform of education for boys as reflected in eighteenth century English literature." (English: Files, H.)

46-588 **McFarlane**, Arthur H. (*McGill*) M.A.: "The prediction of success in technical school courses." (Psychology: Webster, E.)

46-589 **Quinn**, Herbert F. (*Sir George Williams*) M.A.: "The Quebec provincial election of 1944: an analysis of the role of the election in the democratic process." (Political Science: Keirstead, B.)

46-590 **Spurrell**, Althea C. (*McGill*) M.A.: "Towards a 'natural history' of the sociology of art." (Sociology: Dawson, C.)

46-591 **Stewart**, Mary (*McGill*) M.A.: "The relation of ethics and religion in Kierkegard's thought." (Philosophy: MacLennan, R.)

46-592 **Strauss**, Clara (*Queen's*) M.A.: "Rorschach studies of personality problems in the higher age groups." (Psychology: Malmo, R.)

46-593 **Thomson**, Allan (*McGill*) M.A.: "Imperialism in English poetry between 1875 and 1900." (English: Files, H.)

46-594 **Welbourne**, Arthur J. (*Loyola of Montréal*) M.A.: "A study of educational practices in the schools in the island of Montreal." (Education: Currie, A.)

## ANNUAL LISTING

Ph.D. Spring 1947

47-001 **Baird**, David M. (*New Brunswick*) Ph.D.: "Geology of the Burlington peninsula, Newfoundland." (Geological Sciences: Gill, J.)

47-002 **Bryce**, William A. (*Saskatchewan*) Ph D.: "The effect of alternating electrical fields on the polymerization of styrene." (Chemistry: Winkler, C.)

47-003 **Dixon**, John F. (*McGill*) Ph.D.: "Synthesis of carbonyl derivatives of polyhydroxy cyclohexanes." (Chemistry: Purves, C.)

47-004 **Falk**, Hans L. (*McGill*) Ph.D.: "On the synthesis of corticoids and spectrophotometric studies in the steroid hormone group." (Biochemistry: Heard, R.)

47-005 **Genge**, Colin A. (*Alberta*) Ph.D.: "The effects of alternating electrical fields on the polymerization of styrene." (Chemistry: Winkler, C.)

47-006 **Gogek**, Charles J. (*Alberta*) Ph.D.: "Cis-trans isomerism of the polyhydroxy cyclohexane series." (Chemistry: Purves, C.)

47-007 **Hollies**, Norman R. (*Alberta*) Ph.D.: "The dielectric constant of disulfur decafluoride and high pressure instrumentation at high temperatures." (Chemistry: Maass, O.)

47-008 **Johnson**, Herbert (*Saskatchewan*) Ph.D.: "The dielectric constant of adsorbed ethyl chloride." (Chemistry: Maass, O.)

47-009 **Kellaway**, Peter E. (*Occidental*) Ph.D.: "The bioelectric phenomena of the auditory apparatus." (Physiology: Hoff, H.)

47-010 **Lathe**, Grant H. (*McGill*) Ph.D.: "The disturbances of metabolism in wounded men." (Physiology: Hoff, H.)

47-011 **Lorrain**, Paul (*McGill*) Ph.D.: "A low-pressure glow-discharge proton source." (Physics: Foster, J.)

47-012 **Ludwig**, Ralph A. (*Alberta*) Ph.D.: "The physiology of hydromycotic wilting in plants with special reference to tomato wilt." (Plant Pathology: Coulson, J.)

47-013 **MacHutchin**, John G. (*McGill*) Ph.D.: "1. The recovery of glacial acetic acid from the residual liquors of the Bachmann process. 2. The rate of disappearance of hexamine in Bachmann type mixtures and the discovery of DPT. 3. The kinetics of BSX formation." (Chemistry: Winkler, C.)

47-014 **Marchant**, Edwin H. (*Manitoba*) Ph.D.: "Quantitative studies on the larvae of *Trichinella spiralis*." (Parasitology: Cameron, T.)

47-015 **Munn**, Allan M. (*Queen's*) Ph.D.: "A linear electron accelerator." (Physics: Foster, J.)

47-016 **Pringle**, Ross B. (*Alberta*) Ph.D.: "Technical studies on antibiotics with special reference to citrinin." (Agricultural Chemistry: McFarlane, W.)

47-017 **Privett**, Orville S. (*Toronto*) Ph.D.: "Studies on the heat polymerization of linseed oil." (Agricultural Chemistry: McFarlane, W.)

47-018 **Ritchie**, Paul F. (*Mount Allison*) Ph.D.: "The preparation and properties of periodate lignins." (Chemistry: Purves, C.)

47-019 **Trost**, Walter R. (*Alberta*) Ph.D.: "The kinetics of the thermal decomposition of disulfur decafluoride." (Chemistry: Maass, O.)

47-020 **Tuck**, Norman G. (*Alberta*) Ph.D.: "The density of adsorbed layers." (Chemistry: Maass, O.)

47-021 **Wahl**, William G. (*Michigan State*) Ph.D.: "The Canica-Cawatose map area." (Geological Sciences: Osborne, F.)

**Mus.D. Spring 1947**

47-022 **Hanson**, Frank K. (*McGill*) Mus.D.: "Symphony in Canada." (Music: Clark, D.)

**Ph.D. Fall 1947**

47-023 **Campbell**, James A. (*Ontario Agricultural*) Ph.D.: "Studies on the chick assay for vitamin D and some observations on chemical methods for its determination." (Agricultural Chemistry: McFarlane, W.)

47-024 **Christie**, Archibald M. (*McGill*) Ph.D.; "The geology of the Goldfields area, Saskatchewan." (Geological Sciences: Jolliffe, A.)

47-025 **Downes**, Kenneth W. (*Manitoba*) Ph.D.: "Part I. The ammonia-soda process applied to sodium sulphate. Part II. The thermal decomposition of benzoyl peroxide in solvents. Part III. The homogeneous thermal decomposition of acetaldehyde." (Chemistry: Winkler, C.)

47-026 **Farmer**, Florence A. (*McGill*) Ph.D.: "The effect on both mother and offspring of artificial regulation of the metabolic rate of the pregnant and nursing guinea pigs." (Nutrition: Crampton, E.)

47-027 **Gleason**, Clarence H. (*Sir George Williams*) Ph.D.: "Chemical studies in the polyhydric phenol series." (Chemistry: Purves, C.)

47-028 **Gunton**, Robert C. (*Western*) Ph.D.: "Some applications of a Svedberg rotor in ultracentrifuge measurements." (Physics: Foster, J.)

47-029 **Husband**, Robert M. (*Saskatchewan*) Ph.D.: "The action of sodium chlorite and chlorine dioxide on phenolic substances related to lignin." (Chemistry: Purves, C.)

47-030 **Ingraham**, Thomas R. (*Dalhousie*) Ph.D.: "Kinetic studies on the formation and decomposition of hexamethylenetetramine." (Chemistry: Winkler, C.)

47-031 **Jamieson**, James R. (*Alberta*) Ph.D.: "Transformation of the steroid molecule to permit the inclusion of isotopic carbon." (Biochemistry: Heard, R.)

47-032 **Liu**, Chien-kang (*Soochow*, China) Ph.D.: "Origin and growth of the germ cells of *Tubularia crocea* with special reference to the germ-plasm theory." (Zoology: Berrill, N.)

47-033 **Lusena**, Charles V. (*McGill*) Ph.D.: "Studies on the preparation of nucleoproteins and ribonucleic acid from wheat germ." (Agricultural Chemistry: McFarlane, W.)

47-034 **Madras**, Samuel (*Sir George Williams*) Ph.D.: "Cellophane as membrane material." (Chemistry: Maass, O.)

47-035 **Millar**, Charles H. (*Bishop's*) Ph.D.: "Molecular absorption spectra in the 12.5 centimetre region." (Physics: Foster, J.)

47-036 **Spivack**, John D. (*McGill*) Ph.D.: "Reduction of trimethyl gallic acid by sodium and isoamyl alcohol." (Chemistry: Purves, C.)

47-037 **Tasker**, Clinton W. (*Syracuse*) Ph.D.: "p-Toluenesulfonyl and iodo derivatives of some hydroxyethyl ethers." (Chemistry: Purves, C.)

47-038 **Thorn**, George D. (*Alberta*) Ph.D.: "The action of alkaline hypohalites on phenolic substances." (Chemistry: Purves, C.)

47-039 **Yan**, Maxwell M. (*Manitoba*) Ph.D.: "Extraction of woods with sodium bicorbonate-carbon dioxide or with liquid ammonia under pressure." (Chemistry: Purves, C.)

**M.C.L. Spring 1947**

47-500 **Challies**, George S. (*McGill*) M.C.L.: "Expropriation under the law of the Dominion of Canada and the province of Quebec." (Law: Scott, F.)

47-501 **Fergusson**, Neil L. (*Dalhousie*) M.C.L.: "Collective bargaining and Order-in-Council, P.C.1003." (Law: Scott, F.)

**M.Eng. Spring 1947**

47-502 **Cooper**, Howard B. (*McGill*) M.Eng.: "The engineering factors controlling the optimum size of a manufacturing enterprise." (Mechanical Engineering: Coote, J.)

47-503 **Hayes**, John E. (*Queen's*) M.Eng.: "The development of a reflectometer type of standing wave indicator." (Electrical Engineering: Howes, F.)

47-504 **Merson**, Lawrence N. (*McGill*) M.Eng.: "The analysis, design and construction of a null detector for AC impedance bridges." (Electrical Engineering: Howes, F.)

47-505 **Trudeau**, Guy J. (*Nova Scotia Technical*) M.Eng.: "The effect of iron on aluminum bronze." (Metallurgical Engineering: MacEwan, J.)

47-506 **Yorke-Slader**, Geoffrey H. (*McGill*) M.Eng.: "The stability of high voltage power systems." (Electrical Engineering: Christie, C.)

**M.Sc. Spring 1947**

47-507 **Cabbott**, Irwin M. (*McGill*) M.Sc.: "A study of mechanical factors in GR-S bottle polymerization." (Chemistry: Nicholls, R.)

47-508 **Dorken**, Herbert O. (*McGill*) M.Sc.: "Personality factors associated with paraplegia." (Psychology: Alexander, F.)

47-509 **Eiser**, Herman M. (*McGill*) M.Sc.: "Studies on the metabolism of actinomyces griseus in relation to the production of streptomycin." (Agricultural Chemistry: McFarlane, W.)

47-510 **Firlotte**, William R. (*McGill*) M.Sc.: "A survey of ecto- and endo-parasites of brown Norway rat, *Rattus norvegicus*, (Erxleben, 1777), obtained essentially from the region of the 'Quarry' Macdonald College, Quebec, Canada." (Parasitology: Cameron, T.)

47-511 **Fortuyn**, Jan D. (*Amsterdam*, Holland) M.Sc.: "Experimental studies of the thalamo-cortical mechanisms in relation to *petit mal* epilepsy." (Neurology & Neurosurgery: Jasper, H.)

47-512 **Frank**, Julius (*Toronto*) M.Sc.: "The toxic effects of coccidiostatic sulphanamides in chickens." (Parasitology: Cameron, T.)

47-513 **Gilbert**, Joseph E. (*Laval*) M.Sc.: "The acidic intrusives of the Bachelor Lake area." (Geological Sciences: Osborne, F.)

47-514 **Howard**, Robert P. (*McGill*) M.Sc.: "Assays of urinary corticoids: a comparison between results of chemical and biological methods." (Medicine: Venning, E.)

47-515 **Kirkland**, Robert W. (*Saskatchewan*) M.Sc.: "The east ore zone at Giant Yellowknife Mine, N.W.T.:" (Geological Sciences: Jolliffe, A.)

47-516 **Laliberté**, Jacques N. (*Montréal*) M.Sc.: "A study of mineral nutritional effects on carrots." (Horticulture-Botany: Murray, H.)

47-517 **Lord**, Frank T. (*Ontario Agricultural*) M.Sc.: "The influence of the apple spray programme on the natural control of oystershell scale, *Lepidosaphes ulmi* (L)." (Entomology: Brittain, W.)

47-518 **McPherson**, William J. (*Saskatchewan*) M.Sc.: "Critical review of criteria used in the nomenclature and classification of sandstones." (Geological Sciences: Clark, T.)

47-519 **Mahoney**, Gerald M. (*Sir George Williams*) M.Sc.: "The relationship between general mental ability and university achievement." (Psychology: Webster, E.)

47-520 **Manson**, Mary G. (*Toronto*) M.Sc.: "A comparison of three methods of interpreting data from vitamin C bioassay." (Nutrition: Crampton, E.)

47-521 **Moynihan**, Irvin W. (*Ontario Veterinary*) M.Sc.: "The role of the protozoan parasite *Eimeria acervulina* in disease of the domestic chicken." (Parasitology: Cameron, T.)

47-522 **Neilson**, James M. (*Queen's*) M.Sc.: "The stratigraphy and structure of the Mistassini series in the Lake Albanel area." (Geological Sciences: Gill, J.)

47-523 **Proctor**, William C. (*Alberta*) M.Sc.: "The utilization of forage phosphorous by sheep." (Nutrition: Crampton, E.)

47-524 **Rouatt**, James W. (*Saskatchewan*) M.Sc.: "The effects of adding fertilizers and glucose on the morphological and physiological groups of bacteria in soil." (Agricultural Bacteriology: Gray, P.)

47-525 **Scott**, David M. (*McGill*) M.Sc.: "The biology of the yellowtail flounder (*Limanda ferruginea* Storer)." (Zoology: Berrill, N.)

47-526 **Starr**, Harry (*McGill*) M.Sc.: "Experimental alloxan diabetes." (Pathology: Duff, G.)

47-527 **Usher**, John L. (*Saskatchewan*) M.Sc.: "The geology of the St. Dominique Ridge, Bagot county, Que." (Geological Sciences: Clark, T.)

47-528 **Wong**, Esther V. (*Western*) M.Sc.: "Studies on the determination of ascorbic acid." (Agricultural Chemistry: McFarlane, W.)

**M.A. Spring 1947**

47-529 **Arthur**, Elizabeth M. (*Toronto*) M.A.: "Adam Mabane and the French party in Canada, 1760-1791." (History: Adair, E.)

47-530 **Butterfield**, Lee E. (*Hillsdale*) M.A.: "La peinture de la bourgeoise dans 'Les Thibauld' de Roger Martin du Gard." (French: Furness, L.)

47-531 **Elliott**, Harriett E. (*Dalhousie*) M.A.: "Les anglo-saxons dans l'oeuvre de Pierre de Coulevain." (French: Furness, L.)

47-532 **Guter**, Ernest (*McGill*) M.A.: "Consumer credit, consumer spending policies and their effects upon economic fluctuations." (Economics: Higgins, B.)

47-533 **Langlois**, Robert H. (*Michigan*) M.A.: "Shakespeare's influence on Dryden." (English: Files, H.)

47-534 **Lenoir**, Marguerite N. ( ) M.A.: "Le courrier anglais de Stendhal: ses jugements sur la politique et la litterature." (French: Lariviere, H.)

47-535 **MacDonald**, Allister I. (*Acadia*) M.A.: "Shakespeare's treatment of soldiers." (English: Macmillan, C.)

47-536 **MacNeill**, Glorana H. (*Acadia*) M.A.: "Etude comparative de deux traductions anglaise et americaine du roman de Georges Duhamel 'Le Notaire du Havre'." (French: Launay, J.)

47-537 **Martineau**, Jeanne G. (*Ottawa*) M.A.: "La survivance française dans Prescott et Russell." (French: D'Hauteserve, L.)

47-538 **Mindes**, Evelyn (*McGill*) M.A.: "Confederation of Catholic workers of Canada." (Economics: Woods, H.)

47-539 **Prince**, Alma S. (*Vermont*) M.A.: "The relationship between the nobles and the king in France in the late sixteenth and early seventeenth centuries." (History: Adair, E.)

**M.Com. Spring 1947**

47-540 **Burgess**, Charles J. (*McGill*) M.Com.: "An appraisal of the report of the economic policy committee of Jamaica, 1945." (Economics: Beach, E.)

**M.Eng. Fall 1947**

47-541 **Hoyle**, Wilfred G. (*Alberta*) M.Eng.: "Small electronic regulators." (Electrical Engineering: Schippel, W.)

**M.Sc. Fall 1947**

47-542 **Aitken**, Johnstone R. (*Manitoba*) M.Sc.: "A nitrogen balance study of protein supplements in the hog ration." (Nutrition: Crampton, E.)

47-543 **Bercovitch**, Mortimer (*McGill*) M.Sc.: "A new determination of the velocity of sound in air using counter-chronograph and microphones." (Physics: Marshall, J.)

47-544 **Cunnington**, Francis A. (*McGill*) M.Sc.: "Porcupine-Beattie gold belt." (Geological Sciences: Gill, J.)

47-545 **Dechene**, Earl B. (*Sir George Williams*) M.Sc.: "The characterization of a new hydroxy acid isolated from Spanish ergot." (Chemistry: Nicholls, R.)

47-546 **Gass**, James H. (*Mount Allison*) M.Sc.: "Studies in the processing of vegetable oils." (Agricultural Chemistry: McFarlane, W.)

47-547 **Gooding**, Herbert B. (*McGill*) M.Sc.: "Studies in comparative physiology of trees." (Botany: Gibbs, R.)

47-548 **Goss**, George C. (*McGill*) M.Sc.: "The conversion of carotene to vitamin A *in vitro*." (Agricultural Chemistry: McFarlane, W.)

47-549 **Gunn**, Kenrick L. (*Western*) M.Sc.: "Radar echoes from rain showers." (Physics: Marshall, J.)

47-550 **Hare**, John H. (*Ontario Agricultural*) M.Sc.: "The recovery of whey proteins by the use of waste sulfite liquor." (Agricultural Chemistry: McFarlane, W.)

47-551 **Harpur**, Robert P. (*New Zealand*) M.Sc.: "The absorption and oxidation of phenothiazene in the sheep." (Biochemistry: Denstedt, O.)

47-552 **Imbault**, Paul-Emile (*Laval*) M.Sc.: "The acidic plutonic rocks of the Iserhoff River area." (Geological Sciences: Osborne, F.)

47-553 **Jackson**, Ira J. (*New York*) M.Sc.: "Asceptic meningitis due to blood and its breakdown products: an experimental and clinical study." (Neurology & Neurosurgery: Penfield, W.)

47-554 **Johnson**, Arnold L. (*McGill*) M.Sc.: "Heart catheterization in the investigation of congenital heart disease." (Physiology: Hoff, H.)

47-555 **Jooste**, Rene F. (*Witwatersrand*, South Africa) M.Sc.: "The mineralogy of the St. Charles phosphatic titaniferous magnetite deposit." (Geological Sciences: Jolliffe, A.)

47-556 **Loewy**, Ariel G. (*McGill*) M.Sc.: "The infra red total absorption method and its application to some plant physiological problems." (Botany: Scarth, G.)

47-557 **Macbeth**, Robert A. (*Alberta*) M.Sc.: "Factors affecting the thyroid gland and body metabolism." (Endocrinology: Noble, R.)

47-558 **Mackay**, Kathleen I. (*Acadia*) M.Sc.: "Studies on methods for the determination of peroxides in fats and oils." (Agricultural Chemistry: Chapman, R.)

47-559 **McLean**, Chester R. (*Queen's*) M.Sc.: "Experimental studies in the pathology of allergy." (Pathology: Duff, G.)

47-560 **MacPhee**, Albert W. (*McGill*) M.Sc.: "The morphology and bionomics of the predaceous thrips *Haplothrips faurei Hood*." (Entomology: Brittain, W.)

47-561 **Marmur**, Julius (*McGill*) M.Sc.: "A study of the mode of action of chemotherapeutic substances." (Agricultural Bacteriology: Thatcher, F.)

47-562 **Millar**, Myra J. (*McGill*) M.Sc.: "A study on the utilization of different kinds and levels of fat in baked diets." (Nutrition: Crampton, E.)

47-563 **Moster**, Julius B. (*McGill*) M.Sc.: "Studies on the chemical changes in the protein and carbohydrate fractions of milk powders during storage." (Agricultural Chemistry: Chapman, R.)

47-564 **Palmer**, Walter M. (*McGill*) M.Sc.: "Radar echoes from continuous precipitation." (Physics: Marshall, J.)

47-565 **Paul**, Harry (*London*, England) M.Sc.: "Investigation of the effects of flooding on the phosphorous status of soils." (Agricultural Chemistry: DeLong, W.)

47-566 **Phillips**, John H. (*Toronto*) M.Sc.: "The morphology and bionomics of three species of leafhopper inhabiting the cherry." (Entomology: DuPorte, E.)

47-567 **Rabinovitch**, Reuben (*New York*) M.Sc.: "The evolutional pathology of the intervertebral disc." (Neurology & Neurosurgery: MacEachern, D.)

47-568 **Robertson**, William K. (*Ontario Agricultural*) M.Sc.: "A chemical study of some of the factors affecting the availability of potassium in soils." (Agricultural Chemistry: DeLong, W.)

47-569 **Shaw**, Michael (*McGill*) M.Sc.: "Applications of the infra-red absorption technique of measuring gas exchange in plants, to the study of plants exposed to normal and harmful conditions." (Plant Pathology & Botany: Gibbs, R.)

47-570 **Siminovitch**, Helen E. (*Acadia*) M.Sc.: "The validity of physical and chemical tests for determining the quality of flax fibre produced in various types of retting." (Agricultural Chemistry: McFarlane, W.)

47-571 **Stollmeyer**, John E. (*McGill*) M.Sc.: "The metabolism of chorionic gonadotrophin." (Medicine: Hoffman, M.)

47-572 **Tate**, Parr A. (*McGill*) M.Sc.: "A study of high intensity light sources for use in the photography of effects observable in an expansion chamber." (Physics: Terroux, F.)

47-573 **Tiphane**, Marcel (*Montréal*) M.Sc.: "Pershing Township map area." (Geological Sciences: Osborne, F.)

47-574 **Welch**, William K. (*Pittsburgh*) M.Sc.: "A morphological study of human *Glioblastoma multiforme* transplanted to guinea pigs." (Neurology & Neurosurgery: Cone, W.)

47-575 **Wyatt**, Barbara V. (*McGill*) M.Sc.: "Some aspects of experimental cancer." (Endocrinology: Collip, J.)

**M.A. Fall 1947**

47-576 **Bush**, Willard S. (*McMaster*) M.A.: "The effect of World War II upon the financial position of Canadian corporate industry." (Economics: Vineberg, P.)

47-577 **Gilmore**, Robert C. (*Vermont*) M.A.: "Causes of English colonization in America, 1550-1640." (History: Adair, E.)

47-578 **Jackson**, Joan K. (*McGill*) M.A.: "Rehabilitation: a national, institutional and individual crisis." (Sociology: Laviolette, F.)

47-579 **Lynam**, Josephine B. (*New Brunswick*) M.A.: "Educational institutions in New Brunswick, 1830-71." (Education: Hughes, J.)

47-580 **Mills**, George H. (*Bishop's*) M.A.: "The annexation movement of 1849 as seen through the Lower Canadian press." (History: Cooper, J.)

47-581 **Ross**, Harold (*McGill*) M.A.: "The Jew in the educational system of the province of Quebec." (Education: Hughes, J.)

47-582 **Sofin**, Rosalie (*McGill*) M.A.: "The level of aspiration of job applicants." (Psychology: Alexander, F.)

47-583 **Tougas**, Gerard R. (*Alberta*) M.A.: "Anatole France devant la critique americaine." (French: Launay, J.)

47-584 **Wilkinson**, Ida G. (*Manitoba*) M.A.: "Les femmes dans la correspondance de Voltaire." (French: Furness, L.)

## ANNUAL LISTING

**Ph.D. Spring 1948**

48-001 **Albert**, Samuel (*McGill*) Ph.D.: "An attempt to locate steroids in tissues with special emphasis on the distribution of estradiol labeled with $I^{131}$ in cancer-susceptible mice." (Anatomy: Leblond, C.)

48-002 **Bardwell**, John A. (*Western*) Ph.D.: "The formation and properties of three-dimensional polymers." (Chemistry: Winkler, C.)

48-003 **Bell**, Robert E. (*British Columbia*) Ph.D.: "Gamma-rays of neutron capture, studied with beta-ray spectrometer." (Physics: Foster, J.)

48-004 **Friedman**, Constance A. (*McGill*) Ph.D.: "Renal function and experimental hypertension." (Anatomy: Martin, C.)

48-005 **Greenberg**, Louis (*Saskatchewan*) Ph.D.: "The immunizing efficiency of mixed antigens." (Bacteriology: Fleming, D.)

48-006 **Herman**, Lloyd G. (*Toronto*) Ph.D.: "The synergistic action of penicillin, streptomycin, and various sulfonamides on certain germ-negative bacteria." (Agricultural Bacteriology: Thatcher, F.)

48-007 **Kaufman**, Hyman (*McGill*) Ph.D.: "The determination of thermodynamical relations in simple and in complex systems, by the methods of Jacobian analysis." (Physics: Shaw, A.)

48-008 **Macdougall**, Graham R. (*Toronto*) Ph.D.: "A study on the corn gluten of stripper-starch." (Biochemistry: Denstedt, O.)

48-009 **McMillan**, Gardner C. (*McGill*) Ph.D.: "The effect of alloxan diabetes on experimental cholesterol arteriosclerosis in the rabbit." (Pathology: Duff, L.)

48-010 **Rigby**, Francis L. (*Alberta*) Ph.D.: "Studies on acid hydrolysis of proteins." (Agricultural Chemistry: Common, R.)

48-011 **Stewart**, Ronald D. (*McGill*) Ph.D.: "Search for pancreatic alpha-cell hormone." (Biochemistry: Heard, R.)

48-012 **Tomlinson**, Richard H. (*Bishop's*) Ph.D.: "The flow of gases and vapours through adsorbing porous media." (Chemistry: Maass, O.)

48-013 **Wallace**, Raphael H. (*Dalhousie*) Ph.D.: "The nutritional requirements of soil bacteria as influenced by the growth of various crop plants." (Agricultural Bacteriology: Gray, P.)

48-014 **Wolfson**, Joseph L. (*Manitoba*) Ph.D.: "The disintegration of cerium of mass 144." (Physics: Foster, J.)

Ph.D. Fall 1948

48-015 **Bartholomew**, Gilbert (*British Columbia*) Ph.D.: "Energy determination of the hard gamma-ray from gallicum 72 by photodisintegration in a Wilson cloud chamber." (Physics: Terroux, F.)

48-016 **Booth**, Kenneth G. (*British Columbia*) Ph.D.: "Attempted syntheses of a branch-chain cellulose and the unreliability of the periodate method of estimating branching." (Chemistry: Purves, C.)

48-017 **Boulet**, Marcel (*Montréal*) Ph.D.: "A modified method for the determination of lysine and its application to reactions between reducing sugars and amino acids." (Agricultural Chemistry: McFarlane, W.)

48-018 **Brannen**, Eric (*Toronto*) Ph.D.: "The disintegration of hafnium of mass 181." (Physics: Foster, J.)

48-019 **Brunton**, Donald C. (*Queen's*) Ph.D.: "Some aspects of the fission process." (Physics: Foster, J.)

48-020 **Clarke**, Robert L. (*Alberta*) Ph.D.: "The use of the photodisintegration of deuterium in a cloud chamber in the determination of the energy of the hard gamma ray from lanthanum 140." (Physics: Terroux, F.)

48-021 **Coté**, Pierre E. (*Laval*) Ph.D.: "Geology and petrology of the anorthosite and associated rocks of the Chertsey map area." (Geological Sciences: O'Neill, J.)

48-022 **Ellington**, Alton C. (*McGill*) Ph.D.: "The estimation and location of the carbonyl groups in chromium trioxide oxy-starch." (Agricultural Chemistry: Purves, C.)

48-023 **Farmilo**, Charles G. (*Alberta*) Ph.D.: "Synthesis and polymerization of some substituted butadienes." (Chemistry: Nicholls, R.)

48-024 **Girdwood**, Barbara M. (*Toronto*) Ph.D.: "The molecular absorption spectrum of methyl alcohol in the 1.25 cm. region." (Physics: Foster, J.)

48-025 **Greenblatt**, Jayson (*Dalhousie*) Ph.D.: "(a) The reaction between nitrogen atoms and ethylene. (b) The application of diffusion flame techniques to the reaction between nitrogen atoms and ethylene." (Chemistry: Winkler, C.)

48-026 **Hutcheon**, Alan T. (*Saskatchewan*) Ph.D.: "Tree formation in the electrowinning of cadmium and a brief kinetic study of the decomposition of R.D.X. in the system R.D.X.-Al-H2O." (Chemistry: Winkler, C.)

48-027 **Knowles**, John W. (*Toronto*) Ph.D.: "A study of the adsorption of protactinium on manganese oxides." (Physics: Keys, D.)

48-028 **Leslie**, John D. (*British Columbia*) Ph.D.: "The reactions of N- dodecyl mercaptan and potassium persulfate in emulsion systems." (Chemistry: Winkler, C.)

48-029 **MacKenzie**, James S. (*McGill*) Ph.D.: "The electrolytic reduction of ammonium nitrate." (Chemistry: Winkler, C.)

48-030 **MacKenzie**, Kenneth R. (*McGill*) Ph.D.: "Protein metabolism in the rat under the influence of damage, endocrine substances and diet." (Medicine: Browne, J.)

48-031 **Michel**, Walter (*Saskatchewan*) Ph.D.: "A high output, low voltage spread positive ion-source." (Physics: Foster, J.)

48-032 **Montgomery**, Douglas S. (*Toronto*) Ph.D.: "The degradation of polymers." (Chemistry: Winkler, C.)

48-033 **Morrison**, Wesley A. (*Saskatchewan*) Ph.D.: "New types of nuclear disintegrations." (Physics: Foster, J.)

48-034 **Pepper**, Thomas P. (*British Columbia*) Ph.D.: "Study of some nuclear reactions between heavy hydrogen isotopes." (Physics: Foster, J.)

48-035 **Quinn**, Hubert F. (*McGill*) Ph.D.: "The spectrophotometric determination of exhaust gas temperatures in the pulsating jet engine." (Physics: Mordell, D.)

48-036 **Russell**, Stewart H. (*McGill*) Ph.D.: "The effect of high frequency electrical fields on the decomposition of benzoyl peroxide." (Chemistry: Winkler, C.)

48-037 **Saffran**, Judith (*McGill*) Ph.D.: "Studies on the metabolism of steroid hormones." (Biochemistry: Heard, R.)

48-038 **Simard**, Thomas (*Montréal*) Ph.D.: "Studies on the microflora of barley seed and special reference to *Helminthosporium* sativum P.K. and B." (Plant Pathology: Ludwig, R.)

48-039 **Sinclair**, George W. (*Sir George Williams*) Ph.D.: "The biology of the *Gonularida*." (Zoology: Berrill, N.)

48-040 **Stephens-Newsham**, Lloyd G. (*Saskatchewan*) Ph.D.: "The disintegration of thulium." (Physics: Foster, J.)

48-041 **Turner**, Terry E. (*Acadia*) Ph.D.: "The microwave absorption spectrum of methylene chloride." (Physics: Foster, J.)

48-042 **Voyvodic**, Louis (*McGill*) Ph.D.: "Intensity and energy absorption studies on extended gamma-ray sources." (Physics: Foster, J.)

48-043 **Walker**, Jessie M. (*Western*) Ph.D.: "The kinetics of the copolymerization of butadiene and styrene in homogeneous solutions." (Chemistry: Winkler, C.)

48-044 **Warren**, F.G. Ross (*Manitoba*) Ph.D.: "A cold cathode proton source for the synchrocyclotron." (Physics: Foster, J.)

48-045 **Yalden-Thomas,** David C. (*Oxford*, England) Ph.D.: "Hume's moral philosophy in the treatise of human nature." (Philosophy: Maclennan, R.)

**M.C.L. Spring 1948**

48-500 **Aguilar-Mawdsley**, Andres (*Venezuela*) M.C.L.: "De la possession dans le droit civil de la province de Québec." (Law: LeMesurier, C.)

48-501 **Cawadias**, Constantine G. (*Athens*, Greece) M.C.L.: "The arbitration of civil and industrial disputes in Quebec law." (Law: Scott, F.)

48-502 **Lapointe**, Marc C. (*Montréal*) M.C.L.: "The juridical extension of collective agreements in the province of Quebec." (Law: Scott, F.)

**M.Arch. Spring 1948**

48-503 **Papanek**, Rudolf J. (*McGill*) M.Arch.: "Methods of control of the bulk and form of buildings in the central area of cities, with reference to Montreal." (Architecture: Spencer-Sales, H.)

**M.Eng. Spring 1948**

48-504 **Bourne**, James D. (*McGill*) M.Eng.: "A method of reducing harmonic distortion in audio amplifiers." (Electrical Engineering: Howes, F.)

48-505 **Gersovitz**, Benjamin (*McGill*) M.Eng.: "Stresses in a plain plate flat slab reinforced concrete." (Civil Engineering & Applied Mechanics: Dodd, G.)

48-506 **Hall**, J.S. (*Witwatersrand*, South Africa) M.Eng.: "Radio signals masked by noise." (Electrical Engineering: Howes, F.)

48-507 **Kemmett**, Francis W. (*Illinois Institute of Technology*) M.Eng.: "The determination of film co-efficients for condensing vapors." (Chemical Engineering: Phillips, J.)

48-508 **Moore**, William J. (*British Columbia*) M.Eng.: "An electronic synchronous speed regulator." (Electrical Engineering: Schippel, W.)

48-509 **Pavlasek**, Tomas J. (*McGill*) M.Eng.: "Characteristics of composition-type resistors." (Electrical Engineering: Howes, F.)

48-510 **Raju**, B. Sadasiva (*Mysore*, India) M.Eng.: "Concentration of low-grade chromite ores." (Mining Engineering: O'Shaughnessy, M.)

## ANNUAL LISTING

**M.Sc. Spring 1948**

48-511 **Anderson**, George G. (*McGill*) M.Sc.: "The effect of varying quantities of salt upon the microflora of pickled codfish." (Agricultural Bacteriology: Thatcher, F.)

48-512 **Barwick**, Audrey J. (*McGill*) M.Sc.: "A study of the effect of botulinum toxin on the transmission of nerve impulses." (Bacteriology: Stevenson, J.)

48-513 **Boyle**, Willard S. (*McGill*) M.Sc.: "The determination of depths of overburden by sonic echo ranging." (Physics: Watson, H.)

48-514 **Coldwell**, Blake B. (*McGill*) M.Sc.: "Studies on the utilization of open-hearth slag as a fertilizer." (Agricultural Chemistry: DeLong, W.)

48-515 **Crook**, Helen G. (*McGill*) M.Sc.: "The odontoblast method of bioassay versus chemical methods of assaying vitamin C." (Nutrition: Crampton, E.)

48-516 **Cure**, Charles W. (*Indiana*) M.Sc.: "Methods for the induction of epileptiform abnormality in the electroencephalogram of epileptic patients." (Neurology & Neurosurgery: Jasper, H.)

48-517 **Dso**, Li-Liang (*West China Union*, China) M.Sc.: "A study in gastro-intestinal motility." (Physiology: Hoff, H.)

48-518 **Dufresne**, Cyrille (*Laval*) M.Sc.: "Faulting in the St. Lawrence plain." (Geological Sciences: Clark, T.)

48-519 **Durrell**, Winfield B. (*Toronto*) M.Sc.: "A survey of the role of nutrition in sterility of dairy cattle." (Nutrition: Swales, W.)

48-520 **Fochs**, Anita M. (*McGill*) M.Sc.: "Parasites of marine fishes in the Bay of Chaleur area." (Parasitology: Cameron, T.)

48-521 **Gauthier**, Fernand M. (*Laval*) M.Sc.: "A comparison of grain crops grown singly and in combination." (Agronomy: Lods, E.)

48-522 **Gervais**, Paul (*Laval*) M.Sc.: "The effect of several fertilizers and lime on the yield and botanical composition of a pasture sward on a Sherbrooke sandy loam." (Agronomy: Raymond, L.)

48-523 **Gold**, Allen (*McGill*) M.Sc.: "Micro-assay of insulin." (Endocrinology: Noble, R.)

48-524 **Goldfarb**, Lionel (*McGill*) M.Sc.: "The theory of elacticity of aelotropic materials." (Mathematics: Wallace, P.)

48-525 **Hardwick**, David F. (*Saskatchewan*) M.Sc.: "A systematic study of the external male genitalia of the genus *Septis* (*Lepidoptera, Phalaenidae*)." (Entomology: DuPorte, E.)

48-526 **Henrikson**, Arne (*British Columbia*) M.Sc.: "Maintenance of precision standards of electromotive force." (Physics: Shaw, A.)

48-527 **Jardine**, John M. (*Mount Allison*) M.Sc.: "The behavior of tertiary hexadecyl thiol in polymer-emulsion systems." (Chemistry: Nicholls, R.)

48-528 **Kipkie**, George F. (*Queen's*) M.Sc.: "The vascular lesions of renal hypertension in the rabbit." (Pathology: Duff, L.)

48-529 **Kwiecinska-Pappius**, Hanna M. (*McGill*) M.Sc.: "Glycolytic changes in stored blood." (Biochemistry: Denstedt, O.)

48-530 **L'Esperance**, Robert L. (*McGill*) M.Sc.: "A study of the diabase dykes of the Canadian Shield." (Geological Sciences: Gill, J.)

48-531 **Logan**, Ralph A. (*McGill*) M.Sc.: "The theory of relativistic accelerators." (Mathematics: Wallace, P.)

48-532 **McAllister**, Arnold L. (*New Brunswick*) M.Sc.: "A cobalt-tungsten deposit in the Sudbury district." (Geological Sciences: Jolliffe, A.)

48-533 **MacLean**, Angus A. (*McGill*) M.Sc.: "Partition of soil phosphorus as affected by variations of soil properties." (Agricultural Chemistry: DeLong, W.)

48-534 **Mani**, K.V. (*Madras*, India) M.Sc.: "The toxic effect of linseed oil meal in chick rations." (Poultry Husbandry: Nikolaiczuk, N.)

48-535 **Maurer**, Alfred R. (*British Columbia*) M.Sc.: "Some physiological aspects of frozen vegetables." (Horticulture-Botany: Murray, H.)

48-536 **Miller**, Saul (*McGill*) M.Sc.: "The living anatomy of the human lung." (Anatomy: Martin, C.)

48-537 **Millette**, Jean F. (*McGill*) M.Sc.: "The estimation of organic matter in soil profile studies." (Agricultural Chemistry: DeLong, W.)

48-538 **Mulligan**, Robert (*Alberta*) M.Sc.: "The geology of the northern part of the east shore of Great Bear Lake, N.W.T." (Geological Sciences: Jolliffe, A.)

48-539 **Nelson**, William A. (*Alberta*) M.Sc.: "The biology of *Microbracon cephi* Gahan, an important native parasite of the wheat stem sawfly, *Cephus cinctus* Nort." (Entomology: DuPorte, E.)

48-540 **Percival**, Walter L. (*McGill*) M.Sc.: "Rapid exchange of bone salts in the skeleton of newborn animals as shown by an improved autographic technique." (Experimental Surgery: MacKenzie, D.)

48-541 **Prado**, Eline S. (*Sao Paulo*, Brazil) M.Sc.: "Oxidation studies of the steroid ring A." (Biochemistry: Jamieson, R.)

48-542 **Robinson**, Dean B. (*McGill*) M.Sc.: "Studies on barley diseases caused by *Helminthosporium sativum* P.K. and B." (Agronomy & Plant Pathology: Ludwig, R.)

48-543 **Roulty**, Paul M. (*McGill*) M.Sc.: "The influence of a thick neutron detector on the distribution of neutrons in a uniform neutron stream." (Mathematics: Wallace, P.)

48-544 **Ruyter**, Sally A. (*Brown*) M.Sc.: "A comparative study of strains of *Aerobacter* isolated from different sources." (Bacteriology: Murray, E.)

48-545 **Smith**, Alan R. (*British Columbia*) M.Sc.: "A tectonic map of southern British Columbia." (Geological Sciences: Gill, J.)

48-546 **Speakman**, Thomas J. (*Manitoba*) M.Sc.: "Cortical localization of autonomic function." (Neurology & Neurosurgery: Babkin, B.)

48-547 **Stalker**, Archibald M. (*McGill*) M.Sc.: "A study of erosion surfaces in the southern part of the Eastern Townships of Quebec." (Geological Sciences: Gill, J.)

48-548 **Steppler**, Howard A. (*Manitoba*) M.Sc.: "Lignification studies with various grass species." (Agronomy: Raymond, L.)

48-549 **Tower**, Donald B. (*Harvard*) M.Sc.: "Acetylcholine and neuronal activity in craniocerebral trauma and epilepsy." (Neurology & Neurosurgery: McEachern, D.)

48-550 **Van Horne**, William F. (*Bishop's*) M.Sc.: "Fractionation of protein hydrolysates." (Agricultural Chemistry: Baker, B.)

48-551 **Wagner**, Sydney (*McGill*) M.Sc.: "An electron microscope study of the effect of a magnetic field on silver and tin." (Physics: Keys, D.)

48-552 **Webb**, James L. (*McGill*) M.Sc.: "The formation of acetate in brain tissue suspensions." (Biochemistry: Elliott, K.)

48-553 **Wener**, Joseph (*McGill*) M.Sc.: "The neuro-humeral aspects of ulcer formation." (Physiology: Hoff, H.)

48-554 **Whiting**, Francis B. (*British Columbia*) M.Sc.: "An investigation of the Good Hope Mine, Hedley, B.C." (Geological Sciences: O'Neill, J.)

**M.A. Spring 1948**

48-555 **Amyot**, Denis E. (*McGill*) M.A.: "International commodity controls and national policy." (Economics: Higgins, B.)

48-556 **Compton**, Neil M. (*McGill*) M.A.: "The politics of Jonathan Swift." (English: Files, H.)

48-557 **Cox**, Robert W. (*McGill*) M.A.: "The Quebec provincial general elections of 1886." (History: Cooper, J.)

48-558 **Coyle**, James J. (*St. Dunstan's*) M.A.: "A survey of the conflicts in Donne's life and thought which contributed to metaphysical wit." (English: Hemlow, J.)

48-559 **Forgays**, Donald G. (*Dartmouth*) M.A.: "The effect of positive and negative incentives in serial learning: fixation and variability of response as a result of symbolic reward and symbolic punishment." (Psychology: Malmo, R.)

48-560 **Goldberg**, W. (*Queen's*) M.A.: "The ideal in relation to the natural in the political philosophy of Plato." (Philosophy: **)

48-561 **Gottheil**, Edward (*Queen's*) M.A.: "An investigation into the effects of participation in a co-operative as compared to a competitive task on intra-group attitudes of acceptance and rejection." (Psychology: Kellogg, C.)

48-562 **Guardo**, Lea C. (*Marianopolis*) M.A.: "Dante Gabriel Rossetti's translation of Dante's 'Vita Nuova': theory and practice." (English: Noad, A.)

48-563 **Johnston**, Patricia M. (*Dublin*, Ireland) M.A.: "Aspects of the treatment of time in some modern English novelists." (English: Duthie, G.)

48-564 **Kidd**, Dorothy J. (*Western*) M.A.: "Le théâtre d'André Gide." (French: Larivière, P.)

48-565 **McOuat**, D.F. (*Bishop's*) M.A.: "Military policy and organization in New France." (History: Adair, E.)

48-566 **Matthers**, Mary C. (*Villa Maria*) M.A.: "Le cardinal Richelieu dans les romans de Vigny et les romans de Dumas." (French: Furness, L.)

48-567 **Oduber-Quiros**, Daniel (*Costa Rica*) M.A.: "Plato's dialectic." (Philosophy: MacLennan, R.)

48-568 **O'Neill**, Thomas L. (*Bishop's*) M.A.: "British policy in the Italo-Turkish war." (History: Fieldhouse, H.)

48-569 **Polonoff**, Irving I. (*Sir George Williams*) M.A.: "Objectivity and its relation to physical science." (Philosophy: Currie, C.)

48-570 **Willis**, Edith B. (*Stanford*) M.A.: "Factors relating to teacher-child contacts in preschool education." (Psychology: Alexander, F.)

**M.Com. Spring 1948**

48-571 **Van Holsbeek**, Henri M. (*Brussels*, Belgium) M.Com.: "Canada's financial system in war and reconstruction." (Economics: Higgins, B.)

**M.Eng. Fall 1948**

48-572 **Campbell**, Richard H. (*Harvard*) M.Eng.: "Noise from current-carrying resistors." (Electrical Engineering: Chipman, R.)

48-573 **Diamond**, George B. (*McGill*) M.Eng.: "Some factors affecting the capacity and efficiency of a spray drying unit." (Chemical Engineering: Winkler, C.)

## ANNUAL LISTING

M.Sc. Fall 1948

48-574 **Bates**, John I. (*McGill*) M.Sc.: "*In vivo* staining of induced and transplanted brain tumors." (Neurology & Neurosurgery: Penfield, W.)

48-575 **Bencosme**, Sergio (*Montréal*) M.Sc.: "The morphological effects of alloxan injection and the effect of insulin in alloxan diabetes in the rabbit." (Pathology: Leblond, C.)

48-576 **Blake**, Donald A. (*McGill*) M.Sc.: "The Athabaska series at Beaverlodge Lake, Saskatchewan." (Geological Sciences: Hare, F.)

48-577 **Bloomfield**, Solomon S. (*McGill*) M.Sc.: "A study of comparative toxicity of the chemical constituents of urine on the eggs and larvae of horse scierostomes." (Parasitology: Cameron, T.)

48-578 **Brisson**, Germain (*Montréal*) M.Sc.: "Feeding value of the horsebean (*Vicia faba* L.) for chicks." (Nutrition: Nikolaiczuk, N.)

48-579 **Goldman**, Leonard M. (*Cornell*) M.Sc.: "The design and construction of a high voltage generator." (Physics: Terroux, E.)

48-580 **Herer**, Moe L. (*McGill*) M.Sc.: "(a) Lens rupture: a new recessive gene in the mouse. (b) Heredity cataract in mice." (Genetics: Stanley, J.)

48-581 **Hildebrand**, Henry H. (*Kansas*) M.Sc.: "Marine fishes of Arctic Canada." (Zoology: Dunbar, M.)

48-582 **Jeffrey**, Claire O. (*McGill*) M.Sc.: "Electrolytic synthesis of long-chain esters of dicarboxylic acids." (Chemistry: Morton, M.)

48-583 **Kelen**, Andrew (*McGill*) M.Sc.: "Studies on the role of acetylcholine in experimental seizures." (Neurology & Neurosurgery: McEachern, D.)

48-584 **Keys**, John D. (*McGill*) M.Sc.: "An acoustic anemometer." (Physics: Marshall, J.)

48-585 **Langille**, Winston M. (*Acadia*) M.Sc.: "Studies of the availability of the plant nutrient in open hearth slags." (Agricultural Chemistry: DeLong, W.)

48-586 **Leach**, William B. (*Manitoba*) M.Sc.: "The effect of renal hypertension upon the development of experimental cholesterol artheriosclerosis in the rabbit." (Pathology: Duff, G.)

48-587 **Leith**, Wilfred (*Mount Allison*) M.Sc.: "A study on the hypersensitivity in guinea pigs as induced by the inhalation of allergens." (Medicine: Rose, B.)

48-588 **Levitan**, Benjamin A. (*McGill*) M.Sc.: "Action of vitamin P." (Physiology: Hoff, H.)

48-589 **McCorriston**, James R. (*Saskatchewan*) M.Sc.: "(a) Experimental gastric and duodenal ulcer. (b) Reconstructive surgery: experimental use of a skin-lined tube in the greater omentum." (Experimental Surgery: MacKenzie, A.)

48-590 **MacNeill**, Ruby J. (*Acadia*) M.Sc.: "A comparison of basal and resting metabolism in humans and guinea pigs." (Nutrition: Crampton, E.)

48-591 **Murphy**, David R. (*McGill*) M.Sc.: "Investigations dealing with surgery of the heart and lungs in experimental animals." (Experimental Surgery: MacKenzie, D.)

48-592 **Narasinham**, Ramanujaiengar (*Banares Hindu*, India) M.Sc.: "The analysis of the *Typha latifolis* Linn. seed hairs." (Chemistry: Purves, C.)

48-593 **Neilson**, Helen R. (*McGill*) M.Sc.: "A study of the apparent digestibility of indentical diets by different species." (Nutrition: Crampton, E.)

48-594 **Nussey**, Albert N. (*McGill*) M.Sc.: "Some effects of boron on the rooting of softwood cuttings." (Horticulture-Botany: Murray, H.)

48-595 **Rockwell**, Keith R. (*McGill*) M.Sc.: "The production of antibiotic substances by a group of microorginasms with special reference to those active against germ negative bacteria." (Agricultural Bacteriology: Thatcher, F.)

48-596 **Ross**, Winifred M. (*Manitoba*) M.Sc.: "Serological studies in trichinosis in experimental animals." (Parasitology: Cameron, T.)

48-597 **Stranks**, Donald W. (*McMaster*) M.Sc.: "Studies on carbon dioxide assimilation by a cellulose decomposing organism." (Agricultural Bacteriology: McFarlane, W.)

48-598 **Streitfield**, Murray M. (*City College of New York*) M.Sc.: "Studies on the development of resistance to streptomycin by staphlococcus pyogenes." (Bacteriology: Smith, F.)

48-599 **Talvenheimo**, Gerhardt (*McGill*) M.Sc.: "An investigation of the clay fraction of the Ste. Rosalie soil." (Agricultural Chemistry: DeLong, W.)

48-600 **Thurston**, Arthur M. (*McGill*) M.Sc.: "A new bridge for comparing capacitance, mutual inductance and self inductance." (Physics: Watson, H.)

48-601 **Toreson**, Wilfred E. (*McGill*) M.Sc.: "The influence of insulin and of blood sugar level on hydropic degeneration of the islets of Langerhans in alloxan diabetes." (Pathology: Duff, G.)

48-602 **Waugh**, Douglas O. (*McGill*) M.Sc.: "A study of renal lesions produced in rabbits by heterologous plasma protein administration." (Pathology: Smith, F.)

48-603 **Woodford**, Vernon R. (*Charleston*) M.Sc.: "The influence of various factors on glycolysis in human blood during storage." (Biochemistry: Denstedt, O.)

48-604 **Yu**, Pei-Liang (*National Central of Nanking*, China) M.Sc.: "Micro-chemical methods for mineral determination." (Geological Sciences: Jolliff, M.)

48-605 **Zirinsky**, Victor J. (*St. John's*, China) M.Sc.: "The development of a scintillation counter." (Physics: Marshall, J.)

**M.A. Fall 1948**

48-606 **Benn**, Doris E. (*Bryn Mawr*) M.A.: "The philosophical significance of the Ancient Mariner." (Philosophy: Henderson, T.)

48-607 **Bennett**, Richard L. (*Michigan*) M.A.: "The nature of courage." (Philosophy: Klibansky, R.)

48-608 **Bowes**, Walter G. (*Acadia*) M.A.: "L'enfant dans l'oeuvre de Victor Hugo." (French: Furness, L.)

48-609 **Chipman**, John S. (*McGill*) M.A.: "Alternative solutions for the problems of economic regionalism." (Economics: Marsh, D.)

48-610 **Devine**, Francis (*Ottawa*) M.A.: "Les méthodes preconisées pour l'enseignement du français comme langue étrangère de 1850 à 1944." (French: Garbland, E.)

48-611 **Gowdey**, Cecil W. (*McGill*) M.A.: "'Thirty days hath September': a novel." (English: Files, H.)

48-612 **Irvine**, Lucille (*McGill*) M.A.: "Personality structures of truant and delinquent children." (Psychology: Alexander, F.)

48-613 **Keep**, George R. (*London*, England) M.A.: "The Irish migration to Montreal 1847-1867." (History: Cooper, J.)

48-614 **Laing**, Eleanor J. (*McGill*) M.A.: "Etude critique de trois traductions anglaises du premier volume de 'Les Thibault' par Roger Martin du Gard." (French: Darbelnet, J.)

48-615 **MacFarlane**, Joan M. (*McGill*) M.A.: "A comparison of the theories of the educative process of Plato, Aristotle, Dewey and Whitehead." (Education: Currie, A.)

48-616 **McLeish**, John A. (*McGill*) M.A.: "Thomas and Matthew Arnold: their significance for Canadian education." (Education: Hughes, J.)

48-617 **Saunders**, Thomas B. (*Queen's*) M.A.: "The extra-curricular interests and responsibilities of a city principal with reference to the welfare and development of the pupil in the community." (Education: Hughes, J.)

48-618 **Tansey**, Charlotte H. (*Montréal*) M.A.: "Human relations in the fiction of Gertrude Stein." (English: Files, H.)

48-619 **Zakuta**, Leo (*McGill*) M.A.: "The natural areas of the metropolitan community of Montreal, with special reference to the central area." (Sociology: Dawson, C.)

## ANNUAL LISTING

### Ph.D. Spring 1949

49-**001** **Adelstein**, Peter (*McGill*) Ph.D.: "Diffusion studies of high polymer solutions." (Chemistry: Winkler, C.)

49-**002** **Alcock**, Norman Z. (*Queen's*) Ph.D.: "Diffraction of neutrons by gas molecules." (Physics: Foster, J.)

49-**003** **Anderson**, Donald A. (*Mount Allison*) Ph.D.: "The nuclear magnetic moment of boron of mass 11." (Physics: Foster, J.)

49-**004** **Arthur**, Marion E. (*Toronto*) Ph.D.: "The French-Canadian under the British, 1760-1800." (History: Adair, E.)

49-**005** **Brady**, George W. (*Laval*) Ph.D.: "Part I. The kinetics of coagulation of GR-S. latex. Part II. The kinetics of the cis-trans isomerisation of azobenzene." (Chemistry: Winkler, C.)

49-**006** **Carruthers**, James A. (*Western*) Ph.D.: "The ultracentrifuge study of alpha-irradiated albumin." (Physics: Foster, J.)

49-**007** **Christie**, George L. (*Saskatchewan*) Ph.D.: "Equilibrium between copper, zinc, and chlorine at high temperature." (Chemistry: Maass, O.)

49-**008** **Dodds**, John W. (*McGill*) Ph.D.: "Design and construction of K-band resonant slot array." (Physics: Foster, J.)

49-**009** **Douglas**, Donald G. (*Saskatchewan*) Ph.D.: "The disintegration of lutecium of mass 177." (Physics: Foster, J.)

49-**010** **Eager**, Richard L. (*Saskatchewan*) Ph.D.: "The oxidation of mercaptan by potassium persulfate in homogeneous solution." (Chemistry: Winkler, C.)

49-**011** **Funt**, Boris L. (*Dalhousie*) Ph.D.: "Dielectric properties of non-Newtonian liquids." (Chemistry: Maass, O.)

49-**012** **Gilbert**, Joseph E. (*Laval*) Ph.D.: "The geology of the Capsisit Lake area, Abitibi, Quebec." (Geological Sciences: O'Neill, J.)

49-**013** **Goring**, David A. (*London*, England) Ph.D.: "Zeta potentials of cellulose fibres." (Chemistry: Maass, O.)

49-**014** **Gross**, Jack (*McGill*) Ph.D.: "The formation and fate of the thyroid hormone." (Anatomy: Leblond, C.)

49-**015** **Halpern**, Jack (*McGill*) Ph.D.: "Kinetic studies in the solid phase and in solution. Part I. The thermal decomposition of popcorn polymer. Part II. The cis-trans isomerization of azobenzene in solution." (Chemistry: Winkler, C.)

49-**016** **Harwood**, Victor D. (*McGill*) Ph.D.:"The investigation of the ether extract of white spruce bark." (Chemistry: Purves, C.)

49-017 **Henrikson**, Helen A. (*McGill*) Ph.D.: "Potassium deficiency and gastro-intestinal function." (Anatomy: Leblond, C.)

49-018 **Hodgson**, Gordon W. (*Alberta*) Ph.D.: "The exchange of radioiodine between inorganic and organic iodides." (Chemistry: Winkler, C.)

49-019 **Hubley**, Charles E. (*Acadia*) Ph.D.: "Flocculation of cellulose fibre suspensions." (Chemistry: Maass, O.)

49-020 **Hymovitch**, Bernard (*Sir George Williams*) Ph.D.: "Spatial problem-solving in the rat." (Psychology: Hebb, D.)

49-021 **Irvine**, George N. (*Manitoba*) Ph.D.: "A kinetic study of the oxidation of carotenoid pigments during processing of macaroni." (Chemistry: Winkler, C.)

49-022 **Jooste**, Rene F. (*Witwatersrand*, South Africa) Ph.D.: "Geology of the Bourget map area, Chicoutimi county, Quebec." (Geological Sciences: Jolliffe, A.)

49-023 **Kahnka**, Mary J. (*Minnesota*) Ph.D.: "Nucleoproteins of the *Staphylococcus* in connection with immunity." (Bacteriology: MacPherson, C.)

49-024 **Khan**, M. Abdul B. (*Aligarh*, India) Ph.D.: "The morphology and life history of *Strongyloides papillosus*." (Parasitology: Cameron, T.)

49-025 **Kristjanson**, Arnthor M. (*Saskatchewan*) Ph.D.: "Exchange reactions of sodium iodide with aromatic iodides." (Chemistry: Winkler, C.)

49-026 **Logan**, Charles D. (*Mount Allison*) Ph.D.: "Oxidation of polyhydroxyphenols with chlorine dioxide." (Chemistry: Purves, C.)

49-027 **McConnell**, Wallace B. (*Alberta*) Ph.D.: "Effect of addition agents in electrodeposition of copper." (Chemistry: Winkler, C.)

49-028 **McMurray**, Gordon A. (*Bishop's*) Ph.D.: "Psychology and physiology of pain." (Psychology: Malmo, R.)

49-029 **Mahoney**, Gerald M. (*Sir George Williams*) Ph.D.: "The psychological components of morale in an industrial situation." (Psychology: Webster, E.)

49-030 **Milne**, Donald J. (*Saskatchewan*) Ph.D.: "The growth, morphology and relationship of the species of Pacific salmon and the steelhead trout." (Zoology: Berrill, N.)

49-031 **Palmer**, Walter M. (*McGill*) Ph.D.: "Radar echoes from continuous percipitation." (Physics: Marshall, J.)

49-032 **Perlin**, Arthur S. (*McGill*) Ph.D.: "Oxidation of cellulose with chromium trioxide." (Chemistry: Purves, C.)

49-033 **Pinsky**, Alex (*McGill*) Ph.D.: "Studies on the nicotinic acid oxidase of *Pseudomonas flurescens*." (Agricultural Chemistry: Common, R.)

49-034 **Robertson**, Alexander A. (*Alberta*) Ph.D.: "Specific surface and flocculation studies of pulp fibre suspension." (Chemistry: Maass, O.)

49-035 **Roxburgh**, James M. (*Alberta*) Ph.D.: "Overvoltage studies on cadmium cathodes." (Chemistry: Winkler, C.)

49-036 **Saffran**, Murray (*McGill*) Ph.D.: "Metabolism of tricarboxylic acid cycle compounds in kidney and liver tissue." (Biochemistry: Denstedt, O.)

49-037 **Scholefield**, Peter G. (*Wales*) Ph.D.: "Studies in soil metabolism." (Biochemistry: Quastel, J.)

49-038 **Shaw**, Michael (*McGill*) Ph.D.: "Mutual and invironmental relations of photosynthesis transpriation and stomatal opening." (Plant Pathology-Botany: Scarth, G.)

49-039 **Tonks**, David B. (*British Columbia*) Ph.D.: "Alkylations and isomerizations catalysed by an aluminum hydrosilicate." (Chemistry: Nicholls, R.)

**Ph.D. Fall 1949**

49-040 **Aikin**, Archibald M. (*McGill*) Ph.D.: "The emulsion polymerisation of alkybutenes." (Chemistry: Nicholls, R.)

49-041 **Bannard**, Robert A. (*Queen's*) Ph.D.: "A study of certain nitrogen derivatives of methionic acid." (Chemistry: Ross, J.)

49-042 **Bird**, Frederick T. (*McGill*) Ph.D.: "A virus (polyhedral) disease of the European spruce sawfly, *Gilpinia hercyniae* (Hartig)." (Entomology: DuPorte, E.)

49-043 **Birmingham**, Marion K. (*Bennington*) Ph.D.: "Effects of pH and of bicarbonate and CO2 on the respiration and anaerobic golcolysis of rat brain tissue." (Medicine: Browne, J.)

49-044 **Bishop**, Claude T. (*Acadia*) Ph.D.: "The chemical investigation of the aqueous extract of white spruce bark." (Chemistry: Purves, C.)

49-045 **Chapman**, Douglas G. (*Toronto*) Ph.D.: "The influence of gonadal hormones on the composition of blood and liver of the domestic fowl." (Agricultural Chemistry: Common, R.)

49-046 **Fraser**, John S. (*Dalhousie*) Ph.D.: "The beta and gamma radiation of thulium 170." (Physics: Terroux, F. & Foster, J.)

49-047 **Grad**, Bernard (*McGill*) Ph.D.: "The influence of liver and testis on the action of thyroxine in albino rats." (Anatomy: Leblond, C.)

49-048 **Hare**, John H. (*Ontario Agricultural*) Ph.D.: "A study of some chemical changes of proteins of food during storage with particular reference to lysine." (Agricultural Chemistry: Common, R.)

49-**049** **Harpur**, Robert P. (*New Zealand*) Ph.D.: "The relationship of acetylcholine synthesis to carbohydrate metabolism." (Biochemistry: Quastel, J.)

49-**050** **Hayward**, Lloyl D. (*Saskatchewan*) Ph.D.: "Action of hydroxylamine in pyridine on methyl glucose tetranitrate." (Chemistry: Purves, C.)

49-**051** **Keays**, John L. (*British Columbia*) Ph.D.: "Characteristics of various cellulose affecting nitration." (Chemistry: Purves, C.)

49-**052** **Logan**, Kenneth C. (*British Columbia*) Ph.D.: "The electrolytic oxidation of glycol, glucose and lignosulphonic acids." (Chemistry: Purves, C.)

49-**053** **Neubauer**, Lewis G. (*New Zealand*) Ph.D.: "The action of liquid ammonia on maple wood." (Chemistry: Purves, C.)

49-**054** **Read**, Donald E. (*Mount Allison*) Ph.D.: "Properties of the higher benzenepolycarboxylic acids and their isolation." (Chemistry: Purves, C.)

49-**055** **Scott**, David M. (*McGill*) Ph.D.: "The life history and ecology of the cod-worm, *Porrocaecum decipiens* (Krabbe) 1878, in Canadian Altantic waters." (Zoology: Stanley, J.)

49-**056** **Telford**, William M. (*McGill*) Ph.D.: "The radio frequency system of the McGill synchro-cyclotron." (Physics: Terroux, F. & Foster, J.)

49-**057** **Usher**, John L. (*Saskatchewan*) Ph.D.: "The stratigraphy and paleontology of the upper cretaceous rocks." (Geological Sciences: Clark, T.)

49-**058** **Weininger**, Joseph I. (*McGill*) Ph.D.: "The thermal conductivity of gases at high pressure." (Chemistry: Maass, O.)

**M.Eng. Spring 1949**

49-**500** **Attas**, Isaac (*Athens Technical*, Greece) M.Eng.: "Noise of induction motors." (Electrical Engineering: Schippel, W.)

49-**501** **Bennett**, John R. (*McGill*) M.Eng.: "Design of a variable frequency oscillator." (Electrical Engineering: Howes, F.)

49-**502** **Boire**, Paul C. (*McGill*) M.Eng.: "The design of a resonant line impedance measuring device in the frequency range from 100 to 200 MC." (Electrical Engineering: Howes, F.)

49-**503** **Godfrey**, Gerald (*British Columbia*) M.Eng.: "The transmission of facsimile to frequency shift telegraphy." (Electrical Engineering: Chipman, R.)

49-**504** **Goudey**, John F. (*Toronto*) M.Eng.: "Distillation studies in a square column with variable tray design." (Chemical Engineering: Phillips, J.)

49-**505** **Govindaraj**, Sadasiva (*Madras*, India) M.Eng.: "Amplidyne characteristics." (Electrical Engineering: Schippel, W.)

49-506 **Kiang**, Tsch-Kia (*National Chungking*, China) M.Eng.: "Wave propagation through ionized gases." (Electrical Engineering: Chipman, R.)

49-507 **Marshall**, James L. (*Manitoba*) M.Eng.: "Design of ten-conductor, open-wire, transmission line for broadcast frequencies." (Electrical Engineering: Howes, F.)

49-508 **Nachfolger**, Nathan (*McGill*) M.Eng.: "Negative resistance loading of transmission lines." (Electrical Engineering: Howes, F.)

49-509 **Rioux**, Philip G. (*Queen's*) M.Eng.: "The design of discriminators of subminiature frequency modulation transceivers." (Electrical Engineering: Howes, F.)

49-510 **Roach**, Charles L. (*Nova Scotia Technical*) M.Eng.: "The effect of ground-wire currents on low-frequency inductive co-ordination." (Electrical Engineering: Wallace, G.)

**M.Sc. Spring 1949**

49-511 **Antrobus**, Edmund S. (*Cambridge*, England) M.Sc.: "A study of lime-rich metamorphic rocks from Cree Lake, Manitoba." (Geological Sciences: Kranck, E.)

49-512 **Black**, Philip T. (*McGill*) M.Sc.: "Archean sediments in the Canadian Shield." (Geological Sciences: O'Neill, J.)

49-513 **Boswell**, Graeme W. (*Acadia*) M.Sc.: "Investigations on the acidity of leachates from decomposing leaves of deciduous trees." (Agricultural Chemistry: DeLong, W.)

49-514 **Burbidge**, Frederick E. (*Saskatchewan*) M.Sc.: "The modification of continental polar air over Hudson's Bay and eastern Canada." (Geography: Hare, F.)

49-515 **Campbell**, Charles G. (*McGill*) M.Sc.: "Electrolytes in heart disease." (Anatomy: Friedman, S.)

49-516 **Carder**, Alfred C. (*British Columbia*) M.Sc.: "The use of sweet clover in a grain rotation as a means of increasing the fertility of grey-wooded soils." (Agronomy: Cowan, J.)

49-517 **Carter**, Sharon E. (*McGill*) M.Sc.: "The kinds and distribution of fungi in the air over northern Canada above 3000 feet." (Bacteriology: Kelly, C.)

49-518 **Chapman**, John H. (*Western*) M.Sc.: "A critical investigation of tuned audio amplifiers." (Physics: Watson, H.)

49-519 **Chapman**, Robert P. (*Mount Allison*) M.Sc.: "A direct reading phase angle meter." (Physics: Watson, H.)

49-520 **Cinq-Mars**, Lionel (*Laval*) M.Sc.: "Interactions between *Venturia inaequalis* (Cke.) Wint. and saprophytic fungi and bacteria inhabiting apple leaves." (Plant Pathology: Coulson, G.)

49-521 **Connell**, Robert (*Toronto*) M.Sc.: "Studies on *Heterakis gallinea* (Gmelin, 1790; Freeborn, 1923) a nematode vestor of enterohepatitis of turkeys." (Parasitology: Cameron, T.)

49-522 **Davis**, Gordon R. (*McGill*) M.Sc.: "The morphology of certain life-history stages of the birch sawfly, *Arge pectoralis*." (Zoology: Stanley, J.)

49-523 **Eadie**, Frank S. (*McGill*) M.Sc.: "The stopping power for secondary electrons from cobalt 60 in light elements." (Physics: Foster, J.)

49-524 **Eakins**, Peter R. (*McGill*) M.Sc.: "Geology of the Jeep Mine, Rice Lake district, Manitoba." (Geological Sciences: Graham, R.)

49-525 **Fiskell**, John G. (*Ontario Agricultural*) M.Sc.: "The use of radioactive phosphorus in the investigation of fixation and release phenomena in soils." (Agricultural Chemistry: DeLong, W.)

49-526 **Glegg**, Keith C. (*McGill*) M.Sc.: "Theory and design of an improved D-C electronic voltage stabilizer." (Physics: Watson, H.)

49-527 **Gonshor**, Harry (*McGill*) M.Sc.: "The integral solutions of the diophantine equation $y^2=x^3 \div k$." (Mathematics: Rosenthal, E.)

49-528 **Griesbach**, Leonard (*Toronto*) M.Sc.: "The evaluation of the breeding potential of full sisters in the domestic fowl." (Genetics: Boyes, J.)

49-529 **Hawirko**, Roma Z. (*Manitoba*) M.Sc.: "A method for the rapid isolation of *Mycobacterium tuberculosis*." (Bacteriology: Murray, E.)

49-530 **Hodgson**, William A. (*McGill*) M.Sc.: "The effect of dithane sprays on some physiological functions of the plant." (Plant Pathology: Coulson, J.)

49-531 **Hopkins**, Nigel J. (*McGill*) M.Sc.: "Magnetic fields accurately measured from proton magnetic moment." (Physics: Foster, J.)

49-532 **Jaffe**, Frederick A. (*McGill*) M.Sc.: "The quantitative changes in the islets following alloxan." (Pathology: Duff, G.)

49-533 **Karn**, Gordon M. (*McGill*) M.Sc.: "Lymphatic drainage of bone with special reference to osteomyelitis." (Experimental Surgery: Webster, D.)

49-534 **Kite**, William C. (*Oklahoma*) M.Sc.: "The cortical representation of gastric motor function." (Neurology & Neurosurgery: Penfield, W.)

49-535 **Lachance**, Robert A. (*McGill*) M.Sc.: "Bacteriological studies in relation to keeping qualities of eggs." (Agricultural Bacteriology: Thatcher, F.)

49-536 **Langerman**, Helen L. (*McGill*) M.Sc.: "The effect of heat treatment on the nutritive value of some vegetable oils." (Nutrition: Crampton, W.)

49-537 **McDougall**, David J. (*McGill*) M.Sc.: "The pegmatites of Otter Rapids area, Ontario." (Geological Sciences: Jolliffe, A.)

49-538 **McLennan**, Hugh (*McGill*) M.Sc.: "Acetylcholine metabolism in brain tissue." (Biochemistry: Elliott, K.)

49-539 **Margolis**, Bernard (*McGill*) M.Sc.: "A derivation of cross section formulae for resonance scattering and reactions in nuclear processes." (Mathematics: Wallace, P.)

49-540 **Metrakos**, Julius D. (*McGill*) M.Sc.: "The effect of fostering on the growth pattern of the house mouse." (Genetics: Fraser, F.)

49-541 **Meyer**, John S. (*Trinity*) M.Sc.: "Diencephalic function." (Neurology & Neurosurgery: Penfield, W.)

49-542 **Novick**, Seymour (*Chicago*) M.Sc.: "Estimation of aldehydes in rancid fats." (Agricultural Chemistry: Chapman, R.)

49-543 **Pawlikowska**, Anna M. (*McGill*) M.Sc.: "The kinds and distribution of bacteria in the air over northern Canada at altitudes over 5,000 feet." (Bacteriology: Kelly, C.)

49-544 **Rattray**, Basil A. (*McGill*) M.Sc.: "Almost periodic functions of several variables." (Mathematics: Tornhave, H.)

49-545 **Rigby**, Caroline E. (*McGill*) M.Sc.: "A study of vertical motion in radar patterns of rain." (Physics: Marshall, J.)

49-546 **Scott**, David P. (*McGill*) M.Sc.: "A mass of living insects considered as a pseudo-substance, the moving insects acting as pseudo-molecules." (Zoology: Stanley, J.)

49-547 **Stock**, John J. (*Ontario Agricultural*) M.Sc.: "The effect of penicillin on hyaluronidase production by bacteria." (Bacteriology: Smith, F.)

49-548 **Storey**, Winnifred F. (*McGill*) M.Sc.: "The study of renewal rates in the epidermis of the albino rat." (Anatomy: Leblond, C.)

49-549 **Tennant**, Alan D. (*McGill*) M.Sc.: "An investigation of the bacterial flora of the soft shell clam (*Mya arenaria*) in New Brunswick and Nova Scotia." (Agricultural Bacteriology: Thatcher, F.)

49-550 **Trossman**, Walter A. (*McGill*) M.Sc.: "The artificial ripening of mature green tomatoes." (Horticulture: Murray, H.)

49-551 **Veilleux**, Brendan (*Loyola of Montréal*) M.Sc.: "The structure and stratigraphy of the Sherbrooke formation in the Memphremagog area, Eastern Townships, Quebec." (Geological Sciences: Clark, T.)

49-552 **Wallen**, Victor R. (*McGill*) M.Sc.: "A study of the biology and control of ascochyta blights of peas." (Plant Pathology: Coulson, J.)

49-553 **Ziegler**, James E. (*Kansas State*) M.Sc.: "Methods for temporary and reversible paralysis of local areas of the cerebral cortex." (Neurology & Neurosurgery: Jasper, H.)

**M.A. Spring 1949**

49-554 **Blascik**, Frank (*McGill*) M.A.: "An evaluation of item selection method by a criterion of internal consistency." (Psychology: Ferguson, G.)

49-555 **Block**, Victor R. (*McGill*) M.A.: "Untersuchungen zu Goethes 'Römischen Elegien'." (German: Graff, W.)

49-556 **Coultis**, Rosa J. (*Alberta*) M.A.: "La nature dans l'oeuvre de Colette." (French: Larivière, H.)

49-557 **DeShield**, George D. (*Sir George Williams*) M.A.: "Value as a perceptual determinent." (Psychology: Ferguson, G.)

49-558 **Flower**, George E. (*McGill*) M.A.: "A study of the contributions of Dr. E.I. Rexford to education in the province of Quebec." (Education: Hughes, J.)

49-559 **Fox**, Leslie P. (*McGill*) M.A.: "Hannah More, evangelical educationalist." (History: Reid, W.)

49-560 **Geggie**, Mary M. (*McGill*) M.A.: "'Inhabit the garden': a novel." (English: Files, H.)

49-561 **Ghent**, Lila R. (*McGill*) M.A.: "The relationship of experience to the development of hunger." (Psychology: Hebb, D.)

49-562 **Goodin**, Peggy L. (*Michigan*) M.A.: "'Take care of my little girl': a novel." (English: Files, H.)

49-563 **Hampson**, Harold G. (*McGill*) M.A.: "The English navy in the XIVth century." (History: Bayley, C.)

49-564 **Harding**, Lawrence A. (*McGill*) M.A.: "The treatment of social ideas and problems in the plays of John Galsworthy." (English: Files, H.)

49-565 **Hawkins**, Stuart C. (*McGill*) M.A.: "Le réel et l'imaginaire dans contes et romans d'Alexandre Arnoux, 1947." (French: Launay, J.)

49-566 **Hepburn**, Johnston (*Harvard*) M.A.: "La religion du travail dans les romans d'Emile Zola." (French: Launay, J.)

49-567 **Holmes**, Anthony F. (*McGill*) M.A.: "On the properties of distribution of test scores." (Psychology: Ferguson, G.)

49-568 **Howell**, Helen M. (*McGill*) M.A.: "Le monde de Jean Giono." (French: Launay, J.)

49-569 **Lambek**, Hanna W. (*McGill*) M.A.: "Development of racial preferences and self-consciousness as member of a race." (Psychology: Blackburn, J.)

49-570 **Levine**, Albert N. (*McGill*) M.A.: "Ezra Pound and the sense of the past." (English: Anderson, P.)

49-571 **MacCallan**, William D. (*McGill*) M.A.: "The poetic principles of T.S. Eliot." (English: Klein, A.)

49-572 **MacIntosh**, Robert M. (*McGill*) M.A.: "Economic and monetary aspects of national debt retirement." (Economics: James, F.)

49-573 **Mishkin**, Mortimer (*Dartmouth*) M.A.: "Word recognition as a function of retinal locus." (Psychology: Ferguson, G.)

49-574 **O'Sullivan**, Timothy (*National of Ireland*) M.A.: "The religion of Bernard Shaw." (English: Files, H.)

49-575 **Potter**, Harold H. (*Sir George Williams*) M.A.: "Occupations of Negroes in Montreal." (Sociology: Hall, O.)

49-576 **Pratt**, Audrey E. (*British Columbia*) M.A.: "Franz Kafka: der Einfluss des Vater-Sohn Verhaltnisses auf sein Werk." (German: Graff, W.)

49-577 **Purcell**, Donald (*Swarthmore*) M.A.: "'Northern Pastoral': a novel." (English: Files, H.)

49-578 **Rankin**, Winston B. (*McGill*) M.A.: "An exploratory investigation of the relationship between kinesthesis and certain industrial motor skills." (Psychology: Webster, E.)

49-579 **Richard**, O'Neill J. (*Southwestern Louisiana Institute*) M.A.: "Les paysannerie française dans les romans d'Honoré de Balzac." (French: Launay, J.)

49-580 **Stewart**, Mary I. (*McGill*) M.A.: "Le Paris des 'Miserables'." (French: Furness, L.)

49-581 **Wearing**, Parker L. (*McMaster*) M.A.: "Studies in English-Canadian and French-Canadian nature poets." (English: Phelps, A.)

49-582 **Wilson**, James D. (*McGill*) M.A.: "A comparative study of export credits insurance and its operation in Canada." (Economics: Marsh, D.)

**M.C.L. Fall 1949**

49-583 **Camara**, Jose S. (*Minas Gerais*, Brazil) M.C.L.: "The ratification of international treaties." (Law: Cohen, M.)

49-584 **Gazdik**, Julius F. (*Queen Elizabeth*, England) M.C.L.: "Analysis of certain aspects of the law of contracts relating to international carriage of goods by air." (Law: Cohen, M.)

**M.Eng. Fall 1949**

49-585 **Barrett**, George F. (*McGill*) M.Eng.: "An alternative test for the physical properties of arc-weld metal." (Mechanical Engineering: Stafford, P.)

49-586 **Davis**, John F. (*McGill*) M.Eng.: "Integrator-counter for muscle spike-potentials." (Electrical Engineering: Howes, F.)

49-587 **Ellis**, John S. (*Queen's*) M.Eng.: "Diagonal tension reinforcement for 6-inch sections for flat plate construction." (Civil Engineering & Applied Mechanics: Dodd, G.)

49-588 **Eskenazi**, Beno (*Robert of Istanbul*, Turkey) M.Eng.: "Behaviour of a composite slab for the floor of a highway bridge." (Civil Engineering & Applied Mechanics: Dodd, G.)

49-589 **Harris**, Philip J. (*Manitoba*) M.Eng.: "Column strength of an aluminum alloy section." (Civil Engineering & Applied Mechanics: DeStein, J.)

49-590 **Howell**, Allison B. (*McGill*) M.Eng.: "The use of a vaporizer and flame tube combustor in studying combustion of hydrocarbon fuels." (Mechanical Engineering: Mordell, D.)

49-591 **Weeks**, John G. (*Alberta*) M.Eng.: "Dry disk rectifier-motor drives." (Electrical Engineering: Schippel, W.)

M.Sc. Fall 1949

49-592 **Alivisatos**, Spyridon (*Athens*, Greece) M.Sc.: "Changes of the glyoxalase activity of human red blood cells during storage." (Biochemistry: Denstedt, O.)

49-593 **Bagnall**, Richard H. (*McGill*) M.Sc.: "Varietal resistance and immunity of potatoes toward certain viruses." (Plant Pathology: Coulson, J.)

49-594 **Bird**, Allan V. (*Witwatersrand*, South Africa) M.Sc.: "Dural nerve endings and dural sensitivity." (Neurology & Neurosurgery: Young, A.)

49-595 **Castle**, Robert O. (*Stanford*) M.Sc.: "Paleogeological studies in the Maritime provinces." (Geological Sciences: Clark, T.)

49-596 **Cohen**, Harry (*Sir George Williams*) M.Sc.: "The effects of some halogen compounds on the viability of the eggs on schlerostomes found in horses." (Parasitology: Cameron, T.)

49-597 **Collins**, Anne M. (*McGill*) M.Sc.: "The anaerobic bacterial flora of the upper respiratory tract in children." (Bacteriology: Stevenson, J.)

49-598 **Cooperberg**, Abraham A. (*McGill*) M.Sc.: "Studies of the blood volume in some diseases of the blood." (Medicine: Browne, J.)

49-599 **Coulombe**, Louis-Joseph (*Laval*) M.Sc.: "Effect of fusarium toxin on the time-course of photosynthesis, transpiration, stomatal movement in tomato plants." (Plant Pathology: Scarth, G.)

49-600 **Courtois**, Guy A. (*Montréal*) M.Sc.: "Studies of the effect of denervation upon the electrical activity of the cortex." (Neurology & Neurosurgery: Jasper, H.)

49-601 **Dju**, Mei Y. (*Ginling of Nanking*, China) M.Sc.: "The relative nutrition of shredded wheat versus baked ground wheat as measured by digestibility trials by guinea pigs and rats." (Nutrition: Crampton, E.)

49-602 **Gass**, Marcia J. (*Acadia*) M.Sc.: "The vitamin C content of fresh, dehydrated and stored cabbage and potatoes as measured both chemically and biologically." (Nutrition: Crampton, E.)

49-603 **Gerryts**, Edbert (*South Africa*) M.Sc.: "The geology of the Premier (Transvaal) Diamond Mine." (Geological Sciences: Wallace, G.)

49-604 **Gorman**, Thomas W. (*St. Francis Xavier*) M.Sc.: "Effect of intestinal oxygen therapy on portal oxygenation in shock." (Experimental Surgery: Webster, D.)

49-605 **Gourlay**, Robert H. (*McGill*) M.Sc.: "Problems associated with the operation of pneumonectomy." (Experimental Surgery: MacKenzie, D.)

49-606 **Grainger**, Edward H. (*Mount Allison*) M.Sc.: "On the biology of the Arctic char." (Zoology: Cameron, T.)

49-607 **Kobernick**, Sidney D. (*McGill*) M.Sc.: "Cardiac lesions produced in rabbits by foreign serum proteins and adjuvants and their relation to the cardiac lesions of human rheumatic fever." (Pathology: More, R.)

49-608 **Lucas**, Ian A. (*Reading*, England) M.Sc.: "The value of the digestibility trial as an adjunct to growth trial data in indicating the efficiency of hog rations." (Nutrition: Ashton, G.)

49-609 **McKendry**, John B. (*Queen's*) M.Sc.: "Some aspects of choline metabolism." (Experimental Medicine: Hoffman, M.)

49-610 **MacLachlan**, Donald S. (*McGill*) M.Sc.: "Studies in the nutrition of *Corynebacterium sepedonicum*." (Bacteriology: Thatcher, F.)

49-611 **Mahon**, John H. (*McGill*) M.Sc.: "A microbiological study of the amino acid composition of the horsebean (*Vicia faba* L.)." (Agricultural Chemistry: Common, R.)

49-612 **Niloff**, Paul H. (*Bishop's*) M.Sc.: "An experimental study of collateral coronary circulation produced by transplanting the left mammary artery to the left ventricular myocardium." (Experimental Surgery: MacKenzie, D.)

49-613 **Nunes**, Doris S. (*McGill*) M.Sc.: "The evaluation and comparison of the immune response in guinea pigs to infection with pneumococcis type I when treated with sulphonamides and when treated with penicillin." (Bacteriology & Immunology: Murray, E.)

49-614 **Ornstein**, William (*McGill*) M.Sc.: 'Phase measurement in microwave fields." (Physics: Woonton, G.)

49-615 **Rabinovitch**, Mortimer S. (*McGill*) M.Sc.: "Standardization of a closed field intelligence test for rats." (Psychology: Rosvold, H.)

49-616 **Rishikof**, Jack R. (*McGill*) M.Sc.: "Effects of electroconvulsive shocks on the performance of the rat in the closed field test." (Psychology: Rosvold, H.)

49-617 **Roberts**, Henry L. (*Texas*) M.Sc.. "A study of certain alterations in speech during stimulation of specific cortical regions." (Neurology & Neurosurgery: Penfield, W.)

49-618 **Ross**, Roderick C. (*Toronto*) M.Sc.: "A comparison of pathological methods in the diagnosis of cancer of the lung." (Pathology: Duff, G.)

49-619 **Rusted**, Ian E. (*Toronto*) M.Sc.: "The effects of induced asthma-like attacks in man on the intake of oxygen, blood oxygen content and cardiac output." (Experimental Medicine: Rose, B.)

49-620 **Singer**, Bertha (*McGill*) M.Sc.: "Effect of adrenocorticotrophic hormone on the urinary excretion of corticoids in health and disease." (Experimental Medicine: Hoffman, M.)

49-621 **Skinner**, Ralph (*British Columbia*) M.Sc.: "A study of some intrusive rocks and replacement phenomena in the Salmon Arm area, B.C. (Shuswap terrane)." (Geological Sciences: Kranck, E.)

49-622 **Sloan**, Norman (*Manitoba*) M.Sc.: "Studies in 'suppression'." (Neurology & Neurosurgery: Jasper, H.)

49-623 **Summers**, William F. (*Dalhousie*) M.Sc.: "The physical geography of the Avalon Peninsula of Newfoundland." (Geography: Hare, F.)

49-624 **Turner**, Robert C. (*McGill*) M.Sc.: "The diffusion of lead into mercury." (Chemistry: Winkler, C.)

49-625 **Walsh**, George C. (*British Columbia*) M.Sc.: "Glucose and galoctose metabolism in health and disease." (Experimental Medicine: Hoffman, M.)

49-626 **Watson**, Hugh A. (*Toronto*) M.Sc.: "Multiple radiation." (Mathematics: Wallace, P.)

**M.A. Fall 1949**

49-627 **Calvert**, Margaret N. (*Sir George Williams*) M.A.: "Errors of recognition and reproduction of a perceived object." (Psychology: Blackburn, J.)

49-628 **Chan**, Victor O. (*McGill*) M.A.: "Canadian Knights of Labor with special reference to the 1880's." (History: Cooper, J.)

49-629 **Clark**, Mary M. (*New Rochelle*) M.A.: "Willa Cather and the novel *demeublé*." (English: Files, H.)

49-630 **Cree**, George C. (*McGill*) M.A.: "The number theory of a system of hyperbolic complex numbers." (Mathematics: Williams, W.)

49-631 **Gordon**, Thelma G. (*Queen's*) M.A.: "An investigation of some factors influencing the formation of impressions of personality." (Psychology: Hebb, D.)

49-632 **Hanson**, James C. (*New Brunswick*) M.A.: "Collective bargaining in wartime Crown companies in Canada." (Economics: Woods, H.)

49-633 **Heron**, Woodburn (*McGill*) M.A.: "An investigation of latent perceptual learning in the rat." (Psychology: Hebb, D.)

49-634 **Heuser**, Edward A. (*McGill*) M.A.: "An investigation of the poetic imagery of Gerard Manley Hopkins." (English: Anderson, P.)

49-635 **Hoyt**, Ruth (*Boston*) M.A.: "The effects of electroconvulsive shocks on gestation and maternal behaviour in the multiparous rat." (Psychology: Rosvold, H.)

49-636 **Jones**, Taliesin (*Wales*) M.A.: "A survey of Anglo-Welsh poetry: the continuity between seventeenth and twentieth century Anglo-Welsh poets." (English: Duthie, G.)

49-637 **Lash**, Harry N. (*McGill*) M.A.: "A sampling method for the study of rural land use." (Geography: Mackay, J.)

49-638 **Leavitt**, Helen R. (*McGill*) M.A.: "'Threshold': a novel." (English: Files, H.)

49-639 **Leppman**, Wolfgang A. (*McGill*) M.A.: "Das Faust-Mephisto Verhaltnis im 'Urfaust', 'Fragment' und 'Faust I'." (German: Graff, W.)

49-640 **Metcalf**, John F. (*Montana*) M.A.: "Intraparty democracy in the Co-operative Commonwealth Federation." (Political Science: Mallory, J.)

49-641 **Montgomery**, Margaret R. (*Manitoba*) M.A.: "The climate of Labrador and its effects on settlement." (Geography: Hare, K.)

49-642 **Orr**, Paul A. (*Loyola of Montréal*) M.A.: "The artisitic principles of Gerard Manley Hopkins." (English: Anderson, P.)

49-643 **Sloan**, Emmett P. (*McGill*) M.A.: "An experimental investigation of individual differences in tactual perception." (Psychology: Webster, E.)

49-644 **Smith**, Norman E. (*New Brunswick*) M.A.: "The theory of functions of a hyperbolic complex variable." (Mathematics: Williams, W.)

49-645 **Uren**, Philip E. (*McGill*) M.A.: "The historical geography of the St. Maurice Valley." (Geography: Hare, K.)

49-646 **Wolfe**, Nathan (*McGill*) M.A.: "Secular stagnation and economic stability." (Economics: Keirstead, B.)

## ANNUAL LISTING

**Ph.D. Spring 1950**

50-001 **Archer**, William L. (*Western*) Ph.D.: "Permeability of cellophane to liquids and vapours." (Chemistry: Maass, O.)

50-002 **Boyle**, Willard S. (*McGill*) Ph.D.: "The construction of a Dempster type mass spectrometer: its use in the measurement of the diffusion rates of certain alkali metals in tungsten." (Physics: Watson, H.)

50-003 **Butler**, Robert W. (*Imperial*, Trinidad) Ph.D.: "Preparation and properties of cellulose crotonoate and acetate-crotonoates." (Chemistry: Purves, C.)

50-004 **Gunn**, George B. (*Alberta*) Ph.D.: "Rheological properties of non-Newtonian solutions." (Chemistry: Maass, O.)

50-005 **Gunn**, Kenrick L. (*Western*) Ph.D.: "The coalescence of large and small water drops: its effect on rainfall intensity." (Physics: Marshall, J.)

50-006 **Hitschfeld**, Walter (*Toronto*) Ph.D.: "Accretion and thermal processes in the development of precipitation." (Physics: Marshall, J.)

50-007 **Hunten**, Donald M. (*Western*) Ph.D.: "Accurate measurement of nuclear magnetic moments with a radio-frequency bridge." (Physics: Foster, J.)

50-008 **Imbault**, Paul E. (*Laval*) Ph.D.: "The Olga-Geoland Lake area, Abitibi-East county." (Geological Sciences: Gill, J.)

50-009 **Irwin**, Arthur B. (*British Columbia*) Ph.D.: "Geology of the Howson Creek area, Slocal Mining division, B.C." (Geological Sciences: Clark, T.)

50-010 **Jackson**, Ray W. (*Toronto*) Ph.D.: "The synchronizing and monitoring system of the McGill synchro-cyclotron." (Physics: Foster, J.)

50-011 **Kirkland**, Robert W. (*Saskatchewan*) Ph.D.: "A study of part of the Kaniapiskau system northwest of Attilamagen Lake, New Quebec." (Geological Sciences: Gill, J.)

50-012 **Lambek**, Joachim (*McGill*) Ph.D.: "A. Biquaternian vectorfields over Minkowski's space. B. The immersibility of a semi-group into a group." (Mathematics: Zassenhaus, H.)

50-013 **McAllister**, Arnold L. (*New Brunswick*) Ph.D.: "The geology of the Ymir map-area, British Columbia." (Geological Sciences: O'Neill, J.)

50-014 **McDermot**, H. Lloyd (*McGill*) Ph.D.: "The density of water sorbed by charcoal and low pressure adsorption studies." (Chemistry: Maass, O.)

50-015 **McGilvery**, James D. (*McMaster*) Ph.D.: "The mercury photosensitized decomposition of nitric acid." (Chemistry: Winkler, C.)

50-016 **McKerns**, Kenneth W. (*Alberta*) Ph.D.: "A study on the agglutination of erythrocytes." (Biochemistry: Denstedt, O.)

50-017 **Payne**, Torrence P. (*McGill*) Ph.D.: "The serum lipids in relation to the development of experimental cholesterol atherosclerosis." (Pathology: Duff, G.)

50-018 **Pugsley**, William H. (*McGill*) Ph.D.: "The Bank of International Settlement." (Economics: Marsh, D.)

50-019 **Rao**, N.S. Krishna (*Mysore*, India) Ph.D.: "A. Toxonomic studies of the parasites of the sea gull, *Larus argentatus*. B. The intermediate host of *Moniezia expansa* (Rud. 1819)." (Parasitology: Cameron, T.)

50-020 **Stalker**, Archibald M. (*McGill*) Ph.D.: "The geology of the Red Deer area, Alberta, with particular reference to the geomorphology and water supply." (Geological Sciences: Clark, T.)

50-021 **Stobbe**, Peter C. (*Manitoba*) Ph.D.: "Comparative study of the grey-brown podzolic, brown podzolic and brown forest soils of southern Ontario and southern Quebec." (Agricultural Chemistry: DeLong, W.)

50-022 **Van Straten**, Sylvia F. (*McGill*) Ph.D.: "Exchange reactions between alicylic iodides and sodium iodide." (Chemistry: Winkler, C.)

50-023 **Waugh**, Douglas (*McGill*) Ph.D.: "Glomerulonephritis produced in rabbits by massive injections of foreign proteins." (Pathology: More, R.)

**Ph.D. Fall 1950**

50-024 **Belleau**, Fernand B. (*Montreal*) Ph.D.: "Part I. Synthesis of radioactive organic reagents. Part II. Attempted total synthesis in the estrogen series." (Biochemistry: Heard, R.)

50-025 **Bencosme**, Sergia (*Montreal*) Ph.D.: "A comparative historical study of islets of Langerhans in the rabbit under abnormal and normal conditions." (Pathology: Duff, G.)

50-026 **Blades**, H. (*Western*) Ph.D.: "The reaction of nitrogen atoms with methane and ethane." (Chemistry: Wi nkler, C.)

50-027 **Chaplin**, Charles E. (*McGill*) Ph.D.: "Methods of evaluating the germicidal activity of quaternary ammonium compounds." (Agricultural Bacteriology: Gray, P.)

50-028 **Creamer**, George B. (*New York State*) Ph.D.: "3-Hydroxyethyl glucose." (Chemistry: Purves, C.)

50-029 **Dewhurst**, Harold A. (*McGill*) Ph.D.: "The y-ray induced oxidation of $Fr^{+2}$ ion in dilute aqueous solution." (Chemistry: Winkler, C.)

50-030 **Forgays**, Donald G. (*Dartmouth*) Ph.D.: "Reversible disturbances of function following cortical insult." (Psychology: Hebb, D.)

50-031 **Hochster**, Rolf M. (*Sir George Williams*) Ph.D.: "*In vitro* studies of intracellular oxidations and reductions with special reference to sulfhydryl compounds, steroids and related substances." (Biochemistry: Quastel, J.)

50-032 **Jones**, Robert A. (*Western*) Ph.D.: "Reactions in dissociated water vapour." (Chemistry: Winkler, C.)

50-033 **Lansdell**, Herbert C. (*Sir George Williams*) Ph.D.: "The effect of brain damage on rat intelligence." (Psychology: Hebb, D.)

50-034 **Larsson**, Bjorn E. (*Wayne*) Ph.D.: "Studies of ionic polymerization." (Chemistry: Nicholls, R.)

50-035 **Levi**, Leo (*Sir George Williams*) Ph.D.: "Syntheses of vinyl aromatic compounds by pyrolyses over catalysts." (Chemistry: Nicholls, R.)

50-036 **MacFarlane**, Hugh M. (*Manitoba*) Ph.D.: "Studies on the alcoholysis products of sucrose." (Chemistry: Purves, C.)

50-037 **Miller**, David M. (*Alberta*) Ph.D.: "Methyl radical recombination and reactions with metals." (Chemistry: Winkler, C.)

50-038 **Moon**, James H. (*Western*) Ph.D.: "Isotopes produced in gold by high energy protons." (Physics: Foster, J.)

50-039 **Morrow**, Harold F. (*Saskatchewan*) Ph.D.: "The geology of the MacLeod-Cockshutt Gold Mine, Little Long Lac, Ontario." (Geological Sciences: Gill, J.)

50-040 **Reid**, Allana G. (*McGill*) Ph.D.: "The growth and importance of the City of Quebec, 1608-1760." (History: Adair, E.)

50-041 **Robinson**, John (*British Columbia*) Ph.D.: "A possible explanation of microbial halophilism." (Agricultural Bacteriology: Gray, P.)

50-042 **Sims**, Richard P. (*McGill*) Ph.D.: "The decomposition of benzoyl peroxide." (Chemistry: Winkler, C.)

50-043 **Smith**, Alfred A. (*Queen's*) Ph.D.: "An electromyographic study of tension in interrupted and completed tasks." (Psychology: Malmo, R.)

50-044 **Stevens**, Catherine E. (*McGill*) Ph.D.: "Cell turnover of the intestinal epithelium as shown by mitotic counts and the incorporation of $P^{32}$ into desoxyribonucleic acid." (Anatomy: Leblond, C.)

50-045 **Toreson**, Wilfred E. (*McGill*) Ph.D.: "Glycogen infiltration (hydropic degeneration) of the pancreas in diabetes mellitus." (Pathology: Duff, G.)

50-046 **Wagner**, Sydney (*McGill*) Ph.D.: "An x-ray diffraction study of the nuclei of pleochroic haloes." (Physics: Shaw, A.)

50-047 **Wake**, Frank R. (*McGill*) Ph.D.: "Changes of fear with age." (Psychology: Bindra, D.)

50-048 **Walker**, Osman J. (*Alberta*) Ph.D.: "Studies of branched and linear polymers." (Chemistry: Winkler, C.)

50-049 **Webb**, James L. (*McGill*) Ph.D.: "Effects of narcotics and convulsants on brain tissue metabolism." (Biochemistry: Elliott, K.)

**M.C.L. Spring 1950**

50-500 **Benes**, Vaclav (*Charles*, Czechoslovakia) M.C.L.: "Migration for employment: legal and institutional." (Law: Phelan, V.)

**M.Arch. Spring 1950**

50-501 **Weisman**, Brahm (*McGill*) M.Arch.: "The control of residential density." (Architecture: Spence-Sales, H.)

**M.Eng. Spring 1950**

50-502 **Bennett**, Robert M. (*Toronto*) M.Eng.: "Generation of short electrical impulses for gating miniature type vacuum tubes." (Electrical Engineering: Cooke, R.)

50-503 **Carr**, Edward F. (*Rensselaer Polytechnical*) M.Eng.: "The effects of radiation on the properties of quarter-wavelength resonant unshielded parallel-wire transmission lines in frequency range 300 Mc/sec. to 1300 Mc/sec." (Electrical Engineering: Chipman, R.)

50-504 **Cooper**, Ross M. (*McGill*) M.Eng.: "The effect of oxygen enrichment of the air intake of a diesel engine on the exhaust gas composition and the combustion processes." (Chemical Engineering: Gauvin, W.)

50-505 **Fairley**, Randolf D. (*New Brunswick*) M.Eng.: "The design of a dual frequency short wave antenna." (Electrical Engineering: Watson, H.)

50-506 **Hoy**, Norman A. (*Clarkson*) M.Eng.: "The effects of radiation on the properties of half-wavelength resonant unshielded parallel-wire transmission lines, in the frequency range (300-1300) Mc/sec." (Electrical Engineering: Chipman, R.)

50-507 **Knelman**, Fred H. (*Toronto*) M.Eng.: "Relations of the factors in spray drying." (Chemical Engineering: Denstedt, O.)

50-508 **Pavich**, Michael (*British Columbia*) M.Eng.: "Studies of current-noise from small resistors in the frequency range from 20 kc/s. to 500 kc/s." (Electrical Engineering: Chipman, R.)

50-509 **Poznanski**, Zolzislaw (*Bristol*, England) M.Eng.: "Measurements of input admittance of triodes in the frequency range 300 Mc/s. to 900 Mc/s." (Electrical Engineering: Woonton, G.)

50-510 **Woodhouse**, Gordon H. (*McGill*) M.Eng.: "Effect of impurities on lead anodes in the electrolysis of zinc sulphate solutions." (Metallurgical Engineering: Meenie, J.)

M.Sc. Spring 1950

50-511 **Adams**, Glenn N. (*McGill*) M.Sc.: "The air motor as a cloud generator." (Physics: Mordell, D.)

50-512 **Bailey**, W. Robert (*McGill*) M.Sc.: "The effect of pH on the agglutination of H and O suspensions of *Salmonella typhosa* in human and rabbit antisera." (Bacteriology: Murray, E.)

50-513 **Bassett**, Henry G. (*McGill*) M.Sc.: "The Hay River limestone, North West Territories." (Geological Sciences: Berrill, N.)

50-514 **Bekefi**, George (*London*, England) M.Sc.: "Some investigations into the properties of a double-stream, microwave amplifier." (Physics: Woonton, G.)

50-515 **Bloom**, Martin S. (*Chicago*) M.Sc.: "Measurement of heat transfer from precipitation particles to the atmosphere." (Physics: Marshall, J.)

50-516 **Bogoroch**, Rita (*McGill*) M.Sc.: "A theoretical and technical study of autography as a histological method for localization of radioactive elements." (Anatomy: Burgen, A.)

50-517 **Borts**, Robert B. (*McGill*) M.Sc.: "Lens measurement of antenna radiation patterns." (Physics: Miller, G.)

50-518 **Brown**, Frederick T. (*Harvard*) M.Sc.: "A study of the selection of university C.O.T.C. candidates." (Psychology: Ferguson, G.)

50-519 **Campbell**, Joseph D. (*Saskatchewan*) M.Sc.: "The effect of certain mineral nutrients on the yield and quality of tomatoes." (Horticulture: Steppler, H.)

50-520 **Clark**, Barbara E. (*McGill*) M.Sc.: "Studies of the effect of polymerizing temperatures on the nutritive value of linseed and herring oils." (Nutrition: Crampton, E.)

50-521 **Dougherty**, Joan L. (*McGill*) M.Sc.: "Demonstration of a 'steady state' of thyroidal iodine." (Anatomy: MacIntosh, F.)

50-522 **Eade**, Kenneth E. (*Queen's*) M.Sc.: "The Huronian rocks of northwestern Ontario." (Geological Sciences: Clark, T.)

50-523 **Engineer**, Behram B. (*Bombay*, India) M.Sc.: "The iron formation of Snelgrove Lake, Labrador." (Geological Sciences: Holcomb, R.)

50-524 **English**, William D. (*Manitoba*) M.Sc.: "An investigation of disilyl alkanes." (Chemistry: Purves, C.)

50-525 **Girard**, Kenneth F. (*Siena*) M.Sc.: "Attempts to stimulate a sheep erythrocyte agglutination with listeria monocytogenes in laboratory animals." (Bacteriology: Murray, E.)

50-526 **Girvin**, Grace T. (*Hunter*) M.Sc.: "The effect of botulinum toxin upon the bacterial acetylation of choline." (Bacteriology & Immunology: Burgen, A.)

50-527 **Hall**, Nancy C. (*McGill*) M.Sc.: "Antigenic character of pasteurella species from human cases." (Bacteriology: Kalz, G.)

50-528 **Hamilton**, Hugh A. (*McGill*) M.Sc.: "A heterodyne-type bridge detector for ultrasonic frequencies." (Physics: Rowles, W.)

50-529 **Henderson**, Gerald D. (*McGill*) M.Sc.: "Structural studies in an area at the headwaters of the McMurdo Creek, B.C." (Geological Sciences: Wilson, V.)

50-530 **Henneberry**, Gerald (*Dalhousie*) M.Sc.: "The synthesis of phenylalanine labelled with $C^{14}$." (Agricultural Chemistry: Baker, B.)

50-531 **Hoffman**, William H. (*Toronto*) M.Sc.: "An infra-red spectrophotometric investigations of the drying of oils." (Chemistry: Jones, R.)

50-532 **Hogan**, Howard R. (*McGill*) M.Sc.: "The Mina Lake graywacke, Sawyer Lake area, Labrador." (Geological Sciences: Pounder, E.)

50-533 **Holmes**, Stanley W. (*McGill*) M.Sc.: "A petrographic study of basic sills intruding the Howse Series, Labrador." (Geological Sciences: Ross, A.)

50-534 **Hosein**, Esau A. (*McGill*) M.Sc.: "The pharmacology of benezimidazole." (Biochemistry: Melville, K.)

50-535 **Hunter**, John M. (*Sydney*, Australia) M.Sc.: "Epileptoform seizures of thalamic origin." (Neurology & Neurosurgery: Martin, C.)

50-536 **Irwin**, Mary I. (*Saskatchewan*) M.Sc.: "The relative ability of human and the rat to digest identical diets, with particular reference to the techniques of digestion trials." (Nutrition: Neilson, H.)

50-537 **Jacoby**, Arthur W. (*Rutgers*) M.Sc.: "A psuedo-fluid effect exhibited by massed insects." (Zoology: Denstedt, O.)

50-538 **Jardine**, William G. (*Glasgow*, Scotland) M.Sc.: "A critical study of the statistical method in paleontology." (Geological Sciences: Wallace, P.)

50-539 **Johnston**, William W. (*McGill*) M.Sc.: "The inheritance of the growth pattern and certain body characteristics in reciprocal crosses of broad breasted Bronze-Charlevoix turkeys." (Genetics: Boyes, J.)

50-540 **Kassner**, Max H. (*London*, England) M.Sc.: "Screens for the absorption of microwave radiation." (Physics: Chipman, R.)

50-541 **Lewis**, John B. (*McGill*) M.Sc.: "The effect of weather on insect population." (Zoology: Stanley, J.)

50-542 **Lewis**, Revis C. (*McGill*) M.Sc.: "The reaction of oligodendroglia in Wallerina degeneration." (Neurology & Neurosurgery: Kershman, J.)

50-543 **Lloyd**, Lewis E. (*McGill*) M.Sc.: "A quantitative estimation of the effect of rutin on the biological potency of vitamin C." (Nutrition: Denstedt, O.)

50-544 **McIntosh**, Hamish W. (*Cambridge*, England) M.Sc.: "A method for the evaluation of adrenal cortical functions in man." (Experimental Medicine: Cleghorn, R.)

50-545 **MacLaren**, Alexander S. (*Queen's*) M.Sc.: "Some problems in correlation in northwestern Quebec." (Geological Sciences: Gill, J.)

50-546 **Marcus**, Alma (*McGill*) M.Sc.: "Temperature dependence of the mean free path of conduction electrons in graphite." (Mathematics: Opechowski, W.)

50-547 **Margolis**, Leo (*McGill*) M.Sc.: "Aeorbic bacteria in the slime and intestines of some fresh water fish." (Bacteriology: Cameron, T.)

50-548 **Martin**, Helen J. (*McGill*) M.Sc. "Some biotic parameters of an 'ebony' strain of *Tribolium confusum*." (Zoology: DuPorte, E.)

50-549 **Murray**, Thomas K. (*McGill*) M.Sc.: "Studies on the taste of enzymatic digests of proteins." (Agricultural Chemistry: Baker, B.)

50-550 **Patterson**, Donald D. (*McGill*) M.Sc.: "Polarization and absorption lines in solids." (Mathematics: Marshall, J.)

50-551 **Peets**, Ronald C. (*Notre Dame*) M.Sc.: "A quantitative study of thyroid gland growth and function." (Anatomy: Stanley, J.)

50-552 **Proverbs**, Ivor H. (*McGill*) M.Sc.: "A study of the nutritive value of pasture herbage with particular reference to the effects of stage of maturity at the time of harvest." (Nutrition: Raymond, L.)

50-553 **Puxley**, Ann E. (*McGill*) M.Sc.: "The electron optical examination of electric and magnetic fields." (Physics: Howes, F.)

50-554 **Reesal**, Michael R. (*McGill*) M.Sc.: "Helminth parasites of the Trinidad agouti (*Dasyprocta agouti*)." (Parasitology: DuPorte, E.)

50-555 **Robichon**, Jacques (*Ottawa*) M.Sc.: "Entry of radio-phosphorus into the bones of the newborn rat." (Experimental Surgery: Evelyn, K.)

50-556 **Sharp**, Robert T. (*McGill*) M.Sc.: "Electronic structure of boron nitride." (Mathematics: Watson, W.)

50-557 **Stocken**, Charles G. (*Capetown*, South Africa) M.Sc.: "Petrographic methods of determining the source of clastic sediments." (Geological Sciences: Cranck, E.)

50-558 **Whittier**, Angus C. (*Royal Military College*) M.Sc.: "The design and construction of a 100,000 volt linear ion accelerator." (Physics: Mennie, J.)

50-559 **Wigmore**, Robert H. (*Mount Allison*) M.Sc.: "1. A list of *Phalaenidae* of P.E.I. 2. The external morphology of *Apamea americana* Speyer. 3. A study of the external genitalia of 63 species of *Phalaenidae*." (Entomology: DuPorte, E.)

50-560 **Wolfgang**, Robert W. (*Ashland*) M.Sc.: "Parasites of marsupials in Trinidad." (Parasitology: DuPorte, E.)

50-561 **Woods**, James P. (*McGill*) M.Sc.: "A study of the nutritive value of pasture herbage with particular reference to the difference between leaf, stem and head of the plant." (Nutrition: Steppler, H.)

50-562 **Woolverton**, Ralph S. (*Western*) M.Sc.: "The Cambray Discovery Dyke and associated uranium deposits." (Geological Sciences: Jolliffe, A.)

M.A. Spring 1950

50-563 **Capps**, Margaret C. (*McGill*) M.A.: "The dramatic elements in the novels of Jane Austen." (English: Files, H.)

50-564 **Fague**, William R. (*Wesleyan*) M.A.: "'Leaf without shadow': a novel." (English: Files, H.)

50-565 **Fraser**, Arnold W. (*St. Patrick's*) M.A.: "The displaced persons in Canada: a problem in re-education." (Education: Jefferis, J.)

50-566 **Gardner**, Charles W. (*Yankton*) M.A.: "The attitude of the English people towards the introduction of labour-saving machinery during the Industrial Revolution." (History: Usher, A.)

50-567 **Hodge**, Cullen S. (*California*) M.A.: "Existence theorems for ordinary differential equations." (Mathematics: Kozakiewicz, W.)

50-568 **Johnston**, C. Meredith (*McGill*) M.A.: "The historical geography of the Saguenay Valley." (Geography: Kimble, G.)

50-569 **Kushner**, Eva M. (*McGill*) M.A.: "Croce's philosophy of history." (Philosophy: Klibansky, R.)

50-570 **Money-Coutts**, Joanna H. (*Oxford*, England) M.A.: "The noumenal in Kant's ethics." (Philosophy: Noad, A.)

50-571 **Morrow**, James W. (*McGill*) M.A.: "A comparison of the effects of reciprocal dumping with those of F.O.B. Mill pricing." (Economics: Cohen, M.)

50-572 **O'Quinn**, James P. (*St. Francis Xavier*) M.A.: "Le personnage de Vautrin dans l'oeuvre de Balzac." (French: Furness, L.)

50-573 **Paul**, Irving H. (*McGill*) M.A.: "The modified auto-kinetic technique." (Psychology: Tyhurst, J.)

50-574 **Piloto**, Albert E. (*McGill*) M.A.: "An analysis of the ethical and political elements in Sir Philip Sidney's 'New Arcadia'." (English: Hemlow, J.)

50-575 **Portier**, Jacques M. (*Rennes*, France) M.A.: "Les souvenirs personnels de Victor Hugo 'Les Miserables'." (French: Woodhead, W.)

50-576 **Robinson**, Jonathan (*Bishop's*) M.A.: "Bradley's theory of truth." (Philosophy: Sprott, S.)

50-577 **Sakellaropoulos**, Michael (*McGill*) M.A.: "German propaganda during the war: a study of the lack of integration within the Nazi state." (Economics & Political Science: Watkins, F.)

50-578 **Stewart**, Lyall S. (*McGill*) M.A.: "The personality of Virginia Woolf as revealed in her creative work." (English: Files, H.)

50-579 **Wiseman**, Sylvia (*McGill*) M.A.: "An enquiry into the welfare effects arising from the development of the Canadian pulp and paper industry." (Economics: Yajey, B.)

**M.Com. Spring 1950**

50-580 **Poapst**, James V. (*McGill*) M.Com.: "The growth of the life insurance industry in Canada, 1909-1947." (Economics: Byrd, K.)

**LL.M. Fall 1950**

50-581 **Colas**, Emile J. (*McGill*) LL.M.: "The development of the concept of legal personality and trade unions in Canada." (Law: Scott, F.)

**M.Eng. Fall 1950**

50-582 **Bernard**, Gerald A. (*Saskatchewan*) M.Eng.: "The web strength of I-beam sections in light alloys." (Civil Engineering & Applied Mechanics: DeStein, J.)

50-583 **Chant**, Raymond E. (*McGill*) M.Eng.: "The effects of an axial pressure gradient on boundary layer." (Mechanical Engineering: Mordell, D.)

50-584 **Hayles**, Oliver J. (*British Columbia*) M.Eng.: "The absolute measurement of phase difference of low frequency wave forms." (Electrical Engineering: Howes, F.)

50-585 **Javid**, Mansour (*Birmingham*, England) M.Eng.: "Accoustic model of short wave antennas." (Electrical Engineering: Howes, F.)

50-586 **Joly**, George W. (*Loyola of Montreal*) M.Eng.: "Web stability in an all-welded, thin-web, steel plate girder." (Civil Engineering & Applied Mechanics: Jamieson, R.)

50-587 **Keeping**, Kimball J. (*McGill*) M.Eng.: "An apparatus for microwave measurements using resonant cavities." (Electrical Engineering: Chipman, R.)

50-588 **Kuhn**, Bernard G. (*McGill*) M.Eng.: "Impedance measurements on aircraft antennas at medium and high frequencies." (Electrical Engineering: Chipman, R.)

50-589 **Lane**, Alan G. (*McGill*) M.Eng.: "A study of the air ejector." (Mechanical Engineering: Mordell, D.)

50-590 **Levine**, Seymour (*McGill*) M.Eng.: "The effects of turbulence on the spontaneous ignition and combustion of liquid hydrocarbon fuels in a hot gas stream." (Mechanical Engineering: Mordell, D.)

50-591 **Rogers**, James T. (*McGill*) M.Eng.: "The effect of recirculation on the weak limit stability of gas turbine combustion chambers." (Mechanical Engineering: Mordell, D.)

50-592 **Rosen**, Charles A. (*Cooper Union Institute of Technology*) M.Eng.: "The development of a thermistor accoustic probe." (Electrical Engineering: Howes, F.)

50-593 **Smith**, David L. (*Manitoba*) M.Eng.: "Automatic control in frequency shift transmission." (Electrical Engineering: Howes, F.)

50-594 **Stachiewicz**, J.W. (*McGill*) M.Eng.: "Investigations of total carbon formation in the combustion of liquid hydrocarbon fuels." (Mechanical Engineering: Mordell, D.)

**M.Sc. Fall 1950**

50-595 **Bell**, Keith (*McGill*) M.Sc.: "Geology of the Balachey Lake area, Northwest Territories." (Geological Sciences: Gill, J.)

50-596 **Blackmore**, William R. (*Sir George Williams*) M.Sc.: "Specific heats of crystalline solids containing more than one atom per unit cell." (Mathematics: Elliott, H.)

50-597 **Bloom**, Myer (*McGill*) M.Sc.: "Crystallographic investigations using the shape of the nuclear magnetic resonance line." (Physics: Foster, J.)

50-598 **Brochu**, Francis L. (*McGill*) M.Sc.: "The post-natal development of the antero-lateral abdominal wall." (Anatomy: Martin, C.)

50-599 **Chau**, Andrew Y. (*Shanghai National Medical*, China) M.Sc.: "Experimental studies on complete deprivation of arterial supply to the liver, with special reference to Welch bacillus infection." (Experimental Surgery: Webster, D.)

50-600 **Currie**, Donald J. (*Toronto*) M.Sc.: "Part 1. The effect of potassium deficiency on gastric secretion. Part 2. Experimental ulcerative colitis: the effect of bile and/or pancreatic juice on the colon." (Experimental Medicine: Webster, D.)

50-601 **Darrell-McPhee**, Gloria (*Howard*) M.Sc.: "The biology of *Daphnia*." (Zoology: Berrill, N.)

50-602 **De Leeuw**, Nannie K. (*Leiden*, Netherlands) M.Sc.: "Protomine-heparin titration methods for the determination of circulating anti-coagulants." (Experimental Medicine: Lowenstein, L.)

50-603 **Doyle**, James J. (*McGill*) M.Sc.: "Relation of estimates of the availability of phosphorus to soil treatments and to crop yields." (Agronomy: DeLong, W.)

50-604 **Drummond**, Robert N. (*McGill*) M.Sc.: "A traverse of the Romaine River." (Geography: Hare, F.)

50-605 **Dubuc**, Fernand (*Montréal*) M.Sc.: "Map-area west of Timmins Bay, Lake Attikamagen, Labrador." (Geological Sciences: Gill, J.)

50-606 **Elliott**, Bernard B. (*McGill*) M.Sc.: "The properties and kinetics of ascorbic acid oxidase." (Botany: Waygood, G.)

50-607 **Forse**, Raymond F. (*Acadia*) M.Sc.: "The effect of pyridoxine deficiency on gastric secretion." (Experimental Surgery: Miller, G.)

50-608 **Glocklin**, Vera C. (*Toronto*) M.Sc.: "Respiration and utilization of endogenous carbohydrate in *Heterakis gallinea*, a caecal nematode of the domestic fowl." (Biochemistry: Fairbairn, D.)

50-609 **Griffiths**, Herbert D. (*Western*) M.Sc.: "Back scattering of microwave by a conducting circular cylinder." (Physics: Woonton, G.)

50-610 **Harding**, Charles F. (*McGill*) M.Sc.: "The effect of certain minerals nutrients on the ascorbic acid content of leaf lettuce." (Horticulture: Murray, H.)

50-611 **Harrower**, George A. (*Western*) M.Sc.: "A double-stream amplifier for microwave frequencies." (Physics: Woonton, G.)

50-612 **Haskell**, Stanley R. (*McGill*) M.Sc.: "The digestibility of pure samples of barley, of oats, and of wheat with and without admixtures of oats, wheat, barley, wild oats and weed seeds." (Nutrition: Crampton, E.)

50-613 **Hogg**, David C. (*Western*) M.Sc.: "A spectrum analyser for a diffraction field computer." (Physics: Woonton, G.)

50-614 **Julien**, J. Bernard (*Laval*) M.Sc.: "Studies on the seedling disease of barley caused by *Helminthosporium sativum* Pk. and B." (Plant Pathology: Ludwig, R.)

50-615 **Kushner**, Donn J. (*Harvard*) M.Sc.: "The phosphorus content of small arteries." (Biochemistry: Evelyn, K.)

50-616 **Langleben**, Manuel P. (*McGill*) M.Sc.: "The variation of the velocity of sound in air with humidity." (Physics: Marshall, J.)

50-617 **Li**, Choh-luh (*Nanking*, China) M.Sc.: "Anatomical study of fibre connections of the temporal pole in the cat and the monkey." (Neurology & Neurosurgery: Robb, J.)

50-618 **Liberman**, John (*McGill*) M.Sc.: "Some experimental studies on the coat pattern of mice using the skin transplantation technique." (Genetics: Fraser, F.)

50-619 **Lowther**, John S. (*McGill*) M.Sc.: "A critical survey of the Sir William Dawson collection of paleozoic plants with a restudy of *Dadoxylon acadianum* DN." (Botany & Geological Sciences: Clark, T.)

50-620 **McCuaig**, James A. (*McGill*) M.Sc.: "A copper-nickel occurrence in Pardee Township, Thunder Bay district, Ontario." (Geological Sciences: Gill, J.)

50-621 **Maclure**, Kenneth C. (*McGill*) M.Sc.: "Proton induced fission in uranium." (Physics: Foster, J.)

50-622 **Magarvey**, R.H. (*Acadia*) M.Sc.: "Heat transfer from warm falling drops." (Physics: Marshall, J.)

50-623 **Miller**, Walter D. (*Dalhousie*) M.Sc.: "An experimental study on the development of anastomoses between the coronary circulation and the left internal mammary artery implanted into the left ventricular myocardium." (Experimental Surgery: Vineberg, A.)

50-624 **Miller**, William St. C. (*Reading*, England) M.Sc.: "A study of techniques in the evaluation of poultry pastures." (Poultry Husbandry: Nikolaiczuk, N.)

50-625 **Milner**, Peter M. (*Leeds*, England) M.Sc.: "A study of the mode of development of food preferences in rats." (Psychology: Hebb, D.)

50-626 **Nnochiri**, Enyinnaya (*Lincoln*) M.Sc.: "The ecology of the free-living stages of rabbit trichostrongyles." (Parasitology: Cameron, T.)

50-627 **Peron**, Fernand G. (*Sir George Williams*) M.Sc.: "The effect of mechanical treatment on glycolsis in erythrocytes." (Biochemistry: Denstedt, O.)

50-628 **Pump**, Karl K. (*Alberta*) M.Sc.: "The effect of adrenocorticotrophic hormone on respiratory function." (Experimental Medicine: Rose, B.)

50-629 **Radley**, Sidney A. (*Alberta*) M.Sc.: "The design of a pulse generator for a diffraction field computer." (Physics: Woonton, G.)

50-630 **Riddell**, Marion I. (*McGill*) M.Sc.: "The effect of oral streptomycin on faecal bacteria." (Eacteriology: Murray, E.)

50-631 **Rosen**, Harold J. (*McGill*) M.Sc.: "Influence of massage on rate of downgrowth of regenerating axons in injured peripheral nerves: a histological study." (Neurology & Neurosurgery: Cone, W.)

50-632 **Schiff**, Harry (*McGill*) M.Sc.: "On the Bhabha potential." (Mathematics: Wallace, P.)

50-633 **Skoryna**, Stanley C. (*Vienna*, Austria) M.Sc.: "Effects of 2-acetyl-amino-fluorene on the liver of rats." (Experimental Surgery: Webster, D.)

50-634 **Smith**, Donald S. (*McGill*) M.Sc.: "The phase change of light on reflection from thin aluminum films." (Physics: MacPherson, A.)

50-635 **Taylor**, William L. (*McGill*) M.Sc.: "Copper-nickel sulphide deposits of the Bird River, Manitoba and Werner Lake, Ontario areas." (Geological Sciences: O'Neill, J.)

50-636 **Turnau**, Edmund A. (*McGill*) M.Sc.: "A comparison study of the morphology and anatomy of normal *Abies balsamea* and that infected by *Melampsorella cerasti* (Pers.) Schroet." (Botany: Pady, *)

50-637 **Van Buren**, John M. (*Dartmouth*) M.Sc.: "The cortical representation of the feeding reflex." (Neurology & Neurosurgery: Babkin, P.)

50-638 **Wallerstein**, Harvey (*McGill*) M.Sc.: "The role of ego-involvement in perceptual activity." (Psychology: Bindra, D.)

50-639 **Whittall**, Norman S. (*McGill*) M.Sc.: "Oxidations of periodate lignin with alkaline hypoiodite and hypochlorite." (Chemistry: Purves, C.)

50-640 **Wilkinson**, Gordon W. (*Saskatchewan*) M.Sc.: "The deposition of radioactive phosphorus in bones, teeth and healing fractures of rats as shown by autographs and specific activity determinations." (Experimental Surgery: Leblond, C.)

50-641 **Wilmot**, Valerie C. (*Toronto*) M.Sc.: "Blood lipids in relation to diet." (Biochemistry: Swank, R.)

50-642 **Wiseblatt**, Lazare (*McGill*) M.Sc.: "Nutritionally deleterious constituents of heated vegetable oils." (Agricultural Chemistry: Common, R.)

**M.A. Fall 1950**

50-643 **Allen**, Robert L. (*California*) M.A.: "Baudelaire, critique litteraire." (French: Launay, J.)

50-644 **Ariano**, Alphonse (*McGill*) M.A.: "Montaigne et les nouvelletés." (French: Larivière, H.)

50-645 **Ashley**, Leonard (*McGill*) M.A.: "George Peele." (English: Duthie, G.)

50-646 **Betcherman**, Philip (*McGill*) M.A.: "Unions and wage rates in the newsprint industries of Quebec and Ontario, 1909 to 1948: a method of assessing the influence of labour unions on wage rates as exemplified by the Canadian newsprint industry." (Economics: Woods, H.)

50-647 **Blishen**, Bernard R. (*McGill*) M.A.: "A sociological study of three philanthropic financial campaigns in Montreal." (Sociology: Ross, A.)

50-648 **Boulanger**, Jean-Baptiste (*Montréal*) M.A.: "Le drame intime de Marcel Proust et la psychologie de l'amour dans 'A la recherche du temps perdu'." (French: Larivière, H.)

50-649 **Breitenbucher**, Howard E. (*McGill*) M.A.: "Anti-Entente tendencies in French opinion 1904-1912." (History: Fieldhouse, H.)

50-650 **Brougham**, Norma I. (*Western*) M.A.: "Emotional patterns in skin disease." (Psychology: Hebb, D.)

50-651 **Brzezinski**, Zbigniew K. (*McGill*) M.A.: "Russo-Soviet nationalism." (Political Science: Watkins, F.)

50-652 **Dickie**, Robert D. (*Alberta*) M.A.: "An investigation of the motivational factor involved in academic success." (Psychology: Ferguson, G.)

50-653 **Fricker**, Kathleen M. (*McGill*) M.A.: "The leading women characters in the novels of George Eliot." (English: Files, H.)

50-654 **Harrison**, John L. (*Sir George Williams*) M.A.: "Alexander Pope's rhetoric and diction." (English: Files, H.)

50-655 **Jackson**, Jay M. (*McGill*) M.A.: "An experimental investigation of leadership in a work situation using Guttman type scales." (Psychology: Webster, E.)

50-656 **Jones**, Frank E. (*McGill*) M.A.: "Work organization in the structual steel industry: a study of industrial organization and of ethnic relations among structural steelworkers." (Sociology: Hall, O.)

50-657 **Lucas**, Rex A. (*McGill*) M.A.: "Occupational orientation of high school entrants in a bi-ethnic railroad town." (Sociology: Hall, O.)

50-658 **McKay**, Huntly W. (*McGill*) M.A.: "Sociological analysis of a group practice: its effects upon the doctor and the hospital." (Sociology: Hall, O.)

50-659 **Mahon**, R. Kathryn (*Trinity*) M.A.: "Les moeurs et les coutumes rurales au Canada-Français dans le roman canadien-français depuis les origines." (French: Launay, J.)

50-660 **Oliver**, John A. (*McGill*) M.A.: "An analysis of some new tests of disposition rigidity." (Psychology: Ferguson, G.)

50-661 **Oliver**, Michael K. (*McGill*) M.A.: "The theory of social change in the writings of Pierre-Joseph Proudhon." (Economics: Watkins, F.)

50-662 **Orbach**, Jack (*McGill*) M.A.: "A further study of retinal locus as a factor in the recognition of English and Jewish words." (Psychology: Hebb, D.)

50-663 **Pitts**, Mary A. (*McGill*) M.A.: "The literary technique of Aldous Huxley in his novels and short stories." (English: Files, H.)

50-664 **Shipley**, William C. (*McGill*) M.A.: "The economics of assembly and transportation of fluid milk in the Montreal area." (Economics: Burton, G.)

50-665 **Shklar**, Judith (*McGill*) M.A.: "Machiavelli and Rousseau." (Political Science: Watkins, F.)

50-666 **Simon**, Beatrice V. (*McGill*) M.A.: "Autobiographical writings of the North American Indians." (English: Noad, A.)

50-667 **Watson**, Gordon A. (*McGill*) M.A.: "Aristotle's doctrine of practical wisdom." (Philosophy: Maclennan, R.)

50-668 **Westcott**, James W. (*Saskatchewan*) M.A.: "An investigation of some factors influencing the auto-kinetic effect." (Psychology: Luchins, A.)

50-669 **Wilson**, Donald H. (*Bishop's*) M.A.: "Symbolism and W.B. Yeats." (English: Duthie, G.)

**M.Com. Fall 1950**

50-670 **Galbraith**, John A. (*McGill*) M.Com.: "Extensions of contour analysis in economic theory." (Economics: Weldon, J.)

50-671 **Potter**, C.C. (*Sir George Williams*) M.Com.: "The economic significance of Canadian accountancy." (Economics: Byrd, K.)

## ANNUAL LISTING

### Ph.D. Spring 1951

51-001 **Breckon**, Sydney W. (*Queen's*) Ph.D.: "Short proton-induced activities in titanium and iron." (Physics: Foster, J.)

51-002 **Breul**, Frank R. (*Amherst*) Ph.D.: "Family allowances in Canada." (Economics: Mallory, J.)

51-003 **Brown**, Robert M. (*Bishop's*) Ph.D.: "Kinetic studies of a redox polymerization." (Chemistry: Winkler, C.)

51-004 **Chase**, Francis E. (*Ontario Agricultural*) Ph.D.: "Oxidation of organic matter by micro-organisms in the soil." (Agricultural Bacteriology: Gray, P.)

51-005 **Coldwell**, Blake B. (*McGill*) Ph.D.: "An investigation of the chemical composition of the leaf-fall from deciduous forest trees before and after partial decomposition." (Agricultural Chemistry: DeLong, W.)

51-006 **Colter**, John S. (*Alberta*) Ph.D.: "I. Catalytic decomposition of hydroxylamine by hemoglobin. II. Studies of the effects of methyl-bis(beta-chloroethyl) amine and 'anticholine oxidases' on choline metabolism *in vitro*." (Biochemistry: Quastel, J.)

51-007 **Dempster**, John C. (*Manitoba*) Ph.D.: "The effect of potassium bromate on physical properties and structure of flour doughs." (Chemistry: Winkler, C.)

51-008 **Fisher**, Robert W. (*McGill*) Ph.D.: "The importance of the locus of application on the effectiveness of DDT as a contact insecticide for the housefly, *Musca domestica* L. (*Diptera, Muscidae*)." (Entomology: Morrison, F.)

51-009 **Fiskell**, John G. (*Ontario Agricultural*) Ph.D.: "Studies on the relationships between fertilizer phosphate, lants and soils, using neutron-bombarded superphosphate." (Agricultural Chemistry: DeLong, W.)

51-010 **Franklin**, Arthur E. (*McGill*) Ph.D.: "Paper chromatography of proteins." (Biochemistry: Quastel, J.)

51-011 **Gerryts**, Edgert (*South Africa*) Ph.D.: "The petrology of the Kimberlites at the Premier (Transvaal) Diamond Mine, South Africa." (Geological Sciences: Kranck, E.)

51-012 **Gransden**, Max M. (*Western*) Ph.D.: "Properties of new neutron-deficient isotopes of lanthanum." (Physics: Foster, J.)

51-013 **Hawirko**, Roma Z. (*Manitoba*) Ph.D.: "An investigation of oil partition for the isolation of *Mycobacterium tuberculosis* from pathological material." (Bacteriology: Murray, E.)

51-014 **Heyding**, Robert D. (*Saskatchewan*) Ph.D.: "Solvent effect on iodide exchange." (Chemistry: Winkler, C.)

51-015 **Hone**, David W. (*Western*) Ph.D.: "The deflection system of the McGill cyclotron." (Physics: Foster, J.)

51-016 **Hunton**, Vera D. (*Howard*) Ph.D.: "The recognition of disoriented pictures by children." (Psychology: Ferguson, G.)

51-017 **Kobernick**, Sidney D. (*McGill*) Ph.D.: "The pathogenesis of lesions produced in rabbits by administration of foreign serum proteins." (Pathology: More, R.)

51-018 **Levitin**, Norman (*Queen's*) Ph.D.: "Oxidations of periodate lignin with sodium chlorite and chlorine dioxide." (Chemistry: Purves, C.)

51-019 **Lucien**, Harold W. (*Dillard*) Ph.D.: "The synthesis and derivatives of dibenz(1,3)(a,c)cyclohepta-5,7-dione." (Chemistry: Taurins, A.)

51-020 **Luner**, Philip (*Loyola of Montréal*) Ph.D.: "Solvent effects in cis-trans isomerization." (Chemistry: Winkler, C.)

51-021 **McLennan**, Hugh (*McGill*) Ph.D.: "Factors affecting the synthesis of acetylcholine by brain tissue preparations." (Biochemistry: Elliott, K.)

51-022 **Mandelcorn**, Lyon (*New York*) Ph.D.: "Gelatin-halide interaction in copper electro-deposition." (Chemistry: Winkler, C.)

51-023 **Martin**, William M. (*Queen's*) Ph.D.: "Short proton-induced activities in chromium and nickel." (Physics: Foster, J.)

51-024 **Metro**, Stephen J. (*Lebanon Valley*) Ph.D.: "The reaction of 2-bromo-2-nitro-1,3-indandione with pyridine." (Chemistry: Taurins, A.)

51-025 **Mulligan**, Robert (*Alberta*) Ph.D.: "Geology of the Nelson and adjoining part of Salmo map areas, British Columbia." (Geological Sciences: Kranck, E.)

51-026 **Myers**, Gordon E. (*Alberta*) Ph.D.: "An evaluation of certain principles of disinfection." (Bacteriology: Stevenson, J.)

51-027 **Olszewski**, Jerzy (*Freiburg*, West Germany) Ph.D.: "An atlas of the thalamus of *Macaca mulatta* for use with the Horsley-Clarke instrument." (Neurology & Neurosurgery: Penfield, W.)

51-028 **Perry**, Ernest J. (*McGill*) Ph.D.: "Triphenylmethyl radical formation on silver." (Chemistry: Winkler, C.)

51-029 **Ralph**, Arthur O. (*McGill*) Ph.D.: "Study of the effect of ammonium nitrate on the kinetics of the Bachman reaction to produce RDX. The construction and operation of a pilot plant to study the Bachman reaction." (Chemistry: Winkler, C.)

51-030 **Schrage**, Samuel (*Dalhousie*) Ph.D.: "Light scattering in the critical region." (Chemistry: Maass, O.)

51-031 **Smith**, Alan R. (*British Columbia*) Ph.D.: "Occurrence of nickel in igneous rocks." (Geological Sciences: Stevenson, J.)

51-032 **Thomas**, Gordon (*Western*) Ph.D.: "Transport of lead into cathode zinc." (Chemistry: Winkler, C.)

51-033 **Tower**, Donald B. (*Harvard*) Ph.D.: "A study of the acetylcholine system in the cerebral cortex of various mammals and in the human epileptogenic focus and of certain factors which affect its activity." (Neurology & Neurosurgery: Elliott, K.)

51-034 **Trevelyan**, Benjamin J. (*McMaster*) Ph.D.: "The motions of particles in model suspensions subjected to a shear." (Chemistry: Maass, O.)

51-035 **Turner**, Robert C. (*McGill*) Ph.D.: "Studies in electrochemistry." (Chemistry: Winkler, C.)

51-036 **Witty**, Ralph (*McGill*) Ph.D.: "A study of animal and plant transaminases." (Biochemistry: Quastel, J.)

51-037 **Yates**, Claire H. (*Sir George Williams*) Ph.D.: "The preparation of progesterone and desoxycorticosterone acetate labelled in the side chain with radioactive carbon: the metabolism of progesterone." (Biochemistry: Heard, R.)

51-038 **Ziegler**, Peter (*Sir George Williams*) Ph.D.: "Radioactive steroid hormones (ring A labelled)." (Biochemistry: Heard, R.)

51-039 **Zorbach**, William W. (*Bowling Green State*) Ph.D.: "Attempts to label cholesterol in ring B: seco-6-1-cholestan-7-one and seco-6-3(beta)-bromocholestan-7-one: ring A $C^{14}$-labelled cholesterol." (Chemistry: Heard, R. )

**Ph. D. Fall 1951**

51-040 **Alivisatos**, Spyridon (*Athens*, Greece) Ph.D.: "Studies on the enzyme systems of the blood." (Biochemistry: Denstedt, O.)

51-041 **Braganca**, Menezes B. (*Calcutta*, India) Ph.D.: "Biochemical investigations of snake venoms in relation to their neurotoxic effects." (Biochemistry: Quastel, J.)

51-042 **Cabott**, Irving M. (*McGill*) Ph.D.: "Experiments on the pulping of periodate lignin by the sulfite process." (Chemistry: Purves, C.)

51-043 **Chapman**, John H. (*Western*) Ph.D.: "The fading of radio echoes from the ionosphere." (Physics: Woonton, G.)

51-044 **Clark**, Eric N. (*McGill*) Ph.D.: "Beta ray spectra of neutron deficient isotopes of antimony and tellurium." (Physics: Foster, J.)

51-045 **Favis**, Demetrios (*Athens*, Greece) Ph.D.: "Studies of the effect of fibre flocculation on the heterogeneity of paper." (Chemistry: Maass, O.)

51-046 **Forsyth**, Peter A. (*Saskatchewan*) Ph.D.: "A radio investigation of aurora." (Physics: Woonton, G.)

51-047 **Ghent**, Lila R. (*McGill*) Ph.D.: "The effects of varied activities on the post-electroshock electroencephalogram." (Psychology: Hebb, D.)

51-048 **Gillies**, Norman B. (*Dalhousie*) Ph.D.: "The geology of the Canimiti River area, Pontiac County, Quebec." (Geological Sciences: Gill, J.)

51-049 **Harpham**, John A. (*Toronto*) Ph.D.: "Further separations of the water-soluble components of white spruce bark." (Chemistry: Purves, C.)

51-**050** **Henry**, William H. (*Queen's*) Ph.D.: "Study and improvement of the McGill cyclotron." (Physics: Foster, J.)

51-**051** **Keys**, John D. (*McGill*) Ph.D.: "Alpha activity produced by protons of medium energy." (Physics: Foster, J.)

51-**052** **L'Esperance**, Robert L. (*McGill*) Ph.D.: "The geology of Duprat Township and some adjacent areas, northwest Quebec." (Geological Sciences: O'Neill, J.)

51-**053** **McLintock**, John J. (*Manitoba*) Ph.D.: "The continuous laboratory rearing of *Culiseta inornata* (Will.) and a study of the structure and function of the egg-shell and egg-raft (*Diptera*: *Culicidae*)." (Entomology: DuPorte, E.)

51-**054** **Metrakos**, Julius D. (*McGill*) Ph.D.: "The twin method and its application to the study of genetic and environmental factors of some human diseases." (Genetics: Fraser, F.)

51-**055** **Mishkin**, Mortimer (*Dartmouth*) Ph.D.: "Effects of selective ablations of the temporal lobes on the visually guided behavior of monkeys and baboons." (Psychology: Rosvold, H.)

51-**056** **Schalin**, Edmund (*Saskatchewan*) Ph.D.: "Studies on the composition and properties of colloidal fractions isolated from soils." (Agricultural Chemistry: DeLong, W.)

51-**057** **Sherbeck**, Leander A. (*Alberta*) Ph.D.: "The neutral constituents of a Canadian tall oil." (Chemistry: Purves, C.)

51-**058** **Stock**, John J. (*Ontario Agricultural*) Ph.D.: "The imminospecificity of streptococcal hyaluronidases and some of their properties." (Bacteriology: DeVries, J.)

51-**059** **Thompson**, Lloyd M. (*McGill*) Ph.D.: "On the preparation of estrone-16-$C^{14}$ and the study of its metabolism." (Biochemistry: Heard, R.)

51-**060** **Tilley**, Donald E. (*McGill*) Ph.D.: "High energy nuclei emitted under proton bombardment." (Physics: Foster, J.)

**M.Eng. Spring 1951**

51-**500** **Brown**, Donald R. (*McGill*) M.Eng.: "Calibration of variable compression internal combustion engine with standard fuel and investigation of performance with fuel 3GPX22." (Mechanical Engineering: Catway, H.)

51-**501** **Charles**, George E. (*McGill*) M.Eng.: "Heat and mass transfer in dehumidification." (Chemical Engineering: Phillips, J.)

51-**502** **Conrath**, Joseph J. (*McGill*) M.Eng.: "Experimentation on a low speed cascade wind tunnel." (Mechanical Engineering: Mordell, D.)

51-**503** **Ellard**, Christopher (*Athens*, Greece) M.Eng.: "Temperature rise of induction motors." (Electrical Engineering: Schippel, W.)

51-**504** **Lam**, Mathias (*British Columbia*) M.Eng.: "The development of a horizontal Van De Graaff generator." (Electrical Engineering: Wallace, G.)

51-505 **Ross-Ross**, Philip A. (*McGill*) M.Eng.: "A study of the boundary layer in an adverse axial pressure gradient." (Mechanical Engineering: Mordell, D.)

51-506 **Sakellariou**, Theodore (*Athens*, Greece) M.Eng.: "Parasitic torques of induction motors." (Electrical Engineering: Schippel, W.)

51-507 **Tatlock**, John F. (*Manitoba*) M.Eng.: "Dependence of thermistor characteristics on the heat treatment process." (Electrical Engineering: Howes, F.)

M.Sc. Spring 1951

51-508 **Austin**, George M. (*Lafayette*) M.Sc.: "An investigation of the facilitatory and inhibitory activity of the suprabulbar regions of the cat." (Neurology & Neurosurgery: Jasper, H.)

51-509 **Bainborough**, Arthur R. (*Western Ontario*) M.Sc.: "The influence of 2:4 dinitrophenol and thyroxin on the retrogression of experimental cholesterol atherosclerosis in the rabbit." (Pathology: Duff, G.)

51-510 **Barrales**, Hugo L. (*Chile*) M.Sc.: "Photoperiodic reactions of red clover." (Agronomy: White, W.)

51-511 **Beck**, Johannes C. (*McGill*) M.Sc.: "Some metabolic effects of ACTH and cortisone acetate." (Experimental Medicine: Mackenzie, K.)

51-512 **Berryhill**, Florence M. (*Manitoba*) M.Sc.: "The detrimental effects of thermal treatment on the nutritive value of linseed soybean oils." (Nutrition: Crampton, E.)

51-513 **Bertalanffy**, Felix D. (*McGill*) M.Sc.: "The mitotic activity and renewal of the lung." (Anatomy: Leblond, C.)

51-514 **Cain**, Robert M. (*Alabama Polytechnical Institute*) M.Sc.: "A bacteriological survey of institutional dishwashing." (Bacteriology & Immunology: Kelly, C.)

51-515 **Chapman**, Marion H. (*Western*) M.Sc.: "Design and experimental investigation of a radio lens." (Physics: Woonton, G.)

51-516 **Clark**, Gordon M. (*Sir George Williams*) M.Sc.: "The action and use of colchicine in the production of tetraploid fagopyrum esculentum." (Genetics: Boyes, J.)

51-517 **Earle**, Kenneth M. (*Bishop's*) M.Sc.: "The tract of Lissauer and its possible relation to the pain pathway." (Neurology & Neurosurgery: McNaughton, F.)

51-518 **Eartly**, Heidi H. (*McGill*) M.Sc.: "Factors modifying the manifestations of thyroid deficiency in thyroidectomized rats and the influence of other hormones on the action of thyroxine." (Anatomy: Leblond, C.)

51-519 **Fairbairn**, N.J. (*Bishop's*) M.Sc.: "The fractionation of protein hydrolysates by butanol extraction." (Agricultural Chemistry: Baker, B.)

51-520 **Forgus**, Ronald H. (*McGill*) M.Sc.: "An investigation of the relationship between the Einstellung effect and variability." (Psychology: Luchins, A.)

51-521 **Fridhandler**, Louis (*McGill*) M.Sc.: "Billiary obstruction in the rabbit." (Medicine: Mackenzie, K.)

51-522 **Fullerton**, Henry D. (*McGill*) M.Sc.: "A petrographic study of the serpentinized peridotites of the Griffis Lake map area, Quebec." (Geological Sciences: Stevenson, J.)

51-523 **Gallamore**, William A. (*Massachusetts*) M.Sc.: "Studies on the adjuvant action of rutin and ascorbic acid in nutrition." (Nutrition: Crampton, E.)

51-524 **Gibson**, Robert M. (*Glasgow*, Scotland) M.Sc.: "The effect of cortisone in the healing of incised cerebral wounds." (Neurology & Neurosurgery: McNaughton, F.)

51-525 **Howes**, James R. (*London*, England) M.Sc.: "Genetic and physiological differences in the spermatozoa of the domestic fowl." (Genetics: Boyes, J.)

51-526 **Keefe**, Thomas J. (*McGill*) M.Sc.: "Some effects of steroid hormones and thiouracil on storage and mobilization of vitamin A and riboflavin in the domestic fowl." (Agricultural Chemistry: Common, R.)

51-527 **Kennedy**, Byrl J. (*Minnesota*) M.Sc.: "Effects of various substances on protein catabolism." (Experimental Medicine: Mackenzie, K.)

51-528 **Lautsch**, Elizabeth V. (*Manitoba*) M.Sc.: "The accumulation of colloidal substances in the lesions of experimental cholesterol atherosclerosis." (Pathology: McMillan, G.)

51-529 **Lesser**, Elliott (*Brooklyn*) M.Sc.: "Studies on *Entamoeba invadens*." (Parasitology: Cameron, T.)

51-530 **Linis-Linins**, Viktors (*Latvia*) M.Sc.: "Some problems in the theory of univalent functions." (Mathematics: Fox, C.)

51-531 **Loiselle**, Roland (*McGill*) M.Sc.: "Combining ability in corn inbreds." (Agronomy: Raymond, L.)

51-532 **Loomer**, Elijah I. (*McGill*) M.Sc.: "An automatic timing device to adapt a Wilson cloud chamber for use with a cyclotron." (Physics: Terroux, F.)

51-533 **Lutwick**, Laurence E. (*McGill*) M.Sc.: "An investigation of interactions between leachates from decomposing leaves and soil forming materials." (Agricultural Chemistry: DeLong, W.)

51-534 **McGarry**, Eleanor E. (*McGill*) M.Sc.: "Observations on body water and electrolytes following administration of ACTH in man." (Experimental Medicine: Johnson, L.)

51-535 **Meissner**, George F. (*Queen's*) M.Sc.: "The influence of choline on experimental arteriosclerosis." (Pathology: Duff, G.)

51-536 **Melzak**, Zdzislaw A. (*McGill*) M.Sc.: "Some diophantine problems." (Mathematics: Rosenthall, E.)

51-537 **Moore**, Thomas H. (*McGill*) M.Sc.: "Igneous dyke rocks of the Aillik-Makkovik area, Labrador." (Geological Sciences: Kranck, E.)

51-538 **Oliver**, William T. (*Toronto*) M.Sc.: "The effect of humidity on the egg of the caecal worm of chickens." (Parasitology: Cameron, T.)

51-539 **Orvig**, Svenn (*Oslo*, Norway) M.Sc.: "The climate of the ablation-period on the Barnes ice cap, 1950." (Geography: Hare, F.)

51-540 **Owens**, Owen E. (*McGill*) M.Sc.: "The quartz deposits of the Watshishou Knoll area on the north shore of the St. Lawrence River." (Geological Sciences: Gill, J.)

51-541 **Paquin**, Roger (*Laval*) M.Sc.: "Influence of some factors on host invasion by *Corynebacterium sepedonicum* and *Corynebacterium michiganense*." (Plant Pathology: Coulson, J.)

51-542 **Povilaitis**, Bronys (*Lithuania*) M.Sc.: "Study of dormancy in seeds of some important weeds." (Agronomy: Raymond, L.)

51-543 **Richer**, Ruth C. (*McGill*) M.Sc.: "The relation of age to the effect of morphine on the metabolism of mouse brain." (Biochemistry: Quastel, J.)

51-544 **Riley**, George C. (*McGill*) M.Sc.: "The bedrock geology of Makkovik and its relations to the Aillik and Kaipokok series." (Geological Sciences: Kranck, E.)

51-545 **Roper**, Richard B. (*McGill*) M.Sc.: "An embryo-sac study of *Butomus umbellatus*, L." (Botany: Roscoe, M.)

51-546 **Shulman**, R. (*McGill*) M.Sc.: "On some factors influencing mechanization in problem solving." (Psychology: Luchins, A.)

51-547 **Sibalis**, Jack (*McGill*) M.Sc.: "A study of a helminthosporium disease of *Portulaca oleracea* L. and *Portulaca grandiflora* L." (Plant Pathology: Coulson, J.)

51-548 **Siddall**, Margaret I. (*Manitoba*) M.Sc.: "The effect of homogenized condensed fish supplement with or without 'animal protein factor', on the growth of young albino rats fed various basal rations." (Nutrition: Crampton, E.)

51-549 **Slaght**, William H. (*McGill*) M.Sc.: "A petrographic study of the Copper Cliff offser, Sudbury district, Ontario." (Geological Sciences: Stevenson, J.)

51-550 **Slater**, Douglas T. (*McGill*) M.Sc.: "A study of certain agronomic and morphological characteristics of *Lotus corniculatus* and *Lotus uliginosus*." (Agronomy: Steppler, H.)

51-551 **Solomon**, Samuel (*McGill*) M.Sc.: "Diazomethane-$C^{14}$; ring B di-substituted cholestanols." (Biochemistry: Heard, R.)

51-552 **Stevenson**, Ira M. (*McGill*) M.Sc.: "The barite deposit at Brookfield, Nova Scotia." (Geological Sciences: Clark, T.)

51-553 **Stinson**, David A. (*Toronto*) M.Sc.: "The excretion of phenolsulfonphthalein by the kidneys of rabbits." (Experimental Medicine: Evelyn, K.)

51-554 **Stratford**, Joseph G. (*McGill*) M.Sc.: "A study of certain corticothalamic relationships." (Neurology & Neurosurgery: Jasper, H.)

51-555 **Syme**, Andrew M. (*McGill*) M.Sc.: "Glacial features in the vicinity of Knob Lake, Labrador." (Geological Sciences: Gill, J.)

51-556 **Taylor**, Frederick C. (*Western*) M.Sc.: "The petrology of the serpentine bodies in the Matheson district, Ontario." (Geological Sciences: Kranck, E.)

51-557 **Thomson**, Hugh M. (*McGill*) M.Sc.: "Aerobic bacteria associated with the digestive tract of the spruce budworm, *Choristoneura fumiferana* Clem." (Agricultural Bacteriology: Gray, P.)

51-558 **Towers**, George H. (*McGill*) M.Sc.: "Comparative chemistry and taxonomy of plants: the separation and estimation of phenolic aldehydes from the alkaline nitrobenzene oxidation mixtures of plant materials." (Botany: Gibbs, R.)

51-559 **Tremblay**, Mousseau (*Montréal*) M.Sc.: "Structural relations in the Greenville province." (Geological Sciences: O'Neill, J.)

51-560 **Wanklyn**, David I. ( *Oxford,* England) M.Sc.: "A pneumatic stereoscopic camera for the Wilson expansion chamber." (Physics: Terroux, F.)

51-561 **Weigensberg**, Bernard I. (*McGill*) M.Sc.: "Chemical analysis of human arteries and arterioles." (Biochemistry: Evelyn, K.)

51-562 **Whiteside**, John H. (*Toronto*) M.Sc.: "The effect of under-nutrition on experimental cholesterol atherosclerosis." (Pathology: Duff, G.)

51-563 **Young**, William L. (*McGill*) M.Sc.: "The Lucy orebody: its petrology, structure, and origin; Michipicoten district, Ontario, Canada." (Geological Sciences: Gill, J.)

M.A. Spring 1951

51-564 **Brazeau**, Joseph E. (*McGill*) M.A.: "The French-Canadian doctor in Montreal: a study of careers in a profession." (Sociology: Hall, O.)

51-565 **Caralopoulos**, Nicholas (*Athens*, Greece) M.A.: "Fiscal policy in Greece (1917-1930)." (Economics: Higgins, B.)

51-566 **Creighton**, Phyllis (*Wellesley*) M.A.: "The North China plain: a regional study." (Geography: Hare, F.)

51-567 **Currie**, Robert A. (*McGill*) M.A.: "Marlowe's 'Jew of Malta': a critical study." (English: Duthie, G.)

51-568 **Ebbitt**, May (*McGill*) M.A.: "The walls of sense." (English: Files, H.)

51-569 **Johnston**, John A. (*Western*) M.A.: "The Presbyterian College, Montreal, 1865-1915." (History: Cooper, J.)

51-570 **Mills**, Allan W. (*Saskatchewan*) M.A.: "Imitation versus understanding in social learning." (Psychology: Luchins, A.)

51-571 **Mooney**, Craig M. (*Saskatchewan*) M.A.: "Some new closure tests." (Psychology: Ferguson, G.)

51-572 **Nelson**, Arthur J. (*Montréal*) M.A.: "Ambiance spirituelle de Georges Bernanos d'après les thêmes de ses romans." (French: Launay, J.)

51-573 **Paterson**, Laurie A. (*British Columbia*) M.A.: "An isochronic study of Winnipeg and Montreal; peripheral and intervening areas." (Geography: Zaborski, B.)

51-574 **Romaine**, Victor (*San Diego State*) M.A.: "The physical geography of the Two Mountains area, Quebec." (Geography: Zaborski, B.)

51-575 **Senior**, Hereward (*McGill*) M.A.: "The activities of David Urquhart in British diplomacy and politics, 1830-1841." (History: Reid, W.)

51-576 **Westwood**, Mary J. (*British Columbia*) M.A.: "L'element de la souffrance humaine dans l'oeuvre romanesque de Georges Duhamel." (French: Launay, J.)

51-577 **White**, Orville E. (*Alberta*) M.A.: "The history of the practical education courses in Canadian secondary schools." (Education: Currie, A.)

51-578 **Wolfgang**, Mary B. (*Ashland*) M.A.: "L'expression littéraire des sensations olfactives-gustatives dans les romans de Joris-Karl Huysmans." (French: Launay, J.)

**M.C.L. Fall 1951**

51-579 **MacKay**, Kenneth C. (*McGill*) M.C.L.: "The Water Carraige of Goods Act, 1936." (Civil Law: Cohen, M.)

**M.Arch. Fall 1951**

51-580 **Aronin**, Jeffrey E. (*Manitoba*) M.Arch.: "Climate and architecture." (Architecture: Bland, J.)

**M.Eng. Fall 1951**

51-581 **Boucher**, James E. (*Alberta*) M.Eng.: "The resonance characteristics of certain transmission-line circuits." (Electrical Engineering: Chipman, R.)

51-582 **Bradbury**, John S. (*London*, England) M.Eng.: "The effect on pressure surges of pipeline termination." (Civil Engineering & Applied Mechanics: Craig, C.)

51-583 **Coldwell**, Keith L. (*Nova Scotia Technical*) M.Eng.: "Web stresses in an all-welded plate girder." (Civil Engineering & Applied Mechanics: De Stein, J.)

51-584 **Daw**, Geoffrey G. (*London*, England) M.Eng.: "Afterburning in turbojet engines." (Mechanical Engineering: Mordell, D.)

51-585 **Goth**, John W. (*South Dakota School of Mines*) M.Eng.: "An investigation of the electric smelting of copper concentrates." (Metallurgical Engineering: MacEwan, J.)

51-586 **Gribble**, William F. (*Queen's*) M.Eng.: "Impedance of full-wave dipole antennas as a function of center spacing." (Electrical Engineering: Howes, F.)

51-587 **Lyons**, Douglas B. (*McGill*) M.Eng.: "The effects of feed properties on spray drying." (Chemical Engineering: Gauvin, W.)

51-588 **Nenniger**, Emile (*Queen's*) M.Eng.: "Film and dropwise condensation of steam-air mixtures." (Chemical Engineering: Phillips, J.)

51-589 **Rackow**, Alan D. (*Manitoba*) M.Eng.: "Voltage-stabilizing transformers." (Electrical Engineering: Schippel, W.)

51-590 **Tai**, Yue-Shing (*National Kwang-Si*, China) M.Eng.: "The capacitor motor." (Electrical Engineering: Schippel, W.)

51-591 **Walsh**, John H. (*McGill*) M.Eng.: "Statistical analysis of the compositions and related properties of cast steel." (Metallurgical Engineering: Ogilvie, J.)

51-592 **Yurko**, Michael (*Alberta*) M.Eng.: "The radiation resistance of resonant transmission lines." (Electrical Engineering: Chipman, R.)

M.Sc. Fall 1951

51-593 **Alozie**, Obinnaya (*Dubuque*) M.Sc.: "The Helminth parasites of *Catostomus commersonii* in the Quebec area." (Parasitology: Cameron, T.)

51-594 **Anderson**, Francis D. (*New Brunswick*) M.Sc.: "The McDougall-Segur conglomerate." (Geological Sciences: Kranck, E.)

51-595 **Ballem**, Charles M. (*Dalhousie*) M.Sc.: "Studies of gastric secretion." (Experimental Surgery: Webster, D.)

51-596 **Boloten**, M. (*McGill*) M.Sc.: "On Dirac's classical theory of the radiating electron." (Mathematics: Morris, T.)

51-597 **Brodkin**, Elliot (*McGill*) M.Sc.: "Factors affecting the metabolism of acetylcholine in tissue suspensions." (Biochemistry: Elliott, K.)

51-598 **Buck**, Walter K. (*McGill*) M.Sc.: "The geology of the Lake Wasa property, Beauchastel Township, Quebec." (Geological Sciences: Gill, J.)

51-599 **Cann**, Keith E. (*McGill*) M.Sc.: "The effect of certain plant growth regulating substances on early yield and quality of field grown tomatoes." (Horticulture-Botany: Murray, H.)

51-600 **Carr**, Joseph W. (*McGill*) M.Sc.: "Studies on the taste of enzymatic digests of proteins." (Agricultural Chemistry: Baker, B.)

51-601 **Clarke**, Ronald S. (*Sir George Williams*) M.Sc.: "An experimental study of position and object discrimination in the dog." (Psychology: Hebb, D.)

51-602 **Cooper**, Gerald E. (*McGill*) M.Sc.: "The petrology of some syenites and granites in Labrador." (Geological Sciences: Kranck, E.)

51-603 **Corbett**, Wendell O. (*McGill*) M.Sc.: "The effects of benzene hexachloride on bacteria in the rhizosphere of leguminous plants." (Agricultural Bacteriology: Wallace, R.)

51-604 **Crowell**, Clarence R. (*McGill*) M.Sc.: "Precision equipment for measurements on a double-stream microwave amplifier tube." (Physics: Woonton, G.)

51-605 **Dekaban**, Anatole S. (*Warsaw*, Poland) M.Sc.: "The human thalamus: anatomical and developmental study." (Neurology & Neurosurgery: Martin, C.)

51-606 **Fainstat**, Theodore D. (*McGill*) M.Sc.: "Effects of the administration of cortisone during pregnancy on mice and their offspring." (Genetics: Fraser, F.)

51-607 **Francoeur**, Joseph M. (*McGill*) M.Sc.: "Hexosemonophosphate oxidation and methemoglobin reduction in human erythrocytes." (Biochemistry: Denstedt, O.)

51-608 **Greenberg**, Jack S. (*McGill*) M.Sc.: "A study of counting losses due to 'dead-time' of counting circuits." (Physics: Westcott, C.)

51-609 **Hilborn**, John W. (*Toronto*) M.Sc.: "Equilibrium assaying the uranium ore." (Physics: Foster, J.)

51-610 **Klatzo**, Igor (*Freiburg*, West Germany) M.Sc.: "A study of the tumors of the nervous system by the Golgi method." (Neurology & Neurosurgery: Cone, W.)

51-611 **Kalter**, Harold (*Sir George Williams*) M.Sc.: "Incidence, inheritance, and significance of the taste reaction to phenylthiocarbamide (PTO)." (Genetics: Fraser, F.)

51-612 **Laroche**, Joseph R. (*Montréal*) M.Sc.: "Effect of thyroid preparation and iodide administration on young salmon." (Anatomy: Leblond, C.)

51-613 **McKinley**, William P. (*McGill*) M.Sc.: "Investigation on the acidity of leachates from decomposing leaves of deciduous trees." (Agricultural Chemistry: DeLong, W.)

51-614 **Melzack**, Ronald (*McGill*) M.Sc.: "Irrational fears in the dog." (Psychology: Hebb, D.)

51-615 **Moore**, Ralph E. (*McGill*) M.Sc.: "Formation of acetaldehyde and alcohol in frozen peas and their relation to off-flavour development." (Horticulture-Botany: David, J.)

51-616 **Perlman**, Martin M. (*McGill*) M.Sc.: "On the nuclear magnetic resonance determination of the properties of crystals." (Physics: Foster, J.)

51-617 **Pfalzner**, Paul M. (*Toronto*) M.Sc.: "The diffusion of water vapour through wood: an analysis of the adsorption isotherm based on Cassie's theory of sorption." (Physics: Gunn, K.)

51-618 **Popham**, James H. (*McGill*) M.Sc.: "A study in overlearning with human subjects." (Psychology: Ferguson, G.)

51-619 **Poplove**, Myron (*McGill*) M.Sc.: "Studies on the proteolytic enzymes of bacteria." (Agricultural Bacteriology: Gray, P.)

51-620 **Robinson**, Joseph E. (*McGill*) M.Sc.: "A study of the cobalt sediments of Dasserat Township, Quebec." (Geological Sciences: Clark, T.)

51-621 **Rubinstein**, David (*McGill*) M.Sc.: "Studies on the immunochemistry of hemagglutinins." (Biochemistry: Denstedt, O.)

51-622 **Rublee**, J.D. (*Saskatchewan*) M.Sc.: "Dyed antigens and the lesions associated with foreign protein injection." (Pathology: More, R.)

51-623 **Russell**, William J. (*Manitoba*) M.Sc.: "Geography of roads west of Lake Winnipeg inter lake area." (Geography: Zaborski, B.)

51-624 **Schwartz**, Solomon (*McGill*) M.Sc.: "The peripheral distribution and metabolism of thyroxine in mice." (Anatomy: Leblond, C.)

51-625 **Sellen**, John M. (*California Institute of Technology*) M.Sc.: "A determination of the beam current of the McGill synchrocyclotron." (Physics: Foster, J.)

51-626 **Toovey**, Edna W. (*Chicago*) M.Sc.: "Experimental production of gastric neoplasms in the rat." (Experimental Surgery: Webster, D.)

51-627 **Turnbull**, Dorothy K. (*McGill*) M.Sc.: "Studies in iron metabolism." (Biochemistry: Denstedt, O.)

51-628 **Varverikos**, Emmanuel D. (*Sir George Williams*) M.Sc.: "The variability of the vascular supply to the ureter." (Anatomy: Martin, C.)

51-629 **Whitehead**, Howard A. (*Mount Allison*) M.Sc.: "The lethal and mutagenic effects of ultraviolet light on *Escherichia coli*." (Bacteriology: Murray, E.)

**M.A. Fall 1951**

51-630 **Bacarinos**, Eusthathios S. (*Athens*, Greece) M.A.: "State and fiscal monopolies." (Economics: Higgins, B.)

51-631 **Bird**, Thomas C. (*McGill*) M.A.: "Changes in the perception of tachistoscopically presented incomplete figures, in patients receiving electric convulsive therapy." (Psychology: Ferguson, G.)

51-632 **Dickson**, Delphine M. (*London*, England) M.A.: "The contribution of human ecology to physical planning." (Sociology: Dawson, C.)

51-633 **Eccles**, William J. (*McGill*) M.A.: "Jean Bochart de Champigny, intendant of New France 1686-1702." (History: Cooper, J.)

51-634 **Glover**, Thomas W. (*Mount Allison*) M.A.: "Les idées politiques et sociales de Victor Hugo en exil d'après ses discours et sa correspondance." (French: Furness, L.)

51-635 **Haywood**, Bruce (*McGill*) M.A.: "Studien zu Goethes Bearbeitung von Shakespeares 'Romeo und Julia'." (German: Graff, W.)

51-636 **Hersh**, Jacob (*Sir George Williams*) M.A.: "Clergymen in George Eliot and Thomas Hardy." (English: Files, H.)

51-637 **Iversen**, James E. (*McGill*) M.A.: "The social ideas of William Faulkner." (English: Files, H.)

51-638 **Lyman**, Bernard E. (*Grinnell*) M.A.: "Concrete mindedness and rigidity: a comparison of abstract-concrete mindedness in relation to behavioral rigidity." (Psychology: Luchins, A.)

51-639 **Melzak**, Adrienne (*McGill*) M.A.: "Villon et Baudelaire, poètes de Paris." (French: Nardin, P.)

51-640 **Merrill**, Gordon C. (*McGill*) M.A.: "The human geography of the Lesser Slave Lake area of central Alberta." (Geography: Zaborski, B.)

51-641 **Scheier**, Ivan H. (*Union*) M.A.: "A factorial analysis of some tests of rigidity." (Psychology: Ferguson, G.)

51-642 **Sievwright**, Eric C. (*London*, England) M.A.: "The efficacy of advertising expenditures: the consumer's view." (Economics: Beach, E.)

51-643 **Smith**, Charles J. (*Buffalo*) M.A.: "Effect of anterior and posterior lesions in the cerebral cortex of rats on performance in the closed field intelligence test." (Psychology: Hebb, D.)

51-644 **Taylor**, Harland W. (*Hamilton*) M.A.: "The English cloth economy, 1550-1640." (History: Adair, E.)

**M.Com. Fall 1951**

51-645 **Broadbent**, Arnot W. (*New Zealand*) M.Com.: "The impact of international prices on the New Zealand economy." (Economics: Marsh, D.)

## ANNUAL LISTING

**Ph.D. Spring 1952**

52-001 **Baerg**, Abraham P. (*McGill*) Ph.D.: "Silver-silver ion exchange reactions." (Chemistry: Winkler, C.)

52-002 **Batzold**, John S. (*Western*) Ph.D.: "Reactions in dissociated hydrogen peroxide vapour." (Chemistry: Winkler, C.)

52-003 **Baxter**, Robert M. (*Mount Allison*) Ph.D.: "Studies on biotin metabolism." (Biochemistry: Quastel, J.)

52-004 **Bekefi**, George (*London*, England) Ph.D.: "Near-field acoustic diffraction and a comparison with elctro-magnetic waves." (Physics: Woonton, G.)

52-005 **Borts**, Robert B. (*McGill*) Ph.D.: "The effect of the directivity of the probe upon the measurement of near-field diffraction patterns." (Physics: Woonton, G.)

52-006 **Breitman**, Leo (*McGill*) Ph.D.: "The reaction of nitrogen atoms with propane." (Chemistry: Winkler, C.)

52-007 **Campbell**, John D. (*McMaster*) Ph.D.: "The paleobotony and stratigraphic sequence of the Klondike muck deposits." (Botany: Roscoe, M.)

52-008 **Carroll**, Murray N. (*British Columbia*) Ph.D.: "Swelling studies of some natural and synthetic fibers." (Chemistry: Maass, O.)

52-009 **Darlington**, Walter A. (*McGill*) Ph.D.: "Absorption studies with isolated surviving intestine." (Biochemistry: Quastel, J.)

52-010 **Dufresne**, Cyrille (*Laval*) Ph.D.: "A study of the Kaniapiskau system in the Burnt Creek-Goodwood area, New Quebec and Labrador, Newfoundland." (Geological Sciences: Gill, J.)

52-011 **Dugas**, Jean (*Montréal*) Ph.D.: "Geology of the Perth map-area, Lanark and Leeds counties, Ontario." (Geological Sciences: Clark, T.)

52-012 **Eakins**, Peter R. (*McGill*) Ph.D.: "Geological settings of malartic gold deposits, P.Q." (Geological Sciences: Gill, J.)

52-013 **Girard**, Kenneth F. (*Siena*) Ph.D.: "Observations on the influence of a sustained monocytosis upon the anitbody response in rabbits to various antigens." (Bacteriology: Murray, E.)

52-014 **Guthrie**, Donald A. (*Manitoba*) Ph.D.: "Studies on the synthesis of papaverine." (Chemistry: Purves, C.)

52-015 **Hay**, Donald R. (*Western*) Ph.D.: "The measurement and interpretation of the radar cross-sections of aircraft models." (Physics: Woonton, G.)

52-016 **Hiltz**, Arnold A. (*Acadia*) Ph.D.: "Diffusion of radioactive iodoprene in gels." (Chemistry: Winkler, C.)

52-017 **Hopkins**, Nigel J. (*McGill*) Ph.D.: "Scintillation spectrometry with sodium iodide crystals." (Physics: Foster, J.)

52-018 **Hosein**, Esau A. (*McGill*) Ph.D.: "The influence of benzimidazole ontenzyme systems." (Biochemistry: Denstedt, O.)

52-019 **Hoyt**, Ruth (*Boston*) Ph.D.: "Intellectual functioning in schizophrenic patients with lobotomy." (Psychology: Hebb, D.)

52-020 **Johnson**, Frederick A. (*Manitoba*) Ph.D.: "Investigation of radiations from new cadmium and silver isotopes." (Physics: Foster, J.)

52-021 **Johnson**, Willard J. (*McGill*) Ph.D.: "The effects of narcotics and other substances on tissue oxidations and on biological acetylations." (Biochemistry: Quastel, J.)

52-022 **McDougall**, David J. (*McGill*) Ph.D.: "The geology of Southern Pascalis township with special reference to the luminescence of certain minerals of the eruptive rocks." (Geological Sciences: Stevenson, J.)

52-023 **MacIntosh**, Robert M. (*McGill*) Ph.D.: "The finance of housing in Great Britain, 1919-1949." (Economics: Marsh, D.)

52-024 **Nelson**, Samuel J. (*British Columbia*) Ph.D.: "Ordovician palaeontology and stratigraphy of the Churchill and Nelson rivers, Manitoba." (Geological Sciences: Clark, T.)

52-025 **Pappius**, Hanna M. (*McGill*) Ph.D.: "Metabolism of erythrocytes during storage." (Biochemistry: Denstedt, O.)

52-026 **Proverbs**, Maurice D. (*McGill*) Ph.D.: "Residues of organic insecticides in soils." (Entomology: Morrison, F.)

52-027 **Riordon**, Peter H. (*McGill*) Ph.D.: "Geology of the Thetford-Black Lake district of Quebec, with special reference to the asbestos deposits." (Geological Sciences: Gill, J.)

52-028 **Rooney**, Clarence E. (*Saskatchewan*) Ph.D.: "The action of hydroxylamine hydrochloride in pyridine on methyl-beta-D-glucoside tetranitrate." (Chemistry: Purves, C.)

52-029 **Ross**, Mary V. (*Columbia*) Ph.D.: "A comparison of the effect of Einstellunx in different age groups." (Psychology: Luchins, A.)

52-030 **Simpson**, David H. (*McGill*) Ph.D.: "The stratigraphy, structure, and certain mineral deposits at the headwaters of the Spillimacheen River, B.C." (Geological Sciences: Gill, J.)

52-031 **Smith**, Norman E. (*New Brunswick*) Ph.D.: "A statistical problem in the geometry of numbers." (Mathematics: Zassenhaus, H.)

52-032 **Trick**, Gordon S. (*McGill*) Ph.D.: "The reaction of nitrogen atoms with propylene." (Chemistry: Winkler, C.)

52-033 **Vogan**, Eric L. (*Western*) Ph.D.: "An experimental determination of the dielectric properties of a metal-flake dielectric." (Physics: Woonton, G.)

52-034 **Whalley**, Basil J. (*Dalhousie*) Ph.D.: "The oxidation of hydrazobenzene by ammonium persulphate in homogeneous solution." (Chemistry: Winkler, C.)

52-035 **Wiebe**, Allan K. (*McGill*) Ph.D.: "The electrode behaviour of mercury, platinum, and copper." (Chemistry: Winkler, C.)

52-036 **Wolfgang**, Robert W. (*Ashland*) Ph.D.: "*Stephanostomum histrix* (Duj., 1845): taxonomy, morphology and biology of the adult and metacercaria with notes on distribution." (Parasitology: Cameron, T.)

52-037 **Yates**, Havelock H. (*McGill*) Ph.D.: "Physico-chemical effects of radio frequency fields." (Chemistry: Winkler, C.)

**Ph.D. Fall 1952**

52-038 **Biefer**, Gregory J. (*McGill*) Ph.D.: "Electrokinetic measurements on fibrous materials." (Chemistry: Maass, O.)

52-039 **Blake**, Donald A. (*McGill*) Ph.D.: "The geology of the Forget Lake and Nevins Lake map-areas, northern Saskatchewan." (Geological Sciences: Kranck, E.)

52-040 **Brounstein**, Cyril J. (*Saskatchewan*) Ph.D.: "The oxidation of periodate lignin with sodium hypochlorite at pH 12." (Chemistry: Purves, C.)

52-041 **Chaput**, Marcel (*McGill*) Ph.D.: "Calcium and pancreatic alpha cells in metabolism." (Biochemistry: Heard, R.)

52-042 **Cox**, Phoebe L. (*Mount Holyoke*) Ph.D.: "The preparation, distribution, and metabolism of iodo-prolactin labelled with $I^{131}$." (Anatomy: Leblond, C.)

52-043 **Davis**, Gordon R. (*McGill*) Ph.D.: "A nutritional investigation of *Oryzaephilus surinamensis* Linne." (Zoology: Stanley, J.)

52-044 **Eadie**, Frank S. (*McGill*) Ph.D.: "Analysis of protein disintegration under proton bombardment." (Physics: Foster, J.)

52-045 **Gesser**, Hyman (*Loyola of Montréal*) Ph.D.: "The reactions of nitrogen atoms with butenes." (Chemistry: Winkler, C.)

52-046 **Girvin**, Grace T. (*Hunter*) Ph.D.: "The isolation of 'choline acetylase' from *Lactobacillus plantarum*." (Bacteriology: )tevenson, J.)

52-047 **Harrower**, George A. (*Western*) Ph.D.: "The energy spectra of secondary electrons from copper and silver." (Physics: Woonton, G.)

52-048 **Irwin**, Mary I. (*Saskatchewan*) Ph.D.: "The problem of determining physiological fuel values of the primary nutrients of foods, with particular reference to digestibility." (Nutrition: Crampton, E.)

52-049 **Keeping**, Kimball J. (*McGill*) Ph.D.: "Precision microwave measurements using resonance curves." (Electrical Engineering: Chipman, R.)

52-050 **Kushner**, Donn J. (*Harvard*) Ph.D.: "Studies on enzymatic adaptation in micro-organisms." (Biochemistry: Quastel, J.)

52-051 **Lloyd**, Lewis E. (*McGill*) Ph.D.: "Coefficients of apparent digestibility as indices of the nutritional value of rations." (Nutrition: Crampton, E.)

52-052 **Luner**, Charles (*Loyola of Montréal*) Ph.D.: "Part I. Diffusion studies of polyisobutylene. Part II. Kinetic stud6es of hydroxyl free radical. Part III. The reactions of nitrogen atoms with cis-butene-2 and isobutene." (Chemistry: Winkler, C.)

52-053 **McKillican**, Mary E. (*Manitoba*) Ph.D.: "The oxidation of wheat starch with hypochlorous acid." (Chemistry: Purves, C.)

52-054 **Maclure**, Kenneth C. (*McGill*) Ph.D.: "Properties of some neutron deficient isotopes of strontium, indium, and gallium." (Physics: Foster, J.)

52-055 **Manchester**, Donald F. (*Queen's*) Ph.D.: "Oxidation and methylation of the accessible fraction of cellulose." (Chemistry: Purves, C.)

52-056 **Maranda**, Jean-Marie A. (*Montréal*) Ph.D.: "On P-adic integral representations of finite groups." (Mathematics: Zassenhaus, H.)

52-057 **Margolis**, Leo (*McGill*) Ph.D.: "Studies on parasites and diseases of marine and anadromous fish from the Canadian Pacific coast." (Parasitology: Cameron, T.)

52-058 **Milner**, Brenda A. (*Cambridge*, England) Ph.D.: "Intellectual effects of temporal-lobe damage in man." (Psychology: Hebb, D.)

52-059 **Murdock**, James D. (*McGill*) Ph.D.: "Sterols and terpenes from spruce wood bark." (Chemistry: Purves, C.)

52-060 **Roberts**, Henry L. (*Texas*) Ph.D.: "Alterations in speech produced by cerebral stimulation and excision." (Neurology & Neurosurgery: Penfield, W.)

52-061 **Singer**, Bertha (*McGill*) Ph.D.: "Measurement of sodium-retaining substances in human urine." (Experimental Medicine: Venning, E.)

52-062 **Versteeg**, Joseph (*Western*) Ph.D.: "The reaction of nitrogen atoms with ethylene and acetylene." (Chemistry: Winkler, C.)

52-063 **Viron**, Silvio J. (*Queen's*) Ph.D.: "Nitration of 2-aminopyridines and 2-aminothiazoles." (Chemistry: Taurins, A.)

52-064 **Walker**, George W. (*Saskatchewan*) Ph.D.: "Cytology of caryopsis development in *Triticum-Agropyron* amphiploids." (Genetics: Boyes, J.)

52-065 **Wanklyn**, David I. (*Oxford*, England) Ph.D.: "Fast neutron reactions in carbon, oxygen, and neon." (Physics: Terroux, F.)

52-066 **Weldon**, John C. (*McGill*) Ph.D.: "On the theory of distribution." (Economics: Keirstead, B.)

52-067 **Whittier**, Angus C. (*Royal Military College*) Ph.D.: "Fast negative hydrogen ions." (Physics: Terroux, F.)

52-068 **Wigdor**, Blossom T. (*McGill*) Ph.D.: "An approach to personality through the investigation of perceptual behaviour." (Psychology: Luchins, A.)

52-069 **Wu**, Liang Y. (*Lingnan*, China) Ph.D.: "Life history studies on three genera of trematodes found in the Ottawa River." (Parasitology: Cameron, T.)

52-070 **Yaphe**, Wilfred (*McGill*) Ph.D.: "A study of the physiology of *Sporocytophaga* strains isolated from soils." (Agricultural Bacteriology: Gray, P.)

M.Eng. Spring 1952

52-500 **Beauregard**, John P. (*Loyola of Montréal*) M.Eng.: "The mixing of cold air jets with a hot gas stream." (Mechanical Engineering: Mordell, D.)

52-501 **Greenwood**, Stuart W. (*Bristol*, England) M.Eng.: "Instrumentation for flame temperature determination." (Mechanical Engineering: Mordell, D.)

52-502 **Groome**, George R. (*McGill*) M.Eng.: "The frequency conversion properties of transistors between 500 Kc. and 10 Mc." (Electrical Engineering: Howes, F.)

52-503 **LeMesurier**, Kenneth A. (*McGill*) M.Eng.: "The effects on the exhaust gas composition and combustion processes of the addition of oxygen or water vapour to the air intake of a diesel engine." (Chemical Engineering: Mordell, D.)

52-504 **Lorimer** Harry P. (*Manitoba*) M.Eng.: "Oblique impact on soils." (Civil Engineering & Applied Mechanics: Jamieson, R.)

52-505 **Martin**, William S. (*McGill*) M.Eng.: "The measurement and recording of intragastric electromotive force." (Electrical Engineering: Howes, F.)

52-506 **Morton**, Ernest R. (*McGill*) M.Eng.: "Performance of a forced circulation evaporator." (Chemical Engineering: Gauvin, W.)

52-507 **Palsson**, Petur (*McGill*) M.Eng.: "Performance of a cascade refrigerating system." (Chemical Engineering: Gauvin, W.)

52-508 **Phillips**, Lorne A. (*McGill*) M.Eng.: "Operating characteristics of a diesel driven heat pump." (Chemical Engineering: Gauvin, W.)

52-509 **Pinder**, Kenneth L. (*McGill*) M.Eng.: "The fundamentals of spray drying." (Chemical Engineering: Gauvin, W.)

52-510 **Schaus**, Orland O. (*McGill*) M.Eng.: "Heat-transfer coefficients for mixtures of condensable and noncondensable vapours." (Chemical Engineering: Phillips, J.)

M.Sc. Spring 1952

52-511 **Baldwin**, Maitland (*Queen's*) M.Sc.: "Functional representation in the temporal lobe of man: a study of response to electrical stimulation." (Neurology & Neurosurgery: Hebb, D.)

52-512 **Baxter**, James D. (*McGill*) M.Sc.: "The histamine content of allergic and non-allergic human nasal mucous membrane with simultaneous observations on the eosinophils." (Experimental Medicine: Rose, B.)

52-513 **Brown**, Norman E. (*McGill*) M.Sc.: "The geology of the Buchans Junction area, Newfoundland." (Geological Sciences: Riddell, J.)

52-514 **Burgess**, Ralph C. (*McGill*) M.Sc.: "Vitamin requirements for hatchability and early chick growth." (Poultry Husbandry: Nikolaiczuk, N.)

52-515 **Cairns**, Robert R. (*Toronto*) M.Sc.: "A method of conducting agricultural experiments in remote areas." (Agronomy: Steppler, H.)

52-516 **Carroll**, William J. (*Dalhousie*) M.Sc.: "The biology and external morphology of the hemlock looper, Lambdina *fiscellaria fiscellaria* (Guenée), in Newfoundland." (Entomology: DuPorte, E.)

52-517 **Clark**, John (*New Brunswick*) M.Sc.: "The water requirements of yellow birch." (Botany: Gibbs, R.)

52-518 **Clark**, Robert V. (*McGill*) M.Sc.: "Studies on the role of the toxic substances produced by *Helminthosporium sativum* P.K. & B. in its parasitism." (Plant Pathology: Coulson, J.)

52-519 **Comtois**, Romuald D. (*McGill*) M.Sc.: "Differential characterization and selection of staphylococcus bacteriophages." (Bacteriology & Immunology: Kalz, G.)

52-520 **Deland**, Andre N. (*Montréal*) M.Sc.: "The geology of part of the Three Rivers map area, Quebec." (Geological Sciences: Kranck, E.)

52-521 **Dennis**, Donald A. (*McGill*) M.Sc.: "Studies on diethyl quinolate." (Chemistry: Taurins, A.)

52-522 **Dewdney**, John W. (*McMaster*) M.Sc.: "The identification of some radioactive products from the proton bombardment of iodine and iodine salts." (Physics: Foster, J.)

52-523 **Gardiner**, Lorne M. (*New Brunswick*) M.Sc.: "A comparative morphology of *Monochamus notatus* (Drury) and *M. scutellatus* (Say) (*Coleoptera: Cerembycidae*)." (Entomology: DuPorte, E.)

52-524 **Gorham**, Anne L. (*Dalhousie*) M.Sc.: "Developemnt of the female gametophyte and embryo in *Smilacina racemosa* (L) Desf." (Botany: Roscoe, M.)

52-525 **Gorman**, William A. (*McGill*) M.Sc.: "Acid intrusives of the Thetford Mines-Black Lake area." (Geological Sciences: Stevenson, J.)

52-526 **Grant**, Ian C. (*McGill*) M.Sc.: "The tinguaite and related dike rocks of Rosemount quarry." (Geological Sciences: Kranck, E.)

52-527 **Hansen**, Douglas R. (*McGill*) M.Sc.: "Differential growth rates in flax varieties and their relation to other plant characters." (Agronomy: Lods, E.)

52-528 **Hollett**, Charlotte (*McGill*) M.Sc.: "Studies on the absorption and excretion of silicon." (Biochemistry: Denstedt, O.)

52-529 **Jacobs**, Ross D. (*McGill*) M.Sc.: "Study of diphosphopyridine nucleotide in the erythrocytes." (Biochemistry: Denstedt, O.)

52-530 **Kean**, Eccleston A. (*Toronto*) M.Sc.: "Studies on fat digestibility in experimental animals and some factors affecting its estimation." (Nutrition: Crampton, E.)

52-531 **Klinck**, Harold R. (*Toronto*) M.Sc.: "Variation in root development of barley." (Agronomy: Lods, E.)

52-532 **Leroux**, Edgar J. (*Carleton*) M.Sc.: "The effect of various levels of nitrogen, phosphorus and potassium on the fecundity of the two-spotted spider mite *Tetranychus bimaculatus* Harvey." (Entomology: DuPorte, E.)

52-533 **Lyall**, Harold B. (*McGill*) M.Sc.: "Study of the Hornfels collar around Mount Bruno." (Geological Sciences: Clark, T.)

52-534 **Macdonald**, Roderick (*McGill*) M.Sc.: "The synthesis of $C^{14}$ labelled DDT." (Agricultural Chemistry: Baker, B.)

52-535 **MacDougall**, John F. (*McGill*) M.Sc.: "The Birch Lake copper deposit, Saskatchewan." (Geological Sciences: Riddell, J.)

52-536 **Mattinson**, Cyril R. (*Queen's*) M.Sc.: "A study of certain Canadian building and monumental stones of igneous origin." (Geological Sciences: Kranck, E.)

52-537 **Mauer**, Irving (*McGill*) M.Sc.: "Mitotic frequencies in the ganglia of larval stages of *Musca domestica* L. and *Drino bohemica* Mesnil." (Genetics: Boyes, J.)

52-538 **Nommik**, Salme (*Tartu*, Estonia) M.Sc.: "The results with the hemagglutination reaction in various types of tuberculosis." (Bacteriology: Kalz, G.)

52-539 **Richardson**, Howard P. (*Manitoba*) M.Sc.: "The action and efficacy of soil fumigants directed against the currant fruit fly, *Epochra canadensis* Loew (*Diptera: Trupaneidae*)." (Entomology: Morrison, F.)

52-540 **Robinson**, Arthur G. (*Manitoba*) M.Sc.: "A study of *Stethorus punctum* (Lec.) (*Coleoptera: Coccinellidae*) and other predators of mites in Manitoba." (Entomology: DuPorte, E.)

52-541 **Schiller**, Carl (*City College of New York*) M.Sc.: "The effect of ACTH and cortisone on skin and connective tissue." (Experimental Surgery: Baxter, H.)

52-542 **Slipp**, Robert M. (*Dalhousie*) M.Sc.: "The geology of the Round Pond map area, Newfoundland." (Geological Sciences: Riddell, J.)

52-543 **Thomas**, James B. (*New Brunswick*) M.Sc.: "Part I. Bark beetle development and associated insects in white and red pine logging slash. Part II. External anatomy of *Ips pini* (Say) (*Coleoptera: Ipidae*)." (Entomology: DuPorte, E.)

M.A. Spring 1952

52-544 **Adams**, William E. (*McGill*) M.A.: "Economic development and international trade." (Economics: Marsh, D.)

52-545 **Aligwekwe**, Iwuoha E. (*Ohio State*) M.A.: "An evaluation of the 1945 proposals for constitutional change in Nigeria." (Economics: Mallory, J.)

52-546 **Boswell**, William C. (*McGill*) M.A.: "The individual in the novels of Graham Greene." (English: Files, H.)

52-547 **Cobban**, Aileen A. (*McGill*) M.A.: "A regional study of the Richelieu Valley." (Geography: Summers, W.)

52-548 **Coombs**, Donald B. (*Western*) M.A.: "The Hudson Bay lowland, a geographical study." (Geography: Bird, J.)

52-549 **Lithgow**, Robert M. (*Western*) M.A.: "Land settlement in the Richelieu Valley." (Geography: Bird, J.)

52-550 **Meadowcroft**, James W. (*McGill*) M.A.: "The quarto of 'The Merry Wives of Windsor': a critical study, with text and notes." (English: Duthie, G.)

52-551 **Moser**, Shia (*Lemberg*, Poland) M.A.: "Mach and the Vienna Circle." (Philosophy: Klibansky, R.)

52-552 **Munro**, Vivian R. (*McGill*) M.A.: "Les milieux anti-sociaux dans les romans de Francis Carco." (French: Launay, J.)

52-553 **Pochopien**, Kazimierz M. (*Cork*, Ireland) M.A.: "The district of Brome." (Geography: Zaborski, B.)

52-554 **Rabinowitz**, Herbert S. (*City College of New York*) M.A.: "An examination of problem-solving rigidity and abstraction in brain-damaged individuals." (Psychology: Luchins, A.)

52-555 **Saint-Martin**, Fernande (*Montréal*) M.A.: "Les theories de la psychologie du langage et leurs rapports avec les modes d'expression littéraires contemporains." (French: Nardin, P.)

52-556 **Schwartzman**, Alex E. (*McGill*) M.A.: "Lewinian rigidity and the Einstellung test." (Psychology: Luchins, A.)

52-557 **Taggart**, William R. (*Manitoba*) M.A.: "Carlyle's handling of the 'Laws of Nature' concept." (English: Phelps, A.)

52-558 **Tomkins**, George S. (*Sir George Williams*) M.A.: "Some aspects of American influence on Canadian educational thought and practice." (Education: Currie, A.)

52-559 **Whallon**, William W. (*McGill*) M.A.: "The rhythm of the King James Bible." (English: Sprott, S.)

52-560 **Zweig**, Joseph P. (*Sir George Williams*) M.A.: "A comparative study of two remedial methods of group training in effective reading." (Psychology: Ferguson, G.)

## M.Eng. Fall 1952

52-561 **Clark**, George D. (*New Brunswick*) M.Eng.: "The input impedance of a full-wave dipole." (Electrical Engineering: Howes, F.)

52-562 **Drouin**, Paul-Emile (*Polytechnique*) M.Eng.: "The relation between head and discharge in a curved spillway." (Civil Engineering & Applied Mechanics: Craig, C.)

52-563 **Gunnarsson**, Gudni K. (*McGill*) M.Eng.: "Characteristics of an ammonia absorption refrigeration unit." (Chemical Engineering: Gauvin, W.)

52-564 **Kelton**, Michel R. (*McGill*) M.Eng.: "VHF propagation from an antenna located on a mountain." (Electrical Engineering: Howes, F.)

52-565 **Macrakis**, N. (*McGill*) M.Eng.: "Performance characteristics of a countercurrent spray dryer." (Chemical Engineering: Gauvin, W.)

52-566 **Srinivasan**, Malur R. (*Mysore*, India) M.Eng.: "The effect of variation of thermodynamic properties of the working fluid on the performance of compressors." (Mechanical Engineering: Mordell, D.)

## M.Sc. Fall 1952

52-567 **Avery**, Robert J. (*Ontario Veterinary*) M.Sc.: "A study of the methods and conditions for the isolation of pathogenic actinomyces from lesions in animals." (Bacteriology: Murray, E.)

52-568 **Baker**, Harold A. (*New Hampshire*) M.Sc.: "A study of the carotenoid pigments produced on various culture media by a strain of staphylococcus pyogenes." (Bacteriology: Kelly, C.)

52-569 **Bartoshuk**, Alexander K. (*Sir George Williams*) M.Sc.: "An electromyographic study of goal directed activity." (Psychology: Malmo, R.)

52-570 **Bordan**, Jack (*McGill*) M.Sc.: "Radar measurement of rainfall at attenuating wavelengths." (Physics: Marshall, J.)

52-571 **Burgess**, Glenn D. (*Saskatchewan*) M.Sc.: "Haematophagous ectoparasites of *Citellus richardsonii richardsonii* (Sabine) (*Mammalia: Sciuridae*) with notes on biology, distribution and relationship to endemic diseases in southern Saskatchewan." (Parasitology: Cameron, T.)

52-572 **Gold**, Lorne W. (*Saskatchewan*) M.Sc.: "On the relation of snow to meteorology." (Physics: Marshall, J.)

52-573 **Gordon**, Dina (*Toronto*) M.Sc.: "The effect of prolonged cortisone treatment on normal rabbits and on the development of experimental atherosclerosis in rabbits." (Pathology: Kobernick, S.)

52-574 **Grady**, John C. (*McMaster*) M.Sc.: "Distribution of acid volcanics in the Superior province of the Canadian Shield." (Geological Sciences: Gill, J.)

52-575 **Halperin**, Alex H. (*McGill*) M.Sc.: "Bacterial oxidation of bile acids." (Biochemistry: Quastel, J.)

52-576 **Hunten**, Janet L. (*Western*) M.Sc.: "Some optical properties of thin films of selenium." (Physics: McPherson, A.)

52-577 **Jenkins**, Marjorie M. (*Alberta*) M.Sc.: "A study of the accelerated aging of rayon textiles." (Agricultural Chemistry: Common, R.)

52-578 **Johnston**, Constance A. (*McGill*) M.Sc.: "The effect of sulfonamides on guinea pig complement." (Bacteriology: Kalz, G.)

52-579 **Marien**, Breen N. (*McGill*) M.Sc.: "Part A. Effects of resection of massive segments of large and small bowel upon fluid and electrolyte balance. Part B. Effects of spinal anesthesia and different grades of operative trauma upon fluid and electrolyte balance." (Experimental Surgery: Webster, D.)

52-580 **Moen**, H.P. (*Western*) M.Sc.: "Permittivity measurements of solids at frequencies less than 200 megacycles per second." (Physics: Woonton, G.)

52-581 **Moxley**, John E. (*McGill*) M.Sc.: "Studies in the inheritance of persistency in the lactation of dairy cows." (Genetics: Slatis, H.)

52-582 **McMorran**, Arlene R. (*Mount Allison*) M.Sc.: "Morphological and life history studies on *Entamoeba terrapinae* and its comparative morphology with *E. histolytica* and *E. invadens*." (Parasitology: Cameron, T.)

52-583 **Redkevitch**, Zenon (*Massachusetts Institute of Technology*) M.Sc.: "The reaction of 2,3-dibromoindone with pryidine." (Chemistry: Taurins, A.)

52-584 **Rounthwaite**, Harry L. (*McGill*) M.Sc.: "An investigation of the pulmonary circulation during hemorrhagic shock and resuscitation." (Experimental Surgery: Webster, D.)

52-585 **Sabean**, Allan T. (*St. Mary's*) M.Sc.: "A study of the Hantzsch pyridine synthesis." (Chemistry: Taurins, A.)

52-586 **Samuels**, Peter B. (*Hofstra*) M.Sc.: "Venous endothelium: its relation to thrombosis." (Experimental Surgery: Webster, D.)

52-587 **Schad**, Gerhard A. (*Cornell*) M.Sc.: "Helminth parasites in mice of the families *Cricetidea* and *Zapodidae* in eastern Canada." (Parasitology: Cameron, T.)

52-588 **Schnitzer**, Morris (*McGill*) M.Sc.: "Investigation of properties of cation-enriched leaf extracts and leachates." (Agricultural Chemistry: DeLong, W.)

52-589 **Scobie**, Thomas K. (*McGill*) M.Sc.: "Chronic remote vacal stimulation by radiofrequency." (Experimental Surgery: Webster, D.)

52-590 **Segal**, Louis (*McGill*) M.Sc.: "Linear modifications of Maxwell's electrodynamics." (Mathematics: Morris, T.)

52-591 **Shaw**, Walter M. (*Dalhousie*) M.Sc.: "The metabolism of histadine and histamine." (Experimental Medicine: Rose, B.)

52-592 **Stevens**, Bernard A. (*McGill*) M.Sc.: "Frequency modulation to increase radar weather information." (Physics: Marshall, J.)

52-593 **Taylor**, Lester J. (*McGill*) M.Sc.: "The bactericidal and bacteriostatic effects of laurylamine saccharinate." (Agricultural Bacteriology: Gray, P.)

52-594 **Tomiuk**, Daniel (*Loyola of Montréal*) M.Sc.: "Convex and subharmonic functions." (Mathematics: Kozakiewicz, W.)

52-595 **Tyler**, Nancy P. (*Acadia*) M.Sc.: "A study of the seasonal variation in the occurrence of air-borne fungous spores in Montreal." (Botany: Pady, S.)

52-596 **Verdier**, Pamela C. (*McGill*) M.Sc.: "Peptidase activity in the white blood cells of young and old subjects." (Biochemistry: Quastel, J.)

52-597 **Walker**, Bruce E. (*McGill*) M.Sc.: "Somatic chromosome numbers in the mouse." (Genetics: Boothroyd, E.)

52-598 **Wells**, Arthur F. (*McGill*) M.Sc.: "On the separation of nutritionally deleterious and innocuous fractions from the esters of thermally polymerized linseed oil." (Agricultural Chemistry: Common, R.)

52-599 **Willermet**, D.A. (*McGill*) M.Sc.: "Determination of the locus of miniature dominant, a new allele of *Drosophila melanogaster*." (Genetics: Slatis, H.)

M.A. Fall 1952

52-600 **Ballabon**, Maurice B. (*McGill*) M.A.: "A regional study of the Richelieu Valley: the urban centres." (Geography: Hare, F.)

52-601 **Corey**, Earl E. (*McGill*) M.A.: "Le moyen âge dans 'Notre-Dame de Paris'." (French: Furness, L.)

52-602 **Dick**, Helen (*Acadia*) M.A.: "Les heroines du théâtre de Maeterlinck." (French: Nardin, P.)

52-603 **Falk**, John L. (*McGill*) M.A.: "Some factors affecting the judgement of temporal intervals." (Psychology: Bindra, D.)

52-604 **Frankel**, Saul J. (*McGill*) M.A.: "Machiavelli and Hume as forerunners of modern political thought." (Economics: Watkins, F.)

52-605 **Laird**, James T. (*Colgate*) M.A.: "The concept of purpose in Kant's philosophy." (Philosophy: Currie, C.)

52-606 **Mahut**, Helen (*Sir George Williams*) M.A.: "The effect of stimulus position on visual discrimination by the rat." (Psychology: Hebb, D.)

52-607 **Mantzavinos**, A. (*McGill*) M.A.: "Organized labour and economic analysis." (Economics & Political Science: Woods, H.)

52-608 **Mitchell**, Kina M. (*McGill*) M.A.: "Paroles de vivant: la poésie de Saint-John Perse." (French: Nardin, P.)

52-609 **Puhvel**, Jaan (*McGill*) M.A.: "A study of Indo-European compositional prefixes of negative value." (Classics: Carruthers, C.)

52-610 **Walton**, Robert F. (*Western*) M.A.: "Le vocabulaire de la correspondance de Gustave Flaubert de 1854 à 1862." (French: Nardin, P.)

## ANNUAL LISTING

### Ph.D. Spring 1953

53-001 **Carbonneau**, Come (*Laval*) Ph.D.: "Geology of the Big Berry Mountains map-area, Gaspé peninsula, Quebec." (Geological Sciences: Clark, T.)

53-002 **Clermont**, Yves W. (*Montréal*) Ph.D.: "Histology of the seminiferous epithelium of the rat, hamster and monkey." (Anatomy: Leblond, C.)

53-003 **Conn**, John J. (*Manitoba*) Ph.D.: "Reactions and isomerism of beta-aminocrotononitrile and the reaction of aromatic Grignard reagents with beta-aminocrotononitrile." (Chemistry: Taurins, A.)

53-004 **Cooper**, Gerald E. (*McGill*) Ph.D.: "Geology of the Johan Beetz area, Saguenay County, Que." (Geological Sciences: Kranck, E.)

53-005 **Daoust**, Roger J. (*Montréal*) Ph.D.: "The fate of nucleic acids in resting and dividing cells." (Anatomy: Leblond, C.)

53-006 **Eartly**, Heidi H. (*McGill*) Ph.D.: "Separation of the direct effects of thyroxine from those mediated through other endocrine glands." (Anatomy: Leblond, C.)

53-007 **Fishman**, Sherold (*Saskatchewan*) Ph.D.: "The metabolism of electrolytes in preserved blood." (Biochemistry: Denstedt, O.)

53-008 **Greulich**, Richard C. (*Stanford*) Ph.D.: "Radioautographic localization of $C^{14}$ in tissues of rats following administration of $C^{14}$-labelled bicarbonate." (Anatomy: Leblond, C.)

53-009 **Hamilton**, Hugh A. (*McGill*) Ph.D.: "Correlations between high frequency and low frequency noise in a high frequency oscillator." (Physics: Woonton, G.)

53-010 **Henrikson**, Arne (*British Columbia*) Ph.D.: "New isomeric transitions of short life in gold, mercury and thallium." (Physics: Foster, J.)

53-011 **Hogan**, Howard R. (*McGill*) Ph.D.: "The geology of the Nipissis River and Nipisso Lake map-areas." (Geological Sciences: Stevenson, J.)

53-012 **Hogg**, David C. (*Western*) Ph.D.: "An indoor method for measurement of back-scattering co-efficients." (Physics: Woonton, G.)

53-013 **Hospadaruk**, Vladimir (*McGill*) Ph.D.: "The effect of chloride on the deposition of copper, in the presence of arsenic, antimony and bismuth." (Chemistry: Winkler, C.)

53-014 **Jablonski**, Werner L. (*Toronto*) Ph.D.: "Action of liquid ammonia on white spruce bark, extracted with methanol and water." (Chemistry: Purves, C.)

53-015 **Jowsey**, James R. (*Saskatchewan*) Ph.D.: "Calcium metabolism and the reproductive cycle of the fowl." (Agricultural Chemistry: Common, R.)

53-016 **Kalter**, H. (*Sir George Williams*) Ph.D.: "The genetics and physiology of susceptibility to the teratogenic effects of cortisone in mice." (Genetics: Fraser, F.)

53-017 **Kuzmak**, Joseph M. (*Manitoba*) Ph.D.: "Flow of liquids through cellophane." (Chemistry: Mason, S.)

53-018 **Linis-Linins**, Viktors (*Latvia*) Ph.D.: "Analysis in nonarchimedean spaces." (Mathematics: Zassenhaus, H.)

53-019 **Lunde**, Magnus (*British Columbia*) Ph.D.: "The Precambrian and Pleistocene geology of the Grondines map-area, Quebec." (Geological Sciences: Kranck, E.)

53-020 **McCuaig**, James A. (*McGill*) Ph.D.: "Experimental studies in rheomorphism." (Geological Sciences: Kranck, E.)

53-021 **MacLaren**, Alexander S. (*Queen's*) Ph.D.: "Peridotites of northwestern Quebec." (Geological Sciences: Stevenson, J.)

53-022 **MacLeod**, Donald M. (*McGill*) Ph.D.: "Investigations on the form-genera *Beauveria* and *Tritirachium*." (Plant Pathology: Pady, S.)

53-023 **Manley**, Rockliffe St. J. (*McGill*) Ph.D.: "Rotations, collisons and orientations in model suspensions." (Chemistry: Mason, S.)

53-024 **Matuszko**, Anthony J. (*Amherst*) Ph.D.: "Synthesis of 4-(dialkylamino)-pyridines." (Chemistry: Taurins, A.)

53-025 **Milford**, George N. (*Mount Allison*) Ph.D.: "The action of liquid ammonia on spruce chlorite holocellulose." (Chemistry: Purves, C.)

53-026 **Moulds**, Gordon M. (*McGill*) Ph.D.: "The alleged condensation of cellulose nitrate with sodium acetylide." (Chemistry: Purves, C.)

53-027 **Murray**, Francis E. (*Alberta*) Ph.D.: "The physical nature of the critical opalescence." (Chemistry: Maass, O.)

53-028 **Noonan**, Bernard (*Manitoba*) Ph.D.: "Induced representations of lie algebras." (Mathematics: Zassenhaus, H.)

53-029 **Oliver**, William T. (*Toronto*) Ph.D.: "Studies on the effect of phenothiazine, *in vitro*, on *Heterakis gallinae*." (Parasitology: Cameron, T.)

53-030 **Parsons**, Basil I. (*McGill*) Ph.D.: "Oscillographic studies on the effects of addition agents during copper deposition." (Chemistry: Winkler, C.)

53-031 **Pedersen**, Jorgen W. (*Danish Technical*) Ph.D.: "Studies on the hydrolysis of casein." (Agricultural Chemistry: Baker, B.)

53-032 **Peron**, Fernand G. (*Sir George Williams*) Ph.D.: "Biological interconversion reactions of $C^{14}$-desoxycorticosterone acetate and $C^{14}$-progesterone." (Biochemistry: Heard, R.)

53-033 **Reid**, Albert R. (*Dalhousie*) Ph.D.: "The oxidation of cellulose with chromic acid." (Chemistry: Purves, C.)

53-034 **Riddell**, John E. (*McGill*) Ph.D.: "Wall rock alteration around base metal sulphide deposits of northwestern Quebec." (Geological Sciences: Gill, J.)

53-035 **Schiff**, Harry (*McGill*) Ph.D.: "Theoretical calculations of electron capture cross sections." (Mathematics: Jackson, J.)

53-036 **Seidman**, Ruth (*McGill*) Ph.D.: 'Dielectric relaxation in cellulose containing sorbed vapours." (Chemistry: Maass, O.)

53-037 **Sharp**, Robert T. (*McGill*) Ph.D.: "On the diamagnetism of graphite." (Mathematics: Wallace, P.)

53-038 **Vincent**, Donald L. (*Acadia*) Ph.D.: "Xanthate methyl esters of simple alcohols and of cellulose." (Chemistry: Purves, C.)

53-039 **Whitehead**, Howard A. (*Mount Allison*) Ph.D.: "Bacterial response to ultraviolet radiation." (Bacteriology: Murray, E.)

53-040 **Whiteway**, Stirling G. (*Dalhousie*) Ph.D.: "Shapes of coexistence curves in the critical region." (Chemistry: Maass, O.)

**Ph.D. Fall 1953**

53-041 **Adams**, Glenn N. (*McGill*) Ph.D.: "Measurement of recirculation in flame stabilization." (Physics: Marshall, J.)

53-042 **Ashwin**, James G. (*Saskatchewan*) Ph.D.: "Studies on the pharmacology of histamine release." (Physiology: MacIntosh, F.)

53-043 **Back**, Robert A. (*Western*) Ph.D.: "The reactions of nitrogen atoms with the butanes." (Chemistry: Winkler, C.)

53-044 **Bexton**, William H. (*McMaster*) Ph.D.: "Some effects of perceptual limitation in human subjects." (Psychology: Hebb, D.)

53-045 **Boyd**, Donald H. (*Queen's*) Ph.D.: "Studies on the interactions of plasma proteins with ketosteroids: studies on the role of glutathione and ascorbic acid in biological oxidation mechanisms." (Biochemistry: Quastel, J.)

53-046 **Brickman**, William J. (*Alberta*) Ph.D.: "A study of periodate lignin lignosulfonic acids." (Chemistry: Purves, C.)

53-047 **Brownell**, Harold H. (*Queen's*) Ph.D.: "Hydroxyethyl derivatives of glucose and of cellulose." (Chemistry: Purves, C.)

53-048 **Burrow**, Martin D. (*McGill*) Ph.D.: "A generalization of the method of young operators and its use in constructing primitive idempotents for the representations of GL(2,q)." (Mathematics: Zassenhaus, H.)

53-049 **Choquette**, L.P.E. (*Montréal*) Ph.D.: "Studies on some helminths parasitic in the trout *Salvelinus fontinalis* (Mitchill) in Quebec." (Parasitology: Cameron, T.)

53-050 **Dahlstrom**, Carl E. (*Saskatchewan*) Ph.D.: "Neutron deficient isotopes of praseodynium." (Physics: Foster, J.)

53-051 **Francoeur**, Marc (*McGill*) Ph.D.: "Oxidation of carbohydrate in mammalian erythrocytes." (Biochemistry: Denstedt, O.)

53-052 **Fridhandler**, Louis (*McGill*) Ph.D.: "Part I. Chemical absorption from isolated surviving intestine. Part II. Paper chromatography of enzymes and other proteins." (Biochemistry: Quastel, J.)

53-053 **Gérin-Lajoie**, Jean (*Paris*, France) Ph.D.: "Internal financing of post-war investments in Canadian primary textiles." (Economics: Keirstead, B.)

53-054 **Grainger**, Edward H. (*Mount Allison*) Ph.D.: "On the age, growth, migratory habits and reproductive potential of the Arctic char (*Salvelinus alpinus*) of Frobisher Bay." (Zoology: Stanley, J.)

53-055 **Grasberg**, Eugeniusz (*Montréal*) Ph.D.: "On the use of time-concepts in the theory of production and of capital." (Economics: Weldon, J.)

53-056 **Heron**, Woodburn (*McGill*) Ph.D.: "Perception as a function of retinal locus." (Psychology: Ferguson, G.)

53-057 **Karp**, Dorothy (*McGill*) Ph.D.: "Measurement of anticipatory and direct responses to a painful stimulus in schizophrenic patients before and after lobotomy." (Pharmacology: Burns, B.)

53-058 **Kirkaldy**, John S. (*British Columbia*) Ph.D.: "Development of coincidence techniques for the study of high energy proton-induced reactions." (Physics: Westcott, C.)

53-059 **Langleben**, Manuel P. (*McGill*) Ph.D.: "Snow crystal growth and consequent fall pattern." (Physics: Marshall, J.)

53-060 **Lautsch**, Elizabeth V. (*Manitoba*) Ph.D.: "Studies on the histogenesis of experimental artheriosclerosis." (Pathology: McMillan, G.)

53-061 **Lesser**, Elliott (*Brooklyn*) Ph.D.: "The effects of hormones and related compounds on the growth of certain amoebae." (Parasitology: Cameron, T.)

53-062 **McCormick**, Glendon C. (*Dalhousie*) Ph.D.: "An aberration due to the limited aperture of a microwave optical system." (Physics: Woonton, G.)

53-063 **Mahon**, John H. (*McGill*) Ph.D.: "The determination of certain antioxidants in fats and their behavior in food products." (Agricultural Chemistry: Common, R.)

53-064 **Mamelak**, Rose (*McGill*) Ph.D.: "Anaerobic amino acid interactions in Cl. sporogenes." (Biochemistry: Quastel, J.)

53-065 **Moya**, Francisco J. (*Laval*) Ph.D.: "I. Investigation of some factors affecting the pituitary-adrenal system. II. Studies on the glycogenolytic hyperglycemic hormone of the pancreas." (Biochemistry: Heard, R.)

53-066 **Milks**, John E. (*Queen's*) Ph.D.: "The hemicelluloses of aspen wood (*Populus tremuloides*)." (Chemistry: Purves, C.)

53-067 **Peppiatt**, Harry J. (*Toronto*) Ph.D.: "The electromagnetic properties of obstacle-type dielectrics with regular and irregular structures." (Physics: Woonton, G.)

53-068 **Piggott**, Carmen L. (*King's*) Ph.D.: "The Stark effect in silver." (Physics: Foster, J.)

53-069 **Pollak**, John K. (*Sydney*, Australia) Ph.D.: "The nitrogenous components and the amino acid metabolism in the ovaries of *Ascaris lumbricoides*." (Biochemistry: Fairbairn, D.)

53-070 **Ridge**, Frank G. (*McMaster*) Ph.D.: "General principles for the planning of sub-Arctic settlements." (Geography: Hare, F.)

53-071 **Rogers**, James T. (*McGill*) Ph.D.: "Temperature distributions in heat exchanger tube plates." (Mechanical Engineering: Mordell, D.)

53-072 **Rubinstein**, David (*McGill*) Ph.D.: "The respiratory mechanism of the avian erythrocyte." (Biochemistry: Denstedt, O.)

53-073 **Sanderson**, Edwin S. (*Alberta*) Ph.D.: "The substances extracted by water from white spruce bark, pretreated with liquid ammonia." (Chemistry: Purves, C.)

53-074 **Sanyal**, Amiya K. (*Calcutta*, India) Ph.D.: "Xanthate methyl esters of glucose and of cellulose." (Chemistry: Purves, C.)

53-075 **Scheier**, Ivan H. (*Union*) Ph.D.: "An experimental study on the relation between manifest test content and factors." (Psychology: Ferguson, G.)

53-076 **Solomon**, Samuel (*McGill*) Ph.D.: "On the metabolism of ring B unsaturated estrogens and the urinary estrogens in the normal menstrual cycle." (Biochemistry: Heard, R.)

53-077 **Tink**, Roland R. (*Queen's*) Ph.D.: "The electrical conductance of tetraethylammonium bromide and chloride in nitromethane." (Chemistry: Schiff, H.)

53-078 **Weigensberg**, Bernard I. (*McGill*) Ph.D.: "Effect of age, hypertension and arteriosclerosis on the chemical composition of human arterial smooth muscle." (Biochemistry: Evelyn, K.)

53-079 **Wood**, John C. (*Alberta*) Ph.D.: "Purification and properties of methyl and benzyl-D-fructofuranosides and their tetraacetates." (Chemistry: Purves, C.)

53-080 **Woolverton**, Ralph S. (*Western*) Ph.D.: "The Lumby Lake greenstone belt." (Geological Sciences: Gill, J.)

53-081 **Young**, William L. (*McGill*) Ph.D.: "The iron bearing formations of the Michipicoten area, Ontario." (Geological Sciences: Gill, J.)

M.C.L. Spring 1953

53-500 **Glucksthal**, Andrew (*Budapest*, Hungary) M.C.L.: "The liability of the company director." (Law: Anglin, J.)

53-501 **Gyorgy**, Dezso (*Budapest*, Hungary) M.C.L.: "The rights of the minority shareholder." (Law: Anglin, J.)

53-502 **Kallos**, Tibere (*Paris*, France) M.C.L.: "L'enregistrement des droits réels dans la province de Quebec." (Law: Baudouin, L.)

53-503 **Ouimet**, Paul A. (*Mont St. Louis*) M.C.L.: "The law of mining rights in Quebec." (Law: Baudouin, L.)

**S.T.M. Spring 1953**

53-504 **Kingsford**, Maurice R. (*Toronto*) S.T.M.: "Origins of the constitution of the Church of England in Canada, being a study from the beginning of the Church in Canada down to the first provincial synod." (Divinity: Walsh, H.)

**M.Eng. Spring 1953**

53-505 **Bhasin**, Parkash C. (*Panjab*, India) M.Eng.: "Stresses in web and stiffeners in an all-welded plate girder." (Civil Engineering & Applied Mechanics: De Stein, J.)

53-506 **Chow**, David Y. (*National Sun Yat-Sen*, China) M.Eng.: "Thermal contraction and moisture creep in concrete." (Civil Engineering & Applied Mechanics: Jamieson, R.)

53-507 **Kennedy**, David H. (*McGill*) M.Eng.: "Stresses in a thin-webbed steel plate girder." (Civil Engineering & Applied Mechanics: DeStein, J.)

53-508 **McArthur**, Beverley D. (*Queen's*) M.Eng.: "The effect of variation of the thermodynamic properties of the working fluid on the performance of gas turbines." (Mechanical Engineering: Mordell, D.)

53-509 **Tweed**, William J. (*British Columbia*) M.Eng.: "Mechanical aids to control." (Mechanical Engineering: White, J.)

53-510 **Yano**, George E. (*McGill*) M.Eng.: "Pressure drop during evaporation of water in tubes." (Chemical Engineering: Gauvin, W.)

**LL.M. Spring 1953**

53-511 **DeSaussure**, Hamilton (*Yale*) LL.M.: "International law and aerial warfare." (Law: Cooper, J.)

53-512 **Fenston**, John (*Saskatchewan*) LL.M.: "*Res ipsa loquitur*." (Law: Cooper, J.)

53-513 **Hesse**, Nicky E. (*Freiburg*, West Germany) LL.M.: "The aircraft operator's liability." (Law: Cooper, J.)

53-514 **Hubscher**, Frank F. (*Sir George Williams*) LL.M.: "Aviation law in Canada." (Law: Cooper, J.)

53-515 **Martial**, Jean A. (*Bishop's*) LL.M.: "Government control of aviation in Canada." (Law: Cooper, J.)

53-516 **Nemeth**, John (*Budapest*, Hungary) LL.M.: "The nationality of aircraft." (Law: Cooper, J.)

53-517 **Peng**, Ming-Min (*Taiwan*) LL.M.: "Le statut juridique de l'aeronef militaire en temps de paix et en temps de guerre." (Law: Cooper, J.)

M.Sc. Spring 1953

53-518 **Chappel**, Clifford I. (*Ontario Veterinary*) M.Sc.: "The influence of hormones on experimental hepatic lesions." (Experimental Medicine: Johnson, L.)

53-519 **Charles**, Christine M. (*McGill*) M.Sc.: "A lymphocytopenic factor produced by soil bacteria." (Bacteriology: Stevenson, J.)

53-520 **Crysdale**, John H. (*Toronto*) M.Sc.: "An optical system for antenna measurements at microwave frequencies." (Physics: Woonton, G.)

53-521 **Dennis**, Arnett S. (*Acadia*) M.Sc.: "Interactions between continuous showery precipitation." (Physics: Marshall, J.)

53-522 **Densmore**, Arthur A. (*Queen's*) M.Sc.: "The design and construction of a double pulse generator." (Physics: Westcott, C.)

53-523 **Desbarats**, Marie-Louise (*McGill*) M.Sc.: "Studies on brain tissue metabolism: effects of composition of the suspension medium, pentobarbital, and age." (Biochemistry: Birmingham, M.)

53-524 **East**, Thomas W. (*Cambridge*, England) M.Sc.: "Turbulence in clouds as a factor in precipitation." (Physics: Marshall, J.)

53-525 **Etheridge**, David E. (*New Brunswick*) M.Sc.: "Comparative studies of cultural and physiological characteristics of *Fomes annosus* (Fries) Cooke from North American and European localities." (Botany: Pady, S.)

53-526 **Fluss**, Zdenek (*Bristol*, England) M.Sc.: "Pathogensis of atherosclerosis in relation to plasma lipids." (Pathology: Duff, G.)

53-527 **Giroud**, Claude J-P. (*Paris*, France) M.Sc.: "Adrenocorticotrophic hormone and intermedin." (Experimental Medicine: Venning, E.)

53-528 **Godard**, J.D. (*Queen's*) M.Sc.: "Wall-rock alteration of the Bridge River vein deposits." (Geological Sciences: Stevenson, J.)

53-529 **Gottfried**, Kurt (*McGill*) M.Sc.: "On the theory of radiative transitions in heavy nuclei." (Mathematics: Wallace, P.)

53-530 **Goyette**, Louis E. (*McGill*) M.Sc.: "The evaluation of comparative yield trials of maize for silage." (Agronomy: Brawn, R.)

53-531 **Groves**, Trevor K. (*McGill*) M.Sc.: "Mono-kinetic ion source for a single focusing mass spectrograph." (Physics: Foster, J.)

53-532 **Heckman**, Don E. (*McGill*) M.Sc.: "Neutron yields in p,n reactions." (Physics: Pounder, E.)

53-533 **Horlick**, Louis (*McGill*) M.Sc.: "The serum lipids in atherosclerosis." (Experimental Medicine: Duff, G.)

53-534 **Klugman**, Michael A. (*Rhodes*, South Africa) M.Sc.: "A study of post-Pleistocene deposits around Mounts St. Hilaire, St. Bruno, Johnson and Rougemont, Quebec." (Geological Sciences: Riddell, J.)

53-535 **Leeson**, John I. (*Glasgow*, Scotland) M.Sc.: "Petrofabric studies from the Shawbridge area, Quebec." (Geological Sciences: Kranck, E.)

53-536 **McCabe**, James (*Montréal*) M.Sc.: "The reaction of nitrogen atoms with cyclopropane." (Chemistry: Winkler, C.)

53-537 **Marler**, Peter de M. (*McGill*) M.Sc.: "A petrographic study of the base of the intermediate siltstone, Sullivan Mine, Kimberley, British Columbia." (Goelogical Sciences: Stevenson, J.)

53-538 **Martineau**, Real (*Montréal*) M.Sc.: "A study of certain factors affecting the adaptation of bird's-foot trefoil (*Lotus corniculatus* L.)." (Agronomy: Steppler, H.)

53-539 **Melamed**, Samuel (*McGill*) M.Sc.: "On norms of matrices." (Mathematics: Kaufman, H.)

53-540 **Mohiuddin**, Syed D. (*Osmania*, India) M.Sc.: "Cervical fascia: anatomic and clinical." (Anatomy: Martin, C.)

53-541 **Oler**, Norman (*McGill*) M.Sc.: "Fixed point theorems." (Mathematics: Zassenhaus, H.)

53-542 **Phillips**, William E. (*McGill*) M.Sc.: "On the influence of the gonadal hormones on nucleic acid content of the liver and kidneys of the fowl, with some observations on the effect of aminopterin on various responses of the fowl to gonadal hormones." (Agricultural Chemistry: Common, R.)

53-543 **Ross**, Robert G. (*McGill*) M.Sc.: "The microflora of apple leaves and its relationship to *Venturia inaequalis* (CKE) Wint." (Plant Pathology: Coulson, J.)

53-544 **Tiffin**, Brian F. (*Loyola of Montréal*) M.Sc.: "Classical Sturm Liouville expansion theory." (Mathematics: Kozakiewicz, W.)

53-545 **Vosko**, Seymour H. (*McGill*) M.Sc.: "Theoretical interpretation of radiation emitted in neutron capture reactions." (Mathematics: Jackson, J.)

53-546 **Williams**, Roscoe C. (*Manitoba*) M.Sc.: "Linear growth laws in corrosive reactions." (Mathematics: Wallace, P.)

**M.A. Spring 1953**

53-547 **Asimakopulos**, Athanasios (*McGill*) M.A.: "Seasonal variations in employment in Canada." (Economics: Beach, E.)

53-548 **Buchanan**, Donald R. (*Saskatchewan*) M.A.: "Land settlement under the Veterans' Land Act." (Agricultural Economics: MacFarlane, D.)

53-549 **Deitcher**, Samuel (*McGill*) M.A.: "The effect of physical effort on mechanization." (Psychology: Luchins, A.)

53-550 **Fonseca**, Owen W. (*McGill*) M.A.: "Family responses to the crisis of mental illness." (Sociology: Hall, O.)

53-551 **Hurst**, Norman (*McGill*) M.A.: "Education in UNESCO: the first five years." (Education: Hughes, J.)

53-552 **Keirstead**, Marjorie S. (*Oxford*, England) M.A.: "Jealousy in an unproductive society: the treatment of jealousy in some characteristic Restoration comedies." (English: Porter, S.)

53-553 **McGillivray**, R.G. (*McGill*) M.A.: "Trois formes de l'héroisme dans la littérature contemporaine: Bernanos, Malraux, Saint-Exupéry." (French: Larivière, H.)

53-554 **Merrill**, Lesly I. (*British Columbia*) M.A.: "Population distribution in the Riding Mountains, Duck Mountains, and adjacent plains in Manitoba and Saskatchewan, 1870-1946." (Geography: Zaborski, B.)

53-555 **Vallillee**, Gerald A. (*McGill*) M.A.: "Lucretian imagery." (Classics: Carruthers, C.)

**M.C.L. Fall 1953**

53-556 **Gosztonyi**, Paul M. (*Elisabethina*, Hungary) M.C.L.: "Constitutional problems of regional organization." (Law: Cohen, M.)

53-557 **Novotny**, Jan M. (*Prague*, Czechoslovakia) M.C.L.: "Canadian fiscal law." (Law: Cohen, M.)

**M.Arch. Fall 1953**

53-558 **Gordon**, George E. (*Manitoba*) M.Arch.: "An analysis of regulations and standing relating to building." (Architecture: Spence-Sales, H.)

**S.T.M. Fall 1953**

53-559 **Enger**, Knut (*Oslo*, Norway) S.T.M.: "The lay-movement in Norway and the Norwegian church." (Divinity: Thomson, J.)

**M.Eng. Fall 1953**

53-560 **Carruthers**, Frederick R. (*Queen's*) M.Eng.: "The input impedance of a half-wave dipole." (Electrical Engineering: Howes, F.)

53-561 **Geddes**, Leslie A. (*McGill*) M.Eng.: "A line operated electromyograph." (Electrical Engineering: Howes, F.)

53-562 **Lang**, Bernard (*McGill*) M.Eng.: "The engineering and economic aspects of equipment replacement." (Mechanical Engineering: White, J.)

53-563 **Martinek**, Frank (*Brno*, Czechoslovakia) M.Eng.: "Burning of liquid fuel in forced draft." (Mechanical Engineering: Mordell, D.)

53-564 **Matusiak**, Marvin E. (*Toronto*) M.Eng.: "The radiation resistance of resonant parallel strip transmission lines." (Electrical Engineering: Howes, F.)

53-565 **Stachiewicz**, Bogdan R. (*Bristol*, England) M.Eng.: "Design and development of a frequency-shift, voice frequency carrier telegraph without relays." (Electrical Engineering: Howes, F.)

53-566 **Sullivan**, Lorne J. (*Manitoba*) M.Eng.: "The mixing of cold air jets with a hot gas stream in a varying area duct." (Mechanical Engineering: Mordell, D.)

53-567 **Townsend**, David L. (*McGill*) M.Eng.: "Oblique impact on sand." (Civil Engineering & Applied Mechanics: Wilson, W.)

**LL.M. Fall 1953**

53-568 **Abdelmoneim**, Ismail A. (*Farouk*, Egypt) LL.M.: "The law of aviation in Egypt, a review of the basic concepts and future possibilities." (International Air Law: Cooper, J.)

**M.Sc. Fall 1953**

53-569 **Alivisatos**, John (*Athens*, Greece) M.Sc.: "Some aspects of glutathione metabolism." (Experimental Medicine: Mackenzie, K.)

53-570 **Averill**, Edward L. (*Cambridge*, England) M.Sc.: "Some aspects of stress-strain theories and their use in the interpretation of the fracture patterns in rocks." (Geological Sciences: Gill, J.)

53-571 **Baxter**, Donald W. (*Queen's*) M.Sc.: "On the functional and anatomical organization of the neural respiratory mechanisms in the cat." (Neurology & Neurosurgery: Jasper, H.)

53-572 **Beaulieu**, Maurice (*Montréal*) M.Sc.: "The absorption of antibodies *in vitro* by monocytes (large mononuclear leucocytes)." (Bacteriology & Immunology: Murray, E.)

53-573 **Bertrand**, Gilles (*Montréal*) M.Sc.: "Studies on cortical localization in the monkey: the supplementary motor area." (Neurology & Neurosurgery: Penfield, W.)

53-574 **Blake**, Weston (*Dartmouth*) M.Sc.: "Vegetation and physiography of the Goose Bay area, Labrador." (Geography: Hare, F.)

53-575 **Browman**, Mark (*McGill*) M.Sc.: "The effects of compression and the role of the hematoma in fracture healing." (Experimental Surgery: Webster, D.)

53-576 **Buchsbaum**, Solomon J. (*McGill*) M.Sc.: "Diffraction of microwaves by slits and elliptical aperatures." (Physics: Woonton, G.)

53-577 **Bunzl**, Arthur (*McGill*) M.Sc.: "A method for the study of drug action on spinal reflexes in the frog." (Physiology: Burns, B.)

53-578 **Cahn**, Shirley (*McGill*) M.Sc.: "Streptococcus pyogenes in scarlet fever and penicillin sensitivity." (Bacteriology: Kalz, G.)

53-579 **Carballeira**, Andres M. (*Havana*, Cuba) M.Sc.: "Some metabolic effects of pituitary growth hormone in human subjects." (Experimental Medicine: Mackenzie, K.)

53-580 **Clark**, David S. (*McGill*) M.Sc.: "The taxonomy of yeasts from apples." (Agricultural Bacteriology: Wallace, R.)

53-581 **Clifford**, Charles E. (*Carleton*) M.Sc.: "A Wilson cloud chamber study of the reaction $O^{16}$ (n,n alpha) $C^{12}$." (Physics: Terroux, F.)

53-582 **Cloutier**, Joseph A. (*Laval*) M.Sc.: "A scintillation dosimeter for X-rays." (Physics: Foster, J.)

53-583 **Cornwall**, Frederick W. (*Cape Town*, South Africa) M.Sc.: "The distribution of Na, K, Ca, Mg, Fe in metasomatic zones bordering diorite intrusives, and zones of sulphide mineralization, using a revised analytical technique in flame." (Geological Sciences: Riddell, J.)

53-584 **Crawford**, Donna J. (*Manitoba*) M.Sc.: "Studies on the nutritive value of some thermally polymerized edible oils subjected to steam distillation and subsequent urea fractionation." (Nutrition: Crampton, E.)

53-585 **Devitt**, James E. (*Queen's*) M.Sc.: "A study of the tissue mast cell." (Experimental Surgery: Webster, D.)

53-586 **Downer**, John L. (*McGill*) M.Sc.: "The role of the cerebral cortex in temperature discrimination." (Psychology: Zubek, J.)

53-587 **Fernando**, Derrick M. (*Ceylon*) M.Sc.: "A study of the non-susceptibility of buckwheat to microbial attack." (Plant Pathology: Coulson, J.)

53-588 **Francoeur**, Pearl (*Sir George Williams*) M.Sc.: "Studies on the storage of human erythrocytes at low temperatures." (Biochemistry: Denstedt, O.)

53-589 **Godin**, J.J. (*Montréal*) M.Sc.: "A study on some electrical properties of graphite." (Mathematics: **)

53-590 **Hamilton**, Erwin C. (*McGill*) M.Sc.: "Feldspar deposits of the Johan Beitz area." (Geological Sciences: Kranck, E.)

53-591 **Hampson**, Lawrence G. (*McGill*) M.Sc.: "Studies in therapy of hemorrhagic shock with associated myocardial damage." (Experimental Surgery: Webster, D.)

53-592 **Hilchey**, John D. (*McGill*) M.Sc.: "An investigation of potassium fixation by some Canadian soils." (Agricultural Chemistry: DeLong, W.)

53-593 **Ho-Yen**, Basil O. (*McGill*) M.Sc.: "The effect of management on soil organic matter." (Agronomy: DeLong, W.)

53-594 **Hurlbert**, Bernard S. (*Acadia*) M.Sc.: "The syntheses of dimethylaminoalkyl esters of indole-carboxylic acids." (Chemistry: Taurins, A.)

53-595 **Kashket**, Shelby (*McGill*) M.Sc.: "A study of diphosphopyridine nucleotidases in erythrocytes." (Biochemistry: Denstedt, O.)

53-596 **King**, Hamilton D. (*McGill*) M.Sc.: "Bacteria in soil surrounding the roots of barley and oats." (Agricultural Bacteriology: Wallace, R.)

53-597 **Kumamoto**, Yurika (*McGill*) M.Sc.: "Radio-autographic localization of injected calcium 45 and phosphorus in growing teeth of rats." (Anatomy: Leblond, C.)

53-598 **MacLeod**, Lloyd B. (*McGill*) M.Sc.: "Apparent effect of management practices on the phosphorus status of a brown forest soil." (Agronomy: DeLong, W.)

53-599 **McKay**, Gordon A. (*Manitoba*) M.Sc.: "An investigation of August maximum and minimum temperatures at Torbay, Newfoundland." (Geography: Hare, F.)

53-600 **Milne**, Allen R. (*Toronto*) M.Sc.: "The electromagnetic field within circular aperatures." (Physics: Woonton, G.)

53-601 **Neiman**, Gregory M. (*McGill*) M.Sc.: "The effect of adrenocorticotrophin on plasma protein regeneration in the rat following depletion by massive hemorrhage." (Experimental Medicine: Mackenzie, K.)

53-602 **Pedley**, Norah F. (*McGill*) M.Sc.: "A study of the action of some drug on frogs' spinal reflexes." (Physiology: Burns, B.)

53-603 **Prentice**, James D. (*McGill*) M.Sc.: "A study of background in scintillation counters used near the McGill cyclotron." (Physics: Westcott, C.)

53-604 **Rota**, Alexander N. (*Toronto*) M.Sc.: "Surface studies on the arterial intima." (Pathology: Duff, G.)

53-605 **Sangree**, Anne C. (*Wellesley*) M.Sc.: "A geomorphological study of the Stanstead area, Quebec." (Geography: Hare, F.)

53-606 **Shkarofsky**, Issie (*McGill*) M.Sc.: "Near field diffraction patterns on conical rectangular horn radiators." (Physics: Howes, F.)

53-607 **Warren**, George L. (*Manitoba*) M.Sc.: "A study of *Hypomolyx piceus* (De G.) (*Coleoptera*: *Curculionidae*) and its relationship to white spruce, *Picea glauca* (Moench) Voss." (Entomology: DuPorte, E.)

M.A. Fall 1953

53-608 **Collins**, Frank L. (*Indiana*) M.A.: "The impact of the railway brotherhoods on the Canadian National Railways." (Economics: Mallory, J.)

53-609 **Dale**, Frances M. (*McGill*) M.A.: "Osler as a humanist." (English: Hemlow, J.)

53-610 **Ferrabee**, Henry G. (*Queen's*) M.A.: "The educational function of museums in the vicinity of Montreal with special reference to historical museums and sites." (Education: Hughes, J.)

53-611 **Goracz**, Bela A. (*Budapest*, Hungary) M.A.: "Expected utility, risk, and the theory of economic choices." (Economics: Kemp, M.)

53-612 **Hollbach**, Reiner (*Michigan*) M.A.: "Problems of capital formation in underdeveloped countries with special consideration of capital imports and balance of payments problems." (Economics: Marsh, D.)

53-613 **Holt**, Irene M. (*Toronto*) M.A.: "L'esthétique de la Fontaine." (French: Larivière, H.)

53-614 **Jennings**, Peter R. (*McGill*) M.A.: "British foreign policy with regard to the Macedonian Question, 1903-1908." (History: Fieldhouse, N.)

53-615 **Pitt**, Jack A. (*Sir George Williams*) M.A.: "A study in the political and historical essays of Immanuel Kant." (Philosophy: Currie, C.)

53-616 **Rennie**, Douglas L. (*Sir George Williams*) M.A.: "The ethnic division of labour in Montreal, 1931-1951." (Sociology: Hall, O.)

53-617 **Robinson**, Patricia G. (*London*, England) M.A.: "A case study of psychiatry in relation to other medical specialities in a hospital." (Sociology: Hall, O.)

53-618 **Rodman**, Hyman (*McGill*) M.A.: "Informal behaviour of infantry recruits." (Sociology: Hall, O.)

53-619 **Shearman**, George E. (*Queen's*) M.A.: "The response of the secondary school to the needs of the 'non-academic pupil'." (Education: Hughes, J.)

53-620 **Spentzos**, George C. (*McGill*) M.A.: "L'ordre unanimiste de la guerre et le tableau des combattants dans 'Les hommes de bonne volonté'." (French: Launay, J.)

53-621 **Whimster**, Eleanor I. (*McGill*) M.A.: "The course of Butler's literary fame." (English: Dudek, L.)

53-622 **Woodfine**, William J. (*St. Francis Xavier*) M.A.: "The effect of foreign investment - Canada 1946-1951." (Economics: Marsh, D.)

M. Com. Fall 1953

53-623 **May**, Sydney J. (*McGill*) M.Com.: "An econometric model of the Canadian economy." (Economics: Beach, E.)

## ANNUAL LISTING

**Ph.D. Spring 1954**

54-001 **Adamek**, Stephen (*Western*) Ph.D.: "Amino acids as addition agents in the deposition of copper." (Chemistry: Winkler, C.)

54-002 **Adams**, William E. (*McGill*) Ph.D.: "The economics of development." (Economics: Marsh, D.)

54-003 **Andrews**, Douglas H. (*Dalhousie*) Ph.D.: "A new glucoside from the crude phlobaphene fraction of white spruce bark." (Chemistry: Purves, C.)

54-004 **Armstrong**, Donald E. (*Alberta*) Ph.D.: "The acceleration principle." (Economics: Keirstead, B.)

54-005 **Axelrad**, A.A. (*McGill*) Ph.D.: "The role of iodine deficiency in the production of goiter and thyroid tumors." (Anatomy: Leblond, C.)

54-006 **Bartoshuk**, Alexander K. (*Sir George Williams*) Ph.D.: "Electromygraphic gradients in mirror tracing." (Psychology: Malmo, R.)

54-007 **Bertalanffy**, Felix D. (*McGill*) Ph.D.: "Histology and histophysiology of the alveolar lung tissue." (Anatomy: Leblond, C.)

54-008 **Black**, P.T. (*McGill*) Ph.D.: "The geology of Malartic Gold Fields mine." (Geological Sciences: Gill, J.)

54-009 **Coles**, Clifford H. (*Ohio State*) Ph.D.: "Studies on the isolation, purification, and determination of enzymes in succulent plants." (Botany: Waygood, E.)

54-010 **Dunford**, Hugh B. (*Alberta*) Ph.D.: "The reactions of active nitrogen with ethyl, vinyl, propyl and isopropyl chlorides." (Chemistry: Winkler, C.)

54-011 **Faulkner**, Peter (*London*, England) Ph.D.: "Studies on the metabolism of D-glucosamine and N-acetyl-D-glucosamine." (Biochemistry: Quastel, J.)

54-012 **Fox**, Geoffrey E. (*British Columbia*) Ph.D.: "Topology of the field of p-adic numbers." (Mathematics: Zassenhaus, H.)

54-013 **Gendron**, Lucien J. (*Montréal*) Ph.D.: "The structure of butadiene dimers produced by a free-radical chain-transfer mechanism." (Chemistry: Nicholls, R.)

54-014 **Hilborn**, John W. (*Toronto*) Ph.D.: "Beta and gamma spectra of osmium and thenium isotopes." (Physics: Foster, J.)

54-015 **LeRoux**, Edgar J. (*Carleton*) Ph.D.: "The distribution and site of action of DDT applied externally (and internally) to adult house flies *Musca domestica* L. (*Diptera*: *Muscidae*)." (Entomology: Morrison, F.)

54-016 **Levy**, Samuel W. (*McGill*) Ph.D.: "The influence of heparin on fat metabolism." (Physiology: Swank, R.)

54-017 **Li**, Choh-luh (*Nanking*, China) Ph.D.: "Microelectrode studies of the electrical activities of the cerebral cortex." (Neurology & Neurosurgery: Jasper, H.)

54-018 **MacLennan**, Donald F. (*Dalhousie*) Ph.D.: "Double refraction of flow in high polymer solutions." (Chemistry: Mason, S.)

54-019 **Marchessault**, Robert H. (*Loyola of Montréal*) Ph.D.: "The effect of freeze-drying on the physical properties of cellulose fibres and paper. The capillary flow of liquids with entrapped air bubbles." (Chemistry: Mason, S.)

54-020 **Melzack**, Ronald (*McGill*) Ph.D.: "The effects of early experience on the emotional responses to pain." (Psychology: Hebb, D.)

54-021 **Mercer**, John H. (*Cambridge*, England) Ph.D.: "The physiography and glaciology of southernmost Baffin Island." (Geography: Bird, J.)

54-022 **Milner**, Peter M. (*Leeds*, England) Ph.D.: "Effects of intracranial stimulation on rat behavior." (Psychology: Hebb, D.)

54-023 **Morton**, Ernest R. (*McGill*) Ph.D.: "Crystallization of high polymers." (Chemistry: Winkler, C.)

54-024 **Mungall**, Allan G. (*British Columbia*) Ph.D.: "Noise in travelling wave tubes." (Physics: Wagner, S.)

54-025 **O'Donnell**, Vincent J. (*McGill*) Ph.D.: "The biogenesis of cholesterol and the estrogens." (Biochemistry: Heard, R.)

54-026 **Orvig**, Svenn (*Oslo*, Norway) Ph.D.: "Glacial-meteorological observations on icecaps in Baffin Island." (Geography: Hare, F.)

54-027 **Poole**, John B. (*British Columbia*) Ph.D.: "Studies on the micro-environment of the free-living stages of nematodes." (Parasitology: Cameron, T.)

54-028 **Potter**, Calvin C. (*Sir George Williams*) Ph.D.: "An economic analysis of accountancy." (Economics: Beach, E.)

54-029 **Povilaitis**, Bronys (*Lithuania*) Ph.D.: "Fertility in diploid and tetraploid red clover." (Genetics: Boyes, J.)

54-030 **Sampson**, Hubert (*British Columbia*) Ph.D.: "The effects of stress on the performance of individuals varying in responsiveness." (Psychology: Bindra, D.)

54-031 **Schaus**, Orland O. (*McGill*) Ph.D.: "Cathode processes during the electrodeposition of nickel." (Chemical Engineering: Gauvin, W.)

54-032 **Schucher**, Reuben (*McGill*) Ph.D.: "I. Glutamine metabolism in brain. II. Protein synthesis by glandular tissues *in vitro*." (Biochemistry: Quastel, J.)

54-033 **Stevenson**, Ira M. (*McGill*) Ph.D.: "Geology of the Truro map-area, Colchester and Hants counties, Nova Scotia." (Geological Sciences: Clark, T.)

54-034 **Wallen**, Victor R. (*McGill*) Ph.D.: "Antibiosis and some internally seed-hormone pathogens." (Plant Pathology: Coulson, J.)

54-035 **Wallerstein**, Harvey (*McGill*) Ph.D.: "An electromyographic study of attentive listening." (Psychology: Malmo, R.)

**Ph.D. Fall 1954**

54-036 **Antrobus**, Edmund S. (*Cambridge*, England) Ph.D.: "A study of the Witwatersrand system." (Geological Sciences: Clark, T.)

54-037 **Avigan**, Joel (*Hebrew*, Israel) Ph.D.: "Studies on the metabolism of fatty acids in animal tissues." (Biochemistry: Quastel, J.)

54-038 **Baker**, Harold A. (*New Hampshire*) Ph.D.: "The carotenoid pigments of staphylococcus pyogenes." (Bacteriology & Immunology: Stevenson, J.)

54-039 **Beelik**, Andrew (*Hungary*) Ph.D.: "Some new reactions and derivatives of Kojic acid." (Chemistry: Purves, C.)

54-040 **Bigelow**, Robert S. (*McGill*) Ph.D.: "Morphology of the face in the hymenoptera." (Entomology: DuPorte, E.)

54-041 **Brown**, William T. (*McGill*) Ph.D.: "The metabolism of alkylthioacids." (Biochemistry: Quastel, J.)

54-042 **Cipera**, John D. (*Prague*, Czechoslovakia) Ph.D.: "The synthesis of peptide bonds." (Chemistry: Nicholls, R.)

54-043 **Clayton**, Blanche-Petite (*British Columbia*) Ph.D.: "A study of accessory sex structures of the rat and mouse." (Zoology: Scott, C.)

54-044 **Corbett**, David C. (*Toronto*) Ph.D.: "Immigration, population growth and Canadian economic development." (Economics: Keirstead, B.)

54-045 **Crawford**, Gerald J. (*Dalhousie*) Ph.D.: "Studies with spin echoes." (Physics: Foster, J.)

54-046 **Dekaban**, Anatole S. (*Warsaw*, Poland) Ph.D.: "Congenital malformations of the central nervous system." (Neurology & Neurosurgery: McNaughton, F.)

54-047 **Ellis**, Clarence D. (*McGill*) Ph.D.: "Determinative factors in the formation of the *logos* concept in the Johannine literature with particular reference to the prologue of the Fourth Gospel." (Divinity: Caird, G.)

54-048 **Fisher**, Harold D. (*British Columbia*) Ph.D.: "Studies on reproduction in the harp seal (*Phoca groenlandica* Erxleben) in the northwest Atlantic." (Zoology: Dunbar, M.)

54-049 **Frank**, Arlen W. (*Acadia*) Ph.D.: "New syntheses of papaveraldine, isoquinoline and related open-chain compounds." (Chemistry: Purves, C.)

54-050 **Grafstein**, Bernice (*Toronto*) Ph.D.: "Spreading depression in isolated cerebral cortex." (Physiology: Burns, B.)

54-051 **Grossberg**, Allan L. (*California Institute of Technology*) Ph.D.: "Studies on the mechanism of histamine release." (Physiology: MacIntosh, F.)

54-052 **Jacobs**, Ross D. (*McGill*) Ph.D.: "The biogenesis of estrone and cholesterol in the pregnant mare." (Biochemistry: Heard, R.)

54-053 **Kalant**, Norman (*Toronto*) Ph.D.: "Some hormonal effects on ketosis." (Experimental Medicine: Hoffman, M.)

54-054 **Lewis**, John B. (*McGill*) Ph.D.: "The occurrence and vertical distribution of the *Euphausiacea* of the Florida current." (Zoology: Dunbar, M.)

54-055 **MacKay**, Donald C. (*McGill*) Ph.D.: "Cationic interrelationships in the nutrition of the corn plant (*Zea mais*)." (Agricultural Chemistry: DeLong, W.)

54-056 **McKinley**, William P. (*McGill*) Ph.D.: "Studies on the serum proteins of the fowl as affected by gonadal hormones." (Agricultural Chemistry: Common, R.)

54-057 **Mueller**, George V. (*McGill*) Ph.D.: "Experimental work bearing on the origin of hydrous nickel-magnesium silicate minerals." (Geological Sciences: Stevenson, J.)

54-058 **Murray**, Louis G. (*Cape Town*, South Africa) Ph.D.: "Wall rock alteration in the vicinity of base metal sulphide deposits in the Eastern Townships of Quebec." (Geological Sciences: Riddell, J.)

54-059 **Murty**, Grandhi V. (*Andhra*, India) Ph.D.: "A statistical study of concentration in the manufacturing industries of Canada." (Economics: Keirstead, B.)

54-060 **Onyszchuk**, Mario (*McGill*) Ph.D.: "The reaction of active nitrogen with propane, cyclopropane, cyclobutane and neopentane." (Chemistry: Winkler, C.)

54-061 **Prusti**, Bansi D. (*Banaras Hindu*, India) Ph.D.: "Geology of O'Connor Lake area, Northwest Territories with special reference to the mineral deposits." (Geological Sciences: Kranck, E.)

54-062 **Rao**, Bapoje K. (*Osmania*, India) Ph.D.: "The effects of temperature and atmospheric moisture on the behaviour of the horn fly, *Siphona irritans* (L.)." (Entomology: DuPorte, E.)

54-063 **Ravaris**, Charles L. (*Boston*) Ph.D.: "The histochemical localization of esterases in the central nervous system and other tissues of the dog." (Physiology: Burgen, A.)

54-064 **Sacks**, William (*Toronto*) Ph.D.: "Oxidation of spruce periodate lignin with alkaline hypochlorite." (Chemistry: Purves, C.)

54-065 **Scott**, Thomas H. (*New Zealand*) Ph.D.: "Intellectual effects of perceptual isolation." (Psychology: Hebb, D.)

54-066 **Sharpless**, Seth K. (*Chicago*) Ph.D.: "Role of the reticular formation in habituation." (Psychology: Hebb, D.)

54-067 **Smith**, Charles J. (*Buffalo*) Ph.D.: "Problem-solving in brain-injured rats." (Psychology: Hebb, D.)

54-068 **Srinivasan**, Malur R. (*Mysore*, India) Ph.D.: "Flame propagation at elevated temperatures." (Mechanical Engineering: Mordell, D.)

54-069 **Thomas**, James B. (*New Brunswick*) Ph.D.: "The identification of larvae of some species of bark beetles breeding in coniferous trees in eastern Canada." (Entomology: DuPorte, E.)

54-070 **Thompson**, Hugh R. (*Oxford*, England) Ph.D.: "Pangnirtung Pass, Baffin Island: an exploratory regional geomorphology." (Geography: Baird, P.)

54-071 **Thompson**, Norman S. (*Manitoba*) Ph.D.: "Further oxidations of spruce periodate lignin with chlorine dioxide." (Chemistry: Purves, C.)

54-072 **Walker**, Bruce E. (*McGill*) Ph.D.: "Genetico-embryological studies on normal and cleft palates in mice." (Genetics: Fraser, F.)

54-073 **Watts**, Trevor A. (*Manitoba*) Ph.D.: "The alkali-soluble hemicelluloses of black sprucewood." (Chemistry: Purves, C.)

54-074 **Willoughby**, Henry W. (*Ontario Agricultural*) Ph.D.: "Studies of ovary incubations and steroid constituents of the placenta from a mare treated with acetate-1-$C^{14}$." (Biochemistry: Heard, R.)

54-075 **Wiseman**, Sylvia (*McGill*) Ph.D.: "Economic planning for development in economies of arrested development with special reference to the first Indian Five Year plan." (Economics: Keirstead, B.)

**S.T.M. Spring 1954**

54-500 **Sass**, Frederick W. (*Shelton*) S.T.M.: "The nature of God in the writings of Nicolas Berdyaev." (Divinity: Thomson, J.)

**M.Eng. Spring 1954**

54-501 **Anand**, Tilakraj R. (*Panjab*, India) M.Eng.: "Supercritical flow in curved channels." (Civil Engineering & Applied Mechanics: Craig, C.)

54-502 **Cameron**, Edward L. (*McGill*) M.Eng.: "An investigation into some physical properties of rocks and their relationship to pressure problems in mines." (Mining Engineering: Morrison, R.)

54-503 **Coates**, Donald F. (*McGill*) M.Eng.: "Some effects of cation exchange on Leda clay." (Civil Engineering & Applied Mechanics: De Stein, J.)

**LL.M. Spring 1954**

54-504 **DeDongo**, Paul J. (*Budapest*, Hungary) LL.M.: "Progress toward the multilateral exchange of commercial air transport rights." (International Air Law: Cooper, J.)

54-505 **Heller**, Paul P. (*Vienna*, Austria) LL.M.: "Grant and exercise of transit rights in respect of scheduled international air services." (International Air Law: Cooper, J.)

54-506 **Koval**, Joseph (*Saskatchewan*) LL.M.: "Liability to third parties on the surface in air law." (International Air Law: Cooper, J.)

54-507 **Vaisoussis**, Constantine (*Athens*, Greece) LL.M.: "Aviation insurance: passengers and third parties on the surface." (International Air Law: Gasdik, J.)

54-508 **Wine**, Joseph R. (*Montana*) LL.M.: "Aerial warfare and international law." (International Air Law: Cooper, J.)

**M.Sc. Spring 1954**

54-509 **Aron**, Ivan M. (*McGill*) M.Sc.: "A variational approach to the equations of stellar structure." (Mathematics: Morris, T.)

54-510 **Avison**, Arthur T. (*McGill*) M.Sc.: "A study of the internal fractures caused by the deformation of scale models of geological structures." (Geological Sciences: Gill, J.)

54-511 **Carriere**, Rita M. (*McGill*) M.Sc.: "Inter-relations of growth hormone and thyroxine on metabolism and tissue morphology." (Anatomy: Leblond, C.)

54-512 **Carter**, George F. (*McGill*) M.Sc.: "The Dunham dolomite near St. Armand, Quebec." (Geological Sciences: Stearn, C.)

54-513 **Casserly**, Leo M. (*St. Patrick's*) M.Sc.: "The effect of chemical fertilizer treatment on culm diameter, crown development and plant height of three varieties of oats as related to lodging." (Agronomy: Lods, E.)

54-514 **Chambers**, Harriet A. (*Albertus Magnus*) M.Sc.: "Observations and comments on the reaction of *Trichinella spiralis* in hamsters receiving radioactive phosphorus." (Parasitology: Cameron, T.)

54-515 **Coffin**, Althea (*McGill*) M.Sc.: "The preparation and analysis of casein low in vitamins of the B-complex." (Agricultural Chemistry: Baker, B.)

54-516 **Cullen**, Chester F. (*Pittsburgh*) M.Sc.: "Changes produced by alimentary lipemia and large molecular substances in the intact circulation of the hamster: effect on the blood-brain barrier." (Neurology & Neurosurgery: Swank, R.)

54-517 **Cutcliffe**, Jack A. (*McGill*) M.Sc.: "The effect of three levels of nitrogen, phosphorus and potassium on the yield and quality of the canso potato." (Horticulture: Murray, H.)

54-518 **Eadie**, Dorothy A. (*McGill*) M.Sc.: "The metamorphic collar in the sediments around Mount Royal." (Geological Sciences: Saull, V.)

54-519 **Eliopoulos**, Hermes A. (*Salonica*, Greece) M.Sc.: "On a Hamiltonian treatment of fields with non-local interaction." (Mathematics: Wallace, P.)

54-520 **Ellis**, Derek V. (*Edinburgh*, Scotland) M.Sc.: "The littoral transition of eastern Baffin Island." (Zoology: Dunbar, M.)

54-521 **Flower**, Louis G. (*McGill*) M.Sc.: "Interactions of 75-Mev protons with the nuclei of photographic emulsions." (Physics: Foster, J.)

54-522 **Goodwin**, Brian C. (*McGill*) M.Sc.: "Enzyme studies of mitochondria from barley seedlings." (Botany: Waygood, E.)

54-523 **Hudon**, Marcel (*Agricultural Institute of Oka*) M.Sc.: "Biological studies of the onion maggot *Hylemya antiqua* (Meighen) (*Diptera*: *Anthomyiidae*) in the muckland areas of southwestern Quebec." (Entomology: Morrison, F.)

54-524 **Kapica**, L. (*Wales*) M.Sc.: "The purification and properties of pectin methyl esterase from *Cladosporium herbarum* (Pers.) link." (Botony: Pady, S.)

54-525 **Laufer**, Philip J. (*McGill*) M.Sc.: "Basic properties of Banach algebras." (Mathematics: Zassenhaus, H.)

54-526 **Laurin**, Joseph F. (*Montréal*) M.Sc.: "The sulphides and siderite of the Mathieu property, Kewatin Lake area, District of Kenora, Ont." (Geological Sciences: Saull, V.)

54-527 **MacGregor**, Alexander R. (*Galsgow*, Scotland) M.Sc.: "Chazy corals and reefs." (Geological Sciences: Clark, T.)

54-528 **MacLean**, Donald W. (*McGill*) M.Sc.: "Ghost River and related formations between the Athabaska and Smoky Rivers, Alberta." (Geological Sciences: Stearn, C.)

54-529 **MacLean**, Kenneth S. (*Dalhousie*) M.Sc.: "Investigation of carbohydrate-like components of aqueous extracts and leachates from leaves of trees." (Agricultural Chemistry: DeLong, W.)

54-530 **Rogers**, Charles G. (*McGill*) M.Sc.: "Soil bacteria that are resistant to benzenehachloride." (Agricultural Bacteriology: Gray, P.)

54-531 **Simard**, J. ( ) M.Sc.: "Investigations on cabbage yellows induced by *Fusarium oxysporum F. conglutinans* (Wr.) Snyder and Hansen)." (Plant Pathology: Coulson, J.)

54-532 **Stachiewicz**, Evva T. (*McGill*) M.Sc.: "The effect of nitous oxide on enzyme systems." (Biochemistry: Denstedt, O.)

54-533 **Sullivan**, Harry M. (*Queen's*) M.Sc.: "Mass spectrometric analysis of nitrogen." (Physics: Watson, H.)

54-534 **Trasler**, Daphne G. (*McGill*) M.Sc.: "Sex ratio of the offspring of ex-irradiated or nitrogen mustard treated male mice." (Genetics: Fraser, F.)

54-535 **Vessot**, Robert F. (*McGill*) M.Sc.: "Electron guns." (Physics: Wagner, S.)

54-536 **Vulpe**, M. (*Cluj*, Rumania) M.Sc.: "The renewal of the epithelium of the urinary bladder." (Anatomy: Leblond, C.)

54-537 **Waters**, William R. (*Queen's*, Northern Ireland) M.Sc.: "The production of fatty acids by ascaris lumbricoides." (Biochemistry: Fairbairn, D.)

54-538 **Wolofsky**, Leib (*McGill*) M.Sc.: "Geology of the Candego Mine, Gaspé North County, Quebec." (Geological Sciences: Gill, J.)

**M.A. Spring 1954**

54-539 **Armstrong**, Muriel G. (*Alberta*) M.A.: "The Canadian money market." (Economics: Marsh, D.)

54-540 **Brown**, Irving (*Sir George Williams*) M.A.: "Classical economic methodology and its critics." (Economics: Weldon, J.)

54-541 **Edmonds**, William A. (*Yale*) M.A.: "The trend towards secularism in Turkey, as exemplified by its educational development." (Islamic Studies: Berkes, N.)

54-542 **Farrell**, Edna P. (*Sir George Williams*) M.A.: "Guidance in democratic education." (Education: Hughes, J.)

54-543 **Halford**, Charles R. (*Sir George Williams*) M.A.: "Fifty years of life insurance investments." (Economics: Weldon, J.)

54-544 **Harvey**, Mary R. (*Toronto*) M.A.: "Society in the novels of Joyce Cary." (English: Files, H.)

54-545 **Leznoff**, Maurice (*McGill*) M.A.: "The homosexual in urban society." (Sociology: Westley, W.)

54-546 **Marler**, G.E. (*McGill*) M.A.: "Mathematics and matter in motion: a study of Galileo's 'New Science'." (Philosophy: **)

54-547 **Mennie**, William A. (*McGill*) M.A.: "The pattern of local public health organization in Canada." (Economics: Callard, K.)

54-548 **Molson**, Charles R. (*McGill*) M.A.: "The island of Senja in north Norway." (Geography: Hare, F.)

54-549 **Mujahid**, Sharif (*Madras*, India) M.A.: "Al'Afghani: his role in the nineteenth century Muslim awakening." (Islamic Studies: Fazlu-r-Rahman)

54-550 **Nielsen**, Niels H. (*McGill*) M.A.: "Steinberg's: a study in entrepreneurship." (Economics: Keirstead, B.)

54-551 **Pennie**, T.E. (*McGill*) M.A.: "The Canadian market for British exports and investments in the post-war years, 1945-53." (Economics: Keirstead, B.)

54-552 **Price**, John W. (*McMaster*) M.A.: "Education, technology, and the end of man." (Education: Currie, A.)

54-553 **Puhvel**, Martin (*McGill*) M.A.: "The strange case of 'Titus Andronicus'." (English: Duthie, G.)

54-554 **Qaysi**, Abdul W. (*Baghdad*, Iraq) M.A.: "Zahawi's innovations as a thinker and poet." (Islamic Studies: Bagley, F.)

54-555 **Sinclair**, Martin H. (*McGill*) M.A.: "Industrial geography of the Beauharnois canal zone." (Geography: Hare, F.)

54-556 **Van Leight-Frank**, Margit (*McGill*) M.A.: "The principle of individuation in Kierkegard's philosophy." (Philosophy: McKinnon, A.)

54-557 **Walmsley**, Norma E. (*McGill*) M.A.: "Canada's response to the international problem of 'displaced persons', 1947-1951." (Political Science: Callard, K.)

**M.Com. Spring 1954**

54-558 **Hutchison**, John (*Sir George Williams*) M.Com.: "Some considerations on the influence of transport on the economic growth of underdeveloped countries." (Economics: Marsh, D.)

**S.T.M. Fall 1954**

54-559 **Osborne**, Robert E. (*Sir George Williams*) S.T.M.: "The place of the second coming in the theology of the New Testament." (Divinity: Caird, G.)

**M.Eng. Fall 1954**

54-560 **Bula**, Peter J. (*Toronto*) M.Eng.: "The effect of oxygen concentration on flame propagation at elevated temperatures." (Mechanical Engineering: Mordell, D.)

54-561 **Campbell**, Hugh A. (*Manitoba*) M.Eng.: "Flange and stiffener stress in an all-welded plate girder." (Civil Engineering & Applied Mechanics: De Stein, J.)

54-562 **Chess**, Gordon F. (*Toronto*) M.Eng.: "The input inpedance of a full-wave dipole." (Electrical Engineering: Howes, F.)

54-563 **Finlay**, James E. (*Alberta*) M.Eng.: "The recovery of copper from copper matte." (Metallurgical Engineering: MacEwan, J.)

54-564 **Ghitis**, Albert (*Medellin*, Colombia) M.Eng.: "Stresses in the flanges of an all-welded girder." (Civil Engineering & Applied Mechanics: De Stein, J.)

54-565 **MacFarlane**, Ivan C. (*New Brunswick*) M.Eng.: "Oblique impact on sand (II)." (Civil Engineering & Applied Mechanics: Wilson, V.)

54-566 **Penton**, Reginald (*Toronto*) M.Eng.: "The use of Helmholtz resonators in the reduction of ventilation system noise." (Electrical Engineering: Howes, F.)

LL.M. Fall 1954

54-567 **Drion**, Huibert (*Groningen*, Holland) LL.M.: "Limitation of liabilities in international air law." (International Air Law: Cooper, J.)

54-568 **Swan**, John H. (*California*) LL.M.: "Liability for acts of agents and servants in international air law." (International Air Law: Gazdik, J.)

M.Sc. Fall 1954

54-569 **Allen**, Lloyd S. (*Dalhousie*) M.Sc.: "A study of electrogastrophic recordings." (Experimental Surgery: Webster, D.)

54-570 **Armstrong**, Robert A. (*Toronto*) M.Sc.: "Sub-audible noise spectra measurements." (Physics: Woonton, G.)

54-571 **Badior**, Mark A. (*Carleton*) M.Sc.: "A $180^0$ focussing beta ray spectrometer." (Physics: Foster, J.)

54-572 **Baer**, Harold G. (*McGill*) M.Sc.: "The nematodes of Egyptian birds." (Parasitology: Cameron, T.)

54-573 **Beaulieu**, Jacques J. (*McGill*) M.Sc.: "Some experimental investigations of magnetic probes for measurement purposes." (Physics: Bekefi, G.)

54-574 **Belle**, Edward A. (*Lincoln*) M.Sc.: "Nematode parasites of Egyptian reptiles." (Parasitology: Cameron, T.)

54-575 **Birks**, Richard I. (*McGill*) M.Sc.: "Cholinergic transmission in a sympathetic ganglion." (Physiology: MacIntosh, F.)

54-576 **Buller**, William K. (*Western*) M.Sc.: "An experimental study of the internal mammary artery implanted in the left ventricular myocardium, with special reference to variations in the operative procedure as it affects the implant, and to blood flow characteristics through the implant." (Experimental Surgery: Webster, D.)

54-577 **Cadet**, Charles M. (*McGill*) M.Sc.: "The effect of antibiotics in the laying ration upon egg-shell quality." (Poultry Husbandry: Nikolaiczuk, N.)

54-578 **Carriere**, Gilles E. (*Montréal*) M.Sc.: "The geology of the Suffield Mine, Sherbrooke, Que." (Geological Sciences: Riddell, J.)

54-579 **Ciplijauskaite**, Jurate E. (*McGill*) M.Sc.: "The influence of chloramphenicol upon anti-typhoid agglutinin production." (Bacteriology: Murray, E.)

54-580 **Collins**, William B. (*McGill*) M.Sc.: "Boron, calcium and magnesium nutrition of the strawberry as related to strawberry black root." (Horticulture: Taper, C.)

54-581 **Diena**, Benito B. (*Parma*, Italy) M.Sc.: "A toxin neutralizing substance from *penicillium cyaneo fulvum*." (Bacteriology: Stevenson, J.)

54-582 **Endler**, Norman S. (*McGill*) M.Sc.: "The influence of social factors on the autokinetic effect." (Psychology: Luchins, A.)

54-583 **Fontaine**, Marion (*McGill*) M.Sc.: "The planktonic copepods (*Calanoida cyclopoida, monstrilloida*), of Ungava Bay, with special reference to the biology of *Pseudocalanus minutus* and *Calanus finmarchicus*." (Zoology: Dunbar, M.)

54-584 **Freeman**, Peter V. (*Witwatersrand*, South Africa) M.Sc.: "A petrological study of the Munro asbestos 'A' orebody, Màtheson, Ont." (Geological Sciences: Stevenson, J.)

54-585 **Havelka**, Jaroslav (*Milan*, Italy) M.Sc.: "On the motivation of the rat in problem-solving." (Psychology: Thompson, W.)

54-586 **Hayes**, James C. (*Alberta*) M.Sc.: "Gentzen's formalization of the propositional and predicate calculus." (Mathematics: Lambek, J.)

54-587 **Heller**, Irving H. (*McGill*) M.Sc.: "Desoxyribonucleic acid content, cell densities and metabolism of normal brain and human brain tumours." (Neurology & Neurosurgery: Elliott, K.)

54-588 **Hoff**, Theodore F. (*Kansas*)• M.Sc.: "Studies on experimental allergic encephalomyelitis." (Neurology & Neurosurgery: Olszewski, J.)

54-589 **Horan**, Patrick J. (*Dalhousie*) M.Sc.: "An experimental study of the changes both histological and physiological occurring in patches of exteriorized gastric mucosa." (Experimental Surgery: Webster, D.)

54-590 **Isang**, Etim U. (*McGill*) M.Sc.: "The application of the heat unit theory to some cereal crops." (Agronomy: Brawn, R.)

54-591 **Jones**, Alun R. (*Bristol*, England) M.Sc.: "The analysis of the energy spectra of secondary emission from copper and silver." (Physics: Woonton, G.)

54-592 **Kapur**, Kanwal K. (*Panjab*, India) M.Sc.: "Effects of hypophysectomy, growth hormone and 2-acetyl-aminofluorine on pancreatic islets." (Experimental Surgery: Webster, D.)

54-593 **Loughheed**, Thomas C. (*Bishop's*) M.Sc.: "Studies on the taste of enzymatic digests of casein." (Agricultural Chemistry: Baker, B.)

54-594 **Mensah-Dapaa**, W.S. (*New Mexico*) M.Sc.: "Nematode parasites of Egyptian rodents." (Parasitology: Cameron, T.)

54-595 **Menzies**, Margaret H. (*Acadia*) M.Sc.: "The decay of active nitrogen." (Chemistry: Winkler, C.)

54-596 **Mozie**, James O. (*Howard*) M.Sc.: "Responses of *Cladosporium herbarum* (Pers.) link to growth regulating substances." (Botany: Waygood, E.)

54-597 **Nashold**, Blaine S. (*Indiana*) M.Sc.: "Observations on the thalamocortical projections." (Neurology & Neurosurgery: Olszewski, J.)

54-598 **Oborin**, Peter E. (*Saratov*, Russia) M.Sc.: "The role of the sympathomimetic vasomotor innervation of the cat's submaxillary gland." (Physiology: MacIntosh, F.)

54-599 **Pearse**, Charles D. (*British Columbia*) M.Sc.: "High-Q resonant circuits in the frequency range 600 MCS to 1600 MCS using parallel-wire transmission lines." (Electrical Communications: Chipman, R.)

54-600 **Percy**, Edward C. (*McGill*) M.Sc.: "Studies on epiphyseal stimulation." (Experimental Surgery: Webster, D.)

54-601 **Pritchard**, Ernest T. (*Carleton*) M.Sc.: "Observations on fractions prepared from thermally polymerized vegetable oils as related to their effects on the nutrition of the rat." (Agricultural Chemistry: Common, R.)

54-602 **Purvis**, John L. (*McGill*) M.Sc.: "A study of intermedin." (Biochemistry: Denstedt, O.)

54-603 **Simard-Duquesne**, N. (*Montréal*) M.Sc.: "Studies on the metabolism of silicon." (Biochemistry: Denstedt, O.)

54-604 **Stern**, Muriel H. (*McGill*) M.Sc.: "Psychological characteristics of three groups of Caughnawaga Iroquois Indians." (Psychology: Webster, E.)

54-605 **Strachan**, Alison A. (*McGill*) M.Sc.: "A taxonomic study of eye worms (*Thelaziidae*) from Brazilian birds." (Parasitology: Cameron, T.)

54-606 **Yurack**, Joseph A. (*Siena*) M.Sc.: "Antigenic characters in corynebacteria." (Bacteriology: Kalz, G.)

54-607 **Zemel**, Reuben (*McGill*) M.Sc.: "Studies of effect of pressure on bone crystals." (Anatomy: Leblond, C.)

**M.A. Fall 1954**

54-608 **Badgley**, Robin F. (*McGill*) M.A.: "Occupational stratification and evaluation." (Sociology: Elkin, F.)

54-609 **Beauchemin**, C-H. Guy (*Jean-de-Brebeuf*) M.A.: "L'art de la nouvelle chez Prosper Mérimée." (French: Launay, J.)

54-610 **Capelovitch**, Edward M. (*McGill*) M.A.: "Schumpeter's theory of long-run economic change: a study in economics and economic sociology." (Economics: Marsh, D.)

54-611 **Coldhagen**, E. (*Sir George Williams*) M.A.: "The withering away of the state from Marx to Stalin." (Political Science: Brecher, M.)

54-612 **Haydari**, Amir A. (*Tehran*, Iran) M.A.: "Some aspects of Islam in modern Iran, with special reference to the work of Sangalaji and Rashid." (Islamic Studies: Bagley, F.)

54-613 **Kortepeter**, Carl M. (*Harvard*) M.A.: "Turkish language reform: a step in the modernization of Islam in Turkey." (Islamic Studies: Berkes, N.)

54-614 **Lewis**, Herbert (*McGill*) M.A.: "Life and history in the philosophy of Ortega y Gasset." (Philosophy: Currie, C.)

54-615 **McCullough**, Edward E. (*Queen's*) M.A.: "The influence of the invasion of Belgium on Great Britain's entry into the First World War." (History: Fieldhouse, H.)

54-616 **Markson**, Doris M. (*McGill*) M.A.: "Candide chez les anglophones." (French: Launay, J.)

54-617 **Pickup**, T. (*McDonald*) M.A.: "John Donne's knowledge of medicine." (English: Malloch, A.)

54-618 **Piscopo**, Franco A. (*Rome*, Italy) M.A.: "Canadian citizenship." (Economics & Political Science: Mayo, H.)

54-619 **Richardson**, Nigel H. (*McGill*) M.A.: "A study of the relationship between ecological and non-ecological factors in the development of certain natural areas of Montreal." (Sociology: Elkin, F.)

54-620 **Al-Sawi**, Ahmad H. (*Fouad*) M.A.: "Muhammad 'Abduh and Al-Waqa'i' Al-Misriyah." (Islamic Studies: Bagley, F.)

54-621 **Siddiqi**, Mazharuddin (*Madras*, India) M.A.: "The image of the West in Iqbal." (Islamic Studies: Smith, W.)

54-622 **Singer**, David P. (*McGill*) M.A.: "The administration and scope of Canadian anti-monoply policy since the Second World War." (Political Science: Vineberg, P.)

54-623 **Stevenson**, Stanley W. (*Bishop's*) M.A.: "Shakespeare's hand in 'The Spanish Tragedy', 1602." (English: Duthie, G.)

54-624 **Sussman**, David (*McGill*) M.A.: "Matrix representations of the symmetric group in finite fields." (Mathematics: Zassenhaus, H.)

54-625 **Vogel**, Robert (*Sir George Williams*) M.A.: "The diplomatic career of Sir Fairfax Cartwright from 1906 to 1913." (History: Fieldhouse, H.)

54-626 **Walter**, H.A. (*Berlin*, Germany) M.A.: "Kritische Deutung der Stellungnahme Schillers zu Goethes 'Egmont'." (German: Graff, W.)

54-627 **Watts**, Aileen M. (*Toronto*) M.A.: "Le héros contre le milieu dans le roman canadien-français de 1938-1950." (French: Launay, J.)

**M.Com. Fall 1954**

54-628 **Davoud**, Raymond I. (*Cambridge*, England) M.Com.: "The past history, present crisis, and future prospects of the primary textile industry in Canada." (Economics: Kemp, M.)

54-629 **Stenason**, Walter (*McGill*) M.Com.: "Economic analysis of pricing problems in the transportation industry." (Economics: Marsh, D.)

54-630 **Sussman**, Edmond (*London*, England) M.Com.: "Some implications of a customs union: the Benelux case." (Economics: Marsh, D.)

## ANNUAL LISTING

### Ph.D. Spring 1955

55-001 **Anastassiadis**, Phoebus A. (*Athens*, Greece) Ph.D.: "Studies on the hexosamine and hydroxyproline contents of avian tissues." (Agricultural Chemistry: Common, R.)

55-002 **Angus**, Thomas A. (*Toronto*) Ph.D.: "Studies on the toxin of *Bacillus sotto* Ishiwata and on its toxicity against certain insect species." (Agricultural Bacteriology: Gray, P.)

55-003 **Armstrong**, David A. (*McGill*) Ph.D.: "The production of active nitrogen from nitric oxide and ammonia and the reactions of active nitrogen with azomethane and mercury diethyl." (Chemistry: Winkler, C.)

55-004 **Avery**, Robert J. (*Toronto*) Ph.D.: "The classification of the anaerobic actinomyces." (Bacteriology & Immunology: Murray, E.)

55-005 **Bachynski**, Morrel P. (*Saskatchewan*) Ph.D.: "Aberrations in microwave lenses." (Physics: Woonton, G.)

55-006 **Beach**, Horace D. (*Saskatchewan*) Ph.D.: "Drug addiction in rats." (Psychology: Bindra, D.)

55-007 **Bombardieri**, Caurino C. (*Alberta*) Ph.D.: "The study of the Mannich condensation of compounds containing the acidic-NH-group." (Chemistry: Taurins, A.)

55-008 **Bryce**, John R. (*British Columbia*) Ph.D.: "A study of the alkaline extract of white spruce bark pretreated with liquid ammonia." (Chemistry: Purves, C.)

55-009 **Bulani**, Walter (*Saskatchewan*) Ph.D.: "The electrical conductance of some quaternary ammonium halides in solution." (Chemistry: Schiff, H.)

55-010 **Burnett**, Alastair (*British Columbia*) Ph.D.: "Assessment of intelligence in a restricted environment." (Psychology: Ferguson, G.)

55-011 **Cleveland**, Edward M. (*British Columbia*) Ph.D.: "The taxonomy and classification of the corynebacteria." (Bacteriology & Immunology: Stevenson, J.)

55-012 **Crowell**, Clarence R. (*McGill*) Ph.D.: "The temperature dependence of the work functions of the monovalent noble metals." (Physics: Woonton, G.)

55-013 **DeSouza**, John E. (*McGill*) Ph.D.: "Oxidation of mono-methylpyridines and 2-amino-methylpyridines with selenium dioxide." (Chemistry: Taurins, A.)

55-014 **Eade**, Kenneth E. (*Queen's*) Ph.D.: "Petrology of the gneisses of the Clyde area, Baffin Island." (Geological Sciences: Kranck, E.)

55-015 **East**, Thomas W. (*Cambridge*, England) Ph.D.: "Precipitation mechanisms in convective clouds." (Physics: Marshall, J.)

55-016 **Eccles**, William J. (*McGill*) Ph.D.: "Frontenac and New France, 1672-1698." (History: Cooper, J.)

55-017 **Ekler**, Kurt (*McGill*) Ph.D.: "Cathode polarization on copper single crystals." (Chemistry: Winkler, C.)

55-018 **Evans**, Harry G. (*Alberta*) Ph.D.: "Reaction of active nitrogen with methyl chloride." (Chemistry: Winkler, C.)

55-019 **Freeman**, Gordon R. (*Saskatchewan*) Ph.D.: "Reactions of active nitrogen with ammonia, hydrazine and methylamine." (Chemistry: Winkler, C.)

55-020 **Gardiner**, Lorne M. (*New Brunswick*) Ph.D.: "Deterioration of fire-killed pine by wood-boring beetles (*Coleoptera: Cerambycidae*) in the Mississagi region of Ontario." (Entomology: DuPorte, E.)

55-021 **Gardon**, John L. (*Polytechnicum*, Switzerland) Ph.D.: "Physico-chemical properties of lignin sulfonates." (Chemistry: Mason, S.)

55-022 **Husain**, Bilal R. (*Calcutta*, India) Ph.D.: "Semi-micro fossils of the Black River and Trenton groups of Quebec." (Geological Sciences: Clark, T.)

55-023 **Jackson**, Donald S. (*Manitoba*) Ph.D.: "A mass spectral investigation of nitrogen afterglow." (Chemistry: Schiff, H.)

55-024 **Kasman**, Sidney (*Toronto*) Ph.D.: "Investigation of nitraminopyridines and nitraminothiazoles." (Chemistry: Taurins, A.)

55-025 **Lachance**, Robert A. (*McGill*) Ph.D.: "The utilisation of fluorescent plant extracts by bacteria." (Agricultural Bacteriology: Gray, P.)

55-026 **Miller**, Bernard (*Virginia Polytechnical*) Ph.D.: "The influence of the fiber structure on the nitration of cellulose." (Chemistry: Timell, T.)

55-027 **Mossman**, Carolyn E. (*Mount Allison*) Ph.D.: "Surface conductance measurements on pads of fibrous materials." (Chemistry: Mason, S.)

55-028 **Owens**, Owen E. (*McGill*) Ph.D.: "The geology of part of the 'Labrador Trough' south of Leaf Lake, New Quebec." (Geological Sciences: Gill, J.)

55-029 **Pate**, Brian D. (*London*, England) Ph.D.: "Disintegration rate determination by 4pi-counting." (Chemistry: Yaffe, L.)

55-030 **Perlman**, Martin M. (*McGill*) Ph.D.: "The breakdown of proton irradiated proteins." (Physics: Foster, J.)

55-031 **Robertson**, Roderick F. (*British Columbia*) Ph.D.: "A study of the iodine exchange between iodide ions in solution and unimolecular films of alpha-iodostearic acid at the air-water interface." (Chemistry: Mason, S.)

55-032 **Ryan**, Michael T. (*Dublin*, Ireland) Ph.D.: "Studies in ring D oxygenated steroids." (Biochemistry: Heard, R.)

55-033 **Samborski**, Daniel J. (*Saskatchewan*) Ph.D.: "The nature of plant resistance to obligate parasites." (Plant Pathology: Coulson, J.)

55-034 **Schad**, Gerhard (*Cornell*) Ph.D.: "Studies on the genus *Kalicephalus* in snakes." (Parasitology: Cameron, T.)

55-035 **Schnitzer**, Morris (*McGill*) Ph.D.: "Investigations on the interaction of cations with extracts and leachates of forest trees." (Agricultural Chemistry: DeLong, W.)

55-036 **Schonbaum**, Eduard (*Amsterdam*, Netherlands) Ph.D.: "Formation of hormones *in vitro* by adrenal preparations." (Biochemistry: Saffran, M.)

55-037 **Scott**, Peter D. (*McGill*) Ph.D.: "The social and political ideas of T.S. Eliot." (Political Science: Crick, B.)

55-038 **Steppler**, Howard A. (*Manitoba*) Ph.D.: "A study of the combining ability of red clover clones and their use in a breeding program." (Agronomy: Raymond, L.)

55-039 **Stevens**, Bernard A. (*McGill*) Ph.D.: "Radiative transfer theory and the radiance of the horizon sky." (Physics: Marshall, J.)

55-040 **Sukava**, Armas J. (*Manitoba*) Ph.D.: "Thiol and amino addition agents in the electrodeposition of copper." (Chemistry: Winkler, C.)

55-041 **Surwillo**, Walter W. (*Washington*) Ph.D.: "Psychological factors in electromyographic gradients." (Psychology: Malmo, R.)

55-042 **Taylor**, Frederick C. (*Western*) Ph.D.: "The petrology of the serpentine bodies in the Matheson District, Ontario." (Geological Sciences: Stevenson, J.)

55-043 **Tennant**, Alan D. (*McGill*) Ph.D.: "Bacterial indices of pollution in oyster producing areas in Prince Edward Island." (Agricultural Bacteriology: Gray, P.)

55-044 **Verschingel**, Roger H. (*Sir George Williams*) Ph.D.: "I. Investigation of the 'vapour snake' phenomenon. II. A comparison of the production of active nitrogen by the electrodeless and condensed discharges and its reactions with oxygen containing compounds." (Chemistry: Schiff, H.)

**Ph.D. Fall 1955**

55-045 **Bailey**, William R. (*McGill*) Ph.D.: "Applications and limitations of bacteriophage in inducing antigenic and morphological changes in salmonellae." (Bacteriology & Immunology: Murray, E.)

55-046 **Ballabon**, Maurice B. (*McGill*) Ph.D.: "Areal differentiation of the manufacturing belt in central Canada." (Geography: Hare, F.)

55-047 **Beaulieu**, Maurice (*Montréal*) Ph.D.: "*In vitro* production of antibody by menocytes." (Bacteriology & Immunology: Murray, E.)

55-048 **Betts**, Donald D. (*Dalhousie*) Ph.D.: "A theoretical investigation of resonance electron capture cross sections." (Mathematics: Jackson, J.)

55-049 **Brummer**, Johannes J. (*Witwatersrand*, South Africa) Ph.D.: "Geology of the northwest quarter of Holland Township, Gaspé North, Quebec." (Geological Sciences: Riddell, J.)

55-050 **Clifford**, Charles E. (*Carleton*) Ph.D.: "Neutron induced disintegrations in oxygen." (Physics: Terroux, F.)

55-051 **Cloutier**, Joseph A. (*Laval*) Ph.D.: "Study of short-lived proton induced activities." (Physics: Foster, J.)

55-052 **Dennis**, Arnett S. (*Acadia*) Ph.D.: "Measurement of fluctuations in radar echoes from snow." (Physics: Hitschfeld, W.)

55-053 **Doane**, Benjamin K. (*Princeton*) Ph.D.: "Changes in visual function with perceptual isolation." (Psychology: Hebb, D.)

55-054 **Epp**, Edward R. (*Saskatchewan*) Ph.D.: "Study of new isotopes in the osmium region." (Physics: Foster, J.)

55-055 **Forst**, Wendell (*Czechoslovakia Institute of Technology*) Ph.D.: "Reactions of methyl cyanide with hydrogen atoms and with active nitrogen." (Chemistry: Winkler, C.)

55-056 **Gartaganis**, Phoebus (*Salonica*, Greece) Ph.D.: "The reactions of active nitrogen with ethane and methane in the presence of hydrogen atoms." (Chemistry: Winkler, C.)

55-057 **Giroud**, Claude J-P. (*Paris*, France) Ph.D.: "Studies on aldosterone." (Experimental Medicine: Venning, E.)

55-058 **Goldstein**, Fred B. (*Philadelphia*) Ph.D.: "Studies on aromatic acids in relation to phenylpyruvic oligophrenia." (Biochemistry: Quastel, J.)

55-059 **Henry**, James P. (*Cambridge*, England) Ph.D.: "Orthostasis and the kidney." (Experimental Medicine: Rose, B.)

55-060 **Huq**, A.K.M. Fazlul (*Dacca*, Pakistan) Ph.D.: "Investigation of variations in composition of the timothy plant (*Phleum pratense*)." (Agricultural Chemistry: DeLong, W.)

55-061 **Johnston**, John A. (*Western*) Ph.D.: "Factors in the formation of the Presbyterian Church in Canada, 1875." (History: Cooper, J.)

55-062 **Klinck**, Harold R. (*Toronto*) Ph.D.: "Growth studies on the root system of barley." (Agronomy: Lods, E.)

55-063 **Lavallee**, John (*Montréal*) Ph.D.: "Asymptotic theorems in the theory of normal correlation." (Mathematics: Kozakiewicz, W.)

55-064 **Lucas**, Sidney (*McGill*) Ph.D.: "The Peasants Revolt of 1381 in history and legend." (History: Bayley, C.)

55-065 **Mahut**, Helen (*Sir George Williams*) Ph.D.: "Breed differences in the dog's emotional behaviour." (Psychology: Hebb, D.)

55-066 **Maxwell**, Doreen E. (*Queen's*) Ph.D.: "Cytology and correlated morphology of the genus *Neodiprion* Rohwer (*Hemenoptera*: *Symphyta*)." (Genetics: Boyes, J.)

55-067 **Moody**, Harry J. (*Saskatchewan*) Ph.D.: "Total cross section of calcium for neutrons between the energies of 20 and 70 MeV." (Physics: Foster, J.)

55-068 **Mooney**, Craig M. (*Saskatchewan*) Ph.D.: "Perceptual closure with and without eye movements." (Psychology: Hebb, D.)

55-069 **Moore**, Thomas H. (*McGill*) Ph.D.: "A new calorimetric method for determining heats of solution of minerals, and its application." (Geological Sciences: Saull, V.)

55-070 **Nadler**, Norman J. (*McGill*) Ph.D.: "The site and rate of turnover of iodine in the thyroid gland." (Anatomy: Leblond, C.)

55-071 **Paquin**, Roger (*Laval*) Ph.D.: "Host-parasite relationships in tomato fusarium wilt." (Botany: Waygood, E.)

55-072 **Rutherford**, Beth E. (*Toronto*) Ph.D.: "The effect of diet composition on the apparent digestibility and hence on the physiological fuel value of protein." (Nutrition: Crampton, E.)

55-073 **Shaw**, Alan C. (*Alberta*) Ph.D.: "The composition of the oils from some Canadian conifers." (Chemistry: Nicholls, R.)

55-074 **Shyluk**, Walter P. (*Saskatchewan*) Ph.D.: "A study of carboxymethylcellulose and the corresponding glucose derivatives." (Chemistry: Timell, T.)

55-075 **Skarsgard**, Harvey M. (*Saskatchewan*) Ph.D.: "p,xn cross sections in $Pb^{206}$." (Physics: Foster, J.)

55-076 **Snyder**, John L. (*British Columbia*) Ph.D.: "Isolation and properties of native balsam fir cellulose." (Chemistry: Timell, T.)

55-077 **Springbett**, Bruce M. (*Alberta*) Ph.D.: "Series effects in the employment interview." (Psychology: Webster, E.)

55-078 **Taussig**, Andrew (*McGill*) Ph.D.: "The effect of anaerobiosis on phage synthesis by *E. coli.*" (Biochemistry: Quastel, J.)

55-079 **Toby**, Sidney (*London*, England) Ph.D.: "The production of atomic deuterium and its reaction with ethylene." (Chemistry: Schiff, H.)

**S.T.M. Spring 1955**

55-500 **Gough**, Cyril H. (*Dalhousie*) S.T.M.: "The atonement in the sayings of Jesus." (Divinity: Thomson, J.)

55-501 **Perret**, Edmond J. (*Geneva*, Switzerland) S.T.M.: "The Catholic Church in the Apostolic Fathers." (Divinity: Walsh, H.)

**M.Eng. Spring 1955**

55-502 **Adderson**, James N. (*Manitoba*) M.Eng.: "Variables in the manufacture of manganese zinc ferrite." (Electrical Engineering: Howes, F.)

55-503 **Borden**, Byron C. (*McGill*) M.Eng.: "Bridge measurement of junction transistors parameters." (Electrical Engineering: Farnell, G.)

55-504 **Comsa**, Radu P. (*Zurich*, Switzerland) M.Eng.: "Running characteristics of the capacitor-run motor." (Electrical Engineering: Schippel, W.)

55-505 **Girolami**, Renato L. (*McGill*) M.Eng.: "Strength of thin-walled aluminum alloy struts." (Civil Engineering & Applied Mechanics: Wilson, V.)

55-506 **McCutcheon**, John O. (*McGill*) M.Eng.: "Failure mechanism of steel stressed in triaxial tension." (Civil Engineering & Applied Mechanics: Craig, C.)

55-507 **Putnaerglis**, Rudolph (*Latvia*) M.Eng.: "The mechanism of heat transfer across metallic interfaces." (Mechanical Engineering: Mordell, D. & Edis, A.)

**LL.M. Spring 1955**

55-508 **Balachandran**, Ponniah (*Cambridge*, England) LL.M.: "Vicarious liability in air law." (International Air Law: Cooper, J.)

55-509 **McPherson**, Ian E. (*British Columbia*) LL.M.: "The participation of Canada in international aviation agreements." (International Air Law: Cooper, J.)

55-510 **Moursi**, Fouad K. (*Cairo*, Egypt) LL.M.: "Conflict in the competence and jurisdiction of courts of different states to deal with acts and occurrences on board aircraft." (International Air Law: Cooper, J.)

55-511 **Saleh**, Samir (*Beirut*, Lebanon) LL.M.: "Collision between aircraft." (International Air Law: Gazdik, J.)

55-512 **Toepper**, Anton (*Graz*, Austria) LL.M.: "The single forum method and the unification of international private air law: Article 20 of the Rome Convention, 1952." (International Air Law: Gazdik, J.)

**M.Sc. Spring 1955**

55-513 **Assad**, Joseph R. (*Bishop's*) M.Sc.: "The formation of certain granite-like rocks in the footwall of the Sudbury norite, northwest of the Sudbury Basin." (Geological Sciences: Stevenson, J.)

55-514 **Brody**, Harry (*London*, England) M.Sc.: "Effect of hydrogen cyanide on the reaction of active nitrogen with methyl chloride." (Chemistry: Winkler, C.)

55-515 **Carruthers**, Errol W. (*Mount Allison*) M.Sc.: "The fission yield of $Mo^{99}$ in the thermal fission of $U^{235}$." (Chemistry: Yaffe, L.)

55-516 **Cherian**, Kandathil K. (*Madras*, India) M.Sc.: "The specific conductance of fused cryolite-alumina baths." (Metallurgical Engineering: Yates, H.)

55-517 **Cross**, Jean D. (*Mount Holyoke*) M.Sc.: "The effects of anoxia and lack of substrate on the subsequent carbohydrate metabolism of brain tissue." (Biochemistry: Elliott, K.)

55-518 **Findlay**, Wallace I. (*Dalhousie*) M.Sc.: "Investigation of the nutrient status of corn with special reference to nitrogen and phosphorus." (Agronomy: DeLong, W.)

55-519 **Ford**, John D. (*McGill*) M.Sc.: "Calcium balance studies on the fowl with the use of radioactive calcium as tracer." (Agricultural Chemistry: Common, R.)

55-520 **Francis**, Jean B. (*McGill*) M.Sc.: "Embryo sac development in *Cleome spinosa* Jacq." (Botany: Roscoe, M.)

55-521 **Gerard**, Robert D. (*New Mexico*) M.Sc.: "Some aspects of Pleistocene and post-glacial climate change in central Alaska." (Geography: Hare, F.)

55-522 **Ghosh**, Asok C. (*Calcutta*, India) M.Sc.: "The effect of pectic enzymes on tissues stained by Pa-Schiff technique." (Anatomy: Leblond, C.)

55-523 **Guthrie**, John E. (*McGill*) M.Sc.: "Absorption by the isolated surviving small intestine after experimental shock." (Biochemistry: Quastel, J.)

55-524 **Hamilton**, Herman A. (*McGill*) M.Sc.: "Experiments on the extractability of soil phosphorus." (Agricultural Chemistry: DeLong, W.)

55-525 **Jackson**, Garth D. (*McGill*) M.SC.: "A petrographic study of part of the Potsdam sandstone core from the Mallet Well, Ste. Therèse, Que." (Geological Sciences: Clark, T.)

55-526 **Keenan**, Daniel (*McGill*) M.Sc.: "The iodine requirements of the growing chicken." (Poultry Husbandry: Nikolaiczuk, N.)

55-527 **Layne**, Donald St.E. (*McGill*) M.Sc.: "Observations on the effect of gonadal hormones on the nucleic acid contents of the liver and kidneys of the domestic fowl." (Agricultural Chemistry: Common, R.)

55-528 **Loiselle**, Jean-Marie (*Laval*) M.Sc.: "Metabolic changes during acute physiological failure." (Biochemistry: Denstedt, O.)

55-529 **Long**, Harold D. (*New Brunswick*) M.Sc.: "The plant communities of Morgan's Woods." (Botany: Gibbs, R.)

55-530 **McFarlane**, Ross A. (*McMaster*) M.Sc.: "An analyser for velocity modulated electron beams." (Physics: Woonton, G.)

55-531 **McGregor**, John K. (*Toronto*) M.Sc.: "*In vitro* studies of *Histomonas meleagridis* a parasitic protozoan of turkeys." (Parasitology: Cameron, T.)

55-532 **Martin**, William G. (*Carleton*) M.Sc.: "The ultracentrifugal determination of partial specific volumes." (Chemistry: Winkler, C.)

55-533 **Mazurkiewicz**, Irena M. (*Carcow*, Poland) M.Sc.: "Studies on the pharmacology of coronary circulation." (Pharmacology: Melville, K.)

55-534 **Meerovitch**, Eugene B. (*St. John's*, China) M.Sc.: "Studies on *Entamoeba invadens*." (Parasitology: Cameron, T.)

55-535 **Montreuil**, Paul L. (*McGill*) M.Sc.: "Acanthocephala of seals at the Magdalen Islands." (Parasitology: Cameron, T.)

55-536 **Morgante**, Odosca (*Rome*, Italy) M.Sc.: "The isolation of *Mycobacterium tuberculosis* by filtration technique from cerebro-spinal fluid." (Bacteriology & Immunology: Murray, E.)

55-537 **Parsons**, Timothy R. (*McGill*) M.Sc.: "The preparation and analysis of sulphurous acid hydrolysates of casein." (Agricultural Chemistry: Baker, B.)

55-538 **Pollock**, Donald W. (*McGill*) M.Sc.: "The mineralogy of the eastern metals nickel-copper deposit." (Geological Sciences: Stevenson, J.)

55-539 **Schmidt**, Richard C. (*Rhodes*, South Africa) M.Sc.: "Dispersion of copper, lead, and zinc from mineralized zones in an area of moderate relief as indicated by soils and plants." (Geological Sciences: Riddell, J.)

55-540 **Shields**, Ross C. (*Queen's*) M.Sc.: "A detailed investigation of the petrology and ore textures of Mogador Mines Limited." (Geological Sciences: Gill, J.)

55-541 **Taylor**, Robert B. (*Ontario Agricultural*) M.Sc.: "The effects of freezing and cold storage on bacteria in milks." (Agricultural Bacteriology: Gray, P.)

55-542 **Tuffy**, Frank (*Dublin*, Ireland) M.Sc.: "Chert in the ordovician of southern Quebec." (Geological Sciences: Stearn, C.)

55-543 **Vanstone**, William E. (*McGill*) M.Sc.: "Studies on avian serum proteins by zone electrophoresis." (Agricultural Chemistry: Common, R.)

55-544 **Wells**, Doreen E. (*McGill*) M.Sc.: "A cytological study of *Sporormia obliquiseptata* Speg." (Botany: Wilson, C.)

55-545 **Wickson**, Margaret E. (*London*, England) M.Sc.: "Some metabolic interrelationships of *Lilium regale* with reference to gamma-methyleneglutamic acid." (Botany: Towers, G.)

55-546 **Wilson**, Roderic L. (*Western*) M.Sc.: "The barometer coefficient and the mu-messon production spectrum." (Mathematics: Morris, T.)

**M.A. Spring 1955**

55-547 **Clark**, James W. (*McGill*) M.A.: "Factors affecting human response to pain stimulation." (Psychology: Bindra, D.)

55-548 **Gombay**, André M. (*McGill*) M.A.: "The concept of truth in the philosophy of Descartes." (Philosophy: Klibansky, R.)

55-549 **Handelman**, Saul (*Sir George Williams*) M.A.: "'Forty thousand brothers': a novel." (English: Files, H.)

55-550 **Helfield**, Tilya (*McGill*) M.A.: "Attitudes toward love in Spenser." (English: Hemlow, J.)

55-551 **Henry**, Zin A. (*London*, England) M.A.: "A study of Jamaican post-war terms of trade, 1945-1953." (Economics & Political Science: Kemp, M.)

55-552 **Kamali**, Sabih A. (*Aligarh*, India) M.A.: "Ghazzali's 'Tahafut al-Falasifah'." (Islamic Studies: Rahbar, M.)

55-553 **Knaff**, Paul R. (*Champlain*) M.A.: "Some variables affecting complementary subjective color." (Psychology: Bindra, D.)

55-554 **MacKenzie**, Gordon J. (*Alberta*) M.A.: "Victor Hugo et le voyage de 1840 en Allemagne." (French: Launay, J.)

55-555 **Maizel**, Norah L. (*McGill*) M.A.: "A critical study of 'All's Well that Ends Well'." (English: Porter, S.)

55-556 **O'Brien**, John W. (*McGill*) M.A.: "French economic policy and inflation 1944-52." (Economics & Political Science: Weldon, J.)

55-557 **Plunkett**, Thomas (*Sir George Williams*) M.A.: "Local government in Greater Corner Brook, Newfoundland." (Economics & Political Science: Mallory, J.)

55-558 **Polgar**, Sophie (*Geneva*, Switzerland) M.A.: "Voltaire et les Quakers." (French: Launay, J.)

55-559 **Prives**, Moshe Z. (*Sir George Williams*) M.A.: "Incentives in the public service: their role in making it responsive and efficient." (Economics & Political Science: Grasham, W.)

55-560 **Smith**, Irving H. (*Sir George Williams*) M.A.: "Anglo-Russian relations and the Dogger Bank incident, 1902-1905." (History: Fieldhouse, H.)

55-561 **Sutherland**, Ronald (*McGill*) M.A.: "Katherine Mansfield's debt to Chekhov." (English: Beresford-Howe, C.)

55-562 **Vaz**, Edmund W. (*McGill*) M.A.: "The metropolitan taxi-driver; his work and self-conception." (Sociology: Westley, W.)

55-563 **Velay**, Clément C. (*Sir George Williams*) M.A.: "An economic study of the Schuman Plan." (Economics: Dales, J.)

55-564 **Waksberg**, Helene (*McGill*) M.A.: "Serial-position gradient in time estimation." (Psychology: Bindra, D.)

55-565 **Waterhouse**, John (*McGill*) M.A.: "The metronome: a novel." (English: Files, H.)

55-566 **Watson**, William J. (*Carleton*) M.A.: "Muhammad 'Ali and the Khilafat movement." (Islamic Studies: Rahbar, M.)

55-567 **Wipper**, Audrey J. (*McGill*) M.A.: "The occupation of the professional rider." (Sociology: Hall, O.)

**M.Com. Spring 1955**

55-568 **Marshall**, Joyce A. (*Sir George Williams*) M.Com.: "An analysis and appraisal of loss leader selling." (Economics and Political Science: **)

**M.Arch. Fall 1955**

55-569 **Barkham**, J. Brian (*London*, England) M.Arch.: "The development of land settlement and rural architecture in the Province of Quebec." (Architecture: Spence-Sales, H.)

**S.T.M. Fall 1955**

55-570 **Koshy**, Kuttickal I. (*Madras*, India) S.T.M.: "The development of the doctrine of Christ in the light of missionary experience in India." (Divinity: Slater, R.)

55-571 **Poole**, Aquila J. (*McGill*) S.T.M.: "The philosophical theology of William Temple." (Divinity: Thomson, J.)

**M.Eng. Fall 1955**

55-572 **Dodis**, Nicolas G. (*Athens*, Greece) M.Eng.: "Spontaneous ignition measurements of some gaseous fuels injected into a hot air stream." (Mechanical Engineering: Mordell, D.)

55-573 **Goldman**, Carl (*McGill*) M.Eng.: "Torsional resistance of a steel beam having stiffeners." (Civil Engineering & Applied Mechanics: Joly, G.)

55-574 **Gupta**, Makam C. (*Mysore*, India) M.Eng.: "Studies on turbulent flames." (Mechanical Engineering: Mordell, D.)

55-575 **Jakobson**, Gunnar J. (*McGill*) M.Eng.: "Web stresses in a prestressed concrete I-beam." (Civil Engineering & Applied Mechanics: De Stein, J.)

55-576 **Macaulay**, Colin A. (*McGill*) M.Eng.: "The relationship between the physical properties of rocks and underground mining conditions." (Mining Engineering: Morrison, R.)

55-577 **Matsas**, Loucas C. (*Toronto*) M.Eng.: "Compressor-blade vibrations associated with stalling." (Mechanical Engineering: Jackson, J.)

55-578 **Sharratt**, Harold J. (*McGill*) M.Eng.: "The extraction of lithium from spodumene." (Metallurgical Engineering: MacEwan, J.)

55-579 **Tucker**, Henry J. (*McGill*) M.Eng.: "Constant diameter air injector." (Mechanical Engineering: Mordell, D.)

## ANNUAL LISTING

### LL.M. Fall 1955

55-580 **Adelfio**, Antonio (*Palermo*, Italy) LL.M.: "Particular aspects of the Rome Convention of 1952 on damages at the surface." (International Air Law: Gazdik, J.)

55-581 **Hermoso**, J. (*Santo Tomas*, Philippines) LL.M.: "Jurisdiction over acts and occurrences on board an aircraft." (International Air Law: Cooper, J.)

55-582 **Murchison**, John T. (*New Brunswick*) LL.M.: "The contiguous air space zone in international law." (International Air Law: Cooper, J.)

55-583 **Nowak**, Tadeusz C. (*Oxford*, England) LL.M.: "Real rights in aircraft and vessels." (International Air Law: Gazdik, J.)

55-584 **Vlasic**, Ivan (*Zagreb*, Yugoslavia) LL.M.: "The grant of passage and exercise of commercial rights in international air transport." (International Air Law: Cooper, J.)

### M.Sc. Fall 1955

55-585 **Allan**, Charles M. (*McGill*) M.Sc.: "An experimental study of renal damage and electrolyte imbalance following various methods of urinary deviation to the intestine." (Experimental Surgery: Webster, D.)

55-586 **Azima**, Hassan (*California*) M.Sc.: "Studies in body scheme: the effect of perceptual isolation on the experience of the body." (Psychiatry: Scott, W.)

55-587 **Benoit**, Fernand W. (*Montréal*) M.Sc.: "Investigation into the chemical composition of the upper part of the Cape Bon Ami formation and the lower part of the Grande Greve formation." (Geological Sciences: Stearn, C.)

55-588 **Bramlage**, Catharina A. (*Leiden*, Holland) M.Sc.: "The bone marrow in pregnancy and the puerperium." (Experimental Medicine: Lowenstein, L.)

55-589 **Burgoyne**, P. Nicholas W. (*McGill*) M.Sc.: "Cohomology theory in abstract groups." (Mathematics: Zassenhaus, H.)

55-590 **Butler**, Ralph (*Atlantic Union*) M.Sc.: "Distribution and survival of fecal bacteria in sewage polluted water." (Bacteriology & Immunology: Kelly, C.)

55-591 **Butzer**, K.W. (*McGill*) M.Sc.: "Some aspects of postglacial climatic variation in the Near East considered in relation to movements of population." (Meteorology: Hare, F.)

55-592 **Cann**, Malcolm C. (*Sir George Williams*) M.Sc.: "Interconversion reactions of desoxycorticosterone acetate-21-$C^{14}$ by the adrenal cortex." (Biochemistry: Heard, R.)

55-593 **Chiasson**, Thomas C. (*McGill*) M.Sc.: "The effect of various increments of N, P and K on the yield and botanical composition of permanent pastures." (Agronomy: Raymond, L.)

55-594 **Conkie**, William R. (*Toronto*) M.Sc.: "Internal conversion in light nuclei." (Mathematics: Sharp, R.)

55-595 **Coughlin**, Francis R. (*Fordham*) M.Sc.: "Blood volume determinations in surgical patients." (Experimental Surgery: Webster, D.)

55-596 **Crete**, Joseph E. (*Montréal*) M.Sc.: "Studies on the parasitism of *Cercospora beticola* Sacc." (Plant Pathology: Coulson, J.)

55-597 **Deane**, Burton C. (*British Columbia*) M.Sc.: "Life history and importance of the clover root borer, *Hylastinus obscurus* (Marsham) (*Coleoptera*: *Scolytidae*) in Quebec." (Agronomy, Raymond, L.)

55-598 **Drapeau**, Jacqueline U. (*McGill*) M.Sc.: "Studies on the cardiovascular actions of chlorpromazine." (Physiology: Melville, K.)

55-599 **Emo**, Wallace B. (*McGill*) M.Sc.: "The basic intrusives of the Waco Lake area, Saguenay County, P.Q." (Geological Sciences: Kranck, E.)

55-600 **Hagley**, Elmer A. (*McGill*) M.Sc.: "The synergistic action of certain chemicals used in combination with DDT against house fly adults, *Musca domestica* Linn. (*Diptera: Muscidae*)." (Entomology: Morrison, F.)

55-601 **Hardy**, John A. (*Delaware*) M.Sc.: "The oxidation of sucrose with hypochlorous acid." (Chemistry: Purves, C.)

55-602 **Hyndman**, William W. (*McGill*) M.Sc.: "Occlusion of the abdominal aorta above the coeliac axis in hypothermic dogs." (Experimental Surgery: Webster, D.)

55-603 **Johnson**, Thomas A. (*Chicago*) M.Sc.: "Effects of the hypothalamus upon gastric secretion." (Experimental Surgery: Webster, D.)

55-604 **Kochen**, Simon B. (*McGill*) M.Sc.: "Non-standard models for formal languages." (Mathematics: Lambek, J.)

55-605 **Kranck**, Svante H. (*McGill*) M.Sc.: "Geology of the Stony Rapids norite area northern Saskatchewan." (Geological Sciences: Stevenson, J.)

55-606 **Kycia**, Tadeusz F. (*McGill*) M.Sc.: "A study of the feasibility of designing a super-regenerative receiver to meet certain critical requirements." (Physics: Whitehead, J.)

55-607 **Lagnado**, John R. (*Geneva*, Switzerland) M.Sc.: "The effects of ions on monoamine oxidase activity of rat liver." (Biochemistry: Sourkes, T.)

55-608 **Laing**, Charles A. (*McGill*) M.Sc.: "Nutritional studies in totally gastrectomized dogs." (Experimental Surgery: Webster, D.)

55-609 **Lowi**, R. Naomi (*McGill*) M.Sc.: "Blood corticoids in pregnancy." (Experimental Medicine: Venning, E.)

55-610 **McLaren**, Ian A. (*McGill*) M.Sc.: "The biology of the ringed seal (*Phoca hispida* Schreber) in the waters of southwest Baffin Island." (Zoology: Dunbar, M.)

55-611 **Mahatoo**, Winston H. (*McGill*) M.Sc.: "Somesthesis and spatial orientation after perceptual isolation." (Psychology: Webster, E.)

55-612 **Meikle**, Brian K. (*McGill*) M.Sc.: "The geology of the Little River area, Baie d'Espoir, Newfoundland." (Geological Sciences: Gill, J.)

55-613 **Michael**, J. (*McGill*) M.Sc.: "Mathematical principles of statistical quality control." (Mathematics: Timell, T.)

55-614 **Morrell**, Frank (*Columbia*) M.Sc.: "Effect of focal epileptogenic lesions on the connecting function of brain." (Neurology & Neurosurgery: Jasper, H.)

55-615 **Morrison**, E.R. ( ) M.Sc.: "A study of Porphyry Mountain, Holland Township, Quebec." (Geological Sciences: Riddell, J.)

55-616 **Morrison**, Gordon R. (*McGill*) M.Sc. "The relation of rewarding intracranial stimulation to biological drive." (Psychology: Hebb, D.)

55-617 **Ottolenghi**, Paul (*McGill*) M.Sc.: "Enzymes of the mammalian reticulocyte." (Biochemistry: Denstedt, O.)

55-618 **Peckham**, Hugh E. (*Loyola of Montréal*) M.Sc.: "The effect of time on the variation of the apparent digestion coefficients on the proximate principles of a ration fed to sheep." (Nutrition: Crampton, E.)

55-619 **Ramos**, Oswaldo L. (*Sao Paulo*, Brazil) M.Sc.: "Study of the antidiuretic activity of human and rat blood." (Experimental Medicine: Venning, E.)

55-620 **Rothballer**, Alan B. (*Pennsylvania*) M.Sc.: "Studies on the adrenaline-sensitive component of the reticular activating system." (Neurology & Neurosurgery: Jasper, H.)

55-621 **Szabo**, Alexander (*Queen's*) M.Sc.: "Investigations of magnetically focused electron beams." (Physics: Wagner, S.)

55-622 **Whitehead**, Andrew B. (*New Brunswick*) M.Sc.: "The cross section for the nuclear reaction $O^{16}$(p, alpha)$N^{13}$." (Physics: Foster, J.)

55-623 **Williams**, Audrey J. (*Marianopolis*) M.Sc.: "Changes in the microflora of apples during ripening and cold storage." (Agriucltural Bacteriology: Wallace, R.)

**M.A. Fall 1955**

55-624 **Bloomstone**, Shirley S. (*McGill*) M.A.: "Real estate salesmen: study of a sales occupation." (Sociology: Westley, W.)

55-625 **Charteris**, J.N. (*McGill*) M.A.: "Tudor dealings in Scotland between 1488-1524." (History: Reid, W.)

55-626 **Cienciala**, Anna M. (*Liverpool*, England) M.A.: "The Warsaw rising of 1944 in the light of Polish-Soviet relations during World War II." (History: Mladenovic, M.)

55-627 **Dedering**, Christa E. (*Berlin*, Germany) M.A.: "Charles Kingsley's conception and treatment of history in his historical novels: 'Hypatia', 'Westward Ho! ', and 'Hereward the Wake'." (English: Beresford-Howe, C.)

55-628 **Farr**, William (*Wales*) M.A.: "The determination of occupational wage differentials: a comparative analysis." (Economics: Weldon, J.)

55-629 **Friend**, Gregory (*McGill*) M.A.: "A study of the innovations in dramatic construction of George Bernard Shaw with special reference to the technique of his discussion plays." (English: Porter, S.)

55-630 **Gordon**, Llewelyn (*Western Reserve*) M.A.: "A study of the factors which have determined the present stage of economic development in Jamaica." (Geography: Hills, T.)

55-631 **Jonassohn**, Kurt (*Sir George Williams*) M.A.: "The life insurance agent: an occupational study." (Sociology: Elkin, F.)

55-632 **Judges**, Nancy E. (*Richmond*) M.A.: "The British attitude towards the Armenian Question, 1878-1908." (History: Reid, W.)

55-633 **McDonough**, Sheila D. (*McGill*) M.A.: "Eschatology in the Qur'an in the light of recent Biblical criticism." (Comparative Religion: Smith, W.)

55-634 **McFarlane**, Bruce A. (*McGill*) M.A.: "The sociology of sports promotion." (Sociology: Westley, W.)

55-635 **Mu'inu-d-din**, Ahmad K. (*Dacca*, Pakistan) M.A.: "A bibliographical introduction to modern Islamic developments in India and Pakistan." (Islamic Studies: Rahbar, M.)

55-636 **Nashshabah**, Hisham (*Beirut*, Lebanon) M.A.: "Islam and nationalism in the Arab world, a selected and annotated bibliography." (Islamic Studies: Bagley, F.)

55-637 **Oulton**, Rhodes C. (*McGill*) M.A.: "The teaching of geography in Canadian schools: its status, aims, and methods. A critical study." (Education: Hughes, J.)

55-638 **Sebor**, Milos-Marie (*Prague*, Czechoslovakia) M.A.: "A study of geography in the intelligence service." (Geography: Hare, F.)

55-639 **Smith**, Samuel I. (*London*, England) M.A.: "A federated British Caribbean: resource utilisation." (Geography: Hills, T.)

55-640 **Woods**, Helen M. (*McGill*) M.A.: "The treatment of childhood in the major novels of Defoe as a significant factor in the development of English prose fiction." (English: Beresford-Howe, C.)

## ANNUAL LISTING

**Ph.D. Spring 1956**

56-001 **Anderson**, Francis D. (*New Brunswick*) Ph.D.: "The geology of the Woodstock and Millville areas, New Brunswick." (Geological Sciences: Clark, T.)

56-002 **Andrews**, Oliver (*Harvard*) Ph.D.: "Eugéne Dabit, sa vie et son oeuvre." (French: Launay, J.)

56-003 **Bennett**, Clifton F. (*Lewis and Clark*) Ph.D.: "The effect of degree of substitution on the fractional precipitation of cellulose nitrates." (Chemistry: Timell, T.)

56-004 **Black**, William F. (*Manitoba*) Ph.D.: "The *Mydisacea* of the Bras d'Or lakes." (Zoology: Dunbar, M.)

56-005 **Bushuk**, Walter (*Manitoba*) Ph.D.: "Sorption of vapours and gases on flour, starch and gluten." (Chemistry: Winkler, C.)

56-006 **Cornwall**, Frederick W. (*Cape Town*, South Africa) Ph.D.: "Rock alteration and primary base metal dispersion at Barvue, Golden Manitou and New Calumet Mines, Quebec." (Geological Sciences: Riddell, J.)

56-007 **Coulombe**, Louis-Joseph (*Laval*) Ph.D.: "Study of the influence of metabolic products of *Fusarium oxysporum* F. *lycopersici* on certain physiological processes in tomato plants." (Plant Pathology: Coulson, J.)

56-008 **Cumming**, Bruce G. (*Reading*, England) Ph.D.: "A proposed 'growth cycle' in red clover (*Trifolium pratense*, L.) to interpret morphogenetic aspects related to vegetative propagation, photoperiodism, and auxinology." (Agronomy: Steppler, H.)

56-009 **Danby**, Gordon T. (*Carleton*) Ph.D.: "Detailed studies of isotopes of praseodymium and cesium of mass 137." (Physics: Foster, J. & Thompson, A.)

56-010 **Falconer**, Errol L. (*McGill*) Ph.D.: "The location of substituent groups in partially nitrated and in partially xanthated celluloses." (Chemistry: Purves, C.)

56-011 **Findlay**, Marjorie C. (*Cambridge*, England) Ph.D.: "The means of improving the economic situation of the Ungava Bay Eskimos." (Geography: Bird, J.)

56-012 **Frangatos**, Gerassimos (*Athens*, Greece) Ph.D.: "A study of pyridinium betaines." (Chemistry: Taurins, A.)

56-013 **Gorman**, William A. (*McGill*) Ph.D.: "The geology of the Ste. Justine map-area." (Geological Sciences: Stearn, C.)

56-014 **Greenway**, Robert M. (*Oxford*, England) Ph.D.: "The metabolism of choline esters of succinic acid." (Biochemistry: Quastel, J.)

56-015 **Haskell**, Stanley R. (*McGill*) Ph.D.: "A study of the nutritive value of western Canadian barley." (Nutrition: Crampton, E.)

56-016 **Heckman**, Donald E. (*McGill*) Ph.D.: "Neutron energy distributions from proton induced reactions." (Physics: Pounder, E.)

56-017 **Ives**, John D. (*Nottingham*, England) Ph.D.: "Oraefi, south-east Iceland: an essay in regional geomorphology." (Geography: Bird, J.)

56-018 **Jamieson**, James W. (*Queen's*) Ph.D.: "Reactions of atomic hydrogen with ethylenimine, N-methyl ethylenimine and ethylamine." (Chemistry: Winkler, C.)

56-019 **Javid**, Mansour (*Birmingham*, England) Ph.D.: "Performance characteristics of base-line-scanning ambiguity filters for high PRF radars." (Electrical Engineering: Chipman, R.)

56-020 **Kapica**, Lucia (*Wales*) Ph.D.: "Growth of *C. albicans* on keratin as sole source of nitrogen." (Bacteriology & Immunology: Blank, F.)

56-021 **Kashket**, Shelby (*McGill*) Ph.D.: "Hexokinase of the erythrocyte." (Biochemistry: Denstedt, O.)

56-022 **Khan**, Noor A. (*Panjab*, India) Ph.D.: "Studies on the amino acid composition and food value of certain Pakistani pulses." (Agricultural Chemistry: Baker, B.)

56-023 **Klugman**, Michael A. (*South Africa*) Ph.D.: "The geology of an area between Pigou and Sheldrake Rivers, Saguenay County, Quebec, with a detailed study of the anorthosites." (Geological Sciences: Kranck, E.)

56-024 **Korol**, Bernard (*Roosevelt*) Ph.D.: "The correlated effects of drugs on coronary flow, heart action and potassium shifts in the isolated perfused rabbit heart." (Pharmacology: Melville, K.)

56-025 **Lubinsky**, George (*Kiev*, Russia) Ph.D.: "Studies on the evolution of the *Ophryoscolecidae*." (Parasitology: Cameron, T.)

56-026 **Malkin**, Aaron (*Manitoba*) Ph.D.: "The synthesis of diphosphopyridine nucleotide in the erythrocyte." (Biochemistry: Denstedt, O.)

56-027 **Mathison**, James F. (*Saskatchewan*) Ph.D.: "The microwave spectra of carbonyl sulfide and cyanogen chloride in the 8mm. region." (Physics: Foster, J.)

56-028 **Passey**, Richard F. (*Sydney*, Australia) Ph.D.: "Carbohydrate synthesis in embryonating eggs of *Ascaris lumbricoides*." (Biochemistry: Fairbairn, D.)

56-029 **Puhach**, Paul A. (*Alberta*) Ph.D.: "On the contributions of meson exchange currents to the radiative moments of nuclei." (Mathematics: Wallace, P.)

56-030 **Purvis**, John L. (*McGill*) Ph.D.: "Intermedin and tyrosinase." (Biochemistry: Denstedt, O.)

56-031 **Roy**, Louis P. (*Laval*) Ph.D.: "Double neutron capture studies." (Chemistry: Yaffe, L.)

56-032 **Scott**, Robert I. (*British Columbia*) Ph.D.: "Studies on the preparation and reactions of diacylamides and cyclic imides." (Chemistry: Taurins, A.)

56-033 **Screaton**, Rose M. (*Manitoba*) Ph.D.: "The sorption of alkali by Purves lignin." (Chemistry: Mason, S.)

## ANNUAL LISTING

56-034 **Smith**, Donald M. (*McGill*) Ph.D.: "The oxidation of spruce periodate lignosulfonic acids with chlorine dioxide." (Chemistry: Purves, C.)

56-035 **Stennett**, Richard G. (*Western*) Ph.D.: "The arousal continuum." (Psychology: Malmo, R.)

Ph.D. Fall 1956

56-036 **Barton**, Stuart S. (*Toronto*) Ph.D.: "Heats of sorption and adsorption process by isothermal calorimetry." (Chemistry: Mason, S.)

56-037 **Belmont**, Arthur D. (*California*) Ph.D.: "Lower tropospheric inversions at Ice Island T-3." (Geography: Hare, F.)

56-038 **Bleakney**, John S. (*Acadia*) Ph.D.: "A zoogeographical study of the amphibians and reptiles of eastern Canada." (Zoology: Dunbar, M.)

56-039 **Bligh**, Emerson G. (*Acadia*) Ph.D.: "Biogenesis of adrenal cortical steroids." (Biochemistry: Heard, R.)

56-040 **Burley**, Brian J. (*London*, England) Ph.D.: "The physical stability of natrolite." (Geological Sciences: Saull, V.)

56-041 **Cameron**, Austin W. (*Acadia*) Ph.D.: "The mammals of the islands in the Gulf of St. Lawrence." (Zoology: Dunbar, M.)

56-042 **Cameron**, Robert A. (*Dalhousie*) Ph.D.: "An experimental study of the effects of heat, pressure and fluids on sedimentary meterials." (Geological Sciences: Saull, V.)

56-043 **Ciplijauskate**, Jurate E. (*McGill*) Ph.D.: "The influence of chloramphenicol on the antigenic character of *S. typhosa*." (Bacteriology & Immunology: Reed, R.)

56-044 **Diena**, Benito B. (*Parma*, Italy) Ph.D.: "A toxin neutralizing substance from *Penicillium cyaneo-fulvum*." (Bacteriology: Stevenson, J.)

56-045 **Elias**, Lorne (*Carleton*) Ph.D.: "A general direct-current method for the measurement of electrolytic conductance, and its application to nitromethane solutions of quaternary ammonium halides." (Chemistry: Schiff, H.)

56-046 **Estey**, Ralph H. (*McGill*) Ph.D.: "The role of certain factors in the crown and root diseases of red clover." (Plant Pathology: Olsen, O.)

56-047 **Fenyes**, Joseph (*Szeged*, Hungary) Ph.D.: "A study of the reactivity of methylthiazoles." (Chemistry: Taurins, A.)

56-048 **Foster**, Leigh C. (*McGill*) Ph.D.: "Stark effect under high resolution." (Physics: Foster, J.)

56-049 **Frank**, George B. (*City College of New York*) Ph.D.: "The mode of action of veratrine on skeletal muscle." (Physiology: Burns, B.)

56-050 **Ghouri**, Ahmad S. (*Panjab*, India) Ph.D.: "The effect of temperature and nutrition on the the development of the house cricket, *Acheta domesticus* (L.) (*Gryllidae*, *Orthoptera*), and two related species of crickets." (Entomology: DuPorte, E.)

56-051 **Gordon**, Ralph W. (*Toronto*) Ph.D.: "Dielectric relaxation of cellulose nitrate and cellulose." (Chemistry: Mason, S.)

56-052 **Green**, Ralph E. (*Dalhousie*) Ph.D.: "Quenching of triplet positronium by ions in aqueous solutions." (Physics: Foster, J.)

56-053 **Hannan**, Charles K. (*McGill*) Ph.D.: "The cultivation of *M. tuberculosis* recovered by oil partition." (Bacteriology & Immunology: Reed, R.)

56-054 **Hunt**, John W. (*Saskatchewan*) Ph.D.: "Studies of the external beam of the McGill synchro-cyclotron." (Physics: Foster, J.)

56-055 **Kochen**, Joseph A. (*McGill*) Ph.D.: "The effects of the growth of mouse sàrcoma-37 in the chick embryo." (Biochemistry: Quastel, J.)

56-056 **Kumamoto**, Yurika (*McGill*) Ph.D.: "Radioautographic and histochemical studies of young rat tissues with particular attention to dentin." (Anatomy: Leblond, C.)

56-057 **Kushner**, Eva M. (*McGill*) Ph.D.: "Le mythe d'Orphée dans la littérature fran´aise contemporaine." (French: Larivière)

56-058 **Oliver**, Michael K. (*McGill*) Ph.D.: "The social and political ideas of French Canadian nationalists, 1920-1945." (Political Science: Mallory, J.)

56-059 **Pascoe**, Enid (*McGill*) Ph.D.: "Metabolism of short chain fatty acids by *Mycobacterium tuberculosis* var. *bovis* BCG." (Biochemistry: Quastel, J.)

56-060 **Rabinovitch**, William (*McGill*) Ph.D.: "Chemical reactivity in monolayers." (Chemistry: Mason, S.)

56-061 **Rahman**, Mushfequr (*Calcutta*, India) Ph.D.: "A statistical problem in the geometry of numbers: star-shaped domains of quadratic and hexagonal symmetry." (Mathematics: Zassenhaus, H.)

56-062 **Ramamurti**, Dharmapuri V. (*Madras*, India) Ph.D.: "Lysogeny in *M. pyogenes*." (Bacteriology: Kalz, G.)

56-063 **Rao**, Baindur G. (*Madras*, India) Ph.D.: "Metabolism of progesterone and cortisone." (Biochemistry: Heard, R.)

56-064 **Sastry**, Podila-Brahmayya (*Andhra*, India) Ph.D.: "The functional significance of acetylcholine in the brain." (Physiology: MacIntosh, F.)

56-065 **Sayeed**, Kkalid B. (*Madras*, India) Ph.D.: "The central government of Pakistan, 1947-1951." (Political Science: Callard, K.)

56-066 **Schmidt**, Richard C. (*Rhodes*, South Africa) Ph.D.: "Adsorption of copper, lead, and zinc on some common rock forming minerals and its effect on lake sediments." (Geological Sciences: Riddell, J.)

56-067 **Skinner**, Ralph (*British Columbia*) Ph.D.: "Geology of the Tetagouche group, Bathurst, New Brunswick." (Geological Sciences: Clark, T.)

56-068 **Smith**, Lyman A. (*Saskatchewan*) Ph.D.: "The ejection of K-electrons by beta decay." (Mathematics: Sharp, R.)

56-069 **Tremblay**, Mousseau (*Montréal*) Ph.D.: "The geology of the Williamson Diamond Mine, Mwadui, Tanganyika." (Geological Sciences: Kranck, E.)

56-070 **Yurack**, Joseph A. (*Siena*) Ph.D.: "Serological investigation of the corynebacteria." (Bacteriology: Kalz, G.)

**S.T.M. Spring 1956**

56-500 **Kurien**, Vadkumkara T. (*Madras*, India) S.T.M.: "The experience of religious conversion." (Divinity: Rogers, K.)

56-501 **Newman**, Robert S. (*Toronto*) S.T.M.: "The doctrine of the atonement in the writings of James Denney." (Divinity: Thomson, J.)

**M.Eng. Spring 1956**

56-502 **Banks**, Ronald H. (*Saskatchewan*) M.Eng.: "Flexural stresses and deflections of a prestressed concrete I-beam." (Civil Engineering & Applied Mechanics: De Stein, D.)

56-503 **Bernard**, Ernest A. (*Saskatchewan*) M.Eng.: "Spontaneous ignition delays of propane injected into a hot air stream." (Mechanical Engineering: Thompson, A.)

56-504 **Cairnes**, William P. (*Camborne School of Mines*) M.Eng.: "A study of the rupture of rocks under stress with special reference to mine excavations." (Mining Engineering: Morrison, R.)

56-505 **Chakko**, P.C. (*Travancore*, India) M.Eng.: "The mixing of hot subsonic jets with cold air streams." (Mechanical Engineering: Mordell, D.)

56-506 **Goldie**, Hugh J. (*British Columbia*) M.Eng.: "A study of phototransistors." (Electrical Engineering: Farnell, G.)

56-507 **Haberl**, John F. (*McGill*) M.Eng.: "Microwave measurements on high-Q cavities." (Electrical Engineering: Chipman, R.)

56-508 **Kahn**, Juan P. (*Toronto*) M.Eng.: "Study of the properties and behaviour of quartz crystal units with different drive level conditions." (Electrical Engineering: Howes, F.)

56-509 **Rice**, William B. (*McGill*) M.Eng.: "An experimental investigation of the shear angle relationship in metal cutting." (Mechanical Engineering: Bruce, W.)

56-510 **Seguin**, Maurice J. (*Indiana Technical*) M.Eng.: "Job shop planning." (Mechanical Engineering: White, J.)

56-511 **Spratt**, Gordon W. (*McGill*) M.Eng.: "Cold weather effects on fresh concrete." (Civil Engineering & Applied Mechanics: Craig, C.)

M.Sc. Spring 1956

56-512 **Aprile**, Marie A. (*Toronto*) M.Sc.: "Synthesis and metabolism of $C^{14}$-dimethylacrylic acid." (Biochemistry: Heard, R.)

56-513 **Bernstein**, Hyman (*McGill*) M.Sc.: "$F^{19}(p,pn)F^{18}$ excitation function." (Physics: Foster, J.)

56-514 **Blevis**, Earl H. (*Toronto*) M.Sc.: "The focusing of cylindrical electron beams with periodic magnetic fields." (Physics: Wagner, S.)

56-515 **Chapdelaine**, Joseph L. (*Jean de Brébeuf*) M.Sc.: "Scattering of positrons by hydrogen atoms and formation of positronium." (Physics: Jackson, J.)

56-516 **Cloutier**, Gilles G. (*Laval*) M.Sc.: "Scanning characteristics of some aplanatic microwave lenses." (Physics: Bekefi, G.)

56-517 **De Romer**, Henry S. (*McGill*) M.Sc.: "The geology of the eastern border of the Labrador Trough, east of Thevenet Lake, New Quebec." (Geological Sciences: Kranck, E.)

56-518 **Dore**, Burnell V. (*British Columbia*) M.Sc.: "The application of the velocity-jump principle to X-band frequencies." (Physics: Woonton, G.)

56-519 **Gibbs**, Harold C. (*McGill*) M.Sc.: "Some nematode parasites from Egyptian carnivora." (Parasitology: Cameron, T.)

56-520 **Gillett**, Laurie B. (*McGill*) M.Sc.: "Anorthosites and syenites of the Mealy Mountain area, Labrador." (Geological Sciences: Kranck, E.)

56-521 **Huq**, M. Shamsul (*Dacca*, Pakistan) M.Sc.: "Radiation from $Pt^{192}$ and proposed decay scheme." (Physics: Foster, J.)

56-522 **Jenkins**, J.T. (*McGill*) M.Sc.: "Anorthosite-ilmenite-pegmatite relations on the west bank of La Chaloupe River, Saguenay Co., P.Q." (Geological Sciences: Kranck, E.)

56-523 **Lachance**, Charles-Eugène L. (*Laval*) M.Sc.: "A study of certain morphological characters in red clover populations." (Agronomy: Steppler, H.)

56-524 **Legg**, Thomas H. (*British Columbia*) M.Sc.: "The application of microwave lenses to antenna measurements." (Physics: Bekefi, G.)

56-525 **Lende**, Richard A. (*Oregon State*) M.Sc.: "Local spasm in cerebral arteries." (Neurology & Neurosurgery: Jasper, H.)

56-526 **Lukosevicius**, Petras P. (*Bonn*, West Germany) M.Sc.: "The influence of certain environmental factors on loose smut of barley." (Agronomy: Klinck, H.)

56-527 **MacIntosh**, James A. (*McGill*) M.Sc.: "The quartz deposit at St. Donat, Quebec." (Geological Sciences: Gill, J.)

56-528 **MacKay**, Vernon G. (*McGill*) M.Sc.: "Digestible calories versus total digestible nutrients as quantitative measurements of the available energy of swine rations." (Nutrition: Crampton, E.)

56-529 **Mannard**, George W. (*McGill*) M.Sc.: "The geology of the St. Pierre Prospect, Fort Chimo district, Quebec." (Geological Sciences: Gill, J.)

56-530 **Marleau**, Raymond A. (*Montréal*) M.Sc.: "A study of the relation of the Earth's field as presented on aeromagnetic maps to the geology in Beauce area, Quebec." (Geological Sciences: Saull, V.)

56-531 **Massiah**, Thomas F. (*Sir George Williams*) M.Sc.: "The condensation of beta-aminocrotononitrile with cyclohexanones." (Chemistry: Taurins, A.)

56-532 **Maximchuk**, Arlene J. (*Alberta*) M.Sc.: "Age period changes in the composition of the aortic wall in the rabbit." (Biochemistry: Hoffman, M.)

56-533 **Mittelholzer**, Alexander S. (*Laval*) M.Sc.: "An evaluation of certain agronomic characterisitcs of tetraploid Dollard red clover." (Agronomy: Steppler, H.)

56-534 **Read**, Deane C. (*McGill*) M.Sc.: "The root maggots associated with rutabagas in Prince Edward Island: with especial attention to seasonal history and control of the cabbage maggot (*Hylemya brassicae*) (Bouche): *Diptera, Anthomyiidae*)." (Entomology: Morrison, F.)

56-535 **Reeder**, Stewart W. (*McGill*) M.Sc.: "Mineralogy of the sand and clay fractions of two New Brunswick podzols. The Queens series." (Agricultural Chemistry: Dion, H.)

56-536 **Reeves**, Hubert (*Montréal*) M.Sc.: "The formation of positronium in hydrogen and helium gases." (Physics: Jackson, J.)

56-537 **Roumbanis**, Theodore (*McGill*) M.Sc.: "Measurements on periodically-obstructed wave-guides." (Physics: Woonton, G.)

56-538 **Smith**, Robert C. (*Western*) M.Sc.: "A correction to the radiative transition rate occurring in internal conversion." (Mathematics: Jackson, J.)

56-539 **Speers**, Robert (*Toronto*) M.Sc.: "Development of an antigen for macroscopic agglutination of treponemeta." (Bacteriology & Immunology: Kalz, G.)

56-540 **Squires**, Hubert J. (*McGill*) M.Sc.: "Decapod *Crustacea* of the Calanus expeditions in Ungava Bay, 1947-1950." (Zoology: Dunbar, M.)

56-541 **Steele**, Donald H. (*Western*) M.Sc.: "The redfish (*Sebastes marinus* L.) in the Gulf of St. Lawrence." (Zoology: Dunbar, M.)

56-542 **Tanner**, Charles E. (*Purdue*) M.Sc.: "The influence of a mold product on the antigenicity of staphylococcal toxin." (Bacteriology & Immunology: Girvin, G.)

56-543 **Tunis**, Cyril J. (*McGill*) M.Sc.: "An electron gun and beam spreading." (Physics: Wagner, S.)

56-544 **Winter**, Karl A. (*McGill*) M.Sc.: "A study of the effect of physical, botanical and chemical characteristics on the nutritional value of western Canadian oats." (Nutrition: Crampton, E.)

**M.A. Spring 1956**

56-545 **Bider**, Milton A. (*Montréal*) M.A.: "The Anglo-French military and naval staff conversations, 1906-1914." (History: Fieldhouse, H.)

56-546 **Mentha**, Guy (*McGill*) M.A.: "Le jeu de l'illusion et de la réalité dans l'oeuvre de Jean Giraudoux." (French: Launay, J.)

56-547 **Michie**, George H. (*Toronto*) M.A.: "Sept-Iles: Canada's newest seaport." (Geography: Hare, F.)

56-548 **Nemser**, Ruby D. (*McGill*) M.A.: "Spenser and the principle of plenitude." (English: Hemlow, J.)

56-549 **Speyer**, Judith (*McGill*) M.A.: "The nature of political ideals: a study of the political thought of Reinhold Niebuhr." (Political Science: Scott, P.)

56-550 **Steigmann**, Axel H. (*McGill*) M.A.: "The hyper quantity theory of money." (Economics: Beach, E.)

56-551 **Subroto** (*Indonesia*) M.A.: "A study of the post-war terms of trade of Indonesia, 1945-1953." (Economics: Kemp, M.)

**S.T.M. Fall 1956**

56-552 **Skynner**, H.J. (*Manitoba*) S.T.M.: "Natural law in the New Testament." (Divinity: Caird, G.)

**M.Eng. Fall 1956**

56-553 **Balakrishna**, Narasipur H. (*Mysore*, India) M.Eng.: "Some aspects of the spontaneous ignition delay of propane injected into a hot air stream." (Mechanical Engineering: Thompson, A.)

56-554 **Bredahl**, Arve (*Saskatchewan*) M.Eng.: "Designing and testing of microphone windscreens." (Electrical Engineering: Howes, F.)

56-555 **Chipps**, George E. (*McGill*) M.Eng.: "Study of the noise produced by a centrifugal ventilating fan." (Electrical Engineering: Howes, F.)

56-556 **Coll**, David C. (*McGill*) M.Eng.: "Resonance properties of open parallel-wire transmission line sections at 3000 megacycles per second." (Electrical Engineering: Chipman, R.)

56-557 **Fang**, Sin-Kan (*Chiao Tung*, China) M.Eng.: "Spontaneous ignition delays of propane injected into a hot air stream." (Mechanical Engineering: Thompson, A.)

56-558 **Neis**, Vernon V. (*Alberta*) M.Eng.: "Torsional resistance of a steel beam having stiffeners. II." (Civil Engineering & Applied Mechanics: De Stein, J.)

56-559 **Nichols**, Ian O. (*Glasgow*, Scotland) M.Eng.: "Turbulent fluid flow through beds of solid particles." (Chemical Engineering: Gauvin, W.)

56-560 **Pfefferkorn**, Gerhard A. (*Westfalia*, West Germany) M.Eng.: "The transfer of heat from water to a bed of spherical particles." (Mechanical Engineering: Mordell, D.)

56-561 **Pratinidhi**, Shrivivas V. (*Poona*, India) M.Eng.: "An experimental method for measuring heat transfer coefficients in the thermal entrance region of a circular tube." (Mechanical Engineering: Thompson, A.)

56-562 **Shaw**, Gerald A. (*British Columbia*) M.Eng.: "The influence of the angle of impingement on heat transfer coefficients and pressure drops for the flow of air over a tube bank." (Mechanical Engineering: Mordell, D.)

56-563 **Youdelis**, William V. (*Alberta*) M.Eng.: "Inverse segregation in Al-Cu alloys." (Metallurgical Engineering: Kirkaldy, J.)

**LL.M. Fall 1956**

56-564 **Flynn**, Frank J. (*New Hampshire*) LL.M.: "The legal status of the airspace of trusteeship territory." (International Air Law: Cooper, J.)

56-565 **Macbrayne**, Sheila F. (*Glasgow*, Scotland) LL.M.: "Right of innocent passage." (International Air Law: Pépin, E.)

56-566 **Nylen**, Torsten (*Stockholm*, Sweden) LL.M.: "A study of the draft Swedish Civil Aviation Act of 1955." (International Air Law: Pépin, E.)

**M.Sc. Fall 1956**

56-567 **Barnes**, Marion J. (*McMaster*) M.Sc.: "Serological and physiological studies on *Escherichia coli* from cases of gastroenteritis in infants." (Bacteriology: Prissick, F.)

56-568 **Barshaw**, Wilma E. (*McGill*) M.Sc.: "Requirements of a Lancefield group A streptococcus for growth and nephrotoxin production." (Bacteriology & Immunology: Reed, R.)

56-569 **Boyd**, William (*Amherst*) M.Sc.: "The cranial dura and related structures in the region of the hypophyseal fossa in the cow." (Anatomy: Martin, C.)

56-570 **Clark**, Karin H. (*McGill*) M.Sc.: "Factors in the experimental production of congenital cleft palate in mice by cortisone and other agents." (Genetics: Fraser, F.)

56-571 **Coffin**, David E. (*McGill*) M.Sc.: "Investigations on the release of organic matter from the B horizon of podsol soils." (Agricultural Chemistry: DeLong, W.)

56-572 **Dutt**, Nihar R. (*Calcutta*, India) M.Sc.: "Role of histamine in acute radiation syndrome." (Experimental Surgery: Webster, D.)

56-573 **Fabrikant**, Irene B. (*McGill*) M.Sc.: "Methods of differentiating virulent and saprophytic mycobacteria by the slide culture technique." (Bacteriology & Immunology: Reed, R.)

56-574 **Gantchev**, Neno (*Toulouse*, France) M.Sc.: "Nitramines of the pyridinecarboxylic acids series." (Chemistry: Taurins, A.)

56-575 **Givner**, Morris L. (*McGill*) M.Sc.: "Estrogen metabolism in human subjects." (Biochemistry: Bauld, W.)

56-576 **Gleeson**, Christopher F. (*Montréal*) M.Sc.: "The geology and mineralization of the Pegma Lake area in New Quebec." (Geological Sciences: Stevenson, J.)

56-577 **Goodall**, Robert G. (*McGill*) M.Sc.: "An evaluation of hypothermia in hepatic and major abdominal surgery in dogs." (Experimental Surgery: Gurd, F.)

56-578 **Henry**, Vann C. (*McGill*) M.Sc.: "A study of the inheritance of earliness in Gaspé flint and some inbred lines of corn." (Agronomy: Brawn, R.)

56-579 **Hikichi**, Akira (*Toronto*) M.Sc.: "The effect of DDT on codling moth adults (*Carpocapsa pomonella* L.) (*Lepidoptera: Oletheutidae*)." (Entomology: Morrison, F.)

56-580 **Hodgson**, Richard C. (*McGill*) M.Sc.: "Some factors affecting the relationship between prejudice and the ability to identify ethnic group membership." (Psychology: Lambert, W.)

56-581 **Keener**, Ellis B. (*Emory*) M.Sc.: "A study of the reactions of the dura to wounding and loss of substance." (Neurology & Neurosurgery: Cone, W.)

56-582 **Kohler**, Allan C. (*McMaster*) M.Sc.: "The age, growth and maturity of the haddock (*Melanogrammus aeglefinus* L.) from the inshore Lockeport grounds." (Zoology: **)

56-583 **Liszauer**, Susan M. (*Munich*, Germany) M.Sc.: "The use of nephron dissection in the study of human Armanni-Ebstein nephropathy: glycogenic vacualization of renal epithelium." (Pathology: Waugh, D.)

56-584 **McKay**, Ian A. (*McGill*) M.Sc.: "Forest types of the Kenamu-Kenemich drainage basin, Labrador: an interpretation of cover types from an aerial photograph mosaic." (Geography: Hare, F.)

56-585 **McLaughlan**, John M. (*McGill*) M.Sc.: "Vitamin and amino acid interrelationships in the metabolism of a mutant strain of *Escherichia coli*." (Agricultural Bacteriology: Wallace, R.)

56-586 **MacLeod**, Harry A. (*McGill*) M.Sc.: "Studies on the determination of pteroylglutamic acid." (Agricultural Chemistry: Common, R.)

56-587 **MacRae**, Herbert F. (*McGill*) M.Sc.: "Studies on the constitution of casein." (Agricultural Chemistry: Baker, B.)

56-588 **Marsden**, Michael (*Cambridge*, England) M.Sc.: "A geographical study of the south shore of Coronation Gulf between 111°00' W. and 115°45' W." (Geography: Bird, J.)

56-589 **Mercier**, Raymond P. (*McGill*) M.Sc.: "The application of Mellin transforms to statistics." (Mathematics: Fox, C.)

56-590 **Messier**, Bernard H. (*Montréal*) M.Sc.: "Radioautographic localization of some acid soluble phosphorus compounds in tissues of rats injected with $p^{32}$." (Anatomy: Leblond, C.)

56-591 **Morgen**, Robert O. (*Miami*) M.Sc.: "The influence of stress on thyroid function in the rat." (Experimental Medicine: Hoffman, M.)

56-592 **Ogilvy**, William L. (*St. Andrews*, Scotland) M.Sc.: "Vascular changes and direct tissue effects in severe cold injury." (Experimental Surgery: Webster, D.)

56-593 **Peto**, Margaret (*McGill*) M.Sc.: "Free amino acid levels in the yolks of tumour-bearing embryonated eggs." (Biochemistry: Quastel, J.)

56-594 **Pickup**, T. (*McGill*) M.Sc.: "Sample sizes for vegetable seed testing." (Horticulture: Murray, H.)

56-595 **Prillaman**, J.H. ( ) M.Sc.: "The derivation of the chi-square test of goodness of fit." (Mathematics: **)

56-596 **Rochefort**, Joseph G. (*Laval*) M.Sc.: "The distribution of corticotropin in the pituitary gland." (Biochemistry: Saffran, M.)

56-597 **Ronald**, Keith (*McGill*) M.Sc.: "The metazoan parasites of the *Heterosomata* of the Gulf of the St. Lawrence." (Parasitology: Cameron, T.)

56-598 **Rosenberg**, Gilbert (*McGill*) M.Sc.: "A study of certain characteristics of salivary secretion in humans: the relation of adrenal cortical activity to these characteristics." (Experimental Medicine: Hoffman, M.)

56-599 **Rosenfeld**, Michael W. (*McGill*) M.Sc.: "Factors affecting the anaerobic glycolysis of brain tissue and the effects of sodium and potassium on brain metabolism." (Biochemistry: Elliott, K.)

56-600 **Rozdilsky**, Bohdan (*Lvow*, Soviet Union) M.Sc.: "Permeability of cerebral blood vessels to protein molecules in convulsive seizures." (Neurology & Neurosurgery: Olszewski, J.)

56-601 **Seeman**, Philip (*McGill*) M.Sc.: "The exchange of sodium and potassium in salivary glands." (Physiology: Burgen, A.)

56-602 **Segal**, Benny (*McGill*) M.Sc.: "Analysis of a high-speed vacuum system." (Physics: Crowell, C.)

56-603 **Stachenko**, Janine L. (*Bordeaux*, France) M.Sc.: "Production of corticosteroids by rat adrenal tissue *in vitro*." (Investigative Medicine: Venning, E.)

56-604 **Stewart**, Lever F. (*Princeton*) M.Sc.: "Chlorpromazine as an activator of abnormal potentials in the electroencephalograms of patients with seizures." (Neurology & Neurosurgery: Jasper, H.)

56-605 **Sybulski**, Stella (*McGill*) M.Sc.: "An investigation of the urinary corticosteroid pattern in adrenal cortical disease by the technique of paper chromatography." (Investigative Medicine: Venning, E.)

56-606 **Thomas**, George M. (*Annamalai*, India) M.Sc.: "Beta spectroscopic studies with improved sources." (Physics: Foster, J.)

56-607 **Thorne**, Kenrick H. (*McGill*) M.Sc.: "The use of gaseous ammonia as a plant nutrient." (Agronomy: Klinck, H.)

56-608 **Townsend**, Edith E. (*McGill*) M.Sc.: "The fluorimetric measurement of adrenaline and nonadrenaline in human plasma." (Biochemistry: Sourkes, T.)

56-609 **Webster**, Donald C. (*McGill*) M.Sc.: "Sexual reproduction in *Medeola virginiana* L. with some reference to embryo development and endosperm formation." (Botany: Boothroyd, E.)

56-610 **Wiseman**, Miriam H. (*Manitoba*) M.Sc.: "A study of tryptophan metabolism in man." (Biochemistry: Hoffman, M.)

**M.A. Fall 1956**

56-611 **Baumgartner**, Helmut W. (*Giessen*) M.A.: "Problems of resource allocation in Quebec agriculture." (Agricultural Economics: MacFarlane, D.)

56-612 **Brown**, Carl E. (*McGill*) M.A.: "Character-portrayal in the 'Cena Trimalchionis' of Petronius." (Classics: Counsell, E.)

56-613 **Bruck**, Esther R. (*McGill*) M.A.: "The development of William Butler Yeats as a dramatist." (English: Walker, R.)

56-614 **Burnett**, Alvin A. (*McGill*) M.A.: "Measuring the efficiency of agriculture in Quebec." (Agricultural Economics: Kemp, M.)

56-615 **Dowd**, Keith J. (*Carleton*) M.A.: "The first country central school board in Quebec." (Education: Smith, C.)

56-616 **French**, Betty R. (*Boston*) M.A.: "The representations of particular groups." (Mathematics: Burrow, M.)

56-617 **Gyorgy**, Anne M. (*McGill*) M.A.: "Les héroines d'Anouilh." (French: Rigault, A.)

56-618 **Herschorn**, Michael (*McGill*) M.A.: "Uniqueness theorems for ordinary differential equations." (Mathematics: Kaufman, H.)

56-619 **Kyritz**, Heinz G. ( ) M.A.: "Paris als Erlebnis zu Rilkes '3. Stundenbuch' und zu den 'Aufzeichnungen des Malte Laurids Brigge'." (German: Graff, W.)

56-620 **Rosevear**, John N. (*McGill*) M.A.: "Chambly County Protestant Central School Board, 1945-1955." (Education: Smith, C.)

56-621 **Rowlands**, Mary E. (*McGill*) M.A.: "Social satire in the poetry of Robert Henryson." (English: Reid, W.)

56-622 **Rubin**, Gerald M. (*McGill*) M.A.: "Liberal criticism of Sir Edward Grey's foreign policy, 1906-1914." (History: Fieldhouse, H.)

56-623 **Skoll**, Selma D. (*McGill*) M.A.: "Stephen Leacock: the man and his art." (English: MacLennan, H.)

56-624 **Wright**, John M. (*McGill*) M.A.: "The settlement of the Victoria region, British Columbia." (Geography: Hare, F.)

56-625 **Wright**, Ouida (*London*, England) M.A.: "The development of education in Jamaica." (Education: Smith, C.)

## ANNUAL LISTING

### Ph.D. Spring 1957

57-001 **Bartok**, William (*McGill*) Ph.D.: "Rigid and deformable particles in sheared suspensions." (Chemistry: Mason, S.)

57-002 **Belle**, Edward A. (*Lincoln*) Ph.D.: "The effect of microclimate and micro-environment on the free-living stages of *Bunostomum* and *Graphidium* (*Nematoda*)." (Parasitology: Cameron, T.)

57-003 **Birks**, Richard I. (*McGill*) Ph.D.: "Acetylcholine turnover in sympathetic ganglia." (Physiology: MacIntosh, F.)

57-004 **Bubar**, John S. (*McGill*) Ph.D.: "Genetics and cytotaxonomy in birdsfoot trefoil (*Lotus corniculatus* L.)." (Genetics: Boyes, J.)

57-005 **Clark**, David S. (*McGill*) Ph.D.: "The oxidation of carbonaceous compounds by a yeast-like fungus." (Agricultural Bacteriology: Wallace, R.)

57-006 **Dlouhy**, Jan (*McGill*) Ph.D.: "Heat and mass transfer in spray drying." (Chemical Engineering: Gauvin, W.)

57-007 **Douglas**, Richard H. (*Alberta*) Ph.D.: "Snow cells and showers." (Meteorology: Marshall, J.)

57-008 **Edwards**, Donald K. (*British Columbia*) Ph.D.: "A study of acclimatization and other factors affecting respiration and survival in *Tribolium confusum* Duval." (Zoology: Stanley, J.)

57-009 **Ellis**, Derek V. (*Edinburgh*, Scotland) Ph.D.: "Marine infaunal benthos in Arctic North America." (Zoology: Dunbar, M.)

57-010 **Enesco**, Mircea A. (*Roumania*) Ph.D.: "Increase in cell number and size and in extracellular space during postnatal growth of several organs in the albino rat." (Anatomy: Leblond, C.)

57-011 **Freeman**, Peter V. (*Witwatersrand*, South Africa) Ph.D.: "Geology of the Beraud-Mazerac area, Quebec." (Geological Sciences: Kranck, E.)

57-012 **Gloor**, Peter (*Basel*, Switzerland) Ph.D.: "Electrophysiological studies of the amygdala in the cat." (Neurology & Neurosurgery: Jasper, H.)

57-013 **Haering**, Rudolph R. (*British Columbia*) Ph.D.: "The electric and magnetic properties of graphite." (Mathematics: Wallace, P.)

57-014 **Hagley**, Elmer A. (*McGill*) Ph.D.: "The biological activity of some (P-chlorophenyl) compounds synergistic with DDT." (Entomology: McFarlane, J.)

57-015 **Henry**, Zin A. (*London*, England) Ph.D.: "An economic analysis of the guaranteed wage and its application to the Canadian economy." (Economics & Political Science: Woods, H.)

57-016 **Herron**, John T. (*Manitoba*) Ph.D.: "Mass spectrometry of normal oxygen and oxygen subjected to electrical discharge." (Chemistry: Schiff, H.)

57-017 **Hoffman**, John C. (*Toronto*) Ph.D.: "Partial separation of phlobaphenes of white spruce bark by chromatographic methods." (Chemistry: Purves, C.)

57-018 **Hollbach**, Natasha (*Dalhousie*) Ph.D.: "Spallation products formed by the bombardment of cobalt with protons of energies up to 100 Mev." (Chemistry: Yaffe, L.)

57-019 **Horscroft**, Frank D. (*Rhodes*, South Africa) Ph.D.: "The petrology of gabbroic sills in the volcanic series of Roy and McKenzie Townships, Chibougamau Region, Quebec." (Geological Sciences: Kranck, E.)

57-020 **Kornelsen**, Ernest V. (*Saskatchewan*) Ph.D.: "An experimental study of noise processes in an electron gun." (Physics: Woonton, G.)

57-021 **Layne**, Donald S. (*McGill*) Ph.D.: "On the nature of the gonadal hormones of the domestic fowl." (Agricultural Chemistry: Common, R.)

57-022 **Loiselle**, Jean-Marie (*Laval*) Ph.D.: "The behaviour of coenzymes in the liver of the rat during hemorrhagic shock." (Biochemistry: Denstedt, O.)

57-023 **MacEwan**, John R. (*McGill*) Ph.D.: "A study of the rate of self-diffusion of nickel and of the rate of diffusion of nickel into iron, cobalt and two iron-nickel alloys." (Chemistry: MacEwan, J.)

57-024 **Murray**, Thomas K. (*McGill*) Ph.D.: "Studies on the determination of vitamin A and the utilization of vitamin A by the rat." (Agricultural Chemistry: Common, R.)

57-025 **Oler**, Norman (*McGill*) Ph.D.: "An inequality in the geometry of numbers." (Mathematics: Zassenhaus, H.)

57-026 **Pollock**, Donald W. (*McGill*) Ph.D.: "The geology of the Addington-Preston area." (Geological Sciences: Stevenson, J.)

57-027 **Prasad**, Devendra (*Patna*, India) Ph.D.: "Studies on the effect of the micro-environment on the free-living stages of some parasitic nematodes." (Parasitology: Cameron, T.)

57-028 **Riley**, George C. (*McGill*) Ph.D.: "The geology of the Cumberland Sound region, Baffin Island." (Geological Sciences: Kranck, E.)

57-029 **Ross**, Ian K. (*George Washington*) Ph.D.: "The life cycle and cytology of the myxogastres." (Botany: Wilson, C.)

57-030 **Schally**, Andrew V. (*McGill*) Ph.D.: "*In vitro* studies on the control of the release of ACTH." (Biochemistry: Saffran, M.)

57-031 **Shkarofsky**, Issie (*McGill*) Ph.D.: "Behaviour of modulated electron beams subjected to various potential distributions." (Physics: Woonton, G.)

57-032 **Slipp**, Robert M. (*Dalhousie*) Ph.D.: "Base metal deposits in the 'Labrador Trough' between Lake Harveng and Lac Aulneua, New Quebec." (Geological Sciences: Gill, J.)

57-033 **Smart**, Celina (*McGill*) Ph.D.: "Factors affecting the rate of acetic acid production by species of *Acetobacter*." (Agricultural Bacteriology: Wallace, R.)

57-034 **Smith**, David D. (*Sir George Williams*) Ph.D.: "The relationship between abilities and interests: a factorial study." (Psychology: Ferguson, G.)

57-035 **Stuart**, James R. (*McGill*) Ph.D.: "Sodium and potassium concentrations in tissues of rabbits in relation to arterial blood pressure." (Pathology: Waugh, D.)

57-036 **Sullivan**, Calvin R. (*Ontario Agricultural*) Ph.D.: "A biological study of the white pine weevil, *Pissodes strobi* Peck, with special reference to the effect of physical factors on its activity and behaviour." (Entomology: DuPorte, E.)

57-037 **Summers**, William F. (*Dalhousie*) Ph.D.: "A geographical analysis of population trends in Newfoundland." (Geography: Hare, F.)

57-038 **Swan**, Eric P. (*British Columbia*) Ph.D.: "The location of the xanthate groups in partly substituted cellulose xanthates." (Chemistry: Purves, C.)

57-039 **Sweatman**, Gordon K. (*McMaster*) Ph.D.: "Life history, non-specificity and revision of the genus *Chorioptes*, a parasitic mite of herbivores." (Parasitology: Cameron, T.)

57-040 **Thomas**, Telfer L. (*McGill*) Ph.D.: "Constituents of the oleoresin of the American male-fern (*Dryopyeris filix-mas*.)." (Chemistry: Taurins, A.)

57-041 **Vessot**, Robert F. (*McGill*) Ph.D.: "Noise at the anode of an electron gun." (Physics: Woonton, G.)

57-042 **Waid**, Ted H. (*Caen*, France) Ph.D.: "A study of some nitrogen-containing steroids." (Chemistry: Taurins, A.)

57-043 **Wang**, Dalton T. (*Fu Jen*, China) Ph.D.: "Studies on the nature of resistance of plants to disease: alterations in the nitrogen and keto-acid metabolism of resistant and susceptible wheat varieties associated with infection by *Puccinia graminis tritici* Eriks and Henn." (Plant Pathology: Pelletier, R.)

57-044 **Webster**, Gloria A. (*Connecticut*) Ph.D.: "The biology of *Toxocara canis* Werner, 1782." (Parasitology: Cameron, T.)

57-045 **Whitten**, Lloyd K. (*Sydney*, Australia) Ph.D.: "The relationships of nutrition and parasitism." (Parasitology: Cameron, T.)

57-046 **Wiles**, David M. (*McMaster*) Ph.D.: "The reactions of active nitrogen with phosphine and hydrogen chloride." (Chemistry: Winkler, C.)

57-047 **Wolofsky**, Leib (*McGill*) Ph.D.: "Hydrothermal experiments with variable pore pressure and shear stress in part of the MgO2-SiO2-H2O system." (Geological Sciences: Gill, J.)

57-048 **Wright**, Archibald N. (*McGill*) Ph.D.: "The reactions of hydrogen atoms with amines." (Chemistry: Winkler, C.)

**D.Mus. Spring 1957**

57-049 **Frackenpohl**, Arthur R. (*Eastman School of Music*) D.Mus.: "Musical composition: Symphony in D." (Music: Duchow, M.)

## ANNUAL LISTING

**Ph.D. Fall 1957**

57-050 **Armstrong**, Robert A. (*Toronto*) Ph.D.: "The temperature dependence of the work functions of sodium and potassium." (Physics: Crowell, C.)

57-051 **Assaly**, Robert N. (*Saskatchewan*) Ph.D.: "Aberrations and scanning properties of some microwave lens systems." (Physics: Woonton, G.)

57-052 **Bass**, P. (*British Columbia*) Ph.D.: "The role and possible significance of potassium, calcium and magnesium in the cardiac actions of digitalis glycosides." (Pharmacology: Melville, K.)

57-053 **Emo**, Wallace B. (*McGill*) Ph.D.: "The geology of the Wacouno region, Saguenay Co., P.Q." (Geological Sciences: Kranck, E.)

57-054 **Farnell**, Gerald W. (*Toronto*) Ph.D.: "Phase distribution in the focal region of a microwave lens system." (Electrical Engineering: Woonton, G.)

57-055 **Gibson**, Merritt A. (*Acadia*) Ph.D.: "A histochemical and cytological study of the development of membrane bone in the chick (*Gallus domesticus*)." (Zoology: Scott, H.)

57-056 **Huque**, Mohammed M. (*Dacca*, Pakistan) Ph.D.: "Molecular size and configuration of cellulose trinitrate in solution." (Chemistry: Mason, S.)

57-057 **James**, William (*Toronto*) Ph.D.: "Geology of Dungannon and Mayo-Townships in southeastern Ontario." (Geological Sciences: Stevenson, J.)

57-058 **Klassen**, Norman V. (*McGill*) Ph.D.: "The reaction of active nitrogen with cyclopentane." (Chemistry: Winkler, C.)

57-059 **Krupka**, Richard M. (*Saskatchewan*) Ph.D.: "Studies on the keto acid metabolism of wheat seedlings." (Botany: Towers, G.)

57-060 **Kuhn**, Tillo E. (*London*, England) Ph.D.: "The economics of road transport." (Economics: Culliton, J.)

57-061 **Lagnado**, John R. (*Geneva*, Switzerland) Ph.D.: "The role of cofactors in the enzymatic reduction of tetrazolium salts by amines." (Biochemistry: Sourkes, T.)

57-062 **Link**, William T. (*Saskatchewan*) Ph.D.: "Studies of short lived isomeric states of atomic nuclei." (Physics: Foster, J.)

57-063 **MacDougall**, John F. (*McGill*) Ph.D.: 'Experiments bearing on the genesis of sulphide deposits." (Geological Sciences: Gill, J.)

57-064 **Matheson**, Ballem H. (*McGill*) Ph.D.: "A study of the nephritogenic substance produced by type 12 streptococci." (Bacteriology & Immunology: Reed, R.)

57-065 **Mazurkiewicz**, Irena M. (*Jagellon*, Poland) Ph.D.: "Studies of changes in the urinary excretion of adrenaline and noradrenaline with some observations on their possible pharmacological significance." (Pharmacology: Benfey, B.)

57-066 **Meerovitch**, Eugene (*St. John's*, Shanghai) Ph.D.: "Studies on the biology of parasitic amoeba of reptiles." (Parasitology: Cameron, T.)

57-067 **Melamed**, Samuel (*McGill*) Ph.D.: "Qualitative behaviour of non-linear differential equations in the neighbourhood of an isolated singular point." (Mathematics: Kaufman, H.)

57-068 **Morris**, Peter G. (*London*, England) Ph.D.: "A chemical, optical and x-ray study of certain zeolites." (Geological Sciences: Stevenson, J.)

57-069 **Nawab**, Mohammed A. (*Dacca*, Pakistan) Ph.D.: "The viscosity of dilute emulsions and suspensions." (Chemistry: Mason, S.)

57-070 **Nelson**, William A. (*Alberta*) Ph.D.: "Population behaviour of the sheep ked, *Melophagus ovinus* (L.), in relation to endocrine mechanisms in sheep." (Entomology: DuPorte, E.)

57-071 **Nommik**, Salme (*Tartu*, Estonia) Ph.D.: "Serological tests in Canadian hydatid disease." (Parasitology: Cameron, T.)

57-072 **Norman**, Nils (*Oslo*, Norway) Ph.D.: "The participation of bone in the sodium and potassium metabolism of the rat." (Experimental Medicine: Beck, J.)

57-073 **Osborn**, Dale J. (*Colorado*) Ph.D.: "The systematics of certain small mammals of the Quebec peninsula." (Zoology: Dunbar, M.)

57-074 **Ottolenghi**, Paul (*McGill*) Ph.D.: "The lactic dehydrogenase of the mammalian erythrocyte." (Biochemistry: Denstedt, O.)

57-075 **Parmar**, Surendra S. (*Lucknow*, India) Ph.D.: "Carbohydrate metabolism in the central nervous system." (Biochemistry: Quastel, J.)

57-076 **Petrushka**, Evelyn (*McGill*) Ph.D.: "The use of snake venom phospholipase A in a study of mitochondria." (Biochemistry: Quastel, J.)

57-077 **Schnore**, Morris M. (*Western*) Ph.D.: "Individual differences in patterning and level of physiological activity: a study of arousal." (Psychology: Malmo, R.)

57-078 **Sobering**, Simon E. (*Manitoba*) Ph.D.: "The reactions of active nitrogen with chloromethanes." (Chemistry: Winkler, C.)

57-079 **Speers**, Robert (*Toronto*) Ph.D.: "Biological studies on treponemata." (Bacteriology & Immunology: Kalz, G.)

57-080 **Srinivasan**, Swamy A. (*Nagpur*, India) Ph.D.: "Role of aminosugars in glycoside synthesis and in cell metabolism." (Biochemistry: Quastel, J.)

57-081 **Stachiw**, Dennis L. (*Vienna*, Austria) Ph.D.: "Synthesis and reactions of the piperidine spiranes." (Chemistry: Taurins, A.)

57-082 **Stern**, Muriel H. (*McGill*) Ph.D.: "The relation between thyroid function and human temperament." (Psychology: Bindra, D.)

57-083 **Tanner**, Charles E. (*Purdue*) Ph.D.: "The influence of a mold product on the antigenicity of staphylococcal toxin: further studies." (Bacteriology & Immunology: Girvin, G.)

57-084 **Thomson**, Hugh M. (*McGill*) Ph.D.: "*Perezia fumiferanae* Thom., a protozoan parasite of the spruce budworm, *Choristoneura fumiferanae* (Clem.)." (Parasitology: Cameron, T.)

57-085 **Twidale**, Charles R. (*Bristol*, England) Ph.D.: "Development of slopes in central New Quebec-Labrador." (Geography: Bird, J.)

57-086 **Van Steenbergen**, Arie (*Delft*, Netherlands) Ph.D.: "Spin lattice relaxation studies of molecular motions in solids." (Physics: Foster, J.)

57-087 **Velay**, Clement C. (*Sir George Williams*) Ph.D.: "Some aspects of the problem of economic development in underdeveloped countries." (Economics: Weldon, J.)

57-088 **Whitehead**, Andrew B. (*New Brunswick*) Ph.D.: "Cross section studies in carbon, oxygen and fluorine." (Physics: Foster, J.)

57-089 **Wieckowski**, Erwin (*London*, England) Ph.D.: "Action of reducing agents on a limit hypochlorite oxylignin." (Chemistry: Purves, C.)

**M.C.L. Spring 1957**

57-500 **Carisse**, Joseph B. (*Ottawa*) M.C.L.: "La propriété privée et l'urbanisme." (Law: Scott, F.)

**M.Arch. Spring 1957**

57-501 **Leaning**, John D. (*Liverpool*, England) M.Arch.: "The Canadian shopping centre." (Architecture: Spence-Sales, H.)

57-502 **Moriyama**, Raymond J. (*Toronto*) M.Arch.: "Urban renewal planning and design." (Architecture: Spence-Sales, H.)

**S.T.M. Spring 1957**

57-503 **Kirby**, John C. (*McGill*) S.T.M.: "The Exodus in the New Testament." (Divinity: Caird, G.)

**M.Eng. Spring 1957**

57-504 **Charasz**, Jerzy G. (*McGill*) M.Eng.: "An automatic electronic B-H curve plotter for testing magnetic materials over a wide frequency range." (Electrical Engineering: Pavlasek, T.)

57-505 **Davey**, Trevor B. (*Manitoba*) M.Eng.: "Temperature effects on inlet region heat transfer coefficients." (Mechanical Engineering: Stachiewicz, J.)

57-506 **Irwin**, Roland E. (*Queen's*) M.Eng.: "A study of the spontaneous ignition delay of hot lean mixtures of gaseous hydrocarbon fuels and air in a flow system." (Mechanical Engineering: Thompson, A.)

57-507 **Issen**, Lionel (*McGill*) M.Eng.: "A study of prestressed concrete." (Civil Engineering & Applied Mechanics: De Stein, J.)

57-508 **Kubina**, S.J. (*McGill*) M.Eng.: "Design of high-pass acoustic filters with special reference to aircraft engine exhaust manifolds." (Electrical Engineering: Howes, F.)

57-509 **Ortlepp**, William D. (*Witwatersrand*, South Africa) M.Eng.: "An experimental investigation into certain aspects of rock failure." (Mining Engineering: Morrison, R.)

57-510 **Padopulos**, Diogenes (*Chile*) M.Eng.: "Compression of silt under model footings." (Civil Engineering & Applied Mechanics: Coates, D.)

57-511 **Real**, Roderick R. (*Saskatchewan*) M.Eng.: "Noise origin, power and spectra of ducted centrifugal fans." (Electrical Engineering: Howes, F.)

57-512 **Van Walsum**, Ewout (*Delft*, Netherlands) M.Eng.: "Bond of steel wires in prestressed concrete." (Civil Engineering & Applied Mechanics: De Stein, J.)

57-513 **Winship**, R.D. (*McGill*) M.Eng.: "Spontaneous ignition delay of lean hydrocarbon mixtures." (Mechanical Engineering: Thompson, L. & Mordell, D.)

**LL.M. Spring 1957**

57-514 **Ahmad**, Mumtaz (*Panjab*, India) LL.M.: "The law of civil aviation in Pakistan." (International Air Law: Pépin, E.)

57-515 **Ahmed**, Saiyed E. (*Sind*, Pakistan) LL.M.: "The airspace in international air law." (International Air Law: Pépin, E.)

57-516 **Rippon**, Clive L. (*Dalhousie*) LL.M.: "The legal status of military air transport." (International Air Law: Pépin, E.)

57-517 **Wojcik**, Tadeusz Z. (*Cracow*, Poland) LL.M.: "La période de transport dans ses relations avec la responsabilité du transporteur de personnes." (International Air Law: Pépin, E.)

**M.Sc. Spring 1957**

57-518 **Ajemian**, Ann A. (*Western Reserve*) M.Sc.: "Production of a toxin-neutralizing substance by *Penicillium cyaneo-fulvum*." (Bacteriology & Immunology: Girvin, G.)

57-519 **Anderson**, Gordon C. (*McGill*) M.Sc.: "Studies of some factors affecting the establishment of certain forage species." (Agronomy: Steppler, H.)

57-520 **Bahyrycz**, G.S. (*McGill*) M.Sc.: "Geology of the Grey River area, Newfoundland, with special reference to metamorphism." (Geological Sciences: Elson, J.)

57-521 **Burns**, Neal M. (*Illinois*) M.Sc.: "Certain effects of cortical stimulation." (Psychology: Milner, P.)

57-522 **Cambieri**, R. (*McGill*) M.Sc.: "Some nematode parasites of rodents in Egypt." (Parasitology: Cameron, T.)

57-523 **De Freitas**, Anthony S. (*McGill*) M.Sc.: "The effect of heat polymerization on the composition and nutritive value of menhaden oil." (Agricultural Chemistry: Common, R.)

57-524 **Freund**, Gerhard (*Goethe*, West Germany) M.Sc.: "Investigations of methods of determination of human pituitary gonadotropins in urine." (Investigative Medicine: Venning, E.)

57-525 **Gibbs**, Kathleen E. (*McGill*) M.Sc.: "A study of the integument of mites with special attention to that of *Tetranychus telarius* (Linnaeus)." (Entomology: Morrison, F.)

57-526 **Grivas**, John C. (*Athens*, Greece) M.Sc.: "A novel reaction of primary amines with trichloroacetonitrile." (Chemistry: Taurins, A.)

57-527 **Ho-Tung**, Clifton G. (*Syracuse*) M.Sc.: "Ozone formation due to electrical discharges at low pressures." (Chemistry: Schiff, H.)

57-528 **Lawrence**, Charles H. (*McGill*) M.Sc.: "Studies on the parasitism of *Streptomyces scabies* (Thaxt.) Waksman and Henrici." (Plant Pathology: Coulson, J.)

57-529 **Litvak**, John (*Denver*) M.Sc. "Experimental production of gradual vascular occlusions." (Neurology & Neurosurgery: Rasmussen, T.)

57-530 **Lockhart**, Chesley L. (*McGill*) M.Sc.: "Studies concerning the effect of culture filtrates of *Fusarium oxysporum* f., *lycopersici* upon the tomato." (Plant Pathology: Coulson, J.)

57-531 **Longley**, James D. (*British Columbia*) M.Sc.: "A study of the potential difference component of the electrogastrograph." (Experimental Surgery: Burgen, A.)

57-532 **Lotz**, James R. (*Manchester*, England) M.Sc.: "Soils and agricultural possibilities of the Knob Lake area, P.Q." (Geography: Hills, T.)

57-533 **Macpherson**, Andrew H. (*Carleton*) M.Sc.: "A taxonomic study of Canadian Arctic gulls of the genus *Larus*." (Zoology: Dunbar, M.)

57-534 **Paivio**, Allan U. (*McGill*) M.Sc.: "A study of stage fright." (Psychology: Lambert, W.)

57-535 **Rejhon**, George (*New Brunswick*) M.Sc.: "A study of the Ordovician conglomerates near Matane, Que." (Geological Sciences: Stearn, C.)

57-536 **Relly**, Bruce H. (*Rhodes*, South Africa) M.Sc.: "A method for determining the solubility of sulphides." (Geological Sciences: Saull, V.)

57-537 **Singh**, Tej B. (*Agra*, India) M.Sc.: "Studies of endocrine effects on experimental metastatic bone tumours." (Experimental Surgery: Webster, D.)

57-538 **Smith**, Robert E. (*McGill*) M.Sc.: "A study of the mechanism of antibiotic action in eggshell calcification." (Poultry Husbandry: Nikolaiczuk, N.)

57-539 **Sutherland**, Charlotte A. (*Dalhousie*) M.Sc.: "The action of alkaline hypochlorite on simple phenolic substances." (Chemistry: Purves, C.)

57-540 **Vickery**, Vernon R. (*McGill*) M.Sc.: "The *Orthoptera* of Nova Scotia." (Entomology: DuPorte, E.)

57-541 **Wilansky**, Douglas L. (*Dalhousie*) M.Sc.: "The influence of senescence on thyroid function." (Investigative Medicine: Hoffman, M.)

57-542 **Wright**, Leebert A. (*McGill*) M.Sc.: "The effects of thiouracil and progesterone on the responses of the immature pullet to estrogen." (Agricultural Chemistry: Common, R.)

57-543 **Zwartendyk**, Jan (*Amsterdam*, Netherlands) M.Sc.: "A petrographic study of the 'granite wash' in the Clear Hills area, Alberta." (Geological Sciences: Stearn, C.)

**M.A. Spring 1957**

57-544 **Beattie**, Stewart (*Sir George Williams*) M.A.: "Canadian intervention in Russia, 1918-1919." (History: Mladenovic, M.)

57-545 **Birks**, Margaret (*Vassar*) M.A.: "Discrimination among Jewish and Protestant children." (Psychology: Lambert, W.)

57-546 **Caezza**, Concepta Z. (*New York State*) M.A.: "Gilbert Cesbron: romancier chrétien et critique du monde moderne." (French: Launay, J.)

57-547 **Geist**, Paul B. ( ) M.A.: "The social and political theories of Edward Hallett Carr." (Political Science: Brecher, M.)

57-548 **Lachs**, John (*McGill*) M.A.: "Epiphenomenalism: a conflict of science and philosophy." (Philosophy: Henderson, T.)

57-549 **Lieber**, Jack W. (*McGill*) M.A.: "Sir Thomas Elyot and the humanist ideal in education." (Education: Munroe, D.)

57-550 **MacFarlane**, Dougald A. (*St. Francis Xavier*) M.A.: "Labour productivity in the primary fishing industry of the Maritimes and British Columbia." (Agricultural Economics: MacFarlane, D.)

57-551 **Milley**, Chesley B. (*Acadia*) M.A.: "The education of non-Catholic English-speaking physically handicapped children in Montreal." (Education: Smith, C.)

57-552 **Overing**, R.L. (*Sir George Williams*) M.A.: "The educational philosophies of Russell and Whitehead; a comparison and assessment in terms of present day problems." (Education: **)

57-553 **Pineo**, Peter C. (*British Columbia*) M.A.: "Migration and the French Canadian extended family." (Anthropology: Garigue, P.)

**M.Arch. Fall 1957**

57-554 **Lam**, Anna P. (*Hong Kong*) M.Arch.: "The problem of housing density in Hong Kong with reference to decentralization." (Architecture: Spence-Sales, H.)

**S.T.M. Fall 1957**

57-555 **Gerard**, F.R. (*McGill*) S.T.M.: "Le mysticisme de Martin Luther dans la tradition chrétienne." (Divinity: **)

57-556 **Rogers**, A.A. (*Mount Allison*) S.T.M.: "The realm of miracle." (Divinity: Thomson, J.)

57-557 **Zuk**, Michael (*Sir George Williams*) S.T.M.: "The Ukrainian protestant missions in Canada." (Divinity: Walsh, H.)

**M.Eng. Fall 1957**

57-558 **Gilbert**, Jacques (*Laval*) M.Eng.: "Measurements of low frequency small-signal transistor parameters and their relation to theory." (Electrical Engineering: Farnell, G.)

57-559 **Kardos**, Geza (*Saskatchewan*) M.Eng.: "A study of Bourdon tube deflection." (Mechanical Engineering: Edis, A.)

**LL.M. Fall 1957**

57-560 **Arnold**, Stanley R. (*Stanford*) LL.M.: "Sovereign rights in space." (International Air Law: Pépin, E.)

57-561 **Gamacchio**, Giampiero (*Rome*, Italy) LL.M.: "Les premiers resultats de la cooperation aeronautique europèene." (International Air Law: Pépin, E.)

57-562 **Mackintosh**, David D. (*Oxford*, England) LL.M.: "Comparative aspects of airport operators liability in the United Kingdom and the United States." (International Air Law: Cooper, J.)

57-563 **Sheffy**, Menachem (*Hebrew*, Israel) LL.M.: "The Air Navigation Commission of the International Civil Aviation Organization." (International Air Law: Pépin, E.)

M.Sc. Fall 1957

57-564 **Bain**, E.B. (*McGill*) M.Sc.: "Histological, cytological and histochemical studies of the mouse epididymis." (Zoology: Scott, H.)

57-565 **Baines**, Joan D. (*McGill*) M.Sc.: "Studies on the metabolism of the fungus *Ascocybe grovesii*." (Botany: Wilson, C.)

57-566 **Bas-Kraus**, Eva R. (*McGill*) M.Sc.: "The acid phosphatases of rat liver." (Biochemistry: Quastel, J.)

57-567 **Bristow**, John M. (*Leeds*, England) M.Sc.: "Studies of growth types in clones and seed lots of pedigree Kenland, Pennscott, Lasalle and Dollard red clover." (Agronomy: Steppler, H.)

57-568 **Caira**, Eugene G. (*Anderson*, Scotland) M.Sc.: "The experimental production of cholelithiasis and cholecystitis in laboratory animals." (Experimental Surgery: Webster, D.)

57-569 **Cunia**, T. (*Nancy*, France) M.Sc.: "Basic mathematical models in analysis of variance." (Mathematics: **)

57-570 **Dawkins**, Riley A. (*McGill*) M.Sc.: "Studies on two aerobic cellulose decomposing bacteria and their relation to soil organic matter." (Agricultural Bacteriology: Blackwood, A.)

57-571 **Denson**, Marie L. (*McGill*) M.Sc.: "Filament formation in *Candida albicans*." (Bacteriology & Immunology: Blank, F.)

57-572 **Esar**, Rhoda (*McGill*) M.Sc.: "The influence of metabolic activity on the movement of cations across the red blood cell membrane." (Biochemistry: Denstedt, O.)

57-573 **Favreau**, Roger F. (*McGill*) M.Sc.: "Neutron induced reactions in nitrogen." (Physics: Terroux, F.)

57-574 **Goel**, Devendra P. (*Agra*, India) M.Sc.: "The study of the effects of radioactive strontium in laboratory animals." (Experimental Surgery: Webster, D.)

57-575 **Grierson**, John K. (*Liverpool*, England) M.Sc.: "Frequency analysis of whistling atmospherics." (Electrical Communications: Chipman, R.)

57-576 **Haber**, Andrew B. (*McGill*) M.Sc.: "Absorption of amino acids and sugars by the isolated surviving guinea pig small intestine." (Biochemistry: Quastel, J.)

57-577 **Hargrove**, Clifford K. (*New Brunswick*) M.Sc.: "The construction of a curved crystal x-ray spectrometer." (Physics: Foster, J.)

57-578 **Henry**, A.S. ( ) M.Sc.: "Electrophoretic studies on serum gamma-globulins in rheumatic fever." (Biochemistry: Harpur, E. & Denstedt, O.)

57-579 **Idziak**, Edmund S. (*McGill*) M.Sc.: "Bacteriostatic and bactericidal effects of sodium hydroxide and sodium hypochlorite on various bacteria." (Agricultural Bacteriology: Wallace, R.)

57-580 **Inglis**, Frederic G. (*Dalhousie*) M.Sc.: "Studies on chlorpromazine in experimental haemorrhagic shock in dogs." (Experimental Surgery: Webster, D.)

57-581 **Kataria**, Prem N. (*Panjab*, India) M.Sc.: "Studies on experimental production and dissolution of renal calcinosis." (Experimental Surgery: Reid, R.)

57-582 **Kennard**, Charles P. (*McGill*) M.Sc.: "Water absorption and metabolism during the embryonic development of the house cricket *Acheta domesticus* (L.) (*Gryllidae, Orthoptera*)." (Entomology: McFarlane, J.)

57-583 **Kim**, Yoon-Bom (*Seoul*, South Korea) M.Sc.: "The morphological observation of the vessels of the brain of human infants." (Neurology & Neurosurgery: McNaughton, F.)

57-584 **Kouris**, Michael (*Dublin*, Ireland) M.Sc.: "The effect of water removal on the crystallinity of cellulose." (Chemistry: Mason, S.)

57-585 **Lister**, Earle E. (*McGill*) M.Sc.: "Voluntary intake of forage as a measure of its feeding value for ruminants." (Nutrition: Lloyd, L.)

57-586 **Lucis**, Ojars J. (*Sir George Williams*) M.Sc.: "Investigations of the action of hypothalamic and pituitary extracts on adrenocortical function." (Investigative Medicine: Venning, E.)

57-587 **McArdle**, Alice H. (*McGill*) M.Sc.: "The influence of dieldrin on enzyme systems." (Biochemistry: Denstedt, O.)

57-588 **McLeod**, Lionel E. (*Alberta*) M.Sc.: "Experiences in the measurement of various body fluid compartments." (Investigative Medicine: Beck, J.)

57-589 **Menard**, Claude (*Sir George Williams*) M.Sc.: "The kinetics of iodination of some amino acids and phenols." (Chemistry: Sehon, A.)

57-590 **Nebiker**, Walter A. (*Rutgers*) M.Sc.: "Evapotranspiration studies at Knob Lake, Quebec, June-Sept. 1956." (Geography: Orvig, S.)

57-591 **Perey**, Francis G. (*McGill*) M.Sc.: "Microstructure of impure ice." (Physics: Pounder, E.)

57-592 **Pinsky**, Carl (*Sir George Williams*) M.Sc.: "The physiology of the paroxysmal after-discharge." (Physiology: Burgen, A.)

57-593 **Reid**, John E. (*McGill*) M.Sc.: "Factors affecting the rate of fermentation of apple juice." (Agricultural Bacteriology: Clark, D.)

57-594 **Segal**, Mark (*McGill*) M.Sc.: "The antidiuretic, pressor and oxytocic properties of corticotropin-releasing factor (CRF)." (Biochemistry: Saffran, M.)

57-595 **Serrano**, Pedro A. (*Madrid*, Spain) M.Sc.: "Study of a case of adrenal tumour with regard to steroid metabolism." (Experimental Medicine: Venning, E.)

57-596 **Shtern**, I.H. (*Sir George Williams*) M.Sc.: "The Hausdorff and Hamburger one-dimensional moment problem." (Mathematics: **)

57-597 **Thomson**, John A. (*McGill*) M.Sc.: "On the biology of the Arctic char *Slavelinus alpinus* (L.), of Nettilling Lake, Baffin Island, N.W.T." (Zoology: Dunbar, M.)

57-598 **Weiss**, Michael (*McGill*) M.Sc.: "The secretion of proteins by the dog parotid gland." (Physiology: Burgen, A.)

57-599 **Wevrick**, Leonard (*McGill*) M.Sc.: "Subjective certainty as related to psychological test performance." (Psychology: Ferguson, G.)

57-600 **Wilson**, William E. (*McGill*) M.Sc.: "Peripheral circulatory changes in experimental frostbite." (Experimental Surgery: Webster, D.)

M.A. Fall 1957

57-601 **'Abd-al-'ati**, Hammaduh (*Al-Azhar*) M.A.: "The concept of freedom in Muhammad 'Abduh." (Islamic Studies: Bagley, F.)

57-602 **'Abdu-l-Mu'ti**, 'Ali (*Karachi*, Pakistan) M.A.: "The Muhammadijah movement: a bibliographical introduction." (Islamic Studies: Watson, W.)

57-603 **Cureton**, Edward A. (*McGill*) M.A.: "The Lachine Canal." (Geography: Hare, F.)

57-604 **Hogg**, Doreen (*McGill*) M.A.: "Effects of letter position on recognition." (Psychology: Heron, W.)

57-605 **Knowles**, David C. (*McGill*) M.A.: "The American Presbyterian Church of Montreal, 1822-1865." (History: Cooper, J.)

57-606 **Langlois**, Jean-Claude (*Montréal*) M.A.: "L'amenagement des villes à industrie extractive du subarctique." (Geography: Hare, F.)

57-607 **Parker**, T.C. (*McGill*) M.A.: "The foreign trade of Edinburgh, 1500-1542." (History: Reid, W.)

57-608 **Passmore**, Marian R. (*McMaster*) M.A.: "A study of the English-Canadian novel since 1939." (English: MacLennan, H.)

57-609 **Rezek**, G. (*Beirut*, Lebanon) M.A.: "The fiscal system of Jordan." (Economics: Armstrong, D.)

57-610 **Ross**, V.J. ( ) M.A.: "Factors in Scotland affecting the Scottish migrations to Canada between 1840 and 1896." (History: Reid, W.)

57-611 **Wisenthal**, M. (*Sir George Williams*) M.A.: "An examination of some factors which contribute to success in practice teaching." (Education: Crook, F.)

## ANNUAL LISTING

### Ph.D. Spring 1958

58-001 **Andracki**, Stanislaw (*Poznan*, Poland) Ph.D.: "The immigration of Orientals into Canada with special reference to Chinese." (Economics & Political Science: Callard, K.)

58-002 **Assad**, Robert J. (*Bishop's*) Ph.D.: "The geology of the East Sullivan Deposit, Val d'Or, Quebec." (Geological Sciences: Stevenson, J.)

58-003 **Bach**, Glen G. (*Alberta*) Ph.D.: "Three-body forces in hypernuclei." (Mathematics: Sharp, R.)

58-004 **Barth**, Fred W. (*Manitoba*) Ph.D.: "A study of the hemicellulose of milkweed floss (*Asclepias syriaca*, L.)." (Chemistry: Timell, T.)

58-005 **Brodkin**, Elliot (*McGill*) Ph.D.: "Factors affecting the binding and synthesis of acetylcholine." (Biochemistry: Elliott, K.)

58-006 **Byrne**, Anthony W. (*Dublin*, Ireland) Ph.D.: "The stratigraphy and palaeontology of the Beekmantown group in the St. Lawrence lowlands, Quebec." (Geological Sciences: Stearn, C.)

58-007 **Cann**, Malcolm C. (*Sir George Williams*) Ph.D.: "Corticosteroidogenesis." (Biochemistry: Heard, R.)

58-008 **Carter**, Alfred L. (*Dalhousie*) Ph.D.: "Studies of radioactive krypton of low mass." (Physics: Foster, J.)

58-009 **Carter**, George F. (*McGill*) Ph.D.: "Ordovician ostracoda from the St. Lawrence lowlands of Quebec." (Geological Sciences: Clark, T.)

58-010 **Charles**, J. Koilpillai (*Madras*, India) Ph.D.: "Indian economic development: a study in economic history and theory." (Economics: Weldon, J.)

58-011 **Chidzero**, Bernard T. (*South Africa*) Ph.D.: "Tanganyika: influence of international trusteeship on constitutional and political development." (Economics & Political Science: Pratt, R.)

58-012 **Christake**, Anna (*City College of New York*) Ph.D.: "A study of conditioned arousal." (Psychology: Milner, P.)

58-013 **Eidinger**, David (*McGill*) Ph.D.: "Isolation of carbohydrates from periodic acid-Schiff sites." (Anatomy: Leblond, C.)

58-014 **Frankel**, Saul J. (*McGill*) Ph.D.: "Staff relations in the Canadian federal civil service." (Economics & Political Science: Mallory, J.)

58-015 **Gardner**, Prescott E. (*Acadia*) Ph.D.: "A study of the fibrous portion of white spruce bark." (Chemistry: Purves, C.)

58-016 **Gibbs**, Harold C. (*McGill*) Ph.D.: "Studies on *Dochmoides stenocephala* (Railliet, 1884), the northern carnivore hookworm." (Parasitology: Cameron, T.)

58-017 **Glaudemans**, Cornelis P. (*Utrecht*, Netherlands) Ph.D.: "A study of the hemicellulose of white birch (*Betula papyrifera*, Marsh.)." (Chemistry: Timell, T.)

58-018 **Henderson**, John F. (*McGill*) Ph.D.: "The reaction of potassium persulphate with thioglycolic acid in aqueous solution." (Chemistry: Winkler, C.)

58-019 **Herschorn**, Michael (*McGill*) Ph.D.: "Some properties of caratheodory solutions of x' = f(t,x)." (Mathematics: Kaufman, H.)

58-020 **Hollbach**, Reiner (*Michigan*) Ph.D.: "The Canadian primary aluminum industry." (Economics: Beach, E.)

58-021 **Jain**, Abir C. (*Nagpur*, India) Ph.D.: "Studies on the nature of resistance of plants to disease. The effect of *Puccinia graminis tritici* Eriks, and Henn. infection on the respiration and carbon assimilation of resistant and susceptible wheat plants." (Plant Pathology: Coulson, J. & Pelletier, R.)

58-022 **Jayanetti**, Edwin (*Agra*, India) Ph.D.: "Studies on the nature of resistance of plants to disease: the effect of tobacco mosaic virus infection on the organic acid metabolism of resistant and susceptible tobaccos." (Plant Pathology: Coulson, J. & Pelletier, R.)

58-023 **Kelly**, Roger O. (*Saskatchewan*) Ph.D.: "Deactivation processes in active nitrogen." (Chemistry: Winkler, C.)

58-024 **Laufer**, Philip J. (*McGill*) Ph.D.: "The structure of left H-star algebras." (Mathematics: Peck, J.)

58-025 **McKnight**, Theodore S. (*Queen's*) Ph.D.: "Sorptive properties and pore structure of lignin and cellulose." (Chemistry: Mason, S.)

58-026 **Manning**, William P. (*McGill*) Ph.D.: "Heat and mass transfer to decelerating finely-atomized sprays." (Chemical Engineering: Gauvin, W.)

58-027 **Mansfield**, Arthur W. (*Cambridge*, England) Ph.D.: "The biology of the Atlantic walrus *Odobenus rosmarus rosmarus* (Linnaeus), Eastern Canadian Arctic." (Zoology: Dunbar, M.)

58-028 **Martin**, William G. (*Carleton*) Ph.D.: "The partial specific volumes of macromolecules." (Chemistry: Winkler, C.)

58-029 **Mattinson**, Cyril R. (*Queen's*) Ph.D.: "The geology of the Mount Logan area, Gaspé, Quebec." (Geological Sciences: Clark, T.)

58-030 **Mittelholzer**, Alexander S. (*Laval*) Ph.D.: "A study of the utilization of induced tetraploids in the improvement of red clover (*Trifolium pratense* L.)." (Agronomy: Steppler, H.)

58-031 **Monro**, Hector A. (*McGill*) Ph.D.: "The response of *Tenebroides mauritanicus* (L.) in the vacuum fumigation of jute with methyl bromide." (Entomology: DuPorte, E.)

58-032 **Parsons**, Timothy R. (*McGill*) Ph.D.: "The pathogenic nature of finely particulate silica." (Biochemistry: Denstedt, O.)

58-033 **Pavlasek**, Tomas J. (*McGill*) Ph.D.: "An automatic phase plotter for the measurement of microwave fields." (Electrical Engineering: Howes, F.)

58-034 **Premvati**, * (*Banaras Hindu*, India) Ph.D.: "Studies on the genus *Strongyloides* in lower primates." (Parasitology: Cameron, T.)

58-035 **Prives**, Moshe Z. (*Sir George Williams*) Ph.D.: "Career in civil service: Canada, Great Britain and the United States." (Economics & Political Science: Callard, K.)

58-036 **Rayport**, Mark (*Earlham*) Ph.D.: "Micro-electrode studies of experimental epilepsy." (Neurology & Neurosurgery: Jasper, H.)

58-037 **Richter**, Maxwell (*McGill*) Ph.D.: "Studies on the allergens of ragweed pollen." (Biochemistry: Sehon, A.)

58-038 **Riklis**, Emanuel (*Hebrew*, Israel) Ph.D.: "Studies on absorption of sugars by the isolated surviving guinea pig small intestine." (Biochemistry: Quastel, J.)

58-039 **Rochefort**, Guy J. (*Laval*) Ph.D.: "Depletion of pituitary corticotropin by various stress stimuli." (Biochemistry: Saffran, M.)

58-040 **Ronald**, Keith (*McGill*) Ph.D.: "The effects of physical stimuli on the larval stage of *Terranova decipiens* (Krabbe, 1878)." (Parasitology: Cameron, T.)

58-041 **Santry**, Dallas C. (*Dalhousie*) Ph.D.: "Absolute thermal-neutron fission yields of uranium 233." (Chemistry: Yaffe, L.)

58-042 **Schavo**, Anton F. (*Western*) Ph.D.: "The reactions of active nitrogen with acetylene, methylacetylene, and dimethylacetylene." (Chemistry: Winkler, C.)

58-043 **Schmidt**, Stephen C. (*Budapest*, Hungary) Ph.D.: "Models of cyclical fluctuations in farm mortgage credit." (Economics & Political Science: MacFarlane, D.)

58-044 **Sells**, Bruce H. (*Carleton*) Ph.D.: "Mucopolysaccharide metabolism in relation to bleeding disorders." (Biochemistry: Denstedt, O.)

58-045 **Stachenko**, Janine L-M. (*Bordeaux*, France) Ph.D.: "Nature et biogénèse des stéroides sécrétés par les différentes zônes cellulaires du cortex surrénal." (Investigative Medicine: Giroud, C.)

58-046 **Sussman**, David (*McGill*) Ph.D.: "On certain subgroups of algebraic matrix groups at prime characteristic." (Mathematics: Zassenhaus, H.)

58-047 **Sved**, Stephen (*Sir George Williams*) Ph.D.: "The metabolism of amino-acids in the central nervous system." (Biochemistry: Quastel, J.)

58-048 **Sydiaha**, Daniel (*Saskatchewan*) Ph.D.: "The relation between actuarial and descriptive methods in personnel appraisal." (Psychology: Webster, E.)

58-049 **Thomas**, George M. (*Annamalai*, India) Ph.D.: "Radioactive cerium isotope of mass 135 and its decay." (Physics: Foster, J.)

58-050 **Trasler**, Daphne G. (*McGill*) Ph.D.: "Genetic and other factors influencing the pathogenesis of cleft palate in mice." (Genetics: Fraser, F.)

58-051 **Unni**, Ayalur K. (*Annamalai*, India) Ph.D.: "Precision conductance measurements of quaternary ammonium halides in nitromethane." (Chemistry: Schiff, H.)

58-052 **Vanstone**, William E. (*McGill*) Ph.D.: "Studies on the formation of serum proteins in the fowl." (Agricultural Chemistry: Common, R.)

58-053 **Verbeke**, Gentil J. (*Loyola of Montréal*) Ph.D.: "The reactions of active nitrogen with nitric oxide and nitrogen dioxide." (Chemistry: Winkler, C.)

58-054 **Webb**, Tom (*Toronto*) Ph.D.: "Immuno-chemical and physico-chemical studies on the biocolloids in normal human urine." (Biochemistry: Sehon, A.)

**Ph.D. Fall 1958**

58-055 **Hutchinson**, Aleck (*Alberta*) Ph.D.: "Biochemical and physiological studies of *Malus* root-stocks." (Botany-Horticulture: Taper, C. & Towers, G.)

58-056 **Rajalakshmi**, Ramakrishnan (*Bombay*, India) Ph.D.: "Comparative effects of successive and simultaneous presentations on transfer in verbal learning." (Psychology: Ferguson, G.)

58-057 **Woodford**, Vernon R. (*Charleston*) Ph.D.: "The role of nutritional factors in the formation of catecholamines." (Biochemistry: Sourkes, T.)

**M.C.L. Spring 1958**

58-500 **Johnston**, Douglas M. (*St. Andrews*, Scotland) M.C.L.: "A judicial approach to the problems of the world fisheries." (Law: Dunbar, M.)

58-501 **Moughton**, Barry J. (*Oxford*, England) M.C.L.: "The international direction of social security." (Law: Cohen, M.)

**S.T.M. Spring 1958**

58-502 **Davison**, Roy J. (*Boston*) S.T.M.: "The Deuteronomic interpretation of history." (Divinity: Frost, S.)

**M.Eng. Spring 1958**

58-503 **Galbiati**, Ignazio V. (*Pisa*, Italy) M.Eng.: "Shear stresses in diagonally cracked reinforced concrete beams." (Civil Engineering & Applied Mechanics: McCutcheon, J.)

58-504 **Genest**, George L. (*McGill*) M.Eng.: "Compression of silt under model footings." (Civil Engineering & Applied Mechanics: De Stein, J.)

58-505 **Stone**, Samuel A. (*Manitoba*) M.Eng.: "Beyond-the-horizon propagation at microwave frequencies." (Electrical Engineering: Pavlasek, T.)

58-506 **Tao**, Chia-hwa (*Taiwan*) M.Eng.: "The mixing of circular jets." (Mechanical Engineering: Mordell, D.)

58-507 **Yong**, Raymond N. (*Washington and Jefferson*) M.Eng.: "Some physical characteristics of frozen soil." (Civil Engineering & Applied Mechanics: Coates, D.)

M.Sc. Spring 1958

58-508 **Beall**, George H. (*McGill*) M.Sc.: "Some aspects of atmosphere-earth energy relationships." (Geological Sciences: Saull, V.)

58-509 **Berrange**, Jevan P. (*Cape Town*, South Africa) M.Sc.: "Dispersion in humus and moss, of zinc, copper, nickel and lead, from a glaciated precambrian terrain." (Geological Sciences: Riddell, J.)

58-510 **Biard**, J.M. (*McGill*) M.Sc.: "A comparison of embryo sacs and haustoria in selected species of *Impatiens*." (Botany: Wilson, C.)

58-511 **Black**, Ernest D. (*McGill*) M.Sc.: "A petrographic study of the metamorphic rocks of Little Manicouagan Lake area." (Geological Sciences: Stevenson, J.)

58-512 **Boville**, Byron W. (*Toronto*) M.Sc.: "Two-level representation of the atmosphere." (Meteorology: Hare, F.)

58-513 **Branch**, Charles L. (*Vanderbilt*) M.Sc.: "A microelectrode study of Betz cells in the unanesthetized cat." (Neurology & Neurosurgery: Jasper, H.)

58-514 **Bryden**, Mark P. (*Massachusetts Institute of Technology*) M.Sc.: "The role of eye movements in perception." (Psychology: Heron, W.)

58-515 **Dean**, R. S. (*McGill*) M.Sc.: "A compositional study of calcareous Lorraine sedimentary rocks." (Geological Sciences: Webber, G.)

58-516 **Desrochers**, Louis G. (*Montréal*) M.Sc.: "Studies of a new thermionic cathode." (Physics: Stansbury, E.)

58-517 **Ehrlich**, Daniel J. (*Clark*) M.Sc.: "Latency and amplitude of response and the GSR." (Psychology: Bindra, D.)

58-518 **Ferguson**, John (*Witwatersrand*, South Africa) M.Sc.: "A study of metamorphic strata near Fort Chimo, northern Quebec." (Geological Sciences: Kranck, E.)

58-519 **Findlay**, David C. (*McGill*) M.Sc.: "Peridotites of northern Quebec and Ungava." (Geological Sciences: Kranck, E.)

58-520 **Francis**, Lyman E. (*McGill*) M.Sc.: "Studies on the mechanism of gingival hyperplasia induced by diphenylhydantoin." (Pharmacology: Melville, K.)

58-521 **Gardner**, Robert C. (*Alberta*) M.Sc.: "Social factors in second-language acquisition." (Psychology: Lambert, W.)

58-522 **Gustafson**, Jean M. (*McGill*) M.Sc.: "A study of the clover root borer, *Hylastinus obscurus* (Marsham) (*Coleoptera*: *Scholytidae*)." (Entomology: Morrison, F.)

58-523 **Hawkins**, William M. (*Queen's*) M.Sc.: "The geology of the Goshen Copper Prospect, Goshen, New Brunswick." (Geological Sciences: Gill, J.)

58-524 **Hollinger**, Harvey Z. (*McGill*) M.Sc.: "The localization of blocking antibody in the sera of ragweed sensitive patients by starch electrophoresis." (Experimental Medicine: Rose, B.)

58-525 **MacFarlane**, Mona A. (*McGill*) M.Sc.: "Pressure-contour variance and kinetic energy over the Arctic." (Geography: Hare, F.)

58-526 **Morse**, Stearns A. (*Dartmouth*) M.Sc.: "The chemistry, mineralogy, and metamorphism of the standing pond amphibolite, Hanover quadrangle, New Hampshire-Vermont." (Geological Sciences: Webber, G.)

58-527 **Mumtazuddin**, Mohammed (*Aligarh Muslim*, India) M.Sc.: "The geology of the area between Carol Lake and Wabush Lake, Labrador." (Geological Sciences: Elson, J.)

58-528 **Murphy**, Joseph (*McGill*) M.Sc.: "The quantum theory of cyclotron resonance in graphite." (Mathematics: Wallace, P.)

58-529 **Sater**, Geoffrey S. (*Witwatersrand*, South Africa) M.Sc.: "Geology of the McOuat-Gauvin area, Mistassini territory and Roberval electoral district, Quebec." (Geological Sciences: Elson, J.)

58-530 **Sinnott**, Joseph C. (*St. Dunstan's*) M.Sc.: "The control of pulmonary ventilation in physiological hyperpnoea." (Investigative Medicine: MacIntosh, D.)

58-531 **Sosniak**, J. (*McGill*) M.Sc.: "Cross-sections for proton-induced reactions in heavy nuclei." (Physics: Bell, R.)

58-532 **Stairs**, Gordon R. (*New Brunswick*) M.Sc.: "An embryological study of the spruce budworm, *Choristoneura fumiferana* (Clements), (*Lep.*, *Tortricidae*)." (Entomology: DuPorte, E.)

58-533 **Udeaja**, Philip E. (*Manitoba*) M.Sc.: "Studies on the nature of resistance of plants to disease: the effect of growth substances on the resistance of beets to beet leaf-spot (*Cercospora beticola* Sacc.) and of *Phaseolus* beans to bean rust (*Uromyces phaseoli* var. *typica* Arth.)." (Plant Pathology: Pelletier, R.)

58-534 **Vardanis**, Alexandre (*Leeds*, England) M.Sc.: "The effect of lead compounds on the metabolism of the central nervous system." (Genetics: Quastel, J.)

58-535 **Wilson**, Cynthia V. (*London*, England) M.Sc.: "Synoptic régimes in the lower Arctic troposphere during 1955." (Geography: Hare, F.)

M.A. Spring 1958

58-536 **Bale**, Cecil G. (*Royal Military College*) M.A.: "Price and income effects of international capital movements: Canadian case." (Economics & Political Science: Marsh, D.)

58-537 **Clark**, Ian C. (*McGill*) M.A.: "A guide to Ezra Pound, 1885-1920, with special emphasis on his poetic theory and practice." (English: Dudek, L.)

58-538 **Douglas**, Althea M. (*McGill*) M.A.: "Chaucer's use of dress." (English: Hemlow, J.)

58-539 **Duinat**, Blanche E. (*Sir George Williams*) M.A.: "Chateaubriand et le merveilleux chrétien dans *Les martyrs*." (French: Launay, J.)

58-540 **Jacoby**, Barbara J. (*Rochester*) M.A.: "L'enfance dans 'Les hommes de bonne volonté' de Jules Romains." (French: Launay, J.)

58-541 **Jarrette**, Neil M. (*McGill*) M.A.: "The Trinidad cacao industry: its place in the Trinidad economy." (Agricultural Economics: Haviland, W.)

58-542 **Kaal**, Hans (*McGill*) M.A.: "C.I. Lewis' theory of meaning." (Philosophy: Miller, J.)

58-543 **Kabayama**, Joan E. (*McGill*) M.A.: "Educational retardation among non-Roman Catholic Indians at Oka." (Education: Smith, C.)

58-544 **Kinsman**, Michael J. (*McGill*) M.A.: "Space and perception: a critical study of Berkeley's 'new theory of vision'." (Philosophy: Currie, C.)

58-545 **Kovalski**, Voyo (*McGill*) M.A.: "Soviet price mechanisms and economic theory." (Economics: Beach, E.)

58-546 **Martin**, Fernand (*McGill*) M.A.: "Economics of retailing." (Economics & Political Science: Beach, E.)

58-547 **Podgornik**, Louis E. (*Assumption*) M.A.: "L'homme et la mer dans l'oeuvre d'Edouard Peisson." (French: Launay, J.)

58-548 **Szablowski**, Julie A. (*Mount Allison*) M.A.: "L'année 1745 dans la vie et l'oeuvre de Voltaire." (French: Launay, J.)

58-549 **Weller**, Judith A. (*Randolph-Macon Women's*) M.A.: "The government in Rome from 88-82 B.C." (Classics: Gordon, C.)

58-550 **Wilson**, William D. (*Loyola of Montréal*) M.A.: "The demands for motor gasoline and heating oils." (Economics: Culliton, J.)

58-551 **Wimer**, Cynthia C. (*Wellesley*) M.A.: "Stimulus characteristics and verbal learning." (Psychology: Lambert, W.)

M.Arch. Fall 1958

58-552 **Caragianis**, Eva M. (*McGill*) M.Arch.: "The development of urban form through planning administration with specific reference to Oromocto, New Brunswick." (Architecture: Spence-Sales, H.)

58-553 **Walford**, Dorice C. (*Manitoba*) M.Arch.: "Tendencies in the evolution of the centres of Canadian cities." (Architecture: Spence-Sales, H.)

M.Eng. Fall 1958

58-554 **Briggs**, David C. (*McGill*) M.Eng.: "Corrosion behaviour of welded low alloy steel." (Metallurgical Engineering: Yates, H.)

58-555 **Caswell**, Charles F. (*McGill*) M.Eng.: "Investigation of the response of electromechanical servomechanisms in combined linear and non-linear operation." (Electrical Engineering: Pavlasek, T.)

58-556 **Lee**, Ernest S. (*McGill*) M.Eng.: "Electronic analog multiplication using transistors." (Electrical Engineering: Farnell, G.)

58-557 **Lemay**, Henri P. (*Laval*) M.Eng.: "The anodic oxidation of bivalent manganese to tetravalent manganese." (Metallurgical Engineering: MacEwan, J.)

58-558 **Taylor**, George (*Queen's*) M.Eng.: "Turbine performance with varying thermodynamic properties of the working fluid." (Mechanical Engineering: Mordell, D.)

LL.M. Fall 1958

58-559 **Hadjis**, Dimitris (*Athens*, Greece) LL.M.: "Liability limitations in the carriage of passengers and goods by air and sea." (International Air Law: Pépin, E.)

58-560 **Ritchie**, Marguerite E. (*Alberta*) LL.M.: "Crimes aboard aircraft." (International Air Law: Pépin, E.)

M.Sc. Fall 1958

58-561 **Aguilar**, Mary J. (*California*) M.Sc.: "The role of chronic encephalitis in the pathogenesis of epilepsy." (Neurology & Neurosurgery: Rasmussen, T.)

58-562 **Cooke**, Patricia M. (*British Columbia*) M.Sc.: "The purification and anti-viral activities of Noxiversin." (Bacteriology & Immunology: Stevenson, J.)

58-563 **DeMille**, George E. (*New Brunswick*) M.Sc.: "A spectrometer for the analysis of radioactive ores." (Physics: Telford, W.)

58-564 **Donevan**, Richard E. (*Queen's*) M.Sc.: "Studies on pulmonary diffusion." (Experimental Medicine: Bates, D.V.)

58-565 **Fish**, Arthur G. (*Carleton*) M.Sc.: "Pelagic copepoda collected off the west coast of Barbados." (Zoology: Marsden, J.)

58-566 **Freedman**, Arthur N. (*McGill*) M.Sc.: "The surgical treatment of experimental ascites." (Experimental Surgery: Webster, D.)

58-567 **Fulton**, Geraldine E. (*Mount Allison*) M.Sc.: "Some properties of compositions and their applications." (Mathematics: Narayana, T.)

58-568 **Jones**, Graham A. (*Leeds*, England) M.Sc.: "Studies on the activities of rhizosphere microorganisms." (Agricultural Bacteriology: Knowles, R.)

58-569 **Karpishka**, Irene S. (*McGill*) M.Sc.: "Sites of protein synthesis as shown by radioautographic distribution of methionine labelled with $C^{14}$ or $S^{35}$ in mice and rats." (Anatomy: Leblond, C.)

58-570 **Knutti**, Hans J. (*Zurich*, Switzerland) M.Sc.: "Establishment studies of certain forage species in pure and mixed seedings." (Agronomy: Steppler, H.)

58-571 **Lawson**, Norman C. (*Glasgow*, Scotland) M.Sc.: "Inter- and intra-varietal crosses in the improvement of timothy, red clover and birdsfoot trefoil." (Agronomy: Bubar, J.)

58-572 **Lowther**, Ruth L. (*McGill*) M.Sc.: "The effect of ethionine on some plant growth systems." (Botany: Boll, W.)

58-573 **Mahanti**, Biresh C. (*Utkal*, India) M.Sc.: "An experimental study for evaluation of surgical procedures in the treatment of coronary artery insufficiency." (Experimental Surgery: Webster, D.)

58-574 **Murphy**, Frederick G. (*New Brunswick*) M.Sc.: "A study of the effect of partial biliary obstruction in dogs." (Experimental Surgery: Webster, D.)

58-575 **Rao**, C. Kanaka D. (*Andhra*, India) M.Sc.: "Excitation curves for $Cu^{63}(p,n)Zn^{63}$ and $Cu^{63}(p,pn)Cu^{62}$." (Physics: Foster, J.)

58-576 **Reid**, Kenneth H. (*McGill*) M.Sc.: "A closely controlled environment for the growth of snow crystals." (Physics: Gunn, K.)

58-577 **Smith**, Edward R. (*McGill*) M.Sc.: "I. Voluntary intake of forage as a measure of its feeding value for ruminants. II. Ideally cured forages." (Nutrition: Lloyd, L.)

58-578 **Sodhi**, Harbhajan S. (*Panjab*, India) M.Sc.: "Thyroid antibodies and disorders of thyroid physiology and morphology." (Investigative Medicine: Hoffman, M.)

58-579 **Walke**, Lacey (*McGill*) M.Sc.: "Rates of acetic acid formation from ethanol by *Acetobacter suboxydans*." (Agricultural Bacteriology: Blackwood, A.)

58-580 **Warshawski**, Frances G. (*Alberta*) M.Sc.: "Techniques of extracorporeal circulation." (Experimental Surgery: Webster, D.)

## ANNUAL LISTING

### M.A. Fall 1958

58-581 **Bosnitch**, Sava (*Belgrade*, Yugoslavia) M.A.: "The Communist conquest of power in Yugoslavia, 1941-1945." (Economics & Political Science: Brecher, M.)

58-582 **Ferguson**, Donald C. (*Manitoba*) M.A.: "A theorem of Looman-Menchoff." (Mathematics: Kozakiewicz, W.)

58-583 **Glickman**, Rose (*Illinois*) M.A.: "Stalin's concept of the problem of national minorities: theory and practice." (History: Mladenovic, M.)

58-584 **Gwyn**, Julian R. (*Montréal*) M.A.: "The Bosphorus and the Dardanelles, 1902-1923: a study of French and British policies." (History: Fieldhouse, H.)

58-585 **Hoechsmann**, Klaus (*British Columbia*) M.A.: "Radicals and subdirect decompositions." (Mathematics: Zassenhaus, H.)

58-586 **Joos**, Irma (*Sarrebruck*, West Germany) M.A.: "Les artistes dans *A la recherche du temps perdu*." (French: Larivière, H.)

58-587 **Petrogiannis**, Demetrios S. (*Northwestern*) M.A.: "The sterling area as an economic entity." (Economics: Brecher, I.)

58-588 **Pound**, Omar S. (*Hamilton*) M.A.: "The Emperor Akbar as a religious man: six interpretations." (Islamic Studies: Smith, W.)

58-589 **Rymes**, Thomas K. (*Manitoba*) M.A.: "The Canadian short-term capital market." (Economics: Weldon, J.)

58-590 **Sheffy**, Pearl P. (*McGill*) M.A.: "Developing patterns in the plays of Etherege." (English: Cecil, C.)

58-591 **Sproule**, Hugh D. (*Dalhousie*) M.A.: "James Burney to the Right Honourable Earl Spencer: a document in the history of the naval mutinies of 1797." (English: Malloch, A.)

58-592 **Winter**, Jack S. (*McGill*) M.A.: "T.S. Eliot as dramatist in the commercial theatre." (English: Cecil, C.)

58-593 **Wolfe**, Irving (*McGill*) M.A.: "Clifford Odets and the Group Theatre plays in their social context." (English: Cecil, C.)

## ANNUAL LISTING

### Ph.D. Spring 1959

59-001 **Adamek**, Edward G. (*Innsbrück*, Austria) Ph.D.: "The location of xanthate groups in starch xanthates." (Chemistry: Purves, C.)

59-002 **Beacom**, Stanley E. (*Alberta*) Ph.D.: "The effect of grinding on the voluntary consumption and nutrient availability of early vs. late-cut clover and timothy hays when fed to lambs." (Nutrition: Crampton, E.)

59-003 **Benson**, David G. (*New Brunswick*) Ph.D.: "The mineralogy of the New Brunswick sulphide deposits." (Geological Sciences: Webber, G.)

59-004 **Bliss**, James Q. (*Toronto*) Ph.D.: "The individual specificity of dog plasma." (Physiology: Burgen, A.)

59-005 **Boote**, Maurice J. (*Wales*) Ph.D.: "Income retention and fixed capital expansion: a group of Canadian manufacturing corporations, 1932-1953." (Economics & Political Science: Weldon, J.)

59-006 **Boswall**, Graeme W. (*Acadia*) Ph.D.: "Extraction and identification of organic phosphorus compounds of soils." (Agricultural Chemistry: DeLong, W.)

59-007 **Brownstone**, Yehoshua S. (*Manitoba*) Ph.D.: "A pentose phosphate metabolic pathway in human erythrocytes." (Biochemistry: Denstedt, O.)

59-008 **Burns**, Neal M. (*Illinois*) Ph.D.: "Effects of cortical stimulation on learning." (Psychology: Heron, W.)

59-009 **Chappel**, Clifford I. (*Toronto*) Ph.D.: "Factors affecting adrenal-regeneration hypertension in the rat." (Experimental Medicine: Browne, J.)

59-010 **Charles**, George E. (*McGill*) Ph.D.: "Coalescence phenomena at liquid interfaces." (Chemistry: Mason, S.)

59-011 **Clark**, Lloyd A. (*Saskatchewan*) Ph.D.: "Phase relations in the Fe-As-S system." (Geological Sciences: Stevenson, J.)

59-012 **Cloutier**, Gilles G. (*Laval*) Ph.D.: "A monoenergetic electron source for mass spectrometers and its application to the electron impact study of nitric oxide." (Physics: Woonton, G.)

59-013 **Coffin**, David E. (*McGill*) Ph.D.: "Investigation of organic material extracted from a podzol." (Agricultural Chemistry: DeLong, W.)

59-014 **Cumberlidge**, John T. (*Nottingham*, England) Ph.D.: "Some experiments on surface and strain energy in minerals." (Geological Sciences: Saull, V.)

59-015 **Currie**, Allan L. (*Saskatchewan*) Ph.D.: "The hemicellulose of kapok (*Ceiba pentandra*)." (Chemistry: Timell, T.)

59-016 **Das Gupta**, Dyutish C. (*Calcutta*, India) Ph.D.: "Adrenal function in experimental nephrosis." (Investigative Medicine: Giroud, C.)

59-017 **Dean**, William G. (*Toronto*) Ph.D.: "Physiography and vegetation of the Albany River map area, northern Ontario: an aerial photograph reconnaissance." (Geography: Hare, F.)

59-018 **Dondale**, Charles D. (*McGill*) Ph.D.: "Revision of the genus *Philodromus* (*Araneae*: *Thomsidae*) in North America." (Entomology: Bigelow, R.)

59-019 **Eappen**, Collaparambil (*Travancore*, India) Ph.D.: "Radioactive decay of isotopes of mass 182." (Physics: Foster, J.)

59-020 **Eisenbraun**, Allan A. (*Innsbruck*, Austria) Ph.D.: "The oxidation of starch with alkaline hypochlorite." (Chemistry: Purves, C.)

59-021 **Eisenbraun**, Edgar W. (*Bristol*, England) Ph.D.: "The condensation of lignin with formaldehyde." (Chemistry: Purves, C.)

59-022 **Elsdon**, William L. (*Western*) Ph.D.: "An investigation of a spectrophotometric method for the study of crystallization in high polymers." (Chemistry: Winkler, C.)

59-023 **Feldman**, Samuel M. (*Pennsylvania*) Ph.D.: "Differential effect of shock as a function of intensity and cue factors in maze learning." (Psychology: Malmo, R.)

59-024 **Forgacs**, Otto L. (*Manchester*, England) Ph.D.: "Thread-like particles in sheared suspensions." (Chemistry: Mason, S.)

59-025 **Galbraith**, John A. (*McGill*) Ph.D.: "The economics of Canadian banking: an analysis of banking operations and transactions." (Economics: Marsh, D.)

59-026 **George**, Zacheria M. (*Agra*, India) Ph.D.: "The reactions of hydrogen atoms with amines and imines." (Chemistry: Winkler, C.)

59-027 **Gillham**, John K. (*Cambridge*, England) Ph.D.: "Part I: A study of the alpha-cellulose of white birch (*Betula papyrifera*). Part II: A study of the hemicellulose of white elm (*Ulmus americana*)." (Chemistry: Timell, T.)

59-028 **Givner**, Morris L. (*McGill*) Ph.D.: "Estrogen methodology and excretion in human subjects." (Biochemistry: Hobkirk, R.)

59-029 **Glickman**, Stephen (*Brooklyn*) Ph.D.: "Reinforcing properties of arousal." (Psychology: Milner, P.)

59-030 **Gordon**, Julius (*Sir George Williams*) Ph.D.: "Antibody-antigen reactions in allergy." (Biochemistry: Sehon, A.)

59-031 **Griffiths**, James E. (*Manitoba*) Ph.D.: "The preparation and properties of derivatives of germane." (Chemistry: Onyszchuk, M.)

59-032 **Grivas**, John C. (*McGill*) Ph.D.: "Synthesis and structure of amidines." (Chemistry: Taurins, A.)

59-033 **Gupta**, Prem R. (*Banaras*, India) Ph.D.: "Physicochemical studies of alkali lignin." (Chemistry: Mason, S.)

59-034 **Harris**, Seth O. (*Howard*) Ph.D.: "Investigation of the nitraminothiazolecarboxylic acids." (Chemistry: Taurins, A.)

59-035 **Hoffman**, Terrence W. (*Queen's*) Ph.D.: "Theoretical and experimental investigations of the evaporation of stationary droplets and sprays in high temperature surroundings." (Chemical Engineering: Gauvin, W.)

59-036 **Hogarth**, Donald D. (*Toronto*) Ph.D.: "A mineralogical study of pyrochlore and betafite." (Geological Sciences: Stevenson, J.)

59-037 **Hogg**, William A. (*Acadia*) Ph.D.: "Building and industrial stones of eastern Canada." (Geological Sciences: Kranck, E.)

59-038 **Jeffery**, William G. (*Leeds*, England) Ph.D.: "The geology of the Campbell Chibougamau Mine, Quebec." (Geological Sciences: Gill, J.)

59-039 **Kamali**, Sabih A. (*Aligarh*, India) Ph.D.: "The concept of human nature in Hujjat Allah Al-Balighah and its relation to Shah Waliullah's doctrine of *figh*." (Islamic Studies: Adams, C.)

59-040 **Ketcheson**, Barbara G. (*Queen's*) Ph.D.: "The synthesis of nitrogen derivatives of steroids." (Chemistry: Taurins, A.)

59-041 **Kimura**, Douglas S. (*Illinois*) Ph.D.: "Effects of selective hippocampal damage on learning in the rat." (Psychology: Milner, P.)

59-042 **Koppenaal**, Richard J. (*British Columbia*) Ph.D.: "The learning of punished incorrect responses." (Psychology: Bindra, D.)

59-043 **Lang**, Andrew R. (*Melbourne*, Australia) Ph.D.: "Tritium exchange between cellulose and water." (Chemistry: Mason, S.)

59-044 **Larochelle**, Andre (*Laval*) Ph.D.: "A study of the paleomagnetism of rocks from Yamaska and Brome Mountains, Quebec." (Geological Sciences: Saull, V.)

59-045 **Lucis**, Ojars J. (*Sir George Williams*) Ph.D.: "Studies on the influence of various factors on corticosteroid secretion by the adrenal gland *in vitro* with special reference to aldosterone." (Investigative Medicine: Venning, E.)

59-046 **McBride**, Mollie E. (*Dalhousie*) Ph.D.: "Genetic transformation in *Salmonella* with respect to chloramphenicol resistance and antigenic structure." (Bacteriology & Immunology: Stevenson, J.)

59-047 **McFarlane**, Ross A. (*McMaster*) Ph.D.: "Microwave noise in accelerated electron streams." (Physics: Woonton, G.)

59-048 **McIlreath**, Fred J. (*Siena*) Ph.D.: "Studies on the mode of binding of histamine in tissues." (Physiology: Garcia-Arocha, H.)

59-049 **McIntosh**, Bruce A. (*Western*) Ph.D.: "An experimental study of interception noise in electron beams at microwave frequencies." (Physics: Woonton, G.)

59-050 **Mann**, Ernest L. (*Natal*, South Africa) Ph.D.: "The geology of the Seal Lake area, central Labrador." (Geological Sciences: Eakins, P.)

59-051 **Meikle**, Brian K. (*McGill*) Ph.D.: "Experiments with copper sulphides at elevated temperatures." (Geological Sciences: Gill, J.)

59-052 **Miller**, James R. (*Toronto*) Ph.D.: "Experimental and clinical approaches to the biology of congenital defect." (Genetics: Fraser, F.)

59-053 **Mogenson**, Gordon J. (*Saskatchewan*) Ph.D.: "Conditioned responses to cortical stimulation." (Psychology: Hebb, D.)

59-054 **Morgante**, Odosca E. (*Rome*, Italy) Ph.D.: "*In vitro* inactivation of streptomycin and isoniazid action: its practical application in the isolation of mycobacterium tuberculosis from pathological specimens of tuberculous children." (Bacteriology: Reed, R.)

59-055 **Morigi**, Eugene M. (*Bologna*, Italy) Ph.D.: "Biological studies on mycobacteria." (Bacteriology & Immunology: Reed, R.)

59-056 **Myers**, Betty-June (*Ashland*) Ph.D.: "A revision of the subfamily *Anisakinae* with special reference to *Porrocaecum decipiens* and its affinities." (Parasitology: Cameron, T.)

59-057 **Nashshabah**, Hisam A. (*Beirut*, Lebanon) Ph.D.: "Al-Madrasah Al-Mushtansiriyah in Baghdad: a study of Muslim educational institutions." (Islamic Studies: Smith, W.)

59-058 **Nnochiri**, Enyinnaya (*Lincoln*) Ph.D.: "Studies on the micro-environment of rabbit trichostrongyles." (Parasitology: Cameron, T.)

59-059 **Ogryzlo**, Elmer A. (*Manitoba*) Ph.D.: "The use of an isothermal calorimetric detector for the study of electrically discharged O2 and the reaction of O-atoms with NO." (Chemistry: Schiff, H.)

59-060 **Paivio**, Allan U. (*McGill*) Ph.D.: "Child rearing antecedents of audience sensitivity." (Psychology: Lambert, W.)

59-061 **Pasternak**, Israel S. (*McGill*) Ph.D.: "Turbulent convective heat and mass transfer from stationary and accelerating particles." (Chemical Engineering: Gauvin, W.)

59-062 **Peto**, Margaret (*McGill*) Ph.D.: "Protein synthesis of the developing embryo and the effects thereon of tumour growth." (Biochemistry: Quastel, J.)

59-063 **Petruk**, William (*Saskatchewan*) Ph.D.: "The clearwater copper-zinc deposit and its setting, with a special study of mineral zoning around such deposits." (Geological Sciences: Webber, G.)

59-064 **Power**, Geoffrey (*Durham*, England) Ph.D.: "Studies on the Atlantic salmon (*Salmo salar* Linn.) of sub-Arctic Canada." (Zoology: Dunbar, M.)

59-065 **Ramaradhya**, Jakkanahally (*Mysore*, India) Ph.D.: "Studies of some physical and chemical properties of unimolecular films." (Chemistry: Robertson, D.)

59-066 **Ramon-Moliner**, Enrique (*Madrid*, Spain) Ph.D.: "The structure of the postcentral gyrus in the cat." (Neurology & Neurosurgery: McNaughton, M.)

59-067 **Read**, Dale W. (*British Columbia*) Ph.D.: "The degradation of lignosulphonates with sodium in liquid ammonia." (Chemistry: Purves, C.)

59-068 **Salmoiraghi**, Gian C. (*Rome,* Italy) Ph.D.: "The site and behaviour of respiratory neurones in the medula of the cat." (Physiology: Burns, B.)

59-069 **Schieck**, Robert R. (*Toronto*) Ph.D.: "Flow properties of model fibre suspensions." (Mechanical Engineering: Gauvin, W.)

59-070 **Soper**, Robert J. (*Saskatchewan*) Ph.D.: "Characteristics of soil leachates collected under eastern hemlock (*Tsuga canadensis*)." (Agricultural Chemistry: DeLong, W.)

59-071 **Sybulski**, Stella (*McGill*) Ph.D.: "The production and metabolism of corticosteroids in pregnancy." (Investigative Medicine: Venning, E.)

59-072 **Tenenhouse**, Alan (*McGill*) Ph.D.: "The transport of amino acids in Ehrlich ascites cells." (Biochemistry: Quastel, J.)

59-073 **Van Gelder**, Nico M. (*McGill*) Ph.D.: "Metabolism and action of factor I and upsilon-aminobutyric acid." (Biochemistry: Elliott, K.)

59-074 **Vogel**, Robert (*Sir George Williams*) Ph.D.: "British diplomatic Blue Books, 1919-1939." (History: Fieldhouse, H.)

59-075 **Wimer**, Richard E. (*San Jose*) Ph.D.: "Learning and retention in old age." (Psychology: Hebb, D.)

59-076 **Youdelis**, William V. (*Alberta*) Ph.D.: "Mechanisms of solidification in binary alloy castings." (Metallurgical Engineering: MacEwan, J.)

59-077 **Zienius**, Raymond H. (*McGill*) Ph.D.: "Oxidation of pectin and related compounds by bleaching agents." (Chemistry: Purves, C.)

**Ph.D. Fall 1959**

59-078 **Farmakides**, Anna (*Witwatersrand*, South Africa) Ph.D.: "Foreign policy under the 7Bloc des gauches'." (History: Fieldhouse, H.)

59-079 **Haggart**, Catherine (*Montréal*) Ph.D.: "Reactions of active nitrogen with cyanogen and CN radicals." (Chemistry: Winkler, C.)

59-080 **Majchrowicz**, Edward (*Birmingham*, England) Ph.D.: "Effect of aliphatic alcohols on liver metabolism." (Biochemistry: Quastel, J.)

59-081 **Monahan**, Robert L. (*Washington*) Ph.D.: "The development of settlement in the Fairbanks area, Alaska: a study of permanence." (Geography: Bird, J.)

59-082 **Senior**, Hereward (*McGill*) Ph.D.: "The influence of the Orange Lodges on Irish and British politics, 1795-1836." (History: Reid, W.)

59-083 **Townsend**, Edith E. (*McGill*) Ph.D.: "Alternate pathways of tryptophan metabolism in the rat." (Biochemistry: Sourkes, T.)

59-084 **Westbury**, Ronald A. (*McGill*) Ph.D.: "The reactions of active nitrogen with hydrogen sulphide and carbon disulphide." (Chemistry: Winkler, C.)

59-085 **Zaharia**, William (*Manitoba*) Ph.D.: "Cholesterol and acetate as precursors of the adrenal steroids." (Biochemistry: Thomson, D.)

**M.C.L. Spring 1959**

59-500 **Dobson**, Christopher B. (*Cambridge*, England) M.C.L.: "A comparative and historical study of judicial and legislative attitudes towards monopoly in England and Canada." (Civil Law: Cohen, M.)

**M.Arch. Spring 1959**

59-501 **Schoenauer**, Norbert (*Hungary*) M.Arch.: "The influence of urban growth upon surrounding villages, with special reference to Montreal and villages in the Richelieu valley." (Architecture: Spence-Sales, H.)

**M.Eng. Spring 1959**

59-502 **Davies**, John J. (*Witwatersrand*, South Africa) M.Eng.: "Pillars: applications and limitations in underground mining." (Mining Engineering: Morrison, R.)

59-503 **Hyder**, Syed S. (*Aligarh*, India) M.Eng.: "The change in reactivity due to neutron streaming in annular air gaps around fuel rods in a reactor." (Mechanical Engineering: Edis, A.)

59-504 **Sein**, Maung T. (*Rangoon*, Burma) M.Eng.: "Design investigation of a power transmission shaft." (Mechanical Engineering: Edis, A.)

59-505 **Von Hagen**, Wallace M. (*Manitoba*) M.Eng.: "Microwave propagation on overwater paths." (Electrical Engineering: Howes, F.)

59-506 **Waterston**, John R. (*McGill*) M.Eng.: "The analysis of a glued laminated wooden arch." (Civil Engineering & Applied Mechanics: De Stein, J.)

59-507 **Zenner**, Gerhard P. (*British Columbia*) M.Eng.: "A study of avalanche breakdown voltage in silicon diffused p-n junctions." (Electrical Engineering: Howes, F.)

**LL.M. Spring 1959**

59-508 **Leclercq**, Geneviève F. (*Paris*, France) LL.M.: "Les aides à la navigation aérienne: organisation et problèmes juridiques soulèvés par leur fonctionnement." (International Air Law: Pépin, E.)

59-509 **Lureau**, Daniel J. (*Bordeaux*, France) LL.M.: "Exoneration et limitation de responsabilité du transporteur aérien en droit international et en droit comparé." (International Air Law: Pépin, E.)

## ANNUAL LISTING

M.Sc. Spring 1959

59-510 **Bedford**, Frederick W. (*Loyola of Montréal*) M.Sc.: "The arithmetics of linguistic structures." (Mathematics: Lambek, J.)

59-511 **Boright**, Henry A. (*McGill*) M.Sc.: "Diabetic glomerulosclerosis: studies relating to its pathogenesis." (Experimental Medicine: Beck, J.)

59-512 **Buckley**, Ronald A. (*Acadia*) M.Sc.: "The geology of the Weedon Pyrite and Copper Corporation Limited mine." (Geological Sciences: Stevenson, J.)

59-513 **Cavadias**, George (*Athens*, Greece) M.Sc.: "On the minimax theorem and the solution of finite games." (Mathematics: Kozakiewicz, K.)

59-514 **Darragh**, James H. (*McGill*) M.Sc.: "Fat and ketone metabolism in diabetes mellitus." (Experimental Medicine: Bensley, E.)

59-515 **Dawson**, Donald A. (*McGill*) M.Sc.: "The application of information theory to mathematical linguistics." (Mathematics: Lambek, J.)

59-516 **Evans**, John W. (*McGill*) M.Sc.: "Normal stages of the early development of the Barbados flying fish, *Hirundichthys affinis* (Gunther)." (Zoology: Berrill, N.)

59-517 **Guy-Bray**, John V. (*Cambridge*, England) M.Sc.: "Mobility of certain sulphides in sulphur vapour." (Geological Sciences: Saull, V.)

59-518 **Harney**, Patricia M. (*McGill*) M.Sc.: "Cytogenetical effects of seed treatments with maleic hydrazide on tomato plants of the first and second generation." (Horticulture-Genetics: Murray, H.)

59-519 **Hay**, Robert E. (*Queen's*) M.Sc.: "Growth of sulphides in black shales." (Geological Sciences: Saull, V.)

59-520 **Hofmann**, Hans J. (*McGill*) M.Sc.: "The occurrence and petrology of basic intrusions in the northern Mackenzie Mountains, Yukon and North West Territories." (Geological Sciences: Kranck, E.)

59-521 **Iliescu-Constantine**, Rodric (*Bucharest*, Rumania) M.Sc.: "The mechanism of immunorejection in homotransplantation." (Experimental Surgery: Webster, D.)

59-522 **Jackson**, Charles I. (*London*, England) M.Sc.: "Insolation and albedo in Quebec-Labrador." (Geography: Orvig, S.)

59-523 **Laplante**, Charlotte T. (*McGill*) M.Sc.: "Adrenal function in adrenal regeneration hypertension." (Investigative Medicine: Giroud, C.)

59-524 **Leuner**, Wilhelm R. (*Witwatersrand*, South Africa) M.Sc.: "Geology of the west half of La Motte Township, Quebec." (Geological Sciences: Eakins, P.)

59-525 **McCully**, Keith A. (*McGill*) M.Sc.: "Studies of the effects of gonadal hormones on avian mineral metabolism." (Agricultural Chemistry: Common, R.)

59-526 **Machamer**, Jerome F. (*Cornell*) M.Sc.: "The geology of the Forsyth and associated magnetite deposits, Hull Township, province of Quebec." (Geological Sciences: Gill, J.)

59-527 **Millar**, Ronald A. (*Edinburgh*, Scotland) M.Sc.: "The use of a fluorimetric method for the estimation of plasma adrenaline and noradrenaline." (Pharmacology: Benfey, B.)

59-528 **Moore**, Robert B. (*McGill*) M.Sc.: "Studies of neutron deficient radioactive isotopes of xenon." (Physics: Foster, J.)

59-529 **Muller**, Thomas E. (*Budapest*, Hungary) M.Sc.: "Oxidation of xanthate methyl esters of glucose derivatives." (Chemistry: Purves, C.)

59-530 **Parakkal**, Paul F. (*Travancore*, India) M.Sc.: "Regional differences in the pancreas of the albino mouse (*Mus musculus albinus*) as indicated by the distribution of the islets of Langerhans and of alpha and beta cells." (Zoology: Ali, M.)

59-531 **Pilson**, Michael E. (*Bishop's*) M.Sc.: "Studies on casein." (Agricultural Chemistry: Baker, B.)

59-532 **Reynolds**, Lincoln M. (*McGill*) M.Sc.: "Studies on the constitution of casein." (Agricultural Chemistry: Baker, B.)

59-533 **Rosenfeld**, Ze'ev ( ) M.Sc.: "Primitive recursive functions." (Mathematics: Lambek, J.)

59-534 **Roy**, Chitra (*McGill*) M.Sc.: "The synthesis of phenolic glucosides by plant tissues." (Botany: Towers, G.)

59-535 **Sagar**, Richard B. (*London*, England) M.Sc.: "Glacial-meteorological studies in north Ellesmere Island, 1958." (Geography: Orvig, S.)

59-536 **Sinha**, Sharda P. (*Patna*, India) M.Sc.: "The role of the temporal lobe in hearing." (Neurology & Neurosurgery: Jasper, H.)

59-537 **Smith**, David I. (*London*, England) M.Sc.: "Geomorphological studies in the Lake Hazen area, N.W.T." (Geography: Bird, J.)

59-538 **Smith**, Thomas H. (*Manitoba*) M.Sc.: "Auxins and disease in red clover roots." (Plant Pathology: Estey, R.)

59-539 **Spat**, Attilio G. (*McGill*) M.Sc.: "Iron formations and associated rocks in the Mount Wright area, (Quebec)." (Geological Sciences: Stevenson, J.)

59-540 **Uete**, Tetsuo (*Kyoto*, Japan) M.Sc.: "The effect of adrenal steroids on electrolyte excretion." (Investigative Medicine: Venning, E.)

59-541 **Vollo**, Nels B. (*Saskatchewan*) M.Sc.: "The geology of the Henderson Copper deposit, Chibougamau Region, Quebec." (Geological Sciences: Gill, J.)

59-542 **Wallace**, Donald R. (*Bishop's*) M.Sc.: "Occurrence of the Swaine jack-pine sawfly and external anatomy of the mature, feeding larvae." (Entomology: DuPorte, E.)

59-543 **Weaver**, Ralph S. (*New Brunswick*) M.Sc.: "Stark effect in neon under high resolution." (Physics: Foster, J.)

59-544 **Wechsler**, Ann (*Toronto*) M.Sc.: "The secretion of bicarbonate in saliva." (Physiology: Burgen, A.)

M.A. Spring 1959

59-545 **Ansari**, Zafar I. (*Karachi*, Pakistan) M.A.: "An inquiry into the interrelationship between Islam and nationalism in the writings of Egyptians, 1945-56." (Islamic Studies: Adams, C.)

59-546 **Brown**, Ian W. (*McGill*) M.A.: "The Anglican evangelicals in British politics, 1780-1833." (History: Reid, W.)

59-547 **Carson**, Beatrice M. (*Saskatchewan*) M.A.: "The Mevlevi Tarikat considered as organized mysticism in Turkish Islam." (Islamic Studies: Smith, W. & Adams, C.)

59-548 **Feroz**, Muhammad R. (*Panjab*, India) M.A.: "The law of marriage and divorce in Muslim countries." (Islamic Studies: Rasjidi, M.)

59-549 **Foote**, Don C. (*Dartmouth*) M.A.: "Hammerfest, Norway: a study in historical geography." (Geography: Orvig, S.)

59-550 **Frey**, Betty (*Toronto*) M.A.: "Edouard Estaunié et la vie secrète." (French: Lariviere, H.)

59-551 **Goldberg**, Barbara J. (*McGill*) M.A.: "The early novels of D.H. Lawrence." (English: Files, H.)

59-552 **Humphrys**, Graham (*Bristol*, England) M.A.: "Mining activities in Labrador-Ungava." (Geography: Hare, F.)

59-553 **Jaylani**, Tedjaningsih (*Indonesia*) M.A.: "Islamic marriage law in Indonesia." (Islamic Studies: Rasjidi, M.)

59-554 **Jaylani**, Timur (*Indonesia*) M.A.: "The Sarekat Islam movement: its contribution to Indonesian nationalism." (Islamic Studies: Rasjidi, M.)

59-555 **Joos**, Erno (*Grenoble*, France) M.A.: "L'humanisme de Jean Guehenno." (French: Lariviere, H.)

59-556 **Kinsman**, Ronald D. (*Paris*, France) M.A.: "The visit to Canada of 'La Capricieuse' and M. Le Commandant de Belveze in the summer of 1855 as seen through the French-language press of Lower Canada." (History: Cooper, J.)

59-557 **Loeb**, Bernice P. (*Toronto*) M.A.: "The first years of medical practice: a study of the initiation of medical practice by fifty-two Montreal Jewish physicians graduated since 1940." (Sociology & Anthropology: Solomon, D.)

59-558 **Nixon**, Justin W. (*Wyoming*) M.A.: "Monetary velocity in the Canadian economy." (Economics: Armstrong, D.)

59-559 **Polianski**, Alexei N. (*Sir George Williams*) M.A.: "Changes in Canadian labour force participation rates 1946-58: a socio-economic study of the Canadian labour market." (Economics & Political Science: Beach, E.)

59-560 **Raymond**, Charles W. (*McGill*) M.A.: "A land use survey of the Upper St. John River Valley in New Brunswick." (Geography: Bird, J.)

59-561 **Roseman**, Frank (*Sir George Williams*) M.A.: "Anti-combines enforcement in Canada, 1945-58." (Economics: Brecher, I.)

59-562 **Shanks**, Laura E. (*McMaster*) M.A.: "La philosophie de Jean Giraudoux, auteur dramatique." (French: Revershon, M.)

59-563 **Thanos**, Costas A. (*Athens*, Greece) M.A.: "Central banking in Greece." (Economics: Armstrong, D.)

59-564 **Willmott**, William E. (*McGill*) M.A.: "An Eskimo community." (Sociology & Anthropology: Fried, J.)

**S.T.M. Fall 1959**

59-565 **Bertalot**, Renzo (*Waldensian Seminary*, Italy) S.T.M.: "The Roman Catholic modernism and the social gospel: a study of their common premises in the writings of Ernesto Buonaiuti and Walter Rauschenbusch." (Divinity: Walsh, H.)

**M.Eng. Fall 1959**

59-566 **Ahmed**, Syed I. (*Panjab*, India) M.Eng.: "Flow of granular material through orifices." (Civil Engineering & Applied Mechanics: Craig, C.)

59-567 **Blostein**, Maier L. (*McGill*) M.Eng.: "Transistor amplifiers for analogue computers." (Electrical Engineering: Farnell, G.)

59-568 **Chang**, Ching-Ju (*Taiwan*) M.Eng.: "Ignition delay of propane in air between 725-850$^0$C under isothermal conditions." (Mechanical Engineering: Thompson, A.)

59-569 **Hla**, Kyaw (*Rangoon*, Burma) M.Eng.: "Comprehensive analysis of diesel engine performance (Dominion-Crossley diesel engine: Model 6-D/15)." (Mechanical Engineering: Bruce, W.)

59-570 **Mathison**, William (*Glasgow*, Scotland) M.Eng.: "Moment-rotation characteristics of semi-rigid, high-tensile bolted connections." (Civil Engineering & Applied Mechanics: De Stein, J.)

59-571 **Thompson**, Richard D. (*Nova Scotia Technical*) M.Eng.: "Freezing effects on concrete within twenty-four hours of mixing." (Civil Engineering & Applied Mechanics: Wilson, V.)

## ANNUAL LISTING

### LL.M. Fall 1959

59-572 **Dillon**, Joseph G. (*Auckland*, New Zealand) LL.M.: "Agricultural aviation and its regulation." (International Air Law: Pépin, E.)

59-573 **Du Crest**, Maxime M. (*Aix-en-Provence*, France) LL.M.: "L'état et les compagnies de navigation aérienne: les interventions économiques gouvernementales pour l'organisation de la profession de transporteur aérien." (International Air Law: LeDain, G.)

59-574 **MacKneson**, Stephen W. (*McMaster*) LL.M.: "Freedom of flight over the high seas." (International Air Law: Pépin, E.)

### M.Sc. Fall 1959

59-575 **Allington**, Kathleen R. (*London*, England) M.Sc.: "The bogs of central Labrador-Ungava: an examination of their physical characteristics." (Geography: Hare, F.)

59-576 **Barry**, Roger G. (*Liverpool*, England) M.Sc.: "A synoptic climatology for Labrador-Ungava." (Geography: Hare, F.)

59-577 **Beaulieu**, Guy (*Laval*) M.Sc.: "Effect of acetylcholine and nicotine on coronary flow and heart contractions (rate and amplitude) in the isolated perfused heart of the normal and atherosclerotic rabbit." (Pharmacology: Melville, K.)

59-578 **Brody**, Garry S. (*Alberta*) M.Sc.: "Experimental studies in transplantation of small bowel mucosa to the rectum." (Experimental Surgery: Webster, D.)

59-579 **Chiang**, Morgan S-M. (*Taiwan National*) M.Sc.: "Inheritance of growth type, flower and seed color of Dollard red clover." (Agronomy: Brawn, R.)

59-580 **Curtis**, George C. (*Lambuth*) M.Sc.: "The relationship of affect to the excretion of three hormones." (Psychiatry: Cleghorn, R.)

59-581 **Din**, Ghias ud (*New Zealand*) M.Sc.: "Bombardment of zirconium with protons." (Physics: Foster, J.)

59-582 **Eisenstein**, Sam (*Sir George Williams*) M.Sc.: "The effect of ethyl gamma-butyrobetaine on creatine and phosphorous metabolism in rats." (Biochemistry: Hosein, E.)

59-583 **Fessler**, Alfred (*McGill*) M.Sc.: "Transamination in the mammalian erythrocyte." (Biochemistry: Denstedt, O.)

59-584 **Gunn**, Morris W. (*Queensland*, Australia) M.Sc.: "An analogue computer multiplier using transistors." (Electrical Engineering: Farnell, G.)

59-585 **Kingsbury**, Donald M. (*McGill*) M.Sc.: "Canonical languages." (Mathematics: Lambek, J.)

59-586 **Leung**, Philip M-B. (*Taiwan*) M.Sc.: "Composition and nutritive value of heated vegetable oils." (Agricultural Chemistry: Common, R.)

59-587 **Makonnen**, Adunya (*McGill*) M.Sc.: "A study of the pathogenesis of regional enteritis." (Experimental Surgery: Webster, D.)

59-588 **Masson**, David R. (*Manitoba*) M.Sc.: "The scattering of lambda particles by nucleons." (Mathematics: Wallace, P.)

59-589 **Nejedly**, Vladislava J. (*McGill*) M.Sc.: "Histological study of the proximal convoluted tubule in the developing mouse kidney." (Zoology: Ali, M.)

59-590 **Normand**, Gerard L. (*Montréal*) M.Sc.: "An inductive method for the extension of measures." (Physics: Rattray, B.)

59-591 **Page**, Douglas E. (*New Brunswick*) M.Sc.: "Long waves in the Ferrel Westerlies during December 1958." (Meteorology: Hare, F.)

59-592 **Phillips**, Charles O. (*McGill*) M.Sc.: "The nutrition of *Venturia inaequalis* (Cke) Wint." (Plant Pathology: Pelletier, R.)

59-593 **Powell**, Elizabeth A. (*Queen's*) M.Sc.: "The effect of intramuscular injection of gamma butyrobetaine on enzyme movement." (Biochemistry: Hosein, E.)

59-594 **Powell**, John M. (*London*, England) M.Sc.: "The climatic conditions affecting the vegetation of the Lake Hazen area, Ellesmere Island, N.W.T." (Geography: Hare, F.)

59-595 **Richards**, Terence A. (*Western*) M.Sc.: "The results of treatment of haemorrhagic shock on survival, blood volumes and metabolism." (Experimental Surgery: Webster, D.)

59-596 **Samson**, Hugh R. (*Western*) M.Sc.: "Effect of hypothermia on the extent of infarction following middle cerebral occlusion in the monkey." (Neurology & Neurosurgery: Rasmussen, T.)

59-597 **Shah**, Jessie A. (*Oregon State*) M.Sc.: "Haematozoa from some common amphibians of Quebec." (Parasitology: Cameron, T.)

59-598 **Shellabear**, William H. (*Kent State*) M.Sc.: "Evapotranspiration at Point Barrow, Alaska, summer 1956." (Geography: Orvig, S.)

59-599 **Sims**, Walter A. (*Amherst*) M.Sc.: "Sorption of copper, lead, and zinc on American Petroleum Institute reference clays K-4, M-23, and M-25." (Geological Sciences: Eakins, P.)

59-600 **Stanislawski**, Marc (*McGill*) M.Sc.: "Staphylococcal alpha haemolysin fractions and a study of their immunological and biological properties." (Bacteriology & Immunology: Robertson, G.)

59-601 **Taylor**, Allen L. (*Alberta*) M.Sc.: "The temperature dependence of the work function of barium." (Physics: Crowell, C.)

59-602 **Teitlebaum**, Albert D. (*McGill*) M.Sc.: "The fundamental theorem of the theory of games." (Mathematics: Peck, J.)

59-603 **Vanderwolf**, Cornelius H. (*Alberta*) M.Sc.: "The arrest phenomenon and its relation to learning." (Psychology: Hebb, D.)

59-604 **Varma**, Maithili S. (*Agra*, India) M.Sc.: "Studies on carcinogenesis in hamsters." (Experimental Surgery: Webster, D.)

**M.A. Fall 1959**

59-605 **Bartolini**, Angelo E. (*McGill*) M.A.: "La terre, la mer et les hommes dans l'oeuvre d'Henri Queffélec." (French: Launay, J.)

59-606 **Burshtyn**, Hyman (*McGill*) M.A.: "A study of interpersonal persuasion." (Sociology & Anthropology: Westley, W.)

59-607 **Claus**, Hans-Jörg (*Saar*, West Germany) M.A.: "Transfer of training and reactions to novelty." (Psychology: Bindra, D.)

59-608 **Faruqi**, Ziya-ul-Hasan (*Aligarh*, India) M.A.: "Deoband and the demand for Pakistan." (Islamic Studies: Rahman, F.)

59-609 **Hall**, Janet M. (*Wheaton*) M.A.: "Louis Pergaud, animalier." (French: Reverchon, M.)

59-610 **Haugestad**, Per T. (*Oslo*, Norway) M.A.: "Organized multilateral trade: some aspects of the structure and operation of the General Agreement on Tariffs and Trade." (Economics & Political Science: Brecher, M.)

59-611 **Horowitz**, Gad (*Manitoba*) M.A.: "Mosca and Mills: ruling class and power elite." (Economics & Political Science: Frankel, S.)

59-612 **McCarthy**, John J. (*Notre Dame*) M.A.: "Fluctuations in British public opinion concerning Sir Edward Grey's foreign policy during the Balkan Wars, 1912-1913." (History: Fieldhouse, H.)

59-613 **McCrorie**, James N. (*McGill*) M.A.: "The social organization of graduate students in chemistry." (Sociology & Anthropology: Solomon, D.)

59-614 **Mieszkowski**, Peter M. (*McGill*) M.A.: "Canadian import demand for fuels: a study of aggregation bias in econometric research." (Economics: Kemp, M.)

59-615 **Mubarak**, Nasreldin (*London*, England) M.A.: "The Sudan: a study in economic dualisn." (Economics: Brecher, I.)

59-616 **Nemiroff**, Stanley A. (*McGill*) M.A.: "The doubt of material realism." (Philosophy: Miller, J.)

59-617 **Power**, Graham C. (*London*, England) M.A.: "An analysis of geographical factors determining the northern limits of the pulp and paper industry in Northern Ontario." (Geography: Hills, T.)

59-**618** **Ritchie**, Verna F. (*Hunter*) M.A.: "Cecil Rhodes' influence on the British government's policy in South Africa, 1870-1899." (History: Reid, W.)

59-**619** **Romeril**, Paul E. (*British Columbia*) M.A.: "War diplomacy and Turkish Republic: a study in neutrality, 1939-1945." (Islamic Studies: Callard, K.)

59-**620** **Skinner**, James M. (*Acadia*) M.A.: "Indian education on Gilford Island: the factor of anxiety." (Education: Munroe, D.)

# LISTING BY AUTHOR

| AUTHOR | THESIS NUMBER | DEGREE |
|---|---|---|
| 'Abd-al-'ati, Hammaduh | 57-601 | M.A. |
| 'Abdu-l-Mu'ti, 'Ali | 57-602 | M.A. |
| Abdelmoneim, Ismail A. | 53-568 | LL.M. |
| Adair, Thomas H. | 32-507 | M.Sc. |
| Adamek, Edward G. | 59-001 | Ph.D. |
| Adamek, Stephen | 54-001 | Ph.D. |
| Adams, Alfred Byron | 39-001 | Ph.D. |
| Adams, Glenn N. | 50-511 | M.Sc. |
| Adams, Glenn N. | 53-041 | Ph.D. |
| Adams, James R. | 37-501 | M.Sc. |
| Adams, James Russell | 40-500 | Ph.D. |
| Adams, William E. | 54-002 | Ph.D. |
| Adams, William E. | 52-544 | M.A. |
| Adderson, James N. | 55-502 | M.Eng. |
| Adelfio, Antonio | 55-580 | LL.M. |
| Adelstein, Peter | 49-001 | Ph.D. |
| Aguilar-Mawdsley, Andres | 48-500 | M.C.L. |
| Aguilar, Mary J. | 58-561 | M.Sc. |
| Ahmad, Mumtaz | 57-514 | LL.M. |
| Ahmed, Saiyed E. | 57-515 | LL.M. |
| Ahmed, Syed I. | 59-566 | M.Eng. |
| Aikin, Archibald M. | 49-040 | Ph.D. |
| Aikman, Cecil H. | 26-535 | M.A. |
| Aikman, Edward P. | 33-568 | M.Sc. |
| Aikman, Mary E. | 37-542 | M.A. |
| Aikman, William E. P. | 35-001 | Ph.D. |
| Airey, Henry T. | 27-502 | M.Sc. |
| Aitken, Johnstone P. | 47-542 | M.Sc. |
| Ajemian, Ann A. | 57-518 | M.Sc. |
| Al-Sawi, Ahmad H. | 54-620 | M.A. |
| Alarie, Albert M. | 45-001 | Ph.D. |
| Alarie, Albert M. | 43-501 | M.Sc. |
| Albert, Ruth R. | 46-582 | M.A. |
| Albert, Samuel | 48-001 | Ph.D. |
| Alcock, Norman Z. | 49-002 | Ph.D. |
| Alexander, Wendal A. | 38-001 | Ph.D. |
| Aligwekwe, Iwuoha E. | 52-545 | M.A. |
| Alivisatos, John | 53-569 | M.Sc. |
| Alivisatos, Spyridon | 51-040 | Ph.D. |
| Alivisatos, Spyridon | 49-592 | M.Sc. |
| Allan, Charles M. | 55-585 | M.Sc. |
| Allan, John A. | 08-508 | M.Sc. |
| Allan, John M. | 25-505 | M.Sc. |
| Allard, Wilfred Philip | 41-510 | M.A. |
| Allardyce, William J. | 31-001 | Ph.D. |
| Allen, Della Elizabeth | 42-516 | M.Sc. |
| Allen, Gertrude E. | 37-516 | M.A. |
| Allen, John S. | 32-019 | Ph.D. |



| AUTHOR | THESIS NUMBER | DEGREE |
|---|---|---|
| Allen, Lloyd S. | 54-569 | M.Sc. |
| Allen, Marguerite Z. | 31-519 | M.A. |
| Allen, Robert L. | 50-643 | M.A. |
| Allenby, Owen C. | 42-001 | Ph.D. |
| Allington, Kathleen F. | 59-575 | M.Sc. |
| Alozie, Obinnaya | 51-593 | M.Sc. |
| Alward, Frederick P. | 28-527 | M.A. |
| Amaron, Errol C. | 33-572 | M.A. |
| Amsel, Abram | 46-537 | M.A. |
| Amyot, Denis E. | 48-555 | M.A. |
| Anand, Tilakraj R. | 54-501 | M.Eng. |
| Anastassiadis, Phoebus A. | 55-001 | Ph.D. |
| Anderson, Clayton E. | 29-501 | M.Sc. |
| Anderson, Donald A. | 49-003 | Ph.D. |
| Anderson, Ernest Grant | 40-037 | M.Sc. |
| Anderson, Evelyn M. | 34-001 | Ph.D. |
| Anderson, Francis D. | 56-001 | Ph.D. |
| Anderson, Francis D. | 51-594 | M.Sc. |
| Anderson, George G. | 48-511 | M.Sc. |
| Anderson, Gordon C. | 57-519 | M.Sc. |
| Anderson, Joan C. | 44-518 | M.Sc. |
| Anderson, Marian | 20-502 | M.Sc. |
| Anderson, Robert G. | 23-501 | M.Sc. |
| Andracki, Stanislaw | 58-001 | Ph.D. |
| Andreae, Shirley R. | 46-504 | M.Sc. |
| Andreae, Wolfgang A. | 45-014 | Ph.D. |
| Andreae, Wolfgang A. | 43-502 | M.Sc. |
| Andrews, Douglas H. | 54-003 | Ph.D. |
| Andrews, Oliver | 56-002 | Ph.D. |
| Angus, Thomas A. | 55-002 | Ph.D. |
| Ansari, Zafar I. | 59-545 | M.A. |
| Antrobus, Edmund S. | 54-036 | Ph.D. |
| Antrobus, Edmund S. | 49-511 | M.Sc. |
| Aprile, Marie A. | 56-512 | M.Sc. |
| Arcand, Louis J. | 32-500 | M.Eng. |
| Archer, William L. | 50-001 | Ph.D. |
| Argue, George H. | 35-002 | Ph.D. |
| Ariano, Alphonse | 50-644 | M.A. |
| Arkley, Lorne M. | 10-511 | M.Sc. |
| Armour, John C. | 23-502 | M.Sc. |
| Armstrong, Charles A. | 26-536 | M.A. |
| Armstrong, David A. | 55-003 | Ph.D. |
| Armstrong, Donald E. | 54-004 | Ph.D. |
| Armstrong, John G. | 44-014 | Ph.D. |
| Armstrong, John G. | 41-523 | M.Sc. |
| Armstrong, John M. | 33-001 | Ph.D. |
| Armstrong, Muriel G. | 54-539 | M.A. |
| Armstrong, Robert A. | 57-050 | Ph.D. |

| AUTHOR | THESIS NUMBER | DEGREE |
|---|---|---|
| Armstrong, Robert A. | 54-570 | M.Sc. |
| Armstrong, Thomas | 25-506 | M.Sc. |
| Arnell, John C. | 42-002 | Ph.D. |
| Arnold, Stanley R. | 57-560 | LL.M. |
| Aron, Ivan M. | 54-509 | M.Sc. |
| Aronin, Jeffrey E. | 51-580 | M.Arch. |
| Arthur, Elizabeth M. | 49-004 | Ph.D. |
| Arthur, Elizabeth M. | 47-529 | M.A. |
| Asbury, Winfred Nowers | 41-524 | M.Sc. |
| Ashford, Walter R. | 43-001 | Ph.D. |
| Ashley, Leonard | 50-645 | M.A. |
| Ashton, Gordon Clemence | 39-511 | M.Sc. |
| Ashwin, James G. | 53-042 | Ph.D. |
| Asimakopulos, Athanasios | 53-547 | M.A. |
| Askonas, Brigitte A. | 46-557 | M.Sc. |
| Assad, Joseph R. | 55-513 | M.Sc. |
| Assad, Robert J. | 58-002 | Ph.D. |
| Assaly, Robert N. | 57-051 | Ph.D. |
| Astbury, John S. | 38-550 | M.A. |
| Atkinson, Hammond J. | 26-503 | M.Sc. |
| Atkinson, Hammond J. | 34-002 | Ph.D. |
| Atkinson, James T. | 46-505 | M.Sc. |
| Attas, Isaac | 49-500 | M.Eng. |
| Atwell, Ernest A. | 25-507 | M.Sc. |
| Auclair, Lucien | 45-502 | M.Sc. |
| Auld, Jean M. | 29-522 | M.A. |
| Austin, George M. | 51-508 | M.Sc. |
| Averill, Edward L. | 53-570 | M.Sc. |
| Avery, Robert J. | 55-004 | Ph.D. |
| Avery, Robert J. | 52-567 | M.Sc. |
| Avigan, Joel | 54-037 | Ph.D. |
| Avison, Arthur T. | 54-510 | M.Sc. |
| Avison, Henry R. | 40-507 | M.A. |
| Axelrad, A.A. | 54-005 | Ph.D. |
| Ayers, George W. | 37-533 | M.Sc. |
| Aylard, Clara M. | 24-506 | M.Sc. |
| Ayoub, Raymond G. | 46-506 | M.Sc. |
| Azima, Hassan | 55-586 | M.Sc. |
| Bacarinos, Eusthathios S. | 51-630 | M.A. |
| Bach, Glen G. | 58-003 | Ph.D. |
| Bachynski, Morrel P. | 55-005 | Ph.D. |
| Back, Robert A. | 53-043 | Ph.D. |
| Badgley, Robin F. | 54-608 | M.A. |
| Badior, Mark A. | 54-571 | M.Sc. |
| Baer, Harold G. | 54-572 | M.Sc. |
| Baerg, Abraham P. | 52-001 | Ph.D. |
| Bagnall, Richard H. | 49-593 | M.Sc. |
| Bahyrycz, G.S. | 57-520 | M.Sc. |



| AUTHOR | THESIS NUMBER | DEGREE |
|---|---|---|
| Bailey, William R. | 55-045 | Ph.D. |
| Bailey, William P. | 50-512 | M.Sc. |
| Baily, Philip P. | 14-508 | M.Sc. |
| Bain, Archie M. | 29-502 | M.Sc. |
| Bain, F.B. | 57-564 | M.Sc. |
| Bain, George W. | 23-503 | M.Sc. |
| Bainborough, Arthur P. | 51-509 | M.Sc. |
| Baines, Joan D. | 57-565 | M.Sc. |
| Baird, David M. | 47-001 | Ph.D. |
| Baird, John B. | 09-507 | M.Sc. |
| Baker, Alexander D. | 25-508 | M.Sc. |
| Baker, Carrie E. | 34-521 | M.A. |
| Baker, Harold A. | 54-038 | Ph.D. |
| Baker, Harold A. | 52-568 | M.Sc. |
| Baker, Kenneth G. | 33-534 | M.A. |
| Baker, Samuel B. | 43-017 | Ph.D. |
| Balachandran, Ponniah | 55-508 | LL.M. |
| Balakrishna, Narasipur H. | 56-553 | M.Eng. |
| Baldwin, Maitland | 52-511 | M.Sc. |
| Bale, Cecil G. | 58-536 | M.A. |
| Ball, Harry S. | 11-505 | M.Sc. |
| Ball, Ralph H. | 31-002 | Ph.D. |
| Ball, William L. | 35-003 | Ph.D. |
| Ballabon, Maurice B. | 55-046 | Ph.D. |
| Ballabon, Maurice B. | 52-600 | M.A. |
| Ballantyne, Murray G. | 32-559 | M.A. |
| Ballem, Charles M. | 51-595 | M.Sc. |
| Bancroft, Joseph A. | 10-001 | Ph.D. |
| Banfill, Gladys M. | 29-523 | M.A. |
| Banford, Jean E. | 28-528 | M.A. |
| Banks, Ronald H. | 56-502 | M.Eng. |
| Bannard, Robert A. | 49-041 | Ph.D. |
| Bardwell, John A. | 48-002 | Ph.D. |
| Barker, Clifford A. | 45-520 | M.Sc. |
| Barker, Walter E. | 31-011 | Ph.D. |
| Barkham, J. Brian | 55-569 | M.Arch. |
| Barnes, Marion J. | 56-567 | M.Sc. |
| Barnes, William H. | 27-001 | Ph.D. |
| Barnes, William H. | 25-509 | M.Sc. |
| Barnett, Elizabeth S. | 34-522 | M.A. |
| Barrales, Hugo L. | 51-510 | M.Sc. |
| Barrett, Doris Pearl | 41-511 | M.A. |
| Barrett, George F. | 49-585 | M.Eng. |
| Barry, James G. | 46-001 | Ph.D. |
| Barry, Rexford G. | 46-583 | M.A. |
| Barry, Roger G. | 59-576 | M.Sc. |
| Barsha, Jacob | 33-002 | Ph.D. |
| Barshay, [illegible] | [illegible] | M.Sc. |

| AUTHOR | THESIS NUMBER | DEGREE |
|---|---|---|
| Barth, Fred W. | 58-004 | Ph.D. |
| Bartholomew, Gilbert | 48-015 | Ph.D. |
| Bartlett, Harry | 36-523 | M.A. |
| Bartok, William | 57-001 | Ph.D. |
| Bartolini, Angelo E. | 59-605 | M.A. |
| Barton, Stuart S. | 56-036 | Ph.D. |
| Bartoshuk, Alexander K. | 54-006 | Ph.D. |
| Bartoshuk, Alexander K. | 52-569 | M.Sc. |
| Barwick, Audrey J. | 48-512 | M.Sc. |
| Bas-Kraus, Eva R. | 57-566 | M.Sc. |
| Bass, P. | 57-052 | Ph.D. |
| Bassett, Henry G. | 50-513 | M.Sc. |
| Bassinov, Saul | 35-519 | M.A. |
| Bastin, Douglas H. | 46-550 | M.Eng. |
| Bates, Frederick W. | 10-512 | M.Sc. |
| Bates, John I. | 48-574 | M.Sc. |
| Bateson, Nora | 33-535 | M.A. |
| Batzold, John S. | 52-002 | Ph.D. |
| Bauer, Donald de F. | 43-503 | M.Sc. |
| Baumgartner, Helmut W. | 56-611 | M.A. |
| Baxt, Judith Brainin | 41-034 | M.Sc. |
| Baxt, Lawrence M. | 34-507 | M.Sc. |
| Baxter, Donald W. | 53-571 | M.Sc. |
| Baxter, Hamilton A. | 30-501 | M.Sc. |
| Baxter, James D. | 52-512 | M.Sc. |
| Baxter, Robert M. | 52-003 | Ph.D. |
| Baxter, Stewart G. | 32-020 | Ph.D. |
| Bayfield, Edward G. | 24-501 | M.S.A. |
| Bayley, Charles Melville | 39-029 | Ph.D. |
| Beach, Horace D. | 55-006 | Ph.D. |
| Beacom, Stanley E. | 59-002 | Ph.D. |
| Beagley, Thomas G. | 12-507 | M.Sc. |
| Beall, George H. | 58-508 | M.Sc. |
| Beattie, Stewart | 57-544 | M.A. |
| Beatty, Stanley A. | 31-003 | Ph.D. |
| Beauchemin, C-H. Guy | 54-609 | M.A. |
| Beaudet, Lionel | 24-507 | M.Sc. |
| Beaudry, Jean-Romuald | 44-501 | M.Sc. |
| Beaulieu, Andre A. | 38-503 | M.Sc. |
| Beaulieu, Guy | 59-577 | M.Sc. |
| Beaulieu, Jacques J. | 54-573 | M.Sc. |
| Beaulieu, Maurice | 55-047 | Ph.D. |
| Beaulieu, Maurice | 53-572 | M.Sc. |
| Beaupre, Thomas Norbert | 41-035 | M.Sc. |
| Beauregard, John P. | 52-500 | M.Eng. |
| Beauvais, Roxane | 42-508 | M.A. |
| Beazley, Warren B. | 37-001 | Ph.D. |
| Beck, Johannes C. | 51-511 | M.Sc. |



| AUTHOR | THESIS NUMBER | DEGREE |
|---|---|---|
| Becking, John A. | 25-510 | M.Sc. |
| Bedford, Frederick W. | 59-510 | M.Sc. |
| Bedford, Robert H. | 31-004 | Ph.D. |
| Bedoukian, Paul | 41-001 | Ph.D. |
| Bedoukian, Paul | 38-544 | M.Sc. |
| Beebe, Mary Elizabeth | 40-508 | M.A. |
| Beelik, Andrew | 54-039 | Ph.D. |
| Bekefi, George | 52-004 | Ph.D. |
| Bekefi, George | 50-514 | M.Sc. |
| Beland, Eleanor | 46-002 | Ph.D. |
| Bell, Adam C. | 34-003 | Ph.D. |
| Bell, Alan | 37-002 | Ph.D. |
| Bell, John M. | 45-503 | M.Sc. |
| Bell, Keith | 50-595 | M.Sc. |
| Bell, Robert E. | 43-003 | Ph.D. |
| Belle, Edward A. | 57-002 | Ph.D. |
| Belle, Edward A. | 54-574 | M.Sc. |
| Belleau, Fernand B. | 50-024 | Ph.D. |
| Belmont, Arthur D. | 56-037 | Ph.D. |
| Bencosme, Sergio | 50-025 | Ph.D. |
| Bencosme, Sergio | 48-575 | M.Sc. |
| Benes, Vaclav | 50-500 | M.C.L. |
| Benn, Doris E. | 48-606 | M.A. |
| Bennett, Clifton F. | 56-003 | Ph.D. |
| Bennett, John R. | 49-501 | M.Eng. |
| Bennett, Richard L. | 48-607 | M.A. |
| Bennett, Robert D. | 33-508 | M.Sc. |
| Bennett, Robert D. | 35-004 | Ph.D. |
| Bennett, Robert M. | 50-502 | M.Eng. |
| Benning, Paulette | 32-525 | M.A. |
| Benoit, Fernand W. | 55-587 | M.Sc. |
| Benson, David G. | 59-003 | Ph.D. |
| Bercovitch, Mortimer | 47-543 | M.Sc. |
| Bercuson, Leonard | 41-019 | M.A. |
| Beresford-Howe, Constance | 46-538 | M.A. |
| Berger, Julius | 24-536 | M.A. |
| Bergithon, Carl | 31-520 | M.A. |
| Berman, Alfred | 31-521 | M.A. |
| Berman, Doreen | 46-558 | M.Sc. |
| Bernard, Ernest A. | 56-503 | M.Eng. |
| Bernard, Gerald A. | 50-582 | M.Eng. |
| Bernstein, Hyman | 56-513 | M.Sc. |
| Berrange, Jevan P. | 58-509 | M.Sc. |
| Berry, John W. | 33-536 | M.A. |
| Berry, Verne H. | 46-507 | M.Sc. |
| Berry, William G. | 35-520 | M.A. |
| Berryhill, Florence M. | 51-512 | M.Sc. |
| Bertalanffy, Felix D. | 54-007 | Ph.D. |

| AUTHOR | THESIS NUMBER | DEGREE |
|---|---|---|
| Bertalanffy, Felix D. | 51-513 | M.Sc. |
| Bertalot, Renzo | 59-565 | S.T.M. |
| Bertrand, Gilles | 53-573 | M.Sc. |
| Bertrand, Paul | 40-038 | M.Sc. |
| Best, Kathleen E. | 30-517 | M.A. |
| Betcherman, Philip | 50-646 | M.A. |
| Betts, Donald D. | 55-048 | Ph.D. |
| Betts, Robert H. | 45-002 | Ph.D. |
| Bexton, William H. | 53-044 | Ph.D. |
| Bezeau, Louis Manning | 41-036 | M.Sc. |
| Bhasin, Parkash C. | 53-505 | M.Eng. |
| Biard, J.M. | 58-510 | M.Sc. |
| Bickell, William A. | 23-504 | M.Sc. |
| Bider, Milton A. | 56-545 | M.A. |
| Biefer, Gregory J. | 52-038 | Ph.D. |
| Bierler, Etienne S. | 20-503 | M.Sc. |
| Bigelow, Robert S. | 54-040 | Ph.D. |
| Billingsley, Lawrence W. | 37-025 | Ph.D. |
| Billingsley, Lawrence W. | 33-509 | M.Sc. |
| Billington, Edward E. | 13-513 | M.Sc. |
| Binmore, Mary E. | 33-537 | M.A. |
| Birchard, Lucile | 41-020 | M.A. |
| Bird, Allan V. | 49-594 | M.Sc. |
| Bird, Frederick T. | 49-042 | Ph.D. |
| Bird, Joseph N. | 29-501 | M.Sc. |
| Bird, Thomas C. | 51-631 | M.A. |
| Birkett, Winifred L. | 23-520 | M.A. |
| Birks, Margaret | 57-545 | M.A. |
| Birks, Richard I. | 57-003 | Ph.D. |
| Birks, Richard I. | 54-575 | M.Sc. |
| Birmingham, Marion K. | 49-043 | Ph.D. |
| Birmingham, Marion K. | 46-559 | M.Sc. |
| Bishinsky, Charles | 44-015 | Ph.D. |
| Bishop, Annetta C. | 38-525 | M.A. |
| Bishop, Claude T. | 49-044 | Ph.D. |
| Bishop, Eric G. | 27-002 | Ph.D. |
| Bishop, Eric G. | 24-508 | M.Sc. |
| Bishop, Robert F. | 45-521 | M.Sc. |
| Bissell, Harold R. | 23-505 | M.Sc. |
| Bissett, Alice M. | 27-522 | M.A. |
| Bisson, Margaret M. | 31-561 | M.A. |
| Bjorklund, Gordon Herbert | 40-001 | Ph.D. |
| Black, Ernest D. | 58-511 | M.Sc. |
| Black, James M. | 42-003 | Ph.D. |
| Black, P.T. | 54-008 | Ph.D. |
| Black, Percy | 46-508 | M.Sc. |
| Black, Peter T. A. | 35-005 | Ph.D. |
| Black, Philip T. | 49-512 | M.Sc. |



| AUTHOR | THESIS NUMBER | DEGREE |
|---|---|---|
| Black, Robson H. | 46-509 | M.Sc. |
| Black, William F. | 56-004 | Ph.D. |
| Blackader, Alexander D. | 18-501 | M.A. |
| Blackmore, William R. | 50-596 | M.Sc. |
| Blades, H. | 50-026 | Ph.D. |
| Blain, Auray | 45-015 | Ph.D. |
| Blake, Donald A. | 52-039 | Ph.D. |
| Blake, Donald A. | 48-576 | M.Sc. |
| Blake, Weston | 53-574 | M.Sc. |
| Blakely, Sister Claire | 35-521 | M.A. |
| Blampin, Caroline | 20-510 | M.A. |
| Blascik, Frank | 49-554 | M.A. |
| Blau, Abraham | 29-503 | M.Sc. |
| Bleakney, John S. | 56-038 | Ph.D. |
| Blevis, Earl H. | 56-514 | M.Sc. |
| Bligh, Emerson G. | 56-039 | Ph.D. |
| Blishen, Bernard R. | 50-647 | M.A. |
| Bliss, James Q. | 59-004 | Ph.D. |
| Blizzard, Ronald H. | 42-004 | Ph.D. |
| Block, Victor R. | 49-555 | M.A. |
| Bloom, Martin S. | 50-515 | M.Sc. |
| Bloom, Myer | 50-597 | M.Sc. |
| Bloomfield, Arthur I. | 36-524 | M.A. |
| Bloomfield, Morton W. | 35-522 | M.A. |
| Bloomfield, Solomon S. | 48-577 | M.Sc. |
| Bloomstone, Shirley S. | 55-624 | M.A. |
| Blostein, Maier L. | 59-567 | M.Eng. |
| Blouin, Wilhelmine E. | 30-518 | M.A. |
| Blumberg, Perry | 29-504 | M.Sc. |
| Blumenstein, Jacob H. | 25-531 | M.A. |
| Blumenthal, Estelle F. | 35-523 | M.A. |
| Bly, Elsie R. | 36-525 | M.A. |
| Boden, Quinibert P. | 26-537 | M.A. |
| Boehner, Reginald S. | 12-001 | Ph.D. |
| Bogante, Jack R. | 27-523 | M.A. |
| Boger, Dellie Lee | 39-030 | M.A. |
| Bogoroch, Rita | 50-516 | M.Sc. |
| Boire, Paul C. | 49-502 | M.Eng. |
| Bois, Joseph S. | 36-001 | Ph.D. |
| Bois, Joseph S. | 34-544 | M.A. |
| Boldrey, Edwin B. | 36-508 | M.Sc. |
| Bolger, Josephine A. | 42-028 | M.A. |
| Boloten, M. | 51-596 | M.Sc. |
| Bombardieri, Caurino C. | 55-007 | Ph.D. |
| Bonis, Margaret E. | 36-526 | M.A. |
| Boomer, Edward H. | 23-001 | Ph.D. |
| Boomer, Edward H. | 21-501 | M.Sc. |
| Boone, Charles S. | 37-534 | M.Sc. |

| AUTHOR | THESIS NUMBER | DEGREE |
|---|---|---|
| Boos, Albert W. | 28-529 | M.A. |
| Boote, Maurice J. | 59-005 | Ph.D. |
| Booth, Kenneth G. | 48-016 | Ph.D. |
| Boothroyd, Eric R. | 43-002 | Ph.D. |
| Boothroyd, Eric R. | 40-517 | M.Sc. |
| Boothroyd, Raymond A. | 32-508 | M.Sc. |
| Bordan, Jack | 52-570 | M.Sc. |
| Borden, Byron C. | 55-503 | M.Eng. |
| Boright, Henry A. | 59-511 | M.Sc. |
| Bornstein, Murray Bernard | 42-517 | M.Sc. |
| Borts, Robert B. | 52-005 | Ph.D. |
| Borts, Robert B. | 50-517 | M.Sc. |
| Bosnitch, Sava | 58-581 | M.A. |
| Bostock, Hugh S. | 25-511 | M.Sc. |
| Boswell, Graeme W. | 59-006 | Ph.D. |
| Boswell, Graeme W. | 49-513 | M.Sc. |
| Boswell, William C. | 52-546 | M.A. |
| Bott, Raoul H. | 46-551 | M.Eng. |
| Boucher, James E. | 51-581 | M.Eng. |
| Boulanger, Jean-Baptiste | 50-648 | M.A. |
| Boulet, Lucien J. | 37-502 | M.Sc. |
| Boulet, Marcel | 45-504 | M.Sc. |
| Boulet, Marcel | 48-017 | Ph.D. |
| Boulkind, Mabel | 38-526 | M.A. |
| Bourget, Adeline E. | 38-527 | M.A. |
| Bourne, James D. | 48-504 | M.Eng. |
| Bourne, Wesley | 24-509 | M.Sc. |
| Bourns, Arthur N. | 44-001 | Ph.D. |
| Bourque, Leopold | 37-535 | M.Sc. |
| Boville, Byron W. | 58-512 | M.Sc. |
| Bowen, William G. | 45-016 | Ph.D. |
| Bower, John R. | 43-003 | Ph.D. |
| Bowes, Walter G. | 48-608 | M.A. |
| Bowker, Ernest E. | 33-538 | M.A. |
| Boyd, Donald H. | 53-045 | Ph.D. |
| Boyd, Mary L. | 46-003 | Ph.D. |
| Boyd, William | 56-569 | M.Sc. |
| Boyer, Raymond | 33-003 | Ph.D. |
| Boyer, Thomas W. | 45-003 | Ph.D. |
| Boyes, Watson | 25-532 | M.A. |
| Boyle, Robert W. | 09-001 | Ph.D. |
| Boyle, Willard S. | 50-002 | Ph.D. |
| Boyle, Willard S. | 48-513 | M.Sc. |
| Bradbury, John S. | 51-582 | M.Eng. |
| Bradford, Florence E. | 46-584 | M.A. |
| Brady, George W. | 49-005 | Ph.D. |
| Braeuer, Mary A. | 14-501 | M.A. |
| Braganca, Menezes B. | 51-041 | Ph.D. |



| AUTHOR | THESIS NUMBER | DEGREE |
|---|---|---|
| Brais, Roger | 42-005 | Ph.D. |
| Bramlage, Catharina A. | 55-588 | M.Sc. |
| Branch, Charles L. | 58-513 | M.Sc. |
| Branchaud, Sister Mary | 40-509 | M.A. |
| Brannen, Eric | 48-018 | Ph.D. |
| Bray, Alton C. | 29-505 | M.Sc. |
| Bray, Richard C. | 40-039 | M.Sc. |
| Brazeau, Joseph E. | 51-564 | M.A. |
| Breckon, Sydney W. | 51-001 | Ph.D. |
| Bredahl, Arve | 56-554 | M.Eng. |
| Breitenbucher, Howard E. | 50-649 | M.A. |
| Breitman, Leo | 52-006 | Ph.D. |
| Brenhouse, Samuel F. | 34-523 | M.A. |
| Breul, Frank R. | 51-002 | Ph.D. |
| Brewer, Charles P. | 43-018 | Ph.D. |
| Brickman, Leo | 40-002 | Ph.D. |
| Brickman, William J. | 53-046 | Ph.D. |
| Bridgers, William Henry | 41-525 | M.Sc. |
| Brierley, James G. | 29-524 | M.A. |
| Briggs, David C. | 58-554 | M.Eng. |
| Briggs, Janet B. | 42-006 | Ph.D. |
| Brissenden, William G. | 38-500 | M.Eng. |
| Brisson, Germain | 48-578 | M.Sc. |
| Bristow, John M. | 57-567 | M.Sc. |
| Brittain, Isabel E. | 11-501 | M.A. |
| Broadbent, Arnot W. | 51-645 | M.Com. |
| Brochu, Francis L. | 50-598 | M.Sc. |
| Brocklesby, Horace N. | 35-006 | Ph.D. |
| Brodie, Maurice | 31-501 | M.Sc. |
| Brodkin, Elliot | 58-005 | Ph.D. |
| Brodkin, Elliot | 51-597 | M.Sc. |
| Brody, Garry S. | 59-578 | M.Sc. |
| Brody, Harry | 55-514 | M.Sc. |
| Brogden, Clarence L. | 45-505 | M.Sc. |
| Bronner, Frederic J. | 37-517 | M.A. |
| Brooke, Richard O. | 25-512 | M.Sc. |
| Brossard, Leo | 40-040 | M.Sc. |
| Brougham, Norma I. | 50-650 | M.A. |
| Broughton, James W. | 37-003 | Ph.D. |
| Brounstein, Cyril J. | 52-040 | Ph.D. |
| Brow, James B. | 22-501 | M.Sc. |
| Browman, Mark | 53-575 | M.Sc. |
| Brown, Alexander P. | 31-502 | M.Sc. |
| Brown, Arthur G. | 38-002 | Ph.D. |
| Brown, Carl E. | 56-612 | M.A. |
| Brown, Donald P. | 51-500 | M.Eng. |
| Brown, Douglas Frederick | 40-003 | Ph.D. |
| Brown, Ernest A. | 40-004 | Ph.D. |

| AUTHOR | THESIS NUMBER | DEGREE |
|---|---|---|
| Brown, Frederick T. | 50-518 | M.Sc. |
| Brown, George | 31-522 | M.A. |
| Brown, George Osburn | 41-032 | M.Eng. |
| Brown, Ian W. | 59-546 | M.A. |
| Brown, Irving | 54-540 | M.A. |
| Brown, Margaret F. | 36-527 | M.A. |
| Brown, Norman E. | 52-513 | M.Sc. |
| Brown, Richard C. | 27-524 | M.A. |
| Brown, Robert A. | 36-509 | M.Sc. |
| Brown, Robert A. | 39-002 | Ph.D. |
| Brown, Robert K. | 46-020 | Ph.D. |
| Brown, Robert M. | 51-003 | Ph.D. |
| Brown, Robert S. | 36-017 | Ph.D. |
| Brown, Vera L. | 13-501 | M.A. |
| Brown, Walter G. | 06-001 | M.A. |
| Brown, Wilfred H. | 27-525 | M.A. |
| Brown, William T. | 54-041 | Ph.D. |
| Browne, John S. | 32-001 | Ph.D. |
| Brownell, Harold H. | 53-047 | Ph.D. |
| Brownstein, Charles | 25-533 | M.A. |
| Brownstone, Yehoshua S. | 59-007 | Ph.D. |
| Bruck, Esther R. | 56-613 | M.A. |
| Bruger, Moses | 29-506 | M.Sc. |
| Brummer, Johannes J. | 55-049 | Ph.D. |
| Brunner, Godfrey H. | 07-507 | M.Sc. |
| Brunton, Donald C. | 48-019 | Ph.D. |
| Bryce, John R. | 55-008 | Ph.D. |
| Bryce, William A. | 47-002 | Ph.D. |
| Bryden, Mark P. | 58-514 | M.Sc. |
| Brzezinski, Zbigniew K. | 50-651 | M.A. |
| Bubar, John S. | 57-004 | Ph.D. |
| Buchanan, Donald R. | 53-548 | M.A. |
| Buchsbaum, Solomon J. | 53-576 | M.Sc. |
| Buck, Walter K. | 51-598 | M.Sc. |
| Buckland, Francis C. | 37-004 | Ph.D. |
| Buckland, Francis C. | 32-509 | M.Sc. |
| Buckland, Irene K. | 34-004 | Ph.D. |
| Buckley, Bernard P. | 41-501 | Ph.D. |
| Buckley, Ronald A. | 59-512 | M.Sc. |
| Buffam, Basil S. | 24-510 | M.Sc. |
| Bula, Peter J. | 54-560 | M.Eng. |
| Bulani, Walter | 55-009 | Ph.D. |
| Buller, William K. | 54-576 | M.Sc. |
| Bunzl, Arthur | 53-577 | M.Sc. |
| Burbidge, Frederick E. | 49-514 | M.Sc. |
| Burch, George N. | 46-560 | M.Sc. |
| Burgess, Charles J. | 47-540 | M.Com. |
| Burgess, Glenn D. | 52-571 | M.Sc. |



| AUTHOR | THESIS NUMBER | DEGREE |
|---|---|---|
| Burgess, Ralph C. | 52-514 | M.Sc. |
| Burgoyne, P. Nicholas W. | 55-589 | M.Sc. |
| Burk, Christopher A. | 30-519 | M.A. |
| Burke, Hugh E. | 29-001 | Ph.D. |
| Burke, Hugh E. | 25-545 | M.Sc. |
| Burley, Brian J. | 56-040 | Ph.D. |
| Burnett, Alastair | 55-010 | Ph.D. |
| Burnett, Alvin A. | 56-614 | M.A. |
| Burns, Dean K. | 25-534 | M.A. |
| Burns, Neal M. | 59-008 | Ph.D. |
| Burns, Neal M. | 57-521 | M.Sc. |
| Burrow, Martin D. | 46-561 | M.Sc. |
| Burrow, Martin D. | 53-048 | Ph.D. |
| Burshtyn, Hyman | 59-606 | M.A. |
| Burton, Barbara W. | 46-562 | M.Sc. |
| Burton, Frederick R. | 33-004 | Ph.D. |
| Burton, Frederick R. | 28-502 | M.Sc. |
| Burton, Garland G. | 31-523 | M.A. |
| Bush, Willard S. | 47-576 | M.A. |
| Bushuk, Walter | 56-005 | Ph.D. |
| Butler, Keith H. | 28-001 | Ph.D. |
| Butler, Ralph | 55-590 | M.Sc. |
| Butler, Robert W. | 50-003 | Ph.D. |
| Butterfield, Lee F. | 47-530 | M.A. |
| Butzer, K.W. | 55-591 | M.Sc. |
| Buxton, Kenneth S. | 30-015 | Ph.D. |
| Bychowsky, Victor | 39-054 | M.Sc. |
| Byers, Alfred R. | 36-002 | Ph.D. |
| Byers, Alfred R. | 33-510 | M.Sc. |
| Bynoe, Evan T. | 31-503 | M.Sc. |
| Bynoe, Evan T. | 35-007 | Ph.D. |
| Byrne, Anthony W. | 58-006 | Ph.D. |
| Byrne, Joseph Lawrence | 39-055 | M.Sc. |
| Cabbott, Irwin M. | 47-507 | M.Sc. |
| Cabott, Irving M. | 51-042 | Ph.D. |
| Cadet, Charles M. | 54-577 | M.Sc. |
| Caezza, Concepta Z. | 57-546 | M.A. |
| Cahn, Shirley | 53-578 | M.Sc. |
| Cain, Robert M. | 51-514 | M.Sc. |
| Caira, Eugene G. | 57-568 | M.Sc. |
| Cairnes, William P. | 56-504 | M.Eng. |
| Cairns, Robert R. | 52-515 | M.Sc. |
| Calder, Alice D. | 33-539 | M.A. |
| Calder, Douglas S. | 35-008 | Ph.D. |
| Calhoun, John M. | 38-003 | Ph.D. |
| Calvert, Margaret N. | 49-627 | M.A. |
| Camara, Jose S. | 49-583 | M.C.L. |
| Cambieri, R. | 57-522 | M.Sc. |

| AUTHOR | THESIS NUMBER | DEGREE |
|---|---|---|
| Cambron, Adrien | 23-506 | M.Sc. |
| Cambron, Adrien | 28-002 | Ph.D. |
| Camerlain, Homer H. | 30-520 | M.A. |
| Cameron, Alan E. | 14-509 | M.Sc. |
| Cameron, Austin W. | 56-041 | Ph.D. |
| Cameron, Colin D. | 36-510 | M.Sc. |
| Cameron, Douglas Alastair | 40-515 | M.Eng. |
| Cameron, Edward L. | 54-502 | M.Eng. |
| Cameron, Harcourt L. | 45-506 | M.Sc. |
| Cameron, James W. | 32-510 | M.Sc. |
| Cameron, James W. | 38-004 | Ph.D. |
| Cameron, Robert A. | 56-042 | Ph.D. |
| Campbell, Alexander | 26-504 | M.Sc. |
| Campbell, Charles G. | 49-515 | M.Sc. |
| Campbell, Edmund E. | 11-506 | M.Sc. |
| Campbell, Herbert N. | 30-502 | M.Sc. |
| Campbell, Hugh A. | 54-561 | M.Eng. |
| Campbell, James A. | 47-023 | Ph.D. |
| Campbell, James A. | 38-504 | M.Sc. |
| Campbell, John D. | 52-007 | Ph.D. |
| Campbell, Joseph D. | 50-519 | M.Sc. |
| Campbell, Richard H. | 48-572 | M.Eng. |
| Campbell, William B. | 29-002 | Ph.D. |
| Cann, Donald Bruce | 40-041 | M.Sc. |
| Cann, Everett D. | 46-021 | Ph.D. |
| Cann, Keith E. | 51-599 | M.Sc. |
| Cann, Malcolm C. | 58-007 | Ph.D. |
| Cann, Malcolm C. | 55-592 | M.Sc. |
| Cannon, Douglas G. | 38-505 | M.Sc. |
| Cannon, Frederick Merriet | 39-512 | M.Sc. |
| Cannon, John J. | 39-003 | Ph.D. |
| Capelovitch, Edward M. | 54-610 | M.A. |
| Caplan, Benjamin | 31-524 | M.A. |
| Capps, Margaret C. | 50-563 | M.A. |
| Caragianis, Eva M. | 58-552 | M.Arch. |
| Caralopoulos, Nicholas | 51-565 | M.A. |
| Carballeira, Andres M. | 53-579 | M.Sc. |
| Carbonneau, Come | 53-001 | Ph.D. |
| Carder, Alfred C. | 49-516 | M.Sc. |
| Cardonsky, Mary | 29-525 | M.A. |
| Carisse, Joseph B. | 57-500 | M.C.L. |
| Carl, Selma E. | 33-540 | M.A. |
| Carleton, Everett A. | 23-507 | M.Sc. |
| Carlton, Lucille | 45-507 | M.Sc. |
| Carlyle, Arthur W. | 23-508 | M.Sc. |
| Carmichael, Henry G. | 10-513 | M.Sc. |
| Carpenter, Gilbert B. | 28-003 | Ph.D. |
| Carpenter, Lula A. | 33-541 | M.A. |

| AUTHOR | THESIS NUMBER | DEGREE |
|---|---|---|
| Carr, Edward F. | 50-503 | M.Eng. |
| Carr, Joseph W. | 51-600 | M.Sc. |
| Carriere, Gilles E. | 54-578 | M.Sc. |
| Carriere, Rita M. | 54-511 | M.Sc. |
| Carroll, Lovell C. | 30-521 | M.A. |
| Carroll, Murray N. | 52-008 | Ph.D. |
| Carroll, William J. | 52-516 | M.Sc. |
| Carruthers, Errol W. | 55-515 | M.Sc. |
| Carruthers, Frederick P. | 53-560 | M.Eng. |
| Carruthers, James A. | 49-006 | Ph.D. |
| Carson, Beatrice M. | 59-547 | M.A. |
| Carter, Alfred Edward | 42-509 | M.A. |
| Carter, Alfred L. | 58-008 | Ph.D. |
| Carter, George F. | 58-009 | Ph.D. |
| Carter, George F. | 54-512 | M.Sc. |
| Carter, Neal M. | 29-003 | Ph.D. |
| Carter, Sharon F. | 49-517 | M.Sc. |
| Cashin, Martin F. | 26-505 | M.Sc. |
| Casserly, Leo M. | 54-513 | M.Sc. |
| Cassidy, Gordon J. | 25-546 | M.Sc. |
| Castle, Robert O. | 49-595 | M.Sc. |
| Caswell, Charles F. | 58-555 | M.Eng. |
| Cavadias, George | 59-513 | M.Sc. |
| Cave, Allister E. | 25-547 | M.Sc. |
| Cawadias, Constantine G. | 48-501 | M.C.L. |
| Chadillon, Francois J. | 45-519 | M.Eng. |
| Chait, Rachel | 30-522 | M.A. |
| Chakko, P.C. | 56-505 | M.Eng. |
| Chalk, Mary L. | 26-506 | M.Sc. |
| Chalk, Mary L. | 28-004 | Ph.D. |
| Challies, George S. | 47-500 | M.C.L. |
| Challies, George S. | 33-542 | M.A. |
| Chalmers, A. Edith | 45-508 | M.Sc. |
| Chalmers, William | 30-001 | Ph.D. |
| Chambers, Harriet A. | 54-514 | M.Sc. |
| Chan, Allan P. | 46-510 | M.Sc. |
| Chan, Victor C. | 49-628 | M.A. |
| Chang, Ching-Ju | 59-568 | M.Eng. |
| Chang, Lo-ching | 42-048 | M.Eng. |
| Chant, Raymond E. | 50-583 | M.Eng. |
| Chapdelaine, Joseph L. | 56-515 | M.Sc. |
| Chaplin, Charles E. | 50-027 | Ph.D. |
| Chaplin, Charles F. | 46-511 | M.Sc. |
| Chapman, Antony D. | 37-518 | M.A. |
| Chapman, Clifford W. | 35-009 | Ph.D. |
| Chapman, Douglas G. | 49-045 | Ph.D. |
| Chapman, Douglas G. | 45-522 | M.Sc. |
| Chapman, John H. | 51-043 | Ph.D. |

| AUTHOR | THESIS NUMBER | DEGREE |
|---|---|---|
| Chapman, John H. | 49-518 | M.Sc. |
| Chapman, Marion H. | 51-515 | M.Sc. |
| Chapman, Robert P. | 49-519 | M.Sc. |
| Chapman, Ross A. | 44-016 | Ph.D. |
| Chapman, Ross A. | 41-526 | M.Sc. |
| Chappel, Clifford I. | 59-009 | Ph.D. |
| Chappel, Clifford I. | 53-518 | M.Sc. |
| Chaput, Marcel | 52-041 | Ph.D. |
| Charasz, Jerzy G. | 57-504 | M.Eng. |
| Charlap, Gregory | 34-506 | M.C.L. |
| Charles, Christine M. | 53-519 | M.Sc. |
| Charles, George E. | 59-010 | Ph.D. |
| Charles, George E. | 51-501 | M.Eng. |
| Charles, J. Koilpillai | 58-010 | Ph.D. |
| Charteris, J.N. | 55-625 | M.A. |
| Chase, Francis E. | 51-004 | Ph.D. |
| Chataway, Helen D. | 26-001 | Ph.D. |
| Chau, Andrew Y. | 50-599 | M.Sc. |
| Cheasley, Clifford H. | 29-526 | M.A. |
| Cheesbrough, Arthur G. | 10-514 | M.Sc. |
| Chen, Chao-jen | 45-523 | M.Sc. |
| Cherian, Kandathil K. | 55-516 | M.Sc. |
| Chess, Gordon F. | 54-562 | M.Eng. |
| Chiang, Morgan S-M. | 59-579 | M.Sc. |
| Chiasson, Thomas C. | 55-593 | M.Sc. |
| Chidzero, Bernard T. | 58-011 | Ph.D. |
| Chin-Yee, Harold R. | 46-512 | M.Sc. |
| Chipman, Harry R. | 25-001 | Ph.D. |
| Chipman, John S. | 48-609 | M.A. |
| Chipman, Robert A. | 33-500 | M.Eng. |
| Chipps, George E. | 56-555 | M.Eng. |
| Choquette, Laurent P. E. | 53-049 | Ph.D. |
| Choquette, Laurent P. E. | 42-518 | M.Sc. |
| Chorobski, Jerzy | 32-511 | M.Sc. |
| Chow, David Y. | 53-506 | M.Eng. |
| Christake, Anna | 58-012 | Ph.D. |
| Christian, William R. | 46-022 | Ph.D. |
| Christie, Archibald M. | 47-024 | Ph.D. |
| Christie, George L. | 49-007 | Ph.D. |
| Christie, Ronald V. | 33-569 | M.Sc. |
| Cienciala, Anna M. | 55-626 | M.A. |
| Cinq-Mars, Lionel | 49-520 | M.Sc. |
| Cipera, John D. | 54-042 | Ph.D. |
| Ciplijauskate, Jurate E. | 56-043 | Ph.D. |
| Ciplijauskate, Jurate E. | 54-579 | M.Sc. |
| Clark, Annie E. | 33-511 | M.Sc. |
| Clark, Barbara E. | 50-520 | M.Sc. |
| Clark, David S. | 57-005 | Ph.D. |



| AUTHOR | THESIS NUMBER | DEGREE |
|---|---|---|
| Clark, David S. | 53-580 | M.Sc. |
| Clark, Edgar H. Jr. | 35-524 | M.A. |
| Clark, Eric N. | 51-044 | Ph.D. |
| Clark, George D. | 52-561 | M.Eng. |
| Clark, Gordon M. | 51-516 | M.Sc. |
| Clark, Ian C. | 58-537 | M.A. |
| Clark, James W. | 55-547 | M.A. |
| Clark, Jocelyn Godfrey | 39-031 | M.A. |
| Clark, John | 52-517 | M.Sc. |
| Clark, John A. | 26-501 | M.S.A. |
| Clark, Karin H. | 56-570 | M.Sc. |
| Clark, Lloyd A. | 59-011 | Ph.D. |
| Clark, Mary M. | 49-629 | M.A. |
| Clark, Peter A. | 29-530 | M.A. |
| Clark, Robert H. | 45-500 | M.Eng. |
| Clark, Robert V. | 52-518 | M.Sc. |
| Clark, Samuel D. | 35-541 | M.A. |
| Clarke, Douglas B. | 43-521 | M.A. |
| Clarke, George F. | 35-500 | M.Eng. |
| Clarke, Robert L. | 48-020 | Ph.D. |
| Clarke, Ronald S. | 51-601 | M.Sc. |
| Clarkson, Scott F. | 45-509 | M.Sc. |
| Claus, Hans-Jorg | 59-607 | M.A. |
| Claxton, John W. | 27-526 | M.A. |
| Clayton, Blanche-Petite | 54-043 | Ph.D. |
| Cleland, John G. | 26-507 | M.Sc. |
| Clermont, Yves W. | 53-002 | Ph.D. |
| Cleveland, Courtney E. | 40-005 | Ph.D. |
| Cleveland, Courtney E. | 38-506 | M.Sc. |
| Cleveland, Edward M. | 55-011 | Ph.D. |
| Clifford, Charles E. | 55-050 | Ph.D. |
| Clifford, Charles E. | 53-581 | M.Sc. |
| Cloutier, Gilles G. | 59-012 | Ph.D. |
| Cloutier, Gilles G. | 56-516 | M.Sc. |
| Cloutier, Joseph A. | 55-051 | Ph.D. |
| Cloutier, Joseph A. | 53-582 | M.Sc. |
| Coade, Emma L. | 31-562 | M.A. |
| Coates, Donald F. | 54-503 | M.Eng. |
| Cobban, Aileen A. | 52-547 | M.A. |
| Cockfield, Harry R. | 11-502 | M.A. |
| Cockfield, William E. | 15-507 | M.Sc. |
| Coffin, Althea | 54-515 | M.Sc. |
| Coffin, Carl C. | 29-004 | Ph.D. |
| Coffin, David E. | 59-013 | Ph.D. |
| Coffin, David E. | 56-571 | M.Sc. |
| Cohen, Arthur | 36-003 | Ph.D. |
| Cohen, Arthur | 34-508 | M.Sc. |
| Cohen, Bernard B. | 30-523 | M.A. |

| AUTHOR | THESIS NUMBER | DEGREE |
|---|---|---|
| Cohen, Harry | 49-596 | M.Sc. |
| Cohen, Herman | 45-524 | M.Sc. |
| Colas, Emile J. | 50-581 | LL.M. |
| Coldhagen, E. | 54-611 | M.A. |
| Coldwell, Blake B. | 51-005 | Ph.D. |
| Coldwell, Blake B. | 48-514 | M.Sc. |
| Coldwell, Keith L. | 51-583 | M.Eng. |
| Coleman, Charles L. | 28-559 | M.Sc. |
| Coles, Clifford H. | 54-009 | Ph.D. |
| Coll, David C. | 56-556 | M.Eng. |
| Collard, Edgar A. | 37-519 | M.A. |
| Collier, Barbara C. | 42-519 | M.Sc. |
| Collins, Anne M. | 49-597 | M.Sc. |
| Collins, Frank L. | 53-608 | M.A. |
| Collins, Vernon K. | 46-513 | M.Sc. |
| Collins, William B. | 54-580 | M.Sc. |
| Colter, John S. | 51-006 | Ph.D. |
| Common, Frank B. | 14-502 | M.A. |
| Compton, Neil M. | 48-556 | M.A. |
| Comsa, Radu P. | 55-504 | M.Eng. |
| Comtois, Romuald D. | 52-519 | M.Sc. |
| Conkie, William R. | 55-594 | M.Sc. |
| Conklin, Raymond L. | 24-511 | M.Sc. |
| Conn, John J. | 53-003 | Ph.D. |
| Connell, Robert | 49-521 | M.Sc. |
| Connors, Vara M. | 31-525 | M.A. |
| Conrath, Joseph J. | 51-502 | M.Eng. |
| Conroy, Mary P. | 36-528 | M.A. |
| Cooke, Lloyd Miller | 41-002 | Ph.D. |
| Cooke, Patricia M. | 58-562 | M.Sc. |
| Coombs, Donald B. | 52-548 | M.A. |
| Cooper, Corin H. | 13-514 | M.Sc. |
| Cooper, Douglas L. | 31-005 | Ph.D. |
| Cooper, Gerald E. | 51-602 | M.Sc. |
| Cooper, Gerald E. | 53-004 | Ph.D. |
| Cooper, Howard B. | 47-502 | M.Eng. |
| Cooper, John I. | 38-020 | Ph.D. |
| Cooper, Lawrence O. | 31-504 | M.Sc. |
| Cooper, Ross M. | 50-504 | M.Eng. |
| Cooperberg, Abraham A. | 49-598 | M.Sc. |
| Copland, Edward B. | 32-560 | M.A. |
| Corbett, David C. | 54-044 | Ph.D. |
| Corbett, Edward A. | 16-501 | M.A. |
| Corbett, Percy E. | 15-501 | M.A. |
| Corbett, Wendell O. | 51-603 | M.Sc. |
| Cordukes, William E. | 46-514 | M.Sc. |
| Corey, Alfred J. | 36-004 | Ph.D. |
| Corey, Earl E. | 52-601 | M.A. |



| AUTHOR | THESIS NUMBER | DEGREE |
|---|---|---|
| Cornwall, Frederick W. | 56-006 | Ph.D. |
| Cornwall, Frederick W. | 53-583 | M.Sc. |
| Corona, Carlos | 45-525 | M.Sc. |
| Cote, Pierre E. | 48-021 | Ph.D. |
| Coughlin, Clifton Rexford | 39-047 | M.Com. |
| Coughlin, Francis R. | 55-595 | M.Sc. |
| Coulombe, Louis-Joseph | 56-007 | Ph.D. |
| Coulombe, Louis-Joseph | 49-599 | M.Sc. |
| Coultis, Rosa J. | 49-556 | M.A. |
| Courtois, Guy A. | 49-600 | M.Sc. |
| Courtright, Mary N. | 44-002 | Ph.D. |
| Cousins, George V. | 08-501 | M.A. |
| Cownie, Douglas Heron | 41-527 | M.Sc. |
| Cox, Harold A. | 37-503 | M.Sc. |
| Cox, John R. | 11-507 | M.Sc. |
| Cox, Kenneth | 29-552 | M.Sc. |
| Cox, Lionel A. | 46-023 | Ph.D. |
| Cox, Mary D. | 35-525 | M.A. |
| Cox, Phoebe L. | 52-042 | Ph.D. |
| Cox, Robert W. | 48-557 | M.A. |
| Coyle, James J. | 48-558 | M.A. |
| Cragg, Gerald R. | 46-004 | Ph.D. |
| Craig, Carleton | 34-540 | M.Eng. |
| Craig, Glenn H. | 33-543 | M.A. |
| Craig, Grace L. | 34-524 | M.A. |
| Craig, Isabel F. | 37-520 | M.A. |
| Cramer, Archie Barrett | 39-004 | Ph.D. |
| Crawford, Donna J. | 53-584 | M.Sc. |
| Crawford, Gerald J. | 54-045 | Ph.D. |
| Crawford, James M. | 32-501 | M.Eng. |
| Creamer, George B. | 50-028 | Ph.D. |
| Cree, George C. | 49-630 | M.A. |
| Creighton, Edith M. | 26-538 | M.A. |
| Creighton, Phyllis | 51-566 | M.A. |
| Creighton, Robert H. | 43-004 | Ph.D. |
| Cressman, Homer W. | 33-005 | Ph.D. |
| Crete, Joseph E. | 55-596 | M.Sc. |
| Croll, Diane | 42-051 | M.Sc. |
| Cromarty, Robert P. | 17-504 | M.Sc. |
| Cronk, Francis J. | 16-507 | M.Sc. |
| Crook, Helen G. | 48-515 | M.Sc. |
| Cross, Jean D. | 55-517 | M.Sc. |
| Crowe, Marguerite | 28-503 | M.Sc. |
| Crowell, Clarence R. | 55-012 | Ph.D. |
| Crowell, Clarence R. | 51-604 | M.Sc. |
| Crozier, Robert N. | 28-005 | Ph.D. |
| Cruikshank, Marion G. | 31-526 | M.A. |
| Crysdale, John H. | 53-520 | M.Sc. |

| AUTHOR | THESIS NUMBER | DEGREE |
|---|---|---|
| Cuevas Cancino, Francisco | 46-500 | M.C.L. |
| Cullen, Chester F. | 54-516 | M.Sc. |
| Culliton, John T. | 27-527 | M.A. |
| Culver, Eleanor A. | 46-585 | M.A. |
| Cumberlidge, John T. | 59-014 | Ph.D. |
| Cumming, Bruce G. | 56-008 | Ph.D. |
| Cumming, Charles L. | 13-515 | M.Sc. |
| Cumming, Robert S. | 38-528 | M.A. |
| Cunia, T. | 57-569 | M.Sc. |
| Cunningham, Howe S. | 24-502 | M.S.A. |
| Cunningham, Robert L. | 40-006 | Ph.D. |
| Cunnington, Francis A. | 47-544 | M.Sc. |
| Cure, Charles W. | 48-516 | M.Sc. |
| Cureton, Edward A. | 57-603 | M.A. |
| Currie, Allan L. | 59-015 | Ph.D. |
| Currie, Balfour W. | 30-002 | Ph.D. |
| Currie, Cecil | 33-544 | M.A. |
| Currie, Donald J. | 50-600 | M.Sc. |
| Currie, Robert A. | 51-567 | M.A. |
| Curtis, George C. | 59-580 | M.Sc. |
| Çutcliffe, Jack A. | 54-517 | M.Sc. |
| Cuthbertson, Arnold C. | 29-005 | Ph.D. |
| Cuthbertson, Arnold C. | 27-503 | M.Sc. |
| D'Hauteserve, Louis | 29-527 | M.A. |
| Dacey, John Robert | 40-007 | Ph.D. |
| Dahlstrom, Carl E. | 53-050 | Ph.D. |
| Dale, Frances M. | 53-609 | M.A. |
| Danby, Gordon T. | 56-009 | Ph.D. |
| Dando, John A. | 45-543 | M.A. |
| Daniels, Eli | 29-553 | M.Sc. |
| Daoust, Roger J. | 53-005 | Ph.D. |
| Darlington, Walter A. | 52-009 | Ph.D. |
| Darragh, James H. | 59-514 | M.Sc. |
| Darrell-McPhee, Gloria | 50-601 | M.Sc. |
| Darwent, Basil de B. | 43-019 | Ph.D. |
| Das Gupta, Dyutish C. | 59-016 | Ph.D. |
| Davey, Trevor B. | 57-505 | M.Eng. |
| Daviault, Lionel | 28-504 | M.Sc. |
| Davidson, James G. | 25-501 | M.S.A. |
| Davidson, MacFarlane B. | 06-002 | M.A. |
| Davidson, Margaret E. | 46-515 | M.Sc. |
| Davidson, Mary H. | 33-573 | M.A. |
| Davidson, Stanley C. | 25-513 | M.Sc. |
| Davidson, William A. | 14-510 | M.Sc. |
| Davidson, Winnifred H. | 22-526 | M.A. |
| Davies, Frank T. | 28-505 | M.Sc. |
| Davies, John J. | 59-502 | M.Eng. |
| Davies, Thomas R. | 27-528 | M.A. |



| AUTHOR | THESIS NUMBER | DEGREE |
|---|---|---|
| Davies, Vernon R. | 23-509 | M.Sc. |
| Davis, Charles F. | 23-521 | M.A. |
| Davis, Charles W. | 37-504 | M.Sc. |
| Davis, Gordon R. | 52-043 | Ph.D. |
| Davis, Gordon R. | 49-522 | M.Sc. |
| Davis, John | 42-007 | Ph.D. |
| Davis, John F. | 49-586 | M.Eng. |
| Davis, Richard E. | 27-529 | M.A. |
| Davis, Stuart G. | 42-008 | Ph.D. |
| Davison, Roy J. | 58-502 | S.T.M. |
| Davoud, Raymond I. | 54-628 | M.Com. |
| Daw, Geoffrey G. | 51-584 | M.Eng. |
| Dawes, Charles H. | 30-524 | M.A. |
| Dawkins, Riley A. | 57-570 | M.Sc. |
| Dawson, Donald A. | 59-515 | M.Sc. |
| Day, Frank J. | 06-003 | M.A. |
| Day, Franklin H. | 09-508 | M.Sc. |
| De Angelis, Marius L. | 34-500 | M.Eng. |
| De Freitas, Anthony S. | 57-523 | M.Sc. |
| De Hart, Joseph B. | 12-510 | M.Sc. |
| De Jersey, Murray G. | 46-539 | M.A. |
| De Leeuw, Nannie K. | 50-602 | M.Sc. |
| De Montigny, Raimbault | 34-005 | Ph.D. |
| De Romer, Henry | 56-517 | M.Sc. |
| De Stein, Joseph L. | 46-552 | M.Eng. |
| Dean, R. S. | 58-515 | M.Sc. |
| Dean, William G. | 59-017 | Ph.D. |
| Deane, Burton C. | 55-597 | M.Sc. |
| Deans, Sidney A. | 42-009 | Ph.D. |
| Dechene, Earl B. | 47-545 | M.Sc. |
| Dedering, Christa E. | 55-627 | M.A. |
| Deitcher, Samuel | 53-549 | M.A. |
| Dekaban, Anatole S. | 54-046 | Ph.D. |
| Dekaban, Anatole S. | 51-605 | M.Sc. |
| Deland, Andre N. | 52-520 | M.Sc. |
| Dembicki, Steve | 41-033 | M.Eng. |
| Dempster, John C. | 51-007 | Ph.D. |
| Denis, Bertrand T. | 38-005 | Ph.D. |
| Denis, Frank T. | 33-512 | M.Sc. |
| Dennis, Arnett S. | 55-052 | Ph.D. |
| Dennis, Arnett S. | 53-521 | M.Sc. |
| Dennis, Donald A. | 52-521 | M.Sc. |
| Denny, Denison | 34-541 | M.Eng. |
| Densmore, Arthur A. | 53-522 | M.Sc. |
| Denson, Marie L. | 57-571 | M.Sc. |
| Denstedt, Orville F. | 37-026 | Ph.D. |
| Denton, Dorothy May | 41-512 | M.A. |
| Denton, William Ernest | 40-042 | M.Sc. |

| AUTHOR | THESIS NUMBER | DEGREE |
|---|---|---|
| Derick, Russell A. | 23-510 | M.Sc. |
| Desbarats, Marie-Louise | 53-523 | M.Sc. |
| Desrochers, Louis G. | 58-516 | M.Sc. |
| Detlor, W. Lyall | 31-527 | M.A. |
| Devenney, Hartland M. | 34-545 | M.A. |
| Devine, Francis | 48-610 | M.A. |
| Devins, John C. | 46-005 | Ph.D. |
| Devitt, James E. | 53-585 | M.Sc. |
| Dewar, Charles L. | 22-502 | M.Sc. |
| Dewar, Donald James | 40-008 | Ph.D. |
| Dewdney, John W. | 52-522 | M.Sc. |
| Dewey, Alexander G. | 13-502 | M.A. |
| Dewey, George F. | 14-503 | M.A. |
| Dewhurst, Harold A. | 50-029 | Ph.D. |
| DeDongo, Paul J. | 54-504 | LL.M. |
| DeLong, Walter A. | 24-512 | M.Sc. |
| DeLuca, Horace A. | 37-005 | Ph.D. |
| DeMille, George E. | 58-563 | M.Sc. |
| DeSaussure, Hamilton | 53-511 | LL.M. |
| DeShield, George D. | 49-557 | M.A. |
| DeSouza, John E. | 55-013 | Ph.D. |
| Di Florio, Pasquale | 26-539 | M.A. |
| Diamond, George B. | 48-573 | M.Eng. |
| Dick, Helen | 52-602 | M.A. |
| Dick, William J. | 11-508 | M.Sc. |
| Dickie, Robert D. | 50-652 | M.A. |
| Dickieson, Arthur L. | 10-515 | M.Sc. |
| Dickson, Bertram T. | 22-001 | Ph.D. |
| Dickson, Delphine M. | 51-632 | M.A. |
| Diena, Benito B. | 56-044 | Ph.D. |
| Diena, Benito B. | 54-581 | M.Sc. |
| Dike, Mary E. | 37-543 | M.A. |
| Dillon, Joseph G. | 59-572 | LL.M. |
| Dillon, Sister Marie | 37-521 | M.A. |
| Dimmock, Frederick | 26-558 | M.Sc. |
| Din, Ghias ud | 59-581 | M.Sc. |
| Dixon, John F. | 47-003 | Ph.D. |
| Dju, Mei Y. | 49-601 | M.Sc. |
| Dlouhy, Jan | 57-006 | Ph.D. |
| Doane, Benjamin K. | 55-053 | Ph.D. |
| Dobridge, Ronald W. | 29-507 | M.Sc. |
| Dobson, Christopher B. | 59-500 | M.C.L. |
| Dodd, Geoffrey J. | 22-503 | M.Sc. |
| Dodds, John W. | 49-008 | Ph.D. |
| Dodds, John W. | 46-516 | M.Sc. |
| Dodds, Margaret R. | 34-546 | M.A. |
| Dodis, Nicolas G. | 55-572 | M.Eng. |
| Dolan, Desmond Daniel | 39-056 | M.Sc. |



| AUTHOR | THESIS NUMBER | DEGREE |
|---|---|---|
| Dolan, Everett P. | 23-511 | M.Sc. |
| Dolan, John Philip | 41-513 | M.A. |
| Dolid, Jacob | 23-002 | Ph.D. |
| Dolid, Jacob | 21-502 | M.Sc. |
| Donald, Henry G. | 30-525 | M.A. |
| Dondale, Charles D. | 59-018 | Ph.D. |
| Donevan, Richard E. | 58-564 | M.Sc. |
| Dooling, Sister Margaret | 41-514 | M.A. |
| Dore, Burnell V. | 56-518 | M.Sc. |
| Dore, William G. | 35-503 | M.Sc. |
| Dorken, Herbert O. | 47-508 | M.Sc. |
| Dorland, Rodger M. | 39-005 | Ph.D. |
| Dorman, Robert W. | 36-546 | M.Sc. |
| Dosne, Christiane | 42-010 | Ph.D. |
| Doubilet, Henry | 31-505 | M.Sc. |
| Dougherty, Joan L. | 50-521 | M.Sc. |
| Douglas, Allie V. | 26-002 | Ph.D. |
| Douglas, Allie V. | 21-503 | M.Sc. |
| Douglas, Althea M. | 58-538 | M.A. |
| Douglas, Donald E. | 45-017 | Ph.D. |
| Douglas, Donald E. | 43-518 | M.Sc. |
| Douglas, Donald G. | 49-009 | Ph.D. |
| Douglas, George V. | 21-504 | M.Sc. |
| Douglas, John MacDonald | 41-037 | M.Sc. |
| Douglas, Richard H. | 57-007 | Ph.D. |
| Dowd, Keith J. | 56-615 | M.A. |
| Dowler, Vernon B. | 16-508 | M.Sc. |
| Dowling, Donaldson B. | 21-505 | M.Sc. |
| Downer, John L. | 53-586 | M.Sc. |
| Downes, Kenneth W. | 47-025 | Ph.D. |
| Doyle, J. Andre | 42-520 | M.Sc. |
| Doyle, James J. | 50-603 | M.Sc. |
| Drapala, Walter J. | 46-517 | M.Sc. |
| Drapeau, Jacqueline U. | 55-598 | M.Sc. |
| Draper, Herbert L. | 29-528 | M.A. |
| Draper, William B. | 26-508 | M.Sc. |
| Drion, Huibert | 54-567 | LL.M. |
| Drouin, Paul-Emile | 52-562 | M.Eng. |
| Drummond, Robert N. | 50-604 | M.Sc. |
| Drysdale, George A. | 11-509 | M.Sc. |
| Dso, Li-Liang | 48-517 | M.Sc. |
| Du Crest, Maxime M. | 59-573 | LL.M. |
| Dube, Claudia M. | 35-526 | M.A. |
| Dubensky, Alexander | 44-514 | M.A. |
| Dubuc, Fernand | 50-605 | M.Sc. |
| Duckworth, John M. | 28-562 | M.A. |
| Duff, Dorothy | 14-511 | M.Sc. |
| Dufresne, Cyrille | 52-010 | Ph.D. |

| AUTHOR | THESIS NUMBER | DEGREE |
|---|---|---|
| Dufresne, Cyrille | 48-518 | M.Sc. |
| Dufresne, Joseph A. | 13-516 | M.Sc. |
| Dugas, Jean | 52-011 | Ph.D. |
| Duinat, Blanche E. | 58-539 | M.A. |
| Dunbar, Maxwell John | 41-502 | Ph.D. |
| Duncan, Agnes P. | 45-512 | M.A. |
| Duncan, Albert S. | 38-529 | M.A. |
| Duncan, Gaylen F. | 01-002 | M.Sc. |
| Duncan, Joseph | 42-521 | M.Sc. |
| Duncan, Robert Daman | 41-003 | Ph.D. |
| Dunford, Hugh B. | 54-010 | Ph.D. |
| Dunn, William K. | 32-554 | M.Sc. |
| Durrell, Winfield B. | 48-519 | M.Sc. |
| Dussault, H.P. | 46-563 | M.Sc. |
| Dustan, Alan G. | 22-504 | M.Sc. |
| Dutt, Nihar R. | 56-572 | M.Sc. |
| DuPorte, Ernest M. | 21-001 | Ph.D. |
| DuPorte, Ernest M. | 14-512 | M.Sc. |
| Dwyer, Florence Mary | 41-021 | M.A. |
| Dyce, Elton J. | 28-507 | M.Sc. |
| Dyck, Abram J. | 35-028 | Ph.D. |
| Dyer, William J. | 37-536 | M.Sc. |
| Dyer, William J. | 40-009 | Ph.D. |
| Eade, Kenneth E. | 55-014 | Ph.D. |
| Eade, Kenneth E. | 50-522 | M.Sc. |
| Eadie, Dorothy A. | 54-518 | M.Sc. |
| Eadie, Frank S. | 52-044 | Ph.D. |
| Eadie, Frank S. | 49-523 | M.Sc. |
| Eadie, Robert S. | 22-505 | M.Sc. |
| Eager, Richard L. | 49-010 | Ph.D. |
| Eakins, Peter R. | 52-012 | Ph.D. |
| Eakins, Peter R. | 49-524 | M.Sc. |
| Eappen, Collaparambil | 59-019 | Ph.D. |
| Eardley, Eric A. | 32-512 | M.Sc. |
| Earle, Kenneth M. | 51-517 | M.Sc. |
| Eartly, Heidi H. | 51-518 | M.Sc. |
| Eartly, Heidi H. | 53-006 | Ph.D. |
| East, Edith M. | 07-501 | M.A. |
| East, Thomas W. | 55-015 | Ph.D. |
| East, Thomas W. | 53-524 | M.Sc. |
| Eastham, Arthur M. | 43-005 | Ph.D. |
| Eastwood, Thomas A. | 46-006 | Ph.D. |
| Eaton, Ernest L. | 25-502 | M.S.A. |
| Eaton, Mary J. | 09-501 | M.A. |
| Eaves, Charles A. | 37-505 | M.Sc. |
| Ebbitt, May | 51-568 | M.A. |
| Eccles, William J. | 55-016 | Ph.D. |
| Eccles, William J. | 51-633 | M.A. |



| AUTHOR | THESIS NUMBER | DEGREE |
|---|---|---|
| Echlin, Francis Asbury | 39-513 | M.Sc. |
| Edel, Abraham | 28-531 | M.A. |
| Edel, Joseph L. | 28-532 | M.A. |
| Edelstein, Leo J. | 31-506 | M.Sc. |
| Edgar, William S. | 32-526 | M.A. |
| Edmonds, William A. | 54-541 | M.A. |
| Edward, John T. | 42-011 | Ph.D. |
| Edwards, Clifford F. | 45-544 | M.A. |
| Edwards, Donald K. | 57-008 | Ph.D. |
| Edwards, Gordon M. | 21-506 | M.Sc. |
| Edwards, Joseph | 35-010 | Ph.D. |
| Edwards, Margaret C. | 26-540 | M.A. |
| Egan, Marie J. | 43-522 | M.A. |
| Ehrlich, Daniel J. | 58-517 | M.Sc. |
| Eidinger, David | 58-013 | Ph.D. |
| Eiger, Irena Z. | 43-519 | M.Sc. |
| Eisenbraun, Allan A. | 59-020 | Ph.D. |
| Eisenbraun, Edgar W. | 59-021 | Ph.D. |
| Eisenstein, Sam | 59-582 | M.Sc. |
| Eiser, Herman M. | 47-509 | M.Sc. |
| Ekler, Kurt | 55-017 | Ph.D. |
| Elias, Lorne | 56-045 | Ph.D. |
| Eliopoulos, Hermes A. | 54-519 | M.Sc. |
| Eliot, Charles G. | 38-006 | Ph.D. |
| Elkin, Eugene M. | 33-513 | M.Sc. |
| Elkin, Eugene M. | 35-011 | Ph.D. |
| Ellard, Christopher | 51-503 | M.Eng. |
| Ellington, Alton C. | 46-564 | M.Sc. |
| Ellington, Alton C. | 48-022 | Ph.D. |
| Elliott, Bernard B. | 50-606 | M.Sc. |
| Elliott, Harriett E. | 47-531 | M.A. |
| Elliott, Percy H. | 09-509 | M.Sc. |
| Ellis, Clarence D. | 54-047 | Ph.D. |
| Ellis, David H. | 26-509 | M.Sc. |
| Ellis, Derek V. | 57-009 | Ph.D. |
| Ellis, Derek V. | 54-520 | M.Sc. |
| Ellis, John S. | 49-587 | M.Eng. |
| Ellison, Myra K. | 13-503 | M.A. |
| Elsdon, William L. | 59-022 | Ph.D. |
| Elvidge, Arthur R. | 27-003 | Ph.D. |
| Elvidge, Arthur R. | 25-514 | M.Sc. |
| Emmons, William F. | 27-004 | Ph.D. |
| Emmons, William F. | 20-504 | M.Sc. |
| Emo, Wallace B. | 57-053 | Ph.D. |
| Emo, Wallace B. | 55-599 | M.Sc. |
| Endler, Norman S. | 54-582 | M.Sc. |
| Enesco, Mircea A. | 57-010 | Ph.D. |
| Enger, Knut | 53-559 | S.T.M. |

| AUTHOR | THESIS NUMBER | DEGREE |
|---|---|---|
| Engineer, Behram B. | 50-523 | M.Sc. |
| English, William D. | 50-524 | M.Sc. |
| Entin, Martin A. | 42-052 | M.Sc. |
| Epp, Edward R. | 55-054 | Ph.D. |
| Epstein, Elsie | 29-529 | M.A. |
| Epstein, Norman | 46-553 | M.Eng. |
| Epstein, Samuel | 44-017 | Ph.D. |
| Erickson, Theodore C. | 34-509 | M.Sc. |
| Erickson, Theodore C. | 39-006 | Ph.D. |
| Erlenborn, Willi | 21-507 | M.Sc. |
| Erskine, John Steuart | 42-029 | M.A. |
| Esar, Rhoda | 57-572 | M.Sc. |
| Eskenazi, Beno | 49-588 | M.Eng. |
| Estall, Henry M. | 31-528 | M.A. |
| Estey, Ralph H. | 56-046 | Ph.D. |
| Etheridge, David E. | 53-525 | M.Sc. |
| Etziony, Mordecai | 31-529 | M.A. |
| Evans, Arthur B. | 25-515 | M.Sc. |
| Evans, Delano E. | 33-501 | M.Eng. |
| Evans, Gerald T. | 33-514 | M.Sc. |
| Evans, Harry G. | 55-018 | Ph.D. |
| Evans, John W. | 59-516 | M.Sc. |
| Evans, Joseph P. | 37-027 | Ph.D. |
| Evans, Taylor H. | 41-503 | Ph.D. |
| Ewart, Mervyn H. | 46-565 | M.Sc. |
| Fabrikant, Irene B. | 56-573 | M.Sc. |
| Fague, William R. | 50-564 | M.A. |
| Fainstat, Theodore D. | 51-606 | M.Sc. |
| Fair, Louisa M. | 24-537 | M.A. |
| Fairbairn, N.J. | 51-519 | M.Sc. |
| Fairley, Randolf D. | 50-505 | M.Eng. |
| Faith, Willard V. | 24-513 | M.Sc. |
| Falconer, Errol L. | 56-010 | Ph.D. |
| Falk, Hans L. | 47-004 | Ph.D. |
| Falk, John L. | 52-603 | M.A. |
| Falle, George G. | 37-522 | M.A. |
| Fan, Paul C. | 25-516 | M.Sc. |
| Fang, Sin-Kan | 56-557 | M.Eng. |
| Farmakides, Anna | 59-078 | Ph.D. |
| Farmer, Eric W. | 43-500 | M.Eng. |
| Farmer, Florence A. | 47-026 | Ph.D. |
| Farmer, Florence A. | 44-502 | M.Sc. |
| Farmilo, Charles G. | 48-023 | Ph.D. |
| Farnell, Gerald W. | 57-054 | Ph.D. |
| Farr, William | 55-628 | M.A. |
| Farrell, Amelia Mary | 39-032 | M.A. |
| Farrell, Edna P. | 54-542 | M.A. |
| Faruqi, Ziya-ul-Hasan | 59-608 | M.A. |



| AUTHOR | THESIS NUMBER | DEGREE |
|---|---|---|
| Faucher, Joseph Arthur | 42-049 | M.Eng. |
| Faulkner, Peter | 54-011 | Ph.D. |
| Faurot, Jean Hiatt | 40-026 | M.A. |
| Favis, Demetrios | 51-045 | Ph.D. |
| Favreau, Roger F. | 57-573 | M.Sc. |
| Featherston, Florence F. | 29-530 | M.A. |
| Feeny, Harold Francis | 40-518 | M.Sc. |
| Feiner, Abraham | 31-530 | M.A. |
| Feldman, Samuel M. | 59-023 | Ph.D. |
| Fenston, John | 53-512 | LL.M. |
| Fenyes, Joseph | 56-047 | Ph.D. |
| Ferencz, Agnes M. | 45-513 | M.A. |
| Ferguson, Donald C. | 58-582 | M.A. |
| Ferguson, John | 58-518 | M.Sc. |
| Ferguson, William | 32-555 | M.Sc. |
| Fergusson, Neil L. | 47-501 | M.C.L. |
| Fernando, Derrick M. | 53-587 | M.Sc. |
| Feroz, Muhammad P. | 59-548 | M.A. |
| Ferrabee, Henry G. | 53-610 | M.A. |
| Ferrand, Lucy M. | 29-531 | M.A. |
| Fessler, Alfred | 59-583 | M.Sc. |
| Filby, Edgar A. | 32-002 | Ph.D. |
| Filman, Conrad Colton | 42-522 | M.Sc. |
| Filman, Norman J. | 46-554 | M.Eng. |
| Findlay, David C. | 58-519 | M.Sc. |
| Findlay, Gordon H. | 32-556 | M.Sc. |
| Findlay, Gordon H. | 34-019 | Ph.D. |
| Findlay, Marjorie C. | 56-011 | Ph.D. |
| Findlay, Robert A. | 37-006 | Ph.D. |
| Findlay, Wallace I. | 55-518 | M.Sc. |
| Fineman, Manuel N. | 44-003 | Ph.D. |
| Finestone, Harold | 43-523 | M.A. |
| Finlay, James E. | 54-563 | M.Eng. |
| Finlayson, Duncan A. | 34-510 | M.Sc. |
| Finlayson, John N. | 09-510 | M.Sc. |
| Finley, Frederick L. | 24-514 | M.Sc. |
| Finney, William H. | 28-508 | M.Sc. |
| Firestone, Otto Jack | 42-510 | M.A. |
| Firlotte, William R. | 47-510 | M.Sc. |
| Fish, Arthur G. | 58-565 | M.Sc. |
| Fisher, Charles B. | 33-565 | M.Eng. |
| Fisher, Harold D. | 54-048 | Ph.D. |
| Fisher, Herbert E. | 43-020 | Ph.D. |
| Fisher, John Henry | 41-004 | Ph.D. |
| Fisher, Robert W. | 51-008 | Ph.D. |
| Fishman, Sherold | 53-007 | Ph.D. |
| Fiskell, John G. | 51-009 | Ph.D. |
| Fiskell, John G. | 49-525 | M.Sc. |

| AUTHOR | THESIS NUMBER | DEGREE |
|---|---|---|
| Flahault, Elizabeth | 31-531 | M.A. |
| Fleer, Edward Herman | 39-033 | M.A. |
| Fleet, George A. | 24-515 | M.Sc. |
| Flower, George E. | 49-558 | M.A. |
| Flower, Louis G. | 54-521 | M.Sc. |
| Fluss, Zdenek | 53-526 | M.Sc. |
| Flynn, Frank J. | 56-564 | LL.M. |
| Fochs, Anita M. | 48-520 | M.Sc. |
| Fclkins, Hillis O. | 37-506 | M.Sc. |
| Fclkins, Hillis O. | 39-007 | Ph.D. |
| Fonseca, Owen W. | 53-550 | M.A. |
| Fontaine, Marion | 54-583 | M.Sc. |
| Foote, Don C. | 59-549 | M.A. |
| Foran, Herbert P. | 22-506 | M.Sc. |
| Foran, Michael F. | 44-004 | Ph.D. |
| Forbes, Franklin R. | 33-570 | M.Sc. |
| Fcrbes, Frederic J. | 27-530 | M.A. |
| Forbes, John C. | 25-002 | Ph.D. |
| Ford, John D. | 55-519 | M.Sc. |
| Fordyce, Reid George | 39-008 | Ph.D. |
| Forest, Bertrand | 45-526 | M.Sc. |
| Forgacs, Ottc L. | 59-024 | Ph.D. |
| Forgays, Donald G. | 50-030 | Ph.D. |
| Forgays, Donald G. | 48-559 | M.A. |
| Forgus, Ronald H. | 51-520 | M.Sc. |
| Forse, Raymond F. | 50-607 | M.Sc. |
| Fcrsey, Eugene A. | 26-541 | M.A. |
| Forsey, Eugene A. | 41-005 | Ph.D. |
| Forshaw, Robert P. | 38-507 | M.Sc. |
| Fcrst, Wendell | 55-055 | Ph.D. |
| Forster, David S. | 15-502 | M.A. |
| Fcrsyth, Peter A. | 51-046 | Ph.D. |
| Fcrt, Charles A. | 16-509 | M.Sc. |
| Fortier, Mireille | 41-515 | M.A. |
| Fortier, Yves | 41-038 | M.Sc. |
| Fcrtuyn, Jan D. | 47-511 | M.Sc. |
| Foster, Joan M. | 25-535 | M.A. |
| Foster, Leigh C. | 56-048 | Ph.D. |
| Fcwler, Donald E. | 28-509 | M.Sc. |
| Fcwler, Frances L. | 36-005 | Ph.D. |
| Fcwler, Grant M. | 25-517 | M.Sc. |
| Fox, Charles H. | 10-516 | M.Sc. |
| Fox, Geoffrey E. | 54-012 | Ph.D. |
| Fox, Leslie P. | 49-559 | M.A. |
| Fox, Lester L. | 43-517 | M.Com. |
| Fcxlee, Frank H. | 46-024 | Ph.D. |
| Frackenpohl, Arthur R. | 57-049 | D.Mus. |
| Frame, Gordon F. | 32-003 | Ph.D. |



| AUTHOR | THESIS NUMBER | DEGREE |
|---|---|---|
| Francis, Jean B. | 55-520 | M.Sc. |
| Francis, Lyman E. | 58-520 | M.Sc. |
| Francoeur, Joseph M. | 51-607 | M.Sc. |
| Francoeur, Marc | 53-051 | Ph.D. |
| Francoeur, Pearl | 53-588 | M.Sc. |
| Frangatos, Gerassimos | 56-012 | Ph.D. |
| Frank, Arlen W. | 54-049 | Ph.D. |
| Frank, George B. | 56-049 | Ph.D. |
| Frank, Harold | 30-526 | M.A. |
| Frank, Julius | 47-512 | M.Sc. |
| Frankel, Saul J. | 58-014 | Ph.D. |
| Frankel, Saul J. | 52-604 | M.A. |
| Franklin, Arthur F. | 51-010 | Ph.D. |
| Frankton, Clarence | 40-501 | Ph.D. |
| Fraser, Arnold W. | 50-565 | M.A. |
| Fraser, David Robert | 39-034 | M.A. |
| Fraser, Frank C. | 45-004 | Ph.D. |
| Fraser, Frank C. | 41-039 | M.Sc. |
| Fraser, Gordon E. | 37-500 | M.Eng. |
| Fraser, John S. | 49-046 | Ph.D. |
| Freedman, Arthur N. | 58-566 | M.Sc. |
| Freedman, Nathan | 28-560 | M.Sc. |
| Freeman, Gordon R. | 55-019 | Ph.D. |
| Freeman, Paul O. | 46-502 | M.Eng. |
| Freeman, Peter V. | 57-011 | Ph.D. |
| Freeman, Peter V. | 54-584 | M.Sc. |
| French, Betty R. | 56-616 | M.A. |
| Freund, Gerhard | 57-524 | M.Sc. |
| Frey, Betty | 59-550 | M.A. |
| Frey, Flavian F. | 36-529 | M.A. |
| Fricker, Kathleen M. | 50-653 | M.A. |
| Fridhandler, Louis | 51-521 | M.Sc. |
| Fridhandler, Louis | 53-052 | Ph.D. |
| Friedlander, John B. | 46-586 | M.A. |
| Friedman, Constance A. | 48-004 | Ph.D. |
| Friedman, Mac H. | 37-028 | Ph.D. |
| Friedman, Orrie M. | 44-005 | Ph.D. |
| Friedman, Sydney M. | 46-007 | Ph.D. |
| Friedman, Sydney M. | 41-040 | M.Sc. |
| Friend, Gregory | 55-629 | M.A. |
| Fritz, Clara W. | 18-503 | M.Sc. |
| Fry, Margaret Exie | 42-030 | M.A. |
| Fu, Cheng-Yi | 41-041 | M.Sc. |
| Fulford, Llcyd G. | 40-027 | M.A. |
| Fullerton, Douglas H. | 40-033 | M.Com. |
| Fullertcn, Henry P. | 51-522 | M.Sc. |
| Fulton, Geraldine E. | 58-567 | M.Sc. |
| Funt, Boris L. | 49-011 | Ph.D. |

| AUTHOR | THESIS NUMBER | DEGREE |
|---|---|---|
| Gage, Everett L. | 31-551 | M.Sc. |
| Gagnon, Aurele | 42-031 | M.A. |
| Galbiati, Ignazio V. | 58-503 | M.Eng. |
| Galbraith, John A. | 59-025 | Ph.D. |
| Galbraith, John A. | 50-670 | M.Com. |
| Galinsky, Irving | 45-527 | M.Sc. |
| Gallagher, John | 41-516 | M.A. |
| Gallamore, William A. | 51-523 | M.Sc. |
| Gallaugher, Arthur F. | 32-004 | Ph.D. |
| Gallay, Wilfred | 30-003 | Ph.D. |
| Gallay, Wilfred | 28-510 | M.Sc. |
| Galloway, John D. | 12-508 | M.Sc. |
| Gamacchio, Giampiero | 57-561 | LL.M. |
| Gantchev, Neno | 56-574 | M.Sc. |
| Gardiner, Lorne M. | 55-020 | Ph.D. |
| Gardiner, Lorne M. | 52-523 | M.Sc. |
| Gardner, Charles W. | 50-566 | M.A. |
| Gardner, Joseph A. | 44-006 | Ph.D. |
| Gardner, Prescott E. | 58-015 | Ph.D. |
| Gardner, Robert C. | 58-521 | M.Sc. |
| Gardon, John L. | 55-021 | Ph.D. |
| Garland, Sidney G. | 29-532 | M.A. |
| Garmaise, David L. | 45-005 | Ph.D. |
| Gartaganis, Phoebus | 55-056 | Ph.D. |
| Gass, James H. | 47-546 | M.Sc. |
| Gass, Marcia J. | 49-602 | M.Sc. |
| Gauthier, Fernand M. | 48-521 | M.Sc. |
| Gauvin, William | 45-006 | Ph.D. |
| Gauvin, William | 42-515 | M.Eng. |
| Gay, Alice Grace | 41-022 | M.A. |
| Gazdik, Julius F. | 49-584 | M.C.L. |
| Geddes, Amos L. | 36-006 | Ph.D. |
| Geddes, Leslie A. | 53-561 | M.Eng. |
| Gegg, Richard C. | 24-516 | M.Sc. |
| Geggie, Mary M. | 49-560 | M.A. |
| Geist, Paul B. | 57-547 | M.A. |
| Geldard, Walter J. | 17-505 | M.Sc. |
| Geldart, Lloyd Philip | 41-006 | Ph.D. |
| Gendron, Lucien J. | 54-013 | Ph.D. |
| Genereux, Henri G. | 40-043 | M.Sc. |
| Genest, George L. | 58-504 | M.Eng. |
| Genge, Colin A. | 47-005 | Ph.D. |
| George, Zacheria M. | 59-026 | Ph.D. |
| Gerard, F.R. | 57-555 | S.T.M. |
| Gerard, Robert D. | 55-521 | M.Sc. |
| Gerin-Lajoie, Jean | 53-053 | Ph.D. |
| Gerryts, Edbert | 51-011 | Ph.D. |
| Gerryts, Edbert | 49-603 | M.Sc. |



| AUTHOR | THESIS NUMBER | DEGREE |
|---|---|---|
| Gerson, Harold S. | 29-508 | M.Sc. |
| Gersovitz, Benjamin | 48-505 | M.Eng. |
| Gertler, Menard M. | 46-518 | M.Sc. |
| Gervais, Paul | 48-522 | M.Sc. |
| Gesser, Hyman | 52-045 | Ph.D. |
| Gfeller, Frederick | 36-511 | M.Sc. |
| Ghent, Lila R. | 51-047 | Ph.D. |
| Ghent, Lila R. | 49-561 | M.A. |
| Ghitis, Albert | 54-564 | M.Eng. |
| Ghosh, Asok C. | 55-522 | M.Sc. |
| Ghouri, Ahmad S. | 56-050 | Ph.D. |
| Gibbard, Harold A. | 34-547 | M.A. |
| Gibbins, Gwynn G. | 11-510 | M.Sc. |
| Gibbs, Harold C. | 58-016 | Ph.D. |
| Gibbs, Harold C. | 56-519 | M.Sc. |
| Gibbs, Kathleen E. | 57-525 | M.Sc. |
| Gibbs, Ronald D. | 26-510 | M.Sc. |
| Gibson, Merritt A. | 57-055 | Ph.D. |
| Gibson, Robert M. | 51-524 | M.Sc. |
| Gibson, William C. | 36-547 | M.Sc. |
| Giddings, E. W. Garner | 39-049 | M.Eng. |
| Giguere, Paul A. | 37-007 | Ph.D. |
| Gilbert, Harold Adrian | 39-057 | M.Sc. |
| Gilbert, Jacques | 57-558 | M.Eng. |
| Gilbert, Joseph E. | 49-012 | Ph.D. |
| Gilbert, Joseph E. | 47-513 | M.Sc. |
| Gilbert, Margaret R. | 38-508 | M.Sc. |
| Gilbey, John Alfred | 42-523 | M.Sc. |
| Gill, Dorothy A. | 34-525 | M.A. |
| Gillespie, Peter | 12-509 | M.Sc. |
| Gillett, Laurie B. | 56-520 | M.Sc. |
| Gillham, John K. | 59-027 | Ph.D. |
| Gillies, Archibald | 42-012 | Ph.D. |
| Gillies, Elizabeth W. | 41-517 | M.A. |
| Gillies, George A. | 11-511 | M.Sc. |
| Gillies, Norman B. | 51-048 | Ph.D. |
| Gillies, Norman B. | 46-566 | M.Sc. |
| Gillingham, John T. | 46-567 | M.Sc. |
| Gillis, Norman R. | 09-511 | M.Sc. |
| Gilman, Lucius | 36-007 | Ph.D. |
| Gilmore, Laura B. | 31-563 | M.A. |
| Gilmore, Robert C. | 47-577 | M.A. |
| Gilpin, Victor | 44-018 | Ph.D. |
| Gilroy, Geoffrey S. | 34-526 | M.A. |
| Girard, Kenneth F. | 52-013 | Ph.D. |
| Girard, Kenneth F. | 50-525 | M.Sc. |
| Girdwood, Barbara M. | 46-568 | M.Sc. |
| Girdwood, Barbara M. | 48-024 | Ph.D. |

| AUTHOR | THESIS NUMBER | DEGREE |
|---|---|---|
| Girolami, Renato L. | 55-505 | M.Eng. |
| Giroud, Claude J-P. | 55-057 | Ph.D. |
| Giroud, Claude J-P. | 53-527 | M.Sc. |
| Girvin, Grace T. | 52-046 | Ph.D. |
| Girvin, Grace T. | 50-526 | M.Sc. |
| Gishler, Paul E. | 35-012 | Ph.D. |
| Givner, Morris L. | 59-028 | Ph.D. |
| Givner, Morris L. | 56-575 | M.Sc. |
| Glaudemans, Cornelis P. | 58-017 | Ph.D. |
| Gleason, Clarence H. | 47-027 | Ph.D. |
| Gleeson, Christopher F. | 56-576 | M.Sc. |
| Glegg, Keith C. | 49-526 | M.Sc. |
| Glegg, Ronald E. | 46-025 | Ph.D. |
| Glickman, Irwin | 45-528 | M.Sc. |
| Glickman, Rose | 58-583 | M.A. |
| Glickman, Stephen | 59-029 | Ph.D. |
| Gliddon, William G. | 22-507 | M.Sc. |
| Glocklin, Vera C. | 50-608 | M.Sc. |
| Gloor, Peter | 57-012 | Ph.D. |
| Glover, Thomas W. | 51-634 | M.A. |
| Gluckstha1, Andrew | 53-500 | M.C.L. |
| Glynn, John H. | 31-552 | M.Sc. |
| Gobeil, Antoine R. | 35-504 | M.Sc. |
| Gobeil, Antoine R. | 41-007 | Ph.D. |
| Godard, Hugh Phillips | 41-008 | Ph.D. |
| Godard, J.D. | 53-528 | M.Sc. |
| Godbout, Fernand | 29-554 | M.Sc. |
| Godfrey, Gerald | 49-503 | M.Eng. |
| Godin, J.J. | 53-589 | M.Sc. |
| Godine, Morton Robert | 39-035 | M.A. |
| Godwin, Kathleen F. | 22-508 | M.Sc. |
| Goel, Devendra P. | 57-574 | M.Sc. |
| Goforth, John F. | 28-533 | M.A. |
| Goforth, William W. | 32-527 | M.A. |
| Gogek, Charles J. | 47-006 | Ph.D. |
| Going, Margaret C. | 13-504 | M.A. |
| Gold, Allen | 48-523 | M.Sc. |
| Gold, Lorne W. | 52-572 | M.Sc. |
| Gold, M.M.A. | 45-529 | M.Sc. |
| Gold, Rosalynd | 42-511 | M.A. |
| Gold, Samuel | 31-532 | M.A. |
| Gold, Simon | 45-530 | M.Sc. |
| Goldberg, Barbara J. | 59-551 | M.A. |
| Goldberg, Simon Abraham | 40-028 | M.A. |
| Goldberg, W. | 48-560 | M.A. |
| Goldenberg, Hyman C. | 29-533 | M.A. |
| Goldfarb, Lionel | 48-524 | M.Sc. |
| Goldie, Hugh J. | 56-506 | M.Eng. |



| AUTHOR | THESIS NUMBER | DEGREE |
|---|---|---|
| Goldman, Carl | 55-573 | M.Eng. |
| Goldman, Leonard M. | 48-579 | M.Sc. |
| Goldstein, Fred F. | 55-059 | Ph.D. |
| Goldstein, Hildred M. | 16-502 | M.A. |
| Gombay, Andre M. | 55-548 | M.A. |
| Gonshor, Harry | 49-527 | M.Sc. |
| Goodall, Robert G. | 56-577 | M.Sc. |
| Goode, Robert C. | 34-501 | M.Eng. |
| Goodin, Peggy L. | 49-562 | M.A. |
| Gooding, Herbert E. | 47-547 | M.Sc. |
| Goodman, Samuel J. | 32-528 | M.A. |
| Goodwin, Brian C. | 54-522 | M.Sc. |
| Goracz, Bela A. | 53-611 | M.A. |
| Gordon, Dina | 52-573 | M.Sc. |
| Gordon, George E. | 53-558 | M.Arch. |
| Gordon, Julius | 59-030 | Ph.D. |
| Gordon, Llewelyn | 55-630 | M.A. |
| Gordon, Nathan | 09-502 | M.A. |
| Gordon, Ralph W. | 56-051 | Ph.D. |
| Gordon, Thelma G. | 49-631 | M.A. |
| Gordon, Thomas M. | 28-534 | M.A. |
| Gordon, William L. | 24-517 | M.Sc. |
| Gorham, Anne L. | 52-524 | M.Sc. |
| Goring, David A. | 49-013 | Ph.D. |
| Gorman, Thomas W. | 49-604 | M.Sc. |
| Gorman, William A. | 56-013 | Ph.D. |
| Gorman, William A. | 52-525 | M.Sc. |
| Goss, George C. | 47-548 | M.Sc. |
| Gosztonyi, Paul M. | 53-556 | M.C.L. |
| Goth, John W. | 51-585 | M.Eng. |
| Gottfried, Kurt | 53-529 | M.Sc. |
| Gottheil, Edward | 48-561 | M.A. |
| Gottlieb, Rudolf | 30-503 | M.Sc. |
| Goudey, John F. | 49-504 | M.Eng. |
| Gough, Cyril H. | 55-500 | S.T.M. |
| Gough, Roger W. | 30-527 | M.A. |
| Gough, William F. | 27-504 | M.Sc. |
| Gourlay, Robert H. | 49-605 | M.Sc. |
| Govindaraj, Sadasiva | 49-505 | M.Eng. |
| Gowdey, Cecil W. | 48-611 | M.A. |
| Gower, Douglas L. | 26-542 | M.A. |
| Goyette, Louis F. | 53-530 | M.Sc. |
| Grace, Nathaniel H. | 31-006 | Ph.D. |
| Grad, Bernard | 49-047 | Ph.D. |
| Grady, John C. | 52-574 | M.Sc. |
| Grafstein, Bernice | 54-050 | Ph.D. |
| Graham, Annie Philathea | 39-514 | M.Sc. |
| Graham, Archibald R. | 26-511 | M.Sc. |

| AUTHOR | THESIS NUMBER | DEGREE |
|---|---|---|
| Graham, C. R. | 42-512 | M.A. |
| Graham, Gordon B. | 35-542 | M.A. |
| Graham, Kenneth | 37-507 | M.Sc. |
| Graham, Richard P. | 08-509 | M.Sc. |
| Graham, Walter Donald | 42-053 | M.Sc. |
| Graham, Wilfred | 46-026 | Ph.D. |
| Grainger, Edward H. | 49-606 | M.Sc. |
| Grainger, Edward H. | 53-054 | Ph.D. |
| Gransden, Max M. | 51-012 | Ph.D. |
| Grant, Edwin Parkhurst | 40-044 | M.Sc. |
| Grant, Elizabeth R. | 32-021 | Ph.D. |
| Grant, Elizabeth R. | 30-554 | M.A. |
| Grant, Ian C. | 52-526 | M.Sc. |
| Grant, Mary J. | 35-527 | M.A. |
| Grasberg, Eugeniusz | 53-055 | Ph.D. |
| Grassby, James Neil | 40-034 | M.Eng. |
| Grassie, Vernon R. | 46-008 | Ph.D. |
| Gray, Alexander M. | 16-510 | M.Sc. |
| Gray, Kenneth R. | 34-020 | Ph.D. |
| Gray, Leona | 28-563 | M.A. |
| Gray, Nelson M. | 34-542 | M.Sc. |
| Gray, Richard H. | 37-508 | M.Sc. |
| Gray, Richard H. | 40-010 | Ph.D. |
| Greaves, Clifford | 23-003 | Ph.D. |
| Greaves, Clifford | 22-509 | M.Sc. |
| Greaves, Ida C. | 30-528 | M.A. |
| Green, Frederick | 25-518 | M.Sc. |
| Green, Ralph E. | 56-052 | Ph.D. |
| Greenberg, Harry | 27-505 | M.Sc. |
| Greenberg, Harry | 28-009 | Ph.D. |
| Greenberg, Jack S. | 51-608 | M.Sc. |
| Greenberg, Louis | 48-005 | Ph.D. |
| Greenblatt, Jayson | 48-025 | Ph.D. |
| Greenlees, William S. | 33-545 | M.A. |
| Greenway, Robert M. | 56-014 | Ph.D. |
| Greenwood, Stuart W. | 52-501 | M.Eng. |
| Greenwood, Sydney H. | 40-502 | Ph.D. |
| Greig, Edmund W. | 38-509 | M.Sc. |
| Greig, Margaret E. | 32-022 | Ph.D. |
| Greulich, Richard C. | 53-008 | Ph.D. |
| Gribbins, Gordon Henry | 39-050 | M.Eng. |
| Gribble, William F. | 51-586 | M.Eng. |
| Grierson, John K. | 57-575 | M.Sc. |
| Griesbach, Leonard | 49-528 | M.Sc. |
| Grieve, Arthur D. | 32-023 | Ph.D. |
| Griffiths, George H. | 38-501 | M.Eng. |
| Griffiths, Henry J. | 35-505 | M.Sc. |
| Griffiths, Henry J. | 39-009 | Ph.D. |

| AUTHOR | THESIS NUMBER | DEGREE |
|---|---|---|
| Griffiths, Herbert D. | 50-609 | M.Sc. |
| Griffiths, James E. | 59-031 | Ph.D. |
| Grimes-Graeme, Rhoderick | 32-513 | M.Sc. |
| Grimes-Graeme, Rhoderick | 35-013 | Ph.D. |
| Grimes, Evie M. | 13-505 | M.A. |
| Grivas, John C. | 59-032 | Ph.D. |
| Grivas, John C. | 57-526 | M.Sc. |
| Groome, George R. | 52-502 | M.Eng. |
| Gross, Jack | 49-014 | Ph.D. |
| Grossberg, Allan L. | 54-051 | Ph.D. |
| Groves, Trevor K. | 53-531 | M.Sc. |
| Gruchy, Allan G. | 29-534 | M.A. |
| Grummitt, William E. | 43-006 | Ph.D. |
| Guardo, Lea C. | 48-562 | M.A. |
| Guest, Gordon H. | 38-021 | Ph.D. |
| Guest, Rex M. | 44-007 | Ph.D. |
| Guillet, George L. | 09-512 | M.Sc. |
| Gunn, George B. | 50-004 | Ph.D. |
| Gunn, Kenrick L. | 50-005 | Ph.D. |
| Gunn, Kenrick L. | 47-549 | M.Sc. |
| Gunn, Morris W. | 59-584 | M.Sc. |
| Gunnarsson, Gudni K. | 52-563 | M.Eng. |
| Gunton, Robert C. | 47-028 | Ph.D. |
| Gupta, Makam C. | 55-574 | M.Eng. |
| Gupta, Prem R. | 59-033 | Ph.D. |
| Guptill, Ernest W. | 46-009 | Ph.D. |
| Gurd, Frank R. | 46-569 | M.Sc. |
| Gurd, George W. | 32-005 | Ph.D. |
| Gurd, Jean M. | 26-543 | M.A. |
| Gustafson, Jean M. | 58-522 | M.Sc. |
| Guter, Ernest | 47-532 | M.A. |
| Guthrie, Donald A. | 52-014 | Ph.D. |
| Guthrie, John E. | 55-523 | M.Sc. |
| Gutteridge, Harry S. | 35-506 | M.Sc. |
| Guy-Bray, John V. | 59-517 | M.Sc. |
| Guyton, Pauline | 40-510 | M.A. |
| Gwyn, Julian P. | 58-584 | M.A. |
| Gyorgy, Anne M. | 56-617 | M.A. |
| Gyorgy, Dezso | 53-501 | M.C.L. |
| Habeeb, Herbert | 41-009 | Ph.D. |
| Haber, Andrew B. | 57-576 | M.Sc. |
| Haberl, John F. | 56-507 | M.Eng. |
| Hachey, Henry B. | 25-519 | M.Sc. |
| Hadjis, Dimitris | 58-559 | LL.M. |
| Hadrill, Margaret F. | 05-001 | M.A. |
| Haering, Rudolph R. | 57-013 | Ph.D. |
| Hagerman, Verna B. | 34-527 | M.A. |
| Haggart, Catherine | 59-079 | Ph.D. |

| AUTHOR | THESIS NUMBER | DEGREE |
|---|---|---|
| Hagley, Elmer A. | 57-014 | Ph.D. |
| Hagley, Elmer A. | 55-600 | M.Sc. |
| Hague, Helen | 28-535 | M.A. |
| Hague, Owen C. | 14-513 | M.Sc. |
| Halet, Robert A. | 32-514 | M.Sc. |
| Halet, Robert A. | 34-006 | Ph.D. |
| Halford, Charles R. | 54-543 | M.A. |
| Hall, Charles E. | 46-010 | Ph.D. |
| Hall, Charles E. | 42-524 | M.Sc. |
| Hall, Clifton L. | 32-561 | M.A. |
| Hall, George B. | 39-048 | M.Com. |
| Hall, J.S. | 48-506 | M.Eng. |
| Hall, James Dickie | 39-058 | M.Sc. |
| Hall, Janet M. | 59-609 | M.A. |
| Hall, Nancy C. | 50-527 | M.Sc. |
| Hall, Octavia | 46-519 | M.Sc. |
| Hall, Oswald | 37-544 | M.A. |
| Halley, Leroy F. | 37-008 | Ph.D. |
| Hallonquist, Earland G. | 33-006 | Ph.D. |
| Halperin, Alex H. | 52-575 | M.Sc. |
| Halpern, Jack | 49-015 | Ph.D. |
| Halpern, Philip E. | 45-531 | M.Sc. |
| Hamilton, Andrew W. | 30-529 | M.A. |
| Hamilton, Donald M. | 36-500 | M.Eng. |
| Hamilton, Erwin C. | 53-590 | M.Sc. |
| Hamilton, George H. | 33-515 | M.Sc. |
| Hamilton, Herman A. | 55-524 | M.Sc. |
| Hamilton, Hugh A. | 50-528 | M.Sc. |
| Hamilton, Hugh A. | 53-009 | Ph.D. |
| Hamilton, Lorne D. | 45-514 | M.A. |
| Hamilton, Marion M. | 35-543 | M.A. |
| Hamilton, Robert A. | 36-530 | M.A. |
| Hamilton, William B. | 28-561 | M.Sc. |
| Hammond, George H. | 24-518 | M.Sc. |
| Hampson, Harold G. | 49-563 | M.A. |
| Hampson, Lawrence G. | 53-591 | M.Sc. |
| Hampton, William F. | 33-007 | Ph.D. |
| Hampton, William F. | 32-515 | M.Sc. |
| Handelman, Saul | 55-549 | M.A. |
| Hanlan, Leamon H. | 25-503 | M.S.A. |
| Hannan, Charles K. | 56-053 | Ph.D. |
| Hansen, Douglas R. | 52-527 | M.Sc. |
| Hanson, Angus A. | 46-520 | M.Sc. |
| Hanson, Frank K. | 47-022 | Mus.D. |
| Hanson, James C. | 49-632 | M.A. |
| Harbert, Eleanor | 22-527 | M.A. |
| Hardie, Robert H. | 46-570 | M.Sc. |
| Harding, Charles F. | 50-610 | M.Sc. |



| AUTHOR | THESIS NUMBER | DEGREE |
|---|---|---|
| Harding, Ellis G. | 21-508 | M.Sc. |
| Harding, Lawrence A. | 49-564 | M.A. |
| Harding, Stanley R. | 43-504 | M.Sc. |
| Hardwick, David F. | 48-525 | M.Sc. |
| Hardwick, Thomas J. | 44-019 | Ph.D. |
| Hardy, John A. | 55-601 | M.Sc. |
| Hardy, Norah Woodbury | 41-519 | M.A. |
| Hardy, Robert M. | 30-504 | M.Sc. |
| Hare, John H. | 49-048 | Ph.D. |
| Hare, John H. | 47-550 | M.Sc. |
| Hargrove, Clifford K. | 57-577 | M.Sc. |
| Harkness, Harold W. | 30-004 | Ph.D. |
| Harkness, Harold W. | 29-555 | M.Sc. |
| Harlow, Charles M. | 38-007 | Ph.D. |
| Harney, Patricia M. | 59-518 | M.Sc. |
| Harpham, John A. | 51-049 | Ph.D. |
| Harpur, Robert P. | 49-049 | Ph.D. |
| Harpur, Robert P. | 47-551 | M.Sc. |
| Harrington, John L. | 08-510 | M.Sc. |
| Harris, Julius J. | 33-516 | M.Sc. |
| Harris, Norman C. | 11-512 | M.Sc. |
| Harris, Philip J. | 49-589 | M.Eng. |
| Harris, Richard C. | 24-538 | M.A. |
| Harris, Seth O. | 59-034 | Ph.D. |
| Harris, Theodore H. | 28-536 | M.A. |
| Harrison, Donald F. | 22-510 | M.Sc. |
| Harrison, Francis C. | 07-508 | M.Sc. |
| Harrison, John L. | 50-654 | M.A. |
| Harrison, Kenneth A. | 25-520 | M.Sc. |
| Harrison, Sybil M. | 38-510 | M.Sc. |
| Harrower, George A. | 52-047 | Ph.D. |
| Harrower, George A. | 50-611 | M.Sc. |
| Hart, Edward Arthur | 39-059 | M.Sc. |
| Hartwell, Robert M. | 33-546 | M.A. |
| Harvey, John B. | 07-509 | M.Sc. |
| Harvey, Mary R. | 54-544 | M.A. |
| Harvey, Ross B. | 40-011 | Ph.D. |
| Harvie, Jean E. | 36-531 | M.A. |
| Harvie, Robert | 09-513 | M.Sc. |
| Harwood, Robert U. | 32-006 | Ph.D. |
| Harwood, Victor D. | 49-016 | Ph.D. |
| Haskell, Stanley R. | 56-015 | Ph.D. |
| Haskell, Stanley R. | 50-612 | M.Sc. |
| Haslam, Robert N. | 33-008 | Ph.D. |
| Hasley, Isabel J. | 28-537 | M.A. |
| Hatcher, Albert G. | 10-501 | M.A. |
| Hatcher, William H. | 21-002 | Ph.D. |
| Hatcher, William H. | 17-506 | M.Sc. |

| AUTHOR | THESIS NUMBER | DEGREE |
|---|---|---|
| Haugestad, Per T. | 59-610 | M.A. |
| Havelka, Jaroslav | 54-585 | M.Sc. |
| Hawboldt, Lloyd S. | 46-521 | M.Sc. |
| Hawirko, Roma Z. | 51-013 | Ph.D. |
| Hawirko, Roma Z. | 49-529 | M.Sc. |
| Hawkes, Arthur S. | 45-018 | Ph.D. |
| Hawkins, Stuart C. | 49-565 | M.A. |
| Hawkins, Walter L. | 38-008 | Ph.D. |
| Hawkins, William M. | 58-523 | M.Sc. |
| Hay, Alden Wendell | 42-500 | Ph.D. |
| Hay, Donald R. | 52-015 | Ph.D. |
| Hay, Eleanor C. | 43-021 | Ph.D. |
| Hay, Robert E. | 59-519 | M.Sc. |
| Hayakawa, Samuel I. | 28-538 | M.A. |
| Haydari, Amir A. | 54-612 | M.A. |
| Hayden, Amy J. | 09-503 | M.A. |
| Hayes, Albert O. | 10-517 | M.Sc. |
| Hayes, James C. | 54-586 | M.Sc. |
| Hayes, John E. | 47-503 | M.Eng. |
| Hayes, Saul | 28-539 | M.A. |
| Hayles, Oliver J. | 50-584 | M.Eng. |
| Haymaker, Webb | 35-538 | M.Sc. |
| Hayward, Lloyl D. | 49-050 | Ph.D. |
| Haywood, Bruce | 51-635 | M.A. |
| Heard, Jack F. | 32-007 | Ph.D. |
| Heard, Jack F. | 30-530 | M.A. |
| Hearne, Edna M. | 33-028 | Ph.D. |
| Heaton, Phyllis | 32-529 | M.A. |
| Hebb, Catherine O. | 37-009 | Ph.D. |
| Hebb, Donald O. | 32-530 | M.A. |
| Hecht, Maurice | 42-525 | M.Sc. |
| Heckman, Donald E. | 56-016 | Ph.D. |
| Heckman, Donald E. | 53-532 | M.Sc. |
| Heiber, Sol P. | 34-549 | M.Com. |
| Heisler, John Phalen | 41-023 | M.A. |
| Helfield, Tilya | 55-550 | M.A. |
| Heller, Irving H. | 54-587 | M.Sc. |
| Heller, Mildred | 42-032 | M.A. |
| Heller, Nathan | 44-519 | M.Sc. |
| Heller, Paul P. | 54-505 | LL.M. |
| Helwig, Gerald V. | 31-012 | Ph.D. |
| Helwig, Gerald V. | 29-509 | M.Sc. |
| Hemmeon, Ellen C. | 27-531 | M.A. |
| Hemsley, Stuart D. | 44-524 | M.A. |
| Henderson, Ernest H. | 05-002 | M.A. |
| Henderson, Gerald D. | 50-529 | M.Sc. |
| Henderson, Harold Lloyd | 41-024 | M.A. |
| Henderson, Jean T. | 26-512 | M.Sc. |



| AUTHOR | THESIS NUMBER | DEGREE |
|---|---|---|
| Henderson, John F. | 58-018 | Ph.D. |
| Henderson, John T. | 29-511 | M.Sc. |
| Henderson, Thomas G. | 28-540 | M.A. |
| Henery-Logan, Kenneth F. | 46-027 | Ph.D. |
| Henneberry, Gerald | 50-530 | M.Sc. |
| Henrikson, Arne | 48-526 | M.Sc. |
| Henrikson, Arne | 53-010 | Ph.D. |
| Henrikson, Helen A. | 49-017 | Ph.D. |
| Henry, A.S. | 57-578 | M.Sc. |
| Henry, Alice I. | 06-004 | M.A. |
| Henry, Arthur M. | 38-530 | M.A. |
| Henry, Eleanor May | 39-036 | M.A. |
| Henry, Elizabeth V. | 16-511 | M.Sc. |
| Henry, James P. | 55-059 | Ph.D. |
| Henry, James P. | 42-054 | M.Sc. |
| Henry, Vann C. | 56-578 | M.Sc. |
| Henry, William H. | 51-050 | Ph.D. |
| Henry, Zin A. | 57-015 | Ph.D. |
| Henry, Zin A. | 55-551 | M.A. |
| Hepburn, Johnston | 49-566 | M.A. |
| Herer, Moe I. | 48-580 | M.Sc. |
| Herman, Lloyd G. | 48-006 | Ph.D. |
| Hermoso, J. | 55-581 | LL.M. |
| Heron, Woodburn | 49-633 | M.A. |
| Heron, Woodburn | 53-056 | Ph.D. |
| Herron, John T. | 57-016 | Ph.D. |
| Herschorn, Michael | 58-019 | Ph.D. |
| Herschorn, Michael | 56-618 | M.A. |
| Hersh, Jacob | 51-636 | M.A. |
| Herzberg, Otto W. | 18-505 | M.Sc. |
| Herzer, Richard W. | 35-507 | M.Sc. |
| Hess, Ernest | 33-009 | Ph.D. |
| Hesse, Nicky E. | 53-513 | LL.M. |
| Hetherington, Elizabeth M | 36-532 | M.A. |
| Heuser, Edward A. | 49-634 | M.A. |
| Heuser, Heinrich K. | 33-547 | M.A. |
| Hewitt, Frank S. | 31-533 | M.A. |
| Hewson, William B. | 42-013 | Ph.D. |
| Heyding, Robert D. | 51-014 | Ph.D. |
| Heyman, Madeleine C. | 36-533 | M.A. |
| Hicks, Arthur J. | 31-553 | M.Sc. |
| Hicks, Henry B. | 35-501 | M.Eng. |
| Hiebert, Paul G. | 22-511 | M.Sc. |
| Hiebert, Paul G. | 24-001 | Ph.D. |
| Hikichi, Akira | 56-579 | M.Sc. |
| Hilborn, John W. | 54-014 | Ph.D. |
| Hilborn, John W. | 51-609 | M.Sc. |
| Hilchey, John D. | 53-592 | M.Sc. |

| AUTHOR | THESIS NUMBER | DEGREE |
|---|---|---|
| Hildebrand, Henry H. | 48-581 | M.Sc. |
| Hilkert, Marjorie B. | 38-531 | M.A. |
| Hill, Allan C. | 29-006 | Ph.D. |
| Hill, Allan C. | 27-542 | M.Sc. |
| Hill, Eleanor M. | 21-509 | M.Sc. |
| Hill, Hinson | 27-506 | M.Sc. |
| Hill, Lawrence Stanley | 40-045 | M.Sc. |
| Hill, Olive M. | 33-548 | M.A. |
| Hiltz, Arnold A. | 52-016 | Ph.D. |
| Hindley, John G. | 07-502 | M.A. |
| Hinds, Henry E. | 46-522 | M.Sc. |
| Hitschfeld, Walter | 50-006 | Ph.D. |
| Hla, Kyaw | 59-569 | M.Eng. |
| Hc-Tung, Clifton G. | 57-527 | M.Sc. |
| Hc-Yen, Basil O. | 53-593 | M.Sc. |
| Hochster, Rolf M. | 50-031 | Ph.D. |
| Hodge, Cullen S. | 50-567 | M.A. |
| Hodgins, Samuel R. | 29-535 | M.A. |
| Hcdgson, Gordon W. | 49-018 | Ph.D. |
| Hcdgson, Richard C. | 56-580 | M.Sc. |
| Hcdgson, William A. | 49-530 | M.Sc. |
| Hoechsmann, Klaus | 58-585 | M.A. |
| Hoff, Theodore F. | 54-588 | M.Sc. |
| Hoffman, John C. | 57-017 | Ph.D. |
| Hoffman, Martin M. | 43-007 | Ph.D. |
| Hoffman, Terrence W. | 59-035 | Ph.D. |
| Hoffman, William H. | 50-531 | M.Sc. |
| Hcfmann, Hans J. | 59-520 | M.Sc. |
| Hogan, Howard R. | 50-532 | M.Sc. |
| Hogan, Howard R. | 53-011 | Ph.D. |
| Hogarth, Donald D. | 59-036 | Ph.D. |
| Hogg, David C. | 50-613 | M.Sc. |
| Hogg, David C. | 53-012 | Ph.D. |
| Hogg, Doreen | 57-604 | M.A. |
| Hogg, William A. | 59-037 | Ph.D. |
| Hclbrooke, George L. | 28-512 | M.Sc. |
| Hclcomb, Robert K. | 33-010 | Ph.D. |
| Holden, George W. | 27-005 | Ph.D. |
| Hclden, George W. | 24-519 | M.Sc. |
| Holder, Clinton Howard | 39-010 | Ph.D. |
| Hclland, Catherine N. | 34-528 | M.A. |
| Hollbach, Natasha | 57-018 | Ph.D. |
| Hollbach, Reiner | 58-020 | Ph.D. |
| Hollbach, Reiner | 53-612 | M.A. |
| Hollett, Charlctte | 52-528 | M.Sc. |
| Hollies, Norman R. | 47-007 | Ph.D. |
| Hollinger, Harvey Z. | 58-524 | M.Sc. |
| Hollinger, Martin | 42-033 | M.A. |



| AUTHOR | THESIS NUMBER | DEGREE |
|---|---|---|
| Holmes, Anthony F. | 49-567 | M.A. |
| Holmes, Edward L. | 35-029 | Ph.D. |
| Holmes, James M. | 44-008 | Ph.D. |
| Holmes, Stanley W. | 50-533 | M.Sc. |
| Holt, Irene M. | 53-613 | M.A. |
| Home, Maurice S. | 25-548 | M.Sc. |
| Homer, Kenneth C. | 45-515 | M.A. |
| Hone, David W. | 51-015 | Ph.D. |
| Honey, Howard P. | 15-503 | M.A. |
| Hope-Simpson, David | 41-528 | M.Sc. |
| Hopkins, Nigel J. | 52-017 | Ph.D. |
| Hopkins, Nigel J. | 49-531 | M.Sc. |
| Hopper, Ronald V. | 29-510 | M.Sc. |
| Horan, Patrick J. | 54-589 | M.Sc. |
| Horlick, Louis | 53-533 | M.Sc. |
| Horn, Wallace R. | 36-008 | Ph.D. |
| Horowitz, Gad | 59-611 | M.A. |
| Horscroft, Frank D. | 57-019 | Ph.D. |
| Horton, Cyril A. | 37-010 | Ph.D. |
| Horwood, James F. | 33-517 | M.Sc. |
| Horwood, James F. | 35-014 | Ph.D. |
| Hosein, Esau A. | 52-018 | Ph.D. |
| Hosein, Esau A. | 50-534 | M.Sc. |
| Hospadaruk, Vladimir | 53-013 | Ph.D. |
| Hou, Hsiang-Ch'uan | 28-513 | M.Sc. |
| Houghtcn, Edward C. | 27-507 | M.Sc. |
| Howard, Alma C. | 38-009 | Ph.D. |
| Howard, Robert P. | 47-514 | M.Sc. |
| Howard, Waldorf V. | 22-512 | M.Sc. |
| Howard, Waldorf V. | 24-002 | Ph.D. |
| Howat, David | 29-536 | M.A. |
| Howatt, John I. | 31-507 | M.Sc. |
| Howe, Laura I. | 18-504 | M.Sc. |
| Howe, Lawrence M. | 35-502 | M.Eng. |
| Howe, Margaret G. | 45-516 | M.A. |
| Howell, Allison F. | 49-590 | M.Eng. |
| Howell, Helen M. | 49-568 | M.A. |
| Howell, Lucy M. | 12-501 | M.A. |
| Howells, William Crcmpton | 40-012 | Ph.D. |
| Howes, Frederick S. | 26-513 | M.Sc. |
| Howes, James F. | 51-525 | M.Sc. |
| Howie, Ruth J. | 34-529 | M.A. |
| Howland, Frances | 32-024 | Ph.D. |
| Howlett, John G. | 37-509 | M.Sc. |
| Howlett, Leslie E. | 31-007 | Ph.D. |
| Hoy, Norman A. | 50-506 | M.Eng. |
| Hoyle, Wilfred G. | 47-541 | M.Eng. |
| Hoyt, Ruth | 52-019 | Ph.D. |

| AUTHOR | THESIS NUMBER | DEGREE |
|---|---|---|
| Hoyt, Ruth | 49-635 | M.A. |
| Hubley, Charles E. | 49-019 | Ph.D. |
| Hubscher, Frank F. | 53-514 | LL.M. |
| Hudon, Marcel | 54-523 | M.Sc. |
| Hudson, James C. | 28-541 | M.A. |
| Hughes, Frederick G. | 14-504 | M.A. |
| Hughes, Muriel I. | 45-532 | M.Sc. |
| Hughes, Robert Edward | 40-013 | Ph.D. |
| Hugill, John T. | 46-011 | Ph.D. |
| Hum, Thed Klung | 39-051 | M.Eng. |
| Humes, Harold L. | 23-512 | M.Sc. |
| Humphrey, John P. | 45-019 | Ph.D. |
| Humphreys, Storer Plumer | 39-060 | M.Sc. |
| Humphrys, Graham | 59-552 | M.A. |
| Hunt, John W. | 56-054 | Ph.D. |
| Hunten, Donald M. | 50-007 | Ph.D. |
| Hunten, Janet L. | 52-576 | M.Sc. |
| Hunten, Kenneth W. | 26-003 | Ph.D. |
| Hunten, Kenneth W. | 24-520 | M.Sc. |
| Hunter, Albert W. | 37-011 | Ph.D. |
| Hunter, Albert W. | 34-511 | M.Sc. |
| Hunter, Gerald F. | 46-587 | M.A. |
| Hunter, Jean Isobel | 39-506 | M.A. |
| Hunter, John M. | 50-535 | M.Sc. |
| Hunter, Melvin J. | 39-011 | Ph.D. |
| Huntley, Herbert W. | 10-502 | M.A. |
| Hunton, Vera D. | 51-016 | Ph.D. |
| Huq, A.K.M. Fazlul | 55-060 | Ph.D. |
| Huq, M. Shamsul | 56-521 | M.Sc. |
| Huque, Mohammed M. | 57-056 | Ph.D. |
| Hurlbert, Bernard S. | 53-594 | M.Sc. |
| Hurst, Donald G. | 36-009 | Ph.D. |
| Hurst, Donald G. | 34-512 | M.Sc. |
| Hurst, Norman | 53-551 | M.A. |
| Husain, Bilal R. | 55-022 | Ph.D. |
| Husband, Robert M. | 47-029 | Ph.D. |
| Hutcheon, Alan T. | 48-026 | Ph.D. |
| Hutcheson, Maud M. | 27-532 | M.A. |
| Hutchinson, Aleck | 58-055 | Ph.D. |
| Hutchison, John | 54-558 | M.Com. |
| Hutt, Gordon M. | 31-508 | M.Sc. |
| Huxtable, Margaret | 10-503 | M.A. |
| Hyder, Syed S. | 59-503 | M.Eng. |
| Hymovitch, Bernard | 49-020 | Ph.D. |
| Hymovitch, Bernard | 46-523 | M.Sc. |
| Hyndman, William W. | 55-602 | M.Sc. |
| Idziak, Edmund S. | 57-579 | M.Sc. |
| Iliescu-Constantine, Rodr | 59-521 | M.Sc. |



| AUTHOR | THESIS NUMBER | DEGREE |
|---|---|---|
| Illievitz, Abraham B. | 25-521 | M.Sc. |
| Imbault, Paul-Emile | 50-008 | Ph.D. |
| Imbault, Paul-Emile | 47-552 | M.Sc. |
| Inglis, Frederic G. | 57-580 | M.Sc. |
| Ingraham, Thomas R. | 47-030 | Ph.D. |
| Irvine, George N. | 49-021 | Ph.D. |
| Irvine, Lucille | 48-612 | M.A. |
| Irving, William G. | 13-506 | M.A. |
| Irwin, Arthur B. | 50-009 | Ph.D. |
| Irwin, Marion L. | 28-514 | M.Sc. |
| Irwin, Mary I. | 52-048 | Ph.D. |
| Irwin, Mary I. | 50-536 | M.Sc. |
| Irwin, Nora F. | 38-532 | M.A. |
| Irwin, Roland E. | 57-506 | M.Eng. |
| Isang, Etim U. | 54-590 | M.Sc. |
| Israel, Wilfred E. | 28-564 | M.A. |
| Issen, Lionel | 57-507 | M.Eng. |
| Iversen, James E. | 51-637 | M.A. |
| Ives, John D. | 56-017 | Ph.D. |
| Ives, Walter J. | 46-555 | M.Eng. |
| Jablonski, Werner L. | 53-014 | Ph.D. |
| Jack, Lawrence B. | 43-008 | Ph.D. |
| Jackson, Charles I. | 59-522 | M.Sc. |
| Jackson, Donald S. | 55-023 | Ph.D. |
| Jackson, Garth D. | 55-525 | M.Sc. |
| Jackson, Ira J. | 47-553 | M.Sc. |
| Jackson, Ivan R. | 44-503 | M.Sc. |
| Jackson, Jay M. | 50-655 | M.A. |
| Jackson, Joan K. | 47-578 | M.A. |
| Jackson, Joan S. | 43-511 | M.A. |
| Jackson, Naomi C. | 35-544 | M.A. |
| Jackson, Ray W. | 50-010 | Ph.D. |
| Jacobs, Ross D. | 54-052 | Ph.D. |
| Jacobs, Ross D. | 52-529 | M.Sc. |
| Jacobsen, Eric R. | 32-502 | M.Eng. |
| Jacoby, Arthur W. | 50-537 | M.Sc. |
| Jacoby, Barbara J. | 58-540 | M.A. |
| Jaderholm, Henrik W. | 33-502 | M.Eng. |
| Jaffe, Frederick A. | 49-532 | M.Sc. |
| Jahn, Edwin C. | 29-007 | Ph.D. |
| Jahn, Helen L. | 29-537 | M.A. |
| Jain, Abir C. | 58-021 | Ph.D. |
| Jakobson, Gunnar J. | 55-575 | M.Eng. |
| James, Allen P. | 43-520 | M.Sc. |
| James, Clarke B. | 15-508 | M.Sc. |
| James, William | 57-057 | Ph.D. |
| James, William F. | 21-510 | M.Sc. |
| Jamieson, David M. | 33-566 | M.Eng. |

| AUTHOR | THESIS NUMBER | DEGREE |
|---|---|---|
| Jamieson, James R. | 47-031 | Ph.D. |
| Jamieson, James W. | 56-018 | Ph.D. |
| Jamieson, John S. | 08-502 | M.A. |
| Jamieson, Robert E. | 20-505 | M.Sc. |
| Jamieson, Stuart M. | 38-533 | M.A. |
| Jane, Robert S. | 25-003 | Ph.D. |
| Jane, Robert S. | 23-513 | M.Sc. |
| Janes, Henry F. | 27-533 | M.A. |
| Japp, Robert | 30-531 | M.A. |
| Jardine, John M. | 48-527 | M.Sc. |
| Jardine, William G. | 50-538 | M.Sc. |
| Jarrette, Neil M. | 58-541 | M.A. |
| Javid, Mansour | 56-019 | Ph.D. |
| Javid, Mansour | 50-585 | M.Eng. |
| Jayanetti, Edwin | 58-022 | Ph.D. |
| Jaylani, Tedjaningsih | 59-553 | M.A. |
| Jaylani, Timur | 59-554 | M.A. |
| Jefferis, Jeffrey D. | 29-538 | M.A. |
| Jeffery, William G. | 59-038 | Ph.D. |
| Jeffrey, Claire O. | 48-582 | M.Sc. |
| Jehu, Llewellyn | 34-502 | M.Eng. |
| Jenkins, J.T. | 56-522 | M.Sc. |
| Jenkins, Lloyd H. | 30-532 | M.A. |
| Jenkins, Marjorie M. | 52-577 | M.Sc. |
| Jennings, Peter R. | 53-614 | M.A. |
| Jennings, Thomas J. | 35-528 | M.A. |
| Johannson, Oscar K. | 37-029 | Ph.D. |
| Johns, Cyril K. | 26-514 | M.Sc. |
| Johnson, Arnold L. | 47-554 | M.Sc. |
| Johnson, Frederick A. | 52-020 | Ph.D. |
| Johnson, Herbert | 47-008 | Ph.D. |
| Johnson, John S. | 34-530 | M.A. |
| Johnson, Robert E. | 32-516 | M.Sc. |
| Johnson, Thomas A. | 55-603 | M.Sc. |
| Johnson, Willard J. | 52-021 | Ph.D. |
| Johnston, Agnew H. | 29-539 | M.A. |
| Johnston, C. Meredith | 50-568 | M.A. |
| Johnston, Charles F. | 42-034 | M.A. |
| Johnston, Constance A. | 52-578 | M.Sc. |
| Johnston, Douglas M. | 58-500 | M.C.L. |
| Johnston, Harry W. | 29-008 | Ph.D. |
| Johnston, Harry W. | 27-508 | M.Sc. |
| Johnston, John A. | 55-061 | Ph.D. |
| Johnston, John A. | 51-569 | M.A. |
| Johnston, Patricia M. | 48-563 | M.A. |
| Johnston, William W. | 50-539 | M.Sc. |
| Joly, George W. | 50-586 | M.Eng. |
| Jonassohn, Kurt | 55-631 | M.A. |



| AUTHOR | THESIS NUMBER | DEGREE |
|---|---|---|
| Jones, Alun R. | 54-591 | M.Sc. |
| Jones, Donald C. | 37-012 | Ph.D. |
| Jones, Frank E. | 50-656 | M.A. |
| Jones, Graham A. | 58-568 | M.Sc. |
| Jones, Margaret | 38-534 | M.A. |
| Jones, Randolph K. | 24-539 | M.A. |
| Jones, Robert A. | 50-032 | Ph.D. |
| Jones, Taliesin | 49-636 | M.A. |
| Jones, Thomas W. | 21-519 | M.A. |
| Jones, Trevor L. | 35-508 | M.Sc. |
| Joos, Erno | 59-555 | M.A. |
| Joos, Irma | 58-586 | M.A. |
| Jooste, Rene F. | 49-022 | Ph.D. |
| Jooste, Rene F. | 47-555 | M.Sc. |
| Josephson, Vernal | 42-014 | Ph.D. |
| Jowsey, James R. | 53-015 | Ph.D. |
| Judge, Mabel E. | 33-549 | M.A. |
| Judges, Nancy E. | 55-632 | M.A. |
| Julien, J. Bernard | 50-614 | M.Sc. |
| Jull, Morley A. | 19-502 | M.Sc. |
| Kaal, Hans | 58-542 | M.A. |
| Kabayama, Jean E. | 58-543 | M.A. |
| Kahn, Juan F. | 56-508 | M.Eng. |
| Kahnka, Mary J. | 49-023 | Ph.D. |
| Kalant, Norman | 54-053 | Ph.D. |
| Kallos, Tibere | 53-502 | M.C.L. |
| Kalter, Harold | 51-611 | M.Sc. |
| Kalter, Harold | 53-016 | Ph.D. |
| Kamali, Sabih A. | 59-039 | Ph.D. |
| Kamali, Sabih A. | 55-552 | M.A. |
| Kamm, Josephine J. | 29-511 | M.Sc. |
| Kapica, Lucia | 56-020 | Ph.D. |
| Kapica, Lucia | 54-524 | M.Sc. |
| Kaplan, Florence R. | 32-531 | M.A. |
| Kapur, Kanwal K. | 54-592 | M.Sc. |
| Kardos, Geza | 57-559 | M.Eng. |
| Karn, Gordon M. | 49-533 | M.Sc. |
| Karp, Dorothy | 46-571 | M.Sc. |
| Karp, Dorothy | 53-057 | Ph.D. |
| Karpishka, Irene S. | 58-569 | M.Sc. |
| Kashket, Shelby | 56-021 | Ph.D. |
| Kashket, Shelby | 53-595 | M.Sc. |
| Kasman, Sidney | 55-024 | Ph.D. |
| Kassner, Max H. | 50-540 | M.Sc. |
| Kataria, Prem N. | 57-581 | M.Sc. |
| Katz, Morris | 29-017 | Ph.D. |
| Katz, Morris | 27-509 | M.Sc. |
| Katz, Sidney | 37-013 | Ph.D. |

| AUTHOR | THESIS NUMBER | DEGREE |
|---|---|---|
| Katzman, John | 33-011 | Ph.D. |
| Katzman, John | 30-505 | M.Sc. |
| Kaufman, Hyman | 45-533 | M.Sc. |
| Kaufman, Hyman | 48-007 | Ph.D. |
| Kay, Muriel G. | 32-517 | M.Sc. |
| Kean, Eccleston A. | 52-530 | M.Sc. |
| Kearns, Peter J. | 28-515 | M.Sc. |
| Keating, Bernard J. | 37-014 | Ph.D. |
| Keating, Bernard J. | 33-518 | M.Sc. |
| Keays, John L. | 49-051 | Ph.D. |
| Keefe, Thomas J. | 51-526 | M.Sc. |
| Keenan, Daniel | 55-526 | M.Sc. |
| Keener, Ellis B. | 56-581 | M.Sc. |
| Keep, George R. | 48-613 | M.A. |
| Keeping, Kimball J. | 52-049 | Ph.D. |
| Keeping, Kimball J. | 50-587 | M.Eng. |
| Keirstead, Marjorie S. | 53-552 | M.A. |
| Kelen, Andrew | 48-583 | M.Sc. |
| Kelland, Frank J. | 29-540 | M.A. |
| Kellaway, Peter E. | 47-009 | Ph.D. |
| Kelloway, Warwick F. | 25-536 | M.A. |
| Kelly, Ignatius | 38-535 | M.A. |
| Kelly, Marie Ste. Anne | 41-025 | M.A. |
| Kelly, Roger O. | 58-023 | Ph.D. |
| Kelsey, Ernest S. | 33-567 | M.Eng. |
| Kelton, Michel R. | 52-564 | M.Eng. |
| Kemmett, Francis W. | 48-507 | M.Eng. |
| Kenalty, Brendan Joseph | 41-529 | M.Sc. |
| Kennard, Charles P. | 57-582 | M.Sc. |
| Kennedy, Byrl J. | 51-527 | M.Sc. |
| Kennedy, David H. | 53-507 | M.Eng. |
| Kennedy, John Edward | 42-055 | M.Sc. |
| Kennedy, Judith | 38-551 | M.A. |
| Kennedy, Margaret E. | 21-511 | M.Sc. |
| Kennedy, Taylor James | 39-052 | M.Eng. |
| Kent, George Adrian | 42-056 | M.Sc. |
| Kent, Josephine P. | 34-531 | M.A. |
| Kerr, Ernest A. | 41-042 | M.Sc. |
| Kerry, Esther Wilson | 39-037 | M.A. |
| Kershman, John | 33-519 | M.Sc. |
| Ketcheson, Barbara G. | 59-040 | Ph.D. |
| Keys, John D. | 51-051 | Ph.D. |
| Keys, John D. | 48-584 | M.Sc. |
| Khan, M. Abdul B. | 49-024 | Ph.D. |
| Khan, Noor A. | 56-022 | Ph.D. |
| Khaner, Miriam | 35-529 | M.A. |
| Kiang, Tsch-Kia | 49-506 | M.Eng. |
| Kibbe, Doris E. | 38-536 | M.A. |



| AUTHOR | THESIS NUMBER | DEGREE |
|---|---|---|
| Kidd, Dorothy J. | 48-564 | M.A. |
| Kidd, James R. | 44-525 | M.A. |
| Kiefer, Elsie B. | 29-556 | M.A. |
| Kieffer, Michael Ignatius | 39-038 | M.A. |
| Kim, Yoon-Bom | 57-583 | M.Sc. |
| Kimura, Douglas S. | 59-041 | Ph.D. |
| King, Ellis G. | 34-021 | Ph.D. |
| King, Hamilton D. | 53-596 | M.Sc. |
| King, Lucile M. | 10-504 | M.A. |
| King, Robert Henry | 40-519 | M.Sc. |
| King, Thomas Elston | 39-500 | Ph.D. |
| Kingsbury, Donald M. | 59-585 | M.Sc. |
| Kingsford, Maurice P. | 53-504 | S.T.M. |
| Kinnear, Mary E. | 34-532 | M.A. |
| Kinsman, Michael J. | 58-544 | M.A. |
| Kinsman, Ronald D. | 59-556 | M.A. |
| Kipkie, George F. | 48-528 | M.Sc. |
| Kirby, John C. | 57-503 | S.T.M. |
| Kirchschlager, Hellmuth | 40-029 | M.A. |
| Kirk, William D. | 36-545 | M.Eng. |
| Kirkaldy, John S. | 53-058 | Ph.D. |
| Kirkland, Robert W. | 50-011 | Ph.D. |
| Kirkland, Robert W. | 47-515 | M.Sc. |
| Kirkpatrick, Robert | 13-517 | M.Sc. |
| Kirsch, Milton | 45-007 | Ph.D. |
| Kirsch, Simon | 10-002 | Ph.D. |
| Kirsch, Simon | 07-503 | M.A. |
| Kirschberg, Abraham | 29-541 | M.A. |
| Kite, William C. | 49-534 | M.Sc. |
| Klassen, Norman V. | 57-058 | Ph.D. |
| Klatzo, Igor | 51-610 | M.Sc. |
| Klein, Jenny | 36-534 | M.A. |
| Kleiner, George | 37-523 | M.A. |
| Klinck, Harold R. | 55-062 | Ph.D. |
| Klinck, Harold R. | 52-531 | M.Sc. |
| Klineberg, Beatrice A. | 36-535 | M.A. |
| Klugman, Michael A. | 56-023 | Ph.D. |
| Klugman, Michael A. | 53-534 | M.Sc. |
| Knaff, Paul R. | 55-553 | M.A. |
| Knechtel, Max U. | 26-544 | M.A. |
| Knelman, Fred H. | 50-507 | M.Eng. |
| Knight, Enid P. | 44-009 | Ph.D. |
| Knight, Enid P. | 39-515 | M.Sc. |
| Knight, Frederic C. | 15-509 | M.Sc. |
| Knowles, David C. | 57-605 | M.A. |
| Knowles, Eustace C. | 29-542 | M.A. |
| Knowles, John W. | 48-027 | Ph.D. |
| Knutti, Hans J. | 58-570 | M.Sc. |

| AUTHOR | THESIS NUMBER | DEGREE |
|---|---|---|
| Kobernick, Sidney D. | 51-017 | Ph.D. |
| Kobernick, Sidney D. | 49-607 | M.Sc. |
| Kochen, Joseph A. | 56-055 | Ph.D. |
| Kochen, Simon B. | 55-604 | M.Sc. |
| Koenig, Sister Mary G. | 42-035 | M.A. |
| Kohler, Allan C. | 56-582 | M.Sc. |
| Komarov, Simon A. | 31-554 | M.Sc. |
| Komarov, Simon A. | 35-015 | Ph.D. |
| Koppenaal, Richard J. | 59-042 | Ph.D. |
| Korenberg, Sarah M. | 44-504 | M.Sc. |
| Kornelsen, Ernest V. | 57-020 | Ph.D. |
| Korol, Bernard | 56-024 | Ph.D. |
| Kortepeter, Carl M. | 54-613 | M.A. |
| Koshy, Kuttickal I. | 55-570 | S.T.M. |
| Kouris, Michael | 57-584 | M.Sc. |
| Koval, Joseph | 54-506 | LL.M. |
| Kovalski, Voyo | 58-545 | M.A. |
| Kranck, Svante H. | 55-605 | M.Sc. |
| Krieble, Vernon K. | 09-514 | M.Sc. |
| Krieble, Vernon K. | 13-001 | Ph.D. |
| Kristjanson, Arnthor M. | 49-025 | Ph.D. |
| Kronman, Ruth Y. | 33-550 | M.A. |
| Krupka, Richard M. | 57-059 | Ph.D. |
| Kubina, S.J. | 57-508 | M.Eng. |
| Kuhn, Bernard G. | 50-588 | M.Eng. |
| Kuhn, Tillo E. | 57-060 | Ph.D. |
| Kulka, Marshall | 42-501 | Ph.D. |
| Kumamoto, Yurika | 56-056 | Ph.D. |
| Kumamoto, Yurika | 53-597 | M.Sc. |
| Kurien, Vadkumkara T. | 56-500 | S.T.M. |
| Kushner, Donn J. | 52-050 | Ph.D. |
| Kushner, Donn J. | 50-615 | M.Sc. |
| Kushner, Eva M. | 56-057 | Ph.D. |
| Kushner, Eva M. | 50-569 | M.A. |
| Kutz, Russell L. | 33-012 | Ph.D. |
| Kuzmak, Joseph M. | 53-017 | Ph.D. |
| Kwiecinska-Pappius, Hanna | 48-529 | M.Sc. |
| Kycia, Tadeusz F. | 55-606 | M.Sc. |
| Kydd, Mary W. | 24-540 | M.A. |
| Kyritz, Heinz-Georg | 56-619 | M.A. |
| L'Esperance, Robert L. | 51-052 | Ph.D. |
| L'Esperance, Robert L. | 48-530 | M.Sc. |
| L'Herisson, Camille | 30-506 | M.Sc. |
| Lachance, Charles-Eugene | 56-523 | M.Sc. |
| Lachance, Francois de S. | 46-524 | M.Sc. |
| Lachance, Rene O. | 40-014 | Ph.D. |
| Lachance, Rene O. | 39-061 | M.Sc. |
| Lachance, Robert A. | 55-025 | Ph.D. |



| AUTHOR | THESIS NUMBER | DEGREE |
|---|---|---|
| Lachance, Robert A. | 49-535 | M.Sc. |
| Lachs, John | 57-548 | M.A. |
| Lagnado, John R. | 57-061 | Ph.D. |
| Lagnado, John R. | 55-607 | M.Sc. |
| Laing, Charles A. | 55-608 | M.Sc. |
| Laing, Eleanor J. | 48-614 | M.A. |
| Laird, James T. | 52-605 | M.A. |
| Lajoie, Paul | 42-057 | M.Sc. |
| Laliberte, Jacques N. | 47-516 | M.Sc. |
| Lam, Anna P. | 57-554 | M.Arch. |
| Lam, Mathias | 51-504 | M.Eng. |
| Lamal, Mary L. | 37-524 | M.A. |
| Lamb, Cecil A. | 24-503 | M.S.A. |
| Lamb, Henry M. | 13-518 | M.Sc. |
| Lambek, Hanna W. | 49-569 | M.A. |
| Lambek, Joachim | 50-012 | Ph.D. |
| Lambek, Joachim | 46-525 | M.Sc. |
| Lande, Harold B. | 30-533 | M.A. |
| Lane, Alan G. | 50-589 | M.Eng. |
| Lane, Cecil T. | 29-018 | Ph.D. |
| Lane, Cecil T. | 27-510 | M.Sc. |
| Lang, Andrew R. | 59-043 | Ph.D. |
| Lang, Bernard | 53-562 | M.Eng. |
| Lang, John G. | 31-534 | M.A. |
| Lange, Eugene Hausknecht | 39-062 | M.Sc. |
| Langerman, Helen L. | 49-536 | M.Sc. |
| Langille, Winston M. | 48-585 | M.Sc. |
| Langleben, Manuel P. | 50-616 | M.Sc. |
| Langleben, Manuel P. | 53-059 | Ph.D. |
| Langlois, Jean-Claude | 57-606 | M.A. |
| Langlois, Robert H. | 47-533 | M.A. |
| Langstroth, George O. | 30-005 | Ph.D. |
| Lansdell, Herbert C. | 50-033 | Ph.D. |
| Lapin, Murray | 41-519 | M.A. |
| Laplante, Charlotte T. | 59-523 | M.Sc. |
| Lapointe, Marc C. | 48-502 | M.C.L. |
| Laroche, Joseph R. | 51-612 | M.Sc. |
| Larochelle, Andre | 59-044 | Ph.D. |
| Larocque, Gerard L. | 33-520 | M.Sc. |
| Larocque, Gerard L. | 35-016 | Ph.D. |
| Larose, Paul | 25-004 | Ph.D. |
| Larose, Paul | 23-514 | M.Sc. |
| Larsson, Bjorn E. | 50-034 | Ph.D. |
| Lash, Harry N. | 49-637 | M.A. |
| Latham, Allan B. | 27-534 | M.A. |
| Lathe, Frank E. | 15-510 | M.Sc. |
| Lathe, Grant H. | 47-010 | Ph.D. |
| Lathe, Grant H. | 36-548 | M.Sc. |

| AUTHOR | THESIS NUMBER | DEGREE |
|---|---|---|
| Laufer, Philip J. | 58-024 | Ph.D. |
| Laufer, Philip J. | 54-525 | M.Sc. |
| Laurin, Joseph F. | 54-526 | M.Sc. |
| Lautsch, Elizabeth V. | 51-528 | M.Sc. |
| Lautsch, Elizabeth V. | 53-060 | Ph.D. |
| Lavallee, Edouard | 32-518 | M.Sc. |
| Lavallee, John | 55-063 | Ph.D. |
| Lawley, John D. | 31-564 | M.A. |
| Lawrence, Charles H. | 57-528 | M.Sc. |
| Lawrence, Gertrude R. | 30-534 | M.A. |
| Lawson, Norman C. | 58-571 | M.Sc. |
| Laxer, Robert Mendel | 39-507 | M.A. |
| Layhew, John H. | 26-545 | M.A. |
| Layne, Donald St.E. | 57-021 | Ph.D. |
| Layne, Donald St.E. | 55-527 | M.Sc. |
| Layton, Irving | 46-540 | M.A. |
| Leach, William B. | 48-586 | M.Sc. |
| Lead, Harry D. | 37-537 | M.Sc. |
| Leaning, John D. | 57-501 | M.Arch. |
| Leathem, Ronald M. | 36-536 | M.A. |
| Leavitt, Helen R. | 49-638 | M.A. |
| Leblanc, Raymond F. | 40-035 | M.Eng. |
| Leblond, David | 42-058 | M.Sc. |
| Leclercq, Genevieve F. | 59-508 | LL.M. |
| Leduc, Joseph A. | 26-515 | M.Sc. |
| Leduc, Real A. | 45-510 | M.Sc. |
| Lee, Burdett | 46-572 | M.Sc. |
| Lee, Ernest S. | 58-556 | M.Eng. |
| Lees, David | 32-532 | M.A. |
| Leeson, John I. | 53-535 | M.Sc. |
| Legendre, Rosaire | 46-503 | M.Eng. |
| Leger, Francis J. | 38-010 | Ph.D. |
| Legg, Roland E. | 24-521 | M.Sc. |
| Legg, Thomas H. | 56-524 | M.Sc. |
| Legge, Katharine B. | 30-535 | M.A. |
| Legge, Norman R. | 45-008 | Ph.D. |
| Leith, Wilfred | 58-587 | M.Sc. |
| Lemay, Henri P. | 58-557 | M.Eng. |
| Lemieux, Raymond U. | 46-028 | Ph.D. |
| Lende, Richard A. | 56-525 | M.Sc. |
| Lennon, Sister Mary G. | 38-537 | M.A. |
| Lennox, Robert | 35-545 | M.A. |
| Lenoir, Marguerite N. | 47-534 | M.A. |
| Leppman, Wolfgang A. | 49-639 | M.A. |
| Leroux, Edgar J. | 52-532 | M.Sc. |
| Leslie, John D. | 48-028 | Ph.D. |
| Lessard, Henri-Louis | 41-043 | M.Sc. |
| Lesser, Elliott | 51-529 | M.Sc. |



| AUTHOR | THESIS NUMBER | DEGREE |
|---|---|---|
| Lesser, Elliott | 53-061 | Ph.D. |
| Letichevsky, Jack | 41-026 | M.A. |
| Leuner, Wilhelm R. | 59-524 | M.Sc. |
| Leung, Philip M-B. | 59-586 | M.Sc. |
| Levi, Irving | 42-015 | Ph.D. |
| Levi, Leo | 50-035 | Ph.D. |
| Levine, Albert N. | 49-570 | M.A. |
| Levine, Seymour | 50-590 | M.Eng. |
| Levitan, Benjamin A. | 48-588 | M.Sc. |
| Levitin, Norman | 51-018 | Ph.D. |
| Levitsky, Nathan A. | 33-551 | M.A. |
| Levitt, Bella | 41-027 | M.A. |
| Levitt, Jacob | 33-521 | M.Sc. |
| Levitt, Jacob | 35-017 | Ph.D. |
| Levy, Gordon W. | 26-546 | M.A. |
| Levy, Samuel W. | 54-016 | Ph.D. |
| Lewis, David S. | 07-510 | M.Sc. |
| Lewis, Herbert | 54-614 | M.A. |
| Lewis, James Neilson | 39-039 | M.A. |
| Lewis, John B. | 54-054 | Ph.D. |
| Lewis, John B. | 50-541 | M.Sc. |
| Lewis, Revis C. | 50-542 | M.Sc. |
| Leznoff, Maurice | 54-545 | M.A. |
| LeMesurier, Kenneth A. | 52-503 | M.Eng. |
| LeNeveu, Arthur P. | 25-522 | M.Sc. |
| LePage, Inez M. | 32-533 | M.A. |
| LeRoux, Edgar J. | 54-015 | Ph.D. |
| Li, Choh-luh | 54-017 | Ph.D. |
| Li, Choh-luh | 50-617 | M.Sc. |
| Liberman, John | 50-618 | M.Sc. |
| Liebenberg, Louis C. | 25-543 | M.S.A. |
| Lieber, Jack W. | 57-549 | M.A. |
| Lieff, Morris | 38-011 | Ph.D. |
| Lieff, Pearl | 40-030 | M.A. |
| Lin, Shu-Chang | 42-059 | M.Sc. |
| Lin, Wei-cheng | 42-016 | Ph.D. |
| Lindsay, Victor C. | 36-501 | M.Eng. |
| Lindsay, William | 14-505 | M.A. |
| Linis-Linins, Viktors | 51-530 | M.Sc. |
| Linis-Linins, Viktors | 53-018 | Ph.D. |
| Link, William T. | 57-062 | Ph.D. |
| Linton, Everett P. | 32-008 | Ph.D. |
| Linton, Everett P. | 30-507 | M.Sc. |
| Lipman, Julian A. I. | 39-040 | M.A. |
| Lips, Alair | 44-010 | Ph.D. |
| Lipsett, Solomon G. | 27-006 | Ph.D. |
| Lipton, Charles | 39-041 | M.A. |
| Lister, Earle E. | 57-585 | M.Sc. |

| AUTHOR | THESIS NUMBER | DEGREE |
|---|---|---|
| Liszauer, Susan M. | 56-583 | M.Sc. |
| Lithgow, Robert M. | 52-549 | M.A. |
| Little, John W. | 28-542 | M.A. |
| Litvak, John | 57-529 | M.Sc. |
| Liu, Chien-kang | 47-032 | Ph.D. |
| Livingston, William R. | 42-502 | Ph.D. |
| Livingstone, Constance A. | 42-060 | M.Sc. |
| Livinson, Abraham J. | 16-503 | M.A. |
| Lloyd, Lewis E. | 52-051 | Ph.D. |
| Lloyd, Lewis E. | 50-543 | M.Sc. |
| Lockhart, Chesley L. | 57-530 | M.Sc. |
| Lockhead, Allan G. | 19-001 | Ph.D. |
| Lockhead, Allan G. | 12-511 | M.Sc. |
| Lods, Emile A. | 25-504 | M.S.A. |
| Loeb, Bernice P. | 59-557 | M.A. |
| Loewy, Ariel G. | 47-556 | M.Sc. |
| Logan, Charles D. | 49-026 | Ph.D. |
| Logan, John F. | 23-004 | Ph.D. |
| Logan, Kenneth C. | 49-052 | Ph.D. |
| Logan, Ralph A. | 48-531 | M.Sc. |
| Logan, Vaughn Stewart | 39-063 | M.Sc. |
| Loiselle, Jean-Marie | 57-022 | Ph.D. |
| Loiselle, Jean-Marie | 55-528 | M.Sc. |
| Loiselle, Roland | 51-531 | M.Sc. |
| Long, Harold D. | 55-529 | M.Sc. |
| Longan, Virginia L. | 31-565 | M.A. |
| Longley, James D. | 57-531 | M.Sc. |
| Loomer, Elijah I. | 51-532 | M.Sc. |
| Lord, Frank T. | 47-517 | M.Sc. |
| Lorimer, Harry P. | 52-504 | M.Eng. |
| Lorrain, Paul | 47-011 | Ph.D. |
| Lorrain, Paul | 41-530 | M.Sc. |
| Lossing, Frederick P. | 42-017 | Ph.D. |
| Lotz, James R. | 57-532 | M.Sc. |
| Loughheed, Thomas C. | 54-593 | M.Sc. |
| Love, Robert M. | 35-030 | Ph.D. |
| Lovell, Edwin Lister | 40-015 | Ph.D. |
| Lovelock, Margaret K. | 37-545 | M.A. |
| Lowi, R. Naomi | 55-609 | M.Sc. |
| Lowry, Hope | 31-566 | M.A. |
| Lowther, George K. | 35-018 | Ph.D. |
| Lowther, John S. | 50-619 | M.Sc. |
| Lowther, Ruth L. | 58-572 | M.Sc. |
| Lozinsky, Ezra | 23-515 | M.Sc. |
| Lubinsky, George | 56-025 | Ph.D. |
| Lucas, Ian A. | 49-608 | M.Sc. |
| Lucas, Rex A. | 50-657 | M.A. |
| Lucas, Sidney | 55-064 | Ph.D. |



| AUTHOR | THESIS NUMBER | DEGREE |
|---|---|---|
| Lucien, Harold W. | 51-019 | Ph.D. |
| Lucis, Ojars J. | 59-045 | Ph.D. |
| Lucis, Ojars J. | 57-586 | M.Sc. |
| Ludwig, Ralph A. | 47-012 | Ph.D. |
| Lukosevicius, Petras P. | 56-526 | M.Sc. |
| Lumsden, Jean G. | 44-515 | M.A. |
| Lumsden, Stanley G. | 37-525 | M.A. |
| Lunde, Magnus | 53-019 | Ph.D. |
| Luner, Charles | 52-052 | Ph.D. |
| Luner, Philip | 51-020 | Ph.D. |
| Lunn, Alice J. | 34-533 | M.A. |
| Lunn, Alice J. | 42-503 | Ph.D. |
| Lupton, Mac J. | 36-502 | M.Eng. |
| Lureau, Daniel J. | 59-509 | LL.M. |
| Lusby, George R. | 33-029 | Ph.D. |
| Lusena, Charles V. | 47-033 | Ph.D. |
| Lusena, Charles V. | 44-520 | M.Sc. |
| Lusher, David W. | 33-552 | M.A. |
| Lussier, Claude | 46-501 | M.C.L. |
| Lutwick, Laurence E. | 51-533 | M.Sc. |
| Luxton, Edward A. G. | 35-530 | M.A. |
| Lyall, Harold B. | 52-533 | M.Sc. |
| Lyman, Beatrice M. | 29-543 | M.A. |
| Lyman, Bernard E. | 51-638 | M.A. |
| Lyman, Ruth D. | 07-511 | M.Sc. |
| Lynam, Josephine B. | 47-579 | M.A. |
| Lyons, Douglas B. | 51-587 | M.Eng. |
| Lyons, Walter | 32-519 | M.Sc. |
| Lyster, Lynden Laird | 39-064 | M.Sc. |
| Maass, Carol E. | 27-007 | Ph.D. |
| Maass, Otto | 12-512 | M.Sc. |
| Macallum, Alexander D. | 22-513 | M.Sc. |
| Macallum, Alexander D. | 24-003 | Ph.D. |
| Macaulay, Colin A. | 55-576 | M.Eng. |
| Macbeth, Robert A. | 47-557 | M.Sc. |
| Macbrayne, Sheila F. | 56-565 | LL.M. |
| Macdonald, Albert F. | 22-514 | M.Sc. |
| Macdonald, Isabella I. | 20-511 | M.A. |
| Macdonald, Roderick F. | 52-534 | M.Sc. |
| Macdonald, Roderick F. | 46-541 | M.A. |
| Macdougall, Graham R. | 48-008 | Ph.D. |
| Machacek, John E. | 28-006 | Ph.D. |
| Machamer, Jerome F. | 59-526 | M.Sc. |
| Mackay, Kathleen I. | 47-558 | M.Sc. |
| Mackay, Robert de W. | 29-544 | M.A. |
| Mackinney, Herbert W. | 33-522 | M.Sc. |
| Mackinney, Herbert W. | 35-031 | Ph.D. |
| Mackintosh, David D. | 57-562 | LL.M. |

| AUTHOR | THESIS NUMBER | DEGREE |
|---|---|---|
| Macklin, Lionel S. | 32-010 | Ph.D. |
| Maclean, Herbert B. | 10-507 | M.A. |
| Macleod, Annie L. | 10-003 | Ph.D. |
| Maclure, Kenneth C. | 52-054 | Ph.D. |
| Maclure, Kenneth C. | 50-621 | M.Sc. |
| Macnaughton, Ariel M. | 10-508 | M.A. |
| Macphail, Moray S. | 34-534 | M.A. |
| Macpherson, Andrew H. | 57-533 | M.Sc. |
| Macpherson, John | 46-543 | M.A. |
| Macrae, Ruth | 26-516 | M.Sc. |
| Macrakis, N. | 52-565 | M.Eng. |
| MacCallan, William D. | 49-571 | M.A. |
| MacCallum, William J. | 35-509 | M.Sc. |
| MacCrimmon, John R. | 09-504 | M.A. |
| MacDonald, Allister I. | 47-535 | M.A. |
| MacDonald, James L. | 28-516 | M.Sc. |
| MacDonald, Murray V. | 38-511 | M.Sc. |
| MacDougall, Daniel | 44-011 | Ph.D. |
| MacDougall, Daniel | 41-531 | M.Sc. |
| MacDougall, John F. | 57-063 | Ph.D. |
| MacDougall, John F. | 52-535 | M.Sc. |
| MacEwan, John R. | 57-023 | Ph.D. |
| MacFarlane, Dougald A. | 57-550 | M.A. |
| MacFarlane, Hugh M. | 50-036 | Ph.D. |
| MacFarlane, Ivan C. | 54-565 | M.Eng. |
| MacFarlane, Joan M. | 48-615 | M.A. |
| MacFarlane, Mona A. | 58-525 | M.Sc. |
| MacGachen, Freda K. | 31-535 | M.A. |
| MacGregor, Alexander R. | 54-527 | M.Sc. |
| MacGregor, Warren S. | 43-009 | Ph.D. |
| MacHutchin, John G. | 47-013 | Ph.D. |
| MacInnes, Alexander S. | 41-010 | Ph.D. |
| MacIntosh, Frank C. | 37-015 | Ph.D. |
| MacIntosh, James A. | 56-527 | M.Sc. |
| MacIntosh, Robert M. | 52-023 | Ph.D. |
| MacIntosh, Robert M. | 49-572 | M.A. |
| MacIntyre, Thomas Martin | 41-044 | M.Sc. |
| MacKay, Donald C. | 54-055 | Ph.D. |
| MacKay, Donald M. | 36-503 | M.Eng. |
| MacKay, Kenneth C. | 51-579 | M.C.L. |
| MacKay, Margaret E. | 30-006 | Ph.D. |
| MacKay, Vernon G. | 56-528 | M.Sc. |
| MacKeen, Frances C. | 46-542 | M.A. |
| MacKenzie, Francis S. | 16-505 | M.A. |
| MacKenzie, Gordon J. | 55-554 | M.A. |
| MacKenzie, James S. | 48-029 | Ph.D. |
| MacKenzie, John M. | 10-506 | M.A. |
| MacKenzie, Kenneth R. | 48-030 | Ph.D. |



| AUTHOR | THESIS NUMBER | DEGREE |
|---|---|---|
| MacKenzie, Mary E. | 37-526 | M.A. |
| MacKinnon, Patrick A. | 32-536 | M.A. |
| MacKneson, Stephen W. | 59-574 | LL.M. |
| MacLachlan, Donald S. | 49-610 | M.Sc. |
| MacLaggan, Marjorie F. | 31-536 | M.A. |
| MacLaren, Alexander S. | 50-545 | M.Sc. |
| MacLaren, Alexander S. | 53-021 | Ph.D. |
| MacLaren, Margaret J. | 26-548 | M.A. |
| MacLauchlan, Donald W. | 37-030 | Ph.D. |
| MacLean, Alister Joseph | 42-061 | M.Sc. |
| MacLean, Allison R. | 16-001 | Ph.D. |
| MacLean, Allison R. | 12-513 | M.Sc. |
| MacLean, Angus A. | 48-533 | M.Sc. |
| MacLean, David B. | 46-029 | Ph.D. |
| MacLean, Donald W. | 54-528 | M.Sc. |
| MacLean, Kenneth S. | 54-529 | M.Sc. |
| MacLean, Mary W. | 28-546 | M.A. |
| MacLean, Mona G. | 45-517 | M.A. |
| MacLennan, Donald F. | 54-018 | Ph.D. |
| MacLennan, Louise Isabel | 42-062 | M.Sc. |
| MacLennan, Malcolm | 25-537 | M.A. |
| MacLeod, Donald M. | 43-505 | M.Sc. |
| MacLeod, Donald M. | 53-022 | Ph.D. |
| MacLeod, Elmer D. | 26-549 | M.A. |
| MacLeod, Harry A. | 56-586 | M.Sc. |
| MacLeod, Lloyd B. | 53-598 | M.Sc. |
| MacLeod, Malcolm D. | 28-517 | M.Sc. |
| MacLeod, Robert B. | 27-538 | M.A. |
| MacMillan, Donald N. | 30-536 | M.A. |
| MacNeill, Glorana H. | 47-536 | M.A. |
| MacNeill, Ruby J. | 48-590 | M.Sc. |
| MacOdrum, Murdoch M. | 24-541 | M.A. |
| MacPhee, Albert W. | 47-560 | M.Sc. |
| MacPherson, John T. | 28-547 | M.A. |
| MacQueen, David J. | 36-537 | M.A. |
| MacRae, Herbert F. | 56-587 | M.Sc. |
| MacRae, Norman A. | 30-508 | M.Sc. |
| MacSporran, Maysie S. | 30-537 | M.A. |
| MacSween, Florence P. | 15-504 | M.A. |
| MacVicar, Donald H. | 26-550 | M.A. |
| MacVicar, Roderick M. | 34-513 | M.Sc. |
| Madras, Samuel | 47-034 | Ph.D. |
| Magarvey, R.H. | 50-622 | M.Sc. |
| Magee, Arch W. | 43-525 | M.A. |
| Mahanti, Biresh C. | 56-573 | M.Sc. |
| Mahatoo, Winston H. | 55-611 | M.Sc. |
| Mahon, John H. | 49-611 | M.Sc. |
| Mahon, John H. | 53-063 | Ph.D. |

| AUTHOR | THESIS NUMBER | DEGREE |
|---|---|---|
| Mahon, R. Kathryn | 50-659 | M.A. |
| Mahoney, Gerald M. | 49-029 | Ph.D. |
| Mahoney, Gerald M. | 47-519 | M.Sc. |
| Mahut, Helen | 55-065 | Ph.D. |
| Mahut, Helen | 52-606 | M.A. |
| Maizel, Norah L. | 55-555 | M.A. |
| Majchrowicz, Edward | 59-080 | Ph.D. |
| Major, Thomas G. | 22-516 | M.Sc. |
| Makonnen, Adunya | 59-587 | M.Sc. |
| Malcolm, Robert B. | 24-523 | M.Sc. |
| Malkin, Aaron | 56-026 | Ph.D. |
| Mallin, Estelle C. | 36-538 | M.A. |
| Malouf, Stanley E. | 36-512 | M.Sc. |
| Malouf, Stanley E. | 41-504 | Ph.D. |
| Maltais, Jean B. | 28-519 | M.Sc. |
| Mamchur, Stephen W. | 34-548 | M.A. |
| Mamelak, Joseph S. | 46-526 | M.Sc. |
| Mamelak, Rose | 53-064 | Ph.D. |
| Manchester, Donald F. | 52-055 | Ph.D. |
| Mandelcorn, Lyon | 51-022 | Ph.D. |
| Mani, K.V. | 48-534 | M.Sc. |
| Manley, Rockliffe St. J. | 53-023 | Ph.D. |
| Mann, Ernest L. | 59-050 | Ph.D. |
| Mannard, George W. | 56-529 | M.Sc. |
| Manning, Kenneth Raymond | 40-520 | M.Sc. |
| Manning, William P. | 58-026 | Ph.D. |
| Mansfield, Arthur W. | 58-027 | Ph.D. |
| Manson, Mary G. | 47-520 | M.Sc. |
| Mantzavinos, A. | 52-607 | M.A. |
| Maranda, Jean-Marie A. | 52-056 | Ph.D. |
| Marcello, Louis S. | 40-046 | M.Sc. |
| Marchant, Edwin H. | 47-014 | Ph.D. |
| Marchessault, Robert H. | 54-019 | Ph.D. |
| Marcus, Alma | 50-546 | M.Sc. |
| Marcus, Rudolph A. | 46-012 | Ph.D. |
| Margolis, Bernard | 49-539 | M.Sc. |
| Margolis, Leo | 52-057 | Ph.D. |
| Margolis, Leo | 50-547 | M.Sc. |
| Marien, Breen N. | 52-579 | M.Sc. |
| Marion, Leo E. | 29-009 | Ph.D. |
| Markson, Doris M. | 54-616 | M.A. |
| Marleau, Raymond A. | 56-530 | M.Sc. |
| Marler, G.E. | 54-546 | M.A. |
| Marler, Peter de M. | 53-537 | M.Sc. |
| Marmur, Julius | 47-561 | M.Sc. |
| Marsden, James | 36-010 | Ph.D. |
| Marsden, Michael | 56-588 | M.Sc. |
| Marsh, Leonard C. | 33-553 | M.A. |



| AUTHOR | THESIS NUMBER | DEGREE |
|---|---|---|
| Marsh, Leonard C. | 40-016 | Ph.D. |
| Marshall, Harry F. | 34-022 | Ph.D. |
| Marshall, James | 38-013 | Ph.D. |
| Marshall, James I. | 49-507 | M.Eng. |
| Marshall, Joyce A. | 55-569 | M.Com. |
| Marshall, Melville J. | 16-512 | M.Sc. |
| Martial, Jean A. | 53-515 | LL.M. |
| Martin, Fernand | 58-546 | M.A. |
| Martin, Helen J. | 50-548 | M.Sc. |
| Martin, William G. | 58-028 | Ph.D. |
| Martin, William G. | 55-532 | M.Sc. |
| Martin, William M. | 51-023 | Ph.D. |
| Martin, William S. | 52-505 | M.Eng. |
| Martineau, Jeanne G. | 47-537 | M.A. |
| Martineau, Real | 53-538 | M.Sc. |
| Martinek, Frank | 53-563 | M.Eng. |
| Mason, Clarence T. | 33-523 | M.Sc. |
| Mason, Clarence T. | 35-022 | Ph.D. |
| Mason, Stanley George | 39-013 | Ph.D. |
| Massey, Ernest E. | 33-013 | Ph.D. |
| Massiah, Thomas F. | 56-531 | M.Sc. |
| Masson, David R. | 59-588 | M.Sc. |
| Masson, Georges M. | 42-504 | Ph.D. |
| Matheson, Ballem H. | 57-064 | Ph.D. |
| Matheson, George L. | 29-010 | Ph.D. |
| Matheson, George I. | 26-517 | M.Sc. |
| Matheson, Howard W. | 11-513 | M.Sc. |
| Mathewson, Dorothy F. | 24-542 | M.A. |
| Mathison, James F. | 56-027 | Ph.D. |
| Mathison, William | 59-570 | M.Eng. |
| Matsas, Loucas C. | 55-577 | M.Eng. |
| Matthers, Mary C. | 48-566 | M.A. |
| Matthewman, William G. | 39-518 | M.Sc. |
| Matthews, Florida L. | 32-537 | M.A. |
| Matthews, Fred White | 41-011 | Ph.D. |
| Mattinson, Cyril R. | 58-029 | Ph.D. |
| Mattinson, Cyril R. | 52-536 | M.Sc. |
| Matusiak, Marvin E. | 53-564 | M.Eng. |
| Matuszko, Anthony J. | 53-024 | Ph.D. |
| Mauer, Irving | 52-537 | M.Sc. |
| Mauffette, Pierre | 41-045 | M.Sc. |
| Maughan, George P. | 38-512 | M.Sc. |
| Maurer, Alfred R. | 48-535 | M.Sc. |
| Maw, William A. | 25-544 | M.S.A. |
| Maximchuk, Arlene J. | 56-532 | M.Sc. |
| Maxwell, Charles W. | 39-065 | M.Sc. |
| Maxwell, Doreen F. | 55-066 | Ph.D. |
| May, Sydney J. | 53-623 | M.Com. |

| AUTHOR | THESIS NUMBER | DEGREE |
|---|---|---|
| Maytum, Helen E. | 27-511 | M.Sc. |
| Mazurkiewicz, Irena M. | 57-065 | Ph.D. |
| Mazurkiewicz, Irena M. | 55-533 | M.Sc. |
| Mazza, Sister Maria S. | 35-531 | M.A. |
| McAllister, Arnold L. | 50-013 | Ph.D. |
| McAllister, Arnold L. | 48-532 | M.Sc. |
| McArdle, Alice H. | 57-587 | M.Sc. |
| McArthur, Beverley D. | 53-508 | M.Eng. |
| McBain, Alexander R. | 13-507 | M.A. |
| McBain, Mary N. | 21-520 | M.A. |
| McBride, Mollie E. | 59-046 | Ph.D. |
| McCabe, James | 53-536 | M.Sc. |
| McCall, Muriel B. | 28-543 | M.A. |
| McCarthy, John J. | 59-612 | M.A. |
| McCarthy, Joseph L. | 38-012 | Ph.D. |
| McClelland, William R. | 23-516 | M.Sc. |
| McClung, Robert K. | 01-003 | M.A. |
| McConnell, Wallace B. | 49-027 | Ph.D. |
| McCormack, George J. | 16-504 | M.A. |
| McCormick, Glendon C. | 53-062 | Ph.D. |
| McCorriston, James R. | 48-589 | M.Sc. |
| McCoubrey, James Addison | 40-503 | Ph.D. |
| McCracken, Edward J. | 32-534 | M.A. |
| McCrorie, James N. | 59-613 | M.A. |
| McCuaig, James A. | 50-620 | M.Sc. |
| McCuaig, James A. | 53-020 | Ph.D. |
| McCubbin, John W. | 35-019 | Ph.D. |
| McCullagh, Paul F. | 28-544 | M.A. |
| McCullough, Edward E. | 54-615 | M.A. |
| McCully, Keith A. | 59-525 | M.Sc. |
| McCurdy, Lyall R. | 27-513 | M.Sc. |
| McCutcheon, John O. | 55-506 | M.Eng. |
| McDermot, H. Lloyd | 50-014 | Ph.D. |
| McDonald, Cyril P. | 38-538 | M.A. |
| McDonald, Elizabeth | 41-028 | M.A. |
| McDonald, Jessie | 10-505 | M.A. |
| McDonald, Roland D. | 35-020 | Ph.D. |
| McDonough, Sheila D. | 55-633 | M.A. |
| McDougall, David J. | 52-022 | Ph.D. |
| McDougall, David J. | 49-537 | M.Sc. |
| McDougall, John F. | 31-555 | M.Sc. |
| McEvoy, Edward T. | 37-510 | M.Sc. |
| McFarlane, Arthur H. | 46-588 | M.A. |
| McFarlane, Bruce A. | 55-634 | M.A. |
| McFarlane, Duncan H. | 26-547 | M.A. |
| McFarlane, Nathaniel C. | 21-512 | M.Sc. |
| McFarlane, Ross A. | 59-047 | Ph.D. |
| McFarlane, Ross A. | 55-530 | M.Sc. |



| AUTHOR | THESIS NUMBER | DEGREE |
|---|---|---|
| McFee, Malcolm C. | 08-511 | M.Sc. |
| McGarry, Ave Marie | 42-513 | M.A. |
| McGarry, Eleanor E. | 51-534 | M.Sc. |
| McGibbon, Ralph W. | 38-545 | M.Sc. |
| McGill, John J. | 36-544 | M.A. |
| McGillivray, R.G. | 53-553 | M.A. |
| McGilvery, James D. | 50-015 | Ph.D. |
| McGlaughlin, William R. | 22-515 | M.Sc. |
| McGown, Isabella W. | 23-522 | M.A. |
| McGreer, Edgar D. | 23-523 | M.A. |
| McGregor, Claire P. | 05-003 | M.A. |
| McGregor, John K. | 55-531 | M.Sc. |
| McHarg, Muriel S. | 30-555 | M.A. |
| McIlreath, Fred J. | 59-048 | Ph.D. |
| McInnis, Sarah | 28-545 | M.A. |
| McIntosh, Bruce A. | 59-049 | Ph.D. |
| McIntosh, Donald S. | 08-512 | M.Sc. |
| McIntosh, Hamish W. | 50-544 | M.Sc. |
| McIntosh, Robert Lloyd | 39-012 | Ph.D. |
| McIntyre, George D. | 32-535 | M.A. |
| McKay, Gordon A. | 53-599 | M.Sc. |
| McKay, Huntly W. | 50-658 | M.A. |
| McKay, Ian A. | 56-584 | M.Sc. |
| McKay, Kenneth Gardiner | 39-516 | M.Sc. |
| McKendry, John B. | 49-609 | M.Sc. |
| McKeown, Thomas | 35-021 | Ph.D. |
| McKerns, Kenneth W. | 50-016 | Ph.D. |
| McKillican, Mary E. | 52-053 | Ph.D. |
| McKinley, William P. | 54-056 | Ph.D. |
| McKinley, William P. | 51-613 | M.Sc. |
| McKinney, James W. | 23-005 | Ph.D. |
| McKinney, James W. | 20-506 | M.Sc. |
| McKnight, Theodore S. | 58-025 | Ph.D. |
| McLaren, Ian A. | 55-610 | M.Sc. |
| McLaughlan, John M. | 56-585 | M.Sc. |
| McLean, Chester R. | 47-559 | M.Sc. |
| McLean, James Douglas | 41-532 | M.Sc. |
| McLeish, John A. | 48-616 | M.A. |
| McLennan, Hugh | 51-021 | Ph.D. |
| McLennan, Hugh | 49-538 | M.Sc. |
| McLennan, Logan S. | 24-522 | M.Sc. |
| McLeod, Lionel E. | 57-588 | M.Sc. |
| McLeod, Lloyd A. | 44-020 | Ph.D. |
| McLeod, William S. | 43-506 | M.Sc. |
| McLetchie, James K. | 29-545 | M.A. |
| McLintock, John J. | 51-053 | Ph.D. |
| McMaster, Norman B. | 32-520 | M.Sc. |
| McMillan, Gardner C. | 46-573 | M.Sc. |

| AUTHOR | THESIS NUMBER | DEGREE |
|---|---|---|
| McMillan, Gardner C. | 48-009 | Ph.D. |
| McMorran, Arlene R. | 52-582 | M.Sc. |
| McMurray, Gordon A. | 49-028 | Ph.D. |
| McNally, James G. | 27-008 | Ph.D. |
| McNally, William J. | 25-523 | M.Sc. |
| McNamara, Mary F.C. | 40-031 | M.A. |
| McNaughton, Andrew G. | 12-514 | M.Sc. |
| McNaughton, Francis L. | 41-533 | M.Sc. |
| McNeil, John T. | 10-509 | M.A. |
| McNiven, Neal Lindsay | 39-517 | M.Sc. |
| McOuat, D.F. | 48-565 | M.A. |
| McPhail, Murchie K. | 32-009 | Ph.D. |
| McPherson, Anna I. | 23-517 | M.Sc. |
| McPherson, Ian E. | 55-509 | LL.M. |
| McPherson, William J. | 47-518 | M.Sc. |
| McQuillan, Marie B. | 43-524 | M.A. |
| McRae, Duncan R. | 30-007 | Ph.D. |
| McRae, Duncan R. | 28-518 | M.Sc. |
| McVittie, Thomas J. | 14-506 | M.A. |
| Mead, Bruce R. | 43-010 | Ph.D. |
| Meadowcroft, James W. | 52-550 | M.A. |
| Meerovitch, Eugene B. | 57-066 | Ph.D. |
| Meerovitch, Eugene B. | 55-534 | M.Sc. |
| Meikle, Brian K. | 59-051 | Ph.D. |
| Meikle, Brian K. | 55-612 | M.Sc. |
| Meissner, George F. | 51-535 | M.Sc. |
| Melamed, Samuel | 57-067 | Ph.D. |
| Melamed, Samuel | 53-539 | M.Sc. |
| Meldrum, William B. | 10-518 | M.Sc. |
| Melville, Kenneth I. | 31-509 | M.Sc. |
| Melvin, Margaret G. | 19-501 | M.A. |
| Melzack, Ronald | 54-020 | Ph.D. |
| Melzack, Ronald | 51-614 | M.Sc. |
| Melzak, Adrienne | 51-639 | M.A. |
| Melzak, Zdzislaw A. | 51-536 | M.Sc. |
| Menard, Claude | 57-589 | M.Sc. |
| Mendels, Morton M. | 29-546 | M.A. |
| Mennie, John H. | 25-005 | Ph.D. |
| Mennie, William A. | 54-547 | M.A. |
| Mensah-Dapaa, W.S. | 54-594 | M.Sc. |
| Mentha, Guy | 56-546 | M.A. |
| Menzies, Margaret H. | 54-595 | M.Sc. |
| Menzies, Robert G. | 44-505 | M.Sc. |
| Mercer, John H. | 54-021 | Ph.D. |
| Mercier, Raymond P. | 56-589 | M.Sc. |
| Merrill, Gordon C. | 51-640 | M.A. |
| Merrill, Lesly I. | 53-554 | M.A. |
| Merry, Ralph V. | 27-535 | M.A. |



| AUTHOR | THESIS NUMBER | DEGREE |
|---|---|---|
| Merson, Lawrence N. | 47-504 | M.Eng. |
| Messier, Bernard H. | 56-590 | M.Sc. |
| Metcalf, John F. | 49-640 | M.A. |
| Metrakos, Julius D. | 51-054 | Ph.D. |
| Metrakos, Julius D. | 49-540 | M.Sc. |
| Metro, Stephen J. | 51-024 | Ph.D. |
| Meyer, Bertha | 21-521 | M.A. |
| Meyer, John S. | 49-541 | M.Sc. |
| Meyer, Paul H. | 45-545 | M.A. |
| Michael, J. | 55-613 | M.Sc. |
| Michel, Lina J. | 34-535 | M.A. |
| Michel, Walter | 48-031 | Ph.D. |
| Michie, George H. | 56-547 | M.A. |
| Mieszkowski, Peter M. | 59-614 | M.A. |
| Milburne, Kathleen E. | 34-536 | M.A. |
| Miles, Henry J. | 38-513 | M.Sc. |
| Milford, George N. | 53-025 | Ph.D. |
| Milks, John E. | 53-066 | Ph.D. |
| Millar, Charles H. | 47-035 | Ph.D. |
| Millar, Myra J. | 47-562 | M.Sc. |
| Millar, Ronald A. | 59-527 | M.Sc. |
| Miller, Bernard | 55-026 | Ph.D. |
| Miller, Clare B. | 12-502 | M.A. |
| Miller, David M. | 50-037 | Ph.D. |
| Miller, George G. | 26-518 | M.Sc. |
| Miller, Iveson A. | 15-511 | M.Sc. |
| Miller, James R. | 59-052 | Ph.D. |
| Miller, Max J. | 36-513 | M.Sc. |
| Miller, Saul | 48-536 | M.Sc. |
| Miller, Walter D. | 50-623 | M.Sc. |
| Miller, William St. C. | 50-624 | M.Sc. |
| Millette, Jean F. | 48-537 | M.Sc. |
| Milley, Chesley B. | 57-551 | M.A. |
| Millman, Thomas P. | 43-022 | Ph.D. |
| Mills, Allan W. | 51-570 | M.A. |
| Mills, Edward S. | 26-519 | M.Sc. |
| Mills, George H. | 47-580 | M.A. |
| Mills, Margaret F. | 46-527 | M.Sc. |
| Milne, Allen R. | 53-600 | M.Sc. |
| Milne, Donald J. | 49-030 | Ph.D. |
| Milner, Brenda A. | 52-058 | Ph.D. |
| Milner, Peter M. | 54-022 | Ph.D. |
| Milner, Peter M. | 50-625 | M.Sc. |
| Milner, Robert Leopold | 40-017 | Ph.D. |
| Mindes, Evelyn | 47-538 | M.A. |
| Mingie, George W. | 06-005 | M.A. |
| Minshall, William H. | 41-505 | Ph.D. |
| Minshall, William H. | 38-546 | M.Sc. |

| AUTHOR | THESIS NUMBER | DEGREE |
|---|---|---|
| Mirsky, Isadore A. | 29-512 | M.Sc. |
| Mishkin, Mortimer | 51-055 | Ph.D. |
| Mishkin, Mortimer | 49-573 | M.A. |
| Mitchell, Claude R. | 28-520 | M.Sc. |
| Mitchell, Kina M. | 52-608 | M.A. |
| Mitchell, Leonard | 44-012 | Ph.D. |
| Mitchell, Mary V. | 42-063 | M.Sc. |
| Mitchell, Victor E. | 18-001 | D.C.L. |
| Mitchell, William G. | 14-514 | M.Sc. |
| Mittelholzer, Alexander S | 58-030 | Ph.D. |
| Mittelholzer, Alexander S | 56-533 | M.Sc. |
| Moe, George G. | 21-513 | M.Sc. |
| Moellmann, Albert | 35-532 | M.A. |
| Moen, H.P. | 52-580 | M.Sc. |
| Mogenson, Gordon J. | 59-053 | Ph.D. |
| Mohiuddin, Syed D. | 53-540 | M.Sc. |
| Moir, Robert Y. | 46-030 | Ph.D. |
| Molson, Charles R. | 54-548 | M.A. |
| Monahan, Robert L. | 59-081 | Ph.D. |
| Money-Coutts, Joanna H. | 50-570 | M.A. |
| Monro, Hector A. | 58-031 | Ph.D. |
| Monro, Hector A. | 35-510 | M.Sc. |
| Montgomery, Douglas S. | 48-032 | Ph.D. |
| Montgomery, Harriet B. | 33-554 | M.A. |
| Montgomery, Margaret R. | 49-641 | M.A. |
| Montgrain, Clement | 44-506 | M.Sc. |
| Montreuil, Paul L. | 55-535 | M.Sc. |
| Montserin, Blazini G. | 28-521 | M.Sc. |
| Moody, Harry J. | 55-067 | Ph.D. |
| Moon, James H. | 50-038 | Ph.D. |
| Mooney, Craig M. | 55-068 | Ph.D. |
| Mooney, Craig M. | 51-571 | M.A. |
| Mooney, Elizabeth S. | 43-512 | M.A. |
| Moore, Dale H. | 23-524 | M.A. |
| Moore, Leonard P. | 33-014 | Ph.D. |
| Moore, Leonard P. | 30-509 | M.Sc. |
| Moore, Ralph E. | 51-615 | M.Sc. |
| Moore, Ralph G. | 36-018 | Ph.D. |
| Moore, Robert B. | 59-528 | M.Sc. |
| Moore, Ruth E. | 30-538 | M.A. |
| Moore, Thomas H. | 55-069 | Ph.D. |
| Moore, Thomas H. | 51-537 | M.Sc. |
| Moore, William H. | 32-503 | M.Eng. |
| Moore, William J. | 48-508 | M.Eng. |
| Moran, James | 16-513 | M.Sc. |
| Morantz, Daniel J. | 45-534 | M.Sc. |
| More, Robert Hall | 42-526 | M.Sc. |
| Morehouse, Clarence K. | 40-521 | M.Sc. |



| AUTHOR | THESIS NUMBER | DEGREE |
|---|---|---|
| Morehouse, Fred E. | 32-011 | Ph.D. |
| Morehouse, Fred E. | 31-510 | M.Sc. |
| Morgan, Cecil V. | 45-511 | M.Sc. |
| Morgan, Mildred A. | 37-527 | M.A. |
| Morgan, Oliver M. | 30-008 | Ph.D. |
| Morgante, Odosca | 59-054 | Ph.D. |
| Morgante, Odosca | 55-536 | M.Sc. |
| Morgen, Robert O. | 56-591 | M.Sc. |
| Morigi, Eugene M. | 59-055 | Ph.D. |
| Moriyama, Raymond J. | 57-502 | M.Arch. |
| Morley, Peter M. | 38-514 | M.Sc. |
| Morrell, Frank | 55-614 | M.Sc. |
| Morris, Herbert E. | 34-007 | Ph.D. |
| Morris, Peter G. | 57-068 | Ph.D. |
| Morrison, Carson F. | 27-512 | M.Sc. |
| Morrison, Donald M. | 22-517 | M.Sc. |
| Morrison, Donald M. | 24-004 | Ph.D. |
| Morrison, E.R. | 55-615 | M.Sc. |
| Morrison, Earl S. | 44-507 | M.Sc. |
| Morrison, Frank Orville | 39-014 | Ph.D. |
| Morrison, Gordon R. | 55-616 | M.Sc. |
| Morrison, James A. | 43-011 | Ph.D. |
| Morrison, James E. | 26-520 | M.Sc. |
| Morrison, John L. | 37-016 | Ph.D. |
| Morrison, Mary F.M. | 42-527 | M.Sc. |
| Morrison, Thomas J. | 31-511 | M.Sc. |
| Morrison, Wesley A. | 48-033 | Ph.D. |
| Morrow, Harold F. | 50-039 | Ph.D. |
| Morrow, James W. | 50-571 | M.A. |
| Morse, Stearns A. | 58-526 | M.Sc. |
| Morton, Ernest R. | 54-023 | Ph.D. |
| Morton, Ernest R. | 52-506 | M.Eng. |
| Morton, Maurice | 45-009 | Ph.D. |
| Morton, Nelson W. | 33-030 | Ph.D. |
| Morton, Nelson W. | 31-537 | M.A. |
| Morton, Richard | 31-556 | M.Sc. |
| Moser, Shia | 52-551 | M.A. |
| Moss, Albert E. | 37-511 | M.Sc. |
| Moss, Albert E. | 39-501 | Ph.D. |
| Moss, Bernard B. | 39-053 | M.Eng. |
| Mossman, Carolyn E. | 55-027 | Ph.D. |
| Moster, Julius B. | 47-563 | M.Sc. |
| Moughton, Barry J. | 58-501 | M.C.L. |
| Moulds, Gordon M. | 53-026 | Ph.D. |
| Moursi, Fouad K. | 55-510 | LL.M. |
| Mowat, John H. | 42-018 | Ph.D. |
| Moxley, John E. | 52-581 | M.Sc. |
| Moya, Francisco J. | 53-065 | Ph.D. |

| AUTHOR | THESIS NUMBER | DEGREE |
|---|---|---|
| Mcynihan, Irvin W. | 47-521 | M.Sc. |
| Mozie, James O. | 54-596 | M.Sc. |
| Mu'inu-d-din, Ahmad K. | 55-635 | M.A. |
| Mubarak, Nasreldin | 59-615 | M.A. |
| Mueller, George V. | 54-057 | Ph.D. |
| Mueller, William H. | 30-009 | Ph.D. |
| Mueller, William H. | 29-513 | M.Sc. |
| Muir, Allan K. | 25-524 | M.Sc. |
| Muir, William L. | 34-503 | M.Eng. |
| Mujahid, Sharif | 54-549 | M.A. |
| Mullaly, Jessie R. | 28-565 | M.A. |
| Muller, Thomas E. | 59-529 | M.Sc. |
| Mulligan, Robert | 51-025 | Ph.D. |
| Mulligan, Robert | 48-538 | M.Sc. |
| Mumtazuddin, Mchammed | 58-527 | M.Sc. |
| Mungall, Allan G. | 54-024 | Ph.D. |
| Mungen, Richard | 42-019 | Ph.D. |
| Munn, Allan M. | 47-015 | Ph.D. |
| Munn, David W. | 11-514 | M.Sc. |
| Munn, William C. | 05-004 | M.A. |
| Munro, Ferdinand L. | 32-025 | Ph.D. |
| Munro, Lloyd A. | 26-007 | Ph.D. |
| Munro, Vivian R. | 52-552 | M.A. |
| Munroe, David C. | 30-539 | M.A. |
| Munroe, David C. | 38-539 | M.A. |
| Munroe, Eugene Gordon | 41-534 | M.Sc. |
| Munroe, William M. | 46-544 | M.A. |
| Murchison, Jchn T. | 55-582 | LL.M. |
| Murdock, James D. | 52-059 | Ph.D. |
| Murphy, David R. | 48-591 | M.Sc. |
| Murphy, Florence E. | 39-042 | M.A. |
| Murphy, Frederick G. | 58-574 | M.Sc. |
| Murphy, Joseph | 58-528 | M.Sc. |
| Murphy, Sister Marie M. | 42-514 | M.A. |
| Murphy, William H. | 15-512 | M.Sc. |
| Murray, Bertram S. | 27-536 | M.A. |
| Murray, Francis E. | 53-027 | Ph.D. |
| Murray, George E. | 12-515 | M.Sc. |
| Murray, Louis G. | 54-058 | Ph.D. |
| Murray, Mae F. | 28-548 | M.A. |
| Murray, Phyllis M. | 27-537 | M.A. |
| Murray, Sydney G. | 38-540 | M.A. |
| Murray, Thomas K. | 57-024 | Ph.D. |
| Murray, Thomas K. | 50-549 | M.Sc. |
| Murty, Grandhi V. | 54-059 | Ph.D. |
| Myers, Betty-June | 59-056 | Ph.D. |
| Myers, Gordon E. | 51-026 | Ph.D. |
| Nachfolger, Nathan | 49-508 | M.Eng. |



| AUTHOR | THESIS NUMBER | DEGREE |
|---|---|---|
| Nadler, Norman J. | 55-070 | Ph.D. |
| Nakashima, Kimiaki | 46-545 | M.A. |
| Naldrett, Stanley Ncrman | 40-018 | Ph.D. |
| Narasinham, Ramanujaienga | 48-592 | M.Sc. |
| Narod, Miltcn | 43-507 | M.Sc. |
| Nashold, Blaine S. | 54-597 | M.Sc. |
| Nashshabah, Hisham | 59-057 | Ph.D. |
| Nashshabah, Hisham | 55-636 | M.A. |
| Nauss, Arthur William | 40-047 | M.Sc. |
| Nawab, Mohammed A. | 57-069 | Ph.D. |
| Neamtan, Samuel M. | 37-017 | Ph.D. |
| Nebiker, Walter A. | 57-590 | M.Sc. |
| Neeland, William D. | 35-511 | M.Sc. |
| Neilson, Helen R. | 48-593 | M.Sc. |
| Neilson, James M. | 47-522 | M.Sc. |
| Neiman, Gregory M. | 53-601 | M.Sc. |
| Neis, Vernon V. | 56-558 | M.Eng. |
| Neish, Arthur C. | 42-020 | Ph.D. |
| Neish, Arthur Charles | 39-066 | M.Sc. |
| Nejedly, Vladislava J. | 59-589 | M.Sc. |
| Nelles, James G. | 33-563 | M.Com. |
| Nelson, Arthur J. | 51-572 | M.A. |
| Nelscn, Eda M. | 28-549 | M.A. |
| Nelscn, John A. | 45-010 | Ph.D. |
| Nelson, Samuel J. | 52-024 | Ph.D. |
| Nelson, William A. | 57-070 | Ph.D. |
| Nelson, William A. | 48-539 | M.Sc. |
| Nemeth, John | 53-516 | LL.M. |
| Nemiroff, Stanley A. | 59-616 | M.A. |
| Nemser, Ruby D. | 56-548 | M.A. |
| Nenniger, Emile | 51-588 | M.Eng. |
| Neubauer, Lewis G. | 49-053 | Ph.D. |
| Nevitt, Henry J. | 45-501 | M.Eng. |
| Newcombe, Hcward B. | 39-015 | Ph.D. |
| Newman, Robert S. | 56-501 | S.T.M. |
| Newnham, May I. | 21-522 | M.A. |
| Newson, William V. | 01-004 | M.Sc. |
| Newton, Dorcthy F. | 22-518 | M.Sc. |
| Newton, Margaret | 19-503 | M.Sc. |
| Newton, Thecdore F. | 27-543 | M.A. |
| Nichol, Charles A. | 46-528 | M.Sc. |
| Nichol, Helen R. | 21-523 | M.A. |
| Nichol, Jean | 25-538 | M.A. |
| Nicholls, Jchn V. V. | 35-512 | M.Sc. |
| Nicholls, Robert V. V. | 36-019 | Ph.D. |
| Nicholls, Robert V. V. | 35-513 | M.Sc. |
| Nichols, Ian O. | 56-559 | M.Eng. |
| Nichols, Walter M. | 38-547 | M.Sc. |

| AUTHOR | THESIS NUMBER | DEGREE |
|---|---|---|
| Nicolls, Jasper H. | 12-516 | M.Sc. |
| Nielsen, Niels H. | 54-550 | M.A. |
| Niloff, Paul H. | 49-612 | M.Sc. |
| Nixon, Justin W. | 59-558 | M.A. |
| Nnochiri, Enyinnaya | 59-058 | Ph.D. |
| Nnochiri, Enyinnaya | 50-626 | M.Sc. |
| Noad, Algy S. | 21-524 | M.A. |
| Nommik, Salme | 57-071 | Ph.D. |
| Nommik, Salme | 52-538 | M.Sc. |
| Noonan, Bernard | 53-028 | Ph.D. |
| Norcross, Nathan C. | 36-514 | M.Sc. |
| Norman, Nils | 57-072 | Ph.D. |
| Normand, Gerard L. | 59-590 | M.Sc. |
| Normington, James B. | 34-008 | Ph.D. |
| Norris, Kenneth E. | 31-538 | M.A. |
| Norris, Kenneth E. | 39-016 | Ph.D. |
| Novack, Lazare | 46-013 | Ph.D. |
| Novick, Seymour | 49-542 | M.Sc. |
| Novotny, Jan M. | 53-557 | M.C.L. |
| Nowak, Tadeusz C. | 55-583 | LL.M. |
| Nowosad, Frank S. | 33-524 | M.Sc. |
| Noyes, Harry A. Jr. | 38-541 | M.A. |
| Nunes, Doris S. | 49-613 | M.Sc. |
| Nussey, Albert N. | 48-594 | M.Sc. |
| Nylen, Torsten | 56-566 | LL.M. |
| O'Brien, John W. | 55-556 | M.A. |
| O'Brien, Margaret T. | 28-550 | M.A. |
| O'Brien, Michael V. | 37-528 | M.A. |
| O'Connell, Francis J. | 31-512 | M.Sc. |
| O'Donnell, Vincent J. | 54-025 | Ph.D. |
| O'Donovan, Denis K. | 38-014 | Ph.D. |
| O'Heir, Hugh B. | 24-524 | M.Sc. |
| O'Neill, Charles | 24-500 | M.M.A. |
| O'Neill, John J. | 10-519 | M.Sc. |
| O'Neill, Thomas L. | 48-568 | M.A. |
| O'Quinn, James P. | 50-572 | M.A. |
| O'Reilly, Henry J. | 44-508 | M.Sc. |
| O'Shaughnessy, Martin D. | 38-502 | M.Eng. |
| O'Shaughnessy, Michael J. | 33-503 | M.Eng. |
| O'Sullivan, Timothy | 49-574 | M.A. |
| Oborin, Peter E. | 54-598 | M.Sc. |
| Oduber-Quiros, Daniel | 48-567 | M.A. |
| Ogilvie, James D. | 42-021 | Ph.D. |
| Ogilvie, James D. | 40-522 | M.Sc. |
| Ogilvy, Robert F. | 32-504 | M.Eng. |
| Ogilvy, William L. | 56-592 | M.Sc. |
| Ogryzlo, Elmer A. | 59-059 | Ph.D. |
| Okulitch, Vladimir J. | 34-009 | Ph.D. |



| AUTHOR | THESIS NUMBER | DEGREE |
|---|---|---|
| Oldham, Frances K. | 35-514 | M.Sc. |
| Oler, Norman | 57-025 | Ph.D. |
| Oler, Norman | 53-541 | M.Sc. |
| Oliver, John A. | 50-660 | M.A. |
| Oliver, Michael K. | 56-058 | Ph.D. |
| Oliver, Michael K. | 50-661 | M.A. |
| Oliver, William T. | 51-538 | M.Sc. |
| Oliver, William T. | 53-029 | Ph.D. |
| Olszewski, Jerzy | 51-027 | Ph.D. |
| Onyszchuk, Mario | 54-060 | Ph.D. |
| Orbach, Jack | 50-662 | M.A. |
| Orlick, Emanuel | 41-520 | M.A. |
| Ornstein, William | 49-614 | M.Sc. |
| Orr, Paul A. | 49-642 | M.A. |
| Ortlepp, William D. | 57-509 | M.Eng. |
| Orvig, Svenn | 54-026 | Ph.D. |
| Orvig, Svenn | 51-539 | M.Sc. |
| Osborn, Dale J. | 57-073 | Ph.D. |
| Osborne, Robert F. | 54-559 | S.T.M. |
| Ottolenghi, Paul | 57-074 | Ph.D. |
| Ottolenghi, Paul | 55-617 | M.Sc. |
| Ouimet, Paul A. | 53-503 | M.C.L. |
| Oulton, Rhodes C. | 55-637 | M.A. |
| Ounsworth, Leslie Frank | 39-067 | M.Sc. |
| Overbaugh, Sidney C. | 35-023 | Ph.D. |
| Overing, R.I. | 57-552 | M.A. |
| Owen, George R. | 34-537 | M.A. |
| Owens, Owen E. | 55-028 | Ph.D. |
| Owens, Owen E. | 51-540 | M.Sc. |
| Padopulos, Diogenes | 57-510 | M.Eng. |
| Page, Douglas E. | 59-591 | M.Sc. |
| Painter, Richard H. | 29-514 | M.Sc. |
| Paist, Gertrude W. | 36-539 | M.A. |
| Paivio, Allan U. | 59-060 | Ph.D. |
| Paivio, Allan U. | 57-534 | M.Sc. |
| Pall, David Boris | 39-017 | Ph.D. |
| Palmer, Walter M. | 49-031 | Ph.D. |
| Palmer, Walter M. | 47-564 | M.Sc. |
| Palsson, Petur | 52-507 | M.Eng. |
| Panos, Dimitrios | 44-516 | M.A. |
| Panter, Shraga F. | 36-020 | Ph.D. |
| Paour, Peter J. | 36-540 | M.A. |
| Papanek, Rudolf J. | 48-503 | M.Arch. |
| Papineau-Couture, Gilles | 45-011 | Ph.D. |
| Pappius, Hanna M. | 52-025 | Ph.D. |
| Paquet, Arthur | 30-510 | M.Sc. |
| Paquette, Joseph P. | 43-508 | M.Sc. |
| Paquin, Roger | 55-071 | Ph.D. |

| AUTHOR | THESIS NUMBER | DEGREE |
|---|---|---|
| Paquin, Roger | 51-541 | M.Sc. |
| Parakkal, Paul F. | 59-530 | M.Sc. |
| Parent, Robert C. | 24-504 | M.S.A. |
| Parker, David W. | 08-503 | M.A. |
| Parker, T.C. | 57-607 | M.A. |
| Parker, William E. | 37-538 | M.Sc. |
| Parker, William E. | 41-506 | Ph.D. |
| Parlee, Norman A. | 39-018 | Ph.D. |
| Parmar, Surendra S. | 57-075 | Ph.D. |
| Parsons, Basil I. | 53-030 | Ph.D. |
| Parsons, Clarence Reuben | 41-521 | M.A. |
| Parsons, John G. | 46-529 | M.Sc. |
| Parsons, Timothy R. | 58-032 | Ph.D. |
| Parsons, Timothy R. | 55-537 | M.Sc. |
| Parthenais, J. Theodore | 30-540 | M.A. |
| Pascoe, Enid | 56-059 | Ph.D. |
| Passey, Richard F. | 56-028 | Ph.D. |
| Passmore, Marian R. | 57-608 | M.A. |
| Pasternack, David S. | 26-521 | M.Sc. |
| Pasternack, David S. | 28-010 | Ph.D. |
| Pasternak, Israel S. | 59-061 | Ph.D. |
| Pate, Brian D. | 55-029 | Ph.D. |
| Paterson-Smyth, Marjorie | 12-517 | M.Sc. |
| Paterson, Edith L. | 12-503 | M.A. |
| Paterson, Laurie A. | 51-573 | M.A. |
| Pattee, Chauncey J. | 38-548 | M.Sc. |
| Patterson, Arthur L. | 24-525 | M.Sc. |
| Patterson, Arthur L. | 28-011 | Ph.D. |
| Patterson, Donald D. | 50-550 | M.Sc. |
| Patterson, Ralph Francis | 42-505 | Ph.D. |
| Pattison, Irma E. | 31-539 | M.A. |
| Patton, Isabelle J. | 24-550 | M.Sc. |
| Paul, Harry | 47-565 | M.Sc. |
| Paul, Irving H. | 50-573 | M.A. |
| Pavich, Michael | 50-508 | M.Eng. |
| Pavlasek, Tomas J. | 58-033 | Ph.D. |
| Pavlasek, Tomas J. | 48-509 | M.Eng. |
| Pawlikowska, Anna M. | 49-543 | M.Sc. |
| Payette, Albert | 42-528 | M.Sc. |
| Payne, Torrence P. | 50-017 | Ph.D. |
| Pazur, John H. | 46-530 | M.Sc. |
| Pearce, Jesse Arthur | 41-012 | Ph.D. |
| Pearse, Charles D. | 54-599 | M.Sc. |
| Pearson, Mary F. | 07-504 | M.A. |
| Peck, Oswald | 36-021 | Ph.D. |
| Peck, Oswald | 34-514 | M.Sc. |
| Peck, Robert Alfred | 42-036 | M.A. |
| Peckham, Hugh E. | 55-618 | M.Sc. |



| AUTHOR | THESIS NUMBER | DEGREE |
|---|---|---|
| Peden, Gwendolyn W. | 35-546 | M.A. |
| Pedersen, Jorgen W. | 53-031 | Ph.D. |
| Pedley, Norah F. | 53-602 | M.Sc. |
| Peets, Ronald C. | 50-551 | M.Sc. |
| Peiker, Alfred L. | 30-010 | Ph.D. |
| Pellerin, Evelyn | 37-529 | M.A. |
| Pelletier, Alexis D. | 07-505 | M.A. |
| Pelletier, Annie H. | 17-501 | M.A. |
| Pelletier, Joseph R. | 32-557 | M.Sc. |
| Pelletier, Real | 44-521 | M.Sc. |
| Pelletier, Rene A. | 27-009 | Ph.D. |
| Pelletier, Rene A. | 24-526 | M.Sc. |
| Peng, Ming-Min | 53-517 | LL.M. |
| Peniston, Quintin Pearman | 39-019 | Ph.D. |
| Pennie, T.E. | 54-551 | M.A. |
| Penrose, George H. | 45-546 | M.A. |
| Penton, Reginald | 54-566 | M.Eng. |
| Pepper, James M. | 43-023 | Ph.D. |
| Pepper, Thomas P. | 48-034 | Ph.D. |
| Peppiatt, Harry J. | 53-067 | Ph.D. |
| Percival, Walter L. | 48-540 | M.Sc. |
| Percy, Edward C. | 54-600 | M.Sc. |
| Perey, Francis G. | 57-591 | M.Sc. |
| Perlin, Arthur S. | 49-032 | Ph.D. |
| Perlin, Arthur S. | 46-574 | M.Sc. |
| Perlman, Martin M. | 55-030 | Ph.D. |
| Perlman, Martin M. | 51-616 | M.Sc. |
| Peron, Fernand G. | 50-627 | M.Sc. |
| Peron, Fernand G. | 53-032 | Ph.D. |
| Perrault, Charles H. | 46-556 | M.Eng. |
| Perreault, Champlain | 27-514 | M.Sc. |
| Perret, Edmond J. | 55-501 | S.T.M. |
| Perrigard, Elma E. | 36-541 | M.A. |
| Perry, Ernest J. | 51-028 | Ph.D. |
| Perry, Helen M. | 24-527 | M.Sc. |
| Perry, Stanley Z. | 29-515 | M.Sc. |
| Perry, Stanley Z. | 38-022 | Ph.D. |
| Peterson, Frederick O. | 24-543 | M.A. |
| Peto, Margaret | 59-062 | Ph.D. |
| Peto, Margaret | 56-593 | M.Sc. |
| Petrie, Richards J. | 41-013 | Ph.D. |
| Petrogiannis, Demetrios S | 58-587 | M.A. |
| Petruk, William | 59-063 | Ph.D. |
| Petrushka, Evelyn | 57-076 | Ph.D. |
| Pfalzner, Paul M. | 51-617 | M.Sc. |
| Pfefferkorn, Gerhard A. | 56-560 | M.Eng. |
| Phelan, Lewis J. | 29-557 | M.A. |
| Phillips, Charles O. | 59-592 | M.Sc. |

| AUTHOR | THESIS NUMBER | DEGREE |
|---|---|---|
| Phillips, John B. | 30-011 | Ph.D. |
| Phillips, John B. | 28-522 | M.Sc. |
| Phillips, John H. | 47-566 | M.Sc. |
| Phillips, Lorne A. | 52-508 | M.Eng. |
| Phillips, Norman W. | 38-015 | Ph.D. |
| Phillips, William E. | 53-542 | M.Sc. |
| Picard, Robert I. | 32-538 | M.A. |
| Pick, Alfred J. | 37-530 | M.A. |
| Pickel, Margaret B. | 23-525 | M.A. |
| Pickett, Allison D. | 36-515 | M.Sc. |
| Pickup, T. | 56-594 | M.Sc. |
| Pickup, T. | 54-617 | M.A. |
| Pidgeon, Lloyd M. | 29-011 | Ph.D. |
| Pidgeon, Lloyd M. | 27-541 | M.Sc. |
| Pidoux, John L. | 36-504 | M.Eng. |
| Piggott, Carmen L. | 53-068 | Ph.D. |
| Piloto, Albert E. | 50-574 | M.A. |
| Pilson, Michael E. | 59-531 | M.Sc. |
| Pimenoff, Clement J. | 32-553 | M.Eng. |
| Pinder, Kenneth L. | 52-509 | M.Eng. |
| Pineo, Peter C. | 57-553 | M.A. |
| Pinhey, Kathleen F. | 30-012 | Ph.D. |
| Pinsky, Alex | 49-033 | Ph.D. |
| Pinsky, Alex | 46-575 | M.Sc. |
| Pinsky, Carl | 57-592 | M.Sc. |
| Piscopo, Franco A. | 54-618 | M.A. |
| Pitt, Edith S. | 43-513 | M.A. |
| Pitt, Jack A. | 53-615 | M.A. |
| Pitts, Gordon M. | 09-515 | M.Sc. |
| Pitts, Mary A. | 50-663 | M.A. |
| Platt, Muriel E. | 32-012 | Ph.D. |
| Platt, Muriel E. | 29-516 | M.Sc. |
| Plewes, Argyle C. | 34-010 | Ph.D. |
| Plunguian, Mark | 34-023 | Ph.D. |
| Plunkett, Thomas | 55-557 | M.A. |
| Poapst, James V. | 50-580 | M.Com. |
| Pochopien, Kazimierz M. | 52-553 | M.A. |
| Podgornik, Louis E. | 58-547 | M.A. |
| Poirier, Mary A. | 43-526 | M.A. |
| Polgar, Sophie | 55-558 | M.A. |
| Polianski, Alexei N. | 59-559 | M.A. |
| Pollak, John K. | 53-069 | Ph.D. |
| Pollard, Samuel L. | 30-541 | M.A. |
| Polley, John R. | 46-031 | Ph.D. |
| Pollock, Donald W. | 57-026 | Ph.D. |
| Pollock, Donald W. | 55-538 | M.Sc. |
| Polonoff, Irving I. | 48-569 | M.A. |
| Pomerleau, Rene | 27-515 | M.Sc. |



| AUTHOR | THESIS NUMBER | DEGREE |
|---|---|---|
| Ponticello, Eva Edith | 42-037 | M.A. |
| Poole, Aquila J. | 55-571 | S.T.M. |
| Poole, Gordon D. | 36-505 | M.Eng. |
| Poole, John B. | 54-027 | Ph.D. |
| Poole, John P. | 41-046 | M.Sc. |
| Popham, James H. | 51-618 | M.Sc. |
| Popkin, John W. | 37-546 | M.A. |
| Poplove, Myron | 51-619 | M.Sc. |
| Popp, William | 26-522 | M.Sc. |
| Porter, Cecil G. | 13-519 | M.Sc. |
| Portier, Jacques M. | 50-575 | M.A. |
| Potter, Calvin C. | 54-028 | Ph.D. |
| Potter, Calvin C. | 50-671 | M.Com. |
| Potter, Harold H. | 49-575 | M.A. |
| Potter, James G. | 12-504 | M.A. |
| Potvin, Roger | 39-020 | Ph.D. |
| Pound, Omar S. | 58-588 | M.A. |
| Pounder, Elton R. | 37-018 | Ph.D. |
| Povilaitis, Bronys | 54-029 | Ph.D. |
| Povilaitis, Bronys | 51-542 | M.Sc. |
| Powell, Allan T. | 25-525 | M.Sc. |
| Powell, Edward C. | 32-013 | Ph.D. |
| Powell, Elizabeth A. | 59-593 | M.Sc. |
| Powell, John M. | 59-594 | M.Sc. |
| Power, Geoffrey | 59-064 | Ph.D. |
| Power, Graham C. | 59-617 | M.A. |
| Power, Richard M. | 33-525 | M.Sc. |
| Powles, Percival S. | 14-507 | M.A. |
| Poznanski, Zolzislaw | 50-509 | M.Eng. |
| Prado, Eline S. | 48-541 | M.Sc. |
| Prasad, Devendra | 57-027 | Ph.D. |
| Pratinidhi, Shrivivas V. | 56-561 | M.Eng. |
| Pratt, Audrey E. | 49-576 | M.A. |
| Prebble, Malcolm L. | 32-521 | M.Sc. |
| Prebble, Malcolm L. | 40-019 | Ph.D. |
| Premvati, * | 58-034 | Ph.D. |
| Prentice, James D. | 53-603 | M.Sc. |
| Press, Abraham | 27-516 | M.Sc. |
| Preston, George P. | 26-551 | M.A. |
| Price, Aubrey F. | 33-015 | Ph.D. |
| Price, Enid | 20-512 | M.A. |
| Price, Frederick William | 42-038 | M.A. |
| Price, John W. | 54-552 | M.A. |
| Price, Peter | 33-016 | Ph.D. |
| Priestman, Bryan | 29-019 | Ph.D. |
| Priestman, Bryan | 26-523 | M.Sc. |
| Prillaman, J.H. | 56-595 | M.Sc. |
| Prince, Alma S. | 47-539 | M.A. |

| AUTHOR | THESIS NUMBER | DEGREE |
|---|---|---|
| Pringle, Ross B. | 47-016 | Ph.D. |
| Pringle, Ross B. | 45-535 | M.Sc. |
| Pritchard, Ernest T. | 54-601 | M.Sc. |
| Prives, Moshe Z. | 58-035 | Ph.D. |
| Prives, Moshe Z. | 55-559 | M.A. |
| Privett, Orville S. | 47-017 | Ph.D. |
| Privett, Orville S. | 44-509 | M.Sc. |
| Proctor, William C. | 47-523 | M.Sc. |
| Proverbs, Ivor H. | 50-552 | M.Sc. |
| Proverbs, Maurice D. | 52-026 | Ph.D. |
| Proverbs, Maurice D. | 46-531 | M.Sc. |
| Prowse, Alice R. | 32-539 | M.A. |
| Prusti, Bansi D. | 54-061 | Ph.D. |
| Puddington, Ira E. | 36-516 | M.Sc. |
| Puddington, Ira E. | 38-023 | Ph.D. |
| Pudenz, Robert Harry | 41-535 | M.Sc. |
| Pugsley, Leonard I. | 32-014 | Ph.D. |
| Pugsley, Leonard I. | 29-517 | M.Sc. |
| Pugsley, William H. | 50-018 | Ph.D. |
| Puhach, Paul A. | 56-029 | Ph.D. |
| Puhvel, Jaan | 52-609 | M.A. |
| Puhvel, Martin | 54-553 | M.A. |
| Pullman, Joseph C. | 33-526 | M.Sc. |
| Pullman, Joseph C. | 35-032 | Ph.D. |
| Pump, Karl K. | 50-628 | M.Sc. |
| Purcell, Donald | 49-577 | M.A. |
| Purdy, Thomas Lenton | 39-519 | M.Sc. |
| Pursley, Robert | 30-542 | M.A. |
| Purvis, John L. | 56-030 | Ph.D. |
| Purvis, John L. | 54-602 | M.Sc. |
| Putnaerglis, Rudolph | 55-507 | M.Eng. |
| Putnam, Adelaide D. | 33-555 | M.A. |
| Puxley, Ann E. | 50-553 | M.Sc. |
| Pyle, James Johnston | 39-021 | Ph.D. |
| Qaysi, Abdul W. | 54-554 | M.A. |
| Quinn, Herbert F. | 46-589 | M.A. |
| Quinn, Hubert F. | 46-532 | M.Sc. |
| Quinn, Hubert F. | 48-035 | Ph.D. |
| Rabinovitch, Benton S. | 42-022 | Ph.D. |
| Rabinovitch, Mortimer S. | 49-615 | M.Sc. |
| Rabinovitch, Reuben | 47-567 | M.Sc. |
| Rabinovitch, William | 56-060 | Ph.D. |
| Rabinowitz, Herbert S. | 52-554 | M.A. |
| Rackow, Alan D. | 51-589 | M.Eng. |
| Radler, Ruth | 30-543 | M.A. |
| Radley, Sidney A. | 50-629 | M.Sc. |
| Rahman, Mushfequr | 56-061 | Ph.D. |
| Rajalakshmi, Ramakrishnan | 58-056 | Ph.D. |



| AUTHOR | THESIS NUMBER | DEGREE |
|---|---|---|
| Raju, E. Sadasiva | 48-510 | M.Eng. |
| Ralph, Arthur C. | 51-029 | Ph.D. |
| Ramamurti, Dharmapuri V. | 56-062 | Ph.D. |
| Ramaradhya, Jakkanahally | 59-065 | Ph.D. |
| Ramon-Moliner, Enrique | 59-066 | Ph.D. |
| Ramos, Oswaldo L. | 55-619 | M.Sc. |
| Ramsden, Mary E. | 33-574 | M.A. |
| Rand, Frank H. | 32-540 | M.A. |
| Randolf, John H. | 43-527 | M.A. |
| Rankin, Robert A. | 37-512 | M.Sc. |
| Rankin, Robert A. | 33-504 | M.Eng. |
| Rankin, Winston B. | 49-578 | M.A. |
| Rao, Baindur G. | 56-063 | Ph.D. |
| Rao, Bapoje K. | 54-062 | Ph.D. |
| Rao, C. Kanaka D. | 58-575 | M.Sc. |
| Rao, N.S. Krishna | 50-019 | Ph.D. |
| Ratelle, Ruth M. | 39-043 | M.A. |
| Rattray, Basil A. | 49-544 | M.Sc. |
| Ravaris, Charles L. | 54-063 | Ph.D. |
| Rawlinson, Herbert E. | 32-522 | M.Sc. |
| Rawlinson, Herbert E. | 34-024 | Ph.D. |
| Raymond, Charles W. | 59-560 | M.A. |
| Raynauld, Robert | 28-501 | M.S.A. |
| Rayport, Mark | 58-036 | Ph.D. |
| Read, Dale W. | 59-067 | Ph.D. |
| Read, Deane C. | 56-534 | M.Sc. |
| Read, Donald E. | 49-054 | Ph.D. |
| Read, Mary G. | 25-540 | M.A. |
| Read, Stanley M. | 25-539 | M.A. |
| Real, Roderick R. | 57-511 | M.Eng. |
| Redkevitch, Zenon | 52-583 | M.Sc. |
| Reed, Ernest S. | 38-553 | M.A. |
| Reed, John G. | 29-547 | M.A. |
| Reeder, Stewart W. | 56-535 | M.Sc. |
| Reeks, Wilfrid S. | 32-523 | M.Sc. |
| Reesal, Michael R. | 50-554 | M.Sc. |
| Reeve, Herbert A. | 33-017 | Ph.D. |
| Reeve, Herbert A. | 31-557 | M.Sc. |
| Reeves, Hubert | 56-536 | M.Sc. |
| Reich, Nathan | 26-552 | M.A. |
| Reid, Albert R. | 53-033 | Ph.D. |
| Reid, Allana G. | 50-040 | Ph.D. |
| Reid, Allana G. | 45-547 | M.A. |
| Reid, David B. | 46-546 | M.A. |
| Reid, Evans Burton | 40-504 | Ph.D. |
| Reid, Ewart P. | 32-541 | M.A. |
| Reid, Hugh S. | 15-513 | M.Sc. |
| Reid, John F. | 57-593 | M.Sc. |

| AUTHOR | THESIS NUMBER | DEGREE |
|---|---|---|
| Reid, Kenneth H. | 58-576 | M.Sc. |
| Reid, William L. | 38-515 | M.Sc. |
| Reid, William S. | 35-547 | M.A. |
| Reilly, Herschell E. | 14-515 | M.Sc. |
| Reisman, Sol | 42-039 | M.A. |
| Rejhon, George | 57-535 | M.Sc. |
| Relly, Bruce H. | 57-536 | M.Sc. |
| Renaud, Paul E. | 23-526 | M.A. |
| Renaud, Paul E. | 22-500 | LL.M. |
| Rennie, Douglas L. | 53-616 | M.A. |
| Reque, A. Dikka | 24-544 | M.A. |
| Rexford, Laura H. | 34-538 | M.A. |
| Rexford, Orrin B. | 36-552 | M.A. |
| Reynolds, Lincoln M. | 59-532 | M.Sc. |
| Reynolds, Lloyd G. | 33-556 | M.A. |
| Rezek, G. | 57-609 | M.A. |
| Rhoades, Winifred | 31-540 | M.A. |
| Rice, Horace G. | 07-506 | M.A. |
| Rice, William B. | 56-509 | M.Eng. |
| Richard, O'Neill J. | 49-579 | M.A. |
| Richards, Terence A. | 59-595 | M.Sc. |
| Richards, Victor L. | 34-504 | M.Eng. |
| Richardson, Howard P. | 52-539 | M.Sc. |
| Richardson, James K. | 22-519 | M.Sc. |
| Richardson, Laurence R. | 33-527 | M.Sc. |
| Richardson, Laurence R. | 35-024 | Ph.D. |
| Richardson, Lorne N. | 10-520 | M.Sc. |
| Richardson, Nigel H. | 54-619 | M.A. |
| Richardson, Ronald E. | 33-018 | Ph.D. |
| Richardson, Ronald E. | 31-513 | M.Sc. |
| Richer, Ruth C. | 51-543 | M.Sc. |
| Richmond, Hector A. | 35-515 | M.Sc. |
| Richmond, James Hugh | 40-020 | Ph.D. |
| Richter, Maxwell | 58-037 | Ph.D. |
| Riddell, John E. | 36-549 | M.Sc. |
| Riddell, John E. | 53-034 | Ph.D. |
| Riddell, Marion I. | 50-630 | M.Sc. |
| Ridge, Frank G. | 53-070 | Ph.D. |
| Ried, L. | 02-001 | M.Sc. |
| Rigby, Caroline E. | 49-545 | M.Sc. |
| Rigby, Francis L. | 48-010 | Ph.D. |
| Riklis, Emanuel | 58-038 | Ph.D. |
| Riley, George C. | 57-028 | Ph.D. |
| Riley, George C. | 51-544 | M.Sc. |
| Riordon, Charles H. | 27-517 | M.Sc. |
| Riordon, Peter H. | 52-027 | Ph.D. |
| Riordon, Peter H. | 38-518 | M.Sc. |
| Rioux, Philip G. | 49-509 | M.Eng. |



| AUTHOR | THESIS NUMBER | DEGREE |
|---|---|---|
| Rippon, Clive L. | 57-516 | LL.M. |
| Rishikof, Jack R. | 49-616 | M.Sc. |
| Ritchie, Marguerite E. | 58-560 | LL.M. |
| Ritchie, Paul F. | 47-018 | Ph.D. |
| Ritchie, Verna F. | 59-618 | M.A. |
| Rittenhouse, Charles B. J | 38-552 | M.A. |
| Roach, Charles L. | 49-510 | M.Eng. |
| Robb, James P. | 46-533 | M.Sc. |
| Robert, Percy A. | 28-551 | M.A. |
| Roberts, Gwen R. | 32-542 | M.A. |
| Roberts, Henry L. | 52-060 | Ph.D. |
| Roberts, Henry L. | 49-617 | M.Sc. |
| Robertson, Alexander A. | 49-034 | Ph.D. |
| Robertson, Arthur F. | 07-512 | M.Sc. |
| Robertson, Barbara M. | 35-533 | M.A. |
| Robertson, Carol E. | 25-526 | M.Sc. |
| Robertson, Florence F. | 46-534 | M.Sc. |
| Robertson, Foderick F. | 55-031 | Ph.D. |
| Robertson, Ross E. | 44-013 | Ph.D. |
| Robertson, William K. | 47-568 | M.Sc. |
| Robichon, Jacques | 50-555 | M.Sc. |
| Robinson, Arthur G. | 52-540 | M.Sc. |
| Robinson, Bernard S. | 13-508 | M.A. |
| Robinson, Dean B. | 48-542 | M.Sc. |
| Robinson, Donald B. | 43-012 | Ph.D. |
| Robinson, Harold Ross | 42-064 | M.Sc. |
| Robinson, John | 50-041 | Ph.D. |
| Robinson, John | 45-536 | M.Sc. |
| Robinson, Jonathan | 50-576 | M.A. |
| Robinson, Joseph E. | 51-620 | M.Sc. |
| Robinson, Patricia G. | 53-617 | M.A. |
| Robinson, Raymond F. | 38-516 | M.Sc. |
| Robinson, William G. | 41-014 | Ph.D. |
| Robinson, William G. | 38-517 | M.Sc. |
| Robison, Samuel C. | 25-527 | M.Sc. |
| Roche, Mary Nora | 41-047 | M.Sc. |
| Rochefort, Guy J. | 58-039 | Ph.D. |
| Rochefort, Joseph G. | 56-596 | M.Sc. |
| Rochlin, Isidore | 42-529 | M.Sc. |
| Rockwell, Keith R. | 48-595 | M.Sc. |
| Rodman, Hyman | 53-618 | M.A. |
| Roffey, Myles H. | 09-516 | M.Sc. |
| Rogers, A.A. | 57-556 | S.T.M. |
| Rogers, Charles G. | 54-530 | M.Sc. |
| Rogers, David B. | 09-505 | M.A. |
| Rogers, James T. | 50-591 | M.Eng. |
| Rogers, James T. | 53-071 | Ph.D. |
| Rogers, John T. | 24-549 | M.S.A. |

| AUTHOR | THESIS NUMBER | DEGREE |
|---|---|---|
| Rollit, John B. | 32-543 | M.A. |
| Rollit, John B. | 34-011 | Ph.D. |
| Romaine, Victor | 51-574 | M.A. |
| Romeril, Paul E. | 59-619 | M.A. |
| Ronald, Keith | 58-040 | Ph.D. |
| Ronald, Keith | 56-597 | M.Sc. |
| Rooney, Clarence E. | 52-028 | Ph.D. |
| Roper, Richard B. | 51-545 | M.Sc. |
| Rorke, Mabele L. | 08-504 | M.A. |
| Rose, Bram | 37-513 | M.Sc. |
| Rose, Bram | 39-022 | Ph.D. |
| Rose, Harold E. | 20-500 | LL.M. |
| Roseman, Frank | 59-561 | M.A. |
| Rosen, Charles A. | 50-592 | M.Eng. |
| Rosen, Harold J. | 50-631 | M.Sc. |
| Rosenbaum, Saul B. | 26-524 | M.Sc. |
| Rosenberg, Gilbert | 56-598 | M.Sc. |
| Rosenberg, Solomon | 36-011 | Ph.D. |
| Rosenberg, Solomon | 34-515 | M.Sc. |
| Rosenfeld, Michael W. | 56-599 | M.Sc. |
| Rosenfeld, Ze'ev | 59-533 | M.Sc. |
| Rosenthall, Edward | 38-519 | M.Sc. |
| Rosevear, John N. | 56-620 | M.A. |
| Ross-Ross, Philip A. | 51-505 | M.Eng. |
| Ross, Archibald S. | 37-019 | Ph.D. |
| Ross, Charles Alexander | 39-044 | M.A. |
| Ross, Dorothy J. | 32-544 | M.A. |
| Ross, Dorothy J. | 39-023 | Ph.D. |
| Ross, Dorothy V. | 26-553 | M.A. |
| Ross, Douglas A. | 31-514 | M.Sc. |
| Ross, Douglas A. | 34-012 | Ph.D. |
| Ross, Dudley E. | 27-518 | M.Sc. |
| Ross, Harold | 47-581 | M.A. |
| Ross, Henry U. | 38-520 | M.Sc. |
| Ross, Herman R. | 32-545 | M.A. |
| Ross, Ian K. | 57-029 | Ph.D. |
| Ross, Mary C. M. | 35-534 | M.A. |
| Ross, Mary V. | 52-029 | Ph.D. |
| Ross, Robert G. | 53-543 | M.Sc. |
| Ross, Roderick C. | 49-618 | M.Sc. |
| Ross, Sally Chipman | 42-040 | M.A. |
| Ross, V.J. | 57-610 | M.A. |
| Ross, William B. | 33-031 | Ph.D. |
| Ross, William B. | 31-515 | M.Sc. |
| Ross, William B. | 27-519 | M.Sc. |
| Ross, Winifred M. | 48-596 | M.Sc. |
| Rossiter, Maryellen | 42-041 | M.A. |
| Rosten, Jean | 44-522 | M.Sc. |



| AUTHOR | THESIS NUMBER | DEGREE |
|---|---|---|
| Rota, Alexander N. | 53-604 | M.Sc. |
| Rotenberg, Avrahm B. | 41-507 | Ph.D. |
| Rothballer, Alan B. | 55-620 | M.Sc. |
| Rothschild, Fred | 46-549 | M.A. |
| Rouatt, James W. | 47-524 | M.Sc. |
| Roulty, Paul M. | 48-543 | M.Sc. |
| Roumbanis, Theodore | 56-537 | M.Sc. |
| Rounthwaite, Harry L. | 52-584 | M.Sc. |
| Rountree, George M. | 33-557 | M.A. |
| Rowell, Arthur H. | 12-505 | M.A. |
| Rowlands, Mary E. | 56-621 | M.A. |
| Rowles, William | 26-525 | M.Sc. |
| Rowles, William | 28-007 | Ph.D. |
| Rowley, Harry J. | 29-012 | Ph.D. |
| Rowley, Marie Rita | 40-511 | M.A. |
| Roxburgh, James M. | 49-035 | Ph.D. |
| Roy, Chitra | 59-534 | M.Sc. |
| Roy, Esther M. | 37-531 | M.A. |
| Roy, Louis P. | 56-031 | Ph.D. |
| Roy, William J. | 35-548 | M.A. |
| Royer, France M. | 43-514 | M.A. |
| Rozdilsky, Bohdan | 56-600 | M.Sc. |
| Rubin, Gerald M. | 56-622 | M.A. |
| Rubin, Lionel L. | 31-541 | M.A. |
| Rubinstein, David | 51-621 | M.Sc. |
| Rubinstein, David | 53-072 | Ph.D. |
| Rublee, J.D. | 51-622 | M.Sc. |
| Rudoff, Hyman | 37-020 | Ph.D. |
| Russell, Gordon D. | 46-576 | M.Sc. |
| Russell, John | 27-010 | Ph.D. |
| Russell, John | 18-506 | M.Sc. |
| Russell, John K. | 34-013 | Ph.D. |
| Russell, Mary G. | 27-501 | M.S.A. |
| Russell, Stewart H. | 48-036 | Ph.D. |
| Russell, William J. | 51-623 | M.Sc. |
| Rusted, Ian F. | 49-619 | M.Sc. |
| Rutherford, Beth F. | 55-072 | Ph.D. |
| Rutman, Robin L. | 27-539 | M.A. |
| Ruyter, Sally A. | 48-544 | M.Sc. |
| Ryan, Charles C. | 14-516 | M.Sc. |
| Ryan, Michael T. | 55-032 | Ph.D. |
| Rymes, Thomas K. | 56-589 | M.A. |
| Sabean, Allan T. | 52-585 | M.Sc. |
| Sabin, Israel M. | 46-577 | M.Sc. |
| Sacks, Benjamin | 27-540 | M.A. |
| Sacks, William | 54-064 | Ph.D. |
| Sackston, Waldemar E. | 40-523 | M.Sc. |
| Sadler, Wilfrid | 17-507 | M.Sc. |

| AUTHOR | THESIS NUMBER | DEGREE |
|---|---|---|
| Saffran, Judith | 48-037 | Ph.D. |
| Saffran, Murray | 49-036 | Ph.D. |
| Saffran, Murray | 46-578 | M.Sc. |
| Sagar, Richard B. | 59-535 | M.Sc. |
| Saint-Martin, Fernande | 52-555 | M.A. |
| Sainte-Marie, Dorothee L. | 44-510 | M.Sc. |
| Sair, Louis | 37-021 | Ph.D. |
| Sakellariou, Theodore | 51-506 | M.Eng. |
| Sakellaropoulos, Michael | 50-577 | M.A. |
| Saleh, Samir | 55-511 | LL.M. |
| Salisbury, Herbert F. | 39-520 | M.Sc. |
| Sallans, Henry R. | 34-014 | Ph.D. |
| Salman, Mehmet T. | 44-500 | M.Eng. |
| Salmoiraghi, Gian C. | 59-068 | Ph.D. |
| Salt, Alexander E. | 08-505 | M.A. |
| Samborski, Daniel J. | 55-033 | Ph.D. |
| Sampson, Hubert | 54-030 | Ph.D. |
| Samson, Hugh R. | 59-596 | M.Sc. |
| Samuels, Peter B. | 52-586 | M.Sc. |
| Sander, Hans G.F. | 39-024 | Ph.D. |
| Sanders, Herbert L. | 37-022 | Ph.D. |
| Sanders, Herbert L. | 35-516 | M.Sc. |
| Sanderson, Edwin S. | 53-073 | Ph.D. |
| Sangree, Anne C. | 53-605 | M.Sc. |
| Sankey, Charles A. | 30-013 | Ph.D. |
| Sankey, Charles A. | 28-523 | M.Sc. |
| Santry, Dallas C. | 58-041 | Ph.D. |
| Sanyal, Amiya K. | 53-074 | Ph.D. |
| Sass, Frederick W. | 54-500 | S.T.M. |
| Sastry, Podila-Brahmayya | 56-064 | Ph.D. |
| Sater, Geoffrey S. | 58-529 | M.Sc. |
| Saul, Bernard B. | 22-520 | M.Sc. |
| Saunders, James E. | 22-521 | M.Sc. |
| Saunders, Leslie G. | 21-514 | M.Sc. |
| Saunders, Thomas B. | 48-617 | M.A. |
| Saunderson, Hugh H. | 32-015 | Ph.D. |
| Savage, Mae L. | 30-544 | M.A. |
| Savage, Marion C. | 45-537 | M.Sc. |
| Savage, Palmer E. | 34-505 | M.Eng. |
| Savard, Kenneth F.G. | 42-530 | M.Sc. |
| Savile, Douglas B. | 34-543 | M.Sc. |
| Sawyer, William R. | 31-013 | Ph.D. |
| Sayeed, Kkalid B. | 56-065 | Ph.D. |
| Scarrow, James A. | 33-528 | M.Sc. |
| Scarrow, James A. | 34-015 | Ph.D. |
| Schacher, Josephine | 37-539 | M.Sc. |
| Schachter, Melville | 42-531 | M.Sc. |
| Schachter, Ruth | 46-535 | M.Sc. |



| AUTHOR | THESIS NUMBER | DEGREE |
|---|---|---|
| Schad, Gerhard | 55-034 | Ph.D. |
| Schad, Gerhard A. | 52-587 | M.Sc. |
| Schafheitlin, Anna | 13-509 | M.A. |
| Schalin, Edmund | 51-056 | Ph.D. |
| Schally, Andrew V. | 57-030 | Ph.D. |
| Schaus, Orland O. | 54-031 | Ph.D. |
| Schaus, Orland O. | 52-510 | M.Eng. |
| Schavo, Anton F. | 58-042 | Ph.D. |
| Scheier, Ivan H. | 51-641 | M.A. |
| Scheier, Ivan H. | 53-075 | Ph.D. |
| Schenker, Victor | 44-021 | Ph.D. |
| Schieck, Robert F. | 59-069 | Ph.D. |
| Schiessler, Robert Walter | 41-048 | M.Sc. |
| Schiff, Harry | 50-632 | M.Sc. |
| Schiff, Harry | 53-035 | Ph.D. |
| Schiffers, Tania | 42-042 | M.A. |
| Schiffrin, Milton Julius | 41-508 | Ph.D. |
| Schiller, Carl | 52-541 | M.Sc. |
| Schindler, Norman R. | 33-529 | M.Sc. |
| Schindler, Norman R. | 34-016 | Ph.D. |
| Schippel, Walter H. | 36-506 | M.Eng. |
| Schleien, Donna S. | 28-552 | M.A. |
| Schlemm, Leonard G.W. | 39-068 | M.Sc. |
| Schmidt, Richard C. | 56-066 | Ph.D. |
| Schmidt, Richard C. | 55-539 | M.Sc. |
| Schmidt, Stephen C. | 58-043 | Ph.D. |
| Schneider, William George | 41-015 | Ph.D. |
| Schnitzer, Morris | 55-035 | Ph.D. |
| Schnitzer, Morris | 52-588 | M.Sc. |
| Schnore, Morris M. | 57-077 | Ph.D. |
| Schoenauer, Norbert | 59-501 | M.Arch. |
| Scholefield, Peter G. | 49-037 | Ph.D. |
| Schonbaum, Eduard | 55-036 | Ph.D. |
| Schrage, Samuel | 51-030 | Ph.D. |
| Schucher, Reuben | 54-032 | Ph.D. |
| Schurman, David C. | 26-502 | M.S.A. |
| Schwab, Jean G. | 32-546 | M.A. |
| Schwartz, Harry | 39-502 | Ph.D. |
| Schwartz, Solomon | 51-624 | M.Sc. |
| Schwartzman, Alex E. | 52-556 | M.A. |
| Scobie, Thomas K. | 52-589 | M.Sc. |
| Scoggan, Homer J. | 35-517 | M.Sc. |
| Scoggan, Homer J. | 42-023 | Ph.D. |
| Scotcher, Charles W.D. | 39-045 | M.A. |
| Scott, Arthur A. | 13-520 | M.Sc. |
| Scott, Arthur F. | 14-517 | M.Sc. |
| Scott, David M. | 49-055 | Ph.D. |
| Scott, David M. | 47-525 | M.Sc. |

| AUTHOR | THESIS NUMBER | DEGREE |
|---|---|---|
| Scott, David P. | 49-546 | M.Sc. |
| Scott, Donald Burton | 40-021 | Ph.D. |
| Scott, Gordon A. | 24-528 | M.Sc. |
| Scott, Joseph M. | 14-518 | M.Sc. |
| Scott, Mary E. | 28-566 | M.A. |
| Scott, Peter D. | 55-037 | Ph.D. |
| Scott, Robert I. | 56-032 | Ph.D. |
| Scott, Thomas H. | 54-065 | Ph.D. |
| Screaton, Rose M. | 56-033 | Ph.D. |
| Sebor, Milos-Marie | 55-638 | M.A. |
| Seeman, Philip | 56-601 | M.Sc. |
| Segal, Benny | 56-602 | M.Sc. |
| Segal, Louis | 52-590 | M.Sc. |
| Segal, Mark | 57-594 | M.Sc. |
| Segall, Gordon H. | 46-032 | Ph.D. |
| Seguin, Maurice J. | 56-510 | M.Eng. |
| Seidel, Judith | 39-508 | M.A. |
| Seidman, Ruth | 53-036 | Ph.D. |
| Sein, Maung T. | 59-504 | M.Eng. |
| Self, George M. | 38-554 | M.A. |
| Sellen, John M. | 51-625 | M.Sc. |
| Sells, Bruce H. | 58-044 | Ph.D. |
| Selmser, Calbert | 39-069 | M.Sc. |
| Senior, Hereward | 59-082 | Ph.D. |
| Senior, Hereward | 51-575 | M.A. |
| Sergeyeva, Maria A. | 38-549 | M.Sc. |
| Serrano, Pedro A. | 57-595 | M.Sc. |
| Seto, Kin | 40-036 | M.Eng. |
| Seyer, William F. | 20-001 | Ph.D. |
| Seyerd, Henry | 46-547 | M.A. |
| Shah, Jessie A. | 59-597 | M.Sc. |
| Shane, Gerald | 40-022 | Ph.D. |
| Shane, Gerald | 38-521 | M.Sc. |
| Shane, Gerald S. | 42-043 | M.A. |
| Shanks, Laura E. | 59-562 | M.A. |
| Shanly, Eleanor | 14-519 | M.Sc. |
| Shapiro, Clarence H. | 33-505 | M.Eng. |
| Shapiro, Stanley K. | 45-538 | M.Sc. |
| Sharp, Robert T. | 50-556 | M.Sc. |
| Sharp, Robert T. | 53-037 | Ph.D. |
| Sharples, Alice | 25-541 | M.A. |
| Sharpless, Seth K. | 54-066 | Ph.D. |
| Sharratt, Harold J. | 55-578 | M.Eng. |
| Shaw, Alan C. | 55-073 | Ph.D. |
| Shaw, Albert N. | 10-521 | M.Sc. |
| Shaw, Geoffrey T. | 36-012 | Ph.D. |
| Shaw, Geoffrey T. | 33-530 | M.Sc. |
| Shaw, George | 34-516 | M.Sc. |



| AUTHOR | THESIS NUMBER | DEGREE |
|---|---|---|
| Shaw, Gerald A. | 56-562 | M.Eng. |
| Shaw, Gerald E. | 25-549 | M.Sc. |
| Shaw, Hampden C. | 35-539 | M.Sc. |
| Shaw, John Leslie Dickins | 40-505 | Ph.D. |
| Shaw, Michael | 49-038 | Ph.D. |
| Shaw, Michael | 47-569 | M.Sc. |
| Shaw, Thomas P. | 22-522 | M.Sc. |
| Shaw, Walter M. | 52-591 | M.Sc. |
| Shearer, George W. | 08-513 | M.Sc. |
| Shearing, Helen A. | 15-505 | M.A. |
| Shearman, George E. | 53-619 | M.A. |
| Shecter, Una | 39-509 | M.A. |
| Sheffield, Edward Fletche | 40-049 | M.A. |
| Sheffy, Menachem | 57-563 | LL.M. |
| Sheffy, Pearl P. | 58-590 | M.A. |
| Sheldon, Ernest. W. | 05-005 | M.A. |
| Shellabear, William H. | 59-598 | M.Sc. |
| Sheps, Louis J. | 34-025 | Ph.D. |
| Sherbeck, Leander A. | 51-057 | Ph.D. |
| Shewell, Guy E. | 37-540 | M.Sc. |
| Shields, Ross C. | 55-540 | M.Sc. |
| Shipley, John H. | 38-016 | Ph.D. |
| Shipley, William C. | 50-664 | M.A. |
| Shkarofsky, Issie | 57-031 | Ph.D. |
| Shkarofsky, Issie | 53-606 | M.Sc. |
| Shklar, Judith | 50-665 | M.A. |
| Shlakman, Vera | 31-542 | M.A. |
| Shotwell, John S. | 26-559 | M.Sc. |
| Shtern, I.H. | 57-596 | M.Sc. |
| Shugar, David | 40-023 | Ph.D. |
| Shuh, John Edward | 42-065 | M.Sc. |
| Shulman, R. | 51-546 | M.Sc. |
| Shyluk, Walter P. | 55-074 | Ph.D. |
| Sibalis, Jack | 51-547 | M.Sc. |
| Siddall, Margaret I. | 51-548 | M.Sc. |
| Siddigi, Mazharuddin | 54-621 | M.A. |
| Sievwright, Eric C. | 51-642 | M.A. |
| Silver, Edith | 24-545 | M.A. |
| Silver, Helen | 33-558 | M.A. |
| Silver, Ralph C. | 29-519 | M.Sc. |
| Silverman, Beatrice I. | 28-553 | M.A. |
| Simard-Duquesne, N. | 54-603 | M.Sc. |
| Simard, J. | 54-531 | M.Sc. |
| Simard, Lionel R. | 34-517 | M.Sc. |
| Simard, Thomas | 44-511 | M.Sc. |
| Simard, Thomas | 48-038 | Ph.D. |
| Siminovitch, David | 37-541 | M.Sc. |
| Siminovitch, David | 39-025 | Ph.D. |

| AUTHOR | THESIS NUMBER | DEGREE |
|---|---|---|
| Siminovitch, Helen E. | 47-570 | M.Sc. |
| Siminovitch, Louis | 44-022 | Ph.D. |
| Simon, Beatrice V. | 50-666 | M.A. |
| Simpson, David H. | 52-030 | Ph.D. |
| Sims, Richard P. | 50-042 | Ph.D. |
| Sims, Walter A. | 59-599 | M.Sc. |
| Sinclair, George W. | 45-539 | M.Sc. |
| Sinclair, George W. | 48-039 | Ph.D. |
| Sinclair, Martin H. | 54-555 | M.A. |
| Singer, Bertha | 52-061 | Ph.D. |
| Singer, Bertha | 49-620 | M.Sc. |
| Singer, David P. | 54-622 | M.A. |
| Singh, Tej B. | 57-537 | M.Sc. |
| Sinha, Sharda P. | 59-536 | M.Sc. |
| Sinnott, Joseph C. | 58-530 | M.Sc. |
| Sirianni, Aurele F. | 46-033 | Ph.D. |
| Sirken, Irving A. | 43-515 | M.A. |
| Sivertz, Christian | 26-004 | Ph.D. |
| Sivertz, Christian | 24-529 | M.Sc. |
| Sivertz, Victorian | 26-005 | Ph.D. |
| Skarsgard, Harvey M. | 55-075 | Ph.D. |
| Skazin, Lev | 30-511 | M.Sc. |
| Skey, Arthur James | 39-503 | Ph.D. |
| Skinner, James M. | 59-620 | M.A. |
| Skinner, Ralph | 56-067 | Ph.D. |
| Skinner, Ralph | 49-621 | M.Sc. |
| Skoll, Selma D. | 56-623 | M.A. |
| Skoryna, Stanley C. | 50-633 | M.Sc. |
| Skynner, H.J. | 56-552 | S.T.M. |
| Slaght, William H. | 51-549 | M.Sc. |
| Slater, Douglas T. | 51-550 | M.Sc. |
| Slipp, Robert M. | 57-032 | Ph.D. |
| Slipp, Robert M. | 52-542 | M.Sc. |
| Sloan, Emmett P. | 49-643 | M.A. |
| Sloan, Norman | 49-622 | M.Sc. |
| Sloat, Annie P. | 46-548 | M.A. |
| Smart, Celina | 57-033 | Ph.D. |
| Smart, George N. Russell | 45-020 | Ph.D. |
| Smillie, Eleanor A. | 10-510 | M.A. |
| Smith, Alan R. | 51-031 | Ph.D. |
| Smith, Alan R. | 48-545 | M.Sc. |
| Smith, Alfred A. | 50-043 | Ph.D. |
| Smith, Arthur J. | 26-554 | M.A. |
| Smith, Charles J. | 54-067 | Ph.D. |
| Smith, Charles J. | 51-643 | M.A. |
| Smith, David D. | 57-034 | Ph.D. |
| Smith, David I. | 59-537 | M.Sc. |
| Smith, David L. | 50-593 | M.Eng. |



| AUTHOR | THESIS NUMBER | DEGREE |
|---|---|---|
| Smith, Donald M. | 56-034 | Ph.D. |
| Smith, Donald S. | 59-634 | M.Sc. |
| Smith, Edward R. | 58-577 | M.Sc. |
| Smith, Ella L. | 08-506 | M.A. |
| Smith, Esther M. | 06-006 | M.A. |
| Smith, Frederick M. | 24-530 | M.Sc. |
| Smith, George Ransom | 39-504 | Ph.D. |
| Smith, Gladys L. | 30-545 | M.A. |
| Smith, Greig B. | 31-550 | M.Com. |
| Smith, Henry I. | 26-555 | M.A. |
| Smith, Irving H. | 55-560 | M.A. |
| Smith, Lawrence L. | 28-554 | M.A. |
| Smith, Letha A. | 21-515 | M.Sc. |
| Smith, Lyman A. | 56-068 | Ph.D. |
| Smith, Melvin J. | 45-540 | M.Sc. |
| Smith, Norman E. | 52-031 | Ph.D. |
| Smith, Norman E. | 49-644 | M.A. |
| Smith, Philip D. | 36-518 | M.Sc. |
| Smith, Robert C. | 56-538 | M.Sc. |
| Smith, Robert E. | 57-538 | M.Sc. |
| Smith, Samuel I. | 55-639 | M.A. |
| Smith, Stanley Alfred | 42-044 | M.A. |
| Smith, Stanley G. | 36-517 | M.Sc. |
| Smith, Stanley G. | 38-017 | Ph.D. |
| Smith, Thomas H. | 59-538 | M.Sc. |
| Smith, Walter M. | 38-018 | Ph.D. |
| Smyth, Desmond H. | 28-555 | M.A. |
| Snelgrove, Alfred K. | 28-524 | M.Sc. |
| Snell, Arthur H. | 33-019 | Ph.D. |
| Snell, Arthur H. | 31-558 | M.Sc. |
| Snijman, Johan J. | 24-551 | M.Sc. |
| Snyder, John K. | 32-562 | M.A. |
| Snyder, John L. | 55-076 | Ph.D. |
| Sobel, Harry | 46-014 | Ph.D. |
| Sobering, Simon E. | 57-078 | Ph.D. |
| Sodhi, Harbhajan S. | 58-578 | M.Sc. |
| Sofin, Rosalie | 47-582 | M.A. |
| Soley, Russell Clyne | 40-024 | Ph.D. |
| Solin, Cecil D. | 38-542 | M.A. |
| Solomon, David N. | 42-045 | M.A. |
| Solomon, Ernest | 34-017 | Ph.D. |
| Solomon, Samuel | 51-551 | M.Sc. |
| Solomon, Samuel | 53-076 | Ph.D. |
| Soper, Robert J. | 59-070 | Ph.D. |
| Sosniak, J. | 58-531 | M.Sc. |
| Sourkes, Theodore L. | 46-579 | M.Sc. |
| Sowden, Frederick J. | 44-023 | Ph.D. |
| Spanagel, Edgar W. | 33-020 | Ph.D. |

| AUTHOR | THESIS NUMBER | DEGREE |
|---|---|---|
| Sparrow, Arnold H. | 41-016 | Ph.D. |
| Spat, Attilio G. | 59-539 | M.Sc. |
| Speakman, Thomas J. | 48-546 | M.Sc. |
| Spearman, Donald | 43-528 | M.A. |
| Spector, Leo L. | 33-531 | M.Sc. |
| Speers, Robert | 57-079 | Ph.D. |
| Speers, Robert | 56-539 | M.Sc. |
| Spence, Kenneth W. | 30-546 | M.A. |
| Spencer, Roy A. | 15-514 | M.Sc. |
| Spentzos, George C. | 53-620 | M.A. |
| Speyer, Judith | 56-549 | M.A. |
| Spier, Jane D. | 22-523 | M.Sc. |
| Spier, Jane D. | 35-033 | Ph.D. |
| Spivack, John D. | 47-036 | Ph.D. |
| Spratt, Gordon W. | 56-511 | M.Eng. |
| Springbett, Bruce M. | 55-077 | Ph.D. |
| Sproule, Gordon St. G. | 09-517 | M.Sc. |
| Sproule, Hugh D. | 58-591 | M.A. |
| Sproule, William K. | 37-514 | M.Sc. |
| Spurrell, Althea C. | 46-590 | M.A. |
| Squires, Henry D. | 24-531 | M.Sc. |
| Squires, Hubert J. | 56-540 | M.Sc. |
| Srinivasan, Malur R. | 54-068 | Ph.D. |
| Srinivasan, Malur R. | 52-566 | M.Eng. |
| Srinivasan, Swamy A. | 57-080 | Ph.D. |
| Stabler, Ernest | 43-516 | M.A. |
| Stachenko, Janine L-M. | 58-045 | Ph.D. |
| Stachenko, Janine L-M. | 56-603 | M.Sc. |
| Stachiewicz, Bogdan R. | 53-565 | M.Eng. |
| Stachiewicz, Evva T. | 54-532 | M.Sc. |
| Stachiewicz, J.W. | 50-594 | M.Eng. |
| Stachiw, Dennis L. | 57-081 | Ph.D. |
| Stager, Drucilla N. | 26-556 | M.A. |
| Stairs, Gordon R. | 58-532 | M.Sc. |
| Stalker, Archibald | 13-510 | M.A. |
| Stalker, Archibald M. | 50-020 | Ph.D. |
| Stalker, Archibald M. | 48-547 | M.Sc. |
| Stanislawski, Marc | 59-600 | M.Sc. |
| Stanley, Thomas D. | 33-506 | M.Eng. |
| Stansfield, Ellen E. | 31-543 | M.A. |
| Stansfield, John | 29-013 | Ph.D. |
| Stansfield, John | 12-518 | M.Sc. |
| Starr, Harry | 47-526 | M.Sc. |
| Starrock, Murray G. | 29-518 | M.Sc. |
| Stavrakis, George V. | 30-552 | M.Sc. |
| Steacie, Edgar W. | 26-006 | Ph.D. |
| Steacie, Edgar W. | 24-532 | M.Sc. |
| Steacy, Frederick W. | 13-511 | M.A. |



| AUTHOR | THESIS NUMBER | DEGREE |
|---|---|---|
| Steed, Joseph A. | 18-502 | M.A. |
| Steele, Donald H. | 56-541 | M.Sc. |
| Steeves, Allison E. | 37-515 | M.Sc. |
| Steeves, Lewis R. | 33-575 | M.A. |
| Steeves, William H. | 36-013 | Ph.D. |
| Steigmann, Axel H. | 56-550 | M.A. |
| Stenason, Walter | 54-629 | M.Com. |
| Stennett, Richard G. | 56-035 | Ph.D. |
| Stephens-Newsham, Lloyd | 48-040 | Ph.D. |
| Stephens, Henry N. | 23-006 | Ph.D. |
| Steppler, Howard A. | 55-038 | Ph.D. |
| Steppler, Howard A. | 48-548 | M.Sc. |
| Stern, Herbert | 45-012 | Ph.D. |
| Stern, Herbert | 42-066 | M.Sc. |
| Stern, Muriel H. | 57-082 | Ph.D. |
| Stern, Muriel H. | 54-604 | M.Sc. |
| Stevens, Bernard A. | 55-039 | Ph.D. |
| Stevens, Bernard A. | 52-592 | M.Sc. |
| Stevens, Catherine F. | 50-044 | Ph.D. |
| Stevens, Robert L. | 36-550 | M.Sc. |
| Stevens, Thelma V. | 43-509 | M.Sc. |
| Stevens, Valeria Dean | 40-512 | M.A. |
| Stevenson, Ira M. | 54-033 | Ph.D. |
| Stevenson, Ira M. | 51-552 | M.Sc. |
| Stevenson, James A. | 38-555 | M.A. |
| Stevenson, Stanley W. | 54-623 | M.A. |
| Stewart, Gordon Stafford | 40-048 | M.Sc. |
| Stewart, Kenneth F. | 26-526 | M.Sc. |
| Stewart, Lever F. | 56-604 | M.Sc. |
| Stewart, Lyall S. | 50-578 | M.A. |
| Stewart, Mary | 46-591 | M.A. |
| Stewart, Mary I. | 49-580 | M.A. |
| Stewart, Ronald D. | 48-011 | Ph.D. |
| Stewart, William W. | 33-021 | Ph.D. |
| Stewart, William W. | 31-559 | M.Sc. |
| Stidwell, William Francis | 40-516 | M.Eng. |
| Stinson, David A. | 51-553 | M.Sc. |
| Stinton, Arthur W. | 45-541 | M.Sc. |
| Stobart, Walter I. | 32-505 | M.Eng. |
| Stobbe, Peter C. | 50-021 | Ph.D. |
| Stobbe, Peter C. | 34-518 | M.Sc. |
| Stock, John J. | 51-058 | Ph.D. |
| Stock, John J. | 49-547 | M.Sc. |
| Stock, Marie I. | 37-532 | M.A. |
| Stocken, Charles G. | 50-557 | M.Sc. |
| Stollmeyer, John F. | 47-571 | M.Sc. |
| Stone, Fred V. | 33-559 | M.A. |
| Stone, Samuel A. | 59-505 | M.Eng. |

| AUTHOR | THESIS NUMBER | DEGREE |
|---|---|---|
| Storey, Winnifred F. | 49-548 | M.Sc. |
| Stothart, John G. | 36-519 | M.Sc. |
| Stovel, Henry V. | 33-571 | M.Sc. |
| Stovel, Henry V. | 38-019 | Ph.D. |
| Stovel, John Archibald | 41-522 | M.A. |
| Strachan, Alison A. | 54-605 | M.Sc. |
| Strangways, Henry F. | 08-514 | M.Sc. |
| Stranks, Donald W. | 48-597 | M.Sc. |
| Stratford, Joseph G. | 51-554 | M.Sc. |
| Strauss, Clara | 46-592 | M.A. |
| Strean, Lyon P. | 42-506 | Ph.D. |
| Strean, Lyon P. | 40-049 | M.Sc. |
| Streitfield, Murray M. | 48-598 | M.Sc. |
| Stuart, Allan P. | 42-024 | Ph.D. |
| Stuart, James R. | 57-035 | Ph.D. |
| Stultz, Harold T. | 46-580 | M.Sc. |
| Sturrock, Murray G. | 30-014 | Ph.D. |
| Styles, Arthur D. | 35-535 | M.A. |
| Subroto | 56-551 | M.A. |
| Sukava, Armas J. | 55-040 | Ph.D. |
| Sullivan, Calvin R. | 57-036 | Ph.D. |
| Sullivan, Charles T. | 10-522 | M.Sc. |
| Sullivan, Harry M. | 54-533 | M.Sc. |
| Sullivan, Lorne J. | 53-566 | M.Eng. |
| Sullivan, Norah E. | 31-544 | M.A. |
| Summers, William F. | 57-037 | Ph.D. |
| Summers, William F. | 49-623 | M.Sc. |
| Surwillo, Walter W. | 55-041 | Ph.D. |
| Sussman, David | 58-046 | Ph.D. |
| Sussman, David | 54-624 | M.A. |
| Sussman, Edmond | 54-630 | M.Com. |
| Sutherland, Angus J. | 38-522 | M.Sc. |
| Sutherland, Brian P. | 26-527 | M.Sc. |
| Sutherland, Brian P. | 28-008 | Ph.D. |
| Sutherland, Charlotte A. | 57-539 | M.Sc. |
| Sutherland, Francis C. | 15-506 | M.A. |
| Sutherland, George F. | 32-524 | M.Sc. |
| Sutherland, Hugh S. | 31-008 | Ph.D. |
| Sutherland, Hugh S. | 29-520 | M.Sc. |
| Sutherland, John W. | 32-016 | Ph.D. |
| Sutherland, Ronald | 55-561 | M.A. |
| Sved, Stephen | 58-047 | Ph.D. |
| Swales, William E. | 35-025 | Ph.D. |
| Swan, Eric P. | 57-038 | Ph.D. |
| Swan, John H. | 54-568 | LL.M. |
| Swartz, Joseph N. | 37-023 | Ph.D. |
| Sweatman, Gordon K. | 57-039 | Ph.D. |
| Sweny, George W. | 25-528 | M.Sc. |



| AUTHOR | THESIS NUMBER | DEGREE |
|---|---|---|
| Sybulski, Stella | 59-071 | Ph.D. |
| Sybulski, Stella | 56-605 | M.Sc. |
| Sydiaha, Daniel | 59-048 | Ph.D. |
| Sylvester, Elizabeth M. | 46-015 | Ph.D. |
| Syme, Andrew M. | 51-555 | M.Sc. |
| Symons, Jennie L. | 25-006 | Ph.D. |
| Symons, Jennie L. | 21-516 | M.Sc. |
| Szablowski, Julie A. | 58-548 | M.A. |
| Szabo, Alexander | 55-621 | M.Sc. |
| Taggart, William P. | 52-557 | M.A. |
| Tagiuri, Renato | 46-536 | M.Sc. |
| Tai, Yue-Shing | 51-590 | M.Eng. |
| Talpis, Clarence | 30-547 | M.A. |
| Talvenheimo, Gerhardt | 48-599 | M.Sc. |
| Tanner, Charles E. | 57-083 | Ph.D. |
| Tanner, Charles E. | 56-542 | M.Sc. |
| Tanner, Lea E. | 30-548 | M.A. |
| Tansey, Charlotte H. | 49-618 | M.A. |
| Tao, Chia-hwa | 59-506 | M.Eng. |
| Tapp, James S. | 33-022 | Ph.D. |
| Tapp, James S. | 31-567 | M.A. |
| Tarlov, Isadore M. | 32-558 | M.Sc. |
| Tarr, Hugh I. | 31-009 | Ph.D. |
| Tasker, Clinton W. | 47-037 | Ph.D. |
| Tate, Farr A. | 47-572 | M.Sc. |
| Tatlock, John F. | 51-507 | M.Eng. |
| Taussig, Andrew | 55-078 | Ph.D. |
| Taylor, Allen L. | 59-601 | M.Sc. |
| Taylor, Bertram W. | 30-512 | M.Sc. |
| Taylor, Frederick C. | 55-042 | Ph.D. |
| Taylor, Frederick C. | 51-556 | M.Sc. |
| Taylor, George | 59-558 | M.Eng. |
| Taylor, Gordon R. | 33-560 | M.A. |
| Taylor, Harland W. | 51-644 | M.A. |
| Taylor, Kenneth A. | 29-014 | Ph.D. |
| Taylor, Lester J. | 52-593 | M.Sc. |
| Taylor, Margaret E. | 42-046 | M.A. |
| Taylor, Robert B. | 55-541 | M.Sc. |
| Taylor, William Dixon | 40-025 | Ph.D. |
| Taylor, William L. | 59-635 | M.Sc. |
| Teitlebaum, Albert D. | 59-602 | M.Sc. |
| Telford, William M. | 49-056 | Ph.D. |
| Telford, William M. | 41-536 | M.Sc. |
| Tenenhouse, Alan | 59-072 | Ph.D. |
| Tennant, Alan D. | 55-043 | Ph.D. |
| Tennant, Alan D. | 49-549 | M.Sc. |
| Terroux, Fernand R. | 26-528 | M.Sc. |
| Tetrault, Claude Moncel | 40-032 | M.A. |

| AUTHOR | THESIS NUMBER | DEGREE |
|---|---|---|
| Thanos, Costas A. | 59-563 | M.A. |
| Thatcher, Frederick S. | 35-540 | M.Sc. |
| Thatcher, Frederick S. | 39-026 | Ph.D. |
| Thomas, George M. | 58-049 | Ph.D. |
| Thomas, George M. | 56-606 | M.Sc. |
| Thomas, Gordon | 51-032 | Ph.D. |
| Thomas, James B. | 54-069 | Ph.D. |
| Thomas, James B. | 52-543 | M.Sc. |
| Thomas, Telfer L. | 57-040 | Ph.D. |
| Thomas, William | 33-576 | M.A. |
| Thomas, William F. | 31-516 | M.Sc. |
| Thompson, Allan L. | 43-013 | Ph.D. |
| Thompson, Helen Muriel | 39-510 | M.A. |
| Thompson, Hugh R. | 54-070 | Ph.D. |
| Thompson, Lloyd M. | 51-059 | Ph.D. |
| Thompson, Norman S. | 54-071 | Ph.D. |
| Thompson, Richard D. | 59-571 | M.Eng. |
| Thompson, Robert R. | 32-026 | Ph.D. |
| Thompson, Robert R. | 29-521 | M.Sc. |
| Thompson, Winifred | 35-536 | M.A. |
| Thomson, Allan | 46-593 | M.A. |
| Thomson, Herbert F. | 13-512 | M.A. |
| Thomson, Hugh M. | 57-084 | Ph.D. |
| Thomson, Hugh M. | 51-557 | M.Sc. |
| Thomson, John A. | 57-597 | M.Sc. |
| Thomson, Walter W. | 25-007 | Ph.D. |
| Thomson, Walter W. | 23-518 | M.Sc. |
| Thorn, George D. | 47-038 | Ph.D. |
| Thorne, Kenrick H. | 56-607 | M.Sc. |
| Thorne, Oliver | 12-506 | M.A. |
| Thornton, Robert L. | 33-023 | Ph.D. |
| Thorpe, Benjamin J. | 32-547 | M.A. |
| Thorson, Erling | 40-050 | M.Sc. |
| Thurston, Arthur M. | 48-600 | M.Sc. |
| Tidmarsh, Clarence J. | 22-528 | M.A. |
| Tiffin, Brian F. | 53-544 | M.Sc. |
| Tilley, Donald E. | 51-060 | Ph.D. |
| Tink, Roland R. | 53-077 | Ph.D. |
| Tinney, Benjamin F. | 24-505 | M.S.A. |
| Tiphane, Marcel | 47-573 | M.Sc. |
| Toby, Charlotte G. | 46-034 | Ph.D. |
| Toby, Sidney | 55-079 | Ph.D. |
| Toepper, Anton | 55-512 | LL.M. |
| Tombs, Laurence C. | 26-557 | M.A. |
| Tomecko, Joseph Wesely | 40-506 | Ph.D. |
| Tomiuk, Daniel | 52-594 | M.Sc. |
| Tomkins, George S. | 52-558 | M.A. |
| Tomlinson, George H. | 35-026 | Ph.D. |



| AUTHOR | THESIS NUMBER | DEGREE |
|---|---|---|
| Tomlinson, Richard H. | 48-012 | Ph.D. |
| Tonks, David E. | 49-039 | Ph.D. |
| Toole, Francis J. | 29-015 | Ph.D. |
| Toole, Francis J. | 26-529 | M.Sc. |
| Toovey, Edna W. | 51-626 | M.Sc. |
| Topp, Allan C. | 41-017 | Ph.D. |
| Toreson, Wilfred E. | 50-045 | Ph.D. |
| Toreson, Wilfred E. | 48-601 | M.Sc. |
| Tougas, Gerard R. | 47-583 | M.A. |
| Tough, David I. | 32-548 | M.A. |
| Tousaw, Albert A. | 20-507 | M.Sc. |
| Tower, Donald B. | 51-033 | Ph.D. |
| Tower, Donald B. | 48-549 | M.Sc. |
| Towers, George H. | 51-558 | M.Sc. |
| Townsend, Charles T. | 26-530 | M.Sc. |
| Townsend, David L. | 53-567 | M.Eng. |
| Townsend, Edith E. | 59-083 | Ph.D. |
| Townsend, Edith E. | 56-608 | M.Sc. |
| Townsend, Eleanor H. | 29-548 | M.A. |
| Trasler, Daphne G. | 58-050 | Ph.D. |
| Trasler, Daphne G. | 54-534 | M.Sc. |
| Traver, Lillie A. | 29-549 | M.A. |
| Traversy, Eric E. | 15-515 | M.Sc. |
| Treharne, Bryceson | 30-016 | Mus.D. |
| Tremblay, Joseph A. | 11-503 | M.A. |
| Tremblay, Mousseau | 56-069 | Ph.D. |
| Tremblay, Mousseau | 51-559 | M.Sc. |
| Trenholm, Laurence Stuart | 39-070 | M.Sc. |
| Trevelyan, Benjamin J. | 51-034 | Ph.D. |
| Trick, Gordon S. | 52-032 | Ph.D. |
| Trimingham, James H. | 20-508 | M.Sc. |
| Trister, Saul M. | 34-018 | Ph.D. |
| Troop, George R. | 22-529 | M.A. |
| Troop, William H. | 29-550 | M.A. |
| Trossman, Walter A. | 49-550 | M.Sc. |
| Trost, Walter R. | 47-019 | Ph.D. |
| Trotter, Wallace S. | 32-552 | M.Com. |
| Trottier, Bernard | 44-523 | M.Sc. |
| Trudeau, Guy J. | 47-505 | M.Eng. |
| Trueman, James C. | 24-533 | M.Sc. |
| Tuck, Norman G. | 47-020 | Ph.D. |
| Tucker, Henry J. | 55-579 | M.Eng. |
| Tuffy, Frank | 55-542 | M.Sc. |
| Tunis, Cyril J. | 56-543 | M.Sc. |
| Turnau, Edmund A. | 50-636 | M.Sc. |
| Turnbull, Dorothy K. | 51-627 | M.Sc. |
| Turner, Alice W. | 28-556 | M.A. |
| Turner, Robert C. | 51-035 | Ph.D. |

| AUTHOR | THESIS NUMBER | DEGREE |
|---|---|---|
| Turner, Robert C. | 49-624 | M.Sc. |
| Turner, Terry E. | 48-041 | Ph.D. |
| Tuttle, Harry G. | 31-545 | M.A. |
| Tweed, William J. | 53-509 | M.Eng. |
| Twidale, Charles R. | 57-085 | Ph.D. |
| Twinn, Cecil R. | 36-520 | M.Sc. |
| Tyler, Nancy P. | 52-595 | M.Sc. |
| Tyndale, Orville S. | 09-506 | M.A. |
| Udeaja, Philip E. | 58-533 | M.Sc. |
| Udow, Alfred Bernard | 40-524 | M.Sc. |
| Uete, Tetsuo | 59-540 | M.Sc. |
| Ulrichsen, Barbara A. | 35-537 | M.A. |
| Unni, Ayalur K. | 58-051 | Ph.D. |
| Urbain, Joseph V. | 39-046 | M.A. |
| Uren, Philip E. | 49-645 | M.A. |
| Usher, John L. | 49-057 | Ph.D. |
| Usher, John L. | 47-527 | M.Sc. |
| Vaisoussis, Constantine | 54-507 | LL.M. |
| Vallillee, Gerald A. | 53-555 | M.A. |
| Van Barneveld, Charles E. | 16-514 | M.Sc. |
| Van Buren, John M. | 50-637 | M.Sc. |
| Van Gelder, Nico M. | 59-073 | Ph.D. |
| Van Holsbeek, Henri M. | 48-571 | M.Com. |
| Van Horne, William F. | 48-550 | M.Sc. |
| Van Leight-Frank, Margit | 54-556 | M.A. |
| Van Steenbergen, Arie | 57-086 | Ph.D. |
| Van Straten, Sylvia F. | 50-022 | Ph.D. |
| Van Walsum, Ewout | 57-512 | M.Eng. |
| Van_Cleave, Allan B. | 35-027 | Ph.D. |
| Vanderwolf, Cornelius H. | 59-603 | M.Sc. |
| Vanstone, William E. | 58-052 | Ph.D. |
| Vanstone, William E. | 55-543 | M.Sc. |
| Vanterpool, Thomas C. | 25-529 | M.Sc. |
| Vardanis, Alexandre | 58-534 | M.Sc. |
| Varma, Maithili S. | 59-604 | M.Sc. |
| Varverikos, Emmanuel D. | 51-628 | M.Sc. |
| Vasilkioti, Nikolai | 32-506 | M.Eng. |
| Vaz, Edmund W. | 55-562 | M.A. |
| Veilleux, Brendan | 49-551 | M.Sc. |
| Velay, Clement C. | 57-087 | Ph.D. |
| Velay, Clement C. | 55-563 | M.A. |
| Venning, Eleanor M. | 33-032 | Ph.D. |
| Verbeke, Gentil J. | 59-053 | Ph.D. |
| Verdier, Pamela C. | 52-596 | M.Sc. |
| Verschingel, Roger H. | 55-044 | Ph.D. |
| Versteeg, Joseph | 52-062 | Ph.D. |
| Vessot, Charles U. | 22-524 | M.Sc. |
| Vessot, Robert F. | 57-041 | Ph.D. |



| AUTHOR | THESIS NUMBER | DEGREE |
|---|---|---|
| Vessot, Robert F. | 54-535 | M.Sc. |
| Vickery, Vernon R. | 57-540 | M.Sc. |
| Vincent, Donald L. | 53-038 | Ph.D. |
| Vincent, Irving C. | 08-507 | M.A. |
| Vineberg, Arthur M. | 33-033 | Ph.D. |
| Vineberg, Arthur M. | 28-525 | M.Sc. |
| Vineberg, Philip F. | 36-542 | M.A. |
| Vipond, William S. | 09-518 | M.Sc. |
| Viron, Silvio J. | 52-063 | Ph.D. |
| Vlasic, Ivan | 55-584 | LL.M. |
| Vogan, Eric L. | 52-033 | Ph.D. |
| Vogel, Robert | 59-074 | Ph.D. |
| Vogel, Robert | 54-625 | M.A. |
| Vollo, Nels B. | 59-541 | M.Sc. |
| Von Abo, Cecil V. | 22-002 | Ph.D. |
| Von Cardinal, Clive H. | 41-029 | M.A. |
| Von Hagen, Wallace M. | 59-505 | M.Eng. |
| Vosko, Seymour H. | 53-545 | M.Sc. |
| Voyvodic, Louis | 49-042 | Ph.D. |
| Vroom, Alan H. | 45-013 | Ph.D. |
| Vulpe, M. | 54-536 | M.Sc. |
| Wade, Margaret M. | 31-546 | M.A. |
| Wadge, Norman H. | 36-507 | M.Eng. |
| Wagner, Sydney | 50-046 | Ph.D. |
| Wagner, Sydney | 48-551 | M.Sc. |
| Wahl, William G. | 47-021 | Ph.D. |
| Wahl, William G. | 41-050 | M.Sc. |
| Waid, Ted H. | 57-042 | Ph.D. |
| Wake, Frank R. | 50-047 | Ph.D. |
| Waksberg, Helene | 55-564 | M.A. |
| Waldbauer, Louis J. | 23-007 | Ph.D. |
| Waldbauer, Louis J. | 22-525 | M.Sc. |
| Walford, Dorice C. | 58-553 | M.Arch. |
| Walke, Lacey | 58-579 | M.Sc. |
| Walker, Bruce E. | 54-072 | Ph.D. |
| Walker, Bruce E. | 52-597 | M.Sc. |
| Walker, Forestier | 37-024 | Ph.D. |
| Walker, Forestier | 35-518 | M.Sc. |
| Walker, George W. | 52-064 | Ph.D. |
| Walker, Jessie M. | 49-043 | Ph.D. |
| Walker, Laurence Richard | 39-505 | Ph.D. |
| Walker, Margaret G. | 35-549 | M.A. |
| Walker, Osman J. | 50-048 | Ph.D. |
| Walker, Osman J. | 20-002 | Ph.D. |
| Wallace, Alexander B. | 36-551 | M.Sc. |
| Wallace, Donald R. | 59-542 | M.Sc. |
| Wallace, George A. | 21-517 | M.Sc. |
| Wallace, Raphael H. | 46-581 | M.Sc. |

| AUTHOR | THESIS NUMBER | DEGREE |
|---|---|---|
| Wallace, Raphael H. | 48-013 | Ph.D. |
| Wallen, Victor R. | 54-034 | Ph.D. |
| Wallen, Victor R. | 49-552 | M.Sc. |
| Wallerstein, Harvey | 54-035 | Ph.D. |
| Wallerstein, Harvey | 50-638 | M.Sc. |
| Walmsley, Norma E. | 54-557 | M.A. |
| Walsh, George C. | 49-625 | M.Sc. |
| Walsh, John H. | 51-591 | M.Eng. |
| Walter, Albert J. | 26-531 | M.Sc. |
| Walter, Felix H. | 24-546 | M.A. |
| Walter, H.A. | 54-626 | M.A. |
| Walton, Robert F. | 52-610 | M.A. |
| Wang, Dalton T. | 57-043 | Ph.D. |
| Wang, Sheng-Nien | 42-025 | Ph.D. |
| Wanklyn, David I. | 52-065 | Ph.D. |
| Wanklyn, David I. | 51-560 | M.Sc. |
| Warldeworth, Eleanor S. | 31-547 | M.A. |
| Warren, F.G. Ross | 48-044 | Ph.D. |
| Warren, George L. | 53-607 | M.Sc. |
| Warren, Thomas E. | 26-532 | M.Sc. |
| Warshawski, Frances G. | 58-580 | M.Sc. |
| Wasson, Burton K. | 42-026 | Ph.D. |
| Waterhouse, John | 55-565 | M.A. |
| Waters, William R. | 54-537 | M.Sc. |
| Waterston, John R. | 59-506 | M.Eng. |
| Watson, Edmund E. | 26-533 | M.Sc. |
| Watson, Gordon A. | 50-667 | M.A. |
| Watson, Horace G. | 32-027 | Ph.D. |
| Watson, Horace G. | 27-520 | M.Sc. |
| Watson, Hugh A. | 49-626 | M.Sc. |
| Watson, William J. | 55-566 | M.A. |
| Watts, Aileen M. | 54-627 | M.A. |
| Watts, Humphrey Stanley | 40-525 | M.Sc. |
| Watts, Trevor A. | 54-073 | Ph.D. |
| Waugh, Douglas O. | 50-023 | Ph.D. |
| Waugh, Douglas O. | 48-602 | M.Sc. |
| Wearing, Parker L. | 49-581 | M.A. |
| Weaver, Ralph S. | 59-543 | M.Sc. |
| Weaver, William Strathern | 41-509 | Ph.D. |
| Webb, James L. | 50-049 | Ph.D. |
| Webb, James L. | 48-552 | M.Sc. |
| Webb, Tom | 58-054 | Ph.D. |
| Webster, Donald C. | 56-609 | M.Sc. |
| Webster, Donald R. | 33-024 | Ph.D. |
| Webster, Donald R. | 30-513 | M.Sc. |
| Webster, Edward C. | 36-014 | Ph.D. |
| Webster, Edward C. | 33-561 | M.A. |
| Webster, Gloria A. | 57-044 | Ph.D. |



| AUTHOR | THESIS NUMBER | DEGREE |
|---|---|---|
| Wechsler, Ann | 59-544 | M.Sc. |
| Weeks, John G. | 49-591 | M.Eng. |
| Weeks, Marie S. | 32-549 | M.A. |
| Weibel, Louise E. | 23-500 | LL.M. |
| Weigensberg, Bernard I. | 51-561 | M.Sc. |
| Weigensberg, Bernard I. | 53-078 | Ph.D. |
| Weil, Paul Gregory | 41-018 | Ph.D. |
| Weil, Paul Gregory | 39-521 | M.Sc. |
| Weininger, Joseph I. | 49-058 | Ph.D. |
| Weir, Douglas | 10-523 | M.Sc. |
| Weisman, Brahm | 50-501 | M.Arch. |
| Weiss, Michael | 57-598 | M.Sc. |
| Weissenburger, Pierre C. | 33-564 | M.Com. |
| Weisz, Paul | 46-016 | Ph.D. |
| Weisz, Paul | 44-512 | M.Sc. |
| Welbourne, Arthur J. | 46-594 | M.A. |
| Welch, William K. | 47-574 | M.Sc. |
| Weldon, Frederick E. | 30-514 | M.Sc. |
| Weldon, John C. | 52-066 | Ph.D. |
| Weldon, Richard L. | 20-509 | M.Sc. |
| Weldon, Thomas H. | 23-519 | M.Sc. |
| Weller, Judith A. | 58-549 | M.A. |
| Wells, Arthur F. | 52-598 | M.Sc. |
| Wells, Doreen E. | 55-544 | M.Sc. |
| Wells, Franklin B. | 33-034 | Ph.D. |
| Wells, Franklin B. | 31-560 | M.Sc. |
| Welt, Isaac D. | 45-542 | M.Sc. |
| Wendling, Andre V. | 37-031 | Ph.D. |
| Wener, Joseph | 48-553 | M.Sc. |
| Werry, Wilfrid W. | 32-550 | M.A. |
| West, Einar | 42-507 | Ph.D. |
| West, Kenneth A. | 42-027 | Ph.D. |
| Westbury, Ronald A. | 59-084 | Ph.D. |
| Westcott, James W. | 50-668 | M.A. |
| Weston, Grace E. | 34-539 | M.A. |
| Westwood, Mary J. | 51-576 | M.A. |
| Westwood, Robert J. | 33-507 | M.Eng. |
| Wevrick, Leonard | 57-599 | M.Sc. |
| Weyl, Salom | 40-513 | M.A. |
| Whalley, Basil J. | 52-034 | Ph.D. |
| Whallon, William W. | 52-559 | M.A. |
| Wheeler, Nathaniel E. | 11-515 | M.Sc. |
| Whelen, Myron S. | 29-016 | Ph.D. |
| Whimster, Eleanor I. | 53-621 | M.A. |
| Whitby, George S. | 20-003 | Ph.D. |
| Whitby, George S. | 18-507 | M.Sc. |
| White-Stevens, Robert H. | 36-521 | M.Sc. |
| White, Elwood V. | 36-015 | Ph.D. |

| AUTHOR | THESIS NUMBER | DEGREE |
|---|---|---|
| White, Elwood V. | 34-519 | M.Sc. |
| White, Harold | 25-542 | M.A. |
| White, Howard L. | 46-017 | Ph.D. |
| White, Orville E. | 51-577 | M.A. |
| White, Roy M. | 26-534 | M.Sc. |
| White, Thomas N. | 29-020 | Ph.D. |
| White, Thomas N. | 27-521 | M.Sc. |
| White, W. Harold | 43-014 | Ph.D. |
| Whitehead, Andrew B. | 57-088 | Ph.D. |
| Whitehead, Andrew B. | 55-622 | M.Sc. |
| Whitehead, Howard A. | 51-629 | M.Sc. |
| Whitehead, Howard A. | 53-039 | Ph.D. |
| Whitehead, Jean V.H. | 41-030 | M.A. |
| Whitehead, Walter E. | 31-517 | M.Sc. |
| Whiteside, John H. | 51-562 | M.Sc. |
| Whiteway, Stirling G. | 53-040 | Ph.D. |
| Whiting, Francis B. | 48-554 | M.Sc. |
| Whiting, Frank | 43-510 | M.Sc. |
| Whittall, Norman S. | 50-639 | M.Sc. |
| Whittemore, Carl R. | 24-534 | M.Sc. |
| Whitten, Lloyd K. | 57-045 | Ph.D. |
| Whittier, Angus C. | 52-067 | Ph.D. |
| Whittier, Angus C. | 50-558 | M.Sc. |
| Whyte, James H. | 33-532 | M.Sc. |
| Whyte, James H. | 38-024 | Ph.D. |
| Wickenden, Marguerite H. | 28-557 | M.A. |
| Wickson, Margaret E. | 55-545 | M.Sc. |
| Wiebe, Allan K. | 52-035 | Ph.D. |
| Wieckowski, Erwin | 57-089 | Ph.D. |
| Wieland, Walter A. | 18-508 | M.Sc. |
| Wigdor, Blossom T. | 52-068 | Ph.D. |
| Wiggins, Ernest J. | 46-018 | Ph.D. |
| Wigmore, Robert H. | 50-559 | M.Sc. |
| Wilansky, Douglas L. | 57-541 | M.Sc. |
| Wiles, David M. | 57-046 | Ph.D. |
| Wilkinson, George | 25-551 | M.A. |
| Wilkinson, Gordon W. | 50-640 | M.Sc. |
| Wilkinson, Ida G. | 47-584 | M.A. |
| Willard, Eugene W. | 24-547 | M.A. |
| Willermet, D.A. | 52-599 | M.Sc. |
| Williams, Alan R. | 32-017 | Ph.D. |
| Williams, Audrey J. | 55-623 | M.Sc. |
| Williams, Christine S. | 44-517 | M.A. |
| Williams, Frederick H. | 21-518 | M.Sc. |
| Williams, Harry L. | 43-015 | Ph.D. |
| Williams, Ivor David | 42-047 | M.A. |
| Williams, Katharine R. | 36-543 | M.A. |
| Williams, Roscoe C. | 53-546 | M.Sc. |



| AUTHOR | THESIS NUMBER | DEGREE |
|---|---|---|
| Williams, Sydney B. | 36-522 | M.Sc. |
| Williamson, John T. | 33-025 | Ph.D. |
| Williamson, John T. | 30-515 | M.Sc. |
| Willis, Edith B. | 48-570 | M.A. |
| Willis, Helen A. | 17-502 | M.A. |
| Willis, Stewart W. | 31-548 | M.A. |
| Willmott, William E. | 59-564 | M.A. |
| Willoughby, Henry W. | 54-074 | Ph.D. |
| Wilmot, Valerie C. | 50-641 | M.Sc. |
| Wilson, Alice M. | 11-504 | M.A. |
| Wilson, Charles V. | 33-026 | Ph.D. |
| Wilson, Cynthia V. | 59-535 | M.Sc. |
| Wilson, Donald H. | 50-669 | M.A. |
| Wilson, Evelyn C. | 30-556 | M.A. |
| Wilson, George Bernard | 39-027 | Ph.D. |
| Wilson, Harold S. | 25-530 | M.Sc. |
| Wilson, James D. | 49-582 | M.A. |
| Wilson, Norman L. | 33-533 | M.Sc. |
| Wilson, Norman L. | 39-028 | Ph.D. |
| Wilson, Roderic L. | 55-546 | M.Sc. |
| Wilson, William D. | 58-550 | M.A. |
| Wilson, William E. | 57-600 | M.Sc. |
| Wimer, Cynthia C. | 58-551 | M.A. |
| Wimer, Richard E. | 59-075 | Ph.D. |
| Wine, Joseph R. | 54-508 | LL.M. |
| Winkler, Carl A. | 33-027 | Ph.D. |
| Winkler, Louis | 38-543 | M.A. |
| Winship, R.L. | 57-513 | M.Eng. |
| Winter, Jack S. | 58-592 | M.A. |
| Winter, Karl A. | 56-544 | M.Sc. |
| Wipper, Audrey J. | 55-567 | M.A. |
| Wise, Louis M. | 46-019 | Ph.D. |
| Wiseblatt, Lazare | 50-642 | M.Sc. |
| Wiseman, Miriam H. | 56-610 | M.Sc. |
| Wiseman, Solomon | 23-527 | M.A. |
| Wiseman, Sylvia | 54-075 | Ph.D. |
| Wiseman, Sylvia | 50-579 | M.A. |
| Wisenthal, M. | 57-611 | M.A. |
| Wishart, George | 38-523 | M.Sc. |
| Withey, Albert N. | 16-506 | M.A. |
| Witty, Ralph | 51-036 | Ph.D. |
| Wojcik, Tadeusz Z. | 57-517 | LL.M. |
| Wolfe, Irving | 59-593 | M.A. |
| Wolfe, Nathan | 49-646 | M.A. |
| Wolfgang, Mary E. | 51-578 | M.A. |
| Wolfgang, Robert W. | 52-036 | Ph.D. |
| Wolfgang, Robert W. | 50-560 | M.Sc. |
| Wolfson, Joseph L. | 48-014 | Ph.D. |

| AUTHOR | THESIS NUMBER | DEGREE |
| --- | --- | --- |
| Wolofsky, Leib | 57-047 | Ph.D. |
| Wolofsky, Leib | 54-538 | M.Sc. |
| Wong, Esther V. | 47-528 | M.Sc. |
| Woo, Wesley Stewart | 40-514 | M.A. |
| Wood-Legh, Kathleen L. | 24-548 | M.A. |
| Wood, Charles Rowell | 41-051 | M.Sc. |
| Wood, John C. | 53-079 | Ph.D. |
| Woodfine, William J. | 53-622 | M.A. |
| Woodford, Vernon R. | 58-057 | Ph.D. |
| Woodford, Vernon R. | 48-603 | M.Sc. |
| Woodhouse, Gordon H. | 50-510 | M.Eng. |
| Woodley, Elsie C. | 32-551 | M.A. |
| Woods, Harry D. | 31-549 | M.A. |
| Woods, Helen M. | 55-640 | M.A. |
| Woods, James P. | 50-561 | M.Sc. |
| Woolner, Evelyn F. | 45-518 | M.A. |
| Woolsey, Lloyd D. | 44-513 | M.Sc. |
| Woolverton, Ralph S. | 50-562 | M.Sc. |
| Woolverton, Ralph S. | 53-080 | Ph.D. |
| Workman, E. Walter | 34-520 | M.Sc. |
| Worsfold, Henry H. | 17-503 | M.A. |
| Wrenshall, Charlton L. | 36-022 | Ph.D. |
| Wright, Annie Mary | 41-052 | M.Sc. |
| Wright, Archibald N. | 57-048 | Ph.D. |
| Wright, Charles A. | 21-003 | Ph.D. |
| Wright, John M. | 56-624 | M.A. |
| Wright, Leebert A. | 57-542 | M.Sc. |
| Wright, Ouida | 56-625 | M.A. |
| Wright, Robert H. | 31-010 | Ph.D. |
| Wright, Robert H. | 30-516 | M.Sc. |
| Wu, Chow C. | 16-515 | M.Sc. |
| Wu, Liang Y. | 52-069 | Ph.D. |
| Wyatt, Barbara V. | 47-575 | M.Sc. |
| Wykes, Eric R. | 31-518 | M.Sc. |
| Wykes, Neville George | 41-031 | M.A. |
| Wyman, Harold R. | 30-553 | M.Sc. |
| Yaffe, Leo | 43-016 | Ph.D. |
| Yalden-Thomas, David C. | 48-045 | Ph.D. |
| Yan, Maxwell M. | 47-039 | Ph.D. |
| Yano, George E. | 53-510 | M.Eng. |
| Yao, Yu-Lin | 42-050 | M.Eng. |
| Yaphe, Wilfred | 52-070 | Ph.D. |
| Yates, Claire H. | 51-037 | Ph.D. |
| Yates, Havelock H. | 52-037 | Ph.D. |
| Yong, Raymond N. | 58-507 | M.Eng. |
| Yorke-Slader, Geoffrey H. | 47-506 | M.Eng. |
| Yorston, Frederic H. | 24-535 | M.Sc. |
| Yorston, Frederic H. | 28-012 | Ph.D. |



| AUTHOR | THESIS NUMBER | DEGREE |
| --- | --- | --- |
| Youdelis, William V. | 59-076 | Ph.D. |
| Youdelis, William V. | 56-563 | M.Eng. |
| Young, Charles H. | 28-558 | M.A. |
| Young, Donald M. | 36-016 | Ph.D. |
| Young, John M. | 29-526 | M.Sc. |
| Young, William L. | 51-563 | M.Sc. |
| Young, William L. | 53-081 | Ph.D. |
| Younge, Eva R. | 33-562 | M.A. |
| Yu, Pei-Liang | 48-604 | M.Sc. |
| Yuen, Henry B. | 38-524 | M.Sc. |
| Yuill, Harry H. | 10-524 | M.Sc. |
| Yurack, Joseph A. | 56-070 | Ph.D. |
| Yurack, Joseph A. | 54-606 | M.Sc. |
| Yurko, Michael | 51-592 | M.Eng. |
| Zaharia, William | 59-085 | Ph.D. |
| Zakuta, Leo | 48-619 | M.A. |
| Zemel, Reuben | 54-607 | M.Sc. |
| Zenner, Gerhard F. | 59-507 | M.Eng. |
| Ziegler, James E. | 49-553 | M.Sc. |
| Ziegler, Peter | 51-038 | Ph.D. |
| Zienius, Raymond H. | 59-077 | Ph.D. |
| Zirinsky, Victor J. | 48-605 | M.Sc. |
| Zoond, Alexander | 25-550 | M.Sc. |
| Zorbach, William W. | 51-039 | Ph.D. |
| Zuckerman, Abraham | 43-024 | Ph.D. |
| Zuk, Michael | 57-557 | S.T.M. |
| Zwartendyk, Jan | 57-543 | M.Sc. |
| Zweig, David N. | 49-647 | M.A. |
| Zweig, Joseph P. | 52-560 | M.A. |

# LISTING BY DEPARTMENT

| THESIS NUMBER | AUTHOR | DEGREE |
|---|---|---|
| ** | | |
| 15-501 | Corbett, Percy E. | M.A. |
| **Aerodynamics & Engineering** | | |
| 22-507 | Gliddon, William G. | M.Sc. |
| **Agricultural Bacteriology** | | |
| 45-001 | Alarie, Albert M. | Ph.D. |
| 43-501 | Alarie, Albert M. | M.Sc. |
| 48-511 | Anderson, George G. | M.Sc. |
| 55-002 | Angus, Thomas A. | Ph.D. |
| 50-027 | Chaplin, Charles E. | Ph.D. |
| 46-511 | Chaplin, Charles E. | M.Sc. |
| 51-004 | Chase, Francis E. | Ph.D. |
| 57-005 | Clark, David S. | Ph.D. |
| 53-580 | Clark, David S. | M.Sc. |
| 51-603 | Corbett, Wendell O. | M.Sc. |
| 57-570 | Dawkins, Riley A. | M.Sc. |
| 46-563 | Dussault, H.P. | M.Sc. |
| 48-006 | Herman, Lloyd G. | Ph.D. |
| 57-579 | Idziak, Edmund S. | M.Sc. |
| 58-568 | Jones, Graham A. | M.Sc. |
| 53-596 | King, Hamilton D. | M.Sc. |
| 55-025 | Lachance, Robert A. | Ph.D. |
| 49-535 | Lachance, Robert A. | M.Sc. |
| 47-561 | Marmur, Julius | M.Sc. |
| 56-585 | McLaughlan, John M. | M.Sc. |
| 51-619 | Poplove, Myron | M.Sc. |
| 57-593 | Reid, John E. | M.Sc. |
| 50-041 | Robinson, John | Ph.D. |
| 45-536 | Robinson, John | M.Sc. |
| 48-595 | Rockwell, Keith R. | M.Sc. |
| 54-530 | Rogers, Charles G. | M.Sc. |
| 47-524 | Rouatt, James W. | M.Sc. |
| 57-033 | Smart, Celina | Ph.D. |
| 48-597 | Stranks, Donald W. | M.Sc. |
| 52-593 | Taylor, Lester J. | M.Sc. |
| 55-541 | Taylor, Robert B. | M.Sc. |
| 55-043 | Tennant, Alan D. | Ph.D. |
| 49-549 | Tennant, Alan D. | M.Sc. |
| 32-026 | Thompson, Robert R. | Ph.D. |
| 51-557 | Thomson, Hugh M. | M.Sc. |



| THESIS NUMBER | AUTHOR | DEGREE |
|---|---|---|
| **Agricultural Bacteriology** | | |
| 58-579 | Walke, Lacey | M.Sc. |
| 46-581 | Wallace, Raphael H. | M.Sc. |
| 48-013 | Wallace, Raphael H. | Ph.D. |
| 55-623 | Williams, Audrey J. | M.Sc. |
| 52-070 | Yaphe, Wilfred | Ph.D. |
| **Agricultural Chemistry** | | |
| 55-001 | Anastassiadis, Phoebus A. | Ph.D. |
| 45-014 | Andreae, Wolfgang A. | Ph.D. |
| 43-502 | Andreae, Wolfgang A. | M.Sc. |
| 44-014 | Armstrong, John G. | Ph.D. |
| 41-523 | Armstrong, John G. | M.Sc. |
| 26-503 | Atkinson, Hammond J. | M.Sc. |
| 34-002 | Atkinson, Hammond J. | Ph.D. |
| 45-521 | Bishop, Robert F. | M.Sc. |
| 37-534 | Boone, Charles S. | M.Sc. |
| 59-006 | Boswell, Graeme W. | Ph.D. |
| 49-513 | Boswell, Graeme W. | M.Sc. |
| 45-504 | Boulet, Marcel | M.Sc. |
| 48-017 | Boulet, Marcel | Ph.D. |
| 45-505 | Brogden, Clarence L. | M.Sc. |
| 47-023 | Campbell, James A. | Ph.D. |
| 40-041 | Cann, Donald Bruce | M.Sc. |
| 46-021 | Cann, Everett D. | Ph.D. |
| 51-600 | Carr, Joseph W. | M.Sc. |
| 49-045 | Chapman, Douglas G. | Ph.D. |
| 45-522 | Chapman, Douglas G. | M.Sc. |
| 44-016 | Chapman, Ross A. | Ph.D. |
| 41-526 | Chapman, Ross A. | M.Sc. |
| 54-515 | Coffin, Althea | M.Sc. |
| 59-013 | Coffin, David E. | Ph.D. |
| 56-571 | Coffin, David E. | M.Sc. |
| 51-005 | Coldwell, Blake B. | Ph.D. |
| 48-514 | Coldwell, Blake B. | M.Sc. |
| 46-513 | Collins, Vernon K. | M.Sc. |
| 57-523 | De Freitas, Anthony S. | M.Sc. |
| 35-028 | Dyck, Abram J. | Ph.D. |
| 37-536 | Dyer, William J. | M.Sc. |
| 47-509 | Eiser, Herman M. | M.Sc. |
| 46-564 | Ellington, Alton C. | M.Sc. |
| 48-022 | Ellington, Alton C. | Ph.D. |
| 46-565 | Ewart, Mervyn H. | M.Sc. |
| 51-519 | Fairbairn, N.J. | M.Sc. |

Agricultural Chemistry

| THESIS NUMBER | AUTHOR | DEGREE |
|---|---|---|
| 32-556 | Findlay, Gordon H. | M.Sc. |
| 34-019 | Findlay, Gordon H. | Ph.D. |
| 51-009 | Fiskell, John G. | Ph.D. |
| 49-525 | Fiskell, John G. | M.Sc. |
| 33-570 | Forbes, Franklin R. | M.Sc. |
| 55-519 | Ford, John D. | M.Sc. |
| 28-509 | Fowler, Donald F. | M.Sc. |
| 47-546 | Gass, James H. | M.Sc. |
| 46-567 | Gillingham, John T. | M.Sc. |
| 47-548 | Goss, George C. | M.Sc. |
| 42-053 | Graham, Walter Donald | M.Sc. |
| 40-044 | Grant, Edwin Parkhurst | M.Sc. |
| 38-021 | Guest, Gordon H. | Ph.D. |
| 45-531 | Halpern, Philip E. | M.Sc. |
| 55-524 | Hamilton, Herman A. | M.Sc. |
| 49-048 | Hare, John H. | Ph.D. |
| 47-550 | Hare, John H. | M.Sc. |
| 50-530 | Henneberry, Gerald | M.Sc. |
| 53-592 | Hilchey, John D. | M.Sc. |
| 55-060 | Huq, A.K.M. Fazlul | Ph.D. |
| 52-577 | Jenkins, Marjorie M. | M.Sc. |
| 53-015 | Jowsey, James R. | Ph.D. |
| 51-526 | Keefe, Thomas J. | M.Sc. |
| 56-022 | Khan, Noor A. | Ph.D. |
| 44-009 | Knight, Enid P. | Ph.D. |
| 39-515 | Knight, Enid P. | M.Sc. |
| 42-057 | Lajoie, Paul | M.Sc. |
| 48-585 | Langille, Winston M. | M.Sc. |
| 57-021 | Layne, Donald St.E. | Ph.D. |
| 55-527 | Layne, Donald St.E. | M.Sc. |
| 26-515 | Leduc, Joseph A. | M.Sc. |
| 45-510 | Leduc, Real A. | M.Sc. |
| 59-586 | Leung, Philip M-B. | M.Sc. |
| 44-010 | Lips, Alair | Ph.D. |
| 19-001 | Lockhead, Allan G. | Ph.D. |
| 12-511 | Lockhead, Allan G. | M.Sc. |
| 54-593 | Loughheed, Thomas C. | M.Sc. |
| 47-033 | Lusena, Charles V. | Ph.D. |
| 44-520 | Lusena, Charles V. | M.Sc. |
| 51-533 | Lutwick, Laurence E. | M.Sc. |
| 52-534 | Macdonald, Roderick R. | M.Sc. |
| 47-558 | Mackay, Kathleen I. | M.Sc. |
| 44-011 | MacDougall, Daniel | Ph.D. |
| 41-531 | MacDougall, Daniel | M.Sc. |
| 54-055 | MacKay, Donald C. | Ph.D. |



Agricultural Chemistry

| THESIS NUMBER | AUTHOR | DEGREE |
|---|---|---|
| 48-533 | MacLean, Angus A. | M.Sc. |
| 54-529 | MacLean, Kenneth S. | M.Sc. |
| 56-586 | MacLeod, Harry A. | M.Sc. |
| 56-587 | MacRae, Herbert F. | M.Sc. |
| 53-063 | Mahon, John H. | Ph.D. |
| 49-611 | Mahon, John H. | M.Sc. |
| 40-520 | Manning, Kenneth Raymond | M.Sc. |
| 40-046 | Marcello, Louis S. | M.Sc. |
| 59-525 | McCully, Keith A. | M.Sc. |
| 21-512 | McFarlane, Nathaniel C. | M.Sc. |
| 54-056 | McKinley, William P. | Ph.D. |
| 51-613 | McKinley, William P. | M.Sc. |
| 48-537 | Millette, Jean F. | M.Sc. |
| 44-507 | Morrison, Earl S. | M.Sc. |
| 47-563 | Moster, Julius B. | M.Sc. |
| 57-024 | Murray, Thomas K. | Ph.D. |
| 50-549 | Murray, Thomas K. | M.Sc. |
| 39-066 | Neish, Arthur Charles | M.Sc. |
| 45-010 | Nelson, John A. | Ph.D. |
| 46-528 | Nichol, Charles A. | M.Sc. |
| 49-542 | Novick, Seymour | M.Sc. |
| 37-538 | Parker, William E. | M.Sc. |
| 55-537 | Parsons, Timothy R. | M.Sc. |
| 47-565 | Paul, Harry | M.Sc. |
| 46-530 | Pazur, John H. | M.Sc. |
| 53-031 | Pedersen, Jorgen W. | Ph.D. |
| 46-574 | Perlin, Arthur S. | M.Sc. |
| 53-542 | Phillips, William E. | M.Sc. |
| 59-531 | Pilson, Michael E. | M.Sc. |
| 49-033 | Pinsky, Alex | Ph.D. |
| 46-575 | Pinsky, Alex | M.Sc. |
| 47-016 | Pringle, Ross B. | Ph.D. |
| 45-535 | Pringle, Ross B. | M.Sc. |
| 54-601 | Pritchard, Ernest T. | M.Sc. |
| 47-017 | Privett, Orville S. | Ph.D. |
| 44-509 | Privett, Orville S. | M.Sc. |
| 36-516 | Puddington, Ira E. | M.Sc. |
| 29-517 | Pugsley, Leonard I. | M.Sc. |
| 56-535 | Reeder, Stewart W. | M.Sc. |
| 59-532 | Reynolds, Lincoln M. | M.Sc. |
| 48-010 | Rigby, Francis L. | Ph.D. |
| 47-568 | Robertson, William K. | M.Sc. |
| 37-021 | Sair, Louis | Ph.D. |
| 39-520 | Salisbury, Herbert F. | M.Sc. |
| 51-056 | Schalin, Edmund | Ph.D. |

## Agricultural Chemistry

| THESIS NUMBER | AUTHOR | DEGREE |
|---|---|---|
| 55-035 | Schnitzer, Morris | Ph.D. |
| 52-588 | Schnitzer, Morris | M.Sc. |
| 14-518 | Scott, Joseph M. | M.Sc. |
| 33-530 | Shaw, Geoffrey T. | M.Sc. |
| 40-505 | Shaw, John Leslie Dickins | Ph.D. |
| 47-570 | Siminovitch, Helen E. | M.Sc. |
| 30-511 | Skazin, Lev | M.Sc. |
| 39-504 | Smith, George Ransom | Ph.D. |
| 59-070 | Soper, Robert J. | Ph.D. |
| 44-023 | Sowden, Frederick J. | Ph.D. |
| 37-515 | Steeves, Allison E. | M.Sc. |
| 50-021 | Stobbe, Peter C. | Ph.D. |
| 38-522 | Sutherland, Angus J. | M.Sc. |
| 48-599 | Talvenheimo, Gerhardt | M.Sc. |
| 48-550 | Van Horne, William F. | M.Sc. |
| 58-052 | Vanstone, William E. | Ph.D. |
| 55-543 | Vanstone, William E. | M.Sc. |
| 52-598 | Wells, Arthur F. | M.Sc. |
| 50-642 | Wiseblatt, Lazare | M.Sc. |
| 47-528 | Wong, Esther V. | M.Sc. |
| 41-051 | Wood, Charles Rowell | M.Sc. |
| 36-022 | Wrenshall, Charlton L. | Ph.D. |
| 57-542 | Wright, Leebert A. | M.Sc. |

## Agricultural Economics

| THESIS NUMBER | AUTHOR | DEGREE |
|---|---|---|
| 56-611 | Baumgartner, Helmut W. | M.A. |
| 53-548 | Buchanan, Donald R. | M.A. |
| 56-614 | Burnett, Alvin A. | M.A. |
| 58-541 | Jarrette, Neil M. | M.A. |
| 57-550 | MacFarlane, Dougald A. | M.A. |

## Agronomy

| THESIS NUMBER | AUTHOR | DEGREE |
|---|---|---|
| 57-519 | Anderson, Gordon C. | M.Sc. |
| 51-510 | Barrales, Hugo L. | M.Sc. |
| 24-501 | Bayfield, Edward G. | M.S.A. |
| 44-501 | Beaudry, Jean-Romuald | M.Sc. |
| 29-501 | Bird, Joseph N. | M.Sc. |
| 37-502 | Boulet, Lucien J. | M.Sc. |
| 57-567 | Bristow, John M. | M.Sc. |
| 52-515 | Cairns, Robert R. | M.Sc. |
| 49-516 | Carder, Alfred C. | M.Sc. |



## Agronomy

| THESIS NUMBER | AUTHOR | DEGREE |
|---|---|---|
| 54-513 | Casserly, Leo M. | M.Sc. |
| 59-579 | Chiang, Morgan S-M. | M.Sc. |
| 55-593 | Chiasson, Thomas C. | M.Sc. |
| 26-501 | Clark, John A. | M.S.A. |
| 46-514 | Cordukes, William F. | M.Sc. |
| 29-552 | Cox, Kenneth | M.Sc. |
| 56-008 | Cumming, Bruce G. | Ph.D. |
| 24-502 | Cunningham, Howe S. | M.S.A. |
| 25-501 | Davidson, James G. | M.S.A. |
| 55-597 | Deane, Burton C. | M.Sc. |
| 26-558 | Dimmock, Frederick | M.Sc. |
| 35-503 | Dore, William G. | M.Sc. |
| 50-603 | Doyle, James J. | M.Sc. |
| 46-517 | Drapala, Walter J. | M.Sc. |
| 25-502 | Eaton, Ernest L. | M.S.A. |
| 55-518 | Findlay, Wallace I. | M.Sc. |
| 48-521 | Gauthier, Fernand M. | M.Sc. |
| 48-522 | Gervais, Paul | M.Sc. |
| 53-530 | Goyette, Louis F. | M.Sc. |
| 25-503 | Hanlan, Leamon H. | M.S.A. |
| 52-527 | Hansen, Douglas F. | M.Sc. |
| 46-520 | Hanson, Angus A. | M.Sc. |
| 56-578 | Henry, Vann C. | M.Sc. |
| 53-593 | Ho-Yen, Basil C. | M.Sc. |
| 54-590 | Isang, Etim U. | M.Sc. |
| 55-062 | Klinck, Harold R. | Ph.D. |
| 52-531 | Klinck, Harold R. | M.Sc. |
| 58-570 | Knutti, Hans J. | M.Sc. |
| 56-523 | Lachance, Charles-Eugene | M.Sc. |
| 24-503 | Lamb, Cecil A. | M.S.A. |
| 58-571 | Lawson, Norman C. | M.Sc. |
| 25-543 | Liebenberg, Louis C. | M.S.A. |
| 25-504 | Lods, Emile A. | M.S.A. |
| 51-531 | Loiselle, Roland | M.Sc. |
| 56-526 | Lukosevicius, Petras P. | M.Sc. |
| 42-061 | MacLean, Alister Joseph | M.Sc. |
| 53-598 | MacLeod, Lloyd B. | M.Sc. |
| 34-513 | MacVicar, Roderick M. | M.Sc. |
| 53-538 | Martineau, Real | M.Sc. |
| 44-505 | Menzies, Robert G. | M.Sc. |
| 58-030 | Mittelholzer, Alexander S | Ph.D. |
| 56-533 | Mittelholzer, Alexander S | M.Sc. |
| 33-524 | Nowosad, Frank S. | M.Sc. |
| 24-504 | Parent, Robert C. | M.S.A. |
| 32-557 | Pelletier, Joseph R. | M.Sc. |

| THESIS NUMBER | AUTHOR | DEGREE |
|---|---|---|
| **Agronomy** | | |
| 51-542 | Povilaitis, Bronys | M.Sc. |
| 28-501 | Raynauld, Robert | M.S.A. |
| 24-549 | Rogers, John T. | M.S.A. |
| 27-501 | Russell, Mary G. | M.S.A. |
| 26-502 | Schurman, David C. | M.S.A. |
| 42-065 | Shuh, John Edward | M.Sc. |
| 51-550 | Slater, Douglas T. | M.Sc. |
| 55-038 | Steppler, Howard A. | Ph.D. |
| 48-548 | Steppler, Howard A. | M.Sc. |
| 34-518 | Stobbe, Peter C. | M.Sc. |
| 56-607 | Thorne, Kenrick H. | M.Sc. |
| 24-505 | Tinney, Benjamin F. | M.S.A. |
| **Agronomy & Genetics** | | |
| 40-501 | Frankton, Clarence | Ph.D. |
| **Agronomy & Plant Pathology** | | |
| 48-542 | Robinson, Dean B. | M.Sc. |
| **Anatomy** | | |
| 48-001 | Albert, Samuel | Ph.D. |
| 54-005 | Axelrad, A.A. | Ph.D. |
| 46-002 | Beland, Eleanor | Ph.D. |
| 46-558 | Berman, Doreen | M.Sc. |
| 54-007 | Bertalanffy, Felix D. | Ph.D. |
| 51-513 | Bertalanffy, Felix D. | M.Sc. |
| 50-516 | Bogoroch, Rita | M.Sc. |
| 56-569 | Boyd, William | M.Sc. |
| 50-598 | Brochu, Francis L. | M.Sc. |
| 49-515 | Campbell, Charles G. | M.Sc. |
| 54-511 | Carriere, Rita M. | M.Sc. |
| 53-002 | Clermont, Yves W. | Ph.D. |
| 52-042 | Cox, Phoebe L. | Ph.D. |
| 53-005 | Daoust, Roger J. | Ph.D. |
| 42-010 | Dosne, Christiane | Ph.D. |
| 50-521 | Dougherty, Joan L. | M.Sc. |
| 53-006 | Eartly, Heidi H. | Ph.D. |
| 51-518 | Eartly, Heidi H. | M.Sc. |
| 58-013 | Eidinger, David | Ph.D. |



| THESIS NUMBER | AUTHOR | DEGREE |
|---|---|---|
| **Anatomy** | | |
| 57-010 | Enesco, Mircea A. | Ph.D. |
| 48-004 | Friedman, Constance A. | Ph.D. |
| 46-007 | Friedman, Sydney M. | Ph.D. |
| 41-040 | Friedman, Sydney M. | M.Sc. |
| 55-522 | Ghosh, Asok C. | M.Sc. |
| 49-047 | Grad, Bernard | Ph.D. |
| 53-008 | Greulich, Richard C. | Ph.D. |
| 49-014 | Gross, Jack | Ph.D. |
| 46-010 | Hall, Charles E. | Ph.D. |
| 46-519 | Hall, Octavia | M.Sc. |
| 43-021 | Hay, Eleanor C. | Ph.D. |
| 49-017 | Henrikson, Helen A. | Ph.D. |
| 58-569 | Karpishka, Irene S. | M.Sc. |
| 56-056 | Kumamoto, Yurika | Ph.D. |
| 53-597 | Kumamoto, Yurika | M.Sc. |
| 51-612 | Laroche, Joseph E. | M.Sc. |
| 42-060 | Livingstone, Constance [illegible]. | M.Sc. |
| 42-504 | Masson, Georges M. | Ph.D. |
| 41-533 | McNaughton, Francis L. | M.Sc. |
| 56-590 | Messier, Bernard H. | M.Sc. |
| 48-536 | Miller, Saul | M.Sc. |
| 53-540 | Mohiuddin, Syed D. | M.Sc. |
| 55-070 | Nadler, Norman J. | Ph.D. |
| 50-551 | Peets, Ronald C. | M.Sc. |
| 33-525 | Power, Richard M. | M.Sc. |
| 51-624 | Schwartz, Solomon | M.Sc. |
| 50-044 | Stevens, Catherine [illegible]. | Ph.D. |
| 49-548 | Storey, Winnifred [illegible]. | M.Sc. |
| 46-015 | Sylvester, Elizabeth M. | Ph.D. |
| 51-628 | Varverikos, Emmanuel D. | M.Sc. |
| 54-536 | Vulpe, M. | M.Sc. |
| 45-542 | Welt, Isaac D. | M.Sc. |
| 54-607 | Zemel, Reuben | M.Sc. |
| **Animal Nutrition & Breeding** | | |
| 39-511 | Ashton, Gordon Clemence | M.Sc. |
| 41-036 | Bezeau, Louis Manning | M.Sc. |
| 36-510 | Cameron, Colin [illegible]. | M.Sc. |
| 38-504 | Campbell, James [illegible]. | M.Sc. |
| 34-510 | Finlayson, Duncan [illegible]. | M.Sc. |
| 38-507 | Forshaw, Robert [illegible]. | M.Sc. |
| 35-506 | Gutteridge, Harry S. | M.Sc. |
| 40-519 | King, Robert Henry | M.Sc. |

### Animal Nutrition & Breeding

| THESIS NUMBER | AUTHOR | DEGREE |
|---|---|---|
| 39-062 | Lange, Eugene Hausknecht | M.Sc. |
| 41-043 | Lessard, Henri-Louis | M.Sc. |
| 39-063 | Logan, Vaughn Stewart | M.Sc. |
| 41-044 | MacIntyre, Thomas Martin | M.Sc. |
| 39-519 | Purdy, Thomas Lenton | M.Sc. |
| 36-519 | Stothart, John G. | M.Sc. |
| 36-522 | Williams, Sydney B. | M.Sc. |

### Anthropology

| THESIS NUMBER | AUTHOR | DEGREE |
|---|---|---|
| 57-553 | Pineo, Peter C. | M.A. |

### Applied Electricity

| THESIS NUMBER | AUTHOR | DEGREE |
|---|---|---|
| 12-514 | McNaughton, Andrew G. | M.Sc. |

### Architecture

| THESIS NUMBER | AUTHOR | DEGREE |
|---|---|---|
| 51-580 | Aronin, Jeffrey E. | M.Arch. |
| 55-569 | Barkham, J. Brian | M.Arch. |
| 58-552 | Caragianis, Eva M. | M.Arch. |
| 53-558 | Gordon, George E. | M.Arch. |
| 57-554 | Lam, Anna P. | M.Arch. |
| 57-501 | Leaning, John D. | M.Arch. |
| 57-502 | Moriyama, Raymond J. | M.Arch. |
| 48-503 | Papanek, Rudolf J. | M.Arch. |
| 59-501 | Schoenauer, Norbert | M.Arch. |
| 58-553 | Walford, Dorice C. | M.Arch. |
| 50-501 | Weisman, Brahm | M.Arch. |

### Bacteriology

| THESIS NUMBER | AUTHOR | DEGREE |
|---|---|---|
| 20-502 | Anderson, Marian | M.Sc. |
| 52-567 | Avery, Robert J. | M.Sc. |
| 50-512 | Bailey, William R. | M.Sc. |
| 52-568 | Baker, Harold A. | M.Sc. |
| 56-567 | Barnes, Marion J. | M.Sc. |
| 48-512 | Barwick, Audrey J. | M.Sc. |
| 31-004 | Bedford, Robert H. | Ph.D. |
| 29-503 | Blau, Abraham | M.Sc. |
| 31-503 | Bynoe, Evan T. | M.Sc. |



### Bacteriology

| THESIS NUMBER | AUTHOR | DEGREE |
|---|---|---|
| 35-007 | Bynoe, Evan T. | Ph.D. |
| 39-055 | Byrne, Joseph Lawrence | M.Sc. |
| 53-578 | Cahn, Shirley | M.Sc. |
| 49-517 | Carter, Sharon E. | M.Sc. |
| 53-519 | Charles, Christine M. | M.Sc. |
| 54-579 | Ciplijauskate, Jurate E. | M.Sc. |
| 49-597 | Collins, Anne M. | M.Sc. |
| 24-511 | Conklin, Raymond L. | M.Sc. |
| 56-044 | Diena, Benito B. | Ph.D. |
| 54-581 | Diena, Benito B. | M.Sc. |
| 52-013 | Girard, Kenneth F. | Ph.D. |
| 50-525 | Girard, Kenneth F. | M.Sc. |
| 52-046 | Girvin, Grace T. | Ph.D. |
| 31-552 | Glynn, John H. | M.Sc. |
| 27-504 | Gough, William F. | M.Sc. |
| 48-005 | Greenberg, Louis | Ph.D. |
| 50-527 | Hall, Nancy C. | M.Sc. |
| 28-561 | Hamilton, William B. | M.Sc. |
| 07-508 | Harrison, Francis C. | M.Sc. |
| 51-013 | Hawirko, Roma Z. | Ph.D. |
| 49-529 | Hawirko, Roma Z. | M.Sc. |
| 33-009 | Hess, Ernest | Ph.D. |
| 28-514 | Irwin, Marion L. | M.Sc. |
| 26-514 | Johns,Cyril K. | M.Sc. |
| 52-578 | Johnston, Constance A. | M.Sc. |
| 49-023 | Kahnka, Mary J. | Ph.D. |
| 21-511 | Kennedy, Margaret E. | M.Sc. |
| 49-610 | MacLachlan, Donald S. | M.Sc. |
| 42-062 | MacLennan, Louise Isabel | M.Sc. |
| 50-547 | Margolis, Leo | M.Sc. |
| 32-520 | McMaster, Norman B. | M.Sc. |
| 59-054 | Morgante, Odosca | Ph.D. |
| 51-026 | Myers, Gordon E. | Ph.D. |
| 22-518 | Newton, Dorothy E. | M.Sc. |
| 52-538 | Nommik, Salme | M.Sc. |
| 49-543 | Pawlikowska, Anna M. | M.Sc. |
| 24-527 | Perry, Helen M. | M.Sc. |
| 56-062 | Ramamurti, Dharmapuri V. | Ph.D. |
| 50-630 | Riddell, Marion I. | M.Sc. |
| 48-544 | Ruyter, Sally A. | M.Sc. |
| 17-507 | Sadler, Wilfrid | M.Sc. |
| 45-537 | Savage, Marion C. | M.Sc. |
| 14-519 | Shanly, Eleanor | M.Sc. |
| 51-058 | Stock, John J. | Ph.D. |
| 49-547 | Stock, John J. | M.Sc. |

## Bacteriology

| THESIS NUMBER | AUTHOR | DEGREE |
|---|---|---|
| 48-598 | Streitfield, Murray M. | M.Sc. |
| 21-516 | Symons, Jennie L. | M.Sc. |
| 31-009 | Tarr, Hugh L. | Ph.D. |
| 29-521 | Thompson, Robert R. | M.Sc. |
| 26-530 | Townsend, Charles T. | M.Sc. |
| 53-039 | Whitehead, Howard A. | Ph.D. |
| 51-629 | Whitehead, Howard A. | M.Sc. |
| 56-070 | Yurack, Joseph A. | Ph.D. |
| 54-606 | Yurack, Joseph A. | M.Sc. |
| 25-550 | Zoond, Alexander | M.Sc. |

## Bacteriology & Immunology

| THESIS NUMBER | AUTHOR | DEGREE |
|---|---|---|
| 57-518 | Ajemian, Ann A. | M.Sc. |
| 55-004 | Avery, Robert J. | Ph.D. |
| 55-045 | Bailey, William R. | Ph.D. |
| 54-038 | Baker, Harold A. | Ph.D. |
| 56-568 | Barshaw, Wilma E. | M.Sc. |
| 55-047 | Beaulieu, Maurice | Ph.D. |
| 53-572 | Beaulieu, Maurice | M.Sc. |
| 55-590 | Butler, Ralph | M.Sc. |
| 51-514 | Cain, Robert M. | M.Sc. |
| 56-043 | Ciplijauskate, Jurate E. | Ph.D. |
| 55-011 | Cleveland, Edward M. | Ph.D. |
| 52-519 | Comtois, Romuald D. | M.Sc. |
| 58-562 | Cooke, Patricia M. | M.Sc. |
| 57-571 | Denson, Marie L. | M.Sc. |
| 56-573 | Fabrikant, Irene B. | M.Sc. |
| 50-526 | Girvin, Grace T. | M.Sc. |
| 56-053 | Hannan, Charles K. | Ph.D. |
| 56-020 | Kapica, Lucia | Ph.D. |
| 57-064 | Matheson, Ballem H. | Ph.D. |
| 59-046 | McBride, Mollie E. | Ph.D. |
| 55-536 | Morgante, Odosca | M.Sc. |
| 59-055 | Morigi, Eugene M. | Ph.D. |
| 49-613 | Nunes, Doris S. | M.Sc. |
| 57-079 | Speers, Robert | Ph.D. |
| 56-539 | Speers, Robert | M.Sc. |
| 59-600 | Stanislawski, Marc | M.Sc. |
| 42-506 | Strean, Lyon P. | Ph.D. |
| 40-049 | Strean, Lyon P. | M.Sc. |
| 57-083 | Tanner, Charles E. | Ph.D. |
| 56-542 | Tanner, Charles E. | M.Sc. |



## Biochemistry

| THESIS NUMBER | AUTHOR | DEGREE |
|---|---|---|
| 51-040 | Alivisatos, Spyridon | Ph.D. |
| 49-592 | Alivisatos, Spyridon | M.Sc. |
| 31-001 | Allardyce, William J. | Ph.D. |
| 42-516 | Allen, Della Elizabeth | M.Sc. |
| 34-001 | Anderson, Evelyn M. | Ph.D. |
| 46-504 | Andreae, Shirley R. | M.Sc. |
| 56-512 | Aprile, Marie A. | M.Sc. |
| 46-557 | Askonas, Brigitte A. | M.Sc. |
| 54-037 | Avigan, Joel | Ph.D. |
| 57-566 | Bas-Kraus, Eva R. | M.Sc. |
| 52-003 | Baxter, Robert M. | Ph.D. |
| 31-003 | Beatty, Stanley A. | Ph.D. |
| 50-024 | Belleau, Fernand B. | Ph.D. |
| 37-025 | Billingsley, Lawrence W. | Ph.D. |
| 33-509 | Billingsley, Lawrence W. | M.Sc. |
| 35-005 | Black, Peter T. A. | Ph.D. |
| 56-039 | Bligh, Emerson G. | Ph.D. |
| 29-504 | Blumberg, Perry | M.Sc. |
| 53-045 | Boyd, Donald H. | Ph.D. |
| 51-041 | Braganca, Menezes B. | Ph.D. |
| 58-005 | Brodkin, Elliot | Ph.D. |
| 51-597 | Brodkin, Elliot | M.Sc. |
| 54-041 | Brown, William T. | Ph.D. |
| 32-001 | Browne, John S. | Ph.D. |
| 59-007 | Brownstone, Yehoshua S. | Ph.D. |
| 58-007 | Cann, Malcolm C. | Ph.D. |
| 55-592 | Cann, Malcolm C. | M.Sc. |
| 45-507 | Carlton, Lucille | M.Sc. |
| 35-009 | Chapman, Clifford W. | Ph.D. |
| 52-041 | Chaput, Marcel | Ph.D. |
| 25-001 | Chipman, Harry R. | Ph.D. |
| 51-006 | Colter, John S. | Ph.D. |
| 55-517 | Cross, Jean D. | M.Sc. |
| 52-009 | Darlington, Walter A. | Ph.D. |
| 37-026 | Denstedt, Orville F. | Ph.D. |
| 53-523 | Desbarats, Marie-Louise | M.Sc. |
| 45-017 | Douglas, Donald F. | Ph.D. |
| 59-582 | Eisenstein, Sam | M.Sc. |
| 57-572 | Esar, Rhoda | M.Sc. |
| 47-004 | Falk, Hans L. | Ph.D. |
| 54-011 | Faulkner, Peter | Ph.D. |
| 59-583 | Fessler, Alfred | M.Sc. |
| 53-007 | Fishman, Sherold | Ph.D. |
| 25-002 | Forbes, John C. | Ph.D. |
| 51-607 | Francoeur, Joseph M. | M.Sc. |

| THESIS NUMBER | AUTHOR | DEGREE |
|---|---|---|
| **Biochemistry** | | |
| 53-051 | Francoeur, Marc | Ph.D. |
| 53-588 | Francoeur, Pearl | M.Sc. |
| 51-010 | Franklin, Arthur E. | Ph.D. |
| 53-052 | Fridhandler, Louis | Ph.D. |
| 59-028 | Givner, Morris L. | Ph.D. |
| 56-575 | Givner, Morris L. | M.Sc. |
| 50-608 | Glocklin, Vera C. | M.Sc. |
| 55-058 | Goldstein, Fred B. | Ph.D. |
| 59-030 | Gordon, Julius | Ph.D. |
| 30-554 | Grant, Elizabeth R. | M.A. |
| 56-014 | Greenway, Robert M. | Ph.D. |
| 46-569 | Gurd, Frank R. | M.Sc. |
| 55-523 | Guthrie, John F. | M.Sc. |
| 57-576 | Haber, Andrew B. | M.Sc. |
| 52-575 | Halperin, Alex H. | M.Sc. |
| 38-007 | Harlow, Charles M. | Ph.D. |
| 49-049 | Harpur, Robert P. | Ph.D. |
| 47-551 | Harpur, Robert P. | M.Sc. |
| 38-510 | Harrison, Sybil M. | M.Sc. |
| 32-006 | Harwood, Robert U. | Ph.D. |
| 57-578 | Henry, A.S. | M.Sc. |
| 50-031 | Hochster, Rolf M. | Ph.D. |
| 52-528 | Hollett, Charlotte | M.Sc. |
| 52-018 | Hosein, Esau A. | Ph.D. |
| 50-534 | Hosein, Esau A. | M.Sc. |
| 25-521 | Illievitz, Abraham B. | M.Sc. |
| 54-052 | Jacobs, Ross D. | Ph.D. |
| 52-529 | Jacobs, Ross D. | M.Sc. |
| 47-031 | Jamieson, James B. | Ph.D. |
| 52-021 | Johnson, Willard J. | Ph.D. |
| 56-021 | Kashket, Shelby | Ph.D. |
| 53-595 | Kashket, Shelby | M.Sc. |
| 56-055 | Kochen, Joseph A. | Ph.D. |
| 44-504 | Korenberg, Sarah M. | M.Sc. |
| 52-050 | Kushner, Donn J. | Ph.D. |
| 50-615 | Kushner, Donn J. | M.Sc. |
| 33-012 | Kutz, Russell L. | Ph.D. |
| 48-529 | Kwiecinska-Pappius, Hanna | M.Sc. |
| 57-061 | Lagnado, John R. | Ph.D. |
| 55-607 | Lagnado, John R. | M.Sc. |
| 36-548 | Lathe, Grant H. | M.Sc. |
| 57-022 | Loiselle, Jean-Marie | Ph.D. |
| 55-528 | Loiselle, Jean-Marie | M.Sc. |
| 48-008 | Macdougall, Graham R. | Ph.D. |
| 59-080 | Majchrowicz, Edward | Ph.D. |





| THESIS NUMBER | AUTHOR | DEGREE |
|---|---|---|
| **Biochemistry** | | |
| 56-026 | Malkin, Aaron | Ph.D. |
| 53-064 | Mamelak, Rose | Ph.D. |
| 56-532 | Maximchuk, Arlene J. | M.Sc. |
| 27-511 | Maytum, Helen E. | M.Sc. |
| 57-587 | McArdle, Alice H. | M.Sc. |
| 35-021 | McKeown, Thomas | Ph.D. |
| 50-016 | McKerns, Kenneth W. | Ph.D. |
| 51-021 | McLennan, Hugh | Ph.D. |
| 49-538 | McLennan, Hugh | M.Sc. |
| 32-009 | McPhail, Murchie K. | Ph.D. |
| 53-065 | Moya, Francisco J. | Ph.D. |
| 54-025 | O'Donnell, Vincent J. | Ph.D. |
| 38-014 | O'Donovan, Denis K. | Ph.D. |
| 57-074 | Ottolenghi, Paul | Ph.D. |
| 55-617 | Ottolenghi, Paul | M.Sc. |
| 52-025 | Pappius, Hanna M. | Ph.D. |
| 57-075 | Parmar, Surendra S. | Ph.D. |
| 58-032 | Parsons, Timothy R. | Ph.D. |
| 56-059 | Pascoe, Enid | Ph.D. |
| 56-028 | Passey, Richard F. | Ph.D. |
| 53-032 | Peron, Fernand G. | Ph.D. |
| 50-627 | Peron, Fernand G. | M.Sc. |
| 59-062 | Peto, Margaret | Ph.D. |
| 56-593 | Peto, Margaret | M.Sc. |
| 57-076 | Petrushka, Evelyn | Ph.D. |
| 53-069 | Pollak, John K. | Ph.D. |
| 59-593 | Powell, Elizabeth A. | M.Sc. |
| 48-541 | Prado, Eline S. | M.Sc. |
| 32-014 | Pugsley, Leonard I. | Ph.D. |
| 56-030 | Purvis, John L. | Ph.D. |
| 54-602 | Purvis, John L. | M.Sc. |
| 56-063 | Rao, Raindur G. | Ph.D. |
| 51-543 | Richer, Ruth C. | M.Sc. |
| 58-037 | Richter, Maxwell | Ph.D. |
| 58-038 | Riklis, Emanuel | Ph.D. |
| 46-534 | Robertson, Florence E. | M.Sc. |
| 41-047 | Roche, Mary Nora | M.Sc. |
| 59-039 | Rochefort, Guy J. | Ph.D. |
| 56-596 | Rochefort, Joseph G. | M.Sc. |
| 42-529 | Rochlin, Isidore | M.Sc. |
| 56-599 | Rosenfeld, Michael W. | M.Sc. |
| 53-072 | Rubinstein, David | Ph.D. |
| 51-621 | Rubinstein, David | M.Sc. |
| 55-032 | Ryan, Michael T. | Ph.D. |
| 48-037 | Saffran, Judith | Ph.D. |

## Biochemistry

| THESIS NUMBER | AUTHOR | DEGREE |
|---|---|---|
| 49-036 | Saffran, Murray | Ph.D. |
| 46-578 | Saffran, Murray | M.Sc. |
| 44-510 | Sainte-Marie, Dorothee L. | M.Sc. |
| 57-030 | Schally, Andrew V. | Ph.D. |
| 49-037 | Scholefield, Peter G. | Ph.D. |
| 55-036 | Schonbaum, Eduard | Ph.D. |
| 54-032 | Schucher, Reuben | Ph.D. |
| 57-594 | Segal, Mark | M.Sc. |
| 58-044 | Sells, Bruce H. | Ph.D. |
| 54-603 | Simard-Duquesne, N. | M.Sc. |
| 46-014 | Sobel, Harry | Ph.D. |
| 53-076 | Solomon, Samuel | Ph.D. |
| 51-551 | Solomon, Samuel | M.Sc. |
| 57-080 | Srinivasan, Swamy A. | Ph.D. |
| 54-532 | Stachiewicz, Evva T. | M.Sc. |
| 40-048 | Stewart, Gordon Stafford | M.Sc. |
| 48-011 | Stewart, Ronald D. | Ph.D. |
| 58-047 | Sved, Stephen | Ph.D. |
| 55-078 | Taussig, Andrew | Ph.D. |
| 59-072 | Tenenhouse, Alan | Ph.D. |
| 51-059 | Thompson, Lloyd M. | Ph.D. |
| 59-083 | Townsend, Edith E. | Ph.D. |
| 56-608 | Townsend, Edith E. | M.Sc. |
| 51-627 | Turnbull, Dorothy K. | M.Sc. |
| 59-073 | Van Gelder, Nico M. | Ph.D. |
| 52-596 | Verdier, Pamela C. | M.Sc. |
| 28-525 | Vineberg, Arthur M. | M.Sc. |
| 54-537 | Waters, William R. | M.Sc. |
| 50-049 | Webb, James L. | Ph.D. |
| 48-552 | Webb, James L. | M.Sc. |
| 58-054 | Webb, Tom | Ph.D. |
| 53-078 | Weigensberg, Bernard I. | Ph.D. |
| 51-561 | Weigensberg, Bernard I. | M.Sc. |
| 54-074 | Willoughby, Henry W. | Ph.D. |
| 50-641 | Wilmot, Valerie C. | M.Sc. |
| 56-610 | Wiseman, Miriam H. | M.Sc. |
| 51-036 | Witty, Ralph | Ph.D. |
| 58-057 | Woodford, Vernon R. | Ph.D. |
| 48-603 | Woodford, Vernon R. | M.Sc. |
| 51-037 | Yates, Claire H. | Ph.D. |
| 59-085 | Zaharia, William | Ph.D. |
| 51-038 | Ziegler, Peter | Ph.D. |



## Biology

| THESIS NUMBER | AUTHOR | DEGREE |
|---|---|---|
| 14-512 | DuPorte, Ernest M. | M.Sc. |

## Botany

| THESIS NUMBER | AUTHOR | DEGREE |
|---|---|---|
| 40-037 | Anderson, Ernest Grant | M.Sc. |
| 33-001 | Armstrong, John M. | Ph.D. |
| 57-565 | Baines, Joan D. | M.Sc. |
| 58-510 | Biard, J.M. | M.Sc. |
| 31-502 | Brown, Alexander B. | M.Sc. |
| 52-007 | Campbell, John D. | Ph.D. |
| 52-517 | Clark, John | M.Sc. |
| 54-009 | Coles, Clifford H. | Ph.D. |
| 22-001 | Dickson, Bertram T. | Ph.D. |
| 22-504 | Dustan, Alan G. | M.Sc. |
| 37-505 | Eaves, Charles A. | M.Sc. |
| 50-606 | Elliott, Bernard B. | M.Sc. |
| 53-525 | Etheridge, David E. | M.Sc. |
| 32-555 | Ferguson, William | M.Sc. |
| 55-520 | Francis, Jean B. | M.Sc. |
| 18-503 | Fritz, Clara W. | M.Sc. |
| 26-510 | Gibbs, Ronald D. | M.Sc. |
| 47-547 | Gooding, Herbert B. | M.Sc. |
| 54-522 | Goodwin, Brian C. | M.Sc. |
| 52-524 | Gorham, Anne L. | M.Sc. |
| 33-028 | Hearne, Edna M. | Ph.D. |
| 34-511 | Hunter, Albert W. | M.Sc. |
| 32-516 | Johnson, Robert E. | M.Sc. |
| 54-524 | Kapica, Lucia | M.Sc. |
| 10-002 | Kirsch, Simon | Ph.D. |
| 07-503 | Kirsch, Simon | M.A. |
| 57-059 | Krupka, Richard M. | Ph.D. |
| 33-521 | Levitt, Jacob | M.Sc. |
| 35-017 | Levitt, Jacob | Ph.D. |
| 47-556 | Loewy, Ariel G. | M.Sc. |
| 55-529 | Long, Harold D. | M.Sc. |
| 58-572 | Lowther, Ruth L. | M.Sc. |
| 26-516 | Macrae, Ruth | M.Sc. |
| 22-516 | Major, Thomas G. | M.Sc. |
| 12-502 | Miller, Clare E. | M.A. |
| 38-546 | Minshall, William H. | M.Sc. |
| 41-505 | Minshall, William H. | Ph.D. |
| 21-513 | Moe, George G. | M.Sc. |
| 54-596 | Mozie, James O. | M.Sc. |
| 55-071 | Paquin, Roger | Ph.D. |

| THESIS NUMBER | AUTHOR | DEGREE |
|---|---|---|
| **Botany** | | |
| 22-519 | Richardson, James K. | M.Sc. |
| 51-545 | Roper, Richard B. | M.Sc. |
| 57-029 | Ross, Ian K. | Ph.D. |
| 59-534 | Roy, Chitra | M.Sc. |
| 42-023 | Scoggan, Homer J. | Ph.D. |
| 35-517 | Scoggan, Homer J. | M.Sc. |
| 39-025 | Siminovitch, David | Ph.D. |
| 37-541 | Siminovitch, David | M.Sc. |
| 43-509 | Stevens, Thelma V. | M.Sc. |
| 25-006 | Symons, Jennie L. | Ph.D. |
| 51-558 | Towers, George H. | M.Sc. |
| 50-636 | Turnau, Edmund A. | M.Sc. |
| 52-595 | Tyler, Nancy F. | M.Sc. |
| 56-609 | Webster, Donald C. | M.Sc. |
| 55-544 | Wells, Doreen E. | M.Sc. |
| 38-024 | Whyte, James H. | Ph.D. |
| 33-532 | Whyte, James H. | M.Sc. |
| 55-545 | Wickson, Margaret E. | M.Sc. |
| **Botany & Geological Sciences** | | |
| 50-619 | Lowther, John S. | M.Sc. |
| **Botany-Genetics** | | |
| 45-012 | Stern, Herbert | Ph.D. |
| 42-066 | Stern, Herbert | M.Sc. |
| **Botany-Horticulture** | | |
| 41-035 | Beaupre, Thomas Norbert | M.Sc. |
| 58-055 | Hutchinson, Aleck | Ph.D. |
| **Cellulose Chemistry** | | |
| 29-007 | Jahn, Edwin C. | Ph.D. |
| 29-515 | Perry, Stanley Z. | M.Sc. |
| **Chemical Engineering** | | |



| THESIS NUMBER | AUTHOR | DEGREE |
|---|---|---|
| **Chemical Engineering** | | |
| 45-519 | Chadillon, Francois J. | M.Eng. |
| 51-501 | Charles, George E. | M.Eng. |
| 50-504 | Cooper, Ross M. | M.Eng. |
| 48-573 | Diamond, George P. | M.Eng. |
| 57-006 | Dlouhy, Jan | Ph.D. |
| 46-553 | Epstein, Norman | M.Eng. |
| 42-515 | Gauvin, William | M.Eng. |
| 49-504 | Goudey, John F. | M.Eng. |
| 52-563 | Gunnarsson, Gudni K. | M.Eng. |
| 59-035 | Hoffman, Terrence W. | Ph.D. |
| 48-507 | Kemmett, Francis W. | M.Eng. |
| 50-507 | Knelman, Fred H. | M.Eng. |
| 46-503 | Legendre, Rosaire | M.Eng. |
| 52-503 | LeMesurier, Kenneth A. | M.Eng. |
| 51-587 | Lyons, Douglas B. | M.Eng. |
| 52-565 | Macrakis, N. | M.Eng. |
| 58-026 | Manning, William P. | Ph.D. |
| 52-506 | Morton, Ernest R. | M.Eng. |
| 51-588 | Nenniger, Emile | M.Eng. |
| 56-559 | Nichols, Ian O. | M.Eng. |
| 52-507 | Palsson, Petur | M.Eng. |
| 59-061 | Pasternak, Israel S. | Ph.D. |
| 52-508 | Phillips, Lorne A. | M.Eng. |
| 52-509 | Pinder, Kenneth L. | M.Eng. |
| 54-031 | Schaus, Orland O. | Ph.D. |
| 52-510 | Schaus, Orland O. | M.Eng. |
| 40-516 | Stidwell, William Francis | M.Eng. |
| 53-510 | Yano, George E. | M.Eng. |
| **Chemistry** | | |
| 59-001 | Adamek, Edward G. | Ph.D. |
| 54-001 | Adamek, Stephen | Ph.D. |
| 39-001 | Adams, Alfred Byron | Ph.D. |
| 49-001 | Adelstein, Peter | Ph.D. |
| 49-040 | Aikin, Archibald M. | Ph.D. |
| 38-001 | Alexander, Wendal A. | Ph.D. |
| 25-505 | Allan, John M. | M.Sc. |
| 32-019 | Allen, John S. | Ph.D. |
| 42-001 | Allenby, Owen C. | Ph.D. |
| 54-003 | Andrews, Douglas H. | Ph.D. |
| 50-001 | Archer, William L. | Ph.D. |
| 35-002 | Argue, George H. | Ph.D. |
| 55-003 | Armstrong, David A. | Ph.D. |

## Chemistry

| THESIS NUMBER | AUTHOR | DEGREE |
|---|---|---|
| 42-002 | Arnell, John C. | Ph.D. |
| 43-001 | Ashford, Walter R. | Ph.D. |
| 46-505 | Atkinson, James T. | M.Sc. |
| 53-043 | Back, Robert A. | Ph.D. |
| 52-001 | Baerg, Abraham P. | Ph.D. |
| 43-017 | Baker, Samuel B. | Ph.D. |
| 31-002 | Ball, Ralph H. | Ph.D. |
| 35-003 | Ball, William L. | Ph.D. |
| 49-041 | Bannard, Robert A. | Ph.D. |
| 48-002 | Bardwell, John A. | Ph.D. |
| 31-011 | Barker, Walter E. | Ph.D. |
| 27-001 | Barnes, William H. | Ph.D. |
| 25-509 | Barnes, William H. | M.Sc. |
| 46-001 | Barry, James G. | Ph.D. |
| 33-002 | Barsha, Jacob | Ph.D. |
| 58-004 | Barth, Fred W. | Ph.D. |
| 57-001 | Bartok, William | Ph.D. |
| 56-036 | Barton, Stuart S. | Ph.D. |
| 52-002 | Batzold, John S. | Ph.D. |
| 34-507 | Baxt, Lawrence M. | M.Sc. |
| 24-507 | Beaudet, Lionel | M.Sc. |
| 37-001 | Beazley, Warren B. | Ph.D. |
| 38-544 | Bedoukian, Paul | M.Sc. |
| 41-001 | Bedoukian, Paul | Ph.D. |
| 54-039 | Beelik, Andrew | Ph.D. |
| 37-002 | Bell, Alan | Ph.D. |
| 56-003 | Bennett, Clifton F. | Ph.D. |
| 33-508 | Bennett, Robert D. | M.Sc. |
| 35-004 | Bennett, Robert D. | Ph.D. |
| 45-002 | Betts, Robert H. | Ph.D. |
| 52-038 | Biefer, Gregory J. | Ph.D. |
| 44-015 | Bishinsky, Charles | Ph.D. |
| 49-044 | Bishop, Claude T. | Ph.D. |
| 40-001 | Bjorklund, Gordon Herbert | Ph.D. |
| 50-026 | Blades, H. | Ph.D. |
| 42-004 | Blizzard, Ronald H. | Ph.D. |
| 12-001 | Boehner, Reginald S. | Ph.D. |
| 55-007 | Bombardieri, Caurino C. | Ph.D. |
| 23-001 | Boomer, Edward H. | Ph.D. |
| 21-501 | Boomer, Edward H. | M.Sc. |
| 48-016 | Booth, Kenneth G. | Ph.D. |
| 44-001 | Bourns, Arthur N. | Ph.D. |
| 45-016 | Bowen, William G. | Ph.D. |
| 43-003 | Bower, John R. | Ph.D. |
| 46-003 | Boyd, Mary L. | Ph.D. |



## Chemistry

| THESIS NUMBER | AUTHOR | DEGREE |
|---|---|---|
| 33-003 | Boyer, Raymond | Ph.D. |
| 45-003 | Boyer, Thomas W. | Ph.D. |
| 49-005 | Brady, George W. | Ph.D. |
| 42-005 | Brais, Roger | Ph.D. |
| 52-006 | Breitman, Leo | Ph.D. |
| 43-018 | Brewer, Charles F. | Ph.D. |
| 40-002 | Brickman, Leo | Ph.D. |
| 53-046 | Brickman, William J. | Ph.D. |
| 35-006 | Brocklesby, Horace N. | Ph.D. |
| 55-514 | Brody, Harry | M.Sc. |
| 25-512 | Brocke, Richard C. | M.Sc. |
| 37-003 | Broughton, James W. | Ph.D. |
| 52-040 | Brounstein, Cyril J. | Ph.D. |
| 38-002 | Brown, Arthur G. | Ph.D. |
| 40-003 | Brown, Douglas Frederick | Ph.D. |
| 40-004 | Brown, Ernest A. | Ph.D. |
| 39-002 | Brown, Robert A. | Ph.D. |
| 46-020 | Brown, Robert K. | Ph.D. |
| 51-003 | Brown, Robert M. | Ph.D. |
| 36-017 | Brown, Robert S. | Ph.D. |
| 53-047 | Brownell, Harold H. | Ph.D. |
| 55-008 | Bryce, John R. | Ph.D. |
| 47-002 | Bryce, William A. | Ph.D. |
| 34-004 | Buckland, Irene K. | Ph.D. |
| 41-501 | Buckley, Bernard F. | Ph.D. |
| 55-009 | Bulani, Walter | Ph.D. |
| 46-560 | Burch, George N. | M.Sc. |
| 56-005 | Bushuk, Walter | Ph.D. |
| 28-001 | Butler, Keith H. | Ph.D. |
| 50-003 | Butler, Robert W. | Ph.D. |
| 30-015 | Buxton, Kenneth S. | Ph.D. |
| 47-507 | Cabbott, Irwin M. | M.Sc. |
| 51-042 | Cabott, Irving M. | Ph.D. |
| 35-008 | Calder, Douglas S. | Ph.D. |
| 38-003 | Calhoun, John M. | Ph.D. |
| 28-002 | Cambron, Adrien | Ph.D. |
| 23-506 | Cambron, Adrien | M.Sc. |
| 30-502 | Campbell, Herbert N. | M.Sc. |
| 29-002 | Campbell, William E. | Ph.D. |
| 39-003 | Cannon, John J. | Ph.D. |
| 23-507 | Carleton, Everett A. | M.Sc. |
| 28-003 | Carpenter, Gilbert B. | Ph.D. |
| 52-008 | Carroll, Murray N. | Ph.D. |
| 55-515 | Carruthers, Errol W. | M.Sc. |
| 29-003 | Carter, Neal M. | Ph.D. |

| THESIS NUMBER | AUTHOR | DEGREE |
|---|---|---|

Chemistry

| | | |
|---|---|---|
| 30-001 | Chalmers, William | Ph.D. |
| 59-010 | Charles, George E. | Ph.D. |
| 26-001 | Chataway, Helen D. | Ph.D. |
| 10-514 | Cheesbrough, Arthur G. | M.Sc. |
| 46-512 | Chin-Yee, Harold R. | M.Sc. |
| 46-022 | Christian, William R. | Ph.D. |
| 49-007 | Christie, George L. | Ph.D. |
| 54-042 | Cipera, John D. | Ph.D. |
| 29-004 | Coffin, Carl C. | Ph.D. |
| 53-003 | Conn, John J. | Ph.D. |
| 41-002 | Cooke, Lloyd Miller | Ph.D. |
| 31-005 | Cooper, Douglas L. | Ph.D. |
| 36-004 | Corey, Alfred J. | Ph.D. |
| 46-023 | Cox, Lionel A. | Ph.D. |
| 39-004 | Cramer, Archie Barrett | Ph.D. |
| 50-028 | Creamer, George B. | Ph.D. |
| 43-004 | Creighton, Robert H. | Ph.D. |
| 33-005 | Cressman, Homer W. | Ph.D. |
| 28-005 | Crozier, Robert N. | Ph.D. |
| 13-515 | Cumming, Charles L. | M.Sc. |
| 40-006 | Cunningham, Robert L. | Ph.D. |
| 59-015 | Currie, Allan L. | Ph.D. |
| 29-005 | Cuthbertson, Arnold C. | Ph.D. |
| 27-503 | Cuthbertson, Arnold C. | M.Sc. |
| 40-007 | Dacey, John Robert | Ph.D. |
| 43-019 | Darwent, Basil de B. | Ph.D. |
| 42-007 | Davis, John | Ph.D. |
| 42-008 | Davis, Stuart G. | Ph.D. |
| 34-005 | De Montigny, Raimbault | Ph.D. |
| 42-009 | Deans, Sidney A. | Ph.D. |
| 47-545 | Dechene, Earl B. | M.Sc. |
| 51-007 | Dempster, John C. | Ph.D. |
| 52-521 | Dennis, Donald A. | M.Sc. |
| 46-005 | Devins, John C. | Ph.D. |
| 40-008 | Dewar, Donald James | Ph.D. |
| 50-029 | Dewhurst, Harold A. | Ph.D. |
| 24-512 | DeLong, Walter A. | M.Sc. |
| 37-005 | DeLuca, Horace A. | Ph.D. |
| 55-013 | DeSouza, John E. | Ph.D. |
| 47-003 | Dixon, John F. | Ph.D. |
| 39-005 | Dorland, Rodger M. | Ph.D. |
| 36-546 | Dorman, Robert W. | M.Sc. |
| 43-518 | Douglas, Donald E. | M.Sc. |
| 47-025 | Downes, Kenneth W. | Ph.D. |
| 41-003 | Duncan, Robert Daman | Ph.D. |



| THESIS NUMBER | AUTHOR | DEGREE |
|---|---|---|

Chemistry

| | | |
|---|---|---|
| 54-010 | Dunford, Hugh B. | Ph.D. |
| 40-009 | Dyer, William J. | Ph.D. |
| 49-010 | Eager, Richard L. | Ph.D. |
| 43-005 | Eastham, Arthur M. | Ph.D. |
| 46-006 | Eastwood, Thomas A. | Ph.D. |
| 42-011 | Edward, John T. | Ph.D. |
| 35-010 | Edwards, Joseph | Ph.D. |
| 43-519 | Eiger, Irena Z. | M.Sc. |
| 59-020 | Eisenbraun, Allan A. | Ph.D. |
| 59-021 | Eisenbraun, Edgar W. | Ph.D. |
| 55-017 | Ekler, Kurt | Ph.D. |
| 56-045 | Elias, Lorne | Ph.D. |
| 38-006 | Eliot, Charles G. | Ph.D. |
| 33-513 | Elkin, Eugene M. | M.Sc. |
| 35-011 | Elkin, Eugene M. | Ph.D. |
| 59-022 | Elsdon, William I. | Ph.D. |
| 20-504 | Emmons, William F. | M.Sc. |
| 50-524 | English, William D. | M.Sc. |
| 44-017 | Epstein, Samuel | Ph.D. |
| 25-515 | Evans, Arthur P. | M.Sc. |
| 55-018 | Evans, Harry G. | Ph.D. |
| 41-503 | Evans, Taylor H. | Ph.D. |
| 56-010 | Falconer, Errol I. | Ph.D. |
| 48-023 | Farmilo, Charles G. | Ph.D. |
| 51-045 | Favis, Demetrios | Ph.D. |
| 56-047 | Fenyes, Joseph | Ph.D. |
| 32-002 | Filby, Edgar A. | Ph.D. |
| 37-006 | Findlay, Robert A. | Ph.D. |
| 44-003 | Fineman, Manuel N. | Ph.D. |
| 43-020 | Fisher, Herbert E. | Ph.D. |
| 41-004 | Fisher, John Henry | Ph.D. |
| 39-007 | Folkins, Hillis C. | Ph.D. |
| 37-506 | Folkins, Hillis C. | M.Sc. |
| 44-004 | Foran, Michael R. | Ph.D. |
| 39-008 | Fordyce, Reid George | Ph.D. |
| 59-024 | Forgacs, Otto L. | Ph.D. |
| 55-055 | Forst, Wendell | Ph.D. |
| 16-509 | Fort, Charles A. | M.Sc. |
| 36-005 | Fowler, Frances I. | Ph.D. |
| 25-517 | Fowler, Grant M. | M.Sc. |
| 46-024 | Foxlee, Frank H. | Ph.D. |
| 32-003 | Frame, Gordon F. | Ph.D. |
| 56-012 | Frangatos, Gerassimos | Ph.D. |
| 54-049 | Frank, Arlen W. | Ph.D. |
| 55-019 | Freeman, Gordon R. | Ph.D. |

## Chemistry

| THESIS NUMBER | AUTHOR | DEGREE |
|---|---|---|
| 44-005 | Friedman, Orrie M. | Ph.D. |
| 49-011 | Funt, Boris L. | Ph.D. |
| 32-004 | Gallaugher, Arthur F. | Ph.D. |
| 30-003 | Gallay, Wilfred | Ph.D. |
| 56-574 | Gantchev, Neno | M.Sc. |
| 44-006 | Gardner, Joseph A. | Ph.D. |
| 58-015 | Gardner, Prescott E. | Ph.D. |
| 55-021 | Gardon, John L. | Ph.D. |
| 45-005 | Garmaise, David L. | Ph.D. |
| 55-056 | Gartaganis, Phoebus | Ph.D. |
| 45-006 | Gauvin, William | Ph.D. |
| 36-006 | Geddes, Amos I. | Ph.D. |
| 17-505 | Geldard, Walter J. | M.Sc. |
| 54-013 | Gendron, Lucien J. | Ph.D. |
| 47-005 | Genge, Colin A. | Ph.D. |
| 59-026 | George, Zacheria M. | Ph.D. |
| 52-045 | Gesser, Hyman | Ph.D. |
| 39-049 | Giddings, E. W. Garner | M.Eng. |
| 37-007 | Giguere, Paul A. | Ph.D. |
| 38-508 | Gilbert, Margaret R. | M.Sc. |
| 59-027 | Gillham, John K. | Ph.D. |
| 42-012 | Gillies, Archibald | Ph.D. |
| 36-007 | Gilman, Lucius | Ph.D. |
| 44-018 | Gilpin, Victor | Ph.D. |
| 35-012 | Gishler, Paul E. | Ph.D. |
| 58-017 | Glaudemans, Cornelis P. | Ph.D. |
| 47-027 | Gleason, Clarence H. | Ph.D. |
| 46-025 | Glegg, Ronald E. | Ph.D. |
| 41-008 | Godard, Hugh Phillips | Ph.D. |
| 47-006 | Gogek, Charles J. | Ph.D. |
| 56-051 | Gordon, Ralph W. | Ph.D. |
| 49-013 | Goring, David A. | Ph.D. |
| 31-006 | Grace, Nathaniel H. | Ph.D. |
| 35-542 | Graham, Gordon B. | M.A. |
| 46-026 | Graham, Wilfred | Ph.D. |
| 46-008 | Grassie, Vernon R. | Ph.D. |
| 34-020 | Gray, Kenneth R. | Ph.D. |
| 23-003 | Greaves, Clifford | Ph.D. |
| 22-509 | Greaves, Clifford | M.Sc. |
| 28-009 | Greenberg, Harry | Ph.D. |
| 27-505 | Greenberg, Harry | M.Sc. |
| 48-025 | Greenblatt, Jayson | Ph.D. |
| 40-502 | Greenwood, Sydney H. | Ph.D. |
| 32-022 | Greig, Margaret E. | Ph.D. |
| 39-050 | Gribbins, Gordon Henry | M.Eng. |



## Chemistry

| THESIS NUMBER | AUTHOR | DEGREE |
|---|---|---|
| 32-023 | Grieve, Arthur D. | Ph.D. |
| 59-031 | Griffiths, James E. | Ph.D. |
| 59-032 | Grivas, John C. | Ph.D. |
| 57-526 | Grivas, John C. | M.Sc. |
| 43-006 | Grummitt, William E. | Ph.D. |
| 44-007 | Guest, Rex M. | Ph.D. |
| 50-004 | Gunn, George B. | Ph.D. |
| 59-033 | Gupta, Prem R. | Ph.D. |
| 32-005 | Gurd, George W. | Ph.D. |
| 52-014 | Guthrie, Donald A. | Ph.D. |
| 41-009 | Habeeb, Herbert | Ph.D. |
| 59-079 | Haggart, Catherine | Ph.D. |
| 37-008 | Halley, Leroy F. | Ph.D. |
| 33-006 | Hallonquist, Earland G. | Ph.D. |
| 49-015 | Halpern, Jack | Ph.D. |
| 33-007 | Hampton, William F. | Ph.D. |
| 32-515 | Hampton, William F. | M.Sc. |
| 44-019 | Hardwick, Thomas J. | Ph.D. |
| 55-601 | Hardy, John A. | M.Sc. |
| 51-049 | Harpham, John A. | Ph.D. |
| 59-034 | Harris, Seth C. | Ph.D. |
| 40-011 | Harvey, Ross E. | Ph.D. |
| 49-016 | Harwood, Victor D. | Ph.D. |
| 21-002 | Hatcher, William H. | Ph.D. |
| 17-506 | Hatcher, William H. | M.Sc. |
| 45-018 | Hawkes, Arthur S. | Ph.D. |
| 38-008 | Hawkins, Walter I. | Ph.D. |
| 42-500 | Hay, Alden Wendell | Ph.D. |
| 49-050 | Hayward, Lloyl D. | Ph.D. |
| 58-018 | Henderson, John T. | Ph.D. |
| 46-027 | Henery-Logan, Kenneth R. | Ph.D. |
| 57-016 | Herron, John T. | Ph.D. |
| 18-505 | Herzberg, Otto W. | M.Sc. |
| 42-013 | Hewson, William B. | Ph.D. |
| 51-014 | Heyding, Robert D. | Ph.D. |
| 22-511 | Hiebert, Paul G. | M.Sc. |
| 24-001 | Hiebert, Paul G. | Ph.D. |
| 29-006 | Hill, Allan C. | Ph.D. |
| 27-542 | Hill, Allan C. | M.Sc. |
| 21-509 | Hill, Eleanor M. | M.Sc. |
| 52-016 | Hiltz, Arnold A. | Ph.D. |
| 57-527 | Ho-Tung, Clifton G. | M.Sc. |
| 49-018 | Hodgson, Gordon W. | Ph.D. |
| 57-017 | Hoffman, John C. | Ph.D. |
| 50-531 | Hoffman, William H. | M.Sc. |

| THESIS NUMBER | AUTHOR | DEGREE |
|---|---|---|
| Chemistry | | |
| 33-010 | Holcomb, Robert K. | Ph.D. |
| 27-005 | Holden, George W. | Ph.D. |
| 24-519 | Holden, George W. | M.Sc. |
| 39-010 | Holder, Clinton Howard | Ph.D. |
| 57-018 | Hollbach, Natasha | Ph.D. |
| 47-007 | Hollies, Norman R. | Ph.D. |
| 35-029 | Holmes, Edward L. | Ph.D. |
| 44-008 | Holmes, James M. | Ph.D. |
| 36-008 | Horn, Wallace R. | Ph.D. |
| 33-517 | Horwood, James F. | M.Sc. |
| 35-014 | Horwood, James F. | Ph.D. |
| 53-013 | Hospadaruk, Vladimir | Ph.D. |
| 27-507 | Houghton, Edward O. | M.Sc. |
| 18-504 | Howe, Laura I. | M.Sc. |
| 32-024 | Howland, Frances | Ph.D. |
| 49-019 | Hubley, Charles E. | Ph.D. |
| 40-013 | Hughes, Robert Edward | Ph.D. |
| 46-011 | Hugill, John T. | Ph.D. |
| 26-003 | Hunten, Kenneth W. | Ph.D. |
| 24-520 | Hunten, Kenneth W. | M.Sc. |
| 39-011 | Hunter, Melvin J. | Ph.D. |
| 57-056 | Huque, Mohammed M. | Ph.D. |
| 53-594 | Hurlbert, Bernard S. | M.Sc. |
| 47-029 | Husband, Robert M. | Ph.D. |
| 48-026 | Hutcheon, Alan T. | Ph.D. |
| 47-030 | Ingraham, Thomas R. | Ph.D. |
| 49-021 | Irvine, George N. | Ph.D. |
| 53-014 | Jablonski, Werner L. | Ph.D. |
| 55-023 | Jackson, Donald S. | Ph.D. |
| 56-018 | Jamieson, James W. | Ph.D. |
| 25-003 | Jane, Robert S. | Ph.D. |
| 23-513 | Jane, Robert S. | M.Sc. |
| 48-527 | Jardine, John M. | M.Sc. |
| 48-582 | Jeffrey, Claire O. | M.Sc. |
| 37-029 | Johannson, Oscar K. | Ph.D. |
| 47-008 | Johnson, Herbert | Ph.D. |
| 29-008 | Johnston, Harry W. | Ph.D. |
| 27-508 | Johnston, Harry W. | M.Sc. |
| 50-032 | Jones, Robert A. | Ph.D. |
| 42-014 | Josephson, Vernal | Ph.D. |
| 55-024 | Kasman, Sidney | Ph.D. |
| 29-017 | Katz, Morris | Ph.D. |
| 27-509 | Katz, Morris | M.Sc. |
| 37-013 | Katz, Sidney | Ph.D. |
| 32-517 | Kay, Muriel G. | M.Sc. |



| THESIS NUMBER | AUTHOR | DEGREE |
|---|---|---|
| Chemistry | | |
| 49-051 | Keays, John L. | Ph.D. |
| 58-023 | Kelly, Roger O. | Ph.D. |
| 41-529 | Kenalty, Brendan Joseph | M.Sc. |
| 42-056 | Kent, George Adrian | M.Sc. |
| 59-040 | Ketcheson, Barbara G. | Ph.D. |
| 34-021 | King, Ellis G. | Ph.D. |
| 39-500 | King, Thomas Elston | Ph.D. |
| 13-517 | Kirkpatrick, Robert | M.Sc. |
| 45-007 | Kirsch, Milton | Ph.D. |
| 57-058 | Klassen, Norman V. | Ph.D. |
| 57-584 | Kouris, Michael | M.Sc. |
| 09-514 | Krieble, Vernon K. | M.Sc. |
| 13-001 | Krieble, Vernon K. | Ph.D. |
| 49-025 | Kristjanson, Arnthor M. | Ph.D. |
| 42-501 | Kulka, Marshall | Ph.D. |
| 53-017 | Kuzmak, Joseph M. | Ph.D. |
| 59-043 | Lang, Andrew R. | Ph.D. |
| 33-520 | Larocque, Gerard L. | M.Sc. |
| 35-016 | Larocque, Gerard L. | Ph.D. |
| 25-004 | Larose, Paul | Ph.D. |
| 23-514 | Larose, Paul | M.Sc. |
| 50-034 | Larsson, Bjorn E. | Ph.D. |
| 38-010 | Leger, Francis J. | Ph.D. |
| 45-008 | Legge, Norman R. | Ph.D. |
| 46-028 | Lemieux, Raymond U. | Ph.D. |
| 48-028 | Leslie, John D. | Ph.D. |
| 42-015 | Levi, Irving | Ph.D. |
| 50-035 | Levi, Leo | Ph.D. |
| 51-018 | Levitin, Norman | Ph.D. |
| 38-011 | Lieff, Morris | Ph.D. |
| 42-016 | Lin, Wei-cheng | Ph.D. |
| 32-008 | Linton, Everett P. | Ph.D. |
| 30-507 | Linton, Everett P. | M.Sc. |
| 27-006 | Lipsett, Solomon G. | Ph.D. |
| 42-502 | Livingston, William R. | Ph.D. |
| 49-026 | Logan, Charles D. | Ph.D. |
| 23-004 | Logan, John F. | Ph.D. |
| 49-052 | Logan, Kenneth C. | Ph.D. |
| 42-017 | Lossing, Frederick P. | Ph.D. |
| 40-015 | Lovell, Edwin Lister | Ph.D. |
| 51-019 | Lucien, Harold W. | Ph.D. |
| 52-052 | Luner, Charles | Ph.D. |
| 51-020 | Luner, Philip | Ph.D. |
| 33-029 | Lusby, George F. | Ph.D. |
| 27-007 | Maass, Carol E. | Ph.D. |

| THESIS NUMBER | AUTHOR | DEGREE |
|---|---|---|
| **Chemistry** | | |
| 12-512 | Maass, Otto | M.Sc. |
| 22-513 | Macallum, Alexander D. | M.Sc. |
| 24-003 | Macallum, Alexander D. | Ph.D. |
| 33-522 | Mackinney, Herbert W. | M.Sc. |
| 35-031 | Mackinney, Herbert W. | Ph.D. |
| 32-010 | Macklin, Lionel S. | Ph.D. |
| 10-003 | Macleod, Annie L. | Ph.D. |
| 35-509 | MacCallum, William J. | M.Sc. |
| 57-023 | MacEwan, John R. | Ph.D. |
| 50-036 | MacFarlane, Hugh M. | Ph.D. |
| 43-009 | MacGregor, Warren S. | Ph.D. |
| 47-013 | MacHutchin, John G. | Ph.D. |
| 41-010 | MacInnes, Alexander S. | Ph.D. |
| 48-029 | MacKenzie, James S. | Ph.D. |
| 37-030 | MacLauchlan, Donald W. | Ph.D. |
| 16-001 | MacLean, Allison R. | Ph.D. |
| 12-513 | MacLean, Allison R. | M.Sc. |
| 46-029 | MacLean, David B. | Ph.D. |
| 54-018 | MacLennan, Donald F. | Ph.D. |
| 47-034 | Madras, Samuel | Ph.D. |
| 52-055 | Manchester, Donald F. | Ph.D. |
| 51-022 | Mandelcorn, Lyon | Ph.D. |
| 53-023 | Manley, Rockliffe St. J. | Ph.D. |
| 54-019 | Marchessault, Robert H. | Ph.D. |
| 46-012 | Marcus, Rudolph A. | Ph.D. |
| 29-009 | Marion, Leo E. | Ph.D. |
| 36-010 | Marsden, James | Ph.D. |
| 34-022 | Marshall, Harry B. | Ph.D. |
| 16-512 | Marshall, Melville J. | M.Sc. |
| 58-028 | Martin, William G. | Ph.D. |
| 55-532 | Martin, William G. | M.Sc. |
| 33-523 | Mason, Clarence T. | M.Sc. |
| 35-022 | Mason, Clarence T. | Ph.D. |
| 39-013 | Mason, Stanley George | Ph.D. |
| 33-013 | Massey, Ernest E. | Ph.D. |
| 56-531 | Massiah, Thomas F. | M.Sc. |
| 29-010 | Matheson, George L. | Ph.D. |
| 26-517 | Matheson, George L. | M.Sc. |
| 11-513 | Matheson, Howard W. | M.Sc. |
| 41-011 | Matthews, Fred White | Ph.D. |
| 53-024 | Matuszko, Anthony J. | Ph.D. |
| 53-536 | McCabe, James | M.Sc. |
| 38-012 | McCarthy, Joseph L. | Ph.D. |
| 49-027 | McConnell, Wallace B. | Ph.D. |
| 40-503 | McCoubrey, James Addison | Ph.D. |



| THESIS NUMBER | AUTHOR | DEGREE |
|---|---|---|
| **Chemistry** | | |
| 35-019 | McCubbin, John W. | Ph.D. |
| 50-014 | McDermot, H. Lloyd | Ph.D. |
| 35-020 | McDonald, Roland D. | Ph.D. |
| 08-511 | McFee, Malcolm C. | M.Sc. |
| 38-545 | McGibbon, Ralph W. | M.Sc. |
| 50-015 | McGilvery, James D. | Ph.D. |
| 22-515 | McGlaughlin, William R. | M.Sc. |
| 39-012 | McIntosh, Robert Lloyd | Ph.D. |
| 52-053 | McKillican, Mary E. | Ph.D. |
| 23-005 | McKinney, James W. | Ph.D. |
| 20-506 | McKinney, James W. | M.Sc. |
| 58-025 | McKnight, Theodore S. | Ph.D. |
| 41-532 | McLean, James Douglas | M.Sc. |
| 44-020 | McLeod, Lloyd A. | Ph.D. |
| 27-008 | McNally, James G. | Ph.D. |
| 39-517 | McNiven, Neal Lindsay | M.Sc. |
| 43-010 | Mead, Bruce F. | Ph.D. |
| 10-518 | Meldrum, William B. | M.Sc. |
| 57-589 | Menard, Claude | M.Sc. |
| 25-005 | Mennie, John H. | Ph.D. |
| 54-595 | Menzies, Margaret H. | M.Sc. |
| 51-024 | Metro, Stephen J. | Ph.D. |
| 53-025 | Milford, George N. | Ph.D. |
| 53-066 | Milks, John E. | Ph.D. |
| 55-026 | Miller, Bernard | Ph.D. |
| 50-037 | Miller, David M. | Ph.D. |
| 28-520 | Mitchell, Claude R. | M.Sc. |
| 44-012 | Mitchell, Leonard | Ph.D. |
| 46-030 | Moir, Robert Y. | Ph.D. |
| 48-032 | Montgomery, Douglas S. | Ph.D. |
| 33-014 | Moore, Leonard P. | Ph.D. |
| 30-509 | Moore, Leonard P. | M.Sc. |
| 36-018 | Moore, Ralph G. | Ph.D. |
| 45-534 | Morantz, Daniel J. | M.Sc. |
| 40-521 | Morehouse, Clarence K. | M.Sc. |
| 32-011 | Morehouse, Fred R. | Ph.D. |
| 31-510 | Morehouse, Fred R. | M.Sc. |
| 30-008 | Morgan, Oliver M. | Ph.D. |
| 34-007 | Morris, Herbert E. | Ph.D. |
| 22-517 | Morrison, Donald M. | M.Sc. |
| 24-004 | Morrison, Donald M. | Ph.D. |
| 43-011 | Morrison, James A. | Ph.D. |
| 37-016 | Morrison, John L. | Ph.D. |
| 54-023 | Morton, Ernest R. | Ph.D. |
| 45-009 | Morton, Maurice | Ph.D. |

| THESIS NUMBER | AUTHOR | DEGREE |
|---|---|---|
| **Chemistry** | | |
| 31-556 | Morton, Richard | M.Sc. |
| 55-027 | Mossman, Carolyn E. | Ph.D. |
| 53-026 | Moulds, Gordon M. | Ph.D. |
| 42-018 | Mowat, John H. | Ph.D. |
| 30-009 | Mueller, William H. | Ph.D. |
| 29-513 | Mueller, William H. | M.Sc. |
| 59-529 | Muller, Thomas E. | M.Sc. |
| 42-019 | Mungen, Richard | Ph.D. |
| 32-025 | Munro, Ferdinand L. | Ph.D. |
| 26-007 | Munro, Lloyd A. | Ph.D. |
| 52-059 | Murdock, James D. | Ph.D. |
| 53-027 | Murray, Francis E. | Ph.D. |
| 40-018 | Naldrett, Stanley Norman | Ph.D. |
| 48-592 | Narasinham, Ramanujaienga | M.Sc. |
| 57-069 | Nawab, Mohammed A. | Ph.D. |
| 42-020 | Neish, Arthur C. | Ph.D. |
| 49-053 | Neubauer, Lewis G. | Ph.D. |
| 36-019 | Nicholls, Robert V. V. | Ph.D. |
| 35-513 | Nicholls, Robert V. V. | M.Sc. |
| 12-516 | Nicolls, Jasper H. | M.Sc. |
| 34-008 | Normington, James B. | Ph.D. |
| 46-013 | Novack, Lazare | Ph.D. |
| 42-021 | Ogilvie, James D. | Ph.D. |
| 40-522 | Ogilvie, James D. | M.Sc. |
| 59-059 | Ogryzlo, Elmer A. | Ph.D. |
| 54-060 | Onyszchuk, Mario | Ph.D. |
| 35-023 | Overbaugh, Sidney C. | Ph.D. |
| 39-017 | Pall, David Boris | Ph.D. |
| 45-011 | Papineau-Couture, Gilles | Ph.D. |
| 30-510 | Paquet, Arthur | M.Sc. |
| 43-508 | Paquette, Joseph P. | M.Sc. |
| 41-506 | Parker, William E. | Ph.D. |
| 39-018 | Parlee, Norman A. | Ph.D. |
| 53-030 | Parsons, Basil I. | Ph.D. |
| 28-010 | Pasternack, David S. | Ph.D. |
| 26-521 | Pasternack, David S. | M.Sc. |
| 55-029 | Pate, Brian D. | Ph.D. |
| 42-505 | Patterson, Ralph Francis | Ph.D. |
| 24-550 | Patton, Isabelle J. | M.Sc. |
| 41-012 | Pearce, Jesse Arthur | Ph.D. |
| 30-010 | Peiker, Alfred L. | Ph.D. |
| 39-019 | Peniston, Quintin Pearman | Ph.D. |
| 43-023 | Pepper, James M. | Ph.D. |
| 49-032 | Perlin, Arthur S. | Ph.D. |
| 51-028 | Perry, Ernest J. | Ph.D. |



| THESIS NUMBER | AUTHOR | DEGREE |
|---|---|---|
| **Chemistry** | | |
| 38-022 | Perry, Stanley Z. | Ph.D. |
| 30-011 | Phillips, John B. | Ph.D. |
| 28-522 | Phillips, John B. | M.Sc. |
| 38-015 | Phillips, Norman W. | Ph.D. |
| 29-011 | Pidgeon, Lloyd M. | Ph.D. |
| 27-541 | Pidgeon, Lloyd M. | M.Sc. |
| 32-012 | Platt, Muriel E. | Ph.D. |
| 29-516 | Platt, Muriel E. | M.Sc. |
| 34-010 | Plewes, Argyle C. | Ph.D. |
| 34-023 | Plunguian, Mark | Ph.D. |
| 46-031 | Polley, John R. | Ph.D. |
| 39-020 | Potvin, Roger | Ph.D. |
| 32-013 | Powell, Edward C. | Ph.D. |
| 33-015 | Price, Aubrey F. | Ph.D. |
| 38-023 | Puddington, Ira E. | Ph.D. |
| 33-526 | Pullman, Joseph C. | M.Sc. |
| 35-032 | Pullman, Joseph C. | Ph.D. |
| 39-021 | Pyle, James Johnston | Ph.D. |
| 42-022 | Rabinovitch, Benton S. | Ph.D. |
| 56-060 | Rabinovitch, William | Ph.D. |
| 51-029 | Ralph, Arthur O. | Ph.D. |
| 59-065 | Ramaradhya, Jakkanahally | Ph.D. |
| 59-067 | Read, Dale W. | Ph.D. |
| 49-054 | Read, Donald E. | Ph.D. |
| 52-583 | Redkevitch, Zenon | M.Sc. |
| 33-017 | Reeve, Herbert A. | Ph.D. |
| 31-557 | Reeve, Herbert A. | M.Sc. |
| 53-033 | Reid, Albert R. | Ph.D. |
| 40-504 | Reid, Evans Burton | Ph.D. |
| 15-513 | Reid, Hugh S. | M.Sc. |
| 33-018 | Richardson, Ronald E. | Ph.D. |
| 31-513 | Richardson, Ronald E. | M.Sc. |
| 40-020 | Richmond, James Hugh | Ph.D. |
| 47-018 | Ritchie, Paul F. | Ph.D. |
| 49-034 | Robertson, Alexander A. | Ph.D. |
| 07-512 | Robertson, Arthur F. | M.Sc. |
| 25-526 | Robertson, Carol F. | M.Sc. |
| 55-031 | Robertson, Roderick F. | Ph.D. |
| 44-013 | Robertson, Ross E. | Ph.D. |
| 43-012 | Robinson, Donald B. | Ph.D. |
| 25-527 | Robison, Samuel C. | M.Sc. |
| 52-028 | Rooney, Clarence P. | Ph.D. |
| 36-011 | Rosenberg, Solomon | Ph.D. |
| 34-515 | Rosenberg, Solomon | M.Sc. |
| 37-019 | Ross, Archibald S. | Ph.D. |

Chemistry

| THESIS NUMBER | AUTHOR | DEGREE |
|---|---|---|
| 44-522 | Rosten, Jean | M.Sc. |
| 29-012 | Rowley, Harry J. | Ph.D. |
| 49-035 | Roxburgh, James M. | Ph.D. |
| 56-031 | Roy, Louis P. | Ph.D. |
| 37-020 | Rudoff, Hyman | Ph.D. |
| 46-576 | Russell, Gordon D. | M.Sc. |
| 27-010 | Russell, John | Ph.D. |
| 18-506 | Russell, John | M.Sc. |
| 34-013 | Russell, John K. | Ph.D. |
| 48-036 | Russell, Stewart H. | Ph.D. |
| 52-585 | Sabean, Allan T. | M.Sc. |
| 54-064 | Sacks, William | Ph.D. |
| 34-014 | Sallans, Henry R. | Ph.D. |
| 37-022 | Sanders, Herbert L. | Ph.D. |
| 35-516 | Sanders, Herbert L. | M.Sc. |
| 53-073 | Sanderson, Edwin S. | Ph.D. |
| 30-013 | Sankey, Charles A. | Ph.D. |
| 28-523 | Sankey, Charles A. | M.Sc. |
| 58-041 | Santry, Dallas C. | Ph.D. |
| 53-074 | Sanyal, Amiya K. | Ph.D. |
| 22-520 | Saul, Bernard B. | M.Sc. |
| 32-015 | Saunderson, Hugh H. | Ph.D. |
| 42-530 | Savard, Kenneth F.G. | M.Sc. |
| 31-013 | Sawyer, William R. | Ph.D. |
| 33-528 | Scarrow, James A. | M.Sc. |
| 34-015 | Scarrow, James A. | Ph.D. |
| 58-042 | Schavo, Anton F. | Ph.D. |
| 41-048 | Schiessler, Robert Walter | M.Sc. |
| 41-015 | Schneider, William George | Ph.D. |
| 51-030 | Schrage, Samuel | Ph.D. |
| 39-502 | Schwartz, Harry | Ph.D. |
| 56-032 | Scott, Robert I. | Ph.D. |
| 56-033 | Screaton, Rose M. | Ph.D. |
| 46-032 | Segall, Gordon H. | Ph.D. |
| 53-036 | Seidman, Ruth | Ph.D. |
| 20-001 | Seyer, William F. | Ph.D. |
| 40-022 | Shane, Gerald | Ph.D. |
| 38-521 | Shane, Gerald | M.Sc. |
| 55-073 | Shaw, Alan C. | Ph.D. |
| 36-012 | Shaw, Geoffrey T. | Ph.D. |
| 22-522 | Shaw, Thomas P. | M.Sc. |
| 34-025 | Sheps, Louis J. | Ph.D. |
| 51-057 | Sherbeck, Leander A. | Ph.D. |
| 38-016 | Shipley, John H. | Ph.D. |
| 26-559 | Shotwell, John S. | M.Sc. |



Chemistry

| THESIS NUMBER | AUTHOR | DEGREE |
|---|---|---|
| 55-074 | Shyluk, Walter F. | Ph.D. |
| 44-022 | Siminovitch, Louis | Ph.D. |
| 50-042 | Sims, Richard F. | Ph.D. |
| 46-033 | Sirianni, Aurele F. | Ph.D. |
| 26-004 | Sivertz, Christian | Ph.D. |
| 24-529 | Sivertz, Christian | M.Sc. |
| 26-005 | Sivertz, Victorian | Ph.D. |
| 39-503 | Skey, Arthur James | Ph.D. |
| 45-020 | Smart, George N. Russell | Ph.D. |
| 56-034 | Smith, Donald M. | Ph.D. |
| 24-530 | Smith, Frederick M. | M.Sc. |
| 45-540 | Smith, Melvin J. | M.Sc. |
| 38-018 | Smith, Walter M. | Ph.D. |
| 55-076 | Snyder, John L. | Ph.D. |
| 57-078 | Sobering, Simon E. | Ph.D. |
| 40-024 | Soley, Russell Clyne | Ph.D. |
| 34-017 | Solomon, Ernest | Ph.D. |
| 33-020 | Spanagel, Edgar W. | Ph.D. |
| 47-036 | Spivack, John D. | Ph.D. |
| 57-081 | Stachiw, Dennis I. | Ph.D. |
| 29-518 | Starrock, Murray G. | M.Sc. |
| 26-006 | Steacie, Edgar W. | Ph.D. |
| 24-532 | Steacie, Edgar W. | M.Sc. |
| 36-013 | Steeves, William H. | Ph.D. |
| 23-006 | Stephens, Henry N. | Ph.D. |
| 33-021 | Stewart, William W. | Ph.D. |
| 31-559 | Stewart, William W. | M.Sc. |
| 45-541 | Stinton, Arthur W. | M.Sc. |
| 38-019 | Stovel, Henry V. | Ph.D. |
| 33-571 | Stovel, Henry V. | M.Sc. |
| 42-024 | Stuart, Allan P. | Ph.D. |
| 30-014 | Sturrock, Murray G. | Ph.D. |
| 55-040 | Sukava, Armas J. | Ph.D. |
| 28-008 | Sutherland, Brian P. | Ph.D. |
| 26-527 | Sutherland, Brian P. | M.Sc. |
| 57-539 | Sutherland, Charlotte A. | M.Sc. |
| 31-008 | Sutherland, Hugh S. | Ph.D. |
| 29-520 | Sutherland, Hugh S. | M.Sc. |
| 32-016 | Sutherland, John W. | Ph.D. |
| 57-038 | Swan, Eric P. | Ph.D. |
| 37-023 | Swartz, Joseph N. | Ph.D. |
| 33-022 | Tapp, James S. | Ph.D. |
| 31-567 | Tapp, James S. | M.A. |
| 47-037 | Tasker, Clinton W. | Ph.D. |
| 29-014 | Taylor, Kenneth A. | Ph.D. |

Chemistry

| THESIS NUMBER | AUTHOR | DEGREE |
|---|---|---|
| 40-025 | Taylor, William Dixon | Ph.D. |
| 51-032 | Thomas, Gordon | Ph.D. |
| 57-040 | Thomas, Telfer L. | Ph.D. |
| 43-013 | Thompson, Allan L. | Ph.D. |
| 54-071 | Thompson, Norman S. | Ph.D. |
| 25-007 | Thomson, Walter W. | Ph.D. |
| 23-518 | Thomson, Walter W. | M.Sc. |
| 47-038 | Thorn, George D. | Ph.D. |
| 53-077 | Tink, Roland R. | Ph.D. |
| 55-079 | Toby, Sidney | Ph.D. |
| 40-506 | Tomecko, Joseph Wesely | Ph.D. |
| 35-026 | Tomlinson, George H. | Ph.D. |
| 48-012 | Tomlinson, Richard H. | Ph.D. |
| 49-039 | Tonks, David B. | Ph.D. |
| 29-015 | Toole, Francis J. | Ph.D. |
| 26-529 | Toole, Francis J. | M.Sc. |
| 41-017 | Topp, Allan C. | Ph.D. |
| 51-034 | Trevelyan, Benjamin J. | Ph.D. |
| 52-032 | Trick, Gordon S. | Ph.D. |
| 34-018 | Trister, Saul M. | Ph.D. |
| 47-019 | Trost, Walter R. | Ph.D. |
| 44-523 | Trottier, Bernard | M.Sc. |
| 47-020 | Tuck, Norman G. | Ph.D. |
| 51-035 | Turner, Robert C. | Ph.D. |
| 49-624 | Turner, Robert C. | M.Sc. |
| 58-051 | Unni, Ayalur K. | Ph.D. |
| 50-022 | Van Straten, Sylvia F. | Ph.D. |
| 35-027 | Van_Cleave, Allan B. | Ph.D. |
| 58-053 | Verbeke, Gentil J. | Ph.D. |
| 55-044 | Verschingel, Roger H. | Ph.D. |
| 52-062 | Versteeg, Joseph | Ph.D. |
| 53-038 | Vincent, Donald L. | Ph.D. |
| 52-063 | Viron, Silvio J. | Ph.D. |
| 45-013 | Vroom, Alan H. | Ph.D. |
| 57-042 | Waid, Ted H. | Ph.D. |
| 23-007 | Waldbauer, Louis J. | Ph.D. |
| 22-525 | Waldbauer, Louis J. | M.Sc. |
| 37-024 | Walker, Forestier | Ph.D. |
| 35-518 | Walker, Forestier | M.Sc. |
| 48-043 | Walker, Jessie M. | Ph.D. |
| 50-048 | Walker, Osman J. | Ph.D. |
| 20-002 | Walker, Osman J. | Ph.D. |
| 42-025 | Wang, Sheng-Nien | Ph.D. |
| 26-532 | Warren, Thomas R. | M.Sc. |
| 42-026 | Wasson, Burton K. | Ph.D. |



Chemistry

| THESIS NUMBER | AUTHOR | DEGREE |
|---|---|---|
| 40-525 | Watts, Humphrey Stanley | M.Sc. |
| 54-073 | Watts, Trevor A. | Ph.D. |
| 41-509 | Weaver, William Strathern | Ph.D. |
| 49-058 | Weininger, Joseph J. | Ph.D. |
| 33-034 | Wells, Franklin B. | Ph.D. |
| 31-560 | Wells, Franklin B. | M.Sc. |
| 42-507 | West, Einar | Ph.D. |
| 42-027 | West, Kenneth A. | Ph.D. |
| 59-084 | Westbury, Ronald A. | Ph.D. |
| 52-034 | Whalley, Basil J. | Ph.D. |
| 29-016 | Whelen, Myron S. | Ph.D. |
| 20-003 | Whitby, George S. | Ph.D. |
| 18-507 | Whitby, George S. | M.Sc. |
| 36-015 | White, Elwood V. | Ph.D. |
| 34-519 | White, Elwood V. | M.Sc. |
| 46-017 | White, Howard L. | Ph.D. |
| 43-014 | White, W. Harold | Ph.D. |
| 53-040 | Whiteway, Stirling G. | Ph.D. |
| 50-639 | Whittall, Norman S. | M.Sc. |
| 52-035 | Wiebe, Allan K. | Ph.D. |
| 57-089 | Wieckowski, Erwin | Ph.D. |
| 18-508 | Wieland, Walter A. | M.Sc. |
| 46-018 | Wiggins, Ernest J. | Ph.D. |
| 57-046 | Wiles, David M. | Ph.D. |
| 32-017 | Williams, Alan P. | Ph.D. |
| 43-015 | Williams, Harry L. | Ph.D. |
| 33-026 | Wilson, Charles V. | Ph.D. |
| 33-027 | Winkler, Carl A. | Ph.D. |
| 46-019 | Wise, Louis M. | Ph.D. |
| 53-079 | Wood, John C. | Ph.D. |
| 57-048 | Wright, Archibald N. | Ph.D. |
| 21-003 | Wright, Charles A. | Ph.D. |
| 31-010 | Wright, Robert H. | Ph.D. |
| 30-516 | Wright, Robert H. | M.Sc. |
| 30-553 | Wyman, Harold R. | M.Sc. |
| 43-016 | Yaffe, Leo | Ph.D. |
| 47-039 | Yan, Maxwell M. | Ph.D. |
| 52-037 | Yates, Havelock H. | Ph.D. |
| 28-012 | Yorston, Frederic H. | Ph.D. |
| 24-535 | Yorston, Frederic H. | M.Sc. |
| 36-016 | Young, Donald M. | Ph.D. |
| 38-524 | Yuen, Henry B. | M.Sc. |
| 59-077 | Zienius, Raymond H. | Ph.D. |
| 51-039 | Zorbach, William W. | Ph.D. |
| 43-024 | Zuckerman, Abraham | Ph.D. |

| THESIS NUMBER | AUTHOR | DEGREE |
|---|---|---|

## Chemistry

## Chinese Studies

| | | |
|---|---|---|
| 33-560 | Taylor, Gordon R. | M.A. |

## Civil Engineering & Applied Mechanics

| | | |
|---|---|---|
| 59-566 | Ahmed, Syed I. | M.Eng. |
| 54-501 | Anand, Tilakraj R. | M.Eng. |
| 32-500 | Arcand, Louis J. | M.Eng. |
| 56-502 | Banks, Ronald H. | M.Eng. |
| 50-582 | Bernard, Gerald A. | M.Eng. |
| 53-505 | Bhasin, Parkash C. | M.Eng. |
| 51-582 | Bradbury, John S. | M.Eng. |
| 26-504 | Campbell, Alexander | M.Sc. |
| 54-561 | Campbell, Hugh A. | M.Eng. |
| 53-506 | Chow, David Y. | M.Eng. |
| 45-500 | Clark, Robert H. | M.Eng. |
| 54-503 | Coates, Donald F. | M.Eng. |
| 51-583 | Coldwell, Keith L. | M.Eng. |
| 34-540 | Craig, Carleton | M.Eng. |
| 16-507 | Cronk, Francis J. | M.Sc. |
| 46-552 | De Stein, Joseph L. | M.Eng. |
| 52-562 | Drouin, Paul-Emile | M.Eng. |
| 22-505 | Eadie, Robert S. | M.Sc. |
| 49-587 | Ellis, John S. | M.Eng. |
| 49-588 | Eskenazi, Beno | M.Eng. |
| 33-501 | Evans, Delano E. | M.Eng. |
| 46-502 | Freeman, Paul C. | M.Eng. |
| 58-503 | Galbiati, Ignazio V. | M.Eng. |
| 58-504 | Genest, George L. | M.Eng. |
| 48-505 | Gersovitz, Benjamin | M.Eng. |
| 54-564 | Ghitis, Albert | M.Eng. |
| 55-505 | Girolami, Renato L. | M.Eng. |
| 55-573 | Goldman, Carl | M.Eng. |
| 38-501 | Griffiths, George H. | M.Eng. |
| 36-500 | Hamilton, Donald M. | M.Eng. |
| 49-589 | Harris, Philip J. | M.Eng. |
| 39-051 | Hum, Thed Klung | M.Eng. |
| 57-507 | Issen, Lionel | M.Eng. |
| 32-502 | Jacobsen, Eric R. | M.Eng. |
| 55-575 | Jakobson, Gunnar J. | M.Eng. |
| 20-505 | Jamieson, Robert E. | M.Sc. |



| THESIS NUMBER | AUTHOR | DEGREE |
|---|---|---|

## Civil Engineering & Applied Mechanics

| | | |
|---|---|---|
| 34-502 | Jehu, Llewellyn | M.Eng. |
| 50-586 | Joly, George W. | M.Eng. |
| 53-507 | Kennedy, David H. | M.Eng. |
| 36-545 | Kirk, William D. | M.Eng. |
| 52-504 | Lorimer, Harry P. | M.Eng. |
| 36-502 | Lupton, Mac J. | M.Eng. |
| 22-514 | Macdonald, Albert F. | M.Sc. |
| 54-565 | MacFarlane, Ivan C. | M.Eng. |
| 59-570 | Mathison, William | M.Eng. |
| 55-506 | McCutcheon, John C. | M.Eng. |
| 31-555 | McDougall, John F. | M.Sc. |
| 27-512 | Morrison, Carson F. | M.Sc. |
| 56-558 | Neis, Vernon V. | M.Eng. |
| 57-510 | Padopulos, Diogenes | M.Eng. |
| 36-504 | Pidoux, John L. | M.Eng. |
| 32-553 | Pimenoff, Clement J. | M.Eng. |
| 36-505 | Poole, Gordon D. | M.Eng. |
| 34-505 | Savage, Palmer E. | M.Eng. |
| 40-036 | Seto, Kin | M.Eng. |
| 25-549 | Shaw, Gerald F. | M.Sc. |
| 56-511 | Spratt, Gordon W. | M.Eng. |
| 59-571 | Thompson, Richard D. | M.Eng. |
| 53-567 | Townsend, David I. | M.Eng. |
| 57-512 | Van Walsum, Ewout | M.Eng. |
| 59-506 | Waterston, John F. | M.Eng. |
| 58-507 | Yong, Raymond N. | M.Eng. |

## Civil Law

| | | |
|---|---|---|
| 34-506 | Charlap, Gregory | M.C.L. |
| 46-500 | Cuevas Cancino, Francisco | M.C.L. |
| 59-500 | Dobson, Christopher R. | M.C.L. |
| 51-579 | MacKay, Kenneth C. | M.C.L. |

## Classics

| | | |
|---|---|---|
| 56-612 | Brown, Carl P. | M.A. |
| 11-502 | Cockfield, Harry R. | M.A. |
| 35-527 | Grant, Mary J. | M.A. |
| 36-531 | Harvie, Jean E. | M.A. |
| 41-027 | Levitt, Bella | M.A. |
| 37-525 | Lumsden, Stanley G. | M.A. |
| 46-541 | Macdonald, Roderick R. | M.A. |

## Classics

| THESIS NUMBER | AUTHOR | DEGREE |
|---|---|---|
| 46-543 | Macpherson, John | M.A. |
| 16-505 | MacKenzie, Francis S. | M.A. |
| 36-537 | MacQueen, David J. | M.A. |
| 30-538 | Moore, Ruth E. | M.A. |
| 43-513 | Pitt, Edith S. | M.A. |
| 52-609 | Puhvel, Jaan | M.A. |
| 39-045 | Scotcher, Charles W.D. | M.A. |
| 08-506 | Smith, Ella L. | M.A. |
| 42-044 | Smith, Stanley Alfred | M.A. |
| 13-511 | Steacy, Frederick W. | M.A. |
| 53-555 | Vallillee, Gerald A. | M.A. |
| 08-507 | Vincent, Irving O. | M.A. |
| 58-549 | Weller, Judith A. | M.A. |

## Comparative Religion

| THESIS NUMBER | AUTHOR | DEGREE |
|---|---|---|
| 55-633 | McDonough, Sheila D. | M.A. |

## Divinity

| THESIS NUMBER | AUTHOR | DEGREE |
|---|---|---|
| 59-565 | Bertalot, Renzo | S.T.M. |
| 58-502 | Davison, Roy J. | S.T.M. |
| 06-003 | Day, Frank J. | M.A. |
| 54-047 | Ellis, Clarence D. | Ph.D. |
| 53-559 | Enger, Knut | S.T.M. |
| 57-555 | Gerard, F.P. | S.T.M. |
| 55-500 | Gough, Cyril H. | S.T.M. |
| 53-504 | Kingsford, Maurice P. | S.T.M. |
| 57-503 | Kirby, John C. | S.T.M. |
| 55-570 | Koshy, Kuttickal I. | S.T.M. |
| 56-500 | Kurien, Vadkumkara T. | S.T.M. |
| 56-501 | Newman, Robert S. | S.T.M. |
| 54-559 | Osborne, Robert E. | S.T.M. |
| 55-501 | Perret, Edmond J. | S.T.M. |
| 55-571 | Poole, Aquila J. | S.T.M. |
| 07-506 | Rice, Horace G. | M.A. |
| 13-508 | Robinson, Bernard S. | M.A. |
| 57-556 | Rogers, A.A. | S.T.M. |
| 54-500 | Sass, Frederick W. | S.T.M. |
| 56-552 | Skynner, H.J. | S.T.M. |
| 57-557 | Zuk, Michael | S.T.M. |

## Economics

| THESIS NUMBER | AUTHOR | DEGREE |
|---|---|---|
| 54-002 | Adams, William E. | Ph.D. |
| 52-544 | Adams, William F. | M.A. |
| 46-582 | Albert, Ruth P. | M.A. |
| 52-545 | Aligwekwe, Iwucha E. | M.A. |
| 48-555 | Amyot, Denis T. | M.A. |
| 54-004 | Armstrong, Donald F. | Ph.D. |
| 54-539 | Armstrong, Muriel G. | M.A. |
| 53-547 | Asimakopulos, Athanasios | M.A. |
| 51-630 | Bacarinos, Eusthathios S. | M.A. |
| 33-534 | Baker, Kenneth G. | M.A. |
| 30-517 | Best, Kathleen E. | M.A. |
| 50-646 | Betcherman, Philip | M.A. |
| 36-524 | Bloomfield, Arthur I. | M.A. |
| 27-523 | Bogante, Jack F. | M.A. |
| 28-529 | Boos, Albert W. | M.A. |
| 33-538 | Bowker, Ernest F. | M.A. |
| 34-523 | Brenhouse, Samuel F. | M.A. |
| 51-002 | Breul, Frank R. | Ph.D. |
| 51-645 | Broadbent, Arnot W. | M.Com. |
| 54-540 | Brown, Irving | M.A. |
| 47-540 | Burgess, Charles J. | M.Com. |
| 30-519 | Burk, Christopher A. | M.A. |
| 47-576 | Bush, Willard S. | M.A. |
| 30-520 | Camerlain, Homer H. | M.A. |
| 54-610 | Capelovitch, Edward M. | M.A. |
| 51-565 | Caralopoulos, Nicholas | M.A. |
| 30-521 | Carroll, Lovell C. | M.A. |
| 33-542 | Challies, George S. | M.A. |
| 58-010 | Charles, J. Koilpillai | Ph.D. |
| 29-526 | Cheasley, Clifford H. | M.A. |
| 48-609 | Chipman, John S. | M.A. |
| 35-524 | Clark, Edgar H. Jr. | M.A. |
| 39-031 | Clark, Jocelyn Godfrey | M.A. |
| 30-523 | Cohen, Bernard B. | M.A. |
| 53-608 | Collins, Frank I. | M.A. |
| 54-044 | Corbett, David C. | Ph.D. |
| 39-047 | Coughlin, Clifton Rexford | M.Com. |
| 27-527 | Culliton, John T. | M.A. |
| 38-528 | Cumming, Robert S. | M.A. |
| 54-628 | Davoud, Raymond I. | M.Com. |
| 44-514 | Dubensky, Alexander | M.A. |
| 38-529 | Duncan, Albert S. | M.A. |
| 55-628 | Farr, William | M.A. |
| 42-510 | Firestone, Otto Jack | M.A. |
| 43-517 | Fox, Lester L. | M.Com. |

| THESIS NUMBER | AUTHOR | DEGREE |
|---|---|---|
| **Economics** | | |
| 52-604 | Frankel, Saul J. | M.A. |
| 39-034 | Fraser, David Robert | M.A. |
| 46-586 | Friedlander, John B. | M.A. |
| 40-033 | Fullerton, Douglas H. | M.Com. |
| 59-025 | Galbraith, John A. | Ph.D. |
| 50-670 | Galbraith, John A. | M.Com. |
| 53-053 | Gerin-Lajoie, Jean | Ph.D. |
| 41-517 | Gillies, Elizabeth W. | M.A. |
| 34-526 | Gilroy, Geoffrey S. | M.A. |
| 39-035 | Godine, Morton Robert | M.A. |
| 32-527 | Goforth, William W. | M.A. |
| 40-028 | Goldberg, Simon Abraham | M.A. |
| 29-533 | Goldenberg, Hyman C. | M.A. |
| 32-528 | Goodman, Samuel J. | M.A. |
| 53-611 | Goracz, Bela A. | M.A. |
| 28-534 | Gordon, Thomas M. | M.A. |
| 42-512 | Graham, C. R. | M.A. |
| 53-055 | Grasberg, Eugeniusz | Ph.D. |
| 30-528 | Greaves, Ida C. | M.A. |
| 33-545 | Greenlees, William S. | M.A. |
| 29-534 | Gruchy, Allan G. | M.A. |
| 47-532 | Guter, Ernest | M.A. |
| 54-543 | Halford, Charles R. | M.A. |
| 39-048 | Hall, George B. | M.Com. |
| 49-632 | Hanson, James C. | M.A. |
| 28-539 | Hayes, Saul | M.A. |
| 34-549 | Heiber, Sol P. | M.Com. |
| 41-024 | Henderson, Harold Lloyd | M.A. |
| 33-547 | Heuser, Heinrich K. | M.A. |
| 58-020 | Hollbach, Reiner | Ph.D. |
| 53-612 | Hollbach, Reiner | M.A. |
| 42-033 | Hollinger, Martin | M.A. |
| 54-558 | Hutchison, John | M.Com. |
| 43-008 | Jack, Lawrence B. | Ph.D. |
| 27-533 | Janes, Henry F. | M.A. |
| 34-530 | Johnson, John S. | M.A. |
| 29-539 | Johnston, Agnew H. | M.A. |
| 29-540 | Kelland, Frank J. | M.A. |
| 40-029 | Kirchschlager, Hellmuth | M.A. |
| 29-541 | Kirschberg, Abraham | M.A. |
| 37-523 | Kleiner, George | M.A. |
| 58-545 | Kovalski, Voyc | M.A. |
| 57-060 | Kuhn, Tillo E. | Ph.D. |
| 24-540 | Kydd, Mary W. | M.A. |
| 30-533 | Lande, Harold B. | M.A. |



| THESIS NUMBER | AUTHOR | DEGREE |
|---|---|---|
| **Economics** | | |
| 27-534 | Latham, Allan D. | M.A. |
| 26-545 | Layhew, John H. | M.A. |
| 36-536 | Leathem, Ronald M. | M.A. |
| 30-535 | Legge, Katharine B. | M.A. |
| 41-026 | Letichevsky, Jack | M.A. |
| 26-546 | Levy, Gordon W. | M.A. |
| 39-040 | Lipman, Julian A. T. | M.A. |
| 28-542 | Little, John W. | M.A. |
| 33-552 | Lusher, David W. | M.A. |
| 35-530 | Luxton, Edward A. G. | M.A. |
| 20-511 | Macdonald, Isabella L. | M.A. |
| 52-023 | MacIntosh, Robert M. | Ph.D. |
| 49-572 | MacIntosh, Robert M. | M.A. |
| 40-016 | Marsh, Leonard C. | Ph.D. |
| 33-553 | Marsh, Leonard C. | M.A. |
| 53-623 | May, Sydney J. | M.Com. |
| 32-534 | McCracken, Edward J. | M.A. |
| 38-538 | McDonald, Cyril P. | M.A. |
| 36-544 | McGill, John J. | M.A. |
| 32-535 | McIntyre, George D. | M.A. |
| 29-546 | Mendels, Morton M. | M.A. |
| 54-547 | Mennie, William A. | M.A. |
| 59-614 | Mieszkowski, Peter M. | M.A. |
| 47-538 | Mindes, Evelyn | M.A. |
| 50-571 | Morrow, James W. | M.A. |
| 59-615 | Mubarak, Nasreldin | M.A. |
| 30-539 | Munroe, David C. | M.A. |
| 38-540 | Murray, Sydney G. | M.A. |
| 54-059 | Murty, Grandhi V. | Ph.D. |
| 46-545 | Nakashima, Kimiaki | M.A. |
| 33-563 | Nelles, James G. | M.Com. |
| 54-550 | Nielsen, Niels H. | M.A. |
| 59-558 | Nixon, Justin W. | M.A. |
| 38-541 | Noyes, Harry A. Jr. | M.A. |
| 50-661 | Oliver, Michael K. | M.A. |
| 34-537 | Owen, George R. | M.A. |
| 54-551 | Pennie, T.F. | M.A. |
| 24-543 | Peterson, Frederick O. | M.A. |
| 41-013 | Petrie, Richards J. | Ph.D. |
| 58-587 | Petrogiannis, Demetrios S | M.A. |
| 32-538 | Picard, Robert I. | M.A. |
| 37-530 | Pick, Alfred J. | M.A. |
| 50-580 | Poapst, James V. | M.Com. |
| 37-546 | Popkin, John W. | M.A. |
| 54-028 | Potter, Calvin C. | Ph.D. |

## Economics

| THESIS NUMBER | AUTHOR | DEGREE |
|---|---|---|
| 50-671 | Potter, Calvin C. | M.Com. |
| 50-018 | Pugsley, William H. | Ph.D. |
| 43-527 | Randolf, John H. | M.A. |
| 29-547 | Reed, John G. | M.A. |
| 32-541 | Reid, Ewart P. | M.A. |
| 42-039 | Reisman, Sol | M.A. |
| 23-526 | Renaud, Paul E. | M.A. |
| 57-609 | Rezek, G. | M.A. |
| 32-543 | Rollit, John B. | M.A. |
| 34-011 | Rollit, John B. | Ph.D. |
| 59-561 | Roseman, Frank | M.A. |
| 39-044 | Ross, Charles Alexander | M.A. |
| 46-549 | Rothschild, Fred | M.A. |
| 33-557 | Rountree, George M. | M.A. |
| 58-589 | Rymes, Thomas K. | M.A. |
| 30-544 | Savage, Mae L. | M.A. |
| 32-546 | Schwab, Jean G. | M.A. |
| 50-664 | Shipley, William C. | M.A. |
| 51-642 | Sievwright, Eric C. | M.A. |
| 43-515 | Sirken, Irving A. | M.A. |
| 56-550 | Steigmann, Axel H. | M.A. |
| 54-629 | Stenason, Walter | M.Com. |
| 33-559 | Stone, Fred V. | M.A. |
| 41-522 | Stovel, John Archibald | M.A. |
| 35-535 | Styles, Arthur D. | M.A. |
| 56-551 | Subroto | M.A. |
| 54-630 | Sussman, Edmond | M.Com. |
| 40-032 | Tetrault, Claude Moncel | M.A. |
| 59-563 | Thanos, Costas A. | M.A. |
| 22-529 | Troop, George R. | M.A. |
| 29-550 | Troop, William H. | M.A. |
| 32-552 | Trotter, Wallace S. | M.Com. |
| 48-571 | Van Holsbeek, Henri M. | M.Com. |
| 57-087 | Velay, Clement C. | Ph.D. |
| 55-563 | Velay, Clement C. | M.A. |
| 36-542 | Vineberg, Philip F. | M.A. |
| 33-564 | Weissenburger, Pierre C. | M.Com. |
| 52-066 | Weldon, John C. | Ph.D. |
| 24-547 | Willard, Eugene W. | M.A. |
| 49-582 | Wilson, James D. | M.A. |
| 58-550 | Wilson, William D. | M.A. |
| 38-543 | Winkler, Louis | M.A. |
| 54-075 | Wiseman, Sylvia | Ph.D. |
| 50-579 | Wiseman, Sylvia | M.A. |
| 49-646 | Wolfe, Nathan | M.A. |

## Economics

| THESIS NUMBER | AUTHOR | DEGREE |
|---|---|---|
| 53-622 | Woodfine, William J. | M.A. |
| 41-031 | Wykes, Neville George | M.A. |

## Economics & Political Science

| THESIS NUMBER | AUTHOR | DEGREE |
|---|---|---|
| 26-535 | Aikman, Cecil P. | M.A. |
| 58-001 | Andracki, Stanislaw | Ph.D. |
| 58-536 | Bale, Cecil G. | M.A. |
| 31-520 | Bergithon, Carl | M.A. |
| 31-521 | Berman, Alfred | M.A. |
| 25-531 | Blumenstein, Jacob H. | M.A. |
| 59-005 | Boote, Maurice J. | Ph.D. |
| 58-581 | Bosnitch, Sava | M.A. |
| 25-533 | Brownstein, Charles | M.A. |
| 31-524 | Caplan, Benjamin | M.A. |
| 58-011 | Chidzero, Bernard T. | Ph.D. |
| 14-502 | Common, Frank B. | M.A. |
| 22-526 | Davidson, Winnifred H. | M.A. |
| 29-528 | Draper, Herbert I. | M.A. |
| 13-503 | Ellison, Myra K. | M.A. |
| 29-529 | Epstein, Elsie | M.A. |
| 24-537 | Fair, Louisa M. | M.A. |
| 31-530 | Feiner, Abraham | M.A. |
| 27-530 | Forbes, Frederic J. | M.A. |
| 26-541 | Forsey, Eugene A. | M.A. |
| 41-005 | Forsey, Eugene A. | Ph.D. |
| 58-014 | Frankel, Saul J. | Ph.D. |
| 28-533 | Goforth, John F. | M.A. |
| 30-529 | Hamilton, Andrew W. | M.A. |
| 28-536 | Harris, Theodore F. | M.A. |
| 59-610 | Haugestad, Per T. | M.A. |
| 57-015 | Henry, Zin A. | Ph.D. |
| 55-551 | Henry, Zin A. | M.A. |
| 59-611 | Horowitz, Gad | M.A. |
| 24-539 | Jones, Randolph K. | M.A. |
| 52-607 | Mantzavinos, A. | M.A. |
| 55-568 | Marshall, Joyce A. | M.Com. |
| 58-546 | Martin, Fernand | M.A. |
| 21-523 | Nichol, Helen F. | M.A. |
| 55-556 | O'Brien, John W. | M.A. |
| 12-503 | Paterson, Edith L. | M.A. |
| 31-539 | Pattison, Irma E. | M.A. |
| 07-504 | Pearson, Mary F. | M.A. |
| 54-618 | Piscopo, Franco A. | M.A. |

| THESIS NUMBER | AUTHOR | DEGREE |
|---|---|---|
| **Economics & Political Science** | | |
| 55-557 | Plunkett, Thomas | M.A. |
| 59-559 | Polianski, Alexei N. | M.A. |
| 58-035 | Prives, Moshe Z. | Ph.D. |
| 55-559 | Prives, Moshe Z. | M.A. |
| 26-552 | Reich, Nathan | M.A. |
| 31-541 | Rubin, Lionel L. | M.A. |
| 50-577 | Sakellaropoulos, Michael | M.A. |
| 58-043 | Schmidt, Stephen C. | Ph.D. |
| 31-542 | Shlakman, Vera | M.A. |
| 31-550 | Smith, Greig B. | M.Com. |
| 13-510 | Stalker, Archibald | M.A. |
| 26-557 | Tombs, Laurence C. | M.A. |
| 31-548 | Willis, Stewart W. | M.A. |
| 31-549 | Woods, Harry D. | M.A. |
| **Education** | | |
| 38-550 | Astbury, John S. | M.A. |
| 32-525 | Benning, Paulette | M.A. |
| 41-019 | Bercuson, Leonard | M.A. |
| 33-537 | Binmore, Mary E. | M.A. |
| 42-028 | Bolger, Josephine A. | M.A. |
| 38-526 | Boulkind, Mabel | M.A. |
| 11-501 | Brittain, Isabel E. | M.A. |
| 34-545 | Devenney, Hartland M. | M.A. |
| 56-615 | Dowd, Keith J. | M.A. |
| 54-542 | Farrell, Edna P. | M.A. |
| 53-610 | Ferrabee, Henry G. | M.A. |
| 49-558 | Flower, George E. | M.A. |
| 50-565 | Fraser, Arnold W. | M.A. |
| 41-516 | Gallagher, John | M.A. |
| 34-525 | Gill, Dorothy A. | M.A. |
| 45-514 | Hamilton, Lorne D. | M.A. |
| 38-530 | Henry, Arthur M. | M.A. |
| 34-528 | Holland, Catherine N. | M.A. |
| 53-551 | Hurst, Norman | M.A. |
| 21-519 | Jones, Thomas W. | M.A. |
| 58-543 | Kabayama, Joan E. | M.A. |
| 44-525 | Kidd, James R. | M.A. |
| 31-534 | Lang, John G. | M.A. |
| 32-532 | Lees, David | M.A. |
| 57-549 | Lieber, Jack W. | M.A. |
| 16-503 | Livinson, Abraham J. | M.A. |
| 47-579 | Lynam, Josephine B. | M.A. |



| THESIS NUMBER | AUTHOR | DEGREE |
|---|---|---|
| **Education** | | |
| 48-615 | MacFarlane, Joan M. | M.A. |
| 32-536 | MacKinnon, Patrick A. | M.A. |
| 45-517 | MacLean, Mona G. | M.A. |
| 43-525 | Magee, Arch W. | M.A. |
| 48-616 | McLeish, John A. | M.A. |
| 57-551 | Milley, Chesley B. | M.A. |
| 46-544 | Munroe, William M. | M.A. |
| 55-637 | Oulton, Rhodes C. | M.A. |
| 57-552 | Overing, R.I. | M.A. |
| 17-501 | Pelletier, Annie H. | M.A. |
| 45-546 | Penrose, George H. | M.A. |
| 42-038 | Price, Frederick William | M.A. |
| 54-552 | Price, John W. | M.A. |
| 36-552 | Rexford, Orrin B. | M.A. |
| 56-620 | Rosevear, John N. | M.A. |
| 47-581 | Ross, Harold | M.A. |
| 48-617 | Saunders, Thomas B. | M.A. |
| 15-505 | Shearing, Helen A. | M.A. |
| 53-619 | Shearman, George E. | M.A. |
| 40-049 | Sheffield, Edward Fletche | M.A. |
| 59-620 | Skinner, James M. | M.A. |
| 18-502 | Steed, Joseph A. | M.A. |
| 33-575 | Steeves, Lewis R. | M.A. |
| 15-506 | Sutherland, Francis C. | M.A. |
| 35-536 | Thompson, Winifred | M.A. |
| 52-558 | Tomkins, George S. | M.A. |
| 46-594 | Welbourne, Arthur J. | M.A. |
| 51-577 | White, Orville E. | M.A. |
| 11-504 | Wilson, Alice M. | M.A. |
| 57-611 | Wisenthal, M. | M.A. |
| 32-551 | Woodley, Elsie C. | M.A. |
| 17-503 | Worsfold, Henry H. | M.A. |
| 56-625 | Wright, Ouida | M.A. |
| 49-647 | Zweig, David N. | M.A. |
| **Electrical Communications** | | |
| 57-575 | Grierson, John K. | M.Sc. |
| 54-599 | Pearse, Charles D. | M.Sc. |
| **Electrical Engineering** | | |
| 55-502 | Adderson, James N. | M.Eng. |

## Electrical Engineering

| THESIS NUMBER | AUTHOR | DEGREE |
|---|---|---|
| 49-500 | Attas, Isaac | M.Eng. |
| 46-550 | Bastin, Douglas H. | M.Eng. |
| 49-501 | Bennett, John R. | M.Eng. |
| 50-502 | Bennett, Robert M. | M.Eng. |
| 20-503 | Bierler, Etienne S. | M.Sc. |
| 59-567 | Blostein, Maier L. | M.Eng. |
| 49-502 | Boire, Paul C. | M.Eng. |
| 55-503 | Borden, Byron C. | M.Eng. |
| 46-551 | Bott, Raoul H. | M.Eng. |
| 51-581 | Boucher, James E. | M.Eng. |
| 48-504 | Bourne, James D. | M.Eng. |
| 56-554 | Bredahl, Arve | M.Eng. |
| 48-572 | Campbell, Richard H. | M.Eng. |
| 50-503 | Carr, Edward F. | M.Eng. |
| 53-560 | Carruthers, Frederick R. | M.Eng. |
| 58-555 | Caswell, Charles F. | M.Eng. |
| 57-504 | Charasz, Jerzy G. | M.Eng. |
| 54-562 | Chess, Gordon F. | M.Eng. |
| 33-500 | Chipman, Robert A. | M.Eng. |
| 56-555 | Chipps, George E. | M.Eng. |
| 52-561 | Clark, George D. | M.Eng. |
| 56-556 | Coll, David C. | M.Eng. |
| 55-504 | Comsa, Radu P. | M.Eng. |
| 32-501 | Crawford, James M. | M.Eng. |
| 49-586 | Davis, John F. | M.Eng. |
| 34-500 | De Angelis, Marius L. | M.Eng. |
| 51-503 | Ellard, Christopher | M.Eng. |
| 50-505 | Fairley, Randolf D. | M.Eng. |
| 25-516 | Fan, Paul C. | M.Sc. |
| 43-500 | Farmer, Eric W. | M.Eng. |
| 57-054 | Farnell, Gerald W. | Ph.D. |
| 46-554 | Filman, Norman J. | M.Eng. |
| 33-565 | Fisher, Charles B. | M.Eng. |
| 53-561 | Geddes, Leslie A. | M.Eng. |
| 57-558 | Gilbert, Jacques | M.Eng. |
| 49-503 | Godfrey, Gerald | M.Eng. |
| 56-506 | Goldie, Hugh J. | M.Eng. |
| 49-505 | Govindaraj, Sadasiva | M.Eng. |
| 16-510 | Gray, Alexander M. | M.Sc. |
| 51-586 | Gribble, William F. | M.Eng. |
| 52-502 | Groome, George R. | M.Eng. |
| 59-584 | Gunn, Morris W. | M.Sc. |
| 56-507 | Haberl, John F. | M.Eng. |
| 48-506 | Hall, J.S. | M.Eng. |
| 47-503 | Hayes, John E. | M.Eng. |



## Electrical Engineering

| THESIS NUMBER | AUTHOR | DEGREE |
|---|---|---|
| 50-584 | Hayles, Oliver J. | M.Eng. |
| 35-502 | Howe, Lawrence M. | M.Eng. |
| 26-513 | Howes, Frederick S. | M.Sc. |
| 50-506 | Hoy, Norman A. | M.Eng. |
| 47-541 | Hoyle, Wilfred G. | M.Eng. |
| 46-555 | Ives, Walter J. | M.Eng. |
| 33-502 | Jaderholm, Henrik W. | M.Eng. |
| 56-019 | Javid, Mansour | Ph.D. |
| 50-585 | Javid, Mansour | M.Eng. |
| 56-508 | Kahn, Juan P. | M.Eng. |
| 52-049 | Keeping, Kimball J. | Ph.D. |
| 50-587 | Keeping, Kimball J. | M.Eng. |
| 33-567 | Kelsey, Ernest S. | M.Eng. |
| 52-564 | Kelton, Michel E. | M.Eng. |
| 49-506 | Kiang, Tsch-Kia | M.Eng. |
| 57-508 | Kubina, S.J. | M.Eng. |
| 50-588 | Kuhn, Bernard G. | M.Eng. |
| 51-504 | Lam, Mathias | M.Eng. |
| 58-556 | Lee, Ernest S. | M.Eng. |
| 25-522 | LeNeveu, Arthur E. | M.Sc. |
| 49-507 | Marshall, James I. | M.Eng. |
| 52-505 | Martin, William S. | M.Eng. |
| 53-564 | Matusiak, Marvin E. | M.Eng. |
| 47-504 | Merson, Lawrence N. | M.Eng. |
| 32-503 | Moore, William H. | M.Eng. |
| 48-508 | Moore, William J. | M.Eng. |
| 15-512 | Murphy, William H. | M.Sc. |
| 49-508 | Nachfolger, Nathan | M.Eng. |
| 45-501 | Nevitt, Henry J. | M.Eng. |
| 50-508 | Pavich, Michael | M.Eng. |
| 58-033 | Pavlasek, Tomas J. | Ph.D. |
| 48-509 | Pavlasek, Tomas J. | M.Eng. |
| 54-566 | Penton, Reginald | M.Eng. |
| 50-509 | Poznanski, Zolzislaw | M.Eng. |
| 51-589 | Rackow, Alan D. | M.Eng. |
| 57-511 | Real, Roderick E. | M.Eng. |
| 49-509 | Rioux, Philip G. | M.Eng. |
| 49-510 | Roach, Charles I. | M.Eng. |
| 09-516 | Roffey, Myles H. | M.Sc. |
| 50-592 | Rosen, Charles A. | M.Eng. |
| 51-506 | Sakellariou, Theodore | M.Eng. |
| 36-506 | Schippel, Walter H. | M.Eng. |
| 33-505 | Shapiro, Clarence H. | M.Eng. |
| 29-519 | Silver, Ralph C. | M.Sc. |
| 50-593 | Smith, David L. | M.Eng. |

| THESIS NUMBER | AUTHOR | DEGREE |
|---|---|---|
| **Electrical Engineering** | | |
| 53-565 | Stachiewicz, Bogdan R. | M.Eng. |
| 33-506 | Stanley, Thomas D. | M.Eng. |
| 36-550 | Stevens, Robert L. | M.Sc. |
| 58-505 | Stone, Samuel A. | M.Eng. |
| 51-590 | Tai, Yue-Shing | M.Eng. |
| 51-507 | Tatlock, John F. | M.Eng. |
| 20-508 | Trimingham, James H. | M.Sc. |
| 59-505 | Von Hagen, Wallace M. | M.Eng. |
| 21-517 | Wallace, George A. | M.Sc. |
| 49-591 | Weeks, John G. | M.Eng. |
| 47-506 | Yorke-Slader, Geoffrey H. | M.Eng. |
| 51-592 | Yurko, Michael | M.Eng. |
| 59-507 | Zenner, Gerhard P. | M.Eng. |
| **Endocrinology** | | |
| 44-002 | Courtright, Mary N. | Ph.D. |
| 48-523 | Gold, Allen | M.Sc. |
| 47-557 | Macbeth, Robert A. | M.Sc. |
| 46-034 | Toby, Charlotte G. | Ph.D. |
| 47-575 | Wyatt, Barbara V. | M.Sc. |
| **Engine & Machine Design** | | |
| 12-507 | Beagley, Thomas G. | M.Sc. |
| 11-512 | Harris, Norman C. | M.Sc. |
| **Engineering** | | |
| 10-511 | Arkley, Lorne M. | M.Sc. |
| 29-502 | Bain, Archie M. | M.Sc. |
| 11-505 | Ball, Harry S. | M.Sc. |
| 07-507 | Brunner, Godfrey H. | M.Sc. |
| 11-507 | Cox, John R. | M.Sc. |
| 22-503 | Dodd, Geoffrey J. | M.Sc. |
| 10-516 | Fox, Charles H. | M.Sc. |
| 12-509 | Gillespie, Peter | M.Sc. |
| 30-504 | Hardy, Robert M. | M.Sc. |
| 07-509 | Harvey, John B. | M.Sc. |
| 13-518 | Lamb, Henry M. | M.Sc. |
| 09-515 | Pitts, Gordon M. | M.Sc. |
| 15-514 | Spencer, Roy A. | M.Sc. |



| THESIS NUMBER | AUTHOR | DEGREE |
|---|---|---|
| **Engineering** | | |
| 15-515 | Traversy, Eric E. | M.Sc. |
| 24-533 | Trueman, James E. | M.Sc. |
| 22-002 | Von Abo, Cecil V. | Ph.D. |
| **English** | | |
| 37-516 | Allen, Gertrude E. | M.A. |
| 31-519 | Allen, Marguerite Z. | M.A. |
| 33-572 | Amaron, Errol C. | M.A. |
| 50-645 | Ashley, Leonard | M.A. |
| 40-507 | Avison, Henry R. | M.A. |
| 34-522 | Barnett, Elizabeth S. | M.A. |
| 35-519 | Bassinov, Saul | M.A. |
| 46-538 | Beresford-Howe, Constance | M.A. |
| 35-520 | Berry, William G. | M.A. |
| 23-520 | Birkett, Winifred I. | M.A. |
| 38-525 | Bishop, Annetta C. | M.A. |
| 35-522 | Bloomfield, Morton W. | M.A. |
| 35-523 | Blumenthal, Estelle H. | M.A. |
| 36-526 | Bonis, Margaret E. | M.A. |
| 52-546 | Boswell, William C. | M.A. |
| 14-501 | Braeuer, Mary A. | M.A. |
| 29-524 | Brierley, James G. | M.A. |
| 31-522 | Brown, George | M.A. |
| 27-524 | Brown, Richard C. | M.A. |
| 56-613 | Bruck, Esther F. | M.A. |
| 25-534 | Burns, Dean K. | M.A. |
| 33-539 | Calder, Alice D. | M.A. |
| 50-563 | Capps, Margaret C. | M.A. |
| 30-522 | Chait, Rachel | M.A. |
| 37-518 | Chapman, Antony D. | M.A. |
| 58-537 | Clark, Ian C. | M.A. |
| 49-629 | Clark, Mary M. | M.A. |
| 48-556 | Compton, Neil M. | M.A. |
| 36-528 | Conroy, Mary P. | M.A. |
| 48-558 | Coyle, James J. | M.A. |
| 34-524 | Craig, Grace L. | M.A. |
| 31-526 | Cruikshank, Marion G. | M.A. |
| 51-567 | Currie, Robert A. | M.A. |
| 53-609 | Dale, Frances M. | M.A. |
| 45-543 | Dando, John A. | M.A. |
| 27-528 | Davies, Thomas R. | M.A. |
| 23-521 | Davis, Charles F. | M.A. |
| 30-524 | Dawes, Charles H. | M.A. |

| THESIS NUMBER | AUTHOR | DEGREE |
|---|---|---|
| **English** | | |
| 55-627 | Dedering, Christa E. | M.A. |
| 41-512 | Denton, Dorothy May | M.A. |
| 31-527 | Detlor, W. Lyall | M.A. |
| 14-503 | Dewey, George F. | M.A. |
| 37-543 | Dike, Mary E. | M.A. |
| 41-513 | Dolan, John Philip | M.A. |
| 30-525 | Donald, Henry G. | M.A. |
| 58-538 | Douglas, Althea M. | M.A. |
| 45-512 | Duncan, Agnes P. | M.A. |
| 09-501 | Eaton, Mary J. | M.A. |
| 51-568 | Ebbitt, May | M.A. |
| 28-532 | Edel, Joseph L. | M.A. |
| 26-540 | Edwards, Margaret C. | M.A. |
| 50-564 | Fague, William B. | M.A. |
| 37-522 | Falle, George G. | M.A. |
| 50-653 | Fricker, Kathleen M. | M.A. |
| 55-629 | Friend, Gregory | M.A. |
| 42-030 | Fry, Margaret Exie | M.A. |
| 40-027 | Fulford, Lloyd G. | M.A. |
| 49-560 | Geggie, Mary M. | M.A. |
| 59-551 | Goldberg, Barbara J. | M.A. |
| 49-562 | Goodin, Peggy L. | M.A. |
| 30-527 | Gough, Roger W. | M.A. |
| 48-611 | Gowdey, Cecil W. | M.A. |
| 28-563 | Gray, Leona | M.A. |
| 48-562 | Guardo, Lea C. | M.A. |
| 26-543 | Gurd, Jean M. | M.A. |
| 34-527 | Hagerman, Verna B. | M.A. |
| 35-543 | Hamilton, Marion M. | M.A. |
| 36-530 | Hamilton, Robert A. | M.A. |
| 55-549 | Handelman, Saul | M.A. |
| 49-564 | Harding, Lawrence A. | M.A. |
| 24-538 | Harris, Richard C. | M.A. |
| 50-654 | Harrison, John L. | M.A. |
| 33-546 | Hartwell, Robert M. | M.A. |
| 54-544 | Harvey, Mary R. | M.A. |
| 28-537 | Hasley, Isabel J. | M.A. |
| 28-538 | Hayakawa, Samuel I. | M.A. |
| 55-550 | Helfield, Tilya | M.A. |
| 42-032 | Heller, Mildred | M.A. |
| 27-531 | Hemmeon, Ellen C. | M.A. |
| 44-524 | Hemsley, Stuart D. | M.A. |
| 39-036 | Henry, Eleanor May | M.A. |
| 51-636 | Hersh, Jacob | M.A. |
| 36-532 | Hetherington, Elizabeth M | M.A. |



| THESIS NUMBER | AUTHOR | DEGREE |
|---|---|---|
| **English** | | |
| 49-634 | Heuser, Edward A. | M.A. |
| 31-533 | Hewitt, Frank S. | M.A. |
| 33-548 | Hill, Olive M. | M.A. |
| 29-535 | Hodgins, Samuel R. | M.A. |
| 45-515 | Homer, Kenneth C. | M.A. |
| 45-516 | Howe, Margaret G. | M.A. |
| 28-541 | Hudson, James C. | M.A. |
| 14-504 | Hughes, Frederick G. | M.A. |
| 46-587 | Hunter, Gerald F. | M.A. |
| 27-532 | Hutcheson, Maud M. | M.A. |
| 13-506 | Irving, William G. | M.A. |
| 51-637 | Iversen, James E. | M.A. |
| 43-511 | Jackson, Joan S. | M.A. |
| 29-537 | Jahn, Helen I. | M.A. |
| 30-532 | Jenkins, Lloyd H. | M.A. |
| 48-563 | Johnston, Patricia M. | M.A. |
| 49-636 | Jones, Taliesin | M.A. |
| 32-531 | Kaplan, Florence R. | M.A. |
| 53-552 | Keirstead, Marjorie S. | M.A. |
| 38-551 | Kennedy, Judith | M.A. |
| 29-556 | Kiefer, Elsie B. | M.A. |
| 36-534 | Klein, Jenny | M.A. |
| 33-550 | Kronman, Ruth Y. | M.A. |
| 47-533 | Langlois, Robert H. | M.A. |
| 30-534 | Lawrence, Gertrude R. | M.A. |
| 49-638 | Leavitt, Helen R. | M.A. |
| 49-570 | Levine, Albert N. | M.A. |
| 44-515 | Lumsden, Jean G. | M.A. |
| 29-544 | Mackay, Robert de W. | M.A. |
| 10-508 | Macnaughton, Ariel M. | M.A. |
| 49-571 | MacCallan, William D. | M.A. |
| 47-535 | MacDonald, Allister I. | M.A. |
| 31-535 | MacGachen, Freda K. | M.A. |
| 37-526 | MacKenzie, Mary E. | M.A. |
| 31-536 | MacLaggan, Marjorie F. | M.A. |
| 26-548 | MacLaren, Margaret J. | M.A. |
| 25-537 | MacLennan, Malcolm | M.A. |
| 24-541 | MacOdrum, Murdoch M. | M.A. |
| 55-555 | Maizel, Norah L. | M.A. |
| 24-542 | Mathewson, Dorothy R. | M.A. |
| 13-507 | McBain, Alexander R. | M.A. |
| 21-520 | McBain, Mary N. | M.A. |
| 41-028 | McDonald, Elizabeth | M.A. |
| 10-505 | McDonald, Jessie | M.A. |
| 23-523 | McGreer, Edgar D. | M.A. |

## English

| THESIS NUMBER | AUTHOR | DEGREE |
|---|---|---|
| 10-509 | McNeil, John T. | M.A. |
| 52-550 | Meadowcroft, James W. | M.A. |
| 34-536 | Milburne, Kathleen E. | M.A. |
| 33-554 | Montgomery, Harriet R. | M.A. |
| 43-512 | Mooney, Elizabeth S. | M.A. |
| 23-524 | Moore, Dale H. | M.A. |
| 28-565 | Mullaly, Jessie R. | M.A. |
| 27-536 | Murray, Bertram S. | M.A. |
| 28-548 | Murray, Mae F. | M.A. |
| 27-537 | Murray, Phyllis M. | M.A. |
| 28-549 | Nelson, Eda M. | M.A. |
| 56-548 | Nemser, Ruby D. | M.A. |
| 27-543 | Newton, Theodore F. | M.A. |
| 21-524 | Noad, Algy S. | M.A. |
| 28-550 | O'Brien, Margaret T. | M.A. |
| 37-528 | O'Brien, Michael V. | M.A. |
| 49-574 | O'Sullivan, Timothy | M.A. |
| 49-642 | Orr, Paul A. | M.A. |
| 36-539 | Paist, Gertrude W. | M.A. |
| 57-608 | Passmore, Marian R. | M.A. |
| 36-541 | Perrigard, Elma E. | M.A. |
| 29-557 | Phelan, Lewis J. | M.A. |
| 23-525 | Pickel, Margaret B. | M.A. |
| 54-617 | Pickup, T. | M.A. |
| 50-574 | Piloto, Albert E. | M.A. |
| 50-663 | Pitts, Mary A. | M.A. |
| 26-551 | Preston, George P. | M.A. |
| 54-553 | Puhvel, Martin | M.A. |
| 49-577 | Purcell, Donald | M.A. |
| 33-555 | Putnam, Adelaide D. | M.A. |
| 32-540 | Rand, Frank H. | M.A. |
| 25-540 | Read, Mary G. | M.A. |
| 25-539 | Read, Stanley M. | M.A. |
| 38-552 | Rittenhouse, Charles B. J | M.A. |
| 42-040 | Ross, Sally Chipman | M.A. |
| 56-621 | Rowlands, Mary E. | M.A. |
| 28-566 | Scott, Mary E. | M.A. |
| 39-509 | Shecter, Una | M.A. |
| 58-590 | Sheffy, Pearl P. | M.A. |
| 33-558 | Silver, Helen | M.A. |
| 50-666 | Simon, Beatrice V. | M.A. |
| 56-623 | Skoll, Selma D. | M.A. |
| 26-554 | Smith, Arthur J. | M.A. |
| 06-006 | Smith, Esther M. | M.A. |
| 26-555 | Smith, Henry L. | M.A. |



## English

| THESIS NUMBER | AUTHOR | DEGREE |
|---|---|---|
| 28-554 | Smith, Lawrence I. | M.A. |
| 58-591 | Sproule, Hugh D. | M.A. |
| 43-516 | Stabler, Ernest | M.A. |
| 31-543 | Stansfield, Ellen E. | M.A. |
| 40-512 | Stevens, Valeria Dean | M.A. |
| 54-623 | Stevenson, Stanley W. | M.A. |
| 50-578 | Stewart, Lyall S. | M.A. |
| 31-544 | Sullivan, Norah E. | M.A. |
| 55-561 | Sutherland, Ronald | M.A. |
| 52-557 | Taggart, William R. | M.A. |
| 48-618 | Tansey, Charlotte H. | M.A. |
| 46-593 | Thomson, Allan | M.A. |
| 32-547 | Thorpe, Benjamin J. | M.A. |
| 32-548 | Tough, David L. | M.A. |
| 35-537 | Ulrichsen, Barbara A. | M.A. |
| 24-546 | Walter, Felix H. | M.A. |
| 55-565 | Waterhouse, John | M.A. |
| 49-581 | Wearing, Parker I. | M.A. |
| 32-550 | Werry, Wilfrid W. | M.A. |
| 52-559 | Whallon, William W. | M.A. |
| 53-621 | Whimster, Eleanor I. | M.A. |
| 25-542 | White, Harold | M.A. |
| 41-030 | Whitehead, Jean V.H. | M.A. |
| 17-502 | Willis, Helen A. | M.A. |
| 50-669 | Wilson, Donald H. | M.A. |
| 58-592 | Winter, Jack S. | M.A. |
| 58-593 | Wolfe, Irving | M.A. |
| 55-640 | Woods, Helen M. | M.A. |
| 45-518 | Woolner, Evelyn F. | M.A. |

## Entomology

| THESIS NUMBER | AUTHOR | DEGREE |
|---|---|---|
| 25-506 | Armstrong, Thomas | M.Sc. |
| 45-502 | Auclair, Lucien | M.Sc. |
| 25-508 | Baker, Alexander D. | M.Sc. |
| 38-503 | Beaulieu, Andre A. | M.Sc. |
| 54-040 | Bigelow, Robert S. | Ph.D. |
| 49-042 | Bird, Frederick T. | Ph.D. |
| 38-004 | Cameron, James W. | Ph.D. |
| 32-510 | Cameron, James W. | M.Sc. |
| 39-512 | Cannon, Frederick Merriet | M.Sc. |
| 52-516 | Carroll, William J. | M.Sc. |
| 28-504 | Daviault, Lionel | M.Sc. |
| 59-018 | Dondale, Charles D. | Ph.D. |

## Entomology

| THESIS NUMBER | AUTHOR | DEGREE |
|---|---|---|
| 42-520 | Doyle, J. Andre | M.Sc. |
| 42-521 | Duncan, Joseph | M.Sc. |
| 28-507 | Dyce, Elton J. | M.Sc. |
| 51-008 | Fisher, Robert W. | Ph.D. |
| 55-020 | Gardiner, Lorne M. | Ph.D. |
| 52-523 | Gardiner, Lorne M. | M.Sc. |
| 56-050 | Ghouri, Ahmad S. | Ph.D. |
| 57-525 | Gibbs, Kathleen E. | M.Sc. |
| 39-057 | Gilbert, Harold Adrian | M.Sc. |
| 41-007 | Gobeil, Antoine R. | Ph.D. |
| 35-504 | Gobeil, Antoine R. | M.Sc. |
| 26-511 | Graham, Archibald R. | M.Sc. |
| 37-507 | Graham, Kenneth | M.Sc. |
| 58-522 | Gustafson, Jean M. | M.Sc. |
| 57-014 | Hagley, Elmer A. | Ph.D. |
| 55-600 | Hagley, Elmer A. | M.Sc. |
| 24-518 | Hammond, George H. | M.Sc. |
| 48-525 | Hardwick, David F. | M.Sc. |
| 46-521 | Hawboldt, Lloyd S. | M.Sc. |
| 56-579 | Hikichi, Akira | M.Sc. |
| 54-523 | Hudon, Marcel | M.Sc. |
| 57-582 | Kennard, Charles P. | M.Sc. |
| 52-532 | Leroux, Edgar J. | M.Sc. |
| 54-015 | LeRoux, Edgar J. | Ph.D. |
| 47-517 | Lord, Frank T. | M.Sc. |
| 47-560 | MacPhee, Albert W. | M.Sc. |
| 28-519 | Maltais, Jean B. | M.Sc. |
| 38-013 | Marshall, James | Ph.D. |
| 39-518 | Matthewman, William G. | M.Sc. |
| 39-065 | Maxwell, Charles W. | M.Sc. |
| 43-506 | McLeod, William S. | M.Sc. |
| 51-053 | McLintock, John J. | Ph.D. |
| 58-031 | Monro, Hector A. | Ph.D. |
| 45-511 | Morgan, Cecil V. | M.Sc. |
| 38-514 | Morley, Peter M. | M.Sc. |
| 39-014 | Morrison, Frank Orville | Ph.D. |
| 41-534 | Munroe, Eugene Gordon | M.Sc. |
| 57-070 | Nelson, William A. | Ph.D. |
| 48-539 | Nelson, William A. | M.Sc. |
| 29-514 | Painter, Richard H. | M.Sc. |
| 36-021 | Peck, Oswald | Ph.D. |
| 34-514 | Peck, Oswald | M.Sc. |
| 47-566 | Phillips, John H. | M.Sc. |
| 36-515 | Pickett, Allison D. | M.Sc. |
| 40-019 | Prebble, Malcolm L. | Ph.D. |



## Entomology

| THESIS NUMBER | AUTHOR | DEGREE |
|---|---|---|
| 32-521 | Prebble, Malcolm L. | M.Sc. |
| 52-026 | Proverbs, Maurice D. | Ph.D. |
| 46-531 | Proverbs, Maurice D. | M.Sc. |
| 54-062 | Rao, Bapoje K. | Ph.D. |
| 56-534 | Read, Deane C. | M.Sc. |
| 32-523 | Reeks, Wilfrid S. | M.Sc. |
| 52-539 | Richardson, Howard P. | M.Sc. |
| 35-515 | Richmond, Hector A. | M.Sc. |
| 52-540 | Robinson, Arthur G. | M.Sc. |
| 21-514 | Saunders, Leslie G. | M.Sc. |
| 37-540 | Shewell, Guy E. | M.Sc. |
| 58-532 | Stairs, Gordon R. | M.Sc. |
| 26-526 | Stewart, Kenneth E. | M.Sc. |
| 46-580 | Stultz, Harold T. | M.Sc. |
| 57-036 | Sullivan, Calvin R. | Ph.D. |
| 54-069 | Thomas, James B. | Ph.D. |
| 52-543 | Thomas, James B. | M.Sc. |
| 36-520 | Twinn, Cecil R. | M.Sc. |
| 57-540 | Vickery, Vernon R. | M.Sc. |
| 59-542 | Wallace, Donald R. | M.Sc. |
| 53-607 | Warren, George L. | M.Sc. |
| 26-534 | White, Roy M. | M.Sc. |
| 31-517 | Whitehead, Walter E. | M.Sc. |
| 50-559 | Wigmore, Robert H. | M.Sc. |
| 38-523 | Wishart, George | M.Sc. |

## Experimental Medicine

| THESIS NUMBER | AUTHOR | DEGREE |
|---|---|---|
| 53-569 | Alivisatos, John | M.Sc. |
| 52-512 | Baxter, James D. | M.Sc. |
| 51-511 | Beck, Johannes C. | M.Sc. |
| 46-559 | Birmingham, Marion K. | M.Sc. |
| 59-511 | Boright, Henry A. | M.Sc. |
| 55-588 | Bramlage, Catharina A. | M.Sc. |
| 53-579 | Carballeira, Andres M. | M.Sc. |
| 59-009 | Chappel, Clifford I. | Ph.D. |
| 53-518 | Chappel, Clifford I. | M.Sc. |
| 32-511 | Chorobski, Jerzy | M.Sc. |
| 33-569 | Christie, Ronald V. | M.Sc. |
| 42-051 | Croll, Diane | M.Sc. |
| 50-600 | Currie, Donald J. | M.Sc. |
| 59-514 | Darragh, James H. | M.Sc. |
| 50-602 | De Leeuw, Nannie K. | M.Sc. |
| 58-564 | Donevan, Richard E. | M.Sc. |

## Experimental Medicine

| THESIS NUMBER | AUTHOR | DEGREE |
|---|---|---|
| 31-505 | Doubilet, Henry | M.Sc. |
| 34-509 | Erickson, Theodore C. | M.Sc. |
| 33-514 | Evans, Gerald T. | M.Sc. |
| 31-551 | Gage, Everett L. | M.Sc. |
| 55-057 | Giroud, Claude J-P. | Ph.D. |
| 53-527 | Giroud, Claude J-P. | M.Sc. |
| 32-021 | Grant, Elizabeth R. | Ph.D. |
| 44-519 | Heller, Nathan | M.Sc. |
| 55-059 | Henry, James P. | Ph.D. |
| 42-054 | Henry, James P. | M.Sc. |
| 43-007 | Hoffman, Martin M. | Ph.D. |
| 58-524 | Hollinger, Harvey Z. | M.Sc. |
| 53-533 | Horlick, Louis | M.Sc. |
| 37-509 | Howlett, John G. | M.Sc. |
| 54-053 | Kalant, Norman | Ph.D. |
| 51-527 | Kennedy, Byrl J. | M.Sc. |
| 33-519 | Kershman, John | M.Sc. |
| 55-609 | Lowi, R. Naomi | M.Sc. |
| 38-512 | Maughan, George B. | M.Sc. |
| 51-534 | McGarry, Eleanor E. | M.Sc. |
| 50-544 | McIntosh, Hamish W. | M.Sc. |
| 49-609 | McKendry, John B. | M.Sc. |
| 56-591 | Morgen, Robert O. | M.Sc. |
| 53-601 | Neiman, Gregory M. | M.Sc. |
| 57-072 | Norman, Nils | Ph.D. |
| 38-548 | Pattee, Chauncey J. | M.Sc. |
| 50-628 | Pump, Karl K. | M.Sc. |
| 55-619 | Ramos, Oswaldo L. | M.Sc. |
| 39-022 | Rose, Bram | Ph.D. |
| 37-513 | Rose, Bram | M.Sc. |
| 56-598 | Rosenberg, Gilbert | M.Sc. |
| 49-619 | Rusted, Ian E. | M.Sc. |
| 37-539 | Schacher, Josephine | M.Sc. |
| 44-021 | Schenker, Victor | Ph.D. |
| 57-595 | Serrano, Pedro A. | M.Sc. |
| 52-591 | Shaw, Walter M. | M.Sc. |
| 52-061 | Singer, Bertha | Ph.D. |
| 49-620 | Singer, Bertha | M.Sc. |
| 51-553 | Stinson, David A. | M.Sc. |
| 32-558 | Tarlov, Isadore M. | M.Sc. |
| 33-032 | Venning, Eleanor M. | Ph.D. |
| 36-551 | Wallace, Alexander B. | M.Sc. |
| 49-625 | Walsh, George C. | M.Sc. |
| 39-521 | Weil, Paul Gregory | M.Sc. |
| 41-018 | Weil, Paul Gregory | Ph.D. |



## Experimental Medicine

| THESIS NUMBER | AUTHOR | DEGREE |
|---|---|---|
| 34-520 | Workman, F. Walter | M.Sc. |

## Experimental Surgery

| THESIS NUMBER | AUTHOR | DEGREE |
|---|---|---|
| 55-585 | Allan, Charles M. | M.Sc. |
| 54-569 | Allen, Lloyd S. | M.Sc. |
| 51-595 | Ballem, Charles M. | M.Sc. |
| 59-578 | Brody, Garry S. | M.Sc. |
| 53-575 | Browman, Mark | M.Sc. |
| 54-576 | Fuller, William K. | M.Sc. |
| 57-568 | Caira, Eugene G. | M.Sc. |
| 50-599 | Chau, Andrew Y. | M.Sc. |
| 55-595 | Coughlin, Francis R. | M.Sc. |
| 53-585 | Devitt, James E. | M.Sc. |
| 56-572 | Dutt, Nihar R. | M.Sc. |
| 50-607 | Forse, Raymond F. | M.Sc. |
| 58-566 | Freedman, Arthur N. | M.Sc. |
| 57-574 | Goel, Devendra P. | M.Sc. |
| 56-577 | Goodall, Robert G. | M.Sc. |
| 49-604 | Gorman, Thomas W. | M.Sc. |
| 49-605 | Gourlay, Robert H. | M.Sc. |
| 53-591 | Hampson, Lawrence G. | M.Sc. |
| 54-589 | Horan, Patrick J. | M.Sc. |
| 55-602 | Hyndman, William W. | M.Sc. |
| 59-521 | Iliescu-Constantine, Rodr | M.Sc. |
| 57-580 | Inglis, Frederic G. | M.Sc. |
| 55-603 | Johnson, Thomas A. | M.Sc. |
| 54-592 | Kapur, Kanwal K. | M.Sc. |
| 49-533 | Karn, Gordon M. | M.Sc. |
| 57-581 | Kataria, Prem N. | M.Sc. |
| 55-608 | Laing, Charles A. | M.Sc. |
| 57-531 | Longley, James D. | M.Sc. |
| 58-573 | Mahanti, Biresh C. | M.Sc. |
| 59-587 | Makonnen, Adunya | M.Sc. |
| 52-579 | Marien, Breen N. | M.Sc. |
| 48-589 | McCorriston, James R. | M.Sc. |
| 50-623 | Miller, Walter D. | M.Sc. |
| 48-591 | Murphy, David R. | M.Sc. |
| 58-574 | Murphy, Frederick G. | M.Sc. |
| 49-612 | Niloff, Paul H. | M.Sc. |
| 56-592 | Ogilvy, William I. | M.Sc. |
| 48-540 | Percival, Walter I. | M.Sc. |
| 54-600 | Percy, Edward C. | M.Sc. |
| 59-595 | Richards, Terence A. | M.Sc. |

| THESIS NUMBER | AUTHOR | DEGREE |
|---|---|---|
| **Experimental Surgery** | | |
| 50-555 | Robichon, Jacques | M.Sc. |
| 52-584 | Rounthwaite, Harry L. | M.Sc. |
| 52-586 | Samuels, Peter B. | M.Sc. |
| 52-541 | Schiller, Carl | M.Sc. |
| 52-589 | Scobie, Thomas K. | M.Sc. |
| 57-537 | Singh, Tej B. | M.Sc. |
| 50-633 | Skoryna, Stanley C. | M.Sc. |
| 51-626 | Toovey, Edna W. | M.Sc. |
| 59-604 | Varma, Maithili S. | M.Sc. |
| 58-580 | Warshawski, Frances G. | M.Sc. |
| 50-640 | Wilkinson, Gordon W. | M.Sc. |
| 57-600 | Wilson, William E. | M.Sc. |
| **French** | | |
| 41-510 | Allard, Wilfred Philip | M.A. |
| 50-643 | Allen, Robert L. | M.A. |
| 28-527 | Alward, Frederick P. | M.A. |
| 56-002 | Andrews, Oliver | Ph.D. |
| 50-644 | Ariano, Alphonse | M.A. |
| 34-521 | Baker, Carrie E. | M.A. |
| 29-523 | Banfill, Gladys M. | M.A. |
| 36-523 | Bartlett, Harry | M.A. |
| 59-605 | Bartolini, Angelo E. | M.A. |
| 54-609 | Beauchemin, C-H. Guy | M.A. |
| 42-508 | Beauvais, Roxane | M.A. |
| 40-508 | Beebe, Mary Elizabeth | M.A. |
| 41-020 | Birchard, Lucile | M.A. |
| 31-561 | Bisson, Margaret M. | M.A. |
| 35-521 | Blakely, Sister Claire | M.A. |
| 30-518 | Blouin, Wilhelmine E. | M.A. |
| 36-525 | Bly, Elsie R. | M.A. |
| 26-537 | Boden, Quinibert P. | M.A. |
| 39-030 | Boger, Dellie Lee | M.A. |
| 50-648 | Boulanger, Jean-Baptiste | M.A. |
| 38-527 | Bourget, Adeline E. | M.A. |
| 48-608 | Bowes, Walter G. | M.A. |
| 46-584 | Bradford, Florence E. | M.A. |
| 40-509 | Branchaud, Sister Mary | M.A. |
| 37-517 | Bronner, Frederic J. | M.A. |
| 47-530 | Butterfield, Lee E. | M.A. |
| 57-546 | Caezza, Concepta Z. | M.A. |
| 33-541 | Carpenter, Lula A. | M.A. |
| 42-509 | Carter, Alfred Edward | M.A. |



| THESIS NUMBER | AUTHOR | DEGREE |
|---|---|---|
| **French** | | |
| 31-562 | Coade, Emma L. | M.A. |
| 31-525 | Connors, Vara M. | M.A. |
| 52-601 | Corey, Earl E. | M.A. |
| 49-556 | Coultis, Rosa J. | M.A. |
| 35-525 | Cox, Mary D. | M.A. |
| 26-538 | Creighton, Edith M. | M.A. |
| 46-585 | Culver, Eleanor A. | M.A. |
| 29-527 | D'Hauteserve, Louis | M.A. |
| 48-610 | Devine, Francis | M.A. |
| 52-602 | Dick, Helen | M.A. |
| 35-526 | Dube, Claudia M. | M.A. |
| 58-539 | Duinat, Blanche E. | M.A. |
| 41-021 | Dwyer, Florence Mary | M.A. |
| 45-544 | Edwards, Clifford F. | M.A. |
| 43-522 | Egan, Marie J. | M.A. |
| 47-531 | Elliott, Harriett F. | M.A. |
| 42-029 | Erskine, John Steuart | M.A. |
| 39-032 | Farrell, Amelia Mary | M.A. |
| 29-531 | Ferrand, Lucy M. | M.A. |
| 31-531 | Flahault, Elizabeth | M.A. |
| 15-502 | Forster, David S. | M.A. |
| 41-515 | Fortier, Mireille | M.A. |
| 59-550 | Frey, Betty | M.A. |
| 36-529 | Frey, Flavian F. | M.A. |
| 41-022 | Gay, Alice Grace | M.A. |
| 31-563 | Gilmore, Laura B. | M.A. |
| 51-634 | Glover, Thomas W. | M.A. |
| 13-505 | Grimes, Evie M. | M.A. |
| 40-510 | Guyton, Pauline | M.A. |
| 56-617 | Gyorgy, Anne M. | M.A. |
| 32-561 | Hall, Clifton L. | M.A. |
| 59-609 | Hall, Janet M. | M.A. |
| 41-518 | Hardy, Norah Woodbury | M.A. |
| 49-565 | Hawkins, Stuart C. | M.A. |
| 09-503 | Hayden, Amy J. | M.A. |
| 06-004 | Henry, Alice I. | M.A. |
| 49-566 | Hepburn, Johnston | M.A. |
| 36-533 | Heyman, Madeleine C. | M.A. |
| 38-531 | Hilkert, Marjorie R. | M.A. |
| 53-613 | Holt, Irene M. | M.A. |
| 49-568 | Howell, Helen M. | M.A. |
| 34-529 | Howie, Ruth J. | M.A. |
| 38-532 | Irwin, Nora F. | M.A. |
| 58-540 | Jacoby, Barbara J. | M.A. |
| 35-528 | Jennings, Thomas J. | M.A. |

## French

| THESIS NUMBER | AUTHOR | DEGREE |
|---|---|---|
| 42-034 | Johnston, Charles F. | M.A. |
| 38-534 | Jones, Margaret | M.A. |
| 59-555 | Joos, Erno | M.A. |
| 58-586 | Joos, Irma | M.A. |
| 33-549 | Judge, Mabel E. | M.A. |
| 38-535 | Kelly, Ignatius | M.A. |
| 41-025 | Kelly, Marie Ste. Anne | M.A. |
| 34-531 | Kent, Josephine P. | M.A. |
| 38-536 | Kibbe, Doris E. | M.A. |
| 48-564 | Kidd, Dorothy J. | M.A. |
| 39-038 | Kieffer, Michael Ignatius | M.A. |
| 34-532 | Kinnear, Mary E. | M.A. |
| 56-057 | Kushner, Eva M. | Ph.D. |
| 48-614 | Laing, Eleanor J. | M.A. |
| 38-537 | Lennon, Sister Mary G. | M.A. |
| 47-534 | Lenoir, Marguerite N. | M.A. |
| 31-565 | Longan, Virginia L. | M.A. |
| 31-566 | Lowry, Hope | M.A. |
| 46-542 | MacKeen, Frances C. | M.A. |
| 55-554 | MacKenzie, Gordon J. | M.A. |
| 47-536 | MacNeill, Glorana H. | M.A. |
| 15-504 | MacSween, Florence R. | M.A. |
| 50-659 | Mahon, R. Kathryn | M.A. |
| 54-616 | Markson, Doris M. | M.A. |
| 47-537 | Martineau, Jeanne G. | M.A. |
| 48-566 | Matthers, Mary C. | M.A. |
| 32-537 | Matthews, Florida L. | M.A. |
| 35-531 | Mazza, Sister Maria S. | M.A. |
| 42-513 | McGarry, Ave Marie | M.A. |
| 53-553 | McGillivray, P.G. | M.A. |
| 28-545 | McInnis, Sarah | M.A. |
| 43-524 | McQuillan, Marie B. | M.A. |
| 51-639 | Melzak, Adrienne | M.A. |
| 56-546 | Mentha, Guy | M.A. |
| 45-545 | Meyer, Paul H. | M.A. |
| 34-535 | Michel, Lina J. | M.A. |
| 52-608 | Mitchell, Kina M. | M.A. |
| 52-552 | Munro, Vivian R. | M.A. |
| 42-514 | Murphy, Sister Marie M. | M.A. |
| 51-572 | Nelson, Arthur J. | M.A. |
| 21-522 | Newnham, May L. | M.A. |
| 50-572 | O'Quinn, James P. | M.A. |
| 36-540 | Paour, Peter J. | M.A. |
| 41-521 | Parsons, Clarence Reuben | M.A. |
| 30-540 | Parthenais, J. Theodore | M.A. |



## French

| THESIS NUMBER | AUTHOR | DEGREE |
|---|---|---|
| 42-036 | Peck, Robert Alfred | M.A. |
| 58-547 | Podgornik, Louis E. | M.A. |
| 43-526 | Poirier, Mary A. | M.A. |
| 55-558 | Polgar, Sophie | M.A. |
| 42-037 | Ponticello, Eva Edith | M.A. |
| 50-575 | Portier, Jacques M. | M.A. |
| 32-539 | Prowse, Alice B. | M.A. |
| 39-043 | Ratelle, Ruth M. | M.A. |
| 24-544 | Reque, A. Dikka | M.A. |
| 34-538 | Rexford, Laura H. | M.A. |
| 31-540 | Rhoades, Winifred | M.A. |
| 49-579 | Richard, O'Neill J. | M.A. |
| 35-534 | Ross, Mary C. M. | M.A. |
| 42-041 | Rossiter, Maryellen | M.A. |
| 40-511 | Rowley, Marie Rita | M.A. |
| 43-514 | Royer, France M. | M.A. |
| 52-555 | Saint-Martin, Fernande | M.A. |
| 42-042 | Schiffers, Tania | M.A. |
| 59-562 | Shanks, Laura E. | M.A. |
| 25-541 | Sharples, Alice | M.A. |
| 24-545 | Silver, Edith | M.A. |
| 46-548 | Sloat, Annie E. | M.A. |
| 53-620 | Spentzos, George C. | M.A. |
| 26-556 | Stager, Drucilla N. | M.A. |
| 49-580 | Stewart, Mary I. | M.A. |
| 58-548 | Szablowski, Julie A. | M.A. |
| 30-548 | Tanner, Lea F. | M.A. |
| 42-046 | Taylor, Margaret E. | M.A. |
| 39-510 | Thompson, Helen Muriel | M.A. |
| 47-583 | Tougas, Gerard R. | M.A. |
| 29-548 | Townsend, Eleanor H. | M.A. |
| 11-503 | Tremblay, Joseph A. | M.A. |
| 09-506 | Tyndale, Orville S. | M.A. |
| 35-549 | Walker, Margaret G. | M.A. |
| 52-610 | Walton, Robert F. | M.A. |
| 54-627 | Watts, Aileen M. | M.A. |
| 32-549 | Weeks, Marie S. | M.A. |
| 34-539 | Weston, Grace T. | M.A. |
| 51-576 | Westwood, Mary J. | M.A. |
| 28-557 | Wickenden, Marguerite H. | M.A. |
| 47-584 | Wilkinson, Ida G. | M.A. |
| 51-578 | Wolfgang, Mary B. | M.A. |

## French Language & Literature

| THESIS NUMBER | AUTHOR | DEGREE |
|---|---|---|
| 41-511 | Barrett, Doris Pearl | M.A. |
| 37-521 | Dillon, Sister Marie | M.A. |
| 41-514 | Dooling, Sister Margaret | M.A. |
| 42-035 | Koenig, Sister Mary G. | M.A. |
| 37-524 | Lamal, Mary L. | M.A. |
| 37-545 | Lovelock, Margaret K. | M.A. |
| 40-031 | McNamara, Mary F.C. | M.A. |
| 39-042 | Murphy, Florence E. | M.A. |
| 37-529 | Pellerin, Evelyn | M.A. |
| 37-531 | Roy, Esther M. | M.A. |
| 37-532 | Stock, Marie I. | M.A. |
| 39-046 | Urbain, Joseph V. | M.A. |

## Genetics

| THESIS NUMBER | AUTHOR | DEGREE |
|---|---|---|
| 43-503 | Bauer, Donald de F. | M.Sc. |
| 45-015 | Blain, Auray | Ph.D. |
| 43-002 | Boothroyd, Eric R. | Ph.D. |
| 40-517 | Boothroyd, Eric R. | M.Sc. |
| 57-004 | Bubar, John S. | Ph.D. |
| 51-516 | Clark, Gordon M. | M.Sc. |
| 56-570 | Clark, Karin H. | M.Sc. |
| 23-510 | Derick, Russell A. | M.Sc. |
| 51-606 | Fainstat, Theodore D. | M.Sc. |
| 45-004 | Fraser, Frank C. | Ph.D. |
| 41-039 | Fraser, Frank C. | M.Sc. |
| 45-527 | Galinsky, Irving | M.Sc. |
| 36-511 | Gfeller, Frederick | M.Sc. |
| 45-528 | Glickman, Irwin | M.Sc. |
| 49-528 | Griesbach, Leonard | M.Sc. |
| 48-580 | Herer, Moe L. | M.Sc. |
| 38-009 | Howard, Alma C. | Ph.D. |
| 51-525 | Howes, James R. | M.Sc. |
| 37-011 | Hunter, Albert W. | Ph.D. |
| 43-520 | James, Allen P. | M.Sc. |
| 50-539 | Johnston, William W. | M.Sc. |
| 53-016 | Kalter, Harold | Ph.D. |
| 51-611 | Kalter, Harold | M.Sc. |
| 41-042 | Kerr, Ernest A. | M.Sc. |
| 50-618 | Liberman, John | M.Sc. |
| 35-030 | Love, Robert M. | Ph.D. |
| 52-537 | Mauer, Irving | M.Sc. |
| 55-066 | Maxwell, Doreen E. | Ph.D. |
| 51-054 | Metrakos, Julius D. | Ph.D. |



## Genetics

| THESIS NUMBER | AUTHOR | DEGREE |
|---|---|---|
| 49-540 | Metrakos, Julius D. | M.Sc. |
| 59-052 | Miller, James R. | Ph.D. |
| 52-581 | Moxley, John E. | M.Sc. |
| 39-015 | Newcombe, Howard B. | Ph.D. |
| 54-029 | Povilaitis, Bronys | Ph.D. |
| 39-024 | Sander, Hans G.F. | Ph.D. |
| 45-538 | Shapiro, Stanley K. | M.Sc. |
| 38-017 | Smith, Stanley G. | Ph.D. |
| 36-517 | Smith, Stanley G. | M.Sc. |
| 41-016 | Sparrow, Arnold H. | Ph.D. |
| 35-033 | Spier, Jane D. | Ph.D. |
| 58-050 | Trasler, Daphne G. | Ph.D. |
| 54-534 | Trasler, Daphne G. | M.Sc. |
| 58-534 | Vardanis, Alexandre | M.Sc. |
| 54-072 | Walker, Bruce E. | Ph.D. |
| 52-597 | Walker, Bruce E. | M.Sc. |
| 52-064 | Walker, George W. | Ph.D. |
| 52-599 | Willermet, D.A. | M.Sc. |
| 39-027 | Wilson, George Bernard | Ph.D. |
| 41-052 | Wright, Annie Mary | M.Sc. |

## Geography

| THESIS NUMBER | AUTHOR | DEGREE |
|---|---|---|
| 59-575 | Allington, Kathleen R. | M.Sc. |
| 55-046 | Ballabon, Maurice B. | Ph.D. |
| 52-600 | Ballabon, Maurice B. | M.A. |
| 59-576 | Barry, Roger G. | M.Sc. |
| 56-037 | Belmont, Arthur D. | Ph.D. |
| 53-574 | Blake, Weston | M.Sc. |
| 49-514 | Burbidge, Frederick E. | M.Sc. |
| 52-547 | Cobban, Aileen A. | M.A. |
| 52-548 | Coombs, Donald B. | M.A. |
| 51-566 | Creighton, Phyllis | M.A. |
| 57-603 | Cureton, Edward A. | M.A. |
| 59-017 | Dean, William G. | Ph.D. |
| 50-604 | Drummond, Robert N. | M.Sc. |
| 56-011 | Findlay, Marjorie C. | Ph.D. |
| 59-549 | Foote, Don C. | M.A. |
| 55-521 | Gerard, Robert D. | M.Sc. |
| 55-630 | Gordon, Llewelyn | M.A. |
| 59-552 | Humphrys, Graham | M.A. |
| 56-017 | Ives, John D. | Ph.D. |
| 59-522 | Jackson, Charles I. | M.Sc. |
| 50-568 | Johnston, C. Meredith | M.A. |

| THESIS NUMBER | AUTHOR | DEGREE |
|---|---|---|
| **Geography** | | |
| 57-606 | Langlois, Jean-Claude | M.A. |
| 49-637 | Lash, Harry N. | M.A. |
| 52-549 | Lithgow, Robert M. | M.A. |
| 57-532 | Lotz, James R. | M.Sc. |
| 58-525 | MacFarlane, Mona A. | M.Sc. |
| 56-588 | Marsden, Michael | M.Sc. |
| 53-599 | McKay, Gordon A. | M.Sc. |
| 56-584 | McKay, Ian A. | M.Sc. |
| 54-021 | Mercer, John H. | Ph.D. |
| 51-640 | Merrill, Gordon C. | M.A. |
| 53-554 | Merrill, Lesly I. | M.A. |
| 56-547 | Michie, George H. | M.A. |
| 54-548 | Molson, Charles R. | M.A. |
| 59-081 | Monahan, Robert L. | Ph.D. |
| 49-641 | Montgomery, Margaret R. | M.A. |
| 57-590 | Nebiker, Walter A. | M.Sc. |
| 54-026 | Orvig, Svenn | Ph.D. |
| 51-539 | Orvig, Svenn | M.Sc. |
| 51-573 | Paterson, Laurie A. | M.A. |
| 52-553 | Pochopien, Kazimierz M. | M.A. |
| 59-594 | Powell, John M. | M.Sc. |
| 59-617 | Power, Graham C. | M.A. |
| 59-560 | Raymond, Charles W. | M.A. |
| 53-070 | Ridge, Frank G. | Ph.D. |
| 51-574 | Romaine, Victor | M.A. |
| 51-623 | Russell, William J. | M.Sc. |
| 59-535 | Sagar, Richard B. | M.Sc. |
| 53-605 | Sangree, Anne C. | M.Sc. |
| 55-638 | Sebor, Milos-Marie | M.A. |
| 59-598 | Shellabear, William H. | M.Sc. |
| 54-555 | Sinclair, Martin H. | M.A. |
| 59-537 | Smith, David I. | M.Sc. |
| 55-639 | Smith, Samuel I. | M.A. |
| 57-037 | Summers, William F. | Ph.D. |
| 49-623 | Summers, William F. | M.Sc. |
| 54-070 | Thompson, Hugh R. | Ph.D. |
| 57-085 | Twidale, Charles R. | Ph.D. |
| 49-645 | Uren, Philip E. | M.A. |
| 58-535 | Wilson, Cynthia V. | M.Sc. |
| 56-624 | Wright, John M. | M.A. |
| **Geological Sciences** | | |
| 08-508 | Allan, John A. | M.Sc. |



| THESIS NUMBER | AUTHOR | DEGREE |
|---|---|---|
| **Geological Sciences** | | |
| 56-001 | Anderson, Francis D. | Ph.D. |
| 51-594 | Anderson, Francis D. | M.Sc. |
| 54-036 | Antrobus, Edmund S. | Ph.D. |
| 49-511 | Antrobus, Edmund S. | M.Sc. |
| 55-513 | Assad, Joseph F. | M.Sc. |
| 58-002 | Assad, Robert J. | Ph.D. |
| 53-570 | Averill, Edward I. | M.Sc. |
| 54-510 | Avison, Arthur T. | M.Sc. |
| 24-506 | Aylard, Clara M. | M.Sc. |
| 57-520 | Babyrycz, G.S. | M.Sc. |
| 23-503 | Bain, George W. | M.Sc. |
| 47-001 | Baird, David M. | Ph.D. |
| 10-001 | Bancroft, Joseph A. | Ph.D. |
| 50-513 | Bassett, Henry G. | M.Sc. |
| 58-508 | Beall, George H. | M.Sc. |
| 50-595 | Bell, Keith | M.Sc. |
| 55-587 | Benoit, Fernand W. | M.Sc. |
| 59-003 | Benson, David G. | Ph.D. |
| 58-509 | Berrange, Jevan P. | M.Sc. |
| 24-508 | Bishop, Eric G. | M.Sc. |
| 23-505 | Bissell, Harold R. | M.Sc. |
| 58-511 | Black, Ernest D. | M.Sc. |
| 42-003 | Black, James M. | Ph.D. |
| 54-008 | Black, P.T. | Ph.D. |
| 49-512 | Black, Philip T. | M.Sc. |
| 52-039 | Blake, Donald A. | Ph.D. |
| 48-576 | Blake, Donald A. | M.Sc. |
| 29-505 | Bray, Alton C. | M.Sc. |
| 52-513 | Brown, Norman E. | M.Sc. |
| 55-049 | Brummer, Johannes J. | Ph.D. |
| 51-598 | Buck, Walter K. | M.Sc. |
| 32-509 | Buckland, Francis C. | M.Sc. |
| 59-512 | Buckley, Ronald A. | M.Sc. |
| 56-040 | Burley, Brian J. | Ph.D. |
| 33-004 | Burton, Frederick R. | Ph.D. |
| 28-502 | Burton, Frederick R. | M.Sc. |
| 33-510 | Byers, Alfred R. | M.Sc. |
| 58-006 | Byrne, Anthony W. | Ph.D. |
| 45-506 | Cameron, Harcourt L. | M.Sc. |
| 56-042 | Cameron, Robert A. | Ph.D. |
| 53-001 | Carbonneau, Come | Ph.D. |
| 54-578 | Carriere, Gilles E. | M.Sc. |
| 58-009 | Carter, George F. | Ph.D. |
| 54-512 | Carter, George F. | M.Sc. |
| 49-595 | Castle, Robert O. | M.Sc. |

Geological Sciences

| THESIS NUMBER | AUTHOR | DEGREE |
|---|---|---|
| 47-024 | Christie, Archibald M. | Ph.D. |
| 59-011 | Clark, Lloyd A. | Ph.D. |
| 53-004 | Cooper, Gerald E. | Ph.D. |
| 51-602 | Cooper, Gerald E. | M.Sc. |
| 56-006 | Cornwall, Frederick W. | Ph.D. |
| 53-583 | Cornwall, Frederick W. | M.Sc. |
| 48-021 | Cote, Pierre E. | Ph.D. |
| 59-014 | Cumberlidge, John T. | Ph.D. |
| 47-544 | Cunnington, Francis A. | M.Sc. |
| 25-513 | Davidson, Stanley C. | M.Sc. |
| 56-517 | De Romer, Henry | M.Sc. |
| 58-515 | Dean, R. S. | M.Sc. |
| 52-520 | Deland, Andre N. | M.Sc. |
| 33-512 | Denis, Frank T. | M.Sc. |
| 21-505 | Dowling, Donaldson B. | M.Sc. |
| 50-605 | Dubuc, Fernand | M.Sc. |
| 52-010 | Dufresne, Cyrille | Ph.D. |
| 48-518 | Dufresne, Cyrille | M.Sc. |
| 13-516 | Dufresne, Joseph A. | M.Sc. |
| 52-011 | Dugas, Jean | Ph.D. |
| 55-014 | Eade, Kenneth E. | Ph.D. |
| 50-522 | Eade, Kenneth E. | M.Sc. |
| 54-518 | Eadie, Dorothy A. | M.Sc. |
| 52-012 | Eakins, Peter R. | Ph.D. |
| 49-524 | Eakins, Peter R. | M.Sc. |
| 57-053 | Emo, Wallace B. | Ph.D. |
| 55-599 | Emo, Wallace B. | M.Sc. |
| 50-523 | Engineer, Behram B. | M.Sc. |
| 58-518 | Ferguson, John | M.Sc. |
| 58-519 | Findlay, David C. | M.Sc. |
| 57-011 | Freeman, Peter V. | Ph.D. |
| 54-584 | Freeman, Peter V. | M.Sc. |
| 51-522 | Fullerton, Henry D. | M.Sc. |
| 51-011 | Gerryts, Edbert | Ph.D. |
| 49-603 | Gerryts, Edbert | M.Sc. |
| 29-508 | Gerson, Harold S. | M.Sc. |
| 49-012 | Gilbert, Joseph E. | Ph.D. |
| 47-513 | Gilbert, Joseph E. | M.Sc. |
| 56-520 | Gillett, Laurie B. | M.Sc. |
| 51-048 | Gillies, Norman B. | Ph.D. |
| 46-566 | Gillies, Norman B. | M.Sc. |
| 56-576 | Gleeson, Christopher F. | M.Sc. |
| 53-528 | Godard, J.D. | M.Sc. |
| 56-013 | Gorman, William A. | Ph.D. |
| 52-525 | Gorman, William A. | M.Sc. |



Geological Sciences

| THESIS NUMBER | AUTHOR | DEGREE |
|---|---|---|
| 52-574 | Grady, John C. | M.Sc. |
| 52-526 | Grant, Ian C. | M.Sc. |
| 32-513 | Grimes-Graeme, Rhoderick | M.Sc. |
| 59-517 | Guy-Bray, John V. | M.Sc. |
| 32-514 | Halet, Robert A. | M.Sc. |
| 34-006 | Halet, Robert A. | Ph.D. |
| 53-590 | Hamilton, Erwin C. | M.Sc. |
| 43-504 | Harding, Stanley R. | M.Sc. |
| 33-516 | Harris, Julius J. | M.Sc. |
| 09-513 | Harvie, Robert | M.Sc. |
| 58-523 | Hawkins, William M. | M.Sc. |
| 59-519 | Hay, Robert E. | M.Sc. |
| 50-529 | Henderson, Gerald D. | M.Sc. |
| 59-520 | Hofmann, Hans J. | M.Sc. |
| 53-011 | Hogan, Howard R. | Ph.D. |
| 50-532 | Hogan, Howard R. | M.Sc. |
| 59-036 | Hogarth, Donald D. | Ph.D. |
| 59-037 | Hogg, William A. | Ph.D. |
| 28-512 | Holbrocke, George L. | M.Sc. |
| 50-533 | Holmes, Stanley W. | M.Sc. |
| 29-510 | Hopper, Ronald V. | M.Sc. |
| 57-019 | Horscroft, Frank D. | Ph.D. |
| 22-512 | Howard, Waldorf V. | M.Sc. |
| 24-002 | Howard, Waldorf V. | Ph.D. |
| 55-022 | Husain, Bilal R. | Ph.D. |
| 31-508 | Hutt, Gordon M. | M.Sc. |
| 50-008 | Imbault, Paul-Emile | Ph.D. |
| 47-552 | Imbault, Paul-Emile | M.Sc. |
| 50-009 | Irwin, Arthur B. | Ph.D. |
| 55-525 | Jackson, Garth D. | M.Sc. |
| 57-057 | James, William | Ph.D. |
| 50-538 | Jardine, William G. | M.Sc. |
| 59-038 | Jeffery, William G. | Ph.D. |
| 56-522 | Jenkins, J.T. | M.Sc. |
| 49-022 | Jooste, Rene F. | Ph.D. |
| 47-555 | Jooste, Rene F. | M.Sc. |
| 33-518 | Keating, Bernard J. | M.Sc. |
| 50-011 | Kirkland, Robert W. | Ph.D. |
| 47-515 | Kirkland, Robert W. | M.Sc. |
| 56-023 | Klugman, Michael A. | Ph.D. |
| 53-534 | Klugman, Michael A. | M.Sc. |
| 55-605 | Kranck, Svante H. | M.Sc. |
| 51-052 | L'Esperance, Robert L. | Ph.D. |
| 48-530 | L'Esperance, Robert L. | M.Sc. |
| 59-044 | Larochelle, Andre | Ph.D. |

| THESIS NUMBER | AUTHOR | DEGREE |
|---|---|---|

Geological Sciences

| THESIS NUMBER | AUTHOR | DEGREE |
|---|---|---|
| 54-526 | Laurin, Joseph F. | M.Sc. |
| 46-572 | Lee, Burdett | M.Sc. |
| 53-535 | Leeson, John I. | M.Sc. |
| 59-524 | Leuner, Wilhelm R. | M.Sc. |
| 53-019 | Lunde, Magnus | Ph.D. |
| 52-533 | Lyall, Harold B. | M.Sc. |
| 59-526 | Machamer, Jerome F. | M.Sc. |
| 57-063 | MacDougall, John F. | Ph.D. |
| 52-535 | MacDougall, John F. | M.Sc. |
| 54-527 | MacGregor, Alexander R. | M.Sc. |
| 56-527 | MacIntosh, James A. | M.Sc. |
| 53-021 | MacLaren, Alexander S. | Ph.D. |
| 50-545 | MacLaren, Alexander S. | M.Sc. |
| 54-528 | MacLean, Donald W. | M.Sc. |
| 59-050 | Mann, Ernest I. | Ph.D. |
| 56-529 | Mannard, George W. | M.Sc. |
| 56-530 | Marleau, Raymond A. | M.Sc. |
| 53-537 | Marler, Peter de M. | M.Sc. |
| 58-029 | Mattinson, Cyril R. | Ph.D. |
| 52-536 | Mattinson, Cyril R. | M.Sc. |
| 50-013 | McAllister, Arnold L. | Ph.D. |
| 48-532 | McAllister, Arnold L. | M.Sc. |
| 53-020 | McCuaig, James A. | Ph.D. |
| 50-620 | McCuaig, James A. | M.Sc. |
| 52-022 | McDougall, David J. | Ph.D. |
| 49-537 | McDougall, David J. | M.Sc. |
| 08-512 | McIntosh, Donald S. | M.Sc. |
| 47-518 | McPherson, William J. | M.Sc. |
| 59-051 | Meikle, Brian K. | Ph.D. |
| 55-612 | Meikle, Brian K. | M.Sc. |
| 55-069 | Moore, Thomas H. | Ph.D. |
| 51-537 | Moore, Thomas H. | M.Sc. |
| 57-068 | Morris, Peter G. | Ph.D. |
| 55-615 | Morrison, E.R. | M.Sc. |
| 50-039 | Morrow, Harold F. | Ph.D. |
| 58-526 | Morse, Stearns A. | M.Sc. |
| 54-057 | Mueller, George V. | Ph.D. |
| 51-025 | Mulligan, Robert | Ph.D. |
| 48-538 | Mulligan, Robert | M.Sc. |
| 58-527 | Mumtazuddin, Mohammed | M.Sc. |
| 54-058 | Murray, Louis G. | Ph.D. |
| 47-522 | Neilson, James M. | M.Sc. |
| 52-024 | Nelson, Samuel J. | Ph.D. |
| 24-524 | O'Heir, Hugh B. | M.Sc. |
| 10-519 | O'Neill, John J. | M.Sc. |



| THESIS NUMBER | AUTHOR | DEGREE |
|---|---|---|

Geological Sciences

| THESIS NUMBER | AUTHOR | DEGREE |
|---|---|---|
| 34-009 | Okulitch, Vladimir J. | Ph.D. |
| 55-028 | Owens, Owen E. | Ph.D. |
| 51-540 | Owens, Owen E. | M.Sc. |
| 24-526 | Pelletier, Rene A. | M.Sc. |
| 59-063 | Petruk, William | Ph.D. |
| 57-026 | Pollock, Donald W. | Ph.D. |
| 55-538 | Pollock, Donald W. | M.Sc. |
| 33-016 | Price, Peter | Ph.D. |
| 54-061 | Prusti, Bansi D. | Ph.D. |
| 57-535 | Rejhon, George | M.Sc. |
| 57-536 | Relly, Bruce H. | M.Sc. |
| 53-034 | Riddell, John E. | Ph.D. |
| 57-028 | Riley, George C. | Ph.D. |
| 51-544 | Riley, George C. | M.Sc. |
| 52-027 | Riordon, Peter H. | Ph.D. |
| 51-620 | Robinson, Joseph E. | M.Sc. |
| 41-014 | Robinson, William G. | Ph.D. |
| 58-529 | Sater, Geoffrey S. | M.Sc. |
| 33-529 | Schindler, Norman F. | M.Sc. |
| 34-016 | Schindler, Norman F. | Ph.D. |
| 56-066 | Schmidt, Richard C. | Ph.D. |
| 55-539 | Schmidt, Richard C. | M.Sc. |
| 34-516 | Shaw, George | M.Sc. |
| 55-540 | Shields, Ross C. | M.Sc. |
| 34-517 | Simard, Lionel R. | M.Sc. |
| 52-030 | Simpson, David H. | Ph.D. |
| 59-599 | Sims, Walter A. | M.Sc. |
| 56-067 | Skinner, Ralph | Ph.D. |
| 49-621 | Skinner, Ralph | M.Sc. |
| 51-549 | Slaght, William H. | M.Sc. |
| 57-032 | Slipp, Robert M. | Ph.D. |
| 52-542 | Slipp, Robert M. | M.Sc. |
| 51-031 | Smith, Alan R. | Ph.D. |
| 48-545 | Smith, Alan R. | M.Sc. |
| 28-524 | Snelgrove, Alfred K. | M.Sc. |
| 59-539 | Spat, Attilio G. | M.Sc. |
| 24-531 | Squires, Henry D. | M.Sc. |
| 50-020 | Stalker, Archibald M. | Ph.D. |
| 48-547 | Stalker, Archibald M. | M.Sc. |
| 29-013 | Stansfield, John | Ph.D. |
| 12-518 | Stansfield, John | M.Sc. |
| 54-033 | Stevenson, Ira M. | Ph.D. |
| 51-552 | Stevenson, Ira M. | M.Sc. |
| 50-557 | Stocken, Charles G. | M.Sc. |
| 51-555 | Syme, Andrew M. | M.Sc. |

| THESIS NUMBER | AUTHOR | DEGREE |
|---|---|---|

## Geological Sciences

| THESIS NUMBER | AUTHOR | DEGREE |
|---|---|---|
| 55-042 | Taylor, Frederick C. | Ph.D. |
| 51-556 | Taylor, Frederick C. | M.Sc. |
| 50-635 | Taylor, William L. | M.Sc. |
| 47-573 | Tiphane, Marcel | M.Sc. |
| 56-069 | Tremblay, Mousseau | Ph.D. |
| 51-559 | Tremblay, Mousseau | M.Sc. |
| 55-542 | Tuffy, Frank | M.Sc. |
| 49-057 | Usher, John L. | Ph.D. |
| 47-527 | Usher, John L. | M.Sc. |
| 49-551 | Veilleux, Brendan | M.Sc. |
| 59-541 | Vollo, Nels B. | M.Sc. |
| 47-021 | Wahl, William G. | Ph.D. |
| 48-554 | Whiting, Francis B. | M.Sc. |
| 33-025 | Williamson, John T. | Ph.D. |
| 30-515 | Williamson, John T. | M.Sc. |
| 25-530 | Wilson, Harold S. | M.Sc. |
| 33-533 | Wilson, Norman L. | M.Sc. |
| 57-047 | Wolofsky, Leib | Ph.D. |
| 54-538 | Wolofsky, Leib | M.Sc. |
| 53-080 | Woolverton, Ralph S. | Ph.D. |
| 50-562 | Woolverton, Ralph S. | M.Sc. |
| 16-515 | Wu, Chow C. | M.Sc. |
| 31-518 | Wykes, Eric R. | M.Sc. |
| 53-081 | Young, William L. | Ph.D. |
| 51-563 | Young, William L. | M.Sc. |
| 48-604 | Yu, Pei-Liang | M.Sc. |
| 57-543 | Zwartendyk, Jan | M.Sc. |

## Geology

| THESIS NUMBER | AUTHOR | DEGREE |
|---|---|---|
| 41-524 | Asbury, Winfred Nowers | M.Sc. |
| 40-039 | Bray, Richard C. | M.Sc. |
| 40-040 | Brossard, Leo | M.Sc. |
| 36-509 | Brown, Robert A. | M.Sc. |
| 37-004 | Buckland, Francis C. | Ph.D. |
| 36-002 | Byers, Alfred R. | Ph.D. |
| 40-005 | Cleveland, Courtney E. | Ph.D. |
| 38-506 | Cleveland, Courtney E. | M.Sc. |
| 37-504 | Davis, Charles W. | M.Sc. |
| 39-005 | Denis, Bertrand T. | Ph.D. |
| 40-042 | Denton, William Ernest | M.Sc. |
| 41-037 | Douglas, John MacDonald | M.Sc. |
| 41-038 | Fortier, Yves | M.Sc. |
| 40-010 | Gray, Richard H. | Ph.D. |



## Geology

| THESIS NUMBER | AUTHOR | DEGREE |
|---|---|---|
| 37-508 | Gray, Richard H. | M.Sc. |
| 38-509 | Greig, Edmund W. | M.Sc. |
| 35-013 | Grimes-Graeme, Rhoderick | Ph.D. |
| 39-058 | Hall, James Dickie | M.Sc. |
| 39-059 | Hart, Edward Arthur | M.Sc. |
| 40-045 | Hill, Lawrence Stanley | M.Sc. |
| 41-528 | Hope-Simpson, David | M.Sc. |
| 40-012 | Howells, William Crompton | Ph.D. |
| 37-014 | Keating, Bernard J. | Ph.D. |
| 35-018 | Lowther, George K. | Ph.D. |
| 38-511 | MacDonald, Murray V. | M.Sc. |
| 36-512 | Malouf, Stanley F. | M.Sc. |
| 41-504 | Malouf, Stanley E. | Ph.D. |
| 41-045 | Mauffette, Pierre | M.Sc. |
| 40-017 | Milner, Robert Leopold | Ph.D. |
| 06-005 | Mingie, George W. | M.A. |
| 39-501 | Moss, Albert E. | Ph.D. |
| 37-511 | Moss, Albert E. | M.Sc. |
| 40-047 | Nauss, Arthur William | M.Sc. |
| 35-511 | Neeland, William D. | M.Sc. |
| 01-004 | Newson, William V. | M.Sc. |
| 36-549 | Riddell, John E. | M.Sc. |
| 02-001 | Ried, I. | M.Sc. |
| 38-518 | Riordon, Peter H. | M.Sc. |
| 42-064 | Robinson, Harold Ross | M.Sc. |
| 38-516 | Robinson, Raymond F. | M.Sc. |
| 38-517 | Robinson, William G. | M.Sc. |
| 39-068 | Schlemm, Leonard G.W. | M.Sc. |
| 39-069 | Selmser, Calbert | M.Sc. |
| 40-050 | Thorson, Erling | M.Sc. |
| 39-070 | Trenholm, Laurence Stuart | M.Sc. |
| 41-050 | Wahl, William G. | M.Sc. |
| 39-028 | Wilson, Norman L. | Ph.D. |

## Geology & Mineralogy

| THESIS NUMBER | AUTHOR | DEGREE |
|---|---|---|
| 27-002 | Bishop, Eric G. | Ph.D. |
| 25-511 | Bostock, Hugh S. | M.Sc. |
| 24-510 | Buffam, Basil S. | M.Sc. |
| 11-506 | Campbell, Edmund E. | M.Sc. |
| 23-508 | Carlyle, Arthur W. | M.Sc. |
| 11-509 | Dick, William J. | M.Sc. |
| 23-511 | Dolan, Everett P. | M.Sc. |
| 26-509 | Ellis, David H. | M.Sc. |

| THESIS NUMBER | AUTHOR | DEGREE |
|---|---|---|
| **Geology & Mineralogy** | | |
| 24-514 | Finley, Frederick L. | M.Sc. |
| 08-509 | Graham, Richard P. | M.Sc. |
| 21-510 | James, William F. | M.Sc. |
| 27-009 | Pelletier, Rene A. | Ph.D. |
| 27-517 | Riordon, Charles H. | M.Sc. |
| **German** | | |
| 49-555 | Block, Victor P. | M.A. |
| 33-540 | Carl, Selma E. | M.A. |
| 16-502 | Goldstein, Hildred M. | M.A. |
| 51-635 | Haywood, Bruce | M.A. |
| 35-544 | Jackson, Naomi C. | M.A. |
| 10-504 | King, Lucile M. | M.A. |
| 56-619 | Kyritz, Heinz-Georg | M.A. |
| 49-639 | Leppman, Wolfgang A. | M.A. |
| 05-003 | McGregor, Claire R. | M.A. |
| 21-521 | Meyer, Bertha | M.A. |
| 49-576 | Pratt, Audrey E. | M.A. |
| 13-509 | Schafheitlin, Anna | M.A. |
| 28-552 | Schleien, Donna S. | M.A. |
| 28-553 | Silverman, Beatrice I. | M.A. |
| 41-029 | Von Cardinal, Clive H. | M.A. |
| 54-626 | Walter, H.A. | M.A. |
| 40-513 | Weyl, Salcm | M.A. |
| **Greek** | | |
| 29-522 | Auld, Jean M. | M.A. |
| 28-531 | Edel, Abraham | M.A. |
| 10-503 | Huxtable, Margaret | M.A. |
| 28-544 | McCullagh, Paul F. | M.A. |
| **History** | | |
| 49-004 | Arthur, Elizabeth M. | Ph.D. |
| 47-529 | Arthur, Elizabeth M. | M.A. |
| 32-559 | Ballantyne, Murray G. | M.A. |
| 46-583 | Barry, Rexford G. | M.A. |
| 33-535 | Bateson, Nora | M.A. |
| 57-544 | Beattie, Stewart | M.A. |
| 56-545 | Bider, Milton A. | M.A. |



| THESIS NUMBER | AUTHOR | DEGREE |
|---|---|---|
| **History** | | |
| 27-522 | Bissett, Alice M. | M.A. |
| 50-649 | Breitenbucher, Howard E. | M.A. |
| 59-546 | Brown, Ian W. | M.A. |
| 13-501 | Brown, Vera L. | M.A. |
| 49-628 | Chan, Victor O. | M.A. |
| 55-625 | Charteris, J.N. | M.A. |
| 55-626 | Cienciala, Anna M. | M.A. |
| 37-519 | Collard, Edgar A. | M.A. |
| 38-020 | Cooper, John I. | Ph.D. |
| 32-560 | Copland, Edward E. | M.A. |
| 48-557 | Cox, Robert W. | M.A. |
| 46-004 | Cragg, Gerald R. | Ph.D. |
| 37-520 | Craig, Isabel F. | M.A. |
| 06-002 | Davidson, MacFarlane B. | M.A. |
| 13-502 | Dewey, Alexander G. | M.A. |
| 26-539 | Di Floric, Pasquale | M.A. |
| 55-016 | Eccles, William J. | Ph.D. |
| 51-633 | Eccles, William J. | M.A. |
| 32-526 | Edgar, William S. | M.A. |
| 59-078 | Farmakides, Anna | Ph.D. |
| 25-535 | Foster, Joan M. | M.A. |
| 49-559 | Fox, Leslie P. | M.A. |
| 50-566 | Gardner, Charles W. | M.A. |
| 47-577 | Gilmore, Robert C. | M.A. |
| 58-583 | Glickman, Rose | M.A. |
| 26-542 | Gower, Douglas L. | M.A. |
| 58-584 | Gwyn, Julian R. | M.A. |
| 05-001 | Hadrill, Margaret F. | M.A. |
| 28-535 | Hague, Helen | M.A. |
| 49-563 | Hampson, Harold G. | M.A. |
| 22-527 | Harbert, Eleancr | M.A. |
| 41-023 | Heisler, John Phalen | M.A. |
| 12-501 | Howell, Lucy M. | M.A. |
| 53-614 | Jennings, Peter R. | M.A. |
| 55-061 | Johnston, John A. | Ph.D. |
| 51-569 | Johnston, John A. | M.A. |
| 55-632 | Judges, Nancy E. | M.A. |
| 48-613 | Keep, George R. | M.A. |
| 59-556 | Kinsman, Ronald D. | M.A. |
| 57-605 | Knowles, David C. | M.A. |
| 29-542 | Knowles, Eustace C. | M.A. |
| 41-519 | Lapin, Murray | M.A. |
| 55-064 | Lucas, Sidney | Ph.D. |
| 42-503 | Lunn, Alice J. | Ph.D. |
| 34-533 | Lunn, Alice J. | M.A. |

| THESIS NUMBER | AUTHOR | DEGREE |
|---|---|---|
| **History** | | |
| 29-543 | Lyman, Beatrice M. | M.A. |
| 30-537 | MacSporran, Maysie S. | M.A. |
| 59-612 | McCarthy, John J. | M.A. |
| 54-615 | McCullough, Edward E. | M.A. |
| 23-522 | McGown, Isabella W. | M.A. |
| 29-545 | McLetchie, James K. | M.A. |
| 48-565 | McOuat, D.F. | M.A. |
| 43-022 | Millman, Thomas R. | Ph.D. |
| 47-580 | Mills, George H. | M.A. |
| 37-527 | Morgan, Mildred A. | M.A. |
| 05-004 | Munn, William C. | M.A. |
| 38-539 | Munroe, David C. | M.A. |
| 25-538 | Nichol, Jean | M.A. |
| 48-568 | O'Neill, Thomas L. | M.A. |
| 08-503 | Parker, David W. | M.A. |
| 57-607 | Parker, T.C. | M.A. |
| 30-541 | Pollard, Samuel L. | M.A. |
| 20-512 | Price, Enid | M.A. |
| 47-539 | Prince, Alma S. | M.A. |
| 50-040 | Reid, Allana G. | Ph.D. |
| 45-547 | Reid, Allana G. | M.A. |
| 35-547 | Reid, William S. | M.A. |
| 59-618 | Ritchie, Verna F. | M.A. |
| 32-542 | Roberts, Gwen R. | M.A. |
| 08-504 | Rorke, Mabele I. | M.A. |
| 39-023 | Ross, Dorothy J. | Ph.D. |
| 32-544 | Ross, Dorothy J. | M.A. |
| 26-553 | Ross, Dorothy V. | M.A. |
| 57-610 | Ross, V.J. | M.A. |
| 56-622 | Rubin, Gerald M. | M.A. |
| 27-540 | Sacks, Benjamin | M.A. |
| 08-505 | Salt, Alexander E. | M.A. |
| 38-554 | Self, George M. | M.A. |
| 59-082 | Senior, Hereward | Ph.D. |
| 51-575 | Senior, Hereward | M.A. |
| 55-560 | Smith, Irving H. | M.A. |
| 32-562 | Snyder, John K. | M.A. |
| 51-644 | Taylor, Harland W. | M.A. |
| 13-512 | Thomson, Herbert F. | M.A. |
| 12-506 | Thorne, Oliver | M.A. |
| 29-549 | Traver, Lillie A. | M.A. |
| 59-074 | Vogel, Robert | Ph.D. |
| 54-625 | Vogel, Robert | M.A. |
| 31-547 | Warldeworth, Eleanor S. | M.A. |
| 36-543 | Williams, Katharine R. | M.A. |

| THESIS NUMBER | AUTHOR | DEGREE |
|---|---|---|
| **History** | | |
| 30-556 | Wilson, Evelyn C. | M.A. |
| 24-548 | Wood-Legh, Kathleen L. | M.A. |
| **Horticulture** | | |
| 50-519 | Campbell, Joseph D. | M.Sc. |
| 54-580 | Collins, William B. | M.Sc. |
| 54-517 | Cutcliffe, Jack A. | M.Sc. |
| 50-610 | Harding, Charles F. | M.Sc. |
| 56-594 | Pickup, T. | M.Sc. |
| 49-550 | Trossman, Walter A. | M.Sc. |
| **Horticulture-Botany** | | |
| 40-038 | Bertrand, Paul | M.Sc. |
| 37-535 | Bourque, Leopold | M.Sc. |
| 51-599 | Cann, Keith E. | M.Sc. |
| 46-510 | Chan, Allan P. | M.Sc. |
| 42-522 | Filman, Conrad Colton | M.Sc. |
| 45-526 | Forest, Bertrand | M.Sc. |
| 47-516 | Laliberte, Jacques N. | M.Sc. |
| 48-535 | Maurer, Alfred R. | M.Sc. |
| 44-506 | Montgrain, Clement | M.Sc. |
| 51-615 | Moore, Ralph E. | M.Sc. |
| 48-594 | Nussey, Albert N. | M.Sc. |
| 44-508 | O'Reilly, Henry J. | M.Sc. |
| 39-067 | Cunsworth, Leslie Frank | M.Sc. |
| **Horticulture-Genetics** | | |
| 59-518 | Harney, Patricia M. | M.Sc. |
| **Hydraulics** | | |
| 31-504 | Cooper, Lawrence O. | M.Sc. |
| 31-511 | Morrison, Thomas J. | M.Sc. |
| **Hydraulics & Hydrodynamics** | | |
| 23-509 | Davies, Vernon R. | M.Sc. |

| THESIS NUMBER | AUTHOR | DEGREE |
|---|---|---|
| **Hydraulics & Hydrodynamics** | | |
| **Industrial Engineering** | | |
| 32-504 | Ogilvy, Robert F. | M.Eng. |
| 22-524 | Vessot, Charles U. | M.Sc. |
| **International Air Law** | | |
| 53-568 | Abdelmoneim, Ismail A. | LL.M. |
| 55-580 | Adelfio, Antonio | LL.M. |
| 57-514 | Ahmad, Mumtaz | LL.M. |
| 57-515 | Ahmed, Saiyed E. | LL.M. |
| 57-560 | Arnold, Stanley R. | LL.M. |
| 55-508 | Balachandran, Ponniah | LL.M. |
| 54-504 | DeDongo, Paul J. | LL.M. |
| 59-572 | Dillon, Joseph G. | LL.M. |
| 54-567 | Drion, Huibert | LL.M. |
| 59-573 | Du Crest, Maxime M. | LL.M. |
| 56-564 | Flynn, Frank J. | LL.M. |
| 57-561 | Gamacchio, Giampiero | LL.M. |
| 58-559 | Hadjis, Dimitris | LL.M. |
| 54-505 | Heller, Paul P. | LL.M. |
| 55-581 | Hermoso, J. | LL.M. |
| 54-506 | Koval, Joseph | LL.M. |
| 59-508 | Leclercq, Genevieve F. | LL.M. |
| 59-509 | Lureau, Daniel J. | LL.M. |
| 56-565 | Macbrayne, Sheila F. | LL.M. |
| 57-562 | Mackintosh, David D. | LL.M. |
| 59-574 | MacKneson, Stephen W. | LL.M. |
| 55-509 | McPherson, Ian E. | LL.M. |
| 55-510 | Moursi, Fouad K. | LL.M. |
| 55-582 | Murchison, John T. | LL.M. |
| 55-583 | Nowak, Tadeusz C. | LL.M. |
| 56-566 | Nylen, Torsten | LL.M. |
| 57-516 | Rippon, Clive L. | LL.M. |
| 58-560 | Ritchie, Marguerite E. | LL.M. |
| 55-511 | Saleh, Samir | LL.M. |
| 57-563 | Sheffy, Menachem | LL.M. |
| 54-568 | Swan, John H. | LL.M. |
| 55-512 | Toepper, Anton | LL.M. |
| 54-507 | Vaisoussis, Constantine | LL.M. |
| 55-584 | Vlasic, Ivan | LL.M. |
| 54-508 | Wine, Joseph F. | LL.M. |



| THESIS NUMBER | AUTHOR | DEGREE |
|---|---|---|
| **International Air Law** | | |
| 57-517 | Wojcik, Tadeusz Z. | LL.M. |
| **International Law** | | |
| 46-501 | Lussier, Claude | M.C.L. |
| **Invertebrate Morphology** | | |
| 21-001 | DuPorte, Ernest M. | Ph.D. |
| **Investigative Medicine** | | |
| 59-016 | Das Gupta, Dyutish C. | Ph.D. |
| 57-524 | Freund, Gerhard | M.Sc. |
| 59-523 | Laplante, Charlotte T. | M.Sc. |
| 59-045 | Lucis, Ojars J. | Ph.D. |
| 57-586 | Lucis, Ojars J. | M.Sc. |
| 57-588 | McLeod, Lionel E. | M.Sc. |
| 58-530 | Sinnott, Joseph C. | M.Sc. |
| 58-578 | Sodhi, Harbhajan S. | M.Sc. |
| 58-045 | Stachenko, Janine L-M. | Ph.D. |
| 56-603 | Stachenko, Janine L-M. | M.Sc. |
| 59-071 | Sybulski, Stella | Ph.D. |
| 56-605 | Sybulski, Stella | M.Sc. |
| 59-540 | Uete, Tetsuo | M.Sc. |
| 57-541 | Wilansky, Douglas L. | M.Sc. |
| **Islamic Studies** | | |
| 57-601 | 'Abd-al-'ati, Hammaduh | M.A. |
| 57-602 | 'Abdu-l-Mu'ti, 'Ali | M.A. |
| 54-620 | Al-Sawi, Ahmad H. | M.A. |
| 59-545 | Ansari, Zafar I. | M.A. |
| 59-547 | Carson, Beatrice M. | M.A. |
| 54-541 | Edmonds, William A. | M.A. |
| 59-608 | Faruqi, Ziya-ul-Hasan | M.A. |
| 59-548 | Feroz, Muhammad R. | M.A. |
| 54-612 | Haydari, Amir A. | M.A. |
| 59-553 | Jaylani, Tedjaningsih | M.A. |
| 59-554 | Jaylani, Timur | M.A. |
| 59-039 | Kamali, Sabih A. | Ph.D. |

| THESIS NUMBER | AUTHOR | DEGREE |
|---|---|---|
| **Islamic Studies** | | |
| 55-552 | Kamali, Sabih A. | M.A. |
| 54-613 | Kortepeter, Carl M. | M.A. |
| 55-635 | Mu'inu-d-din, Ahmad K. | M.A. |
| 54-549 | Mujahid, Sharif | M.A. |
| 59-057 | Nashshabah, Hisham | Ph.D. |
| 55-636 | Nashshabah, Hisham | M.A. |
| 58-588 | Pound, Omar S. | M.A. |
| 54-554 | Qaysi, Abdul W. | M.A. |
| 59-619 | Romeril, Paul E. | M.A. |
| 54-621 | Siddiqi, Mazharuddin | M.A. |
| 55-566 | Watson, William J. | M.A. |
| **Latin** | | |
| 28-528 | Banford, Jean E. | M.A. |
| 20-510 | Blampin, Caroline | M.A. |
| 36-527 | Brown, Margaret F. | M.A. |
| 28-530 | Clark, Peter A. | M.A. |
| 29-538 | Jefferis, Jeffrey D. | M.A. |
| 31-564 | Lawley, John D. | M.A. |
| 14-505 | Lindsay, William | M.A. |
| 30-555 | McHarg, Muriel S. | M.A. |
| 30-547 | Talpis, Clarence | M.A. |
| **Law** | | |
| 48-500 | Aguilar-Mawdsley, Andres | M.C.L. |
| 50-500 | Benes, Vaclav | M.C.L. |
| 49-583 | Camara, Jose S. | M.C.L. |
| 57-500 | Carisse, Joseph B. | M.C.L. |
| 48-501 | Cawadias, Constantine G. | M.C.L. |
| 47-500 | Challies, George S. | M.C.L. |
| 50-581 | Colas, Emile J. | LL.M. |
| 53-511 | DeSaussure, Hamilton | LL.M. |
| 53-512 | Fenston, John | LL.M. |
| 47-501 | Fergusson, Neil L. | M.C.L. |
| 49-584 | Gazdik, Julius F. | M.C.L. |
| 53-500 | Glucksthal, Andrew | M.C.L. |
| 53-556 | Gosztonyi, Paul M. | M.C.L. |
| 53-501 | Gyorgy, Dezso | M.C.L. |
| 53-513 | Hesse, Nicky E. | LL.M. |
| 53-514 | Hubscher, Frank F. | LL.M. |
| 58-500 | Johnston, Douglas M. | M.C.L. |



| THESIS NUMBER | AUTHOR | DEGREE |
|---|---|---|
| **Law** | | |
| 53-502 | Kallos, Tibere | M.C.L. |
| 48-502 | Lapointe, Marc C. | M.C.L. |
| 53-515 | Martial, Jean A. | LL.M. |
| 18-001 | Mitchell, Victor E. | D.C.L. |
| 58-501 | Moughton, Barry J. | M.C.L. |
| 53-516 | Nemeth, John | LL.M. |
| 53-557 | Novotny, Jan M. | M.C.L. |
| 53-503 | Ouimet, Paul A. | M.C.L. |
| 53-517 | Peng, Ming-Min | LL.M. |
| 22-500 | Renaud, Paul F. | LL.M. |
| 20-500 | Rose, Harold E. | LL.M. |
| 23-500 | Weibel, Louise E. | LL.M. |
| **Machine Design** | | |
| 23-504 | Bickell, William A. | M.Sc. |
| 27-513 | McCurdy, Lyall R. | M.Sc. |
| **Machines & Machine Design** | | |
| 08-510 | Harrington, John I. | M.Sc. |
| **Mathematics** | | |
| 54-509 | Aron, Ivan M. | M.Sc. |
| 46-506 | Ayoub, Raymond G. | M.Sc. |
| 58-003 | Bach, Glen G. | Ph.D. |
| 59-510 | Bedford, Frederick W. | M.Sc. |
| 55-048 | Betts, Donald D. | Ph.D. |
| 50-596 | Blackmore, William R. | M.Sc. |
| 51-596 | Boloten, M. | M.Sc. |
| 55-589 | Burgoyne, P. Nicholas W. | M.Sc. |
| 53-048 | Burrow, Martin D. | Ph.D. |
| 46-561 | Burrow, Martin D. | M.Sc. |
| 59-513 | Cavadias, George | M.Sc. |
| 55-594 | Conkie, William R. | M.Sc. |
| 49-630 | Cree, George C. | M.A. |
| 57-569 | Cunia, T. | M.Sc. |
| 59-515 | Dawson, Donald A. | M.Sc. |
| 54-519 | Eliopoulos, Hermes A. | M.Sc. |
| 58-582 | Ferguson, Donald C. | M.A. |
| 54-012 | Fox, Geoffrey E. | Ph.D. |

| THESIS NUMBER | AUTHOR | DEGREE |
|---|---|---|
| **Mathematics** | | |
| 56-616 | French, Betty R. | M.A. |
| 58-567 | Fulton, Geraldine E. | M.Sc. |
| 53-589 | Godin, J.J. | M.Sc. |
| 31-532 | Gold, Samuel | M.A. |
| 48-524 | Goldfarb, Lionel | M.Sc. |
| 49-527 | Gonshor, Harry | M.Sc. |
| 53-529 | Gottfried, Kurt | M.Sc. |
| 57-013 | Haering, Rudolph R. | Ph.D. |
| 10-501 | Hatcher, Albert G. | M.A. |
| 54-586 | Hayes, James C. | M.Sc. |
| 58-019 | Herschorn, Michael | Ph.D. |
| 56-618 | Herschorn, Michael | M.A. |
| 50-567 | Hodge, Cullen S. | M.A. |
| 58-585 | Hoechsmann, Klaus | M.A. |
| 45-533 | Kaufman, Hyman | M.Sc. |
| 59-585 | Kingsbury, Donald M. | M.Sc. |
| 55-604 | Kochen, Simon B. | M.Sc. |
| 50-012 | Lambek, Joachim | Ph.D. |
| 46-525 | Lambek, Joachim | M.Sc. |
| 58-024 | Laufer, Philip J. | Ph.D. |
| 54-525 | Laufer, Philip J. | M.Sc. |
| 55-063 | Lavallee, John | Ph.D. |
| 53-018 | Linis-Linins, Viktors | Ph.D. |
| 51-530 | Linis-Linins, Viktors | M.Sc. |
| 48-531 | Logan, Ralph A. | M.Sc. |
| 34-534 | Macphail, Moray S. | M.A. |
| 46-526 | Mamelak, Joseph S. | M.Sc. |
| 52-056 | Maranda, Jean-Marie A. | Ph.D. |
| 50-546 | Marcus, Alma | M.Sc. |
| 49-539 | Margolis, Bernard | M.Sc. |
| 59-588 | Masson, David R. | M.Sc. |
| 57-067 | Melamed, Samuel | Ph.D. |
| 53-539 | Melamed, Samuel | M.Sc. |
| 51-536 | Melzak, Zdzislaw A. | M.Sc. |
| 56-589 | Mercier, Raymond P. | M.Sc. |
| 55-613 | Michael, J. | M.Sc. |
| 15-511 | Miller, Iveson A. | M.Sc. |
| 58-528 | Murphy, Joseph | M.Sc. |
| 53-028 | Noonan, Bernard | Ph.D. |
| 57-025 | Oler, Norman | Ph.D. |
| 53-541 | Oler, Norman | M.Sc. |
| 50-550 | Patterson, Donald D. | M.Sc. |
| 56-595 | Prillaman, J.H. | M.Sc. |
| 56-029 | Puhach, Paul A. | Ph.D. |
| 56-061 | Rahman, Mushfequr | Ph.D. |



| THESIS NUMBER | AUTHOR | DEGREE |
|---|---|---|
| **Mathematics** | | |
| 49-544 | Rattray, Basil A. | M.Sc. |
| 10-520 | Richardson, Lorne N. | M.Sc. |
| 59-533 | Rosenfeld, Ze'ev | M.Sc. |
| 38-519 | Rosenthall, Edward | M.Sc. |
| 48-543 | Roulty, Paul M. | M.Sc. |
| 53-035 | Schiff, Harry | Ph.D. |
| 50-632 | Schiff, Harry | M.Sc. |
| 52-590 | Segal, Louis | M.Sc. |
| 53-037 | Sharp, Robert T. | Ph.D. |
| 50-556 | Sharp, Robert T. | M.Sc. |
| 05-005 | Sheldon, Ernest. W. | M.A. |
| 57-596 | Shtern, I.H. | M.Sc. |
| 56-068 | Smith, Lyman A. | Ph.D. |
| 52-031 | Smith, Norman E. | Ph.D. |
| 49-644 | Smith, Norman E. | M.A. |
| 56-538 | Smith, Robert C. | M.Sc. |
| 38-542 | Solin, Cecil D. | M.A. |
| 58-046 | Sussman, David | Ph.D. |
| 54-624 | Sussman, David | M.A. |
| 59-602 | Teitlebaum, Albert D. | M.Sc. |
| 53-544 | Tiffin, Brian F. | M.Sc. |
| 52-594 | Tomiuk, Daniel | M.Sc. |
| 28-556 | Turner, Alice W. | M.A. |
| 53-545 | Vosko, Seymour H. | M.Sc. |
| 49-626 | Watson, Hugh A. | M.Sc. |
| 44-517 | Williams, Christine S. | M.A. |
| 53-546 | Williams, Roscoe C. | M.Sc. |
| 55-546 | Wilson, Roderic I. | M.Sc. |
| **Mathematics & Physics** | | |
| 27-510 | Lane, Cecil T. | M.Sc. |
| 27-520 | Watson, Horace G. | M.Sc. |
| 27-521 | White, Thomas N. | M.Sc. |
| **Mechanical Engineering** | | |
| 56-553 | Balakrishna, Narasipur H. | M.Eng. |
| 49-585 | Barrett, George F. | M.Eng. |
| 52-500 | Beauregard, John P. | M.Eng. |
| 56-503 | Bernard, Ernest A. | M.Eng. |
| 51-500 | Brown, Donald R. | M.Eng. |
| 54-560 | Bula, Peter J. | M.Eng. |

| THESIS NUMBER | AUTHOR | DEGREE |
|---|---|---|
| **Mechanical Engineering** | | |
| 56-505 | Chakko, P.C. | M.Eng. |
| 59-568 | Chang, Ching-Ju | M.Eng. |
| 50-583 | Chant, Raymond E. | M.Eng. |
| 35-500 | Clarke, George F. | M.Eng. |
| 51-502 | Conrath, Joseph J. | M.Eng. |
| 47-502 | Cooper, Howard B. | M.Eng. |
| 57-505 | Davey, Trevor B. | M.Eng. |
| 51-584 | Daw, Geoffrey G. | M.Eng. |
| 55-572 | Dodis, Nicolas G. | M.Eng. |
| 56-557 | Fang, Sin-Kan | M.Eng. |
| 52-501 | Greenwood, Stuart W. | M.Eng. |
| 09-512 | Guillet, George L. | M.Sc. |
| 55-574 | Gupta, Makam C. | M.Eng. |
| 59-569 | Hla, Kyaw | M.Eng. |
| 49-590 | Howell, Allison B. | M.Eng. |
| 59-503 | Hyder, Syed S. | M.Eng. |
| 57-506 | Irwin, Roland F. | M.Eng. |
| 57-559 | Kardos, Geza | M.Eng. |
| 50-589 | Lane, Alan G. | M.Eng. |
| 53-562 | Lang, Bernard | M.Eng. |
| 50-590 | Levine, Seymour | M.Eng. |
| 53-563 | Martinek, Frank | M.Eng. |
| 55-577 | Matsas, Loucas C. | M.Eng. |
| 53-508 | McArthur, Beverley D. | M.Eng. |
| 56-560 | Pfefferkorn, Gerhard A. | M.Eng. |
| 56-561 | Pratinidhi, Shrivivas V. | M.Eng. |
| 55-507 | Putnaerglis, Rudolph | M.Eng. |
| 33-504 | Rankin, Robert A. | M.Eng. |
| 56-509 | Rice, William B. | M.Eng. |
| 34-504 | Richards, Victor L. | M.Eng. |
| 53-071 | Rogers, James T. | Ph.D. |
| 50-591 | Rogers, James T. | M.Eng. |
| 51-505 | Ross-Ross, Philip A. | M.Eng. |
| 59-069 | Schieck, Robert R. | Ph.D. |
| 56-510 | Seguin, Maurice J. | M.Eng. |
| 59-504 | Sein, Maung T. | M.Eng. |
| 56-562 | Shaw, Gerald A. | M.Eng. |
| 54-068 | Srinivasan, Malur R. | Ph.D. |
| 52-566 | Srinivasan, Malur R. | M.Eng. |
| 50-594 | Stachiewicz, J.W. | M.Eng. |
| 53-566 | Sullivan, Lorne J. | M.Eng. |
| 58-506 | Tao, Chia-hwa | M.Eng. |
| 58-558 | Taylor, George | M.Eng. |
| 55-579 | Tucker, Henry J. | M.Eng. |
| 53-509 | Tweed, William J. | M.Eng. |



| THESIS NUMBER | AUTHOR | DEGREE |
|---|---|---|
| **Mechanical Engineering** | | |
| 32-506 | Vasilkioti, Nikolai | M.Eng. |
| 20-509 | Weldon, Richard I. | M.Sc. |
| 57-513 | Winship, F.D. | M.Eng. |
| **Medicine** | | |
| 49-043 | Birmingham, Marion K. | Ph.D. |
| 18-501 | Blackader, Alexander D. | M.A. |
| 45-524 | Cohen, Herman | M.Sc. |
| 49-598 | Cooperberg, Abraham A. | M.Sc. |
| 51-521 | Fridhandler, Louis | M.Sc. |
| 47-514 | Howard, Robert P. | M.Sc. |
| 58-587 | Leith, Wilfred | M.Sc. |
| 48-030 | MacKenzie, Kenneth R. | Ph.D. |
| 46-577 | Sabin, Israel M. | M.Sc. |
| 47-571 | Stollmeyer, John E. | M.Sc. |
| **Metallurgical Engineering** | | |
| 32-507 | Adair, Thomas H. | M.Sc. |
| 58-554 | Briggs, David C. | M.Eng. |
| 42-048 | Chang, Lo-ching | M.Eng. |
| 55-516 | Cherian, Kandathil K. | M.Sc. |
| 11-509 | Drysdale, George A. | M.Sc. |
| 24-513 | Faith, Willard V. | M.Sc. |
| 54-563 | Finlay, James B. | M.Eng. |
| 51-585 | Goth, John W. | M.Eng. |
| 22-510 | Harrison, Donald R. | M.Sc. |
| 23-512 | Humes, Harold L. | M.Sc. |
| 15-510 | Lathe, Frank E. | M.Sc. |
| 58-557 | Lemay, Henri P. | M.Eng. |
| 36-501 | Lindsay, Victor C. | M.Eng. |
| 26-520 | Morrison, James E. | M.Sc. |
| 46-556 | Perrault, Charles H. | M.Eng. |
| 13-519 | Porter, Cecil G. | M.Sc. |
| 55-578 | Sharratt, Harold J. | M.Eng. |
| 09-517 | Sproule, Gordon St. G. | M.Sc. |
| 25-528 | Sweny, George W. | M.Sc. |
| 47-505 | Trudeau, Guy J. | M.Eng. |
| 51-591 | Walsh, John H. | M.Eng. |
| 21-518 | Williams, Frederick H. | M.Sc. |
| 50-510 | Woodhouse, Gordon H. | M.Eng. |
| 59-076 | Youdelis, William V. | Ph.D. |

| THESIS NUMBER | AUTHOR | DEGREE |
|---|---|---|

### Metallurgical Engineering

| | | |
|---|---|---|
| 56-563 | Youdelis, William V. | M.Eng. |

### Metallurgy

| | | |
|---|---|---|
| 40-515 | Cameron, Douglas Alastair | M.Eng. |
| 35-507 | Herzer, Richard W. | M.Sc. |
| 23-516 | McClelland, William P. | M.Sc. |
| 25-525 | Powell, Allan T. | M.Sc. |
| 37-512 | Rankin, Robert A. | M.Sc. |
| 38-520 | Ross, Henry U. | M.Sc. |
| 37-514 | Sproule, William K. | M.Sc. |
| 24-534 | Whittemore, Carl R. | M.Sc. |
| 42-050 | Yao, Yu-Lin | M.Eng. |

### Meteorology

| | | |
|---|---|---|
| 58-512 | Boville, Byron W. | M.Sc. |
| 55-591 | Butzer, K.W. | M.Sc. |
| 57-007 | Douglas, Richard H. | Ph.D. |
| 59-591 | Page, Douglas E. | M.Sc. |

### Mining & Metallurgical Engineering

| | | |
|---|---|---|
| 40-035 | Leblanc, Raymond F. | M.Eng. |

### Mining & Metallurgy

| | | |
|---|---|---|
| 40-034 | Grassby, James Neil | M.Eng. |
| 39-053 | Moss, Bernard B. | M.Eng. |
| 14-517 | Scott, Arthur P. | M.Sc. |

### Mining Engineering

| | | |
|---|---|---|
| 27-502 | Airey, Henry T. | M.Sc. |
| 20-501 | Anderson, Clayton E. | M.Sc. |
| 13-513 | Billington, Edward E. | M.Sc. |
| 38-500 | Brissenden, William G. | M.Eng. |
| 41-032 | Brown, George Osburn | M.Eng. |
| 56-504 | Cairnes, William P. | M.Eng. |
| 14-509 | Cameron, Alan E. | M.Sc. |



| THESIS NUMBER | AUTHOR | DEGREE |
|---|---|---|

### Mining Engineering

| | | |
|---|---|---|
| 54-502 | Cameron, Edward I. | M.Eng. |
| 10-513 | Carmichael, Henry G. | M.Sc. |
| 15-507 | Cockfield, William E. | M.Sc. |
| 28-559 | Coleman, Charles L. | M.Sc. |
| 14-510 | Davidson, William A. | M.Sc. |
| 59-502 | Davies, John J. | M.Eng. |
| 12-510 | De Hart, Joseph E. | M.Sc. |
| 41-033 | Dembicki, Steve | M.Eng. |
| 34-541 | Denny, Denison | M.Eng. |
| 42-049 | Faucher, Joseph Arthur | M.Eng. |
| 37-500 | Fraser, Gordon E. | M.Eng. |
| 11-510 | Gibbins, Gwynn G. | M.Sc. |
| 34-501 | Goode, Robert C. | M.Eng. |
| 21-508 | Harding, Ellis G. | M.Sc. |
| 35-501 | Hicks, Henry B. | M.Eng. |
| 33-566 | Jamieson, David M. | M.Eng. |
| 39-052 | Kennedy, Taylor James | M.Eng. |
| 55-576 | Macaulay, Colin A. | M.Eng. |
| 36-503 | MacKay, Donald M. | M.Eng. |
| 34-503 | Muir, William L. | M.Eng. |
| 12-515 | Murray, George E. | M.Sc. |
| 31-512 | O'Connell, Francis J. | M.Sc. |
| 38-502 | O'Shaughnessy, Martin D. | M.Eng. |
| 33-503 | O'Shaughnessy, Michael J. | M.Eng. |
| 57-509 | Ortlepp, William D. | M.Eng. |
| 48-510 | Raju, B. Sadasiva | M.Eng. |
| 27-519 | Ross, William R. | M.Sc. |
| 44-500 | Salman, Mehmet T. | M.Eng. |
| 32-505 | Stobart, Walter T. | M.Eng. |
| 31-516 | Thomas, William F. | M.Sc. |
| 20-507 | Tousaw, Albert A. | M.Sc. |
| 16-514 | Van Barneveld, Charles F. | M.Sc. |
| 36-507 | Wadge, Norman H. | M.Eng. |
| 26-531 | Walter, Albert J. | M.Sc. |
| 30-514 | Weldon, Frederick E. | M.Sc. |
| 33-507 | Westwood, Robert J. | M.Eng. |

### Music

| | | |
|---|---|---|
| 57-049 | Frackenpohl, Arthur R. | D.Mus. |
| 47-022 | Hanson, Frank K. | Mus.D. |
| 24-500 | O'Neill, Charles | M.M.A. |
| 30-016 | Treharne, Bryceson | Mus.D. |

### Neurology

| THESIS NUMBER | AUTHOR | DEGREE |
|---|---|---|
| 36-508 | Boldrey, Edwin B. | M.Sc. |
| 39-513 | Echlin, Francis Asbury | M.Sc. |
| 39-006 | Erickson, Theodore C. | Ph.D. |
| 37-027 | Evans, Joseph P. | Ph.D. |
| 36-547 | Gibson, William C. | M.Sc. |
| 35-538 | Haymaker, Webb | M.Sc. |
| 38-547 | Nichols, Walter M. | M.Sc. |
| 36-514 | Norcross, Nathan C. | M.Sc. |
| 38-515 | Reid, William L. | M.Sc. |

### Neurology & Neurosurgery

| THESIS NUMBER | AUTHOR | DEGREE |
|---|---|---|
| 58-561 | Aguilar, Mary J. | M.Sc. |
| 51-508 | Austin, George M. | M.Sc. |
| 52-511 | Baldwin, Maitland | M.Sc. |
| 48-574 | Bates, John I. | M.Sc. |
| 53-571 | Baxter, Donald W. | M.Sc. |
| 53-573 | Bertrand, Gilles | M.Sc. |
| 49-594 | Bird, Allan V. | M.Sc. |
| 59-513 | Branch, Charles L. | M.Sc. |
| 45-523 | Chen, Chao-jen | M.Sc. |
| 45-525 | Corona, Carlos | M.Sc. |
| 49-600 | Courtois, Guy A. | M.Sc. |
| 54-516 | Cullen, Chester F. | M.Sc. |
| 48-516 | Cure, Charles W. | M.Sc. |
| 54-046 | Dekaban, Anatole S. | Ph.D. |
| 51-605 | Dekaban, Anatole S. | M.Sc. |
| 51-517 | Earle, Kenneth M. | M.Sc. |
| 47-511 | Fortuyn, Jan D. | M.Sc. |
| 51-524 | Gibson, Robert M. | M.Sc. |
| 57-012 | Gloor, Peter | Ph.D. |
| 54-587 | Heller, Irving H. | M.Sc. |
| 54-588 | Hoff, Theodore F. | M.Sc. |
| 39-060 | Humphreys, Storer Plumer | M.Sc. |
| 50-535 | Hunter, John M. | M.Sc. |
| 47-553 | Jackson, Ira J. | M.Sc. |
| 56-581 | Keener, Ellis B. | M.Sc. |
| 48-583 | Kelen, Andrew | M.Sc. |
| 57-583 | Kim, Yoon-Bom | M.Sc. |
| 49-534 | Kite, William C. | M.Sc. |
| 51-610 | Klatzo, Igor | M.Sc. |
| 56-525 | Lende, Richard A. | M.Sc. |
| 50-542 | Lewis, Revis C. | M.Sc. |
| 54-017 | Li, Choh-luh | Ph.D. |



### Neurology & Neurosurgery

| THESIS NUMBER | AUTHOR | DEGREE |
|---|---|---|
| 50-617 | Li, Choh-luh | M.Sc. |
| 57-529 | Litvak, John | M.Sc. |
| 49-541 | Meyer, John S. | M.Sc. |
| 55-614 | Morrell, Frank | M.Sc. |
| 54-597 | Nashold, Blaine S. | M.Sc. |
| 51-027 | Olszewski, Jerzy | Ph.D. |
| 47-567 | Rabinovitch, Reuben | M.Sc. |
| 59-066 | Ramon-Moliner, Enrique | Ph.D. |
| 58-036 | Rayport, Mark | Ph.D. |
| 46-533 | Robb, James P. | M.Sc. |
| 52-060 | Roberts, Henry L. | Ph.D. |
| 49-617 | Roberts, Henry L. | M.Sc. |
| 50-631 | Rosen, Harold J. | M.Sc. |
| 55-620 | Rothballer, Alan B. | M.Sc. |
| 56-600 | Rozdilsky, Bohdan | M.Sc. |
| 59-596 | Samson, Hugh R. | M.Sc. |
| 59-536 | Sinha, Sharda P. | M.Sc. |
| 49-622 | Sloan, Norman | M.Sc. |
| 48-546 | Speakman, Thomas J. | M.Sc. |
| 56-604 | Stewart, Lever F. | M.Sc. |
| 51-554 | Stratford, Joseph G. | M.Sc. |
| 51-033 | Tower, Donald B. | Ph.D. |
| 48-549 | Tower, Donald B. | M.Sc. |
| 50-637 | Van Buren, John M. | M.Sc. |
| 47-574 | Welch, William K. | M.Sc. |
| 49-553 | Ziegler, James E. | M.Sc. |

### Neurosurgery

| THESIS NUMBER | AUTHOR | DEGREE |
|---|---|---|
| 41-525 | Bridgers, William Henry | M.Sc. |
| 41-535 | Pudenz, Robert Harry | M.Sc. |

### Nutrition

| THESIS NUMBER | AUTHOR | DEGREE |
|---|---|---|
| 47-542 | Aitken, Johnstone R. | M.Sc. |
| 59-002 | Beacom, Stanley E. | Ph.D. |
| 45-503 | Bell, John M. | M.Sc. |
| 51-512 | Berryhill, Florence M. | M.Sc. |
| 48-578 | Brissor, Germain | M.Sc. |
| 46-562 | Burton, Barbara W. | M.Sc. |
| 45-508 | Chalmers, A. Edith | M.Sc. |
| 50-520 | Clark, Barbara E. | M.Sc. |
| 42-519 | Collier, Barbara C. | M.Sc. |

| THESIS NUMBER | AUTHOR | DEGREE |
|---|---|---|

Nutrition

| | | |
|---|---|---|
| 53-584 | Crawford, Donna J. | M.Sc. |
| 48-515 | Crook, Helen G. | M.Sc. |
| 49-601 | Dju, Mei Y. | M.Sc. |
| 48-519 | Durrell, Winfield B. | M.Sc. |
| 47-026 | Farmer, Florence A. | Ph.D. |
| 44-502 | Farmer, Florence A. | M.Sc. |
| 51-523 | Gallamore, William A. | M.Sc. |
| 49-602 | Gass, Marcia J. | M.Sc. |
| 56-015 | Haskell, Stanley R. | Ph.D. |
| 50-612 | Haskell, Stanley R. | M.Sc. |
| 45-532 | Hughes, Muriel I. | M.Sc. |
| 52-048 | Irwin, Mary I. | Ph.D. |
| 50-536 | Irwin, Mary I. | M.Sc. |
| 44-503 | Jackson, Ivan R. | M.Sc. |
| 52-530 | Kean, Eccleston A. | M.Sc. |
| 49-536 | Langerman, Helen L. | M.Sc. |
| 57-585 | Lister, Earle E. | M.Sc. |
| 52-051 | Lloyd, Lewis E. | Ph.D. |
| 50-543 | Lloyd, Lewis E. | M.Sc. |
| 49-608 | Lucas, Ian A. | M.Sc. |
| 56-528 | MacKay, Vernon G. | M.Sc. |
| 48-590 | MacNeill, Ruby J. | M.Sc. |
| 47-520 | Manson, Mary G. | M.Sc. |
| 47-562 | Millar, Myra J. | M.Sc. |
| 46-527 | Mills, Margaret F. | M.Sc. |
| 42-527 | Morrison, Mary F.M. | M.Sc. |
| 43-507 | Narod, Milton | M.Sc. |
| 48-593 | Neilson, Helen R. | M.Sc. |
| 55-618 | Peckham, Hugh E. | M.Sc. |
| 47-523 | Proctor, William C. | M.Sc. |
| 50-552 | Proverbs, Ivor H. | M.Sc. |
| 55-072 | Rutherford, Beth E. | Ph.D. |
| 51-548 | Siddall, Margaret I. | M.Sc. |
| 58-577 | Smith, Edward R. | M.Sc. |
| 46-579 | Sourkes, Theodore L. | M.Sc. |
| 43-510 | Whiting, Frank | M.Sc. |
| 56-544 | Winter, Karl A. | M.Sc. |
| 50-561 | Woods, James P. | M.Sc. |
| 44-513 | Woolsey, Lloyd D. | M.Sc. |

Ore Dressing

| | | |
|---|---|---|
| 23-501 | Anderson, Robert G. | M.Sc. |
| 14-508 | Baily, Philip P. | M.Sc. |



| THESIS NUMBER | AUTHOR | DEGREE |
|---|---|---|

Ore Dressing

| | | |
|---|---|---|
| 25-510 | Becking, John A. | M.Sc. |
| 22-501 | Brow, James B. | M.Sc. |
| 25-547 | Cave, Allister E. | M.Sc. |
| 13-514 | Cooper, Corin H. | M.Sc. |
| 22-502 | Dewar, Charles L. | M.Sc. |
| 21-504 | Douglas, George V. | M.Sc. |
| 21-506 | Edwards, Gordon M. | M.Sc. |
| 21-507 | Erlenborn, Willi | M.Sc. |
| 12-508 | Galloway, John D. | M.Sc. |
| 24-516 | Gegg, Richard C. | M.Sc. |
| 11-511 | Gillies, George A. | M.Sc. |
| 24-521 | Legg, Roland E. | M.Sc. |
| 25-524 | Muir, Allan R. | M.Sc. |
| 22-521 | Saunders, James E. | M.Sc. |
| 24-551 | Snijman, Johan J. | M.Sc. |
| 08-514 | Strangways, Henry F. | M.Sc. |
| 23-519 | Weldon, Thomas H. | M.Sc. |
| 10-524 | Yuill, Harry H. | M.Sc. |

Organic Chemistry

| | | |
|---|---|---|
| 34-003 | Bell, Adam C. | Ph.D. |
| 23-002 | Dolid, Jacob | Ph.D. |
| 21-502 | Dolid, Jacob | M.Sc. |
| 28-510 | Gallay, Wilfred | M.Sc. |
| 07-510 | Lewis, David S. | M.Sc. |

Oriental Languages

| | | |
|---|---|---|
| 24-536 | Berger, Julius | M.A. |
| 25-532 | Boyes, Watson | M.A. |
| 31-523 | Burton, Garland G. | M.A. |
| 35-545 | Lennox, Robert | M.A. |
| 33-551 | Levitsky, Nathan A. | M.A. |
| 33-576 | Thomas, William | M.A. |

Parasitology

| | | |
|---|---|---|
| 51-593 | Alozie, Obinnaya | M.Sc. |
| 54-572 | Baer, Harold G. | M.Sc. |
| 45-520 | Barker, Clifford A. | M.Sc. |
| 57-002 | Belle, Edward A. | Ph.D. |

| THESIS NUMBER | AUTHOR | DEGREE |
|---|---|---|
| **Parasitology** | | |
| 54-574 | Belle, Edward A. | M.Sc. |
| 48-577 | Bloomfield, Solomon S. | M.Sc. |
| 52-571 | Burgess, Glenn D. | M.Sc. |
| 57-522 | Cambieri, R. | M.Sc. |
| 38-505 | Cannon, Douglas G. | M.Sc. |
| 54-514 | Chambers, Harriet A. | M.Sc. |
| 53-049 | Choquette, Laurent P. E. | Ph.D. |
| 42-518 | Choquette, Laurent P. E. | M.Sc. |
| 49-596 | Cohen, Harry | M.Sc. |
| 49-521 | Connell, Robert | M.Sc. |
| 47-510 | Firlotte, William R. | M.Sc. |
| 48-520 | Fochs, Anita M. | M.Sc. |
| 47-512 | Frank, Julius | M.Sc. |
| 58-016 | Gibbs, Harold C. | Ph.D. |
| 56-519 | Gibbs, Harold C. | M.Sc. |
| 39-009 | Griffiths, Henry J. | Ph.D. |
| 35-505 | Griffiths, Henry J. | M.Sc. |
| 35-508 | Jones, Trevor I. | M.Sc. |
| 49-024 | Khan, M. Abdul B. | Ph.D. |
| 46-524 | Lachance, Francois de S. | M.Sc. |
| 53-061 | Lesser, Elliott | Ph.D. |
| 51-529 | Lesser, Elliott | M.Sc. |
| 56-025 | Lubinsky, George | Ph.D. |
| 39-064 | Lyster, Lynden Laird | M.Sc. |
| 47-014 | Marchant, Edwin H. | Ph.D. |
| 52-057 | Margolis, Leo | Ph.D. |
| 55-531 | McGregor, John K. | M.Sc. |
| 52-582 | McMorran, Arlene R. | M.Sc. |
| 57-066 | Meerovitch, Eugene B. | Ph.D. |
| 55-534 | Meerovitch, Eugene B. | M.Sc. |
| 54-594 | Mensah-Dapaa, W.S. | M.Sc. |
| 36-513 | Miller, Max J. | M.Sc. |
| 55-535 | Montreuil, Paul L. | M.Sc. |
| 47-521 | Moynihan, Irvin W. | M.Sc. |
| 59-056 | Myers, Betty-June | Ph.D. |
| 59-058 | Nnochiri, Enyinnaya | Ph.D. |
| 50-626 | Nnochiri, Enyinnaya | M.Sc. |
| 57-071 | Nommik, Salme | Ph.D. |
| 53-029 | Oliver, William T. | Ph.D. |
| 51-538 | Oliver, William T. | M.Sc. |
| 54-027 | Poole, John B. | Ph.D. |
| 41-046 | Poole, John B. | M.Sc. |
| 57-027 | Prasad, Devendra | Ph.D. |
| 58-034 | Premvati, * | Ph.D. |
| 50-019 | Rao, N.S. Krishna | Ph.D. |



| THESIS NUMBER | AUTHOR | DEGREE |
|---|---|---|
| **Parasitology** | | |
| 50-554 | Reesal, Michael R. | M.Sc. |
| 58-040 | Ronald, Keith | Ph.D. |
| 56-597 | Ronald, Keith | M.Sc. |
| 48-596 | Ross, Winifred M. | M.Sc. |
| 55-034 | Schad, Gerhard | Ph.D. |
| 52-587 | Schad, Gerhard A. | M.Sc. |
| 59-597 | Shah, Jessie A. | M.Sc. |
| 54-605 | Strachan, Alison A. | M.Sc. |
| 35-025 | Swales, William E. | Ph.D. |
| 57-039 | Sweatman, Gordon K. | Ph.D. |
| 57-084 | Thomson, Hugh M. | Ph.D. |
| 57-044 | Webster, Gloria A. | Ph.D. |
| 57-045 | Whitten, Lloyd K. | Ph.D. |
| 52-036 | Wolfgang, Robert W. | Ph.D. |
| 50-560 | Wolfgang, Robert W. | M.Sc. |
| 52-069 | Wu, Liang Y. | Ph.D. |
| **Pathology** | | |
| 51-509 | Bainborough, Arthur R. | M.Sc. |
| 50-025 | Bencosme, Sergio | Ph.D. |
| 48-575 | Bencosme, Sergio | M.Sc. |
| 53-526 | Fluss, Zdenek | M.Sc. |
| 45-529 | Gold, M.M.A. | M.Sc. |
| 52-573 | Gordon, Dina | M.Sc. |
| 46-522 | Hinds, Henry E. | M.Sc. |
| 49-532 | Jaffe, Frederick A. | M.Sc. |
| 28-515 | Kearns, Peter J. | M.Sc. |
| 48-528 | Kipkie, George F. | M.Sc. |
| 51-017 | Kobernick, Sidney D. | Ph.D. |
| 49-607 | Kobernick, Sidney D. | M.Sc. |
| 53-060 | Lautsch, Elizabeth V. | Ph.D. |
| 51-528 | Lautsch, Elizabeth V. | M.Sc. |
| 48-586 | Leach, William B. | M.Sc. |
| 56-583 | Liszauer, Susan M. | M.Sc. |
| 47-559 | McLean, Chester R. | M.Sc. |
| 46-573 | McMillan, Gardner C. | M.Sc. |
| 48-009 | McMillan, Gardner C. | Ph.D. |
| 51-535 | Meissner, George F. | M.Sc. |
| 42-526 | More, Robert Hall | M.Sc. |
| 50-017 | Payne, Torrence P. | Ph.D. |
| 26-524 | Rosenbaum, Saul B. | M.Sc. |
| 49-618 | Ross, Roderick C. | M.Sc. |
| 53-604 | Rota, Alexander N. | M.Sc. |

## Pathology

| THESIS NUMBER | AUTHOR | DEGREE |
|---|---|---|
| 51-622 | Rublee, J.D. | M.Sc. |
| 33-531 | Spector, Leo I. | M.Sc. |
| 47-526 | Starr, Harry | M.Sc. |
| 57-035 | Stuart, James R. | Ph.D. |
| 50-045 | Toreson, Wilfred E. | Ph.D. |
| 48-601 | Toreson, Wilfred E. | M.Sc. |
| 50-023 | Waugh, Douglas O. | Ph.D. |
| 48-602 | Waugh, Douglas O. | M.Sc. |
| 51-562 | Whiteside, John H. | M.Sc. |

## Petrography

| THESIS NUMBER | AUTHOR | DEGREE |
|---|---|---|
| 10-517 | Hayes, Albert O. | M.Sc. |

## Pharmacology

| THESIS NUMBER | AUTHOR | DEGREE |
|---|---|---|
| 57-052 | Bass, P. | Ph.D. |
| 59-577 | Beaulieu, Guy | M.Sc. |
| 24-509 | Bourne, Wesley | M.Sc. |
| 29-506 | Bruger, Moses | M.Sc. |
| 26-508 | Draper, William B. | M.Sc. |
| 22-506 | Foran, Herbert P. | M.Sc. |
| 58-520 | Francis, Lyman E. | M.Sc. |
| 53-057 | Karp, Dorothy | Ph.D. |
| 56-024 | Korol, Bernard | Ph.D. |
| 23-515 | Lozinsky, Ezra | M.Sc. |
| 57-065 | Mazurkiewicz, Irena M. | Ph.D. |
| 55-533 | Mazurkiewicz, Irena M. | M.Sc. |
| 31-509 | Melville, Kenneth I. | M.Sc. |
| 59-527 | Millar, Ronald A. | M.Sc. |
| 35-514 | Oldham, Frances K. | M.Sc. |

## Philosophy

| THESIS NUMBER | AUTHOR | DEGREE |
|---|---|---|
| 48-606 | Benn, Doris E. | M.A. |
| 48-607 | Bennett, Richard L. | M.A. |
| 27-526 | Claxton, John W. | M.A. |
| 16-501 | Corbett, Edward A. | M.A. |
| 33-544 | Currie, Cecil | M.A. |
| 31-528 | Estall, Henry M. | M.A. |
| 40-026 | Faurot, Jean Hiatt | M.A. |
| 39-033 | Fleer, Edward Herman | M.A. |



## Philosophy

| THESIS NUMBER | AUTHOR | DEGREE |
|---|---|---|
| 48-560 | Goldberg, W. | M.A. |
| 55-548 | Gombay, Andre M. | M.A. |
| 28-540 | Henderson, Thomas G. | M.A. |
| 07-502 | Hindley, John G. | M.A. |
| 15-503 | Honey, Howard F. | M.A. |
| 58-542 | Kaal, Hans | M.A. |
| 25-536 | Kelloway, Warwick F. | M.A. |
| 58-544 | Kinsman, Michael J. | M.A. |
| 36-535 | Klineberg, Beatrice A. | M.A. |
| 50-569 | Kushner, Eva M. | M.A. |
| 57-548 | Lachs, John | M.A. |
| 52-605 | Laird, James T. | M.A. |
| 54-614 | Lewis, Herbert | M.A. |
| 39-041 | Lipton, Charles | M.A. |
| 10-507 | Maclean, Herbert F. | M.A. |
| 30-536 | MacMillan, Donald N. | M.A. |
| 36-538 | Mallin, Estelle C. | M.A. |
| 54-546 | Marler, G.L. | M.A. |
| 16-504 | McCormack, George J. | M.A. |
| 19-501 | Melvin, Margaret G. | M.A. |
| 50-570 | Money-Coutts, Joanna H. | M.A. |
| 52-551 | Moser, Shia | M.A. |
| 59-616 | Nemiroff, Stanley A. | M.A. |
| 48-567 | Oduber-Quiros, Daniel | M.A. |
| 44-516 | Panos, Dimitrios | M.A. |
| 53-615 | Pitt, Jack A. | M.A. |
| 48-569 | Polonoff, Irving I. | M.A. |
| 14-507 | Powles, Percival S. | M.A. |
| 38-553 | Reed, Ernest S. | M.A. |
| 50-576 | Robinson, Jonathan | M.A. |
| 09-505 | Rogers, David B. | M.A. |
| 46-591 | Stewart, Mary | M.A. |
| 54-556 | Van Leight-Frank, Margit | M.A. |
| 50-667 | Watson, Gordon A. | M.A. |
| 25-551 | Wilkinson, George | M.A. |
| 42-047 | Williams, Ivor David | M.A. |
| 23-527 | Wiseman, Solomon | M.A. |
| 48-045 | Yalden-Thomas, David C. | Ph.D. |

## Physics

| THESIS NUMBER | AUTHOR | DEGREE |
|---|---|---|
| 53-041 | Adams, Glenn N. | Ph.D. |
| 50-511 | Adams, Glenn N. | M.Sc. |
| 33-568 | Aikman, Edward P. | M.Sc. |

| THESIS NUMBER | AUTHOR | DEGREE |
|---|---|---|

Physics

| THESIS NUMBER | AUTHOR | DEGREE |
|---|---|---|
| 35-001 | Aikman, William E. P. | Ph.D. |
| 49-002 | Alcock, Norman Z. | Ph.D. |
| 49-003 | Anderson, Donald A. | Ph.D. |
| 57-050 | Armstrong, Robert A. | Ph.D. |
| 54-570 | Armstrong, Robert A. | M.Sc. |
| 57-051 | Assaly, Robert N. | Ph.D. |
| 55-005 | Bachynski, Morrel P. | Ph.D. |
| 54-571 | Badior, Mark A. | M.Sc. |
| 09-507 | Baird, John B. | M.Sc. |
| 48-015 | Bartholomew, Gilbert | Ph.D. |
| 10-512 | Bates, Frederick W. | M.Sc. |
| 54-573 | Beaulieu, Jacques J. | M.Sc. |
| 52-004 | Bekefi, George | Ph.D. |
| 50-514 | Bekefi, George | M.Sc. |
| 48-003 | Bell, Robert E. | Ph.D. |
| 47-543 | Bercovitch, Mortimer | M.Sc. |
| 56-513 | Bernstein, Hyman | M.Sc. |
| 46-507 | Berry, Verne H. | M.Sc. |
| 46-509 | Black, Robson H. | M.Sc. |
| 56-514 | Blevis, Earl H. | M.Sc. |
| 50-515 | Bloom, Martin S. | M.Sc. |
| 50-597 | Bloom, Myer | M.Sc. |
| 52-570 | Bordan, Jack | M.Sc. |
| 52-005 | Borts, Robert B. | Ph.D. |
| 50-517 | Borts, Robert B. | M.Sc. |
| 09-001 | Boyle, Robert W. | Ph.D. |
| 50-002 | Boyle, Willard S. | Ph.D. |
| 48-513 | Boyle, Willard S. | M.Sc. |
| 48-018 | Brannen, Eric | Ph.D. |
| 51-001 | Breckon, Sydney W. | Ph.D. |
| 48-019 | Brunton, Donald C. | Ph.D. |
| 53-576 | Buchsbaum, Solomon J. | M.Sc. |
| 39-054 | Bychowsky, Victor | M.Sc. |
| 49-006 | Carruthers, James A. | Ph.D. |
| 58-008 | Carter, Alfred L. | Ph.D. |
| 28-004 | Chalk, Mary L. | Ph.D. |
| 26-506 | Chalk, Mary L. | M.Sc. |
| 56-515 | Chapdelaine, Joseph L. | M.Sc. |
| 51-043 | Chapman, John H. | Ph.D. |
| 49-518 | Chapman, John H. | M.Sc. |
| 51-515 | Chapman, Marion H. | M.Sc. |
| 49-519 | Chapman, Robert P. | M.Sc. |
| 51-044 | Clark, Eric N. | Ph.D. |
| 48-020 | Clarke, Robert L. | Ph.D. |
| 55-050 | Clifford, Charles E. | Ph.D. |




| THESIS NUMBER | AUTHOR | DEGREE |
|---|---|---|


Physics

| THESIS NUMBER | AUTHOR | DEGREE |
|---|---|---|
| 53-581 | Clifford, Charles E. | M.Sc. |
| 59-012 | Cloutier, Gilles G. | Ph.D. |
| 56-516 | Cloutier, Gilles G. | M.Sc. |
| 55-051 | Cloutier, Joseph A. | Ph.D. |
| 53-582 | Cloutier, Joseph A. | M.Sc. |
| 54-045 | Crawford, Gerald J. | Ph.D. |
| 28-503 | Crowe, Marguerite | M.Sc. |
| 55-012 | Crowell, Clarence R. | Ph.D. |
| 51-604 | Crowell, Clarence R. | M.Sc. |
| 53-520 | Crysdale, John H. | M.Sc. |
| 30-002 | Currie, Balfour W. | Ph.D. |
| 53-050 | Dahlstrom, Carl E. | Ph.D. |
| 56-009 | Danby, Gordon T. | Ph.D. |
| 09-508 | Day, Franklin H. | M.Sc. |
| 55-052 | Dennis, Arnett S. | Ph.D. |
| 53-521 | Dennis, Arnett S. | M.Sc. |
| 53-522 | Densmore, Arthur A. | M.Sc. |
| 58-516 | Desrochers, Louis G. | M.Sc. |
| 52-522 | Dewdney, John W. | M.Sc. |
| 58-563 | DeMille, George E. | M.Sc. |
| 10-515 | Dickieson, Arthur L. | M.Sc. |
| 59-581 | Din, Ghias ud | M.Sc. |
| 29-507 | Dobridge, Ronald W. | M.Sc. |
| 49-008 | Dodds, John W. | Ph.D. |
| 46-516 | Dodds, John W. | M.Sc. |
| 56-518 | Dore, Purnell V. | M.Sc. |
| 26-002 | Douglas, Allie V. | Ph.D. |
| 21-503 | Douglas, Allie V. | M.Sc. |
| 49-009 | Douglas, Donald G. | Ph.D. |
| 01-002 | Duncan, Gaylen R. | M.Sc. |
| 32-554 | Dunn, William K. | M.Sc. |
| 52-044 | Eadie, Frank S. | Ph.D. |
| 49-523 | Eadie, Frank S. | M.Sc. |
| 59-019 | Eappen, Collaparambil | Ph.D. |
| 55-015 | East, Thomas W. | Ph.D. |
| 53-524 | East, Thomas W. | M.Sc. |
| 09-509 | Elliott, Percy H. | M.Sc. |
| 55-054 | Epp, Edward R. | Ph.D. |
| 57-573 | Favreau, Roger F. | M.Sc. |
| 40-518 | Feeny, Harold Francis | M.Sc. |
| 54-521 | Flower, Louis G. | M.Sc. |
| 51-046 | Forsyth, Peter A. | Ph.D. |
| 56-048 | Foster, Leigh C. | Ph.D. |
| 49-046 | Fraser, John S. | Ph.D. |
| 41-041 | Fu, Cheng-Yi | M.Sc. |

| THESIS NUMBER | AUTHOR | DEGREE |
|---|---|---|
| Physics | | |
| 41-006 | Geldart, Lloyd Philip | Ph.D. |
| 09-511 | Gillis, Norman R. | M.Sc. |
| 46-568 | Girdwood, Barbara M. | M.Sc. |
| 48-024 | Girdwood, Barbara M. | Ph.D. |
| 49-526 | Glegg, Keith C. | M.Sc. |
| 52-572 | Gold, Lorne W. | M.Sc. |
| 48-579 | Goldman, Leonard M. | M.Sc. |
| 51-012 | Gransden, Max M. | Ph.D. |
| 56-052 | Green, Ralph E. | Ph.D. |
| 51-608 | Greenberg, Jack S. | M.Sc. |
| 50-609 | Griffiths, Herbert D. | M.Sc. |
| 53-531 | Groves, Trevor K. | M.Sc. |
| 50-005 | Gunn, Kenrick L. | Ph.D. |
| 47-549 | Gunn, Kenrick L. | M.Sc. |
| 47-028 | Gunton, Robert C. | Ph.D. |
| 46-009 | Guptill, Ernest W. | Ph.D. |
| 25-519 | Hachey, Henry B. | M.Sc. |
| 14-513 | Hague, Owen C. | M.Sc. |
| 53-009 | Hamilton, Hugh A. | Ph.D. |
| 50-528 | Hamilton, Hugh A. | M.Sc. |
| 46-570 | Hardie, Robert H. | M.Sc. |
| 57-577 | Hargrove, Clifford K. | M.Sc. |
| 30-004 | Harkness, Harold W. | Ph.D. |
| 29-555 | Harkness, Harold W. | M.Sc. |
| 52-047 | Harrower, George A. | Ph.D. |
| 50-611 | Harrower, George A. | M.Sc. |
| 33-008 | Haslam, Robert N. | Ph.D. |
| 52-015 | Hay, Donald R. | Ph.D. |
| 32-007 | Heard, Jack F. | Ph.D. |
| 30-530 | Heard, Jack F. | M.A. |
| 42-525 | Hecht, Maurice | M.Sc. |
| 56-016 | Heckman, Donald E. | Ph.D. |
| 53-532 | Heckman, Donald E. | M.Sc. |
| 31-012 | Helwig, Gerald V. | Ph.D. |
| 29-509 | Helwig, Gerald V. | M.Sc. |
| 28-511 | Henderson, John T. | M.Sc. |
| 53-010 | Henrikson, Arne | Ph.D. |
| 48-526 | Henrikson, Arne | M.Sc. |
| 16-511 | Henry, Elizabeth V. | M.Sc. |
| 51-050 | Henry, William H. | Ph.D. |
| 54-014 | Hilborn, John W. | Ph.D. |
| 51-609 | Hilborn, John W. | M.Sc. |
| 50-006 | Hitschfeld, Walter | Ph.D. |
| 53-012 | Hogg, David C. | Ph.D. |
| 50-613 | Hogg, David C. | M.Sc. |



| THESIS NUMBER | AUTHOR | DEGREE |
|---|---|---|
| Physics | | |
| 25-548 | Home, Maurice S. | M.Sc. |
| 51-015 | Hone, David W. | Ph.D. |
| 52-017 | Hopkins, Nigel J. | Ph.D. |
| 49-531 | Hopkins, Nigel J. | M.Sc. |
| 37-010 | Horton, Cyril A. | Ph.D. |
| 31-007 | Howlett, Leslie E. | Ph.D. |
| 56-054 | Hunt, John W. | Ph.D. |
| 50-007 | Hunten, Donald M. | Ph.D. |
| 52-576 | Hunten, Janet L. | M.Sc. |
| 56-521 | Huq, M. Shamsul | M.Sc. |
| 36-009 | Hurst, Donald G. | Ph.D. |
| 34-512 | Hurst, Donald G. | M.Sc. |
| 50-010 | Jackson, Fay W. | Ph.D. |
| 15-508 | James, Clarke E. | M.Sc. |
| 52-020 | Johnson, Frederick A. | Ph.D. |
| 54-591 | Jones, Alun P. | M.Sc. |
| 37-012 | Jones, Donald C. | Ph.D. |
| 50-540 | Kassner, Max H. | M.Sc. |
| 33-011 | Katzman, John | Ph.D. |
| 30-505 | Katzman, John | M.Sc. |
| 48-007 | Kaufman, Hyman | Ph.D. |
| 42-055 | Kennedy, John Edward | M.Sc. |
| 51-051 | Keys, John D. | Ph.D. |
| 48-584 | Keys, John D. | M.Sc. |
| 53-058 | Kirkaldy, John S. | Ph.D. |
| 48-027 | Knowles, John W. | Ph.D. |
| 57-020 | Kornelsen, Ernest V. | Ph.D. |
| 55-606 | Kycia, Tadeusz F. | M.Sc. |
| 29-018 | Lane, Cecil T. | Ph.D. |
| 53-059 | Langleben, Manuel P. | Ph.D. |
| 50-616 | Langleben, Manuel P. | M.Sc. |
| 30-005 | Langstroth, George C. | Ph.D. |
| 56-524 | Legg, Thomas H. | M.Sc. |
| 57-062 | Link, William T. | Ph.D. |
| 51-532 | Loomer, Elijah I. | M.Sc. |
| 47-011 | Lorrain, Paul | Ph.D. |
| 41-530 | Lorrain, Paul | M.Sc. |
| 32-519 | Lyons, Walter | M.Sc. |
| 52-054 | Maclure, Kenneth C. | Ph.D. |
| 50-621 | Maclure, Kenneth C. | M.Sc. |
| 28-516 | MacDonald, James L. | M.Sc. |
| 28-517 | MacLeod, Malcolm D. | M.Sc. |
| 50-622 | Magarvey, R.H. | M.Sc. |
| 51-023 | Martin, William M. | Ph.D. |
| 56-027 | Mathison, James F. | Ph.D. |

Physics

| THESIS NUMBER | AUTHOR | DEGREE |
|---|---|---|
| 01-003 | McClung, Robert K. | M.A. |
| 53-062 | McCormick, Glendon C. | Ph.D. |
| 59-047 | McFarlane, Ross A. | Ph.D. |
| 55-530 | McFarlane, Ross A. | M.Sc. |
| 59-049 | McIntosh, Bruce A. | Ph.D. |
| 39-516 | McKay, Kenneth Gardiner | M.Sc. |
| 23-517 | McPherson, Anna I. | M.Sc. |
| 30-007 | McRae, Duncan R. | Ph.D. |
| 28-518 | McRae, Duncan R. | M.Sc. |
| 49-031 | Michel, Walter | Ph.D. |
| 47-035 | Millar, Charles H. | Ph.D. |
| 53-600 | Milne, Allen R. | M.Sc. |
| 52-580 | Moen, H.P. | M.Sc. |
| 55-067 | Moody, Harry J. | Ph.D. |
| 50-038 | Moon, James H. | Ph.D. |
| 59-528 | Moore, Robert B. | M.Sc. |
| 16-513 | Moran, James | M.Sc. |
| 48-033 | Morrison, Wesley A. | Ph.D. |
| 54-024 | Mungall, Allan G. | Ph.D. |
| 47-015 | Munn, Allan M. | Ph.D. |
| 37-017 | Neamtan, Samuel M. | Ph.D. |
| 59-590 | Normand, Gerard L. | M.Sc. |
| 49-614 | Ornstein, William | M.Sc. |
| 49-031 | Palmer, Walter M. | Ph.D. |
| 47-564 | Palmer, Walter M. | M.Sc. |
| 36-020 | Panter, Shraga F. | Ph.D. |
| 12-517 | Paterson-Smyth, Marjorie | M.Sc. |
| 28-011 | Patterson, Arthur L. | Ph.D. |
| 24-525 | Patterson, Arthur L. | M.Sc. |
| 48-034 | Pepper, Thomas P. | Ph.D. |
| 53-067 | Peppiatt, Harry J. | Ph.D. |
| 57-591 | Perey, Francis G. | M.Sc. |
| 55-030 | Perlman, Martin M. | Ph.D. |
| 51-616 | Perlman, Martin M. | M.Sc. |
| 51-617 | Pfalzner, Paul M. | M.Sc. |
| 53-068 | Piggott, Carmen L. | Ph.D. |
| 37-018 | Pounder, Elton R. | Ph.D. |
| 53-603 | Prentice, James D. | M.Sc. |
| 27-516 | Press, Abraham | M.Sc. |
| 29-019 | Priestman, Bryan | Ph.D. |
| 26-523 | Priestman, Bryan | M.Sc. |
| 50-553 | Puxley, Ann E. | M.Sc. |
| 46-532 | Quinn, Hubert F. | M.Sc. |
| 48-035 | Quinn, Hubert F. | Ph.D. |
| 50-629 | Radley, Sidney A. | M.Sc. |

Physics

| THESIS NUMBER | AUTHOR | DEGREE |
|---|---|---|
| 58-575 | Rao, C. Kanaka D. | M.Sc. |
| 56-536 | Reeves, Hubert | M.Sc. |
| 58-576 | Reid, Kenneth H. | M.Sc. |
| 14-515 | Reilly, Herschell F. | M.Sc. |
| 49-545 | Rigby, Caroline E. | M.Sc. |
| 33-031 | Ross, William B. | Ph.D. |
| 31-515 | Ross, William B. | M.Sc. |
| 41-507 | Rotenberg, Avrahm B. | Ph.D. |
| 56-537 | Roumbanis, Theodore | M.Sc. |
| 28-007 | Rowles, William | Ph.D. |
| 26-525 | Rowles, William | M.Sc. |
| 13-520 | Scott, Arthur A. | M.Sc. |
| 40-021 | Scott, Donald Burton | Ph.D. |
| 56-602 | Segal, Penny | M.Sc. |
| 51-625 | Sellen, John M. | M.Sc. |
| 10-521 | Shaw, Albert N. | M.Sc. |
| 08-513 | Shearer, George W. | M.Sc. |
| 57-031 | Shkarofsky, Issie | Ph.D. |
| 53-606 | Shkarofsky, Issie | M.Sc. |
| 40-023 | Shugar, David | Ph.D. |
| 55-075 | Skarsgard, Harvey M. | Ph.D. |
| 50-634 | Smith, Donald S. | M.Sc. |
| 21-515 | Smith, Letha A. | M.Sc. |
| 36-518 | Smith, Philip D. | M.Sc. |
| 33-019 | Snell, Arthur H. | Ph.D. |
| 31-558 | Snell, Arthur H. | M.Sc. |
| 58-531 | Sosniak, J. | M.Sc. |
| 48-040 | Stephens-Newsham, Lloyd | Ph.D. |
| 55-039 | Stevens, Bernard A. | Ph.D. |
| 52-592 | Stevens, Bernard A. | M.Sc. |
| 10-522 | Sullivan, Charles T. | M.Sc. |
| 54-533 | Sullivan, Harry M. | M.Sc. |
| 55-621 | Szabo, Alexander | M.Sc. |
| 47-572 | Tate, Parr A. | M.Sc. |
| 59-601 | Taylor, Allen L. | M.Sc. |
| 49-056 | Telford, William M. | Ph.D. |
| 41-536 | Telford, William M. | M.Sc. |
| 26-528 | Terroux, Fernand R. | M.Sc. |
| 58-049 | Thomas, George M. | Ph.D. |
| 56-606 | Thomas, George M. | M.Sc. |
| 33-023 | Thornton, Robert L. | Ph.D. |
| 48-600 | Thurston, Arthur M. | M.Sc. |
| 51-060 | Tilley, Donald E. | Ph.D. |
| 56-543 | Tunis, Cyril J. | M.Sc. |
| 48-041 | Turner, Terry E. | Ph.D. |

| THESIS NUMBER | AUTHOR | DEGREE |
|---|---|---|
| **Physics** | | |
| 57-086 | Van Steenbergen, Arie | Ph.D. |
| 57-041 | Vessot, Robert F. | Ph.D. |
| 54-535 | Vessot, Robert F. | M.Sc. |
| 09-518 | Vipond, William S. | M.Sc. |
| 52-033 | Vogan, Eric L. | Ph.D. |
| 48-042 | Voyvodic, Louis | Ph.D. |
| 50-046 | Wagner, Sydney | Ph.D. |
| 48-551 | Wagner, Sydney | M.Sc. |
| 39-505 | Walker, Laurence Richard | Ph.D. |
| 52-065 | Wanklyn, David I. | Ph.D. |
| 51-560 | Wanklyn, David I. | M.Sc. |
| 48-044 | Warren, F.G. Ross | Ph.D. |
| 26-533 | Watson, Edmund E. | M.Sc. |
| 32-027 | Watson, Horace G. | Ph.D. |
| 59-543 | Weaver, Ralph S. | M.Sc. |
| 37-031 | Wendling, Andre V. | Ph.D. |
| 11-515 | Wheeler, Nathaniel E. | M.Sc. |
| 29-020 | White, Thomas N. | Ph.D. |
| 57-088 | Whitehead, Andrew B. | Ph.D. |
| 55-622 | Whitehead, Andrew B. | M.Sc. |
| 52-067 | Whittier, Angus C. | Ph.D. |
| 50-558 | Whittier, Angus C. | M.Sc. |
| 48-014 | Wolfson, Joseph L. | Ph.D. |
| 28-526 | Young, John M. | M.Sc. |
| 48-605 | Zirinsky, Victor J. | M.Sc. |
| **Physiology** | | |
| 23-502 | Armour, John C. | M.Sc. |
| 53-042 | Ashwin, James G. | Ph.D. |
| 41-034 | Baxt, Judith Brainin | M.Sc. |
| 30-501 | Baxter, Hamilton A. | M.Sc. |
| 32-020 | Baxter, Stewart G. | Ph.D. |
| 57-003 | Birks, Richard I. | Ph.D. |
| 54-575 | Birks, Richard I. | M.Sc. |
| 59-004 | Bliss, James Q. | Ph.D. |
| 42-517 | Bornstein, Murray Bernard | M.Sc. |
| 31-501 | Brodie, Maurice | M.Sc. |
| 53-577 | Bunzl, Arthur | M.Sc. |
| 29-001 | Burke, Hugh E. | Ph.D. |
| 25-545 | Burke, Hugh E. | M.Sc. |
| 26-505 | Cashin, Martin F. | M.Sc. |
| 25-546 | Cassidy, Gordon J. | M.Sc. |
| 26-507 | Cleland, John G. | M.Sc. |



| THESIS NUMBER | AUTHOR | DEGREE |
|---|---|---|
| **Physiology** | | |
| 17-504 | Cromarty, Robert F. | M.Sc. |
| 29-553 | Daniels, Eli | M.Sc. |
| 28-505 | Davies, Frank T. | M.Sc. |
| 16-508 | Dowler, Vernon B. | M.Sc. |
| 55-598 | Drapeau, Jacqueline U. | M.Sc. |
| 48-517 | Dso, Li-Liang | M.Sc. |
| 27-003 | Elvidge, Arthur R. | Ph.D. |
| 25-514 | Elvidge, Arthur R. | M.Sc. |
| 27-004 | Emmons, William F. | Ph.D. |
| 28-508 | Finney, William H. | M.Sc. |
| 24-515 | Fleet, George A. | M.Sc. |
| 56-049 | Frank, George B. | Ph.D. |
| 28-560 | Freedman, Nathan | M.Sc. |
| 37-028 | Friedman, Mac H. | Ph.D. |
| 46-518 | Gertler, Menard M. | M.Sc. |
| 45-530 | Gold, Simon | M.Sc. |
| 30-503 | Gottlieb, Rudolf | M.Sc. |
| 54-050 | Grafstein, Bernice | Ph.D. |
| 34-542 | Gray, Nelson M. | M.Sc. |
| 25-518 | Green, Frederick | M.Sc. |
| 54-051 | Grossberg, Allan L. | Ph.D. |
| 37-009 | Hebb, Catherine O. | Ph.D. |
| 28-513 | Hou, Hsiang-Ch'uan | M.Sc. |
| 47-554 | Johnson, Arnold I. | M.Sc. |
| 19-502 | Jull, Morley A. | M.Sc. |
| 46-571 | Karp, Dorothy | M.Sc. |
| 47-009 | Kellaway, Peter E. | Ph.D. |
| 31-554 | Komarov, Simon A. | M.Sc. |
| 35-015 | Komarov, Simon A. | Ph.D. |
| 47-010 | Lathe, Grant H. | Ph.D. |
| 48-588 | Levitan, Benjamin A. | M.Sc. |
| 54-016 | Levy, Samuel W. | Ph.D. |
| 37-015 | MacIntosh, Frank C. | Ph.D. |
| 30-006 | MacKay, Margaret E. | Ph.D. |
| 24-523 | Malcolm, Robert B. | M.Sc. |
| 59-048 | McIlreath, Fred J. | Ph.D. |
| 25-523 | McNally, William J. | M.Sc. |
| 26-518 | Miller, George G. | M.Sc. |
| 26-519 | Mills, Edward S. | M.Sc. |
| 29-512 | Mirsky, Isadore A. | M.Sc. |
| 35-512 | Nicholls, John V. V. | M.Sc. |
| 54-598 | Oborin, Peter E. | M.Sc. |
| 53-602 | Pedley, Norah F. | M.Sc. |
| 57-592 | Pinsky, Carl | M.Sc. |
| 54-063 | Ravaris, Charles L. | Ph.D. |

| THESIS NUMBER | AUTHOR | DEGREE |
|---|---|---|
| **Physiology** | | |
| 32-522 | Rawlinson, Herbert E. | M.Sc. |
| 34-024 | Rawlinson, Herbert E. | Ph.D. |
| 31-514 | Ross, Douglas A. | M.Sc. |
| 34-012 | Ross, Douglas A. | Ph.D. |
| 27-518 | Ross, Dudley E. | M.Sc. |
| 59-068 | Salmoiraghi, Gian C. | Ph.D. |
| 55-064 | Sastry, Podila-Brahmayya | Ph.D. |
| 42-531 | Schachter, Melville | M.Sc. |
| 41-508 | Schiffrin, Milton Julius | Ph.D. |
| 56-601 | Seeman, Philip | M.Sc. |
| 38-549 | Sergeyeva, Maria A. | M.Sc. |
| 30-552 | Stavrakis, George V. | M.Sc. |
| 32-524 | Sutherland, George F. | M.Sc. |
| 22-528 | Tidmarsh, Clarence J. | M.A. |
| 33-033 | Vineberg, Arthur M. | Ph.D. |
| 33-024 | Webster, Donald R. | Ph.D. |
| 30-513 | Webster, Donald R. | M.Sc. |
| 59-544 | Wechsler, Ann | M.Sc. |
| 57-598 | Weiss, Michael | M.Sc. |
| 48-553 | Wener, Joseph | M.Sc. |
| **Plant Anatomy** | | |
| 25-507 | Atwell, Ernest A. | M.Sc. |
| **Plant Morphology** | | |
| 10-523 | Weir, Douglas | M.Sc. |
| **Plant Pathology** | | |
| 37-533 | Ayers, George W. | M.Sc. |
| 49-593 | Bagnall, Richard H. | M.Sc. |
| 32-508 | Boothroyd, Raymond A. | M.Sc. |
| 49-520 | Cinq-Mars, Lionel | M.Sc. |
| 52-518 | Clark, Robert V. | M.Sc. |
| 45-509 | Clarkson, Scott F. | M.Sc. |
| 56-007 | Coulombe, Louis-Joseph | Ph.D. |
| 49-599 | Coulombe, Louis-Joseph | M.Sc. |
| 37-503 | Cox, Harold A. | M.Sc. |
| 55-596 | Crete, Joseph E. | M.Sc. |
| 39-056 | Dolan, Desmond Daniel | M.Sc. |



| THESIS NUMBER | AUTHOR | DEGREE |
|---|---|---|
| **Plant Pathology** | | |
| 32-512 | Eardley, Eric A. | M.Sc. |
| 56-046 | Estey, Ralph H. | Ph.D. |
| 53-587 | Fernando, Derrick M. | M.Sc. |
| 40-043 | Genereux, Henri G. | M.Sc. |
| 42-523 | Gilbey, John Alfred | M.Sc. |
| 29-554 | Godbout, Fernand | M.Sc. |
| 22-508 | Godwin, Kathleen F. | M.Sc. |
| 24-517 | Gordon, William L. | M.Sc. |
| 33-515 | Hamilton, George H. | M.Sc. |
| 25-520 | Harrison, Kenneth A. | M.Sc. |
| 31-553 | Hicks, Arthur J. | M.Sc. |
| 27-506 | Hill, Hinson | M.Sc. |
| 49-530 | Hodgson, William A. | M.Sc. |
| 31-507 | Howatt, John L. | M.Sc. |
| 58-021 | Jain, Abir C. | Ph.D. |
| 58-022 | Jayanetti, Edwin | Ph.D. |
| 50-614 | Julien, J. Bernard | M.Sc. |
| 40-014 | Lachance, Rene C. | Ph.D. |
| 39-061 | Lachance, Rene C. | M.Sc. |
| 32-518 | Lavallee, Edouard | M.Sc. |
| 57-528 | Lawrence, Charles H. | M.Sc. |
| 42-058 | Leblond, David | M.Sc. |
| 57-530 | Lockhart, Chesley L. | M.Sc. |
| 47-012 | Ludwig, Ralph A. | Ph.D. |
| 28-006 | Machacek, John E. | Ph.D. |
| 53-022 | MacLeod, Donald M. | Ph.D. |
| 43-505 | MacLeod, Donald M. | M.Sc. |
| 30-508 | MacRae, Norman A. | M.Sc. |
| 37-510 | McEvoy, Edward T. | M.Sc. |
| 38-513 | Miles, Henry J. | M.Sc. |
| 28-521 | Montserin, Blazini G. | M.Sc. |
| 19-503 | Newton, Margaret | M.Sc. |
| 51-541 | Paquin, Roger | M.Sc. |
| 42-528 | Payette, Albert | M.Sc. |
| 44-521 | Pelletier, Real | M.Sc. |
| 27-514 | Perreault, Champlain | M.Sc. |
| 59-592 | Phillips, Charles O. | M.Sc. |
| 27-515 | Pomerleau, Rene | M.Sc. |
| 26-522 | Popp, William | M.Sc. |
| 53-543 | Ross, Robert G. | M.Sc. |
| 40-523 | Sackston, Waldemar E. | M.Sc. |
| 55-033 | Samborski, Daniel J. | Ph.D. |
| 34-543 | Savile, Douglas B. | M.Sc. |
| 24-528 | Scott, Gordon A. | M.Sc. |
| 51-547 | Sibalis, Jack | M.Sc. |

## Plant Pathology

| THESIS NUMBER | AUTHOR | DEGREE |
|---|---|---|
| 54-531 | Simard, J. | M.Sc. |
| 44-511 | Simard, Thomas | M.Sc. |
| 48-038 | Simard, Thomas | Ph.D. |
| 59-538 | Smith, Thomas H. | M.Sc. |
| 22-523 | Spier, Jane D. | M.Sc. |
| 39-026 | Thatcher, Frederick S. | Ph.D. |
| 35-540 | Thatcher, Frederick S. | M.Sc. |
| 58-533 | Udeaja, Philip E. | M.Sc. |
| 25-529 | Vanterpool, Thomas C. | M.Sc. |
| 54-034 | Wallen, Victor R. | Ph.D. |
| 49-552 | Wallen, Victor R. | M.Sc. |
| 57-043 | Wang, Dalton T. | Ph.D. |
| 36-521 | White-Stevens, Robert H. | M.Sc. |

## Plant Pathology & Botany

| THESIS NUMBER | AUTHOR | DEGREE |
|---|---|---|
| 49-038 | Shaw, Michael | Ph.D. |
| 47-569 | Shaw, Michael | M.Sc. |

## Political Science

| THESIS NUMBER | AUTHOR | DEGREE |
|---|---|---|
| 06-001 | Brown, Walter G. | M.A. |
| 50-651 | Brzezinski, Zbigniew K. | M.A. |
| 54-611 | Coldhagen, E. | M.A. |
| 08-501 | Cousins, George V. | M.A. |
| 57-547 | Geist, Paul B. | M.A. |
| 45-019 | Humphrey, John P. | Ph.D. |
| 08-502 | Jamieson, John S. | M.A. |
| 46-540 | Layton, Irving | M.A. |
| 09-504 | MacCrimmon, John R. | M.A. |
| 49-640 | Metcalf, John F. | M.A. |
| 56-058 | Oliver, Michael K. | Ph.D. |
| 07-505 | Pelletier, Alexis D. | M.A. |
| 46-589 | Quinn, Herbert F. | M.A. |
| 56-065 | Sayeed, Kkalid B. | Ph.D. |
| 55-037 | Scott, Peter D. | Ph.D. |
| 50-665 | Shklar, Judith | M.A. |
| 54-622 | Singer, David P. | M.A. |
| 10-510 | Smillie, Eleanor A. | M.A. |
| 56-549 | Speyer, Judith | M.A. |
| 54-557 | Walmsley, Norma E. | M.A. |



## Poultry Husbandry

| THESIS NUMBER | AUTHOR | DEGREE |
|---|---|---|
| 52-514 | Burgess, Ralph C. | M.Sc. |
| 54-577 | Cadet, Charles M. | M.Sc. |
| 55-526 | Keenan, Daniel | M.Sc. |
| 48-534 | Mani, K.V. | M.Sc. |
| 25-544 | Maw, William A. | M.S.A. |
| 50-624 | Miller, William St. C. | M.Sc. |
| 57-538 | Smith, Robert E. | M.Sc. |

## Psychiatry

| THESIS NUMBER | AUTHOR | DEGREE |
|---|---|---|
| 55-586 | Azima, Hassan | M.Sc. |
| 59-580 | Curtis, George C. | M.Sc. |

## Psychology

| THESIS NUMBER | AUTHOR | DEGREE |
|---|---|---|
| 46-537 | Amsel, Abram | M.A. |
| 26-536 | Armstrong, Charles A. | M.A. |
| 54-006 | Bartoshuk, Alexander K. | Ph.D. |
| 52-569 | Bartoshuk, Alexander K. | M.Sc. |
| 55-006 | Beach, Horace D. | Ph.D. |
| 53-044 | Bexton, William H. | Ph.D. |
| 51-631 | Bird, Thomas C. | M.A. |
| 57-545 | Birks, Margaret | M.A. |
| 46-508 | Black, Percy | M.Sc. |
| 49-554 | Blascik, Frank | M.A. |
| 36-001 | Bois, Joseph S. | Ph.D. |
| 34-544 | Bois, Joseph S. | M.A. |
| 50-650 | Brougham, Norma I. | M.A. |
| 50-518 | Brown, Frederick T. | M.Sc. |
| 58-514 | Bryden, Mark P. | M.Sc. |
| 55-010 | Burnett, Alastair | Ph.D. |
| 59-008 | Burns, Neal M. | Ph.D. |
| 57-521 | Burns, Neal M. | M.Sc. |
| 49-627 | Calvert, Margaret N. | M.A. |
| 29-525 | Cardonsky, Mary | M.A. |
| 58-012 | Christake, Anna | Ph.D. |
| 55-547 | Clark, James W. | M.A. |
| 43-521 | Clarke, Douglas B. | M.A. |
| 51-601 | Clarke, Ronald S. | M.Sc. |
| 59-607 | Claus, Hans-Jorg | M.A. |
| 41-527 | Cownie, Douglas Heron | M.Sc. |
| 46-539 | De Jersey, Murray G. | M.A. |
| 53-549 | Deitcher, Samuel | M.A. |

## Psychology

| THESIS NUMBER | AUTHOR | DEGREE |
|---|---|---|
| 49-557 | DeShield, George D. | M.A. |
| 50-652 | Dickie, Robert D. | M.A. |
| 55-053 | Doane, Benjamin K. | Ph.D. |
| 34-546 | Dodds, Margaret R. | M.A. |
| 47-508 | Dorken, Herbert O. | M.Sc. |
| 53-586 | Downer, John L. | M.Sc. |
| 28-562 | Duckworth, John M. | M.A. |
| 07-501 | East, Edith M. | M.A. |
| 58-517 | Ehrlich, Daniel J. | M.Sc. |
| 54-582 | Endler, Norman S. | M.Sc. |
| 31-529 | Etziony, Mordecai | M.A. |
| 52-603 | Falk, John L. | M.A. |
| 29-530 | Featherston, Florence E. | M.A. |
| 59-023 | Feldman, Samuel M. | Ph.D. |
| 50-030 | Forgays, Donald G. | Ph.D. |
| 48-559 | Forgays, Donald G. | M.A. |
| 51-520 | Forgus, Ronald H. | M.Sc. |
| 30-526 | Frank, Harold | M.A. |
| 42-031 | Gagnon, Aurele | M.A. |
| 58-521 | Gardner, Robert C. | M.Sc. |
| 51-047 | Ghent, Lila R. | Ph.D. |
| 49-561 | Ghent, Lila R. | M.A. |
| 59-029 | Glickman, Stephen | Ph.D. |
| 49-631 | Gordon, Thelma G. | M.A. |
| 48-561 | Gottheil, Edward | M.A. |
| 54-585 | Havelka, Jaroslav | M.Sc. |
| 32-530 | Hebb, Donald O. | M.A. |
| 53-056 | Heron, Woodburn | Ph.D. |
| 49-633 | Heron, Woodburn | M.A. |
| 56-580 | Hodgson, Richard C. | M.Sc. |
| 57-604 | Hogg, Doreen | M.A. |
| 49-567 | Holmes, Anthony F. | M.A. |
| 29-536 | Howat, David | M.A. |
| 52-019 | Hoyt, Ruth | Ph.D. |
| 49-635 | Hoyt, Ruth | M.A. |
| 10-502 | Huntley, Herbert W. | M.A. |
| 51-016 | Hunton, Vera D. | Ph.D. |
| 49-020 | Hymovitch, Bernard | Ph.D. |
| 46-523 | Hymovitch, Bernard | M.Sc. |
| 48-612 | Irvine, Lucille | M.A. |
| 50-655 | Jackson, Jay M. | M.A. |
| 30-531 | Japp, Robert | M.A. |
| 59-041 | Kimura, Douglas S. | Ph.D. |
| 55-553 | Knaff, Paul R. | M.A. |
| 26-544 | Knechtel, Max U. | M.A. |



## Psychology

| THESIS NUMBER | AUTHOR | DEGREE |
|---|---|---|
| 59-042 | Koppenaal, Richard J. | Ph.D. |
| 49-569 | Lambek, Hanna W. | M.A. |
| 50-033 | Lansdell, Herbert C. | Ph.D. |
| 39-507 | Laxer, Robert Mendel | M.A. |
| 51-638 | Lyman, Bernard E. | M.A. |
| 10-506 | MacKenzie, John M. | M.A. |
| 28-546 | MacLean, Mary W. | M.A. |
| 26-549 | MacLeod, Elmer D. | M.A. |
| 27-538 | MacLeod, Robert B. | M.A. |
| 28-547 | MacPherson, John T. | M.A. |
| 26-550 | MacVicar, Donald H. | M.A. |
| 55-611 | Mahatoo, Winston H. | M.Sc. |
| 49-029 | Mahoney, Gerald M. | Ph.D. |
| 47-519 | Mahoney, Gerald M. | M.Sc. |
| 55-065 | Mahut, Helen | Ph.D. |
| 52-606 | Mahut, Helen | M.A. |
| 46-588 | McFarlane, Arthur H. | M.A. |
| 49-028 | McMurray, Gordon A. | Ph.D. |
| 54-020 | Melzack, Ronald | Ph.D. |
| 51-614 | Melzack, Ronald | M.Sc. |
| 27-535 | Merry, Ralph V. | M.A. |
| 51-570 | Mills, Allan W. | M.A. |
| 52-058 | Milner, Brenda A. | Ph.D. |
| 54-022 | Milner, Peter M. | Ph.D. |
| 50-625 | Milner, Peter M. | M.Sc. |
| 51-055 | Mishkin, Mortimer | Ph.D. |
| 49-573 | Mishkin, Mortimer | M.A. |
| 42-063 | Mitchell, Mary V. | M.Sc. |
| 59-053 | Mogenson, Gordon J. | Ph.D. |
| 55-068 | Mooney, Craig M. | Ph.D. |
| 51-571 | Mooney, Craig M. | M.A. |
| 55-616 | Morrison, Gordon F. | M.Sc. |
| 33-030 | Morton, Nelson W. | Ph.D. |
| 31-537 | Morton, Nelson W. | M.A. |
| 39-016 | Norris, Kenneth E. | Ph.D. |
| 31-538 | Norris, Kenneth E. | M.A. |
| 50-660 | Oliver, John A. | M.A. |
| 50-662 | Orbach, Jack | M.A. |
| 41-520 | Orlick, Emanuel | M.A. |
| 59-060 | Paivio, Allan U. | Ph.D. |
| 57-534 | Paivio, Allan U. | M.Sc. |
| 46-529 | Parsons, John G. | M.Sc. |
| 50-573 | Paul, Irving H. | M.A. |
| 35-546 | Peden, Gwendolyn W. | M.A. |
| 51-618 | Popham, James H. | M.Sc. |

| THESIS NUMBER | AUTHOR | DEGREE |
|---|---|---|
| **Psychology** | | |
| 30-542 | Pursley, Robert | M.A. |
| 49-615 | Rabinovitch, Mortimer S. | M.Sc. |
| 52-554 | Rabinowitz, Herbert S. | M.A. |
| 58-056 | Rajalakshmi, Ramakrishnan | Ph.D. |
| 49-578 | Rankin, Winston B. | M.A. |
| 46-546 | Reid, David B. | M.A. |
| 49-616 | Rishikof, Jack R. | M.Sc. |
| 35-533 | Robertson, Barbara M. | M.A. |
| 52-029 | Ross, Mary V. | Ph.D. |
| 12-505 | Rowell, Arthur H. | M.A. |
| 54-030 | Sampson, Hubert | Ph.D. |
| 53-075 | Scheier, Ivan H. | Ph.D. |
| 51-641 | Scheier, Ivan H. | M.A. |
| 57-077 | Schnore, Morris M. | Ph.D. |
| 52-556 | Schwartzman, Alex E. | M.A. |
| 54-065 | Scott, Thomas H. | Ph.D. |
| 42-043 | Shane, Gerald S. | M.A. |
| 54-066 | Sharpless, Seth K. | Ph.D. |
| 35-539 | Shaw, Hampden C. | M.Sc. |
| 51-546 | Shulman, R. | M.Sc. |
| 49-643 | Sloan, Emmett P. | M.A. |
| 50-043 | Smith, Alfred A. | Ph.D. |
| 54-067 | Smith, Charles J. | Ph.D. |
| 51-643 | Smith, Charles J. | M.A. |
| 57-034 | Smith, David D. | Ph.D. |
| 28-555 | Smyth, Desmond H. | M.A. |
| 47-582 | Sofin, Rosalie | M.A. |
| 43-528 | Spearman, Donald | M.A. |
| 30-546 | Spence, Kenneth W. | M.A. |
| 55-077 | Springbett, Bruce M. | Ph.D. |
| 56-035 | Stennett, Richard G. | Ph.D. |
| 57-082 | Stern, Muriel H. | Ph.D. |
| 54-604 | Stern, Muriel H. | M.Sc. |
| 38-555 | Stevenson, James A. | M.A. |
| 46-592 | Strauss, Clara | M.A. |
| 55-041 | Surwillo, Walter W. | Ph.D. |
| 58-048 | Sydiaha, Daniel | Ph.D. |
| 46-536 | Tagiuri, Renato | M.Sc. |
| 40-524 | Udow, Alfred Bernard | M.Sc. |
| 59-603 | Vanderwolf, Cornelius H. | M.Sc. |
| 50-047 | Wake, Frank R. | Ph.D. |
| 55-564 | Waksberg, Helene | M.A. |
| 54-035 | Wallerstein, Harvey | Ph.D. |
| 50-638 | Wallerstein, Harvey | M.Sc. |
| 36-014 | Webster, Edward C. | Ph.D. |



| THESIS NUMBER | AUTHOR | DEGREE |
|---|---|---|
| **Psychology** | | |
| 33-561 | Webster, Edward C. | M.A. |
| 50-668 | Westcott, James W. | M.A. |
| 57-599 | Wevrick, Leonard | M.Sc. |
| 52-068 | Wigdor, Blossom T. | Ph.D. |
| 48-570 | Willis, Edith B. | M.A. |
| 58-551 | Wimer, Cynthia C. | M.A. |
| 59-075 | Wimer, Richard E. | Ph.D. |
| 40-514 | Woo, Wesley Stewart | M.A. |
| 52-560 | Zweig, Joseph P. | M.A. |
| **Reinforced Concrete Construction** | | |
| 09-510 | Finlayson, John N. | M.Sc. |
| **Rock Crushing** | | |
| 14-514 | Mitchell, William G. | M.Sc. |
| **Sanitary Engineering** | | |
| 15-509 | Knight, Frederic C. | M.Sc. |
| **Semitic Studies** | | |
| 09-502 | Gordon, Nathan | M.A. |
| 14-506 | McVittie, Thomas J. | M.A. |
| 12-504 | Potter, James G. | M.A. |
| 16-506 | Withey, Albert N. | M.A. |
| **Social Science** | | |
| 26-547 | McFarlane, Duncan H. | M.A. |
| **Sociology** | | |
| 37-542 | Aikman, Mary E. | M.A. |
| 54-608 | Badgley, Robin F. | M.A. |
| 39-029 | Bayley, Charles Melville | Ph.D. |
| 33-536 | Berry, John W. | M.A. |

| THESIS NUMBER | AUTHOR | DEGREE |
|---|---|---|

Sociology

| | | |
|---|---|---|
| 50-647 | Blishen, Bernard R. | M.A. |
| 55-624 | Bloomstone, Shirley S. | M.A. |
| 51-564 | Brazeau, Joseph E. | M.A. |
| 27-525 | Brown, Wilfred H. | M.A. |
| 35-541 | Clark, Samuel D. | M.A. |
| 33-543 | Craig, Glenn H. | M.A. |
| 33-573 | Davidson, Mary H. | M.A. |
| 27-529 | Davis, Richard E. | M.A. |
| 51-632 | Dickson, Delphine M. | M.A. |
| 45-513 | Ferencz, Agnes M. | M.A. |
| 43-523 | Finestone, Harold | M.A. |
| 53-550 | Fonseca, Owen W. | M.A. |
| 29-532 | Garland, Sidney G. | M.A. |
| 34-547 | Gibbard, Harold A. | M.A. |
| 13-504 | Going, Margaret C. | M.A. |
| 42-511 | Gold, Rosalynd | M.A. |
| 37-544 | Hall, Oswald | M.A. |
| 32-529 | Heaton, Phyllis | M.A. |
| 39-506 | Hunter, Jean Isobel | M.A. |
| 28-564 | Israel, Wilfred E. | M.A. |
| 47-578 | Jackson, Joan K. | M.A. |
| 38-533 | Jamieson, Stuart M. | M.A. |
| 55-631 | Jonassohn, Kurt | M.A. |
| 50-656 | Jones, Frank E. | M.A. |
| 39-037 | Kerry, Esther Wilson | M.A. |
| 39-039 | Lewis, James Neilson | M.A. |
| 54-545 | Leznoff, Maurice | M.A. |
| 32-533 | LePage, Inez M. | M.A. |
| 40-030 | Lieff, Pearl | M.A. |
| 50-657 | Lucas, Rex A. | M.A. |
| 34-548 | Mamchur, Stephen W. | M.A. |
| 28-543 | McCall, Muriel B. | M.A. |
| 55-634 | McFarlane, Bruce A. | M.A. |
| 50-658 | McKay, Huntly W. | M.A. |
| 35-532 | Moellmann, Albert | M.A. |
| 49-575 | Potter, Harold H. | M.A. |
| 30-543 | Radler, Ruth | M.A. |
| 33-574 | Ramsden, Mary E. | M.A. |
| 53-616 | Rennie, Douglas L. | M.A. |
| 33-556 | Reynolds, Lloyd G. | M.A. |
| 54-619 | Richardson, Nigel H. | M.A. |
| 28-551 | Robert, Percy A. | M.A. |
| 53-617 | Robinson, Patricia G. | M.A. |
| 53-618 | Rodman, Hyman | M.A. |
| 32-545 | Ross, Herman R. | M.A. |



| THESIS NUMBER | AUTHOR | DEGREE |
|---|---|---|

Sociology

| | | |
|---|---|---|
| 35-548 | Roy, William J. | M.A. |
| 27-539 | Rutman, Robin L. | M.A. |
| 39-508 | Seidel, Judith | M.A. |
| 46-547 | Seyward, Henry | M.A. |
| 30-545 | Smith, Gladys I. | M.A. |
| 42-045 | Solomon, David N. | M.A. |
| 46-590 | Spurrell, Althea C. | M.A. |
| 31-545 | Tuttle, Harry G. | M.A. |
| 55-562 | Vaz, Edmund W. | M.A. |
| 31-546 | Wade, Margaret M. | M.A. |
| 55-567 | Wipper, Audrey J. | M.A. |
| 28-558 | Young, Charles H. | M.A. |
| 33-562 | Younge, Eva R. | M.A. |
| 48-619 | Zakuta, Leo | M.A. |

Sociology & Anthropology

| | | |
|---|---|---|
| 59-606 | Burshtyn, Hyman | M.A. |
| 59-557 | Loeb, Bernice F. | M.A. |
| 59-613 | McCrorie, James N. | M.A. |
| 59-564 | Willmott, William E. | M.A. |

Theory of Structures

| | | |
|---|---|---|
| 24-522 | McLennan, Logan S. | M.Sc. |

Thermodynamics

| | | |
|---|---|---|
| 11-514 | Munn, David W. | M.Sc. |
| 14-516 | Ryan, Charles C. | M.Sc. |

Zoology

| | | |
|---|---|---|
| 37-501 | Adams, James R. | M.Sc. |
| 40-500 | Adams, James Russell | Ph.D. |
| 44-518 | Anderson, Joan C. | M.Sc. |
| 57-564 | Bain, E.B. | M.Sc. |
| 56-004 | Black, William F. | Ph.D. |
| 56-038 | Bleakney, John S. | Ph.D. |
| 42-006 | Briggs, Janet B. | Ph.D. |
| 56-041 | Cameron, Austin W. | Ph.D. |

## Zoology

| THESIS NUMBER | AUTHOR | DEGREE |
|---|---|---|
| 33-511 | Clark, Annie E. | M.Sc. |
| 54-043 | Clayton, Blanche-Petite | Ph.D. |
| 36-003 | Cohen, Arthur | Ph.D. |
| 34-508 | Cohen, Arthur | M.Sc. |
| 50-601 | Darrell-McPhee, Gloria | M.Sc. |
| 46-515 | Davidson, Margaret E. | M.Sc. |
| 52-043 | Davis, Gordon R. | Ph.D. |
| 49-522 | Davis, Gordon R. | M.Sc. |
| 14-511 | Duff, Dorothy | M.Sc. |
| 41-502 | Dunbar, Maxwell John | Ph.D. |
| 31-506 | Edelstein, Leo J. | M.Sc. |
| 57-008 | Edwards, Donald K. | Ph.D. |
| 57-009 | Ellis, Derek V. | Ph.D. |
| 54-520 | Ellis, Derek V. | M.Sc. |
| 59-516 | Evans, John W. | M.Sc. |
| 58-565 | Fish, Arthur G. | M.Sc. |
| 54-048 | Fisher, Harold D. | Ph.D. |
| 54-583 | Fontaine, Marion | M.Sc. |
| 57-055 | Gibson, Merritt A. | Ph.D. |
| 39-514 | Graham, Annie Philathea | M.Sc. |
| 53-054 | Grainger, Edward H. | Ph.D. |
| 49-606 | Grainger, Edward H. | M.Sc. |
| 42-524 | Hall, Charles E. | M.Sc. |
| 05-002 | Henderson, Ernest H. | M.A. |
| 26-512 | Henderson, Jean T. | M.Sc. |
| 48-581 | Hildebrand, Henry H. | M.Sc. |
| 50-537 | Jacoby, Arthur W. | M.Sc. |
| 29-511 | Kamm, Josephine J. | M.Sc. |
| 35-529 | Khaner, Miriam | M.A. |
| 56-582 | Kohler, Allan C. | M.Sc. |
| 30-506 | L'Herisson, Camille | M.Sc. |
| 37-537 | Lead, Harry D. | M.Sc. |
| 54-054 | Lewis, John B. | Ph.D. |
| 50-541 | Lewis, John B. | M.Sc. |
| 42-059 | Lin, Shu-Chang | M.Sc. |
| 47-032 | Liu, Chien-kang | Ph.D. |
| 07-511 | Lyman, Ruth D. | M.Sc. |
| 57-533 | Macpherson, Andrew H. | M.Sc. |
| 58-027 | Mansfield, Arthur W. | Ph.D. |
| 50-548 | Martin, Helen J. | M.Sc. |
| 55-610 | McLaren, Ian A. | M.Sc. |
| 49-030 | Milne, Donald J. | Ph.D. |
| 35-510 | Monro, Hector A. | M.Sc. |
| 59-589 | Nejedly, Vladislava J. | M.Sc. |
| 57-073 | Osborn, Dale J. | Ph.D. |



## Zoology

| THESIS NUMBER | AUTHOR | DEGREE |
|---|---|---|
| 59-530 | Parakkal, Paul F. | M.Sc. |
| 30-012 | Pinhey, Kathleen F. | Ph.D. |
| 59-064 | Power, Geoffrey | Ph.D. |
| 33-527 | Richardson, Laurence R. | M.Sc. |
| 35-024 | Richardson, Laurence R. | Ph.D. |
| 46-535 | Schachter, Ruth | M.Sc. |
| 49-055 | Scott, David M. | Ph.D. |
| 47-525 | Scott, David M. | M.Sc. |
| 49-546 | Scott, David P. | M.Sc. |
| 45-539 | Sinclair, George W. | M.Sc. |
| 48-039 | Sinclair, George W. | Ph.D. |
| 56-540 | Squires, Hubert J. | M.Sc. |
| 56-541 | Steele, Donald H. | M.Sc. |
| 30-512 | Taylor, Bertram W. | M.Sc. |
| 57-597 | Thomson, John A. | M.Sc. |
| 46-016 | Weisz, Paul | Ph.D. |
| 44-512 | Weisz, Paul | M.Sc. |

## Zoology-Genetics

| THESIS NUMBER | AUTHOR | DEGREE |
|---|---|---|
| 42-052 | Entin, Martin A. | M.Sc. |

# LISTING BY SUPERVISOR

| AUTHOR | DEGREE | THESIS NUMBER |
|---|---|---|
| ** | | |
| Anderson, Marian | M.Sc. | 20-502 |
| Arkley, Lorne M. | M.Sc. | 10-511 |
| Baily, Philip P. | M.Sc. | 14-508 |
| Beagley, Thomas G. | M.Sc. | 12-507 |
| Blackader, Alexander D. | M.A. | 18-501 |
| Braeuer, Mary A. | M.A. | 14-501 |
| Brown, Walter G. | M.A. | 06-001 |
| Campbell, Edmund E. | M.Sc. | 11-506 |
| Common, Frank B. | M.A. | 14-502 |
| Corbett, Percy E. | M.A. | 15-501 |
| Cumming, Charles L. | M.Sc. | 13-515 |
| Davidson, MacFarlane B. | M.A. | 06-002 |
| Davidson, William A. | M.Sc. | 14-510 |
| Day, Frank J. | M.A. | 06-003 |
| Dewey, Alexander G. | M.A. | 13-502 |
| Dewey, George F. | M.A. | 14-503 |
| Duncan, Gaylen R. | M.Sc. | 01-002 |
| Ferencz, Agnes M. | M.A. | 45-513 |
| Fort, Charles A. | M.Sc. | 16-509 |
| Godin, J.J. | M.Sc. | 53-589 |
| Going, Margaret C. | M.A. | 13-504 |
| Goldberg, W. | M.A. | 48-560 |
| Goldstein, Hildred M. | M.A. | 16-502 |
| Hadrill, Margaret F. | M.A. | 05-001 |
| Henry, Alice I. | M.A. | 06-004 |
| Knight, Frederic C. | M.Sc. | 15-509 |
| Lamb, Henry M. | M.Sc. | 13-518 |
| Machacek, John E. | Ph.D. | 28-006 |
| MacKenzie, John M. | M.A. | 10-506 |
| Major, Thomas G. | M.Sc. | 22-516 |
| Mingie, George W. | M.A. | 06-005 |
| Munn, William C. | M.A. | 05-004 |
| Newson, William V. | M.Sc. | 01-004 |
| Nicolls, Jasper H. | M.Sc. | 12-516 |
| Pelletier, Alexis D. | M.A. | 07-505 |
| Pollard, Samuel L. | M.A. | 30-541 |
| Prillaman, J.H. | M.Sc. | 56-595 |
| Ried, L. | M.Sc. | 02-001 |
| Robinson, Bernard S. | M.A. | 13-508 |
| Ross, Dorothy V. | M.A. | 26-553 |
| Scott, Arthur P. | M.Sc. | 14-517 |
| Sheldon, Ernest. W. | M.A. | 05-005 |
| Smith, Esther M. | M.A. | 06-006 |
| Smith, Gladys L. | M.A. | 30-545 |
| Spier, Jane D. | M.Sc. | 22-523 |



| AUTHOR | DEGREE | THESIS NUMBER |
|---|---|---|
| ** | | |
| Van Barneveld, Charles E | M.Sc. | 16-514 |
| Wickenden, Marguerite H. | M.A. | 28-557 |
| Wu, Chow C. | M.Sc. | 16-515 |
| *Yuile, C. | | |
| Gold, M.M.A. | M.Sc. | 45-529 |
| Adair, E. | | |
| Arthur, Elizabeth M. | Ph.D. | 49-004 |
| Arthur, Elizabeth M. | M.A. | 47-529 |
| Ballantyne, Murray G. | M.A. | 32-559 |
| Cragg, Gerald R. | Ph.D. | 46-004 |
| Craig, Isabel F. | M.A. | 37-520 |
| Gilmore, Robert C. | M.A. | 47-577 |
| Heisler, John Phalen | M.A. | 41-023 |
| Lapin, Murray | M.A. | 41-519 |
| Lunn, Alice J. | Ph.D. | 42-503 |
| Lunn, Alice J. | M.A. | 34-533 |
| McOuat, D.F. | M.A. | 48-565 |
| Munroe, David C. | M.A. | 38-539 |
| Prince, Alma S. | M.A. | 47-539 |
| Reid, Allana G. | Ph.D. | 50-040 |
| Reid, Allana G. | M.A. | 45-547 |
| Ross, Dorothy J. | Ph.D. | 39-023 |
| Ross, Dorothy J. | M.A. | 32-544 |
| Taylor, Harland W. | M.A. | 51-644 |
| Warldeworth, Eleanor S. | M.A. | 31-547 |
| Williams, Katharine R. | M.A. | 36-543 |
| Adami, J. | | |
| Harrison, Francis C. | M.Sc. | 07-508 |
| *Shanly, Eleanor | M.Sc. | 14-519 |
| Adams, C. | | |
| Ansari, Zafar I. | M.A. | 59-545 |
| Kamali, Sabih A. | Ph.D. | 59-039 |
| *Carson, Beatrice M. | M.A. | 59-547 |

| AUTHOR | DEGREE | THESIS NUMBER |
|---|---|---|
| **Adams, C.** | | |
| **Adams, F.** | | |
| Allan, John A. | M.Sc. | 08-508 |
| Bain, George W. | M.Sc. | 23-503 |
| Bancroft, Joseph A. | Ph.D. | 10-001 |
| Stansfield, John | Ph.D. | 29-013 |
| Stansfield, John | M.Sc. | 12-518 |
| *Buffam, Basil S. | M.Sc. | 24-510 |
| *Dick, William J. | M.Sc. | 11-508 |
| *DuPorte, Ernest M. | M.Sc. | 14-512 |
| *Ellis, David H. | M.Sc. | 26-509 |
| *Fritz, Clara W. | M.Sc. | 18-503 |
| *Graham, Richard P. | M.Sc. | 08-509 |
| *Gray, Alexander M. | M.Sc. | 16-510 |
| *Harvie, Robert | M.Sc. | 09-513 |
| *Hayes, Albert O. | M.Sc. | 10-517 |
| *Howard, Waldorf V. | M.Sc. | 22-512 |
| *Howard, Waldorf V. | Ph.D. | 24-002 |
| *James, William F. | M.Sc. | 21-510 |
| *Kirsch, Simon | M.A. | 07-503 |
| *Lathe, Frank E. | M.Sc. | 15-510 |
| *McFee, Malcolm C. | M.Sc. | 08-511 |
| *McIntosh, Donald S. | M.Sc. | 08-512 |
| *O'Neill, John J. | M.Sc. | 10-519 |
| *Pelletier, Rene A. | M.Sc. | 24-526 |
| *Priestman, Bryan | Ph.D. | 29-019 |
| *Scott, Joseph M. | M.Sc. | 14-518 |
| *Symons, Jennie L. | M.Sc. | 21-516 |
| *Vessot, Charles U. | M.Sc. | 22-524 |
| *Wheeler, Nathaniel E. | M.Sc. | 11-515 |
| *Whitby, George S. | M.Sc. | 18-507 |
| *Wieland, Walter A. | M.Sc. | 18-508 |
| *Withey, Albert N. | M.A. | 16-506 |
| **Alexander, F.** | | |
| Dorken, Herbert O. | M.Sc. | 47-508 |
| Irvine, Lucille | M.A. | 48-612 |
| Sofin, Rosalie | M.A. | 47-582 |
| Willis, Edith B. | M.A. | 48-570 |



| AUTHOR | DEGREE | THESIS NUMBER |
|---|---|---|
| **Ali, M.** | | |
| Nejedly, Vladislava J. | M.Sc. | 59-589 |
| Parakkal, Paul F. | M.Sc. | 59-530 |
| **Allen, C.** | | |
| Ball, William L. | Ph.D. | 35-003 |
| Barker, Walter F. | Ph.D. | 31-011 |
| Bell, Adam C. | Ph.D. | 34-003 |
| Boyer, Raymond | Ph.D. | 33-003 |
| Cressman, Homer W. | Ph.D. | 33-005 |
| Frame, Gordon F. | Ph.D. | 32-003 |
| Gilman, Lucius | Ph.D. | 36-007 |
| Halley, Leroy F. | Ph.D. | 37-008 |
| Massey, Ernest E. | Ph.D. | 33-013 |
| Nicholls, Robert V. V. | Ph.D. | 36-019 |
| Nicholls, Robert V. V. | M.Sc. | 35-513 |
| Normington, James B. | Ph.D. | 34-008 |
| Overbaugh, Sidney C. | Ph.D. | 35-023 |
| Rudoff, Hyman | Ph.D. | 37-020 |
| Sallans, Henry R. | Ph.D. | 34-014 |
| Scarrow, James A. | M.Sc. | 33-528 |
| Scarrow, James A. | Ph.D. | 34-015 |
| Sheps, Louis J. | Ph.D. | 34-025 |
| Spanagel, Edgar W. | Ph.D. | 33-020 |
| Wells, Franklin B. | Ph.D. | 33-034 |
| Wilson, Charles V. | Ph.D. | 33-026 |
| Young, Donald M. | Ph.D. | 36-016 |
| *Chalmers, William | Ph.D. | 30-001 |
| *Wells, Franklin B. | M.Sc. | 31-560 |
| **Allen, C. .** | | |
| *Skazin, Lev | M.Sc. | 30-511 |
| **Anderson, E.** | | |
| Heuser, Edward A. | M.A. | 49-634 |
| Levine, Albert N. | M.A. | 49-570 |
| Orr, Paul A. | M.A. | 49-642 |

| AUTHOR | DEGREE | THESIS NUMBER |
|---|---|---|
| **Anglin, J.** | | |
| Gluckstbal, Andrew | M.C.L. | 53-500 |
| Gyorgy, Dezso | M.C.L. | 53-501 |
| **Archibald, E.** | | |
| Doubilet, Henry | M.Sc. | 31-505 |
| Miller, George G. | M.Sc. | 26-518 |
| *Ross, Dudley E. | M.Sc. | 27-518 |
| **Armstrong, D.** | | |
| Nixon, Justin W. | M.A. | 59-558 |
| Rezek, G. | M.A. | 57-609 |
| Thanos, Costas A. | M.A. | 59-563 |
| **Ashton, G.** | | |
| Lucas, Ian A. | M.Sc. | 49-608 |
| **Babkin, B.** | | |
| Baxter, Stewart G. | Ph.D. | 32-020 |
| Bornstein, Murray Bernar | M.Sc. | 42-517 |
| Friedman, Mac H. | Ph.D. | 37-028 |
| Gray, Nelson M. | M.Sc. | 34-542 |
| Hebb, Catherine C. | Ph.D. | 37-009 |
| Karp, Dorothy | M.Sc. | 46-571 |
| Komarov, Simon A. | Ph.D. | 35-015 |
| MacIntosh, Frank C. | Ph.D. | 37-015 |
| MacKay, Margaret E. | Ph.D. | 30-006 |
| Nicholls, John V. V. | M.Sc. | 35-512 |
| Rawlinson, Herbert E. | M.Sc. | 32-522 |
| Rawlinson, Herbert E. | Ph.D. | 34-024 |
| Schiffrin, Milton Julius | Ph.D. | 41-508 |
| Sergeyeva, Maria A. | M.Sc. | 38-549 |
| Speakman, Thomas J. | M.Sc. | 48-546 |
| Van Buren, John M. | M.Sc. | 50-637 |
| Vineberg, Arthur M. | Ph.D. | 33-033 |
| Webster, Donald R. | Ph.D. | 33-024 |
| *Gage, Everett L. | M.Sc. | 31-551 |
| *Komarov, Simon A. | M.Sc. | 31-554 |



| AUTHOR | DEGREE | THESIS NUMBER |
|---|---|---|
| **Babkin, B.** | | |
| *Stavrakis, George V. | M.Sc. | 30-552 |
| *Webster, Donald R. | M.Sc. | 30-513 |
| **Bagley, F.** | | |
| 'Abd-al-'ati, Hammaduh | M.A. | 57-601 |
| Al-Sawi, Ahmad H. | M.A. | 54-620 |
| Haydari, Amir A. | M.A. | 54-612 |
| Nashshabah, Hisham | M.A. | 55-636 |
| Qaysi, Abdul W. | M.A. | 54-554 |
| **Baird, P.** | | |
| Thompson, Hugh R. | Ph.D. | 54-070 |
| **Baker, B.** | | |
| Carr, Joseph W. | M.Sc. | 51-600 |
| Coffin, Althea | M.Sc. | 54-515 |
| Fairbairn, N.J. | M.Sc. | 51-519 |
| Henneberry, Gerald | M.Sc. | 50-530 |
| Khan, Noor A. | Ph.D. | 56-022 |
| Loughheed, Thomas C. | M.Sc. | 54-593 |
| Macdonald, Roderick F. | M.Sc. | 52-534 |
| MacRae, Herbert F. | M.Sc. | 56-587 |
| Murray, Thomas K. | M.Sc. | 50-549 |
| Parsons, Timothy R. | M.Sc. | 55-537 |
| Pedersen, Jorgen W. | Ph.D. | 53-031 |
| Pilson, Michael E. | M.Sc. | 59-531 |
| Reynolds, Lincoln M. | M.Sc. | 59-532 |
| Van Horne, William F. | M.Sc. | 48-550 |
| **Bancroft, J.** | | |
| Dufresne, Joseph A. | M.Sc. | 13-516 |
| Pelletier, Rene A. | Ph.D. | 27-009 |
| Squires, Henry D. | M.Sc. | 24-531 |
| *Bishop, Eric G. | Ph.D. | 27-002 |
| *Dolan, Everett P. | M.Sc. | 23-511 |
| *James, William F. | M.Sc. | 21-510 |
| *Wilson, Harold S. | M.Sc. | 25-530 |

| AUTHOR | DEGREE | THESIS NUMBER |
|---|---|---|
| Bancroft, J. | | |
| Barbour, H. | | |
| *Cambron, Adrien | M.Sc. | 23-506 |
| *Jane, Robert S. | M.Sc. | 23-513 |
| *Lozinsky, Ezra | M.Sc. | 23-515 |
| Barnes, H. | | |
| *Bates, Frederick W. | M.Sc. | 10-512 |
| *Boyle, Robert W. | Ph.D. | 09-001 |
| *Cromarty, Robert P. | M.Sc. | 17-504 |
| *Day, Franklin H. | M.Sc. | 09-508 |
| *Dickieson, Arthur L. | M.Sc. | 10-515 |
| *Elliott, Percy H. | M.Sc. | 09-509 |
| *Geldard, Walter J. | M.Sc. | 17-505 |
| *Gillis, Norman R. | M.Sc. | 09-511 |
| *Gray, Alexander M. | M.Sc. | 16-510 |
| *Hague, Owen C. | M.Sc. | 14-513 |
| *Hatcher, William H. | M.Sc. | 17-506 |
| *Henry, Elizabeth V. | M.Sc. | 16-511 |
| *James, Clarke B. | M.Sc. | 15-508 |
| *Kirkpatrick, Robert | M.Sc. | 13-517 |
| *Macleod, Annie L. | Ph.D. | 10-003 |
| *MacLean, Allison R. | Ph.D. | 16-001 |
| *MacLean, Allison R. | M.Sc. | 12-513 |
| *Marshall, Melville J. | M.Sc. | 16-512 |
| *Moran, James | M.Sc. | 16-513 |
| *Murphy, William H. | M.Sc. | 15-512 |
| *Paterson-Smyth, Marjorie | M.Sc. | 12-517 |
| *Reid, Hugh S. | M.Sc. | 15-513 |
| *Reilly, Herschell E. | M.Sc. | 14-515 |
| *Roffey, Myles H. | M.Sc. | 09-516 |
| *Sadler, Wilfrid | M.Sc. | 17-507 |
| *Scott, Arthur A. | M.Sc. | 13-520 |
| *Shearer, George W. | M.Sc. | 08-513 |
| *Vipond, William S. | M.Sc. | 09-518 |
| *Wheeler, Nathaniel E. | M.Sc. | 11-515 |
| Barnes, W. | | |
| Helwig, Gerald V. | Ph.D. | 31-012 |



| AUTHOR | DEGREE | THESIS NUMBER |
|---|---|---|
| Barnes, W. | | |
| Maass, Otto | M.Sc. | 12-512 |
| Matthews, Fred White | Ph.D. | 41-011 |
| Shaw, Albert N. | M.Sc. | 10-521 |
| Sullivan, Charles T. | M.Sc. | 10-522 |
| Wendling, Andre V. | Ph.D. | 37-031 |
| *Brown, Robert S. | Ph.D. | 36-017 |
| Bartown, H. | | |
| *Armour, John C. | M.Sc. | 23-502 |
| Bates, * | | |
| *Spencer, Roy A. | M.Sc. | 15-514 |
| Bates, D.V. | | |
| Donevan, Richard E. | M.Sc. | 58-564 |
| Batho, C. | | |
| *Eadie, Robert S. | M.Sc. | 22-505 |
| *Gliddon, William G. | M.Sc. | 22-507 |
| *Jamieson, Robert E. | M.Sc. | 20-505 |
| *Macdonald, Albert E. | M.Sc. | 22-514 |
| Baudouin, L. | | |
| Kallos, Tibere | M.C.L. | 53-502 |
| Ouimet, Paul A. | M.C.L. | 53-503 |
| Bauld, W. | | |
| Givner, Morris L. | M.Sc. | 56-575 |
| Baxter, H. | | |
| Schiller, Carl | M.Sc. | 52-541 |

| AUTHOR | DEGREE | THESIS NUMBER |
|---|---|---|
| Baxter, H. | | |
| Bayley, C. | | |
| Barry, Rexford G. | M.A. | 46-583 |
| Hampson, Harold G. | M.A. | 49-563 |
| Lucas, Sidney | Ph.D. | 55-064 |
| Beach, E. | | |
| Asimakopulcs, Athanasios | M.A. | 53-547 |
| Burgess, Charles J. | M.Com. | 47-540 |
| Hollbach, Reiner | Ph.D. | 58-020 |
| Kovalski, Voyo | M.A. | 58-545 |
| Martin, Fernand | M.A. | 58-546 |
| May, Sydney J. | M.Com. | 53-623 |
| Polianski, Alexei N. | M.A. | 59-559 |
| Potter, Calvin C. | Ph.D. | 54-028 |
| Sievwright, Eric C. | M.A. | 51-642 |
| Steigmann, Axel H. | M.A. | 56-550 |
| Beck, J. | | |
| Boright, Henry A. | M.Sc. | 59-511 |
| McLeod, Lionel E. | M.Sc. | 57-588 |
| Norman, Nils | Ph.D. | 57-072 |
| Weyl, Salom | M.A. | 40-513 |
| Bekefi, G. | | |
| Beaulieu, Jacques J. | M.Sc. | 54-573 |
| Cloutier, Gilles G. | M.Sc. | 56-516 |
| Legg, Thomas H. | M.Sc. | 56-524 |
| Bell, J. | | |
| Brissenden, William G. | M.Eng. | 38-500 |
| Brown, George Osburn | M.Eng. | 41-032 |
| Cameron, Douglas Alastai | M.Eng. | 40-515 |
| Cooper, Corin H. | M.Sc. | 13-514 |
| Dembicki, Steve | M.Eng. | 41-033 |



| AUTHOR | DEGREE | THESIS NUMBER |
|---|---|---|
| Bell, J. | | |
| Faucher, Joseph Arthur | M.Eng. | 42-049 |
| Fraser, Gordon E. | M.Eng. | 37-500 |
| Goode, Robert C. | M.Eng. | 34-501 |
| Grassby, James Neil | M.Eng. | 40-034 |
| Kennedy, Taylor James | M.Eng. | 39-052 |
| O'Shaughnessy, Martin D. | M.Eng. | 38-502 |
| Westwood, Robert J. | M.Eng. | 33-507 |
| *Anderson, Clayton E. | M.Sc. | 20-501 |
| *Gerson, Harold S. | M.Sc. | 29-508 |
| *Tousaw, Albert A. | M.Sc. | 20-507 |
| Bell, F. | | |
| Sosniak, J. | M.Sc. | 58-531 |
| Benfey, B. | | |
| Mazurkiewicz, Irena M. | Ph.D. | 57-065 |
| Millar, Ronald A. | M.Sc. | 59-527 |
| Benoit, * | | |
| *Alward, Frederick P. | M.A. | 28-527 |
| Bensley, E. | | |
| Darragh, James H. | M.Sc. | 59-514 |
| Beresford-Howe, C. | | |
| Dedering, Christa E. | M.A. | 55-627 |
| Sutherland, Ronald | M.A. | 55-561 |
| Woods, Helen M. | M.A. | 55-640 |
| Berkes, N. | | |
| Edmonds, William A. | M.A. | 54-541 |
| Kortepeter, Carl M. | M.A. | 54-613 |

| AUTHOR | DEGREE | THESIS NUMBER |
|---|---|---|
| Berrill, N. | | |
| Anderson, Joan C. | M.Sc. | 44-518 |
| Bassett, Henry G. | M.Sc. | 50-513 |
| Briggs, Janet B. | Ph.D. | 42-006 |
| Darrell-McPhee, Gloria | M.Sc. | 50-601 |
| Davidson, Margaret E. | M.Sc. | 46-515 |
| Evans, John W. | M.Sc. | 59-516 |
| Lin, Shu-Chang | M.Sc. | 42-059 |
| Liu, Chien-kang | Ph.D. | 47-032 |
| Milne, Donald J. | Ph.D. | 49-030 |
| Richardson, Laurence R. | M.Sc. | 33-527 |
| Schachter, Ruth | M.Sc. | 46-535 |
| Scott, David M. | M.Sc. | 47-525 |
| Sinclair, George W. | Ph.D. | 48-039 |
| Weisz, Paul | Ph.D. | 46-016 |
| Weisz, Paul | M.Sc. | 44-512 |
| *Taylor, Bertram W. | M.Sc. | 30-512 |
| Best, E. | | |
| *Davis, Richard E. | M.A. | 27-529 |
| *Duckworth, John M. | M.A. | 28-562 |
| *Garland, Sidney G. | M.A. | 29-532 |
| *Israel, Wilfred E. | M.A. | 28-564 |
| *McCall, Muriel B. | M.A. | 28-543 |
| *Rutman, Robin L. | M.A. | 27-539 |
| *Wade, Margaret M. | M.A. | 31-546 |
| Beullac, * | | |
| *Gillespie, Peter | M.Sc. | 12-509 |
| Bieler, * | | |
| *Lane, Cecil T. | M.Sc. | 27-510 |
| Bieler, E. | | |
| *Lane, Cecil T. | Ph.D. | 29-018 |



| AUTHOR | DEGREE | THESIS NUMBER |
|---|---|---|
| Bigelow, R. | | |
| Dondale, Charles D. | Ph.D. | 59-018 |
| Bindra, D. | | |
| Beach, Horace D. | Ph.D. | 55-006 |
| Clark, James W. | M.A. | 55-547 |
| Claus, Hans-Jorg | M.A. | 59-607 |
| Ehrlich, Daniel J. | M.Sc. | 58-517 |
| Falk, John L. | M.A. | 52-603 |
| Knaff, Paul R. | M.A. | 55-553 |
| Koppenaal, Richard J. | Ph.D. | 59-042 |
| Sampson, Hubert | Ph.D. | 54-030 |
| Stern, Muriel H. | Ph.D. | 57-082 |
| Wake, Frank R. | Ph.D. | 50-047 |
| Waksberg, Helene | M.A. | 55-564 |
| Wallerstein, Harvey | M.Sc. | 50-638 |
| Bird, J. | | |
| Coombs, Donald B. | M.A. | 52-548 |
| Findlay, Marjorie C. | Ph.D. | 56-011 |
| Ives, John D. | Ph.D. | 56-017 |
| Lithgow, Robert M. | M.A. | 52-549 |
| Marsden, Michael | M.Sc. | 56-588 |
| Mercer, John H. | Ph.D. | 54-021 |
| Monahan, Robert L. | Ph.D. | 59-081 |
| Raymond, Charles W. | M.A. | 59-560 |
| Smith, David I. | M.Sc. | 59-537 |
| Twidale, Charles R. | Ph.D. | 57-085 |
| Birkett, H. | | |
| *McNally, William J. | M.Sc. | 25-523 |
| Birmingham, M. | | |
| Desbarats, Marie-Louise | M.Sc. | 53-523 |
| Blackburn, J. | | |

| AUTHOR | DEGREE | THESIS NUMBER |
|---|---|---|
| **Blackburn, J.** | | |
| Calvert, Margaret N. | M.A. | 49-627 |
| Lambek, Hanna W. | M.A. | 49-569 |
| **Blackwood, A.** | | |
| Dawkins, Riley A. | M.Sc. | 57-570 |
| Walke, Lacey | M.Sc. | 58-579 |
| **Bland, J.** | | |
| Aronin, Jeffrey E. | M.Arch. | 51-580 |
| **Blank, F.** | | |
| Denson, Marie L. | M.Sc. | 57-571 |
| Kapica, Lucia | Ph.D. | 56-020 |
| **Bliss, S.** | | |
| *Greenberg, Harry | M.Sc. | 27-505 |
| *Hill, Allan C. | M.Sc. | 27-542 |
| *Katz, Morris | M.Sc. | 27-509 |
| **Boll, W.** | | |
| Lowther, Ruth L. | M.Sc. | 58-572 |
| **Bonbour, H.** | | |
| *Foran, Herbert P. | M.Sc. | 22-506 |
| **Boothroyd, E.** | | |
| Walker, Bruce E. | M.Sc. | 52-597 |
| Webster, Donald C. | M.Sc. | 56-609 |



| AUTHOR | DEGREE | THESIS NUMBER |
|---|---|---|
| **Bovery, H. D.** | | |
| *Brunner, Godfrey H. | M.Sc. | 07-507 |
| **Boyer, R.** | | |
| Bowen, William G. | Ph.D. | 45-016 |
| Edward, John T. | Ph.D. | 42-011 |
| Friedman, Orrie M. | Ph.D. | 44-005 |
| Garmaise, David L. | Ph.D. | 45-005 |
| Mowat, John H. | Ph.D. | 42-018 |
| Novack, Lazare | Ph.D. | 46-013 |
| Paquette, Joseph P. | M.Sc. | 43-508 |
| White, Howard L. | Ph.D. | 46-017 |
| **Boyes, J.** | | |
| Bubar, John S. | Ph.D. | 57-004 |
| Clark, Gordon M. | M.Sc. | 51-516 |
| Griesbach, Leonard | M.Sc. | 49-528 |
| Howes, James R. | M.Sc. | 51-525 |
| Johnston, William W. | M.Sc. | 50-539 |
| Mauer, Irving | M.Sc. | 52-537 |
| Maxwell, Doreen F. | Ph.D. | 55-066 |
| Povilaitis, Bronys | Ph.D. | 54-029 |
| Walker, George W. | Ph.D. | 52-064 |
| **Boyle, ***| | |
| *Barnes, William H. | Ph.D. | 27-001 |
| **Brady, A.** | | |
| Humphrey, John P. | Ph.D. | 45-019 |
| **Brawn, F.** | | |
| Chiang, Morgan S-M. | M.Sc. | 58-579 |
| Goyette, Louis F. | M.Sc. | 53-530 |
| Henry, Vann C. | M.Sc. | 56-578 |
| Isang, Etim U. | M.Sc. | 54-590 |

| AUTHOR | DEGREE | THESIS NUMBER |
|---|---|---|
| **Brecher, I.** | | |
| Mubarak, Nasreldin | M.A. | 59-615 |
| Petrogiannis, Demetrics | M.A. | 58-587 |
| Roseman, Frank | M.A. | 59-561 |
| **Brecher, M.** | | |
| Bosnitch, Sava | M.A. | 58-581 |
| Coldhagen, E. | M.A. | 54-611 |
| Geist, Paul B. | M.A. | 57-547 |
| Haugestad, Per T. | M.A. | 59-610 |
| **Bridges, J.** | | |
| *MacLeod, Elmer D. | M.A. | 26-549 |
| *MacLeod, Robert B. | M.A. | 27-538 |
| **Brittain, W.** | | |
| Beaulieu, Andre A. | M.Sc. | 38-503 |
| Cameron, James W. | Ph.D. | 38-004 |
| Cannon, Frederick Merrie | M.Sc. | 39-512 |
| Graham, Kenneth | M.Sc. | 37-507 |
| Lord, Frank T. | M.Sc. | 47-517 |
| MacPhee, Albert W. | M.Sc. | 47-560 |
| Marshall, James | Ph.D. | 38-013 |
| Matthewman, William G. | M.Sc. | 39-518 |
| McLeod, William S. | M.Sc. | 43-506 |
| Morley, Peter M. | M.Sc. | 38-514 |
| Pickett, Allison D. | M.Sc. | 36-515 |
| Prebble, Malcolm L. | Ph.D. | 40-019 |
| Prebble, Malcolm L. | M.Sc. | 32-521 |
| Wishart, George | M.Sc. | 38-523 |
| *Painter, Richard H. | M.Sc. | 29-514 |
| **Brockwell, B.** | | |
| *Gordon, Nathan | M.A. | 09-502 |
| **Brockwell, C.** | | |



| AUTHOR | DEGREE | THESIS NUMBER |
|---|---|---|
| **Brockwell, C.** | | |
| Burton, Garland G. | M.A. | 31-523 |
| Lennox, Robert | M.A. | 35-545 |
| Levitsky, Nathan A. | M.A. | 33-551 |
| Thomas, William | M.A. | 33-576 |
| *Berger, Julius | M.A. | 24-536 |
| *Boyes, Watson | M.A. | 25-532 |
| *Davis, Charles F. | M.A. | 23-521 |
| *McVittie, Thomas J. | M.A. | 14-506 |
| *Potter, James G. | M.A. | 12-504 |
| *Withey, Albert N. | M.A. | 16-506 |
| **Brodie, H.** | | |
| McEvoy, Edward T. | M.Sc. | 37-510 |
| **Brown, E.** | | |
| Cooper, Lawrence O. | M.Sc. | 31-504 |
| Davies, Vernon R. | M.Sc. | 23-509 |
| Jacobsen, Eric P. | M.Eng. | 32-502 |
| Morrison, Thomas J. | M.Sc. | 31-511 |
| Savage, Palmer E. | M.Eng. | 34-505 |
| *Brunner, Godfrey H. | M.Sc. | 07-507 |
| *Cronk, Francis J. | M.Sc. | 16-507 |
| *Dodd, Geoffrey J. | M.Sc. | 22-503 |
| *Fox, Charles H. | M.Sc. | 10-516 |
| *Guillet, George L. | M.Sc. | 09-512 |
| *Jamieson, Robert E. | M.Sc. | 20-505 |
| *Traversy, Eric E. | M.Sc. | 15-515 |
| *Watson, Edmund F. | M.Sc. | 26-533 |
| *Watson, Horace G. | M.Sc. | 27-520 |
| **Brown, O.** | | |
| Jamieson, David M. | M.Eng. | 33-566 |
| **Browne, J.** | | |
| Birmingham, Marion K. | Ph.D. | 49-043 |
| Chappel, Clifford I. | Ph.D. | 59-009 |
| Cooperberg, Abraham A. | M.Sc. | 49-598 |

| AUTHOR | DEGREE | THESIS NUMBER |
|---|---|---|
| Browne, J. | | |
| Croll, Diane | M.Sc. | 42-051 |
| Heller, Nathan | M.Sc. | 44-519 |
| Hoffman, Martin M. | Ph.D. | 43-007 |
| Howlett, John G. | M.Sc. | 37-509 |
| MacKenzie, Kenneth R. | Ph.D. | 48-030 |
| Rose, Bram | Ph.D. | 39-022 |
| Rose, Bram | M.Sc. | 37-513 |
| Schacher, Josephine | M.Sc. | 37-539 |
| Schenker, Victor | Ph.D. | 44-021 |
| Venning, Eleanor M. | Ph.D. | 33-032 |
| Weil, Paul Gregory | M.Sc. | 39-521 |
| Weil, Paul Gregory | Ph.D. | 41-018 |
| Bruce, W. | | |
| Hla, Kyaw | M.Eng. | 59-569 |
| Rice, William B. | M.Eng. | 56-509 |
| Bubar, J. | | |
| Lawson, Norman C. | M.Sc. | 58-571 |
| Bunting, T. | | |
| *DeLong, Walter A. | M.Sc. | 24-512 |
| Burgen, A. | | |
| Bliss, James Q. | Ph.D. | 59-004 |
| Bogoroch, Rita | M.Sc. | 50-516 |
| Girvin, Grace T. | M.Sc. | 50-526 |
| Longley, James D. | M.Sc. | 57-531 |
| Pinsky, Carl | M.Sc. | 57-592 |
| Ravaris, Charles L. | Ph.D. | 54-063 |
| Seeman, Philip | M.Sc. | 56-601 |
| Wechsler, Ann | M.Sc. | 59-544 |
| Weiss, Michael | M.Sc. | 57-598 |
| Burns, B. | | |



| AUTHOR | DEGREE | THESIS NUMBER |
|---|---|---|
| Burns, B. | | |
| Bunzl, Arthur | M.Sc. | 53-577 |
| Frank, George B. | Ph.D. | 56-049 |
| Grafstein, Bernice | Ph.D. | 54-050 |
| Karp, Dorothy | Ph.D. | 53-057 |
| Pedley, Norah F. | M.Sc. | 53-602 |
| Salmoiraghi, Gian C. | Ph.D. | 59-068 |
| Burr, E. | | |
| Shapiro, Clarence H. | M.Eng. | 33-505 |
| Burrow, M. | | |
| French, Betty R. | M.A. | 56-616 |
| Burton, G. | | |
| Shipley, William C. | M.A. | 50-664 |
| Byrd, K. | | |
| Poapst, James V. | M.Com. | 50-580 |
| Potter, Calvin C. | M.Com. | 50-671 |
| Caird, G. | | |
| Ellis, Clarence D. | Ph.D. | 54-047 |
| Kirby, John C. | S.T.M. | 57-503 |
| Osborne, Robert E. | S.T.M. | 54-559 |
| Skynner, H.J. | S.T.M. | 56-552 |
| Caldwell, W. | | |
| Corbett, Edward A. | M.A. | 16-501 |
| East, Edith M. | M.A. | 07-501 |
| Rogers, David B. | M.A. | 09-505 |
| *Claxton, John W. | M.A. | 27-526 |
| *Davidson, Winnifred H. | M.A. | 22-526 |
| *Henderson, Thomas G. | M.A. | 28-540 |

| AUTHOR | DEGREE | THESIS NUMBER |
|---|---|---|
| **Caldwell, W.** | | |
| *Hindley, John G. | M.A. | 07-502 |
| *Honey, Howard P. | M.A. | 15-503 |
| *Huntley, Herbert W. | M.A. | 10-502 |
| *Maclean, Herbert B. | M.A. | 10-507 |
| *McCormack, George J. | M.A. | 16-504 |
| *McCullagh, Paul F. | M.A. | 28-544 |
| *Melvin, Margaret G. | M.A. | 19-501 |
| *Powles, Percival S. | M.A. | 14-507 |
| *Renaud, Paul E. | LL.M. | 22-500 |
| *Steed, Joseph A. | M.A. | 18-502 |
| *Wilkinson, George | M.A. | 25-551 |
| **Callard, K.** | | |
| Andracki, Stanislaw | Ph.D. | 58-001 |
| Mennie, William A. | M.A. | 54-547 |
| Prives, Moshe Z. | Ph.D. | 58-035 |
| Romeril, Paul E. | M.A. | 59-619 |
| Sayeed, Kkalid B. | Ph.D. | 56-065 |
| Walmsley, Norma E. | M.A. | 54-557 |
| **Cameron, T.** | | |
| Alozie, Obinnaya | M.Sc. | 51-593 |
| Baer, Harold G. | M.Sc. | 54-572 |
| Barker, Clifford A. | M.Sc. | 45-520 |
| Belle, Edward A. | Ph.D. | 57-002 |
| Belle, Edward A. | M.Sc. | 54-574 |
| Bloomfield, Solomon S. | M.Sc. | 48-577 |
| Burgess, Glenn D. | M.Sc. | 52-571 |
| Cambieri, R. | M.Sc. | 57-522 |
| Cannon, Douglas G. | M.Sc. | 38-505 |
| Chambers, Harriet A. | M.Sc. | 54-514 |
| Choquette, Laurent P. E. | Ph.D. | 53-049 |
| Choquette, Laurent P. E. | M.Sc. | 42-518 |
| Cohen, Harry | M.Sc. | 49-596 |
| Connell, Robert | M.Sc. | 49-521 |
| Firlotte, William R. | M.Sc. | 47-510 |
| Fochs, Anita M. | M.Sc. | 48-520 |
| Frank, Julius | M.Sc. | 47-512 |
| Gibbs, Harold C. | Ph.D. | 58-016 |
| Gibbs, Harold C. | M.Sc. | 56-519 |
| Grainger, Edward H. | M.Sc. | 49-606 |



| AUTHOR | DEGREE | THESIS NUMBER |
|---|---|---|
| **Cameron, T.** | | |
| Griffiths, Henry J. | Ph.D. | 39-009 |
| Griffiths, Henry J. | M.Sc. | 35-505 |
| Jones, Trevor L. | M.Sc. | 35-508 |
| Khan, M. Abdul B. | Ph.D. | 49-024 |
| Lachance, Francois de S. | M.Sc. | 46-524 |
| Lesser, Elliott | Ph.D. | 53-061 |
| Lesser, Elliott | M.Sc. | 51-529 |
| Lubinsky, George | Ph.D. | 56-025 |
| Lyster, Lynden Laird | M.Sc. | 39-064 |
| Marchant, Edwin H. | Ph.D. | 47-014 |
| Margolis, Leo | Ph.D. | 52-057 |
| Margolis, Leo | M.Sc. | 50-547 |
| McGregor, John K. | M.Sc. | 55-531 |
| McMorran, Arlene R. | M.Sc. | 52-582 |
| Meerovitch, Eugene B. | Ph.D. | 57-066 |
| Meerovitch, Eugene B. | M.Sc. | 55-534 |
| Mensah-Dapaa, W.S. | M.Sc. | 54-594 |
| Miller, Max J. | M.Sc. | 36-513 |
| Montreuil, Paul L. | M.Sc. | 55-535 |
| Moynihan, Irvin W. | M.Sc. | 47-521 |
| Myers, Betty-June | Ph.D. | 59-056 |
| Nnochiri, Enyinnaya | Ph.D. | 59-059 |
| Nnochiri, Enyinnaya | M.Sc. | 50-626 |
| Nommik, Salme | Ph.D. | 57-071 |
| Oliver, William T. | Ph.D. | 53-029 |
| Oliver, William T. | M.Sc. | 51-538 |
| Poole, John B. | Ph.D. | 54-027 |
| Poole, John B. | M.Sc. | 41-046 |
| Prasad, Devendra | Ph.D. | 57-027 |
| Premvati, * | Ph.D. | 58-034 |
| Rao, N.S. Krishna | Ph.D. | 50-019 |
| Ronald, Keith | Ph.D. | 58-040 |
| Ronald, Keith | M.Sc. | 56-597 |
| Ross, Winifred M. | M.Sc. | 48-596 |
| Schad, Gerhard | Ph.D. | 55-034 |
| Schad, Gerhard A. | M.Sc. | 52-587 |
| Shah, Jessie A. | M.Sc. | 59-597 |
| Strachan, Alison A. | M.Sc. | 54-605 |
| Swales, William E. | Ph.D. | 35-025 |
| Sweatman, Gordon K. | Ph.D. | 57-039 |
| Thomson, Hugh M. | Ph.D. | 57-084 |
| Webster, Gloria A. | Ph.D. | 57-044 |
| Whitten, Lloyd K. | Ph.D. | 57-045 |
| Wolfgang, Robert W. | Ph.D. | 52-036 |
| Wu, Liang Y. | Ph.D. | 52-069 |

| AUTHOR | DEGREE | THESIS NUMBER |
|---|---|---|
| **Cameron, T.** | | |
| **Campbell, W.** | | |
| Yaffe, Leo | Ph.D. | 43-016 |
| **Carruthers, C.** | | |
| Grant, Mary J. | M.A. | 35-527 |
| Harvie, Jean E. | M.A. | 36-531 |
| Macdonald, Roderick R. | M.A. | 46-541 |
| Puhvel, Jaan | M.A. | 52-609 |
| Smith, Stanley Alfred | M.A. | 42-044 |
| Vallillee, Gerald A. | M.A. | 53-555 |
| *Banford, Jean E. | M.A. | 28-528 |
| *Clark, Peter A. | M.A. | 28-530 |
| *Edel, Abraham | M.A. | 28-531 |
| *Hayakawa, Samuel I. | M.A. | 28-538 |
| *Hemmeon, Ellen C. | M.A. | 27-531 |
| **Catway, H.** | | |
| Brown, Donald R. | M.Eng. | 51-500 |
| **Cecil, C.** | | |
| Sheffy, Pearl P. | M.A. | 58-590 |
| Winter, Jack S. | M.A. | 58-592 |
| Wolfe, Irving | M.A. | 58-593 |
| **Celieres, A.** | | |
| *Coade, Emma L. | M.A. | 31-562 |
| *Longan, Virginia L. | M.A. | 31-565 |
| **Chapman, R.** | | |
| Mackay, Kathleen I. | M.Sc. | 47-558 |
| Moster, Julius B. | M.Sc. | 47-563 |
| Novick, Seymour | M.Sc. | 49-542 |



| AUTHOR | DEGREE | THESIS NUMBER |
|---|---|---|
| **Chapman, R.** | | |
| **Chipman, R.** | | |
| Boucher, James P. | M.Eng. | 51-581 |
| Campbell, Richard H. | M.Eng. | 48-572 |
| Carr, Edward F. | M.Eng. | 50-503 |
| Coll, David C. | M.Eng. | 56-556 |
| Godfrey, Gerald | M.Eng. | 49-503 |
| Grierson, John K. | M.Sc. | 57-575 |
| Haberl, John F. | M.Eng. | 56-507 |
| Hoy, Norman A. | M.Eng. | 50-506 |
| Javid, Mansour | Ph.D. | 56-019 |
| Kassner, Max H. | M.Sc. | 50-540 |
| Keeping, Kimball J. | Ph.D. | 52-049 |
| Keeping, Kimball J. | M.Eng. | 50-587 |
| Kiang, Tsch-Kia | M.Eng. | 49-506 |
| Kuhn, Bernard G. | M.Eng. | 50-588 |
| Pavich, Michael | M.Eng. | 50-508 |
| Pearse, Charles D. | M.Sc. | 54-599 |
| Yurko, Michael | M.Eng. | 51-592 |
| **Chipman, W.** | | |
| *Kearns, Peter J. | M.Sc. | 28-515 |
| **Christie, C.** | | |
| Crawford, James M. | M.Eng. | 32-501 |
| Schippel, Walter H. | M.Eng. | 36-506 |
| Stanley, Thomas D. | M.Eng. | 33-506 |
| Stevens, Robert L. | M.Sc. | 36-550 |
| Yorke-Slader, Geoffrey H | M.Eng. | 47-506 |
| *Fan, Paul C. | M.Sc. | 25-516 |
| *Howes, Frederick S. | M.Sc. | 26-513 |
| *LeNeveu, Arthur P. | M.Sc. | 25-522 |
| *MacLeod, Malcolm D. | M.Sc. | 28-517 |
| *Silver, Ralph C. | M.Sc. | 29-519 |
| **Clark, D.** | | |
| Hanson, Frank K. | Mus.D. | 47-022 |

| AUTHOR | DEGREE | THESIS NUMBER |
|---|---|---|
| **Clark, D.** | | |
| Reid, John E. | M.Sc. | 57-593 |
| **Clark, J.** | | |
| Burton, Frederick R. | Ph.D. | 33-004 |
| Harris, Julius J. | M.Sc. | 33-516 |
| Okulitch, Vladimir J. | Ph.D. | 34-009 |
| *Hopper, Ronald V. | M.Sc. | 29-510 |
| **Clark, T.** | | |
| Anderson, Francis D. | Ph.D. | 56-001 |
| Antrobus, Edmund S. | Ph.D. | 54-036 |
| Brown, Robert A. | Ph.D. | 39-002 |
| Brown, Robert A. | M.Sc. | 36-509 |
| Carbonneau, Come | Ph.D. | 53-001 |
| Carter, George F. | Ph.D. | 58-009 |
| Castle, Robert O. | M.Sc. | 49-595 |
| Dufresne, Cyrille | M.Sc. | 48-518 |
| Dugas, Jean | Ph.D. | 52-011 |
| Eade, Kenneth E. | M.Sc. | 50-522 |
| Gray, Richard H. | M.Sc. | 37-508 |
| Harding, Stanley R. | M.Sc. | 43-504 |
| Husain, Bilal R. | Ph.D. | 55-022 |
| Irwin, Arthur B. | Ph.D. | 50-009 |
| Jackson, Garth D. | M.Sc. | 55-525 |
| Lowther, John S. | M.Sc. | 50-619 |
| Lyall, Harold B. | M.Sc. | 52-533 |
| MacGregor, Alexander R. | M.Sc. | 54-527 |
| Mattinson, Cyril R. | Ph.D. | 58-029 |
| McPherson, William J. | M.Sc. | 47-518 |
| Nelson, Samuel J. | Ph.D. | 52-024 |
| Robinson, Harold Ross | M.Sc. | 42-064 |
| Robinson, Joseph E. | M.Sc. | 51-620 |
| Skinner, Ralph | Ph.D. | 56-067 |
| Stalker, Archibald M. | Ph.D. | 50-020 |
| Stevenson, Ira M. | Ph.D. | 54-033 |
| Stevenson, Ira M. | M.Sc. | 51-552 |
| Usher, John L. | Ph.D. | 49-057 |
| Usher, John L. | M.Sc. | 47-527 |
| Veilleux, Brendan | M.Sc. | 49-551 |



| AUTHOR | DEGREE | THESIS NUMBER |
|---|---|---|
| **Clarke, D.** | | |
| *Treharne, Bryceson | Mus.D. | 30-016 |
| **Clarke, F.** | | |
| Benning, Paulette | M.A. | 32-525 |
| Binmore, Mary E. | M.A. | 33-537 |
| Devenney, Hartland M. | M.A. | 34-545 |
| Gill, Dorothy A. | M.A. | 34-525 |
| Holland, Catherine N. | M.A. | 34-528 |
| Lees, David | M.A. | 32-532 |
| MacKinnon, Patrick A. | M.A. | 32-536 |
| Steeves, Lewis R. | M.A. | 33-575 |
| Woodley, Elsie C. | M.A. | 32-551 |
| *Japp, Robert | M.A. | 30-531 |
| *Lang, John G. | M.A. | 31-534 |
| *Norris, Kenneth E. | M.A. | 31-538 |
| **Cleghorn, R.** | | |
| Curtis, George C. | M.Sc. | 59-580 |
| McIntosh, Hamish W. | M.Sc. | 50-544 |
| **Coates, D.** | | |
| Padopulos, Diogenes | M.Eng. | 57-510 |
| Yong, Raymond N. | M.Eng. | 58-507 |
| **Cohen, M.** | | |
| Camara, Jose S. | M.C.L. | 49-583 |
| Dobson, Christopher B. | M.C.L. | 59-500 |
| Gazdik, Julius F. | M.C.L. | 49-584 |
| Gosztonyi, Paul M. | M.C.L. | 53-556 |
| MacKay, Kenneth C. | M.C.L. | 51-579 |
| Morrow, James W. | M.A. | 50-571 |
| Moughton, Barry J. | M.C.L. | 58-501 |
| Novotny, Jan M. | M.C.L. | 53-557 |
| **Colby, C.** | | |

| AUTHOR | DEGREE | THESIS NUMBER |
|---|---|---|
| **Colby, C.** | | |
| *Cousins, George V. | M.A. | 08-501 |
| *Eaton, Mary J. | M.A. | 09-501 |
| *Jamieson, John S. | M.A. | 08-502 |
| *MacCrimmon, John P. | M.A. | 09-504 |
| *Parker, David W. | M.A. | 08-503 |
| *Pearson, Mary F. | M.A. | 07-504 |
| *Pelletier, Annie H. | M.A. | 17-501 |
| *Rorke, Mabele L. | M.A. | 08-504 |
| *Salt, Alexander E. | M.A. | 08-505 |
| **Collip, J.** | | |
| Allardyce, William J. | Ph.D. | 31-001 |
| Anderson, Evelyn M. | Ph.D. | 34-001 |
| Beatty, Stanley A. | Ph.D. | 31-003 |
| Billingsley, Lawrence W. | Ph.D. | 37-025 |
| Black, Peter T. A. | Ph.D. | 35-005 |
| Browne, John S. | Ph.D. | 32-001 |
| Chapman, Clifford W. | Ph.D. | 35-009 |
| Courtright, Mary N. | Ph.D. | 44-002 |
| Denstedt, Orville F. | Ph.D. | 37-026 |
| Kutz, Pussell L. | Ph.D. | 33-012 |
| Lathe, Grant H. | M.Sc. | 36-548 |
| McPhail, Murchie K. | Ph.D. | 32-009 |
| O'Donovan, Denis K. | Ph.D. | 38-014 |
| Stewart, Gordon Stafford | M.Sc. | 40-048 |
| Toby, Charlotte G. | Ph.D. | 46-034 |
| Wyatt, Barbara V. | M.Sc. | 47-575 |
| *Grant, Elizabeth R. | M.A. | 30-554 |
| *Komarov, Simon A. | M.Sc. | 31-554 |
| *Pugsley, Leonard I. | M.Sc. | 29-517 |
| *Webster, Donald R. | M.Sc. | 30-513 |
| **Collip, J. .** | | |
| *Blumberg, Perry | M.Sc. | 29-504 |
| **Common, R.** | | |
| Anastassiadis, Phoebus A | Ph.D. | 55-001 |
| Chapman, Douglas G. | Ph.D. | 49-045 |
| De Freitas, Anthony S. | M.Sc. | 57-523 |



| AUTHOR | DEGREE | THESIS NUMBER |
|---|---|---|
| **Common, R.** | | |
| Ford, John D. | M.Sc. | 55-519 |
| Hare, John H. | Ph.D. | 49-048 |
| Jenkins, Marjorie M. | M.Sc. | 52-577 |
| Jowsey, James R. | Ph.D. | 53-015 |
| Keefe, Thomas J. | M.Sc. | 51-526 |
| Layne, Donald St.E. | Ph.D. | 57-021 |
| Layne, Donald St.E. | M.Sc. | 55-527 |
| Leung, Philip M-P. | M.Sc. | 59-586 |
| MacLeod, Harry A. | M.Sc. | 56-586 |
| Mahon, John H. | Ph.D. | 53-063 |
| Mahon, John H. | M.Sc. | 49-611 |
| McCully, Keith A. | M.Sc. | 53-525 |
| McKinley, William P. | Ph.D. | 54-056 |
| Murray, Thomas K. | Ph.D. | 57-024 |
| Phillips, William E. | M.Sc. | 53-542 |
| Pinsky, Alex | Ph.D. | 49-033 |
| Pritchard, Ernest T. | M.Sc. | 54-601 |
| Rigby, Francis L. | Ph.D. | 48-010 |
| Vanstone, William E. | Ph.D. | 58-052 |
| Vanstone, William E. | M.Sc. | 55-543 |
| Wells, Arthur F. | M.Sc. | 52-598 |
| Wiseblatt, Lazare | M.Sc. | 50-642 |
| Wright, Leebert A. | M.Sc. | 57-542 |
| **Cone, W.** | | |
| Chen, Chao-jen | M.Sc. | 45-523 |
| Chorobski, Jerzy | M.Sc. | 32-511 |
| Keener, Ellis B. | M.Sc. | 56-581 |
| Kershman, John | M.Sc. | 33-519 |
| Klatzo, Igor | M.Sc. | 51-610 |
| Reid, William L. | M.Sc. | 38-515 |
| Rosen, Harold J. | M.Sc. | 50-631 |
| Welch, William K. | M.Sc. | 47-574 |
| **Conklin, R.** | | |
| Gutteridge, Harry S. | M.Sc. | 35-506 |
| Thompson, Robert R. | M.Sc. | 29-521 |
| Williams, Sydney B. | M.Sc. | 36-522 |

| AUTHOR | DEGREE | THESIS NUMBER |
|---|---|---|
| Conlson, J. | | |
| Thatcher, Frederick S. | M.Sc. | 35-540 |
| Cooke, H. | | |
| *Howard, Waldorf V. | M.Sc. | 22-512 |
| Cooke, R. | | |
| Bennett, Robert M. | M.Eng. | 50-502 |
| Cooper, J. | | |
| Abdelmoneim, Ismail A. | LL.M. | 53-568 |
| Balachandran, Ponniah | LL.M. | 55-508 |
| Chan, Victor O. | M.A. | 49-628 |
| Cox, Robert W. | M.A. | 48-557 |
| DeDongo, Paul J. | LL.M. | 54-504 |
| DeSaussure, Hamilton | LL.M. | 53-511 |
| Drion, Huibert | LL.M. | 54-567 |
| Eccles, William J. | Ph.D. | 55-016 |
| Eccles, William J. | M.A. | 51-633 |
| Fenston, John | LL.M. | 53-512 |
| Flynn, Frank J. | LL.M. | 56-564 |
| Heller, Paul P. | LL.M. | 54-505 |
| Hermoso, J. | LL.M. | 55-581 |
| Hesse, Nicky E. | LL.M. | 53-513 |
| Hubscher, Frank F. | LL.M. | 53-514 |
| Johnston, John A. | Ph.D. | 55-061 |
| Johnston, John A. | M.A. | 51-569 |
| Keep, George R. | M.A. | 48-613 |
| Kinsman, Ronald D. | M.A. | 59-556 |
| Knowles, David C. | M.A. | 57-605 |
| Koval, Joseph | LL.M. | 54-506 |
| Mackintosh, David D. | LL.M. | 57-562 |
| Martial, Jean A. | LL.M. | 53-515 |
| McPherson, Ian E. | LL.M. | 55-509 |
| Millman, Thomas R. | Ph.D. | 43-022 |
| Mills, George H. | M.A. | 47-580 |
| Moursi, Fouad K. | LL.M. | 55-510 |
| Murchison, John T. | LL.M. | 55-582 |
| Nemeth, John | LL.M. | 53-516 |
| Overing, R.L. | M.A. | 57-552 |



| AUTHOR | DEGREE | THESIS NUMBER |
|---|---|---|
| Cooper, J. | | |
| Peng, Ming-Min | LL.M. | 53-517 |
| Vlasic, Ivan | LL.M. | 55-584 |
| Wine, Joseph R. | LL.M. | 54-508 |
| Coote, J. | | |
| Cooper, Howard B. | M.Eng. | 47-502 |
| Corbett, * | | |
| *Foster, Joan M. | M.A. | 25-535 |
| Corbett, P. | | |
| *Clark, Peter A. | M.A. | 28-530 |
| *Morton, Nelson W. | M.A. | 31-537 |
| Coulson, G. | | |
| Ayers, George W. | M.Sc. | 37-533 |
| Bagnall, Richard H. | M.Sc. | 49-593 |
| Cinq-Mars, Lionel | M.Sc. | 49-520 |
| Coulson, J. | | |
| Boothroyd, Raymond A. | M.Sc. | 32-508 |
| Clark, Robert V. | M.Sc. | 52-518 |
| Clarkson, Scott F. | M.Sc. | 45-509 |
| Coulombe, Louis-Joseph | Ph.D. | 56-007 |
| Cox, Harold A. | M.Sc. | 37-503 |
| Crete, Joseph E. | M.Sc. | 55-596 |
| Dolan, Desmond Daniel | M.Sc. | 39-056 |
| Fernando, Derrick M. | M.Sc. | 53-587 |
| Genereux, Henri G. | M.Sc. | 40-043 |
| Gilbey, John Alfred | M.Sc. | 42-523 |
| Hamilton, George H. | M.Sc. | 33-515 |
| Hicks, Arthur J. | M.Sc. | 31-553 |
| Hodgson, William A. | M.Sc. | 49-530 |
| Howatt, John L. | M.Sc. | 31-507 |
| Lachance, Rene C. | Ph.D. | 40-014 |

| AUTHOR | DEGREE | THESIS NUMBER |
|---|---|---|
| **Coulson, J.** | | |
| Lachance, Rene O. | M.Sc. | 39-061 |
| Lavallee, Edouard | M.Sc. | 32-518 |
| Lawrence, Charles H. | M.Sc. | 57-528 |
| Lockhart, Chesley L. | M.Sc. | 57-530 |
| Ludwig, Ralph A. | Ph.D. | 47-012 |
| MacLeod, Donald M. | M.Sc. | 43-505 |
| Miles, Henry J. | M.Sc. | 38-513 |
| Paquin, Roger | M.Sc. | 51-541 |
| Payette, Albert | M.Sc. | 42-528 |
| Pelletier, Real | M.Sc. | 44-521 |
| Ross, Robert G. | M.Sc. | 53-543 |
| Samborski, Daniel J. | Ph.D. | 55-033 |
| Savile, Douglas B. | M.Sc. | 34-543 |
| Sibalis, Jack | M.Sc. | 51-547 |
| Simard, J. | M.Sc. | 54-531 |
| Simard, Thomas | M.Sc. | 44-511 |
| Thatcher, Frederick S. | Ph.D. | 39-026 |
| Wallen, Victor R. | Ph.D. | 54-034 |
| Wallen, Victor R. | M.Sc. | 49-552 |
| *Godbout, Fernand | M.Sc. | 29-554 |
| *Jain, Abir C. | Ph.D. | 58-021 |
| *Jayanetti, Edwin | Ph.D. | 58-022 |
| *MacRae, Norman A. | M.Sc. | 30-508 |
| *Montserin, Blazini G. | M.Sc. | 28-521 |
| **Counsell, E.** | | |
| Brown, Carl E. | M.A. | 56-612 |
| **Coussirat, D.** | | |
| Rice, Horace G. | M.A. | 07-506 |
| *Hindley, John G. | M.A. | 07-502 |
| **Cowan, J.** | | |
| Carder, Alfred C. | M.Sc. | 49-516 |
| **Cox, J.** | | |
| *Baird, John B. | M.Sc. | 09-507 |



| AUTHOR | DEGREE | THESIS NUMBER |
|---|---|---|
| **Cox, J.** | | |
| *Boyle, Robert W. | Ph.D. | 09-001 |
| *Gillis, Norman R. | M.Sc. | 09-511 |
| **Craig, C.** | | |
| Ahmed, Syed I. | M.Eng. | 59-566 |
| Anand, Tilakraj F. | M.Eng. | 54-501 |
| Bradbury, John S. | M.Eng. | 51-582 |
| Drouin, Paul-Emile | M.Eng. | 52-562 |
| McCutcheon, John O. | M.Eng. | 55-506 |
| Spratt, Gordon W. | M.Eng. | 56-511 |
| **Crampton, F.** | | |
| Aitken, Johnstone R. | M.Sc. | 47-542 |
| Ashton, Gordon Clemence | M.Sc. | 39-511 |
| Beacom, Stanley F. | Ph.D. | 59-002 |
| Bell, John M. | M.Sc. | 45-503 |
| Berryhill, Florence M. | M.Sc. | 51-512 |
| Bezeau, Louis Manning | M.Sc. | 41-036 |
| Burton, Barbara W. | M.Sc. | 46-562 |
| Cameron, Colin D. | M.Sc. | 36-510 |
| Campbell, James A. | M.Sc. | 38-504 |
| Chalmers, A. Edith | M.Sc. | 45-508 |
| Clark, Barbara F. | M.Sc. | 50-520 |
| Collier, Barbara C. | M.Sc. | 42-519 |
| Crawford, Donna J. | M.Sc. | 53-584 |
| Crook, Helen G. | M.Sc. | 48-515 |
| Dju, Mei Y. | M.Sc. | 49-601 |
| Farmer, Florence A. | Ph.D. | 47-026 |
| Farmer, Florence A. | M.Sc. | 44-502 |
| Finlayson, Duncan A. | M.Sc. | 34-510 |
| Forshaw, Robert P. | M.Sc. | 38-507 |
| Gallamore, William A. | M.Sc. | 51-523 |
| Gass, Marcia J. | M.Sc. | 49-602 |
| Haskell, Stanley R. | Ph.D. | 56-015 |
| Haskell, Stanley R. | M.Sc. | 50-612 |
| Hughes, Muriel I. | M.Sc. | 45-532 |
| Irwin, Mary I. | Ph.D. | 52-048 |
| Jackson, Ivan P. | M.Sc. | 44-503 |
| Kean, Eccleston A. | M.Sc. | 52-530 |
| King, Robert Henry | M.Sc. | 40-519 |
| Lange, Eugene Hausknecht | M.Sc. | 39-062 |

| AUTHOR | DEGREE | THESIS NUMBER |
|---|---|---|
| **Crampton, E.** | | |
| Langerman, Helen L. | M.Sc. | 49-536 |
| Lessard, Henri-Louis | M.Sc. | 41-043 |
| Lloyd, Lewis E. | Ph.D. | 52-051 |
| Logan, Vaughn Stewart | M.Sc. | 39-063 |
| MacKay, Vernon G. | M.Sc. | 56-528 |
| MacNeill, Ruby J. | M.Sc. | 48-590 |
| Manson, Mary G. | M.Sc. | 47-520 |
| Millar, Myra J. | M.Sc. | 47-562 |
| Mills, Margaret F. | M.Sc. | 46-527 |
| Morrison, Mary F.M. | M.Sc. | 42-527 |
| Neilson, Helen R. | M.Sc. | 48-593 |
| Peckham, Hugh E. | M.Sc. | 55-618 |
| Proctor, William C. | M.Sc. | 47-523 |
| Purdy, Thomas Lenton | M.Sc. | 39-519 |
| Rutherford, Beth E. | Ph.D. | 55-072 |
| Siddall, Margaret I. | M.Sc. | 51-548 |
| Sourkes, Theodore L. | M.Sc. | 46-579 |
| Stothart, John G. | M.Sc. | 36-519 |
| Whiting, Frank | M.Sc. | 43-510 |
| Winter, Karl A. | M.Sc. | 56-544 |
| Woolsey, Lloyd D. | M.Sc. | 44-513 |
| **Cranck, E.** | | |
| Stocken, Charles G. | M.Sc. | 50-557 |
| **Cressey, P.** | | |
| LePage, Inez M. | M.A. | 32-533 |
| Ross, Herman R. | M.A. | 32-545 |
| **Crick, B.** | | |
| Scott, Peter D. | Ph.D. | 55-037 |
| **Crook, F.** | | |
| Wisenthal, M. | M.A. | 57-611 |



| AUTHOR | DEGREE | THESIS NUMBER |
|---|---|---|
| **Crowell, C.** | | |
| Armstrong, Robert A. | Ph.D. | 57-050 |
| Segal, Benny | M.Sc. | 56-602 |
| Taylor, Allen L. | M.Sc. | 59-601 |
| **Crowell, I.** | | |
| Leblond, David | M.Sc. | 42-058 |
| Sackston, Waldemar E. | M.Sc. | 40-523 |
| **Culliton, J.** | | |
| Fullerton, Douglas H. | M.Com. | 40-033 |
| Kuhn, Tillo E. | Ph.D. | 57-060 |
| Lipman, Julian A. I. | M.A. | 39-040 |
| McDonald, Cyril F. | M.A. | 38-538 |
| Popkin, John W. | M.A. | 37-546 |
| Willis, Stewart W. | M.A. | 31-548 |
| Wilson, William D. | M.A. | 58-550 |
| Wykes, Neville George | M.A. | 41-031 |
| **Currie, A.** | | |
| Bolger, Josephine A. | M.A. | 42-028 |
| Kidd, James F. | M.A. | 44-525 |
| MacFarlane, Joan M. | M.A. | 48-615 |
| Magee, Arch W. | M.A. | 43-525 |
| Penrose, George H. | M.A. | 45-546 |
| Price, Frederick William | M.A. | 42-038 |
| Price, John W. | M.A. | 54-552 |
| Tomkins, George S. | M.A. | 52-558 |
| Welbourne, Arthur J. | M.A. | 46-594 |
| White, Orville F. | M.A. | 51-577 |
| **Currie, C.** | | |
| Kinsman, Michael J. | M.A. | 58-544 |
| Laird, James T. | M.A. | 52-605 |
| Lewis, Herbert | M.A. | 54-614 |
| Marler, G.E. | M.A. | 54-546 |
| Pitt, Jack A. | M.A. | 53-615 |
| Polonoff, Irving I. | M.A. | 48-569 |

| AUTHOR | DEGREE | THESIS NUMBER |
|---|---|---|
| Currie, C. | | |
| D'Hauteserve, L. | | |
| Martineau, Jeanne G. | M.A. | 47-537 |
| Ratelle, Ruth M. | M.A. | 39-043 |
| Dale, J. | | |
| Jones, Thomas W. | M.A. | 21-519 |
| *Livinson, Abraham J. | M.A. | 16-503 |
| *Pelletier, Annie H. | M.A. | 17-501 |
| *Rowell, Arthur H. | M.A. | 12-505 |
| *Shearing, Helen A. | M.A. | 15-505 |
| *Steed, Joseph A. | M.A. | 18-502 |
| *Sutherland, Francis C. | M.A. | 15-506 |
| *Wilson, Alice M. | M.A. | 11-504 |
| *Worsfold, Henry H. | M.A. | 17-503 |
| Dales, J. | | |
| Velay, Clement C. | M.A. | 55-563 |
| Darbelnet, J. | | |
| Allard, Wilfred Philip | M.A. | 41-510 |
| Carter, Alfred Edward | M.A. | 42-509 |
| Edwards, Clifford E. | M.A. | 45-544 |
| Fortier, Mireille | M.A. | 41-515 |
| Koenig, Sister Mary G. | M.A. | 42-035 |
| Laing, Eleanor J. | M.A. | 48-614 |
| MacKeen, Frances C. | M.A. | 46-542 |
| Meyer, Paul H. | M.A. | 45-545 |
| Peck, Robert Alfred | M.A. | 42-036 |
| Poirier, Mary A. | M.A. | 43-526 |
| Royer, France M. | M.A. | 43-514 |
| Sloat, Annie P. | M.A. | 46-548 |
| David, J. | | |
| Moore, Ralph E. | M.Sc. | 51-615 |



| AUTHOR | DEGREE | THESIS NUMBER |
|---|---|---|
| David, J. | | |
| Dawson, C. | | |
| Aikman, Mary F. | M.A. | 37-542 |
| Bayley, Charles Melville | Ph.D. | 39-029 |
| Berry, John W. | M.A. | 33-536 |
| Clark, Samuel D. | M.A. | 35-541 |
| Craig, Glenn H. | M.A. | 33-543 |
| Davidson, Mary H. | M.A. | 33-573 |
| Dickson, Delphine M. | M.A. | 51-632 |
| Finestone, Harold | M.A. | 43-523 |
| Gold, Rosalynd | M.A. | 42-511 |
| Hall, Oswald | M.A. | 37-544 |
| Heaton, Phyllis | M.A. | 32-529 |
| Hunter, Jean Isobel | M.A. | 39-506 |
| Lewis, James Neilson | M.A. | 39-039 |
| Mamchur, Stephen W. | M.A. | 34-548 |
| Reynolds, Lloyd G. | M.A. | 33-556 |
| Robert, Percy A. | M.A. | 28-551 |
| Seidel, Judith | M.A. | 39-508 |
| Spurrell, Althea C. | M.A. | 46-590 |
| Younge, Eva R. | M.A. | 33-562 |
| Zakuta, Leo | M.A. | 48-619 |
| *Brown, Wilfred H. | M.A. | 27-525 |
| *Davis, Richard E. | M.A. | 27-529 |
| *Donald, Henry G. | M.A. | 30-525 |
| *Featherston, Florence E. | M.A. | 29-530 |
| *Frank, Harold | M.A. | 30-526 |
| *Garland, Sidney G. | M.A. | 29-532 |
| *Hudson, James C. | M.A. | 28-541 |
| *Israel, Wilfred E. | M.A. | 28-564 |
| *Jahn, Helen L. | M.A. | 29-537 |
| *Knechtel, Max U. | M.A. | 26-544 |
| *Lang, John G. | M.A. | 31-534 |
| *McCall, Muriel B. | M.A. | 28-543 |
| *McFarlane, Duncan H. | M.A. | 26-547 |
| *Preston, George P. | M.A. | 26-551 |
| *Radler, Ruth | M.A. | 30-543 |
| *Rutman, Robin L. | M.A. | 27-539 |
| *Scott, Mary E. | M.A. | 28-566 |
| *Smyth, Desmond H. | M.A. | 28-555 |
| *Wade, Margaret M. | M.A. | 31-546 |
| *Young, Charles H. | M.A. | 28-558 |

| AUTHOR | DEGREE | THESIS NUMBER |
|---|---|---|
| Dawson, C. C. | | |
| *Tuttle, Harry G. | M.A. | 31-545 |
| Day, J. | | |
| Dubensky, Alexander | M.A. | 44-514 |
| Friedlander, John B. | M.A. | 46-586 |
| Hall, George B. | M.Com. | 39-048 |
| Layhew, John H. | M.A. | 26-545 |
| McIntyre, George D. | M.A. | 32-535 |
| Nakashima, Kimiaki | M.A. | 46-545 |
| Nelles, James G. | M.Com. | 33-563 |
| Randolf, John H. | M.A. | 43-527 |
| Ross, Charles Alexander | M.A. | 39-044 |
| Smith, Greig B. | M.Com. | 31-550 |
| Trotter, Wallace S. | M.Com. | 32-552 |
| Vineberg, Philip F. | M.A. | 36-542 |
| *Bogante, Jack R. | M.A. | 27-523 |
| *Savage, Mae L. | M.A. | 30-544 |
| De Long, W. | | |
| Grant, Edwin Parkhurst | M.Sc. | 40-044 |
| De Stein, J. | | |
| Banks, Ronald H. | M.Eng. | 56-502 |
| Bernard, Gerald A. | M.Eng. | 50-582 |
| Bhasin, Parkash C. | M.Eng. | 53-505 |
| Campbell, Hugh A. | M.Eng. | 54-561 |
| Coates, Donald F. | M.Eng. | 54-503 |
| Coldwell, Keith I. | M.Eng. | 51-583 |
| Genest, George L. | M.Eng. | 58-504 |
| Ghitis, Albert | M.Eng. | 54-564 |
| Harris, Philip J. | M.Eng. | 49-589 |
| Issen, Lionel | M.Eng. | 57-507 |
| Jakobson, Gunnar J. | M.Eng. | 55-575 |
| Kennedy, David H. | M.Eng. | 53-507 |
| Mathison, William | M.Eng. | 59-570 |
| Neis, Vernon V. | M.Eng. | 56-558 |
| Van Walsum, Ewout | M.Eng. | 57-512 |
| Waterston, John R. | M.Eng. | 59-506 |



| AUTHOR | DEGREE | THESIS NUMBER |
|---|---|---|
| Denstedt, C. | | |
| Alivisatos, Spyridon | Ph.D. | 51-040 |
| Alivisatos, Spyridon | M.Sc. | 49-592 |
| Andreae, Shirley R. | M.Sc. | 46-504 |
| Brownstone, Yehoshua S. | Ph.D. | 59-007 |
| Carlton, Lucille | M.Sc. | 45-507 |
| Esar, Rhoda | M.Sc. | 57-572 |
| Fessler, Alfred | M.Sc. | 59-583 |
| Fishman, Sherold | Ph.D. | 53-007 |
| Francoeur, Joseph M. | M.Sc. | 51-607 |
| Francoeur, Marc | Ph.D. | 53-051 |
| Francoeur, Pearl | M.Sc. | 53-588 |
| Gurd, Frank R. | M.Sc. | 46-569 |
| Harpur, Robert P. | M.Sc. | 47-551 |
| Hollett, Charlotte | M.Sc. | 52-528 |
| Hosein, Esau A. | Ph.D. | 52-018 |
| Jacobs, Ross D. | M.Sc. | 52-529 |
| Jacoby, Arthur W. | M.Sc. | 50-537 |
| Kashket, Shelby | Ph.D. | 56-021 |
| Kashket, Shelby | M.Sc. | 53-595 |
| Knelman, Fred H. | M.Eng. | 50-507 |
| Kwiecinska-Pappius, Hann | M.Sc. | 48-529 |
| Lloyd, Lewis E. | M.Sc. | 50-543 |
| Loiselle, Jean-Marie | Ph.D. | 57-022 |
| Loiselle, Jean-Marie | M.Sc. | 55-528 |
| Macdougall, Graham R. | Ph.D. | 48-008 |
| Malkin, Aaron | Ph.D. | 56-026 |
| McArdle, Alice H. | M.Sc. | 57-587 |
| McKerns, Kenneth W. | Ph.D. | 50-016 |
| Ottolenghi, Paul | Ph.D. | 57-074 |
| Ottolenghi, Paul | M.Sc. | 55-617 |
| Pappius, Hanna M. | Ph.D. | 52-025 |
| Parsons, Timothy R. | Ph.D. | 58-032 |
| Peron, Fernand G. | M.Sc. | 50-627 |
| Purvis, John L. | Ph.D. | 56-030 |
| Purvis, John L. | M.Sc. | 54-602 |
| Robertson, Florence E. | M.Sc. | 46-534 |
| Roche, Mary Nora | M.Sc. | 41-047 |
| Rochlin, Isidore | M.Sc. | 42-529 |
| Rubinstein, David | Ph.D. | 53-072 |
| Rubinstein, David | M.Sc. | 51-621 |
| Saffran, Murray | Ph.D. | 49-036 |
| Saffran, Murray | M.Sc. | 46-578 |
| Sells, Bruce H. | Ph.D. | 58-044 |
| Simard-Duquesne, N. | M.Sc. | 54-603 |
| Stachiewicz, Evva T. | M.Sc. | 54-532 |

| AUTHOR | DEGREE | THESIS NUMBER |
|---|---|---|
| **Denstedt, O.** | | |
| Turnbull, Dorothy K. | M.Sc. | 51-627 |
| Woodford, Vernon R. | M.Sc. | 48-603 |
| *Henry, A.S. | M.Sc. | 57-578 |
| **Derick, C.** | | |
| *Cardonsky, Mary | M.A. | 29-525 |
| *Derick, Russell A. | M.Sc. | 23-510 |
| *Godwin, Kathleen F. | M.Sc. | 22-508 |
| *Miller, Clare B. | M.A. | 12-502 |
| *Weir, Douglas | M.Sc. | 10-523 |
| **DeLong, W.** | | |
| Armstrong, John G. | M.Sc. | 41-523 |
| Bishop, Robert F. | M.Sc. | 45-521 |
| Boswell, Graeme W. | Ph.D. | 59-006 |
| Boswell, Graeme W. | M.Sc. | 49-513 |
| Brogden, Clarence L. | M.Sc. | 45-505 |
| Cann, Everett D. | Ph.D. | 46-021 |
| Coffin, David E. | Ph.D. | 59-013 |
| Coffin, David E. | M.Sc. | 56-571 |
| Coldwell, Blake B. | Ph.D. | 51-005 |
| Coldwell, Blake B. | M.Sc. | 48-514 |
| Doyle, James J. | M.Sc. | 50-603 |
| Findlay, Wallace I. | M.Sc. | 55-518 |
| Fiskell, John G. | Ph.D. | 51-009 |
| Fiskell, John G. | M.Sc. | 49-525 |
| Gillingham, John T. | M.Sc. | 46-567 |
| Hamilton, Herman A. | M.Sc. | 55-524 |
| Hilchey, John D. | M.Sc. | 53-592 |
| Ho-Yen, Basil O. | M.Sc. | 53-593 |
| Huq, A.K.M. Fazlul | Ph.D. | 55-060 |
| Lajoie, Paul | M.Sc. | 42-057 |
| Langille, Winston M. | M.Sc. | 48-585 |
| Lutwick, Laurence E. | M.Sc. | 51-533 |
| MacDougall, Daniel | Ph.D. | 44-011 |
| MacDougall, Daniel | M.Sc. | 41-531 |
| MacKay, Donald C. | Ph.D. | 54-055 |
| MacLean, Angus A. | M.Sc. | 48-533 |
| MacLean, Kenneth S. | M.Sc. | 54-529 |
| MacLeod, Lloyd B. | M.Sc. | 53-598 |
| Manning, Kenneth Raymond | M.Sc. | 40-520 |



| AUTHOR | DEGREE | THESIS NUMBER |
|---|---|---|
| **DeLong, W.** | | |
| McKinley, William F. | M.Sc. | 51-613 |
| Menzies, Robert G. | M.Sc. | 44-505 |
| Millette, Jean F. | M.Sc. | 48-537 |
| Paul, Harry | M.Sc. | 47-565 |
| Pazur, John H. | M.Sc. | 46-530 |
| Robertson, William K. | M.Sc. | 47-568 |
| Salisbury, Herbert F. | M.Sc. | 39-520 |
| Schalin, Edmund | Ph.D. | 51-056 |
| Schnitzer, Morris | Ph.D. | 55-035 |
| Schnitzer, Morris | M.Sc. | 52-588 |
| Smith, George Ransom | Ph.D. | 39-504 |
| Soper, Robert J. | Ph.D. | 59-070 |
| Sowden, Frederick J. | Ph.D. | 44-023 |
| Steeves, Allison F. | M.Sc. | 37-515 |
| Stobbe, Peter C. | Ph.D. | 50-021 |
| Talvenheimo, Gerhardt | M.Sc. | 48-599 |
| **DeVries, J.** | | |
| Stock, John J. | Ph.D. | 51-058 |
| **Dickson, B.** | | |
| Harrison, Kenneth A. | M.Sc. | 25-520 |
| Hill, Hinson | M.Sc. | 27-506 |
| Perreault, Champlain | M.Sc. | 27-514 |
| Pomerleau, Rene | M.Sc. | 27-515 |
| Popp, William | M.Sc. | 26-522 |
| Richardson, James K. | M.Sc. | 22-519 |
| Scott, Gordon A. | M.Sc. | 24-528 |
| *Atwell, Ernest A. | M.Sc. | 25-507 |
| *Gordon, William I. | M.Sc. | 24-517 |
| *Lamb, Cecil A. | M.S.A. | 24-503 |
| *Iods, Emile A. | M.S.A. | 25-504 |
| *Newton, Dorothy F. | M.Sc. | 22-518 |
| *Tinney, Benjamin F. | M.S.A. | 24-505 |
| *Vanterpool, Thomas C. | M.Sc. | 25-529 |
| **Dion, H.** | | |
| Reeder, Stewart W. | M.Sc. | 56-535 |

| AUTHOR | DEGREE | THESIS NUMBER |
|---|---|---|
| Dodd, G. | | |
| Ellis, John S. | M.Eng. | 49-587 |
| Eskenazi, Beno | M.Eng. | 49-588 |
| Gersovitz, Benjamin | M.Eng. | 48-505 |
| Dombrowski, J. | | |
| *Gilmore, Laura B. | M.A. | 31-563 |
| *Lowry, Hope | M.A. | 31-566 |
| *Sharples, Alice | M.A. | 25-541 |
| *Stager, Drucilla N. | M.A. | 26-556 |
| Downs, A. | | |
| *Cromarty, Robert P. | M.Sc. | 17-504 |
| Du Roure, R. | | |
| Baker, Carrie E. | M.A. | 34-521 |
| Bartlett, Harry | M.A. | 36-523 |
| Beebe, Mary Elizabeth | M.A. | 40-508 |
| Bisson, Margaret M. | M.A. | 31-561 |
| Blakely, Sister Claire | M.A. | 35-521 |
| Bly, Elsie R. | M.A. | 36-525 |
| Boger, Dellie Lee | M.A. | 39-030 |
| Bourget, Adeline F. | M.A. | 38-527 |
| Branchaud, Sister Mary | M.A. | 40-509 |
| Bronner, Frederic J. | M.A. | 37-517 |
| Carpenter, Lula A. | M.A. | 33-541 |
| D'Hauteserve, Louis | M.A. | 29-527 |
| Dillon, Sister Marie | M.A. | 37-521 |
| Dube, Claudia M. | M.A. | 35-526 |
| Frey, Flavian F. | M.A. | 36-529 |
| Heyman, Madeleine C. | M.A. | 36-533 |
| Hilkert, Marjorie B. | M.A. | 38-531 |
| Jennings, Thomas J. | M.A. | 35-528 |
| Jones, Margaret | M.A. | 38-534 |
| Judge, Mabel E. | M.A. | 33-549 |
| Kelly, Ignatius | M.A. | 38-535 |
| Kelly, Marie Ste. Anne | M.A. | 41-025 |
| Kent, Josephine P. | M.A. | 34-531 |
| Kibbe, Doris E. | M.A. | 38-536 |
| Kieffer, Michael Ignatiu | M.A. | 39-038 |



| AUTHOR | DEGREE | THESIS NUMBER |
|---|---|---|
| Du Roure, R. | | |
| Lamal, Mary L. | M.A. | 37-524 |
| Lennon, Sister Mary G. | M.A. | 38-537 |
| Matthews, Florida L. | M.A. | 32-537 |
| Mazza, Sister Maria S. | M.A. | 35-531 |
| McNamara, Mary F.C. | M.A. | 40-031 |
| Michel, Lina J. | M.A. | 34-535 |
| Paour, Peter J. | M.A. | 36-540 |
| Pellerin, Evelyn | M.A. | 37-529 |
| Prowse, Alice E. | M.A. | 32-539 |
| Rexford, Laura H. | M.A. | 34-538 |
| Rowley, Marie Rita | M.A. | 40-511 |
| Roy, Esther M. | M.A. | 37-531 |
| Stock, Marie L. | M.A. | 37-532 |
| Thompson, Helen Muriel | M.A. | 39-510 |
| Urbain, Joseph V. | M.A. | 39-046 |
| Weeks, Marie S. | M.A. | 32-549 |
| *Alward, Frederick P. | M.A. | 28-527 |
| *Blouin, Wilhelmine E. | M.A. | 30-518 |
| *Coade, Emma L. | M.A. | 31-562 |
| *Creighton, Edith M. | M.A. | 26-538 |
| *Ferrand, Lucy M. | M.A. | 29-531 |
| *Gilmore, Laura B. | M.A. | 31-563 |
| *Grimes, Evie M. | M.A. | 13-505 |
| *Longan, Virginia L. | M.A. | 31-565 |
| *Lowry, Hope | M.A. | 31-566 |
| *MacLennan, Malcolm | M.A. | 25-537 |
| *Mathewson, Dorothy R. | M.A. | 24-542 |
| *McInnis, Sarah | M.A. | 28-545 |
| *Murray, Mae F. | M.A. | 28-548 |
| *Newnham, May L. | M.A. | 21-522 |
| *Renaud, Paul E. | M.A. | 23-526 |
| *Reque, A. Dikka | M.A. | 24-544 |
| *Sharples, Alice | M.A. | 25-541 |
| *Silver, Edith | M.A. | 24-545 |
| *Townsend, Eleanor H. | M.A. | 29-548 |
| *Walter, Felix H. | M.A. | 24-546 |
| Duchow, M. | | |
| Frackenpohl, Arthur R. | D.Mus. | 57-049 |
| Dudek, L. | | |

| AUTHOR | DEGREE | THESIS NUMBER |
| --- | --- | --- |
| **Dudek, L.** | | |
| Clark, Ian C. | M.A. | 58-537 |
| Whimster, Eleanor I. | M.A. | 53-621 |
| **Duff, G.** | | |
| Bainborough, Arthur R. | M.Sc. | 51-509 |
| Bencosme, Sergio | Ph.D. | 50-025 |
| Fluss, Zdenek | M.Sc. | 53-526 |
| Hinds, Henry E. | M.Sc. | 46-522 |
| Horlick, Louis | M.Sc. | 53-533 |
| Jaffe, Frederick A. | M.Sc. | 49-532 |
| Kipkie, George F. | M.Sc. | 48-528 |
| Leach, William B. | M.Sc. | 48-586 |
| McLean, Chester R. | M.Sc. | 47-559 |
| McMillan, Gardner C. | M.Sc. | 46-573 |
| McMillan, Gardner C. | Ph.D. | 48-009 |
| Meissner, George F. | M.Sc. | 51-535 |
| More, Robert Hall | M.Sc. | 42-526 |
| Payne, Torrence P. | Ph.D. | 50-017 |
| Ross, Roderick C. | M.Sc. | 49-618 |
| Rota, Alexander N. | M.Sc. | 53-604 |
| Starr, Harry | M.Sc. | 47-526 |
| Toreson, Wilfred E. | Ph.D. | 50-045 |
| Toreson, Wilfred E. | M.Sc. | 48-601 |
| Whiteside, John H. | M.Sc. | 51-562 |
| **Dunbar, M.** | | |
| Black, William F. | Ph.D. | 56-004 |
| Bleakney, John S. | Ph.D. | 56-038 |
| Cameron, Austin W. | Ph.D. | 56-041 |
| Ellis, Derek V. | Ph.D. | 57-009 |
| Ellis, Derek V. | M.Sc. | 54-520 |
| Fisher, Harold D. | Ph.D. | 54-048 |
| Fontaine, Marion | M.Sc. | 54-583 |
| Hildebrand, Henry H. | M.Sc. | 48-581 |
| Johnston, Douglas M. | M.C.L. | 58-500 |
| Kohler, Allan C. | M.Sc. | 56-582 |
| Lewis, John B. | Ph.D. | 54-054 |
| Macpherson, Andrew H. | M.Sc. | 57-533 |
| Mansfield, Arthur W. | Ph.D. | 58-027 |
| McLaren, Ian A. | M.Sc. | 55-610 |
| Osborn, Dale J. | Ph.D. | 57-073 |



| AUTHOR | DEGREE | THESIS NUMBER |
| --- | --- | --- |
| **Dunbar, M.** | | |
| Power, Geoffrey | Ph.D. | 59-064 |
| Squires, Hubert J. | M.Sc. | 56-540 |
| Steele, Donald H. | M.Sc. | 56-541 |
| Thomson, John A. | M.Sc. | 57-597 |
| **Durley, R.** | | |
| Ball, Harry S. | M.Sc. | 11-505 |
| *Dick, William J. | M.Sc. | 11-508 |
| *Finlayson, John N. | M.Sc. | 09-510 |
| *Galloway, John D. | M.Sc. | 12-508 |
| *Gillies, George A. | M.Sc. | 11-511 |
| *Guillet, George I. | M.Sc. | 09-512 |
| *Harrington, John L. | M.Sc. | 08-510 |
| *Harris, Norman C. | M.Sc. | 11-512 |
| *Harvey, John B. | M.Sc. | 07-509 |
| *McNaughton, Andrew G. | M.Sc. | 12-514 |
| *Mitchell, William G. | M.Sc. | 14-514 |
| *Munn, David W. | M.Sc. | 11-514 |
| *Murray, George F. | M.Sc. | 12-515 |
| *Pitts, Gordon M. | M.Sc. | 09-515 |
| *Porter, Cecil G. | M.Sc. | 13-519 |
| *Ryan, Charles C. | M.Sc. | 14-516 |
| *Strangways, Henry F. | M.Sc. | 08-514 |
| *Yuill, Harry H. | M.Sc. | 10-524 |
| **Duthie, G.** | | |
| Ashley, Leonard | M.A. | 50-645 |
| Currie, Robert A. | M.A. | 51-567 |
| Johnston, Patricia M. | M.A. | 48-563 |
| Jones, Taliesin | M.A. | 49-636 |
| Meadowcroft, James W. | M.A. | 52-550 |
| Puhvel, Martin | M.A. | 54-553 |
| Stevenson, Stanley W. | M.A. | 54-623 |
| Wilson, Donald H. | M.A. | 50-669 |
| **DuPorte, E.** | | |
| Auclair, Lucien | M.Sc. | 45-502 |
| Bigelow, Robert S. | Ph.D. | 54-040 |
| Bird, Frederick T. | Ph.D. | 49-042 |

| AUTHOR | DEGREE | THESIS NUMBER |
|---|---|---|
| **DuPorte, E.** | | |
| Cameron, James W. | M.Sc. | 32-510 |
| Carroll, William J. | M.Sc. | 52-516 |
| Daviault, Lionel | M.Sc. | 28-504 |
| Doyle, J. Andre | M.Sc. | 42-520 |
| Duncan, Joseph | M.Sc. | 42-521 |
| Gardiner, Lorne M. | Ph.D. | 55-020 |
| Gardiner, Lorne M. | M.Sc. | 52-523 |
| Ghouri, Ahmad S. | Ph.D. | 56-050 |
| Gilbert, Harold Adrian | M.Sc. | 39-057 |
| Gobeil, Antoine R. | Ph.D. | 41-007 |
| Gobeil, Antoine R. | M.Sc. | 35-504 |
| Hammond, George H. | M.Sc. | 24-518 |
| Hardwick, David F. | M.Sc. | 48-525 |
| Hawboldt, Lloyd S. | M.Sc. | 46-521 |
| Leroux, Edgar J. | M.Sc. | 52-532 |
| Maltais, Jean B. | M.Sc. | 28-519 |
| Martin, Helen J. | M.Sc. | 50-548 |
| Maxwell, Charles W. | M.Sc. | 39-065 |
| McLintock, John J. | Ph.D. | 51-053 |
| Monro, Hector A. | Ph.D. | 58-031 |
| Morgan, Cecil V. | M.Sc. | 45-511 |
| Morrison, Frank Orville | Ph.D. | 39-014 |
| Munroe, Eugene Gordon | M.Sc. | 41-534 |
| Nelson, William A. | Ph.D. | 57-070 |
| Nelson, William A. | M.Sc. | 48-539 |
| Peck, Oswald | Ph.D. | 36-021 |
| Peck, Oswald | M.Sc. | 34-514 |
| Phillips, John H. | M.Sc. | 47-566 |
| Rao, Bapoje K. | Ph.D. | 54-062 |
| Reeks, Wilfrid S. | M.Sc. | 32-523 |
| Reesal, Michael R. | M.Sc. | 50-554 |
| Richmond, Hector A. | M.Sc. | 35-515 |
| Robinson, Arthur G. | M.Sc. | 52-540 |
| Shewell, Guy E. | M.Sc. | 37-540 |
| Stairs, Gordon R. | M.Sc. | 58-532 |
| Stewart, Kenneth E. | M.Sc. | 26-526 |
| Stultz, Harold T. | M.Sc. | 46-580 |
| Sullivan, Calvin R. | Ph.D. | 57-036 |
| Thomas, James B. | Ph.D. | 54-069 |
| Thomas, James B. | M.Sc. | 52-543 |
| Twinn, Cecil R. | M.Sc. | 36-520 |
| Vickery, Vernon R. | M.Sc. | 57-540 |
| Wallace, Donald R. | M.Sc. | 59-542 |
| Warren, George L. | M.Sc. | 53-607 |
| White, Roy M. | M.Sc. | 26-534 |



| AUTHOR | DEGREE | THESIS NUMBER |
|---|---|---|
| **DuPorte, E.** | | |
| Whitehead, Walter E. | M.Sc. | 31-517 |
| Wigmore, Robert H. | M.Sc. | 50-559 |
| Wolfgang, Robert W. | M.Sc. | 50-560 |
| *Armstrong, Thomas | M.Sc. | 25-506 |
| *Baker, Alexander D. | M.Sc. | 25-508 |
| *Dyce, Elton J. | M.Sc. | 28-507 |
| *Graham, Archibald R. | M.Sc. | 26-511 |
| *Maw, William A. | M.S.A. | 25-544 |
| **Dworkin, S.** | | |
| Baxt, Judith Brainin | M.Sc. | 41-034 |
| **Eakins, P.** | | |
| Leuner, Wilhelm D. | M.Sc. | 59-524 |
| Mann, Ernest L. | Ph.D. | 59-050 |
| Sims, Walter A. | M.Sc. | 59-599 |
| **Edis, A.** | | |
| Hyder, Syed S. | M.Eng. | 59-503 |
| Kardos, Geza | M.Eng. | 57-559 |
| Sein, Maung T. | M.Eng. | 59-504 |
| *Putnaerglis, Rudolph | M.Eng. | 55-507 |
| **Elkin, F.** | | |
| Badgley, Robin F. | M.A. | 54-608 |
| Jonassohn, Kurt | M.A. | 55-631 |
| Richardson, Nigel H. | M.A. | 54-619 |
| **Elliott, K.** | | |
| Blackmore, William R. | M.Sc. | 50-596 |
| Brodkin, Elliot | Ph.D. | 58-005 |
| Brodkin, Elliot | M.Sc. | 51-597 |
| Cross, Jean D. | M.Sc. | 55-517 |
| Heller, Irving H. | M.Sc. | 54-597 |
| McLennan, Hugh | Ph.D. | 51-021 |

| AUTHOR | DEGREE | THESIS NUMBER |
|---|---|---|
| **Elliott, K.** | | |
| McLennan, Hugh | M.Sc. | 49-538 |
| Rosenfeld, Michael W. | M.Sc. | 56-599 |
| Tower, Donald B. | Ph.D. | 51-033 |
| Van Gelder, Nico M. | Ph.D. | 59-073 |
| Webb, James L. | Ph.D. | 50-049 |
| Webb, James L. | M.Sc. | 48-552 |
| **Elson, J.** | | |
| Bahyrycz, G.S. | M.Sc. | 57-520 |
| Mumtazuddin, Mohammed | M.Sc. | 58-527 |
| Sater, Geoffrey S. | M.Sc. | 58-529 |
| **Estey, R.** | | |
| Smith, Thomas H. | M.Sc. | 59-538 |
| **Evans, N.** | | |
| *Aylard, Clara M. | M.Sc. | 24-506 |
| *Buffam, Basil S. | M.Sc. | 24-510 |
| *Carlyle, Arthur W. | M.Sc. | 23-508 |
| *Finley, Frederick L. | M.Sc. | 24-514 |
| *Graham, Richard F. | M.Sc. | 08-509 |
| *Harrison, Donald R. | M.Sc. | 22-510 |
| *Pelletier, Rene A. | M.Sc. | 24-526 |
| *Saul, Bernard B. | M.Sc. | 22-520 |
| **Eve, A.** | | |
| Howlett, Leslie E. | Ph.D. | 31-007 |
| Moore, William H. | M.Eng. | 32-503 |
| Patterson, Arthur L. | Ph.D. | 28-011 |
| Ross, William B. | Ph.D. | 33-031 |
| *Anderson, Robert G. | M.Sc. | 23-501 |
| *Bates, Frederick W. | M.Sc. | 10-512 |
| *Bissell, Harold R. | M.Sc. | 23-505 |
| *Boyle, Robert W. | Ph.D. | 09-001 |
| *Brow, James B. | M.Sc. | 22-501 |
| *Chalk, Mary L. | M.Sc. | 26-506 |
| *Currie, Balfour W. | Ph.D. | 30-002 |



| AUTHOR | DEGREE | THESIS NUMBER |
|---|---|---|
| **Eve, A.** | | |
| *Dewar, Charles L. | M.Sc. | 22-502 |
| *Dobridge, Ronald W. | M.Sc. | 29-507 |
| *Douglas, Allie V. | M.Sc. | 21-503 |
| *Hachey, Henry B. | M.Sc. | 25-519 |
| *Larose, Paul | Ph.D. | 25-004 |
| *McPherson, Anna I. | M.Sc. | 23-517 |
| *McRae, Duncan R. | M.Sc. | 28-518 |
| *Mennie, John H. | Ph.D. | 25-005 |
| *Moran, James | M.Sc. | 16-513 |
| *Saunders, James E. | M.Sc. | 22-521 |
| *Smith, Frederick M. | M.Sc. | 24-530 |
| *Smith, Ietha A. | M.Sc. | 21-515 |
| *Stephens, Henry N. | Ph.D. | 23-006 |
| *Terroux, Fernand R. | M.Sc. | 26-528 |
| *Trimingham, James H. | M.Sc. | 20-508 |
| *Wallace, George A. | M.Sc. | 21-517 |
| *White, Thomas N. | M.Sc. | 27-521 |
| *Williams, Frederick H. | M.Sc. | 21-518 |
| *Wright, Charles A. | Ph.D. | 21-003 |
| **Eve, A. B.** | | |
| *Press, Abraham | M.Sc. | 27-516 |
| *Priestman, Bryan | M.Sc. | 26-523 |
| **Eve, A. .** | | |
| *Watson, Edmund E. | M.Sc. | 26-533 |
| **Eve, A. R.** | | |
| *Patterson, Arthur L. | M.Sc. | 24-525 |
| **Eve,A.** | | |
| *Weldon, Thomas H. | M.Sc. | 23-519 |
| **Evelyn, K.** | | |
| Kushner, Donn J. | M.Sc. | 50-615 |

| AUTHOR | DEGREE | THESIS NUMBER |
|---|---|---|
| **Evelyn, K.** | | |
| Robichon, Jacques | M.Sc. | 50-555 |
| Stinson, David A. | M.Sc. | 51-553 |
| Weigensberg, Bernard I. | Ph.D. | 53-078 |
| Weigensberg, Bernard I. | M.Sc. | 51-561 |
| **Fairbairn, D.** | | |
| Glocklin, Vera C. | M.Sc. | 50-608 |
| Passey, Richard F. | Ph.D. | 56-028 |
| Pollak, John K. | Ph.D. | 53-069 |
| Waters, William R. | M.Sc. | 54-537 |
| **Fantham, H.** | | |
| Adams, James R. | M.Sc. | 37-501 |
| Clark, Annie E. | M.Sc. | 33-511 |
| Cohen, Arthur | Ph.D. | 36-003 |
| Cohen, Arthur | M.Sc. | 34-508 |
| Khaner, Miriam | M.A. | 35-529 |
| Lead, Harry D. | M.Sc. | 37-537 |
| Monro, Hector A. | M.Sc. | 35-510 |
| Richardson, Laurence R. | Ph.D. | 35-024 |
| **Farnell, G.** | | |
| Blostein, Maier L. | M.Eng. | 59-567 |
| Borden, Byron C. | M.Eng. | 55-503 |
| Gilbert, Jacques | M.Eng. | 57-558 |
| Goldie, Hugh J. | M.Eng. | 56-506 |
| Gunn, Morris W. | M.Sc. | 59-584 |
| Lee, Ernest S. | M.Eng. | 58-556 |
| **Farthing, J.** | | |
| *Aikman, Cecil H. | M.A. | 26-535 |
| **Fazlu-r-Rahman** | | |
| Mujahid, Sharif | M.A. | 54-549 |



| AUTHOR | DEGREE | THESIS NUMBER |
|---|---|---|
| Ferguson, G. | | |
| Bird, Thomas C. | M.A. | 51-631 |
| Blascik, Frank | M.A. | 49-554 |
| Brown, Frederick T. | M.Sc. | 50-518 |
| Burnett, Alastair | Ph.D. | 55-010 |
| DeShield, George D. | M.A. | 49-557 |
| Dickie, Robert D. | M.A. | 50-652 |
| Heron, Woodburn | Ph.D. | 53-056 |
| Holmes, Anthony F. | M.A. | 49-567 |
| Hunton, Vera D. | Ph.D. | 51-016 |
| Mishkin, Mortimer | M.A. | 49-573 |
| Mooney, Craig M. | M.A. | 51-571 |
| Oliver, John A. | M.A. | 50-660 |
| Popham, James H. | M.Sc. | 51-618 |
| Rajalakshmi, Ramakrishna | Ph.D. | 58-056 |
| Scheier, Ivan H. | Ph.D. | 53-075 |
| Scheier, Ivan H. | M.A. | 51-641 |
| Smith, David D. | Ph.D. | 57-034 |
| Wevrick, Leonard | M.Sc. | 57-599 |
| Zweig, Joseph P. | M.A. | 52-560 |
| Fieldhouse, H. | | |
| Rider, Milton A. | M.A. | 56-545 |
| Breitenbucher, Howard E. | M.A. | 50-649 |
| Farmakides, Anna | Ph.D. | 59-078 |
| Gwyn, Julian R. | M.A. | 58-584 |
| Jennings, Peter E. | M.A. | 53-614 |
| McCarthy, John J. | M.A. | 59-612 |
| McCullough, Edward E. | M.A. | 54-615 |
| O'Neill, Thomas L. | M.A. | 48-568 |
| Rubin, Gerald M. | M.A. | 56-622 |
| Smith, Irving H. | M.A. | 55-560 |
| Vogel, Robert | Ph.D. | 59-074 |
| Vogel, Robert | M.A. | 54-625 |
| Files, H. | | |
| Allen, Gertrude E. | M.A. | 37-516 |
| Amaron, Errol C. | M.A. | 33-572 |
| Beresford-Howe, Constanc | M.A. | 46-538 |
| Berry, William G. | M.A. | 35-520 |
| Blumenthal, Estelle H. | M.A. | 35-523 |
| Boswell, William C. | M.A. | 52-546 |

| AUTHOR | DEGREE | THESIS NUMBER |
|---|---|---|
| Files, H. | | |
| Capps, Margaret C. | M.A. | 50-563 |
| Clark, Mary M. | M.A. | 49-629 |
| Compton, Neil M. | M.A. | 48-556 |
| Denton, Dorothy May | M.A. | 41-512 |
| Dike, Mary E. | M.A. | 37-543 |
| Dolan, John Philip | M.A. | 41-513 |
| Duncan, Agnes P. | M.A. | 45-512 |
| Ebbitt, May | M.A. | 51-568 |
| Fague, William R. | M.A. | 50-564 |
| Falle, George G. | M.A. | 37-522 |
| Fricker, Kathleen M. | M.A. | 50-653 |
| Geggie, Mary M. | M.A. | 49-560 |
| Goldberg, Barbara J. | M.A. | 59-551 |
| Goodin, Peggy L. | M.A. | 49-562 |
| Gowdey, Cecil W. | M.A. | 48-611 |
| Hamilton, Marion M. | M.A. | 35-543 |
| Handelman, Saul | M.A. | 55-549 |
| Harding, Lawrence A. | M.A. | 49-564 |
| Harrison, John L. | M.A. | 50-654 |
| Harvey, Mary R. | M.A. | 54-544 |
| Heller, Mildred | M.A. | 42-032 |
| Hemsley, Stuart D. | M.A. | 44-524 |
| Hersh, Jacob | M.A. | 51-636 |
| Hill, Olive M. | M.A. | 33-548 |
| Homer, Kenneth C. | M.A. | 45-515 |
| Howe, Margaret G. | M.A. | 45-516 |
| Hunter, Gerald F. | M.A. | 46-587 |
| Iversen, James E. | M.A. | 51-637 |
| Kaplan, Florence R. | M.A. | 32-531 |
| Klein, Jenny | M.A. | 36-534 |
| Kronman, Ruth Y. | M.A. | 33-550 |
| Langlois, Robert H. | M.A. | 47-533 |
| Lawrence, Gertrude R. | M.A. | 30-534 |
| Leavitt, Helen R. | M.A. | 49-638 |
| Milburne, Kathleen E. | M.A. | 34-536 |
| Montgomery, Harriet R. | M.A. | 33-554 |
| Mooney, Elizabeth S. | M.A. | 43-512 |
| O'Sullivan, Timothy | M.A. | 49-574 |
| Pitts, Mary A. | M.A. | 50-663 |
| Purcell, Donald | M.A. | 49-577 |
| Stabler, Ernest | M.A. | 43-516 |
| Stewart, Lyall S. | M.A. | 50-578 |
| Tansey, Charlotte H. | M.A. | 48-618 |
| Thomson, Allan | M.A. | 46-593 |
| Waterhouse, John | M.A. | 55-565 |



| AUTHOR | DEGREE | THESIS NUMBER |
|---|---|---|
| Files, H. | | |
| Whitehead, Jean V.H. | M.A. | 41-030 |
| Woolner, Evelyn F. | M.A. | 45-518 |
| *Armstrong, Charles A. | M.A. | 26-536 |
| *Dawes, Charles H. | M.A. | 30-524 |
| *Donald, Henry G. | M.A. | 30-525 |
| *Edel, Abraham | M.A. | 28-531 |
| *Edel, Joseph L. | M.A. | 28-532 |
| *Hayakawa, Samuel I. | M.A. | 28-538 |
| *Jenkins, Lloyd H. | M.A. | 30-532 |
| *Mullaly, Jessie D. | M.A. | 28-565 |
| *Murray, Mae F. | M.A. | 28-548 |
| *Newton, Theodore F. | M.A. | 27-543 |
| *Preston, George P. | M.A. | 26-551 |
| *Read, Mary G. | M.A. | 25-540 |
| *Scott, Mary E. | M.A. | 28-566 |
| *Smith, Arthur J. | M.A. | 26-554 |
| *Smith, Lawrence L. | M.A. | 28-554 |
| Files, H. C. | | |
| *Hewitt, Frank S. | M.A. | 31-533 |
| Fischer, E. | | |
| Boehner, Reginald S. | Ph.D. | 12-001 |
| Fleming, D. | | |
| Greenberg, Louis | Ph.D. | 48-005 |
| Flux, * | | |
| *Pearson, Mary F. | M.A. | 07-504 |
| Forsey, E. | | |
| Bergithon, Carl | M.A. | 31-520 |
| Godine, Morton Robert | M.A. | 39-035 |
| Kleiner, George | M.A. | 37-523 |
| McCracken, Edward J. | M.A. | 32-534 |

| AUTHOR | DEGREE | THESIS NUMBER |
|---|---|---|
| **Forsey, E.** | | |
| *Parthenais, J. Theodore | M.A. | 30-540 |
| **Foster, J.** | | |
| Aikman, Edward P. | M.Sc. | 33-568 |
| Aikman, William E. P. | Ph.D. | 35-001 |
| Alcock, Norman Z. | Ph.D. | 49-002 |
| Anderson, Donald A. | Ph.D. | 49-003 |
| Badior, Mark A. | M.Sc. | 54-571 |
| Bell, Robert E. | Ph.D. | 48-003 |
| Bernstein, Hyman | M.Sc. | 56-513 |
| Bloom, Myer | M.Sc. | 50-597 |
| Brannen, Eric | Ph.D. | 48-018 |
| Breckon, Sydney W. | Ph.D. | 51-001 |
| Brunton, Donald C. | Ph.D. | 48-019 |
| Carruthers, James A. | Ph.D. | 49-006 |
| Carter, Alfred L. | Ph.D. | 58-008 |
| Chalk, Mary L. | Ph.D. | 28-004 |
| Clark, Eric N. | Ph.D. | 51-044 |
| Cloutier, Joseph A. | Ph.D. | 55-051 |
| Cloutier, Joseph A. | M.Sc. | 53-582 |
| Crawford, Gerald J. | Ph.D. | 54-045 |
| Dahlstrom, Carl E. | Ph.D. | 53-050 |
| Dewdney, John W. | M.Sc. | 52-522 |
| Din, Ghias ud | M.Sc. | 59-581 |
| Dodds, John W. | Ph.D. | 49-008 |
| Douglas, Donald G. | Ph.D. | 49-009 |
| Eadie, Frank S. | Ph.D. | 52-044 |
| Eadie, Frank S. | M.Sc. | 49-523 |
| Eappen, Collaparambil | Ph.D. | 59-019 |
| Epp, Edward R. | Ph.D. | 55-054 |
| Feeny, Harold Francis | M.Sc. | 40-518 |
| Flower, Louis G. | M.Sc. | 54-521 |
| Foster, Leigh C. | Ph.D. | 56-048 |
| Geldart, Lloyd Philip | Ph.D. | 41-006 |
| Girdwood, Barbara M. | M.Sc. | 46-568 |
| Girdwood, Barbara M. | Ph.D. | 48-024 |
| Gransden, Max M. | Ph.D. | 51-012 |
| Green, Ralph E. | Ph.D. | 56-052 |
| Groves, Trevor K. | M.Sc. | 53-531 |
| Gunton, Robert C. | Ph.D. | 47-028 |
| Guptill, Ernest W. | Ph.D. | 46-009 |
| Hargrove, Clifford K. | M.Sc. | 57-577 |
| Harkness, Harold W. | Ph.D. | 30-004 |



| AUTHOR | DEGREE | THESIS NUMBER |
|---|---|---|
| **Foster, J.** | | |
| Haslam, Robert N. | Ph.D. | 33-008 |
| Heard, Jack F. | Ph.D. | 32-007 |
| Henrikson, Arne | Ph.D. | 53-010 |
| Henry, William H. | Ph.D. | 51-050 |
| Hilborn, John W. | Ph.D. | 54-014 |
| Hilborn, John W. | M.Sc. | 51-609 |
| Hone, David W. | Ph.D. | 51-015 |
| Hopkins, Nigel J. | Ph.D. | 52-017 |
| Hopkins, Nigel J. | M.Sc. | 49-531 |
| Horton, Cyril A. | Ph.D. | 37-010 |
| Hunt, John W. | Ph.D. | 56-054 |
| Hunten, Donald M. | Ph.D. | 50-007 |
| Huq, M. Shamsul | M.Sc. | 56-521 |
| Jackson, Ray W. | Ph.D. | 50-010 |
| Johnson, Frederick A. | Ph.D. | 52-020 |
| Jones, Donald C. | Ph.D. | 37-012 |
| Kennedy, John Edward | M.Sc. | 42-055 |
| Keys, John D. | Ph.D. | 51-051 |
| Langstroth, George C. | Ph.D. | 30-005 |
| Link, William T. | Ph.D. | 57-062 |
| Lorrain, Paul | Ph.D. | 47-011 |
| Lorrain, Paul | M.Sc. | 41-530 |
| Maclure, Kenneth C. | Ph.D. | 52-054 |
| Maclure, Kenneth C. | M.Sc. | 50-621 |
| Martin, William M. | Ph.D. | 51-023 |
| Mathison, James F. | Ph.D. | 56-027 |
| McKay, Kenneth Gardiner | M.Sc. | 39-516 |
| Michel, Walter | Ph.D. | 48-031 |
| Millar, Charles H. | Ph.D. | 47-035 |
| Moody, Harry J. | Ph.D. | 55-067 |
| Moon, James H. | Ph.D. | 50-038 |
| Moore, Robert B. | M.Sc. | 59-528 |
| Morrison, Wesley A. | Ph.D. | 48-033 |
| Munn, Allan M. | Ph.D. | 47-015 |
| Neamtan, Samuel M. | Ph.D. | 37-017 |
| Panter, Shraga F. | Ph.D. | 36-020 |
| Pepper, Thomas P. | Ph.D. | 48-034 |
| Perlman, Martin M. | Ph.D. | 55-030 |
| Perlman, Martin M. | M.Sc. | 51-616 |
| Piggott, Carmen I. | Ph.D. | 53-068 |
| Pounder, Elton R. | Ph.D. | 37-018 |
| Rao, C. Kanaka D. | M.Sc. | 58-575 |
| Rotenberg, Avrahm B. | Ph.D. | 41-507 |
| Rowles, William | Ph.D. | 28-007 |
| Rowles, William | M.Sc. | 26-525 |

| AUTHOR | DEGREE | THESIS NUMBER |
|---|---|---|
| **Foster, J.** | | |
| Scott, Donald Burton | Ph.D. | 40-021 |
| Sellem, John M. | M.Sc. | 51-625 |
| Shugar, David | Ph.D. | 40-023 |
| Skarsgard, Harvey M. | Ph.D. | 55-075 |
| Snell, Arthur H. | Ph.D. | 33-019 |
| Stephens-Newsham, Lloyd | Ph.D. | 48-040 |
| Telford, William M. | M.Sc. | 41-536 |
| Thomas, George M. | Ph.D. | 58-049 |
| Thomas, George M. | M.Sc. | 56-606 |
| Thornton, Robert L. | Ph.D. | 33-023 |
| Tilley, Donald E. | Ph.D. | 51-060 |
| Turner, Terry E. | Ph.D. | 48-041 |
| Van Steenbergen, Arie | Ph.D. | 57-086 |
| Voyvodic, Louis | Ph.D. | 48-042 |
| Walker, Laurence Richard | Ph.D. | 39-505 |
| Warren, F.G. Ross | Ph.D. | 48-044 |
| Weaver, Ralph S. | M.Sc. | 59-543 |
| Whitehead, Andrew B. | Ph.D. | 57-088 |
| Whitehead, Andrew B. | M.Sc. | 55-622 |
| Wolfson, Joseph L. | Ph.D. | 48-014 |
| *Campbell, Herbert N. | M.Sc. | 30-502 |
| *Fraser, John S. | Ph.D. | 49-046 |
| *MacDonald, James L. | M.Sc. | 28-516 |
| *McRae, Duncan R. | Ph.D. | 30-007 |
| *Reeve, Herbert A. | M.Sc. | 31-557 |
| *Telford, William M. | Ph.D. | 49-056 |
| **Foster, J. .** | | |
| *Danby, Gordon T. | Ph.D. | 56-009 |
| **Fox, C.** | | |
| Linis-Linins, Viktors | M.Sc. | 51-530 |
| Mercier, Raymond P. | M.Sc. | 56-589 |
| **Frances, M.** | | |
| McQuillan, Marie B. | M.A. | 43-524 |



| AUTHOR | DEGREE | THESIS NUMBER |
|---|---|---|
| **Frankel, S.** | | |
| Horowitz, Gad | M.A. | 59-611 |
| **Fraser, *** | | |
| *MacKenzie, Francis S. | M.A. | 16-505 |
| *Murray, Bertram S. | M.A. | 27-536 |
| **Fraser, F.** | | |
| Clark, Karin H. | M.Sc. | 56-570 |
| Fainstat, Theodore D. | M.Sc. | 51-606 |
| Kalter, Harold | Ph.D. | 53-016 |
| Kalter, Harold | M.Sc. | 51-611 |
| Liberman, John | M.Sc. | 50-618 |
| Metrakos, Julius D. | Ph.D. | 51-054 |
| Metrakos, Julius D. | M.Sc. | 49-540 |
| Miller, James R. | Ph.D. | 59-052 |
| Trasler, Daphne G. | Ph.D. | 58-050 |
| Trasler, Daphne G. | M.Sc. | 54-534 |
| Walker, Bruce E. | Ph.D. | 54-072 |
| **Freeman, *** | | |
| Camerlain, Homer H. | M.A. | 30-520 |
| *Epstein, Elsie | M.A. | 29-529 |
| *Reed, John G. | M.A. | 29-547 |
| *Troop, William H. | M.A. | 29-550 |
| **French, R.** | | |
| Arcand, Louis J. | M.Eng. | 32-500 |
| Pidcux, John L. | M.Eng. | 36-504 |
| **Fried, J.** | | |
| Willmott, William E. | M.A. | 59-564 |
| **Friedman, S.** | | |

| AUTHOR | DEGREE | THESIS NUMBER |
|---|---|---|
| **Friedman, S.** | | |
| Campbell, Charles G. | M.Sc. | 49-515 |
| **Frost, S.** | | |
| Davison, Roy J. | S.T.M. | 58-502 |
| **Fryer, C.** | | |
| Bateson, Nora | M.A. | 33-535 |
| Collard, Edgar A. | M.A. | 37-519 |
| Cooper, John I. | Ph.D. | 38-020 |
| Copland, Edward B. | M.A. | 32-560 |
| Edgar, William S. | M.A. | 32-526 |
| Gower, Douglas L. | M.A. | 26-542 |
| Morgan, Mildred A. | M.A. | 37-527 |
| Reid, William S. | M.A. | 35-547 |
| Self, George M. | M.A. | 38-554 |
| Snyder, John K. | M.A. | 32-562 |
| Traver, Lillie A. | M.A. | 29-549 |
| *Bissett, Alice M. | M.A. | 27-522 |
| *Brown, Vera L. | M.A. | 13-501 |
| *Di Florio, Pasquale | M.A. | 26-539 |
| *Ellison, Myra K. | M.A. | 13-503 |
| *Gurd, Jean M. | M.A. | 26-543 |
| *Knowles, Eustace C. | M.A. | 29-542 |
| *MacSporran, Maysie S. | M.A. | 30-537 |
| *McLetchie, James K. | M.A. | 29-545 |
| *Murray, Phyllis M. | M.A. | 27-537 |
| *Nichol, Jean | M.A. | 25-538 |
| *Sacks, Benjamin | M.A. | 27-540 |
| *Smillie, Eleanor A. | M.A. | 10-510 |
| *Steacy, Frederick W. | M.A. | 13-511 |
| *Thomson, Herbert F. | M.A. | 13-512 |
| *Thorne, Oliver | M.A. | 12-506 |
| **Fryer, C. J. and Woodhead, W.** | | |
| *Wilson, Evelyn C. | M.A. | 30-556 |
| **Fryer, C. .** | | |



| AUTHOR | DEGREE | THESIS NUMBER |
|---|---|---|
| **Fryer, C. .** | | |
| *Howell, Lucy M. | M.A. | 12-501 |
| **Furness, L.** | | |
| Barrett, Doris Pearl | M.A. | 41-511 |
| Birchard, Lucile | M.A. | 41-020 |
| Bowes, Walter G. | M.A. | 48-608 |
| Butterfield, Lee E. | M.A. | 47-530 |
| Connors, Vara M. | M.A. | 31-525 |
| Corey, Earl E. | M.A. | 52-601 |
| Dwyer, Florence Mary | M.A. | 41-021 |
| Egan, Marie J. | M.A. | 43-522 |
| Elliott, Harriett E. | M.A. | 47-531 |
| Farrell, Amelia Mary | M.A. | 39-032 |
| Gay, Alice Grace | M.A. | 41-022 |
| Glover, Thomas W. | M.A. | 51-634 |
| Johnston, Charles F. | M.A. | 42-034 |
| Matthers, Mary C. | M.A. | 48-566 |
| McGarry, Ave Marie | M.A. | 42-513 |
| Murphy, Florence E. | M.A. | 39-042 |
| O'Quinn, James P. | M.A. | 50-572 |
| Parsons, Clarence Reuben | M.A. | 41-521 |
| Ponticello, Eva Edith | M.A. | 42-037 |
| Ross, Mary C. M. | M.A. | 35-534 |
| Rossiter, Maryellen | M.A. | 42-041 |
| Stewart, Mary I. | M.A. | 49-580 |
| Taylor, Margaret E. | M.A. | 42-046 |
| Weston, Grace E. | M.A. | 34-539 |
| Wilkinson, Ida G. | M.A. | 47-584 |
| *Banfill, Gladys M. | M.A. | 29-523 |
| *Flahault, Elizabeth | M.A. | 31-531 |
| *Parthenais, J. Theodore | M.A. | 30-540 |
| **Garbland, E.** | | |
| Devine, Francis | M.A. | 48-610 |
| **Garcia-Arocha, H.** | | |
| McIlreath, Fred J. | Ph.D. | 59-048 |

| AUTHOR | DEGREE | THESIS NUMBER |
|---|---|---|
| **Garigue, P.** | | |
| Pineo, Peter C. | M.A. | 57-553 |
| **Gasdik, J.** | | |
| Vaisoussis, Constantine | LL.M. | 54-507 |
| **Gauvin, W.** | | |
| Cooper, Ross M. | M.Eng. | 50-504 |
| Dlouhy, Jan | Ph.D. | 57-006 |
| Epstein, Norman | M.Eng. | 46-553 |
| Gunnarsson, Gudni K. | M.Eng. | 52-563 |
| Hoffman, Terrence W. | Ph.D. | 59-035 |
| Legendre, Rosaire | M.Eng. | 46-503 |
| Lyons, Douglas B. | M.Eng. | 51-587 |
| Macrakis, N. | M.Eng. | 52-565 |
| Manning, William P. | Ph.D. | 58-026 |
| Morton, Ernest R. | M.Eng. | 52-506 |
| Nichols, Ian O. | M.Eng. | 56-559 |
| Palsson, Petur | M.Eng. | 52-507 |
| Pasternak, Israel S. | Ph.D. | 59-061 |
| Phillips, Lorne A. | M.Eng. | 52-508 |
| Pinder, Kenneth L. | M.Eng. | 52-509 |
| Schaus, Orland O. | Ph.D. | 54-031 |
| Schieck, Robert R. | Ph.D. | 59-069 |
| Yano, George E. | M.Eng. | 53-510 |
| **Gazdik, J.** | | |
| Adelfio, Antonio | LL.M. | 55-580 |
| Nowak, Tadeusz C. | LL.M. | 55-583 |
| Saleh, Samir | LL.M. | 55-511 |
| Swan, John H. | LL.M. | 54-568 |
| Toepper, Anton | LL.M. | 55-512 |
| **Gibbs, R.** | | |
| Clark, John | M.Sc. | 52-517 |
| Gooding, Herbert B. | M.Sc. | 47-547 |
| Long, Harold D. | M.Sc. | 55-529 |
| Scoggan, Homer J. | M.Sc. | 35-517 |



| AUTHOR | DEGREE | THESIS NUMBER |
|---|---|---|
| **Gibbs, R.** | | |
| Shaw, Michael | M.Sc. | 47-569 |
| Towers, George H. | M.Sc. | 51-558 |
| **Giles, H.** | | |
| Ross, Sally Chipman | M.A. | 42-040 |
| **Gill, J.** | | |
| Asbury, Winfred Nowers | M.Sc. | 41-524 |
| Averill, Edward L. | M.Sc. | 53-570 |
| Avison, Arthur T. | M.Sc. | 54-510 |
| Baird, David M. | Ph.D. | 47-001 |
| Bell, Keith | M.Sc. | 50-595 |
| Black, F.T. | Ph.D. | 54-008 |
| Brossard, Leo | M.Sc. | 40-040 |
| Buck, Walter K. | M.Sc. | 51-598 |
| Byers, Alfred R. | Ph.D. | 36-002 |
| Byers, Alfred R. | M.Sc. | 33-510 |
| Cameron, Harcourt L. | M.Sc. | 45-506 |
| Cunnington, Francis A. | M.Sc. | 47-544 |
| Dubuc, Fernand | M.Sc. | 50-605 |
| Dufresne, Cyrille | Ph.D. | 52-010 |
| Eakins, Peter R. | Ph.D. | 52-012 |
| Gillies, Norman B. | Ph.D. | 51-048 |
| Grady, John C. | M.Sc. | 52-574 |
| Grimes-Graeme, Rhoderick | M.Sc. | 32-513 |
| Hart, Edward Arthur | M.Sc. | 39-059 |
| Hawkins, William M. | M.Sc. | 58-523 |
| Imbault, Paul-Emile | Ph.D. | 50-008 |
| Jeffery, William G. | Ph.D. | 59-038 |
| Kirkland, Robert W. | Ph.D. | 50-011 |
| L'Esperance, Robert L. | M.Sc. | 48-530 |
| Lee, Burdett | M.Sc. | 46-572 |
| Machamer, Jerome F. | M.Sc. | 59-526 |
| MacDougall, John F. | Ph.D. | 57-063 |
| MacIntosh, James A. | M.Sc. | 56-527 |
| MacLaren, Alexander S. | M.Sc. | 50-545 |
| Malouf, Stanley E. | Ph.D. | 41-504 |
| Mannard, George W. | M.Sc. | 56-529 |
| McCuaig, James A. | M.Sc. | 50-620 |
| Meikle, Brian K. | Ph.D. | 59-051 |
| Meikle, Brian K. | M.Sc. | 55-612 |

| AUTHOR | DEGREE | THESIS NUMBER |
|---|---|---|
| **Gill, J.** | | |
| Morrow, Harold F. | Ph.D. | 50-039 |
| Moss, Albert E. | Ph.D. | 39-501 |
| Nauss, Arthur William | M.Sc. | 40-047 |
| Neilson, James M. | M.Sc. | 47-522 |
| Owens, Owen E. | Ph.D. | 55-028 |
| Owens, Owen E. | M.Sc. | 51-540 |
| Riddell, John E. | Ph.D. | 53-034 |
| Riddell, John E. | M.Sc. | 36-549 |
| Riordon, Peter H. | Ph.D. | 52-027 |
| Robinson, William G. | Ph.D. | 41-014 |
| Schindler, Norman R. | M.Sc. | 33-529 |
| Schindler, Norman R. | Ph.D. | 34-016 |
| Schlemm, Leonard G.W. | M.Sc. | 39-068 |
| Shields, Ross C. | M.Sc. | 55-540 |
| Simpson, David H. | Ph.D. | 52-030 |
| Slipp, Robert M. | Ph.D. | 57-032 |
| Smith, Alan R. | M.Sc. | 48-545 |
| Stalker, Archibald M. | M.Sc. | 48-547 |
| Syme, Andrew M. | M.Sc. | 51-555 |
| Thorson, Erling | M.Sc. | 40-050 |
| Trenholm, Laurence Stuar | M.Sc. | 39-070 |
| Vollo, Nels B. | M.Sc. | 59-541 |
| Wahl, William G. | M.Sc. | 41-050 |
| Wolofsky, Leib | Ph.D. | 57-047 |
| Wolofsky, Leib | M.Sc. | 54-538 |
| Woolverton, Ralph S. | Ph.D. | 53-080 |
| Young, William L. | Ph.D. | 53-081 |
| Young, William L. | M.Sc. | 51-563 |
| **Gillson, A.** | | |
| Mamelak, Joseph S. | M.Sc. | 46-526 |
| *Douglas, Allie V. | Ph.D. | 26-002 |
| *MacDonald, James L. | M.Sc. | 28-516 |
| *Press, Abraham | M.Sc. | 27-516 |
| *Priestman, Bryan | Ph.D. | 29-019 |
| *Priestman, Bryan | M.Sc. | 26-523 |
| *Young, John M. | M.Sc. | 28-526 |
| **Gillson, A..** | | |
| *Home, Maurice S. | M.Sc. | 25-548 |



| AUTHOR | DEGREE | THESIS NUMBER |
|---|---|---|
| **Giroud, C.** | | |
| Das Gupta, Dyutish C. | Ph.D. | 59-016 |
| Laplante, Charlotte T. | M.Sc. | 59-523 |
| Stachenko, Janine I-M. | Ph.D. | 58-045 |
| **Girvin, G.** | | |
| Ajemian, Ann A. | M.Sc. | 57-518 |
| Tanner, Charles E. | Ph.D. | 57-083 |
| Tanner, Charles E. | M.Sc. | 56-542 |
| **Glassford, N.** | | |
| Perrigard, Elma E. | M.A. | 36-541 |
| **Goforth, W.** | | |
| Little, John W. | M.A. | 28-542 |
| *Johnston, Agnew H. | M.A. | 29-539 |
| *Pattison, Irma E. | M.A. | 31-539 |
| *Woods, Harry D. | M.A. | 31-549 |
| **Gordon, A.** | | |
| *McVittie, Thomas J. | M.A. | 14-506 |
| *Withey, Albert N. | M.A. | 16-506 |
| **Gordon, C.** | | |
| Weller, Judith A. | M.A. | 58-549 |
| **Graff, W.** | | |
| Block, Victor R. | M.A. | 49-555 |
| Haywood, Bruce | M.A. | 51-635 |
| Kyritz, Heinz-Georg | M.A. | 56-619 |
| Leppman, Wolfgang A. | M.A. | 49-639 |
| Pratt, Audrey E. | M.A. | 49-576 |
| Von Cardinal, Clive H. | M.A. | 41-029 |
| Walter, H.A. | M.A. | 54-626 |

| AUTHOR | DEGREE | THESIS NUMBER |
|---|---|---|
| Graff, W. | | |
| *Blouin, Wilhelmine E. | M.A. | 30-518 |
| *Chait, Rachel | M.A. | 30-522 |
| *Silverman, Beatrice I. | M.A. | 28-553 |
| *Townsend, Eleanor H. | M.A. | 29-548 |
| Graham, R. | | |
| Bray, Alton C. | M.Sc. | 29-505 |
| Eakins, Peter R. | M.Sc. | 49-524 |
| Halet, Robert A. | M.Sc. | 32-514 |
| Hutt, Gordon M. | M.Sc. | 31-508 |
| Keating, Bernard J. | M.Sc. | 33-518 |
| O'Heir, Hugh B. | M.Sc. | 24-524 |
| Williamson, John T. | M.Sc. | 30-515 |
| *Bostock, Hugh S. | M.Sc. | 25-511 |
| *Carlyle, Arthur W. | M.Sc. | 23-508 |
| *Coleman, Charles L. | M.Sc. | 28-559 |
| *Dolan, Everett P. | M.Sc. | 23-511 |
| *Ellis, David H. | M.Sc. | 26-509 |
| *Finley, Frederick L. | M.Sc. | 24-514 |
| *Riordon, Charles H. | M.Sc. | 27-517 |
| Graham, W. | | |
| *Boyes, Watson | M.A. | 25-532 |
| Grasham, W. | | |
| Prives, Moshe Z. | M.A. | 55-559 |
| Gray, J. | | |
| *Waldbauer, Louis J. | Ph.D. | 23-007 |
| Gray, P. | | |
| Alarie, Albert M. | Ph.D. | 45-001 |
| Alarie, Albert M. | M.Sc. | 43-501 |
| Angus, Thomas A. | Ph.D. | 55-002 |
| Bynoe, Evan T. | M.Sc. | 31-503 |



| AUTHOR | DEGREE | THESIS NUMBER |
|---|---|---|
| Gray, P. | | |
| Chaplin, Charles E. | Ph.D. | 50-027 |
| Chase, Francis E. | Ph.D. | 51-004 |
| Dussault, H.P. | M.Sc. | 46-563 |
| Hess, Ernest | Ph.D. | 33-009 |
| Lachance, Robert A. | Ph.D. | 55-025 |
| McMaster, Norman B. | M.Sc. | 32-520 |
| Poplove, Myron | M.Sc. | 51-619 |
| Robinson, John | Ph.D. | 50-041 |
| Rogers, Charles G. | M.Sc. | 54-530 |
| Rouatt, James W. | M.Sc. | 47-524 |
| Taylor, Lester J. | M.Sc. | 52-593 |
| Taylor, Robert B. | M.Sc. | 55-541 |
| Tennant, Alan D. | Ph.D. | 55-043 |
| Thomson, Hugh M. | M.Sc. | 51-557 |
| Wallace, Raphael H. | M.Sc. | 46-581 |
| Wallace, Raphael H. | Ph.D. | 48-013 |
| Yaphe, Wilfred | Ph.D. | 52-070 |
| Greenshields, * | | |
| *Weibel, Louise E. | LL.M. | 23-500 |
| Gunn, K. | | |
| Pfalzner, Paul M. | M.Sc. | 51-617 |
| Reid, Kenneth H. | M.Sc. | 58-576 |
| Gurd, F. | | |
| Goodall, Robert G. | M.Sc. | 56-577 |
| Hall, C. | | |
| Brazeau, Joseph F. | M.A. | 51-564 |
| Fonseca, Owen W. | M.A. | 53-550 |
| Jones, Frank F. | M.A. | 50-656 |
| Lucas, Rex A. | M.A. | 50-657 |
| McKay, Huntly W. | M.A. | 50-658 |
| Potter, Harold H. | M.A. | 49-575 |
| Rennie, Douglas L. | M.A. | 53-616 |
| Robinson, Patricia G. | M.A. | 53-617 |

| AUTHOR | DEGREE | THESIS NUMBER |
|---|---|---|
| **Hall, O.** | | |
| Rodman, Hyman | M.A. | 53-618 |
| Wipper, Audrey J. | M.A. | 55-567 |
| **Harding, V.** | | |
| Howe, Laura I. | M.Sc. | 18-504 |
| *Dowler, Vernon B. | M.Sc. | 16-508 |
| *MacLean, Allison R. | Ph.D. | 16-001 |
| *Whitby, George S. | Ph.D. | 20-003 |
| *Whitby, George S. | M.Sc. | 18-507 |
| *Wieland, Walter A. | M.Sc. | 18-508 |
| **Hare, F.** | | |
| Allington, Kathleen R. | M.Sc. | 59-575 |
| Ballabon, Maurice B. | Ph.D. | 55-046 |
| Ballabon, Maurice B. | M.A. | 52-600 |
| Barry, Roger G. | M.Sc. | 59-576 |
| Belmont, Arthur D. | Ph.D. | 56-037 |
| Blake, Donald A. | M.Sc. | 48-576 |
| Blake, Weston | M.Sc. | 53-574 |
| Boville, Byron W. | M.Sc. | 58-512 |
| Burbidge, Frederick E. | M.Sc. | 49-514 |
| Butzer, K.W. | M.Sc. | 55-591 |
| Creighton, Phyllis | M.A. | 51-566 |
| Cureton, Edward A. | M.A. | 57-603 |
| Dean, William G. | Ph.D. | 59-017 |
| Drummond, Robert N. | M.Sc. | 50-604 |
| Gerard, Robert D. | M.Sc. | 55-521 |
| Humphrys, Graham | M.A. | 59-552 |
| Langlois, Jean-Claude | M.A. | 57-606 |
| MacFarlane, Mona A. | M.Sc. | 58-525 |
| McKay, Gordon A. | M.Sc. | 53-599 |
| McKay, Ian A. | M.Sc. | 56-584 |
| Michie, George H. | M.A. | 56-547 |
| Molson, Charles R. | M.A. | 54-548 |
| Montgomery, Margaret R. | M.A. | 49-641 |
| Orvig, Svenn | Ph.D. | 54-026 |
| Orvig, Svenn | M.Sc. | 51-539 |
| Page, Douglas E. | M.Sc. | 59-591 |
| Powell, John M. | M.Sc. | 59-594 |
| Ridge, Frank G. | Ph.D. | 53-070 |
| Sangree, Anne C. | M.Sc. | 53-605 |



| AUTHOR | DEGREE | THESIS NUMBER |
|---|---|---|
| **Hare, F.** | | |
| Sebor, Miles-Marie | M.A. | 55-638 |
| Sinclair, Martin H. | M.A. | 54-555 |
| Summers, William F. | Ph.D. | 57-037 |
| Summers, William F. | M.Sc. | 49-623 |
| Uren, Philip E. | M.A. | 49-645 |
| Wilson, Cynthia V. | M.Sc. | 58-535 |
| Wright, John M. | M.A. | 56-624 |
| **Harkness, J.** | | |
| *Gray, Alexander M. | M.Sc. | 16-510 |
| *Grimes, Evie M. | M.A. | 13-505 |
| *Hatcher, Albert G. | M.A. | 10-501 |
| *Honey, Howard P. | M.A. | 15-503 |
| *Lindsay, William | M.A. | 14-505 |
| *MacKenzie, Francis S. | M.A. | 16-505 |
| *MacSween, Florence F. | M.A. | 15-504 |
| *Melvin, Margaret G. | M.A. | 19-501 |
| *Meyer, Bertha | M.A. | 21-521 |
| *Miller, Iveson A. | M.Sc. | 15-511 |
| *Paterson-Smyth, Marjorie | M.Sc. | 12-517 |
| *Richardson, Lorne N. | M.Sc. | 10-520 |
| *Rowell, Arthur H. | M.A. | 12-505 |
| *Schafheitlin, Anna | M.A. | 13-509 |
| *Shanly, Eleanor | M.Sc. | 14-519 |
| *Steacy, Frederick W. | M.A. | 13-511 |
| *Steed, Joseph A. | M.A. | 18-502 |
| *Thorne, Oliver | M.A. | 12-506 |
| *Worsfold, Henry H. | M.A. | 17-503 |
| **Harpur, E.** | | |
| *Henry, A.S. | M.Sc. | 57-578 |
| **Harrison, F.** | | |
| Blau, Abraham | M.Sc. | 29-503 |
| Kennedy, Margaret E. | M.Sc. | 21-511 |
| *Atwell, Ernest A. | M.Sc. | 25-507 |
| *Carleton, Everett A. | M.Sc. | 23-507 |
| *Conklin, Raymond L. | M.Sc. | 24-511 |
| *Dickson, Bertram T. | Ph.D. | 22-001 |

| AUTHOR | DEGREE | THESIS NUMBER |
|---|---|---|
| Harrison, F. | | |
| *Dustan, Alan G. | M.Sc. | 22-504 |
| *Gough, William F. | M.Sc. | 27-504 |
| *Hamilton, William B. | M.Sc. | 28-561 |
| *Irwin, Marion L. | M.Sc. | 28-514 |
| *Johns,Cyril K. | M.Sc. | 26-514 |
| *Newton, Dorothy E. | M.Sc. | 22-518 |
| *Perry, Helen M. | M.Sc. | 24-527 |
| *Sadler, Wilfrid | M.Sc. | 17-507 |
| *Townsend, Charles T. | M.Sc. | 26-530 |
| *Vanterpool, Thomas C. | M.Sc. | 25-529 |
| *Zoond, Alexander | M.Sc. | 25-550 |
| Hatcher, W. | | |
| Bjorklund, Gordon Herber | Ph.D. | 40-001 |
| Hill, Allan C. | Ph.D. | 29-006 |
| Holden, George W. | Ph.D. | 27-005 |
| Horwood, James F. | M.Sc. | 33-517 |
| Horwood, James F. | Ph.D. | 35-014 |
| Hughes, Robert Edward | Ph.D. | 40-013 |
| Kay, Muriel G. | M.Sc. | 32-517 |
| MacLauchlan, Donald W. | Ph.D. | 37-030 |
| Mason, Clarence T. | M.Sc. | 33-523 |
| Mason, Clarence T. | Ph.D. | 35-022 |
| McDonald, Roland D. | Ph.D. | 35-020 |
| McGibbon, Ralph W. | M.Sc. | 38-545 |
| Mueller, William H. | Ph.D. | 30-009 |
| Powell, Edward C. | Ph.D. | 32-013 |
| Savard, Kenneth F.G. | M.Sc. | 42-530 |
| Sturrock, Murray G. | Ph.D. | 30-014 |
| Tomecko, Joseph Wesely | Ph.D. | 40-506 |
| Toole, Francis J. | M.Sc. | 26-529 |
| Weaver, William Strather | Ph.D. | 41-509 |
| *Holden, George W. | M.Sc. | 24-519 |
| *Howland, Frances | Ph.D. | 32-024 |
| *Leduc, Joseph A. | M.Sc. | 26-515 |
| *Mueller, William H. | M.Sc. | 29-513 |
| Haviland, W. | | |
| Jarrette, Neil M. | M.A. | 58-541 |



| AUTHOR | DEGREE | THESIS NUMBER |
|---|---|---|
| Haxter, R. | | |
| *Dustan, Alan G. | M.Sc. | 22-504 |
| Heard, F. | | |
| Aprile, Marie A. | M.Sc. | 56-512 |
| Belleau, Fernand B. | Ph.D. | 50-024 |
| Bligh, Emerson G. | Ph.D. | 56-039 |
| Cann, Malcolm C. | Ph.D. | 58-007 |
| Cann, Malcolm C. | M.Sc. | 55-592 |
| Chaput, Marcel | Ph.D. | 52-041 |
| Douglas, Donald E. | Ph.D. | 45-017 |
| Falk, Hans L. | Ph.D. | 47-004 |
| Jacobs, Ross D. | Ph.D. | 54-052 |
| Jamieson, James R. | Ph.D. | 47-031 |
| Moya, Francisco J. | Ph.D. | 53-065 |
| O'Donnell, Vincent J. | Ph.D. | 54-025 |
| Peron, Fernand G. | Ph.D. | 53-032 |
| Rao, Baindur G. | Ph.D. | 56-063 |
| Ryan, Michael T. | Ph.D. | 55-032 |
| Saffran, Judith | Ph.D. | 48-037 |
| Sainte-Marie, Dorothee L | M.Sc. | 44-510 |
| Sobel, Harry | Ph.D. | 46-014 |
| Solomon, Samuel | Ph.D. | 53-076 |
| Solomon, Samuel | M.Sc. | 51-551 |
| Stewart, Ronald D. | Ph.D. | 48-011 |
| Thompson, Lloyd M. | Ph.D. | 51-059 |
| Willoughby, Henry W. | Ph.D. | 54-074 |
| Yates, Claire H. | Ph.D. | 51-037 |
| Ziegler, Peter | Ph.D. | 51-038 |
| Zorbach, William W. | Ph.D. | 51-039 |
| Hebb, D. | | |
| Baldwin, Maitland | M.Sc. | 52-511 |
| Bexton, William H. | Ph.D. | 53-044 |
| Brougham, Norma I. | M.A. | 50-650 |
| Clarke, Ronald S. | M.Sc. | 51-601 |
| Doane, Benjamin K. | Ph.D. | 55-053 |
| Forgays, Donald G. | Ph.D. | 50-030 |
| Ghent, Lila R. | Ph.D. | 51-047 |
| Ghent, Lila R. | M.A. | 49-561 |
| Gordon, Thelma G. | M.A. | 49-631 |
| Heron, Woodburn | M.A. | 49-633 |

| AUTHOR | DEGREE | THESIS NUMBER |
|---|---|---|
| **Hebb, D.** | | |
| Hoyt, Ruth | Ph.D. | 52-019 |
| Hymovitch, Bernard | Ph.D. | 49-020 |
| Lansdell, Herbert C. | Ph.D. | 50-033 |
| Mahut, Helen | Ph.D. | 55-065 |
| Mahut, Helen | M.A. | 52-606 |
| Melzack, Ronald | Ph.D. | 54-020 |
| Melzack, Ronald | M.Sc. | 51-614 |
| Milner, Brenda A. | Ph.D. | 52-058 |
| Milner, Peter M. | Ph.D. | 54-022 |
| Milner, Peter M. | M.Sc. | 50-625 |
| Mogenson, Gordon J. | Ph.D. | 59-053 |
| Mooney, Craig M. | Ph.D. | 55-068 |
| Morrison, Gordon R. | M.Sc. | 55-616 |
| Orbach, Jack | M.A. | 50-662 |
| Scott, Thomas H. | Ph.D. | 54-065 |
| Sharpless, Seth K. | Ph.D. | 54-066 |
| Smith, Charles J. | Ph.D. | 54-067 |
| Smith, Charles J. | M.A. | 51-643 |
| Vanderwolf, Cornelius H. | M.Sc. | 59-603 |
| Wimer, Richard E. | Ph.D. | 59-075 |
| **Hemlow, J.** | | |
| Coyle, James J. | M.A. | 48-558 |
| Dale, Frances M. | M.A. | 53-609 |
| Douglas, Althea M. | M.A. | 58-538 |
| Helfield, Tilya | M.A. | 55-550 |
| Nemser, Ruby D. | M.A. | 56-548 |
| Piloto, Albert E. | M.A. | 50-574 |
| **Hemmeon, J.** | | |
| Baker, Kenneth G. | M.A. | 33-534 |
| Bloomfield, Arthur I. | M.A. | 36-524 |
| Boos, Albert W. | M.A. | 28-529 |
| Bowker, Ernest E. | M.A. | 33-538 |
| Brenhouse, Samuel E. | M.A. | 34-523 |
| Caplan, Benjamin | M.A. | 31-524 |
| Clark, Edgar H. Jr. | M.A. | 35-524 |
| Clark, Jocelyn Godfrey | M.A. | 39-031 |
| Coughlin, Clifton Rexfor | M.Com. | 39-047 |
| Cumming, Robert S. | M.A. | 38-528 |
| Duncan, Albert S. | M.A. | 38-529 |



| AUTHOR | DEGREE | THESIS NUMBER |
|---|---|---|
| **Hemmeon, J.** | | |
| Firestone, Otto Jack | M.A. | 42-510 |
| Forsey, Eugene A. | Ph.D. | 41-005 |
| Fox, Lester L. | M.Com. | 43-517 |
| Fraser, David Robert | M.A. | 39-034 |
| Gillies, Elizabeth W. | M.A. | 41-517 |
| Gilroy, Geoffrey S. | M.A. | 34-526 |
| Goldberg, Simon Abraham | M.A. | 40-028 |
| Goodman, Samuel J. | M.A. | 32-528 |
| Gordon, Thomas M. | M.A. | 28-534 |
| Graham, C. R. | M.A. | 42-512 |
| Greenlees, William S. | M.A. | 33-545 |
| Harris, Theodore H. | M.A. | 28-536 |
| Henderson, Harold Lloyd | M.A. | 41-024 |
| Hollinger, Martin | M.A. | 42-033 |
| Jack, Lawrence B. | Ph.D. | 43-008 |
| Johnson, John S. | M.A. | 34-530 |
| Jones, Randolph K. | M.A. | 24-539 |
| Kelland, Frank J. | M.A. | 29-540 |
| Kirchschlager, Hellmuth | M.A. | 40-029 |
| Lande, Harold B. | M.A. | 30-533 |
| Latham, Allan B. | M.A. | 27-534 |
| Legge, Katharine B. | M.A. | 30-535 |
| Letichevsky, Jack | M.A. | 41-026 |
| Lusher, David W. | M.A. | 33-552 |
| Luxton, Edward A. G. | M.A. | 35-530 |
| Marsh, Leonard C. | Ph.D. | 40-016 |
| McGill, John J. | M.A. | 36-544 |
| Murray, Sydney G. | M.A. | 38-540 |
| Noyes, Harry A. Jr. | M.A. | 38-541 |
| Owen, George R. | M.A. | 34-537 |
| Petrie, Richards J. | Ph.D. | 41-013 |
| Pick, Alfred J. | M.A. | 37-530 |
| Reid, Ewart P. | M.A. | 32-541 |
| Reisman, Sol | M.A. | 42-039 |
| Rollit, John B. | M.A. | 32-543 |
| Rollit, John B. | Ph.D. | 34-011 |
| Rountree, George M. | M.A. | 33-557 |
| Rubin, Lionel L. | M.A. | 31-541 |
| Sirken, Irving A. | M.A. | 43-515 |
| Stone, Fred V. | M.A. | 33-559 |
| Stovel, John Archibald | M.A. | 41-522 |
| Tetrault, Claude Moncel | M.A. | 40-032 |
| Willard, Eugene W. | M.A. | 24-547 |
| *Best, Kathleen F. | M.A. | 30-517 |
| *Bissett, Alice M. | M.A. | 27-522 |

| AUTHOR | DEGREE | THESIS NUMBER |
|---|---|---|
| **Hemmeon, J.** | | |
| *Brownstein, Charles | M.A. | 25-533 |
| *Carroll, Lovell C. | M.A. | 30-521 |
| *Cheasley, Clifford H. | M.A. | 29-526 |
| *Cohen, Bernard B. | M.A. | 30-523 |
| *Cousins, George V. | M.A. | 08-501 |
| *Draper, Herbert L. | M.A. | 29-528 |
| *Epstein, Elsie | M.A. | 29-529 |
| *Goldenberg, Hyman C. | M.A. | 29-533 |
| *Gruchy, Allan G. | M.A. | 29-534 |
| *Harris, Norman C. | M.Sc. | 11-512 |
| *Jamieson, John S. | M.A. | C8-502 |
| *Janes, Henry F. | M.A. | 27-533 |
| *Kirschberg, Abraham | M.A. | 29-541 |
| *Levy, Gordon W. | M.A. | 26-546 |
| *MacCrimmon, John R. | M.A. | 09-504 |
| *McFarlane, Duncan H. | M.A. | 26-547 |
| *Mendels, Morton M. | M.A. | 29-546 |
| *Nichol, Helen R. | M.A. | 21-523 |
| *Nichol, Jean | M.A. | 25-538 |
| *Peterson, Frederick C. | M.A. | 24-543 |
| *Reed, John G. | M.A. | 29-547 |
| *Renaud, Paul E. | M.A. | 23-526 |
| *Stalker, Archibald | M.A. | 13-510 |
| *Tanner, Lea E. | M.A. | 30-548 |
| *Troop, George R. | M.A. | 22-529 |
| *Troop, William H. | M.A. | 29-550 |
| *Woods, Harry D. | M.A. | 31-549 |
| *Young, Charles H. | M.A. | 28-558 |
| **Hemmeon, J. .** | | |
| *Forsey, Eugene A. | M.A. | 26-541 |
| **Hendel, C.** | | |
| Currie, Cecil | M.A. | 33-544 |
| Fleer, Edward Herman | M.A. | 39-033 |
| Lipton, Charles | M.A. | 39-041 |
| Mallin, Estelle C. | M.A. | 36-538 |
| *Gough, Roger W. | M.A. | 30-527 |
| *Hewitt, Frank S. | M.A. | 31-533 |
| *Jenkins, Lloyd H. | M.A. | 30-532 |
| *MacMillan, Donald N. | M.A. | 30-536 |



| AUTHOR | DEGREE | THESIS NUMBER |
|---|---|---|
| **Hendel, C.** | | |
| *Pursley, Robert | M.A. | 30-542 |
| **Henderson, T.** | | |
| Benn, Doris E. | M.A. | 48-606 |
| Lachs, John | M.A. | 57-548 |
| **Herdt, L.** | | |
| *Bierler, Etienne S. | M.Sc. | 20-503 |
| *Hague, Owen C. | M.Sc. | 14-513 |
| *McNaughton, Andrew G. | M.Sc. | 12-514 |
| *Murphy, William H. | M.Sc. | 15-512 |
| *Scott, Arthur A. | M.Sc. | 13-520 |
| *Trimingham, James H. | M.Sc. | 20-508 |
| *Wallace, George A. | M.Sc. | 21-517 |
| *Williams, Frederick H. | M.Sc. | 21-518 |
| **Heron, W.** | | |
| Bryden, Mark P. | M.Sc. | 58-514 |
| Burns, Neal M. | Ph.D. | 59-008 |
| Hogg, Doreen | M.A. | 57-604 |
| **Hibbert, H.** | | |
| Allen, John S. | Ph.D. | 32-019 |
| Ashford, Walter R. | Ph.D. | 43-001 |
| Baker, Samuel B. | Ph.D. | 43-017 |
| Ball, Ralph H. | Ph.D. | 31-002 |
| Barsha, Jacob | Ph.D. | 33-002 |
| Bell, Alan | Ph.D. | 37-002 |
| Bower, John R. | Ph.D. | 43-003 |
| Brewer, Charles P. | Ph.D. | 43-018 |
| Brickman, Leo | Ph.D. | 40-002 |
| Brocklesby, Horace N. | Ph.D. | 35-006 |
| Buckland, Irene K. | Ph.D. | 34-004 |
| Cocke, Lloyd Miller | Ph.D. | 41-002 |
| Cramer, Archie Barrett | Ph.D. | 39-004 |
| Creighton, Robert H. | Ph.D. | 43-004 |
| Dorland, Rodger M. | Ph.D. | 39-005 |

| AUTHOR | DEGREE | THESIS NUMBER |
|---|---|---|
| Hibbert, H. | | |
| Dorman, Robert W. | M.Sc. | 36-546 |
| Eastham, Arthur M. | Ph.D. | 43-005 |
| Evans, Taylor H. | Ph.D. | 41-503 |
| Fisher, Herbert E. | Ph.D. | 43-020 |
| Fisher, John Henry | Ph.D. | 41-004 |
| Fordyce, Reid George | Ph.D. | 39-008 |
| Fowler, Frances L. | Ph.D. | 36-005 |
| Gallaugher, Arthur F. | Ph.D. | 32-004 |
| Godard, Hugh Phillips | Ph.D. | 41-008 |
| Gray, Kenneth R. | Ph.D. | 34-020 |
| Greig, Margaret E. | Ph.D. | 32-022 |
| Hallonquist, Earland G. | Ph.D. | 33-006 |
| Hawkins, Walter L. | Ph.D. | 38-008 |
| Hewson, William B. | Ph.D. | 42-013 |
| Hunter, Melvin J. | Ph.D. | 39-011 |
| Jahn, Edwin C. | Ph.D. | 29-007 |
| Johnston, Harry W. | M.Sc. | 27-508 |
| King, Ellis G. | Ph.D. | 34-021 |
| Kulka, Marshall | Ph.D. | 42-501 |
| Leger, Francis J. | Ph.D. | 38-010 |
| Levi, Irving | Ph.D. | 42-015 |
| Lieff, Morris | Ph.D. | 38-011 |
| Lovell, Edwin Lister | Ph.D. | 40-015 |
| Mackinney, Herbert W. | M.Sc. | 33-522 |
| Mackinney, Herbert W. | Ph.D. | 35-031 |
| MacGregor, Warren S. | Ph.D. | 43-009 |
| MacInnes, Alexander S. | Ph.D. | 41-010 |
| Marion, Leo E. | Ph.D. | 29-009 |
| Marshall, Harry B. | Ph.D. | 34-022 |
| McCarthy, Joseph L. | Ph.D. | 38-012 |
| Mead, Bruce R. | Ph.D. | 43-010 |
| Moore, Leonard P. | Ph.D. | 33-014 |
| Moore, Ralph G. | Ph.D. | 36-018 |
| Neish, Arthur C. | Ph.D. | 42-020 |
| Paquet, Arthur | M.Sc. | 30-510 |
| Patterson, Ralph Francis | Ph.D. | 42-505 |
| Peniston, Quintin Pearma | Ph.D. | 39-019 |
| Pepper, James M. | Ph.D. | 43-023 |
| Perry, Stanley Z. | Ph.D. | 38-022 |
| Phillips, John B. | Ph.D. | 30-011 |
| Phillips, John B. | M.Sc. | 28-522 |
| Platt, Muriel E. | Ph.D. | 32-012 |
| Platt, Muriel E. | M.Sc. | 29-516 |
| Plunguian, Mark | Ph.D. | 34-023 |
| Pullman, Joseph C. | M.Sc. | 33-526 |



| AUTHOR | DEGREE | THESIS NUMBER |
|---|---|---|
| Hibbert, H. | | |
| Pullman, Joseph C. | Ph.D. | 35-032 |
| Pyle, James Johnston | Ph.D. | 39-021 |
| Powley, Harry J. | Ph.D. | 29-012 |
| Sankey, Charles A. | Ph.D. | 30-013 |
| Sankey, Charles A. | M.Sc. | 28-523 |
| Schwartz, Harry | Ph.D. | 39-502 |
| Starrock, Murray G. | M.Sc. | 29-518 |
| Steeves, William H. | Ph.D. | 36-013 |
| Swartz, Joseph N. | Ph.D. | 37-023 |
| Tarr, Hugh L. | Ph.D. | 31-009 |
| Taylor, Kenneth A. | Ph.D. | 29-014 |
| Tomlinson, George H. | Ph.D. | 35-026 |
| Trister, Saul M. | Ph.D. | 34-018 |
| West, Einar | Ph.D. | 42-507 |
| West, Kenneth A. | Ph.D. | 42-027 |
| Whelen, Myron S. | Ph.D. | 29-016 |
| White, Elwood V. | Ph.D. | 36-015 |
| White, Elwood V. | M.Sc. | 34-519 |
| Zuckerman, Abraham | Ph.D. | 43-024 |
| *Carter, Neal M. | Ph.D. | 29-003 |
| *Gallay, Wilfred | Ph.D. | 30-003 |
| *Hill, Allan C. | M.Sc. | 27-542 |
| *Houghton, Edward O. | M.Sc. | 27-507 |
| *Moore, Leonard P. | M.Sc. | 30-509 |
| *Perry, Stanley Z. | M.Sc. | 29-515 |
| *Pidgeon, Lloyd M. | M.Sc. | 27-541 |
| *Shotwell, John S. | M.Sc. | 26-559 |
| *White, Thomas N. | M.Sc. | 27-521 |
| Hickson, J. | | |
| *Brittain, Isabel E. | M.A. | 11-501 |
| *Honey, Howard P. | M.A. | 15-503 |
| *Livinson, Abraham J. | M.A. | 16-503 |
| *McCormack, George J. | M.A. | 16-504 |
| *Melvin, Margaret G. | M.A. | 19-501 |
| *Powles, Percival S. | M.A. | 14-507 |
| *Wilson, Alice M. | M.A. | 11-504 |
| *Wiseman, Solomon | M.A. | 23-527 |
| Higgins, B. | | |
| Amyot, Denis F. | M.A. | 48-555 |

| AUTHOR | DEGREE | THESIS NUMBER |
|---|---|---|
| **Higgins, B.** | | |
| Bacarinos, Eusthathics S | M.A. | 51-630 |
| Caralopoulos, Nicholas | M.A. | 51-565 |
| Guter, Ernest | M.A. | 47-532 |
| Rothschild, Fred | M.A. | 46-549 |
| Van Holsbeek, Henri M. | M.Com. | 48-571 |
| **Hills, T.** | | |
| Gordon, Llewelyn | M.A. | 55-630 |
| Lotz, James R. | M.Sc. | 57-532 |
| Power, Graham C. | M.A. | 59-617 |
| Smith, Samuel I. | M.A. | 55-639 |
| **Hitschfeld, W.** | | |
| Dennis, Arnett S. | Ph.D. | 55-052 |
| **Hobkirk, R.** | | |
| Givner, Morris L. | Ph.D. | 59-028 |
| **Hoff, H.** | | |
| Dso, Li-Liang | M.Sc. | 48-517 |
| Gertler, Menard M. | M.Sc. | 46-518 |
| Gold, Simon | M.Sc. | 45-530 |
| Johnson, Arnold L. | M.Sc. | 47-554 |
| Kellaway, Peter E. | Ph.D. | 47-009 |
| Lathe, Grant H. | Ph.D. | 47-010 |
| Levitan, Benjamin A. | M.Sc. | 48-588 |
| Wener, Joseph | M.Sc. | 48-553 |
| **Hoffman, M.** | | |
| Cohen, Herman | M.Sc. | 45-524 |
| Kalant, Norman | Ph.D. | 54-053 |
| Maximchuk, Arlene J. | M.Sc. | 56-532 |
| McKendry, John B. | M.Sc. | 49-609 |
| Morgen, Robert O. | M.Sc. | 56-591 |
| Rosenberg, Gilbert | M.Sc. | 56-598 |



| AUTHOR | DEGREE | THESIS NUMBER |
|---|---|---|
| **Hoffman, M.** | | |
| Sabin, Israel M. | M.Sc. | 46-577 |
| Singer, Bertha | M.Sc. | 49-620 |
| Sodhi, Harbhajan S. | M.Sc. | 58-578 |
| Stollmeyer, John F. | M.Sc. | 47-571 |
| Walsh, George C. | M.Sc. | 49-625 |
| Wilansky, Douglas L. | M.Sc. | 57-541 |
| Wiseman, Miriam H. | M.Sc. | 56-610 |
| **Holcomb, R.** | | |
| Engineer, Behram B. | M.Sc. | 50-523 |
| **Hood, E.** | | |
| *Johns,Cyril K. | M.Sc. | 26-514 |
| *Townsend, Charles T. | M.Sc. | 26-530 |
| **Hosein, E.** | | |
| Eisenstein, Sam | M.Sc. | 59-582 |
| Powell, Elizabeth A. | M.Sc. | 59-593 |
| **Howard, *** | | |
| *Brown, Richard C. | M.A. | 27-524 |
| *Renaud, Paul E. | LL.M. | 22-500 |
| **Howard, C.** | | |
| *Mills, Edward S. | M.Sc. | 26-519 |
| **Howes, F.** | | |
| Adderson, James N. | M.Eng. | 55-502 |
| Bastin, Douglas H. | M.Eng. | 46-550 |
| Bennett, John R. | M.Eng. | 49-501 |
| Boire, Paul C. | M.Eng. | 49-502 |
| Bott, Raoul H. | M.Eng. | 46-551 |
| Bourne, James D. | M.Eng. | 48-504 |

| AUTHOR | DEGREE | THESIS NUMBER |
|---|---|---|
| **Howes, F.** | | |
| Bredahl, Arve | M.Eng. | 56-554 |
| Carruthers, Frederick R. | M.Eng. | 53-560 |
| Chess, Gordon F. | M.Eng. | 54-562 |
| Chipman, Robert A. | M.Eng. | 33-500 |
| Chipps, George E. | M.Eng. | 56-555 |
| Clark, George D. | M.Eng. | 52-561 |
| Davis, John F. | M.Eng. | 49-586 |
| Farmer, Eric W. | M.Eng. | 43-500 |
| Filman, Norman J. | M.Eng. | 46-554 |
| Fisher, Charles B. | M.Eng. | 33-565 |
| Geddes, Leslie A. | M.Eng. | 53-561 |
| Gribble, William F. | M.Eng. | 51-586 |
| Groome, George R. | M.Eng. | 52-502 |
| Hall, J.S. | M.Eng. | 48-506 |
| Hayes, John E. | M.Eng. | 47-503 |
| Hayles, Oliver J. | M.Eng. | 50-584 |
| Howe, Lawrence M. | M.Eng. | 35-502 |
| Ives, Walter J. | M.Eng. | 46-555 |
| Jaderholm, Henrik W. | M.Eng. | 33-502 |
| Javid, Mansour | M.Eng. | 50-585 |
| Kahn, Juan P. | M.Eng. | 56-508 |
| Kelsey, Ernest S. | M.Eng. | 33-567 |
| Kelton, Michel R. | M.Eng. | 52-564 |
| Kubina, S.J. | M.Eng. | 57-508 |
| Marshall, James L. | M.Eng. | 49-507 |
| Martin, William S. | M.Eng. | 52-505 |
| Matusiak, Marvin E. | M.Eng. | 53-564 |
| Merson, Lawrence N. | M.Eng. | 47-504 |
| Nachfolger, Nathan | M.Eng. | 49-508 |
| Nevitt, Henry J. | M.Eng. | 45-501 |
| Pavlasek, Tomas J. | Ph.D. | 58-033 |
| Pavlasek, Tomas J. | M.Eng. | 48-509 |
| Penton, Reginald | M.Eng. | 54-566 |
| Puxley, Ann E. | M.Sc. | 50-553 |
| Real, Roderick R. | M.Eng. | 57-511 |
| Rioux, Philip G. | M.Eng. | 49-509 |
| Rosen, Charles A. | M.Eng. | 50-592 |
| Shkarofsky, Issie | M.Sc. | 53-606 |
| Smith, David L. | M.Eng. | 50-593 |
| Stachiewicz, Bogdan F. | M.Eng. | 53-565 |
| Tatlock, John F. | M.Eng. | 51-507 |
| Von Hagen, Wallace M. | M.Eng. | 59-505 |
| Zenner, Gerhard P. | M.Eng. | 59-507 |



| AUTHOR | DEGREE | THESIS NUMBER |
|---|---|---|
| **Hughes, E.** | | |
| Gibbard, Harold A. | M.A. | 34-547 |
| Jamieson, Stuart M. | M.A. | 38-533 |
| Kerry, Esther Wilson | M.A. | 39-037 |
| Lieff, Pearl | M.A. | 40-030 |
| Moellmann, Albert | M.A. | 35-532 |
| Ramsden, Mary E. | M.A. | 33-574 |
| Roy, William J. | M.A. | 35-548 |
| *Stansfield, Ellen F. | M.A. | 31-543 |
| **Hughes, J.** | | |
| Astbury, John S. | M.A. | 38-550 |
| Bercuson, Leonard | M.A. | 41-019 |
| Farrell, Edna P. | M.A. | 54-542 |
| Ferrabee, Henry G. | M.A. | 53-610 |
| Flower, George E. | M.A. | 49-558 |
| Gallagher, John | M.A. | 41-516 |
| Hamilton, Lorne D. | M.A. | 45-514 |
| Henry, Arthur M. | M.A. | 38-530 |
| Hurst, Norman | M.A. | 53-551 |
| Lynam, Josephine B. | M.A. | 47-579 |
| MacLean, Mona G. | M.A. | 45-517 |
| McLeish, John A. | M.A. | 48-616 |
| Munroe, William M. | M.A. | 46-544 |
| Oulton, Rhodes C. | M.A. | 55-637 |
| Rexford, Orrin B. | M.A. | 36-552 |
| Ross, Harold | M.A. | 47-581 |
| Saunders, Thomas B. | M.A. | 48-617 |
| Shearman, George F. | M.A. | 53-619 |
| Sheffield, Edward Fletch | M.A. | 40-049 |
| Thompson, Winifred | M.A. | 35-536 |
| Zweig, David N. | M.A. | 49-647 |
| **Humphrey, J.** | | |
| Lussier, Claude | M.C.L. | 46-501 |
| **Hurlblatt, *** | | |
| *Forster, David S. | M.A. | 45-502 |

Huskins, C.

| AUTHOR | DEGREE | THESIS NUMBER |
|---|---|---|
| Armstrong, John M. | Ph.D. | 33-001 |
| Bauer, Donald de F. | M.Sc. | 43-503 |
| Blain, Auray | Ph.D. | 45-015 |
| Boothroyd, Eric R. | Ph.D. | 43-002 |
| Boothroyd, Eric R. | M.Sc. | 40-517 |
| Entin, Martin A. | M.Sc. | 42-052 |
| Gfeller, Frederick | M.Sc. | 36-511 |
| Glickman, Irwin | M.Sc. | 45-528 |
| Hearne, Edna M. | Ph.D. | 33-028 |
| Hecht, Maurice | M.Sc. | 42-525 |
| Howard, Alma C. | Ph.D. | 38-009 |
| Hunter, Albert W. | Ph.D. | 37-011 |
| Hunter, Albert W. | M.Sc. | 34-511 |
| Johnson, Robert E. | M.Sc. | 32-516 |
| Kerr, Ernest A. | M.Sc. | 41-042 |
| Love, Robert M. | Ph.D. | 35-030 |
| Newcombe, Howard B. | Ph.D. | 39-015 |
| Sander, Hans G.F. | Ph.D. | 39-024 |
| Shapiro, Stanley K. | M.Sc. | 45-538 |
| Smith, Stanley G. | Ph.D. | 38-017 |
| Smith, Stanley G. | M.Sc. | 36-517 |
| Sparrow, Arnold H. | Ph.D. | 41-016 |
| Spier, Jane D. | Ph.D. | 35-033 |
| Wilson, George Bernard | Ph.D. | 39-027 |
| Wright, Annie Mary | M.Sc. | 41-052 |

Jackson, J.

| AUTHOR | DEGREE | THESIS NUMBER |
|---|---|---|
| Betts, Donald D. | Ph.D. | 55-048 |
| Chapdelaine, Joseph L. | M.Sc. | 56-515 |
| Matsas, Loucas C. | M.Eng. | 55-577 |
| Reeves, Hubert | M.Sc. | 56-536 |
| Schiff, Harry | Ph.D. | 53-035 |
| Smith, Robert C. | M.Sc. | 56-538 |
| Vosko, Seymour H. | M.Sc. | 53-545 |

Jacoby, H.

| AUTHOR | DEGREE | THESIS NUMBER |
|---|---|---|
| *Von Abo, Cecil V. | Ph.D. | 22-002 |

James, F.



James, F.

| AUTHOR | DEGREE | THESIS NUMBER |
|---|---|---|
| MacIntosh, Robert M. | M.A. | 49-572 |

Jamieson, F.

| AUTHOR | DEGREE | THESIS NUMBER |
|---|---|---|
| Chow, David Y. | M.Eng. | 53-506 |
| Craig, Carleton | M.Eng. | 34-540 |
| De Stein, Joseph L. | M.Eng. | 46-552 |
| Evans, Delano E. | M.Eng. | 33-501 |
| Freeman, Paul O. | M.Eng. | 46-502 |
| Griffiths, George H. | M.Eng. | 38-501 |
| Hamilton, Donald M. | M.Eng. | 36-500 |
| Hum, Thed Klung | M.Eng. | 39-051 |
| Jehu, Llewellyn | M.Eng. | 34-502 |
| Joly, George W. | M.Eng. | 50-586 |
| Kirk, William D. | M.Eng. | 36-545 |
| Lorimer, Harry F. | M.Eng. | 52-504 |
| Lupton, Mac J. | M.Eng. | 36-502 |
| Pimenoff, Clement J. | M.Eng. | 32-553 |
| Poole, Gordon D. | M.Eng. | 36-505 |
| Prado, Eline S. | M.Sc. | 48-541 |
| Seto, Kin | M.Eng. | 40-036 |
| *McDougall, John F. | M.Sc. | 31-555 |

Jasper, H.

| AUTHOR | DEGREE | THESIS NUMBER |
|---|---|---|
| Austin, George M. | M.Sc. | 51-508 |
| Baxter, Donald W. | M.Sc. | 53-571 |
| Branch, Charles L. | M.Sc. | 58-513 |
| Courtois, Guy A. | M.Sc. | 49-600 |
| Cure, Charles W. | M.Sc. | 48-516 |
| Fortuyn, Jan D. | M.Sc. | 47-511 |
| Gloor, Peter | Ph.D. | 57-012 |
| Lende, Richard A. | M.Sc. | 56-525 |
| Li, Choh-luh | Ph.D. | 54-017 |
| Morrell, Frank | M.Sc. | 55-614 |
| Rayport, Mark | Ph.D. | 58-036 |
| Rothballer, Alan B. | M.Sc. | 55-620 |
| Sinha, Sharda P. | M.Sc. | 59-536 |
| Sloan, Norman | M.Sc. | 49-622 |
| Stewart, Lever F. | M.Sc. | 56-604 |
| Stratford, Joseph G. | M.Sc. | 51-554 |
| Ziegler, James E. | M.Sc. | 49-553 |

| AUTHOR | DEGREE | THESIS NUMBER |
|---|---|---|
| **Jefferis, J.** | | |
| Fraser, Arnold W. | M.A. | 50-565 |
| **Johnson, F.** | | |
| Holcomb, Robert K. | Ph.D. | 33-010 |
| Maass, Carol E. | Ph.D. | 27-007 |
| McCubbin, John W. | Ph.D. | 35-019 |
| Sawyer, William R. | Ph.D. | 31-013 |
| Steacie, Edgar W. | Ph.D. | 26-006 |
| Toole, Francis J. | Ph.D. | 29-015 |
| *Bishop, Eric G. | M.Sc. | 24-508 |
| *Bostock, Hugh S. | M.Sc. | 25-511 |
| *Buxton, Kenneth S. | Ph.D. | 30-015 |
| *Cave, Allister E. | M.Sc. | 25-547 |
| *Davidson, Stanley C. | M.Sc. | 25-513 |
| *Gegg, Richard C. | M.Sc. | 24-516 |
| *Greaves, Clifford | Ph.D. | 23-003 |
| *Greaves, Clifford | M.Sc. | 22-509 |
| *Hachey, Henry B. | M.Sc. | 25-519 |
| *Larose, Paul | Ph.D. | 25-004 |
| *Larose, Paul | M.Sc. | 23-514 |
| *Legg, Roland E. | M.Sc. | 24-521 |
| *McFarlane, Nathaniel C. | M.Sc. | 21-512 |
| *Mitchell, Claude R. | M.Sc. | 28-520 |
| *Munro, Lloyd A. | Ph.D. | 26-007 |
| *Patton, Isabelle J. | M.Sc. | 24-550 |
| *Powell, Allan T. | M.Sc. | 25-525 |
| *Steacie, Edgar W. | M.Sc. | 24-532 |
| *Wilson, Harold S. | M.Sc. | 25-530 |
| **Johnson, L.** | | |
| Chappel, Clifford I. | M.Sc. | 53-518 |
| McGarry, Eleanor E. | M.Sc. | 51-534 |
| **Johnson, W.** | | |
| *Knowles, Eustace C. | M.A. | 29-542 |
| **Jolliffe, A.** | | |



| AUTHOR | DEGREE | THESIS NUMBER |
|---|---|---|
| **Jolliffe, A.** | | |
| Christie, Archibald M. | Ph.D. | 47-024 |
| Jooste, Rene F. | Ph.D. | 49-022 |
| Jooste, Rene F. | M.Sc. | 47-555 |
| Kirkland, Robert W. | M.Sc. | 47-515 |
| McAllister, Arnold I. | M.Sc. | 48-532 |
| McDougall, David J. | M.Sc. | 49-537 |
| Mulligan, Robert | M.Sc. | 48-538 |
| Woolverton, Ralph S. | M.Sc. | 50-562 |
| Yu, Pei-Liang | M.Sc. | 48-604 |
| **Joly, G.** | | |
| Goldman, Carl | M.Eng. | 55-573 |
| **Jones, F.** | | |
| Hoffman, William H. | M.Sc. | 50-531 |
| **Kalz, G.** | | |
| Cahn, Shirley | M.Sc. | 53-578 |
| Comtois, Romuald D. | M.Sc. | 52-519 |
| Hall, Nancy C. | M.Sc. | 50-527 |
| Johnston, Constance A. | M.Sc. | 52-578 |
| Nommik, Salme | M.Sc. | 52-538 |
| Ramamurti, Dharmapuri V. | Ph.D. | 56-062 |
| Speers, Robert | Ph.D. | 57-079 |
| Speers, Robert | M.Sc. | 56-539 |
| Yurack, Joseph A. | Ph.D. | 56-070 |
| Yurack, Joseph A. | M.Sc. | 54-606 |
| **Kaufman, H.** | | |
| Herschorn, Michael | Ph.D. | 58-019 |
| Herschorn, Michael | M.A. | 56-618 |
| Melamed, Samuel | Ph.D. | 57-067 |
| Melamed, Samuel | M.Sc. | 53-539 |
| **Keirstead, B.** | | |

| AUTHOR | DEGREE | THESIS NUMBER |
|---|---|---|
| **Keirstead, B.** | | |
| Albert, Ruth R. | M.A. | 46-582 |
| Armstrong, Donald E. | Ph.D. | 54-004 |
| Corbett, David C. | Ph.D. | 54-044 |
| Gerin-Lajoie, Jean | Ph.D. | 53-053 |
| Murty, Grandhi V. | Ph.D. | 54-059 |
| Nielsen, Niels H. | M.A. | 54-550 |
| Pennie, T.E. | M.A. | 54-551 |
| Quinn, Herbert F. | M.A. | 46-589 |
| Weldon, John C. | Ph.D. | 52-066 |
| Wiseman, Sylvia | Ph.D. | 54-075 |
| Wolfe, Nathan | M.A. | 49-646 |
| **Kellogg, C.** | | |
| Black, Percy | M.Sc. | 46-508 |
| Clarke, Douglas B. | M.A. | 43-521 |
| De Jersey, Murray G. | M.A. | 46-539 |
| Etziony, Mordecai | M.A. | 31-529 |
| Gagnon, Aurele | M.A. | 42-031 |
| Gottheil, Edward | M.A. | 48-561 |
| Hebb, Donald O. | M.A. | 32-530 |
| Laxer, Robert Mendel | M.A. | 39-507 |
| Mitchell, Mary V. | M.Sc. | 42-063 |
| Morton, Nelson W. | Ph.D. | 33-030 |
| Norris, Kenneth E. | Ph.D. | 39-016 |
| Parsons, John G. | M.Sc. | 46-529 |
| Reid, David B. | M.A. | 46-546 |
| Shane, Gerald S. | M.A. | 42-043 |
| Spearman, Donald | M.A. | 43-528 |
| Stevenson, James A. | M.A. | 38-555 |
| Woo, Wesley Stewart | M.A. | 40-514 |
| *Cardonsky, Mary | M.A. | 29-525 |
| *Edel, Joseph L. | M.A. | 28-532 |
| *Howat, David | M.A. | 29-536 |
| *MacPherson, John T. | M.A. | 28-547 |
| *Norris, Kenneth E. | M.A. | 31-538 |
| *Spence, Kenneth W. | M.A. | 30-546 |
| **Kelly, C.** | | |
| Baker, Harold A. | M.Sc. | 52-568 |
| Butler, Ralph | M.Sc. | 55-590 |
| Cain, Robert M. | M.Sc. | 51-514 |



| AUTHOR | DEGREE | THESIS NUMBER |
|---|---|---|
| **Kelly, C.** | | |
| Carter, Sharon E. | M.Sc. | 49-517 |
| MacLennan, Louise Isabel | M.Sc. | 42-062 |
| Pawlikowska, Anna M. | M.Sc. | 49-543 |
| **Kemp, H.** | | |
| *Best, Kathleen E. | M.A. | 30-517 |
| *Blumenstein, Jacob H. | M.A. | 25-531 |
| *Burk, Christopher A. | M.A. | 30-519 |
| *Carroll, Lovell C. | M.A. | 30-521 |
| *Cheasley, Clifford H. | M.A. | 29-526 |
| *Cohen, Bernard B. | M.A. | 30-523 |
| *Forsey, Eugene A. | M.A. | 26-541 |
| *Goldenberg, Hyman C. | M.A. | 29-533 |
| *Greaves, Ida C. | M.A. | 30-528 |
| *Gruchy, Allan G. | M.A. | 29-534 |
| *Hamilton, Andrew W. | M.A. | 30-529 |
| *Johnston, Agnew H. | M.A. | 29-539 |
| *Kirschberg, Abraham | M.A. | 29-541 |
| *Mendels, Morton M. | M.A. | 29-546 |
| *Savage, Mae L. | M.A. | 30-544 |
| **Kemp, H. R.** | | |
| *Draper, Herbert L. | M.A. | 29-528 |
| **Kemp, J.** | | |
| *Dowling, Donaldson B. | M.Sc. | 21-505 |
| **Kemp, M.** | | |
| Burnett, Alvin A. | M.A. | 56-614 |
| Davoud, Raymond I. | M.Com. | 54-628 |
| Goracz, Bela A. | M.A. | 53-611 |
| Henry, Zin A. | M.A. | 55-551 |
| Marshall, Joyce A. | M.Com. | 55-568 |
| Mieszkowski, Peter M. | M.A. | 59-614 |
| Subroto | M.A. | 56-551 |

| AUTHOR | DEGREE | THESIS NUMBER |
|---|---|---|
| **Kershman, J.** | | |
| Lewis, Revis C. | M.Sc. | 50-542 |
| **Keys, D.** | | |
| Black, Robson H. | M.Sc. | 46-509 |
| Fu, Cheng-Yi | M.Sc. | 41-041 |
| Hardie, Robert H. | M.Sc. | 46-570 |
| Heard, Jack F. | M.A. | 30-530 |
| Henderson, John T. | M.Sc. | 28-511 |
| Katzman, John | Ph.D. | 33-011 |
| Katzman, John | M.Sc. | 30-505 |
| Knowles, John W. | Ph.D. | 48-027 |
| Quinn, Hubert F. | M.Sc. | 46-532 |
| Ross, William B. | M.Sc. | 31-515 |
| Smith, Philip D. | M.Sc. | 36-518 |
| Wagner, Sydney | M.Sc. | 48-551 |
| Watson, Horace G. | Ph.D. | 32-027 |
| *Helwig, Gerald V. | M.Sc. | 29-509 |
| *Jane, Robert S. | Ph.D. | 25-003 |
| *MacLeod, Malcolm D. | M.Sc. | 28-517 |
| *Morton, Richard | M.Sc. | 31-556 |
| *Sutherland, Brian P. | M.Sc. | 26-527 |
| *Watson, Horace G. | M.Sc. | 27-520 |
| *Young, John M. | M.Sc. | 28-526 |
| **Kiang, K.** | | |
| Taylor, Gordon R. | M.A. | 33-560 |
| **Kimble, G.** | | |
| Johnston, C. Meredith | M.A. | 50-568 |
| **King, L.** | | |
| Lyons, Walter | M.Sc. | 32-519 |
| *Bierler, Etienne S. | M.Sc. | 20-503 |
| *Douglas, Allie V. | M.Sc. | 21-503 |
| *Flahault, Elizabeth | M.A. | 31-531 |
| *Herzberg, Otto W. | M.Sc. | 18-505 |
| *Lane, Cecil T. | Ph.D. | 29-018 |



| AUTHOR | DEGREE | THESIS NUMBER |
|---|---|---|
| **King, L.** | | |
| *LeNeveu, Arthur P. | M.Sc. | 25-522 |
| *Russell, John | M.Sc. | 18-506 |
| *Silver, Ralph C. | M.Sc. | 29-519 |
| *Smith, Letha A. | M.Sc. | 21-515 |
| **King, L. .** | | |
| *Fan, Paul C. | M.Sc. | 25-516 |
| **Kirkaldy, J.** | | |
| Youdelis, William V. | M.Eng. | 56-563 |
| **Klein, A.** | | |
| MacCallan, William D. | M.A. | 49-571 |
| **Klibansky, R.** | | |
| Bennett, Richard L. | M.A. | 48-607 |
| Gombay, Andre M. | M.A. | 55-548 |
| Kushner, Eva M. | M.A. | 50-569 |
| Moser, Shia | M.A. | 52-551 |
| **Klinck, H.** | | |
| Lukosevicius, Petras P. | M.Sc. | 56-526 |
| Thorne, Kenrick H. | M.Sc. | 56-607 |
| **Knowles, F.** | | |
| Jones, Graham A. | M.Sc. | 58-568 |
| **Kobernick, S.** | | |
| Gordon, Dina | M.Sc. | 52-573 |

| AUTHOR | DEGREE | THESIS NUMBER |
|---|---|---|
| **Kohler, E** | | |
| *Carter, Neal M. | Ph.D. | 29-003 |
| **Kozakiewicz, W.** | | |
| Cavadias, George | M.Sc. | 59-513 |
| Cunia, T. | M.Sc. | 57-569 |
| Ferguson, Donald C. | M.A. | 58-582 |
| Hodge, Cullen S. | M.A. | 50-567 |
| Lavallee, John | Ph.D. | 55-063 |
| Tiffin, Brian F. | M.Sc. | 53-544 |
| Tomiuk, Daniel | M.Sc. | 52-594 |
| **Kranck, E.** | | |
| Anderson, Francis D. | M.Sc. | 51-594 |
| Antrobus, Edmund S. | M.Sc. | 49-511 |
| Blake, Donald A. | Ph.D. | 52-039 |
| Cooper, Gerald E. | Ph.D. | 53-004 |
| Cooper, Gerald E. | M.Sc. | 51-602 |
| De Romer, Henry | M.Sc. | 56-517 |
| Deland, Andre N. | M.Sc. | 52-520 |
| Eade, Kenneth E. | Ph.D. | 55-014 |
| Emo, Wallace B. | Ph.D. | 57-053 |
| Emo, Wallace B. | M.Sc. | 55-599 |
| Ferguson, John | M.Sc. | 58-518 |
| Findlay, David C. | M.Sc. | 58-519 |
| Freeman, Peter V. | Ph.D. | 57-011 |
| Gerryts, Edbert | Ph.D. | 51-011 |
| Gillett, Laurie B. | M.Sc. | 56-520 |
| Grant, Ian C. | M.Sc. | 52-526 |
| Hamilton, Erwin C. | M.Sc. | 53-590 |
| Hofmann, Hans J. | M.Sc. | 59-520 |
| Hogg, William A. | Ph.D. | 59-037 |
| Horscroft, Frank D. | Ph.D. | 57-019 |
| Jenkins, J.T. | M.Sc. | 56-522 |
| Klugman, Michael A. | Ph.D. | 56-023 |
| Leeson, John I. | M.Sc. | 53-535 |
| Lunde, Magnus | Ph.D. | 53-019 |
| Mattinson, Cyril R. | M.Sc. | 52-536 |
| McCuaig, James A. | Ph.D. | 53-020 |
| Moore, Thomas H. | M.Sc. | 51-537 |
| Mulligan, Robert | Ph.D. | 51-025 |
| Prusti, Bansi D. | Ph.D. | 54-061 |



| AUTHOR | DEGREE | THESIS NUMBER |
|---|---|---|
| **Kranck, E.** | | |
| Riley, George C. | Ph.D. | 57-028 |
| Riley, George C. | M.Sc. | 51-544 |
| Skinner, Ralph | M.Sc. | 49-621 |
| Taylor, Frederick C. | M.Sc. | 51-556 |
| Tremblay, Mousseau | Ph.D. | 56-069 |
| **Kreible, V.** | | |
| *Peiker, Alfred L. | Ph.D. | 30-010 |
| **Krieble, V.** | | |
| *McKinney, James W. | M.Sc. | 20-506 |
| *Seyer, William F. | Ph.D. | 20-001 |
| **Lafleur, P.** | | |
| *Davis, Charles F. | M.A. | 23-521 |
| *Eaton, Mary J. | M.A. | 09-501 |
| *Hayden, Amy J. | M.A. | 09-503 |
| *Hughes, Frederick G. | M.A. | 14-504 |
| *Irving, William G. | M.A. | 13-506 |
| *McGreer, Edgar D. | M.A. | 23-523 |
| *Moore, Dale H. | M.A. | 23-524 |
| *Rorke, Mabele L. | M.A. | 08-504 |
| *Tyndale, Orville S. | M.A. | 09-506 |
| **Lambek, J.** | | |
| Bedford, Frederick W. | M.Sc. | 59-510 |
| Dawson, Donald A. | M.Sc. | 59-515 |
| Hayes, James C. | M.Sc. | 54-586 |
| Kingsbury, Donald M. | M.Sc. | 59-585 |
| Kochen, Simon B. | M.Sc. | 55-604 |
| Rosenfeld, Ze'ev | M.Sc. | 59-533 |
| **Lambert, W.** | | |
| Birks, Margaret | M.A. | 57-545 |
| Gardner, Robert C. | M.Sc. | 58-521 |

| AUTHOR | DEGREE | THESIS NUMBER |
|---|---|---|
| **Lambert, W.** | | |
| Hodgson, Richard C. | M.Sc. | 56-580 |
| Paivio, Allan U. | Ph.D. | 59-060 |
| Paivio, Allan U. | M.Sc. | 57-534 |
| Wimer, Cynthia C. | M.A. | 58-551 |
| **Lang, C.** | | |
| Grant, Elizabeth R. | Ph.D. | 32-021 |
| **Lariviere, H.** | | |
| Ariano, Alphonse | M.A. | 50-644 |
| Beauvais, Roxane | M.A. | 42-508 |
| Boulanger, Jean-Baptiste | M.A. | 50-648 |
| Coultis, Rosa J. | M.A. | 49-556 |
| Dooling, Sister Margaret | M.A. | 41-514 |
| Erskine, John Steuart | M.A. | 42-029 |
| Frey, Betty | M.A. | 59-550 |
| Guyton, Pauline | M.A. | 40-510 |
| Hardy, Norah Woodbury | M.A. | 41-518 |
| Holt, Irene M. | M.A. | 53-613 |
| Joos, Erno | M.A. | 59-555 |
| Joos, Irma | M.A. | 58-586 |
| Kidd, Dorothy J. | M.A. | 48-564 |
| Kushner, Eva M. | Ph.D. | 56-057 |
| Lenoir, Marguerite N. | M.A. | 47-534 |
| McGillivray, R.G. | M.A. | 53-553 |
| Murphy, Sister Marie M. | M.A. | 42-514 |
| Schiffers, Tania | M.A. | 42-042 |
| **Latham, G.** | | |
| Allen, Marguerite Z. | M.A. | 31-519 |
| Barnett, Elizabeth S. | M.A. | 34-522 |
| Bloomfield, Morton W. | M.A. | 35-522 |
| Bonis, Margaret E. | M.A. | 36-526 |
| Calder, Alice D. | M.A. | 33-539 |
| Chapman, Antony D. | M.A. | 37-518 |
| Detlor, W. Lyall | M.A. | 31-527 |
| Hagerman, Verna B. | M.A. | 34-527 |
| Hamilton, Robert A. | M.A. | 36-530 |
| Hartwell, Robert M. | M.A. | 33-546 |



| AUTHOR | DEGREE | THESIS NUMBER |
|---|---|---|
| **Latham, G.** | | |
| MacLaren, Margaret J. | M.A. | 26-548 |
| Tough, David L. | M.A. | 32-548 |
| Ulrichsen, Barbara A. | M.A. | 35-537 |
| *Banford, Jean E. | M.A. | 28-528 |
| *Birkett, Winifred L. | M.A. | 23-520 |
| *Brown, Richard C. | M.A. | 27-524 |
| *Chait, Rachel | M.A. | 30-522 |
| *Di Floric, Pasquale | M.A. | 26-539 |
| *Hague, Helen | M.A. | 28-535 |
| *Hemmeon, Ellen C. | M.A. | 27-531 |
| *Hudson, James C. | M.A. | 28-541 |
| *Jahn, Helen L. | M.A. | 29-537 |
| *MacLean, Mary W. | M.A. | 28-546 |
| *MacLennan, Malcolm | M.A. | 25-537 |
| *Radler, Ruth | M.A. | 30-543 |
| *Sacks, Benjamin | M.A. | 27-540 |
| *Silverman, Beatrice I. | M.A. | 28-553 |
| *Smith, Henry L. | M.A. | 26-555 |
| *Tuttle, Harry G. | M.A. | 31-545 |
| *Walter, Felix H. | M.A. | 24-546 |
| *White, Harold | M.A. | 25-542 |
| **Launay, J.** | | |
| Allen, Robert L. | M.A. | 50-643 |
| Andrews, Oliver | Ph.D. | 56-002 |
| Bartolini, Angelo E. | M.A. | 59-605 |
| Beauchemin, C-H. Guy | M.A. | 54-609 |
| Caezza, Concepta Z. | M.A. | 57-546 |
| Culver, Eleanor A. | M.A. | 46-585 |
| Duinat, Blanche E. | M.A. | 58-539 |
| Hawkins, Stuart C. | M.A. | 49-565 |
| Hepburn, Johnston | M.A. | 49-566 |
| Howell, Helen M. | M.A. | 49-568 |
| Jacoby, Barbara J. | M.A. | 58-540 |
| MacKenzie, Gordon J. | M.A. | 55-554 |
| MacNeill, Glorana H. | M.A. | 47-536 |
| Mahon, R. Kathryn | M.A. | 50-659 |
| Markson, Doris M. | M.A. | 54-616 |
| Mentha, Guy | M.A. | 56-546 |
| Munro, Vivian R. | M.A. | 52-552 |
| Nelson, Arthur J. | M.A. | 51-572 |
| Podgornik, Louis E. | M.A. | 58-547 |
| Polgar, Sophie | M.A. | 55-558 |

| AUTHOR | DEGREE | THESIS NUMBER |
|---|---|---|
| **Launay, J.** | | |
| Richard, O'Neill J. | M.A. | 49-579 |
| Spentzos, George C. | M.A. | 53-620 |
| Szablowski, Julie A. | M.A. | 58-548 |
| Tougas, Gerard R. | M.A. | 47-583 |
| Watts, Aileen M. | M.A. | 54-627 |
| Westwood, Mary J. | M.A. | 51-576 |
| Wolfgang, Mary B. | M.A. | 51-578 |
| **Laviolette, F.** | | |
| Jackson, Joan K. | M.A. | 47-578 |
| Seyverd, Henry | M.A. | 46-547 |
| Solomon, David N. | M.A. | 42-045 |
| **Leacock, S.** | | |
| Challies, George S. | M.A. | 33-542 |
| Feiner, Abraham | M.A. | 31-530 |
| Goforth, John F. | M.A. | 28-533 |
| Goforth, William W. | M.A. | 32-527 |
| Hayes, Saul | M.A. | 28-539 |
| Heuser, Heinrich K. | M.A. | 33-547 |
| Leathem, Ronald M. | M.A. | 36-536 |
| Marsh, Leonard C. | M.A. | 33-553 |
| Munroe, David C. | M.A. | 30-539 |
| Picard, Robert I. | M.A. | 32-538 |
| Reich, Nathan | M.A. | 26-552 |
| Schwab, Jean G. | M.A. | 32-546 |
| Styles, Arthur D. | M.A. | 35-535 |
| Tombs, Laurence C. | M.A. | 26-557 |
| Weissenburger, Pierre C. | M.Com. | 33-564 |
| *Blumenstein, Jacob H. | M.A. | 25-531 |
| *Brownstein, Charles | M.A. | 25-533 |
| *Burk, Christopher A. | M.A. | 30-519 |
| *Culliton, John T. | M.A. | 27-527 |
| *Davidson, Winnifred H. | M.A. | 22-526 |
| *Davies, Thomas R. | M.A. | 27-528 |
| *Ellison, Myra K. | M.A. | 13-503 |
| *Fair, Louisa M. | M.A. | 24-537 |
| *Forbes, Frederic J. | M.A. | 27-530 |
| *Greaves, Ida C. | M.A. | 30-528 |
| *Hamilton, Andrew W. | M.A. | 30-529 |
| *Kydd, Mary W. | M.A. | 24-540 |



| AUTHOR | DEGREE | THESIS NUMBER |
|---|---|---|
| **Leacock, S.** | | |
| *Macdonald, Isabella I. | M.A. | 20-511 |
| *McGown, Isabella W. | M.A. | 23-522 |
| *Paterson, Edith L. | M.A. | 12-503 |
| *Pattison, Irma E. | M.A. | 31-539 |
| *Price, Enid | M.A. | 20-512 |
| *Read, Stanley M. | M.A. | 25-539 |
| *Smillie, Eleanor A. | M.A. | 10-510 |
| **Leblond, C.** | | |
| Albert, Samuel | Ph.D. | 48-001 |
| Axelrad, A.A. | Ph.D. | 54-005 |
| Bencosme, Sergio | M.Sc. | 48-575 |
| Bertalanffy, Felix D. | Ph.D. | 54-007 |
| Bertalanffy, Felix D. | M.Sc. | 51-513 |
| Carriere, Rita M. | M.Sc. | 54-511 |
| Clermont, Yves W. | Ph.D. | 53-002 |
| Cox, Phoebe L. | Ph.D. | 52-042 |
| Dacust, Roger J. | Ph.D. | 53-005 |
| Fartly, Heidi H. | Ph.D. | 53-006 |
| Eartly, Heidi H. | M.Sc. | 51-518 |
| Eidinger, David | Ph.D. | 58-013 |
| Enesco, Mircea A. | Ph.D. | 57-010 |
| Ghosh, Asok C. | M.Sc. | 55-522 |
| Grad, Bernard | Ph.D. | 49-047 |
| Greulich, Richard C. | Ph.D. | 53-008 |
| Gross, Jack | Ph.D. | 49-014 |
| Henrikson, Helen A. | Ph.D. | 49-017 |
| Karpishka, Irene S. | M.Sc. | 58-569 |
| Kumamoto, Yurika | Ph.D. | 56-056 |
| Kumamoto, Yurika | M.Sc. | 53-597 |
| Laroche, Joseph R. | M.Sc. | 51-612 |
| Messier, Bernard H. | M.Sc. | 56-590 |
| Nadler, Norman J. | Ph.D. | 55-070 |
| Schwartz, Solomon | M.Sc. | 51-624 |
| Stevens, Catherine E. | Ph.D. | 50-044 |
| Storey, Winnifred F. | M.Sc. | 49-548 |
| Vulpe, M. | M.Sc. | 54-536 |
| Wilkinson, Gordon W. | M.Sc. | 50-640 |
| Zemel, Reuben | M.Sc. | 54-607 |
| **Lee, *** | | |

| AUTHOR | DEGREE | THESIS NUMBER |
|---|---|---|
| Iee, * | | |
| *Macdonald, Isabella L. | M.A. | 20-511 |
| *McCormack, George J. | M.A. | 16-504 |
| *Price, Enid | M.A. | 20-512 |
| *Rose, Harold E. | LL.M. | 20-500 |
| *Willis, Helen A. | M.A. | 17-502 |
| Lemaitre, G. | | |
| Cox, Mary D. | M.A. | 35-525 |
| Hall, Clifton L. | M.A. | 32-561 |
| Howie, Ruth J. | M.A. | 34-529 |
| Irwin, Nora F. | M.A. | 38-532 |
| Kinnear, Mary E. | M.A. | 34-532 |
| Lovelock, Margaret K. | M.A. | 37-545 |
| Walker, Margaret G. | M.A. | 35-549 |
| *Rhoades, Winifred | M.A. | 31-540 |
| *Tanner, Lea E. | M.A. | 30-548 |
| LeDain, G. | | |
| Du Crest, Maxime M. | LL.M. | 59-573 |
| LeMesurier, C. | | |
| Aguilar-Mawdsley, Andres | M.C.L. | 48-500 |
| Lightall, W. | | |
| *MacSporran, Maysie S. | M.A. | 30-537 |
| Lightboll, W. | | |
| *Rose, Harold E. | LL.M. | 20-500 |
| Iighthall, W. | | |
| *McLetchie, James K. | M.A. | 29-545 |



| AUTHOR | DEGREE | THESIS NUMBER |
|---|---|---|
| Lloyd, F. | | |
| Moe, George G. | M.Sc. | 21-513 |
| *Dickson, Bertram T. | Ph.D. | 22-001 |
| *Duff, Dorothy | M.Sc. | 14-511 |
| *Fritz, Clara W. | M.Sc. | 18-503 |
| *Gibbs, Ronald D. | M.Sc. | 26-510 |
| *Godwin, Kathleen F. | M.Sc. | 22-508 |
| *Macrae, Ruth | M.Sc. | 26-516 |
| *Symons, Jennie L. | Ph.D. | 25-006 |
| *Symons, Jennie L. | M.Sc. | 21-516 |
| *Walker, Osman J. | Ph.D. | 20-002 |
| Lloyd, L. | | |
| Lister, Earle E. | M.Sc. | 57-585 |
| Smith, Edward R. | M.Sc. | 58-577 |
| Lockhead, W. | | |
| *DuPorte, Ernest M. | M.Sc. | 14-512 |
| *Jull, Morley A. | M.Sc. | 19-502 |
| *Newton, Margaret | M.Sc. | 19-503 |
| *Weir, Douglas | M.Sc. | 10-523 |
| Lods, E. | | |
| Casserly, Leo M. | M.Sc. | 54-513 |
| Gauthier, Fernand M. | M.Sc. | 48-521 |
| Hansen, Douglas F. | M.Sc. | 52-527 |
| Klinck, Harold R. | Ph.D. | 55-062 |
| Klinck, Harold R. | M.Sc. | 52-531 |
| Raynauld, Robert | M.S.A. | 28-501 |
| *Godbout, Fernand | M.Sc. | 29-554 |
| *MacRae, Norman A. | M.Sc. | 30-508 |
| Lomer, G. | | |
| *Road, Algy S. | M.A. | 21-524 |
| Long, C. | | |

| AUTHOR | DEGREE | THESIS NUMBER |
|---|---|---|
| **Long, C.** | | |
| *Grant, Elizabeth R. | M.A. | 30-554 |
| **Lowenstein, L.** | | |
| Bramlage, Catharina A. | M.Sc. | 55-588 |
| De Leeuw, Nannie K. | M.Sc. | 50-602 |
| **Luchins, A.** | | |
| Deitcher, Samuel | M.A. | 53-549 |
| Endler, Norman S. | M.Sc. | 54-582 |
| Forgus, Ronald H. | M.Sc. | 51-520 |
| Lyman, Bernard E. | M.A. | 51-638 |
| Mills, Allan W. | M.A. | 51-570 |
| Rabinowitz, Herbert S. | M.A. | 52-554 |
| Ross, Mary V. | Ph.D. | 52-029 |
| Schwartzman, Alex E. | M.A. | 52-556 |
| Shulman, R. | M.Sc. | 51-546 |
| Westcott, James W. | M.A. | 50-668 |
| Wigdor, Blossom T. | Ph.D. | 52-068 |
| **Ludwig, R.** | | |
| Julien, J. Bernard | M.Sc. | 50-614 |
| Robinson, Dean B. | M.Sc. | 48-542 |
| Simard, Thomas | Ph.D. | 48-038 |
| **Lynde, C.** | | |
| *Patterson, Arthur L. | M.Sc. | 24-525 |
| **Maass, O.** | | |
| Adams, Alfred Byron | Ph.D. | 39-001 |
| Archer, William L. | Ph.D. | 50-001 |
| Argue, George H. | Ph.D. | 35-002 |
| Arnell, John C. | Ph.D. | 42-002 |
| Beazley, Warren B. | Ph.D. | 37-001 |
| Biefer, Gregory J. | Ph.D. | 52-038 |
| Brais, Roger | Ph.D. | 42-005 |



| AUTHOR | DEGREE | THESIS NUMBER |
|---|---|---|
| **Maass, O.** | | |
| Broughton, James W. | Ph.D. | 37-003 |
| Brown, Arthur G. | Ph.D. | 38-002 |
| Brown, Douglas Frederick | Ph.D. | 40-003 |
| Buckley, Bernard P. | Ph.D. | 41-501 |
| Butler, Keith H. | Ph.D. | 28-001 |
| Calder, Douglas S. | Ph.D. | 35-008 |
| Calhoun, John M. | Ph.D. | 38-003 |
| Campbell, William B. | Ph.D. | 29-002 |
| Cannon, John J. | Ph.D. | 39-003 |
| Carpenter, Gilbert B. | Ph.D. | 28-003 |
| Carroll, Murray N. | Ph.D. | 52-008 |
| Christie, George L. | Ph.D. | 49-007 |
| Coffin, Carl C. | Ph.D. | 29-004 |
| Cooper, Douglas L. | Ph.D. | 31-005 |
| Corey, Alfred J. | Ph.D. | 36-004 |
| Cuthbertson, Arnold C. | Ph.D. | 29-005 |
| Cuthbertson, Arnold C. | M.Sc. | 27-503 |
| Dacey, John Robert | Ph.D. | 40-007 |
| De Montigny, Paimbault | Ph.D. | 34-005 |
| Deluca, Horace A. | Ph.D. | 37-005 |
| Duncan, Robert Daman | Ph.D. | 41-003 |
| Edwards, Joseph | Ph.D. | 35-010 |
| Favis, Demetrios | Ph.D. | 51-045 |
| Filby, Edgar A. | Ph.D. | 32-002 |
| Findlay, Robert A. | Ph.D. | 37-006 |
| Funt, Boris L. | Ph.D. | 49-011 |
| Geddes, Amos L. | Ph.D. | 36-006 |
| Giguere, Paul A. | Ph.D. | 37-007 |
| Gishler, Paul E. | Ph.D. | 35-012 |
| Goring, David A. | Ph.D. | 49-013 |
| Grace, Nathaniel H. | Ph.D. | 31-006 |
| Grieve, Arthur D. | Ph.D. | 32-023 |
| Grummitt, William E. | Ph.D. | 43-006 |
| Gunn, George R. | Ph.D. | 50-004 |
| Gurd, George W. | Ph.D. | 32-005 |
| Harvey, Ross B. | Ph.D. | 40-011 |
| Hiebert, Paul G. | Ph.D. | 24-001 |
| Holder, Clinton Howard | Ph.D. | 39-010 |
| Hollies, Norman F. | Ph.D. | 47-007 |
| Hutley, Charles F. | Ph.D. | 49-019 |
| Hugill, John T. | Ph.D. | 46-011 |
| Hunten, Kenneth W. | Ph.D. | 26-003 |
| Johannson, Oscar K. | Ph.D. | 37-029 |
| Johnson, Herbert | Ph.D. | 47-008 |
| Johnston, Harry W. | Ph.D. | 29-008 |

Maass, O.

| AUTHOR | DEGREE | THESIS NUMBER |
|---|---|---|
| Kenalty, Brendan Joseph | M.Sc. | 41-529 |
| King, Thomas Elston | Ph.D. | 39-500 |
| Larocque, Gerard L. | M.Sc. | 33-520 |
| Larocque, Gerard L. | Ph.D. | 35-016 |
| Linton, Everett P. | Ph.D. | 32-008 |
| Linton, Everett P. | M.Sc. | 30-507 |
| Lipsett, Solomon G. | Ph.D. | 27-006 |
| Livingston, William R. | Ph.D. | 42-502 |
| Lossing, Frederick P. | Ph.D. | 42-017 |
| Lusby, George R. | Ph.D. | 33-029 |
| Macklin, Lionel S. | Ph.D. | 32-010 |
| Madras, Samuel | Ph.D. | 47-034 |
| Marsden, James | Ph.D. | 36-010 |
| Mason, Stanley George | Ph.D. | 39-013 |
| Matheson, George L. | Ph.D. | 29-010 |
| Matheson, George L. | M.Sc. | 26-517 |
| McDermot, H. Lloyd | Ph.D. | 50-014 |
| McIntosh, Robert Lloyd | Ph.D. | 39-012 |
| Morehouse, Fred R. | Ph.D. | 32-011 |
| Morehouse, Fred R. | M.Sc. | 31-510 |
| Morgan, Oliver M. | Ph.D. | 30-008 |
| Morris, Herbert E. | Ph.D. | 34-007 |
| Morrison, Donald M. | Ph.D. | 24-004 |
| Morrison, James A. | Ph.D. | 43-011 |
| Morrison, John L. | Ph.D. | 37-016 |
| Mungen, Richard | Ph.D. | 42-019 |
| Munro, Ferdinand L. | Ph.D. | 32-025 |
| Murray, Francis E. | Ph.D. | 53-027 |
| Naldrett, Stanley Norman | Ph.D. | 40-018 |
| Pall, David Boris | Ph.D. | 39-017 |
| Pearce, Jesse Arthur | Ph.D. | 41-012 |
| Pidgeon, Lloyd M. | Ph.D. | 29-011 |
| Price, Aubrey F. | Ph.D. | 33-015 |
| Richardson, Ronald E. | Ph.D. | 33-018 |
| Richardson, Ronald E. | M.Sc. | 31-513 |
| Robertson, Alexander A. | Ph.D. | 49-034 |
| Ross, Archibald S. | Ph.D. | 37-019 |
| Russell, John | Ph.D. | 27-010 |
| Russell, John K. | Ph.D. | 34-013 |
| Saunderson, Hugh H. | Ph.D. | 32-015 |
| Schneider, William Georg | Ph.D. | 41-015 |
| Schrage, Samuel | Ph.D. | 51-030 |
| Seidman, Ruth | Ph.D. | 53-036 |
| Shaw, Geoffrey T. | Ph.D. | 36-012 |
| Shipley, John H. | Ph.D. | 38-016 |



Maass, O.

| AUTHOR | DEGREE | THESIS NUMBER |
|---|---|---|
| Sirianni, Aurele F. | Ph.D. | 46-033 |
| Skey, Arthur James | Ph.D. | 39-503 |
| Soley, Russell Clyne | Ph.D. | 40-024 |
| Stewart, William W. | Ph.D. | 33-021 |
| Stewart, William W. | M.Sc. | 31-559 |
| Stuart, Allan F. | Ph.D. | 42-024 |
| Sutherland, Brian F. | Ph.D. | 28-008 |
| Sutherland, Hugh S. | Ph.D. | 31-008 |
| Sutherland, Hugh S. | M.Sc. | 29-520 |
| Sutherland, John W. | Ph.D. | 32-016 |
| Taylor, William Dixon | Ph.D. | 40-025 |
| Tomlinson, Richard H. | Ph.D. | 48-012 |
| Topp, Allan C. | Ph.D. | 41-017 |
| Trevelyan, Benjamin J. | Ph.D. | 51-034 |
| Trost, Walter R. | Ph.D. | 47-019 |
| Tuck, Norman G. | Ph.D. | 47-020 |
| Van_Cleave, Allan B. | Ph.D. | 35-027 |
| Walker, Forestier | Ph.D. | 37-024 |
| Walker, Forestier | M.Sc. | 35-518 |
| Weininger, Joseph I. | Ph.D. | 49-058 |
| Whiteway, Stirling G. | Ph.D. | 53-040 |
| Wiggins, Ernest J. | Ph.D. | 46-018 |
| Williams, Alan R. | Ph.D. | 32-017 |
| Winkler, Carl A. | Ph.D. | 33-027 |
| Wise, Louis M. | Ph.D. | 46-019 |
| Wright, Robert H. | Ph.D. | 31-010 |
| Wright, Robert H. | M.Sc. | 30-516 |
| *Barnes, William H. | Ph.D. | 27-001 |
| *Barnes, William H. | M.Sc. | 25-509 |
| *Boomer, Edward H. | Ph.D. | 23-001 |
| *Boomer, Edward H. | M.Sc. | 21-501 |
| *Brown, Robert S. | Ph.D. | 36-017 |
| *Buxton, Kenneth S. | Ph.D. | 30-015 |
| *Chalk, Mary L. | M.Sc. | 26-506 |
| *Crowe, Marguerite | M.Sc. | 28-503 |
| *Faith, Willard V. | M.Sc. | 24-513 |
| *Harkness, Harold W. | M.Sc. | 29-555 |
| *Hatcher, William H. | Ph.D. | 21-002 |
| *Helwig, Gerald V. | M.Sc. | 29-509 |
| *Hiebert, Paul G. | M.Sc. | 22-511 |
| *Humes, Harold L. | M.Sc. | 23-512 |
| *Hunten, Kenneth W. | M.Sc. | 24-520 |
| *Lane, Cecil T. | M.Sc. | 27-510 |
| *McClelland, William R. | M.Sc. | 23-516 |
| *McPherson, Anna I. | M.Sc. | 23-517 |

| AUTHOR | DEGREE | THESIS NUMBER |
|---|---|---|
| Maass, O. | | |
| *McRae, Duncan R. | M.Sc. | 28-518 |
| *Mennie, John H. | Ph.D. | 25-005 |
| *Morrison, James E. | M.Sc. | 26-520 |
| *Muir, Allan K. | M.Sc. | 25-524 |
| *Peiker, Alfred L. | Ph.D. | 30-010 |
| *Robertson, Carol E. | M.Sc. | 25-526 |
| *Sivertz, Christian | Ph.D. | 26-004 |
| *Sivertz, Victorian | Ph.D. | 26-005 |
| *Snell, Arthur H. | M.Sc. | 31-558 |
| *Stephens, Henry N. | Ph.D. | 23-006 |
| *Sweny, George W. | M.Sc. | 25-528 |
| *Tapp, James S. | Ph.D. | 33-022 |
| *Tapp, James S. | M.A. | 31-567 |
| *Terroux, Fernand R. | M.Sc. | 26-528 |
| *Waldbauer, Louis J. | Ph.D. | 23-007 |
| *Watson, Horace G. | M.Sc. | 27-520 |
| *Whittemore, Carl R. | M.Sc. | 24-534 |
| *Wright, Charles A. | Ph.D. | 21-003 |
| *Wyman, Harold B. | M.Sc. | 30-553 |
| Maass, O. . | | |
| *Sivertz, Christian | M.Sc. | 24-529 |
| *Sutherland, Brian P. | M.Sc. | 26-527 |
| Macallum, A. | | |
| *Blumberg, Perry | M.Sc. | 29-504 |
| *Cashin, Martin F. | M.Sc. | 26-505 |
| *Chipman, Harry R. | Ph.D. | 25-001 |
| *Derick, Russell A. | M.Sc. | 23-510 |
| *Dolid, Jacob | Ph.D. | 23-002 |
| *DuPorte, Ernest M. | Ph.D. | 21-001 |
| *Emmons, William F. | Ph.D. | 27-004 |
| *Foran, Herbert P. | M.Sc. | 22-506 |
| *Forbes, John C. | Ph.D. | 25-002 |
| *Fowler, Grant M. | M.Sc. | 25-517 |
| *Henderson, Jean T. | M.Sc. | 26-512 |
| *Hunten, Kenneth W. | M.Sc. | 24-520 |
| *Illievitz, Abraham B. | M.Sc. | 25-521 |
| *Logan, John F. | Ph.D. | 23-004 |
| *Macrae, Ruth | M.Sc. | 26-516 |
| *Malcolm, Robert B. | M.Sc. | 24-523 |



| AUTHOR | DEGREE | THESIS NUMBER |
|---|---|---|
| Macallum, A. | | |
| *Maytum, Helen E. | M.Sc. | 27-511 |
| *Thomson, Walter W. | Ph.D. | 25-007 |
| *Tidmarsh, Clarence J. | M.A. | 22-528 |
| Mackay, H. | | |
| Bain, Archie M. | M.Sc. | 29-502 |
| Cox, John R. | M.Sc. | 11-507 |
| Morrison, Carson F. | M.Sc. | 27-512 |
| *Becking, John A. | M.Sc. | 25-510 |
| *Bickell, William A. | M.Sc. | 23-504 |
| *Billington, Edward E. | M.Sc. | 13-513 |
| *Brunner, Godfrey H. | M.Sc. | 07-507 |
| *Campbell, Alexander | M.Sc. | 26-504 |
| *Cronk, Francis J. | M.Sc. | 16-507 |
| *Dodd, Geoffrey J. | M.Sc. | 22-503 |
| *Douglas, George V. | M.Sc. | 21-504 |
| *Dowler, Vernon B. | M.Sc. | 16-508 |
| *Dowling, Donaldson B. | M.Sc. | 21-505 |
| *Eadie, Robert S. | M.Sc. | 22-505 |
| *Emmons, William F. | M.Sc. | 20-504 |
| *Finlayson, John N. | M.Sc. | 09-510 |
| *Fox, Charles H. | M.Sc. | 10-516 |
| *Gibbins, Gwynn G. | M.Sc. | 11-510 |
| *Gillespie, Peter | M.Sc. | 12-509 |
| *Harding, Ellis G. | M.Sc. | 21-508 |
| *Hardy, Robert M. | M.Sc. | 30-504 |
| *Harrington, John L. | M.Sc. | 08-510 |
| *Herzberg, Otto W. | M.Sc. | 18-505 |
| *Jamieson, Robert E. | M.Sc. | 20-505 |
| *Jull, Morley A. | M.Sc. | 19-502 |
| *Livinson, Abraham J. | M.A. | 16-503 |
| *Lockhead, Allan G. | Ph.D. | 19-001 |
| *Macdonald, Albert E. | M.Sc. | 22-514 |
| *McKinney, James W. | M.Sc. | 20-506 |
| *Mclennan, Logan S. | M.Sc. | 24-522 |
| *McNaughton, Andrew G. | M.Sc. | 12-514 |
| *Newton, Margaret | M.Sc. | 19-503 |
| *Pitts, Gordon M. | M.Sc. | 09-515 |
| *Ross, William B. | M.Sc. | 27-519 |
| *Russell, John | M.Sc. | 18-506 |
| *Shaw, Gerald E. | M.Sc. | 25-549 |
| *Snijman, Johan J. | M.Sc. | 24-551 |
| *Spencer, Roy A. | M.Sc. | 15-514 |

| AUTHOR | DEGREE | THESIS NUMBER |
|---|---|---|
| Mackay, H. | | |
| *Traversy, Eric E. | M.Sc. | 15-515 |
| *Trueman, James C. | M.Sc. | 24-533 |
| *Von Abo, Cecil V. | Ph.D. | 22-002 |
| *Weldon, Richard L. | M.Sc. | 20-509 |
| Mackay, I. | | |
| *Burns, Dean K. | M.A. | 25-534 |
| *Gray, Leona | M.A. | 28-563 |
| *Kelloway, Warwick F. | M.A. | 25-536 |
| *MacOdrum, Murdoch M. | M.A. | 24-541 |
| *MacVicar, Donald H. | M.A. | 26-550 |
| *Mullaly, Jessie R. | M.A. | 28-565 |
| *Nelson, Eda M. | M.A. | 28-549 |
| *Newton, Theodore F. | M.A. | 27-543 |
| *Nichol, Helen R. | M.A. | 21-523 |
| *Renaud, Paul E. | LL.M. | 22-500 |
| *Smith, Arthur J. | M.A. | 26-554 |
| *Troop, George R. | M.A. | 22-529 |
| *Wiseman, Solomon | M.A. | 23-527 |
| Mackay, J. | | |
| Lash, Harry N. | M.A. | 49-637 |
| Mackenzie, K. | | |
| Alivisatcs, John | M.Sc. | 53-569 |
| Beck, Johannes C. | M.Sc. | 51-511 |
| Carballeira, Andres M. | M.Sc. | 53-579 |
| Fridhandler, Louis | M.Sc. | 51-521 |
| Kennedy, Byrl J. | M.Sc. | 51-527 |
| Neiman, Gregory M. | M.Sc. | 53-601 |
| Maclean, R. | | |
| *Atkinson, Hammond J. | M.Sc. | 26-503 |
| Maclennan, R. | | |



| AUTHOR | DEGREE | THESIS NUMBER |
|---|---|---|
| Maclennan, R. | | |
| Faurot, Jean Hiatt | M.A. | 40-026 |
| Klineberg, Beatrice A. | M.A. | 36-535 |
| Oduber-Quiros, Daniel | M.A. | 48-567 |
| Panos, Dimitrios | M.A. | 44-516 |
| Reed, Ernest S. | M.A. | 38-553 |
| Stewart, Mary | M.A. | 46-591 |
| Watson, Gordon A. | M.A. | 50-667 |
| Williams, Ivor David | M.A. | 42-047 |
| Yalden-Thomas, David C. | Ph.D. | 48-045 |
| Macmillan, C. | | |
| Avison, Henry R. | M.A. | 40-507 |
| Bassinov, Saul | M.A. | 35-519 |
| Brierley, James G. | M.A. | 29-524 |
| Conroy, Mary P. | M.A. | 36-528 |
| Craig, Grace L. | M.A. | 34-524 |
| Cruikshank, Marion G. | M.A. | 31-526 |
| Dando, John A. | M.A. | 45-543 |
| Edwards, Margaret C. | M.A. | 26-540 |
| Fulford, Lloyd G. | M.A. | 40-027 |
| Henry, Eleanor May | M.A. | 39-036 |
| Hodgins, Samuel R. | M.A. | 29-535 |
| Jackson, Joan S. | M.A. | 43-511 |
| Kennedy, Judith | M.A. | 38-551 |
| MacDonald, Allister I. | M.A. | 47-535 |
| MacGachen, Freda K. | M.A. | 31-535 |
| MacKenzie, Mary F. | M.A. | 37-526 |
| MacIaggan, Marjorie F. | M.A. | 31-536 |
| McDonald, Elizabeth | M.A. | 41-028 |
| O'Brien, Michael V. | M.A. | 37-528 |
| Paist, Gertrude W. | M.A. | 36-539 |
| Putnam, Adelaide D. | M.A. | 33-555 |
| Rand, Frank H. | M.A. | 32-540 |
| Rittenhouse, Charles E. | M.A. | 38-552 |
| Silver, Helen | M.A. | 33-558 |
| Stevens, Valeria Dean | M.A. | 40-512 |
| Sullivan, Norah E. | M.A. | 31-544 |
| Thorpe, Benjamin J. | M.A. | 32-547 |
| Werry, Wilfrid W. | M.A. | 32-550 |
| *Burns, Dean K. | M.A. | 25-534 |
| *Duff, Dorothy | M.Sc. | 14-511 |
| *Ferrand, Lucy M. | M.A. | 29-531 |
| *Gray, Leona | M.A. | 28-563 |

| AUTHOR | DEGREE | THESIS NUMBER |
|---|---|---|
| **Macmillan, C.** | | |
| *Gurd, Jean M. | M.A. | 26-543 |
| *Harris, Richard C. | M.A. | 24-538 |
| *Hasley, Isabel J. | M.A. | 28-537 |
| *Hughes, Frederick G. | M.A. | 14-504 |
| *Irving, William G. | M.A. | 13-506 |
| *MacOdrum, Murdoch M. | M.A. | 24-541 |
| *Mathewson, Dorothy R. | M.A. | 24-542 |
| *McBain, Alexander R. | M.A. | 13-507 |
| *McBain, Mary N. | M.A. | 21-520 |
| *McInnis, Sarah | M.A. | 28-545 |
| *Murray, Bertram S. | M.A. | 27-536 |
| *Murray, Phyllis M. | M.A. | 27-537 |
| *Nelson, Eda M. | M.A. | 28-549 |
| *O'Brien, Margaret T. | M.A. | 28-550 |
| *O'Neill, Charles | M.M.A. | 24-500 |
| *O'Neill, John J. | M.Sc. | 10-519 |
| *Pickel, Margaret B. | M.A. | 23-525 |
| *Read, Stanley M. | M.A. | 25-539 |
| *Scott, Mary E. | M.A. | 28-566 |
| *Silver, Edith | M.A. | 24-545 |
| *Sutherland, Francis C. | M.A. | 15-506 |
| **Macmillan, L.** | | |
| *Harbert, Eleanor | M.A. | 22-527 |
| **MacBride, *** | | |
| McGregor, Claire R. | M.A. | 05-003 |
| **MacBride, E.** | | |
| *Lewis, David S. | M.Sc. | 07-510 |
| **MacDermot, J. and Woodhead, W.** | | |
| McHarg, Muriel S. | M.A. | 30-555 |
| **MacDermott, J.** | | |



| AUTHOR | DEGREE | THESIS NUMBER |
|---|---|---|
| **MacDermott, J.** | | |
| *Rhoades, Winifred | M.A. | 31-540 |
| **MacDougall, G.** | | |
| Mitchell, Victor E. | D.C.L. | 18-001 |
| **MacEachern, D.** | | |
| Rabinovitch, Reuben | M.Sc. | 47-567 |
| **MacEwan, J.** | | |
| Chang, Io-ching | M.Eng. | 42-048 |
| Finlay, James E. | M.Eng. | 54-563 |
| Goth, John W. | M.Eng. | 51-585 |
| Leblanc, Raymond F. | M.Eng. | 40-035 |
| Lemay, Henri F. | M.Eng. | 58-557 |
| MacEwan, John R. | Ph.D. | 57-023 |
| Moss, Bernard B. | M.Eng. | 39-053 |
| Ross, Henry U. | M.Sc. | 38-520 |
| Sharratt, Harold J. | M.Eng. | 55-578 |
| Sproule, William K. | M.Sc. | 37-514 |
| Trudeau, Guy J. | M.Eng. | 47-505 |
| Yao, Yu-Lin | M.Eng. | 42-050 |
| Youdelis, William V. | Ph.D. | 59-076 |
| **MacFarlane, D.** | | |
| Baumgartner, Helmut W. | M.A. | 56-611 |
| Buchanan, Donald R. | M.A. | 53-548 |
| MacFarlane, Dougald A. | M.A. | 57-550 |
| Schmidt, Stephen C. | Ph.D. | 58-043 |
| **MacIntosh, D.** | | |
| Sinnott, Joseph C. | M.Sc. | 58-530 |
| **MacIntosh, F.** | | |

| AUTHOR | DEGREE | THESIS NUMBER |
|---|---|---|
| **MacIntosh, F.** | | |
| Ashwin, James G. | Ph.D. | 53-042 |
| Birks, Richard I. | Ph.D. | 57-003 |
| Birks, Richard I. | M.Sc. | 54-575 |
| Dougherty, Joan L. | M.Sc. | 50-521 |
| Grossberg, Allan L. | Ph.D. | 54-051 |
| Oborin, Peter E. | M.Sc. | 54-598 |
| Sastry, Podila-Brahmayya | Ph.D. | 56-064 |
| **MacKay, F.** | | |
| Erickson, Theodore C. | M.Sc. | 34-509 |
| **MacKenzie, A.** | | |
| McCorriston, James R. | M.Sc. | 48-589 |
| **MacKenzie, D.** | | |
| Gourlay, Robert H. | M.Sc. | 49-605 |
| Murphy, David R. | M.Sc. | 48-591 |
| Niloff, Paul H. | M.Sc. | 49-612 |
| Percival, Walter L. | M.Sc. | 48-540 |
| Wallace, Alexander B. | M.Sc. | 36-551 |
| **MacLean, R.** | | |
| *Blampin, Caroline | M.A. | 20-510 |
| **MacLennan, H.** | | |
| Passmore, Marian R. | M.A. | 57-608 |
| Skoll, Selma D. | M.A. | 56-623 |
| **MacNaughton, J.** | | |
| Cockfield, Harry R. | M.A. | 11-502 |
| *Gordon, Nathan | M.A. | 09-502 |
| *Huxtable, Margaret | M.A. | 10-503 |
| *King, Lucile M. | M.A. | 10-504 |



| AUTHOR | DEGREE | THESIS NUMBER |
|---|---|---|
| **MacNaughton, J.** | | |
| *Lindsay, William | M.A. | 14-505 |
| *Maclean, Herbert B. | M.A. | 10-507 |
| *MacKenzie, Francis S. | M.A. | 16-505 |
| *Steacy, Frederick W. | M.A. | 13-511 |
| **MacPherson, A.** | | |
| Smith, Donald S. | M.Sc. | 50-634 |
| **MacPherson, C.** | | |
| Kahnka, Mary J. | Ph.D. | 49-023 |
| **Malloch, A.** | | |
| Pickup, T. | M.A. | 54-617 |
| Sproule, Hugh D. | M.A. | 58-591 |
| **Mallory, J.** | | |
| Aligwekwe, Iwuoha E. | M.A. | 52-545 |
| Breul, Frank R. | Ph.D. | 51-002 |
| Collins, Frank L. | M.A. | 53-608 |
| Frankel, Saul J. | Ph.D. | 58-014 |
| Metcalf, John F. | M.A. | 49-640 |
| Oliver, Michael K. | Ph.D. | 56-058 |
| Plunkett, Thomas | M.A. | 55-557 |
| **Malmo, R.** | | |
| Amsel, Abram | M.A. | 46-537 |
| Bartoshuk, Alexander K. | Ph.D. | 54-006 |
| Bartoshuk, Alexander K. | M.Sc. | 52-569 |
| Feldman, Samuel M. | Ph.D. | 59-023 |
| Forgays, Donald G. | M.A. | 48-559 |
| McMurray, Gordon A. | Ph.D. | 49-028 |
| Schnore, Morris M. | Ph.D. | 57-077 |
| Smith, Alfred A. | Ph.D. | 50-043 |
| Stennett, Richard G. | Ph.D. | 56-035 |
| Strauss, Clara | M.A. | 46-592 |

| AUTHOR | DEGREE | THESIS NUMBER |
|---|---|---|
| **Malmo, R.** | | |
| Surwillo, Walter W. | Ph.D. | 55-041 |
| Tagiuri, Renato | M.Sc. | 46-536 |
| Wallerstein, Harvey | Ph.D. | 54-035 |
| **Marsden, J.** | | |
| Fish, Arthur G. | M.Sc. | 58-565 |
| **Marsh, D.** | | |
| Adams, William E. | Ph.D. | 54-002 |
| Adams, William E. | M.A. | 52-544 |
| Armstrong, Muriel G. | M.A. | 54-539 |
| Bale, Cecil G. | M.A. | 58-536 |
| Broadbent, Arnot W. | M.Com. | 51-645 |
| Capelovitch, Edward M. | M.A. | 54-610 |
| Chipman, John S. | M.A. | 48-609 |
| Galbraith, John A. | Ph.D. | 59-025 |
| Hollbach, Reiner | M.A. | 53-612 |
| Hutchison, John | M.Com. | 54-558 |
| MacIntosh, Robert M. | Ph.D. | 52-023 |
| Pugsley, William H. | Ph.D. | 50-018 |
| Stenason, Walter | M.Com. | 54-629 |
| Sussman, Edmond | M.Com. | 54-630 |
| Wilson, James D. | M.A. | 49-582 |
| Woodfine, William J. | M.A. | 53-622 |
| **Marsh, L.** | | |
| Berman, Alfred | M.A. | 31-521 |
| Heiber, Sol P. | M.Com. | 34-549 |
| Shlakman, Vera | M.A. | 31-542 |
| Winkler, Louis | M.A. | 38-543 |
| **Marshall, J.** | | |
| Adams, Glenn N. | Ph.D. | 53-041 |
| Bercovitch, Mortimer | M.Sc. | 47-543 |
| Bloom, Martin S. | M.Sc. | 50-515 |
| Bordan, Jack | M.Sc. | 52-570 |
| Dennis, Arnett S. | M.Sc. | 53-521 |



| AUTHOR | DEGREE | THESIS NUMBER |
|---|---|---|
| **Marshall, J.** | | |
| Douglas, Richard H. | Ph.D. | 57-007 |
| East, Thomas W. | Ph.D. | 55-015 |
| East, Thomas W. | M.Sc. | 53-524 |
| Gold, Lorne W. | M.Sc. | 52-572 |
| Gunn, Kenrick L. | Ph.D. | 50-005 |
| Gunn, Kenrick L. | M.Sc. | 47-549 |
| Hitschfeld, Walter | Ph.D. | 50-006 |
| Keys, John D. | M.Sc. | 48-584 |
| Langleben, Manuel P. | Ph.D. | 53-059 |
| Langleben, Manuel P. | M.Sc. | 50-616 |
| Magarvey, R.H. | M.Sc. | 50-622 |
| Palmer, Walter M. | Ph.D. | 49-031 |
| Palmer, Walter M. | M.Sc. | 47-564 |
| Patterson, Donald D. | M.Sc. | 50-550 |
| Rigby, Caroline F. | M.Sc. | 49-545 |
| Stevens, Bernard A. | Ph.D. | 55-039 |
| Stevens, Bernard A. | M.Sc. | 52-592 |
| Zirinsky, Victor J. | M.Sc. | 48-605 |
| **Martin, C.** | | |
| Boyd, William | M.Sc. | 56-569 |
| Brochu, Francis L. | M.Sc. | 50-598 |
| Dekaban, Anatole S. | M.Sc. | 51-605 |
| Friedman, Constance A. | Ph.D. | 48-004 |
| Friedman, Sydney M. | Ph.D. | 46-007 |
| Hunter, John M. | M.Sc. | 50-535 |
| McNaughton, Francis L. | M.Sc. | 41-533 |
| Miller, Saul | M.Sc. | 48-536 |
| Mohiuddin, Syed D. | M.Sc. | 53-540 |
| Varverikos, Emmanuel D. | M.Sc. | 51-628 |
| **Mason, G.** | | |
| Lumsden, Jean G. | M.A. | 44-515 |
| **Mason, S.** | | |
| Bartok, William | Ph.D. | 57-001 |
| Barton, Stuart S. | Ph.D. | 56-036 |
| Charles, George F. | Ph.D. | 59-010 |
| Forgacs, Otto L. | Ph.D. | 59-024 |

| AUTHOR | DEGREE | THESIS NUMBER |
|---|---|---|
| **Mason, S.** | | |
| Gardon, John L. | Ph.D. | 55-021 |
| Gordon, Ralph W. | Ph.D. | 56-051 |
| Gupta, Prem R. | Ph.D. | 59-033 |
| Huque, Mohammed M. | Ph.D. | 57-056 |
| Kouris, Michael | M.Sc. | 57-584 |
| Kuzmak, Joseph M. | Ph.D. | 53-017 |
| Lang, Andrew R. | Ph.D. | 59-043 |
| MacLennan, Donald F. | Ph.D. | 54-018 |
| Manley, Rockliffe St. J. | Ph.D. | 53-023 |
| Marchessault, Robert H. | Ph.D. | 54-019 |
| McKnight, Theodore S. | Ph.D. | 58-025 |
| Mossman, Carolyn E. | Ph.D. | 55-027 |
| Nawab, Mohammed A. | Ph.D. | 57-069 |
| Rabinovitch, William | Ph.D. | 56-060 |
| Robertson, Roderick F. | Ph.D. | 55-031 |
| Screaton, Rose M. | Ph.D. | 56-033 |
| **Maw, W.** | | |
| MacIntyre, Thomas Martin | M.Sc. | 41-044 |
| Narod, Milton | M.Sc. | 43-507 |
| **Mayo, H.** | | |
| Piscopo, Franco A. | M.A. | 54-618 |
| **McBride, **** | | |
| Henderson, Ernest H. | M.A. | 05-002 |
| **McBride, E.** | | |
| *Lyman, Ruth D. | M.Sc. | 07-511 |
| **McBride, W.** | | |
| Denny, Denison | M.Eng. | 34-541 |
| Hicks, Henry B. | M.Eng. | 35-501 |
| MacKay, Donald M. | M.Eng. | 36-503 |
| Muir, William L. | M.Eng. | 34-503 |



| AUTHOR | DEGREE | THESIS NUMBER |
|---|---|---|
| **McBride, W.** | | |
| O'Connell, Francis J. | M.Sc. | 31-512 |
| O'Shaughnessy, Michael J | M.Eng. | 33-503 |
| Stobart, Walter T. | M.Eng. | 32-505 |
| Thomas, William F. | M.Sc. | 31-516 |
| Wadge, Norman H. | M.Eng. | 36-507 |
| *Coleman, Charles L. | M.Sc. | 28-559 |
| *Holbrocke, George I. | M.Sc. | 28-512 |
| *Hopper, Ronald V. | M.Sc. | 29-510 |
| *Weldon, Frederick E. | M.Sc. | 30-514 |
| **McBride,W.** | | |
| *Snelgrove, Alfred K. | M.Sc. | 28-524 |
| **McCarthy, J.** | | |
| Brooke, Richard O. | M.Sc. | 25-512 |
| Forbes, Franklin R. | M.Sc. | 33-570 |
| *Pugsley, Leonard I. | M.Sc. | 29-517 |
| **McCullagh, *** | | |
| *Banfill, Gladys M. | M.A. | 29-523 |
| **McCutcheon, J.** | | |
| Galbiati, Ignazio V. | M.Eng. | 58-503 |
| **McEachern, D.** | | |
| Kelen, Andrew | M.Sc. | 48-583 |
| Tower, Donald B. | M.Sc. | 48-549 |
| **McFarlane, J.** | | |
| Hagley, Elmer A. | Ph.D. | 57-014 |
| Kennard, Charles P. | M.Sc. | 57-562 |

| AUTHOR | DEGREE | THESIS NUMBER |
|---|---|---|
| **McFarlane, W.** | | |
| Andreae, Wolfgang A. | Ph.D. | 45-014 |
| Andreae, Wolfgang A. | M.Sc. | 43-502 |
| Armstrong, John G. | Ph.D. | 44-014 |
| Boone, Charles S. | M.Sc. | 37-534 |
| Boulet, Marcel | M.Sc. | 45-504 |
| Boulet, Marcel | Ph.D. | 48-017 |
| Campbell, James A. | Ph.D. | 47-023 |
| Chapman, Douglas G. | M.Sc. | 45-522 |
| Chapman, Ross A. | Ph.D. | 44-016 |
| Chapman, Ross A. | M.Sc. | 41-526 |
| Collins, Vernon K. | M.Sc. | 46-513 |
| Eiser, Herman M. | M.Sc. | 47-509 |
| Ellington, Alton C. | M.Sc. | 46-564 |
| Ewart, Mervyn H. | M.Sc. | 46-565 |
| Gass, James H. | M.Sc. | 47-546 |
| Goss, George C. | M.Sc. | 47-548 |
| Graham, Walter Donald | M.Sc. | 42-053 |
| Guest, Gordon H. | Ph.D. | 38-021 |
| Halpern, Philip E. | M.Sc. | 45-531 |
| Hare, John H. | M.Sc. | 47-550 |
| Knight, Enid P. | Ph.D. | 44-009 |
| Knight, Enid P. | M.Sc. | 39-515 |
| Leduc, Real A. | M.Sc. | 45-510 |
| Lips, Alair | Ph.D. | 44-010 |
| Lusena, Charles V. | Ph.D. | 47-033 |
| Lusena, Charles V. | M.Sc. | 44-520 |
| Morrison, Earl S. | M.Sc. | 44-507 |
| Neish, Arthur Charles | M.Sc. | 39-066 |
| Nelson, John A. | Ph.D. | 45-010 |
| Nichol, Charles A. | M.Sc. | 46-528 |
| Parker, William E. | M.Sc. | 37-538 |
| Parker, William E. | Ph.D. | 41-506 |
| Perlin, Arthur S. | M.Sc. | 46-574 |
| Pinsky, Alex | M.Sc. | 46-575 |
| Pringle, Ross B. | Ph.D. | 47-016 |
| Pringle, Ross B. | M.Sc. | 45-535 |
| Privett, Orville S. | Ph.D. | 47-017 |
| Privett, Orville S. | M.Sc. | 44-509 |
| Shaw, John Leslie Dickin | Ph.D. | 40-505 |
| Siminovitch, Helen E. | M.Sc. | 47-570 |
| Stranks, Donald W. | M.Sc. | 48-597 |
| Sutherland, Angus J. | M.Sc. | 38-522 |
| Wong, Esther V. | M.Sc. | 47-528 |
| Wood, Charles Rowell | M.Sc. | 41-051 |



| AUTHOR | DEGREE | THESIS NUMBER |
|---|---|---|
| **McIntosh, D.** | | |
| *Elliott, Percy H. | M.Sc. | 09-509 |
| *James, Clarke B. | M.Sc. | 15-508 |
| *Meldrum, William B. | M.Sc. | 10-518 |
| *Reid, Hugh S. | M.Sc. | 15-513 |
| *Shearer, George W. | M.Sc. | 08-513 |
| *Sivertz, Christian | Ph.D. | 26-004 |
| *Sivertz, Victorian | Ph.D. | 26-005 |
| **McIntosh, J.** | | |
| *Korenberg, Sarah M. | M.Sc. | 44-504 |
| **McIntosh, R.** | | |
| Bishinsky, Charles | Ph.D. | 44-015 |
| Davis, John | Ph.D. | 42-007 |
| Fireman, Manuel N. | Ph.D. | 44-003 |
| Guest, Rex M. | Ph.D. | 44-007 |
| Holmes, James M. | Ph.D. | 44-008 |
| McLeod, Lloyd A. | Ph.D. | 44-020 |
| Robertson, Ross E. | Ph.D. | 44-013 |
| Siminovitch, Louis | Ph.D. | 44-022 |
| **McIntosh,D.** | | |
| *Reilly, Herschell E. | M.Sc. | 14-515 |
| **McKergow, C.** | | |
| Ogilvy, Robert F. | M.Eng. | 32-504 |
| Rankin, Robert A. | M.Eng. | 33-504 |
| Richards, Victor L. | M.Eng. | 34-504 |
| *Rickell, William A. | M.Sc. | 23-504 |
| *Gliddon, William G. | M.Sc. | 22-507 |
| *Ryan, Charles C. | M.Sc. | 14-516 |
| *Vessot, Charles U. | M.Sc. | 22-524 |
| **McKibbin, F.** | | |
| Dyck, Abram J. | Ph.D. | 35-028 |

| AUTHOR | DEGREE | THESIS NUMBER |
|---|---|---|
| McKibbin, R. | | |
| Wrenshall, Charlton L. | Ph.D. | 36-022 |
| McKinnon, A. | | |
| Van Leight-Frank, Margit | M.A. | 54-556 |
| McLeod, C. | | |
| *Baird, John B. | M.Sc. | 09-507 |
| *Harvey, John B. | M.Sc. | 07-509 |
| McMillan, G. | | |
| Lautsch, Elizabeth V. | Ph.D. | 53-060 |
| Lautsch, Elizabeth V. | M.Sc. | 51-528 |
| McNaughton, F. | | |
| Dekaban, Anatole S. | Ph.D. | 54-046 |
| Earle, Kenneth M. | M.Sc. | 51-517 |
| Gibson, Robert M. | M.Sc. | 51-524 |
| Kim, Yoon-Bom | M.Sc. | 57-583 |
| Ramon-Moliner, Enrique | Ph.D. | 59-066 |
| McPherson, A. | | |
| Hunten, Janet L. | M.Sc. | 52-576 |
| McRostie, * | | |
| *Bird, Joseph N. | M.Sc. | 29-501 |
| McTaggart, A. | | |
| Rogers, John T. | M.S.A. | 24-549 |
| *Currie, Balfour W. | Ph.D. | 30-002 |
| *Zoond, Alexander | M.Sc. | 25-550 |



| AUTHOR | DEGREE | THESIS NUMBER |
|---|---|---|
| Meakins, J. | | |
| Christie, Ronald V. | M.Sc. | 33-569 |
| Evans, Gerald T. | M.Sc. | 33-514 |
| Henry, James P. | M.Sc. | 42-054 |
| Maughan, George B. | M.Sc. | 38-512 |
| Pattee, Chauncey J. | M.Sc. | 38-548 |
| Pugsley, Leonard I. | Ph.D. | 32-014 |
| *Cassidy, Gordon J. | M.Sc. | 25-546 |
| *Finney, William H. | M.Sc. | 28-508 |
| Meenie, J. | | |
| Woodhouse, Gordon H. | M.Eng. | 50-510 |
| Melville, K. | | |
| Bass, P. | Ph.D. | 57-052 |
| Beaulieu, Guy | M.Sc. | 59-577 |
| Drapeau, Jacqueline U. | M.Sc. | 55-598 |
| Francis, Lyman E. | M.Sc. | 58-520 |
| Hosein, Esau A. | M.Sc. | 50-534 |
| Korol, Bernard | Ph.D. | 56-024 |
| Mazurkiewicz, Irena M. | M.Sc. | 55-533 |
| Schachter, Melville | M.Sc. | 42-531 |
| Mennie, J. | | |
| Hampton, William F. | Ph.D. | 33-007 |
| Hampton, William F. | M.Sc. | 32-515 |
| Holmes, Edward L. | Ph.D. | 35-029 |
| Horn, Wallace R. | Ph.D. | 36-008 |
| Kent, George Adrian | M.Sc. | 42-056 |
| Lin, Wei-cheng | Ph.D. | 42-016 |
| Morehouse, Clarence K. | M.Sc. | 40-521 |
| Sanders, Herbert L. | Ph.D. | 37-022 |
| Sanders, Herbert L. | M.Sc. | 35-516 |
| Whittier, Angus C. | M.Sc. | 50-558 |
| Messac, * | | |
| *Stager, Drucilla N. | M.A. | 26-556 |

| AUTHOR | DEGREE | THESIS NUMBER |
|---|---|---|
| Messac, R. | | |
| Boden, Quinibert P. | M.A. | 26-537 |
| *Smith, Lawrence L. | M.A. | 28-554 |
| Miller, * | | |
| *Burke, Hugh E. | Ph.D. | 29-001 |
| Miller, G. | | |
| Borts, Robert B. | M.Sc. | 50-517 |
| Forse, Raymond F. | M.Sc. | 50-607 |
| Miller, J. | | |
| Kaal, Hans | M.A. | 58-542 |
| Nemiroff, Stanley A. | M.A. | 59-616 |
| Milner, P. | | |
| Burns, Neal M. | M.Sc. | 57-521 |
| Christake, Anna | Ph.D. | 58-012 |
| Glickman, Stephen | Ph.D. | 59-029 |
| Kimura, Douglas S. | Ph.D. | 59-041 |
| Mladenovic, M. | | |
| Beattie, Stewart | M.A. | 57-544 |
| Cienciala, Anna M. | M.A. | 55-626 |
| Glickman, Rose | M.A. | 58-583 |
| Mordell, D. | | |
| Adams, Glenn N. | M.Sc. | 50-511 |
| Beauregard, John P. | M.Eng. | 52-500 |
| Bula, Peter J. | M.Eng. | 54-560 |
| Chakko, P.C. | M.Eng. | 56-505 |
| Chant, Raymond E. | M.Eng. | 50-583 |
| Conrath, Joseph J. | M.Eng. | 51-502 |
| Daw, Geoffrey G. | M.Eng. | 51-584 |



| AUTHOR | DEGREE | THESIS NUMBER |
|---|---|---|
| Mordell, D. | | |
| Dodis, Nicolas G. | M.Eng. | 55-572 |
| Greenwood, Stuart W. | M.Eng. | 52-501 |
| Gupta, Makam C. | M.Eng. | 55-574 |
| Howell, Allison F. | M.Eng. | 49-590 |
| Lane, Alan G. | M.Eng. | 50-589 |
| Levine, Seymour | M.Eng. | 50-590 |
| LeMesurier, Kenneth A. | M.Eng. | 52-503 |
| Martinek, Frank | M.Eng. | 53-563 |
| McArthur, Beverley D. | M.Eng. | 53-508 |
| Pfefferkorn, Gerhard A. | M.Eng. | 56-560 |
| Quinn, Hubert F. | Ph.D. | 48-035 |
| Rogers, James T. | Ph.D. | 53-071 |
| Rogers, James T. | M.Eng. | 50-591 |
| Ross-Ross, Philip A. | M.Eng. | 51-505 |
| Shaw, Gerald A. | M.Eng. | 56-562 |
| Srinivasan, Malur R. | Ph.D. | 54-068 |
| Srinivasan, Malur R. | M.Eng. | 52-566 |
| Stachiewicz, J.W. | M.Eng. | 50-594 |
| Sullivan, Lorne J. | M.Eng. | 53-566 |
| Tao, Chia-hwa | M.Eng. | 58-506 |
| Taylor, George | M.Eng. | 58-558 |
| Tucker, Henry J. | M.Eng. | 55-579 |
| *Putnaerglis, Rudolph | M.Eng. | 55-507 |
| *Winship, R.D. | M.Eng. | 57-513 |
| More, F. | | |
| Kobernick, Sidney D. | Ph.D. | 51-017 |
| Kobernick, Sidney D. | M.Sc. | 49-607 |
| Rublee, J.D. | M.Sc. | 51-622 |
| Waugh, Douglas O. | Ph.D. | 50-023 |
| Morin, P. | | |
| *Forster, David S. | M.A. | 15-502 |
| *MacSween, Florence R. | M.A. | 15-504 |
| Morris, T. | | |
| Aron, Ivan M. | M.Sc. | 54-509 |
| Boloten, M. | M.Sc. | 51-596 |
| Segal, Louis | M.Sc. | 52-590 |

| AUTHOR | DEGREE | THESIS NUMBER |
|---|---|---|
| **Morris, T.** | | |
| Wilson, Roderic L. | M.Sc. | 55-546 |
| **Morrison, P.** | | |
| Fisher, Robert W. | Ph.D. | 51-008 |
| Gibbs, Kathleen E. | M.Sc. | 57-525 |
| Gustafson, Jean M. | M.Sc. | 58-522 |
| Hagley, Elmer A. | M.Sc. | 55-600 |
| Hikichi, Akira | M.Sc. | 56-579 |
| Hudon, Marcel | M.Sc. | 54-523 |
| LeRoux, Edgar J. | Ph.D. | 54-015 |
| Proverbs, Maurice D. | Ph.D. | 52-026 |
| Proverbs, Maurice D. | M.Sc. | 46-531 |
| Read, Deane C. | M.Sc. | 56-534 |
| Richardson, Howard P. | M.Sc. | 52-539 |
| **Morrison, R.** | | |
| Cairnes, William P. | M.Eng. | 56-504 |
| Cameron, Edward L. | M.Eng. | 54-502 |
| Davies, John J. | M.Eng. | 59-502 |
| Macaulay, Colin A. | M.Eng. | 55-576 |
| Ortlepp, William D. | M.Eng. | 57-509 |
| **Morton, M.** | | |
| Jeffrey, Claire O. | M.Sc. | 48-582 |
| **Mottram, *** | | |
| *Dowler, Vernon B. | M.Sc. | 16-508 |
| **Moyse, C.** | | |
| *Eaton, Mary J. | M.A. | 09-501 |
| *Hughes, Frederick G. | M.A. | 14-504 |
| *Irving, William G. | M.A. | 13-506 |
| *Macnaughton, Ariel M. | M.A. | 10-508 |
| *McBain, Alexander R. | M.A. | 13-507 |
| *McBain, Mary N. | M.A. | 21-520 |



| AUTHOR | DEGREE | THESIS NUMBER |
|---|---|---|
| **Moyse, C.** | | |
| *McDonald, Jessie | M.A. | 10-505 |
| *McNeil, John T. | M.A. | 10-509 |
| *Parker, David W. | M.A. | 08-503 |
| *Willis, Helen A. | M.A. | 17-502 |
| **Munroe, D.** | | |
| Lieber, Jack W. | M.A. | 57-549 |
| Skinner, James M. | M.A. | 59-620 |
| **Murray, *** | | |
| *Hatcher, Albert G. | M.A. | 10-501 |
| *Miller, Iveson A. | M.Sc. | 15-511 |
| *Richardson, Lorne N. | M.Sc. | 10-520 |
| **Murray, E.** | | |
| Avery, Robert J. | Ph.D. | 55-004 |
| Avery, Robert J. | M.Sc. | 52-567 |
| Bailey, William R. | Ph.D. | 55-045 |
| Bailey, William R. | M.Sc. | 50-512 |
| Beaulieu, Maurice | Ph.D. | 55-047 |
| Beaulieu, Maurice | M.Sc. | 53-572 |
| Bedford, Robert H. | Ph.D. | 31-004 |
| Ciplijauskate, Jurate E. | M.Sc. | 54-579 |
| Girard, Kenneth F. | Ph.D. | 52-013 |
| Girard, Kenneth F. | M.Sc. | 50-525 |
| Hawirko, Roma Z. | Ph.D. | 51-013 |
| Hawirko, Roma Z. | M.Sc. | 49-529 |
| Morgante, Odosca | M.Sc. | 55-536 |
| Nunes, Doris S. | M.Sc. | 49-613 |
| Riddell, Marion I. | M.Sc. | 50-630 |
| Ruyter, Sally A. | M.Sc. | 48-544 |
| Thompson, Robert F. | Ph.D. | 32-026 |
| Whitehead, Howard A. | Ph.D. | 53-039 |
| Whitehead, Howard A. | M.Sc. | 51-629 |
| *Glynn, John H. | M.Sc. | 31-552 |
| **Murray, H.** | | |

| AUTHOR | DEGREE | THESIS NUMBER |
|---|---|---|
| **Murray, H.** | | |
| Bourque, Leopold | M.Sc. | 37-535 |
| Cann, Keith E. | M.Sc. | 51-599 |
| Chan, Allan P. | M.Sc. | 46-510 |
| Cutcliffe, Jack A. | M.Sc. | 54-517 |
| Filman, Conrad Colton | M.Sc. | 42-522 |
| Forest, Bertrand | M.Sc. | 45-526 |
| Harding, Charles F. | M.Sc. | 50-610 |
| Harney, Patricia M. | M.Sc. | 59-518 |
| Laliberte, Jacques N. | M.Sc. | 47-516 |
| Maurer, Alfred R. | M.Sc. | 48-535 |
| Montgrain, Clement | M.Sc. | 44-506 |
| Nussey, Albert N. | M.Sc. | 48-594 |
| O'Reilly, Henry J. | M.Sc. | 44-508 |
| Ounsworth, Leslie Frank | M.Sc. | 39-067 |
| Pickup, T. | M.Sc. | 56-594 |
| Trossman, Walter A. | M.Sc. | 49-550 |
| **Narayana, T.** | | |
| Fulton, Geraldine E. | M.Sc. | 58-567 |
| **Nardin, P.** | | |
| Dick, Helen | M.A. | 52-602 |
| Melzak, Adrienne | M.A. | 51-639 |
| Mitchell, Kina M. | M.A. | 52-608 |
| Saint-Martin, Fernande | M.A. | 52-555 |
| Walton, Robert F. | M.A. | 52-610 |
| **Neilson, H.** | | |
| Irwin, Mary I. | M.Sc. | 50-536 |
| **Nichclls, R.** | | |
| Aikin, Archibald M. | Ph.D. | 49-040 |
| Allenby, Owen C. | Ph.D. | 42-001 |
| Blizzard, Ronald H. | Ph.D. | 42-004 |
| Bourns, Arthur N. | Ph.D. | 44-001 |
| Burch, George N. | M.Sc. | 46-560 |
| Cabbott, Irwin M. | M.Sc. | 47-507 |



| AUTHOR | DEGREE | THESIS NUMBER |
|---|---|---|
| **Nicholls, F.** | | |
| Cipera, John D. | Ph.D. | 54-042 |
| Deans, Sidney A. | Ph.D. | 42-009 |
| Dechene, Earl B. | M.Sc. | 47-545 |
| Eiger, Irena Z. | M.Sc. | 43-519 |
| Farmilo, Charles G. | Ph.D. | 48-023 |
| Gendron, Lucien J. | Ph.D. | 54-013 |
| Henery-Logan, Kenneth R. | Ph.D. | 46-027 |
| Jardine, John M. | M.Sc. | 48-527 |
| Larsson, Bjorn E. | Ph.D. | 50-034 |
| Levi, Leo | Ph.D. | 50-035 |
| Maclean, David B. | Ph.D. | 46-029 |
| Morton, Maurice | Ph.D. | 45-009 |
| Polley, John R. | Ph.D. | 46-031 |
| Robinson, Donald B. | Ph.D. | 43-012 |
| Rosten, Jean | M.Sc. | 44-522 |
| Russell, Gordon D. | M.Sc. | 46-576 |
| Shaw, Alan C. | Ph.D. | 55-073 |
| Smart, George N. Russell | Ph.D. | 45-020 |
| Smith, Melvin J. | M.Sc. | 45-540 |
| Stinton, Arthur W. | M.Sc. | 45-541 |
| Tonks, David B. | Ph.D. | 49-039 |
| Wasson, Burton K. | Ph.D. | 42-026 |
| Watts, Humphrey Stanley | M.Sc. | 40-525 |
| **Nikolaiczuk, N.** | | |
| Brisson, Germain | M.Sc. | 48-578 |
| Burgess, Ralph C. | M.Sc. | 52-514 |
| Cadet, Charles M. | M.Sc. | 54-577 |
| Keenan, Daniel | M.Sc. | 55-526 |
| Mani, K.V. | M.Sc. | 48-534 |
| Miller, William St. C. | M.Sc. | 50-624 |
| Smith, Robert F. | M.Sc. | 57-538 |
| **Noad, A.** | | |
| Bishop, Annetta C. | M.A. | 38-525 |
| Brown, George | M.A. | 31-522 |
| Fry, Margaret Exie | M.A. | 42-030 |
| Guardo, Lea C. | M.A. | 48-562 |
| Hetherington, Elizabeth | M.A. | 36-532 |
| Hutcheson, Maud M. | M.A. | 27-532 |
| Money-Coutts, Joanna H. | M.A. | 50-570 |

| AUTHOR | DEGREE | THESIS NUMBER |
|---|---|---|
| **Noad, A.** | | |
| Shecter, Una | M.A. | 39-509 |
| Simon, Beatrice V. | M.A. | 50-666 |
| *Davies, Thomas R. | M.A. | 27-528 |
| *Gough, Roger W. | M.A. | 30-527 |
| *Jefferis, Jeffrey D. | M.A. | 29-538 |
| *Kiefer, Elsie B. | M.A. | 29-556 |
| *Mackay, Robert de W. | M.A. | 29-544 |
| *Moore, Ruth E. | M.A. | 30-538 |
| *Phelan, Lewis J. | M.A. | 29-557 |
| *Stansfield, Ellen E. | M.A. | 31-543 |
| **Noad, A. .** | | |
| *Creighton, Edith M. | M.A. | 26-538 |
| **Noble, R.** | | |
| Gold, Allen | M.Sc. | 48-523 |
| Macbeth, Robert A. | M.Sc. | 47-557 |
| **O'Neil, J.** | | |
| *Aylard, Clara M. | M.Sc. | 24-506 |
| *Bishop, Eric G. | M.Sc. | 24-508 |
| **O'Neill, J.** | | |
| Black, Philip T. | M.Sc. | 49-512 |
| Burton, Frederick R. | M.Sc. | 28-502 |
| Cote, Pierre E. | Ph.D. | 48-021 |
| Gilbert, Joseph E. | Ph.D. | 49-012 |
| Gray, Richard H. | Ph.D. | 40-010 |
| Halet, Robert A. | Ph.D. | 34-006 |
| L'Esperance, Robert L. | Ph.D. | 51-052 |
| McAllister, Arnold L. | Ph.D. | 50-013 |
| Price, Peter | Ph.D. | 33-016 |
| Robinson, Raymond F. | M.Sc. | 38-516 |
| Taylor, William L. | M.Sc. | 50-635 |
| Tremblay, Mousseau | M.Sc. | 51-559 |
| Whiting, Francis B. | M.Sc. | 48-554 |
| Williamson, John T. | Ph.D. | 33-025 |



| AUTHOR | DEGREE | THESIS NUMBER |
|---|---|---|
| **O'Neill, J.** | | |
| *Davidson, Stanley C. | M.Sc. | 25-513 |
| *Gerson, Harold S. | M.Sc. | 29-508 |
| *Holbrocke, George L. | M.Sc. | 28-512 |
| *Snelgrove, Alfred K. | M.Sc. | 28-524 |
| **O'Shaughnessy, M.** | | |
| Raju, B. Sadasiva | M.Eng. | 48-510 |
| Salman, Mehmet T. | M.Eng. | 44-500 |
| **Oertel, H.** | | |
| *Armour, John C. | M.Sc. | 23-502 |
| *Conklin, Raymond L. | M.Sc. | 24-511 |
| *Freedman, Nathan | M.Sc. | 28-560 |
| *Kearns, Peter J. | M.Sc. | 28-515 |
| *McGreer, Edgar D. | M.A. | 23-523 |
| *Perry, Helen M. | M.Sc. | 24-527 |
| *Rosenbaum, Saul F. | M.Sc. | 26-524 |
| **Ogilvie, J.** | | |
| Walsh, John H. | M.Eng. | 51-591 |
| **Olsen, C.** | | |
| Estey, Ralph H. | Ph.D. | 56-046 |
| **Olszewski, J.** | | |
| Hoff, Theodore F. | M.Sc. | 54-588 |
| Nashold, Blaine S. | M.Sc. | 54-597 |
| Rozdilsky, Bohdan | M.Sc. | 56-600 |
| **Onyszchuk, M.** | | |
| Griffiths, James E. | Ph.D. | 59-031 |

| AUTHOR | DEGREE | THESIS NUMBER |
| --- | --- | --- |
| Opechowski, W. | | |
| Marcus, Alma | M.Sc. | 50-546 |
| Orvig, S. | | |
| Foote, Don C. | M.A. | 59-549 |
| Jackson, Charles I. | M.Sc. | 59-522 |
| Nebiker, Walter A. | M.Sc. | 57-590 |
| Sagar, Richard B. | M.Sc. | 59-535 |
| Shellabear, William H. | M.Sc. | 59-598 |
| Osborne, F. | | |
| Black, James M. | Ph.D. | 42-003 |
| Bray, Richard C. | M.Sc. | 40-039 |
| Buckland, Francis C. | Ph.D. | 37-004 |
| Buckland, Francis C. | M.Sc. | 32-509 |
| Cleveland, Courtney E. | Ph.D. | 40-005 |
| Cleveland, Courtney E. | M.Sc. | 38-506 |
| Davis, Charles W. | M.Sc. | 37-504 |
| Denis, Bertrand T. | Ph.D. | 38-005 |
| Denis, Frank T. | M.Sc. | 33-512 |
| Denton, William Ernest | M.Sc. | 40-042 |
| Douglas, John MacDonald | M.Sc. | 41-037 |
| Fortier, Yves | M.Sc. | 41-038 |
| Gilbert, Joseph E. | M.Sc. | 47-513 |
| Gillies, Norman B. | M.Sc. | 46-566 |
| Greig, Edmund W. | M.Sc. | 38-509 |
| Grimes-Graeme, Rhoderick | Ph.D. | 35-013 |
| Hall, James Dickie | M.Sc. | 39-058 |
| Hill, Lawrence Stanley | M.Sc. | 40-045 |
| Hope-Simpson, David | M.Sc. | 41-528 |
| Howells, William Crompto | Ph.D. | 40-012 |
| Imbault, Paul-Emile | M.Sc. | 47-552 |
| Keating, Bernard J. | Ph.D. | 37-014 |
| Lowther, George K. | Ph.D. | 35-018 |
| MacDonald, Murray V. | M.Sc. | 38-511 |
| Malouf, Stanley E. | M.Sc. | 36-512 |
| Mauffette, Pierre | M.Sc. | 41-045 |
| Milner, Robert Leopold | Ph.D. | 40-017 |
| Moss, Albert E. | M.Sc. | 37-511 |
| Neeland, William D. | M.Sc. | 35-511 |
| Riordon, Peter H. | M.Sc. | 38-518 |
| Robinson, William G. | M.Sc. | 38-517 |



| AUTHOR | DEGREE | THESIS NUMBER |
| --- | --- | --- |
| Osborne, F. | | |
| Selmser, Calbert | M.Sc. | 39-069 |
| Shaw, George | M.Sc. | 34-516 |
| Simard, Lionel R. | M.Sc. | 34-517 |
| Tiphane, Marcel | M.Sc. | 47-573 |
| Wahl, William G. | Ph.D. | 47-021 |
| Wilson, Norman L. | M.Sc. | 33-533 |
| Wykes, Eric R. | M.Sc. | 31-518 |
| Osborne, J. | | |
| Wilson, Norman L. | Ph.D. | 39-028 |
| Owens, E. | | |
| *Roffey, Myles H. | M.Sc. | 09-516 |
| Pady, S. | | |
| Etheridge, David E. | M.Sc. | 53-525 |
| Kapica, Lucia | M.Sc. | 54-524 |
| Macleod, Donald M. | Ph.D. | 53-022 |
| Turnau, Edmund A. | M.Sc. | 50-636 |
| Tyler, Nancy P. | M.Sc. | 52-595 |
| Pall, G. | | |
| Lambek, Joachim | M.Sc. | 46-525 |
| Rosenthall, Edward | M.Sc. | 38-519 |
| Solin, Cecil D. | M.A. | 38-542 |
| Williams, Christine S. | M.A. | 44-517 |
| Patterson, E. | | |
| White, Thomas N. | Ph.D. | 29-020 |
| Pavlasek, T. | | |
| Caswell, Charles F. | M.Eng. | 58-555 |
| Charasz, Jerzy G. | M.Eng. | 57-504 |

| AUTHOR | DEGREE | THESIS NUMBER |
|---|---|---|
| **Pavlasek, T.** | | |
| Stone, Samuel A. | M.Eng. | 58-505 |
| **Peck, J.** | | |
| Laufer, Philip J. | Ph.D. | 58-024 |
| Teitlebaum, Albert D. | M.Sc. | 59-602 |
| **Pelletier, R.** | | |
| Phillips, Charles O. | M.Sc. | 59-592 |
| Udeaja, Philip E. | M.Sc. | 58-533 |
| Wang, Dalton T. | Ph.D. | 57-043 |
| *Jain, Abir C. | Ph.D. | 58-021 |
| *Jayanetti, Edwin | Ph.D. | 58-022 |
| **Penfield, W.** | | |
| Bates, John I. | M.Sc. | 48-574 |
| Bertrand, Gilles | M.Sc. | 53-573 |
| Bridgers, William Henry | M.Sc. | 41-525 |
| Corona, Carlos | M.Sc. | 45-525 |
| Echlin, Francis Asbury | M.Sc. | 39-513 |
| Erickson, Theodore C. | Ph.D. | 39-006 |
| Evans, Joseph P. | Ph.D. | 37-027 |
| Gibson, William C. | M.Sc. | 36-547 |
| Haymaker, Webb | M.Sc. | 35-538 |
| Humphreys, Storer Plumer | M.Sc. | 39-060 |
| Jackson, Ira J. | M.Sc. | 47-553 |
| Kite, William C. | M.Sc. | 49-534 |
| Meyer, John S. | M.Sc. | 49-541 |
| Nichols, Walter M. | M.Sc. | 38-547 |
| Norcross, Nathan C. | M.Sc. | 36-514 |
| Olszewski, Jerzy | Ph.D. | 51-027 |
| Pudenz, Robert Harry | M.Sc. | 41-535 |
| Robb, James P. | M.Sc. | 46-533 |
| Roberts, Henry L. | Ph.D. | 52-060 |
| Roberts, Henry L. | M.Sc. | 49-617 |
| Tarlov, Isadore M. | M.Sc. | 32-558 |
| **Penhallon, D.** | | |



| AUTHOR | DEGREE | THESIS NUMBER |
|---|---|---|
| **Penhallon, D.** | | |
| *Harvie, Robert | M.Sc. | 09-513 |
| **Penhallow, D.** | | |
| Kirsch, Simon | Ph.D. | 10-002 |
| *Kirsch, Simon | M.A. | 07-503 |
| **Pepin, F.** | | |
| Ahmad, Mumtaz | LL.M. | 57-514 |
| Ahmed, Saiyed E. | LL.M. | 57-515 |
| Arnold, Stanley F. | LL.M. | 57-560 |
| Dillon, Joseph G. | LL.M. | 59-572 |
| Gamacchio, Giampiero | LL.M. | 57-561 |
| Hadjis, Dimitris | LL.M. | 58-559 |
| Leclercq, Genevieve F. | LL.M. | 59-508 |
| Lureau, Daniel J. | LL.M. | 59-509 |
| Macbrayne, Sheila F. | LL.M. | 56-565 |
| MacKnescn, Stephen W. | LL.M. | 59-574 |
| Nylen, Torsten | LL.M. | 56-566 |
| Rippon, Clive L. | LL.M. | 57-516 |
| Ritchie, Marguerite E. | LL.M. | 58-560 |
| Sheffy, Menachem | LL.M. | 57-563 |
| Wojcik, Tadeusz Z. | LL.M. | 57-517 |
| **Perdriau, M.** | | |
| *Powles, Percival S. | M.A. | 14-507 |
| **Perrin, H.** | | |
| *O'Neill, Charles | M.M.A. | 24-500 |
| *Treharne, Bryceson | Mus.D. | 30-016 |
| **Petersen, J.** | | |
| Boldrey, Edwin E. | M.Sc. | 36-508 |

| AUTHOR | DEGREE | THESIS NUMBER |
|---|---|---|
| **Phelan, V.** | | |
| Benes, Vaclav | M.C.L. | 50-500 |
| **Phelps, A.** | | |
| Taggart, William R. | M.A. | 52-557 |
| Wearing, Parker L. | M.A. | 49-581 |
| **Phillips, J.** | | |
| Bedoukian, Paul | M.Sc. | 38-544 |
| Bennett, Robert D. | M.Sc. | 33-508 |
| Bennett, Robert D. | Ph.D. | 35-004 |
| Chadillon, Francois J. | M.Eng. | 45-519 |
| Charles, George E. | M.Eng. | 51-501 |
| Elkin, Eugene M. | Ph.D. | 35-011 |
| Giddings, E. W. Garner | M.Eng. | 39-049 |
| Goudey, John F. | M.Eng. | 49-504 |
| Gribbins, Gordon Henry | M.Eng. | 39-050 |
| Kemmett, Francis W. | M.Eng. | 48-507 |
| Nenniger, Emile | M.Eng. | 51-588 |
| Schaus, Orland O. | M.Eng. | 52-510 |
| Stidwell, William Franci | M.Eng. | 40-516 |
| Stovel, Henry V. | M.Sc. | 33-571 |
| **Pierce, *** | | |
| *Bogante, Jack R. | M.A. | 27-523 |
| **Porteous, A.** | | |
| Estall, Henry M. | M.A. | 31-528 |
| **Porter, J.** | | |
| Cameron, Alan E. | M.Sc. | 14-509 |
| Carmichael, Henry G. | M.Sc. | 10-513 |
| Cockfield, William E. | M.Sc. | 15-507 |
| De Hart, Joseph B. | M.Sc. | 12-510 |
| Edwards, Gordon M. | M.Sc. | 21-506 |
| Erlenborn, Willi | M.Sc. | 21-507 |



| AUTHOR | DEGREE | THESIS NUMBER |
|---|---|---|
| **Porter, J.** | | |
| *Anderson, Clayton E. | M.Sc. | 20-501 |
| *Anderson, Robert G. | M.Sc. | 23-501 |
| *Becking, John A. | M.Sc. | 25-510 |
| *Billington, Edward E. | M.Sc. | 13-513 |
| *Bissell, Harold R. | M.Sc. | 23-505 |
| *Brow, James B. | M.Sc. | 22-501 |
| *Cave, Allister F. | M.Sc. | 25-547 |
| *Dewar, Charles L. | M.Sc. | 22-502 |
| *Douglas, George V. | M.Sc. | 21-504 |
| *Galloway, John D. | M.Sc. | 12-508 |
| *Gegg, Richard C. | M.Sc. | 24-516 |
| *Gillies, George A. | M.Sc. | 11-511 |
| *Harding, Ellis G. | M.Sc. | 21-508 |
| *Hayes, Albert C. | M.Sc. | 10-517 |
| *Iathe, Frank E. | M.Sc. | 15-510 |
| *Legg, Roland E. | M.Sc. | 24-521 |
| *McKinney, James W. | Ph.D. | 23-005 |
| *Mitchell, William G. | M.Sc. | 14-514 |
| *Muir, Allan K. | M.Sc. | 25-524 |
| *Murray, George E. | M.Sc. | 12-515 |
| *Riordon, Charles H. | M.Sc. | 27-517 |
| *Ross, William E. | M.Sc. | 27-519 |
| *Saunders, James F. | M.Sc. | 22-521 |
| *Snijman, Johan J. | M.Sc. | 24-551 |
| *Spencer, Roy A. | M.Sc. | 15-514 |
| *Strangways, Henry F. | M.Sc. | 08-514 |
| *Tousaw, Albert A. | M.Sc. | 20-507 |
| *Walter, Albert J. | M.Sc. | 26-531 |
| *Weldon, Thomas H. | M.Sc. | 23-519 |
| *Yuill, Harry H. | M.Sc. | 10-524 |
| **Porter, J. A.** | | |
| *Gibbins, Gwynn G. | M.Sc. | 11-510 |
| **Porter, J. .** | | |
| *Airey, Henry T. | M.Sc. | 27-502 |
| **Porter, S.** | | |
| Friend, Gregory | M.A. | 55-629 |

| AUTHOR | DEGREE | THESIS NUMBER |
|---|---|---|
| **Porter, S.** | | |
| Keirstead, Marjorie S. | M.A. | 53-552 |
| Maizel, Norah L. | M.A. | 55-555 |
| **Pounder, E.** | | |
| Heckman, Donald E. | Ph.D. | 56-016 |
| Heckman, Donald E. | M.Sc. | 53-532 |
| Hogan, Howard R. | M.Sc. | 50-532 |
| Perey, Francis G. | M.Sc. | 57-591 |
| **Pratt, R.** | | |
| Chidzero, Bernard T. | Ph.D. | 58-011 |
| **Prince, S.** | | |
| *Brown, Wilfred H. | M.A. | 27-525 |
| **Prissick, F.** | | |
| Barnes, Marion J. | M.Sc. | 56-567 |
| **Purves, C.** | | |
| Adamek, Edward G. | Ph.D. | 59-001 |
| Andrews, Douglas H. | Ph.D. | 54-003 |
| Beelik, Andrew | Ph.D. | 54-039 |
| Bishop, Claude T. | Ph.D. | 49-044 |
| Booth, Kenneth G. | Ph.D. | 48-016 |
| Brickman, William J. | Ph.D. | 53-046 |
| Brounstein, Cyril J. | Ph.D. | 52-040 |
| Brown, Robert K. | Ph.D. | 46-020 |
| Brownell, Harold H. | Ph.D. | 53-047 |
| Bryce, John R. | Ph.D. | 55-008 |
| Butler, Robert W. | Ph.D. | 50-003 |
| Cabott, Irving M. | Ph.D. | 51-042 |
| Christian, William R. | Ph.D. | 46-022 |
| Cox, Lionel A. | Ph.D. | 46-023 |
| Creamer, George B. | Ph.D. | 50-028 |
| Dixon, John P. | Ph.D. | 47-003 |



| AUTHOR | DEGREE | THESIS NUMBER |
|---|---|---|
| **Purves, C.** | | |
| Eisenbraun, Allan A. | Ph.D. | 59-020 |
| Eisenbraun, Edgar W. | Ph.D. | 59-021 |
| Ellington, Alton C. | Ph.D. | 49-022 |
| English, William I. | M.Sc. | 50-524 |
| Falconer, Errol L. | Ph.D. | 56-010 |
| Foxlee, Frank H. | Ph.D. | 46-024 |
| Frank, Arlen W. | Ph.D. | 54-049 |
| Gardner, Joseph A. | Ph.D. | 44-006 |
| Gardner, Prescott E. | Ph.D. | 59-015 |
| Gleason, Clarence H. | Ph.D. | 47-027 |
| Glegg, Ronald E. | Ph.D. | 46-025 |
| Gogek, Charles J. | Ph.D. | 47-006 |
| Grassie, Vernon R. | Ph.D. | 46-008 |
| Guthrie, Donald A. | Ph.D. | 52-014 |
| Hardy, John A. | M.Sc. | 55-601 |
| Harpham, John A. | Ph.D. | 51-049 |
| Harwood, Victor D. | Ph.D. | 49-016 |
| Hayward, Lloyl D. | Ph.D. | 49-050 |
| Hoffman, John C. | Ph.D. | 57-017 |
| Husband, Robert M. | Ph.D. | 47-029 |
| Jablonski, Werner L. | Ph.D. | 53-014 |
| Keays, John L. | Ph.D. | 49-051 |
| Lemieux, Raymond U. | Ph.D. | 46-028 |
| Levitin, Norman | Ph.D. | 51-018 |
| Logan, Charles D. | Ph.D. | 49-026 |
| Logan, Kenneth C. | Ph.D. | 49-052 |
| MacFarlane, Hugh M. | Ph.D. | 50-036 |
| Manchester, Donald F. | Ph.D. | 52-055 |
| McKillican, Mary E. | Ph.D. | 52-053 |
| Milford, George N. | Ph.D. | 53-025 |
| Milks, John E. | Ph.D. | 53-066 |
| Mitchell, Leonard | Ph.D. | 44-012 |
| Moir, Robert Y. | Ph.D. | 46-030 |
| Moulds, Gordon M. | Ph.D. | 53-026 |
| Muller, Thomas E. | M.Sc. | 59-529 |
| Murdock, James D. | Ph.D. | 52-059 |
| Narasinham, Ramanujaieng | M.Sc. | 48-592 |
| Neubauer, Lewis G. | Ph.D. | 49-053 |
| Perlin, Arthur S. | Ph.D. | 49-032 |
| Read, Dale W. | Ph.D. | 59-067 |
| Read, Donald E. | Ph.D. | 49-054 |
| Reid, Albert R. | Ph.D. | 53-033 |
| Ritchie, Paul F. | Ph.D. | 47-018 |
| Rooney, Clarence E. | Ph.D. | 52-028 |
| Sacks, William | Ph.D. | 54-064 |

| AUTHOR | DEGREE | THESIS NUMBER |
|---|---|---|
| **Purves, C.** | | |
| Sanderson, Edwin S. | Ph.D. | 53-073 |
| Sanyal, Amiya K. | Ph.D. | 53-074 |
| Segall, Gordon H. | Ph.D. | 46-032 |
| Sherbeck, Leander A. | Ph.D. | 51-057 |
| Smith, Donald M. | Ph.D. | 56-034 |
| Spivack, John D. | Ph.D. | 47-036 |
| Sutherland, Charlotte A. | M.Sc. | 57-539 |
| Swan, Eric P. | Ph.D. | 57-038 |
| Tasker, Clinton W. | Ph.D. | 47-037 |
| Thompson, Norman S. | Ph.D. | 54-071 |
| Thorn, George D. | Ph.D. | 47-038 |
| Vincent, Donald L. | Ph.D. | 53-038 |
| Watts, Trevor A. | Ph.D. | 54-073 |
| Whittall, Norman S. | M.Sc. | 50-639 |
| Wieckowski, Erwin | Ph.D. | 57-089 |
| Wood, John C. | Ph.D. | 53-079 |
| Yan, Maxwell M. | Ph.D. | 47-039 |
| Zienius, Raymond H. | Ph.D. | 59-077 |
| **Quastel, J.** | | |
| Avigan, Joel | Ph.D. | 54-037 |
| Bas-Kraus, Eva R. | M.Sc. | 57-566 |
| Baxter, Robert M. | Ph.D. | 52-003 |
| Boyd, Donald H. | Ph.D. | 53-045 |
| Braganca, Menezes B. | Ph.D. | 51-041 |
| Brown, William T. | Ph.D. | 54-041 |
| Colter, John S. | Ph.D. | 51-006 |
| Darlington, Walter A. | Ph.D. | 52-009 |
| Faulkner, Peter | Ph.D. | 54-011 |
| Franklin, Arthur E. | Ph.D. | 51-010 |
| Fridhandler, Louis | Ph.D. | 53-052 |
| Goldstein, Fred B. | Ph.D. | 55-058 |
| Greenway, Robert M. | Ph.D. | 56-014 |
| Guthrie, John E. | M.Sc. | 55-523 |
| Haber, Andrew B. | M.Sc. | 57-576 |
| Halperin, Alex H. | M.Sc. | 52-575 |
| Harpur, Robert P. | Ph.D. | 49-049 |
| Hochster, Rolf M. | Ph.D. | 50-031 |
| Johnson, Willard J. | Ph.D. | 52-021 |
| Kochen, Joseph A. | Ph.D. | 56-055 |
| Kushner, Donn J. | Ph.D. | 52-050 |
| Majchrowicz, Edward | Ph.D. | 59-080 |
| Mamelak, Rose | Ph.D. | 53-064 |



| AUTHOR | DEGREE | THESIS NUMBER |
|---|---|---|
| **Quastel, J.** | | |
| Parmar, Surendra S. | Ph.D. | 57-075 |
| Pascoe, Enid | Ph.D. | 56-059 |
| Petc, Margaret | Ph.D. | 59-062 |
| Petc, Margaret | M.Sc. | 56-593 |
| Petrushka, Evelyn | Ph.D. | 57-076 |
| Picher, Ruth C. | M.Sc. | 51-543 |
| Piklis, Emanuel | Ph.D. | 58-038 |
| Scholefield, Peter G. | Ph.D. | 49-037 |
| Schucher, Reuben | Ph.D. | 54-032 |
| Srinivasan, Swamy A. | Ph.D. | 57-080 |
| Sved, Stephen | Ph.D. | 58-047 |
| Taussig, Andrew | Ph.D. | 55-078 |
| Tenenhouse, Alan | Ph.D. | 59-072 |
| Vardanis, Alexandre | M.Sc. | 58-534 |
| Verdier, Pamela C. | M.Sc. | 52-596 |
| Witty, Ralph | Ph.D. | 51-036 |
| **Rabinovitch, I.** | | |
| *Illievitz, Abraham R. | M.Sc. | 25-521 |
| *Maytum, Helen E. | M.Sc. | 27-511 |
| *Vineberg, Arthur M. | M.Sc. | 28-525 |
| **Rahbar, M.** | | |
| Kamali, Sabih A. | M.A. | 55-552 |
| Mu'inu-d-din, Ahmad K. | M.A. | 55-635 |
| Watson, William J. | M.A. | 55-566 |
| **Rahman, F.** | | |
| Faruqi, Ziya-ul-Hasan | M.A. | 59-608 |
| **Rasjidi, M.** | | |
| Feroz, Muhammad R. | M.A. | 59-548 |
| Jaylani, Tedjaningsih | M.A. | 59-553 |
| Jaylani, Timur | M.A. | 59-554 |

| AUTHOR | DEGREE | THESIS NUMBER |
|---|---|---|
| Rasmussen, T. | | |
| Aguilar, Mary J. | M.Sc. | 58-561 |
| Litvak, John | M.Sc. | 57-529 |
| Samson, Hugh R. | M.Sc. | 59-596 |
| Rattray, B. | | |
| Normand, Gerard L. | M.Sc. | 59-590 |
| Raymond, L. | | |
| Boulet, Lucien J. | M.Sc. | 37-502 |
| Chiasson, Thomas C. | M.Sc. | 55-593 |
| Deane, Burton C. | M.Sc. | 55-597 |
| Dimmock, Frederick | M.Sc. | 26-558 |
| Dore, William G. | M.Sc. | 35-503 |
| Drapala, Walter J. | M.Sc. | 46-517 |
| Eaton, Ernest L. | M.S.A. | 25-502 |
| Gervais, Paul | M.Sc. | 48-522 |
| Hanson, Angus A. | M.Sc. | 46-520 |
| Loiselle, Roland | M.Sc. | 51-531 |
| MacVicar, Roderick M. | M.Sc. | 34-513 |
| Nowosad, Frank S. | M.Sc. | 33-524 |
| Povilaitis, Bronys | M.Sc. | 51-542 |
| Proverbs, Ivor H. | M.Sc. | 50-552 |
| Shuh, John Edward | M.Sc. | 42-065 |
| Steppler, Howard A. | Ph.D. | 55-038 |
| Steppler, Howard A. | M.Sc. | 48-548 |
| Stobbe, Peter C. | M.Sc. | 34-518 |
| *Parent, Robert C. | M.S.A. | 24-504 |
| Raymond, L. . | | |
| *Bird, Joseph N. | M.Sc. | 29-501 |
| Reay, * | | |
| *Munn, David W. | M.Sc. | 11-514 |
| Redfield, A. | | |



| AUTHOR | DEGREE | THESIS NUMBER |
|---|---|---|
| Redfield, A. | | |
| *Pinhey, Kathleen F. | Ph.D. | 30-012 |
| Reed, R. | | |
| Barshaw, Wilma E. | M.Sc. | 56-568 |
| Ciplijauskate, Jurate E. | Ph.D. | 56-043 |
| Fabrikant, Irene B. | M.Sc. | 56-573 |
| Hannan, Charles K. | Ph.D. | 56-053 |
| Matheson, Ballem H. | Ph.D. | 57-064 |
| Morgante, Odosca | Ph.D. | 59-054 |
| Morigi, Eugene M. | Ph.D. | 59-055 |
| Reid, F. | | |
| Kataria, Prem N. | M.Sc. | 57-581 |
| Reid, W. | | |
| Brown, Ian W. | M.A. | 59-546 |
| Charteris, J.N. | M.A. | 55-625 |
| Fox, Leslie P. | M.A. | 49-559 |
| Judges, Nancy E. | M.A. | 55-632 |
| Parker, T.C. | M.A. | 57-607 |
| Ritchie, Verna F. | M.A. | 59-618 |
| Ross, V.J. | M.A. | 57-610 |
| Rowlands, Mary F. | M.A. | 56-621 |
| Senior, Hereward | Ph.D. | 59-092 |
| Senior, Hereward | M.A. | 51-575 |
| Reverchon, M. | | |
| Hall, Janet M. | M.A. | 59-609 |
| Shanks, Laura E. | M.A. | 59-562 |
| Rhea, L. | | |
| *Glynn, John H. | M.Sc. | 31-552 |
| *Green, Frederick | M.Sc. | 25-518 |

| AUTHOR | DEGREE | THESIS NUMBER |
|---|---|---|
| **Rice, J.** | | |
| *Maw, William A. | M.S.A. | 25-544 |
| **Riddell, J.** | | |
| Berrange, Jevan P. | M.Sc. | 58-509 |
| Brown, Norman E. | M.Sc. | 52-513 |
| Brummer, Johannes J. | Ph.D. | 55-049 |
| Carriere, Gilles E. | M.Sc. | 54-578 |
| Cornwall, Frederick W. | Ph.D. | 56-006 |
| Cornwall, Frederick W. | M.Sc. | 53-583 |
| Klugman, Michael A. | M.Sc. | 53-534 |
| MacDougall, John F. | M.Sc. | 52-535 |
| Morrison, E.R. | M.Sc. | 55-615 |
| Murray, Louis G. | Ph.D. | 54-058 |
| Schmidt, Richard C. | Ph.D. | 56-066 |
| Schmidt, Richard C. | M.Sc. | 55-539 |
| Slipp, Robert M. | M.Sc. | 52-542 |
| Rigault, A. | | |
| Gyorgy, Anne M. | M.A. | 56-617 |
| Ritchie, D. | | |
| *Kelloway, Warwick F. | M.A. | 25-536 |
| *Wilkinson, George | M.A. | 25-551 |
| Robb, J. | | |
| Li, Choh-luh | M.Sc. | 50-617 |
| Roberts, A. | | |
| Clarke, George F. | M.Eng. | 35-500 |
| McCurdy, Lyall R. | M.Sc. | 27-513 |
| Vasilkioti, Nikolai | M.Eng. | 32-506 |
| *Bickell, William A. | M.Sc. | 23-504 |
| *McLennan, Logan S. | M.Sc. | 24-522 |
| *Shaw, Gerald E. | M.Sc. | 25-549 |
| *Trueman, James C. | M.Sc. | 24-533 |



| AUTHOR | DEGREE | THESIS NUMBER |
|---|---|---|
| Roberts, A. | | |
| *Weldon, Richard L. | M.Sc. | 20-509 |
| Robertson, D. | | |
| Ramaradhya, Jakkanahally | Ph.D. | 59-065 |
| Robertson, G. | | |
| Stanislawski, Marc | M.Sc. | 59-600 |
| Rogers, K. | | |
| Kurien, Vadkumkara T. | S.T.M. | 56-500 |
| Roscoe, M. | | |
| Campbell, John D. | Ph.D. | 52-007 |
| Francis, Jean B. | M.Sc. | 55-520 |
| Gorham, Anne L. | M.Sc. | 52-524 |
| Roper, Richard B. | M.Sc. | 51-545 |
| Stevens, Thelma V. | M.Sc. | 43-509 |
| Rose, * | | |
| *Lindsay, William | M.A. | 14-505 |
| Rose, B. | | |
| Baxter, James D. | M.Sc. | 52-512 |
| Henry, James F. | Ph.D. | 55-059 |
| Hollinger, Harvey Z. | M.Sc. | 58-524 |
| Leith, Wilfred | M.Sc. | 58-587 |
| Pump, Karl K. | M.Sc. | 50-628 |
| Rusted, Ian E. | M.Sc. | 49-619 |
| Shaw, Walter M. | M.Sc. | 52-591 |
| Rosenthall, E. | | |

| AUTHOR | DEGREE | THESIS NUMBER |
|---|---|---|
| Rosenthall, E. | | |
| Burrow, Martin D. | M.Sc. | 46-561 |
| Gonshor, Harry | M.Sc. | 49-527 |
| Melzak, Zdzislaw A. | M.Sc. | 51-536 |
| Shtern, I.H. | M.Sc. | 57-596 |
| Ross, A. | | |
| Blishen, Bernard R. | M.A. | 50-647 |
| Holmes, Stanley W. | M.Sc. | 50-533 |
| Ross, J. | | |
| Bannard, Robert A. | Ph.D. | 49-041 |
| Barry, James G. | Ph.D. | 46-001 |
| Bedoukian, Paul | Ph.D. | 41-001 |
| Schiessler, Robert Walte | M.Sc. | 41-048 |
| Rosvold, H. | | |
| Hoyt, Ruth | M.A. | 49-635 |
| Mishkin, Mortimer | Ph.D. | 51-055 |
| Rabinovitch, Mortimer S. | M.Sc. | 49-615 |
| Rishikof, Jack R. | M.Sc. | 49-616 |
| Rowles, W. | | |
| Hamilton, Hugh A. | M.Sc. | 50-528 |
| Russel, C. | | |
| *Gage, Everett L. | M.Sc. | 31-551 |
| Rutherford, E. | | |
| McClung, Robert K. | M.A. | 01-003 |
| *Robertson, Arthur F. | M.Sc. | 07-512 |



| AUTHOR | DEGREE | THESIS NUMBER |
|---|---|---|
| Ruttan, R. | | |
| Morrison, Donald M. | M.Sc. | 22-517 |
| Thomson, Walter W. | M.Sc. | 23-518 |
| Waldbauer, Louis J. | M.Sc. | 22-525 |
| *Boomer, Edward H. | M.Sc. | 21-501 |
| *Cheesbrough, Arthur G. | M.Sc. | 10-514 |
| *Dolid, Jacob | M.Sc. | 21-502 |
| *Fowler, Grant M. | M.Sc. | 25-517 |
| *Freedman, Nathan | M.Sc. | 28-560 |
| *Geldard, Walter J. | M.Sc. | 17-505 |
| *Greaves, Clifford | M.Sc. | 22-509 |
| *Hatcher, William H. | Ph.D. | 21-002 |
| *Hatcher, William H. | M.Sc. | 17-506 |
| *Herzberg, Otto W. | M.Sc. | 18-505 |
| *Hiebert, Paul G. | M.Sc. | 22-511 |
| *Hill, Eleanor M. | M.Sc. | 21-509 |
| *Howard, Waldorf V. | Ph.D. | 24-002 |
| *Logan, John F. | Ph.D. | 23-004 |
| *Macallum, Alexander D. | M.Sc. | 22-513 |
| *Macleod, Annie L. | Ph.D. | 10-003 |
| *MacLean, Allison R. | Ph.D. | 16-001 |
| *MacLean, Allison R. | M.Sc. | 12-513 |
| *Marshall, Melville J. | M.Sc. | 16-512 |
| *Matheson, Howard W. | M.Sc. | 11-513 |
| *McFarlane, Nathaniel C. | M.Sc. | 21-512 |
| *McGlaughlin, William R. | M.Sc. | 22-515 |
| *McKinney, James W. | Ph.D. | 23-005 |
| *McKinney, James W. | M.Sc. | 20-506 |
| *Reid, Hugh S. | M.Sc. | 15-513 |
| *Robison, Samuel C. | M.Sc. | 25-527 |
| *Russell, John | M.Sc. | 18-506 |
| *Saul, Bernard B. | M.Sc. | 22-520 |
| *Saunders, Leslie G. | M.Sc. | 21-514 |
| *Seyer, William F. | Ph.D. | 20-001 |
| *Shaw, Thomas P. | M.Sc. | 22-522 |
| *Shotwell, John S. | M.Sc. | 26-559 |
| *Thomson, Walter W. | Ph.D. | 25-007 |
| *Walker, Osman J. | Ph.D. | 20-002 |
| *Whitby, George S. | Ph.D. | 20-003 |
| *Whitby, George S. | M.Sc. | 18-507 |
| *Wieland, Walter A. | M.Sc. | 18-508 |
| Ruttan, R. . | | |
| *Kirkpatrick, Robert | M.Sc. | 13-517 |

| AUTHOR | DEGREE | THESIS NUMBER |
|---|---|---|
| Ruttan, R. . | | |
| Saffran, M. | | |
| Rochefort, Guy J. | Ph.D. | 58-039 |
| Rochefort, Joseph G. | M.Sc. | 56-596 |
| Schally, Andrew V. | Ph.D. | 57-030 |
| Schonbaum, Eduard | Ph.D. | 55-036 |
| Segal, Mark | M.Sc. | 57-594 |
| Sanborn, * | | |
| *Gough, William F. | M.Sc. | 27-504 |
| *Hamilton, William B. | M.Sc. | 28-561 |
| *Irwin, Marion L. | M.Sc. | 28-514 |
| *Montserin, Blazini G. | M.Sc. | 28-521 |
| Sander, G. | | |
| James, Allen P. | M.Sc. | 43-520 |
| Sanders, * | | |
| *O'Neill, Charles | M.M.A. | 24-500 |
| Sandwell, B. | | |
| *Aikman, Cecil H. | M.A. | 26-535 |
| *Culliton, John T. | M.A. | 27-527 |
| *Forbes, Frederic J. | M.A. | 27-530 |
| *Janes, Henry F. | M.A. | 27-533 |
| *Levy, Gordon W. | M.A. | 26-546 |
| *Pickel, Margaret B. | M.A. | 23-525 |
| Saull, V. | | |
| Beall, George H. | M.Sc. | 58-508 |
| Burley, Brian J. | Ph.D. | 56-040 |
| Cameron, Robert A. | Ph.D. | 56-042 |
| Cumberlidge, John T. | Ph.D. | 59-014 |



| AUTHOR | DEGREE | THESIS NUMBER |
|---|---|---|
| Saull, V. | | |
| Eadie, Dorothy A. | M.Sc. | 54-518 |
| Guy-Bray, John V. | M.Sc. | 59-517 |
| Hay, Robert F. | M.Sc. | 59-519 |
| Larochelle, Andre | Ph.D. | 59-044 |
| Laurin, Joseph F. | M.Sc. | 54-526 |
| Marleau, Raymond A. | M.Sc. | 56-530 |
| Moore, Thomas H. | Ph.D. | 55-069 |
| Relly, Bruce H. | M.Sc. | 57-536 |
| Saunders, F. | | |
| *McRae, Duncan R. | Ph.D. | 30-007 |
| Scarth, G. | | |
| Anderson, Ernest Grant | M.Sc. | 40-037 |
| Beaupre, Thomas Norbert | M.Sc. | 41-035 |
| Bertrand, Paul | M.Sc. | 40-038 |
| Brown, Alexander B. | M.Sc. | 31-502 |
| Coulombe, Louis-Joseph | M.Sc. | 49-599 |
| Eaves, Charles A. | M.Sc. | 37-505 |
| Ferguson, William | M.Sc. | 32-555 |
| Frankton, Clarence | Ph.D. | 40-501 |
| Levitt, Jacob | M.Sc. | 33-521 |
| Levitt, Jacob | Ph.D. | 35-017 |
| Loewy, Ariel G. | M.Sc. | 47-556 |
| Minshall, William H. | M.Sc. | 38-546 |
| Minshall, William H. | Ph.D. | 41-505 |
| Scoggan, Homer J. | Ph.D. | 42-023 |
| Shaw, Michael | Ph.D. | 49-038 |
| Siminovitch, David | Ph.D. | 39-025 |
| Siminovitch, David | M.Sc. | 37-541 |
| Stern, Herbert | Ph.D. | 45-012 |
| Stern, Herbert | M.Sc. | 42-066 |
| White-Stevens, Robert H. | M.Sc. | 36-521 |
| Whyte, James H. | Ph.D. | 38-024 |
| Whyte, James H. | M.Sc. | 33-532 |
| *Bruger, Moses | M.Sc. | 29-506 |
| *Moore, Leonard P. | M.Sc. | 30-509 |
| *Pasternack, David S. | M.Sc. | 26-521 |
| *Taylor, Bertram W. | M.Sc. | 30-512 |

| AUTHOR | DEGREE | THESIS NUMBER |
|---|---|---|
| **Schiff, H.** | | |
| Bulani, Walter | Ph.D. | 55-009 |
| Elias, Lorne | Ph.D. | 56-045 |
| Herron, John T. | Ph.D. | 57-016 |
| Ho-Tung, Clifton G. | M.Sc. | 57-527 |
| Jackson, Donald S. | Ph.D. | 55-023 |
| Ogryzlo, Elmer A. | Ph.D. | 59-059 |
| Tink, Roland R. | Ph.D. | 53-077 |
| Toby, Sidney | Ph.D. | 55-079 |
| Unni, Ayalur K. | Ph.D. | 58-051 |
| Verschingel, Roger H. | Ph.D. | 55-044 |
| **Schippel, W.** | | |
| Attas, Isaac | M.Eng. | 49-500 |
| Comsa, Radu P. | M.Eng. | 55-504 |
| Ellard, Christopher | M.Eng. | 51-503 |
| Govindaraj, Sadasiva | M.Eng. | 49-505 |
| Hoyle, Wilfred G. | M.Eng. | 47-541 |
| Moore, William J. | M.Eng. | 48-508 |
| Rackow, Alan D. | M.Eng. | 51-589 |
| Sakellariou, Theodore | M.Eng. | 51-506 |
| Tai, Yue-Shing | M.Eng. | 51-590 |
| Weeks, John G. | M.Eng. | 49-591 |
| **Scott, F.** | | |
| Carisse, Joseph B. | M.C.L. | 57-500 |
| Cawadias, Constantine G. | M.C.L. | 48-501 |
| Challies, George S. | M.C.L. | 47-500 |
| Charlap, Gregory | M.C.L. | 34-506 |
| Colas, Emile J. | LL.M. | 50-581 |
| Cuevas Cancino, Francisc | M.C.L. | 46-500 |
| Fergusson, Neil L. | M.C.L. | 47-501 |
| Lapointe, Marc C. | M.C.L. | 48-502 |
| **Scott, H.** | | |
| Bain, E.B. | M.Sc. | 57-564 |
| Clayton, Blanche-Petite | Ph.D. | 54-043 |
| Gibson, Merritt A. | Ph.D. | 57-055 |



| AUTHOR | DEGREE | THESIS NUMBER |
|---|---|---|
| **Scott, P.** | | |
| Speyer, Judith | M.A. | 56-549 |
| **Scott, W.** | | |
| Azima, Hassan | M.Sc. | 55-586 |
| *Hindley, John G. | M.A. | 07-502 |
| *Smith, Ella L. | M.A. | 08-506 |
| *Vincent, Irving C. | M.A. | 08-507 |
| **Scrimger, F.** | | |
| Workman, F. Walter | M.Sc. | 34-520 |
| **Sehon, A.** | | |
| Gordon, Julius | Ph.D. | 59-030 |
| Menard, Claude | M.Sc. | 57-589 |
| Richter, Maxwell | Ph.D. | 58-037 |
| Webb, Tom | Ph.D. | 59-054 |
| **Selye H.** | | |
| Dosne, Christiane | Ph.D. ? | 42-010 |
| **Selye, H.** | | |
| Beland, Eleanor | Ph.D. | 46-002 |
| Berman, Doreen | M.Sc. | 46-558 |
| Friedman, Sydney M. | M.Sc. | 41-040 |
| Hall, Charles E. | Ph.D. | 46-010 |
| Hall, Octavia | M.Sc. | 46-519 |
| Harlow, Charles M. | Ph.D. | 38-007 |
| Hay, Eleanor C. | Ph.D. | 43-021 |
| Livingstone, Constance A | M.Sc. | 42-060 |
| Masson, Georges M. | Ph.D. | 42-504 |
| McKeown, Thomas | Ph.D. | 35-021 |
| Sylvester, Elizabeth M. | Ph.D. | 46-015 |
| Welt, Isaac D. | M.Sc. | 45-542 |

| AUTHOR | DEGREE | THESIS NUMBER |
|---|---|---|
| Sharp, R. | | |
| Bach, Glen G. | Ph.D. | 58-003 |
| Conkie, William R. | M.Sc. | 55-594 |
| Smith, Lyman A. | Ph.D. | 56-068 |
| Shaw, A. | | |
| Dunn, William K. | M.Sc. | 32-554 |
| Henrikson, Arne | M.Sc. | 48-526 |
| Kaufman, Hyman | M.Sc. | 45-533 |
| Kaufman, Hyman | Ph.D. | 48-007 |
| Wagner, Sydney | Ph.D. | 50-046 |
| *Barnes, William H. | M.Sc. | 25-509 |
| *Boomer, Edward H. | Ph.D. | 23-001 |
| *Harkness, Harold W. | M.Sc. | 29-555 |
| *Home, Maurice S. | M.Sc. | 25-548 |
| *Munro, Lloyd A. | Ph.D. | 26-007 |
| *Sivertz, Christian | M.Sc. | 24-529 |
| *Snell, Arthur H. | M.Sc. | 31-558 |
| *Steacie, Edgar W. | M.Sc. | 24-532 |
| *Tapp, James S. | M.A. | 31-567 |
| *Wyman, Harold R. | M.Sc. | 30-553 |
| Shaw, A. , A. | | |
| *Patton, Isabelle J. | M.Sc. | 24-550 |
| Shaw, A. J. | | |
| *Crowe, Marguerite | M.Sc. | 28-503 |
| Simpson, G. | | |
| *Hill, Eleanor M. | M.Sc. | 21-509 |
| *Lozinsky, Ezra | M.Sc. | 23-515 |
| *Yorston, Frederic H. | M.Sc. | 24-535 |
| Simpson, J. | | |
| *Weir, Douglas | M.Sc. | 10-523 |



| AUTHOR | DEGREE | THESIS NUMBER |
|---|---|---|
| Sinclair, S. | | |
| *Brittain, Isabel E. | M.A. | 11-501 |
| *Wilson, Alice M. | M.A. | 11-504 |
| Skirron, * | | |
| *Henry, Elizabeth V. | M.Sc. | 16-511 |
| Slack, S. | | |
| *Blampin, Caroline | M.A. | 20-510 |
| Slater, R. | | |
| Koshy, Kuttickal I. | S.T.M. | 55-570 |
| Slatis, H. | | |
| Moxley, John E. | M.Sc. | 52-581 |
| Willermet, D.A. | M.Sc. | 52-599 |
| Slight, * | | |
| *MacPherson, John T. | M.A. | 28-547 |
| Smith, C. | | |
| Dowd, Keith J. | M.A. | 56-615 |
| Kabayama, Joan E. | M.A. | 58-543 |
| Milley, Chesley P. | M.A. | 57-551 |
| Rosevear, John N. | M.A. | 56-620 |
| Wright, Ouida | M.A. | 56-625 |
| Smith, F. | | |
| Pynoe, Evan T. | Ph.D. | 35-007 |
| Savage, Marion C. | M.Sc. | 45-537 |
| Stock, John J. | M.Sc. | 49-547 |
| Strean, Lyon P. | Ph.D. | 42-506 |

| AUTHOR | DEGREE | THESIS NUMBER |
|---|---|---|
| **Smith, F.** | | |
| Strean, Lyon P. | M.Sc. | 40-049 |
| Streitfield, Murray M. | M.Sc. | 48-598 |
| Waugh, Douglas O. | M.Sc. | 48-602 |
| **Smith, H.** | | |
| *Berger, Julius | M.A. | 24-536 |
| *McBain, Mary N. | M.A. | 21-520 |
| *Wood-Legh, Kathleen L. | M.A. | 24-548 |
| **Smith, J.** | | |
| Byrne, Joseph Lawrence | M.Sc. | 39-055 |
| **Smith, W.** | | |
| McDonough, Sheila D. | M.A. | 55-633 |
| Nashshabah, Hisham | Ph.D. | 59-057 |
| Pound, Omar S. | M.A. | 58-588 |
| Siddiqi, Mazharuddin | M.A. | 54-621 |
| *Carson, Beatrice M. | M.A. | 59-547 |
| **Snell, J.** | | |
| Atkinson, Hammond J. | Ph.D. | 34-002 |
| Findlay, Gordon H. | M.Sc. | 32-556 |
| Findlay, Gordon H. | Ph.D. | 34-019 |
| Lockhead, Allan G. | M.Sc. | 12-511 |
| Puddington, Ira E. | M.Sc. | 36-516 |
| Sair, Louis | Ph.D. | 37-021 |
| Schurman, David C. | M.S.A. | 26-502 |
| Warren, Thomas E. | M.Sc. | 26-532 |
| *Atkinson, Hammond J. | M.Sc. | 26-503 |
| *Bayfield, Edward G. | M.S.A. | 24-501 |
| *Beaudet, Lionel | M.Sc. | 24-507 |
| *Carleton, Everett A. | M.Sc. | 23-507 |
| *Clark, John A. | M.S.A. | 26-501 |
| *DeLong, Walter A. | M.Sc. | 24-512 |
| *Fowler, Donald E. | M.Sc. | 28-509 |
| *Leduc, Joseph A. | M.Sc. | 26-515 |
| *Liebenberg, Louis C. | M.S.A. | 25-543 |



| AUTHOR | DEGREE | THESIS NUMBER |
|---|---|---|
| **Snell, J.** | | |
| *Mueller, William H. | M.Sc. | 29-513 |
| *Parent, Robert C. | M.S.A. | 24-504 |
| *Robison, Samuel C. | M.Sc. | 25-527 |
| *Scott, Joseph M. | M.Sc. | 14-518 |
| *Skazin, Lev | M.Sc. | 30-511 |
| **Snell, J. .** | | |
| *Mitchell, Claude E. | M.Sc. | 28-520 |
| **Solomon, D.** | | |
| Loeb, Bernice F. | M.A. | 59-557 |
| McCrorie, James N. | M.A. | 59-613 |
| **Sourkes, T.** | | |
| Lagnado, John R. | Ph.D. | 57-061 |
| Lagnado, John R. | M.Sc. | 55-607 |
| Townsend, Edith E. | Ph.D. | 59-083 |
| Townsend, Edith E. | M.Sc. | 56-608 |
| Woodford, Vernon R. | Ph.D. | 58-057 |
| **Southam, H.** | | |
| Boulkind, Mabel | M.A. | 38-526 |
| **Spence-Sales, H.** | | |
| Barkham, J. Brian | M.Arch. | 55-569 |
| Caragianis, Eva M. | M.Arch. | 58-552 |
| Gordon, George E. | M.Arch. | 53-558 |
| Lam, Anna P. | M.Arch. | 57-554 |
| Leaning, John D. | M.Arch. | 57-501 |
| Moriyama, Raymond J. | M.Arch. | 57-502 |
| Papanek, Rudolf J. | M.Arch. | 48-503 |
| Schoenauer, Norbert | M.Arch. | 59-501 |
| Walford, Dorice C. | M.Arch. | 58-553 |
| Weisman, Brahm | M.Arch. | 50-501 |

| AUTHOR | DEGREE | THESIS NUMBER |
|---|---|---|
| Sprott, S. | | |
| Robinson, Jonathan | M.A. | 50-576 |
| Whallon, William W. | M.A. | 52-559 |
| Sproule, G. | | |
| Perrault, Charles H. | M.Eng. | 46-556 |
| Stachiewicz, J. | | |
| Davey, Trevor B. | M.Eng. | 57-505 |
| Stafford, P. | | |
| Barrett, George F. | M.Eng. | 49-585 |
| Stanley, C. | | |
| *Henderson, Thomas G. | M.A. | 28-540 |
| *Mackay, Robert de W. | M.A. | 29-544 |
| *MacMillan, Donald N. | M.A. | 30-536 |
| *McCullagh, Paul F. | M.A. | 28-544 |
| *Talpis, Clarence | M.A. | 30-547 |
| *Wilson, Evelyn C. | M.A. | 30-556 |
| Stanley, J. | | |
| Davis, Gordon R. | Ph.D. | 52-043 |
| Davis, Gordon R. | M.Sc. | 49-522 |
| Edwards, Donald K. | Ph.D. | 57-008 |
| Grainger, Edward H. | Ph.D. | 53-054 |
| Herer, Moe L. | M.Sc. | 48-580 |
| Lewis, John B. | M.Sc. | 50-541 |
| Peets, Ronald C. | M.Sc. | 50-551 |
| Scott, David M. | Ph.D. | 49-055 |
| Scott, David P. | M.Sc. | 49-546 |
| Stansbury, E. | | |
| Desrochers, Louis G. | M.Sc. | 58-516 |



| AUTHOR | DEGREE | THESIS NUMBER |
|---|---|---|
| Stansbury, E. | | |
| Stansfield A. | | |
| *McClelland, William P. | M.Sc. | 23-516 |
| Stansfield, A. | | |
| Adair, Thomas H. | M.Sc. | 32-507 |
| Drysdale, George A. | M.Sc. | 11-509 |
| Herzer, Richard W. | M.Sc. | 35-507 |
| Lindsay, Victor C. | M.Eng. | 36-501 |
| Rankin, Robert A. | M.Sc. | 37-512 |
| *Airey, Henry T. | M.Sc. | 27-502 |
| *Faith, Willard V. | M.Sc. | 24-513 |
| *Greaves, Clifford | Ph.D. | 23-003 |
| *Harrison, Donald R. | M.Sc. | 22-510 |
| *Humes, Harold L. | M.Sc. | 23-512 |
| *Larose, Paul | M.Sc. | 23-514 |
| *Lathe, Frank E. | M.Sc. | 15-510 |
| *Morrison, James E. | M.Sc. | 26-520 |
| *Porter, Cecil G. | M.Sc. | 13-519 |
| *Powell, Allan T. | M.Sc. | 25-525 |
| *Sproule, Gordon St. G. | M.Sc. | 09-517 |
| *Sweny, George W. | M.Sc. | 25-528 |
| *Walter, Albert J. | M.Sc. | 26-531 |
| *Weldon, Frederick E. | M.Sc. | 30-514 |
| *Whittemore, Carl R. | M.Sc. | 24-534 |
| *Williams, Frederick H. | M.Sc. | 21-518 |
| Starky, L. | | |
| *Day, Franklin H. | M.Sc. | 09-508 |
| Steacie, E. | | |
| Alexander, Wendal A. | Ph.D. | 38-001 |
| Baxt, Lawrence M. | M.Sc. | 34-507 |
| Brown, Ernest A. | Ph.D. | 40-004 |
| Cunningham, Robert L. | Ph.D. | 40-006 |
| Dewar, Donald James | Ph.D. | 40-008 |
| Elkin, Eugene M. | M.Sc. | 33-513 |

| AUTHOR | DEGREE | THESIS NUMBER |
|---|---|---|
| **Steacie, E.** | | |
| Folkins, Hillis O. | Ph.D. | 39-007 |
| Folkins, Hillis O. | M.Sc. | 37-506 |
| Graham, Gordon B. | M.A. | 35-542 |
| Katz, Sidney | Ph.D. | 37-013 |
| MacCallum, William J. | M.Sc. | 35-509 |
| Parlee, Norman A. | Ph.D. | 39-018 |
| Phillips, Norman W. | Ph.D. | 38-015 |
| Plewes, Argyle C. | Ph.D. | 34-010 |
| Potvin, Roger | Ph.D. | 39-020 |
| Puddington, Ira E. | Ph.D. | 38-023 |
| Reeve, Herbert A. | Ph.D. | 33-017 |
| Rosenberg, Solomon | Ph.D. | 36-011 |
| Rosenberg, Solomon | M.Sc. | 34-515 |
| Shane, Gerald | Ph.D. | 40-022 |
| Shane, Gerald | M.Sc. | 38-521 |
| Shaw, Geoffrey T. | M.Sc. | 33-530 |
| Smith, Walter M. | Ph.D. | 38-018 |
| Solomon, Ernest | Ph.D. | 34-017 |
| Stovel, Henry V. | Ph.D. | 38-019 |
| *Campbell, Herbert N. | M.Sc. | 30-502 |
| *Howland, Frances | Ph.D. | 32-024 |
| *Morton, Richard | M.Sc. | 31-556 |
| *Reeve, Herbert A. | M.Sc. | 31-557 |
| *Tapp, James S. | Ph.D. | 33-022 |
| **Stearn, C.** | | |
| Benoit, Fernand W. | M.Sc. | 55-587 |
| Byrne, Anthony W. | Ph.D. | 58-006 |
| Carter, George F. | M.Sc. | 54-512 |
| Gorman, William A. | Ph.D. | 56-013 |
| MacLean, Donald W. | M.Sc. | 54-528 |
| Rejhon, George | M.Sc. | 57-535 |
| Tuffy, Frank | M.Sc. | 55-542 |
| Zwartendyk, Jan | M.Sc. | 57-543 |
| **Stehle, R.** | | |
| Melville, Kenneth I. | M.Sc. | 31-509 |
| Oldham, Frances K. | M.Sc. | 35-514 |
| *Allan, John M. | M.Sc. | 25-505 |
| *Bourne, Wesley | M.Sc. | 24-509 |
| *Bruger, Moses | M.Sc. | 29-506 |



| AUTHOR | DEGREE | THESIS NUMBER |
|---|---|---|
| **Stehle, R.** | | |
| *Burke, Hugh E. | M.Sc. | 25-545 |
| *Chipman, Harry R. | Ph.D. | 25-001 |
| *Davies, Frank T. | M.Sc. | 28-505 |
| *Draper, William B. | M.Sc. | 26-508 |
| *Fleet, George A. | M.Sc. | 24-515 |
| *Gibbs, Ronald D. | M.Sc. | 26-510 |
| *Holden, George W. | M.Sc. | 24-519 |
| *Houghton, Edward O. | M.Sc. | 27-507 |
| *Macallum, Alexander D. | Ph.D. | 24-003 |
| *Mirsky, Isadore A. | M.Sc. | 29-512 |
| *Perry, Stanley Z. | M.Sc. | 29-515 |
| *Pidgeon, Lloyd M. | M.Sc. | 27-541 |
| *Robertson, Carol F. | M.Sc. | 25-526 |
| *Stavrakis, George V. | M.Sc. | 30-552 |
| *Symons, Jennie L. | Ph.D. | 25-006 |
| *Vineberg, Arthur M. | M.Sc. | 28-525 |
| **Stehle, F.** | | |
| *Forbes, John C. | Ph.D. | 25-002 |
| **Steinberg, A.** | | |
| Fraser, Frank C. | Ph.D. | 45-004 |
| Fraser, Frank C. | M.Sc. | 41-039 |
| **Stephens, S.** | | |
| Galinsky, Irving | M.Sc. | 45-527 |
| **Steppler, H.** | | |
| Anderson, Gordon C. | M.Sc. | 57-519 |
| Bristow, John M. | M.Sc. | 57-567 |
| Cairns, Robert P. | M.Sc. | 52-515 |
| Campbell, Joseph D. | M.Sc. | 50-519 |
| Cumming, Bruce G. | Ph.D. | 56-008 |
| Knutti, Hans J. | M.Sc. | 58-570 |
| Lachance, Charles-Eugene | M.Sc. | 56-523 |
| Martineau, Real | M.Sc. | 53-538 |
| Mittelholzer, Alexander | Ph.D. | 58-030 |

| AUTHOR | DEGREE | THESIS NUMBER |
|---|---|---|
| **Steppler, H.** | | |
| Mittelholzer, Alexander | M.Sc. | 56-533 |
| Slater, Douglas T. | M.Sc. | 51-550 |
| Woods, James P. | M.Sc. | 50-561 |
| **Stevens, P.** | | |
| Eliot, Charles G. | Ph.D. | 38-006 |
| Gilbert, Margaret R. | M.Sc. | 38-508 |
| Greenwood, Sydney H. | Ph.D. | 40-502 |
| McCoubrey, James Addison | Ph.D. | 40-503 |
| McNiven, Neal Lindsay | M.Sc. | 39-517 |
| Reid, Evans Burton | Ph.D. | 40-504 |
| Richmond, James Hugh | Ph.D. | 40-020 |
| Yuen, Henry B. | M.Sc. | 38-524 |
| **Stevenson, J.** | | |
| Assad, Joseph R. | M.Sc. | 55-513 |
| Assad, Robert J. | Ph.D. | 58-002 |
| Baker, Harold A. | Ph.D. | 54-038 |
| Barwick, Audrey J. | M.Sc. | 48-512 |
| Black, Ernest D. | M.Sc. | 58-511 |
| Buckley, Ronald A. | M.Sc. | 59-512 |
| Charles, Christine M. | M.Sc. | 53-519 |
| Clark, Lloyd A. | Ph.D. | 59-011 |
| Cleveland, Edward M. | Ph.D. | 55-011 |
| Collins, Anne M. | M.Sc. | 49-597 |
| Cooke, Patricia M. | M.Sc. | 58-562 |
| Diena, Benito B. | Ph.D. | 56-044 |
| Diena, Benito B. | M.Sc. | 54-581 |
| Freeman, Peter V. | M.Sc. | 54-584 |
| Fullerton, Henry D. | M.Sc. | 51-522 |
| Girvin, Grace T. | Ph.D. | 52-046 |
| Gleeson, Christopher F. | M.Sc. | 56-576 |
| Godard, J.D. | M.Sc. | 53-528 |
| Gorman, William A. | M.Sc. | 52-525 |
| Hogan, Howard R. | Ph.D. | 53-011 |
| Hogarth, Donald D. | Ph.D. | 59-036 |
| James, William | Ph.D. | 57-057 |
| Kranck, Svante H. | M.Sc. | 55-605 |
| MacLaren, Alexander S. | Ph.D. | 53-021 |
| Marler, Peter de M. | M.Sc. | 53-537 |
| McBride, Mollie E. | Ph.D. | 59-046 |



| AUTHOR | DEGREE | THESIS NUMBER |
|---|---|---|
| **Stevenson, J.** | | |
| McDougall, David J. | Ph.D. | 52-022 |
| Morris, Peter G. | Ph.D. | 57-068 |
| Mueller, George V. | Ph.D. | 54-057 |
| Myers, Gordon E. | Ph.D. | 51-026 |
| Pollock, Donald W. | Ph.D. | 57-026 |
| Pollock, Donald W. | M.Sc. | 55-538 |
| Slaght, William H. | M.Sc. | 51-549 |
| Smith, Alan R. | Ph.D. | 51-031 |
| Spat, Attilio G. | M.Sc. | 59-539 |
| Taylor, Frederick C. | Ph.D. | 55-042 |
| **Suit, R.** | | |
| Eardley, Eric A. | M.Sc. | 32-512 |
| **Sullivan C.** | | |
| *McDougall, John F. | M.Sc. | 31-555 |
| **Sullivan, C.** | | |
| Ayoub, Raymond G. | M.Sc. | 46-506 |
| Gold, Samuel | M.A. | 31-532 |
| Turner, Alice W. | M.A. | 28-556 |
| *Campbell, Alexander | M.Sc. | 26-504 |
| *Hardy, Robert M. | M.Sc. | 30-504 |
| *Howat, David | M.A. | 29-536 |
| *O'Brien, Margaret T. | M.A. | 28-550 |
| **Summerby, R.** | | |
| Beaudry, Jean-Romuald | M.Sc. | 44-501 |
| Cordukes, William E. | M.Sc. | 46-514 |
| Cox, Kenneth | M.Sc. | 29-552 |
| Cunningham, Howe S. | M.S.A. | 24-502 |
| Davidson, James G. | M.S.A. | 25-501 |
| Hanlan, Leamon H. | M.S.A. | 25-503 |
| MacLean, Alister Joseph | M.Sc. | 42-061 |
| Pelletier, Joseph R. | M.Sc. | 32-557 |
| Russell, Mary G. | M.S.A. | 27-501 |
| *Bayfield, Edward G. | M.S.A. | 24-501 |

| AUTHOR | DEGREE | THESIS NUMBER |
|---|---|---|
| Summerby, R. | | |
| *Beaudet, Lionel | M.Sc. | 24-507 |
| *Clark, John A. | M.S.A. | 26-501 |
| *Gordon, William L. | M.Sc. | 24-517 |
| *Lamb, Cecil A. | M.S.A. | 24-503 |
| *Liebenberg, Louis C. | M.S.A. | 25-543 |
| *Lods, Emile A. | M.S.A. | 25-504 |
| *Tinney, Benjamin F. | M.S.A. | 24-505 |
| Summers, W. | | |
| Cobban, Aileen A. | M.A. | 52-547 |
| Swales, W. | | |
| Durrell, Winfield B. | M.Sc. | 48-519 |
| Swank, R. | | |
| Cullen, Chester F. | M.Sc. | 54-516 |
| Levy, Samuel W. | Ph.D. | 54-016 |
| Wilmot, Valerie C. | M.Sc. | 50-641 |
| Tait, J. | | |
| Baxter, Hamilton A. | M.Sc. | 30-501 |
| Brodie, Maurice | M.Sc. | 31-501 |
| Cleland, John G. | M.Sc. | 26-507 |
| Daniels, Eli | M.Sc. | 29-553 |
| Elvidge, Arthur R. | Ph.D. | 27-003 |
| Elvidge, Arthur R. | M.Sc. | 25-514 |
| Ross, Douglas A. | M.Sc. | 31-514 |
| Ross, Douglas A. | Ph.D. | 34-012 |
| Sutherland, George F. | M.Sc. | 32-524 |
| *Birkett, Winifred L. | M.A. | 23-520 |
| *Bourne, Wesley | M.Sc. | 24-509 |
| *Burke, Hugh E. | Ph.D. | 29-001 |
| *Burke, Hugh E. | M.Sc. | 25-545 |
| *Cashin, Martin F. | M.Sc. | 26-505 |
| *Cassidy, Gordon J. | M.Sc. | 25-546 |
| *Draper, William B. | M.Sc. | 26-508 |
| *Emmons, William F. | Ph.D. | 27-004 |



| AUTHOR | DEGREE | THESIS NUMBER |
|---|---|---|
| Tait, J. | | |
| *Emmons, William F. | M.Sc. | 20-504 |
| *Finney, William H. | M.Sc. | 28-508 |
| *Fleet, George A. | M.Sc. | 24-515 |
| *Foran, Herbert F. | M.Sc. | 22-506 |
| *Gottlieb, Rudolf | M.Sc. | 30-503 |
| *Green, Frederick | M.Sc. | 25-518 |
| *Hou, Hsiang-Ch'uan | M.Sc. | 28-513 |
| *Malcolm, Robert F. | M.Sc. | 24-523 |
| *McNally, William J. | M.Sc. | 25-523 |
| *Rosenbaum, Saul B. | M.Sc. | 26-524 |
| *Ross, Dudley E. | M.Sc. | 27-518 |
| *Spence, Kenneth W. | M.A. | 30-546 |
| *Tidmarsh, Clarence J. | M.A. | 22-528 |
| Tait, J. . | | |
| *Mirsky, Isadore A. | M.Sc. | 29-512 |
| Tait, J. , E. | | |
| *Mills, Edward S. | M.Sc. | 26-519 |
| Tait, J. E. | | |
| *Davies, Frank T. | M.Sc. | 28-505 |
| Tait, W. | | |
| Bois, Joseph S. | Ph.D. | 36-001 |
| Bois, Joseph S. | M.A. | 34-544 |
| Cownie, Douglas Heron | M.Sc. | 41-527 |
| Dodds, Margaret R. | M.A. | 34-546 |
| Merry, Ralph V. | M.A. | 27-535 |
| Orlick, Emanuel | M.A. | 41-520 |
| Peden, Gwendolyn W. | M.A. | 35-546 |
| Robertson, Barbara M. | M.A. | 35-533 |
| Shaw, Hampden C. | M.Sc. | 35-539 |
| Udow, Alfred Bernard | M.Sc. | 40-524 |
| Webster, Edward C. | Ph.D. | 36-014 |
| Webster, Edward C. | M.A. | 33-561 |
| *Armstrong, Charles A. | M.A. | 26-536 |

| AUTHOR | DEGREE | THESIS NUMBER |
|---|---|---|
| **Tait, W.** | | |
| *Dawes, Charles H. | M.A. | 30-524 |
| *Duckworth, John M. | M.A. | 28-562 |
| *Featherston, Florence E. | M.A. | 29-530 |
| *Frank, Harold | M.A. | 30-526 |
| *Huntley, Herbert W. | M.A. | 10-502 |
| *Japp, Robert | M.A. | 30-531 |
| *Kiefer, Elsie B. | M.A. | 29-556 |
| *Knechtel, Max U. | M.A. | 26-544 |
| *MacLean, Mary W. | M.A. | 28-546 |
| *MacLeod, Robert B. | M.A. | 27-538 |
| *MacVicar, Donald H. | M.A. | 26-550 |
| *Pursley, Robert | M.A. | 30-542 |
| *Read, Mary G. | M.A. | 25-540 |
| *Rowell, Arthur H. | M.A. | 12-505 |
| *Shearing, Helen A. | M.A. | 15-505 |
| *Smith, Henry L. | M.A. | 26-555 |
| *Smyth, Desmond H. | M.A. | 28-555 |
| *Sutherland, Francis C. | M.A. | 15-506 |
| **Tait, W. .** | | |
| *MacLeod, Elmer D. | M.A. | 26-549 |
| **Tait, W. , C.** | | |
| *Cardonsky, Mary | M.A. | 29-525 |
| *Morton, Nelson W. | M.A. | 31-537 |
| **Taper, C.** | | |
| Collins, William B. | M.Sc. | 54-580 |
| *Hutchinson, Aleck | Ph.D. | 58-055 |
| **Taurins, A.** | | |
| Bombardieri, Caurino C. | Ph.D. | 55-007 |
| Conn, John J. | Ph.D. | 53-003 |
| Dennis, Donald A. | M.Sc. | 52-521 |
| DeSouza, John E. | Ph.D. | 55-013 |
| Fenyes, Joseph | Ph.D. | 56-047 |
| Frangatos, Gerassimos | Ph.D. | 56-012 |



| AUTHOR | DEGREE | THESIS NUMBER |
|---|---|---|
| **Taurins, A.** | | |
| Gantchev, Neno | M.Sc. | 56-574 |
| Grivas, John C. | Ph.D. | 59-032 |
| Grivas, John C. | M.Sc. | 57-526 |
| Harris, Seth C. | Ph.D. | 59-034 |
| Hurlbert, Bernard S. | M.Sc. | 53-594 |
| Kasman, Sidney | Ph.D. | 55-024 |
| Ketcheson, Barbara G. | Ph.D. | 59-040 |
| Lucien, Harold W. | Ph.D. | 51-019 |
| Massiah, Thomas F. | M.Sc. | 56-531 |
| Matuszko, Anthony J. | Ph.D. | 53-024 |
| Metro, Stephen J. | Ph.D. | 51-024 |
| Pedkevitch, Zenon | M.Sc. | 52-583 |
| Sabean, Allan T. | M.Sc. | 52-585 |
| Scott, Robert I. | Ph.D. | 56-032 |
| Stachiw, Dennis L. | Ph.D. | 57-081 |
| Thomas, Telfer L. | Ph.D. | 57-040 |
| Viron, Silvio J. | Ph.D. | 52-063 |
| Waid, Ted H. | Ph.D. | 57-042 |
| **Taylor, A.** | | |
| *Salt, Alexander E. | M.A. | 08-505 |
| *Smith, Ella I. | M.A. | 08-506 |
| *Vincent, Irving O. | M.A. | 08-507 |
| **Telford, W.** | | |
| DeMille, George E. | M.Sc. | 58-563 |
| **Terroux, F.** | | |
| Bartholomew, Gilbert | Ph.D. | 48-015 |
| Clarke, Robert L. | Ph.D. | 48-020 |
| Clifford, Charles E. | Ph.D. | 55-050 |
| Clifford, Charles E. | M.Sc. | 53-581 |
| Favreau, Roger F. | M.Sc. | 57-573 |
| Goldman, Leonard M. | M.Sc. | 48-579 |
| Locmer, Elijah I. | M.Sc. | 51-532 |
| Tate, Parr A. | M.Sc. | 47-572 |
| Wanklyn, David I. | Ph.D. | 52-065 |
| Wanklyn, David I. | M.Sc. | 51-560 |
| Whittier, Angus C. | Ph.D. | 52-067 |

| AUTHOR | DEGREE | THESIS NUMBER |
|---|---|---|
| **Terroux, F.** | | |
| *Fraser, John S. | Ph.D. | 49-046 |
| *Telford, William M. | Ph.D. | 49-056 |
| **Thatcher, F.** | | |
| Anderson, George G. | M.Sc. | 48-511 |
| Chaplin, Charles E. | M.Sc. | 46-511 |
| Herman, Lloyd G. | Ph.D. | 48-006 |
| Lachance, Robert A. | M.Sc. | 49-535 |
| MacLachlan, Donald S. | M.Sc. | 49-610 |
| Marmur, Julius | M.Sc. | 47-561 |
| Robinson, John | M.Sc. | 45-536 |
| Rockwell, Keith R. | M.Sc. | 48-595 |
| Tennant, Alan D. | M.Sc. | 49-549 |
| **Thompson, A.** | | |
| Balakrishna, Narasipur H | M.Eng. | 56-553 |
| Bernard, Ernest A. | M.Eng. | 56-503 |
| Brown, Margaret F. | M.A. | 36-527 |
| Chang, Ching-Ju | M.Eng. | 59-568 |
| Fang, Sin-Kan | M.Eng. | 56-557 |
| Irwin, Roland E. | M.Eng. | 57-506 |
| Lawley, John D. | M.A. | 31-564 |
| Lumsden, Stanley G. | M.A. | 37-525 |
| Pratinidhi, Shrivivas V. | M.Eng. | 56-561 |
| *Clark, Peter A. | M.A. | 28-530 |
| *Danby, Gordon T. | Ph.D. | 56-009 |
| *Jefferis, Jeffrey D. | M.A. | 29-538 |
| *Winship, R.D. | M.Eng. | 57-513 |
| **Thompson, W.** | | |
| Havelka, Jaroslav | M.Sc. | 54-585 |
| **Thomson, D.** | | |
| Allen, Della Elizabeth | M.Sc. | 42-516 |
| Askonas, Brigitte A. | M.Sc. | 46-557 |
| Billingsley, Lawrence W. | M.Sc. | 33-509 |
| Harrison, Sybil M. | M.Sc. | 38-510 |



| AUTHOR | DEGREE | THESIS NUMBER |
|---|---|---|
| Thomson, D. | | |
| Harwood, Robert U. | Ph.D. | 32-006 |
| Zaharia, William | Ph.D. | 59-085 |
| *Korenberg, Sarah M. | M.Sc. | 44-504 |
| Thomson, J. | | |
| Enger, Knut | S.T.M. | 53-559 |
| Gerard, F.R. | S.T.M. | 57-555 |
| Gough, Cyril H. | S.T.M. | 55-500 |
| Newman, Robert S. | S.T.M. | 56-501 |
| Poole, Aquila J. | S.T.M. | 55-571 |
| Rogers, A.A. | S.T.M. | 57-556 |
| Sass, Frederick W. | S.T.M. | 54-500 |
| Timell, T. | | |
| Barth, Fred W. | Ph.D. | 58-004 |
| Bennett, Clifton F. | Ph.D. | 56-003 |
| Currie, Allan L. | Ph.D. | 59-015 |
| Gillham, John K. | Ph.D. | 59-027 |
| Glaudemans, Cornelis P. | Ph.D. | 58-017 |
| Michael, J. | M.Sc. | 55-613 |
| Miller, Bernard | Ph.D. | 55-026 |
| Shyluk, Walter P. | Ph.D. | 55-074 |
| Snyder, John L. | Ph.D. | 55-076 |
| Tornhave, H. | | |
| Rattray, Basil A. | M.Sc. | 49-544 |
| Tory, H. | | |
| *Pearson, Mary F. | M.A. | 07-504 |
| Towers, G. | | |
| Krupka, Richard M. | Ph.D. | 57-059 |
| Roy, Chitra | M.Sc. | 59-534 |
| Wickson, Margaret E. | M.Sc. | 55-545 |
| *Hutchinson, Aleck | Ph.D. | 58-055 |

| AUTHOR | DEGREE | THESIS NUMBER |
|---|---|---|
| Towers, G. | | |
| Traquair, * | | |
| *Auld, Jean M. | M.A. | 29-522 |
| Tuck, R. | | |
| Layton, Irving | M.A. | 46-540 |
| Tyhurst, J. | | |
| Paul, Irving H. | M.A. | 50-573 |
| Usher, A. | | |
| Gardner, Charles W. | M.A. | 50-566 |
| Venning, E. | | |
| Birmingham, Marion K. | M.Sc. | 46-559 |
| Freund, Gerhard | M.Sc. | 57-524 |
| Giroud, Claude J-P. | Ph.D. | 55-057 |
| Giroud, Claude J-P. | M.Sc. | 53-527 |
| Howard, Robert P. | M.Sc. | 47-514 |
| Lowi, R. Naomi | M.Sc. | 55-609 |
| Lucis, Ojars J. | Ph.D. | 59-045 |
| Lucis, Ojars J. | M.Sc. | 57-586 |
| Ramos, Oswaldo L. | M.Sc. | 55-619 |
| Serrano, Pedro A. | M.Sc. | 57-595 |
| Singer, Bertha | Ph.D. | 52-061 |
| Stachenko, Janine L-M. | M.Sc. | 56-603 |
| Sybulski, Stella | Ph.D. | 59-071 |
| Sybulski, Stella | M.Sc. | 56-605 |
| Uete, Tetsuo | M.Sc. | 59-540 |
| Vineberg, A. | | |
| Miller, Walter D. | M.Sc. | 50-623 |



| AUTHOR | DEGREE | THESIS NUMBER |
|---|---|---|
| Vineberg, F. | | |
| Bush, Willard S. | M.A. | 47-576 |
| Singer, David P. | M.A. | 54-622 |
| Viner, J. | | |
| *Fair, Louisa M. | M.A. | 24-537 |
| *Kydd, Mary W. | M.A. | 24-540 |
| *Peterson, Frederick O. | M.A. | 24-543 |
| Wagner, S. | | |
| Blevis, Earl H. | M.Sc. | 56-514 |
| Mungall, Allan G. | Ph.D. | 54-024 |
| Szabo, Alexander | M.Sc. | 55-621 |
| Tunis, Cyril J. | M.Sc. | 56-543 |
| Vessot, Robert F. | M.Sc. | 54-535 |
| Wainwright, A. | | |
| *Weibel, Louise E. | LL.M. | 23-500 |
| Walker, J. | | |
| Krieble, Vernon K. | M.Sc. | 09-514 |
| Krieble, Vernon K. | Ph.D. | 13-001 |
| *Cheesbrough, Arthur G. | M.Sc. | 10-514 |
| *Lewis, David S. | M.Sc. | 07-510 |
| *Lyman, Ruth D. | M.Sc. | 07-511 |
| *Matheson, Howard W. | M.Sc. | 11-513 |
| *McIntosh, Donald S. | M.Sc. | 08-512 |
| *Meldrum, William B. | M.Sc. | 10-518 |
| *Robertson, Arthur F. | M.Sc. | 07-512 |
| *Sproule, Gordon St. G. | M.Sc. | 09-517 |
| *Vipond, William S. | M.Sc. | 09-518 |
| Walker, J. D. | | |
| *Macleod, Annie L. | Ph.D. | 10-003 |

| AUTHOR | DEGREE | THESIS NUMBER |
|---|---|---|
| **Walker, R.** | | |
| Bruck, Esther R. | M.A. | 56-613 |
| **Walker, J.** | | |
| *McFee, Malcolm C. | M.Sc. | 08-511 |
| **Wallace, G.** | | |
| De Angelis, Marius L. | M.Eng. | 34-500 |
| Gerryts, Edbert | M.Sc. | 49-603 |
| Lam, Mathias | M.Eng. | 51-504 |
| Roach, Charles L. | M.Eng. | 49-510 |
| *Dobridge, Ronald W. | M.Sc. | 29-507 |
| *Howes, Frederick S. | M.Sc. | 26-513 |
| **Wallace, P.** | | |
| Eliopoulos, Hermes A. | M.Sc. | 54-519 |
| Goldfarb, Lionel | M.Sc. | 48-524 |
| Gottfried, Kurt | M.Sc. | 53-529 |
| Haering, Rudolph R. | Ph.D. | 57-013 |
| Jardine, William G. | M.Sc. | 50-538 |
| Logan, Ralph A. | M.Sc. | 48-531 |
| Margolis, Bernard | M.Sc. | 49-539 |
| Masson, David R. | M.Sc. | 59-588 |
| Murphy, Joseph | M.Sc. | 58-528 |
| Puhach, Paul A. | Ph.D. | 56-029 |
| Roulty, Paul M. | M.Sc. | 48-543 |
| Schiff, Harry | M.Sc. | 50-632 |
| Sharp, Robert T. | Ph.D. | 53-037 |
| Watson, Hugh A. | M.Sc. | 49-626 |
| Williams, Roscoe C. | M.Sc. | 53-546 |
| **Wallace, R.** | | |
| Clark, David S. | Ph.D. | 57-005 |
| Clark, David S. | M.Sc. | 53-580 |
| Corbett, Wendell O. | M.Sc. | 51-603 |
| Idziak, Edmund S. | M.Sc. | 57-579 |
| King, Hamilton D. | M.Sc. | 53-596 |
| McLaughlan, John M. | M.Sc. | 56-585 |



| AUTHOR | DEGREE | THESIS NUMBER |
|---|---|---|
| **Wallace, F.** | | |
| Smart, Celina | Ph.D. | 57-033 |
| Williams, Audrey J. | M.Sc. | 55-623 |
| **Walsh, H.** | | |
| Bertalot, Renzo | S.T.M. | 59-565 |
| Kingsford, Maurice F. | S.T.M. | 53-504 |
| Perret, Edmond J. | S.T.M. | 55-501 |
| Zuk, Michael | S.T.M. | 57-557 |
| **Walter, F.** | | |
| Carl, Selma E. | M.A. | 33-540 |
| Jackson, Naomi C. | M.A. | 35-544 |
| Schleien, Donna S. | M.A. | 28-552 |
| *Ellison, Myra K. | M.A. | 13-503 |
| *Forster, David S. | M.A. | 15-502 |
| *Grimes, Evie M. | M.A. | 13-505 |
| *Harris, Richard C. | M.A. | 24-538 |
| *Hasley, Isabel J. | M.A. | 28-537 |
| *Hayden, Amy J. | M.A. | 09-503 |
| *Huxtable, Margaret | M.A. | 10-503 |
| *King, Lucile M. | M.A. | 10-504 |
| *Lockhead, Allan G. | Ph.D. | 19-001 |
| *Macnaughton, Ariel M. | M.A. | 10-508 |
| *McBain, Alexander F. | M.A. | 13-507 |
| *McDonald, Jessie | M.A. | 10-505 |
| *McVittie, Thomas J. | M.A. | 14-506 |
| *Meyer, Bertha | M.A. | 21-521 |
| *Miller, Clare B. | M.A. | 12-502 |
| *Newnham, May L. | M.A. | 21-522 |
| *Noad, Algy S. | M.A. | 21-524 |
| *Paterson, Edith L. | M.A. | 12-503 |
| *Reque, A. Dikka | M.A. | 24-544 |
| *Schafheitlin, Anna | M.A. | 13-509 |
| *Shearing, Helen A. | M.A. | 15-505 |
| *Tremblay, Joseph A. | M.A. | 11-503 |
| **Walter, H.** | | |
| *Tyndale, Orville S. | M.A. | 09-506 |

| AUTHOR | DEGREE | THESIS NUMBER |
|---|---|---|
| **Walton, F.** | | |
| *Brown, Vera L. | M.A. | 13-501 |
| *Howell, Lucy M. | M.A. | 12-501 |
| *McNeil, John T. | M.A. | 10-509 |
| *Potter, James G. | M.A. | 12-504 |
| *Stalker, Archibald | M.A. | 13-510 |
| *Thomson, Herbert F. | M.A. | 13-512 |
| **Walton, F. , J.** | | |
| *Tremblay, Joseph A. | M.A. | 11-503 |
| **Watkins, F.** | | |
| Brzezinski, Zbigniew K. | M.A. | 50-651 |
| Frankel, Saul J. | M.A. | 52-604 |
| Oliver, Michael K. | M.A. | 50-661 |
| Sakellaropoulos, Michael | M.A. | 50-577 |
| Shklar, Judith | M.A. | 50-665 |
| **Watson, H.** | | |
| Berry, Verne H. | M.Sc. | 46-507 |
| Boyle, Willard S. | Ph.D. | 50-002 |
| Boyle, Willard S. | M.Sc. | 48-513 |
| Chapman, John H. | M.Sc. | 49-518 |
| Chapman, Robert P. | M.Sc. | 49-519 |
| Dodds, John W. | M.Sc. | 46-516 |
| Fairley, Randolf D. | M.Eng. | 50-505 |
| Glegg, Keith C. | M.Sc. | 49-526 |
| Sullivan, Harry M. | M.Sc. | 54-533 |
| Thurston, Arthur M. | M.Sc. | 48-600 |
| **Watson, W.** | | |
| 'Abdu-l-Mu'ti, 'Ali | M.A. | 57-602 |
| Bychowsky, Victor | M.Sc. | 39-054 |
| Hurst, Donald G. | Ph.D. | 36-009 |
| Hurst, Donald G. | M.Sc. | 34-512 |
| Josephson, Vernal | Ph.D. | 42-014 |
| Sharp, Robert T. | M.Sc. | 50-556 |



| AUTHOR | DEGREE | THESIS NUMBER |
|---|---|---|
| **Waugh, I.** | | |
| Liszauer, Susan M. | M.Sc. | 56-583 |
| Stuart, James B. | Ph.D. | 57-035 |
| **Waugh, J.** | | |
| Spector, Leo I. | M.Sc. | 33-531 |
| **Waugh, T.** | | |
| *Gottlieb, Rudolf | M.Sc. | 30-503 |
| *Hague, Helen | M.A. | 28-535 |
| **Waugh, W.** | | |
| Roberts, Gwen B. | M.A. | 32-542 |
| *Lyman, Beatrice M. | M.A. | 29-543 |
| *McGown, Isabella W. | M.A. | 23-522 |
| *Talpis, Clarence | M.A. | 30-547 |
| *White, Harold | M.A. | 25-542 |
| **Waugh, W. .** | | |
| *Wood-Legh, Kathleen I. | M.A. | 24-548 |
| **Waygood, E.** | | |
| Coles, Clifford H. | Ph.D. | 54-009 |
| Goodwin, Brian C. | M.Sc. | 54-522 |
| Mozie, James O. | M.Sc. | 54-596 |
| Paquin, Roger | Ph.D. | 55-071 |
| **Waygood, G.** | | |
| Elliott, Bernard B. | M.Sc. | 50-606 |
| **Webber, G.** | | |
| Benson, David G. | Ph.D. | 59-003 |

| AUTHOR | DEGREE | THESIS NUMBER |
|---|---|---|
| **Webber, G.** | | |
| Dean, R. S. | M.Sc. | 58-515 |
| Morse, Stearns A. | M.Sc. | 58-526 |
| Petruk, William | Ph.D. | 59-063 |
| **Webster, D.** | | |
| Allan, Charles M. | M.Sc. | 55-585 |
| Allen, Lloyd S. | M.Sc. | 54-569 |
| Ballem, Charles M. | M.Sc. | 51-595 |
| Brody, Garry S. | M.Sc. | 59-578 |
| Browman, Mark | M.Sc. | 53-575 |
| Buller, William K. | M.Sc. | 54-576 |
| Caira, Eugene G. | M.Sc. | 57-568 |
| Chau, Andrew Y. | M.Sc. | 50-599 |
| Coughlin, Francis R. | M.Sc. | 55-595 |
| Currie, Donald J. | M.Sc. | 50-600 |
| Devitt, James E. | M.Sc. | 53-585 |
| Dutt, Nihar R. | M.Sc. | 56-572 |
| Freedman, Arthur N. | M.Sc. | 58-566 |
| Goel, Devendra P. | M.Sc. | 57-574 |
| Gorman, Thomas W. | M.Sc. | 49-604 |
| Hampson, Lawrence G. | M.Sc. | 53-591 |
| Horan, Patrick J. | M.Sc. | 54-589 |
| Hyndman, William W. | M.Sc. | 55-602 |
| Iliescu-Constantine, Rod | M.Sc. | 59-521 |
| Inglis, Frederic G. | M.Sc. | 57-580 |
| Johnson, Thomas A. | M.Sc. | 55-603 |
| Kapur, Kanwal K. | M.Sc. | 54-592 |
| Karn, Gordon M. | M.Sc. | 49-533 |
| Laing, Charles A. | M.Sc. | 55-608 |
| Mahanti, Biresh C. | M.Sc. | 58-573 |
| Makonnen, Adunya | M.Sc. | 59-587 |
| Marien, Breen N. | M.Sc. | 52-579 |
| Murphy, Frederick G. | M.Sc. | 58-574 |
| Ogilvy, William L. | M.Sc. | 56-592 |
| Percy, Edward C. | M.Sc. | 54-600 |
| Richards, Terence A. | M.Sc. | 59-595 |
| Rounthwaite, Harry L. | M.Sc. | 52-584 |
| Samuels, Peter B. | M.Sc. | 52-586 |
| Scobie, Thomas K. | M.Sc. | 52-589 |
| Singh, Tej B. | M.Sc. | 57-537 |
| Skoryna, Stanley C. | M.Sc. | 50-633 |
| Toovey, Edna W. | M.Sc. | 51-626 |
| Varma, Maithili S. | M.Sc. | 59-604 |



| AUTHOR | DEGREE | THESIS NUMBER |
|---|---|---|
| **Webster, D.** | | |
| Warshawski, Frances G. | M.Sc. | 58-580 |
| Wilson, William F. | M.Sc. | 57-600 |
| **Webster, E.** | | |
| Hymovitch, Bernard | M.Sc. | 46-523 |
| Jackson, Jay M. | M.A. | 50-655 |
| Mahatoo, Winston H. | M.Sc. | 55-611 |
| Mahoney, Gerald M. | Ph.D. | 49-029 |
| Mahoney, Gerald M. | M.Sc. | 47-519 |
| McFarlane, Arthur H. | M.A. | 46-588 |
| Rankin, Winston B. | M.A. | 49-578 |
| Sloan, Emmett F. | M.A. | 49-643 |
| Springbett, Bruce M. | Ph.D. | 55-077 |
| Stern, Muriel H. | M.Sc. | 54-604 |
| Sydiaha, Daniel | Ph.D. | 58-048 |
| **Weldon, J.** | | |
| Bocte, Maurice J. | Ph.D. | 59-005 |
| Brown, Irving | M.A. | 54-540 |
| Charles, J. Koilpillai | Ph.D. | 58-010 |
| Farr, William | M.A. | 55-628 |
| Galbraith, John A. | M.Com. | 50-670 |
| Grasberg, Eugeniusz | Ph.D. | 53-055 |
| Halford, Charles F. | M.A. | 54-543 |
| O'Brien, John W. | M.A. | 55-556 |
| Rymes, Thomas K. | M.A. | 58-589 |
| Velay, Clement C. | Ph.D. | 57-087 |
| **Welsh, F.** | | |
| *Claxton, John W. | M.A. | 27-526 |
| **Westcott, C.** | | |
| Densmore, Arthur A. | M.Sc. | 53-522 |
| Greenberg, Jack S. | M.Sc. | 51-608 |
| Kirkaldy, John S. | Ph.D. | 53-058 |
| Prentice, James D. | M.Sc. | 53-603 |

| AUTHOR | DEGREE | THESIS NUMBER |
|---|---|---|
| **Westley, W.** | | |
| **Bloomstone, Shirley S.** | **M.A.** | 55-624 |
| **Burshtyn, Hyman** | **M.A.** | 59-606 |
| **Leznoff, Maurice** | **M.A.** | 54-545 |
| **McFarlane, Bruce A.** | **M.A.** | 55-634 |
| **Vaz, Edmund W.** | **M.A.** | 55-562 |
| **Whitby, G.** | | |
| Cambron, Adrien | Ph.D. | 28-002 |
| Chataway, Helen D. | Ph.D. | 26-001 |
| Crozier, Robert N. | Ph.D. | 28-005 |
| Evans, Arthur B. | M.Sc. | 25-515 |
| Gallay, Wilfred | M.Sc. | 28-510 |
| Greenberg, Harry | Ph.D. | 28-009 |
| Katz, Morris | Ph.D. | 29-017 |
| McNally, James G. | Ph.D. | 27-008 |
| Pasternack, David S. | Ph.D. | 28-010 |
| Yorston, Frederic H. | Ph.D. | 28-012 |
| *Allan, John M. | M.Sc. | 25-505 |
| *Cambron, Adrien | M.Sc. | 23-506 |
| *Chalmers, William | Ph.D. | 30-001 |
| *Dolid, Jacob | Ph.D. | 23-002 |
| *Dolid, Jacob | M.Sc. | 21-502 |
| *Fowler, Donald E. | M.Sc. | 28-509 |
| *Gallay, Wilfred | Ph.D. | 30-003 |
| *Greenberg, Harry | M.Sc. | 27-505 |
| *Jane, Robert S. | Ph.D. | 25-003 |
| *Jane, Robert S. | M.Sc. | 23-513 |
| *Katz, Morris | M.Sc. | 27-509 |
| *Macallum, Alexander D. | M.Sc. | 22-513 |
| *Macallum, Alexander D. | Ph.D. | 24-003 |
| *McGlaughlin, William F. | M.Sc. | 22-515 |
| *Pasternack, David S. | M.Sc. | 26-521 |
| *Shaw, Thomas P. | M.Sc. | 22-522 |
| *Smith, Frederick M. | M.Sc. | 24-530 |
| *Yorston, Frederic H. | M.Sc. | 24-535 |
| White, J. | | |
| Lang, Bernard | M.Eng. | 53-562 |
| Seguin, Maurice J. | M.Eng. | 56-510 |
| Tweed, William J. | M.Eng. | 53-509 |



| AUTHOR | DEGREE | THESIS NUMBER |
|---|---|---|
| White, W. | | |
| Barrales, Hugo I. | M.Sc. | 51-510 |
| Whitehead, J. | | |
| Kycia, Tadeusz F. | M.Sc. | 55-606 |
| Whitnall, S. | | |
| Power, Richard M. | M.Sc. | 33-525 |
| Willey, A. | | |
| Edelstein, Leo J. | M.Sc. | 31-506 |
| Kamm, Josephine J. | M.Sc. | 29-511 |
| L'Herisson, Camille | M.Sc. | 30-506 |
| *Armstrong, Thomas | M.Sc. | 25-506 |
| *Baker, Alexander D. | M.Sc. | 25-508 |
| *Duff, Dorothy | M.Sc. | 14-511 |
| *DuPorte, Ernest M. | Ph.D. | 21-001 |
| *DuPorte, Ernest M. | M.Sc. | 14-512 |
| *Dyce, Elton J. | M.Sc. | 28-507 |
| *Graham, Archibald F. | M.Sc. | 26-511 |
| *Henderson, Jean T. | M.Sc. | 26-512 |
| *Hou, Hsiang-Ch'uan | M.Sc. | 28-513 |
| *Jull, Morley A. | M.Sc. | 19-502 |
| *Lyman, Beatrice M. | M.A. | 29-543 |
| *Miller, Clare B. | M.A. | 12-502 |
| *Painter, Richard H. | M.Sc. | 29-514 |
| *Pinhey, Kathleen F. | Ph.D. | 30-012 |
| *Sadler, Wilfrid | M.Sc. | 17-507 |
| *Saunders, Leslie G. | M.Sc. | 21-514 |
| *Sharly, Eleanor | M.Sc. | 14-519 |
| Williams, E. | | |
| *Davidson, Winnifred H. | M.A. | 22-526 |
| *Foster, Joan M. | M.A. | 25-535 |
| *Harbert, Eleanor | M.A. | 22-527 |
| *Moore, Dale H. | M.A. | 23-524 |

| AUTHOR | DEGREE | THESIS NUMBER |
|---|---|---|
| **Williams, W.** | | |
| Cree, George C. | M.A. | 49-630 |
| Macphail, Moray S. | M.A. | 34-534 |
| Smith, Norman E. | M.A. | 49-644 |
| **Wilson, C.** | | |
| Baines, Joan D. | M.Sc. | 57-565 |
| Biard, J.M. | M.Sc. | 58-510 |
| Ross, Ian K. | Ph.D. | 57-029 |
| Wells, Doreen E. | M.Sc. | 55-544 |
| **Wilson, H.** | | |
| *Dickieson, Arthur L. | M.Sc. | 10-515 |
| *Paterson-Smyth, Marjorie | M.Sc. | 12-517 |
| **Wilson, V.** | | |
| Girolami, Renato L. | M.Eng. | 55-505 |
| Henderson, Gerald D. | M.Sc. | 50-529 |
| MacFarlane, Ivan C. | M.Eng. | 54-565 |
| Thompson, Richard D. | M.Eng. | 59-571 |
| Townsend, David L. | M.Eng. | 53-567 |
| **Winkler, C.** | | |
| Adamek, Stephen | Ph.D. | 54-001 |
| Adelstein, Peter | Ph.D. | 49-001 |
| Armstrong, David A. | Ph.D. | 55-003 |
| Atkinson, James T. | M.Sc. | 46-505 |
| Back, Robert A. | Ph.D. | 53-043 |
| Baerg, Abraham P. | Ph.D. | 52-001 |
| Bardwell, John A. | Ph.D. | 48-002 |
| Batzold, John S. | Ph.D. | 52-002 |
| Betts, Robert H. | Ph.D. | 45-002 |
| Blades, H. | Ph.D. | 50-026 |
| Boyd, Mary L. | Ph.D. | 46-003 |
| Boyer, Thomas W. | Ph.D. | 45-003 |
| Brady, George W. | Ph.D. | 49-005 |
| Breitman, Leo | Ph.D. | 52-006 |
| Brody, Harry | M.Sc. | 55-514 |



| AUTHOR | DEGREE | THESIS NUMBER |
|---|---|---|
| **Winkler, C.** | | |
| Brown, Robert M. | Ph.D. | 51-003 |
| Bryce, William A. | Ph.D. | 47-002 |
| Bushuk, Walter | Ph.D. | 56-005 |
| Chin-Yee, Harold R. | M.Sc. | 46-512 |
| Darwent, Basil de B. | Ph.D. | 43-019 |
| Davis, Stuart G. | Ph.D. | 42-008 |
| Dempster, John C. | Ph.D. | 51-007 |
| Devins, John C. | Ph.D. | 46-005 |
| Dewhurst, Harold A. | Ph.D. | 50-029 |
| Diamond, George F. | M.Eng. | 48-573 |
| Douglas, Donald E. | M.Sc. | 43-518 |
| Downes, Kenneth W. | Ph.D. | 47-025 |
| Dunford, Hugh B. | Ph.D. | 54-010 |
| Fager, Richard L. | Ph.D. | 49-010 |
| Eastwood, Thomas A. | Ph.D. | 46-006 |
| Ekler, Kurt | Ph.D. | 55-017 |
| Elsdon, William L. | Ph.D. | 59-022 |
| Epstein, Samuel | Ph.D. | 44-017 |
| Evans, Harry G. | Ph.D. | 55-018 |
| Foran, Michael E. | Ph.D. | 44-004 |
| Forst, Wendell | Ph.D. | 55-055 |
| Freeman, Gordon R. | Ph.D. | 55-019 |
| Gartaganis, Phoebus | Ph.D. | 55-056 |
| Gauvin, William | Ph.D. | 45-006 |
| Gauvin, William | M.Eng. | 42-515 |
| Genge, Colin A. | Ph.D. | 47-005 |
| George, Zacheria M. | Ph.D. | 59-026 |
| Gesser, Hyman | Ph.D. | 52-045 |
| Gillies, Archibald | Ph.D. | 42-012 |
| Gilpin, Victor | Ph.D. | 44-018 |
| Graham, Wilfred | Ph.D. | 46-026 |
| Greenblatt, Jayson | Ph.D. | 48-025 |
| Habeeb, Herbert | Ph.D. | 41-009 |
| Haggart, Catherine | Ph.D. | 59-079 |
| Halpern, Jack | Ph.D. | 49-015 |
| Hardwick, Thomas J. | Ph.D. | 44-019 |
| Hawkes, Arthur S. | Ph.D. | 45-018 |
| Hay, Alden Wendell | Ph.D. | 42-500 |
| Henderson, John F. | Ph.D. | 58-018 |
| Heyding, Robert D. | Ph.D. | 51-014 |
| Hiltz, Arnold A. | Ph.D. | 52-016 |
| Hodgson, Gordon W. | Ph.D. | 49-018 |
| Hospadaruk, Vladimir | Ph.D. | 53-013 |
| Hutcheon, Alan T. | Ph.D. | 48-026 |
| Ingraham, Thomas R. | Ph.D. | 47-030 |

| AUTHOR | DEGREE | THESIS NUMBER |
|---|---|---|
| **Winkler, C.** | | |
| Irvine, George N. | Ph.D. | 49-021 |
| Jamieson, James W. | Ph.D. | 56-018 |
| Jones, Robert A. | Ph.D. | 50-032 |
| Kelly, Roger O. | Ph.D. | 58-023 |
| Kirsch, Milton | Ph.D. | 45-007 |
| Klassen, Norman V. | Ph.D. | 57-058 |
| Kristjanson, Arnthor M. | Ph.D. | 49-025 |
| Legge, Norman R. | Ph.D. | 45-008 |
| Leslie, John D. | Ph.D. | 48-028 |
| Luner, Charles | Ph.D. | 52-052 |
| Luner, Philip | Ph.D. | 51-020 |
| MacHutchin, John G. | Ph.D. | 47-013 |
| MacKenzie, James S. | Ph.D. | 48-029 |
| Mandelcorn, Lyon | Ph.D. | 51-022 |
| Marcus, Rudolph A. | Ph.D. | 46-012 |
| Martin, William G. | Ph.D. | 58-028 |
| Martin, William G. | M.Sc. | 55-532 |
| McCabe, James | M.Sc. | 53-536 |
| McConnell, Wallace B. | Ph.D. | 49-027 |
| McGilvery, James D. | Ph.D. | 50-015 |
| McLean, James Douglas | M.Sc. | 41-532 |
| Menzies, Margaret H. | M.Sc. | 54-595 |
| Miller, David M. | Ph.D. | 50-037 |
| Montgomery, Douglas S. | Ph.D. | 48-032 |
| Morantz, Daniel J. | M.Sc. | 45-534 |
| Morton, Ernest R. | Ph.D. | 54-023 |
| Ogilvie, James D. | Ph.D. | 42-021 |
| Ogilvie, James D. | M.Sc. | 40-522 |
| Onyszchuk, Mario | Ph.D. | 54-060 |
| Papineau-Couture, Gilles | Ph.D. | 45-011 |
| Parsons, Basil I. | Ph.D. | 53-030 |
| Perry, Ernest J. | Ph.D. | 51-028 |
| Rabinovitch, Benton S. | Ph.D. | 42-022 |
| Ralph, Arthur O. | Ph.D. | 51-029 |
| Roxburgh, James M. | Ph.D. | 49-035 |
| Russell, Stewart H. | Ph.D. | 48-036 |
| Schavo, Anton F. | Ph.D. | 58-042 |
| Sims, Richard P. | Ph.D. | 50-042 |
| Sobering, Simon E. | Ph.D. | 57-078 |
| Sukava, Armas J. | Ph.D. | 55-040 |
| Thomas, Gordon | Ph.D. | 51-032 |
| Thompson, Allan L. | Ph.D. | 43-013 |
| Trick, Gordon S. | Ph.D. | 52-032 |
| Trottier, Bernard | M.Sc. | 44-523 |
| Turner, Robert C. | Ph.D. | 51-035 |



| AUTHOR | DEGREE | THESIS NUMBER |
|---|---|---|
| **Winkler, C.** | | |
| Turner, Robert C. | M.Sc. | 49-624 |
| Van Straten, Sylvia F. | Ph.D. | 50-022 |
| Verbeke, Gentil J. | Ph.D. | 58-053 |
| Versteeg, Joseph | Ph.D. | 52-062 |
| Vroom, Alan H. | Ph.D. | 45-013 |
| Walker, Jessie M. | Ph.D. | 49-043 |
| Walker, Osman J. | Ph.D. | 50-049 |
| Wang, Sheng-Nien | Ph.D. | 42-025 |
| Westbury, Ronald A. | Ph.D. | 59-084 |
| Whalley, Basil J. | Ph.D. | 52-034 |
| White, W. Harold | Ph.D. | 43-014 |
| Wiebe, Allan K. | Ph.D. | 52-035 |
| Wiles, David M. | Ph.D. | 57-046 |
| Williams, Harry L. | Ph.D. | 43-015 |
| Wright, Archibald N. | Ph.D. | 57-048 |
| Yates, Havelock H. | Ph.D. | 52-037 |
| **Wood, D.** | | |
| Clark, Robert H. | M.Eng. | 45-500 |
| **Woodhead, W.** | | |
| Bradford, Florence F. | M.A. | 46-584 |
| Levitt, Bella | M.A. | 41-027 |
| Macpherson, John | M.A. | 46-543 |
| MacQueen, David J. | M.A. | 36-537 |
| Pitt, Edith S. | M.A. | 43-513 |
| Portier, Jacques M. | M.A. | 50-575 |
| Scotcher, Charles W.D. | M.A. | 39-045 |
| *Auld, Jean M. | M.A. | 29-522 |
| *Moore, Ruth E. | M.A. | 30-538 |
| *Phelan, Lewis J. | M.A. | 29-557 |
| **Woods, H.** | | |
| Betcherman, Philip | M.A. | 50-646 |
| Hanson, James C. | M.A. | 49-632 |
| Henry, Zin A. | Ph.D. | 57-015 |
| Mantzavinos, A. | M.A. | 52-607 |
| Mindes, Evelyn | M.A. | 47-538 |

| AUTHOR | DEGREE | THESIS NUMBER |
|---|---|---|
| **Woonton, G.** | | |
| Armstrong, Robert A. | M.Sc. | 54-570 |
| Assaly, Robert N. | Ph.D. | 57-051 |
| Bachynski, Morrel P. | Ph.D. | 55-005 |
| Bekefi, George | Ph.D. | 52-004 |
| Bekefi, George | M.Sc. | 50-514 |
| Borts, Robert B. | Ph.D. | 52-005 |
| Buchsbaum, Solomon J. | M.Sc. | 53-576 |
| Chapman, John H. | Ph.D. | 51-043 |
| Chapman, Marion H. | M.Sc. | 51-515 |
| Cloutier, Gilles G. | Ph.D. | 59-012 |
| Crowell, Clarence R. | Ph.D. | 55-012 |
| Crowell, Clarence R. | M.Sc. | 51-604 |
| Crysdale, John H. | M.Sc. | 53-520 |
| Dore, Burnell V. | M.Sc. | 56-518 |
| Farnell, Gerald W. | Ph.D. | 57-054 |
| Forsyth, Peter A. | Ph.D. | 51-046 |
| Griffiths, Herbert D. | M.Sc. | 50-609 |
| Hamilton, Hugh A. | Ph.D. | 53-009 |
| Harrower, George A. | Ph.D. | 52-047 |
| Harrower, George A. | M.Sc. | 50-611 |
| Hay, Donald R. | Ph.D. | 52-015 |
| Hogg, David C. | Ph.D. | 53-012 |
| Hogg, David C. | M.Sc. | 50-613 |
| Jones, Alun R. | M.Sc. | 54-591 |
| Kornelsen, Ernest V. | Ph.D. | 57-020 |
| McCormick, Glendon C. | Ph.D. | 53-062 |
| McFarlane, Ross A. | Ph.D. | 59-047 |
| McFarlane, Ross A. | M.Sc. | 55-530 |
| McIntosh, Bruce A. | Ph.D. | 59-049 |
| Milne, Allen R. | M.Sc. | 53-600 |
| Moen, H.P. | M.Sc. | 52-580 |
| Ornstein, William | M.Sc. | 49-614 |
| Peppiatt, Harry J. | Ph.D. | 53-067 |
| Poznanski, Zolzislaw | M.Eng. | 50-509 |
| Radley, Sidney A. | M.Sc. | 50-629 |
| Roumbanis, Theodore | M.Sc. | 56-537 |
| Shkarofsky, Issie | Ph.D. | 57-031 |
| Vessot, Robert F. | Ph.D. | 57-041 |
| Vogan, Eric L. | Ph.D. | 52-033 |
| **Worrall, D.** | | |
| *Wells, Franklin B. | M.Sc. | 31-560 |



| AUTHOR | DEGREE | THESIS NUMBER |
|---|---|---|
| **Wrenshall, C.** | | |
| Cann, Donald Bruce | M.Sc. | 40-041 |
| Dyer, William J. | Ph.D. | 40-009 |
| Dyer, William J. | M.Sc. | 37-536 |
| Marcello, Louis S. | M.Sc. | 40-046 |
| **Wynne-Edwards, V.** | | |
| Adams, James Russell | Ph.D. | 40-500 |
| Dunbar, Maxwell John | Ph.D. | 41-502 |
| Graham, Annie Philathea | M.Sc. | 39-514 |
| Hall, Charles E. | M.Sc. | 42-524 |
| Sinclair, George W. | M.Sc. | 45-539 |
| **Yaffe, L.** | | |
| Carruthers, Errol W. | M.Sc. | 55-515 |
| Hollbach, Natasha | Ph.D. | 57-018 |
| Bate, Brian D. | Ph.D. | 55-029 |
| Roy, Louis P. | Ph.D. | 56-031 |
| Santry, Dallas C. | Ph.D. | 58-041 |
| **Yajey, B.** | | |
| Wiseman, Sylvia | M.A. | 50-579 |
| **Yates, H.** | | |
| Briggs, David C. | M.Eng. | 59-554 |
| Cherian, Kandathil K. | M.Sc. | 55-516 |
| **Young, A.** | | |
| Bird, Allan V. | M.Sc. | 49-594 |
| **Young, G.** | | |
| *Bishop, Eric G. | Ph.D. | 27-002 |

| AUTHOR | DEGREE | THESIS NUMBER |
|---|---|---|
| Young, R. | | |
| *Douglas, Allie V. | Ph.D. | 26-002 |
| Zaborski, B. | | |
| Merrill, Gordon C. | M.A. | 51-640 |
| Merrill, Lesly I. | M.A. | 53-554 |
| Paterson, Laurie A. | M.A. | 51-573 |
| Pochopien, Kazimierz M. | M.A. | 52-553 |
| Romaine, Victor | M.A. | 51-574 |
| Russell, William J. | M.Sc. | 51-623 |
| Zassenhaus, H. | | |
| Burgoyne, P. Nicholas W. | M.Sc. | 55-589 |
| Burrow, Martin D. | Ph.D. | 53-048 |
| Fox, Geoffrey E. | Ph.D. | 54-012 |
| Hoechsmann, Klaus | M.A. | 58-585 |
| Lambek, Joachim | Ph.D. | 50-012 |
| Laufer, Philip J. | M.Sc. | 54-525 |
| Linis-Linins, Viktors | Ph.D. | 53-018 |
| Maranda, Jean-Marie A. | Ph.D. | 52-056 |
| Noonan, Bernard | Ph.D. | 53-028 |
| Oler, Norman | Ph.D. | 57-025 |
| Oler, Norman | M.Sc. | 53-541 |
| Rahman, Mushfequr | Ph.D. | 56-061 |
| Smith, Norman E. | Ph.D. | 52-031 |
| Sussman, David | Ph.D. | 58-046 |
| Sussman, David | M.A. | 54-624 |
| Zubek, J. | | |
| Downer, John L. | M.Sc. | 53-586 |

# LISTING BY THESIS TITLE

| THESIS | THESIS TITLE |
|---|---|
| ** | |
| 15-501 | |
| Aerodynamics & Engineering | |
| 22-507 | (a) Aeroplane design. (b) The friction of sleigh runners on snow. |
| Agricultural Bacteriology | |
| 32-026 | A study of the distribution of Brucella abortus (Bang) in reacting cows and its isolation from sex organs and from glands. |
| 43-501 | Nitrification and nitrifying organisms in some Quebec soils. |
| 45-001 | A systematic study of amylolytic bacteria, that decompose cellulose, isolated from Quebec soils. |
| 45-536 | The isolation and culture of fungi that produce antibacterial substances. |
| 46-511 | The microflora of the rhizosphere with special reference to the oxidation of manganese. |
| 46-563 | A study of the microflora of sheeps' rumen with special reference to cellulose-decomposing bacteria. |
| 46-581 | Nutritional requirements of cellulolytic bacteria isolated from Quebec soils. |
| 47-524 | The effects of adding fertilizers and glucose on the morphological and physiological groups of bacteria in soil. |
| 47-561 | A study of the mode of action of chemotherapeutic substances. |
| 48-006 | The synergistic action of penicillin, streptomycin, and various sulfonamides on certain germ-negative bacteria. |
| 48-013 | The nutritional requirements of soil bacteria as influenced by the growth of various crop plants. |
| 48-511 | The effect of varying quantities of salt upon the microflora of pickled codfish. |
| 48-595 | The production of antibiotic substances by a group of microorginasms with special reference to those active against germ negative bacteria. |
| 48-597 | Studies on carbon dioxide assimilation by a cellulose decomposing organism. |
| 49-535 | Bacteriological studies in relation to keeping qualities of eggs. |

| THESIS | THESIS TITLE |
|---|---|
| **Agricultural Bacteriology** | |
| 49-549 | An investigation of the bacterial flora of the soft shell clam (Mya arenaria) in New Brunswick and Nova Scotia. |
| 50-027 | Methods of evaluating the germicidal activity of quaternary ammonium compounds. |
| 50-041 | A possible explanation of microbial halophilism. |
| 51-004 | Oxidation of organic matter by micro-organisms in the soil. |
| 51-557 | Aerobic bacteria associated with the digestive tract of the spruce budworm, Choristoneura fumiferana Clem. |
| 51-603 | The effects of benzene hexachloride on bacteria in the rhizosphere of leguminous plants. |
| 51-619 | Studies on the proteolytic enzymes of bacteria. |
| 52-070 | A study of the physiology of Sporocytophaga strains isolated from soils. |
| 52-593 | The bactericidal and bacteriostatic effects of laurylamine saccharinate. |
| 53-580 | The taxonomy of yeasts from apples. |
| 53-596 | Bacteria in soil surrounding the roots of barley and oats. |
| 54-530 | Soil bacteria that are resistant to benzenehachlcride. |
| 55-002 | Studies on the toxin of Bacillus sotto Ishiwata and on its toxicity against certain insect species. |
| 55-025 | The utilisation of fluorescent plant extracts by bacteria. |
| 55-043 | Bacterial indices of pollution in oyster producing areas in Prince Edward Island. |
| 55-541 | The effects of freezing and cold storage on bacteria in milks. |
| 55-623 | Changes in the microflora of apples during ripening and cold storage. |
| 56-585 | Vitamin and amino acid interrelationships in the metabolism of a mutant strain of Escherichia coli. |
| 57-005 | The oxidation of carbonaceous compounds by a yeast-like fungus. |
| 57-033 | Factors affecting the rate of acetic acid production by species of Acetobacter. |

| THESIS | THESIS TITLE |
|---|---|
| **Agricultural Bacteriology** | |
| 57-570 | Studies on two aerobic cellulose decomposing bacteria and their relation to soil organic matter. |
| 57-579 | Bacteriostatic and bactericidal effects of sodium hydroxide and sodium hypochlorite on various bacteria. |
| 57-593 | Factors affecting the rate of fermentation of apple juice. |
| 58-568 | Studies on the activities of rhizosphere microorganisms. |
| 58-579 | Rates of acetic acid formation from ethanol by Acetobacter suboxydans. |
| **Agricultural Chemistry** | |
| 12-511 | Maple sugar sand. |
| 14-518 | The ash constituents and organic acids of maple sugar. |
| 19-001 | Die Zersetzung der Cellulose durch Bakterien. |
| 21-512 | The estimation of malic acid. |
| 26-503 | The detection of adulteration in butter. |
| 26-515 | Turbidity tests on butterfat and its substitutes. |
| 28-509 | A study of the interactions of solutions of maple syrup and basic lead acetate, with particular reference to the Canadian lead number. |
| 29-517 | Studies of bovine amnionic fluid. |
| 30-511 | Studies on maple syrup and maple sugar. |
| 32-556 | Studies on maple sap and syrup. |
| 33-530 | The effect of chemical treatments on the colloidal properties of podsol soils. |
| 33-570 | Chemical studies of bovine foetal fluids during various stages of gestation. |
| 34-002 | Organic matter and acidity in podsol soils. |
| 34-019 | Maple flavour, its nature and origin. |

| THESIS | THESIS TITLE |
|---|---|
| Agricultural Chemistry | |
| 35-028 | Isolation and study of soil organic nitrogen compounds. |
| 36-022 | The condition of the phosphorous of soils. |
| 36-516 | A study of carbonaceous matter of maple syrup which is precipitated by basic lead acetate. |
| 37-021 | The chloroform soluble constituents of maple syrup. |
| 37-515 | An investigation of the iodine content of potatoes and potato soils of the Province of Quebec. |
| 37-534 | A study of the nature of the sulphur compounds in a Quebec peat soil. |
| 37-536 | Photoelectric colorimetry of phosphorus in soil extracts. |
| 37-538 | A study of the distribution of iron in plant tissue. |
| 38-021 | A study of pyrroles in biological materials. |
| 38-522 | Studies on the problem of improving the vitamin A value of winterproduced milk. |
| 39-066 | Studies on the isolation of chloroplasts and their composition. |
| 39-504 | The fractionation of soil phosphorus. |
| 39-515 | A study of the effects of impurities on the accuracy of various methods of sugar analysis. |
| 39-520 | A study of the organic fraction of some Quebec soils. |
| 40-041 | The acid solubility of the inorganic phosphate of Quebec soils. |
| 40-044 | A study of carbohydrate and protein metabolism in relation to blossom-end rot in tomatoes grown under different cultural treatments. |
| 40-046 | The availability and fixation of potassium in pasture soils. |
| 40-505 | Studies on the determination of tryptophane. |
| 40-520 | Studies in lignin: the lignin content of some common vegetables, with observations on methods for the determination of lignin. |
| 41-051 | A study of pigment metabolism in the wheat kernel during ripening. |

| THESIS | THESIS TITLE |
|---|---|
| **Agricultural Chemistry** | |
| 41-523 | Studies on the hemicellulose fraction of plant tissue. |
| 41-526 | Studies on the determination of thiamine and riboflavin in foods. |
| 41-531 | Studies on lignin: the effect of methods of preparation of plant tissue and of conditions of determination on the yield and nature of the apparent lignin obtained. |
| 42-053 | Studies on the determination of vitamin D. |
| 42-057 | Studies on the acid-oxalate fraction of some podzolic soils. |
| 43-502 | Vitamin C fortification of apple juice. |
| 44-009 | Nutritional requirements of trout. |
| 44-010 | Studies on anti-oxidants for lipids and related substances. |
| 44-011 | Studies on the chemical determination of plant lignin. |
| 44-014 | Studies on the hydrogenation of linseed oil in relation to flavour reversion. |
| 44-016 | A study of incipient chemical changes in dried milk powder during storage. |
| 44-023 | Studies on lignin and related compounds in forage and in animal excreta. |
| 44-507 | The use of adsorbents in refining linseed oil. |
| 44-509 | The preparation and antioxidant properties of vitamin E concentrates from wheat-germ oil. |
| 44-520 | Studies on the processing of wheat germ. |
| 45-010 | Studies on the determination of amino acids in protein hydrolysates: a new micro-colorimetric method for the determination of lysine. |
| 45-014 | Studies on vitamin metabolism. |
| 45-504 | A study of the reaction between copper and dithiocarbamic acid, as applied to the determination of copper and amino acids. |
| 45-505 | Variations in the composition of forage plants with special reference to phosphorus and calcium. |
| 45-510 | The stabilization and concentration of vitamin A in cod-liver oil. |

| THESIS | THESIS TITLE |
| --- | --- |
| Agricultural Chemistry | |
| 45-521 | The effect of lime, manure, and certain fertilizers on soil colloids. |
| 45-522 | The chemical determination of free, combined and total choline in biological materials. |
| 45-531 | The nutritive requirements of penicillin notatum. |
| 45-535 | Studies on antibiotics. |
| 46-021 | Fractionation of soil organic matter. |
| 46-513 | Chemical changes in the lipid fraction of wheat germ during storage. |
| 46-528 | A study of an enzymatic method for determination of nicotinic acid in foods. |
| 46-530 | Estimation of lignin in red clover forage: application of triscdium periodate oxidation. |
| 46-564 | Studies on the isolation and quantitative determination of amylose from wheat and cat starch. |
| 46-565 | Production of 2,3-butanediol and the nature of the Bacillus soli fermentation. |
| 46-567 | Studies on the availability of potassium in podzcl soil. |
| 46-574 | Studies on the decomposition of cellulose by micro-organisms. |
| 46-575 | The determination and synthesis of riboflavin in cultures of microorganisms. |
| 47-016 | Technical studies on antibiotics with special reference to citrinin. |
| 47-017 | Studies on the heat polymerization of linseed oil. |
| 47-023 | Studies on the chick assay for vitamin D and some observations on chemical methods for its determination. |
| 47-033 | Studies on the preparation of nucleoproteins and ribonucleic acid from wheat germ. |
| 47-509 | Studies on the metabolism of actinomyces griseus in relation to the production of streptomycin. |
| 47-528 | Studies on the determination of ascorbic acid. |
| 47-546 | Studies in the processing of vegetable oils. |
| 47-548 | The conversion of carotene to vitamin A in vitro. |

| THESIS | THESIS TITLE |
|---|---|
| **Agricultural Chemistry** | |
| 47-550 | The recovery of whey proteins by the use of waste sulfite liquor. |
| 47-558 | Studies on methods for the determination of peroxides in fats and oils. |
| 47-563 | Studies on the chemical changes in the protein and carbohydrate fractions of milk powders during storage. |
| 47-565 | Investigation of the effects of flooding on the phosphorous status of soils. |
| 47-568 | A chemical study of some of the factors affecting the availability of potassium in soils. |
| 47-570 | The validity of physical and chemical tests for determining the quality of flax fibre produced in various types of retting. |
| 48-010 | Studies on acid hydrolysis of proteins. |
| 48-017 | A modified method for the determination of lysine and its application to reactions between reducing sugars and aminc acids. |
| 48-022 | The estimation and location of the carbonyl groups in chromium tricxide oxy-starch. |
| 48-514 | Studies on the utilization of open-hearth slag as a fertilizer. |
| 48-533 | Partition of soil phosphorus as affected by variations of soil properties. |
| 48-537 | The estimation of organic matter in soil profile studies. |
| 48-550 | Fractionation of protein hydrolysates. |
| 48-585 | Studies of the availability of the plant nutrient in open hearth slags. |
| 48-599 | An investigation of the clay fraction of the Ste. Rosalie soil. |
| 49-033 | Studies on the nicotinic acid oxidase of Pseudomonas flurescens. |
| 49-045 | The influence of gonadal hormones on the composition of blood and liver of the domestic fowl. |
| 49-048 | A study of some chemical changes of proteins of food during storage with particular reference to lysine. |
| 49-513 | Investigations on the acidity of leachates from decomposing leaves of deciduous trees. |

| THESIS | THESIS TITLE |
|---|---|
| **Agricultural Chemistry** | |
| 49-525 | The use of radicactive phosphorus in the investigation of fixaticn and release phenomena in soils. |
| 49-542 | Estimation of aldehydes in rancid fats. |
| 49-611 | A microbiological study of the amino acid ccmposition of the horsebean (Vicia faba L.). |
| 50-021 | Comparative study of the grey-brcwn podzolic, brcwn podzolic and brown forest soils cf southern Ontario and southern Quebec. |
| 50-530 | The synthesis of phenylalanine labelled with $C^{14}$. |
| 50-549 | Studies on the taste of enzymatic digests of proteins. |
| 50-642 | Nutritionally deleterious ccnstituents of heated vegetable oils. |
| 51-005 | An investigation of the chemical composition of the leaf-fall frcm deciduous forest trees before and after partial decomposition. |
| 51-009 | Studies on the relationships between fertilizer phosphate, plants and soils, using neutrcn-bcmbarded superphosphate. |
| 51-056 | Studies on the composition and properties of colloidal fractions isclated frcm soils. |
| 51-519 | The fractionaticn of protein hydrolysates by butanol extraction. |
| 51-526 | Some effects of steroid hormones and thiouracil cn storage and mcbilization of vitamin A and riboflavin in the domestic fowl. |
| 51-533 | An investigation of interactions between leachates from decomposing leaves and soil forming materials. |
| 51-600 | Studies on the taste of enzymatic digests of proteins. |
| 51-613 | Investigation on the acidity of leachates from decomposing leaves of deciduous trees. |
| 52-534 | The synthesis of $C^{14}$ labelled DDT. |
| 52-577 | A study of the accelerated aging of rayon textiles. |
| 52-588 | Investigation cf properties of cation-enriched leaf extracts and leachates. |
| 52-598 | On the separation of nutritionally deleterious and innocuous fractions from the esters of thermally polymerized linseed oil. |

| THESIS | THESIS TITLE |
|---|---|
| **Agricultural Chemistry** | |
| 53-015 | Calcium metabolism and the reproductive cycle of the fowl. |
| 53-031 | Studies on the hydrolysis of casein. |
| 53-063 | The determination of certain antioxidants in fats and their behavior in food products. |
| 53-542 | On the influence of the gonadal hormones on nucleic acid content of the liver and kidneys of the fowl, with some observations on the effect of aminopterin on various responses of the fowl to gonadal hormones. |
| 53-592 | An investigation of potassium fixation by some Canadian soils. |
| 54-055 | Cationic interrelationships in the nutrition of the corn plant (Zea mais). |
| 54-056 | Studies on the serum proteins of the fowl as affected by gonadal hormones. |
| 54-515 | The preparation and analysis of casein low in vitamins of the B-complex. |
| 54-529 | Investigation of carbohydrate-like components of aqueous extracts and leachates from leaves of trees. |
| 54-593 | Studies on the taste of enzymatic digests of casein. |
| 54-601 | Observations on fractions prepared from thermally polymerized vegetable oils as related to their effects on the nutrition of the rat. |
| 55-001 | Studies on the hexosamine and hydroxyproline contents of avian tissues. |
| 55-035 | Investigations on the interaction of cations with extracts and leachates of forest trees. |
| 55-060 | Investigation of variations in composition of the timothy plant (Phleum pratense). |
| 55-519 | Calcium balance studies on the fowl with the use of radioactive calcium as tracer. |
| 55-524 | Experiments on the extractability of soil phosphorus. |
| 55-527 | Observations on the effect of gonadal hormones on the nucleic acid contents of the liver and kidneys of the domestic fowl. |
| 55-537 | The preparation and analysis of sulphurous acid hydrolysates of casein. |
| 55-543 | Studies on avian serum proteins by zone electrophoresis. |

| THESIS | THESIS TITLE |
|---|---|
| **Agricultural Chemistry** | |
| 56-022 | Studies on the amino acid composition and food value of certain Pakistani pulses. |
| 56-535 | Mineralogy of the sand and clay fractions of two New Brunswick podzols. The Queens series. |
| 56-571 | Investigations on the release of organic matter from the B horizon of podsol soils. |
| 56-586 | Studies on the determination of pteroylglutamic acid. |
| 56-587 | Studies on the constitution of casein. |
| 57-021 | On the nature of the gonadal hormones of the domestic fowl. |
| 57-024 | Studies on the determination of vitamin A and the utilization of vitamin A by the rat. |
| 57-523 | The effect of heat polymerization on the composition and nutritive value of menhaden oil. |
| 57-542 | The effects of thiouracil and progesterone on the responses of the immature pullet to estrogen. |
| 58-052 | Studies on the formation of serum proteins in the fowl. |
| 59-006 | Extraction and identification of organic phosphorus compounds of soils. |
| 59-013 | Investigation of organic material extracted from a podzol. |
| 59-070 | Characteristics of soil leachates collected under eastern hemlock (Tsuga canadensis). |
| 59-525 | Studies of the effects of gonadal hormones on avian mineral metabolism. |
| 59-531 | Studies on casein. |
| 59-532 | Studies on the constitution of casein. |
| 59-586 | Composition and nutritive value of heated vegetable oils. |
| **Agricultural Economics** | |
| 53-548 | Land settlement under the Veterans' Land Act. |
| 56-611 | Problems of resource allocation in Quebec agriculture. |
| 56-614 | Measuring the efficiency of agriculture in Quebec. |

| THESIS | THESIS TITLE |
|---|---|
| **Agricultural Economics** | |
| 57-550 | Labour productivity in the primary fishing industry of the Maritimes and British Columbia. |
| 58-541 | The Trinidad cacao industry: its place in the Trinidad economy. |
| **Agronomy** | |
| 24-501 | The comparative effect of several systems of fertilization on crop production and soil fertility. |
| 24-502 | Methods of checking and competition in relation to comparative crop tests. |
| 24-503 | The effect of liming, manuring, and burning on certain peat soils, as measured by crop growth. |
| 24-504 | Thickness of planting in corn. |
| 24-505 | Methods of field crop experimentation, with special reference to the duration of the experiments. |
| 24-549 | The relative yield and value of sweet clover under different methods of treatment. |
| 25-501 | The elimination of error in taking yields of forage crops. |
| 25-502 | The effect of frost on germination of corn. |
| 25-503 | The variation in varieties and mixtures of cereal and forage crops with respect to border effect in comparative crop tests. |
| 25-504 | A study of the influence of electric light used to supplement daylight on oats grown as breeding material in the greenhouse during the winter season. |
| 25-543 | The relation of plot yields in one year to those of succeeding years. |
| 26-501 | A study of the influences of several rotations on yield and cost of producing farm crops. |
| 26-502 | Methods of experimentation with corn: elimination of error in plot tests. |
| 26-558 | A comparison of first generation corn hybrids with their parent types. |
| 27-501 | The relation of plot yields of one period with those of another. |
| 28-501 | Study of factors influencing the percentage of hull in oats. |
| 29-501 | Competition between adjacent rows of corn. |

| THESIS | THESIS TITLE |
|---|---|
| Agronomy | |
| 29-552 | A study of the effect of competition on the comparative yields of varieties. |
| 32-557 | Methods of sub-sampling cigar leaf tobacco in relation to accuracy. |
| 33-524 | The effect of some commercial fertilizers on the yield and botanical composition of permanent pastures. |
| 34-513 | Inheritance of seed colour in alfalfa. |
| 34-518 | The effect of some commercial fertilizers on the chemical composition of pasture herbage in the Eastern Townships of Quebec. |
| 35-503 | Ecological aspects of the pasture-conditioned climax in the Eastern Townships of Quebec. |
| 37-502 | Plant ecology and a comparative study of methods of reproduction of certain pasture plants, with an investigation of the soil viable seed flora. |
| 42-061 | Chemical studies in soil variability. |
| 42-065 | I. Fertility studies with the Greensboro loam soil. II. Establishment and succession of seeded pastures as affected by the climatic and biotic factors. |
| 44-501 | The interaction of variaties of crop plants grown in Quebec to localities and seasons. |
| 44-505 | The relation of pH to base saturation in some Quebec soils. |
| 46-514 | Chemical evaluation of the nutrient status of soils with respect to phosphorus and potassium. |
| 46-517 | Lignification studies with red clover. |
| 46-520 | Investigations of brown heart in swedes. |
| 48-521 | A comparison of grain crops grown singly and in combination. |
| 48-522 | The effect of several fertilizers and lime on the yield and botanical composition of a pasture sward on a Sherbrooke sandy loam. |
| 48-548 | Lignification studies with various grass species. |
| 49-516 | The use of sweet clover in a grain rotation as a means of increasing the fertility of grey-wooded soils. |

| THESIS | THESIS TITLE |
|---|---|
| **Agronomy** | |
| 50-603 | Relation of estimates of the availability of phosphorus to soil treatments and to crop yields. |
| 51-510 | Photoperiodic reactions of red clover. |
| 51-531 | Combining ability in corn inbreds. |
| 51-542 | Study of dormancy in seeds of some important weeds. |
| 51-550 | A study of certain agronomic and morphological characteristics of Lotus corniculatus and Lotus uliginosus. |
| 52-515 | A method of conducting agricultural experiments in remote areas. |
| 52-527 | Differential growth rates in flax varieties and their relation to other plant characters. |
| 52-531 | Variation in root development of barley. |
| 53-530 | The evaluation of comparative yield trials of maize for silage. |
| 53-538 | A study of certain factors affecting the adaptation of bird's-foot trefoil (Lotus corniculatus L.). |
| 53-593 | The effect of management on soil organic matter. |
| 53-598 | Apparent effect of management practices on the phosphorus status of a brown forest soil. |
| 54-513 | The effect of chemical fertilizer treatment on culm diameter, crown development and plant height of three varieties of oats as related to lodging. |
| 54-590 | The application of the heat unit theory to some cereal crops. |
| 55-038 | A study of the combining ability of red clover clones and their use in a breeding program. |
| 55-062 | Growth studies on the root system of barley. |
| 55-518 | Investigation of the nutrient status of corn with special reference to nitrogen and phosphorus. |
| 55-593 | The effect of various increments of N, P and K on the yield and botanical composition of permanent pastures. |
| 55-597 | Life history and importance of the clover root borer, Hylastinus obscurus (Marsham) (Coleoptera: Scolytidae) in Quebec. |

| THESIS | THESIS TITLE |
|---|---|
| **Agronomy** | |
| 56-008 | A proposed "growth cycle' in red clover (Trifolium pratense, L.) to interpret morphogenetic aspects related to vegetative propagation, photoperiodism, and auxinology. |
| 56-523 | A study of certain morphological characters in red clover populations. |
| 56-526 | The influence of certain environmental factors on loose smut of barley. |
| 56-533 | An evaluation of certain agronomic characterisitcs of tetraploid Dollard red clover. |
| 56-578 | A study of the inheritance of earliness in Gaspe flint and some inbred lines of corn. |
| 56-607 | The use of gaseous ammonia as a plant nutrient. |
| 57-519 | Studies of some factors affecting the establishment of certain forage species. |
| 57-567 | Studies of growth types in clones and seed lots of pedigree Kenland, Pennscott, Lasalle and Dollard red clover. |
| 58-030 | A study of the utilization of induced tetraploids in the improvement of red clover (Trifolium pratense L.). |
| 58-570 | Establishment studies of certain forage species in pure and mixed seedings. |
| 58-571 | Inter- and intra-varietal crosses in the improvement of timothy, red clover and birdsfoot trefoil. |
| 59-579 | Inheritance of growth type, flower and seed color of Dollard red clover. |
| **Agronomy & Genetics** | |
| 40-501 | Agronomical and ecological research with special reference to the pastures of the Eastern Townships of Quebec. |
| **Agronomy & Plant Pathology** | |
| 48-542 | Studies on barley diseases caused by Helminthosporium sativum P.K. and B. |
| **Anatomy** | |
| 33-525 | The unstriated muscle fibres of the female pelvis. |
| 41-040 | The influence of hormones on renal structure and function. |

| THESIS | THESIS TITLE |
|---|---|
| **Anatomy** | |
| 41-533 | The distribution of sensory nerves to the dura matter and cerebral vessels. |
| 42-010 | The role of the adrenals in general resistance. |
| 42-060 | The adaptation of kidney tests to small laboratory rodents. |
| 42-504 | Experimental investigations on the effect of steroid compounds on the uterus. |
| 43-021 | Morphological studies of steroid metabolism. |
| 45-542 | Influence of dietary constituents upon renal size and structure. |
| 46-002 | The renotropic action of various hormones. |
| 46-007 | The living anatomy of the abdominal alimentary tract. |
| 46-010 | The hormonal production of cardiovascular lesions. |
| 46-015 | The hormonal control of electrolyte metabolism. |
| 46-519 | Hormonal production of arthritis. |
| 46-558 | Hormonal effects on fat deposition in the liver. |
| 48-001 | An attempt to locate steroids in tissues with special emphasis on the distribution of estradiol labeled with $I^{131}$ in cancer-susceptible mice. |
| 48-004 | Renal function and experimental hypertension. |
| 48-536 | The living anatomy of the human lung. |
| 49-014 | The formation and fate of the thyroid hormone. |
| 49-017 | Potassium deficiency and gastro-intestinal function. |
| 49-047 | The influence of liver and testis on the action of thyroxine in albino rats. |
| 49-515 | Electrolytes in heart disease. |
| 49-548 | The study of renewal rates in the epidermis of the albino rat. |
| 50-044 | Cell turnover of the intestinal epithelium as shown by mitotic counts and the incorporation of $P^{32}$ into desoxyribonucleic acid. |

| THESIS | THESIS TITLE |
|---|---|
| **Anatomy** | |
| 50-516 | A theoretical and technical study of autography as a histological method for localization of radioactive elements. |
| 50-521 | Demonstration of a "steady state' of thyroidal iodine. |
| 50-551 | A quantitative study of thyroid gland growth and function. |
| 50-598 | The post-natal development of the antero-lateral abdominal wall. |
| 51-513 | The mitotic activity and renewal of the lung. |
| 51-518 | Factors modifying the manifestations of thyroid deficiency in thyroidectomized rats and the influence of other hormones on the action of thyroxine. |
| 51-612 | Effect of thyroid preparation and iodide administration on young salmon. |
| 51-624 | The peripheral distribution and metabolism of thyroxine in mice. |
| 51-628 | The variability of the vascular supply to the ureter. |
| 52-042 | The preparation, distribution, and metabolism of iodo-prolactin labelled with $I^{131}$. |
| 53-002 | Histology of the seminiferous epithelium of the rat, hamster and monkey. |
| 53-005 | The fate of nucleic acids in resting and dividing cells. |
| 53-006 | Separation of the direct effects of thyroxine from those mediated through other endocrine glands. |
| 53-008 | Radioautographic localization of $C^{14}$ in tissues of rats following administration of $C^{14}$-labelled bicarbonate. |
| 53-540 | Cervical fascia: anatomic and clinical. |
| 53-597 | Radio-autographic localization of injected calcium 45 and phosphorus in growing teeth of rats. |
| 54-005 | The role of iodine deficiency in the production of goiter and thyroid tumors. |
| 54-007 | Histology and histophysiology of the alveolar lung tissue. |
| 54-511 | Inter-relations of growth hormone and thyroxine on metabolism and tissue morphology. |
| 54-536 | The renewal of the epithelium of the urinary bladder. |

| THESIS | THESIS TITLE |
|---|---|
| **Anatomy** | |
| 54-607 | Studies of effect of pressure on bone crystals. |
| 55-070 | The site and rate of turnover of iodine in the thyroid gland. |
| 55-522 | The effect of pectic enzymes on tissues stained by Pa-Schiff technique. |
| 56-056 | Radioautographic and histochemical studies of young rat tissues with particular attention to dentin. |
| 56-569 | The cranial dura and related structures in the region of the hypophyseal fossa in the cow. |
| 56-590 | Radioautographic localization of some acid soluble phosphorus compounds in tissues of rats injected with $P^{32}$. |
| 57-010 | Increase in cell number and size and in extracellular space during postnatal growth of several organs in the albino rat. |
| 58-013 | Isolation of carbohydrates from periodic acid-Schiff sites. |
| 58-569 | Sites of protein synthesis as shown by radioautographic distribution of methionine labelled with $C^{14}$ or $S^{35}$ in mice and rats. |
| **Animal Nutrition & Breeding** | |
| 34-510 | The effect of fertilization on the nutritive value of pasture grass. |
| 35-506 | The effect of feeding deaminized vs. untreated cod liver oils upon growth, egg production, and mortality of poultry. |
| 36-510 | The nutrative value of pasture grasses. |
| 36-519 | An analysis and interpretation of feeding and carcass data of hogs tested under the Canadian Advanced Registry Policy for swine. |
| 36-522 | The comparative nutrative values for poultry of barley, corn, wheat, oats and rye. |
| 38-504 | Studies on the relative ability of steers and rabbits to digest pasture herbage. |
| 38-507 | The intra-seasonal changes in the nutrative value of pasture herbage. |
| 39-062 | The relative ability of steers and rabbits to digest pasture herbage. |
| 39-063 | Milk production in dairy cattle: factors affecting total yield and rate of secretion during lactation period, with particular reference to effect of pregnancy. |

| THESIS | THESIS TITLE |
| --- | --- |
| **Animal Nutrition & Breeding** | |
| 39-511 | The utilization of feed for body weight maintenance and for body weight increase by growing bacon-type swine. |
| 39-519 | A statistical study of the characteristics of the body fat of bacon pigs and some factors which affect them. |
| 40-519 | The relative ability of sheep and rabbits to digest pasture herbage. |
| 41-036 | The relation between chemical composition of ration and its feeding value for bacon hogs. |
| 41-043 | Comparative digestibility by rabbits of ether extract and true fats of feeds. |
| 41-044 | Some factors affecting fat and vitamin A metabolism of fowl with specific reference to the effect of the anterior pituitary. |
| **Anthropology** | |
| 57-553 | Migration and the French Canadian extended family. |
| **Applied Electricity** | |
| 12-514 | Dielectric strength of air, and suspension type insulators. |
| **Architecture** | |
| 48-503 | Methods of control of the bulk and form of buildings in the central area of cities, with reference to Montreal. |
| 50-501 | The control of residential density. |
| 51-580 | Climate and architecture. |
| 53-558 | An analysis of regulations and standing relating to building. |
| 55-569 | The development of land settlement and rural architecture in the Province of Quebec. |
| 57-501 | The Canadian shopping centre. |
| 57-502 | Urban renewal planning and design. |
| 57-554 | The problem of housing density in Hong Kong with reference to decentralization. |

| THESIS | THESIS TITLE |
|---|---|
| **Architecture** | |
| 58-552 | The development of urban form through planning administration with specific reference to Oromocto, New Brunswick. |
| 58-553 | Tendencies in the evolution of the centres of Canadian cities. |
| 59-501 | The influence of urban growth upon surrounding villages, with special reference to Montreal and villages in the Richelieu valley. |
| **Bacteriology** | |
| 07-508 | Published works. |
| 14-519 | On the heat resistance of bacterial spores, with a consideration of the nature of the sporelike bodies seen in B. tuberculosis and allied forms. |
| 17-507 | Studies in marine bacteriology. (1) Bacterial destruction of Copepods. (2) Bacteriology of swelled canned fish. |
| 20-502 | On the relative rate of dextrose fermentation of generations of colon bacteria grown on sugar-free media. |
| 21-511 | The red colouration of dried codfish. |
| 21-516 | Organisms which cause blackening in clams. |
| 22-518 | Marine spore forming bacteria. |
| 24-511 | A sporadic outbreak in cattle resembling tetanus. |
| 24-527 | Media for the lactic acid group of microorganisms. |
| 25-550 | The influence of green manures upon the growth and physiological efficiency of cyotobacter. |
| 26-514 | A rapid method for the determination of mould and yeast counts in creamery butter. |
| 26-530 | A study of bacteria isolated from cases of bovine mastitis. |
| 27-504 | The colon count as a substitute for the numerical count in the examination of a city milk supply. |
| 28-514 | The bacteriology of "process' cheese. |
| 28-561 | Gum production by Azotobacter chroococcum and its physiological significance. |

| THESIS | THESIS TITLE |
|---|---|
| Bacteriology | |
| 29-503 | Studies on microbic dissociation in vibrio comma. |
| 29-521 | The bacterial flora of the pregnant bovine uterus. |
| 31-004 | The vertical distribution of marine bacteria in the northern Pacific Ocean. |
| 31-009 | Studies in bacterial metabolism. |
| 31-503 | A systematic study of the genus mycobacterium. |
| 31-552 | The mechanism of staphylococcus aureus localization in rabbit tissues. |
| 32-520 | The microbiology of air-dried cultivated soils. |
| 33-009 | Effects of sub-optimal temperatures on marine bacteria. |
| 35-007 | Colonial dissociation of saprophytic mycobacteria. |
| 39-055 | The differentiation of salmonella pullorum by fermentation and agglutination reactions. |
| 42-062 | A study of the microorganisms of the genera Staphylococcus and Micrococcus. |
| 45-537 | Enteritis in children. |
| 48-005 | The immunizing efficiency of mixed antigens. |
| 48-512 | A study of the effect of botulinum toxin on the transmission of nerve impulses. |
| 48-544 | A comparative study of strains of Aerobacter isolated from different sources. |
| 48-598 | Studies on the development of resistance to streptomycin by staphlococcus pyogenes. |
| 49-023 | Nucleoproteins of the Staphylococcus in connection with immunity. |
| 49-517 | The kinds and distribution of fungi in the air over northern Canada above 3000 feet. |
| 49-529 | A method for the rapid isolation of Mycobacterium tuberculosis. |
| 49-543 | The kinds and distribution of bacteria in the air over northern Canada at altitudes over 5,000 feet. |
| 49-547 | The effect of penicillin on hyaluronidase production by bacteria. |

| THESIS | THESIS TITLE |
|---|---|
| Bacteriology | |
| 49-597 | The anaerobic bacterial flora of the upper respiratory tract in children. |
| 49-610 | Studies in the nutrition of Corynebacterium sepedonicum. |
| 50-512 | The effect of pH on the agglutination of H and O suspensions of Salmonella typhosa in human and rabbit antisera. |
| 50-525 | Attempts to stimulate a sheep erythrocyte agglutination with listeria monocytogenes in laboratory animals. |
| 50-527 | Antigenic character of pasteurella species from human cases. |
| 50-547 | Aeorbic bacteria in the slime and intestines of some fresh water fish. |
| 50-630 | The effect of oral streptomycin on faecal bacteria. |
| 51-013 | An investigation of oil partition for the isolation of Mycobacterium tuberculosis from pathological material. |
| 51-026 | An evaluation of certain principles of disinfection. |
| 51-058 | The imminospecificity of streptococcal hyaluronidases and some of their properties. |
| 51-629 | The lethal and mutagenic effects of ultraviolet light on Escherichia coli. |
| 52-013 | Observations on the influence of a sustained monocytosis upon the anitbody response in rabbits to various antigens. |
| 52-046 | The isolation of "choline acetylase' from Lactobacillus plantarum. |
| 52-538 | The results with the hemagglutination reaction in various types of tuberculosis. |
| 52-567 | A study of the methods and conditions for the isolation of pathogenic actinomyces from lesions in animals. |
| 52-568 | A study of the carotenoid pigments produced on various culture media by a strain of staphylococcus pyogenes. |
| 52-578 | The effect of sulfonamides on guinea pig complement. |
| 53-039 | Bacterial response to ultraviolet radiation. |

| THESIS | THESIS TITLE |
|---|---|
| **Bacteriology** | |
| 53-519 | A lymphocytopenic factor produced by soil bacteria. |
| 53-578 | Streptococcus pyogenes in scarlet fever and penicillin sensitivity. |
| 54-579 | The influence of Chloramphenicol upon antityphoid agglutinin production. |
| 54-581 | A toxin neutralizing substance from penicillium cyaneo fulvum. |
| 54-606 | Antigenic characters in corynebacteria. |
| 56-044 | A toxin neutralizing substance from Penicillium cyaneo-fulvum. |
| 56-062 | Lysogeny in M. pyogenes. |
| 56-070 | Serological investigation of the corynebacteria. |
| 56-567 | Serological and physiological studies on Escherichia coli from cases of gastroenteritis in infants. |
| 59-054 | In vitro inactivation of streptomycin and isoniazid action: its practical application in the isolation of mycobacterium tuberculosis from pathological specimens of tuberculous children. |
| **Bacteriology & Immunology** | |
| 40-049 | Active and passive immunization with Haemophilus pertussis. |
| 42-506 | Active and passive immunization with Haemophilus pertussis. |
| 49-613 | The evaluation and comparison of the immune response in guinea pigs to infection with pneumococcis type I when treated with sulphonamides and when treated with penicillin. |
| 50-526 | The effect of botulinum toxin upon the bacterial acetylation of choline. |
| 51-514 | A bacteriological survey of institutional dishwashing. |
| 52-519 | Differential characterization and selection of staphylococcus bacteriophages. |
| 53-572 | The absorption of antibodies in vitro by monocytes (large mononuclear leucocytes). |
| 54-038 | The carotenoid pigments of staphylococcus pyogenes. |
| 55-004 | The classification of the anaerobic actinomyces. |

| THESIS | THESIS TITLE |
|---|---|
| Bacteriology & Immunology | |
| 55-011 | The taxonomy and classification of the corynebacteria. |
| 55-045 | Applications and limitations of bacteriophage in inducing antigenic and morphological changes in salmonellae. |
| 55-047 | In vitro production of antibody by monocytes. |
| 55-536 | The isolation of Mycobacterium tuberculosis by filtration technique from cerebro spinal fluid. |
| 55-590 | Distribution and survival of fecal bacteria in sewage polluted water. |
| 56-020 | Growth of C. albicans on keratin as sole source of nitrogen. |
| 56-043 | The influence of chloramphenicol on the antigenic character of S. typhosa. |
| 56-053 | The cultivation of M. tuberculosis recovered by oil partition. |
| 56-539 | Development of an antigen for macroscopic agglutination of treponemeta. |
| 56-542 | The influence of a mold product on the antigenicity of staphylococcal toxin. |
| 56-568 | Requirements of a Lancefield group A streptococcus for growth and nephrotoxin production. |
| 56-573 | Methods of differentiating virulent and saprophytic mycobacteria by the slide culture technique. |
| 57-064 | A study of the nephritogenic substance produced by type 12 streptococci. |
| 57-079 | Biological studies on treponemata. |
| 57-083 | The influence of a mold product on the antigenicity of staphylococcal toxin: further studies. |
| 57-518 | Production of a toxin-neutralizing substance by Penicillium cyaneo-_fulvum. |
| 57-571 | Filament formation in Candida albicans. |
| 58-562 | The purification and anti-viral activities of Noxiversin. |
| 59-046 | Genetic transformation in Salmonella with respect to chloramphenicol resistance and antigenic structure. |
| 59-055 | Biological studies on mycobacteria. |

| THESIS | THESIS TITLE |
|---|---|
| **Bacteriology & Immunology** | |
| 59-600 | Staphylococcal alpha haemolysin fractions and a study of their immunological and biological properties. |
| **Biochemistry** | |
| 25-001 | The heats of solution of certain alkali halides and the specific heats of their solutions. |
| 25-002 | The purification of pepsin and the determination of the chemical constitution and physical characters of the preparations obtained. |
| 25-521 | The relation of kidney activity in diabetes insipidus to the theories of urine excretion. |
| 27-511 | The inorganic chemistry of the nerve fibre as revealed by microchemical methods. |
| 28-525 | Amino acids of blood in pathological conditions. |
| 29-504 | The inorganic constituents of egg yolk. |
| 30-554 | Studies in glycogen metabolism. |
| 31-001 | Chemical and physiological studies of the parathyroid hormone. |
| 31-003 | The chemistry of the soluble proteins of fish muscle and its probable relation to muscular movement and to rigor mortis. |
| 32-001 | Chemical and physiological properties of crystalline oestrogenic hormones. |
| 32-006 | A study of methods for the analysis of bile. |
| 32-009 | Hormonal studies of the placenta and the anterior lobe of the pituitary body. |
| 32-014 | Studies in calcium and phosphorus metabolism. |
| 33-012 | Studies on the physiology of the adrenal cortex. |
| 33-509 | Carotene and vitamin A: the conversion of carotene to vitamin A in vitro. |
| 34-001 | The inter-relationship of the anterior pituitary and the thyroid gland. |
| 35-005 | Anterior pituitary and fat metabolism. |
| 35-009 | On the biological assay of the anterior pituitary-like hormone (A-P-L). |

| THESIS | THESIS TITLE |
|---|---|
| Biochemistry | |
| 35-021 | The hormones, and the nutrition cf the offspring before and after birth. |
| 36-548 | The determinaticn of iodine in the blood. |
| 37-025 | Factors affecting the metabolism of small mammals. |
| 37-026 | An examination cf the lipids cf the anterior pituitary. |
| 38-007 | A haematological and chemical study of the blood during the alarm reaction. |
| 38-014 | A specific metabclic hormone of the pituitary gland and its relaticn to the melancphore-dilating hormone. |
| 38-510 | Homologues of acetoacetic acid. |
| 40-048 | Ketosis. |
| 41-047 | Studies in blood coagulation. |
| 42-516 | The influence of phenothiazine on cellular metabclism. |
| 42-529 | Haemoglobin - a study of its stability in preserved blood. |
| 44-504 | The chemical composition of urinary calculi and its significarce. |
| 44-510 | On the synthesis of the 12-oxygen analcgs cf corticosterone. |
| 45-017 | The reaction of H with amino acids. |
| 45-507 | The fate of intravenously injected colloids. |
| 46-014 | The correlation between neutral urinary reducing lipids and adrenal cortical function. |
| 46-504 | Chemical changes in stored blood. |
| 46-534 | A study of liver function tests on rabbits. |
| 46-557 | Detoxication in psychiatric disorders. |
| 46-569 | Changes in the lipoproteins of human blood serum during processinq. |
| 46-578 | The clearance of injected citrate from the blood. |

| THESIS | THESIS TITLE |
|---|---|
| **Biochemistry** | |
| 47-004 | On the synthesis of corticoids and spectrophotometric studies in the steroid hormone group. |
| 47-031 | Transformation of the steroid molecule to permit the inclusion of isotopic carbon. |
| 47-551 | The absorption and oxidation of phenothiazene in the sheep. |
| 48-008 | A study on the corn gluten of stripper-starch. |
| 48-011 | Search for pancreatic alpha-cell hormone. |
| 48-037 | Studies on the metabolism of steroid hormones. |
| 48-529 | Glycolytic changes in stored blood. |
| 48-541 | Oxidation studies of the steroid ring A. |
| 48-552 | The formation of acetate in brain tissue suspensions. |
| 48-603 | The influence of various factors on glycolysis in human blood during storage. |
| 49-036 | Metabolism of tricarboxylic acid cycle compounds in kidney and liver tissue. |
| 49-037 | Studies in soil metabolism. |
| 49-049 | The relationship of acetylcholine synthesis to carbohydrate metabolism. |
| 49-538 | Acetylcholine metabolism in brain tissue. |
| 49-592 | Changes of the glyoxalase activity of human red blood cells during storage. |
| 50-016 | A study on the agglutination of erythrocytes. |
| 50-024 | Part I. Synthesis of radioactive organic reagents. Part II. Attempted total synthesis in the estrogen series. |
| 50-031 | In vitro studies of intracellular oxidations and reductions with special reference to sulfhydryl compounds, steroids and related substances. |
| 50-049 | Effects of narcotics and convulsants on brain tissue metabolism. |
| 50-534 | The pharmacology of benezimidazole. |

| THESIS | THESIS TITLE |
|---|---|
| **Biochemistry** | |
| 50-608 | Respiration and utilization of endogenous carbohydrate in Heterakis gallinea, a caecal nematode of the domestic fowl. |
| 50-615 | The phosphorus content of small arteries. |
| 50-627 | The effect of mechanical treatment on glycolsis in erythrocytes. |
| 50-641 | Blood lipids in relation to diet. |
| 51-006 | I. Catalytic decomposition of hydroxylamine by hemoglobin. II. Studies of the effects of methyl-bis(beta-chloroethyl) amine and "anticholine oxidases' on choline metabolism in vitro. |
| 51-010 | Paper chromatography of proteins. |
| 51-021 | Factors affecting the synthesis of acetylcholine by brain tissue preparations. |
| 51-036 | A study of animal and plant transaminases. |
| 51-037 | The preparation of progesterone and desoxycorticosterone acetate labelled in the side chain with radioactive carbon: the metabolism of progesterone. |
| 51-038 | Radioactive steroid hormones (ring A labelled). |
| 51-040 | Studies on the enzyme systems of the blood. |
| 51-041 | Biochemical investigations of snake venoms in relation to their neurotoxic effects. |
| 51-059 | On the preparation of estrone-16-$C^{14}$ and the study of its metabolism. |
| 51-543 | The relation of age to the effect of morphine on the metabolism of mouse brain. |
| 51-551 | Diazomethane-$C^{14}$; ring B di-substituted cholestarols. |
| 51-561 | Chemical analysis of human arteries and arterioles. |
| 51-597 | Factors affecting the metabolism of acetylcholine in tissue suspensions. |
| 51-607 | Hexosemonophosphate oxidation and methemoglobin reduction in human erythrocytes. |
| 51-621 | Studies on the immunochemistry of hemagglutinins. |
| 51-627 | Studies in iron metabolism. |

| THESIS | THESIS TITLE |
|---|---|
| Biochemistry | |
| 52-003 | Studies on biotin metabolism. |
| 52-009 | Absorption studies with isolated surviving intestine. |
| 52-018 | The influence of benzimidazole on enzyme systems. |
| 52-021 | The effects of narcotics and other substances on tissue oxidations and on biological acetylations. |
| 52-025 | Metabolism of erythrocytes during storage. |
| 52-041 | Calcium and pancreatic alpha cells in metabolism. |
| 52-050 | Studies on enzymatic adaptation in micro-organisms. |
| 52-528 | Studies on the absorption and excretion of silicon. |
| 52-529 | Study of diphosphopyridine nucleotide in the erythrocytes. |
| 52-575 | Bacterial oxidation of bile acids. |
| 52-596 | Peptidase activity in the white blood cells of young and old subjects. |
| 53-007 | The metabolism of electrolytes in preserved blood. |
| 53-032 | Biological interconversion reactions of $C^{14}$-desoxycorticosterone acetate and $C^{14}$-progesterone. |
| 53-045 | Studies on the interactions of plasma proteins with ketosteroids: studies on the role of glutathione and ascorbic acid in biological oxidation mechanisms. |
| 53-051 | Oxidation of carbohydrate in mammalian erythrocytes. |
| 53-052 | Part I. Chemical absorption from isolated surviving intestine. Part II. Paper chromatography of enzymes and other proteins. |
| 53-064 | Anaerobic amino acid interactions in Cl. sporogenes. |
| 53-065 | I. Investigation of some factors affecting the pituitary-adrenal system. II. Studies on the glycogenolytic hyperglycemic hormone of the pancreas. |
| 53-069 | The nitrogenous components and the amino acid metabolism in the ovaries of Ascaris lumbricoides. |
| 53-072 | The respiratory mechanism of the avian erythrocyte. |

| THESIS | THESIS TITLE |
|---|---|
| **Biochemistry** | |
| 53-076 | On the metabolism of ring B unsaturated estrogens and the urinary estrogens in the normal menstrual cycle. |
| 53-078 | Effect of age, hypertension and arteriosclerosis on the chemical composition of human arterial smooth muscle. |
| 53-523 | Studies on brain tissue metabolism: effects of composition of the suspension medium, pentobarbital, and age. |
| 53-588 | Studies on the storage of human erythrocytes at low temperatures. |
| 53-595 | A study of diphosphopyridine nuclectidases in erythrocytes. |
| 54-011 | Studies on the metabolism of D-glucosamine and N-acetyl-D-glucosamine. |
| 54-025 | The biogenesis of cholesterol and the estrogens. |
| 54-032 | I. Glutamine metabolism in brain. II. Protein synthesis by glandular tissues in vitro. |
| 54-037 | Studies on the metabolism of fatty acids in animal tissues. |
| 54-041 | The metabolism of alkylthioacids. |
| 54-052 | The biogenesis of estrone and cholesterol in the pregnant mare. |
| 54-074 | Studies of ovary incubations and steroid constituents of the placenta from a mare treated with acetate-1-$C^{14}$. |
| 54-532 | The effect of nitous oxide on enzyme systems. |
| 54-537 | The production of fatty acids by ascaris lumbricoides. |
| 54-602 | A study of intermedin. |
| 54-603 | Studies on the metabolism of silicon. |
| 55-032 | Studies in ring D oxygenated steroids. |
| 55-036 | Formation of hormones in vitro by adrenal preparations. |
| 55-058 | Studies on aromatic acids in relation to phenylpyruvic oligophrenia. |

| THESIS | THESIS TITLE |
|---|---|
| **Biochemistry** | |
| 55-078 | The effect of anaerobiosis on phage synthesis by E. coli. |
| 55-517 | The effects of anoxia and lack of substrate on the subsequent carbohydrate metabolism of brain tissue. |
| 55-523 | Absorption by the isolated surviving small intestine after experimental shock. |
| 55-528 | Metabolic changes during acute physiological failure. |
| 55-592 | Interconversion reactions of desoxycorticosterone acetate-21-$C^{14}$ by the adrenal cortex. |
| 55-607 | The effects of ions on monoamine oxidase activity of rat liver. |
| 55-617 | Enzymes of the mammalian reticulocyte. |
| 56-014 | The metabolism of choline esters of succinic acid. |
| 56-021 | Hexokinase of the erythrocyte. |
| 56-026 | The synthesis of diphosphopyridine nucleotide in the erythrocyte. |
| 56-028 | Carbohydrate synthesis in embryonating eggs of Ascaris lumbricoides. |
| 56-030 | Intermedin and tyrosinase. |
| 56-039 | Biogenesis of adrenal cortical steroids. |
| 56-055 | The effects of the growth of mouse sarcoma-37 in the chick embryo. |
| 56-059 | Metabolism of short chain fatty acids by Mycobacterium tuberculosis var. bovis BCG. |
| 56-063 | Metabolism of progesterone and cortisone. |
| 56-512 | Synthesis and metabolism of $C^{14}$-dimethylacrylic acid. |
| 56-532 | Age period changes in the composition of the aortic wall in the rabbit. |
| 56-575 | Estrogen metabolism in human subjects. |
| 56-593 | Free amino acid levels in the yolks of tumour-bearing embryonated eggs. |
| 56-596 | The distribution of corticotropin in the pituitary gland. |

| THESIS | THESIS TITLE |
|---|---|
| **Biochemistry** | |
| 56-599 | Factors affecting the anaerobic glycolysis of brain tissue and the effects of sodium and potassium on brain metabolism. |
| 56-608 | The fluorimetric measurement of adrenaline and noradrenaline in human plasma. |
| 56-610 | A study of tryptophan metabolism in man. |
| 57-022 | The behaviour of coenzymes in the liver of the rat during hemorrhagic shock. |
| 57-030 | In vitro studies on the control of the release of ACTH. |
| 57-061 | The role of cofactors in the enzymatic reduction of tetrazolium salts by amines. |
| 57-074 | The lactic dehydrogenase of the mammalian erythrocyte. |
| 57-075 | Carbohydrate metabolism in the central nervous system. |
| 57-076 | The use of snake venom phospholipase A in a study of mitochondria. |
| 57-080 | Role of aminosugars in glycoside synthesis and in cell metabolism. |
| 57-566 | The acid phosphatases of rat liver. |
| 57-572 | The influence of metabolic activity on the movement of cations across the red blood cell membrane. |
| 57-576 | Absorption of amino acids and sugars by the isolated surviving guinea pig small intestine. |
| 57-578 | Electrophoretic studies on serum gamma-globulins in rheumatic fever. |
| 57-587 | The influence of dieldrin on enzyme systems. |
| 57-594 | The antidiuretic, pressor and oxytocic properties of corticotropin-releasing factor (CRF). |
| 58-005 | Factors affecting the binding and synthesis of acetylcholine. |
| 58-007 | Corticosteroidogenesis. |
| 58-032 | The pathogenic nature of finely particulate silica. |
| 58-037 | Studies on the allergens of ragweed pollen. |
| 58-038 | Studies on absorption of sugars by the isolated surviving guinea pig small intestine. |

| THESIS | THESIS TITLE |
|---|---|
| Biochemistry | |
| 58-039 | Depletion of pituitary corticotropin by varicus stress stimuli. |
| 58-044 | Mucopolysaccharide metabolism in relation to bleeding disorders. |
| 58-047 | The metabolism of amino-acids in the central nervous system. |
| 58-054 | Immuno-chemical and physico-chemical studies on the biocolloids in normal human urine. |
| 58-057 | The role of nutritional factors in the formation of catecholamines. |
| 59-007 | A pentose phosphate metabolic pathway in human erythrocytes. |
| 59-028 | Estrogen methodology and excretion in human subjects. |
| 59-030 | Antibody-antigen reactions in allergy. |
| 59-062 | Protein synthesis of the developing embryo and the effects thereon of tumour growth. |
| 59-072 | The transport of amino acids in Ehrlich ascites cells. |
| 59-073 | Metabolism and action of factor I and upsilon-aminobutyric acid. |
| 59-080 | Effect of aliphatic alcohols on liver metabolism. |
| 59-083 | Alternate pathways of tryptophan metabolism in the rat. |
| 59-085 | Cholesterol and acetate as precursors of the adrenal steroids. |
| 59-582 | The effect of ethyl gamma-butyrobetaine on creatine and phosphorous metabolism in rats. |
| 59-583 | Transamination in the mammalian erythrocyte. |
| 59-593 | The effect of intramuscular injection of gamma butyrobetaine on enzyme movement. |
| Biology | |
| 14-512 | Anatomy of Gryllus pennsylvanicus Burm. |
| Botany | |
| 07-503 | On the development and function of certain structures in the stipe and rhizome of pterisaquihna and other pteridophytes. |

| THESIS | THESIS TITLE |
|---|---|
| Botany | |
| 10-002 | The origin and development of resin canals in the coniferae with special reference to the development of thyloses and their correlation with the thylosal strands of the pteridophytes. |
| 12-502 | Fresh-water algae occurring in the vicinity of Montreal. |
| 18-503 | Plankton diatoms in the vicinity of St Andrew's, N.B. |
| 21-513 | A study in Marquis wheat: a measure of its variability. |
| 22-001 | Studies concerning mosaic diseases. |
| 22-504 | Studies on a new species of Empusa. |
| 22-516 | Cultural reactions of some dry root-rot organisms. |
| 22-519 | A study of bacterial soft rot of iris. |
| 25-006 | Physiological variations in xanthium. |
| 26-510 | Effect of ultra-violet light on spirogyra. |
| 26-516 | The Cyanophyceae: pigments and structure. |
| 31-502 | Effects of temperature on stomata of excised leaves of zebrina pendula. |
| 32-516 | Cytological studies in the genus Hordeum. |
| 32-555 | Some studies on the physiology of cold resistance in plants. |
| 33-001 | Cyto-genetic studies in Matthiola and Triticum. |
| 33-028 | Chromosome studies on the mechanism of meiosis in Melanoplus femur-rubrum. |
| 33-521 | Physiology of cold resistance in plants. |
| 33-532 | The relation of stomatal opening to temperature and other factors. |
| 34-511 | A karyo-systematic investigation in the Gramineae. |
| 35-017 | Cellular changes associated with hardening of plants. |
| 35-517 | Food reserves in trees with special reference to the paper birch Betula alba var. Papyrifera |

| THESIS | THESIS TITLE |
|---|---|
| **Botany** | |
| 37-505 | Physiology of apples in artificial atmospheres. |
| 37-541 | A study of the mechanism of cold injury to plants. |
| 38-024 | A study of factors affecting stomatal movement in the dark. |
| 38-546 | Comparison of the pH requirements of certain lawn grasses and weeds, together with a study of the related physiological differences. |
| 39-025 | Studies on the mechanism of frost injury to plant cells. |
| 40-037 | Changes in germination capacity of weed seeds in storage, and factors influencing it, with special reference to Chenopodium album L. |
| 41-505 | Effects of acidity on growth, structure, and physiology of plants with special reference to root cells. |
| 42-023 | Ecological studies of the Arctic-alpine flora of the Gaspe peninsula and of Bic. |
| 43-509 | Ovule development and parthenocarpy in Polygonum natans. |
| 47-547 | Studies in comparative physiology of trees. |
| 47-556 | The infra red total absorption method and its application to some plant physiological problems. |
| 50-606 | The properties and kinetics of ascorbic acid oxidase. |
| 50-636 | A comparison study of the morphology and anatomy of normal Abies balsamea and that infected by Melampsorella cerastii (Pers.) Schroet. |
| 51-545 | An embryo-sac study of Butomus umbellatus, L. |
| 51-558 | Comparative chemistry and taxonomy of plants: the separation and estimation of phenolic aldehydes from the alkaline nitrobenzene oxidation mixtures of plant materials. |
| 52-007 | The paleobotony and stratigraphic sequence of the Klondike muck deposits. |
| 52-517 | The water requirements of yellow birch. |
| 52-524 | Developemnt of the female gametophyte and embryo in Smilacina racemosa (L) Desf. |
| 52-595 | A study of the seasonal variation in the occurrence of air-borne fungous spores in Montreal. |

| THESIS | THESIS TITLE |
|---|---|
| **Botany** | |
| 53-525 | Comparative studies of cultural and physiological characteristics of Fomes annosus (Fries) Cooke from North American and European localities. |
| 54-009 | Studies on the isolation, purification, and determination of enzymes in succulent plants. |
| 54-522 | Enzyme studies of mitochondria from barley seedlings. |
| 54-524 | The purification and properties of pectin methyl esterase from Cladosporium herbarum (Pers.) link. |
| 54-596 | Responses of Cladosporium herbarum (Pers.) link to growth regulating substances. |
| 55-071 | Host-parasite relationships in tomato fusarium wilt. |
| 55-520 | Embryo sac development in Cleome spinosa Jacq. |
| 55-529 | The plant communities of Morgan's Woods. |
| 55-544 | A cytological study of Sporormia obliquiseptata Speg. |
| 55-545 | Some metabolic interrelationships of Lilium regale with reference to gamma-methyleneglutamic acid. |
| 56-609 | Sexual reproduction in Medeola virginiana L. with some reference to embryo development and endosperm formation. |
| 57-029 | The life cycle and cytology of the myxogastres. |
| 57-059 | Studies on the keto acid metabolism of wheat seedlings. |
| 57-565 | Studies on the metabolism of the fungus Ascocybe grovesii. |
| 58-510 | A comparison of embryo sacs and haustoria in selected species of Impatiens. |
| 58-572 | The effect of ethionine on some plant growth systems. |
| 59-534 | The synthesis of phenolic glucosides by plant tissues. |
| **Botany & Geological Sciences** | |
| 50-619 | A critical survey of the Sir William Dawson collection of paleozoic plants with a restudy of Dadoxylon acadianum DN. |
| **Botany-Genetics** | |

| THESIS | THESIS TITLE |
|---|---|
| **Botany-Genetics** | |
| 42-066 | Micrurgical studies in the physiology of cell division. |
| 45-012 | Physiological and physical changes of protoplasm during meiosis and mitosis in pollen mother-cells of Trillium. |
| **Botany-Horticulture** | |
| 41-035 | Sand culture experiments with spinach. |
| 58-055 | Biochemical and physiological studies of Malus rootstocks. |
| **Cellulose Chemistry** | |
| 29-007 | Nature of the supermolecular state of certain aldehyde and ethylene oxide derivatives. 1:The action of sodium on crotonaldehyde. 2: The ethylene oxide ring in relation to the supermolecular state. |
| 29-515 | (a) Constitution of the so-called tetrabromobutyraltchyde. (b) An investigation into the "super-molecular' structure of polyethyleneoxide and dirinylether. |
| **Chemical Engineering** | |
| 40-516 | An investigation in the recovery of sodium bisulphite cooking liquor. |
| 42-515 | The effect of gelatin on cathode polarization during the electrodeposition of copper. |
| 45-519 | The effect of pulsating air on the rate of drying of porous material. |
| 46-503 | The refining and hydrogenation of fish oils. |
| 46-553 | Non-isothermal friction drop for gas. |
| 48-507 | The determination of film co-efficients for condensing vapors. |
| 48-573 | Some factors affecting the capacity and efficiency of a spray drying unit. |
| 49-504 | Distillation studies in a square column with variable tray design. |
| 50-504 | The effect of oxygen enrichment of the air intake of a diesel engine on the exhaust gas composition and the combustion processes. |
| 50-507 | Relations of the factors in spray drying. |

| THESIS | THESIS TITLE |
|---|---|
| **Chemical Engineering** | |
| 51-501 | Heat and mass transfer in dehumidification. |
| 51-587 | The effects of feed properties on spray drying. |
| 51-588 | Film and dropwise condensation of steam-air mixtures. |
| 52-503 | The effects on the exhaust gas composition and combustion processes of the addition of oxygen or water vapour to the air intake of a diesel engine. |
| 52-506 | Performance of a forced circulation evaporator. |
| 52-507 | Performance of a cascade refrigerating system. |
| 52-508 | Operating characteristics of a diesel driven heat pump. |
| 52-509 | The fundamentals of spray drying. |
| 52-510 | Heat-transfer coefficients for mixtures of condensable and noncondensable vapours. |
| 52-563 | Characteristics of an ammonia absorption refrigeration unit. |
| 52-565 | Performance characteristics of a countercurrent spray dryer. |
| 53-510 | Pressure drop during evaporation of water in tubes. |
| 54-031 | Cathode processes during the electrodeposition of nickel. |
| 56-559 | Turbulent fluid flow through beds of solid particles. |
| 57-006 | Heat and mass transfer in spray drying. |
| 58-026 | Heat and mass transfer to decelerating finely-atomized sprays. |
| 59-035 | Theoretical and experimental investigations of the evaporation of stationary droplets and sprays in high temperature surroundings. |
| 59-061 | Turbulent convective heat and mass transfer from stationary and accelerating particles. |
| **Chemistry** | |
| 07-512 | Notes on some reductions in the presence of finely divided nickel. |

| THESIS | THESIS TITLE |
|---|---|
| Chemistry | |
| 08-511 | The action of thionyl chloride on some organic compounds containing hydroxyl groups, and the physical properties of methyl mandelate. |
| 09-514 | The investigation of amygdalin. |
| 10-003 | A comparison of certain acids containing a conjugated system of of double linkages. |
| 10-514 | Canadian turpentine, and its relation to the French and American varieties. |
| 10-518 | The physical constants of some substituted malonic acids, with special regard to the influence of alkyl sustituents on the electrical conductivity of malonic acids. |
| 11-513 | |
| 12-001 | The hydrolysis of gelatin by baryta. The transformation of glutamine acid into proline. |
| 12-512 | Phase rule studies; organic compounds, containing oxygen, with the halogens and halogen hydrides. |
| 12-513 | Optical studies of the asymmetric aliphatic acids. |
| 12-516 | The hydrates of nickel sulphate. |
| 13-001 | Amygdalins and their inter-reactions with emulsin. |
| 13-515 | Artesian wells of the Island of Montreal. |
| 13-517 | The action of nitric acid upon certain derivatives of gallic acid hi-methyl ether. |
| 15-513 | Molecular weight determinations at low temperatures. |
| 16-001 | A colorimetric method for the estimation of amino acid alpha-nitrogen. |
| 16-509 | Hydrolysis of certain proteins. |
| 16-512 | Chemistry of adipocere. |
| 17-505 | The absorption of ammonia by alumina. |
| 17-506 | Studies in the compounds of phenol and pyridine. |
| 18-504 | Bog butter. Stearic and palmitic esters of propylene and glycol. |

| THESIS | THESIS TITLE |
|---|---|
| **Chemistry** | |
| 18-505 | Study of the preparation and properties of hydrogen peroxide and its aqueous solution. |
| 18-506 | (1) The effect of unsaturation on the formation of molecular compounds. (2) A method for the determination of the densities of gases. |
| 18-507 | The synthesis of mixed triglycerides of palmitic and stearic acids. Observations on the silver salts of the higher fatty acids. |
| 18-508 | The properties of oxynitulase. |
| 20-001 | A chemical investigation of the asphalt in the tar sands of northern Alberta. |
| 20-002 | Investigation of natural and oxidised resins from herea rubber. |
| 20-003 | Contributions to the knowledge of the fats and fatty acids. |
| 20-504 | Further immersion experiments and observations on some of the terrestrial Crustaceae. |
| 20-506 | An investigation of the kerogen in oil shells. |
| 21-002 | The preparation and properties of pure anhydrons, and of pure concentrated solutions of hydrogen peroxide. |
| 21-003 | Physical and chemical properties of the elementary hydrocarbons. |
| 21-501 | An investigation of preparation and properties of ethylene oxide. |
| 21-509 | Autohydrolysis of fats. |
| 22-509 | Beryllium. |
| 22-511 | Properties of pure hydrogen peroxide. |
| 22-513 | Ortho-substituted aromatic antimony compounds. |
| 22-515 | Triglycerides and other fatty derivatives. |
| 22-517 | Tendency towards molecular compound formation of aromatic hydrocarbons with hydrobromic acid. |
| 22-520 | Purification of coal gas with spent "pickle liquor'. |
| 22-522 | The monobromstearic acid from oleic acid and the corresponding monohydroxystearic acids. |

| THESIS | THESIS TITLE |
| --- | --- |
| **Chemistry** | |
| 22-525 | An investigation of the specific and latent heats of fusion at low temperatures. |
| 23-001 | Vapour densities, molecular compound formation and the physical properties of certain organic compounds and their correlation in terms of molecular forces. |
| 23-003 | Beryllium. |
| 23-004 | The protein matter of bile. |
| 23-005 | The kerogen in pyrobituminous shale. |
| 23-006 | Observations relative to the constitution of caoutchouc. |
| 23-007 | An investigation of the specific heats and latent heats of fusion at low temperatures. |
| 23-506 | The preparation of some organic sulphur compounds, and a study of their influence on vulcanization. |
| 23-507 | Soil acidity and lime requirement studies of Quebec soils. |
| 23-513 | Observations on the reaction product between caoutchouc and sulphur. |
| 23-514 | The diffusion of gases through metals. |
| 23-518 | Some derivatives of the diquinolines. |
| 24-001 | The physical and chemical properties of pure hydrogen peroxide. |
| 24-003 | Work on the chemistry of diolefines. |
| 24-004 | A study of molecular forces by means of the gas laws, molecular compound formation, and velocities of reaction. |
| 24-507 | Phosphate deficiency in Quebec soils. |
| 24-512 | Pentosan content in relation to winter hardiness in commercial varieties of the apple. |
| 24-519 | Hydrogen peroxide as an oxidising agent in acid solution. |
| 24-520 | On the examination of anomalous values of the Ramsey-Shields surface tension constant. |
| 24-529 | Reaction velocities and molecular compound formation. |

| THESIS | THESIS TITLE |
|---|---|
| **Chemistry** | |
| 24-530 | Relation between the chemical constitution of organic liquids and their ability to swell certain organic materials: the swelling of rubber. |
| 24-532 | The viscosity of liquid haolgen. |
| 24-535 | A study of the constitution of hevea resin and serum. |
| 24-550 | The relations existing between the degree of unsaturation of an organic compound and the amount of its adsorption by charcoal. |
| 25-003 | A study of the colloidal behaviour of rubber. |
| 25-004 | The diffusion of gases through metals. |
| 25-005 | Vapor densities and molecular attraction. |
| 25-007 | The preparation and the properties of the margarines. |
| 25-505 | A. Preparation of compounds contributory to the study of the mechanism of vulcanization catalysis.<br>B. Acid numbers in raw rubber samples. |
| 25-509 | Some thermal constants of carbon dioxide. |
| 25-512 | A study of the fixation of phosphates by soils. |
| 25-515 | The relation between the chemical constitution of organic liquids and their ability to swell rubber. |
| 25-517 | A method for the determination of halogens in the side chains of aromatic organic compounds. |
| 25-526 | Conductivities of aqueous solutions of sulphur dioxide and other properties of sulphur dioxide. |
| 25-527 | Isolation and identification of the flavouring principle of maple sugar. |
| 26-001 | The sulphuration of fatty oils. |
| 26-003 | Investigation of anomalous values of the Ramsey-Shields constant from the point of view of surface orientation. |
| 26-004 | Reaction velocities and molecular attraction in related systems. |
| 26-005 | Effect of molecular attraction on the total pressure of gas mixtures. |

| THESIS | THESIS TITLE |
|---|---|
| **Chemistry** | |
| 26-006 | The absorbtion of gases in metals. |
| 26-007 | The sorption of vapors by alumina. |
| 26-517 | Some properties of pure hydrogen peroxide. |
| 26-521 | The relation between the polarity of isomeric benzine derivatives and other substances and (a) inhibition by organic colloids; (b) their solvent power. |
| 26-527 | Study of the propylene-halogen hydride reaction. |
| 26-529 | Studies in the oxidation of organic compounds by hydrogen peroxide. |
| 26-532 | Dissociation pressures of the orthophosphates of ammonia. |
| 26-559 | Action of caustic on cellulose: effect of variations in the conditions of manipulation. |
| 27-001 | Some thermal properties of carbon dioxide and of ice. |
| 27-005 | Hydrogen peroxide as an oxidising agent in acid solution. |
| 27-006 | The surface energy and heat of solution of solid sodium chloride. |
| 27-007 | An investigation of the properties of pure sulphur dioxide and its aqueous solutions. |
| 27-008 | Some colloidal and elastic properties of meta styrene and rubber. |
| 27-010 | Molecular attraction. |
| 27-503 | Preparation and properties of pure hydrogen peroxide. |
| 27-505 | 1.The action of potassium cyanide on certain disulphides. 2.Some aspects of the behaviour of pure caoutchouc, with special reference to the influence of protien. |
| 27-507 | Cyclic acetal formation and polymerisation. |
| 27-508 | Fractional distillation on the large laboratory scale as applied to the separation into their components of the binary systems Butanol(1)-Propanol(1), Butatone(2)-Propanone(2) and (2)Butenal(1)-Paraethanal. |
| 27-509 | A study of some polymerizable substances, especially connamylidene fluorene and similar compounds. |

| THESIS | THESIS TITLE |
|---|---|
| **Chemistry** | |
| 27-541 | Mechanism of cyclic acetal formation. |
| 27-542 | Separation and identification of the isomeric ethylidene glycercls. |
| 28-001 | The preparation and properties of the persulphides of hydrogen. |
| 28-002 | A study of the preparation and reactions of some organic sulphides, with special reference to the conversion of dithio carbolkyl disulphides into the corresponding mono sulphides. |
| 28-003 | Aberrations from the ideal gas laws in systems cf one and two ccmponents. |
| 28-005 | An investigaticn of the constituticn of caoutchouc with special reference to the mode of polymerization. |
| 28-008 | Viscosity of gases, and the effect of molecular attraction on the total pressure of gas mixtures. |
| 28-009 | A study of the constituents of the serum of Herea latex. |
| 28-010 | The action of sulphur and sulphur halides on certain unsaturated substances, especially fatty oils. |
| 28-012 | The rotary dispersion of non-tautomeric organic ccmpounds. |
| 28-520 | The influence of the composition of basic lead acetate on the Canadian lead number of maple products. |
| 28-522 | Nature of lignin. |
| 28-523 | Identification of lignin ccnstituents. |
| 29-002 | Proprties of sulphur dioxide solutions above room temperatures. |
| 29-003 | The structural and geometrical isomerism cf cyclic acetals cf glycercl and the migration of groups in glycerol esters and ethers. |
| 29-004 | The effect of molecular attraction upon the velccity of chemical reactions. |
| 29-005 | Preparation and properties cf hydrcgen peroxide. |
| 29-006 | Oxidation of organic compounds, with special reference to hydrogen peroxide. |
| 29-008 | The penetration cf wood by liquids. |

| THESIS | THESIS TITLE |
|---|---|
| **Chemistry** | |
| 29-009 | Isolation and identification of some lignin constituents. |
| 29-010 | Properties of hydrogen peroxide. |
| 29-011 | Adsorption of water by wood. |
| 29-012 | A study of the chemistry of spruce wood lignin and a new method of isolation. |
| 29-014 | The action of hypochlorous acid on lignin and related compounds. |
| 29-015 | The absorption of gases by metals. |
| 29-016 | Studies on the ring structure of cyclic acetals from glycerols. |
| 29-017 | Further observations on the polymerization of indene. The polymerization of styrene, iso-safrole, iso-eugenol and related substances. |
| 29-513 | The oxidation of organic compounds. |
| 29-516 | Ring migration and isomerism in the glycerol cyclic acetals. |
| 29-518 | Cyclic acetal formation. |
| 29-520 | A study of the butylene halogen hydride reactions. |
| 30-001 | Influence of structure upon the ability of organic compounds to polymerize. |
| 30-003 | Studies in polymerization. |
| 30-008 | An investigation of equilibria existing in gas-water systems forming electrolytes. |
| 30-009 | Comparative studies in oxidation. |
| 30-010 | The mechanism for the hydrolysis of hydrogen cyanide. |
| 30-011 | The nature of the resins of Jack pine. |
| 30-013 | The mechanism of the action of sulphurous acid on lignin and related compounds. |
| 30-014 | The mechanism of organic oxidation. |
| 30-015 | Colorimetric measurements in relation to surface phenomena. |

| THESIS | THESIS TITLE |
|---|---|
| **Chemistry** | |
| 30-502 | Kinetics of chemical change in gaseous systems. |
| 30-507 | The preparation and properties of pure hydrogen peroxide. |
| 30-509 | The action of sulphurous acid and bisulphites on cellulose. |
| 30-510 | Mechanism of cyclic formation. |
| 30-516 | On the vapour density of hydrogen sulphide gas. |
| 30-553 | Surface energy relationships. |
| 31-002 | Cellulose ethers. |
| 31-005 | Aberrations from the ideal gas laws and a precision method for the determination of the densities of gases. |
| 31-006 | The sorption of vapors by wood and cellulose. |
| 31-008 | A study of the reactions between unsaturated hydrocarbons and the halogen hydrides. |
| 31-010 | The nature and properties of aqueous solutions of hydrogen sulphide. |
| 31-011 | 1,5-Diketones: addition reactions of phenyl vinyl ketone. |
| 31-013 | Studies in photochemistry. |
| 31-510 | The preparation of ethyl acetylene and a determination of some of its physical constants. |
| 31-513 | Penetration studies: the circulation of alkali reagents into and of reaction products out of the fibre cavity. |
| 31-556 | The kinetics of chemical change in gaseous systems. |
| 31-557 | The kinetics of gas reactions. |
| 31-559 | The viscosity of sulphur dioxide. |
| 31-560 | The preparation of certain organic compounds of nitrogen. |
| 31-567 | Investigation of density of vapors in equilibrium with liquids. |

| THESIS | THESIS TITLE |
|---|---|
| **Chemistry** | |
| 32-002 | The specific volume of cellulose and wood and the density of adsorbed water vapour. |
| 32-003 | Some reactions of gamma ketonic esters. |
| 32-004 | The physical and chemical properties of the polyethylene glycols and their derivatives. |
| 32-005 | Equilibria in the three component system: calcium oxide - sulphur dioxide -water over the temperature range 25°C to 130°C. |
| 32-008 | An investigation of the resonance method for the measurement of dielectric constant. |
| 32-010 | The penetration of sodium hydroxide solutions into spruce wood and the cooking of spruce wood by concentrated sodium hydroxide solutions. |
| 32-011 | Preparation and study of the physical properties of aliphatic acetylenes. |
| 32-012 | Cyclic acetal formation, the ring-partition principle, and their relation to the structure of carbohydrates. |
| 32-013 | Studies in organic peracids. |
| 32-015 | The penetration of aqueous sulphite solutions into spruce wood. |
| 32-016 | Penetration studies: the entry of liquids into the fibre cavity. |
| 32-017 | The surface energy and heat of solution of solid rhombic sulphur and the heat of reaction of S (monoclinic) -- S (rhombic). |
| 32-019 | I. The nature of polymerization and its relation to the dielectric constant. II. The electric moment in relation to the structure of organic compounds. |
| 32-022 | Studies in hydrogen migration. |
| 32-023 | Equilibria in the three-component system: water - calcium oxide - sulphur dioxide over the temperature range 0°C to 25°C. |
| 32-024 | The mechanism of organic reactions in the gaseous state: the kinetics of the oxidation of gaseous acetaldehyde. |
| 32-025 | The relation between particle size and light absorption by suspended particles. |
| 32-515 | Heat capacity of gelatin gels. |

| THESIS | THESIS TITLE |
|---|---|
| Chemistry | |
| 32-517 | Studies in polymerization. |
| 33-002 | The structure of synthetic polysaccharides. |
| 33-003 | The action of sulphuric acid on cyclopropane ketones. |
| 33-005 | Addition reactions of vinyl phenyl ketone III, malonic ester. |
| 33-006 | Synthesis, structure and properties of cyclic and bicyclic acetals. |
| 33-007 | The heat capacity of gelatin gels. |
| 33-010 | The application of densimetric methods to quantitative analysis. |
| 33-013 | Delta-ketonic esters. |
| 33-014 | Action of sulphurous acid on cellulose. |
| 33-015 | An investigation of the reaction between unsaturated hydrocarbons and the halogen hydrides. |
| 33-017 | A comparison of the kinetics of homogeneous and heterogeneous gas reactions. |
| 33-018 | The sorption of sodium hydroxide from liquid phases by various celluloses; and related researches. |
| 33-020 | Anhydroacetonebenzil. |
| 33-021 | The viscosity of gases and its relationship to the gas laws. |
| 33-022 | An investigation of the density of a vapour in equilibrium with a liquid near the critical temperature. |
| 33-026 | Part I. The stereochemistry of certain tertiary amines. Part II. Studies on lactols. |
| 33-027 | Investigation of the continuity of state in one and two component systems. |
| 33-029 | Alkali cooking studies. |
| 33-034 | Part I. The cyanocyclopropanes. Part II. Trivalent asymmetric arsenic. |
| 33-508 | The rate of hydrogenation of certain oils. |
| 33-513 | The kinetics of heterogeneous gas reactions: catalytic de composition of methanol over solid and liquid zinc. |

| THESIS | THESIS TITLE |
|---|---|
| **Chemistry** | |
| 33-517 | Studies in organic oxidation. |
| 33-520 | The determination of the solubility of lime in water and of the sorption of lime on cellulose. |
| 33-522 | A study on the structure of lignin. |
| 33-523 | I. The specific viscosity of acetaldehyde and of acetaldehyde-paraldehyde mixtures. II. A study of the oxidation of allyl alcohol by permanganate in an acid medium. |
| 33-526 | The synthesis of long chain polyethylene ether glycols and the nature of polymerisation. |
| 33-528 | An improved semi-micro Kjeldahl method for estimation of organic nitrogen. |
| 33-571 | The effect of chemical treatments on the structure of cellulose fibers. |
| 34-004 | Phenol derivatives of lignins. |
| 34-005 | Penetration in sulphite cooking. |
| 34-007 | The discontinuity at the critical temperature: adsorption, density and dielectric constant. |
| 34-008 | The condensation of gamma ketonic esters with aromatic aldehydes; ring-chain tautomerism in gamma ketonic acids. |
| 34-010 | The kinetics of the oxidation of mixtures of gaseous hydrocarbons with other substances. |
| 34-013 | A study of the nature of vapour sorption on cellulose. |
| 34-014 | 1,5 - diketones: cyclic compounds containing a carbonyl group; a mechanism for the formation of pyrylium salts. |
| 34-015 | Addition reactions of alpha-methoxybenzalacetophenone. |
| 34-017 | Kinetics of homogeneous gas reactions at high pressures. |
| 34-018 | Cyclic acetal formation and the "Hibbert-Michael' partition principle, and its relation to polysaccharide chemistry. |
| 34-020 | The structure and properties of glycol lignin. |
| 34-021 | The structure and properties of spruce wood lignin and derivatives. |

| THESIS | THESIS TITLE |
|---|---|
| **Chemistry** | |
| 34-022 | The structure and properties of alkali lignin. |
| 34-023 | Preparation, properties and structure of humic acids. Part I. The properties and structure of lignite humic acid. Part II. The preparation, properties and structure of sugar humic acid. |
| 34-025 | Hexendones. |
| 34-507 | The investigation of gaseous oxidation processes by the method of dilute flames. |
| 34-515 | The kinetics of the oxidation of gaseous propionaldehyde. |
| 34-519 | The structure of beech-wood lignin: an investigation into the isolation of lignin by the direct acetylation of beech-wood meal. |
| 35-002 | The nature of adsorption on cellulosic materials from heat of wetting and dielectric constant measurements. |
| 35-003 | The action of ammonia on gamma benzoyl butyric ester. |
| 35-004 | The action of hydrogen on certain oils. |
| 35-006 | The structure and properties of some unsaturated fatty acids, esters and related compounds. |
| 35-008 | Thermal decomposition of alkyl nitrites. |
| 35-010 | On the discontinuity of state at the critical temperature: sorption, density, solubility. |
| 35-011 | Catalytic activity of liquid metals. |
| 35-012 | Studies in the system calcium oxide - sulphur dioxide - water. |
| 35-014 | Studies in organic oxidation. |
| 35-016 | The influence of adsorption and the physical properties of alkaline liquors on the mechanism of cooking of wood. |
| 35-019 | The effects of foreign gases on the kinetics of the decomposition of nitrous oxide on the surface of platinum. |
| 35-020 | The kinetics of some gaseous oxidation reactions. Part I: Oxidations with nitrous oxide. Part II: The oxidation of acetylene. |

| THESIS | THESIS TITLE |
|---|---|
| **Chemistry** | |
| 35-022 | Studies in conductivity. |
| 35-023 | The action of certain Grignard reagents on benzarthrone. |
| 35-026 | The formation of vanillin from lignin sulphonic acids and its relation to the structure of lignin. |
| 35-027 | The viscosity of gases. |
| 35-029 | Reactions of gold and silver in cyanide solutions. |
| 35-031 | Insoluble methanol lignin. |
| 35-032 | Synthesis and properties of polyetylene ether glycols. |
| 35-509 | The kinetics of the oxidation of gaseous hydrogen iodide. |
| 35-513 | Tetrachlorophthalimide as a reagent in qualitative organic analysis. |
| 35-516 | A study of the antimony electrode. |
| 35-518 | Light absorption as a means of measuring particle size and consistency. |
| 35-542 | The sorption of gases by solids: the solubility of water vapour in solid inorganic compounds at high temperatures. |
| 36-004 | A study of the method of the delignification of wood in aqueous acid media. |
| 36-005 | The structure of dextran. |
| 36-006 | An investigation of the pressure, volume and temperature relations of one component systems near the critical point, system ethylene. |
| 36-007 | The action of the Grignard reagent on polynuclear ketones. |
| 36-008 | Calorimetric measurements on gels. |
| 36-010 | The discontinuity at the critical temperature; reaction velocity; dielectric constant. |
| 36-011 | The kinetics of the homogeneous decomposition of diethyl ether at high pressures and other gas reactions. |
| 36-012 | The kinetics of the thermal decomposition of alkyl nitrites. |

| THESIS | THESIS TITLE |
|---|---|
| **Chemistry** | |
| 36-013 | The structure of lignin. |
| 36-015 | Action of chlorine and its derivatives on lignin. |
| 36-016 | Indol formation and dipyrrols. |
| 36-017 | A new adiabatic calorimeter and some thermal properties of deuterium oxide. |
| 36-018 | Degradation products of lignin. |
| 36-019 | The action of basic reagents on a highly phenylated ketolactone. |
| 36-546 | Development of a method for the identification of hydroxyl groups in organic compounds. |
| 37-001 | Equilibria existing in the system calcium oxide - sulphur dioxide - water. |
| 37-002 | Fission products and properties of lignin. |
| 37-003 | Sorption and heat measurements near the critical temperature: a correction equation for the quartz spring balance. |
| 37-005 | The measurement of the dielectric constant of cellulose and that of adsorbed vapour. |
| 37-006 | The development of a method for measuring heat conductivity of colloidal systems under constant humidity conditions. Thermal conductivities of cellulosic materials. |
| 37-007 | The preparation and properties of pure hydrogen peroxide solutions. |
| 37-008 | Aryl iododihalides as halogenating agents. |
| 37-013 | The effect of configuration on unimolecular reaction rates. |
| 37-016 | Measurement of the heats of wetting of liquids and electrolytes on standard cotton and mercerized cotton in relation to theories of mercerization and adsorption. |
| 37-019 | The physical properties of Chlorine and of its aqueous solutions with a view to the elucidation of the equilibria existing in the latter. |
| 37-020 | Cyclopentenolones. |
| 37-022 | Phase boundary potentials. |

| THESIS | THESIS TITLE |
|---|---|
| Chemistry | |
| 37-023 | Bleaching studies. |
| 37-024 | The effects of surrounding media on cellulose. |
| 37-029 | Vapour density of sulphur dioxide at 0.0 degrees C. |
| 37-030 | Properties of hydrogen peroxide. |
| 37-506 | The kinetics of heterogeneous gas reactions: the decomposition of nitrous oxide on a silver catalyst. |
| 38-001 | Free radicals in organic decomposition reactions. |
| 38-002 | An investigation of olefine halogen-hydride reactions in the liquid state. |
| 38-003 | A study of the mechanism of the delignification of wood in aqueous sulphite solutions. |
| 38-006 | 2,3 - diphenylbutadiene. |
| 38-008 | The structure of lignin obtained from hard woods. |
| 38-010 | Some fission products of furans and lignin. |
| 38-011 | The structure of lignin and its relation to other plant constituents. |
| 38-012 | The mechanism of bleaching kraft pulp. |
| 38-015 | Primary processes in the reactions of gaseous hydrocarbons. |
| 38-016 | The heat content of water sorbed on cellulose. |
| 38-018 | The kinetics of organic decomposition reactions. |
| 38-019 | The kinetics of the sorption of gases by solid substances. |
| 38-022 | Nature and mechanism of the polymerization of ethyleneoxide. |
| 38-023 | The thermal decomposition of hydrocarbons. |
| 38-508 | Part I. The structure of dipyrroles and indole formation from pyrroles. Part II. Stereochemistry of linalool. |

| THESIS | THESIS TITLE |
|---|---|
| Chemistry | |
| 38-521 | The kinetics of polymerization of iso-butene. |
| 38-524 | Chrysene and derivatives. |
| 38-544 | Hydrogenation of geraniol and related compounds. |
| 38-545 | Action of phenylmagnesium bromide on anthraquinones. |
| 39-001 | Adiabatic vacuum calorimeter and the precision measurement of specific heats of liquids. |
| 39-002 | The geology of a portion of the Granby Sheet, Que. |
| 39-003 | A study of the mechanism of sulphite cooking. |
| 39-004 | Structure of lignin. |
| 39-005 | The ozonization and structure of lignin in relation to solubility in bisulphite solution. |
| 39-007 | Free radicals in the decomposition of hydrocarbons. |
| 39-008 | The synthesis of polyoxyethylene glycols and the relation of their viscosities to chain length. |
| 39-010 | An investigation of reaction velocity and solubility in the critical temperature region. |
| 39-011 | Ethanolysis of maple wood. |
| 39-012 | An investigation of the transition region of liquid to gas. |
| 39-013 | Transition phenomena in the critical region. |
| 39-017 | The heat capacity and surface tension of ethylene in the critical region. |
| 39-018 | The elementary reactions of the hydrocarbons. |
| 39-019 | The occurrence, isolation, structure and properties of red oak lignin. |
| 39-020 | Cadmium photosensitized reactions. |
| 39-021 | Structure of lignin. |
| 39-049 | The analysis of classified fractions of certain pulps. |

| THESIS | THESIS TITLE |
|---|---|
| **Chemistry** | |
| 39-050 | The recovery of sodium sulphite cooking liquor. |
| 39-500 | The equilibrium existing in the three component system, magnesium oxide -sulphur dioxide - water, over temperature range 25° to 130° C. |
| 39-502 | The colouring matter in Kraft pulp. |
| 39-503 | Heats of wetting of cellulose materials. |
| 39-517 | Reactions of tetrahydrolinalool. |
| 40-001 | The chemical and physical properties of hydrogen peroxide nitric acid solutions. |
| 40-002 | The structure of lignin. |
| 40-003 | The dielectric constants of cellulose and of water sorbed thereon. |
| 40-004 | Elementary reactions of the lower paraffins. |
| 40-006 | The mercury photosensitized reactions of ethane. |
| 40-007 | Pressure, volume, temperature, and density relations in the critical region. |
| 40-008 | The mercury photosensitized reactions of propane. |
| 40-009 | Chemical composition and biological behavior of soil organic phosphorus. |
| 40-011 | The heat capacity of ethylene and carbon dioxide in the critical temperature region. |
| 40-013 | Physical properties and chemical reactions of hydrogen peroxide, nitric acid mixtures. |
| 40-015 | Some properties of long-chain molecules and their solutions. |
| 40-018 | An investigation of the state of aggregation of a one component system in the critical temperature - critical pressure region. |
| 40-020 | The decomposition of quaternary ammonium bases and of xanthate esters. |
| 40-022 | Thermal reactions of the lower hydrocarbons. |
| 40-024 | The influence of environment on the apparent specific volume of cellulose. |

| THESIS | THESIS TITLE |
|---|---|
| **Chemistry** | |
| 40-025 | The effect of surrounding media on the apparent volume of cellulose. |
| 40-502 | The mechanism of intramolecular rearrangements. |
| 40-503 | The Grignard reagent and ethylene oxides. |
| 40-504 | Dimeric ketenes and cyclobutanediones. |
| 40-506 | An investigation of the "leak effect' in measuring dielectric constants. |
| 40-521 | A study of some methods of separation and determination of molybdenum. |
| 40-522 | Kinetics of some gas reactions. |
| 40-525 | The action of ring opening reagents on cyclopropane dicarboxylic acid-1,2. |
| 41-001 | I. Cyclization of 1,5-hexadienes. II. Inactivity of bromine in Bromacetal. |
| 41-002 | High pressure hydrogenation studies of lignin and related materials. |
| 41-003 | Heat of reaction of gaseous sulphur dioxide on moist wood. |
| 41-004 | The synthesis and properties of glycosides related to lignin plant constituents. |
| 41-008 | The hydrogenation of lignin and wood. |
| 41-009 | Zinc photosensitized reactions of ethylene. |
| 41-010 | A comparison of the lignins of plant materials by ethanolysis. |
| 41-011 | X-ray diffraction analysis applied to certain war problems. |
| 41-012 | (1) Water in silica gels. (2) Sodium silicate in water. |
| 41-015 | (1) (a) The preparation and properties of cyanogen fluoride. (b) Measurements of the service time of respirator charcoals for poison gases. (2) The investigation of the physical properties of a two component system in the critical temperature - critical pressure region. |
| 41-017 | (1) The preparation and solubility of phosphorous trifluoride. (2) The preparation of arsine and calcium arsenide. (3) The adsorption of gases by respiratory charcoals. |
| 41-048 | The nitration of paraffin hydrocarbons. |

| THESIS | THESIS TITLE |
|---|---|
| **Chemistry** | |
| 41-501 | The effect of temperature on the scrption of water vapor by cellulosic materials. |
| 41-503 | The chemical structure and antigenicity of Dextran II. |
| 41-506 | Studies on vitamin A and carotene. |
| 41-509 | (1) The ozonization of unsaturated acids. (2) A course in mavstrial crganic analysis. (3) The characterization of mink oil. |
| 41-529 | The reaction of hydrogen atcms with iso-butane. |
| 41-532 | (1) The hydrolysis cf propicnitrile by strong acids. (2) Some reacticns of SF6. |
| 42-001 | The reduction of alpha-bromoisobutyrophenone with aluminium isopropoxide; the nitrartion of p-cymeme. |
| 42-002 | The mechanism of the sorption of gases by charcoal and other research in chemical warfare. |
| 42-004 | 1. Aromatization of petroleum hydrocarbons. 2. Synthesis of cyclopentenedicns. |
| 42-005 | Study of the action of ammonia on phosphorous trifluoride. |
| 42-007 | Sorption of gases by charccal and researches in chemical and explcsive warfare. |
| 42-008 | 1. The proknock activity of vericus compounds. 2. The dynamic scrpticn of ammonia and butane on charcoal. 3. The reaction of hydrogen atoms with prcpylene. |
| 42-009 | 1. The catalytic conversion of p-cymene into toluene. 2. Polyvinyl nitrates. |
| 42-011 | The preparation of RXD by the McGill process. |
| 42-012 | 1. Effect of prcknock substances on butane oxidation. 2. A study of the cyclonite reaction - McGill process. |
| 42-013 | Mechanism of wood ethanolysis and the structure cf lignin. |
| 42-014 | The mesotron component in cosmic rays. |
| 42-015 | The chemical structure of dextran I. |
| 42-016 | Anode potentials cf lead and lead alloys. |

| THESIS | THESIS TITLE |
|---|---|
| Chemistry | |
| 42-017 | 1. The preparation of disulphur decafluoride. 2. The density and viscosity of disulphur decafluoride. 3. The preparation and hydrolysis of aluminium and zinc arsenides. |
| 42-018 | The action of sodium upon highly branched chain ketones. |
| 42-019 | Studies on the compounds of sulphur and fluorine, and the preparation of S2F10, and work on problems in chemical warfare. |
| 42-020 | Studies on the metabolism of normal and tumor tissue of beet-roots. |
| 42-021 | 1. A study of pro-knock activity. 2. The dynamic sorption of ammonia and butane on charcoal. |
| 42-022 | 1. Studies in chemical kinetics. 2. The detection of vesicants. |
| 42-024 | Specific surface measurement of particulate and fibrous materials, and problems of chemical warfare. |
| 42-025 | The thermal decomposition of vinyl ethyl ether. |
| 42-026 | 1. Bentonite as a vapour phase catalyst. 2. The conversion of p-cymene into toluene with ammonium chloride. 3. Synthesis of proknocks. |
| 42-027 | Studies on lignin building units. |
| 42-056 | Problems connected with war research: preparation of calcium arsenate and of arsine and the determination of flourine in urine. |
| 42-500 | (a) The mercury photosensitized decomposition of n-butane. (b) The kinetics of the factors influencing the stability of S. |
| 42-501 | Structure of lignin: isolation of new ethanolysis products from maple wood. |
| 42-502 | A study of the mechanism of the sorption of phosgene by charcoal and other research in chemical warfare. |
| 42-505 | The ultraviolet absorption spectra of lignins and related compounds. |
| 42-507 | The ethanolysis of spruce wood and the structure of lignin. |
| 42-530 | A study of guanyl-nitrourea. |
| 43-001 | Starch nitrates: preparation, properties, and structure. |

| THESIS | THESIS TITLE |
|---|---|
| **Chemistry** | |
| 43-003 | High pressure hydrogenation of wood and related carbohydrates. |
| 43-004 | The oxidation of lignin and related compounds. |
| 43-005 | Studies on lignin progenitors. |
| 43-006 | A.) Viscosity instability in high polymeric systems. B.) Molecular weights from osmotic pressure measurements. C.) The behaviour of various pro-knock compounds. |
| 43-009 | Oxidation of lignins: structural significance. |
| 43-010 | Lignin: structure, extraction, and intratability. |
| 43-011 | The viscosity instability of solutions of high polymers. |
| 43-012 | 1. Reactions of tetrahydrolinalcol. 2. The conversion of N.N. diethyniline to N. ethylaniline. 3. The preparation of picric acid by the oxynitration of benzene. 4. The preparation of RDX. |
| 43-013 | War research problems. A.) The chemistry of methyl-bis B-chlorethylamine and related compounds. B.) Various aspects of pro-knock activity. |
| 43-014 | Part I. The reaction of hydrogen atoms with isobutane and butadiene. Part II. The effect of temperature treatment and moisture content on the quality of dried whole egg powder. |
| 43-015 | A.) Nickel impregnated respirator charcoals. B.) An x-ray investigation of H.M.X. crystals. C.) The kinetics of the reactions to produce R.D.X. |
| 43-016 | Studies on aerosol filtration. |
| 43-017 | Lignin polymers and building units. |
| 43-018 | High pressure hydrogenation of maple wood. |
| 43-019 | The mercury photosensitized reactions of 2-methylpropane (iso-butane). |
| 43-020 | Studies on lignin progenitors. |
| 43-023 | High pressure hydrogenation of maple wood. |
| 43-024 | Wood tissue lignification, plant metabolism and phenol formation. |
| 43-508 | The preparation of 2, 4, 6-trinitrotolyl-3-methyl nitramine from the waste liquor obtained in the purification of T.N.T. |

| THESIS | THESIS TITLE |
|---|---|
| **Chemistry** | |
| 43-518 | The action of hydrogen with amino acids. |
| 43-519 | The synthesis of unsymmetrically disubstituted ethanes. |
| 44-001 | The vapour-phase dehydration of butaniols. |
| 44-003 | Influence of structural factors on the adsorption of gases by charcoal. |
| 44-004 | War research; the sorption of cyanogenchloride on charcoals. |
| 44-005 | An investigation of the chemistry of some polymethylene nitramines. |
| 44-006 | Studies on lignin progenitors. |
| 44-007 | The apparent density and internal structure of activated charcoal. |
| 44-008 | The viscosity stability of high polymers. |
| 44-012 | Studies on lignin progenitors. |
| 44-013 | Characterization of polyvinylacetate by molecular weight determination. |
| 44-015 | The preparation of disulphur decafluoride. |
| 44-017 | The relation between RDX and HMX production in the Bachmann reaction. |
| 44-018 | A.) Thermal decomposition of rossite and picrite in aqueous media. B.) Rate of transition of H.M.X. polymorphs. C.) Thermochemistry of the R.D.X. reactions. |
| 44-019 | A.) The chemistry of methyl bischloroethylamine and related compounds. B.) The deacidifation of RDX-B. |
| 44-020 | The preparation of disulphur decafluoride. |
| 44-022 | The preparation of disulphur decafluoride. |
| 44-522 | The synthesis of 1, 1-diphenylethane from benzene and acetaldehyde. |
| 44-523 | War research. Kinetic studies on the conversion of D.T.P. and P.H.X. to H.M.X. |
| 45-002 | Pilot plant studies on the preparation of RXD-B by the Bachmann reaction. |

| THESIS | THESIS TITLE |
|---|---|
| Chemistry | |
| 45-003 | The recovery of glacial acetic acid from the residual liquors of the Bachmann process. The development of a continuous reactor with which to investigate the Bachmann reaction; a) the U tube reactor, b) the rotating tube reactor. |
| 45-005 | A.) The preparation of 1, 1-Di(4-chlorophenyl) -2, 2, 2-trichloroethane (DDT). B.) The role of hexamine dinitrate in the formation of RDX in the McGill or Ross reaction. |
| 45-006 | Investigation of polarization and effects of addition agents during the electrodeposition of copper. |
| 45-007 | Kinetic studies of the nitrolysis of hexamine in acetic acid and in chloroform and the detonation velocity of axially cavitated cylinders of cast dina. |
| 45-008 | Pilot plant and laboratory studies of the Bachmann reaction for the production of cyclotrimethylenetrinitramine (RDX). |
| 45-009 | The pyrolysis of 1, 1-diphenylethane over bentonite, tertiary mercaptans as modifiers in butadiene-styrene co-polymerization. |
| 45-011 | War research: A.) Thermal decomposition of rossite and picrite in aqueous media. B.) Velocity of detonation of tubular dina. |
| 45-013 | War research: The mechanism of the direct nitrolysis of hexamine. |
| 45-016 | A nitroguanidine-formalehyde explosive polymer of resin type. |
| 45-018 | The thermal detonation of lead azide. |
| 45-020 | The mechanism of RDX fromation in the Bachmann reaction. |
| 45-534 | The reaction of trichloromethylparachlorophenylcarbinol to 1, 1-Di(p-chlorphenyl)-2, 2, -trichloraethane (DDT). |
| 45-540 | The nitration of polyamides. |
| 45-541 | The vapor phase dehydration of ketones and glycols. |
| 46-001 | (a) The action of sulfuric acid on D.D.T. and some related compounds. (b) The synthesis and derivatives of 1-4 chlorophenyl 2,2,2-trichloroethanol. |
| 46-003 | Kinetic studies on the formation of hexamine. |
| 46-005 | The mechanism of popcorn polymer formation. |

| THESIS | THESIS TITLE |
|---|---|
| **Chemistry** | |
| 46-006 | The kinetics of 1,1,1-trichloro-2,2-bis(4-chloro -phenyl)ethane formation. |
| 46-008 | Possible mechanisms for the thermal decomposition of nitrocellulose. |
| 46-011 | The production and study of compounds of sulphur and fluorine for use in chemical warfare, with special reference to disulfur decafluorine, and the physical properties of disulfur decafluorine. |
| 46-012 | Studies on the conversion of PHX to AcAn. |
| 46-013 | The chemistry, the identification, and the quantitative estimation of nitrodicyandiamidine. |
| 46-017 | The resolution of 1-(4-chlorophenyl) -2,2,2-trichloroethanol. Some chemical and insecticidal studies on the separated alcohols. |
| 46-018 | Specific surface of fibrous materials and problems of explosives production. |
| 46-019 | A critical study of osmometers used for macromolecules and the changes of polyvinyl acetate in oxygen. |
| 46-020 | Effects of the accessible fraction of cellulose on some properties of its nitrates. |
| 46-022 | The isometric cis-trans trinitrates of pyrogallitol. |
| 46-023 | Preparations and properties of methyl allyl cellulose. |
| 46-024 | Factors influencing the nitration on polyvinyl alcohol. |
| 46-025 | Studies on the accessible fraction of cellulose. |
| 46-026 | Studies on butadiene polymerization. |
| 46-027 | Studies on the combining ratios of monomers in copolymerization. |
| 46-028 | Hindrance effects in cellulose substitution reactions. |
| 46-029 | Some studies on tertiary hexadecylmercaptan as a modifier in butadiene-styrene copolymerizations. |
| 46-030 | Synthesis of a substituted centralite. |
| 46-031 | Studies on the formation of hexamine from formaldehyde and ammonium salts in aqueous solution. |
| 46-032 | The selective denitration of cellulose nitrates. |

| THESIS | THESIS TITLE |
|---|---|
| **Chemistry** | |
| 46-033 | Molecular weight measurements of macromolecules with an improved osmometer. |
| 46-505 | Studies with the Haring cell. |
| 46-512 | Kinetics of the sulphonation of chlorobenzene. |
| 46-560 | Canadian tall oils and their fatty acids. |
| 46-576 | The reaction of tertiary hexadecyl mercaptan with a butadiene-styrene copolymer. |
| 47-002 | The effect of alternating electrical fields on the polymerization of styrene. |
| 47-003 | Synthesis of carbonyl derivatives of polyhydroxy cyclohexanes. |
| 47-005 | The effects of alternating electrical fields on the polymerization of styrene. |
| 47-006 | Cis-trans isomerism of the polyhydroxy cyclohexane series. |
| 47-007 | The dielectric constant of disulfur decafluoride and high pressure instrumentation at high temperatures. |
| 47-008 | The dielectric constant of adsorbed ethyl chloride. |
| 47-013 | 1. The recovery of glacial acetic acid from the residual liquors of the Bachmann process. 2. The rate of disappearance of hexamine in Bachmann type mixtures and the discovery of DPT. 3. The kinetics of BSX formation. |
| 47-018 | The preparation and properties of periodate lignins. |
| 47-019 | The kinetics of the thermal decomposition of disulfur decafluoride. |
| 47-020 | The density of adsorbed layers. |
| 47-025 | Part I. The ammonia-soda process applied to sodium sulphate. Part II. The thermal decomposition of benzoyl peroxide in solvents. Part III. The homogeneous thermal decomposition of acetaldehyde. |
| 47-027 | Chemical studies in the polyhydric phenol series. |
| 47-029 | The action of sodium chlorite and chlorine dioxide on phenolic substances related to lignin. |
| 47-030 | Kinetic studies on the formation and decomposition of hexamethylenetetramine. |

| THESIS | THESIS TITLE |
|---|---|
| **Chemistry** | |
| 47-034 | Cellophane as membrane material. |
| 47-036 | Reduction of trimethyl gallic acid by sodium and isoamyl alcohol. |
| 47-037 | p-Toluenesulfonyl and iodo derivatives of some hydroxyethyl ethers. |
| 47-038 | The action of alkaline hypohalites on phenolic substances. |
| 47-039 | Extraction of woods with sodium bicorbonate-carbon dioxide or with liquid ammonia under pressure. |
| 47-507 | A study of mechanical factors in GR-S bottle polymerization. |
| 47-545 | The characterization of a new hydroxy acid isolated from Spanish ergot. |
| 48-002 | The formation and properties of three-dimensional polymers. |
| 48-012 | The flow of gases and vapours through adsorbing porous media. |
| 48-016 | Attempted syntheses of a branch-chain cellulose and the unreliability of the periodate method of estimating branching. |
| 48-023 | Synthesis and polymerization of some substituted butadienes. |
| 48-025 | (a) The reaction between nitrogen atoms and ethylene. (b) The application of diffusion flame techniques to the reaction between nitrogen atoms and ethylene. |
| 48-026 | Tree formation in the electrowinning of cadmium and a brief kinetic study of the decomposition of R.D.X. in the system R.D.X.-Al-H2O. |
| 48-028 | The reactions of N-dodecyl mercaptan and potassium persulfate in emulsion systems. |
| 48-029 | The electrolytic reduction of ammonium nitrate. |
| 48-032 | The degradation of polymers. |
| 48-036 | The effect of high frequency electrical fields on the decomposition of benzoyl peroxide. |
| 48-043 | The kinetics of the copolymerization of butadiene and styrene in homogeneous solutions. |
| 48-527 | The behavior of tertiary hexadecyl thiol in polymer-emulsion systems. |
| 48-582 | Electrolytic synthesis of long-chain esters of dicarboxylic acids. |

| THESIS | THESIS TITLE |
|---|---|
| **Chemistry** | |
| 48-592 | The analysis of the Typha latifolis Linn. seed hairs. |
| 49-001 | Diffusion studies of high polymer solutions. |
| 49-005 | Part I. The kinetics of coagulation of GR-S. latex. Part II. The kinetics of the cis-trans isomerisation of azobenzene. |
| 49-007 | Equilibrium between copper, zinc, and chlorine at high temperature. |
| 49-010 | The oxidation of mercaptan by potassium persulfate in homogeneous solution. |
| 49-011 | Dielectric properties of non-Newtonian liquids. |
| 49-013 | Zeta potentials of cellulose fibres. |
| 49-015 | Kinetic studies in the solid phase and in solution. Part I. The thermal decomposition of popcorn polymer. Part II. The cis-trans isomerization of azobenzene in solution. |
| 49-016 | The investigation of the ether extract of white spruce bark. |
| 49-018 | The exchange of radioiodine between inorganic and organic iodides. |
| 49-019 | Flocculation of cellulose fibre suspensions. |
| 49-021 | A kinetic study of the oxidation of carotenoid pigments during processing of macaroni. |
| 49-025 | Exchange reactions of sodium iodide with aromatic iodides. |
| 49-026 | Oxidation of polyhydroxyphenols with chlorine dioxide. |
| 49-027 | Effect of addition agents in electrodeposition of copper. |
| 49-032 | Oxidation of cellulose with chromium trioxide. |
| 49-034 | Specific surface and flocculation studies of pulp fibre suspension. |
| 49-035 | Overvoltage studies on cadmium cathodes. |
| 49-039 | Alkylations and isomerizations catalysed by an aluminum hydrosilicate. |
| 49-040 | The emulsion polymerisation of alkybutenes. |

| THESIS | THESIS TITLE |
|---|---|
| **Chemistry** | |
| 49-041 | A study of certain nitrogen derivatives of methionic acid. |
| 49-044 | The chemical investigation of the aqueous extract of white spruce bark. |
| 49-050 | Action of hydroxylamine in pyridine on methyl glucose tetranitrate. |
| 49-051 | Characteristics of various cellulose affecting nitration. |
| 49-052 | The electrolytic oxidation of glycol, glucose and lignosulphonic acids. |
| 49-053 | The action of liquid ammonia on maple wood. |
| 49-054 | Properties of the higher benzenepolycarboxylic acids and their isolation. |
| 49-058 | The thermal conductivity of gases at high pressure. |
| 49-624 | The diffusion of lead into mercury. |
| 50-001 | Permeability of cellophane to liquids and vapours. |
| 50-003 | Preparation and properties of cellulose crotonoate and acetate-crotonoates. |
| 50-004 | Rheological properties of non-Newtonian solutions. |
| 50-014 | The density of water sorbed by charcoal and low pressure adsorption studies. |
| 50-015 | The mercury photosensitized decomposition of nitric acid. |
| 50-022 | Exchange reactions between alicylic iodides and sodium iodide. |
| 50-026 | The reaction of nitrogen atoms with methane and ethane. |
| 50-028 | 3-Hydroxyethyl glucose. |
| 50-029 | The y-ray induced oxidation of $Fr^{+2}$ ion in dilute aqueous solution. |
| 50-032 | Reactions in dissociated water vapour. |
| 50-034 | Studies of ionic polymerization. |
| 50-035 | Syntheses of vinyl aromatic compounds by pyrolyses over catalysts. |

| THESIS | THESIS TITLE |
|---|---|
| **Chemistry** | |
| 50-036 | Studies on the alcoholysis products of sucrose. |
| 50-037 | Methyl radical recombination and reactions with metals. |
| 50-042 | The decomposition of benzoyl peroxide. |
| 50-048 | Studies of branched and linear polymers. |
| 50-524 | An investigation of disilyl alkanes. |
| 50-531 | An infra-red spectrophotometric investigations of the drying of oils. |
| 50-639 | Oxidations of periodate lignin with alkaline hypoiodite and hypochlorite. |
| 51-003 | Kinetic studies of a redox polymerization. |
| 51-007 | The effect of potassium bromate on physical properties and structure of flour doughs. |
| 51-014 | Solvent effect on iodide exchange. |
| 51-018 | Oxidations of periodate lignin with sodium chlorite and chlorine dioxide. |
| 51-019 | The synthesis and derivatives of dibenz(1,3)(a,c)cycloheptа-5,7-dione. |
| 51-020 | Solvent effects in cis-trans isomerization. |
| 51-022 | Gelatin-halide interaction in copper electrodeposition. |
| 51-024 | The reaction of 2-bromo-2-nitro-1,3-indandione with pyridine. |
| 51-028 | Triphenylmethyl radical formation on silver. |
| 51-029 | Study of the effect of ammonium nitrate on the kinetics of the Bachman reaction to produce RDX. The construction and operation of a pilot plant to study the Bachman reaction. |
| 51-030 | Light scattering in the critical region. |
| 51-032 | Transport of lead into cathode zinc. |
| 51-034 | The motions of particles in model suspensions subjected to a shear. |
| 51-035 | Studies in electrochemistry. |

| THESIS | THESIS TITLE |
|---|---|

**Chemistry**

| | |
|---|---|
| 51-039 | Attempts to label cholesterol in ring B: seco-6-1-cholestan-7-one and seco-6-3(beta)-bromocholestan-7-one: ring A $C^{14}$-labelled cholesterol. |
| 51-042 | Experiments on the pulping of periodate lignin by the sulfite process. |
| 51-045 | Studies of the effect of fibre flocculation on the heterogeneity of paper. |
| 51-049 | Further separations of the water-soluble components of white spruce bark. |
| 51-057 | The neutral constituents of a Canadian tall oil. |
| 52-001 | Silver-silver ion exchange reactions. |
| 52-002 | Reactions in dissociated hydrogen peroxide vapour. |
| 52-006 | The reaction of nitrogen atoms with propane. |
| 52-008 | Swelling studies of some natural and synthetic fibers. |
| 52-014 | Studies on the synthesis of papaverine. |
| 52-016 | Diffusion of radioactive iodoprene in gels. |
| 52-028 | The action of hydroxylamine hydrochloride in pyridine on methyl-beta-D-glucoside tetranitrate. |
| 52-032 | The reaction of nitrogen atoms with propylene. |
| 52-034 | The oxidation of hydrazobenzene by ammonium persulphate in homogeneous solution. |
| 52-035 | The electrode behaviour of mercury, platinum, and copper. |
| 52-037 | Physico-chemical effects of radio frequency fields. |
| 52-038 | Electrokinetic measurements on fibrous materials. |
| 52-040 | The oxidation of periodate lignin with sodium hypochlorite at pH 12. |
| 52-045 | The reactions of nitrogen atoms with butenes. |
| 52-052 | Part I. Diffusion studies of polyisobutylene. Part II. Kinetic studies of hydroxyl free radical. Part III. The reactions of nitrogen atoms with cis-butene-2 and isobutene. |

| THESIS | THESIS TITLE |
|---|---|
| Chemistry | |
| 52-053 | The oxidation of wheat starch with hypochlorous acid. |
| 52-055 | Oxidation and methylation of the accessible fraction of cellulose. |
| 52-059 | Sterols and terpenes from spruce wood bark. |
| 52-062 | The reaction of nitrogen atoms with ethylene and acetylene. |
| 52-063 | Nitration of 2-aminopyridines and 2-aminothiazoles. |
| 52-521 | Studies on diethyl quinolate. |
| 52-583 | The reaction of 2,3-dibromoindone with pryidine. |
| 52-585 | A study of the Hantzsch pyridine synthesis. |
| 53-003 | Reactions and isomerism of beta-aminocrotononitrile and the reaction of aromatic Grignard reagents with beta-aminocrotononitrile. |
| 53-013 | The effect of chloride on the deposition of copper, in the presence of arsenic, antimony and bismuth. |
| 53-014 | Action of liquid ammonia on white spruce bark, extracted with methanol and water. |
| 53-017 | Flow of liquids through cellophane. |
| 53-023 | Rotations, collisons and orientations in model suspensions. |
| 53-024 | Synthesis of 4-(dialkylamino)-pyridines. |
| 53-025 | The action of liquid ammonia on spruce chlorite holocellulose. |
| 53-026 | The alleged condensation of cellulose nitrate with sodium acetylide. |
| 53-027 | The physical nature of the critical opalescence. |
| 53-030 | Oscillographic studies on the effects of addition agents during copper deposition. |
| 53-033 | The oxidation of cellulose with chromic acid. |
| 53-036 | Dielectric relaxation in cellulose containing sorbed vapours. |

| THESIS | THESIS TITLE |
|---|---|
| **Chemistry** | |
| 53-038 | Xanthate methyl esters of simple alcohols and of cellulose. |
| 53-040 | Shapes of coexistence curves in the critical region. |
| 53-043 | The reactions of nitrogen atoms with the butanes. |
| 53-046 | A study of periodate lignin lignosulfonic acids. |
| 53-047 | Hydroxyethyl derivatives of glucose and of cellulose. |
| 53-066 | The hemicelluloses of aspen wood (Populus tremuloides). |
| 53-073 | The substances extracted by water from white spruce bark, pretreated with liquid ammonia. |
| 53-074 | Xanthate methyl esters of glucose and of cellulose. |
| 53-077 | The electrical conductance of tetraethylammonium bromide and chloride in nitromethane. |
| 53-079 | Purification and properties of methyl and benzyl-D-fructofuranosides and their tetraacetates. |
| 53-536 | The reaction of nitrogen atoms with cyclopropane. |
| 53-594 | The syntheses of dimethylaminoalkyl esters of indole-carboxylic acids. |
| 54-001 | Amino acids as addition agents in the deposition of copper. |
| 54-003 | A new glucoside from the crude phlobaphene fraction of white spruce bark. |
| 54-010 | The reactions of active nitrogen with ethyl, vinyl, propyl and isopropyl chlorides. |
| 54-013 | The structure of butadiene dimers produced by a free-radical chain-transfer mechanism. |
| 54-018 | Double refraction of flow in high polymer solutions. |
| 54-019 | The effect of freeze-drying on the physical properties of cellulose fibres and paper. The capillary flow of liquids with entrapped air bubbles. |
| 54-023 | Crystallization of high polymers. |
| 54-039 | Some new reactions and derivatives of Kojic acid. |
| 54-042 | The synthesis of peptide bonds. |

| THESIS | THESIS TITLE |
|---|---|
| **Chemistry** | |
| 54-049 | New syntheses of papaveraldine, iscquinoline and related open-chain compounds. |
| 54-060 | The reaction of active nitrogen with propane, cyclopropane, cyclobutane and neopentane. |
| 54-064 | Oxidation of spruce periodate lignin with alkaline hypochlorite. |
| 54-071 | Further oxidations of spruce periodate lignin with chlorine dioxide. |
| 54-073 | The alkali-soluble hemicelluloses of black sprucewood. |
| 54-595 | The decay of active nitrogen. |
| 55-003 | The production of active nitrogen from nitric oxide and ammonia and the reactions of active nitrogen with azomethane and mercury diethyl. |
| 55-007 | The study of the Mannich condensation of compounds containing the acidic-NH-group. |
| 55-008 | A study of the alkaline extract of white spruce bark pretreated with liquid ammonia. |
| 55-009 | The electrical conductance of some quaternary ammonium halides in solution. |
| 55-013 | Oxidation of mono-methylpyridines and 2-amino-methylpyridines with selenium dioxide. |
| 55-017 | Cathode polarization on copper single crystals. |
| 55-018 | Reaction of active nitrogen with methyl chloride. |
| 55-019 | Reactions of active nitrogen with ammonia, hydrazine and methylamine. |
| 55-021 | Physico-chemical properties of lignin sulfonates. |
| 55-023 | A mass spectral investigation of nitrogen afterglow. |
| 55-024 | Investigation of nitraminopyridines and nitraminothiazoles. |
| 55-026 | The influence of the fiber structure on the nitration of cellulose. |
| 55-027 | Surface conductance measurements on pads of fibrous materials. |
| 55-029 | Disintegration rate determination by 4pi-counting. |
| 55-031 | A study of the iodine exchange between iodide ions in solution and unimolecular films of alpha-iodostearic acid at the air-water interface. |

| THESIS | THESIS TITLE |
|---|---|
| **Chemistry** | |
| 55-040 | Thiol and amino addition agents in the electrodeposition of copper. |
| 55-044 | I. Investigation of the "vapour snake" phenomenon. II. A comparison of the production of active nitrogen by the electrodeless and condensed discharges and its reactions with oxygen containing compounds. |
| 55-055 | Reactions of methyl cyanide with hydrogen atoms and with active nitrogen. |
| 55-056 | The reactions of active nitrogen with ethane and methane in the presence of hydrogen atoms. |
| 55-073 | The composition of the oils from some Canadian conifers. |
| 55-074 | A study of carboxymethylcellulose and the corresponding glucose derivatives. |
| 55-076 | Isolation and properties of native balsam fir cellulose. |
| 55-079 | The production of atomic deuterium and its reaction with ethylene. |
| 55-514 | Effect of hydrogen cyanide on the reaction of active nitrogen with methyl chloride. |
| 55-515 | The fission yield of $Mo^{99}$ in the thermal fission of $U^{235}$. |
| 55-532 | The ultracentrifugal determination of partial specific volumes. |
| 55-601 | The oxidation of sucrose with hypochlorous acid. |
| 56-003 | The effect of degree of substitution on the fractional precipitation of cellulose nitrates. |
| 56-005 | Sorption of vapours and gases on flour, starch and gluten. |
| 56-010 | The location of substituent groups in partially nitrated and in partially xanthated celluloses. |
| 56-012 | A study of pyridinium betaines. |
| 56-018 | Reactions of atomic hydrogen with ethylenimine, N-methyl ethylenimine and ethylamine. |
| 56-031 | Double neutron capture studies. |
| 56-032 | Studies on the preparation and reactions of diacylamides and cyclic imides. |
| 56-033 | The sorption of alkali by Purves lignin. |

| THESIS | THESIS TITLE |
|---|---|
| **Chemistry** | |
| 56-034 | The oxidation of spruce periodate lignosulfonic acids with chlorine dioxide. |
| 56-036 | Heats of sorption and adsorption process by isothermal calorimetry. |
| 56-045 | A general direct-current method for the measurement of electrolytic conductance, and its application to nitromethane solutions of quaternary ammonium halides. |
| 56-047 | A study of the reactivity of methylthiazoles. |
| 56-051 | Dielectric relaxation of cellulose nitrate and cellulose. |
| 56-060 | Chemical reactivity in monolayers. |
| 56-531 | The condensation of beta-aminocrotononitrile with cyclohexanones. |
| 56-574 | Nitramines of the pyridinecarboxylic acids series. |
| 57-001 | Rigid and deformable particles in sheared suspensions. |
| 57-016 | Mass spectrometry of normal oxygen and oxygen subjected to electrical discharge. |
| 57-017 | Partial separation of phlobaphenes of white spruce bark by chromatographic methods. |
| 57-018 | Spallation products formed by the bombardment of cobalt with protons of energies up to 100 Mev. |
| 57-023 | A study of the rate of self-diffusion of nickel and of the rate of diffusion of nickel into iron, cobalt and two iron-nickel alloys. |
| 57-038 | The location of the xanthate groups in partly substituted cellulose xanthates. |
| 57-040 | Constituents of the oleoresin of the American male-fern (Dryopyeris filix-______mas.). |
| 57-042 | A study of some nitrogen-containing steroids. |
| 57-046 | The reactions of active nitrogen with phosphine and hydrogen chloride. |
| 57-048 | The reactions of hydrogen atoms with amines. |
| 57-056 | Molecular size and configuration of cellulose trinitrate in solution. |
| 57-058 | The reaction of active nitrogen with cyclopentane. |

| THESIS | THESIS TITLE |
|---|---|
| Chemistry | |
| 57-069 | The viscosity of dilute emulsions and suspensions. |
| 57-078 | The reactions of active nitrogen with chloromethanes. |
| 57-081 | Synthesis and reactions of the piperidine spiranes. |
| 57-089 | Action of reducing agents on a limit hypochlorite oxylignin. |
| 57-526 | A novel reaction of primary amines with trichloroacetonitrile. |
| 57-527 | Ozone formation due to electrical discharges at low pressures. |
| 57-539 | The action of alkaline hypochlorite on simple phenolic substances. |
| 57-584 | The effect of water removal on the crystallinity of cellulose. |
| 57-589 | The kinetics of iodination of some amino acids and phenols. |
| 58-004 | A study of thé hemicellulose of milkweed floss (Asclepias syriaca, L.). |
| 58-015 | A study of the fibrous portion of white spruce bark. |
| 58-017 | A study of the hemicellulose of white birch (Betula papyrifera, Marsh.). |
| 58-018 | The reaction of potassium persulphate with thioglycolic acid in aqueous solution. |
| 58-023 | Deactivation processes in active nitrogen. |
| 58-025 | Sorptive properties and pore structure of lignin and cellulose. |
| 58-028 | The partial specific volumes of macromolecules. |
| 58-041 | Absolute thermal-neutron fission yields of uranium 233. |
| 58-042 | The reactions of active nitrogen with acetylene, methylacetylene, and dimethylacetylene. |
| 58-051 | Precision conductance measurements of quaternary ammonium halides in nitromethane. |
| 58-053 | The reactions of active nitrogen with nitric oxide and nitrogen dioxide. |
| 59-001 | The location of xanthate groups in starch xanthates. |

| THESIS | THESIS TITLE |
|---|---|
| **Chemistry** | |
| 59-010 | Coalescence phencmena at liquid interfaces. |
| 59-015 | The hemicellulcse of kapok (Ceiba pentandra). |
| 59-020 | The oxidation of starch with alkaline hypochlorite. |
| 59-021 | The condensaticn of lignin with formaldehyde. |
| 59-022 | An investigation cf a spectrophotometric method for the study of crystallizaticn in high polymers. |
| 59-024 | Thread-like particles in sheared suspensions. |
| 59-026 | The reactions of hydrogen atoms with amines and imines. |
| 59-027 | Part I: A study cf the alpha-cellulcse of white birch (Betula papyrifera). Part II: A study of the hemicellulose of white elm (Ulmus americana). |
| 59-031 | The preparation and properties of derivatives of germane. |
| 59-032 | Synthesis and structure cf amidines. |
| 59-033 | Physicochemical studies of alkali lignin. |
| 59-034 | Investigation of the nitraminothiazolecarboxylic acids. |
| 59-040 | The synthesis of nitrogen derivatives cf steroids. |
| 59-043 | Tritium exchange between cellulose and water. |
| 59-059 | The use of an iscthermal calorimetric detector fcr the study of electrically discharged O2 and the reaction of O-atcms with NO. |
| 59-065 | Studies of some physical and chemical properties of unimolecular films. |
| 59-067 | The degradation cf lignosulphonates with sodium in liquid ammonia. |
| 59-077 | Oxidation of pectin and related compounds by bleaching agents. |
| 59-079 | Reactions of active nitrogen with cyanogen and CN radicals. |
| 59-084 | The reactions of active nitrogen with hydrogen sulphide and carbcn disulphide. |

| THESIS | THESIS TITLE |
|---|---|
| **Chemistry** | |
| 59-529 | Oxidation of xanthate methyl esters of glucose derivatives. |
| **Chinese Studies** | |
| 33-560 | An investigation of Chinese schools in Canada. |
| **Civil Engineering & Applied Mechanics** | |
| 16-507 | Concrete columns plain and reinforced. |
| 20-505 | Some considerations on the strength of built-up compression members. |
| 22-505 | A study of the resistances developed in rivetted joints by friction and by rivet bearing. |
| 22-514 | The distribution of stress in a rivetted plate joint of variable section. |
| 25-549 | Continuity in steel I-beams haunched with concrete. |
| 26-504 | An investigation of the secondary stresses in a roof truss having unsymmetrical members. |
| 27-512 | The effect of the manner of support and of certain details of construction on the secondary stresses in a roof truss. |
| 31-555 | The initial stresses in welded joints. |
| 32-500 | Some investigations in reinforced concrete: experimental research on concrete columns with transverse and longitudinal reinforcement. |
| 32-502 | Kane system of composite construction. |
| 32-553 | Theory and application of photo-elasticity. |
| 33-501 | An investigation of the effects produced by electric arc welding on a steel compression member, with an analysis of the distribution of welding stresses in steel plates. |
| 34-502 | An investigation of stress in welded joints. |
| 34-505 | Experiments on cavitation. |
| 34-540 | Temperatures and thermal stresses in welded plates. |
| 36-500 | Preheating effects on residual stresses in arc-welded steel plates. |

| THESIS | THESIS TITLE |
|---|---|
| Civil Engineering & Applied Mechanics | |
| 36-502 | Tension tests for residual stresses in arc-welded steel plates. |
| 36-504 | Physical properties of clay and clay-salt mixtures. |
| 36-505 | An investigation of timber tension splices. |
| 36-545 | The development of bond between a steel beam and a superposed concrete slab. |
| 38-501 | Residual stresses in butt-welded steel plates. |
| 39-051 | The effects of certain factors on the properties of Portland cement concrete. |
| 40-036 | Particle interference in Portland cement concrete. |
| 45-500 | Experiments on water hammer using a Piezo-electric pressure indicator. |
| 46-502 | Triaxial residual stresses in arc-welded steel plates. |
| 46-552 | The structural value of light alloy sections in the plastic range. |
| 48-505 | Stresses in a plain plate flat slab reinforced concrete. |
| 49-587 | Diagonal tension reinforcement for 6-inch sections for flat plate construction. |
| 49-588 | Behaviour of a composite slab for the floor of a highway bridge. |
| 49-589 | Column strength of an aluminum alloy section. |
| 50-582 | The web strength of I-beam sections in light alloys. |
| 50-586 | Web stability in an all-welded, thin-web, steel plate girder. |
| 51-582 | The effect on pressure surges of pipeline termination. |
| 51-583 | Web stresses in an all-welded plate girder. |
| 52-504 | Oblique impact on soils. |
| 52-562 | The relation between head and discharge in a curved spillway. |
| 53-505 | Stresses in web and stiffeners in an all-welded plate girder. |

| THESIS | THESIS TITLE |
|---|---|
| Civil Engineering & Applied Mechanics | |
| 53-506 | Thermal contraction and moisture creep in concrete. |
| 53-507 | Stresses in a thin-webbed steel plate girder. |
| 53-567 | Oblique impact on sand. |
| 54-501 | Supercritical flow in curved channels. |
| 54-503 | Some effects of cation exchange on Leda clay. |
| 54-561 | Flange and stiffener stress in an all-welded plate girder. |
| 54-564 | Stresses in the flanges of an all-welded girder. |
| 54-565 | Oblique impact on sand (II). |
| 55-505 | Strength of thin-walled aluminum alloy struts. |
| 55-506 | Failure mechanism of steel stressed in triaxial tension. |
| 55-573 | Torsional resistance of a steel beam having stiffeners. |
| 55-575 | Web stresses in a prestressed concrete I-beam. |
| 56-502 | Flexural stresses and deflections of a prestressed concrete I-beam. |
| 56-511 | Cold weather effects on fresh concrete. |
| 56-558 | Torsional resistance of a steel beam having stiffeners. II. |
| 57-507 | A study of prestressed concrete. |
| 57-510 | Compression of silt under model footings. |
| 57-512 | Bond of steel wires in prestressed concrete. |
| 58-503 | Shear stresses in diagonally cracked reinforced concrete beams. |
| 58-504 | Compression of silt under model footings. |
| 58-507 | Some physical characteristics of frozen soil. |

| THESIS | THESIS TITLE |
|---|---|
| **Civil Engineering & Applied Mechanics** | |
| 59-506 | The analysis of a glued laminated wooden arch. |
| 59-566 | Flow of granular material through orifices. |
| 59-570 | Moment-rotation characteristics of semi-rigid, high-tensile bolted connections. |
| 59-571 | Freezing effects on concrete within twenty-four hours of mixing. |
| **Civil Law** | |
| 34-506 | The legal status of the worker in Quebec. |
| 46-500 | La nullite des actes juridiques. |
| 51-579 | The Water Carraige of Goods Act, 1936. |
| 59-500 | A comparative and historical study of judicial and legislative attitudes towards monopoly in England and Canada. |
| **Classics** | |
| 08-506 | The dramas of Euripides in their relation to the life and thought of of his time. |
| 08-507 | The relation between the theology of Clement of Alexandria and Greek philosophy. |
| 11-502 | Seneca and his Greek models. |
| 13-511 | St. Paul's philosophy of religion. |
| 16-505 | The virgin birth of Christ. |
| 30-538 | Patriotism and political propaganda in the plays of Euripides. |
| 35-527 | The exposure of infants in ancient Greece from Homeric to Christian times. |
| 36-531 | Imprisonment in Greece. |
| 36-537 | Allegorical interpretation of Homer. |
| 37-525 | Humour in Virgil. |
| 39-045 | The aetiological interest of Euripides. |

| THESIS | THESIS TITLE |
|---|---|
| **Classics** | |
| 41-027 | Supreme political power in Greek literature of the fifth century, B.C. |
| 42-044 | The vocabulary of the non-literary papyri of the Hibeh collection in relation to New Testament language. |
| 43-513 | The political relationship between Caesar and Cicero to the conclusion of the civil war. |
| 46-541 | A revision of Grassmann's law. |
| 46-543 | The origin and development of the Prometheus myth. |
| 52-609 | A study of Indo-European compositional prefixes of negative value. |
| 53-555 | Lucretian imagery. |
| 56-612 | Character-portrayal in the "Cena Trimalchionis' of Petronius. |
| 58-549 | The government in Rome from 88-82 B.C. |
| **Comparative Religion** | |
| 55-633 | Eschatology in the Qur'an in the light of recent Biblical criticism. |
| **Divinity** | |
| 06-003 | The religion of Israel in the eighth and seventh centuries B.C. with special reference to the work of the prophets. |
| 07-506 | The philosophy of the Book of Job. |
| 13-508 | The philosophy of religion as represented in Augustine. |
| 53-504 | Origins of the constitution of the Church of England in Canada, being a study from the beginning of the Church in Canada down to the first provincial synod. |
| 53-559 | The lay-movement in Norway and the Norwegian church. |
| 54-047 | Determinative factors in the formation of the logos concept in the Johannine literature with particular reference to the prologue of the Fourth Gospel. |
| 54-500 | The nature of God in the writings of Nicolas Berdyaev. |

| THESIS | THESIS TITLE |
|---|---|
| **Divinity** | |
| 54-559 | The place of the second coming in the theology of the New Testament. |
| 55-500 | The atonement in the sayings of Jesus. |
| 55-501 | The Catholic Church in the Apostolic Fathers. |
| 55-570 | The development of the doctrine of Christ in the light of missionary experience in India. |
| 55-571 | The philosophical theology of William Temple. |
| 56-500 | The experience of religious conversion. |
| 56-501 | The doctrine of the atonement in the writings of James Denney. |
| 56-552 | Natural law in the New Testament. |
| 57-503 | The Exodus in the New Testament. |
| 57-555 | Le mysticisme de Martin Luther dans la tradition chretienne. |
| 57-556 | The realm of miracle. |
| 57-557 | The Ukrainian protestant missions in Canada. |
| 58-502 | The Deuteronomic interpretation of history. |
| 59-565 | The Roman Catholic modernism and the social gospel: a study of their common premises in the writings of Ernesto Buonaiuti and Walter Rauschenbusch. |
| **Economics** | |
| 20-511 | The status of women in the province of Quebec. |
| 22-529 | Socialism in Canada. |
| 23-526 | Du travail en la Nouvelle France. |
| 24-540 | Alien races in the Canadian West. |
| 24-543 | Corporate finance in Canada. |
| 24-547 | The migration of people from Canada to the United States. |

| THESIS | THESIS TITLE |
|---|---|
| **Economics** | |
| 30-519 | Capital and financial organization in Canada. |
| 30-520 | Economic relations of Canada with the British West Indies. |
| 30-521 | Provincial public finance in Canada. |
| 30-523 | The federal income tax in Canada. |
| 30-528 | The Negro in Canada. |
| 30-533 | Economic factors affecting the trend of language in the Province of Quebec. |
| 30-535 | Labour legislation in Canada affecting women and children. |
| 30-539 | The jurisdiction over merchant shipping within the British empire. |
| 30-544 | Bank credit in Canada. |
| 32-527 | The Canadian tariff: a political instrument and an economic expedient, or, Post-war Canadian tariff. |
| 32-528 | The planned economy in the capitalist state. |
| 32-534 | The steel industry of Nova Scotia. |
| 32-535 | The cellophane industry in Canada and its relations to allied and inter-related industries. |
| 32-538 | Triangular preferential trade. |
| 32-541 | The Doukhobors in Canada. |
| 32-543 | The taxation of motor vehicles. |
| 32-546 | Migration between Canada and the United States with particular reference to professional and intellectual classes. |
| 32-552 | Fluctuations in the exchange value of the Canadian dollar, 1919-1931. |
| 33-534 | Party government in France, with an historical outline of the Third Republic. |
| 33-538 | Unemployment among dock labourers in Montreal. |
| 33-542 | The United States of Europe. |

| THESIS | THESIS TITLE |
|---|---|
| Economics | |
| 26-545 | Public utilities in the Province of Quebec. |
| 26-546 | The "Lemieux' Act and the Privy Council decision of 1925. |
| 27-523 | Government guarantee of bank deposits in Canada. |
| 27-527 | Assisted immigration and land settlement with special reference to Western Canada. |
| 27-533 | Industrial and craft unionism in Canada. |
| 27-534 | The Catholic and National Trade Unions in the province of Quebec. |
| 28-529 | The financial arrangements between the provinces and the Dominion. |
| 28-534 | The Canadian sales tax. |
| 28-539 | Good times and hard times in Canada and their economic environment. |
| 28-542 | Credit and crédit facilities in Canada, with special reference to current commercial practice and merchandising methods. |
| 29-526 | The chain store movement in Canada. |
| 29-533 | The Canadian budgets (1867-1928). |
| 29-534 | Collective bargaining in the building, coalmining and transportation industries of Canada. |
| 29-539 | Diplomatic relations between Canada and Japan, with special reference to underlying economic and political conditions. |
| 29-540 | Public and private ownership in the hydro electric industry of Canada. |
| 29-541 | American investments and control of capital in Canada. |
| 29-546 | The asbestos industry in Canada. |
| 29-547 | The milling industry in Canada. |
| 29-550 | The political and constitutional implications of the 1926 Imperial Conference. |
| 30-517 | Old age pension legislation in Canada. |

| THESIS | THESIS TITLE |
|---|---|
| Economics | |
| 36-542 | The French franc and the gold standard, 1926-1936. |
| 36-544 | The minimum wage and its proposed application in the Dominion of Canada. |
| 37-523 | Capital accumulation in Canada since Confederation. |
| 37-530 | The municipal and financial administration of Paris and Montreal: a comparative study. |
| 37-546 | Trends in the investment of life insurance companies in Canada since 1910, with particular reference to the effects of changing rates of interest. |
| 38-528 | Industrial relations of a typical Canadian company. |
| 38-529 | Unemployment relief in the Prairie Provinces, 1930-1937. |
| 38-538 | The co-operative movement in Nova Scotia. |
| 38-540 | Theories of money, value and trade fluctuations suggested by Canadian monetary and banking history. |
| 38-541 | The history and development of the Committee for Industrial Organization in the United States. |
| 38-543 | The Canadian balance of international payments, 1900-1936. |
| 39-031 | The price of gold since 1931. |
| 39-034 | L'evolution des chemins de fer francais et le probleme canadien. |
| 39-035 | The origin and development of fascist political theory. |
| 39-040 | The relation of the American government to railroads in recent times. |
| 39-044 | The Canadian dollar, its' valuation and control. |
| 39-047 | The newsprint industry in Canada. |
| 39-048 | The demand for and the supply of currency in Canada, as bearing on ultimate credit control. |
| 40-016 | The Canadian working population: an analysis of occupational status divisions and the incidence of unemployment. |
| 40-028 | The French-Canadians and the industrialization of Quebec. |

| THESIS | THESIS TITLE |
|---|---|
| **Economics** | |
| 33-545 | The Canadian export trades and the Depression. |
| 33-547 | A history of trade relations between Canada and France. |
| 33-552 | Some aspects of the Canadian tariff and tariff-making since 1918: protection, and the Canadian cotton yarn and cloth and woollen cloth industries. |
| 33-553 | The problem of seasonal unemployment: a quantitative and comparative survey of seasonal fluctuations in Canadian unemployment. |
| 33-557 | The employment and unemployment problems of the railway industry of Canada, with particular reference to Montreal. |
| 33-559 | Unemployment, and unemployment relief in western Canada. |
| 33-563 | The economic and commercial aspects of aviation in Canada. |
| 33-564 | Wine in Canada: a study of the economic, fiscal and legislative aspects of the production and sale of wine in Canada. |
| 34-011 | Transportation as a national problem. |
| 34-523 | Control of the profit system. |
| 34-526 | A historical survey of economic fluctuations, 1800-1914. |
| 34-530 | History and organization of the Montreal Stock Exchange. |
| 34-537 | La liberte d'opinion: une etude des libertes publiques en France et au Canada. |
| 34-549 | Job-finding and methods of industrial recruitment: a study of a selected group of persons and firms in Montreal. |
| 35-524 | French economic self-sufficiency. |
| 35-530 | Large-scale merchandising in Canada: some economic implications. |
| 35-535 | The interest of Canada in the silver question. |
| 36-524 | Canadian wheat marketing policy: 1929-1936. |
| 36-536 | State control of civil aviation in the British Empire. |

| THESIS | THESIS TITLE |
|---|---|
| Economics | |
| 46-586 | The effect of the War on Canadian foreign trade. |
| 47-532 | Consumer credit, consumer spending policies and their effects upon economic fluctuations. |
| 47-538 | Confederation of Catholic workers of Canada. |
| 47-540 | An appraisal of the report of the economic policy committee of Jamaica, 1945. |
| 47-576 | The effect of World War II upon the financial position of Canadian corporate industry. |
| 48-555 | International commodity controls and national policy. |
| 48-571 | Canada's financial system in war and reconstruction. |
| 48-609 | Alternative solutions for the problems of economic regionalism. |
| 49-572 | Economic and monetary aspects of national debt retirement. |
| 49-582 | A comparative study of export credits insurance and its operation in Canada. |
| 49-632 | Collective bargaining in wartime Crown companies in Canada. |
| 49-646 | Secular stagnation and economic stability. |
| 50-018 | The Bank of International Settlement. |
| 50-571 | A comparison of the effects of reciprocal dumping with those of F.O.B. Mill pricing. |
| 50-579 | An enquiry into the welfare effects arising from the development of the Canadian pulp and paper industry. |
| 50-580 | The growth of the life insurance industry in Canada, 1909-1947. |
| 50-646 | Unions and wage rates in the newsprint industries of Quebec and Ontario, 1909 to 1948: a method of assessing the influence of labour unions on wage rates as exemplified by the Canadian newsprint industry. |
| 50-661 | The theory of social change in the writings of Pierre-Joseph Proudhon. |
| 50-664 | The economics of assembly and transportation of fluid milk in the Montreal area. |
| 50-670 | Extensions of contour analysis in economic theory. |

| THESIS | THESIS TITLE |
|---|---|
| **Economics** | |
| 40-029 | The new trade agreement between the United States and Canada, signed, November 17, 1938. |
| 40-032 | La legislation ouvriere dans la Province de Quebec. |
| 40-033 | The public debt of the Dominion of Canada and associated problems of public finance. |
| 41-013 | The tax systems of Canada. |
| 41-024 | The innovation theory of the trade cycle. |
| 41-026 | Foreign exchange control. |
| 41-031 | The highway transportation problem in Quebec. |
| 41-517 | The asbestos industry since 1929. |
| 41-522 | A study in war finance. |
| 42-033 | The price system, inflation and price control in total war. |
| 42-039 | Internal economic control in wartime: Canada. |
| 42-510 | Development of Mercantilism, a study in government intervention in trade, industry and agriculture in England and France during the sixteenth to eighteenth centuries. |
| 42-512 | Unemployment insurance in Canada. |
| 43-008 | Control of municipal finance in three federal countries: Canada, the United States, and Australia. |
| 43-515 | Wartime labour problems and policies. |
| 43-517 | Prices and wages in Canada since the beginning of the Second World War. |
| 43-527 | Some theories of interest. |
| 44-514 | Some aspects of labour problems in Canadian post-war industry. |
| 46-545 | Economic aspects of Japanese evacuation from the Canadian Pacific coast. |
| 46-549 | Business taxes and investment. |
| 46-582 | A critical evaluation of the theories of economic change of Smith, Ricardo, Marx and Schumpeter. |

| THESIS | THESIS TITLE |
|---|---|
| **Economics** | |
| 54-028 | An economic analysis of accountancy. |
| 54-044 | Immigration, population growth and Canadian economic development. |
| 54-059 | A statistical study of concentration in the manufacturing industries of Canada. |
| 54-075 | Economic planning for development in economies of arrested development with special reference to the first Indian Five Year plan. |
| 54-539 | The Canadian money market. |
| 54-540 | Classical economic methodology and its critics. |
| 54-543 | Fifty years of life insurance investments. |
| 54-547 | The pattern of local public health organization in Canada. |
| 54-550 | Steinberg's: a study in entrepreneurship. |
| 54-551 | The Canadian market for British exports and investments in the post-war years, 1945-53. |
| 54-558 | Some considerations on the influence of transport on the economic growth of underdeveloped countries. |
| 54-610 | Schumpeter's theory of long-run economic change: a study in economics and economic sociology. |
| 54-628 | The past history, present crisis, and future prospects of the primary textile industry in Canada. |
| 54-629 | Economic analysis of pricing problems in the transportation industry. |
| 54-630 | Some implications of a customs union: the Benelux case. |
| 55-563 | An economic study of the Schuman Plan. |
| 55-628 | The determination of occupational wage differentials: a comparative analysis. |
| 56-550 | The hyper quantity theory of money. |
| 56-551 | A study of the post-war terms of trade of Indonesia, 1945-1953. |
| 57-060 | The economics of road transport. |

| THESIS | THESIS TITLE |
|---|---|
| Economics | |
| 50-671 | The economic significance of Canadian accountancy. |
| 51-002 | Family allowances in Canada. |
| 51-565 | Fiscal policy in Greece (1917-1930). |
| 51-630 | State and fiscal monopolies. |
| 51-642 | The efficacy of advertising expenditures: the consumer's view. |
| 51-645 | The impact of international prices on the New Zealand economy. |
| 52-023 | The finance of housing in Great Britain, 1919-1949. |
| 52-066 | On the theory of distribution. |
| 52-544 | Economic development and international trade. |
| 52-545 | An evaluation of the 1945 proposals for constitutional change in Nigeria. |
| 52-604 | Machiavelli and Hume as forerunners of modern political thought. |
| 53-053 | Internal financing of post-war investments in Canadian primary textiles. |
| 53-055 | On the use of time-concepts in the theory of production and of capital. |
| 53-547 | Seasonal variations in employment in Canada. |
| 53-608 | The impact of the railway brotherhoods on the Canadian National Railways. |
| 53-611 | Expected utility, risk, and the theory of economic choices. |
| 53-612 | Problems of capital formation in underdeveloped countries with special consideration of capital imports and balance of payments problems. |
| 53-622 | The effect of foreign investment - Canada 1946-1951. |
| 53-623 | An econometric model of the Canadian economy. |
| 54-002 | The economics of development. |
| 54-004 | The acceleration principle. |

| THESIS | THESIS TITLE |
|---|---|
| **Economics** | |
| 57-087 | Some aspects of the problem of economic development in underdeveloped countries. |
| 57-609 | The fiscal system of Jordan. |
| 58-010 | Indian economic development: a study in economic history and theory. |
| 58-020 | The Canadian primary aluminum industry. |
| 58-545 | Soviet price mechanisms and economic theory. |
| 58-550 | The demands for motor gasoline and heating oils. |
| 58-587 | The sterling area as an economic entity. |
| 58-589 | The Canadian short-term capital market. |
| 59-025 | The economics of Canadian banking: an analysis of banking operations and transactions. |
| 59-558 | Monetary velocity in the Canadian economy. |
| 59-561 | Anti-combines enforcement in Canada, 1945-58. |
| 59-563 | Central banking in Greece. |
| 59-614 | Canadian import demand for fuels: a study of aggregation bias in econometric research. |
| 59-615 | The Sudan: a study in economic dualism. |
| **Economics & Political Science** | |
| 07-504 | Responsible government in Canada and its relation to English opinion 1759-1848. |
| 12-503 | State interference, theory and practice. |
| 13-503 | The Asiatic immigration question in British Columbia. |
| 13-510 | The taxation of land values in Western Canada. |
| 14-502 | The organization of Canadian labour and its relation to the labour movement of the United States. |
| 21-523 | Investigation of labour conditions of children and young persons in Montreal. |

| THESIS | THESIS TITLE |
|---|---|
| **Economics & Political Science** | |
| 22-526 | Wages and prices in the province of Quebec, with special reference to women workers. |
| 24-537 | The transportation of Canadian wheat from the West to the sea. |
| 24-539 | Certain aspects of the economic development of the Dominion of Canada, with special reference to trade relations with the United Kingdom and the United States, and to the effect of tariff policies and investments on the expansion of British North America. |
| 25-531 | The taxation of corporations in Canada. |
| 25-533 | Taxation of income in Canada. |
| 26-535 | The automobile industry in Canada. |
| 26-541 | Economic and social aspects of the Nova Scotia coal industry. |
| 26-552 | The pulp and paper industry in Canada. |
| 26-557 | The port of Montreal. |
| 27-530 | Canada in the League of Nations. |
| 28-533 | The economic and ethnological basis of Canadian confederation. |
| 28-536 | Economic aspects of the Crow's Nest Pass rates agreement. |
| 29-528 | Alberta coal. |
| 29-529 | The minimum wage for women and its application in Canada. |
| 30-529 | Migration of population between Canada and the United States. |
| 31-520 | The problem of social insurance in Canada. |
| 31-521 | The construction industry in Montreal, with special reference to seasonal unemployment. |
| 31-524 | Theories of value from David Hume to John Stuart Mill: a critical study. |
| 31-530 | Factors entering into the use of Canadian wheat in foreign countries. |
| 31-539 | The manufacture and marketing of knitted goods in Canada. |

| THESIS | THESIS TITLE |
|---|---|
| **Economics & Political Science** | |
| 31-541 | The transfer of natural resources to the Prairie Provinces. |
| 31-542 | Unemployment in the men's clothing industry of Montreal. |
| 31-548 | Agricultural credit in Western Canada. |
| 31-549 | Economic relations of the Maritime Provinces to Central Canada. |
| 31-550 | Inter-imperial trade in cotton textiles, 1914-1928. |
| 41-005 | The royal power of dissolution of Parliament in the British Commonwealth. |
| 50-577 | German propaganda during the war: a study of the lack of integration within the Nazi state. |
| 52-607 | Organized labour and economic analysis. |
| 54-618 | Canadian citizenship. |
| 55-551 | A study of Jamaican post-war terms of trade, 1945-1953. |
| 55-556 | French economic policy and inflation 1944-52. |
| 55-557 | Local government in Greater Corner Brook, Newfoundland. |
| 55-559 | Incentives in the public service: their role in making it responsive and efficient. |
| 55-568 | An analysis and appraisal of loss leader selling. |
| 57-015 | An economic analysis of the guaranteed wage and its application to the Canadian economy. |
| 58-001 | The immigration of Orientals into Canada with special reference to Chinese. |
| 58-011 | Tanganyika: influence of international trusteeship on constitutional and political development. |
| 58-014 | Staff relations in the Canadian federal civil service. |
| 58-035 | Career in civil service: Canada, Great Britain and the United States. |
| 58-043 | Models of cyclical fluctuations in farm mortgage credit. |
| 58-536 | Price and income effects of international capital movements: Canadian case. |

| THESIS | THESIS TITLE |
|---|---|
| Economics & Political Science | |
| 58-546 | Economics of retailing. |
| 58-581 | The Communist conquest of power in Yugoslavia, 1941-1945. |
| 59-005 | Income retention and fixed capital expansion: a group of Canadian manufacturing corporations, 1932-1953. |
| 59-559 | Changes in Canadian labour force participation rates 1946-58: a socio-economic study of the Canadian labour market. |
| 59-610 | Organized multilateral trade: some aspects of the structure and operation of the General Agreement on Tariffs and Trade. |
| 59-611 | Mosca and Mills: ruling class and power elite. |
| Education | |
| 11-501 | The development of the sense of beauty. |
| 11-504 | The educational significance of suggestion. |
| 15-505 | The Montessori principles. |
| 15-506 | The church school in the modern state: its province and problems. |
| 16-503 | The pedagogical value and psychical influence of the motion picture on present day educational systems. |
| 17-501 | The relation between the home-maker and the state. |
| 17-503 | The relation of school and university to life. |
| 18-502 | The problem of moral education. |
| 21-519 | Education and industry: their co-relation and development. |
| 31-534 | Educative activities outside the school programme. |
| 32-525 | The question of sex-differentiation in education. |
| 32-532 | The training of teachers: a comparison between Scotland and the province of Quebec. |

| THESIS | THESIS TITLE |
|---|---|
| **Education** | |
| 32-536 | Classification in secondary schools. |
| 32-551 | The history of education in the province of Quebec: a bibliographical guide. |
| 33-537 | The development of appreciation through creative self-expression. |
| 33-575 | The junior high school, with particular reference to Montreal. |
| 34-525 | The drama in secondary education. |
| 34-528 | The relation between arithmetic in the elementary school and mathematics in the secondary school. |
| 34-545 | A critical survey of current opinion on the development of character in physical education. |
| 35-536 | Preliminary work in science in the junior school. |
| 36-552 | Teacher training in the Province of Quebec: a historical study to 1857. |
| 38-526 | Vocational training facilities for women in Montreal. |
| 38-530 | Noegentic abstraction as an essential principle of learning and intelligence. |
| 38-550 | Examinations, with particular reference to their place in secondary schools. |
| 40-049 | College for employed adults. |
| 41-019 | Education in the bloc settlements of western Canada. |
| 41-516 | A study of French influence on Canadian education with special reference to Quebec. |
| 42-028 | A comparative study of the educational traditions of New England with those of French Canada. |
| 42-038 | The use of radio in the school. |
| 43-525 | The work of the Baptists in Canadian education. |
| 44-525 | A study of the influence of Dr. H.M. Tory on educational policy in Canada. |
| 45-514 | The education of Canadian service men. |
| 45-517 | A survey of the education of British women to the nineteenth century. |

| THESIS | THESIS TITLE |
|---|---|
| **Education** | |
| 45-546 | The educational significance of the Home and School movement. |
| 46-544 | The function of music in education. |
| 46-594 | A study of educational practices in the schools in the island of Montreal. |
| 47-579 | Educational institutions in New Brunswick, 1830-71. |
| 47-581 | The Jew in the educational system of the province of Quebec. |
| 48-615 | A comparison of the theories of the educative process of Plato, Aristotle, Dewey and Whitehead. |
| 48-616 | Thomas and Matthew Arnold: their significance for Canadian education. |
| 48-617 | The extra-curricular interests and responsibilities of a city principal with reference to the welfare and development of the pupil in the community. |
| 49-558 | A study of the contributions of Dr. E.I. Rexford to education in the province of Quebec. |
| 49-647 | Jewish education in Canada. |
| 50-565 | The displaced persons in Canada: a problem in re-education. |
| 51-577 | The history of the practical education courses in Canadian secondary schools. |
| 52-558 | Some aspects of American influence on Canadian educational thought and practice. |
| 53-551 | Education in UNESCO: the first five years. |
| 53-610 | The educational function of museums in the vicinity of Montreal with special reference to historical museums and sites. |
| 53-619 | The response of the secondary school to the needs of the "non-academic pupil'. |
| 54-542 | Guidance in democratic education. |
| 54-552 | Education, technology, and the end of man. |
| 55-637 | The teaching of geography in Canadian schools: its status, aims, and methods. A critical study. |
| 56-615 | The first country central school board in Quebec. |

| THESIS | THESIS TITLE |
|---|---|
| Education | |
| 56-620 | Chambly County Protestant Central School Board, 1945-1955. |
| 56-625 | The development of education in Jamaica. |
| 57-549 | Sir Thomas Elyot and the humanist ideal in education. |
| 57-551 | The education of non-Catholic English-speaking physically handicapped children in Montreal. |
| 57-552 | The educational philosophies of Russell and Whitehead; a comparison and assessment in terms of present day problems. |
| 57-611 | An examination of some factors which contribute to success in practice teaching. |
| 58-543 | Educational retardation among non-Roman Catholic Indians at Oka. |
| 59-620 | Indian education on Gilford Island: the factor of anxiety. |
| Electrical Communications | |
| 54-599 | High-Q resonant circuits in the frequency range 600 MCS to 1600 MCS using parallel-wire transmission lines. |
| 57-575 | Frequency analysis of whistling atmospherics. |
| Electrical Engineering | |
| 09-516 | The design and construction of the modern transformer. |
| 15-512 | The production of damped electric waves. |
| 16-510 | Heating and ventilation of electrical machinery. |
| 20-503 | The capacity of high voltage porcelain suspension insulators. |
| 20-508 | Electrical devices used in the anti-submarine campaign. |
| 21-517 | Ratio and phase angle in current transformers. |
| 25-516 | Electric power transmission by alternating currents at high voltage. |
| 25-522 | Transmission of power at high voltages over long distances. |

| THESIS | THESIS TITLE |
|---|---|
| **Electrical Engineering** | |
| 26-513 | Valve oscillator design and characteristics. |
| 29-519 | Electrical power transmission and stability in electrical systems. |
| 32-501 | Stability of generation and transmission systems. |
| 32-503 | Generation and reception of ultra short radio waves. |
| 33-500 | Electron oscillations in thermicnic vacuum tubes. |
| 33-502 | Notes on the design of band pass filters. |
| 33-505 | Relay protection of high voltage electrical power systems. |
| 33-506 | Analysis of three-phase networks by the method of symmetrical ccmponents. |
| 33-565 | Some non-linear vacuum tube topics. |
| 33-567 | The transmission of transient disturbances through linear electrical networks. |
| 34-500 | Regenerative braking of electrical cars and locomotives: a study of its fundamental principles and applications. |
| 35-502 | A study of some problems in radio interference. |
| 36-506 | Electrical power system stability. |
| 36-550 | Effects of unbalanced voltage cn synchronous motcr operation. |
| 43-500 | The design of matching networks for antennas and transmission lines. |
| 45-501 | Design of linear electrical networks to produce waves of given shape from impressed square waves. |
| 46-550 | Problems encountered in the development of a standard test for micrcphones. |
| 46-551 | The design of wide-band matching networks for U.H.F. antennae. |
| 46-554 | A study of the peak values of transient voltages present in the radio-frequency and intermediate-frequency amplifiers of a communicaticn type receiver. |
| [illegible] | The development of a logarithmic indicating instrument for the measurement of radio ncise voltages |

| THESIS | THESIS TITLE |
|---|---|
| Electrical Engineering | |
| 47-503 | The development of a reflectometer type of standing wave indicator. |
| 47-504 | The analysis, design and construction of a null detector for AC impedance bridges. |
| 47-506 | The stability of high voltage power systems. |
| 47-541 | Small electronic regulators. |
| 48-504 | A method of reducing harmonic distortion in audio amplifiers. |
| 48-506 | Radio signals masked by noise. |
| 48-508 | An electronic synchronous speed regulator. |
| 48-509 | Characteristics of composition-type resistors. |
| 48-572 | Noise from current-carrying resistors. |
| 49-500 | Noise of induction motors. |
| 49-501 | Design of a variable frequency oscillator. |
| 49-502 | The design of a resonant line impedance measuring device in the frequency range from 100 to 200 MC. |
| 49-503 | The transmission of facsimile to frequency shift telegraphy. |
| 49-505 | Amplidyne characteristics. |
| 49-506 | Wave propagation through ionized gases. |
| 49-507 | Design of ten-conductor, open-wire, transmission line for broadcast frequencies. |
| 49-508 | Negative resistance loading of transmission lines. |
| 49-509 | The design of discriminators of subminiature frequency modulation transceivers. |
| 49-510 | The effect of ground-wire currents on low-frequency inductive co-ordination. |
| 49-586 | Integrator-counter for muscle spike-potentials. |
| 49-591 | Dry disk rectifier-motor drives. |

| THESIS | THESIS TITLE |
|---|---|
| **Electrical Engineering** | |
| 50-502 | Generation of short electrical impulses for gating miniature type vacuum tubes. |
| 50-503 | The effects of radiation on the properties of quarter-wavelength resonant unshielded parallel-wire transmission lines in frequency range 300 Mc/sec. to 1300 Mc/sec. |
| 50-505 | The design of a dual frequency short wave antenna. |
| 50-506 | The effects of radiation on the properties of half-wavelength resonant unshielded parallel-wire transmission lines, in the frequency range (300-1300) Mc/sec. |
| 50-508 | Studies of current-noise from small resistors in the frequency range from 20 kc/s. to 500 kc/s. |
| 50-509 | Measurements of input admittance of triodes in the frequency range 300 Mc/s. to 900 Mc/s. |
| 50-584 | The absolute measurement of phase difference of low frequency wave forms. |
| 50-585 | Accoustic model of short wave antennas. |
| 50-587 | An apparatus for microwave measurements using resonant cavities. |
| 50-588 | Impedance measurements on aircraft antennas at medium and high frequencies. |
| 50-592 | The development of a thermistor accoustic probe. |
| 50-593 | Automatic control in frequency shift transmission. |
| 51-503 | Temperature rise of induction motors. |
| 51-504 | The development of a horizontal Van De Graaff generator. |
| 51-506 | Parasitic torques of induction motors. |
| 51-507 | Dependence of thermistor characteristics on the heat treatment process. |
| 51-581 | The resonance characteristics of certain transmission-line circuits. |
| 51-586 | Impedance of full-wave dipole antennas as a function of center spacing. |
| 51-589 | Voltage-stabilizing transformers. |
| 51-590 | The capacitor motor. |

| THESIS | THESIS TITLE |
|---|---|
| **Electrical Engineering** | |
| 51-592 | The radiation resistance of resonant transmission lines. |
| 52-049 | Precision microwave measurements using resonance curves. |
| 52-502 | The frequency conversion properties of transistors between 500 Kc. and 10 Mc. |
| 52-505 | The measurement and recording of intragastric electromotive force. |
| 52-561 | The input impedance of a full-wave dipole. |
| 52-564 | VHF propagation from an antenna located on a mountain. |
| 53-560 | The input impedance of a half-wave dipole. |
| 53-561 | A line operated electromyograph. |
| 53-564 | The radiation resistance of resonant parallel strip transmission lines. |
| 53-565 | Design and development of a frequency-shift, voice frequency carrier telegraph without relays. |
| 54-562 | The input inpedance of a full-wave dipole. |
| 54-566 | The use of Helmholtz resonators in the reduction of ventilation system noise. |
| 55-502 | Variables in the manufacture of manganese zinc ferrite. |
| 55-503 | Bridge measurement of junction transistors parameters. |
| 55-504 | Running characteristics of the capacitor-run motor. |
| 56-019 | Performance characteristics of base-line-scanning ambiguity filters for high PRF radars. |
| 56-506 | A study of phototransistors. |
| 56-507 | Microwave measurements on high-Q cavities. |
| 56-508 | Study of the properties and behaviour of quartz crystal units with different drive level conditions. |
| 56-554 | Designing and testing of microphone windscreens. |
| 56-555 | Study of the noise produced by a centrifugal ventilating fan. |

| THESIS | THESIS TITLE |
|---|---|
| **Electrical Engineering** | |
| 56-556 | Resonance properties of open parallel-wire transmission line sections at 3000 megacycles per second. |
| 57-054 | Phase distribution in the focal region of a microwave lens system. |
| 57-504 | An automatic electronic B-H curve plotter for testing magnetic materials over a wide frequency range. |
| 57-508 | Design of high-pass acoustic filters with special reference to aircraft engine exhaust manifolds. |
| 57-511 | Noise origin, power and spectra of ducted centrifugal fans. |
| 57-558 | Measurements of low frequency small-signal transistor parameters and their relation to theory. |
| 58-033 | An automatic phase plotter for the measurement of microwave fields. |
| 58-505 | Beyond-the-horizon propagation at microwave frequencies. |
| 58-555 | Investigation of the response of electromechanical servomechanisms in combined linear and non-linear operation. |
| 58-556 | Electronic analog multiplication using transistors. |
| 59-505 | Microwave propagation on overwater paths. |
| 59-507 | A study of avalanche breakdown voltage in silicon diffused p-n junctions. |
| 59-567 | Transistor amplifiers for analogue computers. |
| 59-584 | An analogue computer multiplier using transistors. |
| **Endocrinology** | |
| 44-002 | Investigation of a method of fractionation of anterior pituitary. |
| 46-034 | Studies on experimental shock. |
| 47-557 | Factors affecting the thyroid gland and body metabolism. |
| 47-575 | Some aspects of experimental cancer. |
| 48-523 | Micro-assay of insulin. |
| **Engine & Machine Design** | |

| THESIS | THESIS TITLE |
|---|---|
| **Engine & Machine Design** | |
| 11-512 | The efficiency of production in industrial plants. |
| 12-507 | Efficiency test of gasoline engines. |
| **Engineering** | |
| 07-507 | The distribution of stress in riveted connections. |
| 07-509 | Train resistance, its causes, measurement and value, and its bearing on locomotive rating and operation. |
| 09-515 | Secondary stresses in bridge trusses induced by riveted joints. |
| 10-511 | The design of a concrete block building with reinforced concrete floors for light manufacturing purposes. |
| 10-516 | Some reinforced concrete designs. |
| 11-505 | An investigation on the economics of tube milling. |
| 11-507 | The efficiency of fine screening devices, with particular reference to the Callow revolving belt screen as a means of preparing crushed ore for treatment upon the Wilfley table. |
| 12-509 | The merits and defects of the concrete column, plain and reinforced, in the light of experimental research. |
| 13-518 | An experimental investigation of the secondary stresses in a fourteen foot Warren truss. |
| 15-514 | An investigation of the strength functions of Nova Scotia mine timbers. |
| 15-515 | Effect of small variations in the proportion of cement upon the strength of some standard mixtures of concrete. |
| 22-002 | A study of certain methods of computing secondary stresses in framed structures, with their adaptation to actual conditions of loading. |
| 22-503 | The water factor in concrete. |
| 24-533 | Investigation of I-beams haunched with concrete with special reference to bond and sheer. |
| 29-502 | Distribution of stress in welded joints. |

| THESIS | THESIS TITLE |
|---|---|
| **Engineering** | |
| 30-504 | Further investigations of the distribution of stresses in welded joints. |
| **English** | |
| 06-006 | Thomas de Quincey and his influence in literature. |
| 09-501 | The element of satire in fiction written by Englishwomen from Miss Burney to George Eliot. |
| 10-505 | The fairy element in English literature. |
| 10-508 | The evolution of the fairy world, with special reference to its treatment in English literature. |
| 10-509 | Partisan poetry of Roundhead and Cavalier. |
| 13-506 | Literary forgeries of the eighteenth century. |
| 13-507 | Historical truth of English chronicle history plays. |
| 14-501 | Spencer and romanticism. |
| 14-503 | English religious memoirs of the seventeenth and eighteenth centuries. |
| 14-504 | Regulation of the English stage from the Restoration to the Licencing Act, 1737. |
| 17-502 | Piers Plowman as an interpretation of fourteenth century life, thought, and literature. |
| 21-520 | The myths and legends of the heroic cycle, and their use in Anglo-Irish literature. |
| 21-524 | Imaginary voyages in English literature: an essay in bibliography. |
| 23-520 | The element of magic in west Highland folklore. |
| 23-521 | Tendencies in English pulpit oratory from Hooker to Tillotson. |
| 23-523 | The satirical aspect of Thackeray's work. |
| 23-524 | A portrayal of the clergyman in the fiction of Jane Austen, Mrs. Gaskell, the Bronte sisters, and George Eliot. |
| 23-525 | Memoirs of the stage. |
| 24-538 | The plays and prefaces of George Bernard Shaw: a study of Shaw the dramatist and his criticism and interpretation of life. |

| THESIS | THESIS TITLE |
|---|---|
| English | |
| 24-541 | Survivals of the English and Scottish popular ballads in Nova Scotia: a study of folk song in Canada. |
| 24-542 | French-Canadian folk songs. |
| 24-546 | Vicente Blasco Ibanez and his relation to the French naturalists. |
| 25-534 | Canadian orators and oratory. |
| 25-537 | Crime and criminals in English and French memoirs. |
| 25-539 | An account of English journalism in Canada from the middle of the eighteenth century to the beginning of the twentieth, with special emphasis being given to the periods prior to Confederation. |
| 25-540 | The treatment of education in the novels of George Eliot, George Meredith and Thomas Hardy. |
| 25-542 | The treatment of immortality by poets of the ninteenth century. |
| 26-540 | Canadian drama, dramatists, and players. |
| 26-543 | The use of the fairy element in the Elizabethan and modern drama: a contrast with special reference to Shakespeare and Barrie. |
| 26-548 | Robert Louis Stevenson and romance: his attitude toward life and his confidence in the essential goodness of man as revealed in his romances. |
| 26-551 | The men and women of Thomas Hardy. |
| 26-554 | The poetry of William Butler Yeats. |
| 26-555 | Tennyson: his relation to Romanticism, with special reference to his political views. |
| 27-524 | The English versions of the Bible, and the various linguistic influences which affected their language and style. |
| 27-528 | Twelve years of the Westminster Review. |
| 27-531 | The rhythm of the new poetry. |
| 27-532 | Rousseau's conception of individualism, as reflected in the poetry of Byron. |
| 27-536 | The writers of the New Testament: a study of style and subject matter in the English Bible. |

| THESIS | THESIS TITLE |
|---|---|
| English | |
| 27-537 | The English novel of the sea from Smollett to Conrad. |
| 27-543 | The development of thought in the poetry of Algernon Charles Swinbourne. |
| 28-532 | Henry James and some recent psychological fiction. |
| 28-537 | Dramatic criticism by playwrights and players. |
| 28-538 | Literary criticism of Matthew Arnold. |
| 28-541 | The social ideals of William Langland. |
| 28-548 | Influence of the French naturalists on the work of George Moore. |
| 28-549 | The literature of the Maritime Provinces of Canada and its bearing on the struggle for education and political freedom. |
| 28-550 | The influence of Irish folk-songs and folk-lore on English literature. |
| 28-554 | Life and letters during the age of Pope:the Dunciad. |
| 28-563 | The development of stage costuming in England. |
| 28-565 | Religious experience of Francis Thompson. |
| 28-566 | The novel of manners as written by women, from Sarah Fielding to Jane Austin. |
| 29-524 | A study of literature in English produced in the province of Quebec prior to Confederation with its historical background. |
| 29-535 | The status of the familiar essay in Canadian literature. |
| 29-537 | The American novel since 1910. |
| 29-544 | The philosophy and poetry of Robert Browning with special reference to his philosophy of immortality; its sources and some conclusions. |
| 29-556 | The development of stage lighting in England and America. |
| 29-557 | Sir Edmund Gosse and the critical portrait. |
| 30-522 | The Cynewulf question. |

| THESIS | THESIS TITLE |
|---|---|
| English | |
| 30-524 | The question of marriage in the novels of 1880-1900. |
| 30-525 | A critical analysis of the writings of Aphra Behn. |
| 30-527 | The political philosophy of Thomas Carlyle, with special emphasis upon his theory of the hero. |
| 30-532 | Dramatic technique and tragic values in the works of Eugene Gladstone O'Neill. |
| 30-534 | The role of Goldsmith and Sheridan in eighteenth century comedy. |
| 31-519 | The Christian implications in Beowulf. |
| 31-522 | The influence on English literature of the "Edinburgh Review' under Francis Jeffrey. |
| 31-526 | The influence of the university on the development of drama in the United States and Canada. |
| 31-527 | The development and influence of Newman's ecclesiastical views. |
| 31-533 | Philosophy in Géorge Eliot's novels. |
| 31-535 | The history and development of scenery on the English stage from mediaeval times to the year 1700. |
| 31-536 | Shakespeare's use of sound and colour. |
| 31-543 | The wonderland in English literature. |
| 31-544 | The purpose and development of the dance in the English drama from 1590 to 1642. |
| 32-531 | Max Beerbohm: an appreciation. |
| 32-540 | Dramatic censorship in France and England, 1843-1909: a study in comparative literature. |
| 32-547 | The Old Testament in English satire. |
| 32-548 | Chaucer's interest in the problem of free will. |
| 32-550 | The theories of Gordon Craig and their relation to the contemporary theatre. |
| 33-539 | New England in American literature since 1900. |
| 33-546 | Arthur Hugh Clough: an impression of a Victorian. |

| THESIS | THESIS TITLE |
|---|---|
| **English** | |
| 33-548 | The English novel of rural life since 1900. |
| 33-550 | William Blake and his forerunners in mysticism. |
| 33-554 | English domestic tragedy from 1731 to 1800. |
| 33-555 | Folklore and balladry in Shakespeare. |
| 33-558 | The significance of Milton's political theories. |
| 33-572 | The development of the idea of religious toleration in England during the Restoration, 1660-1702. |
| 34-522 | The memoirs of pioneer women writers in Ontario. |
| 34-524 | A comparison of some European ballads. |
| 34-527 | The English literature of the Maritime Provinces of Canada: influences and trends. |
| 34-536 | The stream of consciousness in recent English fiction by women. |
| 35-519 | The romantic and realistic in the contemporary British and American drama. |
| 35-520 | Sir William Davenant and the 17th century theatre. |
| 35-522 | "Piers Plowman', annotated, together with an introductory essay. |
| 35-523 | Some recent tendencies in the short story (1914-1934). |
| 35-537 | Democratic tendencies in American poetry of the 19th century. |
| 35-543 | The history of impressionism in English criticism up to the year 1900. |
| 36-526 | Tennyson as the voice of Victorian England. |
| 36-528 | A history of the theatre in Montreal prior to Confederation. |
| 36-530 | American poetry from 1910 to 1935. |
| 36-532 | Spain and the English Romanticists. |
| 36-534 | The history of Johnson's Preface to Shakespeare, 1765-1934. |

| THESIS | THESIS TITLE |
|---|---|
| **English** | |
| 36-539 | The political theories of Alfred Tennyson. |
| 36-541 | The development of properties in drama on the English-speaking stage. |
| 37-516 | Three women letter writers of eighteenth century England: Mrs. Montagu, Mrs. Thrale and Fanny Burney. |
| 37-518 | English folk-carols and the dance. |
| 37-522 | The political fiction of Benjamin Disraeli. |
| 37-526 | The fairness of Byron's judgments. |
| 37-528 | Early Canadian historical literature: the journals of the traders of the North West Co. of Merchants from Canada. |
| 37-543 | Studies of some English mystical poets in the seventeenth and eighteenth centuries. |
| 38-525 | Lady Morgan and her circle. |
| 38-551 | Two New England writers of children's books: Jacob Abbott and Louisa Alcott. |
| 38-552 | Educational dramatics in England in the sixteenth century. |
| 39-036 | Byron: a study of his political theories. |
| 39-509 | Three women autobiographers of the English Civil War period: Mrs. Lucy Hutchinson, Lady Ann Fanshawe, and Margaret, Duchess of Newcastle. |
| 40-027 | The history and development of scenery, costumes and lighting of the English stage from Medieval times to the year 1700. |
| 40-507 | The social and political ideas of John Ruskin. |
| 40-512 | The critic on the hearth; biography as written by the wives of some famous novelists. |
| 41-028 | A pre-Shakesperian drama in pre-Shakesperian and in modern times. |
| 41-030 | Twentieth century poetic drama in English. |
| 41-512 | Studies in humanism: Babbitt, More, and American criticism. |

| THESIS | THESIS TITLE |
|---|---|
| English | |
| 41-513 | The influence of adversity on the career of Henry Wadsworth Longfellow. |
| 42-030 | Gertrude Bell as a literary artist. |
| 42-032 | The significance of Henry Fielding's dramatic works. |
| 42-040 | Huxley's novels of ideas: a study in values. |
| 43-511 | An analysis of Elizabethan and some twentieth century methods of producing Shakespeare's "Hamlet'. |
| 43-512 | The reaction to war and militarism as reflected in the British and American theatre from 1918 to 1942. |
| 43-516 | Bernard Shaw: socialist, reformer and creative evolutionist. |
| 44-515 | The political and social satire of Thomas Love Peacock. |
| 44-524 | English satire since Swift. |
| 45-512 | Some aspects of Ernest Hemingway in his relation to American literary naturalism. |
| 45-515 | James Branch Cabell: an interpretation. |
| 45-516 | The place of Robert Frost in modern American poetry. |
| 45-518 | Humour in the Wessex novels. |
| 45-543 | Some aspects of social drama in America during the thirties. |
| 46-538 | The heroines of Virginia Woolf. |
| 46-587 | The reform of education for boys as reflected in eighteenth century English literature. |
| 46-593 | Imperialism in English poetry between 1875 and 1900. |
| 47-533 | Shakespeare's influence on Dryden. |
| 47-535 | Shakespeare's treatment of soldiers. |
| 48-556 | The politics of Jonathan Swift. |
| 48-558 | A survey of the conflicts in Donne's life and thought which contributed to metaphysical wit. |

| THESIS | THESIS TITLE |
|---|---|
| English | |
| 48-562 | Dante Gabriel Rossetti's translation of Dante's "Vita Nuova': theory and practice. |
| 48-563 | Aspects of the treatment of time in some modern English novelists. |
| 48-611 | "Thirty days hath September': a novel. |
| 48-618 | Human relations in the fiction of Gertrude Stein. |
| 49-560 | "Inhabit the garden': a novel. |
| 49-562 | "Take care of my little girl': a novel. |
| 49-564 | The treatment of social ideas and problems in the plays of John Galsworthy. |
| 49-570 | Ezra Pound and the sense of the past. |
| 49-571 | The poetic principles of T.S. Eliot. |
| 49-574 | The religion of Bernard Shaw. |
| 49-577 | "Northern Pastoral': a novel. |
| 49-581 | Studies in English-Canadian and French-Canadian nature poets. |
| 49-629 | Willa Cather and the novel demeuble. |
| 49-634 | An investigation of the poetic imagery of Gerard Manley Hopkins. |
| 49-636 | A survey of Anglo-Welsh poetry: the continuity between seventeenth and twentieth century Anglo-Welsh poets. |
| 49-638 | "Threshold': a novel. |
| 49-642 | The artisitic principles of Gerard Manley Hopkins. |
| 50-563 | The dramatic elements in the novels of Jane Austen. |
| 50-564 | "Leaf without shadow': a novel. |
| 50-574 | An analysis of the ethical and political elements in Sir Philip Sidney's "New Arcadia'. |
| 50-578 | The personality of Virginia Woolf as revealed in her creative work. |

| THESIS | THESIS TITLE |
|---|---|
| English | |
| 50-645 | George Peele. |
| 50-653 | The leading women characters in the novels of George Eliot. |
| 50-654 | Alexander Pope's rhetoric and diction. |
| 50-663 | The literary technique of Aldous Huxley in his novels and short stories. |
| 50-666 | Autobiographical writings of the North American Indians. |
| 50-669 | Symbolism and W.B. Yeats. |
| 51-567 | Marlowe's "Jew of Malta': a critical study. |
| 51-568 | The walls of sense. |
| 51-636 | Clergymen in George Eliot and Thomas Hardy. |
| 51-637 | The social ideas of William Faulkner. |
| 52-546 | The individual in the novels of Graham Greene. |
| 52-550 | The quarto of "The Merry Wives of Windsor': a critical study, with text and notes. |
| 52-557 | Carlyle's handling of the "Laws of Nature' concept. |
| 52-559 | The rhythm of the King James Bible. |
| 53-552 | Jealousy in an unproductive society: the treatment of jealousy in some characteristic Restoration comedies. |
| 53-609 | Osler as a humanist. |
| 53-621 | The course of Butler's literary fame. |
| 54-544 | Society in the novels of Joyce Cary. |
| 54-553 | The strange case of "Titus Andronicus'. |
| 54-617 | John Donne's knowledge of medicine. |
| 54-623 | Shakespeare's hand in "The Spanish Tragedy', 1602. |

| THESIS | THESIS TITLE |
|---|---|
| **English** | |
| 55-549 | "Forty thousand brothers': a novel. |
| 55-550 | Attitudes toward love in Spenser. |
| 55-555 | A critical study of "All's Well that Ends Well'. |
| 55-561 | Katherine Mansfield's debt to Chekhov. |
| 55-565 | The metronome: a novel. |
| 55-627 | Charles Kingsley's conception and treatment of history in his historical novels: "Hypatia', "Westward Ho!', and "Hereward the Wake'. |
| 55-629 | A study of the innovations in dramatic construction of George Bernard Shaw with special reference to the technique of his discussion plays. |
| 55-640 | The treatment of childhood in the major novels of Defoe as a significant factor in the development of English prose fiction. |
| 56-548 | Spenser and the principle of plenitude. |
| 56-613 | The development of William Butler Yeats as a dramatist. |
| 56-621 | Social satire in the poetry of Robert Henryson. |
| 56-623 | Stephen Leacock: the man and his art. |
| 57-608 | A study of the English-Canadian novel since 1939. |
| 58-537 | A guide to Ezra Pound, 1885-1920, with special emphasis on his poetic theory and practice. |
| 58-538 | Chaucer's use of dress. |
| 58-590 | Developing patterns in the plays of Etherege. |
| 58-591 | James Burney to the Right Honourable Earl Spencer: a document in the history of the naval mutinies of 1797. |
| 58-592 | T.S. Eliot as dramatist in the commercial theatre. |
| 58-593 | Clifford Odets and the Group Theatre plays in their social context. |

| THESIS | THESIS TITLE |
|---|---|
| English | |
| 59-551 | The early novels of D.H. Lawrence. |
| Entomology | |
| 21-514 | The anatomy of Psyllia anali Schneidberger. |
| 24-518 | The genitalia of Graphtolitha (sub-fam. Cucullianae, Noctudae). |
| 25-506 | The description, habits, and life history of the onion maggot, Hylemyia antiga Meit., with special reference to its control in the district of Montreal,Que. |
| 25-508 | A comparative study of the male genitalia of the Canadian Pentatomidae. |
| 26-511 | A morphological study of the genitalia of some Ipidae. |
| 26-526 | A study of the biology and control of the onion maggot. |
| 26-534 | The external anatomy of Camnula pellucida scudder in its various stages. |
| 28-504 | The anatomy, histology and physiology of the digestive canal of crickets. |
| 28-507 | A study of the swarm control of bees. |
| 28-519 | Thoracic sclerites of muscoid diptera. |
| 29-514 | The biology of the tarnished plant bug Lygus pratensis L. |
| 31-517 | The morphology of the head-capsule of some coleopterus larvae. |
| 32-510 | The morphology of Halictus lerouxi, Le P. |
| 32-521 | The biology of Podisus serieventris, with especial reference to its predatory habits. |
| 32-523 | Morphology of the spruce saw-fly, Diprion polytomum Hartig. |
| 34-514 | Some Ichneumonidae of Alberta: a survey of the subfamily Joppinae. |
| 35-504 | Biology of Ips perturbatus Eichh. |
| 35-515 | The morphology of the bark beetle Dendroctonus monticolae Hopk. |
| 36-021 | The genetalia in the Ichneumonidae. |

| THESIS | THESIS TITLE |
|---|---|
| **Entomology** | |
| 36-515 | Studies in Trypetidae with special reference to the genus Rhagoletis. |
| 36-520 | The blackflies of eastern Canada (Simuliidae, Diptera). |
| 37-507 | Development of the confused flour beetle as effected by saturation deficiency and temperature. |
| 37-540 | The Lauxaniidae of eastern Canada. |
| 38-004 | The reactions of the housefly, Musca domestica Linn. to light of different wavelengths. |
| 38-013 | Inverted spray mixtures and their development with reference to codling moth control. |
| 38-503 | Biologie de Carpocapsa pomonella L. en relation avec la temperature et l'humidite. |
| 38-514 | Factors influencing the attractiveness of logs to oviposition by barkbeetles and woodborers. |
| 38-523 | A study of the factors governing the sex ratio in Chelonus annulipes Wesm. a braconid parasite of the European corn borer. |
| 39-014 | A revision of the American species of Gonia Meigen (Diptera: Tachinidae) together with a study of the male genetalia in calyptrate Diptera based on the same genus. |
| 39-057 | The external morphology of the adult of Hydroecia immanis Guenee, with notes on the biology. |
| 39-065 | Studies of the toxicity of nicotine in combination with various adjuvants. |
| 39-512 | Studies in the toxicity of nicotine. |
| 39-518 | The external anatomy of the four-lined leaf bug Poecilocapsus lineatus Fab. |
| 40-019 | The diapause and related phenomena in Diprion polytomum (Hartig). |
| 41-007 | La diapause chez les tenthredes. |
| 41-534 | A study of the genera Callarctia and Apantesis (Lepidoptera: Arctiidae). |
| 42-520 | External morphology of the tarnished plant bug (Lygus pratensis Linn.) |
| 42-521 | Studies on the Pentatomidae of Quebec (Hemiptera: Heteroptera). |
| 43-506 | Further refinement of a technique for testing contact insecticides. |

| THESIS | THESIS TITLE |
|---|---|

## Entomology

| | |
|---|---|
| 45-502 | Biological studies of the Mexican bean beetle, Epilachna varivestis Mulsant, in the province of Quebec. |
| 45-511 | The life history and morphology of the green spruce looper, Semicthisa granitata Gn. |
| 46-521 | Bessa selecta (Meigen) as a parasite of Gilpinia hercyniae (Hartig). |
| 46-531 | Studies on the insecticidal action of DDT (1,1,bis(4,4-dichlorophenyl) 2,2,2-trichloroethane) and related compounds, with a view to correlating this action with chemical structure. |
| 46-580 | The bionomics of the codling moth, Carpocapsae pomonella L., in the Annapolis Valley, Nova Scotia. |
| 47-517 | The influence of the apple spray programme on the natural control of oystershell scale, Lepidosaphes ulmi (L). |
| 47-560 | The morphology and bionomics of the predaceous thrips Haplothrips faurei Hood. |
| 47-566 | The morphology and bionomics of three species of leafhopper inhabiting the cherry. |
| 48-525 | A systematic study of the external male genitalia of the genus Septis (Lepidoptera, Phalaenidae). |
| 48-539 | The biology of Microbracon cephi Gahan, an important native parasite of the wheat stem sawfly, Cephus cinctus Nort. |
| 49-042 | A virus (polyhedral) disease of the European spruce sawfly, Gilpinia hercyniae (Hartig). |
| 50-559 | 1. A list of Phalaenidae of P.E.I. 2. The external morphology of Apamea americana Speyer. 3. A study of the external genitalia of 63 species of Phalaenidae. |
| 51-008 | The importance of the locus of application on the effectiveness of DDT as a contact insecticide for the housefly, Musca domestica L. (Diptera, Muscidae). |
| 51-053 | The continuous laboratory rearing of Culiseta incrnata (Will.) and a study of the structure and function of the egg-shell and egg-raft (Diptera: Culicidae). |
| 52-026 | Residues of organic insecticides in soils. |
| 52-516 | The biology and external morphology of the hemlock looper, Lambdina fiscellaria fiscellaria (Guenee), in Newfoundland. |
| 52-523 | A comparative morphology of Monochamus notatus (Drury) and M. scutellatus (Say) (Coleoptera: Cerembycidae). |

| THESIS | THESIS TITLE |
|---|---|
| **Entomology** | |
| 52-532 | The effect of various levels of nitrogen, phosphorus and potassium on the fecundity of the two-spotted spider mite Tetranychus bimaculatus Harvey. |
| 52-539 | The action and efficacy of soil fumigants directed against the currant fruit fly, Epochra canadensis Loew (Diptera: Trupaneidae). |
| 52-540 | A study of Stethorus punctum (Lec.) (Coleoptera: Coccinellidae) and other predators of mites in Manitoba. |
| 52-543 | Part I. Bark beetle development and associated insects in white and red pine logging slash. Part II. External anatomy of Ips pini (Say) (Coleoptera: Ipidae). |
| 53-607 | A study of Hypomolyx piceus (De G.) (Coleoptera: Curculionidae) and its relationship to white spruce, Picea glauca (Moench) Voss. |
| 54-015 | The distribution and site of action of DDT applied externally (and internally) to adult house flies Musca domestica L. (Diptera: Muscidae). |
| 54-040 | Morphology of the face in the hymenoptera. |
| 54-062 | The effects of temperature and atmospheric moisture on the behaviour of the horn fly, Siphona irritans (L.). |
| 54-069 | The identification of larvae of some species of bark beetles breeding in coniferous trees in eastern Canada. |
| 54-523 | Biological studies of the onion maggot Hylemya antiqua (Meighen) (Diptera: Anthomyiidae) in the muckland areas of southwestern Quebec. |
| 55-020 | Deterioration of fire-killed pine by wood-boring beetles (Coleoptera: Cerambycidae) in the Mississagi region of Ontario. |
| 55-600 | The synergistic action of certain chemicals used in combination with DDT against house fly adults, Musca domestica Linn. (Diptera: Muscidae). |
| 56-050 | The effect of temperature and nutrition on the the development of the house cricket, Acheta domesticus (L.) (Gryllidae, Orthoptera), and two related species of crickets. |
| 56-534 | The root maggots associated with rutabagas in Prince Edward Island: with especial attention to seasonal history and control of the cabbage maggot (Hylemya brassicae) (Bouche): Diptera, Anthomyiidae). |

| THESIS | THESIS TITLE |
|---|---|
| Entcmology | |
| 56-579 | The effect of DDT on codling moth adults (Carpocapsa pomonella L.) (Lepidoptera: Oletheutidae). |
| 57-014 | The biological activity of some (P-chlcrophenyl) compounds synergistic with DDT. |
| 57-036 | A biological study of the white pine weevil, Pisscdes strobi Peck, with special reference to the effect of physical factors on its activity and behaviour. |
| 57-070 | Population behaviour of the sheep ked, Melophagus ovinus (L.), in relaticn tc endocrine mechanisms in sheep. |
| 57-525 | A study of the integument of mites with special attenticn to that of Tetranychus telarius (Linnaeus). |
| 57-540 | The Orthoptera cf Nova Scotia. |
| 57-582 | Water absorption and metabclism during the embrycnic development of the house cricket Acheta domesticus (L.) (Gryllidae, Orthoptera). |
| 58-031 | The response of Tenebroides mauritanicus (L.) in the vacuum fumigaticn of jute with methyl bromide. |
| 58-522 | A study of the clover root borer, Hylastinus obscurus (Marsham) (Coleoptera: Scholytidae). |
| 58-532 | An embryological study of the spruce budworm, Chcristoneura fumiferana (Clements), (Lep., Tortricidae). |
| 59-018 | Revision of the genus Philodromus (Araneae: Thomsidae) in North America. |
| 59-542 | Occurrence of the Swaine jack-pine sawfly and external anatcmy of the mature, feeding larvae. |
| Experimental Medicine | |
| 31-505 | Studies in cholesterosis. |
| 31-551 | The effect of vasomotor nerve secticn on experimental epilepsy. |
| 32-021 | Studies in glyccgen metabolism. |
| 32-511 | Origin, distribution and function of cranial vascular nerves. Part I. A vasodilator nervous pathway to the cerebral vessels from the central nervous system. Part II. On the occurrence cf afferent nerve fibres in the internal carotid plexus. |
| 32-558 | The structural and functional relationships of the cerebrospinal nerve roots. |

| THESIS | THESIS TITLE |
|---|---|
| **Experimental Medicine** | |
| 33-032 | Experimental study of blood fats in health and disease. |
| 33-514 | The glycogen content of the rat heart. |
| 33-519 | The evolution of cell types in the central nervous system - Microglia. |
| 33-569 | The intra-pleural pressure: its significance in health and disease. |
| 34-509 | Neurogenic hyperthermia. |
| 34-520 | The effect of partial tracheal occlusion on the compensatory hypertrophy of autotransplants and remnants of the thyroid gland. |
| 36-551 | The lymphatics of the lower urinary and genital tracts: an experimental study with some special reference to renal infections. |
| 37-509 | Study of water balance in the "alarm reaction'. |
| 37-513 | The determination of histamine in the blood and tissues under various conditions. |
| 37-539 | Metabolism of the sterols related to the female sex glands. |
| 38-512 | A quantitative study of glucuronic acid excretion. |
| 38-548 | The role of the sex hormones in the luteal phase of the menstrual cycle. |
| 39-022 | The metabolism of histamine. |
| 39-521 | The metabolism of the hormone of the adrenal cortex. |
| 41-018 | The adrenal cortex and its role in resistance. |
| 42-051 | Glucuronic acid metabolism. |
| 42-054 | The effects of irradiation of protein antigenicity. |
| 43-007 | Some aspects of the metabolism of the steroid hormone. |
| 44-021 | Nitrogen metabolism in damage and convalescence. |
| 44-519 | The bio-assay of DCA-like substances. |

| THESIS | THESIS TITLE |
|---|---|
| Experimental Medicine | |
| 46-559 | The effect of damage on in vitro protein metabolism. |
| 49-609 | Some aspects of choline metabolism. |
| 49-619 | The effects of induced asthma-like attacks in man on the intake of oxygen, blood oxygen content and cardiac output. |
| 49-620 | Effect of adrenocorticotrophic hormone on the urinary excretion of corticoids in health and disease. |
| 49-625 | Glucose and galactose metabolism in health and disease. |
| 50-544 | A method for the evaluation of adrenal cortical functions in man. |
| 50-600 | Part 1. The effect of potassium deficiency on gastric secretion. Part 2. Experimental ulcerative colitis: the effect of bile and/or pancreatic juice on the colon. |
| 50-602 | Protomine-heparin titration methods for the determination of circulating anti-coagulants. |
| 50-628 | The effect of adrenocorticotrophic hormone on respiratory function. |
| 51-511 | Some metabolic effects of ACTH and cortisone acetate. |
| 51-527 | Effects of various substances on protein catabolism. |
| 51-534 | Observations on body water and electrolytes following administration of ACTH in man. |
| 51-553 | The excretion of phenolsulfonphthalein by the kidneys of rabbits. |
| 52-061 | Measurement of sodium-retaining substances in human urine. |
| 52-512 | The histamine content of allergic and non-allergic human nasal mucous membrane with simultaneous observations on the eosinophils. |
| 52-591 | The metabolism of histadine and histamine. |
| 53-518 | The influence of hormones on experimental hepatic lesions. |
| 53-527 | Adrenocorticotrophic hormone and intermedin. |
| 53-533 | The serum lipids in atherosclerosis. |
| 53-569 | Some aspects of glutathione metabolism. |

| THESIS | THESIS TITLE |
|---|---|
| **Experimental Medicine** | |
| 53-579 | Some metabolic effects of pituitary growth hormone in human subjects. |
| 53-601 | The effect of adrenocorticotrophin on plasma protein regeneration in the rat following depletion by massive hemorrhage. |
| 54-053 | Some hormonal effects on ketosis. |
| 55-057 | Studies on aldosterone. |
| 55-059 | Orthostasis and the kidney. |
| 55-588 | The bone marrow in pregnancy and the puerperium. |
| 55-609 | Blood corticoids in pregnancy. |
| 55-619 | Study of the antidiuretic activity of human and rat blood. |
| 56-591 | The influence of stress on thyroid function in the rat. |
| 56-598 | A study of certain characteristics of salivary secretion in humans: the relation of adrenal cortical activity to these characteristics. |
| 57-072 | The participation of bone in the sodium and potassium metabolism of the rat. |
| 57-595 | Study of a case of adrenal tumour with regard to steroid metabolism. |
| 58-524 | The localization of blocking antibody in the sera of ragweed sensitive patients by starch electrophoresis. |
| 58-564 | Studies on pulmonary diffusion. |
| 59-009 | Factors affecting adrenal-regeneration hypertension in the rat. |
| 59-511 | Diabetic glomerulosclerosis: studies relating to its pathogenesis. |
| 59-514 | Fat and ketone metabolism in diabetes mellitus. |
| **Experimental Surgery** | |
| 48-540 | Rapid exchange of bone salts in the skeleton of newborn animals as shown by an improved autographic technique. |

| THESIS | THESIS TITLE |
|---|---|
| **Experimental Surgery** | |
| 48-589 | (a) Experimental gastric and duodenal ulcer. (b) Reconstructive surgery: experimental use of a skin-lined tube in the greater omentum. |
| 48-591 | Investigations dealing with surgery of the heart and lungs in experimental animals. |
| 49-533 | Lymphatic drainage of bone with special reference to osteomyelitis. |
| 49-604 | Effect of intestinal oxygen therapy on portal oxygenation in shock. |
| 49-605 | Problems associated with the operation of pneumonectomy. |
| 49-612 | An experimental study of collateral coronary circulation produced by transplanting the left mammary artery to the left ventricular myocardium. |
| 50-555 | Entry of radio-phosphorus into the bones of the newborn rat. |
| 50-599 | Experimental studies on complete deprivation of arterial supply to the liver, with special reference to Welch bacillus infection. |
| 50-607 | The effect of pyridoxine deficiency on gastric secretion. |
| 50-623 | An experimental study on the development of anastomoses between the coronary circulation and the left internal mammary artery implanted into the left ventricular myocardium. |
| 50-633 | Effects of 2-acetyl-amino-fluorene on the liver of rats. |
| 50-640 | The deposition of radioactive phosphorus in bones, teeth and healing fractures of rats as shown by autographs and specific activity determinations. |
| 51-595 | Studies of gastric secretion. |
| 51-626 | Experimental production of gastric neoplasms in the rat. |
| 52-541 | The effect of ACTH and cortisone on skin and connective tissue. |
| 52-579 | Part A. Effects of resection of massive segments of large and small bowel upon fluid and electrolyte balance. Part B. Effects of spinal anesthesia and different grades of operative trauma upon fluid and electrolyte balance. |
| 52-584 | An investigation of the pulmonary circulation during hemorrhagic shock and resuscitation. |
| 52-586 | Venous endothelium: its relation to thrombosis. |

| THESIS | THESIS TITLE |
|---|---|
| **Experimental Surgery** | |
| 52-589 | Chronic remote vagal stimulation by radiofrequency. |
| 53-575 | The effects of compression and the role of the hematoma in fracture healing. |
| 53-585 | A study of the tissue mast cell. |
| 53-591 | Studies in therapy of hemorrhagic shock with associated myocardial damage. |
| 54-569 | A study of electrogastrophic recordings. |
| 54-576 | An experimental study of the internal mammary artery implanted in the left ventricular myocardium, with special reference to variations in the operative procedure as it affects the implant, and to blood flow characteristics through the implant. |
| 54-589 | An experimental study of the changes both histological and physiological occurring in patches of exteriorized gastric mucosa. |
| 54-592 | Effects of hypophysectomy, growth hormone and 2-acetyl-aminofluorine on pancreatic islets. |
| 54-600 | Studies on epiphyseal stimulation. |
| 55-585 | An experimental study of renal damage and electrolyte imbalance following various methods of urinary deviation to the intestine. |
| 55-595 | Blood volume determinations in surgical patients. |
| 55-602 | Occlusion of the abdominal aorta above the coeliac axis in hypothermic dogs. |
| 55-603 | Effects of the hypothalamus upon gastric secretion. |
| 55-608 | Nutritional studies in totally gastrectomized dogs. |
| 56-572 | Role of histamine in acute radiation syndrome. |
| 56-577 | An evaluation of hypothermia in hepatic and major abdominal surgery in dogs. |
| 56-592 | Vascular changes and direct tissue effects in severe cold injury. |
| 57-531 | A study of the potential difference component of the electrogastrograph. |
| 57-537 | Studies of endocrine effects on experimental metastatic bone tumours. |

| THESIS | THESIS TITLE |
|---|---|
| Experimental Surgery | |
| 57-568 | The experimental production of cholelithiasis and cholecystitis in laboratory animals. |
| 57-574 | The study of the effects of radioactive strontium in laboratory animals. |
| 57-580 | Studies on chlorpromazine in experimental haemorrhagic shock in dogs. |
| 57-581 | Studies on experimental production and dissolution of renal calcinosis. |
| 57-600 | Peripheral circulatory changes in experimental frostbite. |
| 58-566 | The surgical treatment of experimental ascites. |
| 58-573 | An experimental study for evaluation of surgical procedures in the treatment of coronary artery insufficiency. |
| 58-574 | A study of the effect of partial biliary obstruction in dogs. |
| 58-580 | Techniques of extracorporeal circulation. |
| 59-521 | The mechanism of immuno-rejection in homotransplantation. |
| 59-578 | Experimental studies in transplantation of small bowel mucosa to the rectum. |
| 59-587 | A study of the pathogenesis of regional enteritis. |
| 59-595 | The results of treatment of haemorrhagic shock on survival, blood volumes and metabolism. |
| 59-604 | Studies on carcinogenesis in hamsters. |
| French | |
| 06-004 | Gerard de Nerval. |
| 09-503 | Theophile Gautier as a prose writer. |
| 09-506 | Francois Villon et la poesie lyrique en France au XVe siecle. |
| 11-503 | Emile Zola et l'etude naturaliste des classes de la societe. |
| 13-505 | L'element lyrique dans les drames de Victor Hugo. |
| 15-502 | Les principes de Moliere sur l'education des femmes. |

| THESIS | THESIS TITLE |
|---|---|
| **French** | |
| 15-504 | L'orient musulman dans la litterature francaise au XVIIIe et XIXe siecles. |
| 21-522 | Le sens historique et la couleur locale dans le drame romantique. |
| 24-544 | La critique francaise et le drame norvegien. |
| 24-545 | L'influence de Shakespeare sur le the atre d'Alfred de Musset. |
| 25-541 | "The atre en liberte' de Victor Hugo. |
| 26-537 | La vie intellectuelle des noirs de la Caroline du Nord. |
| 26-538 | Jeanne d'Arc dans le theatre moderne anglais et francais. |
| 26-556 | La legende napoleonienne dans l'oeuvre de Beranger. |
| 28-527 | Le sport dans le roman francais d'apres la guerre. |
| 28-545 | Les caracteres ecclesiastiques dans l'oeuvre d'Anatole France. |
| 28-557 | La presse Franco-Americaine. |
| 29-523 | La theatre de Marie Leneru. |
| 29-527 | La crise de l'adolescence telle qu'elle apparait dans les romans francais parus depuis la guerre de 1914-18. |
| 29-531 | La revendication des femmes chez Brieux. |
| 29-548 | Anatole France critique litteraire. |
| 30-518 | Le catholicisme de M. Paul Bourget etudie dans ses principaux romans et nouvelles. |
| 30-540 | Les origines du journalisme Canadien-Francais. |
| 30-548 | Le travail dans l'oeuvre de Pierre Hamp. |
| 31-525 | Maurice Maeterlinck devant la critique Americaine. |
| 31-531 | La Bretagne dans les lettres contemporaines. |
| 31-540 | La representation de la guerre de 1914-1918 et ses consequences directes par le theatre francais. |

| THESIS | THESIS TITLE |
|---|---|
| French | |
| 31-561 | Le theatre francais a Montreal 1878-1931. |
| 31-562 | La doctrine de l'unanimisme dans les oeuvres de M. Jules Romains. |
| 31-563 | La France d'apres-guerre, jugee par le roman americain. |
| 31-565 | L'Alsace-Lorraine dans le roman francais entre les deux guerres. |
| 31-566 | L'influence francaise sur les poetes hispano-americains de l'ecole "modernista'. |
| 32-537 | Edmond Rostand aux Etats-Unis. |
| 32-539 | L'eau dans l'oeuvre de Lamartine. |
| 32-549 | Les moeurs americaines jugees par les francais d'apres-guerre. |
| 32-561 | Washington Irving et la France. |
| 33-541 | Le juif dans le roman francais d'apres-guerre. |
| 33-549 | Les auteurs francais dans l'enseignement aux Etats-Unis. |
| 34-521 | La participation de la France a l'expedition de Rhode Island en 1778. |
| 34-529 | L'evolution des idees de Romain Rolland sur la vie internationale. |
| 34-531 | Le roman regionaliste depuis la guerre. |
| 34-532 | Les animaux dans Colette. |
| 34-535 | La jeune fille de la bourgeoisie francaise dans le roman d'apres-guerre. |
| 34-538 | Pierre Loti et la Turquie. |
| 34-539 | Quelques interieurs dans les romans d'Honore de Balzac. |
| 35-521 | L'idee religieuse dand l'oeuvre dramatique de Paul Claudel. |
| 35-525 | Les idees dans le theatre de Francois de Curel. |
| 35-526 | La survivance francaise dans la Nouvelle-Angleterre. |

| THESIS | THESIS TITLE |
|---|---|
| **French** | |
| 35-528 | L'histoire du nouveau theatre a New York. |
| 35-531 | L'idee religieuse dans les ceuvres de Charles Peguy. |
| 35-534 | La preciosite dans l'oeuvre dramatique d'Edmond Rcstand. |
| 35-549 | L'histoire dans le theatre d'Alexandre Dumas pere. |
| 36-523 | Guy de Maupassant: sa vie, son oeuvre, et la critique americaine. |
| 36-525 | L'enfant dans le foyer de la bourgeosie francaise d'apres le roman mcderne. |
| 36-529 | L'art unanimiste dans les ceuvres en prose de Jules Romains. |
| 36-533 | Henri Barbusse et son champ de bataille. |
| 36-540 | L'influence de St. Vincent de Paul sur l'elcquence de la chaire. |
| 37-517 | La survivance francaise. |
| 38-527 | Le sentiment de la nature dans le rcmans du XVIIIe siecle. |
| 38-531 | Le developpement de la biographie romancee en France. |
| 38-532 | Le christianisme de Mauriac dans toute son oeuvre. |
| 38-534 | La justice au theatre en France a partir de 1800. |
| 38-535 | L'influence de Francois de Sales sur la preedication de dix-septieme siecle. |
| 38-536 | Les relations de famille dans le roman de Francois Mauriac. |
| 38-537 | Le theatre chretien d'Henri Gheon. |
| 39-030 | Le noir dans le roman francais. |
| 39-032 | Les juifs dans les oetvres des freres Tharaud. |
| 39-038 | L'ecole litteraire de Montreal. |
| 39-043 | Defense et illustration des femmes au quinzieme siecle: "Le champion des dames' de Martin Le Franc. |

| THESIS | THESIS TITLE |
|---|---|
| French | |
| 39-510 | Edmond Demolins: propagateur de l'education anglaise en France. |
| 40-508 | Les sources de l'oeuvre de Marcel Proust. |
| 40-509 | Henri Bremond, critique original des mystiques. |
| 40-510 | La revolte sociale dans le roman d'apres-guerre. |
| 40-511 | Le satanisme dans les oeuvres des auteurs modernes: de Chateaubriand a Georges Bernanos. |
| 41-020 | Madame de Segur, vie, oeuvre et influence sur la litterature enfantine en France. |
| 41-021 | L'Aviation dans la litterature contemporaine. |
| 41-022 | Les livrets d'opera du XIXme siecle tires des chefs-d'oeuvre de la litterature francaise. |
| 41-025 | Le sentiment religieux de Maurice Barres. |
| 41-510 | Le roman d'aventure humoristique de Jean Martet. |
| 41-515 | Le conflit des generations tel que l'illustre le roman francais d'apres-guerre. |
| 41-518 | La peinture de l'amour dans les premiers romans de Paul Bourget. |
| 41-521 | Andre Gide et le communisme. |
| 42-029 | Les historiens canadiens-francais. |
| 42-034 | Deux predicateurs Francais: Adolphe et Wilfred Monod. |
| 42-036 | L'Anglicisme dans les grands quotidiens de Quebec. |
| 42-037 | Les idees dans les prefaces de Francois de Curel. |
| 42-041 | Le theatre de George Sand: sources et influences. |
| 42-042 | Paris, source d'inspiration dans la poesie francaise des origines a Baudelaire. |
| 42-046 | Le roman historique Canadien francais, des origines jusqu'a 1914. |
| 42-508 | Saint Francois de Sales, directeur de conscience. |

| THESIS | THESIS TITLE |
|---|---|
| French | |
| 42-509 | Baudelaire devant la critique de 1857 a 1917. |
| 42-513 | Marie le Franc, romanciere de la Bretagne et du Canada. |
| 42-514 | Ducis, essai sur l'influence de Shakespeare en France jusqu'a l'epoque romantique. |
| 43-514 | Contes populaires et legendes de la province de Quebec. |
| 43-522 | Le sentiment religieux et le sentiment de la nature dans l'oeuvre de Francis Jammes. |
| 43-524 | L'enfant dans l'oeuvre des ecrivains catholiques modernes. |
| 43-526 | L'etude du caractere anglais dans l'oeuvre d'Andre Maurois. |
| 45-544 | La survivance de la culture francaise en Nouvelle-Ecosse. |
| 45-545 | La vie de l'epoque dans les lettres de Mme. de Sevigne. |
| 46-542 | L'actualite politique dans "Les hommes de bonne volonte' (volumes I a XIV) de Jules Romains. |
| 46-548 | La survivance francaise au Nouveau Brunswick. |
| 46-584 | L'histoire du Canada dans l'oeuvre de Maurice Constantin-Weyer. |
| 46-585 | Etude critique de la traduction anglaise du livre de Jules Romains "Le six octobre'. (Premier volume de "Les hommes de bonne volonte'). |
| 47-530 | La peinture de la bourgeoise dans "Les Thibauld' de Roger Martin du Gard. |
| 47-531 | Les anglo-saxons dans l'oeuvre de Pierre de Coulevain. |
| 47-534 | Le courrier anglais de Stendhal: ses jugements sur la politique et la litterature. |
| 47-536 | Etude comparative de deux traductions anglaise et americaine du roman de Georges Duhamel "Le Notaire du Havre'. |
| 47-537 | La survivance francaise dans Prescott et Russell. |
| 47-583 | Anatole France devant la critique americaine. |
| 47-584 | Les femmes dans la correspondance de Voltaire. |

| THESIS | THESIS TITLE |
|---|---|
| French | |
| 48-564 | Le theatre d'Andre Gide. |
| 48-566 | Le cardinal Richelieu dans les romans de Vigny et les romans de Dumas. |
| 48-608 | L'enfant dans l'oeuvre de Victor Hugo. |
| 48-610 | Les methodes preconisees pour l'enseignement du francais comme langue etrangere de 1850 a 1944. |
| 48-614 | Etude critique de trois traductions anglaises du premier volume de "Les Thibault' par Roger Martin du Gard. |
| 49-556 | La nature dans l'oeuvre de Colette. |
| 49-565 | Le reel et l'imaginaire dans contes et romans d'Alexandre Arnoux, 1947. |
| 49-566 | La religion du travail dans les romans d'Emile Zola. |
| 49-568 | Le monde de Jean Giono. |
| 49-579 | Les paysannerie francaise dans les romans d'Honore de Balzac. |
| 49-580 | Le Paris des "Miserables'. |
| 50-572 | Le personnage de Vautrin dans l'oeuvre de Balzac. |
| 50-575 | Les souvenirs personnels de Victor Hugo "Les Miserables'. |
| 50-643 | Baudelaire, critique litteraire. |
| 50-644 | Montaigne et les nouvelletes. |
| 50-648 | Le drame intime de Marcel Proust et la psychologie de l'amour dans "A la recherche du temps perdu'. |
| 50-659 | Les moeurs et les coutumes rurales au Canada-Francais dans le roman canadien-francais depuis les origines. |
| 51-572 | Ambiance spirituelle de Georges Bernanos d'apres les themes de ses romans. |
| 51-576 | L'element de la souffrance humaine dans l'oeuvre romanesque de Georges Duhamel. |
| 51-578 | L'expression litteraire des sensations olfactivesgustatives dans les romans de Joris-Karl Huysmans. |

| THESIS | THESIS TITLE |
|---|---|
| French | |
| 51-634 | Les idees politiques et sociales de Victor Hugo en exil d'apres ses discours et sa correspondance. |
| 51-639 | Villon et Baudelaire, poetes de Paris. |
| 52-552 | Les milieux anti-sociaux dans les romans de Francis Carco. |
| 52-555 | Les theories de la psychologie du langage et leurs rapports avec les modes d'expression litteraires contemporains. |
| 52-601 | Le moyen age dans "Notre-Dame de Paris'. |
| 52-602 | Les heroines du theatre de Maeterlinck. |
| 52-608 | Paroles de vivant: la poesie de Saint-John Perse. |
| 52-610 | Le vocabulaire de la correspondance de Gustave Flaubert de 1854 a 1862. |
| 53-553 | Trois formes de l'heroisme dans la litterature contemporaine: Bernancs, Malraux, Saint-Exupery. |
| 53-613 | L'esthetique de la Fontaine. |
| 53-620 | L'ordre unanimiste de la guerre et le tableau des combattants dans "Les hommes de bonne volonte'. |
| 54-609 | L'art de la nouvelle chez Prosper Merimee. |
| 54-616 | Candide chez les anglophones. |
| 54-627 | Le heros contre le milieu dans le roman canadien-fran]ais de 1938-1950. |
| 55-554 | Victor Hugo et le voyage de 1840 en Allemagne. |
| 55-558 | Voltaire et les Quakers. |
| 56-002 | Eugene Dabit, sa vie et son oeuvre. |
| 56-057 | Le mythe d'Orphee dans la litterature fran]aise contemporaine. |
| 56-546 | Le jeu de l'illusion et de la realite dans l'oeuvre de Jean Giraudoux. |
| 56-617 | Les heroines d'Anouilh. |
| 57-546 | Gilbert Cesbron: romancier chretien et critique du monde moderne. |

| THESIS | THESIS TITLE |
|---|---|
| **French** | |
| 58-539 | Chateaubriand et le merveilleux chretien dans Les martyrs. |
| 58-540 | L'enfance dans "Les hommes de bonne volonte' de Jules Romains. |
| 58-547 | L'homme et la mer dans l'oeuvre d'Edouard Peisson. |
| 58-548 | L'annee 1745 dans la vie et l'oeuvre de Voltaire. |
| 58-586 | Les artistes dans A la recherche du temps perdu. |
| 59-550 | Edouard Estaunie et la vie secrete. |
| 59-555 | L'humanisme de Jean Guehenno. |
| 59-562 | La philosophie de Jean Giraudoux, auteur dramatique. |
| 59-605 | La terre, la mer et les hommes dans l'oeuvre d'Henri Queffelec. |
| 59-609 | Louis Pergaud, animalier. |
| **French Language & Literature** | |
| 37-521 | Etude sur Antoine Frederic Ozanam. |
| 37-524 | L'etude du paysan dans l'oeuvre de Rene Bazin. |
| 37-529 | La langue francaise en Louisiane. |
| 37-531 | L'ecolier et le lyceen dans la litterature francaise contemporaine. |
| 37-532 | Les histoires d'animaux dans la litterature canadienne anglaise. |
| 37-545 | Le cadre et le milieu dans les romans d'Edouard Estaunie. |
| 39-042 | L'influence de Jean-Jacques Rousseau sur la litterature enfantine de 1762 a 1830. |
| 39-046 | Le traditionalisme de Rene Bazin. |
| 40-031 | L'histoire dans la poesie canadienne-francaise de 18601900. |
| 41-511 | La pensee religieuse dans le theatre de Francois de Curel. |

| THESIS | THESIS TITLE |
|---|---|
| **French Language & Literature** | |
| 41-514 | Deux philosophes francais et le renouveau thomiste: l'esprit medieval dans les ceuvres de M. Gilson et de M. Maritair. |
| 42-035 | Les Etats-Unis de 1919 a 1939 vus par les ecrivains francais contemporains. |
| **Genetics** | |
| 23-510 | A study of the genotypic composition of a natural hybrid between Avena sativa and Avena nuda. |
| 35-030 | Cyto-genetic studies of steriloid and sub-fatucid oats. |
| 35-033 | Observations upon chromosome associations. |
| 36-511 | Inheritance studies of earliness, bunt resistance, awns and phenol colour reaction in a spring wheat cross. |
| 36-517 | Cyto-genetic studies of compactoid and speltoid mutations in Triticum vulgare Host. |
| 37-011 | The direction of coiling in the chromonemata of Trillium erectum L. |
| 38-009 | The relation between chromosome behaviour and susceptibility to mammar+ gland cancer in mice. |
| 38-017 | Further studies in the cyto-genetics of compactoid and speltoid mutations in Triticum vulgare host. |
| 39-015 | Chromosome studies in the Liliaceae. I. Chromatid and chiasma interference in Trillium erectum L. |
| 39-024 | Chromosome mutations in avena. |
| 39-027 | The structure and behaviour of chromosomes during meiosis in Trillium erectum L. |
| 40-517 | The interlocking of non-homologous bivalents in Trillium erectum L. |
| 41-016 | Studies on the chromosome spiralization cycle in Trillium. |
| 41-039 | The effects of X chromosome inversions on crossing-over in the third chromosome of Drosophila melanogaster. |
| 41-042 | On the behaviour of the univalents of certain aberrant wheats during microsporogenesis. |
| 41-052 | The expression of rhino, hairless and naked genes in the house mouse. |
| 43-002 | Differential reactivity in the chromosomes of Trillium species. |

| THESIS | THESIS TITLE |
|---|---|
| Genetics | |
| 43-503 | Situs inversus viscerum completus: significance and etiology. |
| 43-520 | An investigation of the cytology of native and Russian species of the genus Taraxacum. |
| 45-004 | The expression and interaction of hereditary factors affecting hair growth in mice. |
| 45-015 | The sexual reproduction of trillium, T. erectum L., T. grandiflorum (Michx) Salisb. |
| 45-527 | A developmental comparison of the normal and wild type floret in avena. |
| 45-528 | An investigation of the relationship of body colour and susceptibility to D.D.T. in Drosophilia melanogaster. |
| 45-538 | Studies on the toxicity of D.D.T. to mice. |
| 48-580 | (a) Lens rupture: a new recessive gene in the mouse. (b) Heredity cataract in mice. |
| 49-528 | The evaluation of the breeding potential of full sisters in the domestic fowl. |
| 49-540 | The effect of fostering on the growth pattern of the house mouse. |
| 50-539 | The inheritance of the growth pattern and certain body characteristics in reciprocal crosses of broad breasted Bronze-Charlevoix turkeys. |
| 50-618 | Some experimental studies on the coat pattern of mice using the skin transplantation technique. |
| 51-054 | The twin method and its application to the study of genetic and environmental factors of some human diseases. |
| 51-516 | The action and use of colchicine in the production of tetraploid fagopyrum esculentum. |
| 51-525 | Genetic and physiological differences in the spermatozoa of the domestic fowl. |
| 51-606 | Effects of the administration of cortisone during pregnancy on mice and their offspring. |
| 51-611 | Incidence, inheritance, and significance of the taste reaction to phenylthiocarbamide (PTO). |
| 52-064 | Cytology of caryopsis development in Triticum-Agropyron amphiploids. |
| 52-537 | Mitotic frequencies in the ganglia of larval stages of Musca domestica L. and Drino bohemica Mesnil. |
| 52-581 | Studies in the inheritance of persistency in the lactation of dairy cows. |

| THESIS | THESIS TITLE |
|---|---|
| **Genetics** | |
| 52-597 | Somatic chromosome numbers in the mouse. |
| 52-599 | Determination of the locus of miniature dominant, a new allele of Drosophila melanogaster. |
| 53-016 | The genetics and physiology of susceptibility to the teratogenic effects of cortisone in mice. |
| 54-029 | Fertility in diploid and tetraploid red clover. |
| 54-072 | Genetico-embryological studies on normal and cleft palates in mice. |
| 54-534 | Sex ratio of the offspring of ex-irradiated or nitrogen mustard treated male mice. |
| 55-066 | Cytology and correlated morphology of the genus Neodiprion Rohwer (Hemenoptera: Symphyta). |
| 56-570 | Factors in the experimental production of congenital cleft palate in mice by cortisone and other agents. |
| 57-004 | Genetics and cytotaxonomy in birdsfoot trefoil (Lotus corniculatus L.). |
| 58-050 | Genetic and other factors influencing the pathogenesis of cleft palate in mice. |
| 58-534 | The effect of lead compounds on the metabolism of the central nervous system. |
| 59-052 | Experimental and clinical approaches to the biology of congenital defect. |
| **Geography** | |
| 49-514 | The modification of continental polar air over Hudson's Bay and eastern Canada. |
| 49-623 | The physical geography of the Avalon Peninsula of Newfoundland. |
| 49-637 | A sampling method for the study of rural land use. |
| 49-641 | The climate of Labrador and its effects on settlement. |
| 49-645 | The historical geography of the St. Maurice Valley. |
| 50-568 | The historical geography of the Saguenay Valley. |
| 50-604 | A traverse of the Romaine River. |
| 51-539 | The climate of the ablation-period on the Barnes ice cap, 1950. |

| THESIS | THESIS TITLE |
|---|---|
| **Geography** | |
| 51-566 | The North China plain: a regional study. |
| 51-573 | An isochronic study of Winnipeg and Montreal; peripheral and intervening areas. |
| 51-574 | The physical geography of the Two Mountains area, Quebec. |
| 51-623 | Geography of roads west of Lake Winnipeg inter lake area. |
| 51-640 | The human geography of the Lesser Slave Lake area of central Alberta. |
| 52-547 | A regional study of the Richelieu Valley. |
| 52-548 | The Hudson Bay lowland, a geographical study. |
| 52-549 | Land settlement in the Richelieu Valley. |
| 52-553 | The district of Brome. |
| 52-600 | A regional study of the Richelieu Valley: the urban centres. |
| 53-070 | General principles for the planning of sub-Arctic settlements. |
| 53-554 | Population distribution in the Riding Mountains, Duck Mountains, and adjacent plains in Manitoba and Saskatchewan, 1870-1946. |
| 53-574 | Vegetation and physiography of the Goose Bay area, Labrador. |
| 53-599 | An investigation of August maximum and minimum temperatures at Torbay, Newfoundland. |
| 53-605 | A geomorphological study of the Stanstead area, Quebec. |
| 54-021 | The physiography and glaciology of southernmost Baffin Island. |
| 54-026 | Glacial-meteorolcgical observations on icecaps in Baffin Island. |
| 54-070 | Pangnirtung Pass, Baffin Island: an exploratory regional geomorphology. |
| 54-548 | The island of Senja in north Norway: an analysis of the fishing and farming occupations and their combination. |
| 54-555 | Industrial geography of the Beauharnois canal zone. |

| THESIS | THESIS TITLE |
|---|---|
| **Geography** | |
| 55-046 | Areal differentiation of the manufacturing belt in central Canada. |
| 55-521 | Some aspects of Pleistocene and post-glacial climate change in central Alaska. |
| 55-630 | A study of the factors which have determined the present stage of economic development in Jamaica. |
| 55-638 | A study of geography in the intelligence service. |
| 55-639 | A federated British Caribbean: resource utilisation. |
| 56-011 | The means of improving the economic situation of the Ungava Bay Eskimos. |
| 56-017 | Oraefi, south-east Iceland: an essay in regional geomorphology. |
| 56-037 | Lower tropospheric inversions at Ice Island T-3. |
| 56-547 | Sept-Iles: Canada's newest seaport. |
| 56-584 | Forest types of the Kenamu-Kenemich drainage basin, Labrador: an interpretation of cover types from an aerial photograph mosaic. |
| 56-588 | A geographical study of the south shore of Coronation Gulf between 111°00' W. and 115°45' W. |
| 56-624 | The settlement of the Victoria region, British Columbia. |
| 57-037 | A geographical analysis of population trends in Newfoundland. |
| 57-085 | Development of slopes in central New Quebec-Labrador. |
| 57-532 | Soils and agricultural possibilities of the Knob Lake area, P.Q. |
| 57-590 | Evapotranspiration studies at Knob Lake, Quebec, June-Sept. 1956. |
| 57-603 | The Lachine Canal. |
| 57-606 | L'amenagement des villes a industrie extractive du subarctique. |
| 58-525 | Pressure-contour variance and kinetic energy over the Arctic. |
| 58-535 | Synoptic regimes in the lower Arctic troposphere during 1955. |
| 59-017 | Physiography and vegetation of the Albany River map area, northern Ontario: an aerial photograph reconnaissance. |

| THESIS | THESIS TITLE |
|---|---|
| **Geography** | |
| 59-081 | The development of settlement in the Fairbanks area, Alaska: a study of permanence. |
| 59-522 | Insolation and albedo in Quebec-Labrador. |
| 59-535 | Glacial-meteorological studies in north Ellesmere Island, 1958. |
| 59-537 | Geomorphological studies in the Lake Hazen area, N.W.T. |
| 59-549 | Hammerfest, Norway: a study in historical geography. |
| 59-552 | Mining activities in Labrador-Ungava. |
| 59-560 | A land use survey of the Upper St. John River Valley in New Brunswick. |
| 59-575 | The bogs of central Labrador-Ungava: an examination of their physical characteristics. |
| 59-576 | A synoptic climatology for Labrador-Ungava. |
| 59-594 | The climatic conditions affecting the vegetation of the Lake Hazen area, Ellesmere Island, N.W.T. |
| 59-598 | Evapotranspiration at Point Barrow, Alaska, summer 1956. |
| 59-617 | An analysis of geographical factors determining the northern limits of the pulp and paper industry in Northern Ontario. |
| **Geological Sciences** | |
| 08-508 | (A) petrographical study of the rocks of Mount Royal. |
| 08-512 | On an occurence of tin ores and associated minerals in Nova Scotia, with a comparative study of tin deposits in other parts of the world. |
| 09-513 | The origin and relations of the Paleozoic breccia of the vicinity of Montreal. |
| 10-001 | Preliminary report on a portion of the coast of British Columbia and the islands adjacent thereto in the Nanaimo district. |
| 10-519 | The diamond-bearing rocks of South Africa. |
| 12-518 | Contributions to the knowledge of the Monteregian petrographical province. |
| 13-516 | Geology of an area in the vicinity of Gull and Olga Lakes, northwestern Quebec. |

| THESIS | THESIS TITLE |
|---|---|
| Geological Sciences | |
| 16-515 | Geology and some of the mineral resources of China. |
| 21-505 | 33 papers and reports. |
| 22-512 | Some outlines of the Montereqian hills. |
| 23-503 | The genesis of the deposits of dolomite and magnesite in Grenville and Olatham Townships, P.Q. |
| 23-505 | The differential flotation of lead, zinc, iron, sulphide ores, employing sub-aeration, i.e. Callow methods, and a comparison of the above with methods based on intermittant mechanical agitation. |
| 24-002 | The Devonian volcanic series in the vicinity of Dalhousie, N.B. |
| 24-506 | Dykes encountered in Mount Royal tunnel. |
| 24-508 | The geology of the Outsider Mine, Portland, B.C. |
| 24-524 | Dykes of Mount Royal tunnel from the West Portal to Station 284+99. |
| 24-526 | Absorption of inclusions of potsdam sandstone by alkalic magma, Mount Royal Heights, Montreal. |
| 24-531 | Dyke rocks of Mount Royal tunnel between East Portal and Station 182-90. |
| 25-513 | Petrographical study of rocks and ores from the Sullivan Mine, Kimberley, B.C. |
| 25-530 | The geology of the tin deposits of Cornwall. |
| 28-502 | A petrographic study of a zinc prospect in Bouchette Township, Que. |
| 28-512 | Petrographic study of the Aldermac mine. |
| 28-524 | The geology of the central mineral belt of Newfoundland: a collation and contribution. |
| 29-013 | Assimilation and petrogrenesis; separation of ores from magmas. |
| 29-505 | A petrographic study of certain corderite-bearing rocks . |
| 29-508 | Investigation of lead-zinc replacements in limestone where there is no apparent connection with igneous activity. |
| 29-510 | The manganese deposits of Tchiatonsi, Georgia, Russia. |

| THESIS | THESIS TITLE |
|---|---|
| Geological Sciences | |
| 30-515 | A detailed petrographic study of ten mile rock occurrence, Hall's Bay Road, Nfld. |
| 31-508 | The whitemud sediments of southern Saskatchewan. |
| 31-518 | The petrology of some crystalline rocks of the Perth Sheet, Ontario. |
| 32-509 | The geology and petrography of a section along the tramway, Mount Royal, Montreal, P. Que. |
| 32-513 | The petrology of certain igneous rocks of Newton township, Ontario. |
| 32-514 | A study of the geology in the vicinity of Corporation Quarry, Mt. Royal, Montreal. |
| 33-004 | Geology of the district about Lake Aylmer, Eastern Townships, Province of Quebec: a report on a detailed investigation of a typical part of this section of the Appalachian region. |
| 33-016 | The geology and ore deposits of the Horne Mine, Noranda, Quebec. |
| 33-025 | The origin and occurrence of the chromite deposits of the Eastern Townships, Quebec. |
| 33-510 | The nature and origin of the glacial and post-glacial deposits lying between the city of Montreal and the Canadian Shield. |
| 33-512 | An investigation of the mineral composition of the ores of Noranda Mines, Limited. |
| 33-516 | The Black River group in the vicinity of Montreal. |
| 33-518 | The pre-carboniferous rocks of the Wentworth section of the Cobequid Hills, N.S. |
| 33-529 | Geology of the Waite-Aikerman-Montgomery property, Duprat and Dufresnoy Townships, Que. |
| 33-533 | A petrological study of Mt. Johnson, Que. |
| 34-006 | The geology and mineral deposits of the Beattie-Galatea area. |
| 34-009 | The geology of the Black River group in the vicinity of Montreal. |
| 34-016 | Igneous rocks of Duprat Lake and Rouyn Lake areas, Quebec. |
| 34-516 | The geology and petrography of Viewmount Ave., Westmount. |
| 34-517 | Pyrrhotite in rocks and mineral deposits. |

| THESIS | THESIS TITLE |
|---|---|
| Geological Sciences | |
| 41-014 | The Flavrian Lake map area and the structural geology of the surrounding district. |
| 42-003 | The Bell River igneous complex. |
| 43-504 | The geology of the lower Lorraine in the vicinity of Montreal. |
| 45-506 | The gold deposits of Fifteen Mile Stream, Nova Scotia. |
| 46-566 | The geology of the Formaque property, Bourlamaque township, Quebec. |
| 46-572 | The place of experimental work in the study of rock structures. |
| 47-001 | Geology of the Burlington peninsula, Newfoundland. |
| 47-021 | The Canica-Cawatose map area. |
| 47-024 | The geology of the Goldfields area, Saskatchewan. |
| 47-513 | The acidic intrusives of the Bachelor Lake area. |
| 47-515 | The east ore zone at Giant Yellowknife Mine, N.W.T.: |
| 47-518 | Critical review of criteria used in the nomenclature and classification of sandstones. |
| 47-522 | The stratigraphy and structure of the Mistassini series in the Lake Albanel area. |
| 47-527 | The geology of the St. Dominique Ridge, Bagot county, Que. |
| 47-544 | Porcupine-Beattie gold belt. |
| 47-552 | The acidic plutonic rocks of the Iserhoff River area. |
| 47-555 | The mineralogy of the St. Charles phosphatic titaniferous magnetite deposit. |
| 47-573 | Pershing Township map area. |
| 48-021 | Geology and petrology of the anorthosite and associated rocks of the Chertsey map area. |
| 48-518 | Faulting in the St. Lawrence plain. |
| 48-530 | A study of the diabase dykes of the Canadian Shield. |

| THESIS | THESIS TITLE |
|---|---|
| Geological Sciences | |
| 48-532 | A cobalt-tungsten deposit in the Sudbury district. |
| 48-538 | The geology of the northern part of the east shore of Great Bear Lake, N.W.T. |
| 48-545 | A tectonic map of southern British Columbia. |
| 48-547 | A study of erosion surfaces in the southern part of the Eastern Townships of Quebec. |
| 48-554 | An investigation of the Good Hope Mine, Hedley, B.C. |
| 48-576 | The Athabaska series at Beaverlodge Lake, Saskatchewan. |
| 48-604 | Micro-chemical methods for mineral determination. |
| 49-012 | The geology of the Capsisit Lake area, Abitibi, Quebec. |
| 49-022 | Geology of the Bourget map area, Chicoutimi county, Quebec. |
| 49-057 | The stratigraphy and paleontology of the upper cretaceous rocks. |
| 49-511 | A study of lime-rich metamorphic rocks from Cree Lake, Manitoba. |
| 49-512 | Archean sediments in the Canadian Shield. |
| 49-524 | Geology of the Jeep Mine, Rice Lake district, Manitoba. |
| 49-537 | The pegmatites of Otter Rapids area, Ontario. |
| 49-551 | The structure and stratigraphy of the Sherbrooke formation in the Memphremagog area, Eastern Townships, Quebec. |
| 49-595 | Paleogeological studies in the Maritime provinces. |
| 49-603 | The geology of the Premier (Transvaal) Diamond Mine. |
| 49-621 | A study of some intrusive rocks and replacement phenomena in the Salmon Arm area, B.C. (Shuswap terrane). |
| 50-008 | The Olga-Geoland Lake area, Abitibi-East county. |
| 50-009 | Geology of the Howson Creek area, Slocal Mining division, B.C. |

| THESIS | THESIS TITLE |
|---|---|
| Geological Sciences | |
| 50-011 | A study of part of the Kaniapiskau system northwest of Attilamagen Lake, New Quebec. |
| 50-013 | The geology of the Ymir map-area, British Columbia. |
| 50-020 | The geology of the Red Deer area, Alberta, with particular reference to the geomorphology and water supply. |
| 50-039 | The geology of the MacLeod-Cockshutt Gold Mine, Little Long Lac, Ontario. |
| 50-513 | The Hay River limestone, North West Territories. |
| 50-522 | The Huronian rocks of northwestern Ontario. |
| 50-523 | The iron formation of Snelgrove Lake, Labrador. |
| 50-529 | Structural studies in an area at the headwaters of the McMurdo Creek, B.C. |
| 50-532 | The Mina Lake graywacke, Sawyer Lake area, Labrador. |
| 50-533 | A petrographic study of basic sills intruding the Howse Series, Labrador. |
| 50-538 | A critical study of the statistical method in paleontology. |
| 50-545 | Some problems in correlation in northwestern Quebec. |
| 50-557 | Petrographic methods of determining the source of clastic sediments. |
| 50-562 | The Cambray Discovery Dyke and associated uranium deposits. |
| 50-595 | Geology of the Balachey Lake area, Northwest Territories. |
| 50-605 | Map-area west of Timmins Bay, Lake Attikamagen, Labrador. |
| 50-620 | A copper-nickel occurrence in Pardee Township, Thunder Bay district, Ontario. |
| 50-635 | Copper-nickel sulphide deposits of the Bird River, Manitoba and Werner Lake, Ontario areas. |
| 51-011 | The petrology of the Kimberlites at the Premier (Transvaal) Diamond Mine, South Africa. |
| 51-025 | Geology of the Nelson and adjoining part of Salmo map areas, British Columbia. |
| 51-031 | Occurrence of nickel in igneous rocks. |

| THESIS | THESIS TITLE |
|---|---|
| Geological Sciences | |
| 51-048 | The geolcgy of the Carimiti River area, Pontiac Ccunty, Quebec. |
| 51-052 | The geology of Duprat Township and some adjacent areas, northwest Quebec. |
| 51-522 | A petrographic study of the serpentinized peridotites of the Griffis Lake map area, Quebec. |
| 51-537 | Igneous dyke rocks of the Aillik-Makkovik area, Labrador. |
| 51-540 | The quartz deposits of the Watshishou Knoll area on the north shore cf the St. Lawrence River. |
| 51-544 | The bedrock geolcgy of Makkovik and its relations to the Aillik and Kaipokck series. |
| 51-549 | A petrographic study of the Copper Cliff offser, Sudbury district, Ontario. |
| 51-552 | The barite deposit at Brookfield, Nova Scotia. |
| 51-555 | Glacial features in the vicinity of Knob Lake, Labrador. |
| 51-556 | The petrology of the serpentine bodies in the Matheson district, Ontario. |
| 51-559 | Structural relations in the Greenville province. |
| 51-563 | The Lucy orebody: its petrology, structure, and origin; Michipiccten district, Ontario, Canada. |
| 51-594 | The McDougall-Segur conglomerate. |
| 51-598 | The geolcgy of the Lake Wasa property, Beauchastel Township, Quebec. |
| 51-602 | The petrology of some syenites and granites in Labrador. |
| 51-620 | A study of the cobalt sediments of Dasserat Township, Quebec. |
| 52-010 | A study of the Kaniapiskau system in the Burnt Creek-Goodwood area, New Quebec and Labrador, Newfoundland. |
| 52-011 | Geology of the Perth map-area, Lanark and Leeds ccunties, Ontario. |
| 52-012 | Geological settings of malartic gold deposits, P.Q. |
| 52-022 | The geology of Scuthern Pascalis township with special reference to the luminescence of certain minerals of the eruptive rocks. |

| THESIS | THESIS TITLE |
|---|---|
| Geological Sciences | |
| 52-024 | Ordovician palaeontology and stratigraphy of the Churchill and Nelson rivers, Manitoba. |
| 52-027 | Geology of the Thetford-Black Lake district of Quebec, with special reference to the asbestos deposits. |
| 52-030 | The stratigraphy, structure, and certain mineral deposits at the headwaters of the Spillimacheen River, B.C. |
| 52-039 | The geology of the Forget Lake and Nevins Lake map-areas, northern Saskatchewan. |
| 52-513 | The geology of the Buchans Junction area, Newfoundland. |
| 52-520 | The geology of part of the Three Rivers map area, Quebec. |
| 52-525 | Acid intrusives of the Thetford Mines-Black Lake area. |
| 52-526 | The tinguaite and related dike rocks of Rosemount quarry. |
| 52-533 | Study of the Hornfels collar around Mount Bruno. |
| 52-535 | The Birch Lake copper deposit, Saskatchewan. |
| 52-536 | A study of certain Canadian building and monumental stones of igneous origin. |
| 52-542 | The geology of the Round Pond map area, Newfoundland. |
| 52-574 | Distribution of acid volcanics in the Superior province of the Canadian Shield. |
| 53-001 | Geology of the Big Berry Mountains map-area, Gaspe peninsula, Quebec. |
| 53-004 | Geology of the Johan Beetz area, Saguenay County, Que. |
| 53-011 | The geology of the Nipissis River and Nipisso Lake map-areas. |
| 53-019 | The Precambrian and Pleistocene geology of the Grondines map-area, Quebec. |
| 53-020 | Experimental studies in rheomorphism. |
| 53-021 | Peridotites of northwestern Quebec. |
| 53-034 | Wall rock alteration around base metal sulphide deposits of northwestern Quebec. |

| THESIS | THESIS TITLE |
|---|---|
| Geological Sciences | |
| 53-080 | The Lumby Lake greenstone belt. |
| 53-081 | The iron bearing formations of the Michipiccten area, Ontario. |
| 53-528 | Wall-rock alteration cf the Bridge River vein deposits. |
| 53-534 | A study of post-Pleistocene deposits around Mounts St. Hilaire, St. Bruno, Johnson and Rougemont, Quebec. |
| 53-535 | Petrofabric studies from the Shawbridge area, Quebec. |
| 53-537 | A petrographic study of the base of the intermediate siltstone, Sullivan Mine, Kimberley, British Columbia. |
| 53-570 | Some aspects of stress-strain theories and their use in the interpretation of the fracture patterns in rocks. |
| 53-583 | The distribution of Na, K, Ca, Mg, Fe in metasomatic zones bordering diorite intrusives, and zones of sulphide mineralization, using a revised analytical technique in flame. |
| 53-590 | Feldspar deposits of the Johan Beitz area. |
| 54-008 | The geology of Malartic Gold Fields mine. |
| 54-033 | Geology of the Truro map-area, Colchester and Hants counties, Ncva Scotia. |
| 54-036 | A study of the Witwatersrand system. |
| 54-057 | Experimental work bearing on the origin of hydrous nickel-magnesium silicate minerals. |
| 54-058 | Wall rock alteration in the vicinity of base metal sulphide depcsits in the Eastern Townships of Quebec. |
| 54-061 | Geology of O'Connor Lake area, Northwest Territories with special reference to the mineral deposits. |
| 54-510 | A study of the internal fractures caused by the deformation of scale models of geological structures. |
| 54-512 | The Dunham dolomite near St. Armand, Quebec. |
| 54-518 | The metamorphic collar in the sediments around Mount Royal. |

| THESIS | THESIS TITLE |
|---|---|
| Geological Sciences | |
| 54-526 | The sulphides and siderite of the Mathieu property, Kewatin Lake area, District of Kenora, Ont. |
| 54-527 | Chazy corals and reefs. |
| 54-528 | Ghost River and related formations between the Athabaska and Smoky Rivers, Alberta. |
| 54-538 | Geology of the Candego Mine, Gaspe North County, Quebec. |
| 54-578 | The geology of the Suffield Mine, Sherbrooke, Que. |
| 54-584 | A petrological study of the Munro asbestos "A' orebody, Matheson, Ont. |
| 55-014 | Petrology of the gneisses of the Clyde area, Baffin Island. |
| 55-022 | Semi-micro fossils of the Black River and Trenton groups of Quebec. |
| 55-028 | The geology of part of the "Labrador Trough' south of Leaf Lake, New Quebec. |
| 55-042 | The petrology of the serpentine bodies in the Matheson District, Ontario. |
| 55-049 | Geology of the northwest quarter of Holland Township, Gaspe North, Quebec. |
| 55-069 | A new calorimetric method for determining heats of solution of minerals, and its application. |
| 55-513 | The formation of certain granite-like rocks in the footwall of the Sudbury norite, northwest of the Sudbury Basin. |
| 55-525 | A petrographic study of part of the Potsdam sandstone core from the Mallet Well, Ste. Therese, Que. |
| 55-538 | The mineralogy of the eastern metals nickel-copper deposit. |
| 55-539 | Dispersion of copper, lead, and zinc from mineralized zones in an area of moderate relief as indicated by soils and plants. |
| 55-540 | A detailed investigation of the petrology and ore textures of Mogador Mines Limited. |
| 55-542 | Chert in the ordovician of southern Quebec. |
| 55-587 | Investigation into the chemical composition of the upper part of the Cape Bon Ami formation and the lower part of the Grande Greve formation. |
| 55-599 | The basic intrusives of the Wacc Lake area, Saguenay County, P.Q. |

| THESIS | THESIS TITLE |
|---|---|
| Geological Sciences | |
| 55-605 | Geology of the Stony Rapids norite area northern Saskatchewan. |
| 55-612 | The geology of the Little River area, Baie d'Espoir, Newfoundland. |
| 55-615 | A study of Porphyry Mountain, Holland Township, Quebec. |
| 56-001 | The geology of the Woodstock and Millville areas, New Brunswick. |
| 56-006 | Rock alteration and primary base metal dispersion at Barvue, Golden Manitou and New Calumet Mines, Quebec. |
| 56-013 | The geology of the Ste. Justine map-area. |
| 56-023 | The geology of an area between Pigou and Sheldrake Rivers, Saguenay County, Quebec, with a detailed study of the anorthosites. |
| 56-040 | The physical stability of natrolite. |
| 56-042 | An experimental study of the effects of heat, pressure and fluids on sedimentary meterials. |
| 56-066 | Adsorption of copper, lead, and zinc on some common rock forming minerals and its effect on lake sediments. |
| 56-067 | Geology of the Tetagouche group, Bathurst, New Brunswick. |
| 56-069 | The geology of the Williamson Diamond Mine, Mwadui, Tanganyika. |
| 56-517 | The geology of the eastern border of the Labrador Trough, east of Thevenet Lake, New Quebec. |
| 56-520 | Anorthosites and syenites of the Mealy Mountain area, Labrador. |
| 56-522 | Anorthosite-ilmenite-pegmatite relations on the west bank of La Chalcupe River, Saguenay Co., P.Q. |
| 56-527 | The quartz deposit at St. Donat, Quebec. |
| 56-529 | The geology of the St. Pierre Prospect, Fort Chimo district, Quebec. |
| 56-530 | A study of the relation of the Earth's field as presented on aeromagnetic maps to the geology in Beauce area, Quebec. |
| 56-576 | The geology and mineralization of the Pegma Lake area in New Quebec. |

| THESIS | THESIS TITLE |
|---|---|
| **Geological Sciences** | |
| 57-011 | Geology of the Beraud-Mazerac area, Quebec. |
| 57-019 | The petrology of gabbroic sills in the volcanic series of Roy and McKenzie Townships, Chibougamau Region, Quebec. |
| 57-026 | The geology of the Addington-Preston area. |
| 57-028 | The geology of the Cumberland Sound region, Baffin Island. |
| 57-032 | Base metal deposits in the "Labrador Trough' between Lake Harveng and Lac Aulneua, New Quebec. |
| 57-047 | Hydrothermal experiments with variable pore pressure and shear stress in part of the MgO2-SiO2-H2O system. |
| 57-053 | The geology of the Wacouno region, Saguenay Co., P.Q. |
| 57-057 | Geology of Dungannon and Mayo-Townships in southeastern Ontario. |
| 57-063 | Experiments bearing on the genesis of sulphide deposits. |
| 57-068 | A chemical, optical and x-ray study of certain zeolites. |
| 57-520 | Geology of the Grey River area, Newfoundland, with special reference to metamorphism. |
| 57-535 | A study of the Ordovician conglomerates near Matane, Que. |
| 57-536 | A method for determining the solubility of sulphides. |
| 57-543 | A petrographic study of the "granite wash' in the Clear Hills area, Alberta. |
| 58-002 | The geology of the East Sullivan Deposit, Val d'Or, Quebec. |
| 58-006 | The stratigraphy and palaeontology of the Beekmantown group in the St. Lawrence lowlands, Quebec. |
| 58-009 | Ordovician ostracoda from the St. Lawrence lowlands of Quebec. |
| 58-029 | The geology of the Mount Logan area, Gaspe, Quebec. |
| 58-508 | Some aspects of atmosphere-earth energy relationships. |
| 58-509 | Dispersion in humus and moss, of zinc, copper, nickel and lead, from a glaciated precambrian terrain. |

| THESIS | THESIS TITLE |
|---|---|
| Geological Sciences | |
| 58-511 | A petrographic study of the metamorphic rocks of Little Manicouagan Lake area. |
| 58-515 | A compositional study of calcareous Lorraine sedimentary rocks. |
| 58-518 | A study of metamorphic strata near Port Chimo, northern Quebec. |
| 58-519 | Peridotites of northern Quebec and Ungava. |
| 58-523 | The geology of the Goshen Copper Prospect, Goshen, New Brunswick. |
| 58-526 | The chemistry, mineralogy, and metamorphism of the standing pond amphibolite, Hanover quadrangle, New Hampshire-Vermont. |
| 58-527 | The geology of the area between Carol Lake and Wabush Lake, Labrador. |
| 58-529 | Geology of the McOuat-Gauvin area, Mistassini territory and Roberval electoral district, Quebec. |
| 59-003 | The mineralogy of the New Brunswick sulphide deposits. |
| 59-011 | Phase relations in the Fe-As-S system. |
| 59-014 | Some experiments on surface and strain energy in minerals. |
| 59-036 | A mineralogical study of pyrochlore and betafite. |
| 59-037 | Building and industrial stones of eastern Canada. |
| 59-038 | The geology of the Campbell Chibougamau Mine, Quebec. |
| 59-044 | A study of the paleomagnetism of rocks from Yamaska and Brome Mountains, Quebec. |
| 59-050 | The geology of the Seal Lake area, central Labrador. |
| 59-051 | Experiments with copper sulphides at elevated temperatures. |
| 59-063 | The clearwater copper-zinc deposit and its setting, with a special study of mineral zoning around such deposits. |
| 59-512 | The geology of the Weedon Pyrite and Copper Corporation Limited mine. |
| 59-517 | Mobility of certain sulphides in sulphur vapour. |

| THESIS | THESIS TITLE |
|---|---|
| **Geological Sciences** | |
| 59-519 | Growth of sulphides in black shales. |
| 59-520 | The occurrence and petrology of basic intrusions in the northern Mackenzie Mountains, Yukon and North West Territories. |
| 59-524 | Geology of the west half of La Motte Township, Quebec. |
| 59-526 | The geology of the Forsyth and associated magnetite deposits, Hull Township, province of Quebec. |
| 59-539 | Iron formations and associated rocks in the Mount Wright area, (Quebec). |
| 59-541 | The geology of the Henderson Copper deposit, Chibougamau Region, Quebec. |
| 59-599 | Sorption of copper, lead, and zinc on American Petroleum Institute reference clays K-4, M-23, and M-25. |
| **Geology** | |
| 01-004 | Certain gabbros and nephthaline syenites of the townships of Monmouth and Glamorgan, Ontario. |
| 02-001 | A petrographical study of the township of Wollaston, Ontario. |
| 06-005 | The influence of the geological structure of Palestine on the development of Jewish history. |
| 35-013 | The origin of the intrusive igneous breccias in the vicinity of Montreal, Quebec. |
| 35-018 | Geology of an area near Shawinigan Falls, Quebec. |
| 35-511 | The petrology of Grenville limestone contacts with certain intrusives. |
| 36-002 | The geology and mineral deposits of the Night Hawk Lake area, Ont. |
| 36-509 | The Sillery Formation in the vicinity of Granby, Quebec. |
| 36-512 | The petrology of a part of Westmount Mountain near Summit Circle, Montreal. |
| 36-549 | The geology of the Buffalo Ankerite Gold Mines, Ltd. |
| 37-004 | The dolomitic magnesite of Grenville Township, Argenteuil Co., P. Que. |
| 37-014 | Geology of the augmentation of Grenville Township, Que. |

| THESIS | THESIS TITLE |
|---|---|
| Geology | |
| 37-504 | The petrography of a section of Westmount Mountain. |
| 37-508 | The Sydney coalfield. |
| 37-511 | Microscopical investigation of certain Quebec ores. Part A. Technique of investigation. |
| 38-005 | Guillet Township map area. |
| 38-506 | The geology of the vicinity of Bralorne Mines, B.C. |
| 38-509 | A description of the Kaniapiskau Series, upper Hamilton River, Newfoundland-Labrador: with a petrographic description of the Dyke Lake volcanics. |
| 38-511 | The Aldermac syenite porphyry stock, Que. |
| 38-516 | The geology of the Orland property, Beauchastel Township, P.Que. |
| 38-517 | The geology of a section of Mount Royal, near the new building of the University of Montreal. |
| 38-518 | The geology of a section of Beauchastel Township, Que. |
| 39-028 | An investigation of the metamorphism of the Orijarvi type with special reference to the zinc-lead deposits at Montauban-lesMines, Que. |
| 39-058 | The geology of the lower 'A' ore-body, Waite-Amulet, as disclosed by diamond drilling. |
| 39-059 | The geology of the Fontana Gold Mines Property, Duverny Township, Quebec. |
| 39-068 | Geology of the Lake Rowan Gold Mines. |
| 39-069 | The petrology of a part of Mount Royal near Cote des Neiges Village. |
| 39-070 | Geology of the Amm Gold Mine, Cadillac Township, Quebec. |
| 39-501 | The geology of the Siscoe Gold Mines, Siscoe, Quebec. |
| 40-005 | The geology of the Empire Mine, Bralorne, B.C. |
| 40-010 | The Sydney coalfield. |
| 40-012 | The Windrum Lake area, Saskatchewan. |

| THESIS | THESIS TITLE |
|---|---|
| **Geology** | |
| 40-017 | Geology and Ore deposits of Barry Lake map-area, Northern Quebec. |
| 40-039 | A comparison of the non-opaque minerals of certain parts of the Waite-Amulet area, Quebec. |
| 40-040 | Geology of the Beaufor Mine. |
| 40-042 | The metamorphism of the Gordon Lake sediments, Northwest Territories. |
| 40-045 | A petrographic study of a basic intrusive sheet in the Yellowknife area, Northwest Territories. |
| 40-047 | The origin and economic possibilities of Canadian manganese deposits. |
| 40-050 | Rocks and rock alteration in part of the Malartic area, Quebec. |
| 41-037 | Mineralography of contrasting mineralization at Gaspe, Quebec. |
| 41-038 | Geology of chromite. |
| 41-045 | Geology of Calumet Mines Ltd. |
| 41-050 | Geology of a part of the north limb of the Marquette syncline. |
| 41-504 | The geology of the Francoeur-Arntfield district, Beauchastel Township, Quebec. |
| 41-524 | Faulting and ore deposition in the Rouyn-Bell River region. |
| 41-528 | Petrogenesis of the silicate minerals associated with copper ores, Gaspe, Quebec. |
| 42-064 | A study of the genus Baculites in the bearpaw formation of Western Canada. |
| **Geology & Mineralogy** | |
| 08-509 | On the properties of krohndite, dausonite and some other Canadian minerals. |
| 11-506 | The exomorphic contact actions of acid igneous intrusions. |
| 11-508 | The influence of igneous intrusions on the development of ore bodies of pneumatolitic origins. |
| 21-510 | The alteration of a quartz diabase dike at the Old Helen Mine. |
| 23-508 | A study of the dyke rocks in Mount Royal Tunnel between Stations 260+00 and 283+00. |

| THESIS | THESIS TITLE |
|---|---|
| Geology & Mineralogy | |
| 23-511 | Metamorphic zone of Mount Royal. |
| 24-510 | The oldest dykes of Mt. Royal, bostonites, tinguaites, etc., and their altered equivalents. |
| 24-514 | The nepheline syenites and pegmatites of Mt. Royal. |
| 25-511 | A petrographic study of the dyke rocks of the Anycx district, B.C. |
| 26-509 | A study of the genesis of the copper and other ores of the Eastern Townships of Quebec. |
| 27-002 | The geology of a section of the Wunnummin Lake area. |
| 27-009 | Geology of the Thurso area, Quebec and Ontario. |
| 27-517 | A study of some of the ignecus rocks and ores of the Slocan Mining District, B.C. |
| German | |
| 05-003 | A study of Goethe's "Faust'. |
| 10-504 | Die Entwicklung des Romans und der Erzahlung in der romantischen Schule. |
| 13-509 | Die deutsche Dorfgeschichte in ihren Haupttypen dargestellt. |
| 16-502 | Die patriotische Poesie der Deutschen im neunzehnten Jahrhundert. |
| 21-521 | Theodor Fontane als Romanschriftsteller. |
| 28-552 | Arthur Schnitzler: eine Studie. |
| 28-553 | P. Heyse und seine Falkentheorie. |
| 33-540 | Grillparzers Tragoedien. |
| 35-544 | Gottfried Keller als Erzahler. |
| 40-513 | A study of the life and works of Conrad Ferdinand Meyer. |
| 41-029 | Maltesches in Rilkes vor-Malteschem Werk. |
| 49-555 | Untersuchungen zu Goethes "Romischen Elegien'. |

| THESIS | THESIS TITLE |
|---|---|
| German | |
| 49-576 | Franz Kafka: der Einfluss des Vater-Sohn Verhaltnisses auf sein Werk. |
| 49-639 | Das Faust-Mephisto Verhaltnis im "Urfaust', "Fragment' und "Faust I'. |
| 51-635 | Studien zu Goethes Bearbeitung von Shakespeares "Romeo und Julia'. |
| 54-626 | Kritische Deutung der Stellungnahme Schillers zu Goethes "Egmont'. |
| 56-619 | Paris als Erlebnis zu Rilkes "3. Stundenbuch' und zu den "Aufzeichnungen des Malte Laurids Brigge'. |
| Greek | |
| 10-503 | The attitude of Euripides to the traditional religion of Greece. |
| 28-531 | Literary decadence and the Alexandrian Callimachus. |
| 28-544 | The idea of evolution in politics in the political writings of Aristotle. |
| 29-522 | The inter-relation between Attic tragedy and Greek art of the Classical period. |
| History | |
| 05-001 | The ecclesiastical policy of Henry IV of France. |
| 05-004 | Quebec in the seventeenth century, a study in social history. |
| 06-002 | Lee's invasion of the north in 1863. |
| 08-503 | Carleton and Burgoyne. |
| 08-504 | The negotiations between General Haldimand and the Allens of Vermont. |
| 08-505 | Quarrels of the religious in the thirteenth century. |
| 12-501 | Sir Bartle Frere's policy in South Africa. |
| 12-506 | A study of the Church of England in its relation to the state, 1688-1760. |
| 13-501 | The history of the Hay-Pauncefote treaty. |
| 13-502 | The first fifteen years of British administration in Montreal, 1760 to 1775. |

| THESIS | THESIS TITLE |
|---|---|
| **History** | |
| 13-512 | Canada's relations with China. |
| 20-512 | Changes in the industrial occupations of women in the environment of Montreal during the period of the war, 1914-1918. |
| 22-527 | Scottish sources of British liberalism. |
| 23-522 | Imperial Federation Movement with special reference to Canada. |
| 24-548 | Parliament in the time of Chaucer. |
| 25-535 | Lord Carteret and the Hanoverian policy of the Georges. |
| 25-538 | James Murray, the military initiator of British civil government in Canada. |
| 26-539 | Peter Martyr: a study in Italian influence upon the English Reformation principally in the reign of Edward VI. |
| 26-542 | The question of a separate Secretary of State for Scotland from the Union of 1707 to the Liberal administration of 1880. |
| 26-553 | British naval obligations to France involved in the Entente of 1904. |
| 27-522 | Lord Palmerston's policy of opposition to the project and to the construction of the Suez Canal. |
| 27-540 | Lord Palmerston's diplomatic partisanship in favour of the Confederate States during the American Civil War, April 1861, October 24, 1862. |
| 28-535 | Heresy in England in the fifteenth century. |
| 29-542 | The English philosophical radicals and Lower Canada, 1822-40. |
| 29-543 | The attitude of the Middle Ages towards animals. |
| 29-545 | Germany's acquisition of South-West Africa: a study in British imperial policy, 1880-1885. |
| 29-549 | Early negotiations for the acquisition of the Hudson's Bay territory by the Union government of Canada. |
| 30-537 | James McGill, a critical biographical study. |
| 30-541 | Fifty years of industrial transition in the British Navy - from sail to steam from wood to iron (1820-70). |

| THESIS | THESIS TITLE |
|---|---|
| **History** | |
| 30-556 | The Seat of Government question,1839-1859. |
| 31-547 | Francois Marie Perrot and the Ile Perrot. |
| 32-526 | Old age pensions: a study of opinion on the subject of state aid to necessitous old age in Great Britain. |
| 32-542 | Popular recreation in the Middle Ages. |
| 32-544 | The position and functions of the Justices of the Peace in England, 1600-1642. |
| 32-559 | Laud and the Church of England. |
| 32-560 | Traces of the influences of the Russo-Japanese War upon the the Chinese revolutionary movement, from 1904-1911. |
| 32-562 | Franklin and Canada. |
| 33-535 | John Neilson of Lower Canada, 1818-1828. |
| 34-533 | Economic development in French Canada, 1740-1760. |
| 35-547 | The struggle of the Church of Scotland for equal rights and privileges with the Church of England in Canada. |
| 36-543 | Social conditions in Nova Scotia, 1749-1783. |
| 37-519 | The origins of the Oxford Movement, with special reference to contemporary English social and intellectual conditions. |
| 37-520 | Economic conditions in Canada, 1763-1783. |
| 37-527 | The office of Receiver-General and its tenure by deputy in the Province of Quebec, 1763-1791. |
| 38-020 | French-Canadian Conservatism in principle and in practice, 1873-1891. |
| 38-539 | The fur trade of New France, down to 1663. |
| 38-554 | The Chartist incident on Kennington Common, April 10th, 1848, critically examined, more particularly in the light of the Home Office Papers at the Public Records Office, London. |
| 39-023 | The country justice in English local government during the first half of the seventeenth century. |

| THESIS | THESIS TITLE |
|---|---|
| History | |
| 41-023 | The county sheriff, 1600-1642. |
| 41-519 | British participation in the sanctions against Italy arising out of the Abyssinian War. |
| 42-503 | Economic development in New France - 1713-1760. |
| 43-022 | Jacob Mountain, first Lord Bishop of Quebec, 1793-1825: a study in Church and state. |
| 45-547 | The importance of the town of Quebec - 1608-1703. |
| 46-004 | The Church and transition, 1660 to 1695. |
| 46-583 | Some aspects of Spencer, Bishop of Norwich. |
| 47-529 | Adam Mabane and the French party in Canada, 1760-1791. |
| 47-539 | The relationship between the nobles and the king in France in the late sixteenth and early seventeenth centuries. |
| 47-577 | Causes of English colonization in America, 1550-1640. |
| 47-580 | The annexation movement of 1849 as seen through the Lower Canadian press. |
| 48-557 | The Quebec provincial general elections of 1886. |
| 48-565 | Military policy and organization in New France. |
| 48-568 | British policy in the Italo-Turkish war. |
| 48-613 | The Irish migration to Montreal 1847-1867. |
| 49-004 | The French-Canadian under the British, 1760-1800. |
| 49-559 | Hannah More, evangelical educationalist. |
| 49-563 | The English navy in the XIVth century. |
| 49-628 | Canadian Knights of Labor with special reference to the 1880's. |
| 50-040 | The growth and importance of the City of Quebec, 1608-1760. |
| 50-566 | The attitude of the English people towards the introduction of labour-saving machinery during the Industrial Revolution. |

| THESIS | THESIS TITLE |
|---|---|
| **History** | |
| 50-649 | Anti-Entente tendencies in French opinion 1904-1912. |
| 51-569 | The Presbyterian College, Montreal, 1865-1915. |
| 51-575 | The activities of David Urquhart in British diplomacy and politics, 1830-1841. |
| 51-633 | Jean Bochart de Champigny, intendant of New France 1686-1702. |
| 51-644 | The English cloth economy, 1550-1640. |
| 53-614 | British foreign policy with regard to the Macedonian Question, 1903-1908. |
| 54-615 | The influence of the invasion of Belgium on Great Britain's entry into the First World War. |
| 54-625 | The diplomatic career of Sir Fairfax Cartwright from 1906 to 1913. |
| 55-016 | Frontenac and New France, 1672-1698. |
| 55-061 | Factors in the formation of the Presbyterian Church in Canada, 1875. |
| 55-064 | The Peasants Revolt of 1381 in history and legend. |
| 55-560 | Anglo-Russian relations and the Dogger Bank incident, 1902-1905. |
| 55-625 | Tudor dealings in Scotland between 1488-1524. |
| 55-626 | The Warsaw rising of 1944 in the light of Polish-Soviet relations during World War II. |
| 55-632 | The British attitude towards the Armenian Question, 1878-1908. |
| 56-545 | The Anglo-French military and naval staff conversations, 1906-1914. |
| 56-622 | Liberal criticism of Sir Edward Grey's foreign policy, 1906-1914. |
| 57-544 | Canadian intervention in Russia, 1918-1919. |
| 57-605 | The American Presbyterian Church of Montreal, 1822-1865. |
| 57-607 | The foreign trade of Edinburgh, 1500-1542. |
| 57-610 | Factors in Scotland affecting the Scottish migrations to Canada between 1840 and 1896. |

| THESIS | THESIS TITLE |
|---|---|
| **History** | |
| 58-583 | Stalin's concept of the problem of national minorities: theory and practice. |
| 58-584 | The Bosphorus and the Dardanelles, 1902-1923: a study of French and British policies. |
| 59-074 | British diplomatic Blue Books, 1919-1939. |
| 59-078 | Foreign policy under the "Bloc des gauches'. |
| 59-082 | The influence of the Orange Lodges on Irish and British politics, 1795-1836. |
| 59-546 | The Anglican evangelicals in British politics, 1780-1833. |
| 59-556 | The visit to Canada of "La Capricieuse' and M. Le Commandant de Belveze in the summer of 1855 as seen through the French-language press of Lower Canada. |
| 59-612 | Fluctuations in British public opinion concerning Sir Edward Grey's foreign policy during the Balkan Wars, 1912-1913. |
| 59-618 | Cecil Rhodes' influence on the British government's policy in South Africa, 1870-1899. |
| **Horticulture** | |
| 49-550 | The artificial ripening of mature green tomatoes. |
| 50-519 | The effect of certain mineral nutrients on the yield and quality of tomatoes. |
| 50-610 | The effect of certain minerals nutrients on the ascorbic acid content of leaf lettuce. |
| 54-517 | The effect of three levels of nitrogen, phosphorus and potassium on the yield and quality of the canso potato. |
| 54-580 | Boron, calcium and magnesium nutrition of the strawberry as related to strawberry black root. |
| 56-594 | Sample sizes for vegetable seed testing. |
| **Horticulture-Botany** | |
| 37-535 | Some investigations with regard to the effect of nitrogen on the storage qualities of celery. |
| 39-067 | Some aspects of the nutrition and storage of celery. |
| 40-038 | Physiological changes in stored celery. |

| THESIS | THESIS TITLE |
|---|---|
| **Horticulture-Botany** | |
| 42-522 | Sand culture experiments with celery. |
| 44-506 | The freezing of celery and its effect upon water loss. |
| 44-508 | Nutrient levels as affecting stringiness in celery. |
| 45-526 | Effects of fertilizer levels on potatoes with respect to yields, specific gravity of tubers and discoloration after cooking. |
| 46-510 | Mineral nutritional effects on head lettuce. |
| 47-516 | A study of mineral nutritional effects on carrots. |
| 48-535 | Some physiological aspects of frozen vegetables. |
| 48-594 | Some effects of boron on the rooting of softwood cuttings. |
| 51-599 | The effect of certain plant growth regulating substances on early yield and quality of field grown tomatoes. |
| 51-615 | Formation of acetaldehyde and alcohol in frozen peas and their relation to off-flavour development. |
| **Horticulture-Genetics** | |
| 59-518 | Cytogenetical effects of seed treatments with maleic hydrazide on tomato plants of the first and second generation. |
| **Hydraulics** | |
| 31-504 | Cavitation phenomena and the flow in diverging tubes. |
| 31-511 | Cavitation phenomena and flow in diverging tubes. |
| **Hydraulics & Hydrodynamics** | |
| 23-509 | Recent advances in hydraulic power development. |
| **Industrial Engineering** | |
| 22-524 | A solution for fibre flax manufacture in Canada. |
| 32-504 | The value of planning in the establishment of large industrial enterprises. |
| **International Air Law** | |

| THESIS | THESIS TITLE |
|---|---|
| **International Air Law** | |
| 53-568 | The law of aviation in Egypt, a review of the basic concepts and future possibilities. |
| 54-504 | Progress toward the multilateral exchange of commercial air transport rights. |
| 54-505 | Grant and exercise of transit rights in respect of scheduled international air services. |
| 54-506 | Liability to third parties on the surface in air law. |
| 54-507 | Aviation insurance: passengers and third parties on the surface. |
| 54-508 | Aerial warfare and international law. |
| 54-567 | Limitation of liabilities in international air law. |
| 54-568 | Liability for acts of agents and servants in international air law. |
| 55-508 | Vicarious liability in air law. |
| 55-509 | The participation of Canada in international aviation agreements. |
| 55-510 | Conflict in the competence and jurisdiction of courts of different states to deal with acts and occurrences on board aircraft. |
| 55-511 | Collision between aircraft. |
| 55-512 | The single forum method and the unification of international private air law: Article 20 of the Rome Convention, 1952. |
| 55-580 | Particular aspects of the Rome Convention of 1952 on damages at the surface. |
| 55-581 | Jurisdiction over acts and occurrences on board an aircraft. |
| 55-582 | The contiguous air space zone in international law. |
| 55-583 | Real rights in aircraft and vessels. |
| 55-584 | The grant of passage and exercise of commercial rights in international air transport. |
| 56-564 | The legal status of the airspace of trusteeship territory. |
| 56-565 | Right of innocent passage. |

| THESIS | THESIS TITLE |
|---|---|
| International Air Law | |
| 56-566 | A study of the draft Swedish Civil Aviation Act of 1955. |
| 57-514 | The law of civil aviation in Pakistan. |
| 57-515 | The airspace in international air law. |
| 57-516 | The legal status of military air transport. |
| 57-517 | La periode de transport dans ses relations avec la responsabilite du transporteur de personnes. |
| 57-560 | Sovereign rights in space. |
| 57-561 | Les premiers resultats de la cooperation aeronautique europeene. |
| 57-562 | Comparative aspects of airport operators liability in the United Kingdom and the United States. |
| 57-563 | The Air Navigation Commission of the International Civil Aviation Organization. |
| 58-559 | Liability limitations in the carriage of passengers and goods by air and sea. |
| 58-560 | Crimes aboard aircraft. |
| 59-508 | Les aides a la navigation aerienne: organisation et problemes juridiques souleves par leur fonctionnement. |
| 59-509 | Exoneration et limitation de responsabilite du transporteur aerien en droit international et en droit compare. |
| 59-572 | Agricultural aviation and its regulation. |
| 59-573 | L'etat et les compagnies de navigation aerienne: les interventions economiques gouvernementales pour l'organisation de la profession de transporteur aerien. |
| 59-574 | Freedom of flight over the high seas. |
| International Law | |
| 46-501 | The revision of international conventions. |
| Invertebrate Morphology | |
| 21-001 | On the muscular system of Gryllus assimilis Fab. (Pennsylvanicus Burm). |
| Investigative Medicine | |

| THESIS | THESIS TITLE |
|---|---|
| **Investigative Medicine** | |
| 56-603 | Production of corticosteroids by rat adrenal tissue in vitro. |
| 56-605 | An investigation of the urinary corticostercid pattern in adrenal cortical disease by the technique of paper chromatcgraphy. |
| 57-524 | Investigations cf methods of determination of human pituitary gcnadotropins in urine. |
| 57-541 | The influence of senescence on thyroid function. |
| 57-586 | Investigations of the action of hypothalamic and pituitary extracts on adrenccortical function. |
| 57-588 | Experiences in the measurement of various body fluid compartments. |
| 58-045 | Nature et biogenese des steroides secretes par les differentes zones cellulaires du cortex surrenal. |
| 58-530 | The control of pulmonary ventilaticn in physiolcgical hyperpnoea. |
| 58-578 | Thyroid antibodies and discrders of thyroid physiology and morphology. |
| 59-016 | Adrenal function in experimental nephrosis. |
| 59-045 | Studies on the influence of varicus factors on ccrticosteroid secretion by the adrenal gland in vitro with special reference to aldcsterone. |
| 59-071 | The production and metabolism of corticosteroids in pregnancy. |
| 59-523 | Adrenal functicn in adrenal regeneraticn hypertension. |
| 59-540 | The effect of adrenal steroids on electrolyte excretion. |
| **Islamic Studies** | |
| 54-541 | The trend towards secularism in Turkey, as exemplified by its educational develcpment. |
| 54-549 | Al'Afghani: his role in the nineteenth century Muslim awakening. |
| 54-554 | Zahawi's innovations as a thinker and poet. |
| 54-612 | Some aspects of Islam in modern Iran, with special reference to the work of Sangalaji and Rashid. |
| 54-613 | Turkish language reform: a step in the modernization of Islam in Turkey. |

| THESIS | THESIS TITLE |
|---|---|
| **Islamic Studies** | |
| 54-620 | Muhammad 'Abduh and Al-Waqa'i' Al-Misriyah. |
| 54-621 | The image of the West in Iqbal. |
| 55-552 | Ghazzali's "Tahafut al-Falasifah'. |
| 55-566 | Muhammad 'Ali and the Khilafat movement. |
| 55-635 | A bibliographical introduction to modern Islamic developments in India and Pakistan. |
| 55-636 | Islam and nationalism in the Arab world, a selected and annotated bibliography. |
| 57-601 | The concept of freedom in Muhammad 'Abduh. |
| 57-602 | The Muhammadijah movement: a bibliographical introduction. |
| 58-588 | The Emperor Akbar as a religious man: six interpretations. |
| 59-039 | The concept of human nature in Hujjat Allah Al-Balighah and its relation to Shah Waliullah's doctrine of fiqh. |
| 59-057 | Al-Madrasah Al-Mushtansiriyah in Baghdad: a study of Muslim educational institutions. |
| 59-545 | An inquiry into the interrelationship between Islam and nationalism in the writings of Egyptians, 1945-56. |
| 59-547 | The Mevlevi Tarikat considered as organized mysticism in Turkish Islam. |
| 59-548 | The law of marriage and divorce in Muslim countries. |
| 59-553 | Islamic marriage law in Indonesia. |
| 59-554 | The Sarekat Islam movement: its contribution to Indonesian nationalism. |
| 59-608 | Deoband and the demand for Pakistan. |
| 59-619 | War diplomacy and Turkish Republic: a study in neutrality, 1939-1945. |
| **Latin** | |
| 14-505 | Alliteration and assonance in Plautus. |

| THESIS | THESIS TITLE |
|---|---|
| **Latin** | |
| 20-510 | Cicero's moral philosophy. |
| 28-528 | Supernatural influence in classical tragedy. |
| 28-530 | The actual and projected legislation of Julius Caesar and its treatment by his successors. |
| 29-538 | Literary indecency in certain Roman satirists. |
| 30-547 | Lucretius and his times. |
| 30-555 | The pauperization of the Roman populace during the Later Republican period, with special reference to frumentation laws and distributions. |
| 31-564 | The attitude of the Roman satirists towards foreigners. |
| 36-527 | The sincerity of the Roman satirists. |
| **Law** | |
| 18-001 | Canadian commericial corporations. |
| 20-500 | Acts of civil status in the province of Quebec. |
| 22-500 | De la personnalite: esquisse d'une theorie d'ensemble. |
| 23-500 | Jurisdiction in matrimonial causes in the Dominion of Canada. |
| 47-500 | Expropriation under the law of the Dominion of Canada and the province of Quebec. |
| 47-501 | Collective bargaining and Order-in-Council, P.C.1003. |
| 48-500 | De la possession dans le droit civil de la province de Quebec. |
| 48-501 | The arbitration of civil and industrial disputes in Quebec law. |
| 48-502 | The juridical extension of collective agreements in the province of Quebec. |
| 49-583 | The ratification of international treaties. |
| 49-584 | Analysis of certain aspects of the law of contracts relating to international carriage of goods by air. |

| THESIS | THESIS TITLE |
|---|---|
| Law | |
| 50-500 | Migration for employment: legal and institutional. |
| 50-581 | The development of the concept of legal personality and trade unions in Canada. |
| 53-500 | The liability of the company director. |
| 53-501 | The rights of the minority shareholder. |
| 53-502 | L'enregistrement des droits reels dans la province de Quebec. |
| 53-503 | The law of mining rights in Quebec. |
| 53-511 | International law and aerial warfare. |
| 53-512 | Res ipsa loquitur. |
| 53-513 | The aircraft operator's liability. |
| 53-514 | Aviation law in Canada. |
| 53-515 | Government control of aviation in Canada. |
| 53-516 | The nationality of aircraft. |
| 53-517 | Le statut juridique de l'aeronef militaire en temps de paix et en temps de guerre. |
| 53-556 | Constitutional problems of regional organization. |
| 53-557 | Canadian fiscal law. |
| 57-500 | La propriete privee et l'urbanisme. |
| 58-500 | A judicial approach to the problems of the world fisheries. |
| 58-501 | The international direction of social security. |
| Machine Design | |
| 23-504 | Friction of a lubricated journal bearing. |
| 27-513 | Journal bearing friction characteristics. |
| Machines & Machine Design | |

| THESIS | THESIS TITLE |
|---|---|
| **Machines & Machine Design** | |
| 08-510 | The operating machinery for the lifting deck of the bridge over the Missouri River at Kansas City, for the Union Depot Bridge and Terminal Railroad Company. |
| **Mathematics** | |
| 05-005 | Spherical trigonometry, orthogonal substitutes and elliptic functions. |
| 10-501 | Numerical evaluation of elliptic functions. |
| 10-520 | Algebraic configurations. |
| 15-511 | The elementary theory of sets of points, with an introductory essay on irrational numbers. |
| 28-556 | Plucker's numbers in the theory of algebraic plane curves. |
| 31-532 | Elementary theory of quadratic forms. |
| 34-534 | On the location in the complex plane of the zeros of a polynomial. |
| 38-519 | Generalized quaternions and the representation of numbers in certain ternary quadratic forms. |
| 38-542 | Representation of numbers in certain regular and irregular ternary quadratics forms. |
| 44-517 | The arithmetic of generalized quaternions. |
| 45-533 | New methods for the derivation of thermodynamical relations for certain complex systems. |
| 46-506 | Transfinite numbers. |
| 46-525 | A non-distributive calculus of numerical functions. |
| 46-526 | Survey of electromagnetic theories. |
| 46-561 | The application of conformal mapping to the solution of electrostatic problems. |
| 48-524 | The theory of elacticity of aelotropic materials. |
| 48-531 | The theory of relativistic accelerators. |
| 48-543 | The influence of a thick neutron detector on the distribution of neutrons in a uniform neutron stream. |

| THESIS | THESIS TITLE |
| --- | --- |
| **Mathematics** | |
| 49-527 | The integral solutions of the diophantine equation y²¢sMathematical type,C¢s x³ ¢sMathematical type,u¢s k. |
| 49-539 | A derivation of cross section formulae for resonance scattering and reactions in nuclear processes. |
| 49-544 | Almost periodic functions of several variables. |
| 49-626 | Multiple radiation. |
| 49-630 | The number theory of a system of hyperbolic complex numbers. |
| 49-644 | The theory of functions of a hyperbolic complex variable. |
| 50-012 | A. Biquaternian vectorfields over Minkowski's space. B. The immersibility of a semi-group into a group. |
| 50-546 | Temperature dependence of the mean free path of conduction electrons in graphite. |
| 50-550 | Polarization and absorption lines in solids. |
| 50-556 | Electronic structure of boron nitride. |
| 50-567 | Existence theorems for ordinary differential equations. |
| 50-596 | Specific heats of crystalline solids containing more than one atom per unit cell. |
| 50-632 | On the Bhabha potential. |
| 51-530 | Some problems in the theory of univalent functions. |
| 51-536 | Some diophantine problems. |
| 51-596 | On Dirac's classical theory of the radiating electron. |
| 52-031 | A statistical problem in the geometry of numbers. |
| 52-056 | On P-adic integral representations of finite groups. |
| 52-590 | Linear modifications of Maxwell's electrodynamics. |
| 52-594 | Convex and subharmonic functions. |

| THESIS | THESIS TITLE |
|---|---|
| **Mathematics** | |
| 53-018 | Analysis in nonarchimedean spaces. |
| 53-028 | Induced representations of lie algebras. |
| 53-035 | Theoretical calculations of electron capture cross sections. |
| 53-037 | On the diamagnetism of graphite. |
| 53-048 | A generalization of the method of young operators and its use in constructing primitive idempotents for the representations of GL(2,q). |
| 53-529 | On the theory of radiative transitions in heavy nuclei. |
| 53-539 | On norms of matrices. |
| 53-541 | Fixed point theorems. |
| 53-544 | Classical Sturm Liouville expansion theory. |
| 53-545 | Theoretical interpretation of radiation emitted in neutron capture reactions. |
| 53-546 | Linear growth laws in corrosive reactions. |
| 53-589 | A study on some electrical properties of graphite. |
| 54-012 | Topology of the field of p-adic numbers. |
| 54-509 | A variational approach to the equations of stellar structure. |
| 54-519 | On a Hamiltonian treatment of fields with non-local interaction. |
| 54-525 | Basic properties of Banach algebras. |
| 54-586 | Gentzen's formalization of the propositional and predicate calculus. |
| 54-624 | Matrix representations of the symmetric group in finite fields. |
| 55-048 | A theoretical investigation of resonance electron capture cross sections. |
| 55-063 | Asymptotic theorems in the theory of normal correlation. |
| 55-546 | The barometer coefficient and the mu-messon production spectrum. |

| THESIS | THESIS TITLE |
|---|---|
| Mathematics | |
| 55-589 | Cohomology theory in abstract groups. |
| 55-594 | Internal conversion in light nuclei. |
| 55-604 | Non-standard models for formal languages. |
| 55-613 | Mathematical principles of statistical quality control. |
| 56-029 | On the contributions of meson exchange currents to the radiative moments of nuclei. |
| 56-061 | A statistical problem in the geometry of numbers: star-shaped domains of quadratic and hexagonal symmetry. |
| 56-068 | The ejection of K-electrons by beta decay. |
| 56-538 | A correction to the radiative transition rate occurring in internal conversion. |
| 56-589 | The application of Mellin transforms to statistics. |
| 56-595 | The derivation of the chi-square test of goodness of fit. |
| 56-616 | The representations of particular groups. |
| 56-618 | Uniqueness theorems for ordinary differential equations. |
| 57-013 | The electric and magnetic properties of graphite. |
| 57-025 | An inequality in the geometry of numbers. |
| 57-067 | Qualitative behaviour of non-linear differential equations in the neighbourhood of an isolated singular point. |
| 57-569 | Basic mathematical models in analysis of variance. |
| 57-596 | The Hausdorff and Hamburger one-dimensional moment problem. |
| 58-003 | Three-body forces in hypernuclei. |
| 58-019 | Some properties of caratheodory solutions of $x' = f(t,x)$. |
| 58-024 | The structure of left H-star algebras. |

| THESIS | THESIS TITLE |
|---|---|
| **Mathematics** | |
| 58-046 | On certain subgroups of algebraic matrix groups at prime characteristic. |
| 58-528 | The quantum theory of cyclotron resonance in graphite. |
| 58-567 | Some properties of compositions and their applications. |
| 58-582 | A theorem of Locman-Menchoff. |
| 58-585 | Radicals and subdirect decompositions. |
| 59-510 | The arithmetics of linguistic structures. |
| 59-513 | On the minimax theorem and the solution of finite games. |
| 59-515 | The application of information theory to mathematical linguistics. |
| 59-533 | Primitive recursive functions. |
| 59-585 | Canonical languages. |
| 59-588 | The scattering of lambda particles by nucleons. |
| 59-602 | The fundamental theorem of the theory of games. |
| **Mathematics & Physics** | |
| 27-510 | An absolute determination of the magnetic susceptibility of potassium in the pure state. |
| 27-520 | The application of the Piezo-electric effect to the measurement of pressures in internal combustion engines. |
| 27-521 | Application of methods of X-ray crystal analysis to a problem in organic chemistry: effect on the X-ray diffraction pattern of stretching meta styrene, as compared with the effect obtained on stretching rubber. |
| **Mechanical Engineering** | |
| 09-512 | The use of alcohol in an internal combustion engine: a comparative series of tests on a Blackstone oil engine using alcohol and coal oil. |
| 20-509 | Internal cooling applied to an internal combustion engine. |

| THESIS | THESIS TITLE |
|---|---|
| **Mechanical Engineering** | |
| 32-506 | Eccentricity and attitude of a full journal bearing. |
| 33-504 | Power supply in industry. |
| 34-504 | The re-design of an iron foundry. |
| 35-500 | The redesign of the sugar mill. |
| 47-502 | The engineering factors controlling the optimum size of a manufacturing enterprise. |
| 49-585 | An alternative test for the physical properties of arc-weld metal. |
| 49-590 | The use of a vaporizer and flame tube combustor in studying combustion of hydrocarbon fuels. |
| 50-583 | The effects of an axial pressure gradient on boundary layer. |
| 50-589 | A study of the air ejector. |
| 50-590 | The effects of turbulence on the spontaneous ignition and combustion of liquid hydrocarbon fuels in a hot gas stream. |
| 50-591 | The effect of recirculation on the weak limit stability of gas turbine combustion chambers. |
| 50-594 | Investigations of total carbon formation in the combustion of liquid hydrocarbon fuels. |
| 51-500 | Calibration of variable compression internal combustion engine with standard fuel and investigation of performance with fuel 3GPX22. |
| 51-502 | Experimentation on a low speed cascade wind tunnel. |
| 51-505 | A study of the boundary layer in an adverse axial pressure gradient. |
| 51-584 | Afterburning in turbojet engines. |
| 52-500 | The mixing of cold air jets with a hot gas stream. |
| 52-501 | Instrumentation for flame temperature determination. |
| 52-566 | The effect of variation of thermodynamic properties of the working fluid on the performance of compressors. |
| 53-071 | Temperature distributions in heat exchanger tube plates. |

| THESIS | THESIS TITLE |
|---|---|
| Mechanical Engineering | |
| 53-508 | The effect of variation of the thermodynamic properties of the working fluid on the performance of gas turbines. |
| 53-509 | Mechanical aids to cortrol. |
| 53-562 | The engineering and economic aspects of equipment replacement. |
| 53-563 | Burning of liquid fuel in forced draft. |
| 53-566 | The mixing of cold air jets with a hot gas stream in a varying area duct. |
| 54-068 | Flame propagation at elevated temperatures. |
| 54-560 | The effect of oxygen concentration on flame propagation at elevated temperatures. |
| 55-507 | The mechanism of heat transfer across metallic interfaces. |
| 55-572 | Spontaneous ignition measurements of some gaseous fuels injected into a hot air stream. |
| 55-574 | Studies on turbulent flames. |
| 55-577 | Compressor-blade vibrations associated with stalling. |
| 55-579 | Constant diameter air injector. |
| 56-503 | Spontaneous ignition delays of propane injected into a hot air stream. |
| 56-505 | The mixing of hot subsonic jets with cold air streams. |
| 56-509 | An experimental investigation of the shear angle relationship in metal cutting. |
| 56-510 | Job shop planning. |
| 56-553 | Some aspects of the spontaneous ignition delay of propane injected into a hot air stream. |
| 56-557 | Spontaneous ignition delays of propane injected into a hot air stream. |
| 56-560 | The transfer of heat from water to a bed of spherical particles. |
| 56-561 | An experimental method for measuring heat transfer coefficients in the thermal entrance region of a circular tube. |

| THESIS | THESIS TITLE |
|---|---|
| **Mechanical Engineering** | |
| 56-562 | The influence of the angle of impingement on heat transfer coefficients and pressure drops for the flow of air over a tube bank. |
| 57-505 | Temperature effects on inlet region heat transfer coefficients. |
| 57-506 | A study of the spontaneous ignition delay of hot lean mixtures of gaseous hydrocarbon fuels and air in a flow system. |
| 57-513 | Spontaneous ignition delay of lean hydrocarbon mixtures. |
| 57-559 | A study of Bourdon tube deflection. |
| 58-506 | The mixing of circular jets. |
| 58-558 | Turbine performance with varying thermodynamic properties of the working fluid. |
| 59-069 | Flow properties of model fibre suspensions. |
| 59-503 | The change in reactivity due to neutron streaming in annular air gaps around fuel rods in a reactor. |
| 59-504 | Design investigation of a power transmission shaft. |
| 59-568 | Ignition delay of propane in air between 725-850°C under isothermal conditions. |
| 59-569 | Comprehensive analysis of diesel engine performance (Dominion-Crossley diesel engine: Model 6-D/15). |
| **Medicine** | |
| 18-501 | Published works. |
| 45-524 | Some aspects of nitrogen metabolism in the rat. |
| 46-577 | The metabolism of testosterone. |
| 47-514 | Assays of urinary corticoids: a comparison between results of chemical and biological methods. |
| 47-571 | The metabolism of chorionic gonadotrophin. |
| 48-030 | Protein metabolism in the rat under the influence of damage, endocrine substances and diet. |
| 49-043 | Effects of pH and of bicarbonate and CO2 on the respiration and anaerobic glcolysis of rat brain tissue. |

| THESIS | THESIS TITLE |
|---|---|
| **Medicine** | |
| 49-598 | Studies of the blood volume in some diseases of the blood. |
| 51-521 | Billiary obstruction in the rabbit. |
| 58-587 | A study on the hypersensitivity in guinea pigs as induced by the inhalation of allergens. |
| **Metallurgical Engineering** | |
| 09-517 | The correlation and standardization of chemical, physical and microscopical methods of testing iron and steel. |
| 11-509 | Chemistry and metallurgy as applied to modern malleable and gray iron foundries. |
| 13-519 | The direct production of steel from iron ore by the Evans-Stansfield process. |
| 15-510 | Metal losses in copper slags. |
| 21-518 | The electric welding of iron and steel. |
| 22-510 | The reduction of iron ores by solid and gaseous reducing reagents at temperatures below that of fusion. |
| 23-512 | The reduction of iron ores by solid and gaseous reducing reagents at temperatures below that of fusion. |
| 24-513 | Some physical properties of copper-nickel mattes. |
| 25-528 | The extraction of copper from its ores by simultaneous leaching and electrolysis. |
| 26-520 | A study of titaniferous blast furnace slags. |
| 32-507 | Sponge iron: some conditions essential for its production. |
| 36-501 | The composition and properties of modern refractory cements. |
| 42-048 | The beneficiation of siderite ores. |
| 46-556 | The effect of aluminum additions on the graphitization rate of white cast iron. |
| 47-505 | The effect of iron on aluminum bronze. |
| 50-510 | Effect of impurities on lead anodes in the electrolysis of zinc sulphate solutions. |

| THESIS | THESIS TITLE |
|---|---|
| **Metallurgical Engineering** | |
| 51-585 | An investigation of the electric smelting of copper concentrates. |
| 51-591 | Statistical analysis of the compositions and related properties of cast steel. |
| 54-563 | The recovery of copper from copper matte. |
| 55-516 | The specific conductance of fused cryolite-alumina baths. |
| 55-578 | The extraction of lithium from spodumene. |
| 56-563 | Inverse segregation in Al-Cu alloys. |
| 58-554 | Corrosion behaviour of welded low alloy steel. |
| 58-557 | The anodic oxidation of bivalent manganese to tetravalent manganese. |
| 59-076 | Mechanisms of solidification in binary alloy castings. |
| **Metallurgy** | |
| 23-516 | A study of the production of iron by electrolysis with special reference to its recovery from sulphide ores. |
| 24-534 | The production of pure titanium oxide. |
| 25-525 | The economic production of titanium oxide from ilmenite. |
| 35-507 | The recovery of copper, gold and silver from sulphide ores and concentrates by processes including roasting, leaching and electrolysis. |
| 37-512 | The design of refractory furnace linings subjected to high temperature and erosion with special reference to oil fired steam generators. |
| 37-514 | Relations between graphite and cementite in pure iron-carbon alloys. |
| 38-520 | Beneficiation of a pyritic siderite ore. |
| 40-515 | Effect of oxygen on the rate of dissolution of gold in cyanide solution. |
| 42-050 | Copper losses in slags. |
| **Meteorology** | |

| THESIS | THESIS TITLE |
|---|---|
| **Meteorology** | |
| 55-591 | Some aspects of postglacial climatic variation in the Near East considered in relation to movements of population. |
| 57-007 | Snow cells and showers. |
| 58-512 | Two-level representation of the atmosphere. |
| 59-591 | Long waves in the Ferrel Westerlies during December 1958. |
| **Mining & Metallurgical Engineering** | |
| 40-035 | The influence of certain factors and impurities on the precipitation of gold from cyanide solutions by zinc dust. |
| **Mining & Metallurgy** | |
| 14-517 | On the open hearth process of steel manufacture: an investigation of the relative methods of an interrupted as distinguished from a continuous process. |
| 39-053 | Recovery of gold from arsenical gold ores. |
| 40-034 | The cyanidation of gold ores, with varying oxygen concentrations. |
| **Mining Engineering** | |
| 10-513 | The mechanical purification of certain Canadian coals. |
| 11-510 | The classification of finely crushed ore with a view of further concentration on the Wilfley table. |
| 12-510 | Spontaneous combustion and weathering of coal. |
| 12-515 | (a) The treatment of the ore from the Sullivan Mine, Kimberley, B.C. and (b) An investigation on the efficiency of the tube mill. |
| 13-513 | The weathering of coal and lignite. |
| 14-509 | The slow combustion of coal. |
| 14-510 | The methods of laying out the underground workings and the haulage systems in the Crow's Nest district. |
| 15-507 | An investigation of the performance of certain rock crushing machines, with a view to finding a method for calculating their efficiency. |

| THESIS | THESIS TITLE |
|---|---|
| **Mining Engineering** | |
| 16-514 | Iron mining in Minnesota. |
| 20-501 | The effect of changes in the design and adjustments of concentrating tables of the Wilfley type and the relation of such changes to the character and efficiency of operation. |
| 20-507 | The effect of changes in the design and adjustments of concentrating tables of Wilfey type, and the relation of such changes to the character and efficiency of operation. |
| 21-508 | An investigation of the mechanical efficiencies of rock crushing machines. |
| 26-531 | Studies in the reduction of telluride ores, with special reference to the ores of Kirkland Lake district, Ontario. |
| 27-502 | The flotation and concentration of certain complex auriferous ores of northern Canada (Kirkland Lake and Porcupine areas). |
| 27-519 | A laboratory investigation of the principles governing the sizing of crushed ores and minerals in sieves. |
| 28-559 | Treatment of complex copper-zinc ores of the Rouyn District. |
| 30-514 | The treatment of gold ore by flotation. |
| 31-512 | The investigation of slime settling in Dorr thickeners. |
| 31-516 | The investigation of slime settling in Dorr thickeners. |
| 32-505 | Flotation of gold and copper in Noranda ore. |
| 33-503 | A study of the factors affecting grinding efficiency in ball mills. |
| 33-507 | An investigation into the chemical reactions that occur during the cyanidation of gold ores. |
| 33-566 | An investigation of the possibilities for air conditioning in hot, deep mines. |
| 34-501 | Probable chemical reactions and their effect on sulphide flotation. |
| 34-503 | Efficiency in the ventilation of metal mines by mechanical means. |
| 34-541 | A study of certain phases of fine grinding. |
| 35-501 | A photoelectric method of measuring the surface of small particles with particular regard to its application to the problems of ore dressing. |

| THESIS | THESIS TITLE |
|---|---|
| **Mining Engineering** | |
| 36-503 | A study of certain phases of fine grinding. |
| 36-507 | A study of certain phases of fine grinding. |
| 37-500 | Fine grinding of ores with particular reference to the surfaces produced. |
| 38-500 | A study of certain phases of fine grinding. |
| 38-502 | Phases of fine grinding. |
| 39-052 | Studies in fine grinding of ores. |
| 41-032 | The effect of oxygen on the cyanidation of gold. |
| 41-033 | Concentration of chromite ores by flotation. |
| 42-049 | Treatment of Lake Rowan gold ore. |
| 44-500 | Flotation of chromite. |
| 48-510 | Concentration of low-grade chromite ores. |
| 54-502 | An investigation into some physical properties of rocks and their relationship to pressure problems in mines. |
| 55-576 | The relationship between the physical properties of rocks and underground mining conditions. |
| 56-504 | A study of the rupture of rocks under stress with special reference to mine excavations. |
| 57-509 | An experimental investigation into certain aspects of rock failure. |
| 59-502 | Pillars: applications and limitations in underground mining. |
| **Music** | |
| 24-500 | A concert overture in F for orchestra. A choral and orchestral setting of "The Ancient Mariner'. |
| 30-016 | Musical compositions. |
| 47-022 | Symphony in Canada. |
| 57-049 | Musical composition: Symphony in D. |
| **Neurology** | |

| THESIS | THESIS TITLE |
|---|---|
| **Neurology** | |
| 35-538 | Tissue culture of the pituitary. |
| 36-508 | The architectonic subdivision of the mammalian cerebral cortex. |
| 36-514 | Studies of cerebral circulation. |
| 36-547 | A morphological study of interneuronal connections. |
| 37-027 | A study of the cerebral cicatrix. |
| 38-515 | The physiology and pathology of herniation of the cerebrum through the incisura tentorii. |
| 38-547 | Changes in the circulation of the brain and spinal cord associated with nervous activity. |
| 39-006 | The nature and spread of the epileptic discharge. |
| 39-513 | Cerebral ischaemia and its relation to epilepsy. |
| **Neurology & Neurosurgery** | |
| 39-060 | Study of the vascular and cytological changes in the cerebral cicatrix. |
| 45-523 | The perineural space of the peripheral nerve. |
| 45-525 | Acute aseptic leptomeningitis postoperative. |
| 46-533 | A study of the effect of cortical excision on speech in patients with previous cerebral injuries. |
| 47-511 | Experimental studies of the thalamo-cortical mechanisms in relation to petit mal epilepsy. |
| 47-553 | Asceptic meningitis due to blood and its breakdown products: an experimental and clinical study. |
| 47-567 | The evolutional pathology of the intervertebral disc. |
| 47-574 | A morphological study of human Glioblastoma multiforme transplanted to guinea pigs. |
| 48-516 | Methods for the induction of epileptiform abnormality in the electroencephalogram of epileptic patients. |
| 48-546 | Cortical localization of autonomic function. |
| 48-549 | Acetylcholine and neuronal activity in craniocerebral trauma and epilepsy. |

| THESIS | THESIS TITLE |
|---|---|
| Neurology & Neurosurgery | |
| 48-574 | In vivo staining of induced and transplanted brain tumors. |
| 48-583 | Studies on the role of acetylcholine in experimental seizures. |
| 49-534 | The cortical representation of gastric motor function. |
| 49-541 | Diencephalic function. |
| 49-553 | Methods for temporary and reversible paralysis of local areas of the cerebral cortex. |
| 49-594 | Dural nerve endings and dural sensitivity. |
| 49-600 | Studies of the effect of denervation upon the electrical activity of the cortex. |
| 49-617 | A study of certain alterations in speech during stimulation of specific cortical regions. |
| 49-622 | Studies in "suppression'. |
| 50-535 | Epileptoform seizures of thalamic origin. |
| 50-542 | The reaction of oligodendroglia in Wallerina degeneration. |
| 50-617 | Anatomical study of fibre connections of the temporal pole in the cat and the monkey. |
| 50-631 | Influence of massage on rate of downgrowth of regenerating axons in injured peripheral nerves: a histological study. |
| 50-637 | The cortical representation of the feeding reflex. |
| 51-027 | An atlas of the thalamus of Macaca mulatta for use with the Horsley-Clarke instrument. |
| 51-033 | A study of the acetylcholine system in the cerebral cortex of various mammals and in the human epileptogenic focus and of certain factors which affect its activity. |
| 51-508 | An investigation of the facilitatory and inhibitory activity of the suprabulbar regions of the cat. |
| 51-517 | The tract of Lissauer and its possible relation to the pain pathway. |
| 51-524 | The effect of cortisone in the healing of incised cerebral wounds. |
| 51-554 | A study of certain corticothalamic relationships. |

| THESIS | THESIS TITLE |
|---|---|
| **Neurology & Neurosurgery** | |
| 51-605 | The human thalamus: anatomical and developmental study. |
| 51-610 | A study of the tumors of the nervous system by the Golgi method. |
| 52-060 | Alterations in speech produced by cerebral stimulation and excision. |
| 52-511 | Functional representation in the temporal lobe of man: a study of response to electrical stimulation. |
| 53-571 | On the functional and anatomical organization of the neural respiratory mechanisms in the cat. |
| 53-573 | Studies on cortical localization in the monkey: the supplementary motor area. |
| 54-017 | Microelectrode studies of the electrical activities of the cerebral cortex. |
| 54-046 | Congenital malformations of the central nervous system. |
| 54-516 | Changes produced by alimentary lipemia and large molecular substances in the intact circulation of the hamster: effect on the blood-brain barrier. |
| 54-587 | Desoxyribonucleic acid content, cell densities and metabolism of normal brain and human brain tumours. |
| 54-588 | Studies on experimental allergic encephalomyelitis. |
| 54-597 | Observations on the thalamocortical projections. |
| 55-614 | Effect of focal epileptogenic lesions on the connecting function of brain. |
| 55-620 | Studies on the adrenaline-sensitive component of the reticular activating system. |
| 56-525 | Local spasm in cerebral arteries. |
| 56-581 | A study of the reactions of the dura to wounding and loss of substance. |
| 56-600 | Permeability of cerebral blood vessels to protein molecules in convulsive seizures. |
| 56-604 | Chlorpromazine as an activator of abnormal potentials in the electroencephalograms of patients with seizures. |
| 57-012 | Electrophysiological studies of the amygdala in the cat. |

| THESIS | THESIS TITLE |
|---|---|
| Neurology & Neurosurgery | |
| 57-529 | Experimental production of gradual vascular occlusions. |
| 57-583 | The morphological observation of the vessels of the brain of human infants. |
| 58-036 | Micro-electrode studies of experimental epilepsy. |
| 58-513 | A microelectrode study of Betz cells in the unanesthetized cat. |
| 58-561 | The role of chronic encephalitis in the pathogenesis of epilepsy. |
| 59-066 | The structure of the postcentral gyrus in the cat. |
| 59-536 | The role of the temporal lobe in hearing. |
| 59-596 | Effect of hypothermia on the extent of infarction following middle cerebral occlusion in the monkey. |
| Neurosurgery | |
| 41-525 | A study of epileptogenic lesions of the brain. |
| 41-535 | The prevention of meningocerebral adhesions. |
| Nutrition | |
| 42-519 | Observations on the guinea pig growth method of vitamin C assay. |
| 42-527 | Studies on the ascorbic acid content of dehydrated vegetables and its retention in cooking. |
| 43-507 | The biological assay of vitamin D. |
| 43-510 | Factors affecting the reliability of digestibility coefficients of livestock feeds. |
| 44-502 | A study of diets intended for use in vitamin C bio-assay, using the guinea pig growth method. |
| 44-503 | The seasonal trend of the chemical composition and digestibility of mixed pasture herbage. |
| 44-513 | Incisor tooth assay of vitamin C: micrometric measurement of the odontoblast cells. |
| 45-503 | Feeding value and digestibility of oats by swine as affected by fineness of grinding. |
| 45-508 | The effect of storage on the vitamin A content of mixed rations as determined by growth of rats. |